www.wadsworth.com

wadsworth.com is the World Wide Web site for Wadsworth Publishing Company and is your direct source to dozens of online resources.

At *wadsworth.com* you can find out about supplements, demonstration software, and student resources. You can also send e-mail to many of our authors and preview new publications and exciting new technologies.

wadsworth.com
Changing the way the world learns®

VOICES OF WISDOM
A Multicultural Philosophy Reader
Fourth Edition

Gary E. Kessler
California State University, Bakersfield

WADSWORTH

THOMSON LEARNING

Australia • Canada • Mexico • Singapore • Spain • United Kingdom • United States

WADSWORTH

THOMSON LEARNING

Philosophy Editor: Peter Adams
Assistant Editor: Kara Kindstrrom
Editorial Assistant: Mark Andrews
Marketing Manager: Dave Garrison
Print Buyer: Barbara Britton
Permissions Editor: Robert Kauser
Production Service: Ruth Cottrell

Text Designers: John Edeen/Lisa Delgado
Copy Editor: Ruth Cottrell
Cover Designer: Annabelle Ison
Cover Image: © Jim Zuckerman/Corbis
Cover Printer: Custom Printing/Von Hoffmann
Compositor: G & S Typesetters, Inc.
Printer: Custom Printing/Von Hoffmann

For permission to use material from this
text, contact us by
  web: http://www.thomsonrights.com
  fax: 1-800-730-2215
  phone: 1-800-730-2214

**Library of Congress
Cataloging-in-Publication Data**
Voices of wisdom : a multicultural
  philosophy reader / [edited by] Gary E.
Kessler.—4th ed.
    p.   cm.
  ISBN 0-534-53572-0
    1. Philosophy—Introductions.   I. Kessler,
Gary E.
  BD21.V59   2000
  100—dc21

                            00-031621

Wadsworth/Thomson Learning
10 Davis Drive
Belmont, CA 94002-3098
USA

For information about our products, contact us:
Thomson Learning Academic Resource Center
1-800-423-0563
http://www.wadsworth.com

International Headquarters
Thomson Learning
International Division
290 Harbor Drive, 2nd Floor
Stamford, CT 06902-7477
USA

UK/Europe/Middle East/South Africa
Thomson Learning
Berkshire House
168–173 High Holborn
London WC1V 7AA
United Kingdom

Asia
Thomson Learning
60 Albert Street, #15-01
Albert Complex
Singapore 189969

Canada
Nelson/Thomson Learning
1120 Birchmount Road
Toronto, Ontario M1K 5G4
Canada

To the memory of Peanut

Contents

Preface

Since the publication of the first edition of *Voices of Wisdom*, I am gratified to note that more introductory textbooks now incorporate a multicultural perspective—a perspective that was unique to this introductory reader when it was first published in 1992. At that time the introductory readers that were available treated philosophy as if it were entirely an Anglo-European male phenomenon. Little or no attention was given to Hindu, Buddhist, Chinese, African, Native American, Latin American, and feminist philosophy. *Voices of Wisdom* helped to change that situation, offering to those who wished it the possibility of assigning significant readings that represent the global nature of philosophizing. This fourth edition continues to offer a multicultural perspective and has benefited from the teaching and learning experiences of the many instructors and students who used the previous editions. Readers have learned that ideas from other cultures are worth careful consideration and that these ideas make important contributions to human understanding.

Philosophy in a Multicultural Perspective

Although I wish to stress the universal nature of philosophizing, I am well aware of the dangers of anachronism. A text of this sort faces not only the problems associated with anachronism in the historical sense but also what we might term "cultural" anachronism. The writings of ancient philosophers mingle with modern texts, and thinkers from different cultures are brought together. The student may get the impression that Plato, Buddha, Nietzsche, Confucius, Descartes, and Aristotle are all contemporaries discussing the same issues with the same concepts in English! There are similarities. But there are also vast differences. Where appropriate, the important similarities and differences are stressed in my introductory remarks.

My selection of issues betrays my own Anglo-European perspective. While many of the topics are fundamental and universal (How should one live? Is knowledge possible? What is really real?), their importance and centrality differ from tradition to tradition. The mind-body problem, the puzzle of freedom and determinism, the problem of moral skepticism—these problems are not necessarily the central ones that gripped the minds of Chinese or Indian philosophers. Just as Anglo-European philosophers have not had much to say about Karma, Buddhist thinkers have not been overly concerned with proving the existence of God.

However, I do believe this Western way of organizing the material is justified in this instance. Even though the significance of the problems and the way they are formulated differ from culture to culture, many of the underlying issues are the same. One cannot reflect for long on Karma and reincarnation without addressing issues relating to freedom and human identity. Furthermore, I think it best, for introductory and practical purposes, to organize the material around traditional Anglo-European philosophical themes. Many students already have some concern with these issues (e.g., the existence of God). In addition, most introductory courses deal with these themes, and this book allows instructors to continue that practice, but some new and different voices are emphasized, thereby enriching philosophical thinking.

It should be noted that there exists no culturally neutral set of categories for organizing the material. If I had used the dominant concerns of, let us say, the Indian tradition (concerns such as release from suffering, duty and the stages of life, and the nature of bondage) to organize the selections, I would not have thereby escaped a cultural perspective. Perhaps, as a multicultural approach becomes more commonplace in introductory courses and as Western philosophy becomes more open and diverse, new categories will emerge. However, until that day, the sources need to be organized in some fashion. What is important is that we are aware of the limitations of our categories and that we continually remind ourselves of the diverse and subtle ways that long-held biases influence the way we select and organize materials.

Historical and cultural comparisons are inevitable, and I encourage them. However, I wish to stress that this reader is not meant to be primarily an exercise in comparative philosophy. It is meant to serve a course that introduces students to *doing* philosophy by drawing on *multicultural* resources. The students who read this text should be impressed with the rich diversity that comprises global philosophizing and should learn the art of philosophizing in a broader and more inclusive context than is usual.

I do wish to stress that it is *global* philosophizing with which I am concerned. Some associate the word "multicultural" almost exclusively with "multiethnic" and "minorities." Those who do so may expect more African American, Latin American, Native American, and feminist philosophers than I have included. These voices also need to be heard, and I have included many. However, my primary concern has been to provide sources that promote an *international* perspective. I believe it is important to educate students for a new century in which an understanding of the interconnectedness of all peoples will be increasingly important in determining the policies and practices of nations.

Topics

Voices of Wisdom includes much philosophical material that has come to be regarded as classic in the West. This material is included for two reasons. First, most students take an introductory philosophy course in conjunction with general education and, as part of that experience, it is important for them to read philosophical writings that are significant to the Western cultural tradition. Second, this writing is good philosophy (that is why it has become classic), and students should experience the ideas of profound philosophical minds. However, profound philosophical minds exist all over the world and, while other styles of thinking and other traditions may be very different, they are no less important.

Part I deals with introductory matters. In Chapter 1, I discuss the nature of philosophy, the meaning of rationality, and provide a new selection dealing with the value of studying philosophy. Chapter 2 focuses on reading skills and offers students practical advice on how to read philosophy. I provide students an opportunity to try out some of my reading suggestions on a new selection (Section 2.3) dealing with the value of a multicultural education. This chapter is new to the fourth edition, although it incorporates some material from the first two editions.

Part II, Ethics, begins by exploring the questions "How Should One Live?" (Chapter 3) and "How Can I Know What Is Right?" (Chapter 4). These are significant questions that, in one form or another, have received much global attention. Furthermore, these are questions with which students can connect personally, and therefore I have found it useful to place them early in the text. In Chapter 3 there are two new selections: Sections 3.3 on Confucius and 3.7 on the meaning of life. Chapter 4 also contains two new selections (Sections 4.3 by Jeremy Bentham and 4.6 by Kwasi Wiredu) along with significant revisions of Sections 4.4 (Nietzsche) and 4.5 (Manning).

I have included two chapters on political and social philosophy in Part II, Ethics, because both deal with issues relating to justice. Chapter 5, "What Makes a Society Just?" includes three new selections: Sections 5.2 by Majid Khadduri, 5.4 by John Rawls, and 5.7 by Ward Churchill. Chapter 6, "Is Justice for All Possible?" is entirely new, covering topics ranging from human rights to animal rights. In this chapter I also discuss issues relating to racism, feminism, affirmative action, environmental ethics, and international business. One essay (Section 6.5) titled "Is Affirmative Action a Second Wrong?" by Warren Kessler is published here for the first time.

Part III, Epistemology, introduces students to the topics "Is Knowledge Possible?" (Chapter 7) and "Does Science Tell Us the Whole Truth and Nothing But the Truth?" (Chapter 8). There is one new selection in Chapter 7 on Classical Indian Epistemology (Section 7.6). The whole of Chapter 8 is new and includes a variety of selections ranging from Thomas Kuhn to Kwame Anthony Appiah.

Part IV on Metaphysics is divided into four chapters: Chapter 9 "What Is Really Real?", Chapter 10 "Are We Free or Determined?", Chapter 11 "What Am I? Who Am I?", and Chapter 12 "Is There a God?" There are two new selections in Chapter 9, one by Paul Churchland on eliminative materialism and another by Jorge Valadez on pre-Columbian cosmologies. Chapter 10 is virtually unchanged, and two new selections appear in Chapter 11: Sections 11.5 on the nature of consciousness by Colin McGinn and 11.7 on social identity by Gloria Anzaldúa. Anselm's version of the ontological argument (Section 12.5) is new to Chapter 12.

In order to include all this new material, I have had to leave out some selections from the last edition. Most notably the chapter on the problem of evil has been eliminated. Regrettably, space precludes including as much as one would like. However, I have tried to be responsive to reviewers' suggestions, thereby, I trust, making *Voices of Wisdom* more useful for introductory courses.

Pedagogical Features

I agree with John Dewey's notion that we learn by doing. In my experience, the more I can get my students to do for themselves, the more they learn. Thus, rather than providing summaries of the selections—a practice that can discourage careful reading by students—I provide the background information they need to understand the selections, and I supply questions that are designed to guide the students' reading *prior* to the selections. This approach encourages students to read the selections for themselves and to formulate their own questions about the material. It also gives instructors an opportunity to require students to answer the questions in a philosophical journal before class meetings. The questions and the students' responses can then be used as the basis for class discussion. Students are thereby encouraged to become actively engaged in the process of figuring out what a text means.

In most chapters the material is arranged chronologically. Sometimes, however, another sort of arrangement is more pedagogically useful, and so I have not restricted myself to the chronological pattern in all cases.

I have put technical terms in bold type on their first occurrence and provided brief definitions. A glossary (Appendix I) provides a convenient reference for these terms and their definitions.

Appendix II provides a brief pronunciation guide to Chinese, Sanskrit, and Arabic words. Foreign words can be daunting to readers and this pronunciation guide should alleviate some of the unease they may feel.

The order of the chapters can, for the most part, be arranged by instructors according to their wishes. I have, in this fourth edition, reordered the chapters into four parts as I indicated above: Introduction (Chapters 1 and 2), Ethics (Chapters 3, 4, 5, and 6), Epistemology (Chapters 7 and 8), and Metaphysics (Chapters 9, 10, 11, and 12). Reviewers' suggestions inspired this new organization, and I hope it proves more useful than the previous organization. Material in one section will sometimes spill over into another because the boundaries between the various fields of philosophy are not airtight and a philosophical issue in one part often leads directly to issues in another area. For example, Paul Churchland's article on eliminative materialism would be equally at home in Chapter 9 or Chapter 11.

I have written the introductory material in an informal, engaging, and, I trust, clear manner. I hope to engage students in the thinking process by connecting the selections to questions and issues students have already begun to encounter. The selections themselves have been classroom-tested and represent different degrees of difficulty. Most will challenge beginning students to think in more depth and in a more precise way.

Acknowledgments

A book like this is written, edited, and revised by many people. Peter Adams, the philosophy editor at Wadsworth, made valuable suggestions. The staff at Wadsworth has been most accommodating and patient. They have kept me from many errors. Ruth Cottrell deserves special thanks for bringing clarity out of the messy prose academics sometimes write. Responsibility for whatever errors and infelicities remain rests on my doorstep.

Student response has been helpful. I have tried to keep students foremost in my mind as this fourth edition evolved. What will work in the classroom and what will stimulate students to engage philosophical issues is of fundamental importance. A special thanks goes to all those students who have shared their concerns, ideas, and suggestions.

The reviewers of my third edition were particularly helpful. I wish it were possible to follow all of their valuable suggestions. I would like to thank the following reviewers for their ideas and comments: Christa Davis Acampora, University of Maine; Roger T.

Ames, University of Hawaii; Charles Brown, Emporia State University; Carol Enns, College of the Sequoias; Linda S. Handelman, Mount San Antonio College; Preston L. McKever-Floyd, Coastal Carolina University; and Don Sievert, University of Missouri.

A very special thanks goes to my wife Katy, whose ideas, insights, and loving support made this book possible. Both she and I dedicate this edition to the memory of our dearly beloved fat, blind cat Peanut. He was a very philosophical cat, and provided many entertaining illustrations of deep philosophical points.

I also wish to thank all of you who used previous editions. Your responses have been gratifying and reinforce my hope that one day a multicultural approach to the study, teaching, and doing of philosophy will be commonplace. I would appreciate hearing your responses to this new edition—about how it works and how it can be improved.

Gary E. Kessler
California State University, Bakersfield
e-mail: gkessler@csub.edu

Part 1

Introduction

Chapter 1

What Is Philosophy?

> . . . those who are eager to learn because they wonder at things are lovers of wisdom (*philosophoi*).
>
> ALEXANDER OF APHRODISIAS

1.1 A Definition of Philosophy

HAVE YOU EVER WONDERED about the purpose of life? Have you ever been curious about what you can reasonably believe? Have you ever marveled at the beauty of nature or been upset by suffering? Have you ever thought that life is unfair? Have you ever been puzzled about what you ought to do?

Perhaps you associate these kinds of questions with philosophy. If you do, why do you? What do you think is philosophical about these questions? When you hear the word *philosophy,* what do you think it means? Think about it awhile and write your answer.

The Greek philosopher Aristotle (384–322 BCE), who asserted that philosophy begins in wonder, was impressed by the ability of human beings to think. In fact, he defined humans as "rational animals." Aristotle maintained that philosophy arises from the human ability to reflect on experience, to wonder and be curious about what happens to us and to others.

Of course, wonder is not the sole cause of philosophizing. Sufficient leisure must be available to engage in reflection, and hence economic and cultural factors play an important role in promoting and influencing human curiosity. However, without the human capacity to wonder and be curious, it is doubtful that philosophical thinking would occur.

I hope this book will stimulate your natural ability to wonder, teach you something of the art of wondering, and help you learn how to live in wonder. Cultivating the art of wondering is important, Aristotle believed, because such an art leads us along the path toward wisdom.

The word *philosophy* comes from a combination of two Greek words—*philos,* meaning "loving" and *sophia,* meaning "wisdom." Etymologically, philosophy means the love of wisdom. To love something is to desire it. So, for many Greeks, the philosopher was the one who desired wisdom. The word *philos* also refers, for the Greeks, to the special kind of love found in close friendship. Hence the philosopher could also be characterized as the "friend of wisdom."

The historical origin of a word, however, often does not help us very much when we are searching for an adequate definition today. The meanings of words change. Also, meanings derived etymologically are sometimes unclear. If the philosopher is the lover or friend of wisdom, then what is wisdom? About that, philosophers—even Greek philosophers—disagree.

Philosophy in Western culture was born in the sixth century BCE among a group of thinkers called the Pre-Socratics. According to tradition, one of these thinkers, Pythagoras (about 570 BCE), coined the word *philosophy*. Along with other Pre-Socratics, he was intensely interested in nature, in knowing how the universe or cosmic order developed, and in figuring out what things were made of. These thinkers disagreed about the stuff out of which things are made (some said earth, some air, others fire, still others water or some combination of these elements), but many of them did think that wisdom consisted of knowledge about nature. To love wisdom, as far as they were concerned, was to search for knowledge about the universe.

A century later, another group of thinkers in Athens offered their services as teachers to those who could afford them. They claimed to teach virtue. The Greek word for virtue (*areté*) means "excellence or power." So to possess virtue is to possess power. Wisdom, they taught, is the possession of virtue. It is to have certain powers or abilities, especially in the social and political realm, to influence people and be successful. Since these teachers claimed to possess this wisdom, they came to be called "Sophists" or "The Wise Ones." For them, philosophy is not a search for knowledge about the universe, nor a *search* for wisdom. Rather, philosophy is the *possession* of wisdom and hence the possession of virtue or excellence, especially in the social and political dimensions of life.

Socrates (470–399 BCE) lived in Athens at the same time as the Sophists. He spent his days wandering around the marketplace, asking people questions about all kinds of things. He found himself perplexed by things other people claimed to know. For example, people claimed to know what knowledge, justice, virtue, and the right way to live are. The Sophists claimed to teach these things. However, under Socrates' relentless critical questioning, the definitions and grand theories that people held about these sorts of things collapsed.

The oracle at Delphi, a well-respected source of divine truth in the ancient world, said that Socrates was the wisest man in Athens. When word of this got to Socrates, he was greatly puzzled. How could he, who knew next to nothing and spent his days asking others, be the wisest? What about the Sophists, the teachers of wisdom? Were not they the wisest? Socrates did believe he knew what virtue is; it is knowledge. But what is knowledge? He had to confess he did not know, so how could he be wise? And yet, he reasoned, the oracle of Delphi could not be lying. It was, after all, the voice of the god Apollo. But the oracle was tricky. You had to figure out what it meant.

Finally, Socrates understood. Wisdom, the oracle was telling him, is knowing that he did not know! Wisdom is the awareness of our ignorance, an awareness of the limitations of knowledge. Let the Sophists claim to be wise; the best Socrates could do was to claim he was a lover of wisdom. He lived his life in the pursuit of wisdom as lovers live their lives in pursuit of the beloved. For him, philosophy was a critical examination of our pretensions to knowledge and the constant search for that final truth that always seems to be just beyond our grasp.

The Greeks were not the only ones to philosophize, for the pursuit of wisdom is common to all cultures. The Greeks were also not the only ones to disagree about the nature of wisdom. For example, in India some philosophers claimed that wisdom is coming to know one's true self as immortal. Yajnavalkya,[1] a wise man described in early Indian literature called the *Upanishads,* tells his wife Maitreyi that wealth will not gain one immortality; only the true self or *atman,* as he called it, is immortal. However, other Indian philosophers disagreed. Wisdom, they said, did not consist in the knowledge of a true immortal self or *atman.* Quite the opposite is the case. Genuine wisdom consists in knowing that there is no such thing as an eternal self or *atman.*

Clearly there are different understandings of what wisdom is and hence there are different understandings of what philosophy is about. No single definition can possibly capture all the nuances of the art of wondering in every place and time in which it appears. This does not mean, however, that we can define philosophy any way we wish, and it does not mean that some definitions are not better than others. Let me offer my definition, which, I think, states something important about philosophizing and helps us distinguish it from other types of thinking: **Philosophy** *is the rational attempt to formulate, understand, and answer fundamental questions.*

Many people think that philosophy is a body of doctrines and that philosophers are people who have answers to difficult questions about the meaning of life. My definition stresses that (1) philosophy is an activity rather than a body of set teachings and (2) philosophers are as concerned with formulating and understanding questions as they are with finding answers.

Formulating questions is very important. What we ask and how we ask it determine, in large part, where we look for answers and the kinds of answers we get. Progress in many fields consists, in part, of an ever-greater refinement of our questions and more precision and sophistication in our methods of interrogation. You will not get good answers if you do not ask the right questions.

For example, the title of this chapter is "What Is Philosophy?" and at the beginning of the chapter I asked you to think about the meaning of the word *philosophy* and to write your answer. Review your answer. Now think about the question, "What is it to philosophize?" If I had formulated the question about your understanding of philosophy as a question about what it is to philosophize and asked you to answer it, would your answer have been any different? If so, how would it have been different?

Understanding what we are after when we ask questions is as important as formulating questions. Words are often ambiguous and vague; we must be as clear as possible about what they mean. If I ask, "What is the meaning of life?" what do I mean? What am I looking for? Is this the best way to put it? What might count as a helpful answer? Where should I look for an answer? Am I asking about the purpose of life? Is life the sort of thing that has a purpose? Or am I interested in what makes life worthwhile? Is the purpose of life (if there is one) the same as what makes life valuable or worthwhile?

The purpose of formulating and understanding questions as precisely as we can is to find answers, but often our answers lead to further questions. Why assume some answer is final? Or why assume all questions we can ask have answers? Also, what counts as an answer? How do I know when I have a good one? Consider this conversation:

1. For a pronunciation guide for Sanskrit, Chinese, and Arabic words see Appendix II. To facilitate reading, I have left out diacritical marks that indicate sounds in other languages that are not normally part of English.

Yolanda: What is the meaning of life?
José: What do you mean by that question?
Yolanda: I mean, what is the purpose of life?
José: Oh, that's easy, its purpose is survival and reproduction. That's what my biology textbook says.

Is José's answer a good one? Is it the sort of answer Yolanda is after? Can this question be answered with factual information, or is it about values? When Yolanda asks, "What is the meaning of life?" is she asking, "What makes life ultimately valuable?" And if she is asking that, then the answer José gives may well miss the mark (unless, of course, Yolanda thinks survival and reproduction are more valuable than anything else).

I said in my definition that philosophers are concerned with *fundamental* questions. The word *fundamental* means "basic" and has to do with what is primary. Fundamental questions are *radical* questions in the sense of pertaining to roots. They are the most basic questions we can ask. Therefore, they are often *abstract* questions that have to do with a wide area of human experience.

However, even though the sorts of questions that concern philosophers are abstract, they are about concepts we employ every day. We are constantly making judgments about good and bad, right and wrong, true and false, reality and fiction, beautiful and ugly, just and unjust. But what is good? By what norms can we distinguish right behavior from wrong? What is truth? How can I distinguish appearance from reality? Is beauty only in the eye of the beholder? What is justice, and is it ever possible to achieve it?

Some of the main branches of Western philosophy are distinguished by the kinds of fundamental questions they ask. Many philosophers have regarded "What is truly real?" as a fundamental question. Note the word *truly.* I did not ask, "What is real?" but "What is *truly* real?" In other words, I am assuming that not everything that appears to be real is real. Or, to put that another way, by asking, "What is truly real?" I am asking how we might distinguish appearance from reality. The branch of philosophy called **metaphysics** deals with this and related issues. One of its purposes, some philosophers have claimed, is to develop a theory of reality or a theory of what is genuinely real. It is also concerned with what might be the most fundamental question we can think of: "Why is there something rather than nothing?"

What is knowledge and what is truth? These seem to be good candidates for fundamental questions because the concepts of knowledge and truth are basic to so much of our thinking, including all that we call science. The branch of Western philosophy known as **epistemology** concerns itself with the issues of knowledge and truth. Epistemologists search for a theory of what knowledge is and how it might be distinguished from opinion. They look for a definition of truth and wonder how we might correctly distinguish truth from error.

Axiology, the third main branch of Western philosophy, has to do with the study of value and the distinction between value and fact. Traditionally, it is divided into two main subdivisions: aesthetics and ethics. **Aesthetics** deals with such questions as: Is beauty a matter of taste, or is it something objective? What standards should be used to judge artistic work? Can we define art? **Ethics** attempts to decide what values and principles we should use to judge human action as morally right or wrong. What is the greatest good? How should one live? Applied ethics applies these values and principles to such social concerns as human rights, racial justice, affirmative action, environmental ethics, and business ethics in order to determine what would be the morally right thing to do.

Fundamental questions are not only basic and abstract; they are also *universal* questions. They are the sorts of questions any thinking person might ask anywhere and at any time. They arise out of our capacity to wonder about ourselves and the world in which we live. They arise naturally, as it were, as we search for wisdom.

Although fundamental questions are universal, or nearly so, it should be noted that the way I have described the organization of the field of philosophy (metaphysics, epistemology, axiology) is decidedly Western. Different societies organize knowledge in different ways. Also, what may seem fundamental in one society may seem far less important in another. For example, some Buddhist philosophers have been suspicious of intellectual speculation about metaphysical matters, especially questions like "Does God exist?" This question, so important to many people, excites little interest among these Buddhist thinkers.

It should also be noted that each of the three main branches of Western philosophy deals with important distinctions that all of us learn to make based on the standards our society teaches us. Hence, metaphysics is concerned with the distinction between *appearance and reality,* epistemology with the distinction between *knowledge and opinion,* and axlology with the distinction between *fact and value.* One important question is whether we can discover criteria that are universal and not merely relative to our own particular time in history and our own particular cultural view for making these distinctions. Fundamental and abstract questions about reality, knowledge, and value—and the distinctions these questions imply—may be universal in the sense that most cultures have developed intellectual traditions concerned with these issues. However, the concrete way the questions are asked, understood, and answered varies a great deal from one tradition to another.

For example, Plato (428–348 BCE) made the distinction between knowledge and opinion, at least in part, by claiming that *opinion* has to do with beliefs about the world, which are based on our sensations, but *knowledge* has to do with the reality we discover through our reason. For him, logic and mathematics constituted examples of knowledge, but information about physical objects based on sensation did not. Under the influence of physical science, many people today would be inclined to say almost the opposite of what Plato said. For instance, many of my students have maintained that knowledge is what empirical science provides, and opinion is a product of abstract speculation like philosophy.

As twenty-first century students living in a highly technological and pluralistic society, we live in a very different world from the ancient Greeks or Indians. Yet we, like them, wonder about life and ask basic questions about what is real, what is true, what is good, and what is beautiful. This is not to say that there are not vast differences among philosophies. There are. Something of this variety you are about to experience firsthand as you read different philosophers from different cultures and different eras.

In sum, I think philosophy is the activity of rationally attempting to formulate, understand, and answer fundamental questions. I have discussed most of the parts of that definition except the word *rational.* Why must it be a rational attempt? And what is it to be rational, anyway? If we cannot agree on what rationality is, how can we know what constitutes a rational attempt to formulate and answer basic questions?

1.2 What Is Rationality?

This fundamental question is one of the most hotly debated issues in philosophy to-day. I cannot hope to settle the puzzles about rationality here, but I can give you some idea about what the issues are, describe some of the different views, and offer a few thoughts of my own.

William James (1842–1910), an important American philosopher, said that "philosophy is the unusually stubborn attempt to think clearly." Now *thinking* is a word with a much broader meaning than the word *rational*. To be rational is to think, but all thinking is not necessarily rational thinking. James does add the qualification "clearly." That narrows the field somewhat. But what is clear thinking, and how do we know it when we see it?

Consider this passage from a Chinese philosopher named Zhuangzi (Chuang Tzu)[2] who lived about 350 BCE.

> Suppose you and I have had an argument. If you have beaten me instead of my beating you, then are you necessarily right and am I necessarily wrong? If I have beaten you instead of your beating me, then am I necessarily right and are you necessarily wrong? Is one of us right and the other wrong? Are both of us right or are both of us wrong? If you and I don't know the answer, then other people are bound to be even more in the dark. Whom shall we get to decide what is right? Shall we get someone who agrees with me? But if he already agrees with me, how can he decide? Shall we get someone who disagrees with both of us? But if he already disagrees with both of us, how can he decide? Shall we get someone who agrees with both of us? But if he already agrees with both of us, how shall he decide? Obviously, then, neither you nor I nor anyone else can know the answer. Shall we wait for still another person?

Zhuangzi wonders how we might decide who is right and who is wrong. You and I are not in a good position to make such a decision, at least not an objective one, because the fact that we are arguing shows we disagree. To bring in a third party to settle the dispute does not seem to help much because he or she will either disagree with you or with me or with both of us, and what was a two-person argument will now become a three-person argument.

Zhuangzi is wondering how we might proceed to settle an argument. What procedures do we have that will eventuate in agreement? Should we appeal to authority? Perhaps some divine revelation? A long-standing tradition? Common sense? Force? Rationality? You might be tempted to say that we should settle it by applying rational standards. If we follow that course, then we can decide which argument is the most rational. Are there, however, objective and universal standards of rationality? Is rationality something entirely subjective or, at the very least, relative to particular historical periods and cultural communities?

Fundamental disagreements about the nature of rationality are very difficult to settle because in initially proceeding to approach the topic we have already made assumptions about what is a rational way to proceed. *Rationality* has to do with the

---

2. There are two methods in wide use today for romanticizing (translating into a Latin-based alphabetical system) Chinese words. One is called Wade-Giles and the other Pinyin. The first time a word or name is introduced, I have used the Pinyin spelling and provided the Wade-Giles spelling in parentheses. See the pronunciation guide for Chinese words in Appendix II. The quotation is from *Chuang Tzu: Basic Writings*, translated by Burton Watson (New York, NY: Columbia University Press, 1996, p. 43).

way we proceed to investigate matters, settle disputes, evaluate evidence, assess people's behaviors, practices, and beliefs. If we could get agreement about the standards of rationality, then the only thing left to argue about would be whether or not these standards were fairly and accurately applied. But how do we proceed if we cannot agree on the standards themselves?

Imagine Zhaungzi's imaginary arguers arguing about the nature of rationality. Not only would they and some third-party find an acceptable settlement of the dispute difficult to obtain, they would not even know how to go about reaching a settlement. What would count as a rational solution to their disagreement if the very nature of rationality is itself the subject of the disagreement? With Zhaungzi we might ask, with more than a mere hint of futility, "Shall we wait for still another person?"

To avoid the futility of endless disagreements, some philosophers maintain that there must be objective and universal standards of rationality. This position on the question of rationality is called **foundationalism**. Generally (there are many different varieties of foundationalism), foundationalists hold that we can decide what is rational by appealing to principles that are undeniable to any rational person. For example, if I maintain that my belief about extraterrestrials visiting Peru is rational, I, according to this view, should be able to present good reasons in support of my belief. The reasons I present will be good ones insofar as they ultimately rest on a set of ideas that are *self-evidently true* for any person who can properly understand them.

What are these foundational principles? Many philosophers have maintained that they are the basic laws of logic and the rules and procedures deducible from those laws. Aristotle, for example, claims that the **law of noncontradiction** (a statement cannot be both true and false) stands at the foundation of all rational reasoning. You cannot rationally assert p (where p stands for any statement) *and* not-p. If you claim p is true, you cannot also claim it is false and be rational. Furthermore, he argues, anyone who denies this law and who is prepared to defend that denial will be unable to advance her or his argument without relying on the very law supposedly rejected.

I must confess that people who argued that the law of noncontradiction is false, and thereby meant that all statements (including their own statement about the falsity of the law of noncontradiction) could be both true and false, I would think either perverse or irrational. You would probably agree with me. However, you might quickly point out that being logical and correctly applying the laws of logic are, at best, necessary conditions of rationality. These are not sufficient. We can imagine someone applying logical procedures and arriving at the most absurd conclusions. If I were clever enough, I could justify my belief in extraterrestrials visiting Peru without violating any logical laws, but is that enough for you to conclude that my belief is rational?

So it would seem we need some fundamental principles, besides the laws of logic, in order to know both the necessary and sufficient conditions of rationality.[3] And here is where the fight really breaks out among foundationalists. Some (usually called *rationalists*) claim that these foundational principles of rationality amount to "clear and distinct ideas" that are innate in the human mind or can be discovered by a careful and critical analysis of our beliefs. Others (usually called *empiricists*) argue that immediate sense impressions form the foundations of rational beliefs. You will

---

3. Something can be sufficient without being necessary and vice versa. A rock hitting a window is sufficient to break it, but not necessary because a baseball might do as well. Milk is necessary to make yogurt, but not sufficient.

encounter something of this debate between rationalists and empiricists as you read this book, so I will not belabor the point here. I only wish you to understand that much philosophical energy has been expended in a search for the foundational principles of rational belief. If we can find such principles, then we will have agreed-upon procedures for sifting through the many different answers to metaphysical questions (What is real?), epistemological questions (What is knowledge?), and axiological questions (What is value?) and settling on those that prove the most rational.

I think you can see the attractiveness of the foundationalist position, especially if you have ever been in one of those arguments where someone keeps asking you, "How do you know that?" At first you are patient and display your reasons. But she or he persists. "How do you know those are good reasons?" You explain why. Again, "Well, how can you be so sure?" About now your blood pressure is rising because you are beginning to see an infinite, bottomless abyss opening up. This could go on forever! But have no fear. Foundationalism can ride to your rescue because foundationalism maintains that regress is not infinite, the pit is not bottomless, and there is a sure foundation of first principles that your questioner will recognize to be rational. There is a way, according to foundationalists, of settling Zhaungzi's imaginary dispute.

However, the foundation you reach on your descent may turn out to be a ledge that gives way under your weight. Why? Because all the philosophical energy that has been spent on the search for foundational principles has ended in disagreement. Thus, many philosophers have declared the modern search for fundamental rational principles bankrupt. Welcome to the postmodern age of *anti-foundationalism.*

Just as there are many varieties of foundationalism, there are also many varieties of anti-foundationalism. In order to remove the negative connotations of the "anti," let us call the critics of foundationalism **constructivists** because many of them maintain that rationality is a social construction.

Some constructivists point to the failure of agreement among foundationalists as proof that the search for objective, universal, self-evident, rational principles is fruitless. Others argue that the so-called self-evident, objective, universal, ahistorical, transcultural foundations of rationality have been shown again and again to be little more than the elevation of the prejudices of an elite class, or of males, or of white culture, or of Western civilization to the honorific title of "self-evident rational principles." What is alleged to be "rational" turns out, after careful critical analysis, to be what Anglo-American European white males value! Foundationalism, this line of criticism maintains, is merely a variety of ethnocentric imperialism disguised with the mask of rationality.

Many constructivists argue that we are all so embedded in our cultures, our traditions, our religions, and our historical situations that we can never find some neutral point, some god's-eye view from which to pass judgment. Not one of our limited viewpoints is privileged. We are hopelessly culture-bound. There is no culturally neutral "third party," as Zhaungzi pointed out so clearly centuries ago, who can settle once and for all our important disputes. There are, of course, cultural procedures for settling disputes. However, it is a grave mistake to elevate such procedures to self-evident, universal marks of rationality.

Still other critics of foundationalism point out that foundationalism is fatally flawed because it is itself based on a contradiction. Foundationalism claims that a rational belief is one supported by good reasons. This means that before I accept your beliefs as rational, I should expect you to be able to display, if questioned, good reasons for such beliefs. If, after you have given me your good reasons, I persist and ask for more, sooner or later I shall have to be content with a belief whose truth is, you claim, "self-evident." So it turns out that good reasons rest on principles that we are asked to accept as self-evidently true and in need of no further support. Such principles would be irrational given the criterion initially assumed to be the hallmark of a rational belief—that is, a belief supported by good reasons.

Displaying the evidence and exploring the subtleties and shifts of argument between foundationalists and constructivists would take us too far afield. However, I should mention one major issue that this debate has engendered because it is particularly relevant to what this book is about. That is the issue of cognitive and ethical relativism. The foundationalists charge the constructivists with both **cognitive relativism** (the denial of universal truths) and **ethical relativism** (the denial of universally valid moral principles). They claim that if one denies the existence of transcultural, universal, objective standards of rationality, then what one is maintaining amounts to the view that there is no such thing as rationality; all there are, are *rationalities*. Eventually, this will lead the constructivist to assert moral relativism as well. One will be led down a slippery slope resulting in the conclusion that any culture's values, any religious tradition, any morality, indeed any set of beliefs, is as good or as rational as anyone else's. However, such relativism is self-defeating. If your view is no better or worse than my view, then all views are of equal merit. Therefore, constructivists can have no justification to support their claim that foundationalism is wrong. Foundationalists' views of rationality as universal and ahistorical are no more rational nor any less rational than constructivists' views of rationalities as local and historical (see Table 1.1).

Table 1.1

FOUNDATIONALISM	CONSTRUCTIVISM
CLAIM	*CLAIM*
One rationality that is universal and objective.	Many rationalities that are local and based on intersubjective agreement.
ARGUMENT	*ARGUMENT*
Beliefs are rational if supported by good reasons.	Rationality is conditioned by history and culture.
If an infinite regress of reasons is to be avoided, there must be a foundation of self-evident beliefs.	Vast amounts of historical, cultural, anthropological, and linguistic evidence supports the above claim.
Such foundational beliefs are: the laws of logic or clear and distinct ideas or beliefs evident to the senses.	
CRITIQUE OF CONSTRUCTIVISM	*CRITIQUE OF FOUNDATIONALISM*
Constructivism amounts to a self-refuting relativism.	Foundationalism cannot agree on what counts as foundational beliefs hence they are not self-evident. Its definition of rational beliefs is contradictory, and its claims amount to ethnocentric imperialism.

This is a powerful response to the constructivist critique of foundationalism. Few of us would argue with others if we thought that all views of morality or all views of truth were of equal worth. Yet we do argue. Few of us would be willing to maintain that programs of "ethnic cleansing," which lamentably characterize so much of human political practice, are as rational or moral as programs that aim at getting human beings to live in peace with one another.

We seem to be caught on the horns of a dilemma. We do not wish to opt for either ethnocentric imperialism or a kind of relativism that advocates "anything goes." Is there any other choice? Is there a way out of this predicament? Much contemporary philosophy is presently concerned with finding a way out of this dilemma, a sort of middle ground that allows us to assert that some answers are better than others but stops short of imposing on others our own local views of what is rational and what is good.

One way to escape the horns of a dilemma is to make careful distinctions. There is a difference between ethnocentrism and ethnocentric *imperialism*. Perhaps it is impossible to totally escape an ethnocentric viewpoint, but we do not have to impose our views on others by presenting them as if they are the only true views.

Likewise some philosophers distinguish between different kinds of relativism. Not all relativism may be self-defeating, contrary to what some foundationalists believe. We must carefully distinguish between relativism in the *strong sense* (the claim there are no universally valid standards) and relativism in the *weak sense* (the claim that standards of rationality and morality are culturally diverse). It seems obvious that standards of rationality and morality are relative to historical and cultural conditions in the sense that they are related to such conditions (weak relativism). Standards of rationality do not float in some timeless, nonhuman space. However, to conclude from this that *all* standards of rationality are of equal value or are equally true (the sort of self-defeating relativism the foundationalists charge the constructivists with) requires a big leap. It does not follow from the fact that there exist different understandings of rationality and morality that all understandings are of equal value, any more than it follows from the fact that there are different understandings of science that all of them are equally good or useful.

However, you might argue that if there are no objective standards of rationality or, at the very least, if we must admit we do not know what they might be, then all we are left with are rationalities bound to historical conditions and local cultural communities, and we have no way of determining which are better. Perhaps you are right. However, I think that we do have some options. We can remain convinced that our community has the last word on the subject and all others are wrong. Or, as we encounter other communities and other cultures, we can listen to them (and they to us) and try to discover ways of settling our disputes *together*. We can expand our conversations, listen to other voices, and together with them ask, What is real? What is knowledge? What is good? As we listen, as we enter into a dialogue, yes, and even as we argue, our standards of rationality will grow and, although we may still disagree in the end, at least we can say we have understood.

Hans-Georg Gadamer, a contemporary German philosopher, argues that truth is an understanding that occurs when there is a "fusion of horizons." Authentic conversation or dialogue occurs when we can recognize our own understanding as a horizon resulting from the perspective or bias we have acquired and when we are willing to risk our horizon in order to allow the horizon of the "other" to appear.

This book is an attempt to expand the philosophical dialogue. A wide variety of sounds will be heard—African American, Latino, Native American, feminist, and even Anglo-American European white males—and hopefully these sounds will turn into meaningful voices of wisdom. We will not agree with all these voices, but we can learn from each, and we may discover wider areas of agreement than we thought possible.

My claim that agreement about what is rational can emerge out of dialogue and expanded cultural communication rests on the assumption that we can understand philosophical views held by people who live in times and places very different from our own and on the hope that learning about ourselves and others is a worthwhile enterprise. Some might argue that we can never understand what others who are very different from us are saying and that my hope is naive. I do not have the space to defend my assumption and my hope, but I do believe that good reasons can be given for them. In any case, we will never find out if we do not try.

Recall that I characterized philosophy as a rational activity of formulating, understanding, and answering fundamental questions. This activity, I wish to stress, relies heavily on the logical skills of analyzing, criticizing, and developing arguments. It is, however, more than this. If the goal of philosophy is to formulate, understand, and answer fundamental questions on both an intellectual and practical level, then we can determine how rational this activity is only by assessing how successfully this goal is achieved by all those who participate in this sort of activity. I do not believe we can rule out any of the profound thinking about fundamental problems that the many peoples of the world have to offer by imposing some predetermined model of rationality. Hence, the very process of assessment is something we must learn as we go.

The Jains of India have a teaching called *syad-vada,* which might be translated as the "perhaps method." This teaching holds that 353 different viewpoints can be held on any question; hence, dogmatic closed-mindedness is inappropriate. To any perspective or any issue, the thoughtful will reply, "Perhaps." This "method" is based on the assumption that no single philosophical view or system can say all there is to be said about reality. It does not mean we should remain silent, nor does it mean that everything that is said (however partial) is of equal worth.

There are times, I think, when we can be a bit more definite than "perhaps," but the flexibility and openness this method recommends is a virtue we all need to practice when we have no privileged viewpoint from which we might settle a matter once and for all. Not all answers are rational. Some are better than others. However, the range of rational responses may be far broader than we realize.

1.3 Does Philosophy Bake Bread?

"Why should I study philosophy?" That is a question I often hear my students ask. It may be a question you are asking. Today many people approach their education pragmatically. They ask, "How will learning this prepare me for a job?" The implication of such a question is that if it does not help me get a job, it is not worth studying. If philosophy bakes no bread, why study it?

You have just read about how we might define philosophy and about some debates over the nature of rationality. What have you learned that is of any importance? When you are interviewed for that first job upon graduation, do you think the interviewer might ask, "All right then, who do you think is right, the foundationalists or the constructivists?"

"Well," you might say, "I certainly don't think that the value of a field of study is completely exhausted by whether or not it leads to gainful employment. However, isn't it the case that philosophy, unlike science, never really settles anything? Philosophers just spin their wheels in endless debate."

It is true that uncertainty haunts the philosopher's study. Indeed, it is uncertainty that keeps the philosophical fires burning. If science could answer all our questions, if putting bread on the table were all there is to a happy life, if religion could provide all the answers we need, then I fear the philosopher in us would soon cease to exist. However, the philosophic wonder of which Aristotle spoke keeps our minds stirring largely because there are so many things about life that are uncertain.

There is an important sense, I think, in which we cannot help but philosophize. Life's circumstances and experiences compel us to think about things beyond our daily bread. If this line of reasoning is right, if we cannot help but philosophize, then should we not learn to do it well? One way of learning how to do it is to listen carefully to others who have philosophized from many different times and places. We can learn by example even when we disagree with the views of those from whom we learn.

We start here with a Western example. Bertrand Russell (1872–1970) is the author of the following selection. He explicitly addressed the issue of the value of philosophy in a book called *The Problems of Philosophy* published in 1912. What he has to say may surprise you. Whatever you may think about his claims, it is clear that the questions about the usefulness of philosophy are neither new nor unimportant.

Russell has been one of the most influential philosophers in the English-speaking world. He helped to establish a type of philosophizing known as *analytic philosophy*. The analytic approach to philosophy is characterized by logical analysis, critique, and clarification of the language we use to express our ideas. Russell made significant contributions to the development of the philosophy of logic, mathematics, and science in the first two decades of the last century. He also became known for his unconventional views on ethical, social, and political issues. Although he came from a long line of privileged English aristocrats, he still lost his teaching appointment at Cambridge University in 1916 because of his opposition to Britain's entering World War I. Throughout his life he lent his considerable talent and brilliant pen to many an anti-war movement, including opposition to the Vietnam War.

As you read what Russell has to say, see if you can answer the following reading questions and identify the passages that support your answers. Discuss in class the questions you had difficulty answering and the ones that stimulated your own thinking about the value of philosophy.

Reading Questions

1. Where, according to Russell, is the value of philosophy to be found?
2. Why does Russell maintain that the "uncertainty of philosophy is more apparent than real"?
3. What does Russell mean when he asserts that the value of philosophy is to be sought in its "very uncertainty"?
4. According to Russell, what may be the chief value of philosophy?

5. What do you think Russell means when he characterizes "true philosophic contemplation" as finding satisfaction in the "enlargement of the not-Self"?
6. How does Russell sum up the value of philosophical study? Do you agree with Russell? Why or why not?

On The Value of Philosophy

BERTRAND RUSSELL

HAVING NOW COME TO THE END of our brief and very incomplete review of the problems of philosophy, it will be well to consider, in conclusion, what is the value of philosophy and why it ought to be studied. It is the more necessary to consider this question, in view of the fact that many men, under the influence of science or of practical affairs, are inclined to doubt whether philosophy is anything better than innocent but useless trifling, hair-splitting distinctions, and controversies on matters concerning which knowledge is impossible.

This view of philosophy appears to result, partly from a wrong conception of the ends of life, partly from a wrong conception of the kind of goods which philosophy strives to achieve. Physical science, through the medium of inventions, is useful to innumerable people who are wholly ignorant of it; thus the study of physical science is to be recommended, not only, or primarily, because of the effect on the student, but rather because of the effect on mankind in general. Thus utility does not belong to philosophy. If the study of philosophy has any value at all for others than students of philosophy, it must be only indirectly, through its effects upon the lives of those who study it. It is in these effects, therefore, if anywhere, that the value of philosophy must be primarily sought.

But further, if we are not to fail in our endeavour to determine the value of philosophy, we must first free our minds from the prejudices of what are wrongly called "practical" men. The "practical" man, as this word is often used, is one who recognizes only material needs, who realizes that men must have food for the body, but is oblivious of the necessity of providing food for the mind. If all men were well off, if poverty and disease had been reduced to their lowest possible point, there would still remain much to be done to produce a valuable society; and even in the existing world the goods of the mind are at least as important as the goods of the body. It is exclusively among the goods of the mind that the value of philosophy is to be found; and only those who are not indifferent to these goods can be persuaded that the study of philosophy is not a waste of time.

Philosophy, like all other studies, aims primarily at knowledge. The knowledge it aims at is the kind of knowledge which gives unity and system to the body of the sciences, and the kind which results from a critical examination of the grounds of our convictions, prejudices, and beliefs. But it cannot be maintained that philosophy has had any very great measure of success in its attempts to provide definite answers to its questions. If you ask a mathematician, a mineralogist, a historian, or any other man of learning, what definite body of truths has been ascertained by his science, his answer will last as long as you are willing to listen. But if you put the same question to a philosopher, he will, if he is candid, have to confess that his study has not achieved posi-

From Bertrand Russell, The Problems of Philosophy, *London: Oxford University Press, 1912, pp. 153–161.*
Reprinted by permission of Oxford University Press.

tive results such as have been achieved by other sciences. It is true that this is partly accounted for by the fact that, as soon as definite knowledge concerning any subject becomes possible, this subject ceases to be called philosophy, and becomes a separate science. The whole study of the heavens, which now belongs to astronomy, was once included in philosophy; Newton's great work was called "the mathematical principles of natural philosophy." Similarly, the study of the human mind, which was a part of philosophy, has now been separated from philosophy and has become the science of psychology. Thus, to a great extent, the uncertainty of philosophy is more apparent than real: those questions which are already capable of definite answers are placed in the sciences, while those only to which, at present, no definite answer can be given, remain to form the residue which is called philosophy.

This is, however, only a part of the truth concerning the uncertainty of philosophy. There are many questions—and among them those that are of the profoundest interest to our spiritual life—which, so far as we can see, must remain insoluble to the human intellect unless its powers become of quite a different order from what they are now. Has the universe any unity of plan or purpose, or is it a fortuitous concourse of atoms? Is consciousness a permanent part of the universe, giving hope of indefinite growth in wisdom, or is it a transitory accident on a small planet on which life must ultimately become impossible? Are good and evil of importance to the universe or only to man? Such questions are asked by philosophy, and variously answered by various philosophers. But it would seem that, whether answers be otherwise discoverable or not, the answers suggested by philosophy are none of them demonstrably true. Yet, however slight may be the hope of discovering an answer, it is part of the business of philosophy to continue the consideration of such questions, to make us aware of their importance, to examine all the approaches to them, and to keep alive that speculative interest in the universe which is apt to be killed by confining ourselves to definitely ascertainable knowledge.

Many philosophers, it is true, have held that philosophy could establish the truth of certain answers to such fundamental questions. They have supposed that what is of most importance in religious beliefs could be proved by strict demonstration to be true. In order to judge of such attempts, it is necessary to take a survey of human knowledge, and to form an opinion as to its methods and its limitations. On such a subject it would be unwise to pronounce dogmatically; but if the investigations of our previous chapters have not led us astray, we shall be compelled to renounce the hope of finding philosophical proofs of religious beliefs. We cannot, therefore, include as part of the value of philosophy any definite set of answers to such questions. Hence, once more, the value of philosophy must not depend upon any supposed body of definitely ascertainable knowledge to be acquired by those who study it.

The value of philosophy is, in fact, to be sought largely in its very uncertainty. The man who has no tincture of philosophy goes through life imprisoned in the prejudices derived from common sense, from the habitual beliefs of his age or his nation, and from convictions which have grown up in his mind without the co-operation or consent of his deliberate reason. To such a man the world tends to become definite, finite, obvious; common objects rouse no questions, and unfamiliar possibilities are contemptuously rejected. As soon as we begin to philosophize, on the contrary, we find . . . that even the most everyday things lead to problems to which only very incomplete answers can be given. Philosophy, though unable to tell us with certainty what is the true answer to the doubts which it raises, is able to suggest many possibilities which enlarge our thoughts and free them from the tyranny of custom. Thus, while diminishing our feeling of certainty as to what things are, it greatly increases our knowledge as to what they may be; it removes the somewhat arrogant dogmatism of those who have never travelled into the region of liberating doubt, and it keeps alive our sense of wonder by showing familiar things in an unfamiliar aspect.

Apart from its utility in showing unsuspected possibilities, philosophy has a value—perhaps its chief value—through the greatness of the objects which it contemplates, and the freedom from narrow and personal aims resulting from this contemplation. The life of the instinctive man is shut up within the circle of his private interests: family and friends may be included, but the outer world is not regarded except as it may help or hinder what comes within the circle of instinctive wishes. In such a life there is something feverish and confined, in comparison with which the philosophic life is calm and free. The private world of instinctive interests is a small one, set in the midst of a great and powerful world which must, sooner or later, lay our private world in ruins. Unless we can so enlarge our interests as to include the whole outer world, we remain like a garrison in a beleaguered fortress, knowing that the enemy prevents escape and that ultimate surrender is inevitable. In such a life there is no peace, but a constant strife between the insistence of desire and the powerlessness of will. In one way or another, if our life is to be great and free, we must escape this prison and this strife.

One way of escape is by philosophic contemplation. Philosophic contemplation does not, in its widest survey, divide the universe into two hostile camps—friends and foes, helpful and hostile, good and bad—it views the whole impartially. Philosophic contemplation, when it is unalloyed, does not aim at proving that the rest of the universe is akin to man. All acquisition of knowledge is an enlargement of the Self, but this enlargement is best attained when it is not directly sought. It is obtained when the desire for knowledge is alone operative, by a study which does not wish in advance that its objects should have this or that character, but adapts the Self to the characters which it finds in its objects. This enlargement of Self is not obtained when, taking the Self as it is, we try to show that the world is so similar to this Self that knowledge of it is possible without any admission of what seems alien. The desire to prove this is a form of self-assertion and, like all self-assertion, it is an obstacle to the growth of Self which it desires, and of which the Self knows that it is capable. Self-assertion, in philosophic speculation as elsewhere, views the world as a means to its own ends; thus it makes

the world of less account than Self, and the Self sets bounds to the greatness of its goods. In contemplation, on the contrary, we start from the not-Self, and through its greatness the boundaries of Self are enlarged; through the infinity of the universe the mind which contemplates it achieves some share in infinity.

For this reason greatness of soul is not fostered by those philosophies which assimilate the universe to Man. Knowledge is a form of union of Self and not-Self; like all union, it is impaired by dominion, and therefore by any attempt to force the universe into conformity with what we find in ourselves. There is a widespread philosophical tendency towards the view which tells us that Man is the measure of all things, that truth is man-made, that space and time and the world of universals are properties of the mind, and that, if there be anything not created by the mind, it is unknowable and of no account for us. This view, if our previous discussions were correct, is untrue; but in addition to being untrue, it has the effect of robbing philosophic contemplation of all that gives it value, since it fetters contemplation to Self. What it calls knowledge is not a union with the not-Self, but a set of prejudices, habits, and desires, making an impenetrable veil between us and the world beyond. The man who finds pleasure in such a theory of knowledge is like the man who never leaves the domestic circle for fear his word might not be law.

The true philosophic contemplation, on the contrary, finds its satisfaction in every enlargement of the not-Self, in everything that magnifies the objects contemplated, and thereby the subject contemplating. Everything, in contemplation, that is personal or private, everything that depends upon habit, self-interest, or desire, distorts the object, and hence impairs the union which the intellect seeks. By thus making a barrier between subject and object, such personal and private things become a prison to the intellect. The free intellect will see as God might see, without a *here* and *now*, without hopes and fears, without the trammels of customary beliefs and traditional prejudices, calmly, dispassionately, in the sole and exclusive desire of knowledge—knowledge as impersonal, as purely contemplative, as it is possible for man to attain. Hence also the free intellect will value more the abstract and universal knowledge into which the accidents of private history do not enter, than the knowledge brought by the senses, and dependent, as such knowledge must be, upon an exclusive and personal point of view and a body whose sense-organs distort as much as they reveal.

The mind which has become accustomed to the freedom and impartiality of philosophic contemplation will preserve something of the same freedom and impartiality in the world of action and emotion. It will view its purposes and desires as parts of the whole, with the absence of insistence that results from seeing them as infinitesimal fragments in a world of which all the rest is unaffected by any one man's deeds. The impartiality which, in contemplation, is the unalloyed desire for truth, is the very same quality of mind which, in action, is justice, and in emotion is that universal love which can be given to all, and not only to those who are judged useful or admirable.

Thus contemplation enlarges not only the objects of our thoughts, but also the objects of our actions and our affections: it makes us citizens of the universe, not only of one walled city at war with all the rest. In this citizenship of the universe consists man's true freedom, and his liberation from the thraldom of narrow hopes and fears.

Thus, to sum up our discussion of the value of philosophy: Philosophy is to be studied, not for the sake of any definite answers to its questions, since no definite answers can, as a rule, be known to be true, but rather for the sake of the questions themselves; because these questions enlarge our conception of what is possible, enrich our intellectual imagination and diminish the dogmatic assurance which closes the mind against speculation; but above all because, through the greatness of the universe which philosophy contemplates, the mind also is rendered great, and becomes capable of that union with the universe which constitutes its highest good.

Suggestions for Further Reading

John Passmore's article on "Philosophy" in Volume 6 of *The Encyclopedia of Philosophy* (New York: Macmillan/Free Press, 1967) is a good place to start for an overview of different conceptions of what philosophy is.

For a discussion of philosophy and philosophizing in a global context, see the introduction to *World Philosophies: An Historical Introduction* by David E. Cooper (Oxford, UK: Blackwell, 1996) and the first chapter of *World Philosophies* by Ninian Smart (London: Routledge, 1999).

Relativism: Interpretation and Confrontation, edited by Michael Krauz (Notre Dame, IN: University of Notre Dame Press, 1989) and *Rationality and Relativism,* edited by M. Hollis and S. Lukes (Cambridge, MA: MIT Press, 1982) will take you deeper into the rationality/relativism debate.

The opening chapter of *Whose Justice? Which Rationality?* by Alasdair MacIntyre (Notre Dame, IN: University of Notre Dame Press, 1988) is also useful in stimulating you to think about the importance of tradition in providing a context for agreement, and Donald Davidson's "On the Very Idea of a Conceptual Scheme," from *Inquiries Into Truth and Interpretation* (New York: Oxford University Press, 1985), is a much discussed essay on these issues.

See William James's "The Sentiment of Rationality," in *Essays on Faith and Morals* (New York: World, 1962), pp. 63–110, for a classic statement about what sort of philosophy might create feelings of rationality.

Genevieve Lloyd's *The Man of Reason: "Male" and "Female" in Western Philosophy* (Minneapolis: University of Minnesota Press, 1984) shows how gender has influenced our views of rationality.

See Hans-Georg Gadamer's *Truth and Method* (New York: Seabury Press, 1975) for his notion of truth as the "fusion of horizons."

Videos

The Gods Must Be Crazy (109 minutes, produced by CBS/Fox) compares an encounter between modern technological society and a society of hunter-gatherers in South Africa. Within the first 15 to 20 minutes, you will be able to see how what appears rational to one kind of society appears to be quite "crazy" from the point of view of a very different kind of society.

The instructional videos on "Rationality" and the one on "Relativism," which are part of the premier philosophy television program *No Dogs or Philosophers Allowed* (NDOPA), should stimulate discussion and thought on these topics. They are 60 minutes each and available from Philosophy Documentation Center, Bowling Green State University, Bowling Green, OH 43403-0189.

 You can locate InfoTrac-College Edition articles about this chapter by accessing the InfoTrac-College Edition website (http://www.infotrac-college.com/wadsworth/). Using the InfoTrac-College Edition subject guide, enter the search terms relevant to this chapter, and then read abstracts for relevant articles.

Chapter 2

How Should We Read Philosophy?

> **Learning without thought is labor lost; thought without learning is perilous.**
>
> CONFUCIUS

2.1 Getting Started

READING PHILOSOPHY is both exciting and rewarding. Philosophy provides intellectual stimulation: the pleasure of discovering new ideas, the fascination of following the thread of a provocative argument, the challenge of rethinking inherited beliefs. For these reasons, reading philosophy can be enjoyable, but often it is not easy. Much philosophical writing presents trains of reasoning. To fully appreciate such writing, you must learn to think along with the author. This requires concentration, and so it is best to read philosophy when you are refreshed and alert.

Philosophical texts come in a wide variety of types, ranging from technical essays to dramatic dialogues. They come from different cultures and different historical periods, and they are written in different languages. It is not easy to adjust to this variety. It takes practice to appreciate and understand ancient Greek dialogues, Buddhist fables, seventeenth-century French essays, and Chinese poetry.

Many of us are accustomed to reading *secondary* sources that explain the ideas of others. Textbooks digest what others say, explain it, underline the important points, present summaries, and define technical words. Because much of our education has centered on reading textbooks, we may not be accustomed to wrestling with *primary* sources—the original texts and words—even in translation. If we are not used to digesting material on our own, explaining it to ourselves, learning how to do our own summaries, and looking up words and references we do not understand, then we will find it difficult, at first, to read primary sources. Like anything else that is new, it will take some practice and some help from an instructor.

Voices of Wisdom is a combination of secondary material (my introductions to each chapter and to each selection in the chapters) and primary material (selections from the writings of philosophers past and present). Reading the primary texts may, in some cases, prove a rather difficult task. You will need to learn how to read analytically and critically.

The purpose of *analytical reading* is to find out what the text says and to understand it as best you can. This will require analysis on your part. To analyze something is to break it into parts or smaller units. Thus you will need to distinguish main ideas from supporting ideas and to determine what the author is trying to accomplish.

Critical reading involves evaluation. Your evaluation may be positive, negative, or some mixture of the two. Criticism requires you to make the effort to think about the ideas, analogies, arguments, evidence, and metaphors presented in the text as well as the implications and assumptions.

Here are some suggestions that will help you understand philosophical texts and develop the skills of critical analysis.

1. Read the material at least twice. First, skim it rapidly to get the lay of the land. Pick out the main points to determine with what the author is primarily concerned and what is the overall point of the writing. It is helpful, when doing this, to read the first sentence of every paragraph somewhat carefully on the assumption that it is the topic sentence that tells you what the paragraph is about. Then skim the rest of the paragraph. After skimming the selection reread more carefully, looking for answers to particular reading questions and noting the details.

2. Read actively and with a purpose. Engage the text in a conversation. Imagine the author is speaking directly to you and, as in any conversation, respond to what is being said. Ask questions, look for answers, evaluate, and seek more information about puzzling ideas.

3. Read analytically and sympathetically. Your first task in reading is to analyze and comprehend what the author is saying. Make a list in your own words of the important ideas. See if you can find a short quotation that best expresses the author's main argument. Try to understand the author's viewpoint and the goal he or she is attempting to accomplish. Do not expect to understand everything. Make an "I-don't-understand" list and discuss it in class. It is no sin not to understand and there is nothing wrong with asking questions. That is how we learn.

- Here are some *analytical questions* that you can ask and answer as you read. They will help you understand the selections: (a) What is the thesis (the central idea or main point)? (b) What are the major points made in developing and supporting the thesis? (c) How are key terms defined? (d) What are the basic assumptions made by the author? (e) What are the important implications of the author's position?

In *Voices of Wisdom,* I have provided an introduction to the issues, background material for each of the selections, definitions of key terms (in both the text and a glossary), and a list of reading questions after the introductions and prior to each selection. Make use of this material to help you understand the selection. In addition to your answers to the general analytic questions listed above and the critical questions listed below, write down your answers to the reading questions. Note the ones you could not answer, and discuss them in class.

4. Read critically. Do not believe everything you read. If something seems wrong, it may well be wrong. Formulate, as best you can, *why* something seems wrong to you. If possible, figure out what could be changed to improve the idea or the argument. Make an "I-don't-agree-and-here's-why" list and discuss it in class.

· Here are some *critical questions* that will help you evaluate the strengths and weaknesses of the selections. (a) Is what is said clear? If not, how is it unclear? (b) Are adequate definitions given for important concepts? Can you think of counterexamples?[1] (c) Are the arguments adequate to support the claims; e.g., are the premises true? the assumptions dubious?[2] (d) Do the implications of the text lead to absurd or false consequences? (e) Are important aspects of the issue overlooked? (f) How well did the author accomplish her or his goal?

5. After you have finished, review what you have read. Avoid getting lost in the trees. Stand back and try to see the forest. Can you summarize what you have read in your own words in a single brief paragraph? You may find it helpful to write a critical précis (see below).

6. It is a good idea to keep a "philosophical notebook" in which you record your notes on the readings. This notebook should contain your answers to the reading questions (both the ones I ask in the text and the ones you ask), your "I-don't-understand" list, your "I-don't-agree-and-here's-why" list, your critical précis, and any other thoughts relating to the reading that you wish to record.

2.2 The Critical Précis

Adapting an idea from what Margaret K. Woodworth (1988) calls a "rhetorical précis," we can characterize a *critical précis* as a brief paragraph made up of the following elements. In the first sentence you record the name of the author, the title of the work, appropriate publishing information, a rhetorically accurate verb such as *argues, believes,* or *reports,* and a "that" clause containing the author's thesis or major assertion. The second part explains briefly and accurately how the author supports and develops his or her thesis. Try to keep this to a single sentence if possible. The third part should be a single sentence that states the author's *purpose* for writing. The fourth part is a single sentence describing the author's audience. The fifth part of your critical précis contains your critique or evaluation of what the author says. Once

---

1. The use of counterexamples is a powerful tool for checking the adequacy of definitions. A *counterexample* shares the alleged characteristics of the *definiendum* but is not an example of it, or it is an example of the *definiendum* but does not have the characteristics stated in the definition. A *definiendum* is the idea or concept that is being defined. For example, if I define a human being as a rational animal, someone might point to recent research among advanced primates, such as apes, that indicates these non-human animals can reason rationally as a counterexample of the first type that renders my definition inadequate because it is too broad; that is, it includes animals that are not human. Or someone might cite a newborn human infant as a counterexample of the second type that renders my definition inadequate because it is too narrow; that is, it excludes some things we normally call human.

2. *Statements* are sentences that assert something to be true or false. Notice that all sentences (for example, questions) are not statements in this narrow sense. An *argument* is a sequence of statements used to support, back up, prove, or give reasons for something. A *conclusion* is a statement in an argument that is supported or backed by other statements. A *premise* is a statement in an argument that supports, provides evidence, or gives the reasons for a conclusion. Arguments are inadequate if the premises fail in some way to give adequate support or good reasons why we should think the conclusion true.

again, keep your evaluation brief. Limit it to a single sentence if possible. If feasible, incorporate both a positive and negative evaluation in your brief critique.

As an example of a critical précis, let us re-examine the selection by Bertrand Russell in Section 1.3. The numbers in parentheses correspond to the parts of the critical précis I described in the last paragraph. Before reading my example, review that selection and your answers to the reading questions.

Critical Précis

(1) In "On the Value of Philosophy," from *The Problems of Philosophy* (Oxford, 1912, pp. 153–161) reprinted in Gary E. Kessler, *Voices of Wisdom: A Multicultural Philosophy Reader,* Fourth edition, (Belmont, CA: Wadsworth, 2000, pp. 14–17), Bertrand Russell asserts that the value of philosophy is primarily found in the effect it has on those who study it. (2) He supports his thesis by arguing that if our focus is on attaining knowledge that leads to immediate, material goods, then we will miss the value of philosophical study because such study will supply other types of goods, namely goods that "enlarge our conception of what is possible, enrich our intellectual imagination," diminish dogmatism, and render humans capable of "union with the universe," a union that is the "highest good" of the human mind. (3) Russell's purpose is to convince the reader that the true value of philosophy resides in a type of mental contemplation that makes humans less selfish and narrow-minded. (4) The author appears to be writing to a popular audience of non-philosophers who question the value of philosophical study because they are "practically" minded. (5) Although I think that Russell is right in drawing attention to the contemplative value of philosophy, he fails to sufficiently appreciate its practical value of teaching analytical and critical skills that can be applied to many different concerns.

When constructing the first sentence of the critical précis, it is important to avoid general words like "writes" or "states." Use more specific words that accurately describe what the author is *doing.* Is the author arguing, reporting, indicating, contending, suggesting, or insisting? Also, be sure to use the word *that* rather than words like *how* or *about* after the verb in order to focus on stating the author's *thesis* rather than the *topic* the author is writing about. The thesis is the position or idea the author advocates, whereas the topic is the subject about which the author is writing. Russell's thesis is that the value of philosophical study is to be found in its transforming effect on the life of the student. Russell's topic is the value of philosophy.

The second part of the critical précis requires careful thought and depends, in part, on getting the thesis or major point right. If you cannot figure out what the main point or thesis is, then you will not be able to see how that thesis is developed and supported. If the author is writing in a conventional format, then the main point is usually stated early in the essay, and the middle part of the essay contains the points made in support of the major contention. Often the author will summarize his or her ideas at the end and this will provide a helpful clue to the main ideas and supporting ideas. Notice how heavily I relied on Russell's own summary in constructing part 2 of the précis. Your answers to the analytical questions discussed in Section 2.1 above will help you grasp the author's thesis and the way it is developed.

Figuring out the author's purpose or goal (part 3 of the précis) will help you discern the author's thesis and key ideas. Frequently, particularly in conventional philosophical writing, the goal will be to persuade the reader of the truth of some idea or set of ideas. Ask yourself, "What does the author want me to think or to believe about the topic under consideration?" The answer to that question will often make the author's thesis or major contention clear.

Likewise, identifying the audience in part 4 of the critical précis will enable you to better grasp the author's intent. Sometimes the author will identify the audience explicitly, but frequently you will have to offer your best guess based on the way the material is presented. Learn to read between the lines, as it were, listening for such rhetorical devices as "many men, under the influence of science or of practical affairs, are inclined to doubt. . . ." Russell opens his essay by mentioning these "doubters" of the value of philosophy, and it is a safe assumption that he is addressing these doubters in order to make them believers. If you can figure out to whom the author is writing, you are in a better position to understand such rhetorical characteristics of the author's writing as word choice, order of presentation, choice of examples, use of analogies, and the like. As critical readers we must be sensitive to both *what* is said and *how* it is said.

The fifth and final section of the critical précis requires that you become sensitive to your own reactions to what you have read. As you were reading, when did you hear yourself saying, "Right on. You tell 'em, Bertie." When did you say to yourself, "What on earth is he talking about?" At what point in the essay did you think, "This sounds kinda fishy to me"? Go back over these places and see if you can be more specific about why you agreed or disagreed. This can become the basis of part 5. Also, be sure to ask yourself, "What has the author left out"? Or, "If I were writing on this topic, what would I say?" The answers to the critical questions listed in the last section will help you in writing the fifth part of the critical précis.

Learning the skills of analytical and critical reading will not only help you understand philosophical texts better but also help you understand other kinds of writing as well. Learning to read analytically and critically will move you along the road of independent thinking so that you will find it easier to think through issues and formulate your own ideas about matters that interest you. Becoming an independent thinker requires that you learn to interrogate the texts, to enjoy their insights, and to search for more information, thereby coming to appreciate the stimulation and challenge of reading philosophy. Therefore, you may wish, as time permits, to do further reading relating to the material you have read. At the end of each selection in *Voices of Wisdom* I provide suggestions for further reading that you can pursue if you desire more information about the topic or further clarification and development of important ideas. You can also go to the library or check out the WWW for additional material.

2.3 A Test Case

John Dewey (1859–1952), an American philosopher who had a deep and abiding impact on educational theory and who, along with William James (see Section 7.5), contributed to the development of a type of philosophy called *pragmatism,* argued that we learn by doing. The best way to learn the analytic and critical reading skills discussed above is to apply them. The next selection, by Lawrence A. Blum, a professor of philosophy at the University of Massachusetts at Amherst, provides us with an opportunity to check our understanding of the procedures I have just outlined.

Blum's essay is particularly appropriate because he focuses on the values of multicultural education, which is also the focus of *Voices of Wisdom.* For the most part textbooks that introduce students to philosophy focus on the Western philosophical tradition. European and Anglo-American philosophy and philosophers dominate the standard introductory approaches. However, since 1992 when the first edition of this book appeared, recognition of the value of a multicultural approach to beginning philosophy has been increasing.

Why? What is the particular value of multiculturalism in philosophical education? Are there not some decided drawbacks to lumping African, Native American, and Asian thought with philosophical ideas from Europe and England? Should students not learn the core philosophical writings that have had the greatest impact on the development of professional philosophy as now practiced in most major universities? These core writings are predominately European and Anglo-American—not Asian, African, or even Latin American.

How one evaluates the importance of multiculturalism depends on one's educational goals. Blum argues that in a pluralistic society made up of diverse peoples from different cultural traditions, education should pursue the goal of developing the values of antiracism, multiculturalism, interracial community, and respect for persons as individuals. In the essay that follows, he focuses on the first three values.

First, read the selection rapidly, looking for the main ideas. Second, reread it more carefully and write your answers to the following analytical questions: (1) What is the thesis (the central idea or main point)? (2) What are the major points made in developing and supporting the thesis? (3) How are key terms defined? (4) What are the basic assumptions made by the author? (5) What are the important implications of the author's position? Second, if there are parts of the article you do not understand, indicate them on your "I-don't-understand" list. Third, as you reread, write your answers to the following critical questions: (1) Is what is said clear? If not, how is it unclear? (2) Are adequate definitions given for important concepts? Can you think of counterexamples? (3) Are the arguments adequate to support the claims, e.g., are the premises true? the assumptions dubious? (4) Do the implications of the text lead to absurd or false consequences? (5) Are important aspects of the issue overlooked? (6) How well did the author accomplish her or his goal? Fourth, create an "I-don't-agree and here's why" list.

You should now be in a good position to write a critical précis quickly and easily. Using the instructions and the model provided in Section 2.2 above, write a critical précis of Lawrence A. Blum's article, "Antiracism, Multiculturalism, and Interracial Community: Three Educational Values for a Multicultural Society."

Check your answers to the analytical and critical questions and compare your critical précis with those your classmates have written. In your discussions, focus on the differences and the areas of difficulty. Doing all this may be time-consuming and difficult at first, but after a little practice you will be able to do it more easily and more quickly. Your confidence in your reading ability will increase, and your comprehension of philosophical writing (as well as other types of writing) will improve.

Antiracism, Multiculturalism, and Interracial Community: Three Educational Values for a Multicultural Society

LAWRENCE A. BLUM

I WANT TO ARGUE that there are a plurality of values that one would want taught in schools and families. None of these can be reduced to the others, nor can any take the place of the others. Without claiming comprehensiveness for my list I want to suggest that there are at least four values, or families of values, essential to a program of value education for a multiracial society. . . .

The first value is *antiracism* or *opposition* to racism:

Racism is the denial of the fundamental moral equality of all human beings. It involves the expression of attitudes of superior worth or merit justifying or underpinning the domination or unjust advantage of some groups over others. Antiracism as a value involves striving to be without racist attitudes oneself as well as being prepared to work against both racist attitudes in others and racial injustice in society more generally.

The second value is *multiculturalism:*

Multiculturalism involves an understanding, appreciation and valuing of one's own culture, and an informed respect and curiosity about the ethnic culture of others. It involves a valuing of other cultures, not in the sense of approving of all aspects of those cultures, but of attempting to see how a given culture can express value to its own members.

The third value is a sense of *community*, and in particular an *interracial community:*

This involves a sense, not necessarily explicit or articulated, that one possesses human bonds with persons of other races and ethnicities. The bonds may, and ideally should, be so broad as to

encompass all of humanity; but they may also be limited to the bonds formed in friendships, schools, workplaces, and the like.

The fourth value is *treating persons as individuals:*

This involves recognizing the individuality of each person—specifically, that while an individual person is a member of an ethnic or racial group, and while that aspect may be an important part of who she is, she is more than that ethnic or racial identity. It is the lived appreciation of this individuality, not simply paying lip service to it, that constitutes the value I will call treating persons as individuals. . . .

Again, I claim that these four are distinct though related values, and that all of them are essential to multicultural value education. Failure to appreciate their distinctness poses the danger that one of them will be neglected in a value education program. At the same time there are natural convergences and complementarities among the four values taken in any combination; there are ways of teaching each value that support the promotion of each one of the other values. On the other hand, I will claim, there can also be tensions, both practical and theoretical, between various of the values; that is, some ways of teaching one of the values may work against the conveying of one of the others. Since the values can be either convergent or in tension, it will be crucial to search for ways of teaching them that minimize the tension and support the convergences.

I have designated *antiracism* as the first value for this value education. In contrast to the three others, this one is stated negatively—in opposition to something rather than as a positive goal to be striven for. Why do I not refer to this value positively as "racial equality" or "racial justice"? One reason is that the oppositional definition brings out that a central aspect of the value of antiracism involves countering an evil and not just promoting a good. An important component of what children need to be taught is how to notice, to confront, to oppose, and to work toward the elimination of manifestations of racism. Particular moral abilities and traits of character, involving certain forms of empowerment, are required for activities of *opposition* that are not required merely for the promotion of a good goal. Of course, antiracism does presuppose the positive value of racial justice; hence, the positive element is implicitly contained in the value of antiracism.

To understand the value of antiracism we must first understand *racism*. The term racism, while a highly charged and condemnatory one, has no generally agreed upon meaning. On the one hand all can agree that using a racial slur, telling a Chicano student that one does not like Chicanos and wishes they were not in one's school, or carving "KKK" on . . . [an] African-American student's door, are racist acts. At the same time the conservative writer Dinesh D'Souza has given voice to a suspicion, shared I am sure by others, that the term "racism" is in danger of losing its meaning and moral force through a too broad usage.

I agree that there has sometimes been a tendency to inflate the meaning of the word racism so it becomes virtually a catchall term for any behavior concerning race or race relations that its user strongly condemns. This development ill serves those like myself who wish racism to be taken more seriously than it presently is. Like the boy who cried "wolf," the inflation of the concept of racism to encompass phenomena with questionable connection to its core meaning desensitizes people to the danger, horror, and wrongfulness of true racism.

Here is my definition of racism, which I present without further defense: Racism refers both to an institutional or social structure of racial domination or injustice—as when we speak of a racist institution—and also to individual actions, beliefs, and attitudes, whether consciously held or not, which express, support or justify the superiority of one racial group to another. Thus, on both the individual and institutional levels, racism involves denying or violating the equal dignity and worth of all human beings independent of race; and, on both levels, racism is bound up with dominance and hierarchy.

There are three components of (the value of) *antiracism* as I see it.

One is the belief in the equal worth of all persons regardless of race, not just as an intellectual matter, but rooted more deeply in one's attitudes and emotions; this is to have what one might call a *nonracist* moral consciousness. But it is not enough to learn to be nonracist as an individual; students must also be taught to *understand* the particularity of racism as a psychological and historical phenomenon. This is partly because one aspect of antiracism is learning to perceive racism and to recognize when it is occurring. Just being nonracist cannot guarantee this. For one may sincerely subscribe to the right principles of racial justice and yet not see particular instances of racism right under one's nose, in either institutional or individual forms; for example, not recognizing unintended patterns of exclusion of people of color, or not recognizing a racial stereotype.

There are three components to this second feature of antiracism (understanding racism). The first is the *psychological* dynamic of racism, such as scapegoating and stereotyping, rigidity and fear of difference, rationalization of privilege and power, projecting of unwanted wishes onto others, and other psychological processes contributing to racist attitudes. The second is the *historical* dynamic of racism in its particular forms: slavery, colonialism, segregation, Nazism, the mistreatment of native Americans, and the like. Involved also must be learning about movements *against* racism, such as abolitionism, civil rights movements, and the black power movement; and learning about institutional racism as well. The third component is the role of *individuals* in sustaining or resisting racist institutions, patterns, and systems—how individuals can change racist structures; how they may contribute to or help to perpetuate racist patterns even if they themselves are not actually racist.

Studying the historical dynamics of racism necessarily involves teaching the victimization of some groups by others. While some conservative critics of multicultural education ridicule and derogate focusing on a group's history as victims of racism, it would nevertheless be intellectually irresponsible not to do so. One can hardly understand the historical experience of African-Americans without slavery, of Jews without the Holocaust, of Asian-Americans without the historic barriers to citizenship and to family life and without the World War II internment camps.

Nevertheless, from the point of view of historical accuracy as well as that of value education, it is vital not to *confine* the presentation of a group to its status as victim. One needs to see subordinate groups as agents in their own history—not just as suffering victimization but as responding to it, sometimes by active resistance both cultural and political, sometimes by passive resistance, sometimes by accommodation. The study of social history is invaluable here in providing the framework for seeing that victims made their own history in the face of their victimization, and for giving concrete embodiment to the philosophical truth that human beings retain the capacity for agency even when oppressed and dominated by others.

The third component of antiracist education (in addition to nonracism and understanding racism) is *opposition to racism;* for nonracism implies only that one does all one can to avoid racism in *one's own* actions and attitudes. This is insufficient, for students need also to develop a sense of responsibility concerning manifestations of racism in other persons and in the society more generally. For example, since students will almost inevitably witness racist acts, to confine their own responsibility simply to ensuring that they individually do not participate in such actions themselves is to give students a mixed message about how seriously they are being asked to take racism.

• • •

The second educational value, *multiculturalism,* encompasses the following three subvalues: (a) affirming one's own cultural identity; learning

about and valuing one's own cultural heritage; (b) respecting and desiring to understand and learn about (and from) cultures other than one's own; (c) valuing and taking delight in cultural diversity itself; that is, regarding the existence of distinct cultural groups within one's own society as a positive good to be treasured and nurtured. The kind of respect involved in the second condition (respecting others) is meant to be an informed (and not uncritical) respect grounded in an understanding of another culture. It involves an attempt to see the culture from the point of view of its members and in particular to see how members of that culture value the expression of their own culture. It involves an active interest in and ability in some way to enter into and to enjoy the cultural expressions of other groups.

Such an understanding of another culture in no way requires an affirmation of every feature of that culture as positively good, as some critics of multiculturalism fear (or at least charge). It does not preclude criticism, on the basis either of norms of that culture itself which particular practices in that culture might violate, or of standards external to that culture. Of course when it is legitimate to use a standard external to a culture (e.g., a particular standard of equality between men and women drawn from the Western liberal tradition) is a complex issue. And multiculturalism always warns both against using a legitimate criticism of some feature of a culture as moral leverage to condemn the culture as a whole—declaring it not worthy of serious curricular attention, or disqualifying it as a source of moral insight to those outside that culture, for example—as well as alerting us to the difficult-to-avoid failure to scrutinize the basis of that criticism for its own cultural bias. Nevertheless, multiculturalism need not and should not identify itself with the view that members of one culture never have the moral standing to make an informed criticism of the practices of another culture.

The outward directedness of the second feature of multiculturalism (respecting other cultures) is an important complement to the inward focus of the first feature (learning about and valuing one's own culture). This dual orientation meets the criticism sometimes made of multi-culturalism that it creates divisions between students. For the second feature prescribes a reaching out beyond one's own group and thus explicitly counters the balkanizing effect of the first dimension of multiculturalism alone. Nevertheless, that first feature—learning about and valuing one's own culture—is an integral part of multiculturalism, not merely something to be tolerated, treated as a response to political pressure, or justified simply on the grounds of boosting self-esteem. An individual's cultural identity is a deeply significant element of herself, and understanding of her own culture should be a vital part of the task of education. An understanding of one's own culture as contributing to the society of which one is a part is a significant part of that first element of multiculturalism.

The third component of multiculturalism is the valuing of diversity itself. Not only do we want our young people to respect specific other cultures but also to value a school, a city, a society in which diverse cultural groups exist. While this diversity may certainly present problems for young people, one wants them to see the diversity primarily as something to value, prefer, and cherish.

Three dimensions of culture seem to be deserving of curricular and other forms of educational attention in schools. The first is the *ancestor culture* of the ethnic group, nation, or civilization of origin. For Chinese-Americans this would involve understanding Chinese culture, including ancient Chinese cultures, philosophies, religions, and the like. For Irish-Americans it would be Irish history and culture. For Mexican-Americans it would include attention to some of the diverse cultures of Mexico—the Aztec, the Mayan, as well as the Spanish, and then the hybrid Spanish/indigenous culture which forms modern Mexican culture.

While all ethnic cultures have an ancestor culture, not all current groups bear the same relationship to that ancestor culture. For example, African-Americans' connection to their ancestor culture is importantly different from that of immigrant groups like Italians, Eastern European Jews, and Irish. Although scholars disagree about the actual extent of influence of various African

cultures on current African-American cultural forms, it was a general feature of American slavery systematically to attempt to deprive African slaves of their African culture. By contrast voluntary immigrant groups brought with them an intact culture, which they renegotiated in the new conditions of the United States. In fact the label "African-American" can be seen as an attempt to forge a stronger analogy between the experience of black Americans and that of other immigrant groups than do other expressions, such as "black" or even "Afro-American." The former conceptualization emphasizes that American blacks are not simply a product of America but do indeed possess an ancestor culture, no matter how brutally that culture was attacked. Note, however, that there is an important difference between this use of "African-American" and that applied, for example, to "second-generation Ethiopian-Americans." The latter is truer parallel to white ethnic "hyphenate Americans."

Other differences among groups, such as the current ethnic group's distance in time from its original emigration, variations and pressures to assimilate once in the United States, and the effects of racism affect the significance of the ancestor for culture for a current ethnic group. Nevertheless ancestor culture plays some role for every group.

A second dimension of culture to be encompassed by multicultural education is the *historical experience* of the ethnic group within the United States. Generally it will attend to the historical experiences, ways of life, triumphs and setbacks, art and literature, contributions and achievements, of ethnic groups in the United States. The latter point is uncontroversial; all proponents of multicultural education agree in the need to correct the omission in traditional curricula, and text books of many ethnic groups' experiences and contributions to our national life. But distinguishing this dimension from the ancestor culture and giving attention to both of them is crucial. For the culture of the Chinese-American is *not* the same as the culture of traditional or modern China; it is a culture with its own integrity: neither the purer form of ancestor culture nor that of middle-America. It can be called "intercultural," influenced by more than one culture (as indeed the ancestor culture itself may have been), yet forming a culture in its own right.

A third dimension of culture is the *current ethnic culture* of the group in question. This is the dimension most directly embodied in the student member of that culture. This current ethnic culture—family ethnic rituals, foods, customs regarding family roles and interactions, values, musical and other cultural preferences, philosophies of life, and the like—bears complex relationships to the ancestor culture as well as to the group's historical ethnic experience in the United States. It changes over time and is affected in myriad ways by the outer society. As with ancestor culture and historical ethnic experience, the student's current ethnic culture must be given respect. What such respect consists in is a complex matter, as the following examples indicate.

In one case respect can involve allowing Arab girls to wear traditional headgear in school if they so desire. In another it can mean seeing a child's remark in class as containing insight stemming from her cultural perspective that might otherwise be missed or seem off the mark. Another form of respect for culture involves, for example, recognizing that a Vietnamese child's failure to look a teacher in the eye is not a sign of evasiveness or lack of interest but a way of expressing a deference to teachers and authority, culturally regarded as appropriate. Thus, respect for ethnic cultures sometimes involves a direct valorizing of a part of that culture; at other times neither valorizing nor disvaluing, but allowing for its expression because it is important to the student. In another context, it can involve reshaping one's own sense of what is educationally essential, to take into account another culture's difference. Finally, it can sometimes involve seeing a cultural manifestation as a genuine obstacle to learning but respecting the cultural setting in which it is embedded and the student's own attachment to that cultural feature, and finding ways to work with or around that obstacle to accomplish an educational goal.

In summary, ancestor culture, ethnic historical experience in the United States, and current ethnic culture are three dimensions of ethnic culture requiring attention in a multicultural education. They are all dimensions that children need to be taught and taught to respect—both in their own and other's cultures.

The context of multicultural education presupposes a larger society consisting of various cultures. Thus, teaching an attitude of appreciation toward a particular one of these cultures in the three dimensions just mentioned will have both a particular and general aspect. We will want students to appreciate cultures in their own right, but also in their relationship to the larger society. This simple point can help us to avoid two familiar, and contrasting, pitfalls of multicultural education, that can be illustrated with the example of Martin Luther King, Jr.

One pitfall would be exemplified by a teacher who portrayed King as an important leader of the black community, but who failed to emphasize that he should be seen as a great *American* leader more generally—as a true hero for all Americans, indeed for all humanity, and not *only* for or of African-Americans. The teacher fails to show the non-African-American students that they too have a connection with King simply as Americans.

Yet an exactly opposite pitfall is to teach appreciation of the contribution of members of particular cultures *only* insofar as those contributions can be seen in universal terms or in terms of benefiting the entire society. This pitfall would be exemplified by seeing Dr. King only in terms of his contribution to humanity or to American society more generally, but *not* acknowledging him as a product and leader specifically of the African-American community. Multicultural education needs to enable non-African-American students (whether white or not) to be able to appreciate a leader of the African-American community in that role itself, and not *only* by showing that the leader in question made a contribution to everyone in the society. Thus, multicultural education needs to emphasize both the general or full society dimension of each culture's contributions and heroes and also the particular or culture-specific dimension.

Many people associate multiculturalism with the idea of moral *relativism* or cultural relativism and specifically with the view that because no one from one culture is in a position to judge another culture, no one is in a position to say which culture should be given priority in the allocation of respect, curricular inclusion, and the like. Therefore, according to this way of thinking, every culture has a claim to equal inclusion and respect, because no one is in a position to say which ones are *more* worthy of respect. While the philosophic relativism on which this version of multiculturalism rests needs to be taken seriously—it has a long and distinguished philosophic history—there is an alternative, quite different and non-relativistic, philosophic foundation for multiculturalism as well. This view—which might be called *pluralistic*—agrees that cultures manifest different values but affirms that the values of a given culture can be, or can come to be, appreciated (as well as assessed) by someone from a different culture. Thus, while cultures are different, they are at least partly accessible to one another.

According to this pluralist, nonrelativist line of thought, multicultural education should involve exposing students to, and helping them to appreciate the range of, values embodied in different cultures. Both whites and Cambodian immigrant students can come to appreciate Toni Morrison's novels of black life in America. African-American students can come to understand and appreciate Confucian philosophy. This pluralist view should not minimize the work often necessary to see beyond the parochial assumptions and perspectives of one's own culture in order to appreciate the values of another culture. Indeed, one of the undoubted contributions of the multicultural movement has been to reveal those obstacles as well as the dominant culture's resistance to acknowledging them. Nevertheless, the fact that such an effort can be even partially successful provides a goal of multicultural education that is barely conceivable within the pure relativist position.

• • •

The third value for an educational program that I want to discuss is the *sense of community*—specifically a sense of community that embraces racial and cultural differences. While the idea of a multiracial integrated community has historically been linked with the struggle against racism, I think there is reason for focusing on it as a value distinct from antiracism. The sense of community that I mean involves a sense of bond with other persons, a sense of shared identification with the community in question (be it a class, a school or workplace), a sense of loyalty to and involvement with this community. I will make the further assumption that the experience of interracial community in such institutions is an important contributor to being able fully to experience members of other races and cultures as fellow citizens and fellow human beings throughout one's life.

It is true that the achievement of or the experience of interracial community is likely to contribute to a firm commitment to nonracist and antiracist values. Nevertheless, there is an important difference between the two families of values. A sense of community is defeated not only by racist attitudes, in which members of one group feel themselves superior to members of another group, but simply by experiencing members of other races and cultural groups as *other,* as distant from oneself, as people with whom one does not feel comfortable, and has little in common. . . . What defeats a sense of community is to see members of a group primarily as *they,* as a kind of undifferentiated group counterposed to a *we,* defined by the group one identifies with oneself. One becomes blind to the individuality of members of the *they* group. One experiences this group as deeply different from oneself, even if one cannot always account for or explain that sense of difference. This anticommunal consciousness can exist in the absence of actual racist attitudes towards the other group, although the former is a natural stepping stone toward the latter. I think many students in schools, of all races and cultures, never do achieve the experience of interracial community, never learn to feel comfortable with members of other racial and ethnic groups, even though these students do not really have racist attitudes in the strict sense. Rather, the sense of group difference simply overwhelms any experiencing of commonality and sharing that is necessary for developing a sense of community.

Fortunately, we need not choose between the values of interracial community and antiracism; rather, we should search for ways of teaching antiracist values that minimize the potential for harming or preventing interracial community. I will briefly mention two general guidelines in this regard. One is constantly to emphasize the internal variety within a group being studied; not to say "whites" and "blacks" all the time as if these were monolithic groups. For example, in discussing slavery, make clear that not all blacks were slaves during the period of slavery, that there were many free blacks. Similarly, most whites did *not* own slaves, and a few whites even actively aligned themselves with the cause of abolition, aiding free blacks who organized the underground railroads and the like. Exhibiting such internal variety within "white," "black," and other groups helps to prevent the formation of rigid or undifferentiated images of racial groups that lend themselves readily to a *we/they* consciousness that undermines community.

A second guideline is to try to give students the experience (in imagination at least) of being both discriminated against, excluded, or demeaned, and also being the discriminator, the excluder, the advantaged one. . . .

Encouraging students to attempt as much as possible to experience the vantage points of advantaged and disadvantaged, included and excluded, and the like, provides an important buffer to a "we/they" consciousness in the racial domain. This buffering is accomplished not so much by encouraging, as the first guideline does, the appreciation of internal diversity in a given group, as by bridging the gulf between the experience of the dominant and that of the subordinate. This is achieved by showing children that there is at least *some* dimension of life on which they occupy the dominant, and on others the subordinate, position (even if these dimensions are not of equal significance). . . .

Finally, our conception of interracial community must itself allow for the recognition of difference. A powerful, but misleading, tradition in our thinking about community is that people only feel a sense of community when they think of themselves as "the same" as the other members of the community. But, as Robert Bellah[1] and his colleagues argue in *Habits of the Heart,* the kind of community needed in the United States is *pluralistic* community, one which involves a sense of bond and connection stemming from shared activity, condition, task, location, and the like—and grounded ultimately in an experience of shared humanity—yet recognizing and valuing cultural differences (and other kinds of differences as well).

1. Robert Bellah, et al., *Habits of the Heart: Individualism and Commitment in American Life* (Berkeley: University of California Press, 1985).

Suggestions for Further Reading

The following will provide more information on the skill of reading effectively: Andrew Harnack, "Reading Critically" in *Writing Research Papers: A Student Guide for Use with OPPOS-ING VOICES®* (San Diego, CA: Greenhaven Press, 1994. 1–13); E. D. Klemke, et. al. "Introduction: Philosophy and the Study of Philosophy" in *Philosophy: The Basic Issues.* Third Edition (New York: St. Martin's Press, 1990. 1–24); Jay F. Rosenberg, "Six Ways to Read a Philosopher," *The Practice of Philosophy: A Handbook for Beginners.* Third Edition (Upper Saddle River, NJ: Prentice Hall, 1996. 110–113); and Margaret K. Woodworth, "The Rhetorical Précis." *Rhetoric Review* 7:1 (Fall 1988): 156–63.

Those wishing to pursue the topic of multiculturalism should consult *Multiculturalism: Examining the Politics of Recognition,* expanded edition, edited by Amy Gutmann (Princeton, NJ: Princeton University Press, 1994); *Multiculturalism: A Critical Reader,* edited by David Theo Goldberg (Cambridge, MA: Basil Blackwell, 1994); and *Campus Wars: Multiculturalism and the Politics of Difference,* edited by John Arthur and Amy Shapiro (Boulder, CO: Westview Press, 1995).

Is Multiculturalism Bad For Women?, edited by Joshua Cohen, et. al., features a lead essay by Susan Moller Okin followed by responses on issues of tolerating cultures that have oppressive practices (Princeton, NJ: Princeton University Press, 1999).

Videos

Both *Cross-Cultural Communication in Diverse Settings* (60 minutes) and *Valuing Diversity: Multicultural Communication* (19 minutes) probe the difficulties of communicating across cultures and are available from Insight Media, 2162 Broadway, New York, NY 10024. *What Should an Educated Person Know?* (30 minutes) is Bill Moyers's interview with John Searle. Searle advocates a core of Western works with "some" works from other cultures as long as they meet certain criteria. Available from Films for the Humanities and Sciences, PO Box 2053, Princeton, NJ 08543.

 You can locate InfoTrac-College Edition articles about this chapter by accessing the InfoTrac-College Edition website (http://www.infotrac-college.com/wadsworth/). Using the InfoTrac-College Edition subject guide, enter the search terms relevant to this chapter, and then read abstracts for relevant articles.

Ethics

Chapter 3

How Should One Live?

> **The superior person is open-minded and not partisan.**
> CONFUCIUS

3.1 Introduction

Have you ever wondered about how one should live? Should we live compassionately, pursuing a wisdom that liberates us from suffering? Should we live a virtuous and sincere life of balance, harmony, and family loyalty? Perhaps we should live a life of critical reflection, searching for truth and following an argument wherever it may lead. Should we live in pursuit of happiness? What exactly is happiness? How can we attain it? Perhaps we must unselfishly do what duty demands in devotion to God. Few of us would deny that we should live a meaningful life. A life without meaning and purpose is not desirable. However, what is a meaningful life, and how can it be pursued in a world that constantly threatens boredom if not meaninglessness?

The question of how one should live is fundamental to human existence. It is a question that has concerned ancient and modern peoples, Eastern and Western cultures. What do you understand by the question? If you had to write an essay on the topic, how would you begin? "One should live the good life," you might say. That seems a sensible way to start. The next question is, of course, what is the good life? Notice that the term "the good life" is both **ambiguous** (it can mean many different things and often it is not clear precisely to what it refers) and **vague** because the line between a good life and a bad life is not always clear. Is the good life one that is personally satisfying or a life possessing moral merit? Can it be both? Should it be both?

Let us assume that the good life is both, namely a personally satisfying life and a life of moral worth. Proceeding on this assumption you can continue your essay by exploring what is most important to you. What sorts of things do you value the most? Health? Wealth? Pleasure? However, just because you desire certain things, does that mean you *ought* to desire them? Desiring something is one thing, but claiming you ought to desire it is something else. The search for what is personally satisfying sooner or later runs into the issue of moral merit, and, if we assume the good life should be both personally satisfying and morally worthwhile, we must now explore the question in more depth.

What does *ought* have to do with this question about conducting one's life? "How *should* one live?" is not the same question as "How *ought* one to live?" You might say "I should go to the store," but that does not mean that you "ought" to in the sense that you are morally obligated to do so. Even so your sense of what you are morally obligated to do often grows out of your sense of what you should do.

Who is the "one" whom this question addresses? It is an impersonal one. "How should *one* live?" is not the same question as "How should *I* live?" So does your answer hold good for you alone? What about others? Is there one way we all ought to live? Writing an essay about how you think you should live is one thing. Writing an essay about how you think everyone ought to live is another matter. For one thing, the latter essay is a lot more difficult to write.*

If you have ever wondered about how you or anyone else ought to live, you have been concerned with what philosophers call *ethics* or *moral philosophy*. Ethics comes from the Greek word *ethos,* which means "character." For the Greeks, ethics had to do with developing a virtuous character. They believed that if you develop such a character, you will not only know the right thing to do but also do it.

Today we use the word *ethics* in many different ways. Sometimes it refers to moral rules or a way of life based on a religiously inspired moral code. We speak of "Christian ethics" or "Buddhist ethics." However, sometimes it refers to the secular study of moral values and a search for the principles of right moral action. As a branch of philosophy, "ethics" is used in this latter sense to refer to reflection on or study of moral issues. It is concerned with such questions as: What is the morally right way to live? How can I know what is morally right? How can I decide morally difficult cases? What makes a society just?

We can answer moral questions in different ways. One way is **descriptive**. We might *describe* the kinds of values people have and the sorts of principles they use in making moral judgments. Another way is **normative**. Normative reflection has to do with trying to discover *norms* or principles by which we *ought* to live. Many philosophers maintain that ethics is primarily a normative study. It is not only a description of what people find morally good and morally bad; it also seeks to discover norms that ought to guide our actions.

Although we can distinguish the kinds of questions moral philosophers ask, the answers often blend into one another. An answer to the question about how one should live will sooner or later have to address such issues as how we can know what is right, whether justice is possible, whether God exists, whether there is life after death, and many more. The readings in this chapter directly address the question of how one should live, in a broad sense, but this same question is addressed, in one way or another, by many of the other readings in *Voices of Wisdom*.

One useful way to approach the brief sampling of answers (which follow) to the question about how one should live is to see if you can find, explicitly or implicitly, answers to a set of what, how, and why questions. *What* is the good life? That is, what, according to the philosophers sampled here, is the goal of human life? Is the good life understood to be one that is primarily personally fulfilling or one of moral value? Is it understood to be both? *How* is the good life attained? That is, what are

---

*See Chapter 1, "Socrates' Question," in *Ethics and the Limits of Philosophy* by Bernard Williams (Cambridge, MA: Harvard University Press, 1985) for a discussion of the various ways the question "How should one live?" can be understood and for Williams's recommendation that we *not* take it in the sense of a question about obligation. He argues that Western philosophy would do well to return to this question as the starting point of ethical reflection. Also see John Kekes, *The Morality of Pluralism* (Princeton, NJ: Princeton University Press, 1993) for an argument in support of moral pluralism (there are many good ways to live) and against moral monism (there is only one good way to live).

the means that the author recommends that would lead one (presumably) to the goal of living a good life. *Why* is the life as described a good one? That is, is the goal of human life the author envisions appropriate and right? Why is the means recommended appropriate? That is, what reasons (if any) does the author give for thinking that the means will in fact lead to the goal? The "why" question asks you to find out how the philosopher justifies his or her answer. At least two sorts of justification are called for: (1) a justification of the goal and (2) a justification of the means. You may wish to set up a grid on which you can write brief answers to these questions based on your reading and then compare the answers that are given.

Table 2.1

	BUDDHA	CONFUCIUS	SOCRATES	ARISTOTLE	GITA	KOLAK & MARTIN
What						
How						
Why						

Analyzing the answers in this way not only allows you to discern differences and similarities among the answers but also provides an opportunity for you to evaluate the answers. Is the good life as described or presupposed truly good? Can you think of a better one? Are the justifications adequate? Why should we think that the way to live (the means) will result in a good life? Maybe there is something the authors have overlooked. What about luck? Maybe living a good life is not a matter of choice but dumb luck. Can we attain a good life if we live in a horrible society? Does social harmony or social disintegration have anything to do with it? What about illness or poverty? Are these significant factors?

As you read and think through these questions, your own understanding of the question and the issues should deepen, and your own answer should become clearer. What do you think the good life is, and how do you think it can be attained?

3.2 The Buddha and the Middle Way

The word *Buddha,* which means "the Enlightened One," is the title bestowed on Siddhartha Gautama, who was born into a royal family in Nepal around 563 BCE. He lived a life of luxury and pleasure in the palace. On a trip outside the palace, he became aware of the suffering (*dukkha*) of humans. He witnessed people experiencing disease, old age, and death. At the age of twenty-nine, he left his life of comfort and became an ascetic in search of the solution to the problem of suffering.

Siddhartha studied with the sages of his day and practiced extreme austerities. Ironically, he nearly starved himself to death in his search for the answer to suffering. However, he found no satisfactory answer, either from his teachers or from his extreme ascetic practices. Eventually, he went his own way. One evening, he seated himself under a tree (later called the Bo-tree, or Tree of Enlightenment) and resolved not to stir from meditation until he discovered how to overcome suffering. He attained enlightenment and henceforth was called the Buddha.

After his enlightenment, he taught the wisdom he had realized and the practice for attaining that wisdom because he wished to help others gain **nirvana**, the release from suffering. He was convinced, based on his experience, that human beings should live free from suffering and that such a life was possible. He taught for forty-five years and founded an order of monks. He died at the age of eighty, in 483 BCE, thirteen years before Socrates (see Section 3.4 below) was born. From his teachings, a religion called Buddhism has grown and spread throughout Asia and much of the rest of the world. It is divided into three main groups: Theravada (Way of the Elders), Mahayana (Greater Vehicle), and Vajrayana (Diamond Vehicle). His teachings also inspired philosophical reflection, and various philosophical schools have also developed. Here we are primarily interested in Buddha, the philosopher or lover of wisdom, rather than Buddha, the religious founder.

What follows is one selection from the "Long Discourses" (*Digha Nikaya*, Sutta 22:18–22), attributed to the Buddha himself, concerning the **Four Noble Truths**. These constitute the heart of his message and presumably express, in condensed form, what he learned under the Bo-tree. The second selection is a commentary, from a Theravadan viewpoint, on the Fourth Noble Truth (also called the **Middle Way** or the **Eightfold Path**) by a contemporary Sri Lankan Buddhist scholar, Dr. Walpola Rahula.

Reading Questions

As you read the first selection, see if you can answer these questions:
1. What is *suffering?*
2. What is the relationship between *craving* and *pleasure?*
3. Why does the Buddha teach that the cessation of suffering (Third Noble Truth) is the extinction of craving?
   As you read the commentary by Rahula, see if you can answer these questions:
4. Why is the Fourth Noble Truth called the Middle Path?
5. What is the relationship between compassion and wisdom?
6. What is the difference between *knowing accordingly* and *penetration?* Can you give an example of each from your own experience?
7. What is the good life, according to the Buddha, and how would he answer the question, "How should one live?" Do you agree? Why, or why not?

The Four Noble Truths

THE BUDDHA

17. "AGAIN, MONKS, a monk abides contemplating mind-objects as mind-objects in respect of the Four Noble Truths. How does he do so?

Here, a monk knows as it really is: 'This is suffering'; he knows as it really is: 'This is the origin of suffering'; he knows as it really is: 'This is

From Thus Have I Heard: The Long Discourses of the Buddha: Digha Nikaya, *translated by Maurice Walshe, 1987, pp. 344–349. Reprinted by permission of Wisdom Publications, Boston.*

the cessation of suffering'; he knows as it really is: 'This is the way of practice leading to the cessation of suffering.'

18. "And what, monks, is the Noble Truth of Suffering? Birth is suffering, aging is suffering, death is suffering, sorrow, lamentation, pain, sadness and distress are suffering. Being attached to the unloved is suffering, being separated from the loved is suffering, not getting what one wants is suffering. In short, the five aggregates of grasping are suffering. . . .

"And how, monks, in short, are the five aggregates of grasping suffering? They are as follows: the aggregate of grasping that is form, the aggregate of grasping that is feeling, the aggregate of grasping that is perception, the aggregate of grasping that is the mental formations, the aggregate of grasping that is consciousness. These are, in short, the five aggregates of grasping that are suffering.[1] And that, monks, is called the Noble Truth of Suffering.

19. "And what, monks, is the Noble Truth of the Origin of Suffering? It is that craving which gives rise to rebirth, bound up with pleasure and lust, finding fresh delight now here, now there: that is to say sensual craving, craving for existence, and craving for non-existence.

"And where does this craving arise and establish itself? Wherever in the world there is anything agreeable and pleasurable, there this craving arises and establishes itself.

"And what is there in the world that is agreeable and pleasurable? The eye in the world is agreeable and pleasurable, the ear . . . , the nose . . . , the tongue . . . , the body . . . , the mind in the world is agreeable and pleasurable, and there this craving arises and establishes itself. Sights, sounds, smells, tastes, tangibles, mind-objects in the world are agreeable and pleasurable, and there this craving arises and establishes itself.

"The craving for sights, sounds, smells, tastes, tangibles, mind-objects in the world is agreeable and pleasurable, and there this craving arises and establishes itself.[2]

"Thinking of sights, sounds, smells, tastes, tangibles, mind-objects in the world is agreeable and pleasurable, and there this craving arises and establishes itself.

"Pondering on sights, sounds, smells, tastes, tangibles and mind-objects in the world is agreeable and pleasurable, and there this craving arises and establishes itself. And that, monks, is called the Noble Truth of the Origin of Suffering.

20. "And what, monks, is the Noble Truth of the Cessation of Suffering? It is the complete fading-away and extinction of this craving, its forsaking and abandonment, liberation from it, detachment from it. And how does this craving come to be abandoned, how does its cessation come about? . . .

21. "And what, monks, is the Noble Truth of the Way of Practice Leading to the Cessation of Suffering? It is just this Noble Eightfold Path, namely:—Right View, Right Thought; Right Speech, Right Action, Right Livelihood; Right Effort, Right Mindfulness, Right Concentration.

"And what, monks, is Right View? It is, monks, the knowledge of suffering, the knowledge of the origin of suffering, the knowledge of the cessation of suffering, and the knowledge of the way of practice leading to the cessation of suffering. This is called Right View.

"And what, monks, is Right Thought? The thought of renunciation, the thought of non-ill-will, the thought of harmlessness. This, monks, is called Right Thought.

"And what, monks, is Right Speech? Refraining from lying, refraining from slander, refraining from harsh speech, refraining from frivolous speech. This is called Right Speech.

"And what, monks, is Right Action? Refraining from taking life, refraining from taking what is not given, refraining from sexual misconduct. This is called Right Action.

---

1. [The five aggregates constitute the components of the individual human being. *Form* refers to the physical, *feelings* to the sensations that arise from the operation of the senses, *perception* to the cognition or awareness of sensation, *mental formations* to the emotions and dispositions to act based on sensations, and *consciousness* to the product or result of the interaction of the other four aggregates.—Ed.]

2. [In the West, we classify five senses as sight, sound, smell, taste, and touch. Buddhism adds a sixth, the mind.—Ed.]

"And what, monks, is Right Livelihood? Here, monks, the Ariyan disciple, having given up wrong livelihood, keeps himself by right livelihood.

"And what, monks, is Right Effort? Here, monks, a monk rouses his will, makes an effort, stirs up energy, exerts his mind and strives to prevent the arising of unarisen evil unwholesome mental states. He rouses his will . . . and strives to overcome evil unwholesome mental states that have arisen. He rouses his will . . . and strives to produce unarisen wholesome mental states. He rouses his will, makes an effort, stirs up energy, exerts his mind and strives to maintain wholesome mental states that have arisen, not to let them fade away, to bring them to greater growth, to the full perfection of development. This is called Right Effort.

"And what, monks, is Right Mindfulness? Here, monks, a monk abides contemplating body as body, ardent, clearly aware and mindful, having put aside hankering and fretting for the world; he abides contemplating feelings as feelings . . . ; he abides contemplating mind as mind . . . ; he abides contemplating mind-objects as mind-objects, ardent, clearly aware and mindful, having put aside hankering and fretting for the world. This is called Right Mindfulness.

"And what, monks, is Right Concentration? Here, a monk, detached from sense-desires, detached from unwholesome mental states, enters and remains in the first jhāna,[3] which is with thinking and pondering, born of detachment, filled with delight and joy. And with the subsiding of thinking and pondering, by gaining inner tranquillity and oneness of mind, he enters and remains in the second jhāna, which is without thinking and pondering, born of concentration, filled with delight and joy. And with the fading away of delight, remaining imperturbable, mindful and clearly aware, he experiences in himself the joy of which the Noble Ones say: 'Happy is he who dwells with equanimity and mindfulness,' he enters the third jhāna. And, having given up pleasure and pain, and with the disappearance of former gladness and sadness, he enters and remains in the fourth jhāna, which is beyond pleasure and pain, and purified by equanimity and mindfulness. This is called Right Concentration. And that, monks, is called the way of practice leading to the cessation of suffering."

3. [*Jhāna* (or *dhyana*) refers to altered states of consciousness that occur in meditation.—Ed.]

The Fourth Noble Truth

WALPOLA RAHULA

THE FOURTH NOBLE TRUTH is that of the Way leading to the Cessation of *Dukkha* [suffering]. This is known as the "Middle Path," because it avoids two extremes: one extreme being the search for happiness through the pleasures of the senses, which is "low, common, unprofitable and the way of the ordinary people"; the other being the search for happiness through self-mortification in different forms of asceticism, which is "painful, unworthy and unprofitable." Having himself first tried these two extremes, and having found them to be useless, the Buddha discovered through personal experience the Middle Path "which gives vision and knowledge, which leads to Calm, Insight, Enlightenment, Nirvāna." This Middle Path is generally referred to as the Noble Eightfold Path, because it is composed of eight categories or divisions: namely,

1. Right Understanding,
2. Right Thought,
3. Right Speech,
4. Right Action,
5. Right Livelihood,
6. Right Effort,
7. Right Mindfulness,
8. Right Concentration.

Practically the whole teaching of the Buddha, to which he devoted himself during 45 years, deals in some way or other with this Path. He explained it in different ways and in different words to different people, according to the stage of their development and their capacity to understand and follow him. But the essence of those many thousand discourses scattered in the Buddhist Scriptures is found in the Noble Eightfold Path.

It should not be thought that the eight categories or divisions of the Path should be followed and practised one after the other in the numerical order as given in the usual list above. But they are to be developed more or less simultaneously, as far as possible according to the capacity of each individual. They are all linked together and each helps the cultivation of the others.

These eight factors aim at promoting and perfecting the three essentials of Buddhist training and discipline: namely: (*a*) Ethical Conduct, (*b*) Mental Discipline and (*c*) Wisdom. It will therefore be more helpful for a coherent and better understanding of the eight divisions of the Path, if we group them and explain them according to these three heads.

Ethical Conduct is built on the vast conception of universal love and compassion for all living beings, on which the Buddha's teaching is based. It is regrettable that many scholars forget this great ideal of the Buddha's teaching, and indulge in only dry philosophical and metaphysical divagations when they talk and write about Buddhism. The Buddha gave his teaching "for the good of the many, for the happiness of the many, out of compassion for the world."

According to Buddhism, for a man to be perfect there are two qualities that he should develop equally: compassion on one side, and wisdom on the other. Here compassion represents love, charity, kindness, tolerance and such noble qualities on the emotional side, or qualities of the heart, while wisdom would stand for the intellectual side or the qualities of the mind. If one develops only the emotional neglecting the intellectual, one may become a good-hearted fool; while to develop only the intellectual side neglecting the emotional may turn one into a hard-hearted intellect without feeling for others. Therefore, to be perfect one has to develop both equally. That is the aim of the Buddhist way of life: in it wisdom and compassion are inseparably linked together, as we shall see later.

Now, in Ethical Conduct, based on love and compassion, are included three factors of the Noble Eightfold Path: namely, Right Speech, Right Action and Right Livelihood. (Nos. 3, 4 and 5 in the list).

Right Speech means abstention (1) from telling lies, (2) from backbiting and slander and talk that may bring about hatred, enmity, disunity and disharmony among individuals or groups of people, (3) from harsh, rude, impolite, malicious and abusive language, and (4) from idle, useless and foolish babble and gossip. When one abstains from these forms of wrong and harmful speech one naturally has to speak the truth, has to use words that are friendly and benevolent, pleasant and gentle, meaningful and useful. One should not speak carelessly: speech should be at the right time and place. If one cannot say something useful, one should keep "noble silence."

Right Action aims at promoting moral, honourable and peaceful conduct. It admonishes us that we should abstain from destroying life, from stealing, from dishonest dealings, from illegitimate sexual intercourse, and that we should also help others to lead a peaceful and honourable life in the right way.

Right Livelihood means that one should abstain from making one's living through a profession that brings harm to others, such as trading in arms and lethal weapons, intoxicating drinks, poisons, killing animals, cheating, etc., and should live by a profession which is honourable, blameless and innocent of harm to others. One can clearly see here that Buddhism is strongly opposed to any kind of war, when it lays down that trade in arms and lethal weapons is an evil and unjust means of livelihood.

These three factors (Right Speech, Right Action and Right Livelihood) of the Eightfold Path constitute Ethical Conduct. It should be realized that the Buddhist ethical and moral conduct aims at promoting a happy and harmonious life both for the individual and for society. This moral conduct is considered as the indispensable foundation for all higher spiritual attainments. No spiritual development is possible without this moral basis.

Next comes Mental Discipline, in which are included three other factors of the Eightfold Path: namely, Right Effort, Right Mindfulness (or Attentiveness) and Right Concentration. (Nos. 6, 7 and 8 in the list).

Right Effort is the energetic will (1) to prevent evil and unwholesome states of mind from arising, and (2) to get rid of such evil and unwholesome states that have already arisen within a man, and also (3) to produce, to cause to arise, good and wholesome states of mind not yet arisen, and (4) to develop and bring to perfection the good and wholesome states of mind already present in a man.

Right Mindfulness (or Attentiveness) is to be diligently aware, mindful and attentive with regard to (1) the activities of the body, (2) sensations or feelings, (3) the activities of the mind and (4) ideas, thoughts, conceptions and things.

The practice of concentration on breathing is one of the well-known exercises, connected with the body, for mental development. There are several other ways of developing attentiveness in relation to the body—as modes of meditation.

With regard to sensations and feelings, one should be clearly aware of all forms of feelings and sensations, pleasant, unpleasant and neutral, of how they appear and disappear within oneself.

Concerning the activities of mind, one should be aware whether one's mind is lustful or not, given to hatred or not, deluded or not, distracted or concentrated, etc. In this way one should be aware of all movements of mind, how they arise and disappear.

As regards ideas, thoughts, conceptions and things, one should know their nature, how they appear and disappear, how they are developed, how they are suppressed, and destroyed, and so on. These four forms of mental culture or meditation are treated in detail in the *Setting-up of Mindfulness*.

The third and last factor of Mental Discipline is Right Concentration leading to the four stages of *Dhyāna,* generally called trance or *recueillement.* In the first stage of *Dhyāna,* passionate desires and certain unwholesome thoughts like sensuous lust, ill-will, languor, worry, restlessness, and sceptical doubt are discarded, and feelings of joy and happiness are maintained, along with certain mental activities. In the second stage, all intellectual activities are suppressed, tranquillity and "one-pointedness" of mind developed, and the feelings of joy and happiness are still retained. In the third stage, the feeling of joy, which is an active sensation, also disappears, while the disposition of happiness still remains in addition to mindful equanimity. In the fourth stage of *Dhyāna,* all sensations, even of happiness and unhappiness, of joy and sorrow, disappear, only pure equanimity and awareness remaining.

Thus the mind is trained and disciplined and developed through Right Effort, Right Mindfulness, and Right Concentration. The remaining two factors, namely Right Thought and Right Understanding, go to constitute Wisdom.

Right Thought denotes the thoughts of selfless renunciation or detachment, thoughts of love and thoughts of non-violence, which are extended to all beings. It is very interesting and important to note here that thoughts of selfless detachment, love and non-violence are grouped on the side of wisdom. This clearly shows that true wisdom is endowed with these noble qualities, and that all thoughts of selfish desire, ill-will, hatred and violence are the result of a lack of wisdom—in all spheres of life whether individual, social, or political.

Right Understanding is the understanding of things as they are, and it is the Four Noble Truths that explain things as they really are. Right Understanding, therefore, is ultimately reduced to the understanding of the Four Noble Truths.

This understanding is the highest wisdom which sees the Ultimate Reality. According to Buddhism there are two sorts of understanding: What we generally call understanding is knowledge, an accumulated memory, an intellectual grasping of a subject according to certain given data. This is called "knowing accordingly." It is not very deep. Real deep understanding is called "penetration," seeing a thing in its true nature, without name and label. This penetration is possible only when the mind is free from all impurities and is fully developed through meditation.

From this brief account of the Path, one may see that it is a way of life to be followed, practised and developed by each individual. It is self-discipline in body, word and mind, self-development and self-purification. It has nothing to do with belief, prayer, worship or ceremony. In that sense, it has nothing which may popularly be called "religious." It is a Path leading to the realization of Ultimate Reality, to complete freedom, happiness and peace through moral, spiritual and intellectual perfection.

In Buddhist countries there are simple and beautiful customs and ceremonies on religious occasions. They have little to do with the real Path. But they have their value in satisfying certain religious emotions and the needs of those who are less advanced, and helping them gradually along the Path.

With regard to the Four Noble Truths we have four functions to perform:

The First Noble Truth is *Dukkha*, the nature of life, its suffering, its sorrows and joys, its imperfection and unsatisfactoriness, its impermanence and insubstantiality. With regard to this, our function is to understand it as a fact, clearly and completely.

The Second Noble Truth is the Origin of *Dukkha*, which is desire, "thirst," accompanied by all other passions, defilements and impurities. A mere understanding of this fact is not sufficient. Here our function is to discard it, to eliminate, to destroy and eradicate it.

The Third Noble Truth is the Cessation of *Dukkha*, Nirvāna, the Absolute Truth, the Ultimate Reality. Here our function is to realize it.

The Fourth Noble Truth is the Path leading to the realization of Nirvāna. A mere knowledge of the Path, however complete, will not do. In this case, our function is to follow it and keep to it.

Suggestions for Further Reading

For a brief introduction to religious Buddhism, see Bradley K. Hawkins, *Buddhism* (Upper Saddle River, NJ: Prentice-Hall, 1999).

Herman Hesse's *Siddhartha,* translated by Hilda Rosner (New York: New Directions, 1951), is an entertaining and thought-provoking fictional account of the Buddha's life. It promotes the values of self-realization and independence of thought.

Several articles in *A Companion to World Philosophies* edited by Eliot Deutsche and Ron Bontekoe (Oxford: Blackwell, 1997) provide helpful overviews on different topics in Buddhist philosophy including ideas of the good.

The second volume of the *Routledge Encyclopedia of Philosophy* edited by Edward Craig (London: Routledge, 1998, pp. 51–118) contains articles on various aspects of Buddhism along with good bibliographies.

Videos

Buddhism: The Path to Enlightenment (35 minutes) traces the life of the Buddha. *Buddhism: The Middle Way of Compassion* (25 minutes) discusses karma and the Eightfold Path. *Buddhism* (50 minutes) explores the history behind the philosophy of Buddhism and Sylvia

Boorstein discusses the four noble truths in *Embodying Buddhism* (60 minutes). These videos are available from Insight Media, 2162 Broadway, New York, NY 10024.

Buddhism: Footprints of the Buddha (TimeLife Videos) enhances student understanding of Buddhism.

3.3 Confucius and the Life of Virtue

Twelve years after the Buddha was born in India, Confucius (551–479 BCE) was born in the state of Lu in China. ("Confucius" is the latinization of Kong Fuzi (K'ung Fu Tzu),* which means "Master Kong.") He lived at a time when Chinese society had disintegrated into social and political chaos. Because of these circumstances, he became interested in the question of how the well-being of society could best be achieved and how this was related to the good life.

Biographical information is uncertain, but tradition tells us that Confucius was from the nobility. When he was three years old, his father died. At age nineteen he married and sought a government career. However, he was to make his name as an educator, not as a politician. He provided what we today would call a "humanistic" education to commoners and nobles alike, and he taught what might be termed a "humanistic social philosophy"—"social" because of his concern for achieving a good social order and "humanistic" because of his concern to cultivate humane qualities in the human spirit. His reputation in China became so immense that on the popular level he was deified, while among scholars he was venerated as a great sage.

Ren (*jen*) is one of the central ideas of his thought. It has been translated in a variety of ways: "goodness," "humanity," "benevolence," and "humanheartedness," to name only a few. The concept is so rich and used in such a variety of ways that no simple English translation captures its meaning. *Ren* is not something we are, but something we become by cultivating our aesthetic, moral, cognitive, and spiritual sensibilities. These qualities develop in social or community contexts involving ordered and ritualized relationships. *Ren* is closely related to the principle of reciprocity, which ought to govern relationships among humans. We should not, Confucius contended, do to others what we would not have them do to us. Long before Judaism and Christianity, Confucius had articulated a form of the "Golden Rule."

Li (pronounced "lee") is another central concept in Confucian philosophy. It can mean rules of proper behavior, ritual or rite, custom, etiquette, ceremony, worship, and propriety. Humans should behave appropriately. The models for appropriate behavior came, according to Confucius, from the traditional rites and customs handed down from the past Golden Age. He regarded himself as a traditionalist and spent much of his time teaching and interpreting the cultural classics (called the "Six Disciplines") from China's past. Tradition is important in his view because it provides an external check on what one may subjectively believe to be the right way to act and is a repository of the wisdom of the past with regard to proper conduct. However,

---

*There are two widely used methods for romanticizing (translating into a Latin-based alphabetical system) Chinese words. One is called Wade-Giles and the other Pinyin. The first time a word or name is introduced, I have used the Pinyin spelling and provided the Wade-Giles spelling in parentheses. See the pronunciation guide for Chinese words in Appendix II.

tradition must be personally appropriated and made one's own. Otherwise rituals become dead ceremonies performed mechanically and without meaning.

One of the major traditional virtues in China associated with Confucianism is **xiao** (hsiao) (pronounced "shee-ow"). *Xiao* is often translated as filial piety and involves the practice of kindness, honor, respect, and loyalty among family members. Confucius believed that a strong family is the basis of a strong society. In fact, the family is the microcosmic version of society. Society ought to be one large family, and ultimately *xiao* should be extended to the whole human community. Family harmony contributes to a wider social harmony and a social harmony supports family harmony.

Yi (pronounced "yee") is often translated as "rightness" and sometimes as "morals" or "morality." Many interpreters of Confucius, including the author of our next selection, D. C. Lau, think *yi,* or morality, becomes the primary concern of Confucius as he searches for the best way to live. While there is no denying that Confucius was concerned with what we today would call moral issues, the concept of *yi* is broader than morality. *Yi* refers to what is appropriate or fitting to do in a given situation. Hence it has aesthetic, political, social, and religious implications as well as moral ones.

Although it is usual to interpret Confucius as primarily concerned with moral, social, and political values, the aesthetic dimension of his thought needs to be emphasized as well. Ethics has to do with moral value; aesthetics has to do with artistic value or beauty. The Confucian concern with balance, harmony, and appropriateness reflects aesthetic values. Indeed, the very division between moral and aesthetic value is something Confucius probably did not recognize. For him to call an action right was not merely to pass a moral judgment, but an aesthetic judgment as well. Moral order is aesthetic order. The good and the beautiful are one.

Education plays a key role in the process of becoming a virtuous person because knowledge of the past is a clue to proper action in the present. Since becoming a virtuous person or developing good character is a process, it is something we must *learn* how to do. Hence, proper instruction and good education is one of the keys to self-cultivation.

Because of present-day concerns with individual self-realization associated with the human potential movement and because of the "cult of individual privacy and freedom" that has developed in U.S. society, it is tempting to read Confucius as if he were concerned exclusively with the self-improvement of the individual. However, the individual can never be abstracted from society. Ultimately, for Confucius, there could be no absolute separation between the public and private realms of life. If *ren* is the foundation of one's individual life, it is also the foundation of society. His vision of the ideal world is one in which the world is like a home shared by all. Trust among all prevails and "all people love and respect their parents and children . . . there is caring for the old . . . sharing replaces selfishness and materialistic greed . . . and the door to every home need never be locked and bolted by day or night" (*The Record of Rites,* Book IX).

I have chosen to use a secondary source to introduce us to Confucius because it is rather difficult for a modern reader who has little or no background in Confucian philosophy to understand primary sources. Our guide to Confucius is D. C. Lau, respected translator and interpreter of Confucian thought. The following comes from the introduction to his widely used translation of Confucius' *Analects.*

Reading Questions

(Note: I have used the Wade-Giles spelling of Chinese terms in my questions because Lau uses Wade-Giles.)

1. What, according to Lau, is the most fundamental message of Confucius?
2. What is the difference between the *chün tzu* and the *hsiao jen?*
3. Can anyone become a *chün tzu?*
4. What is *jen* and how is it related to *chung* and *shu?*
5. Why are the obligations we owe others proportionate to the closeness of our relationship to them?
6. If benevolence requires the overcoming of self-interest, then why should our obligations to others be proportionate to the benefits we receive from them?
7. What is the relationship between *jen* and *li?*

Confucius and Moral Character

D. C. LAU

BEFORE WE PROCEED to look at what Confucius has to say about moral character, it is convenient, first of all, to dispose of two concepts which were already current in Confucius' time, viz., the Way (*tao*) and virtue (*te*). The importance Confucius attached to the Way can be seen from his remark, "He has not lived in vain who dies the day he is told about the Way" (IV.8). Used in this sense, the Way seems to cover the sum total of truths about the universe and man, and not only the individual but also the state is said either to possess or not to possess the Way. As it is something which can be transmitted from teacher to disciple, it must be something that can be put into words. There is another slightly different sense in which the term is used. The way is said also to be someone's way, for instance, "the ways of the Former Kings" (I.12), "the way of King Wen and King Wu" (XIX.22), or "the way of the Master" (IV.15). When thus specified, the way naturally can only be taken to mean the way followed by the person in question. As

for the Way, rival schools would each claim to have discovered it even though what each school claimed to have discovered turned out to be very different. The Way, then, is a highly emotive term and comes very close to the term "Truth" as found in philosophical and religious writings in the West.

There seems to be little doubt that the word *te*, virtue, is cognate with the word *te*, to get. Virtue is an endowment men get from Heaven. The word was used in this sense when Confucius, facing a threat to his life, said, "Heaven is author of the virtue that is in me" (VII.23), but this usage is rare in the *Analects*. By the time of Confucius, the term must have already become a moral term. It is something one cultivates, and it enables one to govern a state well. One of the things that caused him concern was, according to Confucius, his failure to cultivate his virtue (VII.3). He also said that if one guided the common people by virtue they would not only reform themselves but have a sense of shame (II.3).

From D. C. Lau, *The Analects*, London: Penguin Books, 1979, pp. 11–22. Copyright © D. C. Lau, 1979. *Reprinted by permission.*

Both the Way and virtue were concepts current before Confucius' time and, by then, they must have already acquired a certain aura. They both, in some way, stem from Heaven. It is, perhaps, for this reason that though he said little of a concrete and specific nature about either of these concepts, Confucius, nevertheless, gave them high precedence in his scheme of things. He said, "I set my heart on the Way, base myself on virtue, lean upon benevolence for support and take my recreation in the arts" (VII.6). Benevolence is something the achievement of which is totally dependent upon our own efforts, but virtue is partly a gift from Heaven.

Behind Confucius' pursuit of the ideal moral character lies the unspoken, and therefore, unquestioned, assumption that the only purpose a man can have and also the only worthwhile thing a man can do is to become as good a man as possible. This is something that has to be pursued for its own sake and with complete indifference to success or failure. Unlike religious teachers, Confucius could hold out no hope of rewards either in this world or in the next. As far as survival after death is concerned, Confucius' attitude can, at best, be described as agnostic. When Tzu-lu asked how gods and spirits of the dead should be served, the Master answered that as he was not able even to serve man how could he serve the spirits, and when Tzu-lu further asked about death, the Master answered that as he did not understand even life how could he understand death (XI.12). This shows, at least, a reluctance on the part of Confucius to commit himself on the subject of survival after death. While giving men no assurance of an after life, Confucius, nevertheless, made great moral demands upon them. He said of the Gentleman[1] of purpose and the benevolent man that "while it is inconceivable that they should seek to stay alive at the expense of benevolence, it may happen that they have to accept death in order to have benevolence accomplished" (XV.9). When such demands are made on men, little wonder that one of Confucius' disciples should have considered that a Gentleman's "burden is heavy and the road is long," for his burden was benevolence and the road came to an end only with death (VIII.7).

If a man cannot be assured of a reward after death, neither can he be guaranteed success in his moral endeavours in this life. The gatekeeper at the Stone Gate asked Tzu-lu, "Is that the K'ung who keeps working towards a goal the realization of which he knows to be hopeless?" (XIV.38). On another occasion, after an encounter with a recluse, Tzu-lu was moved to remark, "The gentleman takes office in order to do his duty. As for putting the Way into practice, he knows all along that it is hopeless" (XVIII.7). Since in being moral one can neither be assured of a reward nor guaranteed success, morality must be pursued for its own sake. This is, perhaps, the most fundamental message in Confucius' teachings, a message that marked his teachings from other schools of thought in ancient China.

For Confucius there is not one single ideal character but quite a variety. The highest is the sage (*sheng jen*). This ideal is so high that it is hardly ever realized. Confucius claimed neither to be a sage himself nor even to have seen such a man. He said, "How dare I claim to be a sage or a benevolent man?" (VII.34) and, on another occasion, "I have no hopes of meeting a sage" (VII.26). The only time he indicated the kind of man that would deserve the epithet was when Tzu-kung asked him, "If there were a man who gave extensively to the common people and brought help to the multitude, what would you think of him? Could he be called benevolent?" Confucius' answer was, "It is no longer a matter of benevolence with such a man. If you must describe him, 'sage' is, perhaps, the right word" (VI.30).

Lower down the scale there are the good man (*shan jen*) and the complete man (*ch'eng jen*). Even the good man Confucius said he had not seen, but the term "good man" seems to apply essentially to men in charge of government, as he said, for instance, "How true is the saying that

---

1. Throughout this book, "Gentleman" is used as an equivalent for *shih* while "gentleman" is mad for *chün tzu*. *Shih* was the lowest rank of officials while *chün tzu* denoted either a men of moral excellence or a man in authority. . . .

after a state has been ruled for a hundred years by good men it is possible to get the better of cruelty and to do away with killing" (XIII.11), and "After a good man has trained the common people for seven years, they should be ready to take up arms" (XIII.29). On the one occasion when he was asked about the way of the good man, Confucius' answer was somewhat obscure (XI.20). As for the complete man, he is described in terms applied not exclusively to him. He "remembers what is right at the sight of profit," and "is ready to lay down his life in the face of danger" (XIV.12). Similar terms are used to describe the Gentleman (XIX.1).

There is no doubt, however, that the ideal moral character for Confucius is the *chün tzu* (gentleman), as he is discussed in more than eighty chapters in the *Analects*. *Chün tzu* and *hsiao jen* (small man) are correlative and contrasted terms. The former is used of men in authority while the latter of those who are ruled. In the *Analects,* however, *chün tzu* and *hsiao jen* are essentially moral terms. The *chün tzu* is the man with a cultivated moral character, while the *hsiao jen* is the opposite. It is worth adding that the two usages indicating the social and moral status are not exclusive, and, in individual cases, it is difficult to be sure whether, besides their moral connotations, these terms may not also carry their usual social connotations as well.

As the gentleman is the ideal moral character, it is not to be expected that a man can become a gentleman without a great deal of hard work or cultivation, as the Chinese called it. There is a considerable number of virtues a gentleman is supposed to have and the essence of these virtues is often summed up in a precept. In order to have a full understanding of the complete moral character of the gentleman, we have to take a detailed look at the various virtues he is supposed to possess.

Benevolence (*jen*) is the most important moral quality a man can possess. Although the use of this term was not an innovation on the part of Confucius, it is almost certain that the complexity of its content and the pre-eminence it attained amongst moral qualities were due to Confucius.

That it is *the* moral quality a gentleman must possess is clear from the following saying.

> If the gentleman forsakes benevolence, in what way can he make a name for himself? The gentleman never deserts benevolence, not even for as long as it takes to eat a meal. If he hurries and stumbles, one may be sure that it is in benevolence that he does so. (IV.5)

In some contexts "the gentleman" and "the benevolent man" are almost interchangeable terms. For instance, it is said in one place that "a gentleman is free from worries and fears" (XII.4), while elsewhere it is the benevolent man who is said not to have worries (IX.29, XIV.28). As benevolence is so central a concept, we naturally expect Confucius to have a great deal to say about it. In this we are not disappointed. There are no less than six occasions on which Confucius answered direct questions about benevolence, and as Confucius had the habit of framing his answers with the specific needs of the inquirer in mind, these answers, taken together, give us a reasonably complete picture.

The essential point about benevolence is to be found in Confucius' answer to Chung-kung:

> Do not impose on others what you yourself do not desire. (XII.2)

These words were repeated on another occasion.

> Tzu-kung asked, "Is there a single word which can be a guide to conduct throughout one's life?" The Master said, "It is perhaps the word 'shu'. Do not impose on others what you yourself do not desire." (XV.24)

By taking the two sayings together we can see that *shu* forms part of benevolence and, as such, is of great significance in the teachings of Confucius. This is confirmed by a saying of Tseng Tzu's. To the Master's remark that there was a single thread binding his way together, Tseng Tzu added the explanation, "The way of the Master consists in *chung* and *shu*. That is all" (IV.15). There is another saying which is, in fact, also about *shu*. In answer to a question from Tzu-kung, Confucius said,

A benevolent man helps others to take their stand in so far as he himself wishes to take his stand, and gets others there in so far as he himself wishes to get there. The ability to take as analogy what is near at hand can be called the method of benevolence. (VI.30)

From this we can see that *shu* is the method of discovering what other people wish or do not wish done to them. The method consists in taking oneself—"what is near at hand"— as an analogy[2] and asking oneself what one would like or dislike were one in the position of the person at the receiving end. *Shu*, however, cannot be the whole of benevolence as it is only its method. Having found out what the other person wants or does not want, whether we go on to do to him what we believe he wants and refrain from doing to him what we believe he does not want must depend on something other than *shu*. As the way of the Master consists of *chung* and *shu*, in *chung* we have the other component of benevolence. *Chung* is the doing of one's best and it is through *chung* that one puts into effect what one had found out by the method of *shu*. Tseng Tzu said on another occasion, "Every day I examine myself on three counts," and of these the first is "In what I have undertaken on another's behalf, have I failed to be *chung*?" (I.4). Again, when asked how a subject should serve his ruler, Confucius' answer was that he "should serve his ruler with *chung*" (III.19). Finally, it is also said that in dealing with others one should be *chung* (XIII.19). In all these cases there is no doubt at all that *chung* means "doing one's best."

Another answer Confucius gave to the question about benevolence was, "Love your fellow men" (XII.22). As he did not elaborate, his meaning is not very clear. But fortunately he used this phrase again on two other occasions. In I.5 he said, "In guiding a state of a thousand chariots . . . avoid excesses in expenditure and love your fellow men; employ the labour of the common people in the right seasons." Again, the Master, according to Tzu-yu, once said "that the gentleman instructed in the Way loves his fellow men and that the small man instructed in the Way is easy to command" (XVII.4). In the first case, the love for one's fellow men (*jen*) is contrasted with the employment of the common people (*min*) in the right seasons, while in the second the gentleman's loving his fellow men is contrasted with the small man's being easy to command. If we remember that the small man was probably different from the common people, we cannot rule out the possibility that when Confucius defined benevolence in terms of loving one's fellow men he did not have the common people in mind as well. Even if this is the case, it is perhaps not as strange as it may seem at first sight, and in order to see it in perspective, we should first take a look at the basis of Confucius' system of morals.

Confucius had a profound admiration for the Duke of Chou who, as regent in the early part of the reign of his young nephew, King Ch'eng, was the architect of the Chou feudal system some five hundred years before Confucius' time. It is beyond the scope of this introduction to discuss in detail the influence of the Duke on Chinese society and the Chinese political system. It is sufficient simply to single out for mention his most important contribution, the clan inheritance system known as *tsung fa*. Under this system, succession passes to the eldest son by the principal wife. Younger sons or sons by concubines become founders of their own noble houses. Thus the feudal lord stands to the king in a double relationship. In terms of political relationship he is a vassal while in terms of blood ties he is the head of a cadet branch of the royal clan. Political allegiance has as its foundation family allegiance. This social system founded by the Duke of Chou proved its soundness by the durability of the Chou Dynasty.

Following the footsteps of the Duke of Chou, Confucius made the natural love and obligations obtaining between members of the family the

---

2. There is a more explicit definition of *shu* in one of the philosophers of the Warring States period. The *Shih tzu* says, "By '*shu*' is meant using oneself as a measure." (*Ch'ün shu chih yao*, 36.19b).

basis of a general morality. The two most important relationships within the family are those between father and son and between elder and younger brother. The love one owes to one's parents is *hsiao* while the respect due one's elder brother is *t'i*. If a man is a good son and a good younger brother at home, he can be counted on to behave correctly in society. Tzu-yu said,

> It is rare for a man whose character is such that he is good as a son (*hsiao*) and obedient as a young man (*t'i*) to have the inclination to transgress against his superiors; it is unheard of for one who has no such inclination to be inclined to start a rebellion.(I.2)

He goes on to draw the logical conclusion that "being good as a son and obedient as a young man is, perhaps, the root of a man's character."

In later Confucianism an undue emphasis was put on being a good son, but we can see here that even in early Confucian teachings *hsiao* was one of the most basic virtues.

If being a good son makes a good subject, being a good father will also make a good ruler. Love for people outside one's family is looked upon as an extension of the love for members of one's own family. One consequence of this view is that the love, and so the obligation to love, decreases by degrees as it extends outwards. Geographically, one loves members of one's own family more than one's neighbours, one's neighbours more than one's fellow villagers, and so on. Socially, one loves members of one's own social class more than those of another class. Thus it would not be surprising if benevolence was confined to one's fellow men (*jen*), but what is much more important to remember is that this does not mean that one does not love the common people at all. One loves them, but to a lesser degree and, perhaps, in a different manner. In Confucius' terminology, one should be generous (*hui*) to the common people (V.16). This is in keeping with Confucius' general attitude towards obligations. Our obligation towards others should be in proportion to the benefit we have received from them. This seems to be the case even between parents and children. In commenting on Tsai Yü who wanted to cut short the three-year mourning period, Confucius said, "Was Yü not given three years' love by his parents?" (XVII.21). This may be taken to mean that the observance of the three-year mourning period is, in some sense, a repayment of the love received from one's parents in the first years of one's life. If this is so, it is not difficult to see why the obligations we owe to other people should also be in proportion to the closeness of our relationship to them. As to how a ruler should treat the common people, this is a topic to which we shall return.

Concerning the nature of benevolence, there is another answer given by Confucius which is of great importance because the question was put to him by his most talented disciple.

> Yen Yüan asked about benevolence. The Master said, "To return to the observance of the rites through overcoming the self constitutes benevolence. If for a single day a man could return to the observance of the rites through overcoming himself, then the whole Empire would consider benevolence to be his. However, the practice of benevolence depends on oneself alone, and not on others." (XII.1)

There are two points in this definition of benevolence which deserve attention. First, benevolence consists in overcoming the self. Second, to be benevolent one has to return to the observance of the rites.

Take the first point first. It is a central tenet in the teachings of Confucius that being moral has nothing to do with self-interest. To be more precise, to say that two things have nothing to do with each other is to say that there is no relationship whatsoever between them, either positive or negative. If being moral has nothing to do with pursuing one's own interest, neither has it anything to do with deliberately going against it. Why, then, it may be asked, is it so important to emphasize this lack of relationship between the two? The answer is this. Of all the things that are likely to distort a man's moral judgement and deflect him from his moral purpose, self-interest is the strongest, the most persistent and the most insidious. Confucius was well aware of this. That is why he said, more than once, that at the sight of profit one should think of what is right (XIV.12, XVI.10 and XIX.1). In another context he warned men in their old age against acquisitiveness (XVI.7). He also asked, "Is it really possible to work side by side with a mean fellow in the service of a lord? Before he gets what he wants, he worries lest he should not get it. After he has got it, he worries lest he should lose it, and when that happens he will not stop at anything" (XVII.15). Confucius came to the conclusion that he would not remain in undeserved wealth or position in spite of their being desirable objects (IV.5).

The point about returning to the observance of the rites is equally important. The rites (*li*) were a body of rules governing action in every aspect of life and they were the repository of past insights into morality. It is, therefore, important that one should, unless there are strong reasons to the contrary, observe them. Though there is no guarantee that observance of the rites necessarily leads, in every case, to behaviour that is right, the chances are it will, in fact, do so. To this point we shall return. For the moment, it is enough to say that Confucius had great respect for the body of rules which went under the name of *li*. That is why when Yen Yüan pressed for more specific details, he was told not to look or listen, speak or move, unless it was in accordance with the rites (XII.1). This, in Confucius' view, was no easy task, so much so that "if for a single day a man could return to the observance of the rites through overcoming himself, then the whole Empire would consider benevolence to be his."

There are two occasions when answers are given which emphasize another aspect of benevolence. When Fan Ch'ih asked about benevolence, the Master said, "The benevolent man reaps the benefit only after overcoming difficulties" (VI.22). Similarly, when Ssu-ma Niu asked about benevolence, the Master said, "The mark of the benevolent man is that he is loath to speak," and then went on to explain, "When to act is difficult, is it any wonder that one is loath to speak?" (XII.3). That he considered benevolence difficult

can be seen from his reluctance to grant that anyone was benevolent. He would not commit himself when asked whether Tzu-lu, Jan Ch'iu and Kung-hsi Ch'ih were benevolent (V.8). Nor would he grant that either Ling Yin Tzu-wen or Ch'en Wen Tzu was benevolent (V.19). He refused to claim benevolence for himself (VII.32). This is no more than one would expect from a man of modesty. However, he did say of Yen Yüan, "in his heart for three months at a time Hui does not lapse from benevolence," while "the others attain benevolence merely by fits and starts" (VI.7). This emphasis on the difficulty of practising benevolence is echoed, as we have seen, by Tseng Tzu who described benevolence as "a heavy burden" (VIII.7). But although Confucius emphasized the difficulty of practising benevolence, he also made it abundantly clear that whether we succeed or not depends solely on ourselves. As we have already seen, he said in answer to Yen Yüan's question that "the practice of benevolence depends on oneself alone, and not on others" (XII.1). He was quite clear that failure to practise benevolence was not due to lack of strength to carry it through. He said, "Is there a man who, for the space of a single day, is able to devote all his strength to benevolence? I have not come across such a man whose strength proves insufficient for the task" (IV.6). Thus when Jan Ch'iu excused himself by saying, "It is not that I am not pleased with your way, but rather that my strength gives out," Confucius' comment was, "A man whose strength gives out collapses along the course. In your case you set the limits beforehand" (VI.12). Confucius stated his conviction unambiguously when he said, "Is benevolence really far away? No sooner do I desire it than it is here" (VII.30). On the lines of the *Odes*

> The flowers of the cherry tree,
> How they wave about!
> It's not that I do not think of you,
> But your home is so far away,

Confucius commented, "He did not really think of her. If he did, there is no such thing as being far away" (IX.31). He must have made this comment with its possible application to benevolence in mind. . . .

Suggestions for Further Reading

A. S. Cua's article "Confucian Philosophy, Chinese" in volume 2 of the *Routledge Encyclopedia of Philosophy* (London: Routledge, 1998, pp. 538–543) provides a good introduction to key Confucian ideas.

Herbert Fingarette in *Confucius: The Secular as Sacred* (Waveland Press, 1998) brilliantly explores the philosophical importance of Confucius' ideas in a clear and readable style.

Also see *Thinking Through Confucius* (New York: State University of New York Press, 1987) by David L. Hall and Roger T. Ames. This book is advanced, but it brings out the philosophical importance of Confucius for our time.

The introduction to *The Analects of Confucious: A Philosophical Translation* (New York: Ballantine Books, 1998) by Roger T. Ames and Henry Rosemont, Jr. addresses some of the difficulties involved in translating Chinese concepts into English.

See "*Jen* and *Li* in the *Analects*" by Kwong-loi Shun in *Philosophy East and West: A Quarterly of Comparative Philosophy* 43 (July 1993): 457–479, for a detailed discussion of these central Confucian concepts.

Chad Hansen has provided a clear introduction to Confucian ethics in "Classical Chinese Ethics," found in *A Companion to Ethics,* edited by Peter Singer (Oxford: Blackwell, 1991), pp. 69–81.

See Chung M. Tse's "Confucianism and Contemporary Ethical Issues" in *World Religions and Global Ethics,* edited by S. Cromwell Crawford (New York: Paragon House, 1989), pp. 91–125, for an application of Confucian principles to such contemporary moral issues as punishment, justice, racism, sexism, and economic fairness.

Videos

A Confucian Life in America: Tu Wei-ming (30 minutes) features the Confucian scholar Tu Wei-ming discussing with Bill Moyers the relevance of Confucius for today. *Confucianism* (58 minutes) features Houstin Smith discussing Confucianism, Taoism, and Buddhism in China. Both of these are available from Films for the Humanities and Sciences, PO Box 2053, Princeton, NJ 08543-2053.

Confucius (50 minutes) traces Confucius' life and is available from Insight Media, 2162 Broadway, New York, NY 10024-0621.

3.4 Socrates on Living the Examined Life

Socrates (470–399 BCE), born in Athens nine years after Confucius died, lived during the golden era of Greek culture in a city that had become the intellectual and cultural center of the Mediterranean world. Many consider him the father of Western philosophy.

We have inherited contradictory pictures of Socrates. Plato, his most famous student and author of the dialogues in which Socrates stars, portrays him as the ideal philosopher. Aristophanes, in his play *The Clouds,* pictures him as a buffoon. Unlike the Pre-Socratics (see Section 1.1), Socrates showed little interest in natural philosophy. Like the Sophists (see Section 1.1), he was intensely interested in ethical and political problems. To many, he appeared to be just another Sophist, teaching the youth virtue. Plato contrasts him with the Sophists, however, claiming that he took no fee for his instruction and that his instruction was not a matter of *telling* others the truth but, like the activity of a midwife, of helping others give birth to and critically examine their own ideas.

His method (the **Socratic method**) consisted of asking people questions about matters they presumably knew something about. Socrates would usually begin by asking for a definition of a concept like justice. Once a definition was offered, he analyzed its meaning and critically examined it. Some defect was found, and the definition was reformulated to avoid the defect. Then this new definition was critically examined until another defect appeared. The process went on as long as Socrates could keep the other parties talking.

As an example, let's consider the dialogue called *Euthyphro*. Socrates is at the courthouse in Athens because he has been charged with corrupting the youth and inventing new gods. The latter charge amounts to a charge of impiety, and so he is anxious to talk with Euthyphro, who has appeared at the courthouse on his way to prosecute his own father for the impious act of murder. He asks Euthyphro, who claims to be something of an expert in these matters, to define piety. Euthyphro responds by offering his own action of prosecuting his father for murder as an example of piety.

Socrates points out that this is an *example* of piety, but it is not the sort of definition he is seeking. He wants to know the *essential* characteristics of piety. So Euthyphro tries again and defines piety as whatever is pleasing to the gods. This definition is soon found wanting when Socrates points out that the gods are often pleased by different things. What pleases Zeus does not always please his wife, Hera. So Euthyphro amends his definition. Piety is what is pleasing to *all* the gods. Socrates responds to this reformulation by asking, "Do the gods love piety because it is pious, or is it pious because the gods love it?" What is at issue is whether piety has some intrinsic characteristic that accounts for the fact that the gods love it, or whether the essential trait that determines piety is simply the fact that the gods love it. Euthyphro replies that the gods love piety because it is pious. Then Socrates shows him that he has not yet offered a good definition of piety itself, but only stated an effect of piety— namely that, whatever it is essentially, piety has the effect of pleasing all the gods. So Euthyphro, getting rather upset, offers another definition. This one, too, proves inadequate, but Euthyphro manages to make an excuse and leave before Socrates can drag yet another definition from him and demolish it. The dialogue ends, as so many do, with the issue of what piety is still up in the air. However, progress has been made. We now know more about what piety is not, but no positive, agreed-on definition has been formulated.

This dialogue not only illustrates the Socratic method but also probes the interesting and complex problem of the foundation of ethics. If we substitute the word *good* for the word *piety* and the word *will* for the word *love*, then, following Socrates' lead, we can ask, "Does God will the good because it is good, or is something good because God wills it?" In other words, is moral goodness an independent value, or is it something that depends on something else (like the will or command of God)? Some Jewish, Christian, and Islamic theologians have argued in favor of the **divine command theory** of ethics. According to this theory, God's command or will makes something morally right. Such a theory implies that the Ten Commandments, for example, are good only because God decreed them. Hence murder is not morally wrong in itself, but only if God should happen to forbid it. However, this sort of theory appears to make morality a matter of divine whim. If God decides to command just the opposite of the Ten Commandments, then this new set of commandments would become morally right. Surely we want to say that there is something intrinsically wrong about certain actions like murder, no matter what God might happen to command.

Socrates got into trouble with the people of Athens and was brought to trial in 399 BCE. Three Athenians—Meletus, Anytus, and Lycon—brought charges. There were 501 citizens on the jury. *The Apology,* which you are about to read, is Plato's account of the trial and Socrates' defense. It provides a dramatic statement of why Socrates believes that the pursuit of truth by the critical methods of rational inquiry is the way one should live. However, we should be cautious about interpreting Socrates' views in a purely intellectual way. He is concerned with the pursuit of wisdom and truth through the critical use of reason; there can be no doubt about that. However, this way of living is not unrelated to moral concerns. As he says at one point, his teaching has always been "not to take thought of yourself or your properties, but to care about the improvement of your soul." This "improvement of soul" is not acquired by money but by the practice of virtue. Indeed, he claims that "from virtue come money and every other good of man, public as well as private."

Reading Questions

1. What is the main point Socrates makes by telling the story about the oracle of Delphi?
2. How does Socrates defend himself against the charge of corrupting the youth and the charge of atheism?
3. At one point Socrates compares himself to a gadfly (horsefly) and the Athenians to a thoroughbred horse. What is the point of this comparison?
4. Socrates asserts that the unexamined life is not worth living. Imagine living your life using the Socratic method to examine your own beliefs and actions as well as the beliefs and actions of others. Would this be a good way to live? Why, or why not?
5. What are some basic assumptions made by Socrates in his response to the verdict of death?
6. How do you think Socrates would answer the question, "How should one live?"

The Apology

PLATO

Socrates: HOW YOU HAVE FELT, O men of Athens, hearing the speeches of my accusers, I cannot tell. I know their persuasive words almost made me forget who I was, such was their effect. Yet they hardly spoke a word of truth. But many as their falsehoods were, there was one of them which quite amazed me—I mean when they told you to be on your guard and not let yourselves

The translation is based on Benjamin Jowett's nineteenth-century translation as updated and revised by Christopher Biffle, A Guided Tour of Five Works by Plato *(Mountain View, CA: Mayfield, 1988), pp. 30–50. Reprinted by permission of Mayfield Publishing Company. Footnotes deleted.*

be deceived by the force of my eloquence. They ought to have been ashamed of saying this, because they were sure to be detected as soon as I opened my lips and displayed my deficiency. They certainly did appear to be most shameless in saying this, unless by the force of eloquence they mean the force of truth; for then I do indeed admit that I am eloquent. But in how different a way from theirs!

Well, as I was saying, they have hardly uttered a word, or not more than a word, of truth. You shall hear from me the whole truth: not, however, delivered in their manner, in an oration ornamented with words and phrases. No, indeed! I shall use the words and arguments which occur to me at the moment. I am certain this is right, and at my time of life I should not appear before you, O men of Athens, in the character of a juvenile orator—let no one expect this of me. And I must beg you to grant me one favor, which is this—if you hear me using the same words in my defense which I have been in the habit of using, and which most of you may have heard in the agora, and at the tables of the money-changers, or anywhere else, I ask you not to be surprised at this, and not to interrupt me. I am more than 70 years of age and this is the first time I have ever appeared in a court of law, and I am a stranger to the ways of this place. Therefore I would have you regard me as if I was really a stranger whom you would excuse if he spoke in his native tongue and after the fashion of his country. That, I think, is not an unfair request. Never mind the way I speak, which may or may not be good, but think only of the justice of my cause, and give heed to that. Let the judge decide justly and the speaker speak truly.

First, I have to reply to the older charges and to my first accusers, and then I will go on to the later ones. I have had many accusers who accused me in the past and their false charges have continued during many years. I am more afraid of them than of Anytus and his associates, who are dangerous, too, in their own way. But far more dangerous are these, who began when you were children, and took possession of your minds with their falsehoods, telling of Socrates, a wise man, who speculated about the heavens

above, and searched into the earth beneath, and made the worse argument defeat the better. These are the accusers whom I fear because they are the circulators of this rumor and their listeners are too likely to believe that speculators of this sort do not believe in the gods. My accusers are many and their charges against me are of ancient date. They made them in days when you were impressionable—in childhood, or perhaps in youth—and the charges went by unanswered for there was none to answer. Hardest of all, their names I do not know and cannot tell, unless in the chance case of a comic poet. But the main body of these slanderers who from envy and malice have convinced you—and there are some of them who are convinced themselves, and impart their convictions to others—all these, I say, are most difficult to deal with. I cannot have them up here and examine them. Therefore, I must simply fight with shadows in my own defense and examine when there is no one who answers. I will ask you then to assume with me that my opponents are of two kinds: one more recent, the other from the past. I will answer the latter first, for these accusations you heard long before the others, and much more often.

Well, then, I will make my defense, and I will try in the short time allowed to do away with this evil opinion of me which you have held for such a long time. I hope I may succeed, if this be well for you and me, and that my words may find favor with you. But I know to accomplish this is not easy—I see the nature of the task. Let the event be as the gods will; in obedience to the law I make my defense.

I will begin at the beginning and ask what the accusation is which has given rise to this slander of me and which has encouraged Meletus to proceed against me. What do the slanderers say? They shall be my prosecutors and I will sum up their words in an affidavit. "Socrates is an evil-doer and a curious person, who searches into things under the earth and in the heavens. He makes the weaker argument defeat the stronger and he teaches these doctrines to others." That is the nature of the accusation, and that is what you have seen in the comedy of Aristophanes. He introduced a man whom he calls Socrates, going about and saying he can walk in the air, and talking a lot of nonsense concerning matters which I do not pretend to know anything about—however, I mean to say nothing disparaging of anyone who is a student of such knowledge. I should be very sorry if Meletus could add that to my charge. But the simple truth is, O Athenians, I have nothing to do with these studies. Very many of those here are witnesses to the truth of this and to them I appeal. Speak then, you who have heard me, and tell your neighbors whether any of you ever heard me hold forth in few words or in many upon matters of this sort. . . . You hear their answer. And from what they say you will be able to judge the truth of the rest.

There is the same foundation for the report I am a teacher, and take money; that is no more true than the other. Although, if a man is able to teach, I honor him for being paid. There is Gorgias of Leontium, Prodicus of Ceos, and Hippias of Elis, who go round the cities and are able to persuade young men to leave their own citizens, by whom they might be taught for nothing, and come to them, whom they not only pay but are thankful if they may be allowed to pay them.

There is actually a Parian philosopher residing in Athens who charges fees. I came to hear of him in this way: I met a man who spent a world of money on the sophists, Callias, the son of Hipponicus, and knowing he had sons, I asked him: "Callias," I said, "if your two sons were foals or calves, there would be no difficulty in finding someone to raise them. We would hire a trainer of horses, or a farmer probably, who would improve and perfect them in their own proper virtue and excellence. But, as they are human beings, whom are you thinking of placing over them? Is there anyone who understands human and political virtue? You must have thought about this because you have sons. Is there anyone?"

"There is," he said.

"Who is he?" said I. "And of what country? And what does he charge?"

"Evenus the Parian," he replied. "He is the man and his charge is five minae."

Happy is Evenus, I said to myself, if he really has this wisdom and teaches at such a modest charge. Had I the same, I would have been very proud and conceited; but the truth is I have no knowledge like this, O Athenians.

I am sure someone will ask the question, "Why is this, Socrates, and what is the origin of these accusations of you: for there must have been something strange which you have been doing? All this great fame and talk about you would never have come up if you had been like other men. Tell us then, why this is, as we should be sorry to judge you too quickly."

I regard this as a fair challenge, and I will try to explain to you the origin of this name of "wise," and of this evil fame. Please attend then and although some of you may think I am joking, I declare I will tell you the entire truth. Men of Athens, this reputation of mine has come from a certain kind of wisdom which I possess. If you ask me what kind of wisdom, I reply, such wisdom as is attainable by man, for to that extent I am inclined to believe I am wise. Whereas, the persons of whom I was speaking have a superhuman wisdom which I may fail to describe, because I do not have it. He who says I have, speaks false, and slanders me.

O men of Athens, I must beg you not to interrupt me, even if I seem to say something extravagant. For the word which I will speak is not mine. I will refer you to a wisdom which is worthy of credit, and will tell you about my wisdom—whether I have any, and of what sort—and that witness shall be the god of Delphi. You must have known Chaerephon. He was a friend of mine and also a friend of yours, for he shared in the exile of the people and returned with you. Well, Chaerephon, as you know, was very impetuous in all his doings, and he went to Delphi and boldly asked the oracle to tell him whether—as I said, I must beg you not to interrupt—he asked the oracle to tell him whether there was anyone wiser than I was. The Pythian prophetess answered, there was no man wiser. Chaerephon is dead, himself, but his brother, who is in court, will confirm the truth of this story.

Why do I mention this? Because I am going to explain to you why I have such an evil name. When I heard the answer, I said to myself, "What can the god mean and what is the interpretation of this riddle? I know I have no wisdom, great or small. What can he mean when he says I am the wisest of men? And yet he is a god, and cannot lie; that would be against his nature." After long consideration, I at last thought of a method of answering the question.

I reflected if I could only find a man wiser than myself then I might go to the god with a refutation in my hand. I would say to him, "Here is a man who is wiser than I am, but you said I was the wisest." Accordingly I went to one who had the reputation of wisdom, and observed him— his name I need not mention; he was a politician whom I selected for examination. When I began to talk with him I could not help thinking he was not really wise, although he was thought wise by many, and wiser still by himself. I tried to explain to him that he thought himself wise, but was not really wise. The result was he hated me and his hatred was shared by several who were present who heard me. So I left him, saying to myself, as I went away: "Well, although I do not suppose either of us knows anything really beautiful and good, I am better off than he is—for he knows nothing and thinks that he knows. I neither know nor think that I know. In this latter, then, I seem to have an advantage over him." Then I went to another who had still higher philosophical pretensions and my conclusion was exactly the same. I made another enemy of him and of many others besides him.

After this I went to one man after another, being aware of the anger which I provoked and I lamented and feared this, but necessity was laid upon me. The word of the god, I thought, ought to be considered first. And I said to myself, "I must go to all who appear to know, and find out the meaning of the oracle." And I swear to you Athenians, by the dog, I swear!, the result of my mission was this: I found the men with the highest reputations were all nearly the most foolish and some inferior men were really wiser and better.

I will tell you the tale of my wanderings and of the Herculean labors, as I may call them, which I endured only to find at last the oracle was right. When I left the politicians, I went to the poets: tragic, dithyrambic, and all sorts. There, I said to

myself, you will be detected. Now you will find out you are more ignorant than they are. Accordingly, I took them some of the most elaborate passages in their own writings, and asked what was the meaning of them—thinking the poets would teach me something. Will you believe me? I am almost ashamed to say this, but I must say there is hardly a person present who would not have talked better about their poetry than the poets did themselves. That quickly showed me poets do not write poetry by wisdom, but by a sort of inspiration. They are like soothsayers who also say many fine things, but do not understand the meaning of what they say. The poets appeared to me to be much the same and I further observed that upon the strength of their poetry they believed themselves to be the wisest of men in other things in which they were not wise. So I departed, conceiving myself to be superior to them for the same reason I was superior to the politicians.

At last I went to the artisans, because I was conscious I knew nothing at all and I was sure they knew many fine things. In this I was not mistaken, for they did know many things of which I was ignorant, and in this they certainly were wiser than I was. But I observed even the good artisans fell into the same error as the poets. Because they were good workmen, they thought they also knew all sorts of high matters and this defect in them overshadowed their wisdom. Therefore, I asked myself on behalf of the oracle whether I would like to be as I was, having neither their knowledge nor their ignorance, or like them in both. I answered myself and the oracle that I was better off as I was.

This investigation led to my having many enemies of the worst and most dangerous kind and has given rise also to many falsehoods. I am called wise because my listeners always imagine I possess the wisdom which I do not find in others. The truth is, O men of Athens, the gods only are wise and in this oracle they mean to say wisdom of men is little or nothing. They are not speaking of Socrates, only using my name as an illustration, as if they said, "He, O men, is the wisest who, like Socrates, knows his wisdom is in truth worth nothing." And so I go my way, obedient to the gods, and seek wisdom of anyone, whether citizen or stranger, who appears to be wise. If he is not wise, then in support of the oracle I show him he is not wise. This occupation quite absorbs me, and I have no time to give either to any public matter of interest or to any concern of my own, but I am in utter poverty by reason of my devotion to the gods.

There is another thing. Young men of the richer classes, who have little to do, gather around me of their own accord. They like to hear the pretenders examined. They often imitate me and examine others themselves. There are plenty of persons, as they soon enough discover, who think they know something, but really know little or nothing. Then those who are examined by the young men instead of being angry with themselves are angry with me. "This confounded Socrates," they say, "this villainous misleader of youth!" Then if somebody asks them, "Why, what evil does he practice or teach?," they do not know and cannot tell. But so they may not appear ignorant, they repeat the readymade charges which are used against all philosophers about teaching things up in the clouds and under the earth, and having no gods, and making the worse argument defeat the stronger. They do not like to confess their pretense to knowledge has been detected, which it has. They are numerous, ambitious, energetic and are all in battle array and have persuasive tongues. They have filled your ears with their loud and determined slanders. This is the reason why my three accusers, Meletus and Anytus and Lycon, have set upon me. Meletus has a quarrel with me on behalf of the poets, Anytus, on behalf of the craftsmen, Lycon, on behalf of the orators. As I said at the beginning, I cannot expect to get rid of this mass of slander all in a moment.

This, O men of Athens, is the truth and the whole truth. I have concealed nothing. And yet, I know this plainness of speech makes my accusers hate me and what is their hatred but a proof that I am speaking the truth? This is the reason for their slander of me, as you will find out either in this or in any future inquiry.

I have said enough in my defense against the first class of my accusers. I turn to the second class who are headed by Meletus, that good and patriotic man, as he calls himself. Now I will try to defend myself against them: These new accusers must also have their affidavit read. What do they say? Something of this sort: "Socrates is a doer of evil and corrupter of the youth, and he does not believe in the gods of the state. He has other new divinities of his own." That is their charge and now let us examine the particular counts. He says I am a doer of evil, who corrupts the youth but I say, O men of Athens, Meletus is a doer of evil and the evil is that he makes a joke of a serious matter. He is too ready to bring other men to trial from a pretended zeal and interest about matters in which he really never had the smallest interest. And the truth of this I will try to prove to you.

Come here, Meletus, and let me ask a question of you. You think a great deal about the improvement of youth?

Meletus: Yes I do.

Socrates: Tell the judges, then, who is their improver. You must know, as you have taken the pains to discover their corruptor and are accusing me before them. Speak then, and tell the judges who their improver is. Observe, Meletus, that you are silent and have nothing to say. But is this not rather disgraceful and a very great proof of what I was saying, that you have no interest in the matter? Speak up, friend, and tell us who their improver is.

Mel: The laws.

Soc: But that, my good sir, is not my meaning. I want to know who the person is, who, in the first place, knows the laws.

Mel: The jury, Socrates, who are present in court.

Soc: Do you mean to say, Meletus, they are able to instruct and improve youth?

Mel: Certainly they are.

Soc: All of them, or only some and not others?

Mel: All of them.

Soc: By the goddess Hera, that is good news! There are plenty of improvers, then. And what do you say of the audience—do they improve them?

Mel: Yes, they do.

Soc: And the senators?

Mel: Yes, the senators improve them.

Soc: But perhaps the members of the Assembly corrupt them? Or do they too improve them?

Mel: They improve them.

Soc: Then every Athenian improves and elevates them, all with the exception of myself. I alone am their corruptor? Is that what you say?

Mel: Most definitely.

Soc: I am very unfortunate if that is true. But suppose I ask you a question. Would you say that this also holds true in the case of horses? Does one man do them harm and everyone else good? Is not the exact opposite of this true? One man is able to do them good and not the many. The trainer of horses, that is to say, does them good, and others who deal with horses injure them? Is that not true, Meletus, of horses or any other animals? Yes, certainly. Whether you and Anytus say yes or no, that is no matter. Fortunate indeed would be the condition of youth if they had one corruptor only and all the rest of the world were their improvers. You, Meletus, have sufficiently shown you never had a thought about the young. Your carelessness is seen in your not caring about the matters spoken of in this very indictment.

And now, Meletus, I must ask you another question: Which is better, to live among bad citizens or among good ones? Answer, friend, I say, for that is a question which may be easily answered. Do not the good do their neighbors good and the bad do them evil?

Mel: Certainly.

Soc: And is there anyone who would rather be injured than benefited by those who associate with him? Answer, my good friend, the law requires you to answer—does anyone like to be injured?

Mel: Certainly not.

Soc: And when you accuse me of corrupting the youth, do you charge I corrupt them intentionally or unintentionally?

Mel: Intentionally, I say.

Soc: But you just admitted that the good do their neighbors good, and the evil do them evil. Now, is that a truth which your superior wisdom has recognized thus early in life, and am I, at my age, in such ignorance as not to know if a man with whom I associate is corrupted by me, I am

very likely to be harmed by him? Yet you say I corrupt him, and intentionally too; of that you will never persuade me or any other human being. But either I do not corrupt them, or I corrupt them unintentionally, so that on either view of the case you lie. If my offense is unintentional, the law does not mention unintentional offenses. You ought to have taken me aside and warned me, because if I had been better advised, I should have stopped doing what I only did unintentionally—no doubt I should. Instead, you hated to talk with me or teach me and you indicted me in this court, which is a place not of instruction, but of punishment.

I have shown, Athenians, as I was saying, Meletus has no care at all, great or small, about the matter. But still I should like to know, Meletus, in what way do I corrupt the young. I suppose you mean, as I infer from your indictment, I teach them not to acknowledge the gods which the state acknowledges, but some other new divinities or spiritual agencies instead. These are the lessons which corrupt the youth, as you say.

Mel: Yes, I say that emphatically.

Soc: Then, by the gods, Meletus, of whom we are speaking, tell me and the court, in somewhat plainer terms, what you mean! I do not understand whether you charge I teach others to acknowledge some gods, and therefore do believe in gods, and am not an entire atheist—but only that they are not the same gods which the city recognizes, or, do you mean to say that I am atheist simply, and a teacher of atheism?

Mel: I mean the latter—that you are a complete atheist.

Soc: That is an extraordinary statement, Meletus. Why do you say that? Do you mean that I do not believe the sun or moon are gods, which is the common belief of all men?

Mel: I assure you, jurymen, he does not believe in them. He says the sun is stone and the moon, earth.

Soc: Friend Meletus, you think you are accusing Anaxagoras and you have a bad opinion of the jury, if you believe they do not know these doctrines are found in the books of Anaxagoras the Clazomenian. These are the doctrines which the youth are said to learn from Socrates, when these doctrines can be bought in the marketplace. The youth might cheaply purchase them and laugh at Socrates if he pretends to father such eccentricities. And so, Meletus, you really think that I do not believe in any god?

Mel: I swear by Zeus that you absolutely believe in none at all.

Soc: You are a liar, Meletus, not believed even by yourself. I cannot help thinking, O men of Athens, Meletus is reckless and impudent and has written this indictment in a spirit of wantonness and youthful bravado. He has made a riddle, thinking to fool me. He said to himself: "I shall see whether this wise Socrates will discover my ingenious contradiction, or whether I shall be able to deceive him and the rest of them." For he certainly does appear to me to contradict himself in the indictment as much as if he said that Socrates is guilty of not believing in the gods, and yet of believing in them—but this surely is a piece of nonsense.

I should like you, O men of Athens, to join me in examining what I conceive to be his inconsistency and you, Meletus, answer. And I must remind you not to interrupt me if I speak in my accustomed manner.

Did any man, Meletus, ever believe in the existence of human things, and not human beings? . . . I wish, men of Athens, that he would answer and not be always trying to create an interruption. Did ever any man believe in horsemanship and not in horses? Or in flute playing and not in flute players? No, my friend, I will answer for you and to the court, as you refuse to answer for yourself. There is no man who ever did. But now, please answer the next question. Can a man believe in spiritual and divine activities and not in divine beings?

Mel: He cannot.

Soc: I am glad I have extracted that answer, by the assistance of the court. Nevertheless you swear in the indictment that I teach and believe in divine activities (new or old, no matter for that). At any rate, I believe in divine activities, as you swear in the affidavit, but if I believe in divine activities, I must believe in divine beings. Is that not true? Yes, that is true, for I may assume that your silence gives assent to that. Now what

are divine beings? Are they not either gods or the sons of gods? Is that true?

Mel: Yes, that is true.

Soc: But this is just the ingenious riddle of which I was speaking. The divine beings are gods and you say first that I don't believe in gods, and then again that I do believe in gods; that is, if I believe in divine beings. For if the divine beings are the illegitimate sons of gods, whether by the nymphs or by any other mothers, as is thought, that, as all men will agree, necessarily implies the existence of their parents. You might as well affirm the existence of mules, and deny the existence of horses and donkeys. Such nonsense, Meletus, could only have been intended by you as a test of me. You have put this into the indictment because you have no real charge against me. But no one who has a particle of understanding will ever be convinced by you that the same men can believe in divine and superhuman activities, and yet not believe that there are gods and demigods.

I have said enough in answer to the charge of Meletus. Any elaborate defense is unnecessary but, as I was saying before, I certainly have many enemies and this will be my destruction if I am destroyed; of that I am certain—not Meletus, nor Anytus, but the envy and slander of the world, which has been the death of many good men and will probably be the death of many more. I will not be the last of them.

Someone will say: Are you not ashamed, Socrates, of a way of life which is likely to bring you to an untimely end? To him I answer: There you are mistaken, a man who is good for anything should not calculate the chance of living or dying. He should only consider whether in doing anything he is doing right or wrong and acting the part of a good man or of a bad. Whereas, according to your view, the heroes who fell at Troy were not good for much, and the son of Thetis above all, who altogether despised danger in comparison with disgrace. His goddess mother said to him, in his eagerness to slay Hector, that if he avenged his companion Patroclus, and slew Hector, he would die himself.

"Fate," as she said, "waits upon you next after Hector."

He, hearing this, utterly despised danger and death, and instead of fearing them, feared rather to live in dishonor and not to avenge his friend.

"Let me die next," he replied, "and be avenged of my enemy, rather than stay here by the beaked ships to be mocked and a burden on the earth."

Had Achilles any thought of death and danger? For wherever a man's place is, whether the place which he has chosen or that in which he has been placed by a commander, there he should remain in the hour of danger. He should not consider death or anything else but only disgrace. And this, O men of Athens, is a true saying.

My conduct would be strange, O men of Athens, if I, who was ordered by the generals you chose to command me at Potidaea, Amphipolis, and Delium, remained where they placed me, like any other man facing death, should know when, as I believe, God orders me to fulfil the philosopher's mission of searching into myself and other men, desert my post through fear of death, or any other fear. That would indeed be strange, and I might be justly arraigned in court for denying the existence of the gods, if I disobeyed the oracle because I was afraid of death. Then I should be supposing I was wise when I was not wise.

This fear of death is indeed the imitation of wisdom, and not real wisdom, being the appearance of knowing the unknown. No one knows whether death, which they in their fear believe to be the greatest evil, may not be the greatest good. Is there not here the pretense of knowledge, which is a disgraceful sort of ignorance? This is the point that, as I think, I am superior to men in general and in which I might believe myself wiser than other men. Whereas I know little of the other world, I do not suppose that I know. But I do know that injustice and disobedience to a better, whether god or man, is evil and dishonorable, and I will never fear or avoid a possible good rather than a certain evil. Therefore if you let me go now, reject the advice of Anytus, who said if I were not put to death I should not have been prosecuted, and that if I escape now, your sons will all be utterly ruined by listening to my words. If you say to me, Socrates, this time we will not listen to Anytus and will let you off, but upon one condition, you are not to inquire and speculate in this way any more and if you are caught doing this again you shall die. If this was the condition on which you let me go, I would reply: Men of Athens, I honor and love you but I shall obey the god rather than you. While I have life and strength I shall never cease from practicing and teaching philosophy, exhorting anyone whom I meet in my usual way and convincing him, saying: O my friend, why do you, who are a citizen of the great and wise city of Athens, care so much about laying up the greatest amount of money, honor and reputation, and so little about wisdom, truth and the greatest improvement of the soul, which you never regard or heed at all? Are you not ashamed of this? If the person with whom I am arguing says: Yes, but I do care; I do not depart or let him go at once. I question, examine and cross-examine him, and if I think he has no virtue, but only says he has, I reproach him with undervaluing the greater, and overvaluing the lesser. This I would say to everyone I meet, young and old, citizen and alien, but especially to the citizens, inasmuch as they are my brethren. This is the command of the god, as I would have you know and I believe that to this day no greater good has ever happened in the state than my service to the god.

I do nothing but go about persuading you all, old and young alike, not to take thought of yourself or your properties, but to care about the improvement of your soul. I tell you virtue is not acquired with money, but that from virtue come money and every other good of man, public as well as private. This is my teaching, and if this is the doctrine which corrupts the young, my influence is certainly ruinous. If anyone says this is not my teaching, he is speaking a lie. Therefore, O men of Athens, I say to you, do as Anytus bids or not as Anytus bids, and either acquit me or not; but whatever you do, know that I shall never change my ways, not even if I have to die many times.

Men of Athens, do not interrupt, but hear me. There was an agreement between us that you should hear me out. I think what I am going to say will do you good: for I have something more to say, which you may be inclined to interrupt but I ask you not to do this.

I want you to know if you kill someone like me, you will injure yourselves more than you will injure me. Meletus and Anytus will not injure me. They cannot because it is not possible that a bad man should injure someone better than himself. I do not deny he may, perhaps, kill him, or drive him into exile, or deprive him of civil rights. He may imagine, and others may imagine, he is doing him a great injury but I do not agree with him. The evil of doing as Anytus is doing—of unjustly taking away another man's life is far greater.

Now, Athenians, I am not going to argue for my own sake, as you may think, but for yours, that you may not sin against the gods or lightly reject their favor by condemning me. If you kill me you will not easily find another like me, who, if I may use such a ludicrous figure of speech, am a sort of gadfly, given to the State by the gods. The State is like a great and noble steed who is slow in his motions owing to his very size and needs to be stirred into life. I am that gadfly which the gods have given the State and all day long and in all places am always fastening upon you, arousing, persuading, and reproaching you. As you will not easily find another like me, I would advise you to spare me. I believe you may feel irritated at being suddenly awakened when you are caught napping. You may think if you were to strike me dead, as Anytus advises, which you easily might, then you would sleep on for the remainder of your lives, unless the god in his care of you gives you another gadfly. That I am given to you by the god is proved by this: if I had been like other men, I should not have neglected my own concerns all these years, and been occupied with yours, coming to you individually like a father or elder brother, exhorting you to think about virtue. This, I say, would not be like human nature. If I had gained anything, or if my exhortations had been paid, there would be some sense in that; but now, as you see not even my accusers dare to say I have ever sought pay from anyone. They have no witnesses for that. I have a witness of the truth of what I say; my poverty is my witness.

Someone may wonder why I go about in private giving advice and busying myself with the concerns of others, but do not come forward in public and advise the state. I will tell you the reason for this. You have often heard me speak of an oracle or sign which comes to me and is the divinity which Meletus ridicules in the indictment. This sign I have had ever since I was a child. The sign is a voice which comes to me and always forbids me to do something which I am going to do, but never commands me to do anything. This is what stands in the way of my being a politician. And correctly I think. For I am certain, O men of Athens, if I had engaged in politics, I would have perished long ago, and done no good either to you or to myself. Do not be offended at my telling you the truth. The truth is no man who goes to war with you or any other multitude, honestly struggling against acts of unrighteousness in the state, will save his life. He who will really fight for the right, if he would live even for a little while, must have a private station and not a public one.

I can give you proofs of this, not words only, but deeds, which you value more than words. Let me tell you a part of my own life which will prove to you I would never have yielded to injustice from any fear of death, and that if I had not yielded I should have died at once. I will tell you a story—tasteless perhaps and commonplace, but nevertheless true. . . .

The only office of state which I ever held, O men of Athens, was when I served on the council. The clan Antiochis, which is my clan, had the presidency at the trial of the generals who had not taken up the bodies of the slain after the battle of Arginusae. You proposed to try them all together, which was illegal, as you all thought afterwards, but at the time I was the only one of the committee who was opposed to the illegality. I gave my vote against you. When the orators threatened to impeach and arrest me and have me taken away, and you called and shouted, I made up my mind I would run the risk, having law and justice with me, rather than take part in your injustice because I feared imprisonment and death. This happened in the days of the democracy. But when the oligarchy of the Thirty was in power, they brought me and four others into the rotunda, and told us to bring in Leon from Salamis because they wanted to execute him. This was an example of the sort of commands which they were always giving in order to implicate as many as possible in their crimes. Then I showed, not in word only but in deed, if I may be allowed to use such an expression, I cared not a straw for death, and my only fear was the fear of doing an unrighteous or unholy thing. The strong arm of that oppressive power did not frighten me into doing wrong. When we came out of the rotunda the other four went to Salamis and fetched Leon, but I went quietly home. For this I might have lost my life, had not the power of the Thirty shortly afterwards come to an end. And to this many will witness.

Now do you really imagine I could have survived all these years if I had led a public life, supposing that like a good man I always supported the right and made justice, as I should, the first thing? No indeed, men of Athens, neither I nor any other. I have been always the same in all my actions, public as well as private, and never have yielded to any base agreement with those who are slanderously termed my disciples, or to any other. The truth is I have no regular disciples but if anyone likes to come and hear me while I am pursuing my mission, whether he be young or old, he may freely come. Nor do I converse with those who pay only, and not with those who do not pay; but anyone, whether he be rich or poor, may question and answer me and listen to my words. If he turns out to be a bad man or a good one, I am not responsible, as I never taught him anything. If anyone says he has ever learned or heard anything from me in private which all the world has not heard, I would like you to know that he is lying.

I will be asked, why do people delight in continually conversing with you? I have told you already, Athenians, the whole truth about this. They like to hear the cross-examination of the pretenders to wisdom; there is amusement in this. This is a duty which the gods have imposed upon me, as I am assured by oracles, visions, and in every sort of way which the will of divine power was ever made plain to anyone. This is true, O

Athenians or, if not true, would be soon refuted. If I am really corrupting the youth and have corrupted some of them already, those who have grown up and are aware I gave them bad advice in the days of their youth should come forward as accusers and take their revenge. If they do not like to come themselves, some of their relatives, fathers, brothers, or other kinsmen, should say what evil their families suffered at my hands. Now is their time. I see many of them in the court.

There is Crito, who is of the same age and of the same township as myself, and there is Critobulus, his son, whom I also see. There is Lysanias of Sphettus, who is the father of Aeschines—he is present; and also there is Antiphon of Cephisus, who is the father of Epigenes; and there are the brothers of several who have associated with me. There is Nicostratus, the son of Theosdotides, and the brother of Theodotus (not Theodotus himself—he is dead, and therefore, he will not seek to stop him). There is Paralus, the son of Demodocus, who had a brother Theages; and Adeimantus, the son of Ariston, whose brother Plato is present; and Aeantodorus, who is the brother of Apollodorus, whom I also see. I might mention a great many others, any of whom Meletus could have produced as witnesses in the course of his speech. Let him still produce them, if he has forgotten—I will make way for him. Let him speak, if he has any testimony of this sort which he can produce. Nay, Athenians, the very opposite is the truth. For all these are ready to witness on behalf of the corruptor, of the destroyer of their kindred, as Meletus and Anytus call me; not the corrupted youth only— there might have been a motive for that—but their uncorrupted elder relatives. Why should they, too, support me with their testimony? Why indeed, except for the reason of truth and justice, and because they know I am speaking the truth and Meletus is lying.

Well, Athenians, this and similar to this is nearly all the defense I have to offer. Yet a word more. Perhaps there may be someone who is offended by me, when he calls to mind how he himself on a similar, or even a less serious occasion, had recourse to prayers and supplications with many tears, and how he produced his children in court, which was a moving spectacle, together with a group of his relations and friends. I, who am probably in danger of my life, will do none of these things. Perhaps this may come into his mind and he may be set against me, and vote in anger because he is displeased at this. Now if there is such a person among you I reply to him: My friend, I am a man, and like other men, a creature of flesh and blood and not of wood or stone, as Homer says. I have a family, yes, and sons, O Athenians, three in number, one of whom is growing up, and two others who are still young. Yet I will not bring any of them here in order to beg you for an acquittal. And why not? Not from any self-will or disregard of you. Whether I am, or am not, afraid of death is another question, of which I will not now speak. My reason is that I feel such conduct to be discreditable to myself, you and the whole state. One who has reached my years and who has a name for wisdom, whether deserved or not, should not lower himself. The world has decided that Socrates is in some way superior to other men. And if those among you who are said to be superior in wisdom, courage and any other virtue, lower themselves in this way, how shameful is their conduct!

I have seen men of reputation, when they have been condemned, behaving in the strangest manner. They seemed to believe they were going to suffer something dreadful if they died, and they could be immortal if you only allowed them to live. I think they were a dishonor to the state, and any stranger coming in would say the most eminent men of Athens, to whom the Athenians themselves give honor and command, are no better than women. I say these things ought not to be done by those of us who are of reputation; and if they are done, you ought not to permit them. You ought to show you are more inclined to condemn, not the man who is quiet, but the man who gets up a doleful scene and makes the city ridiculous.

Setting aside the question of dishonor, there seems to be something wrong in begging a judge and thus procuring an acquittal instead of informing and convincing him. For his duty is not to make a present of justice, but to give judgment. He has sworn he will judge according to the laws and not according to his own good pleasure. Neither he nor we should get into the habit of perjuring ourselves—there can be no piety in that. Do not require me to do what I consider dishonorable, impious and wrong, especially now, when I am being tried for impiety on the indictment of Meletus. For if, O men of Athens, by force of persuasion and entreaty, I could overpower your oaths, then I should be teaching you to believe there are no gods, and convict myself in my own defense of not believing in them. But that is not the case. I do believe there are gods and in a far higher sense than any of my accusers believe in them. To you and to the gods I commit my cause, to be determined by you as is best for you and me.

(The jury returns a guilty verdict and Meletus proposes death as a punishment.)

There are many reasons why I am not grieved, O men of Athens, at the vote of condemnation. I expected this and am only surprised the votes are so nearly equal. I thought the majority against me would have been far larger, but now, had thirty votes gone over to the other side, I would have been acquitted. And I may say I have escaped Meletus' charges. And I may say more; without the assistance of Anytus and Lycon, he would not have had a fifth part of the votes, as the law requires, in which case he would have incurred a fine of a thousand drachmae.

He proposes death as the penalty. What shall I propose on my part, O men of Athens? Clearly what is my due. What is that which I ought to pay or to receive? What shall be done to the man who has never been idle during his whole life, but has been careless of what the many care about—wealth, family interests, military offices and speaking in the Assembly, and courts, plots, and parties. Believing I was really too honest a man to follow in this way and live, I did not go where I could do no good to you or to myself. I went where I could do the greatest good privately to every one of you. I sought to persuade every man among you that he must look to himself and seek virtue and wisdom before he looks to his private interests, and look to the welfare of the State before he looks to the wealth of the

State. This should be the order which he observes in all his actions. What shall be done to someone like me? Doubtless some good thing, O men of Athens, if he has his reward and the good should be suitable to him. What would be a reward suitable to a poor man who is your benefactor, who desires to instruct you? There can be no more fitting reward than maintenance in the Prytaneum, O men of Athens, a reward which he deserves far more than the citizen who wins the prize at Olympia in the horse or chariot race, whether the chariots were drawn by two horses or many. For I am in need and he has enough. He only gives you the appearance of happiness and I give you the reality. Thus, if I am to estimate the penalty justly, I say maintenance in the Prytaneum is just.

Perhaps you think I am mocking you in saying this, as in what I said before about the tears and prayers. But that is not the case. I speak because I am convinced I never intentionally wronged anyone, although I cannot convince you of that—for we have had a short conversation only. If there were a law at Athens, such as there is in other cities, that a case involving the death penalty should not be decided in one day, then I believe I would have convinced you. Now the time is too short. I cannot quickly refute great slanders and, as I am convinced that I never wronged another, I will assuredly not wrong myself. I will not say of myself that I deserve any evil, nor propose any penalty. Why should I? Because I am afraid of the penalty of death which Meletus proposes? When I do not know whether death is a good or an evil, why should I propose a penalty which would certainly be an evil? Shall I say imprisonment? And why should I live in prison, and be the slave of the judges of the year—of the Eleven? Or shall the penalty be a fine, and imprisonment until the fine is paid? There is the same objection. I should have to stay in prison for I have no money and cannot pay. And if I say exile, and this may be the penalty which you will affix, I must indeed be blinded by love of life, if I do not realize that you, who are my own citizens, cannot endure my words and have found them so hateful you want to silence them, others are likely to endure me. No indeed,

men of Athens, that is not very likely. And what a life should I lead, at my age, wandering from city to city, living in ever-changing exile and always being driven out! For I am quite sure that whatever place I go, the young men will come to me. If I drive them away, their elders will drive me out. And, if I let them come, their fathers and friends will drive me out for their sakes.

Someone will say: Yes, Socrates, but can you not hold your tongue, and then go into a foreign city, and no one will interfere with you? Now I have great difficulty in making you understand my answer to this. If I tell you this would be a disobedience to a divine command, and therefore I cannot hold my tongue, you will not believe I am serious. If I say again that greatest good is daily to converse about virtue, and all that concerning which you hear me examining myself and others, and that the life which is unexamined is not worth living—that you are still less likely to believe. And yet what I say is true, although it is hard for me to persuade you. Moreover, I am not accustomed to thinking I deserve any punishment. Had I money I might have proposed to give you what I had and would have been none the worse. But you see I have none and can only ask you to proportion the fine to my means. However, I think I could afford a mina, and therefore I propose that penalty. Plato, Crito, Critobulus, and Apollodorus, my friends here, bid me say 30 minae and they will pay the fine. Well, then, say 30 minae, let that be the penalty for that they will be ample security to you.

(The jury votes again to decide between Socrates' proposal of a fine and Meletus' proposal of the death penalty. The verdict is death.)

Not much time will be gained, O Athenians, in return for the evil name you will get from the enemies of the city, who will say you killed Socrates, a wise man. They will call me wise even though I am not wise when they want to reproach you. If you waited a little while, your desire would have been fulfilled in the course of nature. I am far advanced in years, as you may perceive, and not far from death. I am speaking now only to those of you who have condemned me to death. And I have another thing to say to them: You think I was convicted through deficiency of words—I mean, if I had thought fit to leave nothing undone, nothing unsaid, I might have gained an acquittal. Not so, the deficiency which led to my conviction was not of words—certainly not. I did not have the boldness or impudence or inclination to address you as you would have liked me to address you, weeping, wailing, and lamenting, and saying and doing many things which you have been accustomed to hear from others, and which, as I say, are unworthy of me. I believed I should not do anything common or cowardly in the hour of danger. I do not now repent the manner of my defense. I would rather die having spoken after my manner than speak in your manner and live. Neither in war nor yet at law ought any man to use every way of escaping death. Often in battle there is no doubt if a man will throw away his arms and fall on his knees before his pursuers, he may escape death. In other dangers there are other ways of escaping death, if a man is willing to say and do anything.

The difficulty, my friends, is not in avoiding death, but in avoiding evil; for evil runs faster than death. I am old and move slowly, and the slower runner has overtaken me, and my accusers are keen and quick, and the faster runner, who is evil, has overtaken them. And now I depart hence condemned by you to suffer the penalty of death, and they, too, go their ways condemned by the truth to suffer the penalty of wickedness. I must abide by my award—let them abide by theirs. I suppose these things may be regarded as fated—and I think things are as they should be.

And now, O men who have condemned me, I would prophesy to you. I am about to die and that is the hour in which men are gifted with prophetic power. I prophesy to you who are my murderers that, immediately after my death, punishment far heavier than you have inflicted on me will await you. You have killed me because you wanted to escape the accuser, and not to give an account of your lives. That will not be as you suppose. I say there will be more accusers of you than there are now, accusers I have restrained: and as they are younger they will be more severe with you and you will be more offended at them. For if you

think that by killing men you can avoid the accuser censuring your lives, you are mistaken; that is not a way of escape which is either possible or honorable. The easiest, noblest way is not to be crushing others but to be improving yourselves. This is the prophecy which I utter before my departure to the members of the jury who have condemned me.

Friends, who have acquitted me, I would like also to talk with you about this thing which has happened, while the judges are busy, and before I go to the place where I must die. Stay awhile, for we may as well talk with one another while there is time. You are my friends and I would like to show you the meaning of this event which has happened to me. O my judges—for you I may truly call judges—I should like to tell you of a wonderful occurrence. Before this, the familiar oracle within me has constantly been in the habit of opposing me even about trifles, if I was going to make a slip or error about anything. Now, as you see there has come upon me that which may be thought, and is generally believed to be, the last and worst evil. But the oracle made no sign of opposition, either as I was leaving my house and going out in the morning, or when I was going up into this court, or while I was speaking at anything I was going to say. I have often been stopped in the middle of a speech, but now in nothing I either said or did has the oracle opposed me. Why is this? I will tell you. I regard this as a proof that what has happened to me is a good, and that those of us who think that death is an evil are in error. This is a great proof to me of what I am saying, for the customary sign would surely have opposed me had I been going to evil and not to good.

Let us reflect in another way, and we shall see there is great reason to hope that death is a good. Either death is a state of nothingness and utter unconsciousness, or, as men say, there is a change and migration of the soul from this world to another. Now if you suppose there is no consciousness, but a sleep like the sleep of him who is undisturbed even by the sight of dreams, death will be an unspeakable gain. If a person were to select the night in which his sleep was undisturbed even by dreams and were to compare this with the other days and nights of his life, and then were to tell us how many days and nights he passed in the course of his life better and more pleasantly than this one, I think any man, even a great king, will not find many such days or nights, when compared with the others. Now if death is like this, I say to die is to gain, for eternity is then only a single night. But if death is the journey to another place, and there, as men say, all the dead are, what good, O my friends and judges, can be greater than this? If indeed when the traveler arrives in the other world, he is delivered from the false judges in this world, and finds the true judges who are said to give judgment there, Minos, Rhadamanthus, Aeacus, and Triptolemus, and other sons of the gods who were righteous in their own life, that journey will be worth making. What would a man give if he might converse with Orpheus and Masaeus and Hesiod and Homer? Nay, if this is true, let me die again and again. I, too, shall have a wonderful interest in a place where I can converse with Palamedes, and Ajax, the son of Telamon, and other heroes of old who have suffered death through an unjust judgment. I think there will be pleasure, in comparing my own sufferings with theirs. Above all, I shall be able to continue my search into true and false knowledge. As in this world, so also in that; I shall find out who is wise, and who pretends to be wise but is not. What would a man give, O judges, to be able to examine the leader of the great Trojan expedition; or Odysseus or Sisy-

phus, or numberless others, men and women too! What infinite delight would there be in conversing with them and asking them questions! For in that world they do not put a man to death for such investigations, certainly not. For besides being happier in that world than in this, they will be immortal, if what is said is true.

Wherefore, O judges, be of good cheer about death, and know this truth—no evil can happen to a good man, either in life or after death. He and his are not neglected by the gods nor has my own approaching end happened by mere chance. I see clearly that to die and be released was better for me and therefore the oracle gave no sign. Because of this also, I am not angry with my accusers or my condemners. They have done me no harm, although neither of them meant to do me any good; and for this I gently blame them.

Still I have a favor to ask of them. When my sons are grown up, I would ask you, O my friends, to punish them. I would have you trouble them, as I troubled you, if they seem to care about riches, or anything, more than virtue. Or, if they pretend to be something when they are really nothing, then chastise them, as I chastised you, for not caring about what they ought to care, and thinking they are something when they are really nothing. And if you do this, I and my sons will have received justice at your hands. The hour of departure has arrived, and we go on our different ways—I to die, and you to live. Which is better only the god knows.

Suggestions for Further Reading

A good place to start is with John M. Cooper's "Socrates," in volume 9 of *Routledge Encyclopedia of Philosophy* (London: Routledge, 1998, pp. 8–18).

For recent studies of Socrates and his thought, see Hugh H. Benson (ed.), *Essays on the Philosophy of Socrates* (New York: Oxford University Press, 1992).

You may have noticed that Plato does not give an account of the prosecution's case. If you are interested in a controversial reconstruction of the Athenian side by one of America's great journalists, try I. F. Stone's *The Trial of Socrates* (Boston: Little, Brown, 1988). Stone's footnotes will take you deep into the literature, and his intriguing account will puncture some of the most sacred and cherished myths about Socrates.

Gregory Vlastos's *Socrates, Ironist and Moral Philosopher* (Ithaca, NY: Cornell University Press, 1991) challenges some traditional views of Socrates but is advanced.

Videos

In *Plato's Apology: The Life and Teachings of Socrates* (30 minutes), M. Adler explains his view of Socrates' method and teaching by examining key passages in *The Apology. The Trial of Socrates* (29 minutes) provides a dramatic reenactment. Both are available from Insight Media, 2162 Broadway, New York, NY 10024.

Maxwell Anderson's *Barefoot in Athens* (76 minutes) is a play that centers on Socrates' trial. It is available from Films for the Humanities and Sciences, PO Box 2053, Princeton, NJ 08543.

3.5 Aristotle on Happiness and the Life of Moderation

Aristotle (384–322 BCE) was a student of Plato and is recognized, along with Plato, as one of the greatest philosophic minds of the ancient Western world. He made significant contributions to all areas of philosophy, as well as to the natural sciences. He founded a school in Athens called the Lyceum. His students became known as the Peripatetics (which means "to walk around") because of his habit of strolling in the garden of the school while giving instruction.

Aristotle was from Macedonia and, while living there, tutored Alexander, the son of the king. Alexander the Great, as he was later called, established a vast empire. Legend has it that as he traveled toward India on his conquests, Alexander sent plant and animal specimens back to Aristotle. Alexander's death in 323 triggered anti-Macedonian sentiment in Athens. Realizing that his life might be in danger, Aristotle left in a hurry and, recalling what happened to Socrates, reputedly made the comment that he was leaving lest he provide an opportunity for the Athenians to "sin twice against philosophy."

Aristotle was a **teleologist**. He believed that all existing things have a purpose (in Greek the word for "end," "goal," or "purpose" is *telos*) and that their purpose constitutes their good. So, when seeking to answer the question "How should one live?" Aristotle naturally considers the issue of what is the good for humans. Notice he does not ask what is his good. He is not concerned with individual good but with the good for all humans. He calls this good **eudaimonia**, which is here translated as "happiness." This translation is somewhat misleading because in English happiness refers to a feeling. For Aristotle happiness is more than a feeling; it is also a way of acting and living. Hence, some have translated it as human "flourishing." Since flourishing involves achieving excellence, any discussion of *eudaimonia* or human flourishing must pay attention to the notion of virtue.

The word *virtue* (*areté* in Greek) refers to an excellence. The excellence of a thing is the full development of the potentials of its essential nature. Because the human animal is essentially a "rational" animal according to Aristotle, the good for humans must involve the realization of their rational natures. For Aristotle, a life of moderation accords best with reason. He views moral virtue as a mean between extremes and vice as either a deficiency or an excess. For example, courage is the mean between rashness (the vice of excess in confidence) and cowardice (the vice of deficiency in confidence). However, Aristotle does recognize that some actions have no mean. For example, there is no mean for the act of murder. How do you murder someone with moderation?

The selection that follows is from the first two books of the *Nicomachean Ethics,* which consists of lectures on *ethos* (character, habit) supposedly edited by Aristotle's son, Nicomachus. In the first book, Aristotle presents an argument in support of his claim that happiness is the chief end of humans and searches for a precise definition. In the second, he examines the question of virtue and proposes a theory about the nature of moral virtue. He argues that living a morally virtuous life is essential to being happy. Unfortunately, there is not enough space to include the rest of what he has to say here, but the following summary will tell you where his discussion leads.

The third and fourth books continue the discussion of moral virtue and introduce the issue of whether humans are free to choose to live a virtuous life. Book 5 examines the virtue of justice. This is the highest social value because, Aristotle argues, the good life cannot be lived apart from a good society. In Book 6, Aristotle shifts his attention from moral virtue to intellectual virtue. Humans are concerned with both theoretical and practical wisdom. Practical wisdom is essential to happiness because in order to live our lives well we must exercise good judgment. Books 7–9 deal with issues of moral strength and weakness, pleasure, and friendship. Pleasure is not the highest good, he argues, but it is part of the highest good. We also need good friends to be happy. In the final chapter, Aristotle focuses on theoretical wisdom and argues that the highest human happiness is the contemplation of truth. Hence, only theoretical wisdom can lead to "primary" happiness, while practical wisdom can lead to "secondary" happiness.

Reading Aristotle will test your reading skills. He is not easy to read, in part because you are reading the translation of lecture notes edited by someone else. However, he is also dealing with issues about how to live at a profound level, and one must get into his mind, so to speak, in order to follow his line of reasoning. The effort will, however, be repaid as you learn to think about the issue of how to conduct one's life at a deeper level.

Be sure to activate your "I-don't-understand" list and go over it with a classmate or in class for clarification.

Reading Questions

1. What, according to Aristotle, has the good been declared by others to be?
2. Why must the chief good be desired for its own sake?
3. Aristotle says that on a very abstract level, happiness can be considered as "living well and doing well." If so, the next question becomes "In what specifically does this consist?" Aristotle argues that whatever it is it must be something final, chosen for its own sake, self-sufficient, and an end of action. If this is so, why will not health or wealth or pleasure or honor (all of which are goods) count as the chief good or happiness?
4. How does Aristotle arrive at the conclusion that the human good (happiness) is an activity of soul in accordance with virtue? (*Hint:* His argument begins with the notion that human beings have a function.)
5. Given what Aristotle says in Book 1, Section 9, about how happiness is acquired, how do you think he would respond to the question "Can someone be happy even if he or she suffers bad luck?"

6. What are the two kinds of virtue, and do the moral virtues arise by nature (are we born with them?) or by learning and practice?

7. Why does Aristotle conclude that virtue must be a state of character?

8. State in your own words what Aristotle means when he claims, "Virtue, then, is a state of character concerned with choice, lying in a mean, i.e., the mean relative to us, this being determined by a rational principle, and by that principle by which the man of practical wisdom would determine it."

9. What are the excesses, deficiencies, and the means with respect to (a) feelings of fear and confidence, (b) giving and taking of money, (c) honor and dishonor, and (d) anger?

10. In Book 2, Section 9, Aristotle gives some advice for those who wish to practice virtue (hit the mean). Summarize his advice.

11. What are the similarities and differences between how a Confucian (see Section 3.3 above) would answer the question "How should one live?" and how Aristotle would answer it?

Nicomachean Ethics

ARISTOTLE

Book I

1.

EVERY ART AND EVERY INQUIRY, and similarly every action and pursuit, is thought to aim at some good; and for this reason the good has rightly been declared to be that at which all things aim. But a certain difference is found among ends; some are activities, others are products apart from the activities that produce them. Where there are ends apart from the actions, it is the nature of the products to be better than the activities. Now, as there are many actions, arts, and sciences, their ends also are many; the end of the medical art is health, that of shipbuilding a vessel, that of strategy victory, that of economics wealth. But where such arts fall under a single capacity—as bridlemaking and the other arts concerned with the equipment of horses fall under the art of riding, and this and every military action under strategy, in the same way other arts

fall under yet others—in all of these the ends of the master arts are to be preferred to all the subordinate ends; for it is for the sake of the former that the latter are pursued. It makes no difference whether the activities themselves are the ends of the actions, or something else apart from the activities, as in the case of the sciences just mentioned.

2.

If, then, there is some end of the things we do, which we desire for its own sake (everything else being desired for the sake of this), and if we do not choose everything for the sake of something else (for at that rate the process would go on to infinity, so that our desire would be empty and vain), clearly this must be the good and the chief good. Will not the knowledge of it, then, have a great influence on life? Shall we not, like archers who have a mark to aim at, be more likely to hit

Reprinted from Nicomachean Ethics, *translated by W. D. Ross (1925), by permission of Oxford University Press. Footnotes deleted.*

upon what is right? If so, we must try, in outline at least to determine what it is, and of which of the sciences or capacities it is the object. . . .

4.

Let us resume our inquiry and state, in view of the fact that all knowledge and every pursuit aims at some good, . . . what is the highest of all goods achievable by action. Verbally there is very general agreement; for both the general run of men and people of superior refinement say that it is happiness, and identify living well and doing well with being happy; but with regard to what happiness is they differ, and the many do not give the same account as the wise. For the former think it is some plain and obvious thing, like pleasure, wealth, or honour; they differ, however, from one another—and often even the same man identifies it with different things, with health when he is ill, with wealth when he is poor; but, conscious of their ignorance, they admire those who proclaim some great ideal that is above their comprehension. Now some thought that apart from these many goods there is another which is self-subsistent and causes the goodness of all these as well. To examine all the opinions that have been held were perhaps somewhat fruitless; enough to examine those that are most prevalent or that seem to be arguable. . . .

5.

Let us, however, resume our discussion from the point at which we digressed. To judge from the lives that men lead, most men, and men of the most vulgar type, seem (not without some ground) to identify the good, or happiness, with pleasure; which is the reason why they love the life of enjoyment. For there are, we may say, three prominent types of life—that just mentioned, the political, and thirdly the contemplative life. Now the mass of mankind are evidently quite slavish in their tastes, preferring a life suitable to beasts, but they get some ground for their view from the fact that many of those in high places share the tastes of Sardanapallus. A consideration of the prominent types of life shows that people of superior refinement and of active disposition identify happiness with honour; for this is, roughly speaking, the end of the political life. But it seems too superficial to be what we are looking for, since it is thought to depend on those who bestow honour rather than on him who receives it, but the good we divine to be something proper to a man and not easily taken from him. Further, men seem to pursue honour in order that they may be assured of their goodness; at least it is by men of practical wisdom that they seek to be honoured, and among those who know them, and on the ground of their virtue; clearly, then, according to them, at any rate, virtue is better. And perhaps one might even suppose this to be, rather than honour, the end of the political life. But even this appears somewhat incomplete; for possession of virtue seems actually compatible with being asleep, or with life-long inactivity, and, further, with the greatest sufferings and misfortunes; but a man who was living so no one would call happy, unless he were maintaining a thesis at all costs. But enough of this; for the subject has been sufficiently treated even in the current discussions. Third comes the contemplative life, which we shall consider later. The life of money-making is one undertaken under compulsion, and wealth is evidently not the good we are seeking; for it is merely useful and for the sake of something else. And so one might rather take the aforenamed objects to be ends; for they are loved for themselves. But it is evident that not even these are ends; yet many arguments have been thrown away in support of them. Let us leave this subject, then. . . .

7.

Let us again return to the good we are seeking, and ask what it can be. It seems different in different actions and arts; it is different in medicine, in strategy, and in the other arts likewise. What then is the good of each? Surely that for whose sake everything else is done. In medicine this is health, in strategy victory, in architecture a house, in any other sphere something else, and in every action and pursuit the end; for it is for the sake of this that all men do whatever else they do. Therefore, if there is an end for all that we do, this will be the good achievable by action, and if there are more than one, these will be the goods achievable by action.

So the argument has by a different course reached the same point; but we must try to state this even more clearly. Since there are evidently more than one end, and we choose some of these (e.g., wealth, flutes, and in general instruments) for the sake of something else, clearly not all ends are final ends; but the chief good is evidently something final. Therefore, if there is only one final end, this will be what we are seeking, and if there are more than one, the most final of these will be what we are seeking. Now we call that which is in itself worthy of pursuit more final than that which is worthy of pursuit for the sake of something else, and that which is never desirable for the sake of something else more final than the things that are desirable both in themselves and for the sake of that other thing, and therefore we call final without qualification that which is always desirable in itself and never for the sake of something else.

Now such a thing happiness, above all else, is held to be; for this we choose always for itself and never for the sake of something else, but honour, pleasure, reason, and every virtue we choose indeed for themselves (for if nothing resulted from them we should still choose each of them), but we choose them also for the sake of happiness, judging that by means of them we shall be happy. Happiness, on the other hand, no one chooses for the sake of these, nor, in general, for anything other than itself.

From the point of view of self-sufficiency the same result seems to follow; for the final good is thought to be self-sufficient. Now by self-sufficient we do not mean that which is sufficient for a man by himself, for one who lives a solitary life, but also for parents, children, wife, and in general for his friends and fellow citizens, since man is born for citizenship. But some limit must be set to this; for if we extend our requirement to ancestors and descendants and friends' friends we are in for an infinite series. Let us examine this question, however, on another occasion; the

self-sufficient we now define as that which when isolated makes life desirable and lacking in nothing; and such we think happiness to be; and further we think it most desirable of all things, without being counted as one good thing among others—if it were so counted it would clearly be made more desirable by the addition of even the least of goods; for that which is added becomes an excess of goods, and of goods the greater is always more desirable. Happiness, then, is something final and self-sufficient, and is the end of action.

Presumably, however, to say that happiness is the chief good seems a platitude, and a clearer account of what it is is still desired. This might perhaps be given, if we could first ascertain the function of man. For just as for a flute-player, a sculptor, or any artist, and, in general, for all things that have a function or activity, the good and the "well" is thought to reside in the function, so would it seem to be for man, if he has a function. Have the carpenter, then, and the tanner certain functions or activities, and has man none? Is he born without a function? Or as eye, hand, foot, and in general each of the parts evidently has a function, may one lay it down that man similarly has a function apart from all these? What then can this be? Life seems to be common even to plants, but we are seeking what is peculiar to man. Let us exclude, therefore, the life of nutrition and growth. Next there would be a life of perception, but it also seems to be common even to the horse, the ox, and every animal. There remains, then, an active life of the element that has a rational principle; of this, one part has such a principle in the sense of being obedient to one, the other in the sense of possessing one and exercising thought. And, as "life of the rational element" also has two meanings, we must state that life in the sense of activity is what we mean; for this seems to be the more proper sense of the term. Now if the function of man is an activity of soul which follows or implies a rational principle, and if we say "a so-and-so" and "a good so-and-so" have a function which is the same in kind, e.g., a lyre-player and a good lyre-player, and so without qualification in all cases, eminence in respect of goodness being added to the name of the function (for the function of a lyre-player is to play the lyre, and that of a good lyre-player is to do so well): if this is the case, [and we state the function of man to be a certain kind of life, and this to be an activity or actions of the soul implying a rational principle, and the function of a good man to be the good and noble performance of these, and if any action is well performed when it is performed in accordance with the appropriate excellence: if this is the case,] human good turns out to be activity of soul in accordance with virtue, and if there are more than one virtue, in accordance with the best and most complete.

But we must add "in a complete life." For one swallow does not make a summer, nor does one day; and so too one day, or a short time, does not make a man blessed and happy. . . .

[*Editor's Note:* In Section 8, here omitted, Aristotle compares his view of happiness as living well and doing well with what most people say. He finds that many who have expressed their views on this topic agree in general with his own views. He takes this as confirmation that he is on the right track. Many regard happiness as consisting of three kinds of goods: worldly goods, bodily goods, and goods of the soul. While Aristotle wishes to stress in his account that happiness resides primarily in goods of the soul (the virtues), he acknowledges that we are not likely to call someone happy if they lack entirely worldly goods (wealth, friends, political influence) and bodily goods (noble family, handsome appearance, long life, and children). But both worldly goods and bodily goods often depend on circumstances beyond one's control. Can one be happy, even if misfortune diminishes some worldly and bodily goods? Some would say that happiness depends on good fortune. Others that it is a matter of acquiring virtue or excellence.]

9.

For this reason also the question is asked, whether happiness is to be acquired by learning or by habituation or some other sort of training, or comes in virtue of some divine providence or again by chance. Now if there is any gift of the gods to men, it is reasonable that happiness should be god-given, and most surely god-given of all human things inasmuch as it is the best. But this question would perhaps be more appropriate to another inquiry; happiness seems, however, even if it is not god-sent but comes as a result of virtue and some process of learning or training, to be among the most god-like things; for that which is the prize and end of virtue seems to be the best thing in the world, and something god-like and blessed.

It will also on this view be very generally shared; for all who are not maimed as regards their potentiality for virtue may win it by a certain kind of study and care. But if it is better to be happy thus than by chance, it is reasonable that the facts should be so, since everything that depends on the action of nature is by nature as good as it can be, and similarly everything that depends on art or any rational cause, and especially if it depends on the best of all causes. To entrust to chance what is greatest and most noble would be a very defective arrangement.

The answer to the question we are asking is plain also from the definition of happiness; for it has been said to be a virtuous activity of soul, of a certain kind. Of the remaining goods, some must necessarily pre-exist as conditions of happiness, and others are naturally co-operative and useful as instruments. And this will be found to agree with what we said at the outset; for we stated the end of political science to be the best end, and political science spends most of its pains on making the citizens to be of a certain character, viz. good and capable of noble acts.

It is natural, then, that we call neither ox nor horse nor any other of the animals happy; for none of them is capable of sharing in such activity. For this reason also a boy is not happy; for he is not yet capable of such acts, owing to his age; and boys who are called happy are being congratulated by reason of the hopes we have for them. For there is required, as we said, not only complete virtue but also a complete life, since many changes occur in life, and all manner of chances, and the most prosperous may fall into great misfortunes in old age, as is told of Priam in the Trojan Cycle; and one who has experienced such chances and has ended wretchedly no one calls happy. . . .

13.

Since happiness is an activity of soul in accordance with perfect virtue, we must consider the nature of virtue; for perhaps we shall thus see better the nature of happiness. . . .

Book II
1.

Virtue, then, being of two kinds, intellectual and moral, intellectual virtue in the main owes both its birth and its growth to teaching (for which reason it requires experience and time), while moral virtue comes about as a result of habit, whence also its name *ethiké* is one that is formed by a slight variation from the word *ethos* (habit). From this it is also plain that none of the moral virtues arises in us by nature; for nothing that exists by nature can form a habit contrary to its nature. For instance the stone which by nature moves downwards cannot be habituated to move upwards, not even if one tries to train it by throwing it up ten thousand times; nor can fire be habituated to move downwards, nor can anything else that by nature behaves in one way be trained to behave in another. Neither by nature, then, nor contrary to nature do the virtues arise in us; rather we are adapted by nature to receive them, and are made perfect by habit.

Again, of all the things that come to us by nature we first acquire the potentiality and later exhibit the activity (this is plain in the case of the senses; for it was not by often seeing or often hearing that we got these senses, but on the contrary we had them before we used them, and did not come to have them by using them); but the virtues we get by first exercising them, as also happens in the case of the arts as well. For the things we have to learn before we can do them, we learn by doing them, e.g., men become builders by building and lyre-players by playing

the lyre; so too we become just by doing just acts, temperate by doing temperate acts, brave by doing brave acts.

This is confirmed by what happens in states; for legislators make the citizens good by forming habits in them, and this is the wish of every legislator, and those who do not effect it miss their mark, and it is in this that a good constitution differs from a bad one.

Again, it is from the same causes and by the same means that every virtue is both produced and destroyed, and similarly every art; for it is from playing the lyre that both good and bad lyre-players are produced. And the corresponding statement is true of builders and of all the rest; men will be good or bad builders as a result of building well or badly. For if this were not so, there would have been no need of a teacher, but all men would have been born good or bad at their craft. This, then, is the case with the virtues also; by doing the acts that we do in our transactions with other men we become just or unjust, and by doing the acts that we do in the presence of danger, and being habituated to feel fear or confidence, we become brave or cowardly. The same is true of appetites and feelings of anger; some men become temperate and good-tempered, others self-indulgent and irascible, by behaving in one way or the other in the appropriate circumstances. Thus, in one word, states of character arise out of like activities. This is why the activities we exhibit must be of a certain kind; it is because the states of character correspond to the differences between these. It makes no small difference, then, whether we form habits of one kind or of another from our very youth; it makes a very great difference, or rather *all* the difference. . . .

5.

Next we must consider what virtue is. Since things that are found in the soul are of three kinds—passions, faculties, states of character, virtue must be one of these. By passions I mean appetite, anger, fear, confidence, envy, joy, friendly feeling, hatred, longing, emulation, pity, and in general the feelings that are accompanied by pleasure or pain; by faculties the things in virtue of which we are said to be capable of feeling these, e.g., of becoming angry or being pained or feeling pity; by states of character the things in virtue of which we stand well or badly with reference to the passions, e.g., with reference to anger we stand badly if we feel it violently or too weakly, and well if we feel it moderately; and similarly with reference to the other passions.

Now neither the virtues nor the vices are *passions,* because we are not called good or bad on the ground of our passions, but are so called on the ground of our virtues and our vices, and because we are neither praised nor blamed for our passions (for the man who feels fear or anger is not praised, nor is the man who simply feels anger blamed, but the man who feels it in a certain way), but for our virtues and our vices we are praised or blamed.

Again, we feel anger and fear without choice, but the virtues are modes of choice or involve choice. Further, in respect of the passions we are said to be moved, but in respect of the virtues and the vices we are said not to be moved but to be disposed in a particular way.

For these reasons also they are not *faculties;* for we are neither called good nor bad, nor praised nor blamed, for the simple capacity of feeling the passions; again, we have the faculties by nature, but we are not made good or bad by nature; we have spoken of this before.

If, then, the virtues are neither passions nor faculties, all that remains is that they should be *states of character.*

Thus we have stated what virtue is in respect of its genus.

6.

We must, however, not only describe virtue as a state of character, but also say what sort of state it is. We may remark, then, that every virtue or excellence both brings into good condition the thing of which it is the excellence and makes the work of that thing be done well; e.g., the excellence of the eye makes both the eye and its work good; for it is by the excellence of the eye that we see well. Similarly the excellence of the horse makes a horse both good in itself and good at running and at carrying its rider and at awaiting the attack of the enemy. Therefore, if this is true in every case, the virtue of man also will be the state of character which makes a man good and which makes him do his own work well.

How this is to happen we have stated already, but it will be made plain also by the following consideration of the specific nature of virtue. In everything that is continuous and divisible it is possible to take more, less, or an equal amount, and that either in terms of the thing itself or relative to us; and the equal is an intermediate between excess and defect. By the intermediate in the object I mean that which is equidistant from each of the extremes, which is one and the same for all men; by the intermediate relative to us that which is neither too much nor too little—and this is not one, nor the same for all. For instance, if ten is many and two is few, six is the intermediate, taken in terms of the object; for it exceeds and is exceeded by an equal amount; this is intermediate according to arithmetical proportion. But the intermediate relative to us is not to be taken so; if ten pounds are too much for a particular person to eat and two too little, it does not follow that the trainer will order six pounds; for this also is perhaps too much for the person who is to take it, or too little—too little for Milo, too much for the beginner in athletic exercises. The same is true of running and wrestling. Thus a master of any art avoids excess and defect, but seeks the intermediate and chooses this—the intermediate not in the object but relative to us. If it is thus, then, that every art does its work well—by looking to the intermediate and judging its works by this standard (so that we often say of good works of art that it is not possible either to take away or to add anything, implying that excess and defect destroy the goodness of works of art, while the mean preserves it; and good artists, as we say, look to this in their work), and if, further, virtue is more exact and better than any art, as nature also is, then virtue must have the quality of aiming at the intermediate. I mean moral virtue; for it is this that is concerned with passions and actions, and in these there is excess, defect, and the intermediate. For instance, both fear and confidence and appetite and anger and pity and in general pleasure and pain may be felt both too much and too little, and in both cases not well; but to feel them at the right times, with reference to the right objects, towards the right people, with the right motive, and in the right way, is what is both intermediate and best, and this is characteristic of virtue. Similarly with regard to actions also there is excess, defect, and the intermediate. Now virtue is concerned with passions and actions, in which excess is a form of failure, and so is defect, while the intermediate is praised and is a form of success; and being praised and being successful are both characteristics of virtue. Therefore virtue is a kind of mean, since, as we have seen, it aims at what is intermediate.

Again, it is possible to fail in many ways (for evil belongs to the class of the unlimited, as the Pythagoreans conjectured, and good to that of the limited), while to succeed is possible only in one way (for which reason also one is easy and the other difficult—to miss the mark easy, to hit it difficult); for these reasons also, then, excess and defect are characteristic of vice, and the mean of virtue;

> For men are good in but one way, but bad in many.

Virtue, then, is a state of character concerned with choice, lying in a mean, i.e., the mean relative to us, this being determined by a rational principle, and by that principle by which the man of practical wisdom would determine it. Now it is a mean between two vices, that which depends on excess and that which depends on defect; and again it is a mean because the vices respectively fall short of or exceed what is right in both passions and actions, while virtue both finds and chooses that which is intermediate. Hence in respect of its substance and the definition which states its essence virtue is a mean, with regard to what is best and right an extreme.

But not every action nor every passion admits of a mean; for some have names that already imply badness, e.g., spite, shamelessness, envy, and in the case of actions adultery, theft, murder; for all of these and suchlike things imply by their names that they are themselves bad, and not the excesses or deficiencies of them. It is not possible, then, ever to be right with regard to them; one must always be wrong. Nor does goodness or badness with regard to such things depend on committing adultery with the right woman, at the right time, and in the right way, but simply to do any of them is to go wrong. It would be equally absurd, then, to expect that in unjust, cowardly, and voluptuous action there should be a mean, an excess, and a deficiency; for at that rate there would be a mean of excess and of deficiency, an excess of excess, and a deficiency of deficiency. But as there is no excess and deficiency of temperance and courage because what is intermediate is in a sense an extreme, so too of the actions we have mentioned there is no mean nor any excess and deficiency, but however they are done they are wrong; for in general there is neither a mean of excess and deficiency, nor excess and deficiency of a mean.

7.

We must, however, not only make this general statement, but also apply it to the individual facts. For among statements about conduct those which are general apply more widely, but those which are particular are more genuine, since conduct has to do with individual cases, and our statements must harmonize with the facts in these cases. We may take these cases from our table. With regard to feelings of fear and confidence courage is the mean; of the people who exceed, he who exceeds in fearlessness has no name (many of the states have no name), while the man who exceeds in confidence is rash, and he who exceeds in fear and falls short in confidence is a coward. With regard to pleasures and pains—not all of them, and not so much with regard to the pains—the mean is temperance, the excess self-indulgence. Persons deficient with regard to the pleasures are not often found; hence such persons also have received no name. But let us call them "insensible."

With regard to giving and taking of money, the mean is liberality, the excess and the defect prodigality and meanness. In these actions people exceed and fall short in contrary ways; the prodigal exceeds in spending and falls short in taking, while the mean man exceeds in taking and falls short in spending. (At present we are giving a mere outline or summary, and are satisfied with this; later these states will be more exactly determined.) With regard to money there are also other dispositions—a mean, magnificence (for the magnificent man differs from the liberal man; the former deals with large sums, the latter with small ones), and excess, tastelessness and vulgarity, and a deficiency, niggardliness; these differ from the states opposed to liberality, and the mode of their difference will be stated later.

With regard to honour and dishonour the mean is proper pride, the excess is known as a sort of "empty vanity," and the deficiency is undue humility; and as we said liberality was related to magnificence, differing from it by dealing with small sums, so there is a state similarly related to proper pride, being concerned with small honours while that is concerned with great. For it is possible to desire honour as one ought, and more than one ought, and less, and the man who exceeds in his desires is called ambitious, the man who falls short unambitious, while the intermediate person has no name. The dispositions also are nameless, except that that of the ambitious man is called ambition. Hence the people who are at the extremes lay claim to the middle place; and we ourselves sometimes call the intermediate person ambitious and sometimes unambitious, and sometimes praise the ambitious man and sometimes the unambitious. The reason of our doing this will be stated in what follows; but now let us speak of the remaining states according to the method which has been indicated.

With regard to anger also there is an excess, a deficiency, and a mean. Although they can scarcely be said to have names, yet since we call the intermediate person good-tempered let us call the mean good temper; of the persons at the extremes let the one who exceeds be called irascible, and his vice irascibility, and the man who falls short an inirascible sort of person, and the deficiency inirascibility. . . .

9.

That moral virtue is a mean, then, and in what sense it is so, and that it is a mean between two vices, the one involving excess, the other deficiency, and that it is such because its character is to aim at what is intermediate in passions and in actions, has been sufficiently stated. Hence also it is no easy task to be good. For in everything it is no easy task to find the middle, e.g., to find the middle of a circle is not for everyone but for him who knows; so, too, any one can get angry—that is easy—or give or spend money; but to do this to the right person, to the right extent, at the right time, with the right motive, and in the right way, *that* is not for everyone, nor is it easy; wherefore goodness is both rare and laudable and noble. Hence he who aims at the intermediate must first depart from what is the more contrary to it, as Calypso advises—

Hold the ship out beyond that surf and spray.

For of the extremes one is more erroneous, one less so; therefore, since to hit the mean is hard in the extreme, we must as a second best, as people say, take the least of the evils; and this will be done best in the way we describe.

But we must consider the things towards which we ourselves also are easily carried away; for some of us tend to one thing, some to another; and this will be recognizable from the pleasure and the pain we feel. We must drag ourselves away to the contrary extreme; for we shall get into the intermediate state by drawing well away from error, as people do in straightening sticks that are bent.

Now in everything the pleasant or pleasure is most to be guarded against; for we do not judge it impartially. We ought, then, to feel towards pleasure as the elders of the people felt towards Helen, and in all circumstances repeat their saying; for if we dismiss pleasure thus we are less likely to go astray. It is by doing this, then, (to sum the matter up) that we shall best be able to hit the mean.

But this is no doubt difficult, and especially in individual cases; for it is not easy to determine both how and with whom and on what provocation and how long one should be angry; for we too sometimes praise those who fall short and call them good-tempered, but sometimes we praise those who get angry and call them manly. The man, however, who deviates little from goodness is not blamed, whether he do so in the direction of the more or of the less, but only the man who deviates more widely; for *he* does not fail to be noticed. But up to what point and to what extent a man must deviate before he becomes blame-worthy it is not easy to determine by reasoning, any more than anything else that is perceived by the senses; such things depend on particular facts, and the decision rests with perception. So much, then, is plain, that the intermediate state is in all things to be praised, but that we must incline sometimes towards the excess, sometimes towards the deficiency; for so shall we most easily hit the mean and what is right.

Suggestions for Further Reading

The article on "Aristotle" by T. H. Irwin in volume 1 of *Routledge Encyclopedia of Philosophy* (London: Routledge, 1998, pp. 415–435) provides a brief overview of Aristotle's thought, including a section on his ethical views.

For a summary of the *Nicomachean Ethics,* see Marvin Easterling's essay in *World Philosophy* (Volume 1), edited by Frank N. Magill (Englewood Cliffs, NJ: Salem Press, 1961, 1982), pp. 369–380.

See Stephen A. White's *Sovereign Virtue: Aristotle on the Relation Between Happiness and Prosperity* (Stanford, CA: Stanford University Press, 1992) for a careful analysis of Aristotle's views on the good life and the conditions that make it possible.

J. O. Urmson's *Aristotle's Ethics* (Oxford: Blackwell, 1988), Richard Kraut's *Aristotle on the Human Good* (Princeton, NJ: Princeton University Press, 1989), and Nancy Sherman's *The Fabric of Character: Aristotle's Theory of Virtue* (Oxford: Clarendon Press, 1989) will also prove helpful.

Contemporary virtue ethics builds on Aristotle's ideas. A good introduction to the contemporary debate can be found in *How Should One Live?: Essays on the Virtues,* edited by Roger Crisp (New York: Oxford University Press, 1996).

Videos

In *Aristotle's Ethics: The Theory of Happiness* (36 minutes), M. Adler concentrates on the first two books, discussing his understanding of Aristotle's views on the good life. Available from Insight Media, 2162 Broadway, New York, NY 10024.

Applying the Lessons of Ancient Greece: Martha Nussbaum (30 minutes) from Films for the Humanities and Sciences (PO Box 2053, Princeton, NJ 08543) draws on Aristotle and Greek tragedy to describe the fragility of human goodness.

3.6 The Song of God

Have you ever faced a conflict of duties? For example, have you ever been torn between your duty to be loyal to a friend and your obligation to tell the truth? Have you ever confronted a situation in which, in order to do right, you had to do wrong? Have you ever been faced with options, neither of which were morally desirable? Have you ever felt sad because you live in a world where so often you must choose between doing the "lesser of two evils"?

In this same world, we are taught that we should strive for moral perfection. Reason demands that we should always do what is right and good, never what is wrong. Yes, we must face temptation and wrestle with evil, but in the end are we not expected to triumph over sin? Jesus reportedly said, "Be perfect, as your Father in heaven is perfect." But moral perfection, be it demanded by reason or by God, is impossible. Try as we might, we cannot make this a morally black-and-white world; too many choices are various shades of moral gray.

If you have ever faced moral conflicts or wondered how moral perfection is possible in a morally imperfect world, you ought to be able to identify with Arjuna, one of the main characters in the *Bhagavad-Gita* (*Song of God*). This Hindu poem forms part of India's greatest epic poem, *Mahabharata.* It was written sometime between the fourth and second centuries BCE. Much of the *Gita* is a conversation between Arjuna, who is a member of the warrior caste and a leader of the Pandava family, and Sri (Lord) Krishna, his cousin and the incarnation of the god Vishnu (Vishnu is the god responsible, according to traditional Hindu mythology, for sustaining the universe after it has been created by the god Brahman). This conversation is narrated by Sanjaya, a poet and charioteer. It takes place just before a horrendous battle, which is part of a civil war started by some of Arjuna's relatives. Krishna attempts to get Arjuna to do his duty, which, since he is a warrior and since he is on the side of right in this war, is to fight. However, Arjuna is reluctant because those whom he must fight and kill are his relatives and friends. We can formulate Arjuna's conflict as a dilemma:

1. Either Arjuna ought to fight or he ought not to fight.
2. If he fights, he will violate his duty to protect his relatives.
3. If he does not fight, he will violate his duty as a warrior and his obligation to fight in a just war.
4. Therefore, either he violates one set of duties or he violates another set of duties.

To appreciate the depth of this dilemma in the Indian context, we need some background information about Hinduism. The word for duty is **dharma**, which means, among other things, the order or law underlying the cosmos and embodied in social and ethical law codes. In this context, to violate one's duty is to violate *dharma* and thus to upset the natural, cosmic order. An immoral act has a negative impact on the whole universe. According to Hindu moral theory, there is a moral and natural law called the law of **karma**. Karma comes from the Sanskrit word *karman,* which means "action" or "the consequences of action." The law of *karma* states, "what you sow, so shall you reap." If you do good deeds, you will experience good things sometime in this or a future life; and if you act wrongly, you will suffer accordingly. The ultimate goal in life is to escape **samsara**, the cycle of rebirth, death, and suffering that characterizes human life. Our *karma* traps us in *samsara* because it determines our **reincarnation**, or rebirth into a new physical body. If the full consequences of our karma do not come in this life, we must live another life, and another, and another, and another, until there is no *karma* left and we get it right. In this context, the question of how one should live takes on added urgency because a wrong answer affects both the order of the universe and your future lives.

However, how can "getting it right" be possible? If, like Arjuna, we are faced with situations in which no matter what we do we will get bad *karma,* there seems no hope of breaking the cycle. Arjuna is doomed if he fights and doomed if he does not fight. We live in a morally imperfect world, and we can never hope to achieve moral perfection. However, even if we could, even if all our actions produced good *karma,* we would still be reborn. If we do evil, we are reborn to reap the bad consequences. If we do good, we are reborn to reap the good consequences.

We have now uncovered a more universal form of Arjuna's dilemma, what A. L. Herman calls the "dilemma of action." We can express it as follows:

1. Either you do good acts or you do bad acts.
2. If you do good acts, you are bound to be reborn to reap the good results.
3. If you do bad acts, you are bound to be reborn to reap the bad results.
4. Therefore, you reap good results or bad results, but, in either case, you are reborn.

We may not believe that transgressions of moral codes violate the natural order of things, and we may not believe in the law of *karma* or the idea of reincarnation. Nevertheless, each of us in his or her own way faces a form of Arjuna's dilemma—the conflict of duties, the necessity to do wrong in order to do right, the lack of moral perfection.

Is there a way out of these moral dilemmas? Krishna teaches that freedom from these dilemmas is found in the practice of disciplined action (*karmayoga*). All action is to be performed detached from the consequences of action. Or, to put it another way, act unselfishly. Do what is right because it is right, not because the consequences will bring benefit or harm. How can this be done? One can do this by first gaining knowledge (*jnanayoga*) of our true natures (an eternal, unchanging self) and by dedicating the fruits of our actions in devotion (*bhaktiyoga*) to God. These three yogas or disciplines (*karma, jnana,* and *bhakti*) are interconnected. To live the good life requires acting in an appropriate way (unselfishly), knowing who you really are (an eternal self), and being devoted to God.

The first book describes Arjuna's state of mind and the dilemma in which he finds himself. The second book states the assumptions on which Krishna's advice is based: (1) The self is eternal and survives bodily death, and (2) one must do one's moral duty. Although this selection ends with the second book, the rest of the *Gita* goes on to elaborate the themes found in the second book. The third and fourth books develop the relationship between sacrifice and action, and the fifth and sixth books examine the tension between a life of renunciation (withdrawal from action) and action. In the final six books, Krishna recapitulates his basic teaching and integrates it with the need for religious devotion. The climax comes with Krishna's awe-inspiring theophany (revelation of his divinity).

The *Gita* is the "Song of God." Hence it is meant to be sung aloud. Lacking the music, we can and should speak it aloud in order to appreciate its poetic qualities as well as its meaning. Read it aloud dramatically and its meaning will be clearer to you.

Reading Questions

1. Why does Arjuna declare, "We don't know which weight is worse to bear—our conquering them or their conquering us"?
2. What reasons does Krishna present to Arjuna in support of his advice to fight?

3. What is the method of "spiritual discipline" (*karmayoga*)?

4. What are the characteristics, according to Krishna, of a person "deep in contemplation whose insight and thought are sure"?

5. How would following Krishna's advice solve Arjuna's dilemma?

6. Do you think living the sort of life Krishna recommends (knowing the true nature of the self, doing one's moral duty, being unconcerned about the results of one's action, devotion to the divine) would be a good way to live? Why, or why not?

Bhagavad-Gita

I. The First Teaching: Arjuna's Dejection

Arjuna, his war flag a rampant monkey,
saw Dhritarashtra's sons assembled
as weapons were ready to clash,
and he lifted his bow.

He told his charioteer:
"Krishna,
halt my chariot
between the armies!

Far enough for me to see
these men who lust for war,
ready to fight with me
in the strain of battle.

I see men gathered here,
eager to fight,
bent on serving the folly
of Dhritarashtra's son."

When Arjuna had spoken,
Krishna halted
their splendid chariot
between the armies.

Facing Bhishma and Drona
and all the great kings,
he said, "Arjuna, see
the Kuru men assembled here!"

Arjuna saw them standing there:
fathers, grandfathers, teachers,
uncles, brothers, sons,
grandsons, and friends.

He surveyed his elders
and companions in both armies,
all his kinsmen
assembled together.

The greed that distorts their reason
blinds them to the sin they commit
in ruining the family, blinds them
to the crime of betraying friends.

How can we ignore the wisdom
of turning from this evil
when we see the sin
of family destruction, Krishna?

When the family is ruined,
the timeless laws of family duty
perish; and when duty is lost,
chaos overwhelms the family.

In overwhelming chaos, Krishna,
women of the family are corrupted;
and when women are corrupted,
disorder is born in society.

This discord drags the violators
and the family itself to hell;
for ancestors fall when rites
of offering rice and water lapse.

The sins of men who violate
the family create disorder in society

that undermines the constant laws
of caste and family duty.

Krishna, we have heard
that a place in hell
is reserved for men
who undermine family duties.

I lament the great sin
we commit when our greed
for kingship and pleasures
drives us to kill our kinsmen.

Dejected, filled with strange pity,
he said this:

"Krishna, I see my kinsmen
gathered here, wanting war.

My limbs sink,
my mouth is parched,
my body trembles,
the hair bristles on my flesh.

The magic bow slips
from my hand, my skin burns,
I cannot stand still,
my mind reels.

I see omens of chaos,
Krishna; I see no good
in killing my kinsmen
in battle.

Krishna, I seek no victory,
or kingship or pleasures.
What use to us are kingship,
delights, or life itself?

We sought kingship, delights,
and pleasures for the sake of those
assembled to abandon their lives
and fortunes in battle.

They are teachers, fathers, sons,
and grandfathers, uncles, grandsons,
fathers and brothers of wives,
and other men of our family.

I do not want to kill them
even if I am killed, Krishna;
not for kingship of all three worlds,
much less for the earth!

What joy is there for us, Krishna,
in killing Dhritarashtra's sons?
Evil will haunt us if we kill them,
though their bows are drawn to kill.

Honor forbids us to kill
our cousins, Dhritarashtra's sons;
how can we know happiness
if we kill our own kinsmen?

If Dhritarashtra's armed sons
kill me in battle when I am unarmed
and offer no resistance,
it will be my reward."

Saying this in the time of war,
Arjuna slumped into the chariot
and laid down his bow and arrows,
his mind tormented by grief.

The Second Teaching

PHILOSOPHY AND SPIRITUAL DISCIPLINE

Sanjaya

Arjuna sat dejected,
filled with pity,
his sad eyes blurred by tears.
Krishna gave him counsel.

Lord Krishna

Why this cowardice
in time of crisis, Arjuna?
The coward is ignoble, shameful,
foreign to the ways of heaven.

Don't yield to impotence!
It is unnatural in you!
Banish this petty weakness from your heart.
Rise to the fight, Arjuna!

Arjuna

Krishna, how can I fight
against Bhishma and Drona
with arrows
when they deserve my worship?

It is better in this world
to beg for scraps of food

than to eat meals
smeared with the blood
of elders I killed
at the height of their power
while their goals
were still desires.

We don't know which weight
is worse to bear—
our conquering them
or their conquering us.
We will not want to live
if we kill
the sons of Dhritarashtra
assembled before us.

The flaw of pity
blights my very being;
conflicting sacred duties
confound my reason.
I ask you to tell me
decisively—Which is better?
I am your pupil.
Teach me what I seek!

I see nothing
that could drive away
the grief
that withers my senses;
even if I won kingdoms
of unrivaled wealth
on earth
and sovereignty over gods.

Sanjaya

Arjuna told this
to Krishna—then saying,
"I shall not fight,"
he fell silent.

Mocking him gently,
Krishna gave this counsel
as Arjuna sat dejected,
between the two armies.

Lord Krishna

You grieve for those beyond grief;
and you speak words of insight;
but learned men do not grieve
for the dead or the living.

Never have I not existed,
nor you, nor these kings;
and never in the future
shall we cease to exist.

Just as the embodied self
enters childhood, youth, and old age,
so does it enter another body;
this does not confound a steadfast man.

Contacts with matter make us feel
heat and cold, pleasure and pain.
Arjuna, you must learn to endure
fleeting things—they come and go!

When these cannot torment a man,
when suffering and joy are equal
for him and he has courage,
he is fit for immortality.

Nothing of nonbeing comes to be,
nor does being cease to exist;
the boundary between these two
is seen by men who see reality.

Indestructible is the presence
that pervades all this;
no one can destroy
this unchanging reality.

Our bodies are known to end,
but the embodied self is enduring,
indestructible, and immeasurable;
therefore, Arjuna, fight the battle!

He who thinks this self a killer
and he who thinks it killed,
both fail to understand;
it does not kill, nor is it killed.

It is not born,
it does not die;
having been,
it will never not be;
unborn, enduring,
constant, and primordial,
it is not killed
when the body is killed.

Arjuna, when a man knows the self
to be indestructible, enduring, unborn,
unchanging, how does he kill
or cause anyone to kill?

As a man discards
worn-out clothes
to put on new
and different ones,
so the embodied self
discards
its worn-out bodies
to take on other new ones.

Weapons do not cut it,
fire does not burn it,
waters do not wet it,
wind does not wither it.

It cannot be cut or burned;
it cannot be wet or withered;
it is enduring, all-pervasive,
fixed, immovable, and timeless.

It is called unmanifest,
inconceivable, and immutable;
since you know that to be so,
you should not grieve!

If you think of its birth
and death as ever-recurring,
then too, Great Warrior,
you have no cause to grieve!

Death is certain for anyone born,
and birth is certain for the dead;
since the cycle is inevitable,
you have no cause to grieve!

Creatures are unmanifest in origin,
manifest in the midst of life,
and unmanifest again in the end.
Since this is so, why do you lament?

Rarely someone
sees it,
rarely another
speaks it,
rarely anyone
hears it—
even hearing it,
no one really knows it.

The self embodied in the body
of every being is indestructible;
you have no cause to grieve
for all these creatures, Arjuna!

Look to your own duty;
do not tremble before it;
nothing is better for a warrior
than a battle of sacred duty.

The doors of heaven open
for warriors who rejoice
to have a battle like this
thrust on them by chance.

If you fail to wage this war
of sacred duty,
you will abandon your own duty
and fame only to gain evil.

People will tell
of your undying shame,
and for a man of honor
shame is worse than death.

The great chariot warriors will think
you deserted in fear of battle;
you will be despised
by those who held you in esteem.

Your enemies will slander you,
scorning your skill
in so many unspeakable ways—
could any suffering be worse?

If you are killed, you win heaven;
if you triumph, you enjoy the earth;
therefore, Arjuna, stand up
and resolve to fight the battle!

Impartial to joy and suffering,
gain and loss, victory and defeat,
arm yourself for the battle,
lest you fall into evil.

Understanding is defined in terms
     of philosophy;
now hear it in spiritual discipline.
Armed with this understanding, Arjuna,
you will escape the bondage of action.

No effort in this world
is lost or wasted;
a fragment of sacred duty
saves you from great fear.

This understanding is unique
in its inner core of resolve;

diffuse and pointless are the ways
irresolute men understand.

Undiscerning men who delight
in the tenets of ritual lore
utter florid speech, proclaiming,
"There is nothing else!"

Driven by desire, they strive after heaven
and contrive to win powers and delights,
but their intricate ritual language
bears only the fruit of action in rebirth.

Obsessed with powers and delights,
their reason lost in words,
they do not find in contemplation
this understanding of inner resolve.

Arjuna, the realm of sacred lore
is nature—beyond its triad of qualities,
dualities, and mundane rewards,
be forever lucid, alive to your self.

For the discerning priest,
all of sacred lore
has no more value than a well
when water flows everywhere.

Be intent on action,
not on the fruits of action;
avoid attraction to the fruits
and attachment to inaction!

Perform actions, firm in discipline,
relinquishing attachment;
be impartial to failure and success—
this equanimity is called discipline.

Arjuna, action is far inferior
to the discipline of understanding;
so seek refuge in understanding—pitiful
are men drawn by fruits of action.

Disciplined by understanding,
one abandons both good and evil deeds;
so arm yourself for discipline—
discipline is skill in actions.

Wise men disciplined by understanding
relinquish the fruit born of action;
freed from these bonds of rebirth,
they reach a place beyond decay.

When your understanding passes beyond
the swamp of delusion,
you will be indifferent to all
that is heard in sacred lore.

When your understanding turns
from sacred lore to stand fixed,
immovable in contemplation,
then you will reach discipline.

Arjuna

Krishna, what defines a man
deep in contemplation whose insight
and thought are sure? How would he speak?
How would he sit? How would he move?

Lord Krishna

When he gives up desires in his mind,
is content with the self within himself,
then he is said to be a man
whose insight is sure, Arjuna.

When suffering does not disturb his mind,
when his craving for pleasures has vanished,
when attraction, fear, and anger are gone,
he is called a sage whose thought is sure.

When he shows no preference
in fortune or misfortune
and neither exults nor hates,
his insight is sure.

When, like a tortoise retracting
its limbs, he withdraws his senses
completely from sensuous objects,
his insight is sure.

Sensuous objects fade
when the embodied self abstains from food;
the taste lingers, but it too fades
in the vision of higher truth.

Even when a man of wisdom
tries to control them, Arjuna,
the bewildering senses
attack his mind with violence.

Controlling them all,
with discipline he should focus on me;
when his senses are under control,
his insight is sure.

Brooding about sensuous objects
makes attachment to them grow;
from attachment desire arises,
from desire anger is born.

From anger comes confusion;
from confusion memory lapses;
from broken memory understanding is lost;
from loss of understanding, he is ruined.

But a man of inner strength
whose senses experience objects
without attraction and hatred,
in self-control, finds serenity.

In serenity, all his sorrows
dissolve;
his reason becomes serene,
his understanding sure.

Without discipline,
he has no understanding or inner power;
without inner power, he has no peace;
and without peace where is joy?

If his mind submits to the play
of the senses,
they drive away insight,
as wind drives a ship on water.

So, Great Warrior, when withdrawal
of the senses
from sense objects is complete,
discernment is firm.

When it is night for all creatures,
a master of restraint is awake;
when they are awake, it is night
for the sage who sees reality.

As the mountainous depths
of the ocean
are unmoved when waters
rush into it,
so the man unmoved
when desires enter him
attains a peace that eludes
the man of many desires.

When he renounces all desires
and acts without craving,
possessiveness,
or individuality, he finds peace.

This is the place of the infinite spirit;
achieving it, one is freed from delusion;
abiding in it even at the time of death,
one finds the pure calm of infinity.

Suggestions for Further Reading

If you want a general overview of Hindu philosophy, see the introduction to *The Sourcebook in Indian Philosophy*, edited by S. Radhakrishnan and Charles A. Moore (Princeton, NJ: Princeton University Press, 1957).

For a careful philosophical analysis of the *Gita*, see A. L. Herman, *An Introduction to Indian Thought* (Englewood Cliffs, NJ: Prentice-Hall, 1976).

Another helpful and philosophically sophisticated discussion can be found in Ronald M. Green, *Religious Reason* (New York: Oxford University Press, 1978), p. 238ff.

See also the introduction to Miller's translation (the one I have used here) and the introduction found in *The Bhagavadgita in the Mahabharata: Text and Translation* (Chicago: University of Chicago Press, 1981) by J. A. B. van Buitenen.

Ramesh N. Patel's *Philosophy of the Gita* (New York: Peter Lang, 1991) provides a difficult but innovative treatment. See pp. 101–115 in particular.

Videos

Hinduism and the Song of God: A Modern Interpretation of the Bhagavad Gita (30 minutes) is an award-winning video that explains the four yogas, the four stages of life, karma, and how the *Gita* describes the purpose of human life. Available from the Hartley Film Foundation, 59 Cat Rock Rd., Cos Cob, CT 06807.

The Mahabharata is available in a 3-hour version from Audio-Forum, 96 Broad St., Guilford, CT 06437.

3.7 Does Life Have Meaning?

Most of you have probably seen a cartoon of someone climbing a mountain and reaching a bearded guru in order to ask, "What is the meaning of life?" The answer is usually unexpected and slightly humorous.

Imagine a variation. Imagine the seeker reaching the guru and asking, "Why must life have a meaning?" Perhaps the guru is suddenly dumbfounded in this new version so the seeker continues, "I mean, isn't it all right for life to be pointless?"

This second version may seem odd because we all assume that life must have a meaning and that it is important that it does. The second version does not make that assumption. Instead it wonders about why we think it necessary or important that life have a meaning.

Imagine a third version of the cartoon. The seeker reaches the guru and asks, "What does it mean to ask what is the meaning of life?" Perhaps this time the guru is not dumbfounded, but answers, "You have been studying too much philosophy." That may be true. You have already learned to question questions by asking how they might best be understood and formulated. So what are we to make of the question about the meaning of life? What does it mean?

If you think about it, it is a rather odd question. If what we do, think, and believe as we live our lives makes sense, why must life as a whole make sense? If there are good reasons for how I live my life in its details, why do I need a reason for my life taken as a whole? However, is the question even a question about *my* life? Is it not a question about every life? If we interpret the question this way, as a question about the whole of every human life (should we include animals and plants?), then the answer becomes both more difficult and more questionable. How could there be a good reason for every life that will ever be lived? Why should we think there is such a reason? Just because something supports my computer, why should I presume that there is something that supports everything in the universe?

I have assumed that the question about the meaning of life is a question about finding a good reason for living. Shift your focus a bit and think about what might be a "good reason" for living. Is there only one? Could there be many? How is the search for a good reason for living connected to the search for the good life? Does the answer to the question, "How should one live?" also provide an answer to the question, "What is the meaning of life?" If life has no meaning, no good reason, and no point, does it make any sense to worry about how we should conduct our lives?

Daniel Kolak, Director of the Cognitive Science Laboratory at William Paterson University, and Raymond Martin, professor of philosophy at the University of Maryland, explore questions about the meaning and purpose of human life in the following essay. They suggest that many of us often look in the wrong place for an answer. Finding a satisfactory answer involves a reorientation in our thinking about how best to conduct our lives.

Reading Questions

1. What is the difference between the problem of the meaning of life and the problem of life?
2. What is the pattern of internal struggle?
3. What are two ways to stop internal struggle, and what are the advantages of accepting yourself just as you are?
4. Can you think of any counterexamples to the authors' claim that success depends upon pleasing others?
5. In what sense is our desire for independence the "glue of social cohesion"?
6. Give an example of connecting "directly to an activity."
7. What is the main point of this essay?
8. What are some of the assumptions made by the authors?
9. How well did the authors accomplish their goal?

Meaning

DANIEL KOLAK and RAYMOND MARTIN

WHAT IS IT ALL ABOUT? Why are we here? Is there some purpose, or meaning, to life?

At one time or another, everyone asks such questions. As children and as old people, especially, we wonder: Why? What does it all mean? Most of the rest of the time, we're so busy trying to be successful we don't worry about meaning. But even then, in the back of our minds, we may still wonder. And when we do, what is it we really want to know?

Suppose you're at a party. You love being with the people there; they love having you there. The music is terrific, the food and drinks are delicious, and everything is paid for. No one has to go anywhere, do anything, be any particular way. Everyone is having a wonderful time. Suddenly someone turns to you and asks, "Why are we here? What is the meaning of this party?" You'd probably consider the question irrelevant. Suppose, on the other hand, the party is terrible. Then you might think the question has a point.

So also with the question "What is the meaning of life?" When life is wonderful, we don't ask what it means—we're too busy enjoying it. When life is a painful struggle, the question forces itself upon us not so much because we want to answer the question of the meaning of life but, rather, because we want to end our struggle. We don't then care about solving the problem of the *meaning* of life. We care about solving the problem of *life*.

Everyone wants to have a good time. And it seems everyone has a recipe. Yet nearly everyone is involved in a painful struggle. There must be something wrong with the recipes.

Nearly everyone *is* struggling, not only in the poorest parts of the world but everywhere. Poor people struggle just to survive, but even affluent people struggle. Everywhere, nearly everyone is *always* struggling. Why? What can we do about it? Isn't that what we usually want to know, when the question of the meaning of life bothers us?

Theoretical answers might be of theoretical interest. But even after all the philosophy books, novels, songs, poems, and movies, people are still struggling. Lots of answers have been given— some serious, some funny, some clever, some

From *Daniel Kolak and Raymond Martin,* Wisdom Without Answers: A Guide to the Experience of Philosophy. *Belmont, CA: Wadsworth, 1989, pp. 80–90. Reprinted by permission of Wadsworth/Thomson Learning.*

stupid—but they haven't ended the struggle. On the other hand, knowing *why* life is a struggle could change things a great deal. It might even lessen the struggle enough to enable us to live more meaningful lives.

Everyone knows it takes two to have a fight. You can't be involved in a struggle unless someone or something is resisting. The resistance might come from the outside or from the inside—either you are divided from someone else, or from your environment, or from yourself. Without division there can be no resistance. Without resistance there can be no struggle.

So the way to stop struggling is to end the fragmentation that leads to resistance. The problem is that we don't want to stop struggling at the cost of being dominated. If we drop all resistance, someone else is sure to dominate us. But even people who no one is trying to dominate, even those in control, are struggling. In some places in the world, and at some times, struggle comes from the outside. But at all places in the world, and at all times, struggle comes from the inside.

What is *your* internal struggle? You're reading this book. Chances are no one is trying to shoot you. Chances are, though, that you are bothered by some internal struggle. How can you live without internal struggle? When you're bothered by questions about the meaning of life, isn't that what you usually want to know?

External and internal struggle both can be stopped in the same way: Drop all resistance. The problem with this simple answer in the case of external struggle is that we're afraid of being dominated. But no such problem exists in the case of internal struggle. In fact, just the opposite is the case. The reason you're bothered by internal struggle in the first place is that you're trying to dominate yourself—one part of you is trying to dominate another part of you.

Consider the simplest possible example of internal struggle. Suppose you drink too much alcohol and it bothers you. Part of you wants to continue. Another part of you wants to quit. If *all* of you wants to continue drinking, there is no struggle, you just drink. If *all* of you wants to quit, there is no struggle, you just quit. The

problem is how to decide which part of yourself should prevail—in this case, the drinker or the nondrinker—and then how to get the other part to stop resisting.

Almost all internal struggle follows the same pattern. There is what you *are* and there is what you think you *should* be. That is the essence of internal conflict. So, which part should prevail—the actual you, who exists right now, or the ideal you, who might exist sometime in the future?

You can end your internal struggle in two ways: by eventually becoming the ideal you, or by accepting yourself exactly as you are right now and dropping all notions of how you should be. The first way, you continue struggling with yourself in the hope your struggle will end some day. The second way, you stop struggling right away.

It is difficult to drop being the way you are. It is easier to drop all notions of how you should be. You might eventually be able to change the way you are, but "trying to change" is a sure formula for perpetuating the struggle.

So, in the simple case of the drinker versus the nondrinker, who wins? For the time being, the drinker wins. That doesn't necessarily mean that the drinker will *always* be a drinker. Maybe—but not necessarily. Accepting the fact of being a drinker, accepting it without condition that you might change, may, as we shall see, be an effective way to become a nondrinker. The evolution might not take place, but there is a *chance* it will. One thing is certain: If the evolution does take place, it will be effortless.

But what if the drinker is addicted? Won't surrendering all resistance mean oblivion and death? Perhaps. But continuing to struggle with addiction might also mean oblivion and death—after great effort and pain! If one must drink oneself to death, isn't it better to do it effortlessly, rather than with great struggle and pain?

We are all addicted to one thing or another. Accepting ourselves as we are without any condition that we change can give us insight into the causes of our addictions. For instance, one major reason people enjoy alcohol is that it makes them less inhibited. But why are they inhibited in the first place? Isn't that kind of inhibition just their own resistance against what they themselves really are? The alcohol takes away the inhibition and allows the inhibited part to come out. Often self-destructive behavior is the inhibited part of you, ordinarily repressed by the ideal you, finally exerting itself and saying, "If you don't let me out, I'll kill you!" So the drinker who allows self-acceptance might become less inhibited—even without alcohol—and, in turn, might be less prone to drug abuse.

But if we all cease struggling, won't we just lie around all day? What will move us to act? Perhaps nothing. We might lie around all day. But one thing that *could* move us to act is love of some activity. We don't need to be coerced into doing what we love to do.

So whatever your struggle, the way out of that struggle is to accept yourself as you are without any condition that you change. The alternative is to keep struggling. That's the alternative most of us take because, deep down, we believe that struggle is the price we must pay for success. Without struggle, we think, we could never go from being what we are now to being the successful person we would someday like to be. But there is something suspicious about this strategy: Nearly everyone is struggling, yet few are successful.

Ordinarily, when we call someone successful, we're talking about career. That is only one kind of success. You can also be successful as a person—for instance, by being happy and by contributing to the happiness of others. Professional and personal success don't necessarily go together. We all know people who are successful in their careers but failures as persons and people who have failed in their careers but are successful as persons. Struggling does not ensure either kind of success. Does anything?

There may be no single key to having a successful career. But there is a common element: The farmer who becomes a successful farmer, the doctor who becomes a successful doctor, the playwright who becomes a successful playwright, and so on, all become successful, if they do, by pleasing others. To make money, for instance, you have to sell something or provide a service

that someone else wants to buy. Somewhere down the line, all types of professional success require pleasing others.

What, then, of being successful as a person? Oddly enough, here too success requires pleasing others. Being happy at work, being a good friend, a good parent, a good lover, and so on, all ultimately involve pleasing others.

Few of us are hermits. Even pleasing ourselves involves pleasing others. We may like to think of ourselves as individualists. The truth is that being successful as a person—being happy and contributing to the happiness of others—almost always involves pleasing others. So a common element to both professional and personal success seems to be: pleasing others.

Instinctively we already know this. But we may not like to admit it. We tend to view ourselves through the lens of an idealized self-image, part of which is our belief that we are not dependent on the approval of others, that we are the masters of our own destinies. We don't like to think of ourselves as dependent, even for our happiness, upon other people's approval. We like to think that it doesn't matter what people think of us. The truth is it does matter.

We need the approval of others, but we don't want to need it. So we often pretend that we don't need it. We resist needing it. This creates a tension within us, an internal struggle between the part of us that wants approval and the part that wants independence from the need for approval.

There is an ironic twist to this tension within us. We think the way to independence is through success. But the way to success is almost always through the approval of others. The student, the architect, the actor, the grocer, the football player, are all dependent on the approval of bosses, clients, fans, and so on, to gain greater independence from their need for approval.

We're all in the same boat. For instance, the authors of this book think that if this book is a great success, they will become more independent and will be better able to go where they want, do what they want, write what they want, and so on, without having to worry about what others think. The authors want to free themselves from the need for approval. How are they going to do it? Like everyone else, they will gain their independence from the need for the approval of others by gaining the approval of others. How smart!

This truth about success cuts deeply into all of our lives. Consider, for example, the way power is distributed in a romantic relationship. The one who is more powerful is the one who is less dependent on the other. How do you get less dependent? Usually by having more choice as to who you are with. The better you are at pleasing others, all else being equal, the more choice you have as to who you are with. The more choice you have, the more independent you are. So even in romantic relationships the way to independence is through pleasing others. Ironically, the way to independence is through dependence.

Such are society's mechanisms for keeping all of us in line. Without our need to seek the approval of others, society would collapse. The very structure of society—no matter what the society's particular mores are—depends on social cohesion. One way society ensures this cohesion is by linking our need to be independent with our need for approval. Society breeds the desire for independence into us to ensure that, as individuals, we will be dependent on the approval of others, thereby ensuring social cohesion. We depend on approval because only through approval can we hope to achieve independence. Our desire for independence is part of the very glue of social cohesion.

It may seem, then, from what we've just said, that seeking approval is the key to success. If success is impossible without approval, then the way to success would seem to be to aim directly for it. That is what most of us do.

This strategy can't be completely wrong. After all, we've just seen that the approval of others is necessary for success. For instance, most students want to get good grades. That is their criterion of success. Students instinctively know that the surest way to get good grades is to get approval from their teachers by agreeing with them.

This strategy works—but only to a point. It often, but not always, ensures that the student gets good grades. But merely getting good grades is a mediocre level of success. As every good teacher knows, those students who reach a high level of success in school—academic excellence—develop the capacity for *independent* thought. Getting good grades, on the other hand, usually doesn't ensure that a student has developed this capacity.

Students who agree with their teachers tend to get good grades partly because imitating their teachers' views on the material they are studying is the first level of connecting to that material. The best students then go on to challenge the opinions of their teachers in creative ways. The best students, once they have achieved the initial connection between themselves and the subject matter through imitating the teacher, then go on to connect to the subject matter directly. This requires taking risks—in particular, risking the disapproval of their teachers. Ultimately, what must matter most to these students is not the connection between themselves and their teachers, but the connection between themselves and their subject matter.

Seeking approval is the first step to success. But it only goes so far. In the end, it is even limiting. If you want to reach the higher levels of success, you must win approval not by seeking it but rather by achieving some level of excellence through connecting directly to the activity you are involved in. The ironic twist is that such a level of excellence through direct connecting to an activity can never be attained so long as one is primarily concerned with seeking approval. One must drop the quest for approval in order to attain success in its fullest form.

In other words, people tend to think that success has something to do with pleasing others because that is itself an indirect way of connecting with an activity. But pleasing others is also a byproduct of connecting directly with an activity. In the end, what matters most is not approval but connecting directly with an activity, for that is the way to attain a high level of success. For instance, you might get a promotion by pleasing your boss, a job as an actor by pleasing a director, a lucrative business contract by pleasing a client, and so on. All these initial successes are like the student getting a good grade by pleasing the teacher. Whether or not you are successful in your new job once you have it, whether or not you are successful as an actor, grocer, teacher, or whatever, will ultimately depend on how you connect to whatever activity your job requires.

What does it mean to connect directly to an activity? First, consider professional success. The purpose of all professions is to make a product. For instance, doctors cultivate health, architects design buildings, playwrights write plays, and so on. Many people view their work-related activities merely as instruments for producing products. They don't value the process that leads to the product as an end in itself. The ones who do, however, are the ones who become most successful. The student who loves to study, the boxer who loves to box, the runner who loves to run, the farmer who loves to farm, all experience the same joy of activity. They love the *process,* not just the product, and so they succeed to a much greater degree.

Suppose you repair bicycles. Fixing bicycles is the process. A fixed bicycle is the product. You want to be a successful bicycle repairman. How? You can't be successful unless you please your clients. You must turn damaged or faulty bicycles into good ones, and you must do it efficiently and well. You can do this at a minimal level if you merely want to please your customers. You can do it much better if you love to repair bicycles.

But every activity, every process, it would seem, has its drudgery. In bicycle repair, you have to repack the ball bearings, grease the chains, adjust the cables. Ordinarily, such chores are drudgery because, as we do them, we focus on getting them done instead of on doing them. When we focus on getting them done we are not all there. Our hands are there and perhaps part of our minds are there, but another part of us constantly projects into the future. If we are completely there, focused on our activity, paying at-

tention to everything we do, our activity, no matter what it is, will rarely be drudgery. Almost always, our desire to get it over with makes it drudgery.

Suppose, for instance, you are told to set up and then dismantle a toy city. It will take hours and hours of patient, detailed work to set up the city, only to destroy it in the end. How would you react? As you were doing it, you'd probably be thinking: What is the purpose of this? I want to finish, get some sleep before I have to go to work, and so on.

Yet when we were children, we played like that for hours on end. Did we worry then about the purpose of building toy cities, only to dismantle them as soon as we finished? What was the purpose of building them? Wasn't it simply the act of doing it? When we were children, we played games not to be done with them, but to do them. That's why we enjoyed them so much. Isn't that the very source of the magic of childhood?

Living is a series of activities that involves everything you do, including your job. Living is your activity. The product is *you.* Being connected to your life means, ultimately, being connected to all the activities of your life. These activities continually produce new versions of you. Being connected means valuing these activities not merely as a means to an end—as a means to producing a certain type of you—but rather as ends in themselves.

Consider, for example, the activity of keeping yourself physically fit. It can be done primarily as an end in itself. Or it can be done as a mere means to fitness. Ask yourself this: Who will be more physically fit after five years—the person who flogs himself into jogging every morning, or the person who so enjoys the physical act of running that she does it willingly every day?

If in all your activities the thing you focus on is the finished product—the read book, the fixed bicycle, the delivered mail, the ideal you—happiness will elude you. Happiness might surface after you have completed something, but then it is usually time to start something else. Then you rush through the next project, struggling with yourself because you don't really want to be doing it either. You just want to have done it, to be finished.

If you are connected to the process, the main reward isn't with the finishing. It's with the doing. The finishing may even have a sorrowful aspect to it because it will signify the end of a particular process. For the authors of this book, for instance, when the last word is written, when the final revision is sent off to the publisher, there will be joy. There will also be sorrow because a process they love will have ended. There might be other books, other processes. But *this* particular process will have ended forever.

So also with the process of being a person. When a life that has been good is nearing completion, there will be sorrow. There might also be the joy of completion. There might even be other lives. But *this* life, *this* particular process, will end forever.

The key to success in life, then, is connecting, not with a product, but with a process: ultimately, with the process of being ourselves. Where there is genuine connection to a process, there will be success.

Success, like a good party, has its own intrinsic value. It makes our lives rich and full of meaning. And where there is success, there will ultimately also be sorrow because it is the nature of all processes to change, and by changing they end.

Suggestions for Further Reading

See the article by Jason Gaiger on "Lebensphilosophie" (philosophy of life) in volume 5 of the *Routledge Encyclopedia of Philosophy,* edited by Edward Craig (London: Routledge, 1998, pp. 487–489) for some historical background.

A classic essay by William James, "Is life Worth Living?" can be found in *Essays on Faith and Morals* (New York: The World Publishing Company, 1962). James gives an emphatically positive answer and admonishes his readers "Be not afraid of life."

The last chapter in Thomas Nagel's *What Does it All Mean? A Very Short Introduction to Philosophy* (Oxford: Oxford University Press, 1987) explicitly addresses the issue of what sort of meaning life might have.

John Wisdom sorts out the many meanings of the question about the meaning of life in *Paradox and Discovery* (Oxford: Basil Blackwell, 1968, pp. 38–42), and the famous existentialist philosopher, Albert Camus, addresses issues of absurdity and suicide in the now classic *The Myth of Sisyphus and Other Essays* (New York: Alfred A. Knopf, Inc., 1955).

For a collection of some of the best writings on the meaning of life, see *The Meaning of Life,* edited by E. D. Klemke (2nd ed., New York: Oxford University Press, 2000).

 You can locate InfoTrac-College Edition articles about this chapter by accessing the InfoTrac-College Edition website (http://www.infotrac-college.com/wadsworth/). Using the InfoTrac-College Edition subject guide, enter the search terms relevant to this chapter, and then read abstracts for relevant articles.

Chapter 4

How Can I Know What Is Right?

> Ethics is limitations on freedom of action in the struggle for existence.
>
> ALDO LEOPOLD

4.1 Introduction

HAVE YOU EVER WONDERED how you can know what is morally right? You have been told to do the right thing. But what is the *right* thing? Sometimes it is very hard to figure out. Sometimes our duties conflict. We know we should be loyal to our friends, but shouldn't we report them for cheating? Sometimes we must choose between alternatives, both of which seem wrong.

To know what is the right thing to do, we need to know what makes an action right. How can we know that? Do my motives make my actions right? If I intend to do my moral duty as best I understand it, isn't that enough? We call that acting out of a good will. However, maybe a good will is not enough. Maybe it is not my motives but the consequences of what I do that count. If my actions result in good things for most people, isn't that sufficient to justify my actions?

You might reply, "What about the act itself? It is surely either right or wrong in itself, no matter what my motives are or the consequences. Aren't some things just plain wrong? It is not right to steal even if my motives are good or the consequences will benefit some. Stealing is just plain wrong."

The philosopher wonders why it is "just plain wrong." What *makes* it wrong? How do I know that it is wrong?

We all know that people have different values and believe different things to be right. Are your moral beliefs any better than anyone else's? Some people are **ethical skeptics**. They doubt whether there is any such thing as moral truth. For them, there is no way we can know that stealing is wrong. It may be, but we cannot know that. To show that the ethical skeptic is mistaken, you would have to show how we can arrive at moral knowledge.

Some people are **ethical relativists**. They deny that there are any universally valid moral principles. Even stealing can be "right" if some culture recognizes it to be "right," even though others might think it "wrong." However, if we subscribe to ethical relativism, it appears that we must give up any basis for condemning someone like Hitler. Morally deplorable actions such as "ethnic cleansing" become "right" if some culture thinks them to be right. Surely there must be some moral absolutes.

93

While ethical skeptics doubt that we can know any moral absolutes, if there should happen to be any, and ethical relativists claim that there are, in fact, no such absolutes, **ethical absolutists** claim there are. Moral values, they argue, are objective. They transcend time and place. What is right is right, regardless of what anyone may think. Stealing is wrong, even if it might be justified in some circumstances by some higher good and even if some culture might think it is "cool."

If you have wondered about these issues, you have been asking some important questions that have to do with the very foundations of morality. In this chapter, we explore some different answers to this question: How can we know what is right?

4.2 Kant and the Categorical Imperative

Immanuel Kant (1724–1804) was born, spent his entire life, and died in Königsberg, Prussia. He studied natural science, mathematics, history, and philosophy at the University of Königsberg. After graduation he worked for a while as a tutor to the children of Prussian aristocrats, eventually landing a job as *Privatdozent* at the university. This meant that he was licensed by the university to offer lectures, but the university did not pay him. Rather, he was paid by the students who attended his lectures. For more than a dozen years, Kant lectured on a wide variety of subjects for up to 21 hours a week in order to make enough money to live.

Kant's monetary fortunes improved when he was finally appointed professor of logic and metaphysics in 1770 and was paid a decent wage by the university. In 1781 one of his many books appeared, *The Critique of Pure Reason,* which was destined to revolutionize Western philosophy. It earned Kant the reputation of being one of the greatest philosophical minds of the modern period. In this book Kant was concerned with epistemological as well as metaphysical issues. Does the world conform to our ideas, or do our ideas conform to the world? Most people thought that true ideas are those that conform to the world. However, Kant argued just the opposite, namely, that the world conforms to our ideas.

We do not have time to go into Kant's complex proof nor the radical implications of this contention. I note it in passing to indicate that Kant made contributions to philosophy in other areas besides moral philosophy, even though we will be concerned here primarily with his ethical ideas. According to Kant, we cannot know what is the morally right thing to do unless we can know what *makes* an action morally right.

Before we can know what might make an action right, we have to do a little bit of thinking about the parts of an action. It is evident that actions have consequences. So we might wonder whether the consequences or the results of an action make it right. People who advocate the view that consequences determine the rightness of an action support what philosophers call **teleological ethical theories**.

There is more to action, however, than its consequences. There is also the motive for the action, and it is worth asking whether motives, not consequences, make an action morally right. We know that people can do something that has good results, but do it for the wrong reasons. I may refrain from cheating on a test because I am afraid I will get caught. Not cheating has good consequences because it makes the test fair for all. However, is it right to praise me for being morally good simply because I was afraid to cheat? Should I not do the right thing because it is the right thing? Moral theories that advocate doing what is good because it is good, regardless of the consequences, are called **deontological ethical theories** (from the Greek *deon,* meaning "duty," and *logos,* meaning "science" or "study of").

Kant wondered about the sorts of questions we have been discussing. His answers constitute a deontological theory. He argues that the only thing that is unconditionally good is a good will. What makes a good will good is not the consequences that result from its acts, nor the inclinations and desires that *in fact* influence it, but its freely willing to do what *duty* requires.

And what does duty require? It requires that we act in accord with the **categorical imperative**, which can be formulated, "Act only on that maxim through which you can at the same time will that it should become a universal law." For example, if you are wondering whether you should tell the truth, you should formulate a maxim, "Always tell the truth," and ask whether you can will that such a rule become a universal law—that is, a law everyone ought to obey. Note that this imperative, or command, is *categorical,* that is, unconditional. It is not a *hypothetical,* or conditional, command. Kant does *not* say, "Act only on that maxim if. . . ." Kant believed that this imperative is equivalent to a rule that requires us always to treat persons as ends in themselves rather than as means to some other end, such as the production of pleasure, happiness, or wealth.

An action is right, Kant argues, if it is done from a good will, and a will is good if it meets three conditions:

1. The maxim on which its action is based can be universalized.
2. It freely accepts (what Kant called *autonomy*) its duty.
3. It treats people as ends, not means.

Kant was looking for a rational foundation for morality. He opposed ethical relativism and disagreed with those who were skeptical of moral truth. Kant was an ethical absolutist. Moral truth is objective, he contended, and morality has a rational foundation revealing that some things are morally right no matter what anyone thinks or what any society claims.

The selection that follows is from *Groundwork of the Metaphysics of Morals,* which Kant published in 1785. He intended it to be a brief introduction to his theory, which he later elaborated in the *Critique of Practical Reason.* Even though this work is introductory, it is not easy to read. Take your time, think about what Kant is saying, and answer the following questions.

Reading Questions

1. What is good without qualification?
2. Do the consequences or results of a good will make it good?
3. According to Kant, a good will is manifested in acting for the sake of duty. He contends that "the worth of character begins to show" when a person "does good, not from inclination, but from duty." Why does Kant claim this? Do you agree? Why, or why not?
4. Where, according to Kant, does the moral value or worth of an action done from duty reside? In the results of the action? In the actual motive a person may in fact have (the *material principle*)? If not in these, where?
5. What do you think Kant meant when he said, "Duty is the necessity to act out of reverence for the law"?

6. What is the *categorical imperative?*
7. Kant claimed we can will to lie, but we cannot will a universal law of lying. Do you agree? Why, or why not?
8. Kant said that if you want to know whether an action is morally right, determine the maxim or subjective principle on which it is based and then ask, "Can I also will that my maxim should become a universal law?" If the answer is no, it is not the right thing to do. Apply Kant's advice to the following case: You are a bright individual who usually gets good grades. You want to go to law school, and you need good grades to get accepted at a good law school. You find yourself taking a philosophy test for which you are not well prepared, and you have an opportunity to cheat without being caught. By cheating, you will definitely improve your final grade for the course. Should you cheat? If you were a Kantian (a follower of Kant's theory), what would be your answer, and what would be your reasoning?
9. How did Kant answer the question "How can I know what is right?"

Groundwork of the Metaphysics of Morals

IMMANUEL KANT

The Good Will

IT IS IMPOSSIBLE to conceive anything at all in the world, or even out of it, which can be taken as good without qualification, except a *good will.* Intelligence, wit, judgment, and any other *talents* of the mind we may care to name, or courage, resolution, and constancy of purpose, as qualities of *temperament,* are without doubt good and desirable in many respects; but they can also be extremely bad and hurtful when the will is not good which has to make use of these gifts of nature, and which for this reason has the term "*character*" applied to its peculiar quality. It is exactly the same with *gifts of fortune.* Power, wealth, honour, even health and that complete well-being and contentment with one's state which goes by the name of "*happiness,*" produce boldness, and as a consequence often over-boldness as well, unless a good will is present by which their influence on the mind—and so, too, the whole principle of action—may be corrected and adjusted to universal ends; not to mention that a rational and impartial spectator can never feel approval in contemplating the uninterrupted prosperity of a being graced by no touch of a pure and good will, and that consequently a good will seems to constitute the indispensable condition of our very worthiness to be happy.

Some qualities are even helpful to this good will itself and can make its task very much easier. They have none the less no inner unconditioned worth, but rather presuppose a good will which sets a limit to the esteem in which they are rightly held and does not permit us to regard them as absolutely good. Moderation in affections and passions, self-control, and sober reflexion are not only good in many respects: they may even seem to constitute part of the *inner* worth of a person. Yet they are far from being properly described as good without qualification (however unconditionally they have been commended by the ancients). For without the principles of a good will they may become exceedingly bad; and the very coolness of a scoundrel makes him, not merely more dangerous, but also immediately more abominable in our eyes than we should have taken him to be without it.

From I. Kant, Groundwork of the Metaphysics of Morals, *translated by H. J. Paton (New York: Harper & Row, 1964), pp. 61–62; 64–71. Reprinted by permission of Unwin Hyman, Ltd. Translator's footnotes deleted.*

The Good Will and Its Results

A good will is not good because of what it effects or accomplishes—because of its fitness for attaining some proposed end: it is good through its willing alone—that is, good in itself. Considered in itself it is to be esteemed beyond comparison as far higher than anything it could ever bring about merely in order to favour some inclination or, if you like, the sum total of inclinations. Even if, by some special disfavour of destiny or by the niggardly endowment of step-motherly nature, this will is entirely lacking in power to carry out its intentions; if by its utmost effort it still accomplishes nothing, and only good will is left (not, admittedly, as a mere wish, but as the straining of every means so far as they are in our control); even then it would still shine like a jewel for its own sake as something which has its full value in itself. Its usefulness or fruitlessness can neither add to, nor subtract from, this value. Its usefulness would be merely, as it were, the setting which enables us to handle it better in our ordinary dealings or to attract the attention of those not yet sufficiently expert, but not to commend it to experts or to determine its value. . . .

The Good Will and Duty

We have now to elucidate the concept of a will estimable in itself and good apart from any further end. This concept, which is already present in a sound natural understanding and requires not so much to be taught as merely to be clarified, always holds the highest place in estimating the total worth of our actions and constitutes the condition of all the rest. We will therefore take up the concept of *duty*, which includes that of a good will, exposed, however, to certain subjective limitations and obstacles. These, so far from hiding a good will or disguising it, rather bring it out by contrast and make it shine forth more brightly.

The Motive of Duty

I will here pass over all actions already recognized as contrary to duty, however useful they may be with a view to this or that end; for about these the question does not even arise whether they could have been done *for the sake of duty* inasmuch as they are directly opposed to it. I will also set aside actions which in fact accord with duty, yet for which men have *no immediate inclination,* but perform them because impelled to do so by some other inclination. For there it is easy to decide whether the action which accords with duty has been done *from duty* or from some purpose of self-interest. This distinction is far more difficult to perceive when the action accords with duty and the subject has in addition an *immediate* inclination to the action. For example, it certainly accords with duty that a grocer should not overcharge his inexperienced customer; and where there is much competition a sensible shopkeeper refrains from so doing and keeps to a fixed and general price for everybody so that a child can buy from him just as well as anyone else. Thus people are served *honestly;* but this is not nearly enough to justify us in believing that the shopkeeper has acted in this way from duty or from principles of fair dealing; his interests required him to do so. We cannot assume him to have in addition an immediate inclination towards his customers, leading him, as it were out of love, to give no man preference over another in the matter of price. Thus the action was done neither from duty nor from immediate inclination, but solely from purposes of self-interest.

On the other hand, to preserve one's life is a duty, and besides this every one has also an immediate inclination to do so. But on account of this the often-anxious precautions taken by the greater part of mankind for this purpose have no inner worth, and the maxim of their action is without moral content. They do protect their lives *in conformity with duty,* but not *from the motive of duty.* When on the contrary, disappointments and hopeless misery have quite taken away the taste for life; when a wretched man, strong in soul and more angered at his fate than faint-hearted or cast down, longs for death and still preserves his life without loving it—not from inclination or fear but from duty; then indeed his maxim has a moral content.

To help others where one can is a duty, and besides this there are many spirits of so sympathetic a temper that, without any further motive of vanity or self-interest, they find an inner pleasure in spreading happiness around them and can take delight in the contentment of others as their own work. Yet I maintain that in such a case an action of this kind, however right and however amiable it may be, has still no genuinely moral worth. It stands on the same footing as other inclinations—for example, the inclination for honour, which if fortunate enough to hit on something beneficial and right and consequently honorable, deserves praise and encouragement, but not esteem; for its maxim lacks moral content, namely, the performance of such actions, not from inclination, but *from duty.* Suppose then that the mind of this friend of man were overclouded by sorrows of his own which extinguished all sympathy with the fate of others, but that he still had power to help those in distress, though no longer stirred by the need of others because sufficiently occupied with his own; and suppose that, when no longer moved by any inclination, he tears himself out of this deadly insensibility and does the action without any inclination for the sake of duty alone; then for the first time his action has its genuine moral worth. Still further: if nature had implanted little sympathy in this or that man's heart; if (being in other respects an honest fellow) he were cold in temperament and indifferent to the sufferings of others—perhaps because, being endowed with the special gift of patience and robust endurance in his own sufferings, he assumed the like in others or even demanded it; if such a man (who would in truth not be the worst product of nature) were not exactly fashioned by her to be a philanthropist, would he not still find in himself a source from which he might draw a worth far higher than any that a good-natured temperament can have? Assuredly he would. It is precisely in this that the worth of character begins to show—a moral worth and beyond all comparison the highest—namely, that he does good, not from inclination, but from duty.

To assure one's own happiness is a duty (at least indirectly); for discontent with one's state, in a press of cares and amidst unsatisfied wants, might easily become a great *temptation to the transgression of duty.* But here also, apart from regard to duty, all men have already of themselves the strongest and deepest inclination towards happiness, because precisely in this idea of happiness all inclinations are combined into a sum total. The prescription for happiness is, however, often so constituted as greatly to interfere with some inclinations, and yet men cannot form under the name of "happiness" any determinate and assured conception of the satisfaction of all inclinations as a sum. Hence it is not to be wondered at that a single inclination which is determinate as to what it promises and as to the time of its satisfaction may outweigh a wavering idea; and that a man, for example, a sufferer from gout, may choose to enjoy what he fancies and put up with what he can—on the ground that on balance he has here at least not killed the enjoyment of the present moment because of some possibly groundless expectations of the good fortune supposed to attach to soundness of health. But in this case also, when the universal inclination towards happiness has failed to determine his will, when good health, at least for him, has not entered into his calculations as so necessary, what remains over, here as in other cases, is a law—the law of furthering his happiness, not from inclination, but from duty; and in this for the first time his conduct has a real moral worth.

It is doubtless in this sense that we should understand too the passages from Scripture in which we are commanded to love our neighbour and even our enemy. For love out of inclination cannot be commanded; but kindness done from duty—although no inclination impels us, and even although natural and unconquerable disinclination stands in our way—is *practical,* and not *pathological,* love, residing in the will and not in the propensions [propensity] of feeling, in principles of action and not of melting compassion; and it is this practical love alone which can be an object of command.

The Formal Principle of Duty

Our second proposition is this: An action done from duty has its moral worth, *not in the purpose to be attained by it,* but in the maxim in accordance with which it is decided upon; it depends therefore, not on the realization of the object of the action, but solely on the *principle of volition* in accordance with which, irrespective of all objects of the faculty of desire, the action has been performed. That the purposes we may have in our actions, and also their effects considered as ends and motives of the will, can give to actions no unconditioned and moral worth is clear from what has gone before. Where then can this worth be found if we are not to find it in the will's relation to the effect hoped for from the action? It can be found nowhere but *in the principle of the will,* irrespective of the ends which can be brought about by such an action; for between its *a priori* principle, which is formal, and its *a posteriori* motive, which is material, the will stands, so to speak, at a parting of the ways; and since it must be determined by some principle, it will have to be determined by the formal principle of volition when an action is done from duty, where, as we have seen, every material principle is taken away from it.

Reverence for the Law

Our third proposition, as an inference from the two preceding, I would express thus: *Duty is the necessity to act out of reverence for the law.* For an object as the effect of my proposed action I can have an *inclination,* but *never reverence,* precisely because it is merely the effect, and not the activity, of a will. Similarly for inclination as such, whether my own or that of another, I cannot have reverence: I can at most in the first case approve, and in the second case sometimes even love—that is, regard it as favourable to my own advantage. Only something which is conjoined with my will solely as a ground and never as an effect—something which does not serve my inclination, but outweighs it or at least leaves it entirely out of account in my choice—and therefore only bare law for its own sake, can be an object of reverence and therewith a command. Now an action done from duty has to set aside altogether the influence of inclination, and along with inclination every object of the will; so there is nothing left able to determine the will except

objectively the *law* and subjectively *pure reverence* for this practical law, and therefore the maxim[1] of obeying this law even to the detriment of all my inclinations.

Thus the moral worth of an action does not depend on the result expected from it, and so too does not depend on any principle of action that needs to borrow its motive from this expected result. For all these results (agreeable states and even the promotion of happiness in others) could have been brought about by other causes as well, and consequently their production did not require the will of a rational being, in which, however, the highest and unconditioned good can alone be found. Therefore nothing but the *idea of the law* in itself, *which admittedly is present only in a rational being*—so far as it, and not an expected result, is the ground determining the will—can constitute that pre-eminent good which we call moral, a good which is already present in the person acting on this idea and has not to be awaited merely from the result.[2]

---

1. A *maxim* is the subjective principle of a volition: an objective principle (that is, one which would also serve subjectively as a practical principle for all rational beings if reason had full control over the faculty of desire) is a practical *law*.
2. It might be urged against me that I have merely tried, under cover of the word "*reverence,*" to take refuge in an obscure feeling instead of giving a clearly articulated answer to the question by means of a concept of reason. Yet, although reverence is a feeling, it is not a feeling *received* through outside influence, but one *self-produced* by a rational concept, and therefore specifically distinct from feelings of the first kind, all of which can be reduced to inclination or fear. What I recognize immediately as law for me, I recognize with reverence, which means merely consciousness of the *subordination* of my will to a law without the mediation of external influences on my senses. Immediate determination of the will by the law and consciousness of this determination is called "*reverence,*" so that reverence is regarded as the *effect* of the law on the subject and not as the *cause* of the law. Reverence is properly awareness of a value which demolishes my self-love. Hence, there is something which is regarded neither as an object of inclination nor as an object of fear, though it has at the same time some analogy with both. The *object* of reverence is the *law* alone—that law which we impose *on ourselves* but yet as necessary in itself. Considered as a law, we are subject to it without any consultation of self-love; considered as self-imposed it is a consequence of our will. In the first respect it is analogous to fear, in the second to inclination. All reverence for a person is properly only reverence for the law (of honesty and so on) of which that person gives us an

The Categorical Imperative

But what kind of law can this be the thought of which, even without regard to the results expected from it, has to determine the will if this is to be called good absolutely and without qualification? Since I have robbed the will of every inducement that might arise for it as a consequence of obeying any particular law, nothing is left but the conformity of actions to universal law as such, and this alone must serve the will as its principle. That is to say, I ought never to act except in such a way *that I can also will that my maxim should become a universal law.* Here bare conformity to universal law as such (without having as its base any law prescribing particular actions) is what serves the will as its principle, and must so serve it if duty is not to be everywhere an empty delusion and a chimerical concept. The ordinary reason of mankind also agrees with this completely in its practical judgments and always has the aforesaid principle before its eyes.

Take this question, for example. May I not, when I am hard pressed, make a promise with the intention of not keeping it? Here I readily distinguish the two senses which the question can have—Is it prudent, or is it right, to make a false promise? The first no doubt can often be the case. I do indeed see that it is not enough for me to extricate myself from present embarrassment by this subterfuge: I have to consider whether from this lie there may not subsequently accrue to me much greater inconvenience than that from which I now escape, and also—since, with all my supposed *astuteness,* to foresee the consequences is not so easy that I can be sure there is no chance, once confidence in me is lost, of this proving far more disadvantageous than all the ills I now think to avoid—whether it may not be a *more prudent* action to proceed here on a general maxim and make it my habit not to give a promise except

with the intention of keeping it. Yet it becomes clear to me at once that such a maxim is always founded solely on fear of consequences. To tell the truth for the sake of duty is something entirely different from doing so out of concern for inconvenient results; for in the first case the concept of the action already contains in itself a law for me, while in the second case I have first of all to look around elsewhere in order to see what effects may be bound up with it for me. When I deviate from the principle of duty, this is quite certainly bad; but if I desert my prudential maxim, this can often be greatly to my advantage, though it is admittedly safer to stick to it. Suppose I seek, however, to learn in the quickest way and yet unerringly how to solve the problem "Does a lying promise accord with duty?" I have then to ask myself "Should I really be content that my maxim (the maxim of getting out of a difficulty by a false promise) should hold as a universal law (one valid both for myself and others)?" And could I really say to myself that everyone may make a false promise if he finds himself in a difficulty from which he can extricate himself in no other way? I then become aware at once that I can indeed will to lie, but I can by no means will a universal law of lying; for by such a law there could properly be no promises at all, since it would be futile to profess a will for future action to others who would not believe my profession or who, if they did so over-hastily, would pay me back in like coin; and consequently my maxim, as soon as it was made a universal law, would be bound to annul itself.

Thus I need no far-reaching ingenuity to find out what I have to do in order to possess a good will. Inexperienced in the course of world affairs and incapable of being prepared for all the chances that happen in it, I ask myself only "Can you also will that your maxim should become a universal law?" Where you cannot, it is to be rejected, and that not because of a prospective loss to you or even to others, but because it cannot fit as a principle into a possible enactment of universal law. For such an enactment reason compels my immediate reverence, into whose grounds (which the philosopher may investigate) I have as yet no *insight,* although I do at least under-

---

example. Because we regard the development of our talents as a duty, we see too in a man of talent a sort of *example of the law* (the law of becoming like him by practice), and this is what constitutes our reverence for him. All moral *interest,* so-called, consists solely in *reverence* for the law.

stand this much: reverence is the assessment of a worth which far outweighs all the worth of what is commended by inclination, and the necessity for me to act out of *pure* reverence for the prac- tical law is what constitutes duty, to which every other motive must give way because it is the condition of a will good *in itself,* whose value is above all else.

Suggestions for Further Reading

The articles on Kant in *The Encyclopedia of Philosophy* (New York: Macmillan, 1967) and *Routledge Encyclopedia of Philosophy* (London: Routledge, 1998) will provide further infor- mation on Kant in general and on his ethical theory in particular.

H. J. Paton, in his translation of Kant's *Groundwork,* also provides a commentary on each major section of Kant's text. This commentary will help you figure out what Kant means.

Also *Masterpieces of World Philosophy* edited by Frank N. Magill (New York: Harper- Collins, 1990, p. 336ff.) provides a brief summary.

For an introductory explanation of Kant's views, see Douglas J. Soccio's *Archetypes of Wisdom,* 2nd ed. (Belmont, CA: Wadsworth, 1995), p. 392ff.

Videos

So, This Is Philosophy? (24 minutes) uses dramatic dialogue to explore how people distin- guish right from wrong. *Philosophy and Human Values* features Professor Rick Roderick discussing the moral values of Socrates, Kant, Hegel, Mill, and more (eight lectures given in 1991; 45 minutes each). All videos are available from Insight Media, 2162 Broadway, New York, NY 10024.

4.3 Utilitarianism

Suppose you have to decide whether your loveable cat, who has been your compan- ion for many years and is now very sick, should be "put to sleep," as we euphemisti- cally say. How would you go about making the decision? Would you consider how much pain your cat (let's call her Jenny) is suffering? Would you consider Jenny's chances of recovery? Would and *should* you think about your own pain and loss if you put Jenny to sleep?

Now suppose that Jenny is your mother, not your cat. Suppose further that you lived in a state that allowed physician-assisted suicide. Suppose your mother is not able to tell a physician what she wants, and you must make a decision. How would you go about it? Would the same questions that occurred to you in the case of your cat also occur to you in this case? Would those questions be relevant? Should the de- cision-making process be essentially the same in both cases?

Now suppose that Jenny is the name you have selected for your newborn daughter who is so severely retarded and incapable of thought or action that she will be nothing but a burden to you and your family for as long as she may live. She will never know you, or have the capacity to love you. Suppose further that you live in a state that permits euthanasia. Should Jenny be "put to sleep"? How would you decide?

Are the same sorts of considerations that you agonized about in the first two cases relevant to this case? Is there any way of thinking about these cases that might help us know what is right?

Jeremy Bentham (1748–1832), a British philosopher and social reformer, thinks he can provide you with some help in deciding these difficult cases. He believes that a rational and scientific approach to social and moral issues is possible if we learn to apply what he called "the principle of utility."

Bentham's ethical theory is called **utilitarianism**. Classified as a teleological theory, it maintains that what makes an action right are its consequences. If the consequences are good, then the action is right. However, what are good consequences? Bentham answers that good consequences are those that result in the greatest amount of pleasure (happiness) for the "party whose interest is in question." The party may be the collection of individuals we call a community insofar as they share common interests or it may be a particular individual.

John Stuart Mill (1806–1873), a follower of Bentham, interpreted Bentham's discussion of the interests of the community to mean that Bentham was talking about the greatest happiness for the greatest number of people who are affected by the action in question. Whether this is what Bentham meant is a matter of scholarly dispute. However, it is clear that Bentham's principle of utility is intended to guide legislative (and individual) decision-making by focusing attention on the amount of pleasure that might result from a particular law or course of action.

Because Bentham believes that the good is pleasure, his utilitarian theory is also a variety of **hedonism**. According to hedonistic theories, the highest good is pleasure. Morality is thus grounded in feelings that are natural to the human animal. We, like all animals, act in order to avoid pain and maximize pleasure.

While much traditional morality counsels us to disassociate the pleasurable from the morally good, Bentham thinks this is a mistake. A principle of asceticism, as he calls it, that not only disassociates moral goodness from pleasure, but also equates the denial of pleasure with what is morally good, is hopelessly unscientific and irrational as far as Bentham is concerned. The principle of asceticism can provide no objective standards for moral decision-making in the way that the principle of utility can. Indeed these objective standards can, Bentham argues, be reduced to a kind of moral calculus that allows us to quantify our moral and legislative decision-making process.

Ethicists who follow a Kantian deontological theory (see the previous selection) usually criticize utilitarianism for its failure to provide an adequate theory of justice. Some argue, for example, that it would be possible to justify slavery on utilitarian grounds because that may give more pleasure to the community in general. In other words, Kantians argue that it would be possible to deny people their rights given the utilitarian viewpoint. An adequate theory of justice, they claim, can be based only on the recognition that people have rights simply because they are people. That is, rights are intrinsic, and Kant's categorical imperative acknowledges this. However, utilitarianism does not hold that people have rights just because they are people. People have rights only if granting them rights produces greater happiness to the community.

The following selection is from Bentham's most important work, *An Introduction to the Principles of Morals and Legislation*, first published in 1789. Read it and make up your own mind about whether the deontological focus on doing one's duty and recognizing the rights of others is a better moral approach than Bentham's utilitaranism.

Reading Questions

1. What is the relationship between the principle of utiltiy and pleasure and pain?
2. How does Bentham define the "interest of the community"?
3. According to Bentham, what do *ought, right,* and *wrong* mean?
4. How does Bentham support his claim that the proof of the principle of utility is unnecessary?
5. How does Bentham refute the principle of asceticism?
6. What are the seven criteria Bentham provides for determining the value of pleasure and pain?
7. Create the broad outlines of a governmental policy or law on physician-assisted suicide by using Bentham's utilitarian calculus. Is the calculus helpful? Are you satisfied with the results? Why, or why not?
8. How does Bentham answer the question, "How can I know what is right?"

Of the Principle of Utility

JEREMY BENTHAM

I. NATURE HAS PLACED MANKIND under the governance of two sovereign masters, *pain* and *pleasure*. It is for them alone to point out what we ought to do, as well as to determine what we shall do. On the one hand the standard of right and wrong, on the other the chain of causes and effects, are fastened to their throne. They govern us in all we do, in all we say, in all we think: every effort we can make to throw off our subjection, will serve but to demonstrate and confirm it. In words a man may pretend to abjure their empire: but in reality he will remain subject to it all the while. The *principle of utility* recognises this subjection, and assumes it for the foundation of that system, the object of which is to rear the fabric of felicity by the hands of reason and of law. Systems which attempt to question it, deal in sounds instead of sense, in caprice instead of reason, in darkness instead of light.

But enough of metaphor and declamation: it is not by such means that moral science is to be improved.

II. The principle of utility is the foundation of the present work: it will be proper therefore at the outset to give an explicit and determinate account of what is meant by it. By the principle* of utility is meant that principle which approves or disapproves of every action whatsoever, according to the tendency which it appears to have to augment or diminish the happiness of the party whose interest is in question: or, what is the same thing in other words, to promote or to oppose that happiness. I say of every action whatsoever; and therefore not only of every action of a private individual, but of every measure of government.

III. By utility is meant that property in any object, whereby it tends to produce benefit, advantage, pleasure, good, or happiness, (all this in the present case comes to the same thing) or (what comes again to the same thing) to prevent the happening of mischief, pain, evil, or unhappiness to the party whose interest is considered:

---

*The principle here in question may be taken for an act of the mind; a sentiment; a sentiment of approbation; a sentiment which, when applied to an action, approves of its utility, as that quality of it by which the measure of approbation or disapprobation bestowed upon it ought to be governed.

From An Introduction to the Principles of Morals and Legislation *(London: Clarendon Press, 1907). Some footnotes have been omitted.*

if that party be the community in general, then the happiness of the community: if a particular individual, then the happiness of that individual.

IV. The interest of the community is one of the most general expressions that can occur in the phraseology of morals: no wonder that the meaning of it is often lost. When it has a meaning, it is this. The community is a fictitious *body,* composed of the individual persons who are considered as constituting as it were its *members.* The interest of the community then is, what?—the sum of the interests of the several members who compose it.

V. It is in vain to talk of the interest of the community, without understanding what is the interest of the individual. A thing is said to promote the interest, or to be *for* the interest, of an individual, when it tends to add to the sum total of his pleasures: or, what comes to the same thing, to diminish the sum total of his pains.

VI. An action then may be said to be conformable to the principle of utility, or, for shortness sake, to utility, (meaning with respect to the community at large) when the tendency it has to augment the happiness of the community is greater than any it has to diminish it.

VII. A measure of government (which is but a particular kind of action, performed by a particular person or persons) may be said to be conformable to or dictated by the principle of utility, when in like manner the tendency which it has to augment the happiness of the community is greater than any which it has to diminish it. . . .

X. Of an action that is conformable to the principle of utility one may always say either that it is one that ought to be done, or at least that it is not one that ought not to be done. One may say also, that it is right it should be done; at least that it is not wrong it should be done: that it is a right action; at least that it is not a wrong action. When thus interpreted, the words *ought,* and *right* and *wrong,* and others of that stamp, have a meaning: when otherwise, they have none.

XI. Has the rectitude of this principle been ever formally contested? It should seem that it had, by those who have not known what they have been meaning. Is it susceptible of any direct proof? it should seem not: for that which is used

to prove every thing else, cannot itself be proved: a gain of proofs must have their commencement somewhere. To give such proof is as impossible as it is needless.

XII. Not that there is or ever has been that human creature breathing, however stupid or perverse, who has not on many, perhaps on most occasions of his life, deferred to it. By the natural constitution of the human frame, on most occasions of their lives men in general embrace this principle, without thinking of it: if not for the ordering of their own actions, yet for the trying of their own actions, as well as of those of other men. There have been, at the same time, not many, perhaps, even of the most intelligent, who have been disposed to embrace it purely and without reserve. There are even few who have not taken some occasion or other to quarrel with it, either on account of their not understanding always how to apply it, or on account of some prejudice or other which they were afraid to examine into, or could not bear to part with. For such is the stuff that man is made of: in principle and in practice, in a right track and in a wrong one, the rarest of all human qualities is consistency.

XIII. When a man attempts to combat the principle of utility, it is with reasons drawn, without his being aware of it, from that very principle itself.* His arguments, if they prove any thing, prove not that the principle is *wrong,* but that, according to the applications he supposes to be made of it, it is *misapplied.* Is it possible for a man to move the earth? Yes; but he must first find out another earth to stand upon. . . .

. . . Admitting any other principle than the principle of utility to be a right principle, a principle that it is right for a man to pursue; admitting (what is not true) that the word *right* can have a meaning without reference to utility, let him say whether there is any such thing as a *motive* that a man can have to pursue the dictates of it: if there is, let him say what that motive is, and

---

*"The principle of utility, (I have heard it said) is a dangerous principle: it is dangerous on certain occasions to consult it." This is as much as to say, what? that it is not consonant to utility, to consult utility: in short, that it is *not* consulting it, to consult it.

how it is to be distinguished from those which enforce the dictates of utility: if not, then lastly let him say what it is this other principle can be good for?

Of Principles Adverse to That of Utility

I. If the principle of utility be a right principle to be governed by, and that in all cases, it follows from what has been just observed, that whatever principle differs from it in any case must necessarily be a wrong one. To prove any other principle, therefore, to be a wrong one, there needs no more than just to show it to be what it is, a principle of which the dictates are in some point or other different from those of the principle of utility: to state it is to confute it. . . .

V. There are two classes of men of very different complexions, by whom the principle of asceticism appears to have been embraced; the one a set of moralists, the other a set of religionists. Different accordingly have been the motives which appear to have recommended it to the notice of these different parties. Hope, that is the prospect of pleasure, seems to have animated the former: hope, the aliment of philosophic pride: the hope of honour and reputation at the hands of men. Fear, that is the prospect of pain, the latter: fear, the offspring of superstitious fancy: the fear of future punishment at the hands of a splenetic and revengeful Deity. I say in this case fear: for of the invisible future, fear is more powerful than hope. These circumstances characterize the two different parties among the partisans of the principle of asceticism; the parties and their motives different, the principle the same.

Value of a Lot of Pleasure or Pain, How to Be Measured

I. Pleasures then, and the avoidance of pains, are the *ends* which the legislator has in view: it behooves him therefore to understand their *value*. Pleasures and pains are the *instruments* he has to work with: it behooves him therefore to understand their force, which is again, in other words, their value.

II. To a person considered *by himself,* the value of a pleasure or pain considered *by itself,* will be greater or less, according to the four following circumstances:*

1. Its *intensity*.
2. Its *duration*.
3. Its *certainty* or *uncertainty*.
4. Its *propinquity* or *remoteness*.

III. These are the circumstances which are to be considered in estimating a pleasure or a pain considered each of them by itself. But when the value of any pleasure or pain is considered for the purpose of estimating the tendency of any *act* by which it is produced, there are two other circumstances to be taken into the account; these are,

5. Its *fecundity,* or the chance it has of being followed by sensations of the *same* kind: that is, pleasures, if it be a pleasure: pains, if it be a pain.
6. Its *purity,* or the chance it has of *not* being followed by sensations of the *opposite* kind: that is, pains, if it be a pleasure: pleasures, if it be a pain.

These two last, however, are in strictness scarcely to be deemed properties of the pleasure or the pain itself; they are not, therefore, in strictness to be taken into the account of the value of that pleasure of that pain. They are in strictness to be deemed properties only of the act, or other event, by which such pleasure or pain has been produced; and accordingly are only to be taken into the account of the tendency of such act or such event.

IV. To a *number* of persons, with reference to each of whom the value of a pleasure or a pain is considered, it will be greater or less, according to seven circumstances: to wit, the six preceding ones; *viz.*

1. Its *intensity*.
2. Its *duration*.
3. Its *certainty* or *uncertainty*.
4. Its *propinquity* or *remoteness*.
5. Its *fecundity*.
6. Its *purity*.

*These circumstances have since been demonstrated *elements* or *dimensions of value* in a pleasure or a pain.

And one other; to wit:

7. Its *extent;* that is, the number of persons to whom it *extends;* or (in other words) who are affected by it.

V. To take an exact account then of the general tendency of any act, by which the interests of a community are affected, proceed as follows. Begin with any one person of those whose interests seem most immediately to be affected by it: and take an account,

1. Of the value of each distinguishable *pleasure* which appears to be produced by it in the *first* instance.
2. Of the value of each *pain* which appears to be produced by it in the *first* instance.
3. Of the value of each pleasure which appears to be produced by it *after* the first. This constitutes the *fecundity* of the first *pleasure* and the *impurity* of the first *pain.*
4. Of the value of each *pain* which appears to be produced by it after the first. This constitutes the *fecundity* of the first *pain,* and the *impurity* of the first pleasure.
5. Sum up all of the values of all the *pleasures* on the one side, and those of all the pains on the other. The balance, if it be on the side of pleasure, will give the *good* tendency of the act upon the whole, with respect to the interests of that *individual* person; if on the side of pain, the *bad* tendency of it upon the whole.

6. Take an account of the *number* of persons whose interests appear to be concerned; and repeat the above process with respect to each. *Sum up* the numbers expressive of the degrees of *good* tendency, which the act has, with respect to each individual, in regard to whom the tendency of it is *good* upon the whole: do this again with respect to each individual, in regard to whom the tendency of it is *good* upon the whole: do this again with respect to each individual, in regard to whom the tendency of it is *bad* upon the whole. Take the *balance;* which, if on the side of *pleasure,* will give the general *good tendency* of the act, with respect to the total number or community of individuals concerned; if on the side of pain, the general *evil tendency,* with respect to the same community.

VI. It is not to be expected that this process should be strictly pursued previously to every moral judgment, or to every legislative or judicial operation. It may, however, be always kept in view: and as near as the process actually pursued on these occasions approaches to it, so near will such process approach to the character of an exact one. . . .

Suggestions for Further Reading

Mary P. Mack's *Jeremy Bentham: An Odyssey of Ideas* (New York: Columbia University Press, 1963) provides a full-scale intellectual biography.

Masterpieces of World Philosophy edited by Frank N. Magill (New York: HarperCollins, 1990, p. 344ff.) summarizes the principle ideas of Bentham's utilitarianism and provides an account of some of the controversy over how we should interpret Bentham.

For a collection of essays on utilitarianism in general, see *Utilitarianism and Its Critics,* edited by Jonathan Glover (New York: Macmillan, 1990). You can check out Bentham on the web at http://www.utm.edu/research/iep/b/bentham.htm, courtesy of the *Internet Encyclopedia of Philosophy.*

Videos

Insight Media (2162 Broadway, New York, NY 10024) offers *Utilitarianism,* a 25-minute discussion by Professor Bernard Williams.

In *Moral Philosophy* (45 minutes), R. M. Hare examines the utilitarianism of Bentham, Mill, and Sidgwick. Available from Films for the Humanities and Sciences (www.film.com).

4.4 Revaluation of Values

Consideration of the question "How can I know what is right?" leads to thinking about other questions, such as what makes an action right. The "what" in both these questions initiates a search for a "something" that not only makes for moral rightness but also is something we can know. Pondering what this "something" might be sends our minds along a path searching for what some have called the foundations of morality. Where does morality come from? What supports it? Why, in our struggle for existence, should we limit our behavior in any way, or at least in any way that might be called moral? Why be moral?

Many people have found a close association between religion and morality. Not only are the moral values we hold historically derived from certain religions like Judaism, Christianity, Islam, Hinduism, Confucianism, and others, but many have held that there must be some sort of divine source or foundation for morality. So some might say that the shortest answer to the question "How can I know what is right?" is "What does God say?"

This line of thought reflects a divine command theory of ethics (see Section 3.4). What is good is what God commands. However, this short answer is problematic. Which "god" are we talking about? How do we know what are the divine commands? Wars have been fought with both sides claiming they were acting according to God's will. And, as Socrates pointed out, if God's command or will determines what is good, then nothing is good in itself, but only if God should happen to will it. If the meaning of the concept "moral goodness" is equivalent to the meaning "God commands," then we have no independent standards for judging whether what God commands is good. It is good by definition. So, for example, if I believe God has commanded me to allow my diabetic child to go without medical treatment, then that is a good thing to do—by definition.

Another problem arises if we ask, "How do we know the divine will won't change?" One day murder may be wrong (forbidden by God) and the next day right (commanded by God). One can always counter that God is unchanging. The divine mind will never change with respect to morality. Of course, saying this is one thing; proving it is quite another. Thus this divine foundation of morality is beginning to appear very unstable, and moral goodness is beginning to look like little more than obedience to a superior power.

Some might say that if there is no God, then anything is morally permissible. There is no reason at all to limit our freedom to do what we want. Both Kant and Bentham (see the two previous sections) were concerned with the issue of the foundation of morality and wanted to make a rational case for morality. If we cannot rely entirely on a religious answer to our question, perhaps human reason itself, without relying on alleged revelations of God's will, can supply an answer.

What if human reason should fail? What if Kant's categorical imperative and Bentham's principle of utility turn out to be inadequate answers? Where might we turn next? Perhaps there is no answer (a view some have dubbed **ethical nihilism**) or, if there is, we cannot not know it (ethical skepticism).

Friedrich Nietzsche (1844–1900), a German philosopher, thought both the religious answer and the reliance on human reason failed. If all religious and rational accounts of morality fail, what are we left with? Some have argued that Nietzsche gave a negative answer. We are left with nothing (nihilism). Others have argued that

Nietzsche tries to overcome ethical nihilism with a theory of his own. Exactly how to characterize this theory, however, is problematic. For some it amounts to a version of **ethical emotivism**, or the claim that moral judgments express the appraiser's attitudes of approval or disapproval. "A (where A is some action) is good" becomes, according to an emotivist theory, "I like A." It is a short step, some philosophers have argued, from this position to the view that people ought to do what is in their own self-interest (**ethical egoism**) since it is in our self-interest to do what we like. Ethical egoism is often contrasted with **altruism** (the view that people ought, at least sometimes, to do what is in the interest of others). Much of the morality we have inherited stresses an altruistic viewpoint and Kant, as we have seen, finds selfishness at the root of immorality.

In order to understand Nietzsche, we must make a distinction between morality and ethics. The word morality can be used in both a wide and a narrow sense. In its wider sense it refers to any code of conduct or system of values. In this sense it is equivalent to the term *ethics.* In its narrow sense morality refers to a specific code or value system. Thus we speak about "honor among thieves" as a moral code, albeit one beyond morality as we normally think of it. In other words, morality in the narrow sense is only one of the possibilities for an ethical life (morality in the wider sense).

Nietzsche's approach to morality is naturalistic in the sense that an explanation of its existence requires no reference to some world beyond nature, be that a supernatural world containing some god who gives commands to humans or a metaphysical world of elaborate rationalistic theories that explain good and evil. The practices and associated feelings that we call ethical are quite natural to the human species. How we interpret or understand those practices (morality in the narrow sense) changes with time. What has happened, according to Nietzsche, is that an ascetic ideal of self-denial has come to dominate morality as we think of it. This has come about because of what he calls a "slave revolt" led by priests that transformed a noble idea of virtue or excellence into our conventional or herd ideas of moral virtue. This ascetic ideal will no longer work as an adequate interpretation of human ethical practice. The religious and traditional moral establishment that has supported it is becoming (for a variety of very complex reasons) increasingly weak. Its capacity to convince us that it is the right interpretation of our ethical practices is waning. What is needed is a new interpretation, a new moral ideal, if you will, that takes us beyond the conventional moral understandings of good and evil.

Exactly what this new ideal would be, Nietzsche, I think, did not clearly see. It was something that was arriving, a future that he only had glimpses of prior to his death in 1900. What he did know was that it was not a divine command theory, or a categorical imperative, or a principle of utility, or a principle of asceticism. It was a principle of a new nobility, a new type of humanity, that we have yet to realize. This new moral ideal affirms not the pleasure principle of the utilitarians, or the English psychologists as Nietzsche calls them, but the "will to power" that affirms life, the whole of life with all its pleasures and all its pains.

The selection that follows incorporates material from two of Nietzsche's most influential books, *Beyond Good and Evil,* first published in 1886, and *On the Genealogy of Morality,* first published in 1887. According to Nietzsche, the *Genealogy* was a "clarification and supplement to my last book, *Beyond Good and Evil.*" In both books Nietzsche wants to show how the values of a noble and ruling class were revaluated by the slave classes led by priests (Nietzsche singles out the role the Jews played early in this process, but his remarks should not be construed as anti-Semitic) and motivated by hatred directed at the ruling class. Once we realize that our own life-denying morality that counsels us to sacrifice our self for the sake of others is the product of a historical process of revaluation, the way will be opened for another revaluation and the creation of a life-affirming morality that counsels us to respect ourselves and all who affirm life.

Reading Questions

1. How does Nietzsche characterize the pre-moral, moral, and extra-moral periods of human history?
2. What is wrong, according to Nietzsche, with past philosophical attempts to find the rational ground of morality?
3. What do you think Nietzsche means when he says, "moralities too are only *a sign-language of the emotions*"?
4. What is the difference between the "will to the denial of life" and the "will to power"?
5. What are some of the basic differences between *slave morality* and *master morality?*
6. What is noble?
7. What is the "English psychologists'" theory of the origin of the concept "good" and why is it wrong?
8. What, according to Nietzsche, is the real origin of the concepts good and bad?
9. Under what conditions does the opposition between unegoistic (altruistic) and egoistic (selfish) arise?
10. According to Nietzsche, what role does the priestly class play in the development of morality?
11. What role does *ressentiment* (grudge-bearing resentment) play in the creation of slave morality?
12. What do you think Nietzsche means when he says that "bad" is of noble origin and "evil" is the "true *deed*" of a slave morality?
13. What do you think about some of the things Nietzsche says? Do you think he is right or wrong? Could the conventional morality we follow today have a history rooted in class conflict and resentment?

Beyond Good and Evil

FRIEDRICH NIETZSCHE

32.

THROUGHOUT THE LONGEST PART of human history—it is called prehistoric times—the value or non-value of an action was derived from its consequences: the action itself came as little into consideration as did its origin, but, in much the same way as today in China a distinction or disgrace reflects back from the child onto its parents,

From Friedrich Nietzsche, Beyond Good and Evil: Prelude to a Philosophy of the Future, *translated by R. J. Hollingdale. London: Penguin Books, 1990. Copyright © R. J. Hollingdale, 1973, 1990. Reprinted by permission.*

so it was the retroactive force of success or failure which led men to think well or ill of an action. Let us call this period the *pre-moral* period of mankind: the imperative "know thyself" was then still unknown. Over the past ten thousand years, on the other hand, one has in a few large tracts of the earth come step by step to the point at which it is no longer the consequences but the origin of the action which determines its value: a great event, taken as a whole, a considerable refinement of vision and standard, the unconscious after-effect of the sovereignty of aristocratic values and of belief in "origins," the sign of a period which may be called the *moral* in the narrower sense: the first attempt at self-knowledge has been made. Instead of the consequences, the origin: what an inversion of perspectives! And certainly one achieved only after protracted struggles and vacillations! To be sure, a fateful new superstition, a peculiar narrowness of interpretation therewith became dominant: men interpreted the origin of an action in the most definite sense as origin in an *intention;* men became *unanimous* in the belief that the value of an action resided in the value of the intention behind it. The intention as the whole origin and prehistory of an action: it is under the sway of this prejudice that one has morally praised, blamed, judged and philosophized on earth almost to the present day.—But ought we not today to have arrived at the necessity of once again determining upon an inversion and shift of values, thanks to another self-examination and deepening on the part of man—ought we not to stand on the threshold of a period which should be called, negatively at first, the *extra-moral:* today, when among us immoralists at least the suspicion has arisen that the decisive value of an action resides in precisely that which is *not intentional* in it, and that all that in it which is intentional, all of it that can be seen, known, "conscious," still belongs to its surface and skin—which, like every skin, betrays something but *conceals* still more? In brief, we believe that the intention is only a sign and symptom that needs interpreting, and a sign, moreover, that signifies too many things and which thus taken by itself signifies practically nothing—that morality

in the sense in which it has been understood hitherto, that is to say the morality of intentions, has been a prejudice, a precipitancy, perhaps something provisional and precursory, perhaps something of the order of astronomy and alchemy, but in any event something that must be overcome. The overcoming of morality, in a certain sense even the self-overcoming of morality: let this be the name for that protracted secret labour which has been reserved for the subtlest, most honest and also most malicious consciences as living touchstones of the soul. . . .

Part Five: On the Natural History of Morals

186.

. . . Philosophers one and all have, with a strait laced seriousness that provokes laughter, demanded something much higher, more pretentious, more solemn of themselves as soon as they have concerned themselves with morality as a science: they wanted to furnish the *rational ground* of morality—and every philosopher hitherto has believed he has furnished this rational ground; morality itself, however, was taken as "given." How far from their clumsy pride was that apparently insignificant task left in dust and mildew, the task of description, although the most delicate hands and senses could hardly be delicate enough for it! It was precisely because moral philosophers knew the facts of morality only somewhat vaguely in an arbitrary extract or as a chance abridgement, as morality of their environment, their class, their church, the spirit of their times, their climate and zone of the earth, for instance— it was precisely because they were ill informed and not even very inquisitive about other peoples, ages and former times, that they did not so much as catch sight of the real problems of morality—for these come into view only if we compare *many* moralities. Strange though it may sound, in all "science of morals" hitherto the problem of morality itself has been *lacking:* the suspicion was lacking that there was anything problematic here. What philosophers called "the rational ground of morality" and sought to furnish was, viewed in the proper light, only a scholarly form of *faith* in the prevailing morality, a new way of *expressing* it, and thus itself a fact within a certain morality, indeed even in the last resort a kind of denial that this morality *ought* to be conceived of as a problem—and in any event the opposite of a testing, analysis, doubting and vivisection of this faith. . . .

187.

Quite apart from the value of such assertions as "there exists in us a categorical imperative" one can still ask: what does such an assertion say of the man who asserts it? There are moralities which are intended to justify their authors before others; other moralities are intended to calm him and make him content with himself; with others he wants to crucify and humiliate himself; with others he wants to wreak vengeance, with others hide himself, with others transfigure himself and set himself on high; this morality serves to make its author forget, that to make him or something about him forgotten; many moralists would like to exercise power and their creative moods on mankind; others, Kant perhaps among them, give to understand with their morality: "what is worthy of respect in me is that I know how to obey—and things *ought* to be no different with you!"—in short, moralities too are only a *sign-language of the emotions.* . . .

259.

To refrain from mutual injury, mutual violence, mutual exploitation, to equate one's own will with that of another: this may in a certain rough sense become good manners between individuals if the conditions for it are present (namely if their strength and value standards are in fact similar and they both belong to *one* body). As soon as there is a desire to take this principle further, however, and if possible even as the *fundamental principle of society,* it at once reveals itself for what it is: as the will to the *denial* of life, as the

principle of dissolution and decay. One has to think this matter thoroughly through to the bottom and resist all sentimental weakness: life itself is *essentially* appropriation, injury, overpowering of the strange and weaker, suppression, severity, imposition of one's own forms, incorporation and, at the least and mildest, exploitation—but why should one always have to employ precisely those words which have from of old been stamped with a slanderous intention? Even that body within which, as was previously assumed, individuals treat one another as equals—this happens in every healthy aristocracy—must, if it is a living and not a decaying body, itself do all that to other bodies which the individuals within it refrain from doing to one another: it will have to be the will to power incarnate, it will want to grow, expand, draw to itself, gain ascendancy—not out of any morality or immorality, but because it *lives,* and because life *is* will to power. On no point, however, is the common European consciousness more reluctant to learn than it is here; everywhere one enthuses, even under scientific disguises, about coming states of society in which there will be "no more exploitation"—that sounds to my ears like promising a life in which there will be no organic functions. "Exploitation" does not pertain to a corrupt or imperfect or primitive society: it pertains to the *essence* of the living thing as a fundamental organic function, it is a consequence of the intrinsic will to power which is precisely the will of life.—Granted this is a novelty as a theory—as a reality it is the *primordial fact* of all history: let us be at least that honest with ourselves!—

260.

In a tour of the many finer and coarser moralities which have ruled or still rule on earth I found certain traits regularly recurring together and bound up with one another: until at length two basic types were revealed and a basic distinction emerged. There is *master morality* and *slave morality*—I add at once that in all higher and mixed cultures attempts at mediation between the two are apparent and more frequently confusion and mutual misunderstanding between them, indeed sometimes their harsh juxtaposition—even within the same man, within *one* soul. The moral value-distinctions have arisen either among a ruling order which was pleasurably conscious of its distinction from the ruled—or among the ruled, the slaves and dependants of every degree. In the former case, when it is the rulers who determine the concept "good," it is the exalted, proud states of soul which are considered distinguishing and determine the order of rank. The noble human being separates from himself those natures in which the opposite of such exalted proud states find expression: he despises them. It should be noted at once that in this first type of morality the antithesis "good" and "bad" means the same thing as "noble" and "despicable"—the antithesis "good" and "*evil*" originates elsewhere. The cowardly, the timid, the petty, and those who think only of narrow utility are despised; as are the mistrustful with their constricted glance, those who abase themselves, the dog-like type of man who lets himself be mistreated, the fawning flatterer, above all the liar—it is a fundamental belief of all aristocrats that the common people are liars. "We who are truthful"—thus did the nobility of ancient Greece designate themselves. It is immediately obvious that designations of moral value were everywhere first applied to *human beings,* and only later and derivatively to *actions:* which is why it is a grave error when moral historians start from such questions as "why has the compassionate action been praised?" The noble type of man feels *himself* to be the determiner of values, he does not need to be approved of, he judges "what harms me is harmful in itself," he knows himself to be that which in general first accords honour to things, he *creates values.* Everything he knows to be part of himself, he honours: such a morality is self-glorification. In the foreground stands the feeling of plenitude, of power which seeks to overflow, the happiness of high tension, the consciousness of a wealth which would like to give away and bestow—the noble human being too aids the unfortunate but not, or almost not, from pity, but more from an urge begotten by superfluity of power. The noble human being honours in himself the man of power, also the man who has power over himself, who understands how to speak and how to keep silent, who enjoys practising severity and harshness upon himself and feels reverence for all that is severe and harsh. "A hard heart has Wotan set in my breast," it says in an old Scandinavian saga: a just expression coming from the soul of a proud Viking. A man of this type is actually proud that he is *not* made for pity: which is why the hero of the saga adds as a warning: "he whose heart is not hard in youth will never have a hard heart." Brave and noble men who think that they are at the farthest remove from that morality which sees the mark of the moral precisely in pity or in acting for others or in *désintéressement;* belief in oneself, pride in oneself, a fundamental hostility and irony for "selflessness" belong just as definitely to noble morality as does a mild contempt for and caution against sympathy and the "warm heart."—It is the powerful who *understand* how to honour, that is their art, their realm of invention. Deep reverence for age and the traditional—all law rests on this twofold reverence—belief in and prejudice in favour of ancestors and against descendants, is typical of the morality of the powerful; and when, conversely, men of "modern ideas" believe almost instinctively in "progress" and "the future" and show an increasing lack of respect for age, this reveals clearly enough the ignoble origin of these "ideas." A morality of the rulers is, however, most alien and painful to contemporary taste in the severity of its principle that one has duties only towards one's equals; that towards beings of a lower rank, towards everything alien, one may act as one wishes or "as the heart dictates" and in any case "beyond good and evil"—: it is here that pity and the like can have a place. The capacity for and the duty of protracted gratitude and protracted revenge—both only among one's equals—subtlety in requittal, a refined conception of friendship, a certain need to have enemies (as conduit systems, as it were, for the emotions of envy, quarrelsomeness, arrogance—fundamentally so as to be able to be a good *friend*): all these are typical marks of noble morality which, as previously indicated, is not the morality of "modern ideas" and is therefore hard to enter into today, also hard to unearth and uncover.—It is otherwise with the second type of morality, *slave morality*. Suppose the abused, oppressed, suffering, unfree, those uncertain of themselves and weary should moralize: what would their moral evaluations have in common? Probably a pessimistic mistrust of the entire situation of man will find expression, perhaps a condemnation of man together with his situation. The slave is suspicious of the virtues of the powerful: he is sceptical and mistrustful, *keenly* mistrustful, of everything "good" that is honoured among them—he would like to convince himself that happiness itself is not genuine among them. On the other hand, those qualities which serve to make easier the existence of the suffering will be brought into prominence and flooded with light: here it is that pity, the kind and helping hand, the warm heart, patience, industriousness, humility, friendliness come into honour—for here these are the most useful qualities and virtually the only means of enduring the burden of existence. Slave morality is essentially the morality of utility. Here is the source of the famous antithesis "good" and "*evil*"—power and danger were felt to exist in evil, a certain dreadfulness, subtlety and strength which could not admit of contempt. Thus, according to slave morality the "evil" inspire fear; according to master morality it is precisely the "good" who inspire fear and want to inspire it, while the "bad" man is judged contemptible. The antithesis reaches its height when, consistently with slave morality, a breath of disdain finally also comes to be attached to the "good" of this morality—it may be a slight and benevolent disdain—because within the slaves' way of thinking the good man has in any event to be a *harmless* man: he is good-natured, easy to deceive, perhaps a bit stupid, *un bonhomme*. Wherever slave morality comes to predominate, language exhibits a tendency to bring the words "good" and "stupid" closer to each other.—A final fundamental distinction: the longing for *freedom*, the instinct for the happiness and the refinements of the feeling of freedom, belong just as necessarily to slave morality and morals as the art of reverence and devotion and the enthusiasm for them are the regular symptom of an aristocratic mode of thinking and valuating.— This makes it clear without further ado why love *as passion*—it is our European speciality—absolutely must be of aristocratic origin: it was, as is well known, invented by the poet-knights of Provence, those splendid, inventive men of the "*gai saber*" to whom Europe owes so much and, indeed, almost itself.— . . .

287.

—What is noble? What does the word "noble" mean to us today? What, beneath this heavy, overcast sky of the beginning rule of the rabble which makes everything leaden and opaque, betrays and makes evident the noble human being?—It is not his actions which reveal him—actions are always ambiguous, always unfathomable—; neither is it his "works." One finds today among artists and scholars sufficient who reveal by their works that they are driven on by a profound desire for the noble: but precisely this need *for* the noble is fundamentally different from the needs of the noble soul itself, and in fact an eloquent and dangerous sign of its lack. It is not the works, it is the *faith* which is decisive here, which determines the order of rank here, to employ an old religious formula in a new and deeper sense: some fundamental certainty which a noble soul possesses in regard to itself, something which may not be sought or found and perhaps may not be lost either.—*The noble soul has reverence for itself.*—. . .

On the Genealogy of Morality

FRIEDRICH NIETZSCHE

First Treatise: "Good and Evil," "Good and Bad"

1.

—These English psychologists whom we also have to thank for the only attempts so far to produce a history of the genesis of morality—they themselves are no small riddle for us; I confess, in fact, that precisely as riddles in the flesh they have something substantial over their books—*they themselves are interesting!* These English psychologists—what do they actually want? One finds them, whether voluntarily or involuntarily, always at the same task, namely of pushing the *partie honteuse** of our inner world into the foreground and of seeking that which is actually effective, leading, decisive for our development, precisely where the intellectual pride of man would least of all *wish* to find it (for example in the *vis inertiae*† of habit or in forgetfulness or in a blind and accidental interlacing and mechanism of ideas or in anything purely passive, automatic, reflexive, molecular, and fundamentally mindless)—what is it actually that always drives these psychologists in precisely *this* direction? Is it a secret, malicious, base instinct to belittle mankind, one that perhaps cannot be acknowledged even to itself? Or, say, a pessimistic suspicion, the mistrust of disappointed, gloomy idealists who have become poisonous and green? Or a little subterranean animosity and rancor against Christianity (and Plato) that has perhaps not yet made it past the threshold of consciousness? Or even a lasciv-

ious taste for the disconcerting, for the painful-paradoxical, for the questionable and nonsensical aspects of existence? Or finally—a little of everything, a little meanness, a little gloominess, a little anti-Christianity, a little tickle and need for pepper? . . . But I am told that they are simply old, cold, boring frogs who creep and hop around on human beings, into human beings, as if they were really in their element there, namely in a *swamp*. I resist this, still more, I don't believe it; and if one is permitted to wish where one cannot know, then I wish from my heart that the reverse may be the case with them—that these explorers and microscopists of the soul are basically brave, magnanimous, and proud animals who know how to keep a rein on their hearts as well as their pain and have trained themselves to sacrifice all desirability to truth, to *every* truth, even plain, harsh, ugly, unpleasant, unchristian, immoral truth . . . For there are such truths.—

2.

Hats off then to whatever good spirits may be at work in these historians of morality! Unfortunately, however, it is certain that they lack the *historical spirit* itself, that they have been left in the lurch precisely by all the good spirits of history! As is simply the age-old practice among philosophers, they all think *essentially* ahistorically; of this there is no doubt. The ineptitude of their moral genealogy is exposed right at the beginning, where it is a matter of determining the origins of the concept and judgment "good." "Originally"—so they decree—"unegoistic actions were praised and called good from the perspective of those to whom they were rendered, hence for whom they were *useful;* later one *forgot* this origin of the praise and, simply because

*partie honteuse] shameful part (in the plural, this expression is the equivalent of the English "private parts").
†*vis inertiae*] force of inactivity. In Newtonian physics, this term denotes the resistance offered by matter to any force tending to alter its state of rest or motion.

unegoistic actions were *as a matter of habit* always praised as good, one also felt them to be good—as if they were something good in themselves." One sees immediately: this first derivation already contains all the characteristic traits of the idiosyncrasy of English psychologists—we have "usefulness," "forgetting," "habit," and in the end "error," all as basis for a valuation of which the higher human being has until now been proud as if it were some kind of distinctive prerogative of humankind. This pride *must* be humbled, this valuation devalued: has this been achieved? . . . Now in the first place it is obvious to me that the actual genesis of the concept "good" is sought and fixed in the wrong place by this theory: the judgment "good" does *not* stem from those to whom "goodness" is rendered! Rather it was "the good" themselves, that is the noble, powerful, higher-ranking, and high-minded who felt and ranked themselves and their doings as good, which is to say, as of the first rank, in contrast to everything base, low-minded, common, and vulgar. Out of this *pathos of distance* they first took for themselves the right to create values, to coin names for values: what did they care about usefulness! The viewpoint of utility is as foreign and inappropriate as possible, especially in relation to so hot an outpouring of highest rank-ordering, rank-distinguishing value judgments: for here feeling has arrived at an opposite of that low degree of warmth presupposed by every calculating prudence, every assessment of utility—and not just for once, for an hour of exception, but rather for the long run. As was stated, the pathos of nobility and distance, this lasting and dominant collective and basic feeling of a higher ruling nature in relation to a lower nature, to a "below"—*that* is the origin of the opposition "good" and "bad." (The right of lords to give names goes so far that we should allow ourselves to comprehend the origin of language itself as an expression of power on the part of those who rule: they say "this *is* such and such," they seal each thing and happening with a sound and thus, as it were, take possession of it.) It is because of this origin that from the outset the word "good" does *not* necessarily attach itself to "unegoistic" actions—as is the supersti-

tion of those genealogists of morality. On the contrary, only when aristocratic value judgments begin to *decline* does this entire opposition "egoistic" "unegoistic" impose itself more and more on the human conscience—to make use of my language, it is *the herd instinct* that finally finds a voice (also *words*) in this opposition. And even then it takes a long time until this instinct becomes dominant to such an extent that moral valuation in effect gets caught and stuck at that opposition (as is the case in present-day Europe: today the prejudice that takes "moral," "unegoistic," "*désintéressé*"* to be concepts of equal value already rules with the force of an "*idée fixe*" † and sickness in the head).

3.

In the second place, however: quite apart from the historical untenability of that hypothesis concerning the origins of the value judgment "good," it suffers from an inherent psychological absurdity. The usefulness of the unegoistic action is supposed to be the origin of its praise, and this origin is supposed to have been *forgotten:*—how is this forgetting even *possible*? Did the usefulness of such actions cease at some point? The opposite is the case: this usefulness has been the everyday experience in all ages, something therefore that was continually underscored anew; accordingly, instead of disappearing from consciousness, instead of becoming forgettable, it could not help but impress itself upon consciousness with ever greater clarity. How much more reasonable is that opposing theory (it is not therefore truer—) advocated for example by Herbert Spencer—which ranks the concept "good" as essentially identical with the concept "useful," "purposive," so that in the judgments "good" and "bad" humanity has summed up and sanctioned its *unforgotten* and *unforgettable* experiences concerning what is useful-purposive, what is injurious-nonpurposive. Good, according to this theory, is whatever has proved itself as useful from time immemorial: it may thus claim validity

---

*_désintéressé_] disinterested, unselfish, selfless.
† "_idée fixe_"] obsession; literally: a fixed idea.

as "valuable in the highest degree," as "valuable in itself." This path of explanation is also false, as noted above, but at least the explanation is in itself reasonable and psychologically tenable.

4.

—The pointer to the *right* path was given to me by the question: what do the terms coined for "good" in the various languages actually mean from an etymological viewpoint? Here I found that they all lead back to the *same conceptual transformation*—that everywhere the basic concept is "noble," "aristocratic" in the sense related to the estates, out of which "good" in the sense of "noble of soul," "high-natured of soul," "privileged of soul" necessarily develops: a development that always runs parallel to that other one which makes "common," "vulgar," "base" pass over finally into the concept "bad." The most eloquent example of the latter is the German word "*schlecht*" [bad] itself: which is identical with "*schlicht*" [plain, simple]—compare "*schlechtweg*," "*schlechterdings*" [simply or downright]—and originally designated the plain, the common man, as yet without a suspecting sideward glance, simply in opposition to the noble one. Around the time of the Thirty-Years' War, in other words late enough, this sense shifts into the one now commonly used.—With respect to morality's genealogy this appears to me to be an *essential* insight; that it is only now being discovered is due to the inhibiting influence that democratic prejudice exercises in the modern world with regard to all questions of origins. And this influence extends all the way into that seemingly most objective realm of natural science and physiology, as I shall merely hint at here. But the nonsense that this prejudice—once unleashed to the point of hate—is able to inflict, especially on morality and history, is shown by Buckle's notorious case; the *plebeianism* of the modern spirit, which is of English descent, sprang forth there once again on its native ground, vehemently like a muddy volcano and with that oversalted, overloud, common eloquence with which until now all volcanoes have spoken.— . . .

7.

—One will already have guessed how easily the priestly manner of valuation can branch off from the knightly-aristocratic and then develop into its opposite; this process is especially given an impetus every time the priestly caste and the warrior caste confront each other jealously and are unable to agree on a price. The knightly-aristocratic value judgments have as their presupposition a powerful physicality, a blossoming, rich, even overflowing health, together with that which is required for its preservation: war, adventure, the hunt, dance, athletic contests, and in general everything which includes strong, free, cheerful-hearted activity. The priestly-noble manner of valuation—as we have seen—has other presuppositions: too bad for it when it comes to war! Priests are, as is well known, the *most evil enemies*—why is that? Because they are the most powerless. Out of their powerlessness their hate grows into something enormous and uncanny, into something most spiritual and most poisonous. The truly great haters in the history of the world have always been priests, also the most ingenious haters:—compared with the spirit of priestly revenge all the rest of spirit taken together hardly merits consideration. Human history would be much too stupid an affair without the spirit that has entered into it through the powerless:—let us turn right to the greatest example. Of all that has been done on earth against "the noble," "the mighty," "the lords," "the power-holders," nothing is worthy of mention in comparison with that which the *Jews* have done against them: the Jews, that priestly people who in the end were only able to obtain satisfaction from their enemies and conquerors through a radical revaluation of their values, that is, through an act of *spiritual revenge*. This was the only way that suited a priestly people, the people of the most suppressed priestly desire for revenge. It was the Jews who in opposition to the aristocratic value equation (good = noble = powerful = beautiful = happy = beloved of God) dared its inversion, with fear-inspiring consistency, and held it fast with teeth of the most unfathomable hate (the hate of powerlessness), namely: "the miserable alone are the good; the poor, powerless, lowly alone are the good; the suffering, deprived, sick, ugly are also the only pious, the only blessed in God, for them alone is there blessedness,—whereas you, you noble and powerful ones, you are in all eternity the evil, the cruel, the lustful, the insatiable, the godless, you will eternally be the wretched, accursed, and damned!". . . We know *who* inherited this Jewish revaluation. . . . In connection with the enormous and immeasurably doom-laden initiative provided by the Jews with this most fundamental of all declarations of war, I call attention to the proposition which I arrived at on another occasion ("Beyond Good and Evil" section 195)—namely, that with the Jews *the slave revolt in morality* begins: that revolt which has a two-thousand-year history behind it and which has only moved out of our sight today because it—has been victorious. . . .

10.

The slave revolt in morality begins when *ressentiment* itself becomes creative and gives birth to values: the *ressentiment* of beings denied the true reaction, that of the deed, who recover their losses only through an imaginary revenge. Whereas all noble morality grows out of a triumphant yes-saying to oneself, from the outset slave morality says "no" to an "outside," to a "different," to a "not-self": and *this* "no" is its creative deed. This reversal of the value-establishing glance—this *necessary* direction toward the outside instead of back onto oneself—belongs to the very nature of *ressentiment:* in order to come into being, slave-morality always needs an opposite and external world; it needs, psychologically speaking, external stimuli in order to be able to act at all,—its action is, from the ground up, reaction. The reverse is the case with the noble manner of valuation: it acts and grows spontaneously, it seeks out its opposite only in order to say "yes" to itself still more gratefully and more jubilantly—its negative concept "low" "common" "bad" is only an after-birth, a pale contrast-

image in relation to its positive basic concept, saturated through and through with life and passion: "we noble ones, we good ones, we beautiful ones, we happy ones!" When the noble manner of valuation lays a hand on reality and sins against it, this occurs relative to the sphere with which it is *not* sufficiently acquainted, indeed against a real knowledge of which it rigidly defends itself: in some cases it forms a wrong idea of the sphere it holds in contempt, that of the common man, of the lower people; on the other hand, consider that the affect of contempt, of looking down on, of the superior glance—assuming that it does *falsify* the image of the one held in contempt—will in any case fall far short of the falsification with which the suppressed hate, the revenge of the powerless, lays a hand on its opponent—in effigy, of course. Indeed there is too much carelessness in contempt, too much taking-lightly, too much looking-away and impatience mixed in, even too much of a feeling of cheer in oneself; for it to be capable of transforming its object into a real caricature. . . . For the *ressentiment* of the noble human being, when it appears in him, runs its course and exhausts itself in an immediate reaction, therefore it does not *poison*—on the other hand it does not appear at all in countless cases where it is unavoidable in all the weak and powerless. To be unable for any length of time to take his enemies, his accidents, his *misdeeds* themselves seriously—that is the sign of strong, full natures in which there is an excess of formative, reconstructive, healing power that also makes one forget (a good example of this from the modern world is Mirabeau, who had no memory for insults and base deeds committed against him and who was only unable to forgive because he—forgot). Such a human is simply able to shake off with a single shrug a collection of worms that in others would dig itself in; here alone is also possible—assuming that it is at all possible on earth—the true "*love* of one's enemies." What great reverence for his enemies a noble human being has!—and such reverence is already a bridge to love. . . . After all, he demands his enemy for himself, as his distinction; he can stand no other enemy than one in whom there is nothing to hold in contempt and *a very great deal* to honor! On the other hand, imagine "the enemy" as the human being of *ressentiment* conceives of him—and precisely here is his deed, his creation: he has conceived of "the evil enemy," "*the evil one*," and this indeed as the basic concept, starting from which he now also thinks up, as reaction and counterpart, a "good one"—himself! . . .

11.

Precisely the reverse, therefore, of the case of the noble one, who conceives the basic concept "good" in advance and spontaneously, starting from himself that is, and from there first creates for himself an idea of "bad"! This "bad" of noble origin and that "evil" out of the brewing cauldron of unsatiated hate—the first, an after-creation, something on the side, a complementary color; the second, in contrast, the original, the beginning, the true *deed* in the conception of a slave morality—how differently the two words "bad" and "evil" stand there, seemingly set in opposition to the same concept "good"! But it is *not* the same concept "good": on the contrary, just ask yourself *who* is actually "evil" in the sense of the morality of *ressentiment*. To answer in all strictness: *precisely* the "good one" of the other morality, precisely the noble, the powerful, the ruling one, only recolored, only reinterpreted, only reseen through the poisonous eye of *ressentiment*. There is one point we wish to deny least of all here: whoever encounters those "good ones" only as enemies encounters nothing but *evil enemies*, and the same humans who are kept so strictly within limits *inter pares*, by mores, worship, custom, gratitude, still more by mutual surveillance, by jealousy, and who on the other hand in their conduct towards each other prove themselves so inventive in consideration, self-control, tact, loyalty, pride, and friendship,—they are not much better than uncaged beasts of prey toward the outside world, where that which is foreign, the foreign world, begins. There they enjoy freedom from all social constraint; in the wilderness they recover the losses incurred through the tension that comes from a long enclosure and fencing-in within the peace of the community; they step *back* into the innocence of the beast-of-prey conscience, as jubilant monsters, who perhaps walk away from a hideous succession of murder, arson, rape, torture with such high spirits and equanimity that it seems as if they have only played a student prank, convinced that for years to come the poets will again have something to sing and to praise. . . .

Suggestions for Further Reading

The article on Nietzsche by Maudemarie Clark in volume 6 of *Routledge Encyclopedia of Philosophy,* edited by Edward Cragg (London: Routledge, 1998), provides a brief overview of Nietzsche's philosophy as does the online *Stanford Encyclopedia of Philosophy* at http://plato.stanford.edu/entries/nietzsche/.

Walter Kaufmann's *Nietzsche: Philosopher, Psychologist, Antichrist* (Princeton, NJ: Princeton University Press, 1950), while dated, still provides one of the most thorough studies in English.

Nietzsche: A Collection of Critical Essays, edited by Robert C. Solomon (Garden City, NY: Anchor Books, 1973), provides a good collection of essays written from various perspectives.

Kai Nielson's *Ethics Without God* (Buffalo, NY: Prometheus Books, 1973) explores some of the issues concerning the relationship of religion and morality.

If you are interested in pursuing the divine command theory, see *Divine Commands and Morality,* edited by Paul Helm (Oxford: Oxford University Press, 1981), for a good sampling of the range of views.

Videos

Ethics in the Twentieth Century features Robert Solomon discussing the apparent loss of firm ground for making moral judgments in our century (six lectures given in 1993; 29 minutes each). *Existentialism* presents an overview of the movement, including discussions of Kierkegaard, Nietzsche, and Sartre (35 minutes). Both videos are available from Insight Media, 2162 Broadway, New York, NY 10024.

A 45-minute video devoted entirely to a discussion by J. P. Stern of Nietzsche's ideas is available from Films for the Humanities and Sciences (www.films.com) as part of their Great Philosophers series.

4.5 Toward a Feminist Ethic

In 1982, Carol Gilligan, a developmental psychologist, published a book entitled *In a Different Voice.* She pointed out that empirical research into moral reasoning and moral development used samples consisting of mostly male subjects. Thus, most of the major psychological theories of moral reasoning took male reasoning and male development as the norm.

Gilligan began to listen to women and discovered that their approach to moral issues was different from the male approach. The male perspective toward relationships tends to emphasize reciprocity. Equality, justice, rights, impartiality, objectivity, generalization, fair rules, and logical reasoning emerge as central concerns of males when dealing with moral dilemmas. For example, an 11-year-old boy, Jake, is given the Heinz dilemma. A man named Heinz considers whether to steal a drug that he cannot afford to buy because the drug is essential for saving the life of his wife. Jake is confident that Heinz should steal the drug because this is a clear-cut case of a conflict between the values of property and life. Logically, he argues, since life is irreplaceable, it must be given greater priority than property.

The female approach to moral problems, according to Gilligan, tends to be responsive. Care, love, trust, dealing with specific persons who have specific needs, compassion, mercy, forgiveness, the importance of not hurting anyone, and the authority of feeling in solving problems emerge as central concerns of females when dealing with moral issues. For example, Amy, also 11 years old, when given the Heinz dilemma, says she is not sure whether Heinz should steal the drug since that would harm the druggist. Also, Heinz might harm himself if he is caught and has to go to jail. That would also harm his wife who needs him to take care of her. Of course, she shouldn't be allowed to die either. Some other way needs to be found (borrow the money, work out installment payments), and she suggests they all get together, talk about the problem, and find a solution acceptable to all concerned.

Lawrence Kohlberg, who originally designed the study and developed the theory to which Gilligan is responding, construed the Heinz dilemma as a conflict between life and property and thus would regard Jake's response as indicative of a higher level of moral reasoning than Amy's. Gilligan remarks that one is not "higher" than the other—they are just different.

The major and most influential theories in moral philosophy have been developed by men. They reflect what Gilligan sees as the male concern with logical consistency, impartiality, rights, and obligations. Gilligan's work in descriptive psychology inspired the development of *feminist ethical theories* by philosophers. These feminist theories often begin with a critique of the sexism hidden in traditional moral theories and then go on to develop theories that take seriously caring and nurturing.

However, some feminist philosophers have been critical of this development for several reasons. First, an ethics of care may itself be sexist by elevating to philosophic status gender stereotypes of women as more self-sacrificing and more nurturing than men. This can work against women by reinforcing the idea that women are best suited to raising children and working in the "caring" professions, thereby restricting their opportunities. Second, an ethics of care cannot be divorced from an ethics of justice without severe consequences. Justice demands that we treat people fairly, and this is an ethical notion that has played an important role in the women's movement for liberation. For example, the "Seneca Falls Declaration" that resulted from the 1848 conference convened by Elizabeth Cady Stanton and Lucretia Mott in Seneca Falls, New York, to consider the "rights of women" states that "these truths [are] self-evident: that all men and *women* are created equal. . . ." The implicit reference to the "Declaration of Independence" and the adding of the word *women* anchored the claim to equal rights in the values already widely accepted in the United States and thereby made it far more difficult for men to deny women fundamental rights (such as the right to vote). Whatever we may think about the ethical importance of caring for people, caring without justice leaves us with a very one-sided moral theory.

Rita Manning teaches philosophy at San Jose State University. The selection that follows comes from her book, *Speaking From the Heart,* in which she defends "an ethic of care both as an adequate and as a feminist moral philosophy." She thinks that in responding to people who need care we should not appeal to abstract principles, such as obligation and utilitarian theories do, but rather we need to "pay attention to the concrete other in his or her real situation."

Reading Questions

1. What are the two elements of an ethic of caring?
2. In what sort of situation am I obligated to care, and in what situation can I choose when and how to care? Give an example of each.
3. Does the ethic of caring require feeling a particular emotion toward the one in need?
4. What is the difference between *subsistence needs* and *psychological needs?* Give an example of each.
5. If one's obligation to care arises from the existence of helplessness, why should I, according to Manning, care for values, institutions, and objects other than persons and animals?
6. What is the main point of Section III, "Caring and Human Nature"?
7. Why is the distinction between natural caring and ethical caring useful, and is it related to "moral imagination"?
8. How does Manning defend a "general obligation to care"?
9. What, according to Manning, is Nodding's position on the relationship between an ethic of care and rule-based ethical theories? Why does Manning reject Nodding's first two arguments, and how does she modify her third argument?
10. How does Manning defend her views against the arguments of Houston, O'Neill, Flanagan, and Jackson? Do you think her defense is successful? Why, or why not?
11. In the conclusion, Manning mentions several advantages to an ethic of care. Do you think her arguments are adequate to support this conclusion? Why, or why not?

Just Caring

RITA MANNING

. . . I SHALL SKETCH A MODEL of ethical considerations which I shall call, following Nel Noddings, an ethic of caring.[1] . . .

I must confess at the outset that this model owes more to my experience as a woman, a teacher, and a mother than it does to my training and experience in moral philosophy. Over the years, my students have convinced me of the barrenness of standard ethical theories. It has occurred to me only very recently that, in sketching a more adequate model, I might appeal to my own experience as a moral person. I credit Hume,[2] Annette Baier,[3] and Carol Gilligan,[4] with waking me from my dogmatic slumber and Nel Noddings with allowing me to take caring, which is central to my moral experience, seriously.

An ethic of caring, as I shall defend it, includes two elements. First is a disposition to care. This is a willingness to receive others, a willingness to give the lucid attention required to appropriately fill the needs of others. In this sense, an ethic of care is contextual; my actions must be guided by this lucid attention.[5] I see this disposition to care

as nourished by a spiritual awareness similar to the awareness argued for by proponents of the women's spirituality movement. As Starhawk describes this awareness: "Immanent justice rests on the first principle of magic: all things are interconnected. All is relationship. Perhaps the ultimate ethic of immanence is to choose to make that relationship one of love . . . love for all the eternally self-creating world, love of the light and the mysterious darkness, and raging love against all that would diminish the unspeakable beauty of the world."[6]

This disposition to care assumes a commitment to an ideal of caring; the ethically preferred world is one in which creatures are caring and cared for. Its institutions support and sustain caring while simultaneously reducing the need for care by eliminating the poverty, despair, and indifference that create a need for care.

Second, in addition to being sensitive to one's place in the world and to one's general obligation to be a caring person, one is also obligated to care for. (I am following Noddings in using "care for" to indicate caring as expressed in action.) In the paradigm case, caring for involves acting in some appropriate way to respond to the needs of persons and animals, but can also be extended to responding to the needs of communities, values, or objects.

We are obligated to adopt this model of caring, insofar as we can, in our moral deliberations. This qualification refers not only to physical,

1. Nel Noddings, *Caring: A Feminine Approach to Ethics and Moral Education* (Berkeley: University of California Press, 1984).

2. Hume argued that the task of moral philosophy ought to be to look reflectively at actual moral practice. This conception also can be seen, though to a lesser extent, in Aristotle, and in Alasdair MacIntyre, *After Virtue* (Notre Dame, Ind.: University of Notre Dame Press, 1981).

3. Annette Baier argues forcefully that we should pay exclusive attention to reforming current moral practices. See *Postures of the Mind: Essays on Mind and Morals,* especially chapters 11–15 (Minneapolis: University of Minnesota Press, 1985).

4. Carol Gilligan, *In a Different Voice* (Cambridge, Mass.: Harvard University Press, 1982).

5. Marilyn Friedman and Margaret Urban Walker point out that there are two separate theses in Gilligan: that care and responsibility moral reasoning is extremely sensitive to context and that the appropriate response is care and responsibility. See Marilyn Friedman, "Care and Context in Moral

Reasoning," in Eva Kittay and Diana Meyers, eds., *Women and Moral Theory* (Totowa, N.J.: Rowman and Littlefield, 1987) and Margaret Urban Walker, "What Does the Different Voice Say?: Gilligan's Women and Moral Philosophy," *The Journal of Value Inquiry* 23 (1989): 123–34.

6. Starhawk, *Dreaming the Dark* (Boston: Beacon Press, 1989) 44.

emotional, and psychological incapacity, but to the larger inability to simply adopt a moral life, which is radically different from the way of life we have participated in all our lives. This is a kind of incapacity that we all share. We simply cannot choose to have another's moral sensibilities, even if we are convinced that they are finer in some sense than our own. It doesn't follow that we have no obligations to become more morally sensitive; the point here is that we cannot simply will ourselves to begin to see the moral universe in some radically new way. But even where we can adopt a model of caring, we are morally permitted and sometimes morally obliged to appeal to rules and rights. In Gilligan's idiom, we are required to listen to the voices of both care and justice.

In what follows, I shall first fill in some of the details of this model. Specifically, I shall discuss what it is to care for someone or something and when we are obligated to care for. Next, I shall say something about the role of rules and rights in this model. . . .

I. Caring

I have often wondered if taking a class in moral philosophy was the best way for students to become sensitive to moral concerns. It seemed to me that a better way would be to have students work in soup kitchens or shelters for the homeless.[7] Taking care of my children has made me more open to moral concerns. In taking care of the hungry, homeless, and helpless, we are engaged in caring for. In the standard case, caring for is immediate; it admits of no surrogates. When we directly care for some creature, we are in physical contact. Our eyes meet, our hands touch. However, not every need can be met in this immediate way, and sometimes we must accept surrogates. Not every need can be met by individual action; in such cases, we must seek collective action.[8] But when we can do the car-

ing for directly, we ought to do so, at least some of the time. The need of the other may sometimes require that a particular person do the caring for. If my child needs my attention, I cannot meet this need by sending her to a therapist. Even when the needs of the other do not require our personal attention, we must provide some of the caring for directly in order to develop and sustain our ability to care.

Day-to-day interactions with other persons create a web of reciprocal caring. In these interactions, one is obliged to be a caring person. One is free, to a certain extent, to choose when and how to care for these others. One's choice is limited by one's relationships with these others and by their needs. A pressing need calls up an immediate obligation to care for; roles and responsibilities call up an obligation to respond in a caring manner. In the first case, one is obligated (though this obligation can be limited by a principle of supererogation) to respond; in the second, one can choose, within limits, when and how to care.

A creature in need who is unable to meet this need without help calls for a caring response on my part. This response need not always be direct. Sometimes it is better to organize a political response. (Many, for example, who are confronted on the street by homeless people are unsure about how to respond, convinced that their immediate response will not be enough, and might even be counterproductive.) Certain relationships obligate us to provide direct caring for. When my daughter falls and asks me to "kiss it and make it better" I can't send her to my neighbor for the kiss.

Our roles (e.g., as mother, as teacher, as volunteer) put us in particular relationships to others.[9] These roles require and sustain caring. Obligations to infant children and animals involve meeting their basic needs for physical sustenance (food, shelter, clothing, health care) and for companionship and love. Obligations to stu-

7. Richard Schubert, one of my creative and courageous colleagues, gives such assignments.
8. See my "The Random Collective as a Moral Agent" for a further discussion of collective action and obligation. *Social Theory and Practice* 11 (Spring 1985): 97–105.

9. Alasdair McIntyre, following Aristotle, made much of this notion of role responsibility. See *After Virtue*. See also Virginia Held, *Rights and Goods* (New York: The Free Press, 1984).

dents are grounded upon roles of teacher and philosopher and the students' psychological needs to discover who they are and how they can live with integrity. Here, one ought to feel a connection with the students but also with teaching and philosophy. But if a student needs another kind of care, we may be obligated to provide it, though not single-handedly. The response depends upon one's ability to care for, one's obligation to care for oneself, and one's sense of the appropriateness of the need and the best way to meet it.

In discharging obligations to care for, which are based on role responsibility, one should be conscious of the need to fill those roles conscientiously. The role of teacher, for example, requires a certain impartiality; the role of mother requires a fierce devotion to each particular child. But one is free, to a certain extent, to choose roles. In adopting or reshaping roles, one should be sensitive to the need to be cared for as well as the capacity to care. In critiquing socially designed and assigned roles, we should aim for roles and divisions of roles that make caring more likely to occur.

Caring for can involve a measure of self-sacrifice. The rescuers of Jessica McLure, the little girl who fell into a well, who went without sleep for days, the parents of an infant who go without uninterrupted sleep for months, are involved in caring for.

Caring for involves an openness to the one cared for; it requires seeing the real need and satisfying it insofar as we are able. In satisfying it, we should be sensitive not just to the need but to the feelings of those in need.

Caring for does not require feeling any particular emotion toward the one cared for, but an openness to the possibility that some emotional attachment may form in the process of caring for. Nor does it require an ongoing relationship with the one cared for.[10] One may meet the one

10. Noddings makes much of the requirement that caring requires an ongoing relationship. It is on this basis that she denies that we can have an obligation to care for the starving children in Africa, and animals. In an October 1988 talk to the Society for Women in Philosophy, she allowed that caring for does not exhaust our obligations, so we could have other obligations to the starving children in Africa. I would

cared for as stranger, though the caring for will change that.

Obviously, a model of caring along the lines I am defending must include an account of needs. An account of needs must recognize that needs are in some sense social, so identifying needs requires an understanding of biology, psychology, and other relevant social sciences.

Such an account would draw a distinction between subsistence needs and psychological needs. Subsistence needs will usually be needs that must be filled if physical existence is to continue, while psychological needs are needs that must be filled if human flourishing is to occur. Filling subsistence needs does not automatically benefit both the carer and the cared for. Rather, the carer is likely to feel burdened by filling such needs, though the recognition that one has filled such needs often creates a sense of virtue in the carer. Filling psychological needs can often be more fulfilling. It is more likely to be done in a reciprocal relationship, and in such a relationship filling psychological needs requires that both parties share the roles of carer and cared for.

Finally, one need not respond to every need. In choosing how and when to respond, one should consider the seriousness of the need, the benefit to the one needing care of filling this particular need, one's own capacity to fill the need, and the competing needs of others, including oneself, that will be affected by filling this particular need.

II. *Objects of Care*

One can care for persons, animals, ideas, values, institutions, and objects. Later, I will discuss caring for persons and animals in some detail, but here I want to make some brief remarks about caring for ideas, values, institutions, and objects. In caring for ideas, values, and institutions, one devotes oneself to their survival, growth, and flourishing in much the same way as we devote

prefer to say that we have obligations to care for the starving children and animals, but that not all caring obligations require direct care.

ourselves to the growth and flourishing of a child. In doing so, we are caring for ourselves (insofar as these are our ideas and values) and persons and animals (insofar as these ideas and values support a network of care that embraces persons and animals). In caring for objects, one is devoted primarily to their survival (although some objects, trees, for example, can be said to grow and flourish). The choice of objects of care should reflect our own need to be cared for and our capacity to care. But decisions about what to care for should not depend exclusively upon our own needs and capacities. We should also be sensitive to the needs that summon the obligation to care for. If we understand our obligation to care for as following from the existence of need and helplessness, we should care for ideas, institutions, values, objects, and practices that would diminish such needs. One might argue that we could virtually eliminate the need to care for by creating appropriate institutions, values, and practices and hence undermine our capacity to care. But even in a perfectly just world, children would need care, and people and animals would get sick. Furthermore, human needs include more than needs for physical sustenance. Human needs for companionship and intimacy would exist even in a world free from the horrors of war, homelessness, sickness, and disease.

III. Caring and Human Nature

Alasdair MacIntyre argues that morality has historically been defended by appeal either to "the ghost of conceptions of divine law" or "the ghost of conceptions of human nature and activity." Since neither conception is "at home in the modern world,"[11] morality lacks a foundation. Since morality lacks a foundation, relativism and emotivism have gained a secure foothold, at least in the popular culture.[12]

Though I sympathize with the postmodern rejection of essentialist theories of human na-

ture, I do not agree that there is nothing beyond mere historically conditioned, relatively pervasive human traits. The truth lies somewhere in between. While conceptions of human nature are too often overgeneralizations made on the basis of one's situated experience, one needn't reject the very possibility of finding sufficiently general human characteristics and experiences. Since there are such sufficiently general characteristics and experiences, we need not reject conceptions of human nature as providing a foundation for morality, though we do need to examine such conceptions. Conceptions of human nature generate a picture of the good life. The good life involves overcoming human nature, liberating human nature, or a combination of both: overcoming what is base and liberating what is pure. In this way, conceptions of human nature inform morality.

Many have argued that liberal ethical theories and political philosophies have assumed an unflattering and inaccurate picture of human nature. Marx, for example, criticizes the "individualistic monad"[13] lurking behind defenses of rights. A similar criticism has recently been made by Elizabeth Wolgast in her attacks on "social atomism"[14] and Alison Jaggar in her criticism of "abstract individualism."[15]

Jaggar identifies abstract individualism as the theory of human nature which underlies liberal political philosophy. I think we can assume that this theory provides a foundation for ethical theory as well. Abstract individualism is the view that essential human characteristics are properties of individuals and are given independently of the social context. This theory, as Jaggar describes it, is committed to the following claims.

1. Rationality is a mental capacity of individuals rather than groups and is possessed in approx-

---

11. MacIntyre, *After Virtue*, 105.

12. We can see how one would defend morality by appeal to divine law, and why such an appeal might fail. The *Meno* is a good example of such an appeal.

13. Karl Marx, "On the Jewish Question," in T. B. Bottomore, ed., *Karl Marx: Early Writings* (New York: McGraw Hill, 1964).

14. Elizabeth Wolgast, *The Grammar of Justice* (Ithaca, N.Y.: Cornell University Press, 1987), chap. 1.

15. Alison Jaggar, *Feminist Politics and Human Nature* (Totowa, N.J.: Rowman & Allanheld, 1983) throughout, but see Chapter Three.

imately equal measure by all humans, though this capacity can be more or less developed.

2. Rationality is our most valuable capacity.
3. Each individual is intrinsically valuable because of this ability to reason.
4. Each human's desires can in principle be fulfilled separately from the desires of other humans.
5. People typically seek to maximize their individual self-interest.
6. Resources for fulfilling desires are limited.
7. Because of the value of rationality and the existence of scarcity and desires to possess certain goods, autonomy is protected by the good society.[16]

One can argue about whether Jaggar has accurately described liberal political and moral philosophy here, but even if we grant that the picture is overdrawn, a version of it undergirds Kantian and utilitarian moral theories. We can see how this conception supports Kantian ethics with its emphasis on duty. If one is unconnected to others, and basically self-interested, no other motivation to be moral could exist.

Utilitarianism is also a rational alternative if abstract individualism is true. An unconnected, basically self-interested individual would admit that social life is not worth living without some constraints on the self-interest of others. It is then rational to adopt a system of mutual restraint, as long as one's own interests will count. In this way, the rational person can protect his interests.

An ethic of care rejects the abstract individualism criticized by Jaggar. On this view, we are all connected, and, as Noddings puts it, "the primary aim is caring and being cared for. . . ."[17] This caring can take place only in potentially reciprocal relationships between human beings. The good society protects this aim and allows for the full development of our best selves, which are those selves represented by "our most caring and tender moments."[18] Since caring is not a totally rational process, although it is partly this, an ethic of care would reject claims number two and

three. Rationality is not our most valuable capacity; the capacity for caring represents our "best selves." It would also reject claim four. If our primary desires are to care and be cared for in relationships with other humans, then we cannot fulfill our desires independently of other humans. We should not be seen as seeking to maximize self-interest either, because caring involves the suspension of self-interest in many cases, so she would reject claim number five as well. Claim number six is noncontroversial, but claim number seven would also be rejected because it follows from number three.

We can see that an ethic of care requires a new conception of human nature, and such an account would involve a picture of humans as essentially involved in relationships with other humans.

IV. Knowing How and When to Care

It is not unreasonable to expect an ethic to give us some guidance about how to act, though as I have argued . . . it is unreasonable to expect a calculus. An ethic of care, then, ought to give us some guidance about how and when to care.

Noddings explicitly acknowledges her great debt to Hume, as do I. It seems reasonable then to begin by looking at Hume's answer to this question. Hume saw morality as resting upon a human capacity for sympathetic identification with others.[19] When we see someone suffering, for example, we feel the suffering almost as if it were our own. Our desire to do something to relieve the suffering springs naturally from this empathic response. This natural sentiment is supplanted by an appeal to justice when the sentiment is lacking. Suppose, for example, that the suffering is taking place in a distant place and we are merely aware of it. Our awareness does not excite in us the same empathic response that the immediate perception of the suffering would. What

16. Ibid.
17. Noddings, *Caring,* 174.
18. Ibid., 104.

19. David Hume, *An Enquiry Concerning the Principles of Morals,* sect. 3. L. A. Selby-Biggs, ed., (Oxford: Oxford University Press, 1962); *A Treatise on Human Nature,* bk. 3, pt. 20, L. A. Selby-Biggs, ed. (Oxford: Oxford University Press, 1964).

we must do in this case is remind ourselves that although we do not know the sufferer, we can assume that the sufferer shares essential characteristics with someone who is close to us. Since we cannot find any reason to reject the appeal of the one while desiring to respond to the other, we recognize the demands made on us by the absent sufferer. Here what we see is sentiment, colored by reflection. This reflection results in rather general principles, though the principles are seen as derivative of our experience and our sentiments.

Noddings makes a similar move when she distinguishes natural from ethical caring.[20] Natural caring is the caring that one is inclined to do, that springs from ties of affection to others. In the absence of such inclination, one must summon up ethical caring. Both Hume and Noddings are vague about precisely what caring demands in any particular situation. Hume suggests that, at least with respect to general principles, we let experience be our guide; we look for those principles that will make the world more comfortable for the social creatures we are. Noddings rejects an appeal to general principles, but offers instead a strategy for deciding what to do. When natural caring is absent, one should ask oneself what the ideal caring self would do in this situation. She is not suggesting that we appeal to an impartial observer here. Instead, she asks us to remember a situation in which we were ideally caring; we appeal here to our own ideal of caring.

What is implied in both Hume and Noddings is that when sentiment and natural caring do motivate us, we freely follow their dictates. Both of them admit that this capacity can stagnate and die or it can flourish, and, accordingly, we have an obligation to support this capacity in ourselves. Noddings argues that we can only learn to care if we have been cared for as children, and if we have been given opportunities to care. If we have been, then, as adults, we sustain and enrich this capacity by continuing to seek opportunities to care actively for others.

Assuming we are caring persons, both Hume and Noddings suggest that we can trust our impulses; our instincts will guide us toward proper caring, at least when we are caring in the context of a fully present other. There is, of course, an additional requirement that Noddings in particular pays attention to: that we know how the other feels and what the other wants and how the other is likely to be affected by our actions.

Martha Nussbaum combines both sentiment and awareness in her notion of moral imagination. She describes moral imagination as the ability to see "a complex, concrete reality in a highly lucid and richly responsive way . . . taking in what is there, with imagination and feeling."[21]

I agree with Hume, Noddings, and Nussbaum that our interactions with others can and should be guided by our moral imaginations, by our sentiments balanced by our rich understanding of the context. Obviously our responses to strangers will not be guided by the same degree of understanding and sentiment as our responses to those close to us. However, Hume and Noddings are right to suggest that we imagine ourselves in contact with them, that we try to become as aware as we can be of their situations, that we allow this awareness to occasion an emotional response, and that we act, in the full knowledge that our actions, based as they are on insufficient understanding and often less than vibrant sentiment, might not be the right ones. I also agree with Nussbaum and Hume that general principles have a role to play. We appeal to our experiences with intimate others to generate a set of general principles, though we keep in mind that these are merely rules of thumb, based on past experience. But in the absence of understanding and rich emotional response, this might be the only way to guide our actions toward strangers.

V. Defense of a General Obligation to Care

I am inclined to see the obligation to care as moral bedrock. If it can be said to rest on anything, it rests on our human capacity for caring interaction. Rather than offer a defense of care in

20. Noddings, *Caring,* chap. 4.

21. Martha Nussbaum, "Finely Aware and Richly Responsible: Literature and the Moral Imagination," *The Journal of Philosophy* 82 (1985): 516–29.

terms of appeals to general principles, I would offer a defense of something like general principles in terms of care. Still, for those who find the appeal to general principles more compelling than the obligation to care, I offer a defense of care in terms of such suitably general principles.

The obligation to respond as carer when appropriate can be defended on three grounds. The first is the need. Here one might appeal to Peter Singer's principle, "If it is in our power to prevent something very bad happening without thereby sacrificing anything of comparable moral significance, we ought to do it."[22]

The second is the recognition that human relationships require a continuous kind of caring. This caring involves three components: being receptive to the other, being accepting of the other, and being on call for the other when he/she is in need.[23] Unless we want to do away with human relationships, we must be open to the demands of caring that such relationships require. But caring in human relationships is, as human relationships are, reciprocal.

The third defense is that we cannot develop and sustain the ability to care unless we do some active caring. This is an empirical claim, and we must look both to social science and to our own experience in evaluating it, but there is an obvious way in which caring for enhances our ability to care. When we make the real attempt to care for, we must understand the needs of the one cared for. We must also see how that one wants the needs to be addressed. This ability to notice needs and wants and to empathize as well as sympathize is developed through caring. Of course, one might ask here why one should want to develop this capacity to care. It seems to me that the right response is to point out that human lives devoid of caring impulses and responses would be nasty, brutish, short, and lonely.

Nel Noddings offers a different defense of the general obligation to care, one which seems to offer some problematic consequences. Noddings's theory is that morality essentially involves one obligation: the obligation to care. Caring involves two elements: natural caring and ethical caring. Natural caring requires engrossment in the other, "seeing the other's reality as possible for me,"[24] and the motivation to act "based on recognition of the other's wants and desires and . . . the objective elements of his problematic situation."[25] Ethical caring involves summoning natural caring by remembering "our most caring and tender moments"[26] and recognizing that these moments represent our best self. Ethical caring can only be achieved in situations where dynamic, mutual relationships are possible.

This analysis provides, according to Noddings, an analysis of obligation.

> I can be obligated to P if: (1) There exists or is potential a relation between P and me; (2) There exists the dynamic potential for growth in relation, including the potential for increased reciprocity and mutuality.

We are only obligated when these conditions obtain because, in her view, it is only under these conditions that caring can occur. Noddings denies that "universal caring" is a possibility[27] and admits to the following three consequences of her analysis. First, "I am not obligated to starving children in Africa."[28] Her argument for this is not exactly clear, but it appears that she would want to say that my ongoing relationships confer obligations that are primary. She says that fulfilling obligations to the starving children in Africa would require me to "abandon my obligations"[29] to those to whom I am already related. Second, we have no obligations to animals because there is no possibility for genuine mutuality from animals.[30] Third, the life of one caring (the ethically preferred life for all according to Noddings) must, in some sense, be a private life. "Her public life is limited by her insistence upon

22. Peter Singer, *Practical Ethics* (Cambridge: Cambridge University Press, 1979), 168.
23. This analysis is from Milton Mayeroff, *On Caring* (New York: Perennial Library, 1971).
24. Noddings, *Caring,* 14.
25. Ibid., 24.
26. Ibid., 86.
27. Ibid.
28. Ibid.
29. Ibid.
30. Ibid., 87.

meeting the other as one caring . . . when reaching out destroys or drastically reduces her actual caring, she retreats and renews her contact with those who address her."[31]

I want to take issue with each of these consequences, but I don't think that by doing so I am rejecting Noddings's account. Indeed, I am puzzled about why Noddings thought she was committed to them. It seems to be that a sympathetic reading of her could justify the exactly opposite conclusions.[32]

Noddings needn't grant that helping the starving in Africa requires abandoning obligations to those to whom one is related. However, I suspect that she would still want to insist that I am not obligated to the starving in Africa. There is no present relationship between me and the starving children in Africa, nor is it likely that such a relationship will begin in the future. She gives us the example of a missionary who decides to go to Africa to help the starving. She says that this person might well have such obligations because this person will begin to have such relationships.[33]

I don't agree that we have no obligations to the starving in Africa, in part because I don't accept Noddings's assumption about the primacy of current obligations. It seems to me that we have self-interested reasons for wanting to meet the obligations to those with whom we share a relationship. First, the possibility and hence the expectation of reciprocity gives us a self-interested reason for meeting these obligations first. Second, if we are truly "engrossed" by the persons for whom we care, we will receive some pleasure in meeting these obligations. I don't want to argue that no moral reasons can be offered where reasons of self-interest naturally obtain, but I do think that we should be suspicious of ethical theories that restrict our obligations to those duties that we have a self-interested reason to perform.

Noddings might have argued that we can have mutually reciprocal relationships with animals, or she might have taken the same stance with regard to animals that she takes with regard to abortion. In the latter case, she argues that the prospective mother can grant "sanctity" to the first-trimester fetus by viewing it as a "product of love between a man deeply cared-for and me,"[34] and, as such, "joined to others through formal chains of caring."[35] Because the caring exists for this mother, abortion would be immoral. If the mother chooses not to sanctify the fetus, no such relationship exists in the first trimester, and hence abortion would not be immoral. As the fetus begins to develop, it becomes "more nearly capable of response as cared-for."[36] At this point the relationship begins to exist and grow, and abortion is again immoral. It sounds like she is saying that if I choose to view myself as involved in a relationship with a fetus, then I have obligations toward it, even if it is not now capable of having a mutually reciprocal relationship with me.[37] Why can't I then choose to see myself as involved in a relationship with animals, or at least with some animals? If I choose to see the animal this way, then I do have an obligation toward the animal. But this is not a very satisfactory consequence for a defender of animal rights; according to this view, if I don't choose to view myself as in a relationship with animals, I am free to treat them any way I want. I would be inclined to say that if we do have obligations toward animals, and I think we do, it is in virtue of qualities that the animals possess, for example the ability to suffer, and not in virtue of our willingness to recognize such qualities.

The claim that one must withdraw from the public sphere and retreat to the private when neglecting those to whom one is already related strikes me as a classic defense of the stereotypical role of the housewife. It tends to reinforce both

---

31. Ibid., 89.
32. Noddings has since given up these consequences. See her response to critics, "A Response," *Hypatia* 5 (1990): 120–26.
33. Noddings, *Caring*, 86.
34. Ibid., 87.
35. Ibid.
36. Ibid.
37. For other discussions of abortion from the perspective of an ethic of care, see Janet Smith, "Abortion and Moral Development Theory: Listening with Different Ears," *International Philosophical Quarterly* 28 (1988): 31–51 and Celia Wolf-Devine, "Abortion and the 'Feminine Voice'," *Public Affairs Quarterly* 3 (1989): 81–97.

self-interest and moral cowardice in the face of injustice, inequality, and suffering outside our own little worlds.

What is objectionable about all these consequences is the implication that one can choose all one's obligations. While obligations are created through voluntary commitments, this does not exhaust the possibilities. Further, Noddings's desire to thus limit our obligations is incompatible with the distinction she makes between natural and ethical caring. If one is obligated to do some ethical caring, and this involves calling upon one's ideal caring self, won't this ideal caring self feel some obligation toward animals and starving children in Africa? I'm convinced that it would, for much the same reasons that Hume thinks that the demands of justice will assert themselves after some reflection. We can come to recognize that the starving children in Africa share crucial characteristics with the children we know and love; we can see that animals share important characteristics as well. Surely, our ideal caring selves will not ignore this.

VI. Limitations on Obligations to Care

I don't think that we are obligated to be like Mother Teresa, who cares for continuously.[38] But how are we to limit our obligation to care? One strategy for limiting our obligation to care for focuses on the defenses of this obligation. First, we have a *prima facie* obligation to care for when we come across a creature in need who is unable to meet that need without help, when our caring is called upon as a part of a reciprocal relationship, or when caring is indicated as part of our role responsibility. Actual obligations rest upon the seriousness of the need, the assessment of the appropriateness of filling the need, and the ability to do something about filling it. But we must also recognize that we are persons who

must be cared for and who deserve such care. The continuous caring for required to respond to needs for physical sustenance is, for most of us, incompatible with caring for ourselves. But not all caring for involves responding to physical needs. The caring for required to sustain relationships, which is usually reciprocal, can be a source of great strength to the person doing the caring for. And finally, allowing ourselves to suffer caring burnout also diminishes our ability to care for others in the future. I don't mean to argue that caring for requires no sacrifice. Indeed, where the need is great and the ability to meet it sufficient, we are required to sacrifice. But one is not required to adopt this as a form of life.

The obligation to care for is not an all-or-nothing thing. Being unable to care for now does not eliminate the possibility that one may be obligated to meet this need later. This is a general point about obligations. I might owe someone money and be unable to pay it back now, through no fault of my own. If I later come into a windfall, I am obligated to pay the money back then. In addition, there is no one right way to care for. Our assessment of the appropriateness of the need, our ability to meet the need, and our sense of the most successful way of doing so provide some guidance here. Perhaps immediate caring for is the best way to meet a need in one case, and cooperative political activity the most successful way of meeting other needs. I would want to leave these kinds of choices up to the agent.

VII. Rules and Rights

Larry Blum offers a useful taxonomy of the relation between what he calls impartialist positions and an ethic of care. He defines an impartialist position as one based on "impartiality, impersonality, justice, formal rationality, and universal principle."[39] He discusses seven different impartialist responses to an ethic of care, ranging from absolute dismissal to acceptance of an ethic of care as a subsidiary of an impartialist ethic. I

---

38. The inappropriateness of slavish caring has long been a theme in feminist thought. Betty Friedan called thinking that one's role in life requires such caring "the problem that has no name." See *The Feminine Mystique* (New York: Dell Publishing Co., 1963).

39. Lawrence A. Blum, "Gilligan and Kohlberg: Implications for Moral Theory," *Ethics* 98 (April 1988): 472–91.

want to turn the tables here and offer a defense of rules and rights in terms of care.

In my model, rules and rights serve three purposes. They can be used to persuade, to sketch a moral minimum below which no one should fall and beyond which behavior is condemned, and they can be used to deliberate in some cases.

The attention to rules and rights here does not reflect an unwillingness to make appeals to virtues and practices. I do include virtues and practices as fulfilling each of the three functions that rules and rights play in my model. We certainly can and do persuade by reminding others of virtues: "Would an honest man do that?" We likewise persuade by pointing to practices: "Native Americans don't have that kind of an attitude about the earth." Virtues and practices can serve as minimums: "I can see that you won't be doing me any favors, but at least give me the courtesy of a honest reply."

We don't live in a caring world. By that I mean that not everyone recognizes his or her obligation to care. Our society does not encourage the flourishing of this capacity, but undermines it in various ways. In a world notable for its lack of caring, we need tools of persuasion to protect the helpless. This is one of the roles that rules and rights fill. We can reason in the language of rules with those who lack a sufficient degree of caring. If their natural sympathies are not engaged by the presence of suffering, we can attempt to appeal to reason: How would you want to be treated if you were in their place? What would be the consequences of such behavior on a large scale? I am not convinced of the effect of such persuasion, and it is, I think, an empirical question whether such appeals would persuade where caring did not, but I suspect that such socially agreed upon minimums could serve as persuasive appeals.

Rules and rights provide a minimum below which no one should fall and beyond which behavior is morally condemned. Rules provide a minimum standard for morality. Rights provide a measure of protection for the helpless. But, on this level of moral discourse, morality is, like politics, the art of the possible. In the face of large-scale selfishness and inattention, perhaps the best

we can hope for is a minimum below which no one should fall and beyond which behavior is roundly condemned. But we should not fool ourselves into thinking that staying above this minimum is a sufficient condition for being a morally decent person. I don't want to deny the importance of these socially agreed upon minimums; in a less than perfect world, they provide some real protection. They are not, in principle, incompatible with caring, but can, I think, encourage caring. Much caring requires collective action, and without a shared sense of moral minimums it will be difficult to organize such collective action.

Elizabeth Wolgast, in *The Grammar of Justice,* argues against the view that treating patients in a moral fashion is entirely a matter of respecting their rights.[40] She points out that patients are often sick and in need of care. In this situation, she argues, we want doctors and other health care workers to care for the patient. This involves far more than respecting rights. One could talk, I suppose, about a patient's right to be cared for, but, as Wolgast points out, rights talk suggests a minimum below which the doctor should not fall, and in this case, we are less interested in the minimum than in the maximum. We want all our moral citizens to be open to the obligation to care for.

Rules and rights can also be used to deliberate under some conditions. Often we don't need to appeal to rules in deciding whom to care for and how to care for them. A creature's need and our ability to meet it identifies it as a candidate for caring for. We decide how to care for by appeal to the need, the strategies for meeting it, and the desires of the one in need about how best to meet the need. But when we are not in direct contact with the objects of care, our actions cannot be guided by the expressed and observed desires of those cared for, and hence we might want to appeal to rules. In these cases, we must make assumptions about their desires, and we can assume that they do not wish to fall below some minimum. Rules that provide a minimum standard for acceptable behavior ought to be

40. See Elizabeth Wolgast, *The Grammar of Justice,* chap. 3.

sensitive to the general desires and aims of creatures, so we may take these into consideration.

In some cases, we might be justified in appealing to our needs for care and on that basis decide that we do not wish to violate some socially approved minimum standard of behavior. Suppose, for example, that I think that you want me to lie to you and I also think that it would be better for you if I did lie. But we have an audience, and I know that our audience would disapprove of my lying. Am I justified in telling the truth? (One of the virtues of an ethic of care is that it allows us to frame this question.) It seems to me that it depends on how you and I will be affected by the lie, but the existence of a social rule about honesty can be taken into consideration.

We might also appeal to rules and rights when care must be allocated. For example, in a hospital emergency room we must make sure that the needs of the first accident victim of the night do not cause us to ignore the later victims. . . .

Finally, since rules and rights can express a consensus about morally acceptable behavior, we should be sensitive to the expectations generated in the one cared for by the public recognition of such rules and rights. For example, suppose I want to make sure that my family and friends are happy and involved in the wedding of my son. I might be tempted to ignore the rules of etiquette in making sure that my guests are uniquely provided for. But if the mother of the bride feels slighted because I didn't treat her the way she expected to be treated (i.e., as the etiquette rules say you should treat the mother of the bride), then I haven't really responded to her in a caring manner.

One might argue here that meeting some expressed needs might violate the moral minimums in our society. I am willing to grant that this can happen. If it does, we must remember that the rules do not have a life of their own, but are guides. They help us to formulate a caring response because they speak to us of what most of us would want as a caring response in a similar situation. If the one needing care does not want the response suggested by the appropriate rule, we should listen to them very carefully and be willing to ignore the rule. For example, suppose

someone wanted us to help him/her commit suicide. I suspect that ideally we could and should settle this kind of a case without appealing to rules. Instead, we should appeal to the facts of the case. Is the person terminally ill or merely depressed? These conditions require different remedies. In the first case, one might be doing the right thing by aiding in the suicide. Here one must count the cost to oneself, as well as the needs and desires of the one cared for. In the second case, we appeal beyond the expressed needs to the unexpressed needs. This person probably needs some other care. Here we make every attempt to listen to this person, to understand his or her pain, but we also remind ourselves that suicide is the final option for dealing with pain. We make this decision, not by appeal to a rule, but by reminding ourselves of the times when we or someone we know came close to suicide. We remember how it felt and how it was resolved.

In some cases, though, we cannot respond as one caring. As we approach caring burnout, we appeal to rules and rights. We do not want our behavior to fall below some minimum standard, nor do we want the one in need of care to fall below some moral minimum.

In the ideal caring society with sufficient resources to meet needs and to provide for some sort of flourishing, each of us would spend roughly the same amount of time being cared for. We would experience this as children and as adults. Hence, we would be surrounded by a nexus of caring. We would be persons who cared for and were supported by a history of being cared for. We would be free, to some extent, to choose whom to care for because there would be others to provide for needs and for flourishing. We would not be totally free, because social roles would commit us to some responsibilities to care. It is not clear that rules and rights would play a very big part in this world, but this is certainly not the world in which we live.

The people in our world differ in their ability and their willingness to care for others. Since I am both a creature who can care and who needs care, I would, if I were committed to caring, be faced with enormous needs for care while sometimes suffering from a lack of caring for myself.

This is true even if we grant that the kind of caring (in particular, psychological caring) involved in reciprocal relationships sustains all parties in the relationship. But since such relationships don't come easily and naturally, I would have to spend some time and energy establishing a nexus of care to support myself. In creating and maintaining this nexus of care, I would be developing bonds and responsibilities of care.

But spending much of one's time getting one's own needs for care satisfied leaves little time for caring for others. At the same time, everyone else is in much the same boat, and the gross inequality in the distribution of resources means that many slip between the caring cracks and into dire need. This puts the caring person in a bind. Real need presents itself to a person who is often running a caring deficit of his or her own. Caring burnout results. The only way to effectively reduce caring burnout is to change cultural and social institutions toward a model of caring. This is not the path that our culture has taken. Instead we careen from me-first philosophies to paroxysms of guilt about the tremendous needs that have resulted. We make renewed commitments to care which are rejected as soft-headed a generation later.

What are caring persons to do? Caring persons should try to respond to need by caring for, but they must pay attention to their own needs for care. They must navigate through an uncaring world without falling into total caring burnout. They should work for institutions, cultures, and practices that would reduce subsistence needs by redistributing resources and increasing the supply of caretakers, and they should encourage social change toward a culture of reciprocity in meeting psychological needs. But while struggling in our pre-caring world, caring persons are not obligated to continue caring until they slip into caring burnout. This denies their own status as persons who deserve care and is counterproductive, and it diminishes, in the long run, the amount of care they can provide. As they approach caring burnout, they should refill their care tanks by taking care of their own needs. During this period of renewal, they are still required to respect the moral minimums represented by rules and rights.

I want to look now at Nel Noddings's claim that an ethic of care cannot make any appeal to rules. Clearly, she does not want to enrich traditional ethical theory with an account of caring; she wants to supplant it and thus argues that we must reject all rule-based ethical theories. Noddings offers three separate arguments, which I will examine in turn. The first argument looks like this:

1. Rule-based ethical theories require moral rules that are universalizable.
2. In order to accept the principle of universalizability, we must establish that human predicaments exhibit sufficient sameness.
3. We can only establish that human predicaments exhibit sufficient sameness by abstracting away those qualities that reveal the sameness.
4. If we abstract away the qualities that reveal the sameness, the situation no longer seems to reveal a moral question.[41]

I have filled in the gaps in this argument by adding the following claims:

5. Therefore, moral rules cannot be universalizable.
6. Therefore, rule-based ethical theories must either reject universalizability or be rejected.
7. But universalizability is the only criterion that distinguishes moral rules from nonmoral rules.
8. Therefore, without universalizability, rule-based moral theories are not moral theories at all.
9. Therefore, we must reject rule-based moral theories.

This argument depends upon premise three. Seyla Benhabib makes an even stronger claim, that, in the absence of the particularity of the moral situation, no rule could ever be applied

---

41. I reconstructed these arguments from comments that Noddings makes throughout, but especially in chapters one and two.

since we wouldn't know what kind of a situation we are dealing with.[42] I'm not convinced that premise three is right. Consider the following two examples. Mary is told a malicious lie on Friday. "The company is going out of business. You're out of a job." Mary has worked hard for this job, very much wants to keep it, and there are no companies in the area that do similar work. Mary is committed to the area, loves her job, and needs the money. On Monday, Mary finds out that it was a lie. John is told on Friday by a malicious technician that the results of his wife's amniocentesis are that the baby has a neural tube defect. This is their first baby, and they both want the baby. They are in their mid-forties and fear that it would be extremely hard to have another one. On Monday, John finds out that it was a malicious lie.

What do we abstract away to uncover the similarities between these cases? Specifics such as who told the lie and the precise consequences of the lie, etc., would be abstracted away. What's left is that it was a deliberate lie and that suffering was caused by the belief that a heartfelt desire was to be thwarted. But these are just the qualities that make these moral situations.

Her second argument is the following:

1. To care is to act out of affection and regard.
2. If I am acting out of affection and regard, my actions will be unpredictable because they will spring from engrossment in a particular person, in a particular situation.
3. If I am acting by appeal to rules, my behavior would be predictable.
4. Therefore, to care is to reject an appeal to rules.[43]

What could premise two mean? The following interpretations suggest themselves: (a) an outsider wouldn't be able to predict my actions because she would lack knowledge of the individual and the situation; (b) I would be unable to predict my future actions because I do not now have knowledge of the situation.

But both of these claims are true about rule-based action as well. How can I or an observer know what rule I will apply if I don't yet know the situation?

The last argument is:

1. Caring requires an engrossment in the one cared for and a desire to help the one cared for.
2. Rule-based moral reasoning shifts our focus away from the particular individual and toward an abstract problem.
3. When we turn our attention away from a particular individual, self-interest may tempt us to rationalize the situation in a way that ignores the needs of the particular individual.[44]

This argument turns upon claim three, but three says only that self-interest may allow us to misapply the rules. This is not necessarily a criticism of rule-based ethical theories unless the temptation exists only for rule-based ethical theories. But self-interest may tempt us to do what is in the interest of the one most cared for when there is a conflict, so the care model can also be subverted by self-interest.

I have other reservations about rule-based moral reasoning . . . but here I would support a version of this argument with an amended third premise:

3. When we focus our attention primarily on rules, we fail to see the complexity of the moral situation. This can result in our doing harm to others involved in the situation.

There are two worries here. One is that the commitment to the impartialist position is incompatible with a strong degree of empathy. This is, in part, an empirical claim, which Alfred Bloom shed some light on in a study of the inclination to adopt impartialist or empathic responses. He concluded that "there was a very weak correlation between inclination to assume an autonomous stance and level of empathic

---

42. Seyla Benhabib, "The Generalized and the Concrete Other: The Kohlberg-Gilligan Controversy and Feminist Theory," *Praxis International* 5 (January 1986): 402–24.
43. Noddings, *Caring,* chaps. 1 and 2.

44. Ibid.

response."[45] Empathy was most closely associated with a strongly supportive emotional environment in childhood. Obviously, this does not show that it is impossible to be both empathic and impartialist, but it does show that the commitment to the impartialist position does not guarantee empathy. The second worry is that even if one is both empathic and committed to the impartialist position, the commitment to principle undermines the motivation to take a close look at the situation. This is so because it doesn't really matter what the details are if you have already decided to follow your principles no matter what. You only need enough detail to tell which principle obtains. At this point, both Noddings and Benhabib would respond that it is impossible to tell which principle obtains unless we already take a very detailed look at the situation, but as I argued earlier, I think they are wrong about this.

I think that we can construct a sympathetic account of Noddings's theory which will allow us to avoid this last criticism as well as the three consequences mentioned earlier (that if we adopt her caring perspective we cannot care about strangers or animals). Her theory can be seen as an attempt to describe the moral perspective. A rule-based moral theory would tell us to make moral decisions by seeing which rule applies and applying it. A perspectivist theory would say that we should instead adopt a particular perspective and see what kind of a decision would emerge from that perspective. Noddings suggests that we adopt the perspective of the ideal caring self. When we are confronted with a moral decision, we recall that self and ask ourselves what that self would do in this situation. Notice that we ought to be able to adopt this perspective even if we are dealing with strangers or animals. We simply remind ourselves how we would act if we were our ideal caring selves dealing with a cared for one. Hence, this theory does not require, as Noddings thinks it does, that we are in an ongoing caring relationship with the object of our moral

deliberation. Adopting this perspective in all cases, whether they involve friends or strangers, would make this perspective less likely to lead to self-interested decisions.

This strategy, interestingly enough, resembles the position taken by neo-Kantians such as Barbara Herman and Marcia Baron who see the categorical imperative as a test for maxims rather than a strategy for developing maxims which are then to be applied without exception.[46] I agree that this is a more sympathetic rendering of Kant, though I doubt that he would have much sympathy for it. In any case, it is not clear to me how testing the maxim of my action at the moment of deliberation is very different from stopping and adopting a particular perspective, since it is not clear to me what role the maxim is serving here.

I think that we could simply conceive our maxims as rules of thumb which are based on sentiment and past experience and which require constant reevaluation. I agree with Noddings that we should not allow our attention to maxims to become rule fetishism, but should appeal to them only when our moral imagination flags.

Some have argued that unless rules have some priority over care, we won't know what kind of caring is appropriate. As Barbara Houston puts it:

> The philosophical point here is simply that if we stick to a formal account of caring, then we have no way to rule out undesirable caring relations. We must appeal to other values to keep caring morally decent. Caring is not an ethic that can stand alone:[47]

Onora O'Neill makes a similar point:

> To show love or concern to others, or to maintain loyalty and fidelity is not just a matter of responding to the particularities of situations in some way or another (villains may do that!), but of responding to those particularities in a principled way.[48]

---

45. Alfred H. Bloom, "Psychological Ingredients of High-Level Moral Thinking," *Journal for the Theory of Social Behavior* 16 (March 1986): 89–103.

46. Barbara Herman, "Integrity and Impartiality," *Monist* 66 (1983): 233–50; Marcia Baron, "The Alleged Repugnance of Acting from Duty," *Inquiry* 26 (1984): 387–405.

47. Barbara Houston, "Caring and Exploitation," *Hypatia* 5 (1990): 115–19.

48. Onora O'Neill, "Virtuous Lives and Just Societies," *Journal of Social Philosophy* 20 (1989): 25–30.

I agree with Houston and O'Neill that defective caring can occur. I do not think, though, that we need to appeal to rules to tell us which is the appropriate care. In the first place, we would have the same problem with the rules: How do we tell which are the right rules? I think we can judge an instance of care by appeal to our ideal of caring. Here, we can look to Noddings's ideal caring self and to my ideal of a caring world.

Owen Flanagan and Kathryn Jackson offer a different criticism of the priority of care over rules.

> Imagine someone who sees the problem of repaying foreign loans as an issue of love between nations; or a mother who construes all positive interactions with her children as something they are owed.[49]

Virginia Held makes a similar point.[50] The point here is that there are some settings in which care is appropriate and other settings in which rules should prevail. Although I agree about the example of the mother, I disagree about the example of nations. We should see the problem of repaying foreign loans as an issue of love, though not between nations. Thinking of it as an issue between nations blinds us to the reality that real persons are affected. Instead, we should understand the consequences of repaying or not repaying foreign loans on real persons. Consider the budget deficit of the United States, for example. If we think of it abstractly, merely in terms of obeying the appropriate rules, we wouldn't hesitate to say that we should pay the debts of the United States, especially if we conflate foreign banks with foreign nations. But let us reconceive this in terms of the people who would be getting the payment and the people who would be making the payments. The debtors in this case are the taxpayers. Since the bulk of taxes are paid by poor and middle-class taxpayers, the debtors are mostly poor or middle class. The holders of the bonds, on the other hand, are most often wealthy (those who would benefit from tax-exempt re-

turns) and often wealthy foreign nationals. If the United States slides into a serious recession, the idea of writing off some of our government obligations doesn't sound so bad. The alternative would be to increase the disparity between rich and poor at a time when being poor has disastrous consequences. Imagine now the situation for some desperate debtor countries, tempted to borrow cheap dollars and forced to repay with expensive dollars.

Notice how differently we think about this case when we reconceive it in terms of an ethic of care. I think this example supports Noddings's claim that conceiving situations in terms of abstract principles blinds us to morally relevant facts.

My conclusion about rules is that appealing to moral rules, where moral rules are seen as rules of thumb, is morally acceptable in the following cases: to create socially recognized moral minimums, to respond to the expectations of others where such expectations are colored by moral rules, and where moral attention flags, for reasons which are beyond our control.

I have not yet talked about what the rules and rights should be. In drafting a set of rules and rights, I should be sensitive to two considerations. The first is that rules and rights provide a moral minimum. The second is that rules and rights reflect a consensus about moral minimums. In this sense, morality is the art of the possible.

The morally preferred way to live is to appeal to caring. This suggests that rules and rights should reflect a sense of what counts as need, a conception of flourishing, and a recognition of what would usually be accepted, by the ones cared for, as appropriate ways of responding to need and providing for flourishing. Notions of need and flourishing ought to be sensitive to empirical considerations, about human nature, interaction, social organization, etc., but they also have an irreducible normative component. A defense of rules and rights would need to defend this normative component. We would also want rules and rights that would provide a climate for moral growth toward a caring society.

Rules and rights do play an important role in my ethics of caring, but we should not forget

49. Owen Flanagan and Kathryn Jackson, "Justice, Care, and Gender: The Kohlberg-Gilligan Debate Revisited," *Ethics* 97 (1987): 622–37.
50. Held, *Rights and Goods.*

that our primary responsibility is to care for. If this means that we are often unsure about just what to do, then we must live with this uncertainty. Discovering what to do requires that we listen carefully to the ones cared for. We should also recognize that it is often painful to be confronted by those in need, and even by those whom we could enrich. Appealing to rules provides a measure of security for ourselves, but we should not allow it to distance us from the objects of care.

VIII. Caring and Other Ethical Theories

. . . [C]aring as I describe it is not an ethical theory in any full-blown sense. I have just now argued that it is not an ethical theory in the sense of a set of rules to be rigidly applied. Still, one might wonder if it could be compared to virtue theory or what I call perspectivism.

Hume's influence is broad and obvious. I have adopted both his picture of what a moral philosophy should be (the art of suggesting and testing moral strategies in light of our real world experience) and his conviction that humans have a capacity for care and that this capacity explains the force morality has for humans (and perhaps other animals).

One might think that I am simply defending virtue ethics, but I don't believe so. Virtue ethics require that the virtue not enter into the deliberations of the virtuous person. The brave person does not do an act because it is the act that would be chosen by a brave person. She does it because she thinks it is the right thing to do and because she is more interested in the rightness of the act than the personal consequences of doing so. In Noddings's and my view, caring does and must enter into the deliberation of the caring person. The caring person must sometimes ask herself what her ideal caring self would do in the situation. Still, an ethic of care has much in common with virtue theory. They both emphasize the importance of habit and inclination. Neither pretends to provide a calculus for moral decision making; rather they

insist that the context coupled with the character of the actor and some general rules of thumb will provide all the cues.

Nietzsche offers a model that is similar in some respects to an ethic of care. Both Nietzsche and an ethic of care suggest that we answer questions about how to live our lives by taking a particular perspective. He advocates taking an "eternal recurrence" perspective.[51] He invites us to imagine living our lives over and over again, eternally. We can then ask ourselves, "If I were to live this moment over, eternally, what would I have wanted to do?" An ethic of care invites us to take the perspective of our ideal caring selves. Both views share with the virtue tradition the belief that the ideal moral agent should internalize this perspective to a certain extent so that one's actions flow naturally from a settled disposition. Nietzsche's view is broader than an ethic of care because he is concerned with how we live our lives and not just how we make moral decisions. . . .

An ethic of care is holistic in two ways. First, it recognizes that we are embedded in connections of care and that our self-identity is, in large part, a function of our role in these complex interconnections. In this sense, we see ourselves as part of a larger whole, and inseparable from this whole. An ethic of care, as I conceive it, is holistic in a larger sense as well. It assumes an underlying picture of the earth as one body, and of ourselves as part of this body. It sees an attitude of awe as the appropriate response to the recognition that we are part of this sacred body. Not every version of an ethic of care need be holistic in this second sense. Nel Noddings, for example, is not committed to this. But I think it allows us to escape from the parochialism of an ethic of care that is grounded only in human attachments.

---

51. While I am inclined to see eternal recurrence as a normative principle, others have interpreted it differently. Bernd Magnus, for example, sees it as a description of a certain attitude, the attitude that an Ubermensch would take toward life. See *Nietzsche's Existential Imperative* (Indianapolis: Indiana University Press, 1978).

So, while both ethics are holistic, they are holistic in different ways. There is a second way in which they differ. A land ethic, as Callicott describes it, is indifferent to the value that humans put on other humans and certain animals.

Both a land ethic and an ethic of care are ethics for and from the perspective of humans. In this sense, neither can escape from human psychology. If an ethic is seen as providing guidance for living a good human life, then we must recognize important features of human psychology—the attachments of humans to other humans and certain animals, for example. While Callicott tries to ignore this, an ethic of care takes it as central.

IX. *Conclusion*

An ethic of care has many advantages. It allows us to reconceptualize, and thereby better understand, many moral quandaries, such as that of the porcupine and the moles. It strikes many, and women in particular, as a truer picture of their own moral intuitions. It assumes a theory of human nature that is an improvement upon abstract individualism. It generates a theory of moral education which focuses on the enhancement of the capacity to care. Finally, and most importantly, it might, if widely adopted, make the world a better place.

Suggestions for Further Reading

Since Gilligan's research has inspired some of the ethical theories developed by feminist philosophers, it is helpful to read Gilligan's *In a Different Voice* (Cambridge, MA: Harvard University Press, 1982).

See *An Ethics of Care: Feminist and Interdisciplinary Perspectives,* edited by Mary Jeanne Larrabee (New York: Routledge, 1993), for an excellent collection of articles critiquing and extending Gilligan's work.

Nel Noddings, *Caring: A Feminine Approach to Ethics and Moral Education* (Berkeley: University of California Press, 1984), has had a major impact on the field.

See Chapter 5 of Eve Browning Cole's *Philosophy and Feminist Criticism: An Introduction* (New York: Paragon House, 1993) for an overview of feminist ethics written for the beginning student. She also includes an excellent bibliography.

See Chapter 7 of Jean Crimshaw's *Philosophy and Feminist Thinking* (Minneapolis: University of Minnesota Press, 1986) for a critique of some of the ideas associated with feminist ethical theories.

Feminist Ethics, edited by Claudia Card (Lawrence: University Press of Kansas, 1991), contains a good collection of essays.

See Cynthia W. Crysdale, "Gilligan and the Ethics of Care: An Update," *Religious Studies Review* 20 (January 1994): 21ff., for a summary of the discussion to that date.

See Michael Slote's "The Justice of Caring," in *Social Philosophy and Policy* 15 (Winter 1998) 171–195, for a restatement of the ethic of caring in virtue-ethical terms and a defense of the ethic from standard critiques of its inadequacy.

4.6 Some African and Western Conceptions of Morals

Have you ever thought about the difference between morality and custom? Societies have rules intended to control and shape human behavior. How can we tell which of these rules are moral and which custom? Is respect for elders a custom or is it a moral rule?

It is important to be able to distinguish custom from morality because most of us rely on social rules to tell us what is right and what is wrong. While the rules of custom tell us what is customary in any given society, they do not tell us what is *morally* right. For example, if you lived in a society where it was customary to take off one's shoes when entering a home, you would probably be offended if guests did not do that, but it is doubtful you would consider their failure to observe this custom a moral failure. However, if you were confused about the difference between custom and morality, you might consider this impolite behavior as immoral behavior and respond accordingly. Morality seems much more serious than mere custom. Being impolite is one thing; being immoral is quite another.

If we do not understand the difference between morality and custom, we cannot progress very far in seeking an answer to the question of how we can know what is morally right. We also cannot progress very far in understanding the morality of different cultures. A case in point is Africa.

Eurocentric intellectuals, including philosophers, have often viewed the peoples of Africa as "primitive." European colonialism and the African slave trade shaped the thinking of many about what an African is, and what an African society is like. The distorted thinking that resulted meant that African social rules were often viewed as "mere custom" in contrast to the "moral" rules of Westerners. The superiority of Western society with its morality and the inferiority of African society with its customs was clearly embedded in that contrast.

This simple contrast between "us" and "them" turns out, as most simple contrasts do, to be mistaken. Some traditional African social rules do constitute customs, as do some Western social rules. However, not all social rules are customs, either in Africa or in the West. Some do constitute moral rules. Kwasi Wiredu, who teaches philosophy at the University of South Florida, points out, in the next selection, how we can make a distinction between custom and morality.

Wiredu is well aware, however, that even if one can make the distinction between rules that are moral and those that constitute custom, the question of how we go about justifying moral rules still remains. In other words, we do not discover the ethical theory that tells us our moral rules are the right rules by discovering how we can make the distinction between custom and morality. Wiredu's exploration of ethical theory uncovers some interesting contrasts between African ethics as represented by the Akan people, the largest ethnic group in Ghana, and Western ethical theory. Contrary to Eurocentric expectations, the Akan not only have a morality, but also they have a humanistic ethical justification for their moral rules, a justification that contrasts with some nonhumanistic and supernaturalistic theories found in the West.

Reading Questions

1. What is the difference between morality and custom?
2. Outline Wiredu's argument for locating the "universal obligatoriness of moral rules" in social existence.
3. How does a humanistic ethic differ from "ethical supernaturalism"?
4. How do the misidentification of the point of view of morality with some transcendent point of view and the misidentification of good conduct with moral uprightness help open the door to moral relativism?
5. What is the difference between a communalistic viewpoint and an individualistic one?

6. How do the Akan and Christian understandings of ethics differ?

7. Wiredu analyzes the Ten Commandments, putting them into the categories of moral rules, customs, and taboos. Do you agree with his analysis? Why, or why not?

8. In your opinion, does Christianity "reduce morality to the status of taboo"? Why, or why not?

9. Given what Wiredu says about Akan ethics, how do you think they would answer the question, "How can I know what is morally right" and how do you think that answer would differ from the answer given by Christianity as Wiredu interprets it?

10. What is the most important thing you have learned from Wiredu's essay?

Custom and Morality

KWASI WIREDU

CONTEMPORARY AFRICAN EXPERIENCE is marked by a certain intellectual anomaly. The African today, as a rule, lives in a cultural flux characterized by a confused interplay between an indigenous cultural heritage and a foreign cultural legacy of a colonial origin. Implicated at the deepest reaches of this cultural amalgam is the superimposition of Western conceptions of the good on African thought and conduct. The issues involved here are of the utmost existential urgency, for it may well be that many of the instabilities of contemporary African society are traceable to this circumstance.

But, first, to fundamentals. Rules are absolutely essential to human communities. At the very least there must be some linguistic rules— rules of syntax and semantics—for without some interaction you do not have the communion implied by the concept of community, and without language you do not have the communication presupposed by human interaction. Only a little reflection is required to see that there also has to be a whole host of other kinds of rules for defining, regulating, and facilitating interactions and relationships. For example, if we drive, we must have traffic rules; if we buy and sell, we must have

rules not only to regulate these activities but also to define them in the first place, and so on, indefinitely.

The mention of rules of traffic and of commerce naturally brings to mind the concept of law. Laws are promulgated or acknowledged rules that are enforced or, at least, intended to be enforced by a recognized authority having sanctions, usually physical force, at its disposal. Laws are, of course, a feature of the *modus operandi* of governments. But there are other, more informal, rules such as are prescribed by custom, tradition, convention, fashion, and etiquette. Most likely, any human society will have rules of this sort whether or not it is organized in the manner of political governance. There is still, however, one category of rules of the most extreme importance to human society that we have not mentioned so far, at least, not explicitly. This is the category of moral rules. Morality and law do intersect, for some laws are simply moral rules formalized and backed up with the authority of the state. But there are also laws that are clearly not moral rules. Think of traffic rules, for example.

The question now is, How may we distinguish between moral rules and all the rest? This

From Kwasi Wiredu, "Custom and Morality: A Comparative Analysis of Some African and Western Conceptions of Morals" in African Philosophy: Selected Readings *by Albert G. Mosley. Englewood Cliffs, NJ: Prentice-Hall, 1995, pp. 390–406. Endnotes deleted. Reprinted by permission.*

question is important because moral rules seem to have an *intrinsic* obligatoriness which is lacking in other kinds of rules. In warming up toward an answer it would perhaps help if we cleared up some points of usage. The word *moral* and its cognates are frequently used with such broad signification as to cover matters that might also be brought under custom, tradition, or even convention, all of which, for the sake of conceptual economy, might be called simply *custom*. Thus, in discussing the morals of a given people, one might mention such things as their rules of marriage and sex conduct generally, their manner of organizing mutual aid, their. way of defining and evaluating success in life, their system of reward and punishment, and so forth. Considerations of this kind should certainly reveal a lot about their values, but the point is that not all those values are moral values.

Consider some particulars. Among the Akans of Ghana, a value is placed on beauty of speech that might well appear extraordinary to other people. Beauty of speech here refers not just to beauty of delivery but also, and more particularly, to a characteristic of speech deriving from both logical and rhetorical factors. Beautiful speech is one that develops a coherent and persuasive argument, clinching points—and this is crucial—with striking and decisive proverbs. Anybody not possessed of such a tongue can forget any ambitions of high office at the court of a traditional Akan ruler. There is, surely, nothing immoral in adhering to much less proverbial criteria for this kind of recruitment.

Or consider a somewhat simpler case. In Akan society, one just does not address a person or group without first greeting them. Failure to observe this rule is regarded as a very serious lapse from good behavior. Persistent default will cost any individual his or her reputation. A related rule is this. If in the course of greeting people, one has occasion to shake hands with or wave to more than one person, one absolutely must always proceed from right to left. Again, nonconformity is regarded as an error so grave as to be capable of radically compromising a person's standing in the society. These rules are motivated by values that are not universal either generically or in terms of degree; they can hardly be called moral rules.

This should become apparent from the following thought experiment. Compare any of the rules just mentioned with the rule of truth telling. One cannot contemplate the latter for any length of time without a renewed sense of its unconditional imperativeness. An Akan living in Akanland is expected, as a matter of course, to observe, for example, Akan rules of greeting. It goes without saying that other people living in other lands need not feel any such obligation. On the other hand, whether you are a Ghanaian or an American or a Chinese or of any other nationality, race, or culture, truth telling is an indefeasible obligation on you. To trifle with such an imperative is, quite plainly, to be immoral in a very strict sense. It seems, then, that if we could elucidate the unconditional or universal obligatoriness of moral rules, we would be able to make at least a start at drawing an illuminating distinction between rules of conduct that are moral in the strict sense and those that are not moral or are so only by courtesy of some linguistic idiom.

In this project it might be useful to start with another thought experiment. Let us revert to the rule of truth telling and ask ourselves if we can imagine any circumstances in which it might be feasible to base conduct in human society on its reversal. To so much as pose this question is to realize that the answer must be "No!" Any such situation would be a situation of the breakdown of human community; for if truth telling were, by open common avowal, not binding, and everybody could tell lies without let or hindrance, no one could depend on anyone's word, and social life would become intolerably Hobbesian. By contrast, it is a visible fact that life without rules like the Akan rules of greeting mentioned above is not intolerable. This suggests the following condition for the identification of moral rules in the strict sense: A rule of conduct is not a moral rule unless its nonexistence or reversal would bring about the collapse of human community.

It should be observed that the kind of contra-truth-telling situation that we imagined a moment ago is not merely one in which many people tell lies in various circumstances. This, unfortunately, is the actual state of affairs in which we all live, move, and have our struggles. On the contrary, the imagined scenario is the more drastic one in which, to use Kantian language, the maxim "Tell lies whenever convenient" has become a universal rule of conduct. Apart from flirting a little with Kantian terminology, there is an obvious formal analogy between our emerging characterization of moral rules and Kant's use of his "categorical imperative" to the same purpose. In one formulation, the principle of the categorical imperative says, "Act only on that maxim through which you can at the same time will that it should become a universal law." Now, for Kant, the decisive consideration is that one cannot *consistently* will the maxim of an action that is contrary to good morals to be universalized. This elevation of pure consistency in the realm of morals is quite germane but still insufficient as the foundation of morals. If it were, the principle of noncontradiction would be the supreme law of morals, but it is not.

It is important, however, to note that the principle of noncontradiction satisfies the condition so far specified for moral rules. Certainly, if that principle were to be generally and studiously discarded—a scale of noncompliance not dreamed of by even the most enthusiastic paraconsistentist—there would no longer be any such thing as a human community, for communication would become impossible; and without communication, as we earlier saw, there is no human community. It follows that the condition in question is not a sufficient condition for a rule being a moral rule but only a necessary one.

How, then, may we attain sufficiency in the characterization of the rules of morality? What we need is, I think, to exhibit the necessary connection between morality and human interests. This connection almost leaps into the eye when we consider what sort of motivation might lead an individual to break a rule such as that of truth telling. This can only be the desire of the individual to pursue his or her own interests in deliberate indifference to the interests of others. Its short name is selfishness. The point becomes even more clear if we take concrete examples of moral imperatives such as "Do not steal" or "Do not

pursue your neighbor's wife." It must dawn on us, from such considerations, that the rationale of a moral rule is the harmonization of the interests of the individual with the interests of others in society, and its motivation is the sympathetic appreciation of those interests, a frame of mind that facilitates the mind's ability to contemplate with equanimity the possible abridgement of one's own interests in deference to the interests of others. The rationale discloses the objective, and the motivation the subjective, aspects of morals; both aspects are essential to the constitution of morality. And this accounts for the important distinction between scrupulous action and a merely prudential one. An individual is not deserving of moral approbation merely because he or she did something that promotes the requisite harmony of interests; he or she has to have done it in the requisite spirit.

This last remark must again remind us of Kant. The sage insisted that doing your duty is not morally meritorious unless it is done out of respect for duty. But our depiction of morals has also an un-Kantian implication. Kant spurned any suggestion that human well-being could be the motto of the moral life. On the other hand, by our lights, human well-being is an irreducible presupposition of all morality. Not, of course, that every quest for human well-being is a moral enterprise; but every moral endeavor is a certain kind of quest for human well-being. It is the kind that seeks its objective through the empathetic harmonization of human interests. Empathetic or not, a certain minimum of harmonization of interests is indispensable to any tolerable form of human social existence. Hence morality, at least, on its objective side, is humanly essential. Herein lies the universal obligatoriness of moral rules.

Perhaps no one can be the ultimate authority on the origins of his or her opinions, but I find these thoughts on the necessary connection between morality and human well-being totally attuned to the moral thinking pervasive in the culture in which I was born and raised, namely, the culture of the Akans of Ghana. The first axiom of all Akan axiological thinking is that man or woman is the measure of all value. (*"Onipa na ohia."*) And every Akan maxim about the specifically moral values that I know, explicitly or implicitly, postulates the harmonization of interests as the means, and the securing of human well-being as the end, of all moral endeavor.

On the strength of the last remark, we may characterize Akan ethics as humanistic. In this, of course, the Akans are not unique. There are humanistic strands in Western ethical thought, too. But it is significant to note that there is also in the West, in contrast to the situation in Akan thought, a highly influential tradition of ethical supernaturalism. Indeed, if you take account of popular as well technical thought, it may justly be said that the dominant bent of Western ethics is nonhumanistic. I hasten to point out that I use the word *nonhumanistic* as the strict contradictory of *humanistic* in the sense just indicated. I do not mean *nonhumanistic* in the sense of wicked or anything like that. As for wickedness, I suspect that, by and large, it is evenly distributed among all the different tribes of humankind. It is, besides, worthy of note that not all nonhumanistic ethics in the West are supernaturalistic. Kant's ethics, for example, are sharply nonhumanistic; he expressly disavows any *necessary* connection between morality and human interests. Yet, his conception of morality is equally sharply non-supernaturalistic. He defines moral worth, purely by the lights of human reason, in terms of respect for the categorical imperative. God, indeed, has a place in the total scheme of Kant's ethics, but only as the legislative and executive source of compensation, in the afterlife, for virtue unrequited in this life. God's very existence, incidentally, is ("from a practical point of view") established—believe it or not—by the alleged necessity of this eschatological compensation. As distinct from this kind of logically extrinsic status for God in ethics, ethical supernaturalism bases the very essence of morality on the will of God. On that view, what is morally right is, by definition, what is in accord with the will of God. This view of ethics is particularly popular, though not universal, among Christians. I have already remarked on its absence from Akan ethical thinking and will return to the point in due course.

Meanwhile, there is a judicious flexibility in humanistic ethics to which attention should be called at this point. It consists in the fact that from such an ethical standpoint it is easy to see that and to see why, although moral rules are unconditionally imperative, they are not necessarily exceptionless. Probably everyone has had his or her moral imagination teased by the following classical poser: What do you do if confronted by a sword-brandishing psychopath who inquires of your mother's whereabouts with the unambiguous purpose of promptly hacking her to pieces? By virtual common consent, moral uprightness does not require sacrificing your mother on the altar of truth-telling under this kind of duress. But on nonhumanistic premises it is not clear why not. On the other hand, if the moral end is the evenhanded securing of human interests, then some tempering with the truth in the harrowing encounter imagined is easily recognized as a rational adjustment of principle to special circumstance. The reason why such an adjustment does not smack of opportunistic casuistry is that it is obvious that everybody's interests are, on the whole, best served by withholding the truth in question from a lunatic on the rampage. It might be said, accordingly, that what we have here is only an exception to the rule of truth telling, not an overturning of it; and if the exception proves this rule, it is because in the very act of seeming to evade it we are, in fact, reaffirming its rationale. It emerges, by an obvious generalization, that moral rules are susceptible to exceptions but not to reversal, and the admissible exceptions can only be ones that uphold their rationale.

In Western philosophy, Kant is certainly one of the thinkers who had the strongest sense of the irreversibility of moral rules. But he seems to have conflated this irreversibility with exceptionlessness. He thus made himself an uninviting exception to the apparent consensus in regard to the permissibility of telling a lie to save one's mother in the terrible situation visualized a moment ago. As is well-known, he earnestly maintained, in the teeth of this specific example, that one is in duty bound to yield the truth, come what maniac may. I cannot help suspecting that the powerful mind of Kant was trapped into so irrational an inflexibility by the dead weight of his nonhumanistic approach to ethics.

But this is speculation. Let us return to the question of the distinction between custom and morality, this time more concretely. In the light of the foregoing discussion, it is clear that, for example, the Akan rule of greeting mentioned earlier is a rule of custom rather than of morality, strictly speaking. It is not unimportant on that account, but it lacks the unconditional obligatoriness of a moral rule; an honest person can envisage its absence from human social intercourse with composure. It is only putting the same point in different words to say that the obligatoriness of custom may be relative to a particular culture or society or to an even lesser grouping. Perhaps this might be called a form of relativism. If so, it will have to be recognized as a rather limited and atypical form of relativism that does not really conform to the acceptation of that word, for it does not rule out the possibility that the rationale of a custom might become interculturally appreciated once it has been situated in the context of its own habitat.

However, the question of rationale does not always arise in connection with custom. Some customs seem to originate in accidental or even subconscious circumstances. It may well be, for example, that the unique set of phonetic articulations used in a particular language out of the myriads of possibilities owes its origins to a process in which, as Ruth Benedict suggests in her classic "Anthropology and the Abnormal," accidental and subconscious factors play a decisive role. In regard to customs of such accidental origins, which are, I think, more important in the differentiation of cultures than the cross-culturally explicable ones, propriety or impropriety is even more strikingly relative to culture.

As an example of a cross-culturally intelligible custom, consider the rule of respect for elders. Probably every culture enjoins it with some degree of urgency. But the differences of degree from one society to another in this continuum of urgency can be extremely significant. One of the Ten Commandments says, "Honor thy father and thy mother: that thy days may be long upon the land which the Lord thy God giveth thee" (Exodus 20:12). From other bible stories, such as, for example, the story of the fate that befell

the mischievous infants who made fun of an old man who seemed to be making heavy weather of walking up a trivial hill (remember the Almighty dispatched some wild beasts to devour them), one may safely generalize the quoted commandment into a pretty rigorous requirement of respect for those of ripe age. Now, this particular imperative is a major feature of the traditional Akan ethic. In this respect, therefore, there is an obvious similarity between Akan morals and the morals of ancient Judea, from where both the commandment and the story originate. In this same respect, however, there is a noticeable dissimilarity between the dictates of Akan and Judean morality, on the one hand, and those of, say American morality, on the other, as far as I can see. Notice, by the way, that in this paragraph I have used the concept of morals in its broad signification.

To return to the comparison of morals, it cannot be said, of course, that people are not expected to respect their elders in the United States of America. But the fact is that the deference that is considered to be due to age in Akan traditional society is much greater than is required in the American social environment. The difference is, indeed, so great that one might almost call it one of kind rather than of degree. In consequence, one can foresee quite serious disparities in the moral characterization of relevant actions, reactions, and attitudes. Thus, a traditional Akan elder freshly transported into American society would be likely to find the attitude of American youth to their elders to be marked, or more strictly, marred by an unbearable offhandedness; while, for their part, American youth in a converse shift of environment would be likely to feel that traditional Akan society demands nothing short of grovelling docility from the young in their relations with the old.

This difference is, in fact, easy to understand. Traditional Akan society, as presumably its Judean counterpart, was a society in which science, technology, and industry had not reached any very high level of development. In such societies, knowledge is likely to be, on the whole, more a possession of the old than of the young. Prestige and influence will naturally go along with knowledge, more especially, knowledge of a practical kind. Under such conditions, the high respect accorded to age is not gratuitous. The position is apt, however, to change in a highly industrialized, technological society. Respect for age is still in place, but it is unlikely to reach the high levels obtaining in a traditional society, nor, in view of the all-too-human tendency to overcompensation in major transitions of outlook, will it always reach a reasonable level.

In all this, what is of crucial significance is that the differences noted, whatever their explanation, appertain to custom rather than morality in the narrow sense. To repeat, this observation does not imply any diminution in the importance of custom as such. Still less does it imply that customs are necessarily inaccessible to transcultural evaluation from either a moral or utilitarian standpoint. Morality, in particular, can override anything, saving only its own rationale. Nevertheless, it is of the last consequence to realize that the merits or demerits of a particular custom may be independent of any specifically moral considerations. Many customs are, indeed, designed to achieve the well-being of given societies, and we may suppose that some do actually succeed in this. But in itself, this is not a moral fact. Furthermore, there is plenty of room for variability in the efficacy of customs. A custom that is good in one society may be the contrary in another. Or it may be good in a given society at a given time without being so in a changed era. Thus, for the same sorts of reasons as those previously rehearsed, the high respect demanded for age in Akan traditional society is giving rise to intergenerational tensions in contemporary semi-industrialized Akan society.

This susceptibility to being overtaken by changing time, place, or circumstance is one of the marks of custom as distinct from morality. Yet, because there is, as already remarked, a broad concept of morality within which custom is a moral topic, it has been easy for some students of the great variety of customs among the different cultures of the world to conclude that all morality is *relative* in the specific sense that moral rightness consists in being approved by a given culture, society, group, or epoch. This, of course, is an egregious error. Even with respect to custom, there are quite definite limits to relativity. Any custom that leads to needless suffering, for example, is bad wherever and whenever it exists. True, it may not be easy to show that a particular instance of suffering is needless, for the issue may be entangled in the web of a complex system of cosmological beliefs. But it is a fact of history that even the most entrenched belief systems can change under the pressure of recalcitrant facts.

An interesting thing about the confusion of the norms of custom, which may be relative to time, place, or circumstance, with the norms of morality, which are not, is that it has two sides of opposite attractions. The first consists in treating morality as if it is of a piece with custom, while the second consists in treating custom as if it is of a piece with morality. The relativist wades into the error by the first side, while a sanctimonious antirelativist is apt to tumble into the same error by the second.

Relativism seems to be enjoying something of a revival in recent philosophy. This is not due to any intrinsic intellectual merit of that standpoint. It is due, I think, to the fact that, ironically, antirelativism is liable, through a certain adulteration of logic with psychology, to be transformed into some form of authoritarian absolutism, which turns off many intellectuals who have their hearts in the right place. The transformation is roughly like this. From the fact that morality is not relative to culture or circumstance, it is inferred that it is not dependent on anything human. The way is then open to the antirelativist, full of a sense of the importance of morals, to suppose that morality is only correctly conceived from a divine or some suitably Olympian perspective. The thinkers or nonthinkers who thus align themselves with a point of view so infinitely superior to any merely human point of view easily gain a sense of infallibility (by association) in their own self-perception. Accordingly, their own norms of conduct are seen as ineluctable models of the right and the good in the sphere of all morals. The divergent ways of life of other individuals or peoples, except perhaps the most inconsequential, are therefore wrong, immoral, impermissible; they constitute an execrable affront to righteousness. It should now be clear how antirelativism, ill conceived, can become a particularly insidious enemy of that open-mindedness in the face of the diversity of ways of life among the different peoples of the world, which cultural pluralism seeks to foster.

Two misidentifications are touched on, explicitly or implicitly, in this diagnosis. There is the misidentification of the point of view of morality with some transcendent point of view, and there is the misidentification of good conduct with moral uprightness. I shall return to the first in more concrete terms later. Let me try, at this stage, to bring some concrete observations to bear on the second. It may be conceded at once, in apparent mitigation of the grossness of the error here in question, that it is not always easy to distinguish between custom and morality in specific cases. A particular case of considerable intercultural interest is the question of the legitimacy or illegitimacy of polygamy. It is well-known that in Africa and some other parts of the world polygamy is regarded as a legitimate marriage arrangement. On the other hand, the Christian missionaries who came to Africa to "save" our souls, perceiving the practice to be incompatible with their own norms of good conduct, condemned it inexorably as immoral and worked assiduously to eradicate it. They have had a measure of success in this. But there has been a certain superficiality about that success, which has been responsible for a kind of ethical schizophrenia in the consciousness of many of our people. However sincere the African convert has been in his avowal of the foreign faith, he has too often not been able to erase from all the recesses of his consciousness a predisposition to many of the cultural habits ingrained in him in the course of his domestic and community socialization. In the upshot, many noble and pious Africans have been known to operate a subtle compromise of an official monogamy supplemented with informal but quite stable and demographically significant amorous relationships. Needless to say, the "pagan" sections of our populations have never been able to view this dual system of behavior as anything but a somewhat amusing form of emergency pragmatism.

Be that as it may, the question is, How are we to analyze this whole situation from the point of view of the philosophy of morals? If, in keeping with our earlier thought experiment, we consider whether circumstances are conceivable in which polygamy might come, everywhere, to be seen as a more reasonable connubial institution than monogamy, little imagination would be needed to conjure up a scenario to motivate an affirmative answer. Suppose, for example, that by some unanticipated combination of persisting causes women were to come to outnumber men by, say, fifty to one. Make it a hundred to one or worse, if you foresee greater resistance to the impending suggestion, which is that in such a state of affairs to insist on a policy of one-man-one-wife would mean, as a matter of simple arithmetic that the overwhelming majority of women would go through life in the most drastic sexual deprivation and, very probably, in deep emotional distress on account of the inevitable frustration of related instincts. Common decency would everywhere recommend polygamy or something substantially similar to that system under such conditions.

Or reverse the experiment. Imagine that, through equally inscrutable changes in the phenomena of our world, men come to outnumber women by the aforementioned factor. Then, by similar and perhaps more urgent considerations, good sense would urge an analogous revision of marriage system: polyandry in place of monogamy! Rational flexibility would be more urgent in this hypothetical case than in the previous one, only because, if in the new circumstances the principle were to be pressed that only one man could be the recipient of all the married attentions of one woman, you could infallibly predict that the resultant sexual and emotional famine among men would quickly drive them to a war of all men against all men. An obvious general lesson here is that rules of conduct were made for man or woman, not the other way round; but a more particular lesson is that, purely in itself, the issue of polygamy versus its contraries is one of custom rather than morality in the strict sense.

Again, from this last point, it cannot be inferred that polygamy enjoys any relativistic immunity from cross-cultural evaluation. On the contrary, it can still, in principle, be scrutinized from, at least, a utilitarian point of view. And, in any case, as a human institution, its actual operation by any given group of persons will undoubtedly generate moral issues. The point is only that the self-righteous blanket denunciation of polygamy in Africa by the Christian missionaries was, if nothing else, oblivious to philosophical considerations of considerable practical import. In fact, polygamy, like monogamy to be sure, is open to all sorts of moral abuses from both sides of the relationship, and the Akans are extremely sensitive to this fact, as shown in their folklore, for example. They have also been alive to the sociological implications of a changing economy. The generality of Akans have perceived that industrialization, even such as it has been, has brought in its trail conditions severely uncongenial to polygamy, and the practice is currently on the wane. Practical considerations rather than moralistic preachments are what have proved really decisive. And this is as it should be, having regard both to the true nature of the issue and the humanistic basis of the Akan outlook on the rules of human conduct.

Industrialization, by the way, has made a morally more debatable inroad into another aspect of the Akan ethic. The word *communalist* might be used to characterize the bent of that ethic. This alludes to the fact that in that outlook the norms of morality are defined in terms of the adjustment of the interests of the individual to the interests of society rather than in terms of the adjustment of the interests of society to those of the individual. The latter way of viewing morality may be taken to be characteristic of individualism. From a logical point of view, pure morality still remains a constant in this variation of outlook; for, however the adjustment of interests is arrived at, its actual existence satisfies the objective conditions of morality. But psychologically, the accent on the community in a communalist orientation can provide an added incentive to the moral motivation. Unfortunately, the apparent concomitants of industrialization are eroding this mechanism for the reinforcement of morals.

The most threatening circumstance in this regard is the urbanization that has attended industrialization. African residents of large cities no longer have the benefits of either the support or the sanctions of the system of caring that was the mainstay of traditional community life. The circles of obligations, rights, and privileges, which irradiated from the center of household relations of kinship to the larger circumferences of lineage and clan affinities, provided a natural school for training in the practice of sympathetic impartiality, which, in its most generalized form, is the root of all moral virtue. The integration of individuality into community in African traditional society is so thoroughgoing that, as is too rarely noted, the very concept of a person has a normative layer of meaning. A person is not just an individual of human parentage, but also one evincing in his or her projects and achievements an adequate sense of social responsibility. Bereft of the traditional underpinnings of this sense of responsibility, city dwellers are left with nothing but their basic sense of human sympathy in their moral dealings with the great numbers of strangers encountered in and out of the work environment. The well-known crime rate in the cities is proof of the limited capabilities of that moral equipment. Thus, by and large, industrialization seems to be proving deleterious to that system of communal caring and solidarity that was a strong point of traditional communalism. One of the greatest problems facing us in Africa is how to reap the benefits of industrialization without incurring the more unlovable of its apparent fallouts, such as the ethic of austere individualism.

When the Akan or, in general, the African traditional social outlook is described as *communalist,* is it unusual to contrast it with that of Western society by calling it *individualistic.* There is a certain obvious anthropological validity in this comparison. But some riders are necessary. First, it should be repeated that this does not disclose a difference with respect to the actual content of morality. Aside from the difference in the manner of viewing the adjustment of interests required by morality, the real difference between communalism and individualism has to do with custom and life-style rather than anything else. Although the notion of custom tends to evoke imageries of social practice, while life-style is more readily associated with individual lives, both are, conceptually, of a kind and are distinct from morality in the strict sense. While on this, it might be of some use to note that histories of Western ethics regularly allot generous space to certain classical portrayals of different life-styles. Aristotle's treatments of ethics, for example, or the discourses of the epicureans and the stoics, consist largely of (reasoned) recommendations of particular life-styles and only deal with questions of pure morality when they touch, relatively briefly, on such topics as justice. Had our communalist forebears preserved in print their thoughts on the same range of subjects, we may be sure that mutual aid would have loomed larger in their meditations than most of the concerns of the classical moralists.

Second, the distinction between communalism and individualism is one of degree only; a considerable value may [be] attached to communality in individualistic societies, just as individuality is not necessarily trivialized within communalism. Finally, the two orientations can coexist in different sectors of the same society. Thus, for example, intimations of a communalist outlook are discernible in the life-styles of the rural folks of individualistic America.

Perhaps the sphere of conduct in which the conflict between Akan morals and Western morality, or more strictly, the Christian form of it, has been acutest is the sphere of sexual morality. Christianity, as it came to us in Africa through the missionaries, proscribed premarital sex as totally incompatible with morality. Contrast this with Akan conceptions of marriage. This is conceived of as a union in which the parties are a pair of individuals and their respective families, and the purpose is principally, though not exclusively, procreation. As such, it is not a relationship lightly to be entered into. Considerable mutual knowledge between both principals, including "carnal" knowledge, is regarded as a common-sense requirement. Indeed, prior intimacy is viewed not only as educative but also as prag-

matic. Akan men and women usually seek visible signs of fertility before committing themselves to the union in question. Thus, far from something like pregnancy before marriage being looked on as a scandal, it is welcomed as an auspicious omen.

But a man does not just fall on a woman and impregnate her on the off chance of a possible marriage. The thing is governed by rigorous and well-structured rules. A man who takes a comprehensive fancy to a woman has, if his advances are reciprocated, to reveal the fact, in the first instance, to his own family and, in the second, to the woman's. To the latter, he goes in due time in the company of his father with offerings of schnapps and a message of the following tenor: The man has been very strongly impressed with your royal and would like to see a lot more of her. He has, in fact, been seeing her for a little while. This offering is only an earnest of his sentiments and intentions. All being well, he will come back later in due style. Meanwhile, he begs to suggest that if you look for her and you do not readily find her, you may check with him. Unless the woman's family, who, on their side, would already have done some research on the prospective suitor, have well-founded moral or medical objections to him, they will give their blessing to the association, knowing full well that the two will not stop short of sex, though, at this stage, there would be no absolute guarantee of marriage. Of course, if all goes well, the man will come again to seal the relationship with due ceremony.

On the other hand, if a man, heedless to custom, should unceremoniously put a woman in the family way—reckless individuals exist in all cultures—he would be declared to have "stolen" her and would be liable to quite severe fines and concerted and equally severe reprimands from all concerned on both kinship sides. The premarital arrangements just recounted are, obviously, radically different from anything that was officially countenanced in orthodox Christian circles. Still, in light of our distinction between custom and morality, there is no question but that what we have here are just different customs. To the Christian authorities, however, the Akan system involved living in sin.

It is a fact, of course, that in the last three decades or so orthodox Christian precepts of pre-marital chastity have been massively overtaken by "permissive" practices in Western society. For the time being, however, the significant difference between the Akan and Christian milieus remains, for it makes sense to speak of permissiveness in this connection only in environments where there is a background of previously authoritative commandments to the contrary. In Akan society, the practice in question is not permissive; it is the permitted. At all events this difference illustrates the kind of plurality of ways of life in the world that a reasonable mind ought to be able to contemplate without pique or panic.

So far we have not encountered any difference of morality in the strict sense between Akan and Western ways of life. This is not accidental. If the concern of morality is the harmonization of the interests of the individual with the interests of society, this is exactly what is to be expected, for none but the most brutish form of existence could be foreseen among any group of individuals who standardly disavowed and disregarded any such concerns. It is true that individuals and groups may differ in their degree of inclination or dedication to such aims; but this is a fact of practice, not of precept.

Nevertheless, without prejudice to the last reflection, there may be philosophically important differences in the ways in which various individuals, groups, or peoples conceive of morality in the strict sense; and I would like to comment on a difference of this sort between Akan and certain influential Western conceptions of morals. The Western intellectual situation is characterized by a great diversity of philosophic persuasions, and prudence dictates abstention from unqualified generalizations. Yet, there is a certain recognizable metaethical orientation in some very important forms of Christian thinking that might approximately be called orthodox. This is the understanding of ethics, which sees its basis in religion. Certainly, the influence of this way of viewing morality is very pervasive in popular Christian thinking and is, surely, not unconnected with the semantical fact that the adjective

"un-Christian" imputes some measure of moral degeneracy. That this way of thinking about morality is popular, even if not universal, in Western society is undoubtedly a noteworthy fact about Western moral thinking. And in any case, the Christian evangelism that was brought to Africa was of this outlook.

In regard to this notion of the dependence of morality on religion, we encounter a rather striking contrast, for it does not even make sense in the Akan context. This brings us back to some matters previously touched on, namely, the antithesis in ethics between humanism, on the one hand, and antihumanism with its subspecies of supernaturalism, on the other. As noted earlier, in Akan thought, what is moral is, by definition, what promotes the well-being of society by way of the harmonization of interests. Logically, the existence of God is irrelevant to the essence of morality as so conceived. It is, indeed, a fact that the Akans, like *most* other African peoples, believe in the existence of a Supreme Being, who might be called God, provided this nomenclature is not taken to imply an identity of attributes with the Christian God. This Supreme Being is regarded as supremely good; but, from the Akan point of view, it would just be compounding ambiguity with obscurity to suggest that "good" here means anything other than what it means in mundane semantics. In particular, to say that "morally good" means "in conformity with the will of God" would leave it *logically* possible that the morally good could conceivably be at variance with the harmonious ordering of human interests, a veritable contradiction in Akan terms. Yet, in orthodox Christianity, specifically, this is the kind of dependence that morality is supposed to have on religion. The relation is not merely a motivational dependence; it is a conceptual one: moral rightness just connotes accordance with the will of God.

The only area of Akan thinking where any kind of rightness or wrongness is defined in this sort of way—that is, in terms of the will of an extra-human being—is the area of taboo. A taboo is a prohibition expressing the dislike of some extra-human being believed capable of punishing noncompliance with disasters, sometimes quite severe and widespread. The idea here is that what a taboo prohibits is *ipso facto* bad; it is not supposed to be prohibited because it is bad, rather, it is regarded as bad solely because it is thus prohibited.

Two observations are urgent at this point. First, in view of the humanistic conception of morals in Akan thinking, any concept of badness defined in terms of taboo falls outside the pale of morality in the strict sense. Second, there is evidence to suggest that taboo is not an irreducible category in the Akan system of norms of conduct. It is arguable that the taboos are a pedagogical expedient designed by our sages of old to concentrate ordinary minds on the path of desirable behavior.

Consider two frequently cited taboos of Akan society. One is, "Do not work your farm on Thursdays" and the other, "Never have sex in the bush." The taboo-style explanation of the first is that Thursday is the day after which the earth goddess is named. Her name is *Asaase Yaa*. The word *Asaase* means the earth, and *Yaa* is the first name given to any female born on Thursday. Thus, the two words together mean something like, "Madam Earth whose day is Thursday," and the madam apparently regards working on that day as an act of disrespect to her. Now, the Akans credit their ancestors not only with wisdom but also with ingenuity. Our ancestors are reputed generally to have had good practical reasons for their prescriptions and proscriptions. If so, one must suspect some lost rationale, in this case, perhaps communally regularized respite from toil.

We are on stronger grounds with respect to the second taboo. The common explanation is that bush sex is a pastime that the earth goddess simply finds insupportable and will punish with soil infertility. But why? After all, sex in the bedroom is as much a kind of commotion on some earth surface as sex in the bush. In fact, a practical rationale is not far to seek and is known to be proffered by those who do not rest content with the ideas of the populace. The freedom of unaccompanied females from unorthodox sexual invasion in isolated areas could hardly have been far from the motivation of the ancestors who laid down this rule. Other taboos would seem to be susceptible to similarly intelligible explanations.

Not only, then, are taboos not a component of the Akan system of morals, strictly so-called, but also they would seem not to constitute *as such* any *essential* part of the Akan repertoire of customs and usages. The rules themselves, of course, remain an ingredient of the Akan ethos, but the apparent irrationality of their genesis would seem to be dissolvable.

On the other hand, taboos seem to have quite a secure place in the orthodox Christian ethic alongside the moral rules proper. Take the decalogue again, and recall the following injunctions. (1) Thou shalt not kill. (2) Thou shalt not commit adultery. (3) Thou shalt not steal. (4) Thou shalt not bear false witness against they neighbor. (5) Thou shalt not covet they neighbor's house, thou shalt not covet they neighbor's wife, nor his manservant, nor his maidservant, nor his ox, nor his ass, nor anything that is thy neighbor's. (Exodus 20:13–17. Numbering not in biblical sequence.) Subject to reasonable qualifications with respect to the first and some refinements and updating here and there, these are straightforward moral rules in the narrow sense under our definition of morality. They, obviously, do not differentiate the Christian ethic from the Akan counterpart. In their essential meaning, all these rules can be effortlessly duplicated in the Akan stock of ethical sayings. Indeed, it is difficult to see how such moral truisms could differentiate the moralities of any pair of human groups.

Recall next the following: (6) Honor thy father and thy mother (etc.). (7) Thou shalt not take the name of the LORD thy God in vain (etc.). The first of this pair, as we have already discussed, is a custom—one that is invested with comparable importance in both traditional Judean and Akan society but is rather less touted in places such as the United States. The second is perhaps a special case of the first.

But, now, reflect on the remaining commandments, which run as follows. (8) Thou shalt have no other gods before me. (9) Thou shalt not make onto thee any graven image or any likeness of anything that is in heaven above or that is in the earth beneath or that is in the water under the earth. (10) Remember the sabbath day to keep it holy. These have all the distinctive marks of taboos. They are, as far as one can see, rules whose entire normative force consists in expressing the likes and dislikes of an extra-human being.

What do these taboos look like from the perspective of the Akan traditional worldview? Let us begin with the first two, namely, those prohibiting any trafficking in other gods. These are unlikely to convey much meaning to a traditional Akan. In his cosmology he believes that there exist, as *regular* parts of the world order fashioned out (not "created") by the Supreme Being, a great variety of extra-human beings and forces which are capable of aiding humans if properly tapped or approached. The more impersonal of these forces are, on this view, as intrinsic to the scheme of things in this world as electricity or rainfall, and the relatively personalized ones are viewed much like we view other minds, except that they are differently localized and, in some cases, are supposed to be endowed (by God) with striking powers. Thus it must sound very paradoxical indeed to the Akan to suggest that it could possibly occur to God to take offence at his dealings with those forces. Some of the more remarkable aspects of the Christian conversion of large masses of traditional Akans have to do with how they were persuaded to make verbal commitments to commandments such as the ones now under discussion. The fact, in any case, is that the traditional beliefs usually remained psychologically operative in spite of everything.

What of the taboo relating to the sabbath? This is likely to make some sense to the Akan, because in some ways it appears analogous to the Akan taboo against farm work on Thursdays. However,

an important question immediately arises: Would the orthodox Christian take kindly to any attempt to find a practical, nonsupernaturalistic rationale for the sabbath commandment? If, as I suspect, the answer is likely to be "no," then this Christian taboo and the others are revealed as taboos in a more irreducible sense than the Akan ones.

The foregoing reflection has an even more remarkable implication for the characterization of Christian morals. If Christians do not shy away from calling moral rules in the strict sense commandments of God whose moral rightness logically consists in the sheer fact of being the will of God, it would follow, from the definition of taboo, that they reduce morality to the status of taboo. Such a reduction is, surely, unfortunate. It is fortunate, however, that in analyzing a set of rules of conduct, such as the Ten Commandments, one can, if one has a clear criterion for the purpose, separate custom from morality, and, even within custom, distinguish the rationally explicable elements from the normative surds. In this way, one is enabled to recognize in the ways of life of different peoples those ethical norms of universal applicability that underlie the possibility of orderly dialogue and interaction between different peoples, groups, or individuals, while, at the same time, understanding the basis of the great variety of norms by which people live.

On the preceding showing, it is apparent that the distinction between custom and morality is of more than a theoretic interest. Failure on the part of some benefactors of Africa to make or observe the distinction in all its subtlety has not served the continent well. But it is not only in Africa that the distinction can have practical consequences. Inattention to it can result, everywhere, in authoritarian moralism.

Suggestions for Further Reading

If you are interested in an overview of African thought, see Parker English and Kibujjo M. Kalumba, *African Philosophy: A Classical Approach* (Upper Saddle River, NJ: Prentice-Hall, 1996) and *An Introduction to African Philosophy* by Samuel Oluoch Imbo (Lanham, Maryland: Rowman and Littlefield, 1998). The rest of the essays in *African Philosophy: Selected Readings* by Albert B. Mosley (Englewood Cliffs, NJ: Prentice Hall, 1995) will also prove useful.

For a collection of essays exploring the development of African philosophy and identifying four main trends (ethnophilosophy, professional philosophy, philosophic sagacity, and nationalist-ideological philosophy), see *African Philosophy: The Essential Readings,* edited by Tsenay Serequebertan (New York: Paragon House, 1991).

For a collection that includes African American philosophy as well, see *African Philosophy: An Anthology* edited by Emmanuel Chkukwudi Eze (Malden, MA: Blackwell, 1998).

Kwame Anthony Appiah's *In My Father's House: Africa in the Philosophy of Culture* (London: Methuen, 1992) is a thoughtful and careful reflection on a variety of issues surrounding African philosophy. See especially Chapter 6 for a careful consideration of rationality in a cross-cultural context. Likewise, Chapter 6 on morality and community in *The African Philosophy Reader,* edited by P. M. Coetzee and A. P. J. Roux (New York: Routledge, 1998) will prove helpful.

See Bruce B. Janz's *African Philosophy Resources* at http://www.augustana.ab.ca/~janzb/afphilpage.htm with links to all kinds of interesting sources.

 You can locate InfoTrac-College Edition articles about this chapter by accessing the InfoTrac-College Edition website (http://www.infotrac-college.com/wadsworth/). Using the InfoTrac-College Edition subject guide, enter the search terms relevant to this chapter, and then read abstracts for relevant articles.

Chapter 5

What Makes a Society Just?

> **The problem of setting up a state can be solved even by a nation of devils.**
>
> IMMANUEL KANT

5.1 Introduction

HAVE YOU EVER WONDERED, "What is justice?" Have you been curious about why we have governments? What is the best form of government? Who should rule? Where does the authority to rule come from? Have you ever thought, "Why should there be laws and why should we obey them? Are all people naturally wicked and do they need to be restrained from doing bad or forced to do good? Is it morally justifiable to break the law?" Have you noticed that we talk a lot about liberty, equality, and justice but have a hard time defining these concepts? Should liberty be sacrificed to promote equality? Or should liberty be protected at all costs, even if it means some people will not get an equal opportunity?

Have you wondered, "What should the government give the people—what they want or what is good for them? Who knows what is good for them? Should the state serve the interests of the individual, or should the interests of the individual be subordinate to the interests of the state?"

If you have thought about these sorts of questions, you have been concerned with the kinds of issues and problems that are normally studied by social and political philosophers. Political and social philosophy deal with issues of moral value at the level of the group. **Political philosophy** is primarily concerned with the justification of governmental authority to rule and with the nature of government or the state. **Social philosophy** is primarily concerned with who gets what and how.

Your pursuit of your own good occurs within a social context—that is, within a context in which others are also pursuing their own good. In such a social context, issues of fairness, social rights and responsibilities, the limits of political and economic power, and the welfare of your fellow human beings inevitably arise.

Like ethics, social-political philosophy is primarily *normative* rather than *descriptive*. For example, one goal of political philosophy is not just to describe the kinds of governments there are and how they function, but also to figure out which are the best forms of government and by what standards such a judgment can be made.

There are many issues and problems relating to social-political philosophy, and we can do no more than investigate a few of them in this chapter. However, two concepts are central to many of the debates in this field: authority and justice. A government is the exercise of power and coercive force by one person or group over the rest in a society. A fundamental political question has to do with what gives one group the authority to exercise such power. **Anarchism** is the position that governments are by nature immoral and should not be established. Those who argue in favor of anarchism maintain that each individual has the ultimate moral authority to live and act as he or she chooses. It is immoral for one group to rule another, and it is immoral of you, as an individual, to surrender your moral responsibility for the conduct of your own life to another. Of course, many people believe that anarchism would lead to social chaos, and so government of some kind seems necessary. But the question remains, by whose authority does one person or group rule another? And even if we grant that some kind of government is needed, the issues of what kind and the limits of its power must be answered.

Some people have argued that one of the purposes of government is to ensure justice. Philosophers often distinguish among **compensatory justice**, **retributive justice**, and **distributive justice**. Affirmative action programs, which may provide for preferential treatment, constitute examples of compensatory (also called "corrective") justice because they involve providing benefits to persons who have suffered undeserved hardships or who have been denied benefits they deserve. The imposition of legal penalties (e.g., putting someone in prison) is an example of retributive justice because it involves placing burdens on people who have enjoyed benefits they did not deserve or who are guilty of failing to fulfill their responsibilities. Distributive justice is the fair distribution of both burdens and benefits to persons in situations of conflict of interest and relative scarcity. For example, not everyone can get into medical school, so how can we decide who should be accepted in a manner fair to all?

These three notions—compensation, retribution, and fair distribution—indicate that the concepts of fairness and desert are central to the concept of justice. What about the notion of equality? Isn't treating everyone equally the same as treating them justly? **Egalitarians** argue that all persons, simply because they are persons, should share equally in the distribution of all benefits and burdens. Yet treating everyone equally may not always be the just thing to do. Paying Harry $50,000 and paying Chong the same, even though Harry has worked only 5 years for the company and has a poor performance record whereas Chong is a 15-year veteran with an excellent record, does not seem just. Harry and Chong are both persons, but in the case of salary should this be the primary consideration? However, allowing some people, because of good luck or birth, to become extremely wealthy and others, because of misfortune or birth, to become extremely poor does not seem fair either. Is there a fair way to distribute wealth?

5.2   God and Justice

Who ought to have the ultimate authority to rule? In other words, who is sovereign or has the right to exercise sovereignty? Should it be one person, several, or all people? If we need rulers, which type of rule is best? What criteria would help us decide the issue?

Plato, in the *Republic* (see Section 9.3), describes an ideal society in which only the lovers of wisdom (philosophers) rule. Justice is achieved, according to Plato, when each of the classes of his ideal republic do well what they are best suited to do. Justice shall reign when the rulers rule wisely, the guardians protect courageously, and the producers produce and consume goods moderately. Plato's vision of a just society has been widely influential. However, his pupil Aristotle (see Section 9.5) modified his teacher's political ideas.

Aristotle divided governments into three types: rule of one, rule of some, and rule of all. He divided these types again into those that were good because they had the common good in view and those that were bad because they had only self-interest or special interests in mind.

TYPE	GOOD	BAD
One	Monarchy	Tyranny
Some	Aristocracy	Oligarchy
All	Polity	Democracy

It might surprise you to find **democracy** (rule by the people) listed as the bad form of the rule of all, but Aristotle believed that democracies did not promote the common good. Rather, they promote the special interests of those who are able to exercise the most influence. For Aristotle, the moral entitlement to rule derives from whether those in power have their own interest in view or the interests of all segments of society. In other words, good governments promote the common good, and they do this by making human flourishing possible.

Aristotle did not list **theocracy** (the theory that only God has the right to rule) among his governmental types, but this has been a widespread and long-lasting theory of sovereignty. The Hebrew Bible (called by Christians the Old Testament) endorses a theocratic state in which a king rules with God's proxy. The monarchs of the ancient world ruled as divine stand-ins, and the emperors of China had the mandate of heaven as their charter. During the Middle Ages, the divine right of kings was a widely held political theory, which said, in effect, that the moral entitlement to exercise the power to rule is a divine right, but this right can be granted by God to those of his (her?) choice. The great monarchies of Europe were founded on this principle, and their power maintained by the support of the Roman Catholic Church. Even today in the United States, one hears talk of the "restoration" of a theocratic state among fundamentalist Protestants, and the modern world is not without its theocracies.

The notion that God alone is sovereign is an idea that is found not only in ancient Judaism and Christianity but also in Islam. Muhammad (570–632) is considered by Muslims to be a prophet of **Allah** (God). A **Muslim** is one who submits to the will of Allah, and Islam is the name of a religious community that seeks to obey the commands of Allah. According to Islam, Allah revealed his will to the prophet Muhammad. Those revelations are recorded in the *Qur'an,* the holy book of Islam. Central to Islamic practice are the **five pillars of Islam**: witnessing that there is no God but Allah and that Muhammad is his Apostle; mandatory prayers, or *salat;* mandatory alms (*zakat*); fasting during the month of Ramadan; and *hajj,* or pilgrimage to Mecca.

Throughout Islamic history there has been and there continues to be considerable debate about the best type of government. The fundamental presupposition of this debate is that the right to rule belongs to God because only God is the perfectly just creator of all that exists. All parties agree on this theistic understanding of sovereignty. The disputes center on the political implications of divine sovereignty.

After the death of Muhammad, various schools of Islamic thought developed. Two of these schools—the **Sunni** and **Shi'i**—agreed that, since God does not rule human society directly, humans must devise governments that strive to realize as nearly as humans can the divine ideal of justice. According to the Sunni, a caliph (successor to the Prophet) should be selected or elected to provide political and military leadership. This caliphate would have, according to the Sunni, limited religious power although, ideally, the caliph himself would be a descendant from Muhammad's tribe if not from Muhammad himself. The Shi'i argued that leadership should be vested in an imam (leader) who is the direct descendant of the Prophet and his cousin and son-in-law Ali, who, according to the Shi'i, is the first true imam after the Prophet himself. The imam is a divinely inspired religious *and* political leader.

Islamic philosophers, while well aware of the debates within Islam over legitimate political succession, tended to take a different approach to the issue of what makes a society just. While acknowledging the sovereignty of Allah and the authority of revelation, philosophers such as Abu al-Walid Ibn Rushd (d. 595/1198), known in the West by his Latin name of Averroes, introduced ideas derived from both Aristotle and Plato into the debate. Criteria derived from reasonable reflection on the issues must also be considered. Proper genealogy is not enough. Just rulers are rational rulers, whatever may be their connection to the Prophet.

Majid Khadduri, author of the next selection, is professor emeritus of The School of Advanced International Studies of the Johns Hopkins University. After some general comments about the view of justice found in Islamic sources, he summarizes Ibn Rushd's views.

Reading Questions

1. What is the difference between positive justice and revelational justice?
2. What are the three sources of justice in Islamic tradition?
3. Why is it more accurate to call the Islamic state a Divine nomocracy rather than a theocracy?
4. What is the literal meaning of *'adl?*
5. How does Ibn Rushd draw on the ideas of Plato and Aristotle?
6. According to Ibn Rushd, why should the ruler of a just state be a philosopher (lover of wisdom)?
7. What are unjust states like, and why does Ibn Rushd consider democracy one of them?

The Islamic Conception of Justice

MAJID KHADDURI

And fill up the measure when you measure, and with the just balance; that it better and fairer in the issue.

—Q. XVII, 37

And when you speak, be just, even if it should be to a kinsman.

—Q. VI, 153

JUSTICE IS ESSENTIALLY a relative concept. Whenever a man asserts that which he considers his just claim, were it to be valid, it must be relevant to an established public order under which a certain scale of justice is acknowledged. Scales of justice vary considerably from land to land, and each scale is defined and ultimately determined by society in accordance with the public order of that society. Yet no matter how scales differ one from another, they all seem to have certain elements in common and, broadly speaking, may be divided into two major categories.

One category is to be found in societies which assume that men are capable of determining their individual or collective interests and know that which they may need or to which they may aspire; they therefore can, individually or collectively, establish a public order under which a certain scale or scales of justice are likely to evolve by tacit agreement or by formal action. This kind of justice, a product of the interaction between expectations and existing conditions, may be called positive justice. It is admittedly imperfect and men always endeavor to refine and improve it by a continuing process of social change. The ideal or perfect justice is a mirage, and the real one develops by improvisation from generation to generation.

In a society which presupposes that man is essentially weak and therefore incapable of rising above personal failings, the idea that fallible human beings can determine what their collective interests are and lay down an impartial standard of justice is scarcely acceptable. In such a society a superhuman or divine authority is invoked to provide either the sources or the basic principles of the public order under which a certain standard of justice is established. Whether the superhuman authority is exercised by a gifted sage or an inspired prophet, the kind of justice that flows from such a source commands respect and can have a lasting impact on the administration of justice. Some of the ancient societies—the Hebrew, the Christian and the Islamic are but three examples—were committed to this viewpoint: God disclosed Himself through Revelations, communicated to men through prophets, in which His justice is embodied. The justice which flows from such a high divine source is considered applicable to all men and forms another category of justice. In contrast with positive justice, it may be called Divine or Revelational justice. It is the product of intuition, or divine inspiration, and is closely interwoven with religion and ethics. It coincides with Reason and may well fall in the category of natural justice. Aristotle used the term "natural justice" in the sense that it is the product not of social but of natural forces. Following Aristotle, scholars often equated Divine or God's justice with natural justice, but, unlike the natural-law scholars who were concerned with the relation of justice to society, Christian and Muslim scholars focused their primary concern on the concept of justice in relation to God's Will and related it to the destiny of man. Both held that Divine Justice is the ultimate objective of the Revelation, expressed in its early form in the sacred laws of Christianity and Islam. In the *Summa Theologica*, St. Thomas Aquinas termed the sacred law of Christianity the Eternal Law,

From *Majid Khadduri*, The Islamic Conception of Justice. *Baltimore, MD: The Johns Hopkins University Press,* 1984, pp. 1–6, 8–11, 97–101. © 1984 by The Johns Hopkins University Press. Reprinted by permission. Notes deleted.

and Muslim scholars called their Eternal Law simply the "pathway" (Sharī'a). The concept of justice embodied in the Religion and Law of Islam, not to speak of Christian justice, evoked an endless debate among scholars concerning both its scope and character and how its standard is to be realized on Earth.

The Sources of Justice

In Islam, Divine Justice is enshrined in the Revelation and Divine Wisdom which the Prophet Muhammad communicated to his people. The Revelation, transmitted in God's words, is to be found in the Qur'ān; and the Divine Wisdom, inspired to the Prophet, was uttered in the Prophet's own words and promulgated as the Sunna, which subsequently came to be known as the Hadīth, or the Prophet's Traditions. These two authoritative or "textual sources," the embodiment of God's Will and Justice, provided the raw material on the basis of which the scholars, through the use of a third "derivative source" of human reasoning called ijtihād, laid down the Law and the Creed. The fundamental principles of the Law and the Creed, and the creative works of succeeding generations, formed the foundation of the renowned Islamic public order. . . .

In Islamic theory, God is the Sovereign of the community of believers; He is its ultimate Ruler and Legislator. The Revelation and Divine Wisdom are the primary sources of the developing public order, presuming to meet the community's growing needs and expectations. The principles and maxims of justice derived from the Revelation and Divine Wisdom were considered infallible and inviolable, designed for all time and potentially capable of application to all men. In principle, the Law laid down by the Divine Legislator is an ideal and perfect system. But the public order, composed of the Law as well as state acts and the rulings (furū') and opinions of the scholars on all matters arrived at through human reasoning (ijtihād), are by necessity subject to adaptation and refinement to meet changing conditions and the growing needs of the community.

Since the Divine Legislator did not rule directly over the believers, the enthronement of a Ruler to represent God on Earth, to whom God's authority was delegated, had become necessary to put the Law into practice and to rule with Justice. A new form of government had thus been established based on Divine Law and Justice. This form of government, often called theocracy, is obviously not based on the principle that authority is exercised directly by God (whether as a Pharaoh or a Caesar) but by a representative who derives his authority not directly from God but from God's Law. It is therefore the Law, embodying the principles of Divine authority, which indeed rules and therefore the state becomes not, strictly speaking, a theocracy, but a form of nomocracy. The Islamic State, whose constitution and source of authority is a Divine Law, might be called a Divine nomocracy.

The textual sources, consisting of the Revelation and Divine Wisdom, are the Qur'ān and the Sunna. To these constitutional instruments, the proximate source of authority, all the political leaders and contending parties appealed to assert their conflicting claims to power. Likewise, on the strength of these sources, the scholars sought to legitimize one claim against another by diverse arguments—theological, legal, and others—on the grounds of justice. Although the scholars agreed on the Divine nature of justice, they disagreed on how it should be realized on Earth and formulated various doctrines of justice reflecting the conflicting interests, local traditions, and aspirations of rival leaders and groups in their struggle for power. Legitimacy and justice were often used interchangeably by political leaders, and the scholars, in an attempt to rationalize the legitimacy of rival groups, provided one scale of justice or another drawn from the emerging public order. . . .

At the outset the debate on justice began on the political level. In a community founded on religion, it was indeed in the nature of things that public concern should focus first on the question of legitimacy and the qualification of the Ruler whose primary task was to put God's Law and Justice into practice. Since the Prophet, the first Ruler, died without providing a rule for succession, the question of legitimacy became crucial. Should any pretender to the throne seize power without a valid claim, his act would naturally be considered a travesty to Divine Justice. The debate thus was bound to center on the procedural question of the choice of the person who would have a legitimate claim to succeed the Prophet in accordance with the standard of political justice embodied in the textual sources.

Once the debate on political justice started, it never really ended. Like Pandora's box, it became exceedingly difficult to bring political differences under control. It led to schism in the body politic and the rise of rival credal groups and sects, each seeking to rationalize its standard of political justice on one credal ground or another. From the political level the debate gradually shifted to other levels—theological, legal, and others—although ulterior political motivation continued to reassert itself in one form or another. As the Islamic public order advanced, the debate moved to higher levels of sophistication, and scholars in fields other than theology and law—philosophers and other men of learning—were very soon drawn into it. For no great thinker, whether in Islam or in any other community, could possibly remain indifferent to a debate on a subject as engaging and central as justice. But before we proceed further, perhaps a clarification of the literary meaning of justice and other related terms would be in order.

The Literary Meaning of Justice

The meaning of the common usage of words expressing the notions of justice or injustice is not only important in the abstract sense, but also illuminating for an understanding of the manifold aspects of justice; since the literal meaning of words is ultimately the outgrowth of their social or every-day meaning, the writers and thinkers are likely to be influenced by it in the articulation and rationalization of man's needs and expectations in the struggle to achieve justice and other human ideals. Classical Arabic is renowned for its richness in vocabulary and literary expressions. Indeed, it is no exaggeration to say that for every concept or action describing or identifying a particular human activity, perhaps a dozen words

in the major lexicons are likely to be found, notwithstanding that each word is not necessarily a synonym, as it may often imply a slightly different shade of meaning from the other. For instance, for the name of God (although this is not a typical example), it may be interesting to note, there are ninety-nine words called the asmā' al-ḥusna (the beautiful names), each denoting or expressing the meaning of one of His manifold attributes.

For every aspect of justice there are several words and the most common in usage is the word "'adl." . . . The antonym of 'adl is not a modified spelling of the word 'adl denoting its negative meaning—as is the counter word "injustice" to "justice" in English—but an entirely different word called "jawr." . . .

Literally, the word 'adl is an abstract noun, derived from the verb 'adala, which means: First, to straighten or to sit straight, to amend or modify; second, to run away, depart or deflect from one (wrong) path to the other (right) one; third, to be equal or equivalent, to be equal or match, or to equalize; fourth, to balance or counterbalance, to weigh, or to be in a state of equilibrium. Finally, 'adl (or 'idl) may also mean example or alike (Q. V, 96), a literal expression which is indirectly related to justice. . . .

The literal meaning of 'adl in classical Arabic is thus a combination of moral and social values denoting fairness, balance, temperance and straightforwardness. Logically, Divine Justice would be a synthesis of all these values and virtues; indeed such a conceptual meaning is the theme of the debate among theologians, jurists and philosophers and will be the subject of our inquiry in the pages to follow.

The Notion of Justice in the Qur'ān and Traditions

The Prophet Muhammad, who seems to have been endowed with a deep sense of justice, found widespread inequity and oppression in the society in which he had grown up, and he sought to establish order and harmony within which a distinct standard of justice would be acknowledged.

As a Prophet, he naturally stressed religious values, but he was also a social reformer, and his decisions provided precedents on the strength of which the issues that were to arise in succeeding generations were resolved. The idea of justice was of particular interest to him, and he dealt with the problems of his day with uprightness, balance, and fairness. Nor was he indifferent to discrimination and inhuman acts, as exemplified in the legislation for the improvement of the status of women, emancipation of slaves (though slavery as a system was not abolished), and prohibition of infanticide and other unjust acts and practices. Moreover, he himself valued certain virtues honored by his followers and he incorporated them in his teachings. As he said in one of his often quoted utterances, his call was not to abolish but to "further the good morals" (li utammim makārim al-akhlāq) that had been in existence in society, and he felt compelled to confirm them.

In the tribal society of Arabia, where survival was perhaps the tribesman's primary concern, such virtues as honor, courage, and liberality were more highly prized than other virtues. These were epitomized in the word "muruwwa," consisting of everything that was taken to be praiseworthy and which may be called the Arab *summum bonum*. The muruwwa continued to be viewed so high in Arab eyes in subsequent centuries that al-Maqqarī (d. 770/1369) in his definition of justice, stated that no one could claim to be just were he to compromise the virtue of muruwwa. But in the exhibition of honor and courage the tribesmen were often brutal and oppressive, especially in the pursuit of *vendetta*, with the consequent subordination of the virtues of fairness and moderation to arbitrary rules of order. The poet 'Amr B. Kulthūm, composer of one of the well-known Seven Odes (al-Mu'allaqāt al-Sab'a) was not the only one who sang the praise of brutality and oppression attributed to his tribe. The absence of a coherent social order and political unity in the tribal society of Arabia necessarily subordinated the scale of justice to the requirements of survival, and consequently the appeal to justice took the negative form of retribution, such as retaliation and the payment of blood-money, rather than the positive forms of fairness, balance, and temperance.

The Prophet, while conceding the value of courage and other virtues, felt keenly the need to assert religious and moral values to temper cruelty and harshness. For this reason, the Qur'ān and Traditions often warned believers against bigotry and oppression, and admonished them that in the fulfillment of their religious obligations they must above all be just. In the Qur'ān there are over two hundred admonitions against injustice expressed in such words as zulm, ithm, dalāl, and others, and no less than almost a hundred expressions embodying the notion of justice, either directly in such words as 'adl, qist, mizān, and others . . . or in a variety of indirect expressions.

Second only to the existence of the One God, no other religious or moral principles are more emphasized in the Qur'ān and Traditions than the principles of uprightness, equity, and temperance, partly because of their intrinsic value but mainly because of the reaction against the pre-Islamic social order which paid little or no attention to justice. The most important Quranic references to justice are as follows:

> God commands justice and good-doing . . . and He forbids indecency, dishonor and insolence. (Q. XV, 92)
> God commands you to deliver trusts back to their owners, and when you judge among men, you should judge with justice. (Q. IV, 61)
> Of those We created are a people who guide by the truth, and by it act with justice. (Q. VIII, 180)

In the Traditions, the Prophet sought to explain the meaning of the abstract maxims of justice enunciated in the Qur'ān by specific examples, expressed in legal and ethical terms, to distinguish between just and unjust acts as well as to set underlying rules indicating what the scale of justice ought to be. Since the Prophet dealt essentially with practical questions, the theologians and other scholars found in the Traditions precedents on the strength of which they formulated their theories of justice. However, neither in the Qur'ān nor in the Traditions are there specific measures to indicate what are the constituent elements of justice or how justice can be realized on Earth. Thus the task of working out what the standard of justice ought to be fell upon the scholars who sought to draw its elements from the diverse authoritative sources and the rulings and acts embodied in the works of commentators.

The religious character of the public order, however, imposed by its very nature certain restraints, and the community of believers, distrustful of the capacity of fallible men to legislate for society, discouraged radical departure from the literal meaning of textual sources. Small wonder that many scholars, under popular pressures, were often forced to renounce doctrines seemingly inconsistent with the literal meaning of the authoritative sources, despite the growing needs of society for innovations. However, most scholars felt that they were duty-bound to accept the interpretation of the standard of justice laid down by their predecessors more strictly than by those who sought radical changes. . . .

Having established the harmony of Reason and Revelation, Ibn Rushd proceeded to discuss his ideas of justice making a distinction between the Divine and Human justice (Rational Justice). He made it clear that despite differences in sources (Greek and Islamic), the notion of justice embodied in both is ultimately the same. In setting forth his theory of human justice, Ibn Rushd has drawn on both Plato and Aristotle, making a distinction between the theoretical and practical forms of justice with an emphasis on the latter. Justice, like other virtues, does not exist in its perfect form in a vacuum, said Ibn Rushd; it attains its perfection only when men are citizens of the state. Just as virtues are faculties of the soul, he added, justice is the highest virtue of man as a citizen. But justice is not just one virtue; it is, as Plato said, the sum of all virtues. "It consists," he said, "in no more than every citizen following the activity for which he is best qualified by nature." He went on to explain that this is conceivable only when the state is functioning in accordance with the guidance provided by the speculative science (philosophy) and governed by its masters. These are the ruling classes of the state just as the

intellect is the ruling part of the soul. So justice means that each man (or class) does what he (or the class) has to do in proper measure and time.

Ibn Rushd distinguishes between virtues like wisdom and courage which are closely connected with one class only, and virtues like justice and temperance ('iffa) which are manifestly connected with all classes of the state. In agreement with Aristotle, he says that the virtue of temperance is connected with all, although Plato insists that temperance is a virtue confined to craftsmen. Justice is the virtue necessary for all.

In the realization of justice—indeed, in the realization of all virtues—Ibn Rushd said, in agreement with Aristotle, that three conditions are required. First, it is not only knowledge of the nature of virtues that is necessary; action is even more important. Second, the souls of the young must be inculcated with these virtues and cultivated to the point of perfection; if evil is ever in possession of some, it must be removed. Third, the qualities and virtues, whenever they are combined and render other virtues perfect, must be specified.

Ibn Rushd then turned to the question of how to inculcate and cultivate these virtues into the souls of the citizens. There are obviously two methods: First, by persuasion, either rhetorical and poetical for the multitude or the rational (speculative) for the elect; and second, by force. The first method is for the citizens who had already been accustomed to it from youth, and the other is for the adversaries and all those who are not sensitive to the appeals of virtue. The latter is evidently not for the citizens of the Virtuous State; it is for states whose public order is not based on virtues. In dealing with these states, whose rulers resort to force to correct their citizens, there is no other way than to resort to war. The Law, says Ibn Rushd, indicates how the two methods can be applied. If persuasion is not heeded, war becomes just (jihād) against rebels as well as unbelievers. Since preparation for war is impossible without the cultivation of the virtue of courage, the citizens should cultivate this virtue in preparedness for war when it becomes necessary. Just as wisdom is the virtue necessary for the realization of justice within the state, so courage is necessary for the realization of justice in the relationship between nations.

Ibn Rushd, in agreement with Plato, maintains that justice can be realized only in a state founded upon a set of virtues, namely, wisdom, courage, temperance, and justice. Whenever these virtues are fully cultivated, the state becomes an ideal state. A few words about each virtue may be called for.

Wisdom includes possession of theoretical and practical knowledge concerning governance and Law. Men who are endowed with this rare quality are very few; they may be found only among the philosophers and those who are capable of governing the State. The rulers of the Ideal State, said Ibn Rushd in agreement with Plato, "are necessarily the Philosophers."

Courage as a virtue is the quality of strength against such emotions as fear and desire, which can be attained by education, especially in music and gymnastics. This virtue is most needed by the guardians whose responsibility is to maintain order and protect the state from its enemies.

Temperance and justice are in a different category from wisdom and courage. Whereas the last two are ordinarily found among rulers and guardians, temperance and justice are virtues necessary for all men. Temperance may be defined as the middle or the mean in human behavior—in eating, drinking, sexual intercourse, and others—and the man who is temperate "is he who can, of his own accord, remain permanently in this middle position." He can control himself and restrain "the soul from pleasures and desire." "It is said," Ibn Rushd adds, "that the temperate man is the most courageous and master over himself." Just as the man who is by his intellect the master over the inferior, so is the temperate state more courageous than others and a master over itself. In order to attain such a quality, temperance should exist not only in one class but in all—the rulers and the ruled alike.

Finally, justice as a virtue is the quality of fairness and self-control. It is the quality by which the state can survive and claims to continue as long as the rulers and the multitude are in agreement "to keep that which the laws demand," namely, that "everyone . . . does that business for

which he is fitted by nature, and does not long for what he does not possess." In other words, the ideal state is the Just State by reason of the quality of justness with which all its citizens are clothed, just as wrongdoings reduce other states to "states of injustice" or "erring states."

Justice is maintained in the state as long as each citizen pursues the virtue most fitting to his class. The Just State is characterized as wise, courageous, and temperate, provided that these virtues exist in the state in their true measure, so that the rational faculty (Reason) rules over the other faculties.

Justice, in order to endure, is dependent on the Ruler who presides over the destiny of the state. Such a Ruler must be a philosopher, because he is the only one who desires knowledge and investigates its nature (separated from matter) and is able to teach it. Knowledge may be taught to the few either by the rational or demonstrative argument; the multitude can be taught only by rhetorical and poetical methods. In order to succeed, the philosopher should master both the theoretical and the practical arts, just as the king, in order to perfect the art of governance, is in need of the qualities of wisdom and intellect. The lawgiver obviously needs the same qualities. Indeed, the qualities of the philosopher, the king, and the lawgiver are the same. The Imām, Ruler of the Islamic state, must possess all of these qualities.

Should the ruler be a prophet? Ibn Rushd's answer to this question in general is in the affirmative. Apart from being a prophet or a philosopher, however, the Ruler must be endowed with a set of natural qualifications such as disposition to theoretical knowledge, love for the truth, high-mindedness, courage, fluency in speech, good memory, control over desires that are not proper for rulers (like sensual desires and love for money), and—last but not least—justice. Since the existence of the prophet is a rarity, . . . Ibn Rushd stressed the personal qualities of the Ruler upon whom the survival of the state is dependent. Thus it would be tempting to conclude that were the state to be a just state it should be presided over by a Ruler possessing the theoretical and practical qualities without having first been ruled by a prophet. In such a state Rational Justice may be equated with the *jus naturale*.

The opposite of the Just State are the erring or wrongdoing states where injustice prevails. Like Plato, Ibn Rushd identifies four types of states apart from the Ideal State; in each a different scale of justice is maintained. The first is the state whose order is based on honor, which is called timocracy. In such a state, justice is subordinate to honor and to other qualities. As an end, honor may be combined with wealth and power and may tempt men to overpower each other and do evil and injustice. Men of honor are masters and their status corresponds generally to the degree of honor they attain. Rulers possess the ability to distribute honors in pursuit of the measures that preserve their control. This, says Ibn Rushd, is the kind of justice that exists in timocracy.

The second type, called plutocracy, is ruled by a few whose power rests on wealth. So wealth, not virtue, is the measure of the quality of men. The Ruler, the most powerful and perhaps the richest, combines with wealth an ability to govern successfully and consequently he is the master of the state, provided he allows his men to acquire wealth and let them enjoy it indefinitely. Wealth and power are the privilege of the few, but the majority, possessing no claim to privilege, are poor and oppressed.

The third type is the democratic state in which everybody is free from restraints and each is entitled to do whatever his heart desires. The aims and qualities of men vary—some love honor, others wealth, and still others tyranny. But there may be some who possess a few virtues and are moved by them. All arts and dispositions come into being, and it is possible that an "ideal state" as well as other types of states may emerge out of these varied dispositions. The man who is truly just is the one who has the power of leadership. The majority, at the mercy of whoever becomes the master, are plundered and oppressed by the more powerful, but these are often tempted to commit excesses "just as it happens in our own time and in our own state." When the conditions deteriorate and the rulers can no longer distribute wealth among supporters, they resort to imposing heavy taxes. Consequently the common run of men, encouraged by dissatisfied supporters, try to shake off the oppressors, but the masters seek control by force. The State, supported by a few (including religious leaders), becomes tyrannical. The end of such a state is reduced to nothing more than to serve the master and to fulfill his wishes. This state is obviously the opposite of the Just State. Only in the Just State can the citizen attain justice equal to his natural abilities. . . .

Suggestions for Further Reading

A good introduction to Islam is *Concept of Islam* by Mahmoud Abu-Saud (Indianapolis: American Trust Publications, 1983). Chapter 8 deals with Islamic social order.

John L. Esposito's *Islam: The Straight Path,* 3rd Edition (New York: Oxford University Press, 1998) is an up-to-date, authoritative source. Esposito's earlier book, *Islam and Politics* (Syracuse, NY: Syracuse University Press, 1984) concentrates on political issues.

Chapter 3 of Fazlu Rahman's *Major Themes of the Qur'an* (Minneapolis: Bibliotheca Islamica, 1980) discusses Qur'anic views of society.

Also see Chapter 8, "Questions of Modern Time," in Kenneth Craig and R. Marston Splight, *The House of Islam,* 3rd Edition (Belmont, CA: Wadsworth, 1988).

Voices of Resurgent Islam, edited by John L. Esposito (New York: Oxford University Press, 1983), and *Islam in Transition: Muslim Perspectives,* edited by John J. Donohue and John L. Esposito (New York: Oxford University Press, 1982), provide a good sampling of writings on Islamic political and social theory in the modern world.

Ibn Khaldun was one of the greatest sociological thinkers in Islam. For a discussion of his ideas see Fuad Baali's *Society, State, and Urbanism: Ibn Khaldun's Sociological Thought* (Albany: State University of New York Press, 1988).

Videos

Islam: There Is No God but God (52 minutes) explores the appeal of Islam, one of the fastest growing religions today. *The Story of Islam* (120 minutes) traces its history and both *Shiites: Followers of Ali* (27 minutes) and *Sunnis and the Prohibited Mecca* (27 minutes) explore the differences between the two major groups. A six-part BBC series called *Living Islam* describes the history and practices of Islam (50 minutes each). All videos are available from Insight Media, 2162 Broadway, New York, NY 10024.

For a brief (15 minutes) introduction to Islam see *Islam: Sacrifice to Allah. Islam Today* (30 minutes) recounts the conflicts between traditional Islamic values and modern values and lifestyles. *The Islamic Mind: Seyyed Hossein Nasr* explores how Islam and the West can coexist. *Islamic Conversations* is a six-part series dealing with the Islamic state, women in Islam, Islam and pluralism, and more. Each video is 30 minutes and is available from Films for Humanities and Sciences, PO Box 2053, Princeton, NJ 08543.

5.3 Capitalism and Exploitation

Should people be allowed to own property? That may be a startling question. We are so used to the notion of private property that it seems absurd to even ask such a question. Of course, we should be able to own property and, furthermore, do with it as we see fit. However, think a moment. Which society is better: One in which the wealthy are allowed to accumulate as much wealth as they can, or one in which the state regulates the distribution of wealth for the sake of the common good? Remember— we are *not* all born equal. Some of us are born into wealth and privilege. We can afford a good education, good medical care, excellent legal representation. Others of us are born into poverty. We cannot afford education, medical care, and legal counsel. Is that fair?

Adam Smith (1723–1790), in his influential book *The Wealth of Nations,* published in 1776, argued for an economic philosophy called **laissez-faire capitalism**. He believed that, in the long run, a free competitive market would work for the common good. Smith thought that even though we are all selfish by nature, the laws that guided self-interested competitors would work like an "invisible hand" to the benefit of all.

Smith argued that the value of a commodity equals the amount of labor it commands (the labor theory of value). Those who acquire capital or "stock" can hire labor to produce a product. If a division of labor is efficiently established (in a famous example, Smith divided the process of making pins into eighteen different jobs, thereby increasing the number of pins per worker that could be produced), a *surplus* value over and above the expense of wages and materials will result. This profit is a repayment to the capitalists for their efforts and ingenuity.

Central to this theory is the concept of private property. John Locke (1632– 1704), an English philosopher, articulated this concept long before Smith. He wrote in *Concerning Civil Government* that God gave "nature to humans to use for their benefit." The use of nature involves human labor. Once labor is mixed with the material God has given to humans, private property results. He wrote, "Whatsoever then, he [a human being] removes out of a state that nature hath provided and left it in, he hath mixed his labor with, and joined to it something that is his own, and thereby makes it his property." Since this property is private (owned by the individual), the individual should be free to use it as he or she sees fit. Thus, Locke argued for certain individual rights, among them the right to life, liberty, and the preservation of property. If those words sound at least partly familiar, it is because Thomas Jefferson (1743–1826) in the *Declaration of Independence* of the United States borrowed them from Locke but made one change, substituting the "pursuit of happiness" for "preservation of property."

The view that the freedom of the individual takes priority over the group is subject to some serious objections. For one thing, a community is more than an atomistic collection of individuals. It is an organic whole, and the good of each is not necessarily the good of all. In addition, the notion of "human rights" implies more than leaving people alone to compete with one another. Human rights include an equal opportunity to participate in and contribute to society. The right to work under safe conditions, to have access to education, to obtain adequate medical care, to enjoy a decent standard of living and a secure retirement—there is no provision for such rights in laissez-faire capitalism. And what about the intrinsic value of cooperation? Should not society promote cooperation? Laissez-faire capitalism promotes competition. Alienation, envy, corruption, greed—such can be the results when petty self-interest prevails.

Karl Marx (1818–1883) and Friedrich Engels (1820–1895) saw the results of Adam Smith's economic theory. They saw workers abused and degraded, children exploited, and society divided into two antagonistic classes: the proletariat (an urban population of wage-earning workers) and the bourgeoisie (the owners of production, along with bankers and financiers). All this was the result of the activity of capitalists whose primary interest was to maximize profits.

Marx and Engels argued that the division of labor results in meaningless repetitive jobs that alienate workers from the product of their labors. The workers, even though they have "mixed" their labor with natural materials, do not own the result. The capitalist owns the product and can dispose of it as she or he wishes. They also argued that wage labor is necessarily exploitation because workers give more than they receive. If this were not the case, it would be crazy for a capitalist to hire a worker because the value produced by an hour's labor would not be worth more than the money paid for that hour's worth of work (plus materials and overhead). The so-called "surplus value" from which the capitalist makes a profit is, in fact, created by paying workers less than full value for their efforts.

Marx and Engels advocated **socialism** in place of capitalism. All citizens should own the means of production, and there should be rational planning of economic investment and growth. Production should exist for the sake of human need, not private profit. There should be a just distribution of goods and services. At first, a strong governmental role is needed to create such a system. Eventually, however, as full equality and universal prosperity are achieved, the classes will disappear and a society of naturally cooperative individuals will emerge. The need for a state will simply wither away. When this happens, **communism**, in its ideal form, will be achieved.

There are some serious objections to this position. For one thing, socialism, at least in centrally planned, one-party **totalitarian** states, does not seem to work well.

The collapse of the Soviet Union is a case in point. People do not work very hard when they lack economic incentives. Voluntary cooperation is one thing, but forced cooperation is entirely different. The notion that eventually a classless society will be in place and government will disappear seems to be wishful thinking. If anything, government may get stronger and more absolute. Abuse of power may increase as control increases. The state may become more totalitarian and, while the human rights to education, employment, medical care, and shelter are ensured, the human rights of free assembly, free speech, and freedom of religion are often denied.

Neither sacrificing the interests of the individual completely to the interests of the community nor sacrificing the interests of the community completely to the interests of the individual seems to be the best way to produce a just society. Perhaps this is why many economic systems have moved in a mixed direction—that is, creating a mixture of capitalism and socialism.

Both Marx and Engels believed that the revolution that could bring about economic justice needed to be led by the workers—those most exploited by capitalism. They wrote the *Manifesto of the Communist Party* in 1848, not only to explain their views and defend them, but also to call on the workers of the world to unite and throw off the chains of capitalistic exploitation. As you read parts of this manifesto, answer the questions and engage Marx and Engels in a critical dialogue about what makes a society just.

Reading Questions

1. Do you think that the description of bourgeois society as *essentially* exploitive is accurate? Why, or why not?
2. What is the *proletariat,* and how does it differ from the *bourgeoisie?*
3. What objections have been made to communism, and how do Marx and Engels answer those objections? Do you find their responses convincing? Why, or why not?
4. Do you think the measures Marx and Engels outline for wresting power from the bourgeoisie will eventually result in the end of class struggles and the arrival of a just society? Why, or why not?
5. How would Marx and Engels answer the question, "What makes a society just?"

Manifesto of the Communist Party

KARL MARX AND FRIEDRICH ENGELS

I. *Bourgeois and Proletarians*

THE HISTORY OF ALL HITHERTO EXISTING SOCIETY is the history of class struggles.

Freeman and slave, patrician and plebeian, lord and serf, guild master and journeyman, in a word, oppressor and oppressed, stood in constant opposition to one another, carried on an uninterrupted, now hidden, now open fight—a fight that each time ended either in a revolutionary reconstitution of society at large, or in the common ruin of the contending classes.

In the earlier epochs of history, we find almost everywhere a complicated arrangement of society into various orders, a manifold gradation of

Selections from Manifesto of the Communist Party, *first published in English by Friedrich Engels in 1888.*

social rank. In ancient Rome, we have patricians, knights, plebeians, slaves; in the Middle Ages, feudal lords, vassals, guild masters, journeymen, apprentices, serfs; in almost all of these classes, again, subordinate gradations.

The modern bourgeois society that has sprouted from the ruins of feudal society has not done away with class antagonisms. It has but established new classes, new conditions of oppression, new forms of struggle in place of the old ones.

Our epoch, the epoch of the bourgeoisie, possesses, however, this distinctive feature: it has simplified the class antagonisms. Society as a whole is more and more splitting up into two great hostile camps, into two great classes directly facing each other: bourgeoisie and proletariat.

From the serfs of the Middle Ages sprang the chartered burghers of the earliest towns. From these burgesses the first elements of the bourgeoisie were developed.

The discovery of America, the rounding of the Cape, opened up fresh ground for the rising bourgeoisie. The East Indian and Chinese markets, the colonisation of America, trade with the colonies, the increase in the means of exchange and in commodities generally, gave to commerce, to navigation, to industry, an impulse never before known, and thereby, to the revolutionary element in the tottering feudal society, a rapid development.

The feudal system of industry, under which industrial production was monopolised by closed guilds, now no longer sufficed for the growing wants of the new markets. The manufacturing system took its place. The guild masters were pushed on one side by the manufacturing middle class; division of labour between the different corporate guilds vanished in the face of division of labour in each single workshop.

Meantime the markets kept ever growing, the demand ever rising. Even manufacture no longer sufficed. Thereupon, steam and machinery revolutionised industrial production. The place of manufacture was taken by the giant, modern industry; the place of the industrial middle class, by industrial millionaires, the leaders of whole industrial armies, the modern bourgeois.

Modern industry has established the world market, for which the discovery of America paved the way. This market has given an immense development to commerce, to navigation, to communication by land. This development has, in its turn, reacted on the extension of industry; and in proportion as industry, commerce, navigation, railways extended, in the same proportion the bourgeoisie developed, increased its capital, and pushed into the background every class handed down from the Middle Ages.

We see, therefore, how the modern bourgeoisie is itself the product of a long course of development, of a series of revolutions in the modes of production and of exchange. . . .

The bourgeoisie, historically, has played a most revolutionary part.

The bourgeoisie, wherever it has got the upper hand, has put an end to all feudal, patriarchal, idyllic relations. It has pitilessly torn asunder the motley feudal ties that bound man to his "natural superiors," and has left remaining no other nexus between man and man than naked self-interest, than callous "cash payment." It has drowned the most heavenly ecstasies of religious fervour, of chivalrous enthusiasm, of philistine sentimentalism, in the icy water of egotistical calculation. It has resolved personal worth into exchange value, and in place of the numberless indefeasible chartered freedoms, has set up that single, unconscionable freedom—free trade. In one word, for exploitation veiled by religious and political illusions, it has substituted naked, shameless, direct, brutal exploitation.

The bourgeoisie has stripped of its halo every occupation hitherto honoured and looked up to with reverent awe. It has converted the physician, the lawyer, the priest, the poet, the man of science, into its paid wage-labourers.

The bourgeoisie has torn away from the family its sentimental veil, and has reduced the family relation to a mere money relation. . . .

The bourgeoisie cannot exist without constantly revolutionising the instruments of production, and thereby the relations of production, and with them the whole relations of society. Conservation of the old modes of production in unaltered form was, on the contrary, the first condition of existence for all earlier industrial classes. Constant revolutionising of production, uninterrupted disturbance of all social conditions, everlasting uncertainty and agitation, distinguish the bourgeois epoch from all earlier ones. All fixed, fast-frozen relations, with their train of ancient and venerable prejudices and opinions, are swept away; all new-formed ones become antiquated before they can ossify. All that is solid melts into air, all that is holy is profaned, and man is at last compelled to face with sober senses his real conditions of life and his relations with his kind.

The need of a constantly expanding market for its products chases the bourgeoisie over the whole surface of the globe. It must nestle everywhere, settle everywhere, establish connexions everywhere.

The bourgeoisie has through its exploitation of the world market given a cosmopolitan character to production and consumption in every country. To the great chagrin of reactionists, it has drawn from under the feet of industry the national ground on which it stood. All old-established national industries have been destroyed or are daily being destroyed. They are dislodged by new industries, whose introduction becomes a life and death question for all civilised nations, by industries that no longer work up indigenous raw material, but raw material drawn from the remotest zones; industries whose products are consumed not only at home, but in every quarter of the globe. In place of the old wants, satisfied by the productions of the country, we find new wants, requiring for their satisfaction the products of distant lands and climes. In place of the old local and national seclusion and self-sufficiency, we have intercourse in every direction, universal interdependence of nations. And as in material, so also in intellectual production. The intellectual creations of individual nations become common property. National one-sidedness and narrow-mindedness become more and more impossible, and from the numerous national and local literatures there arises a world literature.

The bourgeoisie, by the rapid improvement of all instruments of production, by the immensely facilitated means of communication, draws all, even the most barbarian, nations into civilisation. The cheap prices of its commodities are the heavy artillery with which it batters down all Chinese walls, with which it forces the barbarians' intensely obstinate hatred of foreigners to capitulate. It compels all nations, on pain of extinction, to adopt the bourgeois mode of production; it compels them to introduce what it calls civilisation into their midst, that is, to become bourgeois themselves. In one word, it creates a world after its own image. . . .

Modern bourgeois society with its relations of production, of exchange, and of property, a society that has conjured up such gigantic means of production and of exchange, is like the sorcerer who is no longer able to control the powers of the nether world whom he has called up by his spells. For many a decade past, the history of industry and commerce is but the history of the revolt of modern productive forces against modern conditions of production, against the property relations that are the conditions for the existence of the bourgeoisie and of its rule. It is enough to mention the commercial crises that by their periodical return put on its trial, each time more threateningly, the existence of the entire bourgeois society. In these crises a great part not only of the existing products, but also of the previously created productive forces, are periodically destroyed. In these crises there breaks out an epidemic that, in all earlier epochs, would have seemed an absurdity—the epidemic of overproduction. Society suddenly finds itself put back into a state of momentary barbarism; it appears as if a famine, a universal war of devastation, had cut off the supply of every means of subsistence; industry and commerce seem to be destroyed. And why? Because there is too much civilisation, too much means of subsistence, too much industry, too much commerce. The productive forces at the disposal of society no longer tend to further the development of the conditions of bourgeois property; on the contrary, they have become too powerful for these conditions by which they are fettered, and so soon as they overcome these fetters, they bring disorder into the whole of bourgeois society, endanger the existence of bourgeois property. The conditions of bourgeois society are too narrow to comprise the wealth created by them. And how does the bourgeoisie get over these crises? On the one hand, by enforced destruction of a mass of productive forces; on the other, by the conquest of new markets and by the more thorough exploitation of the old ones. That is to say, by paving the way for more extensive and more destructive crises, and by diminishing the means whereby crises are prevented.

The weapons with which the bourgeoisie felled feudalism to the ground are now turned against the bourgeoisie itself.

But not only has the bourgeoisie forged the weapons that bring death to itself; it has also called into existence the men who are to wield those weapons—the modern working class, the proletarians.

In proportion as the bourgeoisie, that is, capital, is developed, in the same proportion is the proletariat, the modern working class, developed—a class of labourers who live only so long as they find work and who find work only so long as their labour increases capital. These labourers, who must sell themselves piecemeal, are a commodity like every other article of commerce, and are consequently exposed to all the vicissitudes of competition, to all the fluctuations of the market.

Owing to the extensive use of machinery and to division of labour, the work of the proletarians has lost all individual character and, consequently, all charm for the workman. He becomes an appendage of the machine, and it is only the most simple, most monotonous, and most easily acquired knack that is required of him. Hence, the cost of production of a workman is restricted, almost entirely, to the means of subsistence that he requires for his maintenance and for the propagation of his race. But the price of a commodity, and therefore also of labour, is equal to its cost of production. In proportion, therefore, as the repulsiveness of the work increases, the wage decreases. Nay more, in proportion as the use of machinery and division of labour increases, in the same proportion the burden of toil also increases, whether by prolongation of the working hours, by increase of the

work exacted in a given time, or by increased speed of the machinery, etc. . . .

But with the development of industry the proletariat not only increases in number; it becomes concentrated in greater masses, its strength grows, and it feels that strength more. The various interests and conditions of life within the ranks of the proletariat are more and more equalised, in proportion as machinery obliterates all distinctions of labour, and nearly everywhere reduces wages to the same low level. The growing competition among the bourgeois, and the resulting commercial crises, make the wages of the workers ever more fluctuating. The unceasing improvement of machinery, ever more rapidly developing, makes their livelihood more and more precarious; the collisions between individual workmen and individual bourgeois take more and more the character of collisions between two classes. Thereupon the workers begin to form combinations (Trades Unions) against the bourgeois; they club together in order to keep up the rate of wages; they found permanent associations in order to make provision beforehand for these occasional revolts. Here and there the contest breaks out into riots. . . .

In the conditions of the proletariat, those of old society at large are already virtually swamped. The proletarian is without property; his relation to his wife and children has no longer anything in common with the bourgeois family-relations; modern industrial labour, modern subjection to capital, the same in England as in France, in America as in Germany, has stripped him of every trace of national character. Law, morality, religion, are to him so many bourgeois prejudices, behind which lurk in ambush just as many bourgeois interests.

All the preceding classes that got the upper hand, sought to fortify their already acquired status by subjecting society at large to their conditions of appropriation. The proletarians cannot become masters of the productive forces of society, except by abolishing their own previous mode of appropriation, and thereby also every other previous mode of appropriation. They have nothing of their own to secure and to fortify; their mission is to destroy all previous securities for, and insurances of, individual property.

All previous historical movements were movements of minorities, or in the interests of minorities. The proletarian movement is the self-conscious, independent movement of the immense majority, in the interests of the immense majority. The proletariat, the lowest stratum of our present society, cannot stir, cannot raise itself up, without the whole superincumbent strata of official society being sprung into the air.

Though not in substance, yet in form, the struggle of the proletariat with the bourgeoisie is at first a national struggle. The proletariat of each country must, of course, first of all settle matters with its own bourgeoisie.

In depicting the most general phases of the development of the proletariat, we traced the more or less veiled civil war, raging within existing society, up to the point where that war breaks out into open revolution, and where the violent overthrow of the bourgeoisie lays the foundation for the sway of the proletariat. . . .

All property relations in the past have continually been subject to historical change consequent upon the change in historical conditions.

The French Revolution, for example, abolished feudal property in favour of bourgeois property.

The distinguishing feature of Communism is not the abolition of property generally, but the abolition of bourgeois property. But modern bourgeois private property is the final and most complete expression of the system of producing and appropriating products, that is based on class antagonisms, on the exploitation of the many by the few.

In this sense, the theory of the Communists may be summed up in the single sentence: Abolition of private property.

We Communists have been reproached with the desire of abolishing the right of personally acquiring property as the fruit of a man's own labour, which property is alleged to be the groundwork of all personal freedom, activity and independence.

Hard-won, self-acquired, self-earned property! Do you mean the property of the petty artisan and of the small peasant, a form of property that preceded the bourgeois form? There is no need to abolish that; the development of industry has to a great extent already destroyed it, and is still destroying it daily.

Or do you mean modern bourgeois private property?

But does wage-labour create any property for the labourer? Not a bit. It creates capital, *i.e.,* that kind of property which exploits wage-labour, and which cannot increase except upon condition of begetting a new supply of wage-labour for fresh exploitation. Property, in its present form, is based on the antagonism of capital and wage-labour. Let us examine both sides of this antagonism.

To be a capitalist, is to have not only a purely personal, but a social *status* in production. Capital is a collective product, and only by the united action of many members, nay, in the last resort, only by the united action of all members of society, can it be set in motion.

Capital is, therefore, not a personal, it is a social power.

When, therefore, capital is converted into common property, into the property of all members of society, personal property is not thereby transformed into social property. It is only the social character of the property that is changed. It loses its class-character.

Let us now take wage-labour.

The average price of wage-labour is the minimum wage, *i.e.,* that quantum of the means of subsistence, which is absolutely requisite to keep the labourer in bare existence as a labourer. What, therefore, the wage-labourer appropriates by means of his labour, merely suffices to prolong and reproduce a bare existence. We by no means intend to abolish this personal appropriation of the products of labour, an appropriation that is made for the maintenance and reproduction of human life, and that leaves no surplus wherewith to command the labour of others. All that we want to do away with, is the miserable character of this appropriation, under which the labourer lives merely to increase capital, and is allowed to live only in so far as the interest of the ruling class requires it.

In bourgeois society, living labour is but a means to increase accumulated labour. In Communist society, accumulated labour is but a means to widen, to enrich, to promote the existence of the labourer.

In bourgeois society, therefore, the past dominates the present; in Communist society, the present dominates the past. In bourgeois society capital is independent and has individuality, while the living person is dependent and has no individuality.

And the abolition of this state of things is called by the bourgeois, abolition of individuality and freedom! And rightly so. The abolition of bourgeois individuality, bourgeois independence, and bourgeois freedom is undoubtedly aimed at.

By freedom is meant, under the present bourgeois conditions of production, free trade, free selling and buying.

But if selling and buying disappears, free selling and buying disappears also. This talk about free selling and buying, and all the other "brave words" of our bourgeoisie about freedom in general, have a meaning, if any, only in contrast with restricted selling and buying, with the fettered traders of the Middle Ages, but have no meaning when opposed to the Communistic abolition of buying and selling, of the bourgeois conditions of production, and of the bourgeoisie itself.

You are horrified at our intending to do away with private property. But in your existing society, private property is already done away with for nine-tenths of the population; its existence for the few is solely due to its non-existence in the hands of those nine-tenths. You reproach us, therefore, with intending to do away with a form of property, the necessary condition for whose existence is the non-existence of any property for the immense majority of society.

In one word, you reproach us with intending to do away with your property. Precisely so; that is just what we intend.

From the moment when labour can no longer be converted into capital, money, or rent, into a social power capable of being monopolised, *i.e.,* from the moment when individual property can no longer be transformed into bourgeois property, into capital, from that moment, you say, individuality vanishes.

You must, therefore, confess that by "individual" you mean no other person than the bourgeois, than the middle-class owner of property. This person must, indeed, be swept out of the way, and made impossible.

Communism deprives no man of the power to appropriate the products of society; all that it does is to deprive him of the power to subjugate the labour of others by means of such appropriation.

It has been objected that upon the abolition of private property all work will cease, and universal laziness will overtake us.

According to this, bourgeois society ought long ago to have gone to the dogs through sheer idleness; for those of its members who work, acquire nothing, and those who acquire anything, do not work. The whole of this objection is but another expression of the tautology: that there can no longer be any wage-labour when there is no longer any capital.

All objections urged against the Communistic mode of producing and appropriating material products, have, in the same way, been urged against the Communistic modes of producing and appropriating intellectual products. Just as, to the bourgeois, the disappearance of class property is the disappearance of production itself, so the disappearance of class culture is to him identical with the disappearance of all culture.

That culture, the loss of which he laments, is, for the enormous majority, a mere training to act as a machine.

But don't wrangle with us so long as you apply, to our intended abolition of bourgeois property, the standard of your bourgeois notions of freedom, culture, law, &c. Your very ideas are but the outgrowth of the conditions of your bourgeois production and bourgeois property, just as your jurisprudence is but the will of your class made into a law for all, a will, whose essential character and direction are determined by the economical conditions of existence of your class.

The selfish misconception that induces you to transform into eternal laws of nature and of reason, the social forms springing from your present mode of production and form of property—historical relations that rise and disappear in the progress of production—this misconception you share with every ruling class that has preceded you. What you see clearly in the case of ancient property, what you admit in the case of feudal property, you are of course forbidden to admit in the case of your own bourgeois form of property.

Abolition of the family! Even the most radical flare up at this infamous proposal of the Communists.

On what foundation is the present family, the bourgeois family, based? On capital, on private gain. In its completely developed form this family exists only among the bourgeoisie. But this state of things finds its complement in the practical absence of the family among the proletarians, and in public prostitution.

The bourgeois family will vanish as a matter of course when its complement vanishes, and both will vanish with the vanishing of capital.

Do you charge us with wanting to stop the exploitation of children by their parents? To this crime we plead guilty.

But, you will say, we destroy the most hallowed of relations, when we replace home education by social.

And your education! Is not that also social, and determined by the social conditions under which you educate, by the intervention, direct or indirect, of society, by means of schools, etc.? The Communists have not invented the intervention of society in education; they do but seek to alter the character of that intervention, and to rescue education from the influence of the ruling class. The bourgeois clap-trap about the family and education, about the hallowed co-relation of parent and child, becomes all the more disgusting, the more, by the action of Modern In-

dustry, all family ties among the proletarians are torn asunder, and their children transformed into simple articles of commerce and instruments of labour.

But you Communists would introduce community of women, screams the whole bourgeoisie in chorus.

The bourgeois sees in his wife a mere instrument of production. He hears that the instruments of production are to be exploited in common, and, naturally, can come to no other conclusion than that the lot of being common to all will likewise fall to the women.

He has not even a suspicion that the real point aimed at is to do away with the status of women as mere instruments of production.

For the rest, nothing is more ridiculous than the virtuous indignation of our bourgeois at the community of women, which, they pretend, is to be openly and officially established by the Communists. The Communists have no need to introduce community of women; it has existed almost from time immemorial.

Our bourgeois, not content with having the wives and daughters of their proletarians at their disposal, not to speak of common prostitutes, take the greatest pleasure in seducing each other's wives.

Bourgeois marriage is in reality a system of wives in common and thus, at the most, what the Communists might possibly be reproached with, is that they desire to introduce, in substitution for a hypocritically concealed, an openly legalised community of women. For the rest, it is self-evident that the abolition of the present system of production must bring with it the abolition of the community of women springing from that system, *i.e.,* of prostitution both public and private.

The Communists are further reproached with desiring to abolish countries and nationality.

The working men have no country. We cannot take from them what they have not got. Since the proletariat must first of all acquire political supremacy, must rise to be the leading class of the nation, must constitute itself *the* nation, it is, so far, itself national, though not in the bourgeois sense of the word.

National differences and antagonisms between peoples are daily more and more vanishing, owing to the development of the bourgeoisie, to freedom of commerce, to the world-market, to uniformity in the mode of production and in the conditions of life corresponding thereto.

The supremacy of the proletariat will cause them to vanish still faster. United action, of the leading civilised countries at least, is one of the first conditions for the emancipation of the proletariat.

In proportion as the exploitation of one individual by another is put an end to, the exploitation of one nation by another will also be put an end to. In proportion as the antagonism between classes within the nation vanishes, the hostility of one nation to another will come to an end.

The charges against Communism made from a religious, a philosophical, and, generally, from an ideological standpoint, are not deserving of serious examination.

Does it require deep intuition to comprehend that man's ideas, views and conceptions, in one word, man's consciousness, changes with every change in the conditions of his material existence, in his social relations and in his social life? What else does the history of ideas prove, than that intellectual production changes its character in proportion as material production is changed? The ruling ideas of each age have ever been the ideas of its ruling class.

When people speak of ideas that revolutionise society, they do but express the fact, that within the old society, the elements of a new one have been created, and that the dissolution of the old ideas keeps even pace with the dissolution of the old conditions of existence.

When the ancient world was in its last throes, the ancient religions were overcome by Christianity. When Christian ideas succumbed in the 18th century to rationalist ideas, feudal society fought its death battle with the then revolutionary bourgeoisie. The ideas of religious liberty and freedom of conscience merely gave expression to the sway of free competition within the domain of knowledge.

"Undoubtedly," it will be said, "religious, moral, philosophical and juridical ideas have been modified in the course of historical development. But religion, morality, philosophy, political science, and law, constantly survived this change."

"There are, besides, eternal truths, such as Freedom, Justice, etc., that are common to all states of society. But Communism abolishes eternal truths, it abolishes all religion, and all morality, instead of constituting them on a new basis; it therefore acts in contradiction to all past historical experience."

What does this accusation reduce itself to? The history of all past society has consisted in the development of class antagonisms, antagonisms that assumed different forms at different epochs.

But whatever form they may have taken, one fact is common to all past ages, *viz.*, the exploitation of one part of society by the other. No wonder, then, that the social consciousness of past ages, despite all the multiplicity and variety it displays, moves within certain common forms, or general ideas, which cannot completely vanish except with the total disappearance of class antagonisms.

The Communist revolution is the most radical rupture with traditional property relations; no wonder that its development involves the most radical rupture with traditional ideas.

But let us have done with the bourgeois objections to Communism.

We have seen above, that the first step in the revolution by the working class, is to raise the proletariat to the position of ruling class, to win the battle of democracy.

The proletariat will use its political supremacy to wrest, by degrees, all capital from the bourgeoisie, to centralise all instruments of production in the hands of the State, *i.e.,* of the proletariat organised as the ruling class; and to increase the total of productive forces as rapidly as possible.

Of course, in the beginning, this cannot be effected except by means of despotic inroads on the rights of property, and on the conditions of bourgeois production; by means of measures, therefore, which appear economically insufficient and untenable, but which, in the course of the movement, outstrip themselves, necessitate further inroads upon the old social order, and are unavoidable as a means of entirely revolutionising the mode of production.

These measures will of course be different in different countries.

Nevertheless in the most advanced countries, the following will be pretty generally applicable.

1. Abolition of property in land and application of all rents of land to public purposes.
2. A heavy progressive or graduated income tax.
3. Abolition of all right of inheritance.
4. Confiscation of the property of all emigrants and rebels.
5. Centralisation of credit in the hands of the State, by means of a national bank with State capital and an exclusive monopoly.
6. Centralisation of the means of communication and transport in the hands of the State.
7. Extension of factories and instruments of production owned by the State; the bringing into cultivation of wastelands, and the improvement of the soil generally in accordance with a common plan.
8. Equal liability of all to labour. Establishment of industrial armies, especially for agriculture.
9. Combination of agriculture with manufacturing industries; gradual abolition of the distinction between town and country, by a more equable distribution of the population over the country.
10. Free education for all children in public schools. Abolition of children's factory labour in its present form. Combination of education with industrial production etc., etc.

When, in the course of development, class distinctions have disappeared, and all production has been concentrated in the hands of a vast association of the whole nation, the public power will lose its political character. Political power, properly so called, is merely the organised power of one class for oppressing another. If the proletariat during its contest with the bourgeoisie is compelled, by the force of circumstances, to organise itself as a class, if, by means of a revolution, it makes itself the ruling class, and, as such, sweeps away by force the old conditions of production, then it will, along with these conditions, have swept away the conditions for the existence of class antagonisms and of classes generally, and will thereby have abolished its own supremacy as a class.

In place of the old bourgeois society, with its classes and class antagonisms, we shall have an association, in which the free development of each is the condition for the free development of all.

IV. Position of the Communists in Relation to the Various Existing Opposition Parties

. . . The Communists everywhere support every revolutionary movement against the existing social and political order of things.

In all these movements they bring to the front, as the leading question in each, the property question, no matter what its degree of development at the time.

Finally, they labour everywhere for the union and agreement of the democratic parties of all countries.

The Communists disdain to conceal their views and aims. They openly declare that their ends can be attained only by the forcible overthrow of all existing social conditions. Let the ruling classes tremble at a Communistic revolution. The proletarians have nothing to lose but their chains. They have a world to win.

WORKING MEN OF ALL COUNTRIES, UNITE!

Suggestions for Further Reading

See Jean Baechler's *The Origins of Capitalism,* translated by Barry Cooper (New York: St. Martin's Press, 1976), for a discussion of the nature and history of capitalism.

Karl Marx: Selected Writings, edited by Lawrence H. Simon (Indianapolis, IN: Hackett, 1994), provides a good selection of sources with a helpful introduction.

See also http://www.epistemelinks.com/Pers/MarxPers.htm for good links to all kinds of information on Marx.

Marx and Marxism, edited by G. H. R. Parkinson (New York: Cambridge University Press, 1982), provides a critical collection of essays.

See Tom Bottomore's edited collection of essays on Marx in *Karl Marx* (Englewood Cliffs, NJ: Prentice-Hall, 1973).

Videos

The Self-Made Society (26 minutes) explores the tension between individualism and the common good. *Karl Marx and Marxism* shows the impact of Marx on the twentieth century (52 minutes), and *John Locke* (52 minutes) explores Locke's ideas against the political background of his day. See *Marxist Philosophy* (45 minutes) for Charles Taylor's assessment of the appeal and flaws of Marxist philosophy. These videos are available from Films for the Humanities and Sciences, PO Box 2053, Princeton, NJ 08543.

5.4 The Original Position

What is the role of justice in a society? Is it very important or not so important? Is it more important than anything else? Should all the laws and all the major institutions of a society be changed or rejected if they are unjust?

You can imagine arguments on both sides of the issue. Someone might say that the promotion of law and order is of primary importance for any government. Justice must sometimes take a back seat to these more important goals. One could counter that law and order without justice is a sham. Peace and social stability at any price are just not worth it. There is no greater social good than justice.

If you read Kant (see Section 4.2), you might recognize a Kantian theme in the claim that justice is the highest social good. If you read Bentham (see Section 4.3), you might recognize a utilitarian theme in the claim that justice must sometimes take a back seat to a greater good. So where do we go from here? How can we decide whether justice is the most important social good? Surely we must know what justice is before we can decide how important it is? What is justice?

Philosophers distinguish between the material principle of justice and the formal principle of justice. The **material principle of justice** is some particular trait that is used as a basis for distributing benefits and burdens. If someone claimed that race, ethnic background, sex, or sexual orientation is the basis on which he or she decided to deny (or give) someone a job, what would you say? Is this fair? If someone claimed that seniority, skill, or a record of good performance is the basis on which she or he decided to deny (or give) someone a job, what would you say? Is this fair? The **formal principle of justice** requires that benefits and burdens be distributed fairly according to *relevant* differences and similarities. So if I decide to award an A to all my students who wear something red on the first Tuesday of each month, is that fair?

"But," you might properly retort, "that is not relevant."

Why isn't it?

"Because," you say, "it has nothing to do with how well they perform on the exams."

That is a reasonable response. However, why is performance on exams relevant? How do we decide what is relevant and fair?

Imagine that you are faced with the task of creating a new society. You are in the dark about your status in that new society. You do not know if you will be rich or poor. You do not know if you will be healthy or sick. You do not know your race or gender or sexual orientation or religion. Not knowing any of these things, what sort of society would you create? What sort of government would it have? How would its laws be enacted? What would its public policies be like?

The philosopher John Rawls thinks he knows what kind of society you would create in such a situation. You would create a just society. In 1971 Rawls, professor of philosophy at Harvard University, published a now famous and influential book called *A Theory of Justice*. Below you will read some selections from that book in which Rawls answers some of the questions we have been thinking about here.

Reading Questions

1. What is the role of justice?
2. What is the subject of justice?
3. What is the main idea of Rawls's theory of justice?
4. What role does the original position play in justifying different principles of justice?
5. What does Rawls mean by "reflective equilibrium"?
6. What two principles of justice would persons in the original position be likely to choose? How are these principles related?
7. What is the "veil of ignorance," and why is it important in developing a contractarian theory of justice?
8. Given what you have read, what do you think is wrong with Rawls's theory of justice? Why do you think it is wrong?
9. How would Rawls answer the question, "What makes a society just?"

A Theory of Justice

JOHN RAWLS

1. The Role of Justice

JUSTICE IS THE FIRST VIRTUE of social institutions, as truth is of systems of thought. A theory however elegant and economical must be rejected or revised if it is untrue; likewise laws and institutions no matter how efficient and well-arranged must be reformed or abolished if they are unjust. Each person possesses an inviolability founded on justice that even the welfare of

From John Rawls, A Theory of Justice, *Cambridge, MA: Harvard University Press, 1971, pp. 3–5, 7, 11–15, 17–22, 60–62, 136–142. © Copyright 1971 by the President and Fellows of Harvard College. Footnotes edited.*

society as a whole cannot override. For this reason justice denies that the loss of freedom for some is made right by a greater good shared by others. It does not allow that the sacrifices imposed on a few are outweighed by the larger sum of advantages enjoyed by many. Therefore in a just society the liberties of equal citizenship are taken as settled; the rights secured by justice are not subject to political bargaining or to the calculus of social interests. The only thing that permits us to acquiesce in an erroneous theory is the lack of a better one; analogously, an injustice is tolerable only when it is necessary to avoid an even greater injustice. Being first virtues of human activities, truth and justice are uncompromising.

These propositions seem to express our intuitive conviction of the primacy of justice. No doubt they are expressed too strongly. In any event I wish to inquire whether these contentions or others similar to them are sound, and if so how they can be accounted for. To this end, it is necessary to work out a theory of justice in the light of which these assertions can be interpreted and assessed. I shall begin by considering the role of the principles of justice. Let us assume, to fix ideas, that a society is a more or less self-sufficient association of persons who in their relations to one another recognize certain rules of conduct as binding and who for the most part act in accordance with them. Suppose further that these rules specify a system of cooperation designed to advance the good of those taking part in it. Then, although a society is a cooperative venture for mutual advantage, it is typically marked by a conflict as well as by an identity of interests. There is an identity of interests since social cooperation makes possible a better life for all than any would have if each were to live solely by his own efforts. There is a conflict of interests since persons are not indifferent as to how the greater benefits produced by their collaboration are distributed, for in order to pursue their ends they each prefer a larger to a lesser share. A set of principles is required for choosing among the various social arrangements which determine this division of advantages and for underwriting an agreement on the proper distributive shares. These principles are the principles of social jus-

tice: they provide a way of assigning rights and duties in the basic institutions of society and they define the appropriate distribution of the benefits and burdens of social cooperation.

Now let us say that a society is well-ordered when it is not only designed to advance the good of its members but when it is also effectively regulated by a public conception of justice. That is, it is a society in which (1) everyone accepts and knows that the others accept the same principles of justice, and (2) the basic social institutions generally satisfy and are generally known to satisfy these principles. In this case while men may put forth excessive demands on one another, they nevertheless acknowledge a common point of view from which their claims may be adjudicated. If men's inclination to self-interest makes their vigilance against one another necessary, their public sense of justice makes their secure association together possible. Among individuals with disparate aims and purposes a shared conception of justice establishes the bonds of civic friendship; the general desire for justice limits the pursuit of other ends. One may think of a public conception of justice as constituting the fundamental charter of a well-ordered human association. . . .

2. *The Subject of Justice*

Many different kinds of things are said to be just and unjust: not only laws, institutions, and social systems, but also particular actions of many kinds, including decisions, judgments, and imputations. We also call the attitudes and dispositions of persons, and persons themselves, just and unjust. Our topic, however, is that of social justice. For us the primary subject of justice is the basic structure of society, or more exactly, the way in which the major social institutions distribute fundamental rights and duties and determine the division of advantages from social cooperation. By major institutions I understand the political constitution and the principal economic and social arrangements. Thus the legal protection of freedom of thought and liberty of conscience, competitive markets, private property in the means of production, and the monogamous family are examples of major social institutions. Taken together as one scheme, the major institutions define men's rights and duties and influence their life-prospects, what they can expect to be and how well they can hope to do. The basic structure is the primary subject of justice because its effects are so profound and present from the start. The intuitive notion here is that this structure contains various social positions and that men born into different positions have different expectations of life determined, in part, by the political system as well as by economic and social circumstances. In this way the institutions of society favor certain starting places over others. These are especially deep inequalities. Not only are they pervasive, but they affect men's initial chances in life; yet they cannot possibly be justified by an appeal to the notions of merit or desert. It is these inequalities, presumably inevitable in the basic structure of any society, to which the principles of social justice must in the first instance apply. These principles, then, regulate the choice of a political constitution and the main elements of the economic and social system. The justice of a social scheme depends essentially on how fundamental rights and duties are assigned and on the economic opportunities and social conditions in the various sectors of society. . . .

3. The Main Idea of the Theory of Justice

My aim is to present a conception of justice which generalizes and carries to a higher level of abstraction the familiar theory of the social contract as found, say, in Locke, Rousseau, and Kant.[1] In order to do this we are not to think of the original contract as one to enter a particular society or to set up a particular form of government. Rather, the guiding idea is that the principles of justice for the basic structure of society are the object of the original agreement. They are the principles that free and rational persons concerned to further their own interests would accept in an initial position of equality as defining the fundamental terms of their association. These principles are to regulate all further agreements; they specify the kinds of social cooperation that can be entered into and the forms of government that can be established. This way of regarding the principles of justice I shall call justice as fairness.

Thus we are to imagine that those who engage in social cooperation choose together, in one joint act, the principles which are to assign basic rights and duties and to determine the division of social benefits. Men are to decide in advance how they are to regulate their claims against one another and what is to be the foundation charter of their society. Just as each person must decide by rational reflection what constitutes his good, that is, the system of ends which it is rational for him to pursue, so a group of persons must decide once and for all what is to count among them as just and unjust. The choice which rational men would make in this hypothetical situation of equal liberty, assuming for the present that this choice problem has a solution, determines the principles of justice.

In justice as fairness the original position of equality corresponds to the state of nature in the traditional theory of the social contract. This original position is not, of course, thought of as an actual historical state of affairs, much less as a primitive condition of culture. It is understood as a purely hypothetical situation characterized so as to lead to a certain conception of justice. Among the essential features of this situation is that no one knows his place in society, his class position or social status, nor does any one know his fortune in the distribution of natural assets

---

1. As the text suggests, I shall regard Locke's *Second Treatise of Government,* Rousseau's *The Social Contract,* and Kant's ethical works beginning with *The Foundations of the Metaphysics of Morals* as definitive of the contract tradition. For all of its greatness, Hobbes's *Leviathan* raises special problems. A general historical survey is provided by J. W. Gough, *The Social Contract,* 2nd ed. (Oxford, The Clarendon Press, 1957), and Otto Gierke, *Natural Law and the Theory of Society,* trans. with an introduction by Ernest Barker (Cambridge, The University Press, 1934). A presentation of the contract view as primarily an ethical theory is to be found in

G. R. Grice, *The Grounds of Moral Judgment* (Cambridge, The University Press, 1967). . . .

and abilities, his intelligence, strength, and the like. I shall even assume that the parties do not know their conceptions of the good or their special psychological propensities. The principles of justice are chosen behind a veil of ignorance. This ensures that no one is advantaged or disadvantaged in the choice of principles by the outcome of natural chance or the contingency of social circumstances. Since all are similarly situated and no one is able to design principles to favor his particular condition, the principles of justice are the result of a fair agreement or bargain. For given the circumstances of the original position, the symmetry of everyone's relations to each other, this initial situation is fair between individuals as moral persons, that is, as rational beings with their own ends and capable, I shall assume, of a sense of justice. The original position is, one might say, the appropriate initial status quo, and thus the fundamental agreements reached in it are fair. This explains the propriety of the name "justice as fairness": it conveys the idea that the principles of justice are agreed to in an initial situation that is fair. The name does not mean that the concepts of justice and fairness are the same, any more than the phrase "poetry as metaphor" means that the concepts of poetry and metaphor are the same.

Justice as fairness begins, as I have said, with one of the most general of all choices which persons might make together, namely, with the choice of the first principles of a conception of justice which is to regulate all subsequent criticism and reform of institutions. Then, having chosen a conception of justice, we can suppose that they are to choose a constitution and a legislature to enact laws, and so on, all in accordance with the principles of justice initially agreed upon. Our social situation is just if it is such that by this sequence of hypothetical agreements we would have contracted into the general system of rules which defines it. Moreover, assuming that the original position does determine a set of principles (that is, that a particular conception of justice would be chosen), it will then be true that whenever social institutions satisfy these principles those engaged in them can say to one another that they are cooperating on terms to which they would agree if they were free and equal persons whose relations with respect to one another were fair. They could all view their arrangements as meeting the stipulations which they would acknowledge in an initial situation that embodies widely accepted and reasonable constraints on the choice of principles. The general recognition of this fact would provide the basis for a public acceptance of the corresponding principles of justice. No society can, of course, be a scheme of cooperation which men enter voluntarily in a literal sense; each person finds himself placed at birth in some particular position in some particular society, and the nature of this position materially affects his life prospects. Yet a society satisfying the principles of justice as fairness comes as close as a society can to being a voluntary scheme, for it meets the principles which free and equal persons would assent to under circumstances that are fair. In this sense its members are autonomous and the obligations they recognize self-imposed.

One feature of justice as fairness is to think of the parties in the initial situation as rational and mutually disinterested. This does not mean that the parties are egoists, that is, individuals with only certain kinds of interests, say in wealth, prestige, and domination. But they are conceived as not taking an interest in one another's interests. They are to presume that even their spiritual aims may be opposed, in the way that the aims of those of different religions may be opposed. Moreover, the concept of rationality must be interpreted as far as possible in the narrow sense, standard in economic theory, of taking the most effective means to given ends. I shall modify this concept to some extent, . . . but one must try to avoid introducing into it any controversial ethical elements. The initial situation must be characterized by stipulations that are widely accepted.

In working out the conception of justice as fairness one main task clearly is to determine which principles of justice would be chosen in the original position. To do this we must describe this situation in some detail and formulate with care the problem of choice which it presents. These matters I shall take up in the immediately succeeding chapters. It may be observed, however, that once the principles of justice are thought of as arising from an original agreement in a situation of equality, it is an open question whether the principle of utility would be acknowledged. Offhand it hardly seems likely that persons who view themselves as equals, entitled to press their claims upon one another, would agree to a principle which may require lesser life prospects for some simply for the sake of a greater sum of advantages enjoyed by others. Since each desires to protect his interests, his capacity to advance his conception of the good, no one has a reason to acquiesce in an enduring loss for himself in order to bring about a greater net balance of satisfaction. In the absence of strong and lasting benevolent impulses, a rational man would not accept a basic structure merely because it maximized the algebraic sum of advantages irrespective of its permanent effects on his own basic rights and interests. Thus it seems that the principle of utility is incompatible with the conception of social cooperation among equals for mutual advantage. It appears to be inconsistent with the idea of reciprocity implicit in the notion of a well-ordered society. Or, at any rate, so I shall argue.

I shall maintain instead that the persons in the initial situation would choose two rather different principles: the first requires equality in the assignment of basic rights and duties, while the second holds that social and economic inequalities, for example inequalities of wealth and authority, are just only if they result in compensating benefits for everyone, and in particular for the least advantaged members of society. These principles rule out justifying institutions on the grounds that the hardships of some are offset by a greater good in the aggregate. It may be expedient but it is not just that some should have less in order that others may prosper. But there is no injustice in the greater benefits earned by a few provided that the situation of persons not so fortunate is thereby improved. The intuitive idea is that since everyone's well-being depends upon a scheme of cooperation without which no one could have a satisfactory life, the division of advantages should be such as to draw forth the willing cooperation of everyone taking part in it, including those less well situated. Yet this can be expected only if reasonable terms are proposed. The two principles mentioned seem to be a fair agreement on the basis of which those better endowed, or more fortunate in their social position, neither of which we can be said to deserve, could expect the willing cooperation of others when some workable scheme is a necessary condition of the welfare of all. Once we decide to look for a conception of justice that nullifies the accidents of natural endowment and the contingencies of social circumstance as counters in quest for political and economic advantage, we are led to these principles. They express the result of leaving aside those aspects of the social world that seem arbitrary from a moral point of view. . . .

4. The Original Position and Justification

I have said that the original position is the appropriate initial status quo which insures that the fundamental agreements reached in it are fair. This fact yields the name "justice as fairness." It is clear, then, that I want to say that one conception of justice is more reasonable than another, or justifiable with respect to it, if rational persons in the initial situation would choose its principles over those of the other for the role of justice. Conceptions of justice are to be ranked by their acceptability to persons so circumstanced. Understood in this way the question of justification is settled by working out a problem of deliberation: we have to ascertain which principles it would be rational to adopt given the contractual situation. This connects the theory of justice with the theory of rational choice.

If this view of the problem of justification is to succeed, we must, of course, describe in some detail the nature of this choice problem. A problem of rational decision has a definite answer only if we know the beliefs and interests of the parties, their relations with respect to one another, the alternatives between which they are to choose, the procedure whereby they make up their minds, and so on. As the circumstances are presented in different ways, correspondingly different principles are accepted. The concept of the original position, as I shall refer to it, is that of the most philosophically favored interpretation of this initial choice situation for the purposes of a theory of justice.

But how are we to decide what is the most favored interpretation? I assume, for one thing, that there is a broad measure of agreement that principles of justice should be chosen under certain conditions. To justify a particular description of the initial situation one shows that it incorporates these commonly shared presumptions. One argues from widely accepted but weak premises to more specific conclusions. Each of the presumptions should by itself be natural and plausible; some of them may seem innocuous or even trivial. The aim of the contract approach is to establish that taken together they impose significant bounds on acceptable principles of justice. The ideal outcome would be that these conditions determine a unique set of principles; but I shall be satisfied if they suffice to rank the main traditional conceptions of social justice.

One should not be misled, then, by the somewhat unusual conditions which characterize the original position. The idea here is simply to make vivid to ourselves the restrictions that it seems reasonable to impose on arguments for principles of justice, and therefore on these principles themselves. Thus it seems reasonable and generally acceptable that no one should be advantaged or disadvantaged by natural fortune or social circumstances in the choice of principles. It also seems widely agreed that it should be impossible to tailor principles to the circumstances of one's own case. We should insure further that particular inclinations and aspirations, and persons' conceptions of their good do not affect the principles adopted. The aim is to rule out those principles that it would be rational to propose for acceptance, however little the chance of success, only if one knew certain things that are irrelevant from the standpoint of justice. For example, if a man knew that he was wealthy, he might find it rational to advance the principle that various taxes for welfare measures be counted unjust; if he knew that he was poor, he would most likely

propose the contrary principle. To represent the desired restrictions one imagines a situation in which everyone is deprived of this sort of information. One excludes the knowledge of those contingencies which sets men at odds and allows them to be guided by their prejudices. In this manner the veil of ignorance is arrived at in a natural way. This concept should cause no difficulty if we keep in mind the constraints on arguments that it is meant to express. At any time we can enter the original position, so to speak, simply by following a certain procedure, namely, by arguing for principles of justice in accordance with these restrictions.

It seems reasonable to suppose that the parties in the original position are equal. That is, all have the same rights in the procedure for choosing principles; each can make proposals, submit reasons for their acceptance, and so on. Obviously the purpose of these conditions is to represent equality between human beings as moral persons, as creatures having a conception of their good and capable of a sense of justice. The basis of equality is taken to be similarity in these two respects. Systems of ends are not ranked in value; and each man is presumed to have the requisite ability to understand and to act upon whatever principles are adopted. Together with the veil of ignorance, these conditions define the principles of justice as those which rational persons concerned to advance their interests would consent to as equals when none are known to be advantaged or disadvantaged by social and natural contingencies.

There is, however, another side to justifying a particular description of the original position. This is to see if the principles which would be chosen match our considered convictions of justice or extend them in an acceptable way. We can note whether applying these principles would lead us to make the same judgments about the basic structure of society which we now make intuitively and in which we have the greatest confidence; or whether, in cases where our present judgments are in doubt and given with hesitation, these principles offer a resolution which we can affirm on reflection. There are questions which we feel sure must be answered in a certain way. For example, we are confident that religious intolerance and racial discrimination are unjust. We think that we have examined these things with care and have reached what we believe is an impartial judgment not likely to be distorted by an excessive attention to our own interests. These convictions are provisional fixed points which we presume any conception of justice must fit. But we have much less assurance as to what is the correct distribution of wealth and authority. Here we may be looking for a way to remove our doubts. We can check an interpretation of the initial situation, then, by the capacity of its principles to accommodate our firmest convictions and to provide guidance where guidance is needed.

In searching for the most favored description of this situation we work from both ends. We begin by describing it so that it represents generally shared and preferably weak conditions. We then see if these conditions are strong enough to yield a significant set of principles. If not, we look for further premises equally reasonable. But if so, and these principles match our considered convictions of justice, then so far well and good. But presumably there will be discrepancies. In this case we have a choice. We can either modify the account of the initial situation or we can revise our existing judgments, for even the judgments we take provisionally as fixed points are liable to revision. By going back and forth, sometimes altering the conditions of the contractual circumstances, at others withdrawing our judgments and conforming them to principle, I assume that eventually we shall find a description of the initial situation that both expresses reasonable conditions and yields principles which match our considered judgments duly pruned and adjusted. This state of affairs I refer to as reflective equilibrium. It is an equilibrium because at last our principles and judgments coincide; and it is reflective since we know to what principles our judgments conform and the premises of their derivation. At the moment everything is in order. But this equilibrium is not necessarily stable. It is liable to be upset by further examination of the conditions which should be imposed on the contractual situation and by particular cases which may lead us to revise our judgments. Yet for the time being we have done what we can to render coherent and to justify our convictions of social justice. We have reached a conception of the original position.

I shall not, of course, actually work through this process. Still, we may think of the interpretation of the original position that I shall present as the result of such a hypothetical course of reflection. It represents the attempt to accommodate within one scheme both reasonable philosophical conditions on principles as well as our considered judgments of justice. In arriving at the favored interpretation of the initial situation there is no point at which an appeal is made to self-evidence in the traditional sense either of general conceptions or particular convictions. I do not claim for the principles of justice proposed that they are necessary truths or derivable from such truths. A conception of justice cannot be deduced from self-evident premises or conditions on principles; instead, its justification is a matter of the mutual support of many considerations, of everything fitting together into one coherent view.

A final comment. We shall want to say that certain principles of justice are justified because they would be agreed to in an initial situation of equality. I have emphasized that this original position is purely hypothetical. It is natural to ask why, if this agreement is never actually entered into, we should take any interest in these principles, moral or otherwise. The answer is that the conditions embodied in the description of the original position are ones that we do in fact accept. Or if we do not, then perhaps we can be persuaded to do so by philosophical reflection. Each aspect of the contractual situation can be given supporting grounds. Thus what we shall do is to collect together into one conception a number of conditions on principles that we are ready upon due consideration to recognize as reasonable. These constraints express what we are prepared to regard as limits on fair terms of social cooperation. One way to look at the idea of the original position, therefore, is to see it as an expository device which sums up the meaning of these conditions and helps us to extract their consequences. On the other hand, this conception is also an intuitive notion that suggests its own elaboration, so that led on by it we are drawn to define more clearly the standpoint from which we can best interpret moral relationships. We need a conception that enables us to envision our objective from afar: the intuitive notion of the original position is to do this for us. . . .

11. *Two Principles of Justice*

I shall now state in a provisional form the two principles of justice that I believe would be chosen in the original position. . . .

The first statement of the two principles reads as follows.

> First: each person is to have an equal right to the most extensive basic liberty compatible with a similar liberty for others.
>
> Second: social and economic inequalities are to be arranged so that they are both (a) reasonably expected to be to everyone's advantage, and (b) attached to positions and offices open to all.

There are two ambiguous phrases in the second principle, namely "everyone's advantage" and "open to all." . . .

By way of general comment, these principles primarily apply, as I have said, to the basic structure of society. They are to govern the assignment of rights and duties and to regulate the distribution of social and economic advantages. As their formulation suggests, these principles presuppose that the social structure can be divided into two more or less distinct parts, the first principle applying to the one, the second to the other. They distinguish between those aspects of the social system that define and secure the equal liberties of citizenship and those that specify and establish social and economic inequalities. The basic liberties of citizens are, roughly speaking, political liberty (the right to vote and to be eligible for public office) together with freedom of speech and assembly; liberty of conscience and freedom of thought; freedom of the person along with the right to hold (personal) property; and freedom from arbitrary arrest and seizure as defined by the concept of the rule of law. These liberties are all required to be equal by the first principle, since citizens of a just society are to have the same basic rights.

The second principle applies, in the first approximation, to the distribution of income and wealth and to the design of organizations that make use of differences in authority and responsibility, or chains of command. While the distribution of wealth and income need not be equal, it must be to everyone's advantage, and at the same time, positions of authority and offices of command must be accessible to all. One applies the second principle by holding positions open, and then, subject to this constraint, arranges social and economic inequalities so that everyone benefits.

These principles are to be arranged in a serial order with the first principle prior to the second. This ordering means that a departure from the institutions of equal liberty required by the first principle cannot be justified by, or compensated for, by greater social and economic advantages. The distribution of wealth and income, and the hierarchies of authority, must be consistent with both the liberties of equal citizenship and equality of opportunity.

It is clear that these principles are rather specific in their content, and their acceptance rests on certain assumptions that I must eventually try to explain and justify. A theory of justice depends upon a theory of society in ways that will become evident as we proceed. For the present, it should be observed that the two principles (and this holds for all formulations) are a special case of a more general conception of justice that can be expressed as follows.

> All social values—liberty and opportunity, income and wealth, and the bases of self-respect—are to be distributed equally unless an unequal distribution of any, or all, of these values is to everyone's advantage.

Injustice, then, is simply inequalities that are not to the benefit of all. Of course, this conception is extremely vague and requires interpretation.

As a first step, suppose that the basic structure of society distributes certain primary goods, that is, things that every rational man is presumed to want. These goods normally have a use whatever a person's rational plan of life. For simplicity, assume that the chief primary goods at the disposition of society are rights and liberties, powers and opportunities, income and wealth. . . . These are the social primary goods. Other primary goods such as health and vigor, intelligence and imagination, are natural goods; although their possession is influenced by the basic structure, they are not so directly under its control. Imagine, then, a hypothetical initial arrangement in which all the social primary goods are equally distributed: everyone has similar rights and duties, and income and wealth are evenly shared. This state of affairs provides a benchmark for judging improvements. If certain inequalities of wealth and organizational powers would make everyone better off than in this hypothetical starting situation, then they accord with the general conception.

Now it is possible, at least theoretically, that by giving up some of their fundamental liberties men are sufficiently compensated by the resulting social and economic gains. The general conception of justice imposes no restrictions on what sort of inequalities are permissible; it only requires that everyone's position be improved. We need not suppose anything so drastic as consenting to a condition of slavery. Imagine instead that men forego certain political rights when the economic returns are significant and their capacity to influence the course of policy by the exercise of these rights would be marginal in any case. It is this kind of exchange which the two principles as stated rule out; being arranged in serial order they do not permit exchanges between basic liberties and economic and social gains. The serial ordering of principles expresses an underlying preference among primary social goods. When this preference is rational so likewise is the choice of these principles in this order. . . .

24. The Veil of Ignorance

The idea of the original position is to set up a fair procedure so that any principles agreed to will be just. The aim is to use the notion of pure proce-

dural justice as a basis of theory. Somehow we must nullify the effects of specific contingencies which put men at odds and tempt them to exploit social and natural circumstances to their own advantage. Now in order to do this I assume that the parties are situated behind a veil of ignorance. They do not know how the various alternatives will affect their own particular case and they are obliged to evaluate principles solely on the basis of general considerations.

It is assumed, then, that the parties do not know certain kinds of particular facts. First of all, no one knows his place in society, his class position or social status; nor does he know his fortune in the distribution of natural assets and abilities, his intelligence and strength, and the like. Nor, again, does anyone know his conception of the good, the particulars of his rational plan of life, or even the special features of his psychology such as his aversion to risk or liability to optimism or pessimism. More than this, I assume that the parties do not know the particular circumstances of their own society. That is, they do not know its economic or political situation, or the level of civilization and culture it has been able to achieve. The persons in the original position have no information as to which generation they belong. These broader restrictions on knowledge are appropriate in part because questions of social justice arise between generations as well as within them, for example, the question of the appropriate rate of capital saving and of the conservation of natural resources and the environment of nature. There is also, theoretically anyway, the question of a reasonable genetic policy. In these cases too, in order to carry through the idea of the original position, the parties must not know the contingencies that set them in opposition. They must choose principles the consequences of which they are prepared to live with whatever generation they turn out to belong to.

As far as possible, then, the only particular facts which the parties know is that their society is subject to the circumstances of justice and whatever this implies. It is taken for granted, however, that they know the general facts about human society. They understand political affairs and the principles of economic theory; they know the basis of social organization and the laws of human psychology. Indeed, the parties are presumed to know whatever general facts affect the choice of the principles of justice. There are no limitations on general information, that is, on general laws and theories, since conceptions of justice must be adjusted to the characteristics of the systems of social cooperation which they are to regulate, and there is no reason to rule out these facts. It is, for example, a consideration against a conception of justice that, in view of the laws of moral psychology, men would not acquire a desire to act upon it even when the institutions of their society satisfied it. For in this case there would be difficulty in securing the stability of social cooperation. It is an important feature of a conception of justice that it should generate its own support. That is, its principles should be such that when they are embodied in the basic structure of society men tend to acquire the corresponding sense of justice. Given the principles of moral learning, men develop a desire to act in accordance with its principles. In this case a conception of justice is stable. This kind of general information is admissible in the original position.

The notion of the veil of ignorance raises several difficulties. Some may object that the exclusion of nearly all particular information makes it difficult to grasp what is meant by the original position. Thus it may be helpful to observe that one or more persons can at any time enter this position, or perhaps, better, simulate the deliberations of this hypothetical situation, simply by reasoning in accordance with the appropriate restrictions. In arguing for a conception of justice we must be sure that it is among the permitted alternatives and satisfies the stipulated formal constraints. No considerations can be advanced in its favor unless they would be rational ones for us to urge were we to lack the kind of knowledge that is excluded. The evaluation of principles must proceed in terms of the general consequences of their public recognition and universal application, it being assumed that they will be complied with by everyone. To say that a certain conception of justice would be chosen in the original position is equivalent to saying that ra-

tional deliberation satisfying certain conditions and restrictions would reach a certain conclusion. If necessary, the argument to this result could be set out more formally. I shall, however, speak throughout in terms of the notion of the original position. It is more economical and suggestive, and brings out certain essential features that otherwise one might easily overlook.

These remarks show that the original position is not to be thought of as a general assembly which includes at one moment everyone who will live at some time; or, much less, as an assembly of everyone who could live at some time. It is not a gathering of all actual or possible persons. To conceive of the original position in either of these ways is to stretch fantasy too far; the conception would cease to be a natural guide to intuition. In any case, it is important that the original position be interpreted so that one can at any time adopt its perspective. It must make no difference when one takes up this viewpoint, or who does so: the restrictions must be such that the same principles are always chosen. The veil of ignorance is a key condition in meeting this requirement. It insures not only that the information available is relevant, but that it is at all times the same.

It may be protested that the condition of the veil of ignorance is irrational. Surely, some may object, principles should be chosen in the light of all the knowledge available. There are various replies to this contention. Here I shall sketch those which emphasize the simplifications that need to be made if one is to have any theory at all. . . . To begin with, it is clear that since the differences among the parties are unknown to them, and everyone is equally rational and similarly situated, each is convinced by the same arguments. Therefore, we can view the choice in the original position from the standpoint of one person selected at random. If anyone after due reflection prefers a conception of justice to another, then they all do, and a unanimous agreement can be reached. We can, to make the circumstances more vivid, imagine that the parties are required to communicate with each other through a referee as intermediary, and that he is to announce which alternatives have been suggested and the reasons offered in their support.

He forbids the attempt to form coalitions, and he informs the parties when they have come to an understanding. But such a referee is actually superfluous, assuming that the deliberations of the parties must be similar.

Thus there follows the very important consequence that the parties have no basis for bargaining in the usual sense. No one knows his situation in society nor his natural assets, and therefore no one is in a position to tailor principles to his advantage. We might imagine that one of the contractees threatens to hold out unless the others agree to principles favorable to him. But how does he know which principles are especially in his interests? The same holds for the formation of coalitions: if a group were to decide to band together to the disadvantage of the others, they would not know how to favor themselves in the choice of principles. Even if they could get everyone to agree to their proposal, they would have no assurance that it was to their advantage, since they cannot identify themselves either by name or description. The one case where this conclusion fails is that of saving. Since the persons in the original position know that they are contemporaries (taking the present time of entry interpretation), they can favor their generation by refusing to make any sacrifices at all for their successors; they simply acknowledge the principle that no one has a duty to save for posterity. Previous generations have saved or they have not; there is nothing the parties can now do to affect that. So in this instance the veil of ignorance fails to secure the desired result. Therefore I resolve the question of justice between generations in a different way by altering the motivation assumption. But with this adjustment no one is able to formulate principles especially designed to advance his own cause. Whatever his temporal position, each is forced to choose for everyone.

The restrictions on particular information in the original position are, then, of fundamental importance. Without them we would not be able to work out any definite theory of justice at all. We would have to be content with a vague formula stating that justice is what would be agreed to without being able to say much, if anything, about the substance of the agreement itself. The formal constraints of the concept of right, those applying to principles directly, are not sufficient for our purpose. The veil of ignorance makes possible a unanimous choice of a particular conception of justice. Without these limitations on knowledge the bargaining problem of the original position would be hopelessly complicated. Even if theoretically a solution were to exist, we would not, at present anyway, be able to determine it.

The notion of the veil of ignorance is implicit, I think, in Kant's ethics. . . . Nevertheless the problem of defining the knowledge of the parties and of characterizing the alternatives open to them has often been passed over, even by contract theories. Sometimes the situation definitive of moral deliberation is presented in such an indeterminate way that one cannot ascertain how it will turn out. Thus Perry's doctrine is essentially contractarian: he holds that social and personal integration must proceed by entirely different principles, the latter by rational prudence, the former by the concurrence of persons of good will. He would appear to reject utilitarianism on much the same grounds suggested earlier: namely, that it improperly extends the principle of choice for one person to choices facing society. The right course of action is characterized as that which best advances social aims as these would be formulated by reflective agreement given that the parties have full knowledge of the circumstances and are moved by a benevolent concern for one another's interests. No effort is made, however, to specify in any precise way the possible outcomes of this sort of agreement. Indeed, without a far more elaborate account, no conclusions can be drawn. I do not wish here to criticize others; rather, I want to explain the necessity for what may seem at times like so many irrelevant details.

Now the reasons for the veil of ignorance go beyond mere simplicity. We want to define the original position so that we get the desired solution. If a knowledge of particulars is allowed, then the outcome is biased by arbitrary contingencies. As already observed, to each according to his threat advantage is not a principle of justice. If the original position is to yield agreements that are just, the parties must be fairly situated and treated equally as moral persons. The arbitrariness of the world must be corrected for by adjusting the circumstances of the initial contractual situation. Moreover, if in choosing principles we required unanimity even when there is full information, only a few rather obvious cases could be decided. A conception of justice based on unanimity in these circumstances would indeed be weak and trivial. But once knowledge is excluded, the requirement of unanimity is not out of place and the fact that it can be satisfied is of great importance. It enables us to say of the preferred conception of justice that it represents a genuine reconciliation of interests.

A final comment. For the most part I shall suppose that the parties possess all general information. No general facts are closed to them. I do this mainly to avoid complications. Nevertheless a conception of justice is to be the public basis of the terms of social cooperation. Since common understanding necessitates certain bounds on the complexity of principles, there may likewise be limits on the use of theoretical knowledge in the original position. Now clearly it would be very difficult to classify and to grade for complexity the various sorts of general facts. I shall make no attempt to do this. We do however recognize an intricate theoretical construction when we meet one. Thus it seems reasonable to say that other things equal one conception of justice is to be preferred to another when it is founded upon markedly simpler general facts, and its choice does not depend upon elaborate calculations in the light of a vast array of theoretically defined possibilities. It is desirable that the grounds for a public conception of justice should be evident to everyone when circumstances permit. This consideration favors, I believe, the two principles of justice over the criterion of utility. . . .

Suggestions for Further Reading

See *Masterpieces of World Philosophy,* edited by Frank N. Magill (New York: HarperCollins, 1990, p. 678ff), for a summary of Rawls's theory and some criticisms.

In *Anarchy, State, and Utopia* (New York: Basic Books, 1974) Robert Nozick gives a particularly insightful critique of Rawls's argument and advances the antithesis of Rawls's view of the role of the state in achieving a good society.

Also see the article by Paul Smith, "Incentives and Justice: G.A. Cohen's Egalitarian Critique of Rawls," in *Social Theory and Practice* (Summer 1998: p. 205ff), for a discussion of Rawls's views in relationship to Marxism.

If you are interested in how Rawls's views relate to theocratic views of justice, see "Rawls and the Challenge of Theocracy to Freedom" by Robert B. Thigpen and Lyle A. Downing in *Journal of Church and State* (Vol. 40, Autumn 1998: p. 757ff.)

See http://info.bris.ac.uk/~plcdib/tj.html for a reading list and course outline exploring some of the issues relating to Rawls's theory of justice. Rawls has updated and revised his theory in *Political Liberalism* (New York: Columbia University Press, 1996).

Justice, edited by Jonathan Westphal (Indianapolis, IN: Hackett, 1996), provides an excellent collection of philosophical ideas about justice ranging from Plato to Rawls and beyond.

Videos

Michael Sandel: Can Self-Government Survive? (30 minutes) explores views of justice in relationship to issues of democracy. *What Is Justice?* (30 minutes) examines the views of Aristotle, Marx, Rawls, and Nozick. Rawls's updated version of the social contract, among other topics, is explored in *What Justifies the State?* (30 minutes). These videos are available from Insight Media, 2162 Broadway, New York, NY 10024.

In the series "No Dogs or Philosophers Allowed," the topic of justice is discussed in *Justice: Critical Legal Theory.* Available from Philosophy Documentation Center, Bowling Green State University, Bowling Green, OH 13103.

5.5 Our Obligation to the State

In Chapter 3, we left Socrates condemned to death by the Athenian court. His execution was delayed because of a religious festival, and his friends made plans for his escape from prison. Crito went to Socrates in prison and tried to persuade him to escape. Socrates argued that the right thing for him to do was to obey the law. This argument was surprising because in the *Apology* he made it quite clear that his mission to search for the truth was of more value than conforming to the laws of Athens. Even if the Athenians should order him to stop his activities, he would continue because, as he so dramatically put it, "the unexamined life is not worth living."

So why did Socrates now argue that he should obey the laws of Athens and drink the hemlock? Should all laws be obeyed just because they are legally established? Where do governments get the authority to pass laws? Where do they get the authority to take a human life? If the laws are bad laws, isn't it right to break them? If someone is unjustly condemned, isn't it right to try to escape punishment? Or is it morally right to suffer the consequences of your actions, even if what you did was right?

At one point in his argument, Socrates made an allusion to an implied agreement that he had with the state. According to this agreement, the city-state of Athens had provided him and his family with certain benefits in return for his promise to keep the laws. By living in Athens, he had tacitly entered into a contract, and to break that contract now would be dishonest. Here we find the seeds for what has emerged as one of the dominant modern Western theories of political authority, the theory of the social contract (see Rawls's appeal to a contractarian position in the previous selection).

Social contract theory states that the authority of government derives from a voluntary agreement among all the people to form a political community and to obey the laws passed by a government they collectively select. Thomas Hobbes (1588–1679), in his book *Leviathan,* imagined a state of nature that was pre-social. This condition he characterized as a "war of all against all" in which people pursued their own self-interest and the only right was the right to self-preservation. The desire for self-preservation eventually made it clear that peace was a desirable goal and that the only way to secure this was to give the "sword of sovereignty" to someone who could guarantee order.

Jean-Jacques Rousseau (1712–1778), in his book *Social Contract,* rejected Hobbes's view that humans are by nature selfish and warlike. Human nature is basically good, he argued; evil arises with society. Civilization corrupts us. However, even though we are born free and good, we are bound together in a social contract and obliged to obey the decisions of the group to which our agreement has bound us. Individually, we have unique desires and interests that express our individual will. But as voting citizens of a community, we manifest the "general will" of the group, and it is this general will that forms the foundation of political authority.

Social contract theory makes clear how closely political theories are tied to theories of human nature. If we think humans are by nature evil, governments will be seen as necessary goods that restrain evil and prevent chaos. Governments provide law and order. The stronger the government, the better. If we think humans are by nature good, governments will be seen as necessary evils that hamper free and spontaneous expression. Governments restrict our freedom, and the less government, the better.

Notice how different social contract theory is from the theocratic and successionist theories of early Islam and the Platonically inspired philosophical theories of the philosopher king discussed in the first selection in this chapter. The right to rule derives not from God or wisdom, according to this view, but from an agreement of the people. If sovereignty derives from agreement of citizens, can not those citizens break such an agreement when they deem it necessary?

Reading Questions

1. What are Crito's main arguments in favor of Socrates' escape?
2. Socrates first responds by stating certain principles with which he gets Crito to agree. What are these principles?
3. Socrates imagines that the laws of Athens are speaking to him. In this speech, what are the most important points in support of not escaping?
4. Socrates asserts that "the really important thing is not to live, but to live well." Do you agree? Why, or why not?
5. Assume you are Crito. Offer Socrates your best argument for escaping that does not cause him to violate his principles.
6. Do you think the government is, as Socrates asserts, like your parents? Why?
7. Does living in a country amount to a tacit promise on your part to obey *all* its laws? Why, or why not?
8. What do you think Socrates should do and why?
9. Based on your reading of the *Crito,* how do you think Socrates would answer the question, "What makes a society just?"

Crito

PLATO

Socrates: Why have you come at this hour, Crito? It must be quite early?

Crito: Yes, it certainly is.

Soc: What time is it?

Cr: The dawn is breaking.

Soc: I am surprised the keeper of the prison let you in.

Cr: He knows me because I come often, Socrates, and he owes me a favor.

Soc: Did you just get here?

The original translation is by Benjamin Jowett and has been revised and updated by Christopher Biffle, A Guided Tour of Five Works of Plato *(Mountain View, CA: Mayfield, 1988), pp. 57–67. Reprinted by permission of Mayfield Publishing Company.*

Cr: No, I came some time ago.

Soc: Why did you sit and say nothing instead of waking me at once?

Cr: Why, indeed, Socrates, I myself would rather not have all this sleeplessness and sorrow. I have been wondering at your peaceful slumber and that was the reason why I did not (wake) you. I wanted you to be out of pain. I always thought you fortunate in your calm temperament but I never saw anything like the easy, cheerful way you bear this calamity.

Soc: Crito, when a man reaches my age he should not fear approaching death.

Cr: Other men of your age in similar situations fear death.

Soc: That may be. But you have not told me why you come at this early hour.

Cr: I bring you a sad and painful message; not sad, as I believe, for you, but to all of us who are your friends and saddest of all to me.

Soc: Has the ship come from Delos, on the arrival of which I am to die?

Cr: No, the ship has not actually arrived, but it will probably be here today because people who came from Sunium tell me they left it there. Therefore tomorrow, Socrates, will be the last day of your life.

Soc: Very well, Crito. If it is the will of the gods, I am willing but I believe there will be a delay of a day.

Cr: Why do you say that?

Soc: I will tell you. I am to die on the day after the arrival of the ship?

Cr: Yes, that is what the authorities say.

Soc: I do not think the ship will be here until tomorrow. I had a dream last night, or rather only just now, when you fortunately allowed me to sleep.

Cr: What was your dream?

Soc: I saw the image of a wondrously beautiful woman, clothed in white robes, who called to me and said: "O Socrates, the third day hence to fertile Phthia shalt thou go."

Cr: What a strange dream, Socrates!

Soc: I think there can be no doubt about the meaning, Crito.

Cr: Perhaps the meaning is clear to you. But, oh my beloved Socrates, let me beg you once more to take my advice and escape! If you die I shall not only lose a friend who can never be replaced, but there is another evil: People who do not know you and me will believe I might have saved you if I had been willing to spend money, but I did not care to do so. Now, can there be a worse disgrace than this—that I should be thought to value money more than the life of a friend? The many will not be persuaded I wanted you to escape and you refused.

Soc: But why, my dear Crito, should we care about the opinion of the many? Good men, and they are the only persons worth considering, will think of these things as they happened.

Cr: But do you see, Socrates, the opinion of the many must be regarded, as is clear in your own case, because they can do the very greatest evil to anyone who has lost their good opinion.

Soc: I only wish, Crito, they could. Then they could also do the greatest good and that would be excellent. The truth is, they can do neither good nor evil. They cannot make a man wise or make him foolish and whatever they do is the result of chance.

Cr: Well, I will not argue about that. But please tell me, Socrates, if you are acting out of concern for me and your other friends. Are you afraid if you escape we may get into trouble with the informers for having stolen you away and lose either the whole or a great part of our property, or even a worse evil may happen to us? Now, if this is your fear, be at ease. In order to save you we should surely run this, or even a greater, risk. Be persuaded, then, and do as I say.

Soc: Yes, Crito, that is one fear which you mention, but by no means the only one.

Cr: Do not be afraid. There are persons who at no great cost are willing to save you and bring you out of prison. As for the informers, they are reasonable in their demands, a little money will satisfy them. My resources, which are ample, are at your service and if you are troubled about spending all mine, there are strangers who will give you theirs. One of them, Simmias the Theban, brought a sum of money for this very purpose. Cebes and many others are willing to spend their money, too. I say therefore, do not hesitate about making your escape and do not say, as you did in the court, you will have difficulty in knowing what to do with yourself if you escape. Men will love you in other places you may go and not only in Athens. There are friends of mine in Thessaly, if you wish to go to them, who will value and protect you and no Thessalian will give you any trouble. Nor can I think you are justified, Socrates, in betraying your own life when you might be saved. This is playing into the hands of your enemies and destroyers. Besides, I say you are betraying your children. You should bring them up and educate them; instead you go away and leave them, and they will have to grow up on their own. If they do not meet with the usual fate of orphans, there will be small thanks to you. No man should bring children into the world who is unwilling to continue their nurture and education. You are choosing the easier part, as I think, not the better and manlier, which you should as one who professes virtue in all his actions. Indeed, I am ashamed not only of you, but of us, your friends, when I think this entire business of yours will be attributed to our lack of courage. The trial need never have started or might have been brought to another conclusion. The end of it all, which is the crowning absurdity, will seem to have been permitted by us, through cowardice and baseness, who might have saved you. You might have saved yourself, if we had been good for anything, for there was no difficulty in escaping, and we did not see how disgraceful, Socrates, and also miserable all this will be to us as well as to you. Make up your mind then. Or rather, have your mind already made up, for the time of deliberation is over. There is only one thing to be done, which must be done if at all this very night, and which any delay will render all but impossible. I plead with you therefore, Socrates, to be persuaded by me, and do as I say.

Soc: Dear Crito, your zeal is invaluable if right. If wrong, the greater the zeal, the greater the evil. Therefore we must consider whether these things should be done or not. I am, and always have been, someone who must be guided by reason, whatever the reason may be which, upon reflection, appears to me to be the best. Now that this misfortune has come upon me, I cannot put away my old beliefs. The principles I honored and revered I still honor and unless we can find other and better principles, I will not agree with you. I would not even if the power of the multitude could inflict many more imprisonments, confiscations and deaths, frightening us like children with foolish terrors.

What will be the best way of considering the question? Shall I return to your old argument about the opinions of men, some of which should be considered, and others, as we were saying, are not to be considered. Now were we right in maintaining this before I was condemned? And has the argument which was once good, now proved to be talk for the sake of talking—in fact an amusement only and altogether foolish? That is what I want to consider with your help, Crito: whether, under my present circumstances, the argument appears to be in any way different or not and is to be followed by me or abandoned. That argument, I believe, is held by many who claim to be authorities, was to the effect, that the opinions of some men are to be considered and of other men not to be considered. Now you, Crito, are not going to die tomorrow—at least, there is no probability of this. You are therefore not likely to be deceived by the circumstances in which you are placed. Tell me, then, whether I am right in saying that some opinions are to be valued and other opinions are not to be valued. I ask you whether I was right in believing this?

Cr: Certainly.

Soc: The good opinions are to be believed and not the bad?

Cr: Yes.

Soc: And the opinions of the wise are good and the opinions of the foolish are evil?

Cr: Certainly.

Soc: And what was said about another matter? Is the gymnastics student supposed to attend to the praise and blame and opinion of every man, or of one man only—his physician or trainer, whoever that is?

Cr: Of one man only.

Soc: And he should fear the blame and welcome praise of that one only, and not of the many?

Cr: That is clear.

Soc: He should live and train, eat and drink in the way which seems good to his single teacher who has understanding, rather than according to the opinion of all other men put together?

Cr: True.

Soc: And if he disobeys and rejects the opinion and approval of the one, and accepts the opinion of the many who have no understanding, will he not suffer evil?

Cr: Certainly he will.

Soc: And how will the evil affect the disobedient student?

Cr: Clearly, it will affect his body; that is what is destroyed by the evil.

Soc: Very good. Is this not true, Crito, of other things which we need not separately consider? In the matter of the just and unjust, the fair and foul, the good and evil, which are the subjects of our present discussion, should we follow the opinion of the many and fear them, or the opinion of the one man who has understanding? Is he the one we ought to fear and honor more than all the rest of the world? If we leave him, we shall destroy and injure that principle in us which may be assumed to be improved by justice and deteriorated by injustice? Is there not such a principle?

Cr: Certainly there is, Socrates.

Soc: Take a similar case. If, acting under the advice of men who have no understanding, we ruined what is improved by health and destroyed by disease—when the body has been destroyed, I say, would life be worth having?

Cr: Yes.

Soc: Could we live having an evil and corrupted body?

Cr: Certainly not.

Soc: And will life be worth having, if the soul is crippled, which is improved by justice and harmed by injustice? Do we suppose the soul to be inferior to the body?

Cr: Certainly not.

Soc: More important, then?

Cr: Far more important.

Soc: Then, my friend, we must not consider what the many say of us, but what he, the one man who has understanding of the just and unjust will say, and what the truth will say. Therefore you begin in error when you suggest we should consider the opinion of the many about the just and unjust, the good and evil, the honorable and dishonorable, but what if someone says, "But the many can kill us."

Cr: Yes, Socrates, that will clearly be the answer.

Soc: Still I believe our old argument is unshaken. I would like to know whether I may say the same of another proposition—that not life, but a good life, is to be chiefly valued?

Cr: Yes, that is also true.

Soc: And a good life is equivalent to a just and honorable one—that is also true?

Cr: Yes, that is true.

Soc: From these beliefs I am ready to consider whether I should or should not try to escape without the consent of the Athenians. If I am clearly right in escaping, then I will make the attempt, but if not, I will remain here. The other considerations which you mention, of money and loss of reputation and the duty of educating children, are, I fear, only the beliefs of the many, who would be as ready to bring people to life, if they were able, as they are to put them to death. The only question remaining to be considered is whether we shall do right escaping or allowing others to aid our escape and paying them money and thanks or whether we shall not do right. If the latter, then death or any other calamity which may result from my remaining here must not be allowed to influence us.

Cr: I think you are right, Socrates. But, how shall we proceed?

Soc: Let us consider the matter together and either refute me if you can and I will be convinced; or else cease, my dear friend, from repeating to me that I ought to escape against the wishes of the Athenians. I am extremely eager to be persuaded by you, but not against my own better judgment. And now please consider my first position and do your best to answer me.

Cr: I will do my best.

Soc: Are we to say we are never intentionally to do wrong, or that in one way we should and in another way we should not do wrong? Or is doing wrong always evil and dishonorable, as I was just now saying? Are all our former admissions to be thrown away because of these last few days? Have we, at our age, been earnestly discoursing with one another all our life long only to discover we are no better than children? Or, are we convinced in spite of the opinion of the many and in spite of consequences of the truth of what we said, that injustice is always an evil and dishonor to him who acts unjustly? Shall we agree to that?

Cr: Yes.

Soc: Then we must do no wrong?

Cr: Certainly not.

Soc: Nor when injured should we injure in return, as the many imagine. We must injure no one at all?

Cr: Clearly not.

Soc: Again, Crito, can we do evil?

Cr: Surely not, Socrates.

Soc: And what of doing evil in return for evil, which is the morality of the many—is that just or not?

Cr: Not just.

Soc: For doing evil to another is the same as injuring him.

Cr: Very true.

Soc: Then we ought not to retaliate or render evil for evil to any one, whatever evil we may have suffered from him. But I would have you consider, Crito, whether you really mean what you are saying. For this opinion has never been held, and never will be held, by many people. Those who are agreed and those who are not agreed upon this point have no common ground, and can only despise one another when they see how widely they differ. Tell me, then, whether you agree with my first principle, that neither injury nor retaliation nor returning evil for evil is ever right. Shall that be the premise of our argument? Or do you disagree? For this has been and still is my opinion; but, if you are of another opinion, let me hear what you have to say. If, however, you remain of the same mind as formerly, I will go to the next step.

Cr: You may proceed, for I have not changed my mind.

Soc: The next step may be put in the form of a question: Ought a man to do what he admits to be right, or ought he to betray the right?

Cr: He ought to do what he thinks right.

Soc: But if this is true, what is the application? In leaving the prison against the will of the Athenians, do I wrong anyone? Or do I wrong those whom I ought least to wrong? Do I abandon the principles which were acknowledged by us to be just. What do you say?

Cr: I cannot tell, Socrates, because I do not know.

Soc: Then consider the matter in this way— imagine I am about to escape, and the Laws and the State come and interrogate me: "Tell us, Socrates," they say, "what are you doing? Are you going to overturn us—the Laws and the State, as far as you are able? Do you imagine that a State can continue and not be overthrown, in which the decisions of Law have no power, but are set aside and overthrown by individuals?"

What will be our answer, Crito, to these and similar words? Anyone, and especially a clever orator, will have a good deal to say about the evil of setting aside the Law which requires a sentence to be carried out. We might reply, "Yes, but the State has injured us and given an unjust sentence." Suppose I say that?

Cr: Very good, Socrates.

Soc: "And was that our agreement with you?" the Law would say, "Or were you to abide by the sentence of the State?" And if I was surprised at their saying this, the Law would probably add: "Answer, Socrates, instead of opening your eyes: you are in the habit of asking and answering questions. Tell us what complaint you have against us which justifies you in attempting to destroy us and the State? In the first place did we not bring you into existence? Your father married your mother by our aid and conceived you. Say whether you have any objection against those of us who regulate marriage?" None, I should reply. "Or against those of us who regulate the system of care and education of children in which you were trained? Were not the Laws, who have the charge of this, right in commanding your father to train you in the arts and exercise?" Yes, I should reply.

"Well then, since you were brought into the world, nurtured and educated by us, can you deny in the first place that you are our child and slave, as your fathers were before you? And if this is true you are not on equal terms with us. Nor can you think you have a right to do to us what we are doing to you. Would you have any right to strike or do any other evil to a father or to your master, if you had one, when you have been struck or received some other evil at his hands? And because we think it is right to destroy you, do you think that you have any right to destroy us in return, and your country so far as you are able? And will you, O expounder of virtue, say you are justified in this? Has a philosopher like you failed to discover your country is more to be valued and higher and holier by far than mother and father or any ancestor, and more regarded in the eyes of the gods and of men of understanding? It should be soothed and gently and reverently entreated when angry, even more than a father, and if not persuaded, it should be obeyed. And when we are punished by the State, whether with imprisonment or whipping, the punishment is to be endured in silence. If the State leads us to wounds or death in battle, we follow as is right; no one can yield or leave his rank, but whether in battle or in a court of law, or in any other place, he must do what his city and his country order him. Or, he must change their view of what is just. If he may do no violence to his father or mother, much less may he do violence to his country." What answer shall we make to this, Crito? Do the Laws speak truly, or do they not?

Cr: I think that they do.

Soc: Then the Laws will say: "Consider, Socrates, if this is true, that in your present attempt you are going to do us wrong. For, after having brought you into the world, nurtured and educated you, and given you and every other citizen a share in every good we had to give, we further give the right to every Athenian, if he does not like us when he has come of age and has seen the ways of the city, he may go wherever else he pleases and take his goods with him. None of us Laws will forbid or interfere with him. Any of you who does not like us and the city, and who wants to go to a colony or to any other city, may go where he likes, and take his possessions with him. But he who has experience of the way we order justice and administer the State, and still remains, has entered into an implied contract to do as we command him. He who disobeys us is, as we maintain, triply wrong; first, because in disobeying us he is disobeying his parents; second, because we are the authors of his education; third, because he has made an agreement with us that he will duly obey our commands. He neither obeys them nor convinces us our commands are wrong. We do not rudely impose our commands but give each person the alternative of obeying or convincing us. That is what we offer and he does neither. These are the sort of accusations to which, as we were saying, Socrates, you will be exposed if you do as you were intending; you, above all other Athenians."

Suppose I ask, why is this? They will justly answer that I above all other men have acknowledged the agreement.

"There is clear proof," they will say, "Socrates, that we and the city were not displeasing to you. Of all Athenians you have been the most constant resident in the city, which, as you never leave, you appear to love. You never went out of the city either to see the games, except once when you went to the Isthmus, or to any other place unless you were on military service; nor did you travel as other men do. Nor had you any curiosity to know other States or their Laws: Your affections did not go beyond us and our State; we were your special favorites and you agreed in our government of you. This is the State in which you conceived your children, which is a proof of your satisfaction. Moreover, you might, if you wished, have fixed the penalty at banishment in the course of the trial—the State which refuses to let you go now would have let you go then. You pretended you preferred death to exile and that you were not grieved at death. And now you have forgotten these fine sentiments and pay no respect to us, the Laws, who you destroy. You are doing what only a miserable slave would do, running away and turning your back upon the agreements which you made as a citizen. First of all, answer this very question: Are we right in saying you agreed to be governed according to us in deed, and not in word only? Is that true or not?"

How shall we answer that, Crito? Must we not agree?

Cr: We must, Socrates.

Soc: Then will the Laws say: "You, Socrates, are breaking the agreements which you made with us at your leisure, not in any haste or under any compulsion or deception, but having had 70 years to think of them, during which time you were at liberty to leave the city, if we were not to your liking, or if our covenants appeared to you to be unfair. You might have gone either to Lacedaemon or Crete, which you often praise for their good government, or to some other Hellenic or foreign state. You, above all other Athenians, seemed to be so fond of the State and of us, her Laws, that you never left her. The lame, the blind, the maimed were not more stationary in the State than you were. Now you run away and forsake your agreements. Now, Socrates, if you will take our advice; do not make yourself ridiculous by escaping out of the city.

"Just consider, if you do evil in this way, what good will you do either yourself or your friends? That your friends will be driven into exile and lose their citizenship, or will lose their property, is reasonably certain. You yourself, if you fly to one of the neighboring cities, like Thebes or Megara, both of which are well-governed cities, will come to them as an enemy, Socrates. Their government will be against you and all patriotic citizens will cast suspicious eye upon you as a destroyer of the laws. You will confirm in the minds of the judges the justice of their own condemnation of you. For he who is a corruptor of the laws is more than likely to be corruptor of the young. Will you then flee from well-ordered cities and virtuous men? Is existence worth having on these terms? Or will you go to these cities without shame and talk to them, Socrates? And what will you say to them? Will you say what you say here about virtue, justice, institutions and laws being the best things among men? Would that be decent of you? Surely not.

"If you go away from well-governed states to Crito's friends in Thessaly, where there is a great disorder and immorality, they will be charmed to have the tale of your escape from prison, set off with ludicrous particulars of the manner in which you were wrapped in a goatskin or some other disguise and metamorphosed as the fashion of runaways is—that is very likely. But will there be no one to remind you in your old age you violated the most sacred laws from a miserable desire of a little more life. Perhaps not, if you keep them in a good temper. But if they are angry you will hear many degrading things; you will live, but how? As the flatterer of all men, and the servant of all men. And doing what? Eating and drinking in Thessaly, having gone abroad in order that you may get a dinner. Where will your fine sentiments about justice and virtue be then? Say that you wish to live for the sake of your children, that you may bring them up and educate them—will you take them into Thessaly and deprive them of Athenian citizenship? Is that the benefit which you would confer upon them? Or are you under the impression that they will be better cared for and educated here if you are still alive, although absent from them because your friends will take care of them? Do you think if you are an inhabitant of Thessaly they will take care of them, and if you are an inhabitant of the other world they will not take care of them? No, if they who call themselves friends are truly friends, they surely will.

"Listen, then, Socrates, to us who have brought you up. Think not of life and children first, and of justice afterwards, but of justice first, that you may be justified before the rulers of the other world. For neither will you nor your children be happier or holier in this life, or happier in another, if you do as Crito bids. Now you depart in innocence, a sufferer and not a doer of evil; a victim, not of the Laws, but of men. But if you escape, returning evil for evil and injury for injury, breaking the agreements which you have made with us, and wronging those whom you ought least to wrong, that is to say, yourself, your friends, your country, and us, we shall be angry with you while you live. Our brethren, the Laws in the other world, will receive you as an enemy because they will know you have done your best to destroy us. Listen, then, to us and not to Crito."

This is the voice which I seem to hear murmuring in my ears, like the sound of a divine flute in the ears of the mystic. That voice, I say, is humming in my ears and prevents me from hearing any other. I know anything more which you may say will be useless. Yet speak, if you have anything to say.

Cr: I have nothing to say, Socrates.

Soc: Then let me follow what seems to be the will of the gods.

Suggestions for Further Reading

See John Locke's *Two Treatises on Government* (originally published in 1689; available in a critical edition, edited by Peter Laslett (Cambridge: Cambridge University Press, 1963), for a classic treatment of the issues of political authority, the justification of property and punishment, the social contract theory, and the idea of tacit consent.

Society and the Individual: Readings in Political and Social Philosophy, edited by Richard T. Garner and Andrew Oldenquist (Belmont, CA: Wadsworth, 1990), provides a good selection of texts on issues of liberty, equality, and authority.

At http://classics.mit.edu/Plato/crito.html you will find the text of the *Crito* as well as comments by readers. You can even add your own interpretation for others to read.

Video

The Trial of Socrates (29 minutes) covers both the trial and death of Socrates, including material from the *Crito,* and is available from Insight Media, 2162 Broadway, New York, NY 10024.

5.6 Civil Disobedience

Are there times when disobeying the law is morally justified? What are the responsibilities of a citizen? The dialogue *Crito* raised these issues, but in one way or another we have been asking these questions whenever the issue of governmental authority has arisen. The issue of civil disobedience also raises fundamental questions about the rule of law. Why do we need laws?

A case against the rule of law might go something like this: Laws limit human freedom and hinder spontaneity; they are sometimes unfair and repressive; common sense, social custom, and religion already provide enough guidance; and morality can never be legislated.

Many of course believe that the rule of law is both good and necessary. Laws protect people, create social stability, and provide opportunities to develop rights that people might not otherwise enjoy. The rights to life, liberty, and the pursuit of happiness need to be protected and defined by laws. In pluralistic societies, we cannot depend on customs and traditions to unite people. Nor can we depend on the virtue and goodwill of our leaders.

Only the rule of law can prevent abuse of power, but how can we tell the difference between good laws and bad laws? Are there minimal conditions for good laws? We might argue that good laws guarantee access to the resources necessary to live, provide for enforcement of contracts, and give security from violence. Such laws should be fairly enforced, adjudicated in courts free from prejudice, provide for due process, and be free from vagueness and ambiguity. Should we also add that the right of civil disobedience be granted, or would such a right undermine entirely the rule of law?

Civil disobedience has played and continues to play a major role in effecting political and legal change. In the nineteenth century, Henry David Thoreau went to jail for refusing to pay taxes to a government that supported slavery. He argued that conscience constitutes a higher law than the law of any land. We all have a moral duty to obey our consciences, but how many of us are willing to pay the legal penalty for disobeying the law?

Civil disobedience became a political strategy in many nations in the twentieth century. Gandhi used it to liberate India from British colonial rule. He carried a copy of Thoreau's *On Civil Disobedience* with him and used it as a blueprint for nonviolent resistance. Nelson Mandela used civil disobedience to change the apartheid system of South Africa. But when does civil disobedience become political revolution? When violence is used? Must one be willing to suffer the consequences of breaking the law in order to engage in a morally justifiable act of civil disobedience? Is *uncivil* disobedience morally justified? What makes disobedience civil rather than uncivil?

Martin Luther King, Jr. (1929–1968), a Baptist minister and winner of the Nobel Peace Prize, devoted his life to the struggle for racial justice in the United States. Like Thoreau and Gandhi, he argued for nonviolent methods. As a result, he found himself opposing those African Americans who did advocate the use of violence. He died from an assassin's bullet in Memphis, Tennessee.

A year before he won the Nobel Peace Prize and five years before his death, he served a sentence in the Birmingham, Alabama, jail for participating in a civil rights demonstration. Eight prominent Alabama clergy wrote an open letter critical of King's methods. In his famous "Letter from Birmingham Jail," King responds to their criticisms and, in the process, writes a moving justification of civil disobedience.

In light of the first selection in this chapter (Section 5.2) on ideas of justice in Islam, it is interesting to note the role that a religious conception of justice plays in King's argument and the role of religious institutions in promoting or retarding racial justice in the United States. Some people often appeal to notions of a "higher law" that is explicitly linked to God when they engage in social criticism and reform.

Reading Questions

1. Do you agree with King's claim that "injustice anywhere is a threat to justice everywhere"? Why, or why not?
2. Do you think groups are more immoral than individuals? Why?
3. What are the differences, according to King, between unjust laws and just laws? Are all the differences compatible? For example, could not a law code passed and obeyed by the majority that respects the rights of the minority be unjust in the sense that it is not in harmony with God's law? Can you think of an example?
4. Under what conditions is it permissible, according to King, to break the law? Do you agree? Why?
5. According to King, what is the purpose of law and order? Do you agree?
6. According to King, what is the proper role of the Christian Church with respect to issues of social justice? Do you think he is right? Why, or why not?

7. Write a brief letter in response to King from the point of view of the clergy who originally criticized him.
8. How do you think King would answer the question, "What makes a society just?"

Letter from Birmingham Jail

MARTIN LUTHER KING, JR.

MY DEAR FELLOW CLERGYMEN,
While confined here in the Birmingham city jail, I came across your recent statement calling our present activities "unwise and untimely." Seldom, if ever, do I pause to answer criticism of my work and ideas. If I sought to answer all of the criticisms that cross my desk, my secretaries would be engaged in little else in the course of the day, and I would have no time for constructive work. But since I feel that you are men of genuine good will and your criticisms are sincerely set forth, I would like to answer your statement in what I hope will be patient and reasonable terms.

I think I should give the reason for my being in Birmingham, since you have been influenced by the argument of "outsiders coming in." I have the honor of serving as president of the Southern Christian Leadership Conference, an organization operating in every southern state, with headquarters in Atlanta, Georgia. We have some 85 affiliate organizations all across the South— one being the Alabama Christian Movement for Human Rights. Whenever necessary and possible we share staff, educational and financial resources with our affiliates. Several months ago our local affiliate here in Birmingham invited us to be on call to engage in a nonviolent direct-action program if such were deemed necessary. We readily consented and when the hour came we lived up to our promises. So I am here, along with several members of my staff, because we were invited here. I am here because I have basic organizational ties here.

Beyond this, I am in Birmingham because injustice is here. Just as the eighth century prophets left their little villages and carried their "thus saith the Lord" far beyond the boundaries of their hometowns; and just as the Apostle Paul left his little village of Tarsus and carried the gospel of Jesus Christ to practically every hamlet and city of the Graeco-Roman world, I too am compelled to carry the gospel of freedom beyond my particular hometown. Like Paul, I must constantly respond to the Macedonian call for aid.

Moreover, I am cognizant of the interrelatedness of all communities and states. I cannot sit idly by in Atlanta and not be concerned about what happens in Birmingham. Injustice anywhere is a threat to justice everywhere. We are caught in an inescapable network of mutuality, tied in a single garment of destiny. Whatever affects one directly affects all indirectly. Never again can we afford to live with the narrow, provincial "outside agitator" idea. Anyone who lives in the United States can never be considered an outsider anywhere in this country.

You deplore the demonstrations that are presently taking place in Birmingham. But I am sorry that your statement did not express a similar concern for the conditions that brought the demonstrations into being. I am sure that each of you would want to go beyond the superficial social analyst who looks merely at effects, and does not grapple with underlying causes. I would not hesitate to say that it is unfortunate that so-called demonstrations are taking place in Birmingham at this time, but I would say in more emphatic terms that it is even more unfortunate that the white power structure of this city left the Negro community with no other alternative.

In any nonviolent campaign there are four basic steps: (1) collection of the facts to determine whether injustices are alive, (2) negotiation, (3) self-purification, and (4) direct action. We have gone through all of these steps in Birmingham. There can be no gainsaying of the fact that racial injustice engulfs this community.

Birmingham is probably the most thoroughly segregated city in the United States. Its ugly record of police brutality is known in every section of this country. Its unjust treatment of Negroes in the courts is a notorious reality. There have been more unsolved bombings of Negro homes and churches in Birmingham than any city in this nation. These are the hard, brutal and unbelievable facts. On the basis of these conditions Negro leaders sought to negotiate with the city fathers. But the political leaders consistently refused to engage in good faith negotiation.

Then came the opportunity last September to talk with some of the leaders of the economic community. In these negotiating sessions certain promises were made by the merchants—such as the promise to remove the humiliating racial signs from the stores. On the basis of these promises Rev. Shuttlesworth and the leaders of the Alabama Christian Movement for Human Rights agreed to call a moratorium on any type of demonstrations. As the weeks and months unfolded we realized that we were the victims of a broken promise. The signs remained. Like so many experiences of the past we were confronted with blasted hopes, and the dark shadow of a deep disappointment settled upon us. So we had no alternative except that of preparing for direct action, whereby we would present our very bodies as a means of laying our case before the conscience of the local and national community. We were not unmindful of the difficulties involved.

So we decided to go through a process of self-purification. We started having workshops on nonviolence and repeatedly asked ourselves the questions, "Are you able to accept blows without retaliating?" "Are you able to endure the ordeals of jail?" We decided to set our direct-action program around the Easter season, realizing that with the exception of Christmas, this was the largest shopping period of the year. Knowing that a strong economic withdrawal program would be the by-product of direct action, we felt that this was the best time to bring pressure on the merchants for the needed changes. Then it occurred to us that the March election was ahead and so we speedily decided to postpone action until after election day. When we discovered that Mr. Connor was in the run-off, we decided again to postpone action so that the demonstrations could not be used to cloud the issues. At this time we agreed to begin our nonviolent witness the day after the run-off.

This reveals that we did not move irresponsibly into direct action. We, too, wanted to see Mr. Connor defeated; so we went through postponement after postponement to aid in this community need. After this we felt that direct action could be delayed no longer.

You may well ask, "Why direct action? Why sit-ins, marches, etc.? Isn't negotiation a better path?" You are exactly right in your call for negotiation. Indeed, this is the purpose of direct action. Nonviolent direct action seeks to create such a crisis and establish such creative tension that a community that has constantly refused to negotiate is forced to confront the issue. It seeks so to dramatize the issue that it can no longer be ignored. I just referred to the creation of tension as a part of the work of the nonviolent resister. This may sound rather shocking. But I must confess that I am not afraid of the word tension. I have earnestly worked and preached against violent tension, but there is a type of constructive nonviolent tension that is necessary for growth. Just as Socrates felt that it was necessary to create a tension in the mind so that individuals could rise from the bondage of myths and half-truths to the unfettered realm of creative analysis and objective appraisal, we must see the need of having nonviolent gadflies to create the kind of tension in society that will help men to rise from the dark depths of prejudice and racism to the majestic heights of understanding and brotherhood. So the purpose of the direct action is to create a situation so crisis-packed that it will inevitably open the door to negotiation. We, therefore, concur with you in your call for negotiation. Too long has our beloved Southland been bogged down in the tragic attempt to live in monologue rather than dialogue.

One of the basic points in your statement is that our acts are untimely. Some have asked, "Why didn't you give the new administration time to act?" The only answer that I can give to this inquiry is that the new administration must be prodded about as much as the outgoing one before it acts. We will be sadly mistaken if we feel that the election of Mr. Boutwell will bring the millennium to Birmingham. While Mr. Boutwell is much more articulate and gentle than Mr. Connor, they are both segregationists, dedicated to the task of maintaining the status quo. The hope I see in Mr. Boutwell is that he will be reasonable enough to see the futility of massive resistance to desegregation. But he will not see this without pressure from the devotees of civil rights. My friends, I must say to you that we have not made a single gain in civil rights without determined legal and nonviolent pressure. History is the long and tragic story of the fact that privileged groups seldom give up their privileges voluntarily. Individuals may see the moral light and voluntarily give up their unjust posture; but as Reinhold Niebuhr has reminded us, groups are more immoral than individuals.

We know through painful experience that freedom is never voluntarily given by the oppressor; it must be demanded by the oppressed. Frankly, I have never yet engaged in a direct action movement that was "well-timed," according to the timetable of those who have not suffered unduly from the disease of segregation. For years now I have heard the words "Wait!" It rings in the ear of every Negro with a piercing familiarity. This "Wait" has almost always meant "Never." It has been a tranquilizing thalidomide, relieving the emotional stress for a mo-ment, only to give birth to an ill-formed infant of frustration. We must come to see with the distinguished jurist of yesterday that "justice too long delayed is justice denied." We have waited for more than 340 years for our constitutional and God-given rights. The nations of Asia and Africa are moving with jetlike speed toward the goal of political independence, and we still creep at horse and buggy pace toward the gaining of a cup of coffee at a lunch counter. I guess it is easy for those who have never felt the stinging darts of segregation to say, "Wait." But when you have seen vicious mobs lynch your mothers and fathers at will and drown your sisters and brothers at whim; when you have seen hate-filled policemen curse, kick, brutalize and even kill your black brothers and sisters with impunity; when you see the vast majority of your twenty million Negro brothers smothering in an airtight cage of poverty in the midst of an affluent society; when you suddenly find your tongue twisted and your speech stammering as you seek to explain to your six-year-old daughter why she can't go to the public amusement park that has just been advertised on television, and see tears welling up in her little eyes when she is told that Funtown is closed to colored children, and see the depressing clouds of inferiority begin to form in her little mental sky, and see her begin to distort her little personality by unconsciously developing a bitterness toward white people; when you have to concoct an answer for a five-year-old son asking in agonizing pathos: "Daddy, why do white people treat colored people so mean?"; when you take a cross-country drive and find it necessary to sleep night after night in the uncomfortable corners of your automobile because no motel will accept you; when you are humiliated day in and day out by nagging signs reading "white" and "colored"; when your first name becomes "nigger" and your middle name becomes "boy" (however old you are) and your last name becomes "John," and when your wife and mother are never given the respected title "Mrs."; when you are harried by day and haunted by night by the fact that you are a Negro, living constantly at tiptoe stance never quite knowing what to expect next, and plagued with inner fears and outer resentments; when you are forever fighting a degenerating sense of "nobodiness"; then you will understand why we find it difficult to wait. There comes a time when the cup of endurance runs over, and men are no longer willing to be plunged into an abyss of injustice where they experience the blackness of corroding despair. I hope, sirs, you can understand our legitimate and unavoidable impatience.

You express a great deal of anxiety over our willingness to break laws. This is certainly a legitimate concern. Since we so diligently urge people to obey the Supreme Court's decision of 1954 outlawing segregation in the public schools, it is rather strange and paradoxical to find us consciously breaking laws. One may well ask, "How can you advocate breaking some laws and obeying others?" The answer is found in the fact that there are two types of laws: there are *just* and there are *unjust* laws. I would agree with Saint Augustine that "An unjust law is no law at all."

Now what is the difference between the two? How does one determine when a law is just or unjust? A just law is a man-made code that squares with the moral law or the law of God. An unjust law is a code that is out of harmony with the moral law. To put it in the terms of Saint Thomas Aquinas, an unjust law is a human law that is not rooted in eternal and natural law. Any law that uplifts human personality is just. Any law that degrades human personality is unjust. All segregation statutes are unjust because segregation distorts the soul and damages the personality. It gives the segregator a false sense of superiority, and the segregated a false sense of inferiority. To use the words of Martin Buber, the great Jewish philosopher, segregation substitutes an "I–it" relationship for the "I–thou" relationship, and ends up relegating persons to the status of things. So segregation is not only politically, economically and sociologically unsound, but it is morally wrong and sinful. Paul Tillich has said that sin is separation. Isn't segregation an existential expression of man's tragic separation, an expression of his awful estrangement, his terrible sinfulness? So I can urge men to disobey segregation ordinances because they are morally wrong.

Let us turn to a more concrete example of just and unjust laws. An unjust law is a code that a majority inflicts on a minority that is not binding on itself. This is difference made legal. On the other hand a just law is a code that a majority compels a minority to follow that it is willing to follow itself. This is sameness made legal.

Let me give another explanation. An unjust law is a code inflicted upon a minority which that minority had no part in enacting or creating because they did not have the unhampered right to vote. Who can say that the legislature of Alabama which set up the segregation laws was democratically elected? Throughout the state of Alabama all types of conniving methods are used to prevent Negroes from becoming registered voters and there are some counties without a single Negro registered to vote despite the fact that the Negro constitutes a majority of the population. Can any law set up in such a state be considered democratically structured?

These are just a few examples of unjust and just laws. There are some instances when a law is just on its face and unjust in its application. For instance, I was arrested Friday on a charge of parading without a permit. Now there is nothing wrong with an ordinance which requires a permit for a parade, but when the ordinance is used to preserve segregation and to deny citizens the First Amendment privilege of peaceful assembly and peaceful protest, then it becomes unjust.

I hope you can see the distinction I am trying to point out. In no sense do I advocate evading or defying the law as the rabid segregationist would do. This would lead to anarchy. One who breaks an unjust law must do it *openly, lovingly* (not hatefully as the white mothers did in New Orleans when they were seen on television screaming, "nigger, nigger, nigger"), and with a willingness to accept the penalty. I submit that an individual who breaks a law that conscience tells him is unjust, and willingly accepts the penalty by staying in jail to arouse the conscience of the community over its injustice, is in reality expressing the very highest respect for law.

Of course, there is nothing new about this kind of civil disobedience. It was seen sublimely in the refusal of Shadrach, Meshach and Abednego to obey the laws of Nebuchadnezzar because a higher moral law was involved. It was practiced superbly by the early Christians who were willing to face hungry lions and the excruciating pain of chopping blocks, before submitting to certain unjust laws of the Roman Empire. To a degree academic freedom is a reality today because Socrates practiced civil disobedience.

We can never forget that everything Hitler did in Germany was "legal" and everything the Hungarian freedom fighters did in Hungary was "illegal." It was "illegal" to aid and comfort a Jew in Hitler's Germany. But I am sure that if I had lived in Germany during that time I would have aided and comforted my Jewish brothers even though it was illegal. If I lived in a Communist country today where certain principles dear to the Christian faith are suppressed, I believe I would openly advocate disobeying these antireligious laws. I must make two honest confessions to you, my Christian and Jewish brothers. First, I must confess that over the last few years I have been gravely disappointed with the white moderate. I have almost reached the regrettable conclusion that the Negro's great stumbling block in the stride toward freedom is not the White Citizen's Councieler or the Ku Klux Klanner, but the white moderate who is more devoted to "order" than to justice; who prefers a negative peace which is the absence of tension to a positive peace which is the presence of justice; who constantly says, "I agree with you in the goal you seek, but I can't agree with your methods of direct action"; who paternalistically feels that he can set the timetable for another man's freedom; who lives by the myth of time and who constantly advised the Negro to wait until a "more convenient season." Shallow understanding from people of good will is more frustrating than absolute misunderstanding from people of ill will. Lukewarm acceptance is much more bewildering than outright rejection.

I had hoped that the white moderate would understand that law and order exist for the purpose of establishing justice, and that when they fail to do this they become dangerously structured dams that block the flow of social progress.

I had hoped that the white moderate would understand that the present tension of the South is merely a necessary phase of the transition from an obnoxious negative peace, where the Negro passively accepted his unjust plight, to a substance-filled positive peace, where all men will respect the dignity and worth of human personality. Actually, we who engage in nonviolent direct action are not the creators of tension. We merely bring to the surface the hidden tension that is already alive. We bring it out in the open where it can be seen and dealt with. Like a boil that can never be cured as long as it is covered up but must be opened with all its pus-flowing ugliness to the natural medicines of air and light, injustice must likewise be exposed, with all of the tension its exposing creates, to the light of human conscience and the air of national opinion before it can be cured.

In your statement you asserted that our actions, even though peaceful, must be condemned because they precipitate violence. But can this assertion be logically made? Isn't this like condemning the robbed man because his possession of money precipitated the evil act of robbery? Isn't this like condemning Socrates because his unswerving commitment to truth and his philosophical delvings precipitated the misguided popular mind to make him drink the hemlock? Isn't this like condemning Jesus because His unique God-consciousness and never-ceasing devotion to His will precipitated the evil act of crucifixion? We must come to see, as federal courts have consistently affirmed, that it is immoral to urge an individual to withdraw his efforts to gain his basic constitutional rights because the quest precipitates violence. Society must protect the robbed and punish the robber.

I had also hoped that the white moderate would reject the myth of time. I received a letter this morning from a white brother in Texas which said: "All Christians know that the colored people will receive equal rights eventually, but it is possible that you are in too great of a religious hurry. It has taken Christianity almost two thousand years to accomplish what it has. The teachings of Christ take time to come to earth." All that is said here grows out of a tragic misconception of time. It is the strangely irrational notion that there is something in the very flow of time that will inevitably cure all ills. Actually time is neutral. It can be used either destructively or constructively. I am coming to feel that the people of ill will have used time much more effectively than the people of good will. We will have to repent in this generation not merely for the vitriolic words and actions of the bad people, but for the appalling silence of the good people. We must come to see that human progress never rolls in on wheels of inevitability. It comes through the tireless efforts and persistent work of men willing to be co-workers with God, and without this hard work time itself becomes an ally of the forces of social stagnation. We must use time creatively, and forever realize that the time is always ripe to do right. Now is the time to make real the promise of democracy, and transform our pending national elegy into a creative psalm of brotherhood. Now is the time to lift our national policy from the quicksand of racial injustice to the solid rock of human dignity.

You spoke of our activity in Birmingham as extreme. At first I was rather disappointed that fellow clergymen would see my nonviolent efforts as those of the extremist. I started thinking about the fact that I stand in the middle of two opposing forces in the Negro community. One is a force of complacency made up of Negroes who, as a result of long years of oppression, have been so completely drained of self-respect and a sense of "somebodiness" that they have adjusted to segregation, and, of a few Negroes in the middle class who, because of a degree of academic and economic security, and because at points they profit by segregation, have unconsciously become insensitive to the problems of the masses. The other force is one of bitterness and hatred, and comes perilously close to advocating violence. It is expressed in the various black nationalist groups that are springing up over the nation, the largest and best known being Elijah Muhammad's Muslim movement. This movement is nourished by the contemporary frustration over the continued existence of racial discrimination. It is made up of people who have lost faith in America, who have absolutely repudiated Christianity, and who have concluded that the white man is an incurable "devil." I have tried to stand between these two forces, saying that we need not follow the "do-nothingism" of the complacent or the hatred and despair of the black nationalist. There is the more excellent way of love and nonviolent protest. I'm grateful to God that, through the Negro church, the dimension of nonviolence entered our struggle. If this philosophy had not emerged, I am convinced that by now many streets of the South would be flowing with floods of blood. And I am further convinced that if our white brothers dismiss us as "rabble-rousers" and "outside agitators" those of us who are working through the channels of nonviolent direct action and refuse to support our nonviolent efforts, millions of Negroes, out of frustration and despair, will seek solace and security in black nationalist ideologies, a development that will lead inevitably to a frightening racial nightmare.

Oppressed people cannot remain oppressed forever. The urge for freedom will eventually come. This is what happened to the American Negro. Something within has reminded him of his birthright of freedom; something without has reminded him that he can gain it. Consciously and unconsciously, he has been swept in by what the Germans call the *Zeitgeist,* and with his black brothers of Africa, and his brown and yellow brothers of Asia, South America and the Caribbean, he is moving with a sense of cosmic urgency toward the promised land of racial justice. Recognizing this vital urge that has engulfed the Negro community, one should readily understand public demonstrations. The Negro has many pent-up resentments and latent frustrations. He has to get them out. So let him march sometime; let him have his prayer pilgrimages to the city hall; understand why he must have sit-ins and freedom rides. If his repressed emotions do not come out in these nonviolent ways, they will come out in ominous expressions of violence. This is not a threat; it is a fact of history. So I have not said to my people "get rid of your discontent." But I have tried to say that this normal and healthy discontent can be channelized through the creative outlet of nonviolent direct action. Now this approach is being dismissed as extremist. I must admit that I was initially disappointed in being so categorized.

But as I continued to think about the matter, I gradually gained a bit of satisfaction from being considered an extremist. Was not Jesus an extremist in love—"Love your enemies, bless them that curse you, pray for them that despitefully use you." Was not Amos an extremist for justice—"Let justice roll down like waters and righteousness like a mighty stream." Was not Paul an extremist for the gospel of Jesus Christ—"I bear in my body the marks of the Lord Jesus." Was not Martin Luther an extremist—"Here I stand; I can do none other so help me God." Was not John Bunyan an extremist—"I will stay in jail to the end of my days before I make a butchery of my conscience." Was not Abraham Lincoln an extremist—"This nation cannot survive half slave and half free." Was not Thomas Jefferson an extremist—"We hold these truths to be self-evident, that all men are created equal." So the question is not whether we will be extremist but what kind of extremist will we be. Will we be extremists for hate or will we be extremists for love? Will we be extremists for the preservation of injustice—or will we be extremists for the cause of justice? In that dramatic scene on Calvary's hill, three men were crucified. We must not forget that all three were crucified for the same crime—the crime of extremism. Two were extremists for immorality, and thusly fell below their environment. The other, Jesus Christ, was an extremist for love, truth and goodness, and thereby rose above his environment. So, after all, maybe the South, the nation and the world are in dire need of creative extremists.

I had hoped that the white moderate would see this. Maybe I was too optimistic. Maybe I expected too much. I guess I should have realized that few members of a race that has oppressed another race can understand or appreciate the deep groans and passionate yearnings of those that have been oppressed and still fewer have the vision to see that injustice must be rooted out by strong, persistent and determined action. I am thankful, however, that some of our white broth-

ers have grasped the meaning of this social revolution and committed themselves to it. They are still all too small in quantity, but they are big in quality. Some like Ralph McGill, Lillian Smith, Harry Golden and James Dabbs have written about our struggle in eloquent, prophetic and understanding terms. Others have marched with us down nameless streets of the South. They have languished in filthy roach-infested jails, suffering the abuse and brutality of angry policemen who see them as "dirty nigger-lovers." They, unlike so many of their moderate brothers and sisters, have recognized the urgency of the moment and sensed the need for powerful "action" antidotes to combat the disease of segregation.

Let me rush on to mention my other disappointment. I have been so greatly disappointed with the white church and its leadership. Of course, there are some notable exceptions. I am not unmindful of the fact that each of you has taken some significant stands on this issue. I commend you, Rev. Stallings, for your Christian stance on this past Sunday, in welcoming Negroes to your worship service on a non-segregated basis. I commend the Catholic leaders of this state for integrating Springhill College several years ago.

But despite these notable exceptions I must honestly reiterate that I have been disappointed with the church. I do not say that as one of the negative critics who can always find something wrong with the church. I say it as a minister of the gospel, who loves the church; who was nurtured in its bosom; who has been sustained by its spiritual blessings and who will remain true to it as long as the cord of life shall lengthen.

I had the strange feeling when I was suddenly catapulted into the leadership of the bus protest in Montgomery several years ago that we would have the support of the white church. I felt that the white ministers, priests and rabbis of the South would be some of our strongest allies. Instead, some have been outright opponents, refusing to understand the freedom movement and misrepresenting its leaders; all too many others have been more cautious than courageous and have remained silent behind the anesthetizing security of the stained-glass windows.

In spite of my shattered dreams of the past, I came to Birmingham with the hope that the white religious leadership of this community would see the justice of our cause, and with deep moral concern, serve as the channel through which our just grievances would get to the power structure. I had hoped that each of you would understand. But again I have been disappointed. I have heard numerous religious leaders of the South call upon their worshippers to comply with a desegregation decision because it is the *law,* but I have longed to hear white ministers say, "Follow this decree because integration is morally *right* and the Negro is your brother." In the midst of blatant injustices inflicted upon the Negro, I have watched white churches stand on the sideline and merely mouth pious irrelevancies and sanctimonious trivialities. In the midst of a mighty struggle to rid our nation of racial and economic injustice, I have heard so many ministers say, "Those are social issues with which the gospel has no real concern," and I have watched so many churches commit themselves to a completely otherworldly religion which made a strange distinction between body and soul, the sacred and the secular.

So here we are moving toward the exit of the twentieth century with a religious community largely adjusted to the status quo, standing as a taillight behind other community agencies rather than a headlight leading men to higher levels of justice.

I have traveled the length and breadth of Alabama, Mississippi and all the other southern states. On sweltering summer days and crisp autumn mornings I have looked at her beautiful churches with their lofty spires pointing heavenward. I have beheld the impressive outlay of her massive religious education buildings. Over and over again I have found myself asking: "What kind of people worship here? Who is their God? Where were their voices when the lips of Governor Barnett dripped with words of interposition and nullification? Where were they when Governor Wallace gave the clarion call for defiance and hatred? Where were their voices of support when tired, bruised and weary Negro men and women

decided to rise from the dark dungeons of complacency to the bright hills of creative protest?"

Yes, these questions are still in my mind. In deep disappointment, I have wept over the laxity of the church. But be assured that my tears have been tears of love. There can be no deep disappointment where there is not deep love. Yes, I love the church; I love her sacred walls. How could I do otherwise? I am in the rather unique position of being the son, the grandson and the great-grandson of preachers. Yes, I see the church as the body of Christ. But, oh! How we have blemished and scarred that body through social neglect and fear of being nonconformists.

There was a time when the church was very powerful. It was during that period when the early Christians rejoiced when they were deemed worthy to suffer for what they believed. In those days the church was not merely a thermometer that recorded the ideas and principles of popular opinion; it was a thermostat that transformed the mores of society. Wherever the early Christians entered a town the power structure got disturbed and immediately sought to convict them for being "disturbers of the peace" and "outside agitators." But they went on with the conviction that they were "a colony of heaven," and had to obey God rather than man. They were small in number but big in commitment. They were too God-intoxicated to be "astronomically intimidated." They brought an end to such ancient evils as infanticide and gladiatorial contest.

Things are different now. The contemporary church is often a weak, ineffectual voice with an uncertain sound. It is so often the arch-supporter of the status quo. Far from being disturbed by the presence of the church, the power structure of the average community is consoled by the church's silent and often vocal sanction of things as they are.

But the judgment of God is upon the church as never before. If the church of today does not recapture the sacrificial spirit of the early church, it will lose its authentic ring, forfeit the loyalty of millions, and be dismissed as an irrelevant social club with no meaning for the twentieth century. I am meeting young people every day whose disappointment with the church has risen to outright disgust.

Maybe again, I have been too optimistic. Is organized religion too inextricably bound to the status quo to save our nation and the world? Maybe I must turn my faith to the inner spiritual church, the church within the church, as the true *ecclesia* and the hope of the world. But again I am thankful to God that some noble souls from the ranks of organized religion have broken loose from the paralyzing chains of conformity and joined us as active partners in the struggle for freedom. They have left their secure congregations and walked the streets of Albany, Georgia, with us. They have gone through the highways of the South on tortuous rides for freedom. Yes, they have gone to jail with us. Some have been kicked out of their churches, and lost support of their bishops and fellow ministers. But they have gone with the faith that right defeated is stronger than evil triumphant. These men have been the leaven in the lump of the race. Their witness has been the spiritual salt that has preserved the true meaning of the gospel in these troubled times. They have carved a tunnel of hope through the dark mountain of disappointment.

I hope the church as a whole will meet the challenge of this decisive hour. But even if the church does not come to the aid of justice, I have no despair about the future. I have no fear about the outcome of our struggle in Birmingham, even if our motives are presently misunderstood. We will reach the goal of freedom in Birmingham and all over the nation, because the goal of America is freedom. Abused and scorned though we may be, our destiny is tied up with the destiny of America. Before the Pilgrims landed at Plymouth, we were here. Before the pen of Jefferson etched across the pages of history the majestic words of the Declaration of Independence, we were here. For more than two centuries our foreparents labored in this country without wages; they made cotton king; and they built the homes of their masters in the midst of brutal injustice and shameful humiliation—and yet out of a bottomless vitality they continued to thrive and develop. If the inexpressible cruelties of slav-

ery could not stop us, the opposition we now face will surely fail. We will win our freedom because the sacred heritage of our nation and the eternal will of God are embodied in our echoing demands.

I must close now. But before closing I am impelled to mention one other point in your statement that troubled me profoundly. You warmly commended the Birmingham police force for keeping "order" and "preventing violence." I don't believe you would have so warmly commended the police force if you had seen its angry violent dogs literally biting six unarmed, nonviolent Negroes. I don't believe you would so quickly commend the policemen if you would observe their ugly and inhuman treatment of Negroes here in the city jail; if you would watch them push and curse old Negro women and young Negro girls; if you would see them slap and kick old Negro men and young boys; if you will observe them, as they did on two occasions, refuse to give us food because we wanted to sing our grace together. I'm sorry that I can't join you in your praise for the police department.

It is true that they have been rather disciplined in their public handling of the demonstrators. In this sense they have been rather publicly "nonviolent." But for what purpose? To preserve the evil system of segregation. Over the last few years I have consistently preached that nonviolence demands that the means we use must be as pure as the ends we seek. So I have tried to make it clear that it is wrong to use immoral means to attain moral ends. But now I must affirm that it is just as wrong, or even more so, to use moral means to preserve immoral ends. Maybe Mr. Connor and his policemen have been rather publicly nonviolent, as Chief Pritchett was in Albany, Georgia, but they have used the moral means of nonviolence to maintain the immoral end of flagrant racial injustice. T. S. Eliot has said that there is no greater treason than to do the right deed for the wrong reason.

I wish you had commended the Negro sit-inners and demonstrators of Birmingham for their sublime courage, their willingness to suffer and their amazing discipline in the midst of the most inhuman provocation. One day the South will recognize its real heroes. They will be the James Merediths, courageously and with a majestic sense of purpose facing jeering and hostile mobs and the agonizing loneliness that characterizes the life of the pioneer. They will be old, oppressed, battered Negro women, symbolized in a seventy-two-year-old woman of Montgomery, Alabama, who rose up with a sense of dignity and with her people decided not to ride the segregated buses, and responded to one who inquired about her tiredness with ungrammatical profundity: "My feet is tired, but my soul is rested." They will be the young high school and college students, young ministers of the gospel and a host of their elders courageously and nonviolently sitting-in at lunch counters and willingly going to jail for conscience's sake. One day the South will know that when these disinherited children of God sat down at lunch counters they were in reality standing up for the best in the American dream and the most sacred values in our Judeo-Christian heritage, and thusly, carrying our whole nation back to those great wells of democracy which were dug deep by the Founding Fathers in the formulation of the Constitution and the Declaration of Independence.

Never before have I written a letter this long (or should I say a book?). I'm afraid that it is much too long to take your precious time. I can assure you that it would have been much shorter if I had been writing from a comfortable desk, but what else is there to do when you are alone for days in the dull monotony of a narrow jail cell other than write long letters, think strange thoughts, and pray long prayers?

If I have said anything in this letter that is an overstatement of the truth and is indicative of an unreasonable impatience, I beg you to forgive me. If I have said anything in this letter that is an understatement of the truth and is indicative of my having a patience that makes me patient with anything less than brotherhood, I beg God to forgive me.

I hope this letter finds you strong in the faith. I also hope that circumstances will soon make it possible for me to meet each of you, not as an integrationist or a civil rights leader, but as a fellow clergyman and a Christian brother. Let us all hope that the dark clouds of racial prejudice will soon pass away and the deep fog of misunderstanding will be lifted from our fear-drenched communities and in some not too distant tomorrow the radiant stars of love and brotherhood will shine over our great nation with all of their scintillating beauty.

Yours for the cause of Peace and Brotherhood,
Martin Luther King, Jr.

Suggestions for Further Reading

Henry David Thoreau's *On Civil Disobedience* is a classic. See *Civil Disobedience,* edited by Hugo Bedau (New York: Pegasus, 1969), for a collection of essays on the topic.

Hannah Arendt's *Crises of the Republic* (New York: Harcourt Brace Jovanovich, 1969) deals with a number of issues ranging from civil disobedience and violence to political revolution.

Ronald Dworkin, in *Taking Rights Seriously* (Cambridge, MA: Harvard University Press, 1970), argues that any society that recognizes rights must abandon "the notion of a general duty to obey the law that holds in all cases."

Martin Luther King, Jr., was using civil disobedience to gain African American liberation and a racially integrated society. There is an immense literature on the topic of racism and black liberation. For starters, see Frantz Fanon, *The Wretched of the Earth* (New York: Grove Press, 1965); *Philosophy and Opinions of Marcus Garvey,* Volume I of *The American Negro: His History and Literature* (Salem, NH: Arno Press, 1968); Eldridge Cleaver's famous *Soul on Ice* (New York: Dell, 1968); *The Autobiography of Malcolm X* (New York: Grove Press, 1965); and S. Carmichael and C. Hamilton's *Black Power* (New York: Vintage Press, 1967).

William R. Jones, "Liberation Strategies in Black Theology: Mao, Martin, or Malcolm?" in *Philosophy Born of Struggle: Anthology of Afro-American Philosophy from 1917,* edited by Leonard Harris (Dubuque, IA.: Kendell/Hunt, 1983), pp. 229–241, argues that for non-violent civil disobedience to work, the oppressor must accept the co-humanity of the oppressed. But in a racist society, this presupposition is absent, and so self-sacrificing love will not have its intended effect.

For the perspective of an African-American woman, see Angela Davis, *Women, Race, and Class* (New York: Random House, 1982).

Videos

Martin Luther King, Jr.: A Personal Portrait (53 minutes; produced by Michaelis Tapes).

Martin Luther King, Jr.: I Have a Dream (28 minutes; produced by API) shows King's "I Have a Dream" speech on the steps of the Lincoln memorial.

Eyes on the Prize: No Easy Walk 1961–63 (1986, PBS Video).

A video of King's speeches, *Promised Land* (50 minutes; Filmmakers Library), is a recollection of the promise and legacy of the civil rights movement. Also, from the same source, *Are We Different?* (27 minutes) shows African American students talking about race, racism, and race relations.

The Meeting (60 minutes; PBS Video) is a dramatization of a fictional secret meeting between Dr. King and Malcom X in which they debate the use of violence versus nonviolence in attaining just social ends.

Ethnic Notions (57 minutes; California Newsreel) traces the development of black stereotypes.

See *Racism on Campus* (210 minutes; Governor's State University) for an examination of racism on college campuses from both an historical and contemporary perspective.

For more information, see your Media Services Catalog.

5.7 Sovereignty and Justice: An Indigenist's Viewpoint

Have you ever wondered why oppression exists? Have you wondered how oppression might be eliminated? Surely one of the features of societies that makes them unjust is the existence of oppression. Oppression can take many forms: economic, racial, sexual. The rich dominate the poor and get richer at their expense. In the United States and elsewhere, whites discriminate against blacks. Men limit the opportunities for women. Gays and lesbians are denied the rights and opportunities others enjoy. Native Americans have suffered near extinction and cultural destruction at the hands of the European invaders and their descendants. Mexican Americans have been brutally exploited as farm laborers, and prevented, until recently, from gaining any significant political power. Unfortunately, I could go on and on recounting example after example.

Oppressors need to justify their position, and so they convince themselves that those whom they oppress are inferior, immoral, heathen, lazy, stupid, dirty, or somehow deserving of their lot in life. In effect, they dehumanize the oppressed while keeping for themselves the image of full humanity. For example, during the westward expansion in the United States, it was often said that "The only good Indian is a dead Indian."

Oppressors also need to justify their positions by legal means. If what one does is immoral, that fact can be disguised by making it appear legal. Exactly how the U.S government has made it legal to take and occupy land once occupied by others is the subject of the next selection by Ward Churchill.

Ward Churchill (Creek/Cherokee Metis), one of the most influential voices of native resistance in North America, is a professor of Communications and Coordinator of American Indian Studies at the University of Colorado at Boulder. He is also co-director of the Colorado chapter of the American Indian Movement (AIM) that is active in seeking justice for the descendants of the first peoples to inhabit North America.

Before you read Churchill's argument, imagine that you are a judge and have been asked to rule in a case. The facts of the case appear simple enough. A group of people many years ago occupied land that was taken from them by force and fraud. This land has changed hands many times and today the descendants of those who took the land occupy it. Now the descendants of the original people are demanding that justice be done. Your task is to decide what constitutes justice in this case. What must be done now to make a society in which this happened a more just society?

Reading Questions

1. What is the "Discovery Doctrine"?
2. What is the "Norman Yoke," and how does it change the Discovery Doctrine?
3. What is the main point Churchill makes in the section on "Treaties as Tools of the State"?
4. Explain the logic supporting the "Marshall Doctrine."
5. What is the "Allotment Act," and what were its consequences?
6. According to Churchill, what was the purpose of the IRA?
7. What is the "Blue Water Thesis," and what role did it play in countering the claims of AIM?
8. What are some of Churchill's conclusions?
9. Assuming Churchill is right, how can justice be done with respect to indigenous peoples and to those who now occupy and control much of their former land and its wealth?

Perversions of Justice

WARD CHURCHILL

FROM THE OUTSET of the "Age of Discovery" precipitated by the Columbian voyages, the European powers, eager to obtain uncontested title to at least some portion of the lands their emissaries were encountering, quickly recognized the need to establish a formal code of juridical standards to legitimate what they acquired. This lent a patina of "civilized" legality to the actions of the European Crowns. More importantly, the system was envisioned to resolve disputes be-

From *Ward Churchill,* Struggle for the Land. *Monroe, ME: Common Courage Press, 1993, pp. 34–49, 53– 54, 59–63. Copyright © 1993 Ward Churchill. Reprinted by permission. Footnotes omitted.*

tween the Crowns themselves, each vying with the others in a rapacious battle over the wealth accruing through ownership of given regions in the "New World."

In order for any such regulatory code to be considered effectively binding by all Old World parties, it was vital that it be sanctioned by the Church. A theme begun with a series of Papal Bulls begun by Pope Innocent IV during the late thirteenth century First Crusade was used to define the proper ("lawful") relationship between Christians and "Infidels" in worldly matters such as property rights. Beginning in the early sixteenth century, Spanish jurists in particular did much to develop this theory into what have come to be known as the "Doctrine of Discovery" and an attendant dogma, the "Rights of Conquest." Through the efforts of legal scholars such as Franciscus de Vitoria and Matías de Paz, Spanish articulations of Discovery Doctrine, endorsed by the Pope, rapidly evolved to hold the following as primary tenets of international law:

- Outright ownership of land accrued to the Crown represented by a given Christian (European) discoverer only when the land discovered proved to be uninhabited (territorium res nullius).
- Title to inhabited lands discovered by Crown representatives was recognized as belonging inherently to the indigenous people encountered, but rights to acquire land from, and to trade with the natives of the region accrued exclusively to the discovering Crown *vis-à-vis* other European powers. In exchange for this right, the discovering power committed itself to proselytizing the Christian gospel among the natives.
- Acquisition of land title from indigenous peoples could occur only by their consent—by an agreement usually involving purchase—rather than through force of arms, so long as the natives did not arbitrarily decline to trade with Crown representatives, refuse to admit missionaries among them, or inflict gratuitous violence upon citizens of the Crown.
- Absent these last three conditions, utilization of armed force to acquire aboriginally held

territory was considered unjust and claims to land title accruing therefrom to be correspondingly invalid.
- Should one or more of the three conditions be present, then the Crown had a legal right to use whatever force was required to subdue native resistance and impound their property as compensation. Land title gained by prosecution of such "Just Wars" was considered valid.

Although this legal perspective was hotly debated at the time (it still is, in certain quarters), and saw considerable violation by European colonists, it was generally acknowledged as the standard against which international conduct would be weighed. By the early seventeenth century, the requirements of the Discovery Doctrine had led the European states, England in particular, to adopt a policy of entering into formal treaties with native nations. These full-fledged international instruments officially recognized the sovereignty of the indigenous parties to such agreements as equivalent to that of the respective Crowns. They became an expedient to obtaining legally valid land titles from American Indian peoples, first in what is now the state of Virginia, and then in areas further north. Treaties concerning trade, professions of peace and friendship, and to consummate military alliances were also quite common.

Undeniably, there is a certain overweening arrogance imbedded in the proposition that Europeans were somehow intrinsically imbued with an authority to unilaterally restrict the range of those to whom Native Americans might sell their property, assuming they wished to sell it at all. Nonetheless, the legal posture of early European colonialism in recognizing that indigenous peoples constituted bona fide nations holding essentially the same rights to land and sovereignty as any other, seems rather advanced and refined in retrospect. In these respects, the Doctrine of Discovery is widely viewed as one of the more important cornerstones of modern international law and diplomacy.

With its adoption of Protestantism, however, Britain had already begun to mark its independence from papal regulation by adding an element of its own, usually termed the "Norman Yoke," to the doctrine. Land rights were said to rest in large part upon the extent to which owners demonstrate a willingness and ability to "develop" their territories in accordance with a scriptural obligation to exercise "dominium" over nature. Thus, entitlement is restricted to the quantity of real estate which the individual or people can convert from "wilderness" to a "domesticated" state. This criterion bestowed on English settlers an inherent right to dispossess native people of all land other than that which the latter might be "reasonably expected" to put to such "proper" uses as cultivation. More importantly at this time, this doctrinal innovation automatically placed the British Crown on a legal footing from which it could contest the discovery rights of any European power not adhering to the requirement of "overcoming the wilderness."

This allowed England simultaneously to "abide by the law" and directly confront Catholic France for ascendancy in the Atlantic regions of North America. After a series of "French and Indian Wars" beginning in the late 1600s and lasting nearly a century, the British were victorious, but at a cost greater than the expected financial benefits to the Crown of launching its colonial venture in the first place. As one major consequence, King George II, in a move intended to preclude further warfare with indigenous nations, issued the Proclamation of 1763. This royal edict stipulated that all settlement or other forms of land acquisition by British subjects west of a line running along the Allegheny and Appalachian Mountains from Canada to the Spanish colony of Florida would be suspended indefinitely, and perhaps permanently. English expansion on the North American continent was thereby brought to an abrupt halt.

Treaties as Tools of the State

The new British proclamation conflicted sharply with the desires for personal gain growing among a voracious élite within the seaboard colonial population. Most of the colonies held some pretense of title to "western" lands, much of it conveyed by earlier Crown grant, and had planned to use it as a means of bolstering their respective economic positions. Similarly, members of the landed gentry such as George Washington, Thomas Jefferson, John Adams, James Madison and Anthony Wayne all possessed considerable speculative interests in land parcels on the far side of the 1763 demarcation line. The only way in which these could be converted into profit was for the parcels to be settled and developed. Vociferous contestation and frequent violation of the proclamation, eventually enforced by George III, became quite common. This dynamic became a powerful precipitating factor in the American Revolution, during which many rank-and-file rebels were convinced to fight against the Crown by promises of western land grants "for services rendered" in the event their revolt was successful.

But successful revolt does not necessarily bring legitimacy. The United States emerged from its decolonization struggle against Britain—perhaps the most grievous offense which could be perpetrated by any subject people under then prevailing law—as a pariah, an outlaw state that was shunned as an utterly illegitimate entity by most other countries. Desperate to establish itself as a legitimate nation, and lacking other viable alternatives with which to demonstrate its aptitude for complying with international legality, the new government was virtually compelled to observe the strictest of protocols in its dealings with Indians. Indeed, what the Continental Congress needed more than anything at the time was for indigenous nations, already recognized as respectable sovereignties via their treaties with the European states, to bestow a comparable recognition upon the fledgling U.S. by entering into treaties with *it*. The urgency of the matter was compounded by the fact that the Indians maintained military parity with, and in some cases superiority to, the U.S. Army all along the frontier.

As a result, both the Articles of Confederation and subsequent Constitution of the United States contained clauses explicitly and exclusively restricting relations with indigenous nations to the federal government, insofar as the former were recognized as enjoying the same politico-legal status as any other foreign power. The U.S.

also officially renounced, in the 1789 Northwest Ordinance and elsewhere, any aggressive intent concerning indigenous nations, especially with regard to their respective landbases:

> The utmost good faith shall always be observed towards the Indians; their land and property shall never be taken from them without their consent; and in their property, rights, and liberty, they shall never be disturbed . . . but laws founded in justice and humanity shall from time to time be made, for wrongs done to them, and for peace and friendship with them.

This rhetorical stance, reflecting an impeccable observance of international legality, was also incorporated into agreements between the U.S. and European states during its formative years. For instance, in the 1803 "Louisiana" Purchase of much of North America west of the Mississippi from France, the federal government solemnly pledged itself to protect "the inhabitants of the ceded territory . . . in the free enjoyment of their liberty, property and the religion they profess." Other sections of the purchase agreement make it clear that federal authorities understood they were acquiring from the French, not the land itself, but France's monopolistic trade rights and prerogatives to buy any acreage within the area its indigenous owners wished to sell.

The same understanding certainly pertained to all unceded Indian Country claimed by Britain under Discovery Doctrine east of the Mississippi, once it was quit-claimed by George III in the Treaty of Paris concluding the Revolution. Even if English discovery rights somehow "passed" to the new republic by virtue of this royal action, an extremely dubious premise in itself, there still remained the matter of obtaining native consent to U.S. ownership of any area beyond the 1763 proclamation line. Hence, in addition to the legitimacy gained by signing treaties with the indigenous nations, and the military goals of some such instruments, the U.S. actively pursued treaties to procure indigenous agreement to land cessions. This comprised the main currency of American diplomacy throughout the immediate post-revolutionary period. Moreover, the need to secure valid land title from native people through treaties far outlasted the motivations of diplomatic and military necessity, these having been greatly diminished in importance after U.S. victories over Tecumseh's alliance in 1794 and 1811, Britain in the War of 1812, and the Red Stick Confederacy during 1813 and 1814. The treaties were and remain the basic real estate documents anchoring U.S. claims to land title—and thus to rights of occupancy—in North America.

But, while these treaties solved some issues such as legitimacy for the newly born state, they created new problems. In gaining diplomatic recognition and land cessions from indigenous nations through treaties, the U.S. was simultaneously admitting not only that Indians ultimately owned virtually all of the territory coveted by the U.S., but that they were also under no obligation to part with it. As William Wirt, an early attorney general, put it in 1821:

> [Legally speaking,] so long as a tribe exists and remains in possession of its lands, its title and possession are sovereign and exclusive. We treat with them as separate sovereignties, and while an Indian nation continues to exist within its acknowledged limits, we have no more right to enter upon their territory than we have to enter upon the territory of a foreign prince.

A few years later, Wirt amplified his point:

> The point, once conceded, that the Indians are independent to the purpose of treating, their independence is to that purpose as absolute as any other nation. Being competent to bind themselves by treaty, they are equally competent to bind the party that treats with them. Such party cannot take benefit of [a] treaty with the Indians, and then deny them the reciprocal benefits of the treaty on the grounds that they are not independent nations to all intents and purposes. . . . Nor can it be conceded that their independence as a nation is a limited independence. Like all other independent nations, they have the absolute power of war and peace. Like all other independent nations, their territories are inviolate by any other sovereignty. . . . They are entirely self-governed, self-directed. They treat, or refuse to treat, at their pleasure; and there is no human power that can rightly control

them in the exercise of their discretion in this respect.

For twenty years following the revolution (roughly 1790 to 1810), such acknowledgment of these genuine indigenous sovereign rights and status considerably retarded the acquisition of land grants by revolutionary soldiers, as well as consummation of the plans of the élite caste of prerevolutionary land speculators. Over the next two decades (1810 to 1830), the issue assumed an ever increasing policy importance: native sovereignty replaced Crown policy as the preeminent barrier to U.S. territorial consolidation east of the Mississippi. Worse, as Chief Justice John Marshall pointed out in 1822, any real adherence to the rule of law in regard to native rights might not only block U.S. expansion, but—since not all the territory therein had been secured through Crown treaties—cloud title to significant portions of the original thirteen states as well. Perhaps predictably, it was perceived in juridical circles that the only means of circumventing this dilemma was through construction of a legal theory—a subterfuge, as it were—by which the more inconvenient implications of international law might be voided even while the republic maintained an appearance of holding to its doctrinal requirements.

The Marshall Doctrine: "Legal" Justification of an Outlaw State

The task of forging the required "interpretation" of existing law fell to Chief Justice Marshall, widely considered one of the great legal minds of his time. Whatever his scholarly qualifications, the Chief Justice was hardly a disinterested party. His ideological advocacy of the rebel cause before and during the revolution was vociferous. More important, both he and his father were consequent recipients of 10,000 acre grants west of the Appalachians, in what is now the state of West Virginia. His first serious foray into land rights law thus centered in devising a conceptual basis to secure title for his own and similar grants. In the 1810 *Fletcher v. Peck* case, he invoked the Norman Yoke tradition in a manner which far exceeded previous British applications, advancing the patently absurd contention that the areas involved were effectively "vacant" even though very much occupied—and in many instances stoutly defended—by indigenous inhabitants. On this basis, he declared individual Euroamerican deeds within recognized Indian territories might be considered valid whether or not native consent was obtained.

While *Peck* was obviously useful from the U.S. point of view, resolving a number of short-term difficulties in meeting obligations already incurred by the government with regard to individual citizens, it was a tactical opinion, falling far short of accommodating the country's overall territorial goals and objectives. In the 1823 *Johnson v. McIntosh* case, however, Marshall followed up with a more clearly strategic enunciation, reaching to the core issues. Here, he opined that, because Discovery Rights purportedly constricted native discretion in disposing of property, the sovereignty of discoverers was to that extent inherently superior to that of indigenous nations. From this point of departure, he then proceeded to invert all conventional understandings of the Discovery Doctrine, ultimately asserting that native people occupied land within discovered regions at the sufferance of their discoverers rather than the other way around. A preliminary rationalization was thus contrived by which to explain the fact that the U.S. had already begun depicting its borders as encompassing vast portions of unceded Indian Country.

Undoubtedly aware that neither *Peck* nor *McIntosh* was likely to withstand the gaze of even minimal international scrutiny, Marshall next moved to bolster the logic undergirding his position. In the two so-called "Cherokee Cases" of the early 1830s, he hammered out the thesis that native nations within North America were "nations like any other" in the sense that they possessed both territories they were capable of ceding, and recognizable governmental bodies empowered to cede these areas through treaties. However, he argued on the basis of the reasoning deployed in *McIntosh*, they were nations of a "peculiar type," both "domestic to" and "dependent upon" the United States, and therefore possessed of a degree of sovereignty intrinsically less than that enjoyed by the U.S. itself. Thus while native peoples are entitled to exercise some range of autonomy in managing their affairs within their own territories, both the limits of that autonomy and the extent of the territories involved can be "naturally" and unilaterally established by the federal government. At base, this is little more than a judicial description of the classic relationship between colonizer and colonized, put forth in such a way as to seem at first glance to be the exact opposite.

While it might be contended (and has been, routinely enough) that Marshall's framing of the circumstances pertaining to the Cherokee Nation, already completely surrounded by the territoriality of the United States by 1830, bore some genuine relationship to then prevailing reality, he did not confine his observations to the situation of the Cherokees, or even to native nations east of the Mississippi. Rather, he purported to articulate the legal status of *all* indigenous nations, including those west of the Mississippi—the Lakota, Cheyenne, Arapaho, Comanche, Kiowa, Navajo and Chiricahua Apache, to name but a few—which had not yet encountered the U.S. in any appreciable way. Self-evidently, these nations could not have been described with the faintest accuracy as domestic to or dependent upon the United States. The clear intent belied by Marshall's formulation was that they be *made so* in the future. The doctrine completed with elaboration of the Cherokee Cases was thus the pivotal official attempt to rationalize and legitimate the future campaign of conquest and colonization which was absolutely contrary to the customary law of the period.

The doctrine was not complete without a final inversion of accepted international legal norms and definitions of "Just" and "Unjust" warfare. Within Marshall's convoluted and falsely premised reasoning, it became arguable that indigenous nations acted unlawfully whenever and wherever they attempted to physically prevent exercise of the U.S. "right" to expropriate their property. Resistance to invasion of indigenous homelands could then be construed as "aggression" against the United States. In this sense, the

U.S. could declare itself to be waging a "Just"— and therefore lawful—War against native people on any occasion where force of arms was required to realize its territorial ambitions. *Ipso facto,* all efforts of native people to defend themselves against systematic dispossession and subordination could thereby be categorized as "unjust"— and thus unlawful—by the United States.

In sum, the Marshall Doctrine shredded significant elements of the existing Laws of Nations. Given the historical records of federal judicial officials such as Attorney General Wirt and Marshall himself, and the embodiment of such understandings in the Constitution and formative federal statutes, this breach was not unintentional or inadvertent. Instead, with calculated juridical cynicism, the Chief Justice deliberately confused and deformed accepted legal principles to "justify" his country's pursuit of a thoroughly illegitimate course of territorial acquisition. Insofar as federal courts and policymakers elected to adopt his doctrine as the predicate to all subsequent relations with American Indians, the posture of the United States as an outlaw state was rendered permanent.

From Treaty Violation to Extermination

The Cherokee Cases were followed by a half-century hiatus in important judicial determinations regarding American Indians. On the foundation provided by the Marshall Doctrine, the government felt confident in entering into the great bulk of the more than 370 treaties with indigenous nations by which it professed to have gained the consent of Indians in ceding huge portions of the native landbase. With its self-anointed position of superior sovereignty, it would be under "no legal obligation" to live up to its end of the various bargains struck. Well before the end of the nineteenth century, the United States stood in default on virtually every treaty agreement it had made with native people, and there is considerable evidence in many instances that this was intended from the outset. Aside from the fraudulent nature of U.S. participation in the treaty process, there is an ample record that many of the instruments of cession were militarily coerced while the government implemented Marshall's version of Just Wars against Indians. As the U.S. Census Bureau put it in 1894:

> The Indian wars under the United States government have been about 40 in number [most of them occurring after 1835]. They have cost the lives of . . . about 30,000 Indians [at a minimum]. . . . The actual number of killed and wounded Indians must be very much greater than the number given, as they conceal, where possible, their actual loss in battle. . . . Fifty percent additional would be a safe number to add to the numbers given.

The same report noted that some number "very much more" than 8,500 Indians were known to have been killed by government-sanctioned private citizen action—dubbed "individual affairs"—during the course of U.S./ Indian warfare. In fact, such citizen action was primarily responsible for reducing the native population of Texas from about 100,000 in 1828 to less than 10,000 in 1880. Similarly, in California, an aggregate indigenous population which still numbered approximately 300,000 had been reduced to fewer than 35,000 by 1860, mainly because of "the cruelties and wholesale massacres perpetrated by [American] miners and early settlers." Either of these illustrations offers a death toll several times the total number officially recognized as accruing through individual affairs in the 48 contiguous states.

Even while this slaughter was occurring, the government was conducting, by its own admission, a "policy of extermination" in its conduct of wars against those indigenous nations which proved "recalcitrant" in giving up their land and liberty. This manifested itself in a lengthy series of massacres of native people—men, women, children, and old people alike—at the hands of U.S. troops. Among the worst were those at Blue River (Nebraska, 1854), Bear River (Idaho, 1863), Sand Creek (Colorado, 1864), Washita River (Oklahoma, 1868), Sappa Creek (Kansas, 1875), Camp Robinson (Nebraska, 1878), and Wounded Knee (South Dakota, 1890). Some-

what different, but comparable, methods of destroying indigenous peoples included the forced march of the entire Cherokee Nation along the "Trail of Tears" to Oklahoma during the 1830s (55 percent did not survive), and the internment of the bulk of the Navajo Nation under abysmal conditions at the Bosque Redondo from 1864 to 1868 (35 to 50 percent died). Such atrocities were coupled with an equally systematic extermination of an entire animal species, the buffalo or North American Bison, as part of a military strategy to starve resistant Indians into submission by "destroying their commissary."

It is probable that more than a quarter-million Indians perished as a direct result of U.S. extermination campaigns. By the turn of the century, only 237,196 native people were recorded by census as still being alive with the United States, perhaps 2 percent of the total indigenous population of the U.S. portion of North America at the point of first contact with Europeans. Correlating rather precisely with this genocidal reduction in the number of native inhabitants was an erosion of Indian land holdings to approximately 2.5 percent of the "lower 48" states. Admiring its effectiveness, barely thirty years later, Adolf Hitler would explicitly anchor his concept of *lebensraumpolitik* ("politics of living space") directly upon U.S. practice against American Indians.

Justice as a "Pulverizing Engine"

Even as the census figures were being tallied, the United States had already moved beyond the "Manifest Destiny" embodied in the conquest phase of its continental expansion, and was emphasizing the development of colonial administration over residual indigenous land and lives through the Bureau of Indian Affairs (BIA), a subpart of the War Department which had been reassigned for this purpose to the Department of Interior.

This was begun as early as 1871, when Congress—having determined that the military capacity of indigenous nations had finally been sufficiently reduced by incessant wars of attrition—elected to consecrate Marshall's description of their "domestic" status by suspending further treaty-making with them. In 1885, the U.S. began for the first time to directly extend its internal jurisdiction over reserved Indian territories ("reservations") through passage of the Major Crimes Act. When this was immediately challenged as a violation of international standards, Supreme Court Justice Samuel F. Miller rendered an opinion which consolidated and extended Marshall's earlier assertion of federal plenary power over native nations, contending that the government held an "incontrovertible right" to exercise authority over Indians as it saw fit and "for their own good." Miller also concluded that Indians lacked legal recourse in matters of federal interest, their sovereignty being defined as whatever Congress did not remove through specific legislation. This decision opened the door to enactment of more than 5,000 statutes regulating affairs in Indian Country by the present day.

One of the first of these was the General Allotment Act of 1887, "which unilaterally negated Indian control over land tenure patterns within the reservations, forcibly replacing the traditional mode of collective use and occupancy with the Anglo-Saxon system of individual property ownership." The Act also imposed for the first time a formal eugenics code—dubbed "blood quantum"—by which American Indian identity would be federally defined on racial grounds rather than by native nations themselves on the basis of group membership/citizenship.

The Allotment Act stipulated that each officially recognized American Indian would receive an allotment of land according to the following formula: 160 acres for family heads, eighty acres for single persons over eighteen years of age and orphans under eighteen, and forty acres for non-orphan children under eighteen. "Mixed blood" Indians received title by fee simple patent; "full bloods" were issued "trust patents," meaning they had no control over their property for a period of 25 years. Once each person recognized by the government as belonging to a given Indian nation had received his or her allotment, the "surplus" acreage was "opened" to non-Indian homesteading or conversion into the emerging system of national parks, forests, and grasslands. . . .

Given the contours of federal policy towards American Indians, how is it that the indigenous nations were not obliterated long ago? The answer is ironic. Unbeknownst to the policymakers who implemented allotment policy against Indians during the late nineteenth century, much of the ostensibly useless land to which native people were consigned turned out to be some of the most mineral rich on earth. It is presently estimated that as much as two-thirds of all known U.S. "domestic" uranium reserves lie beneath reservation lands, as well as perhaps a quarter of the readily accessible low sulphur coal and about a fifth of the oil and natural gas. In addition, the reservations are now known to hold substantial deposits of copper, zinc, iron, nickel, molybdenum, bauxite, zeolite and gold.

Such matters were becoming known by the early 1920s. Federal economic planners quickly discerned a distinct advantage in retaining these abundant resources within the framework of governmental trust control. In contrast to land held privately, this arrangement was an expedient to awarding extractive leases, mining licenses and the like to preferred corporate entities. Granting these rights might have proven impossible had the reservations been liquidated altogether. Hence, beginning in 1921, it was determined that selected indigenous nations should be maintained. Washington began to experiment with the creation of "tribal governments" intended to administer what was left of Indian Country on behalf of an emerging complex of interlocking federal/corporate interests. In 1934, this resulted in the passage of the Indian Reorganization Act (IRA), a bill which served to supplant virtually every remaining traditional indigenous government in the country, replacing them with federally designed "Tribal Councils" structured along the lines of corporate boards and empowered primarily to sign off on mineral leases and similar instruments.

The arrangement led to a recapitulation of the Marshall Doctrine's principle of indigenous "quasi-sovereignty" in slightly revised form: now, native nations were cast as being sovereign enough to legitimate Euroamerican mineral exploitation on their reservations, never sovereign enough to prevent it. Predictably, under such circumstances the BIA negotiated mining leases, duly endorsed by the puppet governments it had installed, "on behalf of" its "Indian wards" which have typically paid native people 15 percent or less of market royalty rates on minerals taken from their lands. The "super profits" thus generated for major corporations have had a significant positive effect on U.S. economic growth since 1950, a matter amplified by the BIA "neglecting" to include land restoration and other environmental cleanup clauses into contracts pertaining to reservation land. (Currently, Indians are construed as sovereign enough to waive environmental protection regulations but never sovereign enough to enforce them). One consequence of this trend is that, on reservations where uranium mining has occurred, Indian Country has become so contaminated by radioactive substances that the government has actively considered designating them as "National Sacrifice Areas" unfit for human habitation. Planning is also afoot to utilize several reservations as dump sites for high level nuclear wastes and toxic chemical substances which cannot be otherwise disposed of conveniently. . . .

A Legal Raft in Blue Water

During the 1970s, the American Indian Movement (AIM), an organization militantly devoted to the national liberation of Native North America, emerged in the United States. In part, the group attempted the physical decolonization of the Pine Ridge Reservation in South Dakota (home of the Oglala Lakota people), but was met with a counterinsurgency war waged by federal agencies such as the FBI and U.S. Marshals Service, and surrogates associated with the reservation's IRA Council. Although unsuccessful in achieving a resumption of indigenous self-determination at Pine Ridge, the tenacity of AIM's struggle (and the ferocity of the government's repression of it) attracted considerable international attention. This led, in 1980, to the establishment of a United Nations Working Group

on Indigenous Populations, under auspices of the U.N. Economic and Social Council (ECOSOC), an entity mandated to assess the situation of native peoples globally and produce a universal declaration of their rights as a binding element of international law.

Within this arena, the United States, joined by Canada, has consistently sought to defend its relations with indigenous nations by trotting out the Marshall Doctrine's rationalization that the U.S. has assumed a trust responsibility rather than outright colonial domination over Native North America. American Indian delegates have countered, correctly, that trust prerogatives, in order to be valid under international law, must be tied to some clearly articulated time interval after which the subordinate nations resume independent existence. This has been successfully contrasted to the federal (and Canadian) government's presumption that it enjoys a permanent trust authority over indigenous nations; assumption of *permanent* plenary authority over another nation's affairs and property is the essential definition of colonialism, it is argued, and is illegal under a number of international covenants.

The U.S. and Canada have responded with prevarication, contending that their relationship to Native North America cannot be one of colonialism insofar as United Nations Resolution 1541 (XV), the so-called "Blue Water Thesis," specifies that in order to be defined as a colony a nation must be separated from its colonizer by at least thirty miles of open ocean. The representatives of both countries have also done everything in their power to delay or prevent completion of the Universal Declaration of the Rights of Indigenous Peoples, arguing, among other things, that the term "peoples," when applied to native populations, should not carry the force of law implied by its use in such international legal instruments as the Universal Declaration of Human Rights (1948), Covenant on Civil and Political Rights (1978), and the International Convention on Elimination of All Forms of Racial Discrimination (1978). The United States in particular has implied that it will not abide by any declaration of indigenous rights which runs counter to what it perceives as its own interests, a matter which would replicate its posture with regard to the authority of the International Court of Justice (the "World Court") and elements of international law such as the 1948 Convention on Prevention and Punishment of the Crime of Genocide.

Meanwhile, the U.S. has set out to "resolve things internally" through what may be intended as a capstone extrapolation of the Marshall Doctrine. This has assumed the shape of a drive to convince Indians to accept the premise that, rather than struggling to regain the self-determining rights to separate sovereign existence embodied in their national histories and treaty relationships, they should voluntarily merge themselves with the U.S. polity. In this scenario, the IRA administrative apparatus created during the 1930s would assume a position as a "third level of the federal government," finally making indigenous rights within the U.S. inseparable from those of the citizenry as a whole. This final assimilation of native people into the "American sociopolitical mainstream" would obviously void most (or perhaps all) potential utility for Indian rights which exist in or might emerge from international law over the next few years. The option is therefore being seriously pursued by a Senate Select Committee on Indian Affairs, chaired by Hawaii Senator Daniel Inouye (who has already done much to undermine the last vestiges of rights held by the native people of his own state).

The Marshall Doctrine on a Global Scale

During the fall of 1990, President George Bush stepped onto the world stage beating the drums for what he termed a "Just War" to roll back what he described as the "naked aggression" of Iraq's invasion and occupation of neighboring Kuwait. Claiming to articulate "universal principles of international relations and human decency," Bush stated that such aggression "cannot stand," that "occupied territory must be liberated, legitimate governments must be reinstated, the benefits of their aggression must be denied to aggressive powers." Given the tone

and tenor of this Bushian rhetoric—and the undeniable fact that Iraq had a far better claim to Kuwait (its nineteenth province, separated from the Iraqis by the British as an administrative measure following World War I), than the U.S. has to virtually any part of North America—one might logically expect the American president to call airstrikes in upon his own capitol as a means of forcing his government to withdraw from Indian Country. Since he did not, the nature of his "New World Order" is clear: it is based on the rule of force, not on the rule of law.

The United States does not now possess, nor has it ever had, a legitimate right to occupancy in at least half the territory it claims as its own on this continent. It began its existence as an outlaw state and, given the nature of its expansion to its present size, it has adamantly remained so through the present moment. In order to make things appear otherwise, its legal scholars and its legislators have persistently and often grotesquely manipulated and deformed accepted and sound legal principles, both internationally and domestically. They have done so in precisely the same fashion, and on the same basis, as the [N]azi leaders they stood at the forefront in condemning for Crimes Against Humanity at Nuremberg.

In no small part because of its past achievements in consolidating its position on other peoples' land in North America, the United States may well continue to succeed where the [N]azis failed. With the collapse of the Soviet Union, it has emerged as the ascendant military power on the planet during the late twentieth century. As the sheer margin of its victory over Iraq has revealed, it now possesses the capacity to extend essentially the same sort of relationships it has already imposed upon American Indians to the remainder of the world. And, given the experience it has acquired in Indian Affairs over the years, it is undoubtedly capable of garbing this process of planetary subordination in a legalistic attire symbolizing its deep-seated concern with international freedom and dignity, the sovereignty of other nations, and the human rights of all peoples. At a number of levels, the Marshall Doctrine reckons to become truly globalized in the years ahead.

This is likely to remain the case, unless and until significant numbers of people within and without the United States recognize the danger, and the philosophical system underpinning it, for what it is. More importantly, any genuine alternative to a consummation of the Bushian vision of world order is predicated upon these same people acting upon their insights, opposing the order implicit to the U.S. status quo both at home and abroad. Ultimately, the dynamic represented by the Marshall Doctrine must be reversed, and the structure it fostered dismantled, within the territorial corpus of the United States itself. In this, nothing can be more central than the restoration of indigenous land and indigenous national rights in the fullest sense of the term. The U.S.—at least as it has come to be known, and in the sense that it knows itself—must be driven from North America. In its stead resides the possibility, likely the only possibility, of a truly just and liberatory future for all humanity.

Suggestions for Further Reading

See Ward Churchill and Howard Zinn, *From a Native Son: Selected Essays on Indigenism, 1985–1995* (Cambridge, MA: South End Press, 1996) for a powerful discussion of issues of injustice effecting indigenous peoples.

Dee Brown's *Bury My Heart at Wounded Knee* (New York: Henry Holt and Co., 1971) is a classic account of how the West was invaded by the whites who stole it.

Custer Died For Your Sins by Vine Deloria, Jr (New York: Avon Books, 1969) is nothing less than an Indian manifesto.

Also see Vine Deloria, Jr. and Clifford M. Lytle, *The Nations Within: The Past and Future of American Indian Sovereignty* (New York: Pantheon Press, 1984).

The Destruction of California Indians by Robert F. Heizer (Lincoln: University of Nebraska Press, 1974) reveals how thousands of California natives died from 1847 to 1865 so that white Americans could reap the wealth of the land.

An index to Native American sites on the web can be found at http://www.indirect.com/www/akers/resources.html. Also see http://www2.hmc.edu/~tbeckman/indian.html for links to sites containing a variety of resources on Native Americans.

Videos

Wiping the Tears of Seven Generations (60 minutes) won many documentary awards for a careful examination of U.S. history through the eyes of the Lakota Sioux (KIFARU Productions, San Francisco, CA).

A series of videos (about 50 minutes each), entitled *The Native Americans,* deals with their history, experiences, and the diversity of their traditions. The series is available from Turner Home Entertainment, 1 CNN Center, Atlanta, GA 30303.

 You can locate InfoTrac-College Edition articles about this chapter by accessing the InfoTrac-College Edition website (http://www.infotrac-college.com/wadsworth/). Using the InfoTrac-College Edition subject guide, enter the search terms relevant to this chapter, and then read abstracts for relevant articles.

Chapter 6

Is Justice for All Possible?

> **Live compassionately.**
> THE BUDDHA

6.1 Introduction

WHEN I ASK STUDENTS to write a brief essay on whether they think a just society is possible, the responses I get are overwhelmingly negative. They do not think a just society is possible because, as one student put it, "Someone will always be unhappy with the way things are."

The United States, as well as other countries, faces a number of complex issues requiring some sort of legislation. Yet every time a law is passed or a judicial decision is made, someone is going to feel cheated. Even so, decisions must be made, and we can only hope that the decisions make good moral sense even if someone may be "unhappy."

The issue of human rights is a case in point. Do humans have certain rights just because they are human? Are such rights universal or local? Does some international agency have the right to enforce certain human rights in countries that do not recognize such rights? Should trade decisions be based on the "human rights record" of countries?

Racism and sexism have plagued many countries. Can they be eliminated? Is a society that tolerates racism and sexism a just society? Can there ever be justice for those who have been victims of racism and sexism? Are affirmative action programs justified? One often hears such programs justified on the grounds of compensatory justice (see Section 5.1). However, many argue that the correction of a past injustice leads to a present injustice.

If humans have rights, do other animals have rights? Would you support the abolition of the use of animals in laboratory testing? Would you, if you had the power, prohibit commercial and sport hunting? Is justice for other-than-human animals possible?

Environmental issues appear in the news almost daily. As we move into the twenty-first century, many predict that a good portion of our time and resources will be spent cleaning up the mess left by the last century's insensitivity to the environment. As international businesses expand and globalization becomes more and more entrenched, the temptations to exploit humans, other-than-human animals, and our environment in the name of "progress" (read "profit") will multiply.

Social philosophy discusses these sorts of issues (and many more). Philosophers try to illuminate the issues, sort out the reasonable positions, and argue for policies that make moral sense. We will become a part of some of these discussions in this chapter, and, I trust, our thinking about them will deepen. We may, in some cases, still be uncertain about what is the best thing to do, and we still may realize that some people will be unhappy no matter what is done, but at least our vision of social justice in some areas may become clearer.

6.2 Universal Human Rights

If I asked you to come up with a list of universal human rights, could you? For example, does everyone have the right to life and liberty? Does everyone have the right to own property? Does everyone have the right to work?

Did you know that before the mid-twentieth century, there were very few restraints on what states could do to their citizens? The relationship between citizens and states was, for the most part, thought to be a domestic, internal affair. The genocide, ethnic cleansings, and other human atrocities that increased to an unprecedented degree in the last century eventually led to the adoption by the United Nations on December 10, 1948 of a Universal Declaration of Human Rights. Forty-eight nations ratified the Declaration and eight abstained (South Africa, Saudi Arabia, and six members of the Soviet bloc at that time).

Eleanor Roosevelt chaired the international commission that wrote the Declaration. She was deeply interested in social issues, particularly racial equality and women's rights. She represented the United States at the United Nations and worked tirelessly to get the Declaration drafted and passed.

Below you will find an edited version of the United Nations Declaration following a brief article by René Trujillo. Trujillo, a professor at San Jose State University, writes about the moral reflection that occurred as the Spanish conquered the indigenous peoples in the "New World." He points out that, contrary to what we might expect, issues of human rights and human dignity played an important role in the thinking of some Spanish philosophers of the day.

"Little good it did the native peoples," you might say. In the same vein, some have wondered whether the United Nations Declaration has done much good. Indeed it seems that a universal declaration of human rights will do little good because governments and greedy corporations ignore the human rights of others whenever it is to their advantage to do so. There is no doubt that some states have repeatedly violated many of the specific provisions of the Declaration. However, over the years many have come to see the Declaration as a useful gauge for progress on the issue of human rights. Virtually every national constitution incorporates some of its provisions, and human rights organizations refer to the Declaration as a standard of rights and freedoms.

Reading Project and Questions

1. Write a critical précis (see Section 2.2) for Trujillo's article.
2. What do you think is left out of UN *Universal Declaration of Human Rights* that should be included, and what do you think is included that should be left out? Give reasons for your answer.
3. Do you see any links between these two selections? If so, what are they?

Human Rights in the "Age of Discovery"

RENÉ TRUJILLO

AS WE REMEMBER the "Age of Discovery" of the "New World," in terms of the brutality that attended it for the indigenous peoples of the Western Hemisphere, let us also remember what effect it had on conscientious European thinkers of the day. Let us learn not only from the mistakes of the conquest, but from the moral reflection that it occasioned.

In reply to the theology and philosophy of repression prevalent in his day, Francisco de Vitoria (1485–1546) proposed an alternative in his *Carta Constitucional de los Indios*. The major thesis of this work was expressed in three fundamental principles. First, the indigenous peoples had a fundamental right based on their humanity—that is, based on the fact that they were human beings—to be treated as free people. Second, they had a fundamental right to defend their own sovereignty. Third, and finally, they enjoyed the fundamental right of all peoples to work toward and to make peace and international solidarity. It was in light of these three beliefs that Vitoria both determined and evaluated the rights and concomitant obligations of the Spanish Crown to be in and remain in the "new" world. Ultimately, considering the transgressions suffered by the indigenous peoples, he concluded that Spain owed restitution to the natives.

The dispute that ensued between Juan Gines de Sepulveda (1490–1573), the official defender of the monarch, and Vitoria was based on the concept of the just war. They were concerned with the justifications for the actions of the Spanish Crown against the integrity of the societies of indigenous peoples with whom the Spanish conquerors had contact. More broadly, these two men were concerned with the concept of "justice" in general as it pertained to human rights and obligations.

The constitutional principles of Vitoria's alternative perspective can be understood on the basis of five points. In the first place, the Spaniards and indigenous peoples had to be understood as equal with regards to their humanity. This consideration spanned both actual and potential human characteristics. Second, any assertion of inhumanity in the indigenous peoples had to be understood as due to a lack of education and to their resultant barbaric customs. Some European thinkers of the day were enlightened enough to see that this same point might be leveled against the European communities within which they found themselves. Third, the indigenous peoples, in the same fashion as the Spanish, had property rights to their possessions and as such could not be dispossessed of them by virtue of any charge of lack of culture. This would follow for the same reasons as those which would serve to protect an uncultured individual in Spain. Fourth—and this might be very controversial today—the indigenous peoples might be entrusted to the tutelage of the Spaniards while still in an "underdeveloped state." This provision, of course, assumes that the aim of the tutelage would be the eventual autonomy of the indigenous peoples, and that the Spaniards had the requisite moral character and skill to undertake such a position. Finally, the consent of the indigenous peoples and their free choice were the ultimate grounds for any just Spanish intervention in the "new" world.

To better understand these assertions, and to see their relevance to us today, we must understand the motivation behind them. We might

From Social Justice in a Diverse Society, *edited by Rita C. Manning and René Trujillo. Mountain View, CA: Mayfield Publishing Company, 1996, pp. 66–67. Copyright © 1966 Mayfield Publishing Company. Reprinted by permission.*

appropriately ask, What question do they answer? All demands placed on the indigenous peoples were justified in the minds of the Spanish based on their belief in the universal power of the Roman Catholic Church. Specifically, the appropriateness of their actions followed from the world authority of the pope, who, they thought, had sovereign power over all spiritual and temporal concerns. The papal "donation" of the Indies to the Catholic Kings (Fernando II el Catolico, king of Aragon and Castilla and Isabel I la Catolica, queen of Castilla) conferred the status of vassals (in a feudal sense) to the indigenous peoples, and established sovereignty for Spain over the "new" world. This condition of servitude was understood in Spain as "natural" and as having ample historical precedent. The latter belief was certainly clearly true; however, the issue of servitude, natural or otherwise, was to create a significant theological and moral crisis.

Along with their papal authority to govern came the mandate to evangelize the indigenous peoples, that is, to seek their free conversion to Christendom. It was understood as the duty of the indigenous peoples to accept evangelization—but what would this imply about the nature and humanity of these peoples? The Spanish monarchy wished to justify its wars against the indigenous peoples by establishing papal authority, Spanish sovereignty, and the right to evangelize. It wanted to be able to establish the submission, occupation, and enslavement of these peoples as the natural and inevitable consequence of the just war waged against indigenous rebellion and resistance. Much of this policy, however, rested on the notion that these indigenous individuals had some *duty* to comply. The resistance to these ideas, as evidenced in Vitoria's position, was based on a reevaluation of the necessary preconditions for moral duty. What sort of being has moral duties?

The resounding answer was "human beings." But human beings have not only moral duties and responsibilities, they have moral rights. They have human rights. Can one be held responsible for one's moral duties in the face of the systematic infringement of one's moral rights? Can one be morally disenfranchised within the commu-

nity of moral beings, and still be expected to comply with moral law? These were some of the questions that motivated the opposition to come out against the policies and actions of the crown.

Today it is true, as it was five hundred years ago, that duty and obligation imply rights and benefits if they are to be considered just. To have the duties of a human being, one must be able to enjoy the rights that attend the human condition. If there are any moral duties to be defined within such a state, there must also be a sense of moral rights. The conclusion I draw from these observations is that morality requires humanity, and humanity depends on the recognition and observance of dignity. In the case of human beings, dignity is achieved not only through our duties and obligations to others, but also through the obligations and duties of others to ourselves. Human duties to ourselves or others only make sense in a reflective equilibrium that defines the rights that follow from these duties.

In today's communities there is an overabundance of duties talk in the face of a paucity of rights talk. When we do speak of rights, it is overwhelmingly in terms of personal rights and not the rights of others. We may in word understand that these rights depend on each other, but our deeds rarely conform to this understanding. If we are to secure the rights of any individuals whatsoever, we must secure the rights of all. If we are to establish the duties of any one person, we must confirm the basis for such a duty as rooted in the enjoyment of some right or privilege. Otherwise, we commit ourselves to the irrational: we ask of all disenfranchised human beings that they act systematically and freely against their own interests and that they trust in the beneficence of those who force them into such a dilemma.

Until we recognize that humanity manifests itself variously, we are in no position to judge either ourselves or others. Race, gender, class, and sexual orientation have historically been used as the basis for different duties and rights. These duties and rights have always been determined by the politically strong and the duties exacted with vengeance from the politically subordinate. We see continued evidence of this trend today. Take the recent Colorado state initiative to repeal all antigay discrimination protection legislation (as currently on the books in Boulder, Denver, and Aspen). How can we ask individuals to fully participate in a community where they are not deemed worthy of their full human rights with all the protection society is willing to offer others? The answer is, we cannot. To support the quality of our lives, each and every one of us must be committed to the quality of all lives. Otherwise, we will suffer the consequences.

United Nations Universal Declaration of Human Rights

The General Assembly

PROCLAIMS

This universal declaration of human rights as a common standard of achievement for all peoples and all nations, to the end that every individual and every organ of society, keeping this Declaration constantly in mind, shall strive by teaching and education to promote respect for these rights and freedoms and by progressive measures, national and international, to secure their universal and effective recognition and observance, both among the peoples of Member States themselves and among the peoples of territories under their jurisdiction.

ARTICLE 1

All human beings are born free and equal in dignity and rights. They are endowed with reason and conscience and should act towards one another in a spirit of brotherhood.

ARTICLE 2

Everyone is entitled to all the rights and freedoms set forth in this Declaration, without distinction of any kind, such as race, colour, sex, language, religion, political or other opinion, national or social origin, property, birth or other status.

Furthermore, no distinction shall be made on the basis of the political, jurisdictional or international status of the country or territory to which a person belongs, whether it be independent, trust, non-self-governing or under any other limitation of sovereignty.

ARTICLE 3

Everyone has the right to life, liberty and security of person.

ARTICLE 4

No one shall be held in slavery or servitude; slavery and the slave trade shall be prohibited in all their forms.

ARTICLE 5

No one shall be subjected to torture or to cruel, inhuman or degrading treatment or punishment.

ARTICLE 6

Everyone has the right to recognition everywhere as a person before the law.

ARTICLE 7

All are equal before the law and are entitled without any discrimination to equal protection of the law. All are entitled to equal protection against any discrimination in violation of this Declaration and against any incitement to such discrimination.

ARTICLE 8

Everyone has the right to an effective remedy by the competent national tribunals for acts violating the fundamental rights granted him by the constitution or by law.

ARTICLE 9

No one shall be subjected to arbitrary arrest, detention or exile.

ARTICLE 10

Everyone is entitled in full equality to a fair and public hearing by an independent and impartial tribunal, in the determination of his rights and obligations and of any criminal charge against him.

ARTICLE 11

1. Everyone charged with a penal offence has the right to be presumed innocent until proved guilty according to law in a public trial at which he has had all the guarantees necessary for his defence.

2. No one shall be held guilty of any penal offence on account of any act or omission which did not constitute a penal offence, under national or international law, at the time when it was committed. Nor shall a heavier penalty be imposed than the one that was applicable at the time the penal offence was committed.

ARTICLE 12

No one shall be subjected to arbitrary interference with his privacy, family, home or correspondence, nor to attacks upon his honour and reputation. Everyone has the right to the protection of the law against such interference or attacks.

ARTICLE 13

1. Everyone has the right to freedom of movement and residence within the borders of each state.

2. Everyone has the right to leave any country, including his own, and to return to his country.

ARTICLE 14

1. Everyone has the right to seek and to enjoy in other countries asylum from persecution.

2. This right may not be invoked in the case of prosecutions genuinely arising from non-political crimes or from acts contrary to the purposes and principles of the United Nations.

ARTICLE 15

1. Everyone has the right to a nationality.

2. No one shall be arbitrarily deprived of his nationality nor denied the right to change his nationality.

ARTICLE 16

1. Men and women of full age, without any limitation due to race, nationality or religion, have the right to marry and to found a family. They are entitled to equal rights as to marriage, during marriage and at its dissolution.

2. Marriage shall be entered into only with the free and full consent of the intending spouses.

3. The family is the natural and fundamental group unit of society and is entitled to protection by society and the State.

ARTICLE 17

1. Everyone has the right to own property alone as well as in association with others.

2. No one shall be arbitrarily deprived of his property.

ARTICLE 18

Everyone has the right to freedom of thought, conscience and religion; this right includes freedom to change his religion or belief, and freedom, either alone or in community with others and in public or private, to manifest his religion or belief in teaching, practice, worship and observance.

ARTICLE 19

Everyone has the right to freedom of opinion and expression; this right includes freedom to hold opinions without interference and to seek, receive and impart information and ideas through any media and regardless of frontiers.

ARTICLE 20

1. Everyone has the right to freedom of peaceful assembly and association.

2. No one may be compelled to belong to an association.

ARTICLE 21

1. Everyone has the right to take part in the government of his country, directly or through freely chosen representatives.

2. Everyone has the right of equal access to public service in his country.

3. The will of the people shall be the basis of the authority of government; this will shall be expressed in periodic and genuine elections which shall be by universal and equal suffrage and shall be held by secret vote or by equivalent free voting procedures.

ARTICLE 22

Everyone, as a member of society, has the right to social security and is entitled to realization, through national effort and international cooperation and in accordance with the organization and resources of each State, of the economic, social and cultural rights indispensable for his dignity and the free development of his personality.

ARTICLE 23

1. Everyone has the right to work, to free choice of employment, to just and favourable conditions of work and to protection against unemployment.

2. Everyone, without any discrimination, has the right to equal pay for equal work.

3. Everyone who works has the right to just and favourable remuneration ensuring for himself and his family an existence worthy of human dignity, and supplemented, if necessary, by other means of social protection.

4. Everyone has the right to form and to join trade unions for the protection of his interests.

ARTICLE 24

Everyone has the right to rest and leisure, including reasonable limitation of working hours and periodic holidays with pay.

ARTICLE 25

Everyone has the right to a standard of living adequate for the health and well-being of himself and of his family, including food, clothing, housing and medical care and necessary social services, and the right to security in the event of unemployment, sickness, disability, widowhood, old age or other lack of livelihood in circumstances beyond his control.

1. Motherhood and childhood are entitled to special care and assistance. All children, whether born in or out of wedlock, shall enjoy the same social protection.

ARTICLE 26

1. Everyone has the right to education. Education shall be free, at least in the elementary and fundamental stages. Elementary education shall be compulsory. Technical and professional education shall be made generally available and higher education shall be equally accessible to all on the basis of merit.

2. Education shall be directed to the full development of the human personality and to the strengthening of respect for human rights and fundamental freedoms. It shall promote understanding, tolerance and friendship among all nations, racial or religious groups, and shall further

the activities of the United Nations for the maintenance of peace.

3. Parents have a prior right to choose the kind of education that shall be given to their children.

ARTICLE 27

1. Everyone has the right freely to participate in the cultural life of the community, to enjoy the arts and to share in scientific advancement and its benefits.

2. Everyone has the right to the protection of the moral and material interests resulting from any scientific, literary or artistic production of which he is the author.

ARTICLE 28

Everyone is entitled to a social and international order in which the rights and freedoms set forth in this Declaration can be fully realized.

ARTICLE 29

1. Everyone has duties to the community in which alone the free and full development of his personality is possible.

2. In the exercise of his rights and freedoms, everyone shall be subject only to such limitations as are determined by law solely for the purpose of securing due recognition and respect for the rights and freedoms of others and of meeting the just requirements of morality, public order and the general welfare in a democratic society.

3. These rights and freedoms may in no case be exercised contrary to the purposes and principles of the United Nations.

ARTICLE 30

Nothing in this Declaration may be interpreted as implying for any State, group or person any right to engage in any activity or to perform any act aimed at the destruction of any of the rights and freedoms set forth herein.

Suggestions for Further Reading

See Alan R. White's *Rights* (Oxford: Oxford University Press, 1984) for a discussion of four different answers to the question of who has moral rights.

Gerald Dworkin, in *The Theory and Practice of Autonomy* (Cambridge: Cambridge University Press, 1988), argues that the protection of autonomy is a necessary requirement of a just state.

For a collection of articles dealing with human rights and justice, see Part I of *Applied Ethics: A Multicultural Approach,* edited by Larry May, Shari Collins-Chobanian, and Kai Wong, 2nd Edition (Upper Saddle River, NJ: Prentice-Hall, 1998).

In *The Idea of Human Rights: Four Inquiries* Michael J. Perry (New York: Oxford University Press, 1998) argues that, from a purely secular viewpoint, the idea of universal human rights makes little sense. It is tied, he thinks, to the idea of a universal God.

For a collection of lectures addressing various aspects of the issue, see *On Human Rights—The Oxford Amnesty Lectures, 1993* (New York: Basic Books, 1993).

See Michael Ignatieff's "Human Rights: The Midlife Crisis" in *New York Review of Books,* Volume XLVI (May 20, 1999), 58–62 for a review of several books dealing with the Universal Declaration of Human Rights.

Thomas W. Pogge explores the link between "Human Flourishing and Universal Justice" (*Social Philosophy and Policy,* Vol. 16, Winter 1999: 333–361) in a nuanced and careful manner.

For the full text of the *Declaration* see http://www.un.org/rights/50/decla.htm. For a list of extensive connections to a variety of documents relating to human rights, see http://www.tufts.edu/departments/fletcher/multi/humanRights.html.

Videos

Human Rights and Moral Practice (35 minutes) was released by Mystic Fire Studio in 1994 and is available from Amazon.com.

6.3 Are Human Rights Universal?

Let's start with a problem. Suppose some company wants to do business with a company you own and you want to do business with it. Suppose further that this company treats its employees dreadfully by your standards. The sorts of rights that you give your employees are denied to theirs. When you discuss the matter with representatives of the other company, they respond by saying that their employees have rights but that their rights are not the same as the ones your employees enjoy because their company operates with a different set of values than yours. They add that you do not have the right to impose your values on their company.

What would you say? What would you do? Would you do business anyway, acknowledging the diversity of values as legitimate? Would you argue that your values are right and that until they change the way they treat their employees, you will not do business with them? Does the severity of the treatment make any difference? What if they exploited the labor of children and made people work in unsafe conditions? What if they denied the right of complaint to their employees, so that no grievance could be brought against the company for unfair treatment?

In my discussion of rationality in Section 1.2, I contrasted a foundationalist viewpoint that claimed there is one universal set of rational standards with the constructivist viewpoint that claimed there are many local rationalities. A very similar discussion is going on today about human rights.

Some philosophers and others maintain that human rights are universal. This is certainly the belief behind the United Nation's *Declaration* (see Section 6.2). However, today there are others who argue that rights are culturally specific. Each culture has its own set of values, and these different local values determine not only whether humans are thought to have rights, but also what sort of rights they might have. For example, some argue that in many Asian countries that have felt the influence of Confucianism (see Section 3.3), it is quite natural to place more emphasis on the good of the community as a whole. Hence, when the good of the community conflicts with the good of the individual, the communal good should be given preference.

This emphasis on the value of community can be seen in the constitution of the People's Republic of China. The constitution aims at promoting social harmony rather than providing mechanisms for settling disputes among individuals. It is also clear that any rights citizens enjoy derive from their membership in the community. In the United Nations *Declaration,* rights are enjoyed by individual humans just because they are humans, not because they happen to be citizens of some particular state.

Xiaorong Li, in the following selection, discusses the issue of whether human rights are universal in the context of the Asian values debate. Ms. Li is a research scholar at the Institute for Philosophy and Public Policy at the University of Maryland. She is Vice-Chair of Human Rights in China and, in 1998, while visiting her parents, was arrested and deported by the Chinese.

As you may know, many have urged the U.S. government not to grant most favored nation status to China for purposes of trade because of the Chinese record on human rights. The Chinese have often responded by arguing that human rights are culturally specific and that the Chinese have their rights which, although different from those of the West, are nevertheless appropriate to Chinese society. Li carefully analyzes and evaluates the various claims and arguments. Do your answers to the problem of doing business with which I started this section match what Li says?

Reading Questions

1. What is the supposed "Asian view" of human rights?
2. What is the "genetic fallacy," and what role does it play in the argument over cultural specificity?
3. What is wrong, according to Li, with the claim that in Asia more value is rightly placed on community rather than on the individual?
4. Why does Li think the claim that rights to economic development have priority over civil rights is a false dilemma?
5. Do you think Li is correct when she argues that political and civil rights cannot be separated from social, economic, and cultural rights? Why, or why not?
6. In what senses might a right be universal, and which of these senses is most important for the debate between cultural relativists and universalists?
7. Is the argument that any idea that has survived rigorous cross-cultural examination is universally valid convincing? Why, or why not?

"Asian Values" and the Universality of Human Rights

XIAORONG LI

ORIENTALIST SCHOLARSHIP in the nineteenth century perceived Asians as the mysterious and backward people of the Far East. Ironically, as this century draws to a close, leaders of prosperous and entrepreneurial East and Southeast Asian countries eagerly stress Asia's incommensurable differences from the West and demand special treatment of their human rights record by the international community. They reject outright the globalization of human rights and claim that Asia has a unique set of values, which, as Singapore's ambassador to the United Nations has urged, provide the basis for Asia's different understanding of human rights and justify the "exceptional" handling of rights by Asian governments.

Is this assertion of "Asian values" simply a cloak for arrogant regimes whose newly gained confidence from rapidly growing economic power makes them all the more resistant to outside criticism? Does it have any intellectual substance? What challenges has the "Asian values" debate posed to a human rights movement committed to globalism?

Though scholars have explored the understanding of human rights in various Asian contexts, the concept of "Asian values" gains politi-

From Report from the Institute for Philosophy and Public Policy, *Volume 16 (Spring 1996), 18–23.*
Reprinted by permission.

cal prominence only when it is articulated in government rhetoric and official statements. In asserting these values, leaders from the region find that they have a convenient tool to silence internal criticism and to fan anti-Western nationalist sentiments. At the same time, the concept is welcomed by cultural relativists, cultural supremacists, and isolationists alike, as fresh evidence for their various positions against a political liberalism that defends universal human rights and democracy. Thus, the "Asian values" debate provides an occasion to reinvigorate deliberation about the foundations of human rights, the sources of political legitimacy, and the relation between modernity and cultural identity.

This essay makes a preliminary attempt to identify the myths, misconceptions, and fallacies that have gone into creating an "Asian view" of human rights. By sorting out the various threads in the notions of "cultural specificity" and "universality," it shows that the claim to "Asian values" hardly constitutes a serious threat to the universal validity of human rights.

Defining the "Asian View"

To speak of an "Asian view" of human rights that has supposedly emanated from Asian perspectives or values is itself problematic: it is impossible to defend the "Asianness" of this view and its legitimacy in representing Asian culture(s). "Asia" in our ordinary language designates large geographic areas which house diverse political entities (states) and their people, with drastically different cultures and religions, and unevenly developed (or undeveloped) economies and political systems. Those who assert commonly shared "Asian values" cannot reconcile their claims with the immense diversity of Asia—a heterogeneity that extends to its people, their social-political practices and ethnic-cultural identities. Nonetheless, official statements by governments in the region typically make the following claims about the so-called "Asian view" of human rights:

Claim I: Rights are "culturally specific." Human rights emerge in the context of particular social, economic, cultural and political conditions. The circumstances that prompted the institu-tionalization of human rights in the West do not exist in Asia. China's 1991 White Paper stated that "[o]wing to tremendous differences in historical background, social system, cultural tradition and economic development, countries differ in their understanding and practice of human rights." In the Bangkok Governmental Declaration, endorsed at the 1993 Asian regional preparatory meeting for the Vienna World Conference on Human Rights, governments agreed that human rights "must be considered in the context of a dynamic and evolving process of international norm-setting, bearing in mind the significance of national and regional peculiarities and various historical, cultural, and religious backgrounds."

Claim II: The community takes precedence over individuals. The importance of the community in Asian culture is incompatible with the primacy of the individual, upon which the Western notion of human rights rests. The relationship between individuals and communities constitutes the key difference between Asian and Western cultural "values." An official statement of the Singapore government, *Shared Values* (1991), stated that "[a]n emphasis on the community has been a key survival value for Singapore." Human rights and the rule of law, according to the "Asian view," are individualistic by nature and hence destructive of Asia's social mechanism. Increasing rates of violent crime, family breakdown, homelessness, and drug abuse are cited as evidence that Western individualism (particularly the American variety) has failed.

Claim III: Social and economic rights take precedence over civil and political rights. Asian societies rank social and economic rights and "the right to economic development" over individuals' political and civil rights. The Chinese White Paper (1991) stated that "[t]o eat their fill and dress warmly were the fundamental demands of the Chinese people who had long suffered cold and hunger." Political and civil rights, on this view, do not make sense to poor and illiterate multitudes; such rights are not meaningful under destitute and unstable conditions. The right of workers to form independent unions, for example, is not as urgent as stability and efficient production. Implicit here is the promise that once people's basic needs are met—once they are adequately fed, clothed, and educated—and the social order is stable, the luxury of civil and political rights will be extended to them. In the meantime, economic development will be achieved more efficiently if the leaders are authorized to restrict individuals' political and civil rights for the sake of political stability.

Claim IV: Rights are a matter of national sovereignty. The right of a nation to self-determination includes a government's domestic jurisdiction over human rights. Human rights are internal affairs, not to be interfered with by foreign states or multinational agencies. In its 1991 White Paper, China stated that "the issue of human rights falls by and large within the sovereignty of each state." In 1995, the Chinese government confirmed its opposition to "some countries' hegemonic acts of using a double standard for the human rights of other countries . . . and imposing their own pattern on others, or interfering in the internal affairs of other countries by using 'human rights' as a pretext." The West's attempt to apply universal standards of human rights to developing countries is disguised cultural imperialism and an attempt to obstruct their development.

Elsewhere and Here

In this essay I address the first three claims that make up the "Asian view," particularly the argument that rights are "culturally specific." This argument implies that social norms originating in other cultures should not be adopted in Asian culture. But, in practice, advocates of the "Asian view" often do not consistently adhere to this rule. Leaders from the region pick and choose freely from other cultures, adopting whatever is in their political interest. They seem to have no qualms about embracing such things as capitalist markets and consumerist culture. What troubles them about the concept of human rights, then, turns out to have little to do with its Western cultural origin.

In any case, there are no grounds for believing that norms originating *elsewhere* should be inherently unsuitable for solving problems *here*.

Such a belief commits the "genetic fallacy" in that it assumes that a norm is suitable only to the culture of its origin. But the origin of an idea in one culture does not entail its unsuitability to another culture. If, for example, there are good reasons for protecting the free expression of Asian people, free expression should be respected, no matter whether the idea of free expression originated in the West or Asia, or how long it has been a viable idea. And in fact, Asian countries may have now entered into historical circumstances where the affirmation and protection of human rights is not only possible but desirable.

In some contemporary Asian societies, we find economic, social, cultural, and political conditions that foster demands for human rights as the norm-setting criteria for the treatment of individual persons and the communities they form. National aggregate growth and distribution, often under the control of authoritarian governments, have not benefited individuals from vulnerable social groups—including workers, women, children, and indigenous or minority populations. Social and economic disparities are rapidly expanding. Newly introduced market forces, in the absence of rights protection and the rule of law, have further exploited and disadvantaged these groups and created anxiety even among more privileged sectors—professionals and business owners, as well as foreign corporations—in places where corruption, disrespect for property rights, and arbitrary rule are the norm. Political dissidents, intellectuals and opposition groups who dare to challenge the system face persecution. Meanwhile, with the expansion of communications technology and improvements in literacy, information about repression and injustice has become more accessible both within and beyond previously isolated communities; it is increasingly known that the notion of universal rights has been embraced by people in many Latin American, African, and some East and Southeast Asian countries (Japan, South Korea, Taiwan, and the Philippines). Finally, the international human rights movement has developed robust non-Western notions of human rights, including economic, social, and cultural rights, providing individuals in Asia with powerful tools to fight against poverty, corruption, military repression, discrimination, cultural and community destruction, as well as social, ethnic, and religious violence. Together, these new circumstances make human rights relevant and implementable in Asian societies.

Culture, Community, and the State

The second claim, that Asians value community over individuality, obscures more than it reveals about community, its relations to the state and individuals, and the conditions congenial to its flourishing. The so-called Asian value of "community harmony" is used as an illustration of "cultural" differences between Asian and Western societies, in order to show that the idea of individuals' inalienable rights does not suit Asian societies. This "Asian communitarianism" is a direct challenge to what is perceived as the essence of human rights, i.e., its individual-centered approach, and it suggests that Asia's community-centered approach is superior.

However, the "Asian view" creates confusions by collapsing "community" into the state and the state into the (current) regime. When equations are drawn between community, the state and the regime, any criticisms of the regime become crimes against the nation-state, the community, and the people. The "Asian view" relies on such a conceptual maneuver to dismiss individual rights that conflict with the regime's interest, allowing the condemnation of individual rights as anti-communal, destructive of social harmony, and seditionist against the sovereign state.

At the same time, this view denies the existence of conflicting interests between the state (understood as a political entity) and communities (understood as voluntary, civil associations) in Asian societies. What begins as an endorsement of the value of community and social harmony ends in an assertion of the supreme status of the regime and its leaders. Such a regime is capable of dissolving any non-governmental organizations it dislikes in the name of "community interest," often citing traditional Confucian values of social harmony to defend restrictions on the right to free association and expression, and thus wields

ever more pervasive control over unorganized individual workers and dissenters. A Confucian communitarian, however, would find that the bleak, homogeneous society that these governments try to shape through draconian practices— criminal prosecutions for "counterrevolutionary activities," administrative detention, censorship, and military curfew—has little in common with her ideal of social harmony.

Contrary to the "Asian view," individual freedom is not intrinsically opposed to and destructive of community. Free association, free expression, and tolerance are vital to the well-being of communities. Through open public deliberations, marginalized and vulnerable social groups can voice their concerns and expose the discrimination and unfair treatment they encounter. In a liberal democratic society, which is mocked and denounced by some Asian leaders for its individualist excess, a degree of separation between the state and civil society provides a public space for the flourishing of communities.

A False Dilemma

The third claim of the "Asian view," that economic development rights have a priority over political and civil rights, supposes that the starving and illiterate masses have to choose between starvation and oppression. It then concludes that "a full belly" would no doubt be the natural choice. Setting aside the paternalism of this assumption, the question arises of whether the apparent trade-off—freedom in exchange for food—actually brings an end to deprivation, and whether people must in fact choose between these two miserable states of affairs.

When it is authoritarian leaders who pose this dilemma, one should be particularly suspicious. The oppressors, after all, are well-positioned to amass wealth for themselves, and their declared project of enabling people to "get rich" may increase the disparity between the haves and the have-nots. Moreover, the most immediate victims of oppression—those subjected to imprisonment or torture—are often those who have spoken out against the errors or the incompetence of authorities who have failed to alleviate deprivation, or who in fact have made it worse. The sad truth is that an authoritarian regime can practice political repression and starve the poor at the same time. Conversely, an end to oppression often means the alleviation of poverty—as when, to borrow Amartya Sen's example, accountable governments manage to avert famine by heeding the warnings of a free press.

One assumption behind this false dilemma is that "the right to development" is a state's sovereign right and that it is one and the same as the "social-economic rights" assigned to individuals under international covenants. But the right of individuals and communities to participate in and enjoy the fruit of economic development should not be identified with the right of nation-states to pursue national pro-development policies, even if such policies set the stage for individual citizens to exercise their economic rights. Even when "the right to development" is understood as a sovereign state right, as is sometimes implied in the international politics of development, it belongs to a separate and distinct realm from that of "social-economic rights."

The distinction between economic rights and the state's right to development goes beyond the issue of who holds these particular rights. National development is an altogether different matter from securing the economic rights of vulnerable members of society. National economic growth does not guarantee that basic subsistence for the poor will be secured. While the right to development (narrowly understood) enables the nation-state as a unit to grow economically, social-economic rights are concerned with empowering the poor and vulnerable, preventing their marginalization and exploitation, and securing their basic subsistence. What the right of development, when asserted by an authoritarian state, tends to disregard, but what social-economic rights aspire to protect, is fair economic equality or social equity. Unfortunately, Asia's development programs have not particularly enabled the poor and vulnerable to control their basic livelihood, especially where development is narrowly understood as the creation of markets and measured by national aggregate growth rates.

A more plausible argument for ranking social and economic rights above political and civil rights is that poor and illiterate people cannot really exercise their civil-political rights. Yet the poor and illiterate may benefit from civil and political freedom by speaking, without fear, of their discontent. Meanwhile, as we have seen, political repression does not guarantee better living conditions and education for the poor and illiterate. The leaders who are in a position to encroach upon citizens' rights to express political opinions will also be beyond reproach and accountability for failures to protect citizens' social-economic rights.

Political-civil rights and social-economic-cultural rights are in many ways indivisible. Each is indispensable for the effective exercise of the other. If citizens' civil-political rights are unprotected, their opportunities to "get rich" can be taken away just as arbitrarily as they are bestowed; if citizens have no real opportunity to exercise their social-economic rights, their rights to political participation and free expression will be severely undermined. For centuries, poverty has stripped away the human dignity of Asia's poor masses, making them vulnerable to violations of their cultural and civil-political rights. Today, a free press and the rule of law are likely to enhance Asians' economic opportunity. Political-civil rights are not a mere luxury of rich nations, as some Asian leaders have told their people, but a safety net for marginalized and vulnerable people in dramatically changing Asian societies.

Universality Unbroken

The threat posed by "Asian values" to the universality of human rights seems ominous. If Asian cultural relativism prevails, there can be no universal standards to adjudicate between competing conceptions of human rights. But one may pause and ask whether the "Asian values" debate has created any really troubling threat to universal human rights—that is, serious enough to justify the alarm that it has touched off.

The answer, I argue, depends on how one understands the concepts of universality and cultural specificity. In essence, there are three ways in which a value can be universal or culturally specific. First, these terms may refer to the *origin* of a value. In this sense, they represent a claim about whether a value has developed only within specific cultures, or whether it has arisen within the basic ideas of every culture.

No one on either side of the "Asian values" debate thinks that human rights are universal with respect to their origin. It is accepted that the idea of human rights originated in Western traditions. The universalist does not disagree with the cultural relativist on this point—though they would disagree about its significance—and it is not in this sense that human rights are understood as having universality.

Second, a value may be culturally specific or universal with respect to its prospects for *effective (immediate) implementation*. That is, a value may find favorable conditions for its implementation only within certain cultures, or it may find such conditions everywhere in the world.

Now, I don't think that the universalist would insist that human rights can be immediately or effectively implemented in all societies, given their vastly different conditions. No one imagines that human rights will be fully protected in societies that are ravaged by violent conflict or warfare; where political power is so unevenly distributed that the ruling forces can crush any opposition; where social mobility is impossible, and people segregated by class, caste system, or cultural taboos are isolated and uninformed; where most people are on the verge of starvation and where survival is the pressing concern. The list could go on. However, to acknowledge that the prospects for effective implementation of human rights differ according to circumstances is not to legitimize violations under these unfavorable conditions, nor is it to deny the universal applicability or validity of human rights (as defined below) to all human beings no matter what circumstances they face.

Third, a value may be understood as culturally specific by people who think it is *valid* only within certain cultures. According to this understanding, a value can be explained or defended only by appealing to assumptions already accepted by a given culture; in cultures that do not share those assumptions, the validity of such a value will become questionable. Since there are few universally shared cultural assumptions that can be invoked in defense of the concept of human rights, the universal validity of human rights is problematic.

The proponents of this view suppose that the validity of human rights can only be assessed in an intracultural conversation where certain beliefs or assumptions are commonly shared and not open to scrutiny. However, an intercultural conversation about the validity of human rights is now taking place among people with different cultural assumptions: it is a conversation that proceeds by opening those assumptions to reflection and reexamination. Its participants begin with some minimal shared beliefs: for example, that genocide, slavery, and racism are wrong. They accept some basic rules of argumentation to reveal hidden presuppositions, disclose inconsistencies between ideas, clarify conceptual ambiguity and confusions, and expose conclusions based on insufficient evidence and oversimplified generalizations. In such a conversation based on public reasoning, people may come to agree on a greater range of issues than seemed possible when they began. They may revise or reinterpret their old beliefs. The plausibility of such a conversation suggests a way of establishing universal validity: that is, by referring to public reason in defense of a particular conception or value.

If the concept of human rights can survive the scrutiny of public reason in such a cross-cultural conversation, its universal validity will be confirmed. An idea that has survived the test of rigorous scrutiny will be reasonable or valid not just within the boundaries of particular cultures, but reasonable in a non-relativistic fashion. The deliberation and public reasoning will continue, and it may always be possible for the concept of human rights to become doubtful and subject to revision. But the best available public reasons so far seem to support its universal validity. Such public reasons include the arguments against genocide, slavery, and racial discrimination. Others have emerged from the kind of reasoning that reveals fallacies, confusions, and mistakes involved in the defense of Asian cultural exceptionalism.

Suggestions for Further Reading

See *Confucianism and Human Rights,* edited by Wm. Theodore de Bary and Tu Wei-ming (New York: Columbia University Press, 1998) for a collection of 18 essays by philosophers, historians, and legal scholars based on papers given at two conferences held at the East-West Center in Honolulu.

For the connections between conceptions of human rights and different religious traditions, see *Human Rights and the World's Religions* edited by Leroy Rouner (Notre Dame, IN: University of Notre Dame Press, 1988).

Asian Perspectives on Human Rights, edited by Claude E. Welch, Jr., and Virginia A. Leary (Boulder, CO: Westview Press, 1990), offers a collection of essays by various scholars relating to Asian cultural traditions and the human rights question.

Volume 50 of *Philosophy East and West* (January 2000) contains two articles relevant to the human rights issues: "Dramatic Intervention: Human Rights from a Buddhist Perspective" by Peter D. Hershock and "The Limits of Irony: Rorty and the China Challenge" by Randall Peerenboom.

For information on human rights in China from a Chinese perspective, see *Human Rights in China* (Information Office, The State Council of the People's Republic of China, 1991). For an opposing view, see Fang Lizhi, "Keeping the Faith," *The New York Review of Books,* Vol. XXXV (December 1989), 43–44.

Also on the issue of China, see *Human Rights and Chinese Values,* edited by Michael Davis (New York: Oxford University Press, 1995).

For information on this issue on the Web see http://www.mtholyoke.edu/acad/intrel/freefor.htm.

6.4 Racism and Feminism

Suppose I ask you to list five types of the most common social injustices. I would wager that both racism and sexism are somewhere on that list. Both these social wrongs appear to be so widespread and difficult to eliminate because race and sex are such fundamental features of human existence. However, it clearly is not possible to achieve justice for all as long as racial prejudice and sexual discrimination exist.

It is important to distinguish individual racism and sexism from institutional forms. The first kind involves negative attitudes and beliefs about someone of another race or sex that often results in negative actions such as racial epithets and sexual harassment. The second kind, institutional racism and sexism, involves intitutions' traditional ways of doing things that mistreat people because of their race or sex. For example, for many years blacks and women were not allowed to serve on police forces or in the military in the United States and other countries. Women were not allowed to vote in the United States until 1920, and they are still not allowed to vote in Saudi Arabia. Institutional racism and sexism unfairly create disadvantages for some and advantages for others on irrelevant grounds and thus violate the formal principle of justice (see Section 5.4).

Combating both individual and institutional racism and sexism is the goal of various liberation movements. One thinks of the black power movement or the women's liberation movement of the 1960s and 1970s. Both were intended to empower the victims of racism and sexism. The ideas they spawned—racial equality and feminism—have continued to shape social policy in many countries to the present day.

It has proven very difficult to eliminate the injustices of racism and sexism. Just when we think progress is being made, new forms of both are discovered. In part this is due to our tendencies to see the world from an egocentric viewpoint. In part it is due to the power, prestige, and benefits that result from being in the advantaged group. In part, perhaps in large part, it is due to the elitism that infects all societies. Even efforts devoted to the liberation of one group can mask negative beliefs and attitudes toward other groups. Thus black men fighting for liberation have often excluded women from leadership positions, and white women fighting for sexual equality have discriminated against black women.

The author of our next selection is bell hooks, a professor of English at City College of New York. She was born Gloria Watkins but writes under the name of her great-grandmother in order to pay homage to the unheard voices of black women, past and present. She writes her name all in lowercase, thereby symbolizing her skepticism about the importance of fame even though her book, *Ain't I a Woman,* from which the following selection is taken, brought her fame as an author, activist, and important social critic.

Reading Project and Question

1. Write a critical précis (see Section 2.2) of the selection by bell hooks.
2. What did you learn from reading this selection that you did not know before?

Ain't I a Woman

BELL HOOKS

IN A RETROSPECTIVE EXAMINATION of the black female slave experience, sexism looms as large as racism as an oppressive force in the lives of black women. Institutionalized sexism—that is, patriarchy—formed the base of the American social structure along with racial imperialism. Sexism was an integral part of the social and political order white colonizers brought with them from their European homelands, and it was to have a grave impact on the fate of enslaved black women. In its earliest stages, the slave trade focused primarily on the importation of laborers; the emphasis at that time was on the black male. The black female slave was not as valued as the black male slave. On the average, it cost more money to buy a male slave than a female slave. The scarcity of workers coupled with the relatively few numbers of black women in American colonies caused some white male planters to encourage, persuade, and coerce immigrant white females to engage in sexual relationships with black male slaves as a means of producing new workers. In Maryland, in the year 1664, the first anti-amalgamation law was passed; it was aimed at curtailing sexual relationships between white women and enslaved black men. One part of the preamble of this document stated:

That whatsoever freeborn woman shall intermarry with any slave, from and after the last day

From bell hooks, Ain't I a Woman: Black Women and Feminism, *Boston, MA: South End Press, 1981, pp. 15–19, 87–90, 119–124, 159–161, 194–196. Copyright © 1981 by Gloria Watkins. Reprinted by permission.*

of the present assembly, shall serve the masters of such slaves during the life of her husband; and that all the issue of such free born women, so married shall be slaves as their fathers were.

The most celebrated case of this time was that of Irish Nell, an indentured servant sold by Lord Baltimore to a southern planter who encouraged her to marry a black man named Butler. Lord Baltimore, on hearing of the fate of Irish Nell, was so appalled that white women were either by choice or coercion co-habiting sexually with black male slaves that he had the law repealed. The new law stated that the offspring of relationships between white women and black men would be free. As efforts on the part of outraged white men to curtail inter-racial relationships between black men and white women succeeded, the black female slave acquired a new status. Planters recognized the economic gain they could amass by breeding black slave women. The virulent attacks on slave importation also led to more emphasis on slave breeding. Unlike the offspring of relationships between black men and white women, the offspring of any black slave woman regardless of the race of her mate would be legally slaves, and therefore the property of the owner to whom the female slave belonged. As the market value of the black female slave increased, larger numbers were stolen or purchased by white slave traders.

White male observers of African culture in the 18th and 19th centuries were astounded and impressed by the African male's subjugation of the African female. They were not accustomed to a patriarchal social order that demanded not only that women accept an inferior status, but that they participate actively in the community labor force. Amanda Berry Smith, a 19th century black missionary, visited African communities and reported on the condition of African women:

> The poor women of Africa, like those of India, have a hard time. As a rule, they have all the hard work to do. They have to cut and carry all the wood, carry all the water on their heads, and plant all the rice. The men and boys cut and burn the bush, with the help of the women; but sowing the rice, and planting the cassava, the women have to do.

> You will often see a great, big man walking ahead with nothing in his hand but a cutlass (as they always carry that or a spear), and a woman, his wife, coming on behind with a great big child on her back, and a load on her head.

> No matter how tired she is, her lord would not think of bringing her a jar of water, to cook his supper with, or of beating the rice, no, she must do that.

The African woman schooled in the art of obedience to a higher authority by the tradition of her society was probably seen by the white male slaver as an ideal subject for slavery. As much of the work to be done in the American colonies was in the area of hoe-agriculture, it undoubtedly occurred to slavers that the African female, accustomed to performing arduous work in the fields while also performing a wide variety of tasks in the domestic household, would be very useful on the American plantation. While only a few African women were aboard the first ships bringing slaves to the new world, as the slave trade gathered momentum, females made up one-third of the human cargo aboard most ships. Because they could not effectively resist capture at the hands of thieves and kidnappers, African women became frequent targets for white male slavers. Slavers also used the capture of women important to the tribe, like the daughter of a king, as a means of luring African men into situations where they could be easily captured. Other African women were sold into slavery as punishment for breaking tribal laws. A woman found guilty of committing an act of adultery might be sold into bondage.

White male slavers did not regard the African female as a threat, so often aboard slave ships black women were stored without being shackled while black men were chained to one another. The slavers believed their own safety to be threatened by enslaved African men, but they had no such fear of the African female. The placing of African men in chains was to prevent possible uprisings. As white slavers feared resistance and retaliation at the hands of African men, they placed as much distance between themselves and black male slaves as was possible on board. It was only in relationship to the black female slave that the white slaver could exercise freely absolute power, for he could brutalize and exploit her without fear of harmful retaliation. Black female slaves moving freely about the decks were a ready target for any white male who might choose to physically abuse and torment them. Initially every slave on board the ship was branded with a hot iron. A cat-o'-nine-tails was used by the slavers to lash those Africans that cried out in pain or resisted the torture. Women were lashed severely for crying. They were stripped of their clothing and beaten on all parts of their body. Ruth and Jacob Weldon, an African couple who experienced the horrors of the slave passage, saw "mothers with babes at their breasts basely branded and scarred, till it would seem as if the very heavens might smite the infernal tormentors with the doom they so richly merited." After the branding all slaves were stripped of any clothing. The nakedness of the African female served as a constant reminder of her sexual vulnerability. Rape was a common method of torture slavers used to subdue recalcitrant black women. The threat of rape or other physical brutalization inspired terror in the psyches of displaced African females. Robert Shufeldt, an observer of the slave trade, documented the prevalence of rape on slave ships. He asserts, "In those days many a negress was landed upon our shore already impregnated by someone of the demonic crew that brought her over."

Many African women were pregnant prior to their capture or purchase. They were forced to endure pregnancy without any care given to their diet, without any exercise, and without any assistance during the labor. In their own communities African women had been accustomed to much pampering and care during pregnancy, so the barbaric nature of childbearing on the slave ship was both physically harmful and psychologically demoralizing. Annals of history record that the American slave ship Pongas carried 250 women, many of them pregnant, who were squeezed into a compartment of 16 by 18 feet. The women who survived the initial stages of pregnancy gave birth aboard ship with their bodies exposed to either the scorching sun or the freezing cold. The numbers of black women who died during childbirth

or the number of stillborn children will never be known. Black women with children on board the slave ships were ridiculed, mocked, and treated contemptuously by the slaver crew. Often the slavers brutalized children to watch the anguish of their mothers. In their personal account of life aboard a slave ship, the Weldons recounted an incident in which a child of nine months was flogged continuously for refusing to eat. When beating failed to force the child to eat, the captain ordered that the child be placed feet first into a pot of boiling water. After trying other torturous methods with no success, the captain dropped the child and caused its death. Not deriving enough satisfaction from this sadistic act, he then commanded the mother to throw the body of the child overboard. The mother refused but was beaten until she submitted. . . .

Chapter Three

THE IMPERIALISM OF PATRIARCHY

When the contemporary movement toward feminism began, there was little discussion of the impact of sexism on the social status of black women. The upper and middle class white women who were at the forefront of the movement made no effort to emphasize that patriarchal power, the power men use to dominate women, is not just the privilege of upper and middle class white men, but the privilege of all men in our society regardless of their class or race. White feminists so focused on the disparity between white male/white female economic status as an indication of the negative impact of sexism that they drew no attention to the fact that poor and lower-class men are as able to oppress and brutalize women as any other group of men in American society. The feminist tendency to make synonymous male possession of economic power with being an oppressor caused white men to be labeled "the" enemy. The labeling of the white male patriarch as "chauvinist pig" provided a convenient scapegoat for black male sexists. They could join with white and black women to protest against white male oppression and divert attention away from their sexism, their support of patriarchy, and their sexist exploitation of women. Black leaders, male and female, have been unwilling to acknowledge black male sexist oppression of black women because they do not want to acknowledge that racism is not the only oppressive force in our lives. Nor do they wish to complicate efforts to resist racism by acknowledging that black men can be victimized by racism but at the same time act as sexist oppressors of black women. Consequently there is little acknowledgement of sexist oppression in black male/female relationships as a serious problem. Exaggerated emphasis on the impact of racism on black men has evoked an image of the black male as effete, emasculated, crippled. And so intensely does this image dominate American thinking that people are absolutely unwilling to admit that the damaging effects of racism on black men neither prevents them from being sexist oppressors nor excuses or justifies their sexist oppression of black women.

Black male sexism existed long before American slavery. The sexist politics of white-ruled and colonized America merely reinforced in the minds of enslaved black people existing beliefs that men were the superiors of women. In an earlier discussion of the slave sub-culture I noted that the patriarchal social structure gave the enslaved male higher status than the enslaved female. Historiographers have not been willing to acknowledge either the higher status of the enslaved male in the black sub-culture or the fact that sex-based differentiation of work roles as assigned by white masters reflected a bias towards the male (i.e., black women required to perform "male" tasks but black men not required to perform "female" tasks—women labor in fields but men do no childcare). In modern times, the emphasis on the sexist definition of the male role as that of protector and provider has caused scholars to argue that the most damaging impact of slavery on black people was that it did not allow black men to assume the traditional male role. But the inability of black men to assume the role of protector and provider did not change the reality that men in patriarchal society automatically have higher status than women—they are not

obliged to earn that status. Consequently, the enslaved black male, though obviously deprived of the social status that would enable him to protect and provide for himself and others, had a higher status than the black female slave based solely on his being male. This higher status did not always lead to preferential treatment but it was overtly acknowledged by sex-role differentiation.

Sexist discrimination against all women in the labor force and in higher educational spheres throughout 19th century America meant that of those black people who aspired to leadership roles, either during slavery or at manumission, black men were the more likely candidates. As black men dominated leadership roles, they shaped the early black liberation movement so that it reflected a patriarchal bias. Courageous black women leaders like Sojourner Truth and Harriet Tubman did not represent the norm; they were exceptional individuals who dared to challenge the male vanguard to struggle for freedom. At public appearances, rallies, luncheons, and dinners black male leaders spoke in support of patriarchal rule. They did not talk directly about discriminating against women. Their sexism was shrouded in romantic visions of black men lifting black women to pedestals. Outspoken black nationalist leader Martin Delaney in his political treatise, *The Condition, Elevation, Emigration, and Destiny of the Colored People of the United States,* which was first published in 1852, advocated distinct sex role patterns for black women and men:

> Let our young men and women prepare themselves for usefulness and business; that the men may enter into merchandise, trading, and other things of importance; the young women may become teachers of various kinds, and otherwise fill places of usefulness. . . .
>
> Our females must be qualified, because they are to be the mothers of our children. As mothers are the first nurse and instructors of children; from them children consequently, get their first impression, which being always the most lasting, should be the more correct. Raise the mothers above the level of degradation, and the offspring is elevated with them. In a word, instead of our young men, transcribing in their

blank books recipes for Cooking, we desire to see them making the transfer of Invoices and Merchandise.

Frederick Douglass saw the entire racial dilemma in America as a struggle between white men and black men. In 1865 he published an essay titled "What the Black Man Wants" which argued in favor of black men gaining the vote while women remained disenfranchised:

> Shall we at this moment justify the deprivation of the Negro of the right to vote, because some one else is deprived of that privilege? I hold that women, as well as men, have the right to vote, and my heart and my voice go with the movement to extend suffrage to women; but the question rests on another basis than that on which our rights rest. We may be asked, I say, why we want it. I will tell you why we want it. We want it because it is our right, first of all. No class of men can, without insulting their own nature, be content with any deprivation of their rights.

It is evident in this statement that to Douglass the "negro" was synonymous with the black male. And though he claims in his essay to support woman suffrage, he clearly believed it was more appropriate and fitting that men be given the right to vote. By emphasizing that the right to vote was more important to men than women, Douglass and other black male activists allied themselves with white male patriarchs on the basis of shared sexism. . . .

Chapter Four

RACISM AND FEMINISM:
THE ISSUE OF ACCOUNTABILITY

American women of all races are socialized to think of racism solely in the context of race hatred. Specifically in the case of black and white people, the term racism is usually seen as synonymous with discrimination or prejudice against black people by white people. For most women, the first knowledge of racism as institutionalized oppression is engendered either by direct personal experience or through information gleaned from conversations, books, television, or movies.

Consequently, the American woman's understanding of racism as a political tool of colonialism and imperialism is severely limited. To experience the pain of race hatred or to witness that pain is not to understand its origin, evolution, or impact on world history. The inability of American women to understand racism in the context of American politics is not due to any inherent deficiency in woman's psyche. It merely reflects the extent of our victimization.

No history books used in public schools informed us about racial imperialism. Instead we were given romantic notions of the "new world," the "American dream," America as the great melting pot where all races come together as one. We were taught that Columbus *discovered* America; that "Indians" were scalphunters, killers of innocent women and children; that black people were enslaved because of the biblical curse of Ham, that God "himself" had decreed they would be hewers of wood, tillers of the field, and bringers of water. No one talked of Africa as the cradle of civilization, of the African and Asian people who came to America before Columbus. No one mentioned mass murders of Native Americans as genocide, or the rape of Native American and African women as terrorism. No one discussed slavery as a foundation for the growth of capitalism. No one described the forced breeding of white wives to increase the white population as sexist oppression.

I am a black woman. I attended all-black public schools. I grew up in the south where all around me was the fact of racial discrimination, hatred, and forced segregation. Yet my education as to the politics of race in American society was not that different from that of white female students I met in integrated high schools, in college, or in various women's groups. The majority of us understood racism as a social evil perpetuated by prejudiced white people that could be overcome through bonding between blacks and liberal whites, through militant protest, changing of laws or racial integration. Higher educational institutions did nothing to increase our limited understanding of racism as a political ideology. Instead professors systematically denied us truth, teaching us to accept racial polarity in the form of white supremacy and sexual polarity in the form of male dominance.

American women have been socialized, even brainwashed, to accept a version of American history that was created to uphold and maintain racial imperialism in the form of white supremacy and sexual imperialism in the form of patriarchy. One measure of the success of such indoctrination is that we perpetuate both consciously and unconsciously the very evils that oppress us. I am certain that the black female sixth grade teacher who taught us history, who taught us to identify with the American government, who loved those students who could best recite the pledge of allegiance to the American flag was not aware of the contradiction; that we should love this government that segregated us, that failed to send schools with all black students supplies that went to schools with only white pupils. Unknowingly she implanted in our psyches a seed of the racial imperialism that would keep us forever in bondage. For how does one overthrow, change, or even challenge a system that you have been taught to admire, to love, to believe in? Her innocence does not change the reality that she was teaching black children to embrace the very system that oppressed us, that she encouraged us to support it, to stand in awe of it, to die for it.

That American women, irrespective of their education, economic status, or racial identification, have undergone years of sexist and racist socialization that has taught us to blindly trust our knowledge of history and its effect on present reality, even though that knowledge has been formed and shaped by an oppressive system, is nowhere more evident than in the recent feminist movement. The group of college-educated white middle and upper class women who came together to organize a women's movement brought a new energy to the concept of women's rights in America. They were not merely advocating social equality with men. They demanded a transformation of society, a revolution, a change in the American social structure. Yet as they attempted to take feminism beyond the realm of radical rhetoric and into the realm of American life, they revealed that they had not changed, had not undone the sexist and racist brainwashing that had taught them to regard women unlike themselves as Others. Consequently, the Sisterhood they talked about has not become a reality, and the women's movement they envisioned would have a transformative effect on American culture has not emerged. Instead, the hierarchical pattern of race and sex relationships already established in American society merely took a different form under "feminism": the form of women being classed as an oppressed group under affirmative action programs further perpetuating the myth that the social status of all women in America is the same; the form of women's studies programs being established with all-white faculty teaching literature almost exclusively by white women about white women and frequently from racist perspectives; the form of white women writing books that purport to be about the experience of American women when in fact they concentrate solely on the experience of white women; and finally the form of endless argument and debate as to whether or not racism was a feminist issue.

If the white women who organized the contemporary movement toward feminism were at all remotely aware of racial politics in American history, they would have known that overcoming barriers that separate women from one another would entail confronting the reality of racism, and not just racism as a general evil in society but the race hatred they might harbor in their own psyches. Despite the predominance of patriarchal rule in American society, America was colonized on a racially imperialistic base and not on a sexually imperialistic base. No degree of patriarchal bonding between white male colonizers and Native American men overshadowed white racial imperialism. Racism took precedence over sexual alliances in both the white world's interaction with Native Americans and African Americans, just as racism overshadowed any bonding between black women and white women on the basis of sex. Tunisian writer Albert Memmi emphasizes in *The Colonizer and the Colonized* the impact of racism as a tool of imperialism:

> Racism appears . . . not as an incidental detail, but as a consubstantial part of colonialism. It is the highest expression of the colonial system and one of the most significant features of the

colonialist. Not only does it establish a fundamental discrimination between colonizer and colonized, a sine qua non of colonial life, but it also lays the foundation for the immutability of this life.

While those feminists who argue that sexual imperialism is more endemic to all societies than racial imperialism are probably correct, American society is one in which racial imperialism supersedes sexual imperialism.

In America, the social status of black and white women has never been the same. In 19th and early 20th century America, few if any similarities could be found between the life experiences of the two female groups. Although they were both subject to sexist victimization, as victims of racism black women were subjected to oppressions no white woman was forced to endure. In fact, white racial imperialism granted all white women, however victimized by sexist oppression they might be, the right to assume the role of oppressor in relationship to black women and black men. From the onset of the contemporary move toward feminist revolution, white female organizers attempted to minimize their position in the racial caste hierarchy of American society. In their efforts to disassociate themselves from white men (to deny connections based on shared racial caste), white women involved in the move toward feminism have charged that racism is endemic to white male patriarchy and have argued that they cannot be held responsible for racist oppression. Commenting on the issue of white female accountability in her essay "'Disloyal to Civilization': Feminism, Racism, and Gynephobia," radical feminist Adrienne Rich contends:

> If Black and White feminists are going to speak of female accountability, I believe the word racism must be seized, grasped in our bare hands, ripped out of the sterile or defensive consciousness in which it so often grows, and transplanted so that it can yield new insights for our lives and our movement. An analysis that places the guilt for active domination, physical and institutional violence, and the justifications embedded in myth and language, on white women not only compounds false consciousness; it allows us all to deny or neglect the charged connection among black and white women from the historical conditions of slavery on, and it impedes any real discussion of women's instrumentality in a system which oppresses all women and in which hatred of women is also embedded in myth, folklore, and language.

No reader of Rich's essay could doubt that she is concerned that women who are committed to feminism work to overcome barriers that separate black and white women. However, she fails to understand that from a black female perspective, if white women are denying the existence of black women, writing "feminist" scholarship as if black women are not a part of the collective group American women, or discriminating against black women, then it matters less that North America was colonized by white patriarchal *men* who institutionalized a racially imperialistic social order than that white women who purport to be feminists support and actively perpetuate anti-black racism.

To black women the issue is not whether white women are more or less racist than white men, but that they are racist. If women committed to feminist revolution, be they black or white, are to achieve any understanding of the "charged connections" between white women and black women, we must first be willing to examine woman's relationship to society, to race, and to American culture as it is and not as we would ideally have it be. That means confronting the reality of white female racism. Sexist discrimination has prevented white women from assuming the dominant role in the perpetuation of white racial imperialism, but it has not prevented white women from absorbing, supporting, and advocating racist ideology or acting individually as racist oppressors in various spheres of American life. . . .

Chapter Five

BLACK WOMEN AND FEMINISM

More than a hundred years have passed since the day Sojourner Truth stood before an assembled body of white women and men at an anti-slavery rally in Indiana and bared her breasts to prove that she was indeed a woman. To Sojourner, who had traveled the long road from slavery to freedom, the baring of her breasts was a small matter. She faced her audience without fear, without shame, proud of having been born black and female. Yet the white man who yelled at Sojourner, "I don't believe you really are a woman," unwittingly voiced America's contempt and disrespect for black womanhood. In the eyes of the 19th century white public, the black female was a creature unworthy of the title woman; she was mere chattel, a thing, an animal. When Sojourner Truth stood before the second annual convention of the women's rights movement in Akron, Ohio, in 1852, white women who deemed it unfitting that a black woman should speak on a public platform in their presence screamed: "Don't let her speak! Don't let her speak! Don't let her speak!" Sojourner endured their protests and became one of the first feminists to call their attention to the lot of the black slave woman who, compelled by circumstance to labor alongside black men, was a living embodiment of the truth that women could be the work-equals of men.

It was no mere coincidence that Sojourner Truth was allowed on stage after a white male spoke against the idea of equal rights for women, basing his argument on the notion that woman was too weak to perform her share of manual labor—that she was innately the physical inferior to man. Sojourner quickly responded to his argument, telling her audience:

> . . . Well, children, whar dar is so much racket dar must be something out o' kilter. I tink dat 'twixt de niggers of de Souf and de women at de Norf all a talkin 'bout rights, de white men will be in a fix pretty soon. But what's all dis here talkin' 'bout? Dat man ober dar say dat women needs to be helped into carriages, and lifted ober ditches, and to have de best places . . . and ain't I a woman? Look at me! Look at my arm! . . . I have plowed, and planted, and gathered into barns, and no man could head me—and ain't I a woman? I could work as much as any man (when I could get it), and bear de lash as well—and ain't I a woman? I have borne five children and I seen 'em mos all sold off into slavery, and when I cried out with a mother's grief, none but Jesus hear—and ain't I a woman?

Unlike most white women's rights advocates, Sojourner Truth could refer to her own personal life experience as evidence of woman's ability to function as a parent; to be the work equal of man; to undergo persecution, physical abuse, rape, torture; and to not only survive but emerge triumphant.

Sojourner Truth was not the only black woman to advocate social equality for women. Her eagerness to speak publicly in favor of women's rights despite public disapproval and resistance paved the way for other politically-minded black women to express their views. Sexism and racism have so informed the perspective of American historiographers that they have tended to overlook and exclude the effort of black women in discussions of the American women's rights movement. White female scholars who support feminist ideology have also ignored the contribution of black women. In contemporary works, like *The Remembered Gate: Origins of American Feminism* by Barbara Berg; *Herstory* by June Sochen, *Hidden from History* by Sheila Rowbothan, *The Women's Movement* by Barbara Deckard, to name a few, the role black women played as advocates for women's rights in the 19th century is never mentioned. Eleanor Flexner's *Century of Struggle*, which was first published in 1959, remains one of the very few book-length historical works on the women's rights movement that documents the participation of black women.

Most women involved in the recent move toward a feminist revolution assume that white women have initiated all feminist resistance to male chauvinism in American society, and further assume that black women are not interested in women's liberation. While it is true that white women have led every movement toward feminist revolution in American society, their dominance is less a sign of black female disinterest in feminist struggle than an indication that the politics of colonization and racial imperialism have made it historically impossible for black women in the United States to lead a women's movement. . . .

Feminism is an ideology in the making. According to the Oxford English Dictionary the term "feminism" was first used in the latter part of the 19th century and it was defined as having the "qualities of females." The meaning of the term has been gradually transformed and the 20th century dictionary definition of feminism is a "theory of the political, economic, and social equality of the sexes." To many women this definition is inadequate. In the introduction to *The Remembered Gate: Origins of American Feminism* Barbara Berg defines feminism as a "broad movement embracing numerous phases of woman's emancipation." She further states:

> It is the freedom to decide her own destiny; freedom from sex-determined role; freedom from society's oppressive restrictions; freedom to express her thoughts fully and to convert them freely to actions. Feminism demands the acceptance of woman's right to individual conscience and judgment. It postulates that woman's essential worth stems from her common humanity and does not depend on the other relationships of her life.

Her expanded definition of feminism is useful but limited. Many women have found that neither the struggle for "social equality" nor the focus on an "ideology of woman as an autonomous being" are enough to rid society of sexism and male domination. To me feminism is not simply a struggle to end male chauvinism or a movement to ensure that women will have equal rights with men; it is a commitment to eradicating the ideology of domination that permeates Western culture on various levels—sex, race, and class, to name a few—and a commitment to reorganizing U.S. society so that the self-development of people can take precedence over imperialism, economic expansion, and material desires. Writers of a feminist pamphlet published anonymously in 1976 urged women to develop political consciousness:

> In all these struggles we must be assertive and challenging, combating the deep-seated tendency in Americans to be liberal, that is, to evade struggling over questions of principle for fear of creating tensions or becoming unpopular. Instead we must live by the fundamental dialectical principle: that progress comes only from struggling to resolve contradictions.

It is a contradiction that white females have structured a women's liberation movement that is racist and excludes many non-white women. However, the existence of that contradiction should not lead any woman to ignore feminist issues. Oftentimes I am asked by black women to explain why I would call myself a feminist and by using that term ally myself with a movement that is racist. I say, "The question we must ask again and again is how can racist women call themselves feminists." It is obvious that many women have appropriated feminism to serve their own ends, especially those white women who have been at the forefront of the movement; but rather than resigning myself to this appropriation I choose to re-appropriate the term "feminism," to focus on the fact that to be "feminist" in any authentic sense of the term is to want for all people, female and male, liberation from sexist role patterns, domination, and oppression.

Today masses of black women in the U.S. refuse to acknowledge that they have much to gain by feminist struggle. They fear feminism. They have stood in place so long that they are afraid to move. They fear change. They fear losing what little they have. They are afraid to openly confront white feminists with their racism or black males with their sexism, not to mention confronting white men with their racism and sexism. I have sat in many a kitchen and heard black women express a belief in feminism and eloquently critique the women's movement explaining their refusal to participate. I have witnessed their refusal to express these same views in a public setting. I know their fear exists because they have seen us trampled upon, raped, abused, slaughtered, ridiculed and mocked. Only a few black women have rekindled the spirit of feminist struggle that stirred the hearts and minds of our 19th century sisters. We, black women who advocate feminist ideology, are pioneers. We are clearing a path for ourselves and our sisters. We hope that as they see us reach our goal—no longer victimized, no longer unrecognized, no longer afraid—they will take courage and follow.

Suggestions for Further Reading

See *Remembered Rapture* by bell hooks (New York: Henry Holt & Company, 1999) for a collection of essays illuminating writing and women's issues.

The selected bibliography in *Ain't I a Woman* will take you deeper into the literature that informed hooks.

Esther Chow's "The Feminist Movement: Where Are All the Asian American Women?" in *From Different Shores: Perspectives on Race and Ethnicity in America,* edited by Ronald Takaki, 2nd Edition (New York: Oxford University Press, 1994), will add an Asian perspective.

For an excellent collection of articles and a good bibliography on women's subordination as it relates to race and class, see Part 3 of *Feminist Frameworks: Alternative Theoretical Accounts of the Relations between Women and Men,* edited by Alison M. Jaggar and Paula S. Rothenberg, 3rd Edition (New York: McGraw-Hill, Inc, 1993).

See "Bell Hooks Resources" at http://www.gpc.peachnet.edu/~mnunes/hooks.html for information on hooks and links to web sites dealing with issues of racism, feminism, and classism.

Videos

See *Understanding Prejudice* (50 minutes) and *Racism in the 20th Century* (48 minutes) for treatments of some of the issues associated with racism. Both are available from Films for the Humanities and Sciences, PO Box 2053, Princeton, NJ 08543. A historically illuminating treatment of the early days of the women's movement in the United States can be seen in *The Story of Elizabeth Cady Stanton and Susan B. Anthony* (3 hours) by Ken Burns and Paul Barnes. Available from PBS at www.pbs.org/shop.

6.5 The Affirmative Action Debate

I am sure that all of you would agree that discrimination based on sex, race, ethnicity, religion, and sexual preference has occurred in many countries. You also recognize that there is widespread agreement today that hiring, promotion, housing, and educational practices that routinely work to the disadvantage of African Americans, women, Mexican Americans, Native Americans, Asians, and others because of their race, sex, or ethnicity are morally wrong.

But why are they are morally wrong? Having learned some moral philosophy, you might say that discrimination of the sort I have mentioned is wrong because it violates the formal principle of justice, which requires that we make decisions based on relevant criteria. It is simply not fair to refuse to hire someone just because he or she is black or brown or a he or a she when that person can do a job perfectly well.

In recognition of past wrongs and in the hope of producing a more just society, *affirmative action* programs were started. There are a wide variety of such programs, but some of the most controversial are often called "preferential treatment" programs. Such programs require that "all things being equal," preferential treatment should be given to minority and female applicants.

Such preferential treatment programs are often justified by appeal to the principle of compensatory justice, which states that whenever an injustice has happened, a just compensation must be made to those who have been injured. If Mexican Americans, for example, have been "disadvantaged" in the past because of their ethnicity, it is only right to "advantage" them now. Sometimes such programs are justified by appeal to the *principle of utility,* which states that when the interests of everyone affected are given equal weight, the action that is morally correct will, on balance, produce better consequences than any alternative.

It would appear that preferential treatment programs can disadvantage one group because of its race, sex, or ethnicity and advantage another because of these same factors. This has led some to charge that such programs amount to *reverse discrimination.* If past discrimination based on sex, ethnicity, or race was wrong because it violated the formal principle of justice, then present discrimination based on those factors is also wrong and wrong for the same reason.

However, are affirmative action programs really a second wrong? In the first selection, Warren Kessler, professor of philosophy at Fresno State University, argues that they are not. He considers some of the standard arguments against affirmative action and finds them wanting.

Even if these standard criticisms fail, however, there may be other considerations. In the second selection, Shelby Steele, professor of English at San Jose State University and author of the award-winning book *The Content of Our Character* (1990), argues that current affirmative action policies perpetuate, rather than alleviate, the very harm such policies are meant to eliminate.

Reading Project and Question

1. Write a critical précis (see Section 2.2) of both selections.
2. What did you learn that you did not know before from reading these two selections?

Is Affirmative Action a Second Wrong?

WARREN KESSLER

1. PHILOSOPHICAL ARGUMENTS against affirmative action have been raised since the creation of this controversial social policy in 1973. They have become even more significant since the backlash against affirmative action found advocates on the Supreme Court and among Republican party leaders, who have seen the critique of affirmative action both as a matter of program and tactic. Recently two significant events reflect objections to affirmative action: the passage of Proposition 209 in California and the Supreme

Court's decision in a University of Texas case, banning the use of race in admissions decisions.[1]

As with any significant ethical issue or public policy question worthy of debate, there are good arguments and good people on both sides of the affirmative action issue. Yet it is amazing how many bad arguments there are surrounding this subject, not only bad arguments out in the body

1. *Hopwood v. Texas* May 19, 1996.

This paper was delivered at the 27th Annual Conference on Value Inquiry: Twentieth-Century Values, April 1999, at Central Missouri State University and at the Central Valley [CA] Philosophy Association on October 23, 1999. Reprinted by permission of the author.

politic and the media talk shows, but in the discourse of generally superb philosophers.

In this paper I will concentrate on the most prominent charge that affirmative action is itself unjust because it is a form of "reverse discrimination" or "discrimination based on race or gender."

2. The charge that affirmative action is reverse discrimination emerged concurrently with the policy itself and has become the mantra of affirmative action's critics in and out of philosophy. At the heart of the argument is the belief that affirmative action excludes well-qualified white men from jobs, promotions, college admissions, graduate programs, and opportunities to enter professions based solely on their race and gender. The critics also argue that the preferential treatment affirmative action programs give to certain women and men of color works to the disadvantage of many women or members of various ethnic groups who are not favored by affirmative action.

In one of the earliest and most prominently published statements of this argument, Lisa Newton claims that giving a preference of any sort to women and people of color based on affirmative action is a form of discrimination, an injustice, and that this is wrong per se, whether or not the discrimination is "reverse discrimination."

> . . . all discrimination is wrong *prima facie* because it violates justice, and that goes for reverse discrimination too. No violation of justice among citizens may be justified (may overcome the *prima facie* objection) by appeal to the ideal of equality, for that ideal is logically dependent upon the ideal of justice.[2]

> When the southern employer refuses to hire blacks in white collar jobs, when Wall Street will only hire women as secretaries with new titles, when Mississippi high schools routinely flunk all black boys above ninth grade, we have examples of injustice. . . . But of course, when the employers and the schools *favor* women and blacks the same injustice is done.[3]

Newton argues, following Aristotle, that political justice is equal treatment before the law. Any unequal treatment based on race or gender, rather than on behavior, performance or ability is an improper form of unequal treatment under law and is therefore unjust.

3. One problem in common to all of the arguments alleging that affirmative action is reverse discrimination is that they rarely specify how the discrimination occurs. Critics such as Governor Wilson allege that "Today, affirmative action preferences are actually quotas based on race and gender."[4] Yet, in fact, EEOC guidelines have never required quotas, but only goals and timetables, when under representation of women or other protected classes has been demonstrated.

The Supreme Court allows quotas only in rare circumstances. These are always in the context of legal findings of overt discrimination or a consent decree in which an employer admits to having discriminated and accepts the quota as a remedy for past discrimination. In a sense, the quota is a punishment for the employer's past discrimination. It is only when the past and present discrimination are so clear that quotas are used or allowed. The employer is charged with remedying the discrimination in a systematic way and is not trusted to work with less formal goals and timetables in good faith.

When only goals and timetables are used, it is not at all evident that any kind of discrimination occurs at all under affirmative action. Affirmative action requires that an organization examine its outreach efforts to assure that its advertising is reaching women and minorities. It requires that the business evaluate its job criteria to be sure that they are functionally related to the ability to do the job and do not discriminate even unintentionally against women or minorities.

An example of such inadvertent discrimination occurred in Newark, New Jersey before their 1967 riot. In analyzing the causes of the riot, city officials heard many Puerto Ricans argue angrily that there were no Puerto Rican police officers in the entire city. Police officials were

---

2. Newton, Lisa, "Reverse Discrimination is Unjustified," *Ethics* 83 (1973), 310.
3. Ibid., p. 310.

4. *Los Angeles Times,* September 1996, comment on Proposition 209.

puzzled, because they had been trying to recruit some Puerto Rican officers. What they discovered was that a height requirement was excluding Puerto Ricans, even though the city wanted to hire them and they had applied.

Affirmative action is working for business. When the Bush administration sought to repeal affirmative action, the U.S. Chamber of Commerce opposed the plan. The Chamber argued that, although its members hadn't wanted affirmative action in the first place, it was working effectively to diversify their work force, overcome racial and gender bigotry at work, and bring talented women and minorities into a wide range of positions from which they had previously been excluded.

In a recent testimony before Congress, Deval L. Patrick, Assistant Attorney General of the Justice Department's Civil Rights Division, stated that the evidence does not bear out the myth that "there are unqualified, undeserving women and minorities who are getting the benefits that ought to go to qualified and deserving men."[5] He said affirmative action laws allow consideration of minority status only in cases where applicants' job or academic qualifications are comparable, and where the quality of the resulting pool of students or workers would not be compromised.

Anecdotes are legion in which unsuccessful white male applicants were told by a boss or a personnel director that they would have been given a job or promotion except for the fact that "we had to give it to a minority." Yet why, in the absence of a court order or consent decree, would any employer in his or her right mind turn away the person they thought best qualified "just to hire a minority member"?[6] In all probability, the employer has chosen the person he or she believes is best qualified for the job, but does not

have the integrity to state that honestly to disappointed applicants.

4. The beauty of an argument like Newton's is its appeal to our straightforward sense that, whatever the benefits of a policy or course of action, two wrongs do not make a right. If it is wrong for southern employers to discriminate against blacks, Newton claims, it is just as wrong for us to discriminate in favor of blacks, however benevolent our reasons might be. It does not matter how much good can be done by an injustice, as critics of utilitarianism have argued for centuries. Punishing people we know to be innocent would be wrong even if it reduced crime by some deterrent effect.

Although it is clearly wrong to do something wrong because someone else has, it does not follow that when we do something like what a wrongdoer does to respond to his wrongdoing, we are always committing a second wrong. It is extremely interesting that the two wrongs argument has such appeal with affirmative action and not in a whole host of other situations. If a police officer shoots at a bank robber who has shot customers and is firing at police in a getaway, we do not accuse the police of "reverse shooting." If an orthopedic surgeon breaks a broken leg in order to set it properly, we do not accuse the doctor of "reverse leg breaking." In the paradigm case of "fighting fire with fire," when firefighters in forest fires set backfires to stop the rush of a fire, we do not accuse the firefighters of "reverse arson." Why not? Because we usually accept the purposes for which they are acting as they do. We consider the tactic they employ to be justified, even though in some sense it would be *prima facie* wrong without an appropriate context, precisely because there is an appropriate context, because we consider the tactic being employed to be the best way of achieving acceptable or important goals, even though they would be wrongs in other contexts—e.g., if the police fired at an unarmed criminal or a criminal who had surrendered.

An analogy I find illuminating is insurance. Most of us who own cars have automobile insurance. Yet in any given year, most car owners do not have serious claims to make on their

5. *New York Times*, July 12, 1996.

6. In reality what is often occurring is that the employer is having it both ways, getting the best person for the job, diversifying a work force in demographic conditions that make this valuable, and continuing to stir the fires of racism or sexism by encouraging those they turn away to blame women and minorities rather than the employer.

insurance. Innocent as they may be, and good drivers at that, they pay out premiums to businesses that keep some portion for operations, some for profit and then pass the balance on to total strangers whom they never harmed. Only a bad reader of Ayn Rand or a good reader of John Hospers would call this "a coercive program of income redistribution" or "a confiscatory tax to subsidize or compensate people we have never harmed."[7]

We accept insurance as a practice, in part because we are covered by it ourselves and could benefit from participation in the pooled fund if we suffered an accident or a theft. However, most of us do not suffer an accident or theft in a given year, and so we see our funds get funneled to others year after year. Why do we accept this? An obvious consideration is that we have agreed to pool liability and that we realize that those who are actually harmed by accident or theft or injury need help.

We do not whine and mutter because others did the harm, not us—the equivalent of saying, "I never owned slaves. I don't discriminate." We see other members of society injured, we realize they need help, and we have found insurance an acceptable way of sharing risks, sharing responsibility and helping those in need.

It is difficult to escape the implication that the kicking and screaming about reverse discrimination from many of its sources rest in a rejection of the goals of affirmative action. It entails a denial of real and continuing discrimination against women and people of color, this despite abundant evidence of glass ceilings, 70 percent pay for women doing work comparable to men, etc. Men and women with a remarkable number of social and educational advantages continue to argue that they have nothing to do with past or continuing discrimination. They have had the advantage of going to good schools in relatively segregated neighborhoods, schools that receive preferential funding because of the reliance of the school system on property tax. They also have had access to better reading materials, media, and culture at home because of the socioeconomic advantages of their parents. Critics of affirmative action continue to push near total reliance for college admissions on SAT scores and grades, though parental income is the most consistent variable associated with SAT scoring differences.

The photos and films of Citadel cadets jumping for joy at the withdrawal of the first woman cadet in their history are worth a thousand words. If we were perfectly honest, we would admit that faculty committees and departments have jumped with similar joy emotionally when they have made affirmative action fail—e.g., when they could manipulate a hiring process so that a white male was appointed over affirmative action candidates they put on the short list to appease their administration, or when their first woman or black did not get tenure or left on his or her own after sensing the hostility and distance that oozed through the professional veneer of their "colleagues."

5. The two-wrongs criticism gains some of its force from the realization that discrimination in its normal, pernicious form is totally arbitrary—that is, it involves biases that are either totally baseless or a function of hasty generalizations about a group. For affirmative action, the charge that it is a form of "reverse" discrimination seems connected with the view that ethnicity and gender are not related to the ability to do a job or be a good student. While it is true that being a woman per se does not imbue someone with special insight or sensitivity of any sort—for example, employers and schools are increasingly aware of the benefits diversity brings to a workplace or college. Just a day after the University of California Regents voted to repeal their affirmative action policies, major employers in my community were asserting that they would continue to seek diversity despite decisions by organizations like the U.C. to end affirmative action or even court decisions barring quotas and set asides. A spokesperson for Pacific Gas and Electric, California's largest utility, said PG&E remained committed to diversity for two reasons. "It's the right thing to do, and it makes good

7. Ayn Rand, *The Virtue of Selfishness*, reissue edition. (New York: New American Library, 1989); John Hospers, "What Libertarianism Is," in *The Libertarian Alternative*, ed. by Tibor Machan (New York: Prentice-Hall), 1974.

business sense." The human resource manager of a Dow Chemical factory said, "Diversity is just good business. We want to be a good corporate citizen and we should represent the ethnic makeup of the work force."[8]

Critics of affirmative action fail to consider that the experience of a woman or a black man might actually improve their contribution to a business meeting or the capacity of an academic department to encourage, advise, and teach students. Businesses that are trying to reach Hispanic customers frequently fall victim to quirks of translation they do not recognize because they do not have anyone conversant with Spanish or Mexican dialects to check their work. The Chevy Nova ran into unexpected difficulty in South America because "*no va*" in Spanish means "doesn't go."[9] Police departments are frequently charged with racism because they send all white police into black neighborhoods or have no one from a Southeast Asian background to interact with citizens in a neighborhood filled with new Southeast Asian immigrants.

If a quota or point system is used in such a way as to bar white men from serious consideration for a job in the event that qualified women or people of color are in the pool, one might make a case that race or gender are being used in a discriminatory way. No doubt affirmative action is sometimes applied—or more accurately—*mis*-

applied that way. If, however, white men receive honest and fair consideration, but women and minorities are preferred among comparable candidates because their presence on a job or in a class or in a meeting would add depth and dimension to deliberations and help the organization do its job more effectively, merit is still paramount and there is no invidious discrimination. It is not height discrimination for the NBA to want centers close to seven feet tall. Employers are no more to be faulted if they have reason to believe that women and people of color will be assets to their organization and that diversity is a strength.

6. There are a few considerations that I need to mention in closing. First, most defenders of affirmative action realize that it is an imperfect system at best and that in an ideal world it would not be needed. It does not follow, of course, that because a policy is needed in a less than ideal world that it is immoral or unjust. Tom Beauchamp is particularly articulate on this point. He concedes that there may be elements of injustice toward white men in the affirmative action process. Certainly some white men experience degrees of hardship they would not if employers and schools were not using affirmative action programs. But Beauchamp presents abundant evidence of continuing discrimination against women and minorities. He argues that, as with many social policies and laws, we are warranted in accepting the *prima facie* wrong done to some men and women for the greater good of society. This greater good requires that we end artificial barriers to the employment, education and advancement of women and people of color.

Of course, this is a utilitarian argument, and it is at the heart of many criticisms of affirmative action that utilitarianism is rejected in favor of a deontology of some sort in which a harm or injustice to even one white male is considered sufficient to repudiate the whole affirmative action project. While rejecting utilitarianism is fashionable for philosophers, the alternative does not really look so good when it smacks of Kant's absolutism.

Critics of affirmative action who will not tolerate one iota of harm or inconvenience to a white

---

8. *Fresno Bee,* July 14, 1996.

9. Ford had a similar problem in Brazil when the Pinto flopped. The company found out that Pinto was Brazilian slang for tiny male genitals. Ford pried all the nameplates off and substituted Corcel, which means horse. Similarly, after printing thousands of signs in China, Coca-Cola discovered that, depending on the dialect, the phrase means bite the wax tadpole or female horse stuffed with wax. In Taiwan, the translation of the Pepsi slogan "Come alive with the Pepsi Generation" came out as "Pepsi will bring your ancestors back from the dead." Also in China, the Kentucky Fried Chicken slogan "fingerlickin good" came out as "eat your fingers off." The American slogan for Salem cigarettes, "Salem—Feeling Free," got translated in the Japanese market into "When smoking Salem, you feel so refreshed that your mind seems to be free and empty." In France, Colgate introduced a toothpaste called Cue, the name of a notorious porno magazine. In Italy, a campaign for Schweppes tonic water translated the name into Schweppes toilet water. (Michael O'Horo, Jaffe Associates, Inc., *A Virtual Consultancy*)

male or white woman recoil in outrage when liberals say they would rather that a thousand guilty criminals go free than that an innocent person is found guilty for lack of due process, procedural error, or inadequate representation. They are often willing to execute criminals who represent no clear and present danger and place a limit on the number of appeals someone might have if convicted, while they scream bloody murder about the absolute injustice of counting race or gender in employment or college admission.

As with insurance, which we have come to accept because we find it a decent way to handle real problems, we have come to accept the x-raying of baggage and the emptying of our pockets at airport terminals to quell skyjacking and terrorism. We do not hear mass outcries from the critics of affirmative action that such x-raying and searching are an injustice to the millions of travelers who are not skyjackers or terrorists and have given no one probable cause to believe that they have weapons or bombs with them. Because we have accepted the fundamental goal of protecting the airlines against these crimes, we accept the justice of what would have previously been considered an injustice.

It is evident that the largest part of the rejection of affirmative action as "reverse discrimination" and "injustice" does not rest on any consistent commitment to justice or a consistent rejection of utilitarian approaches to law and law enforcement. Except for a highly principled few, it reflects a rejection of the goals of affirmative action, the opening of employment and educational opportunity, not merely at entry levels but at all levels of management and professional status.

Affirmative action is not a second wrong or a wrong against justice. It is an imperfect response to deep and endemic patterns of social, political, economic, and cultural oppression.

Like tools used in fighting other evils, it has unsavory aspects and can always be improved. Yet it will remain important and morally justified to consider gender and ethnic differences as a means of remedying both past and continuing discrimination, to take differences into account until such differences no longer make a difference to the detriment of women, people of color, and our entire society.

The Price of Preference

SHELBY STEELE

IN A FEW SHORT YEARS, when my two children will be applying to college, the affirmative action policies by which most universities offer black students some form of preferential treatment will present me with a dilemma. I am a middle-class black, a college professor, far from wealthy, but also well-removed from the kind of deprivation that would qualify my children for the label "disadvantaged." Both of them have endured racial insensitivity from whites. They have been called names, have suffered slights, and have experienced first-hand the peculiar malevolence that racism brings out in people. Yet, they have never experienced racial discrimination, have never been stopped by their race on any path they have chosen to follow. Still, their society now tells them that if they will only designate themselves as black on their college applications, they

From The Content of our Character: A New Vision of Race in America *by Shelby Steele. New York: St. Martin's Press, pp. 111–125. Copyright © 1990 by Shelby Steele. Reprinted by permission of St. Martin's Press Incorporated.*

will likely do better in the college lottery than if they conceal this fact. I think there is something of a Faustian bargain in this.

Of course, many blacks and a considerable number of whites would say that I was sanctimoniously making affirmative action into a test of character. They would say that this small preference is the meagerest recompense for centuries of unrelieved oppression. And to these arguments other very obvious facts must be added. In America, many marginally competent or flatly incompetent whites are hired everyday—some because their white skin suits the conscious or unconscious racial preference of their employer. The white children of alumni are often grandfathered into elite universities in what can only be seen as a residual benefit of historic white privilege. Worse, white incompetence is always an individual matter, while for blacks it is often confirmation of ugly stereotypes. The Peter Principle was not conceived with only blacks in mind. Given that unfairness cuts both ways, doesn't it only balance the scales of history that my children now receive a slight preference over whites? Doesn't this repay, in a small way, the systematic denial under which their grandfather lived out his days?

So, in theory, affirmative action certainly has all the moral symmetry that fairness requires—the injustice of historical and even contemporary white advantage is offset with black advantage; preference replaces prejudice, inclusion answers exclusion. It is reformist and corrective, even repentant and redemptive. And I would never sneer at these good intentions. Born in the late forties in Chicago, I started my education (a charitable term in this case) in a segregated school and suffered all the indignities that come to blacks in a segregated society. My father, born in the South, only made it to the third grade before the white man's fields took permanent priority over his formal education. And though he educated himself into an advanced reader with an almost professional authority, he could only drive a truck for a living and never earned more than ninety dollars a week in his entire life. So, yes, it is crucial to my sense of citizenship, to my ability to identify with the spirit and the interests of America, to know

that this country, however imperfectly, recognizes its past sins and wishes to correct them.

Yet good intentions, because of the opportunity for innocence they offer us, are very seductive and can blind us to the effects they generate when implemented. In our society, affirmative action is, among other things, a testament to white goodwill and to black power, and in the midst of these heavy investments, its effects can be hard to see. But after twenty years of implementation, I think affirmative action has shown itself to be more bad than good and that blacks—whom I will focus on in this essay—now stand to lose more from it than they gain.

In talking with affirmative action administrators and with blacks and whites in general, it is clear that supporters of affirmative action focus on its good intentions while detractors emphasize its negative effects. Proponents talk about "diversity" and "pluralism"; opponents speak of "reverse discrimination," the unfairness of quotas and set-asides. It was virtually impossible to find people outside either camp. The closest I came was a white male manager at a large computer company who said, "I think it amounts to reverse discrimination, but I'll put up with a little of that for a little more diversity." I'll live with a little of the effect to gain a little of the intention, he seemed to be saying. But this only makes him a halfhearted supporter of affirmative action. I think many people who don't really like affirmative action support it to one degree or another anyway.

I believe they do this because of what happened to white and black Americans in the crucible of the sixties when whites were confronted with their racial guilt and blacks tasted their first real power. In this stormy time white absolution and black power coalesced into virtual mandates for society. Affirmative action became a meeting ground for these mandates in the law, and in the late sixties and early seventies it underwent a remarkable escalation of its mission from simple anti-discrimination enforcement to social engineering by means of quotas, goals, timetables, set-asides, and other forms of preferential treatment.

Legally, this was achieved through a series of executive orders and EEOC guidelines that allowed racial imbalances in the workplace to stand as proof of racial discrimination. Once it could be assumed that discrimination explained racial imbalances, it became easy to justify group remedies to presumed discrimination, rather than the normal case-by-case redress for proven discrimination. Preferential treatment through quotas, goals, and so on is designed to correct imbalances based on the assumption that they always indicate discrimination. This expansion of what constitutes discrimination allowed affirmative action to escalate into the business of social engineering in the name of anti-discrimination, to push society toward statistically proportionate racial representation, without any obligation of proving actual discrimination.

What accounted for this shift, I believe, was the white mandate to achieve a new racial innocence and the black mandate to gain power. Even though blacks had made great advances during the sixties without quotas, these mandates, which came to a head in the very late sixties, could no longer be satisfied by anything less than racial preferences. I don't think these mandates in themselves were wrong, since whites clearly needed to do better by blacks and blacks needed more real power in society. But, as they came together in affirmative action, their effect was to distort our understanding of racial discrimination in a way that allowed us to offer the remediation of preference on the basis of mere color rather than actual injury. By making black the color of preference, these mandates have re-burdened society with the very marriage of color and preference (in reverse) that we set out to eradicate. The old sin is reaffirmed in a new guise.

But the essential problem with this form of affirmative action is the way it leaps over the hard business of developing a formerly oppressed people to the point where they can achieve proportionate representation on their own (given equal opportunity) and goes straight for the proportionate representation. This may satisfy some whites of their innocence and some blacks of

their power, but it does very little to truly uplift blacks.

A white female affirmative action officer at an Ivy League university told me what many supporters of affirmative action now say: "We're after diversity. We ideally want a student body where racial and ethnic groups are represented according to their proportion in society." When affirmative action escalated into social engineering, diversity became a golden word. It grants whites an egalitarian fairness (innocence) and blacks an entitlement to proportionate representation (power). *Diversity* is a term that applies democratic principles to races and cultures rather than to citizens, despite the fact that there is nothing to indicate that real diversity is the same thing as proportionate representation. Too often the result of this on campus (for example) has been a democracy of colors rather than of people, an artificial diversity that gives the appearance of an educational parity between black and white students that has not yet been achieved in reality. Here again, racial preferences allow society to leapfrog over the difficult problem of developing blacks to parity with whites and into a cosmetic diversity that covers the blemish of disparity—a full six years after admission, only about 26 percent of black students graduate from college.

Racial representation is not the same thing as racial development, yet affirmative action fosters a confusion of these very difficult needs. Representation can be manufactured; development is always hard-earned. However, it is the music of innocence and power that we hear in affirmative action that causes us to cling to it and to its distracting emphasis on representation. The fact is that after twenty years of racial preferences, the gap between white and black median income is greater than it was in the seventies. None of this is to say that blacks don't need policies that ensure our right to equal opportunity, but what we need more is the development that will let us take advantage of society's efforts to include us.

I think that one of the most troubling effects of racial preferences for blacks is a kind of demoralization, or put another way, an enlargement of self-doubt. Under affirmative action the quality that earns us preferential treatment is an implied inferiority. However this inferiority is explained—it is still inferiority. There are explanations, and then there is the fact. And the fact must be borne by the individual as a condition apart from the explanation, apart even from the fact that others like himself also bear this condition. In integrated situations where blacks must compete with whites who may be better prepared these explanations may quickly wear thin and expose the individual to racial as well as personal self-doubt.

All of this is compounded by the cultural myth of black inferiority that blacks have always lived with. What this means in practical terms is that when blacks deliver themselves into integrated situations, they encounter a nasty little reflex in whites, a mindless, atavistic reflex that responds to the color black with alarm. Attributions may follow this alarm if the white cares to indulge them, and if they do, they will most likely be negative—one such attribution is intellectual ineptness. I think this reflex and the attributions that may follow it embarrass most whites today; therefore, it is usually quickly repressed. Nevertheless, on an equally atavistic level, the black will be aware of the reflex his color triggers and will feel a stab of horror at seeing himself reflected in this way. He, too, will do a quick repression, but a lifetime of such stabbings is what constitutes his inner realm of racial doubt.

The effects of this may be a subject for another essay. The point here is that the implication of inferiority that racial preferences engender in both the white and black mind expands rather than contracts this doubt. Even when the black sees no implication of inferiority in racial preferences, he knows that whites do, so that—consciously or unconsciously—the result is virtually the same. The effect of preferential treatment—the lowering of normal standards to increase black representation—puts blacks at war with an expanded realm of debilitating doubt, so that the doubt itself becomes an unrecognized preoccupation that undermines their ability to perform, especially in integrated situations. On largely white campuses, blacks are five times more likely to drop out than whites. Preferential treatment, no matter how it is justified in the light of day, subjects blacks to a midnight of self-doubt, and so often transforms their advantage into a revolving door.

Another liability of affirmative action comes from the fact that it indirectly encourages blacks to exploit their own past victimization as a source of power and privilege. Victimization, like implied inferiority, is what justifies preference, so that to receive the benefits of preferential treatment one must, to some extent, become invested in the view of one's self as a victim. In this way, affirmative action nurtures a victim-focused identity in blacks. The obvious irony here is that we become inadvertently invested in the very condition we are trying to overcome. Racial preferences send us the message that there is more power in our past suffering than our present achievements—none of which could bring us a *preference* over others.

When power itself grows out of suffering, then blacks are encouraged to expand the boundaries of what qualifies as racial oppression, a situation that can lead us to paint our victimization in vivid colors, even as we receive the benefits of preference. The same corporations and institutions that give us preference are also seen as our oppressors. At Stanford University minority students—some of whom enjoy as much as $15,000 a year in financial aid—recently took over the president's office demanding, among other things, more financial aid. The power to be found in victimization, like any power, is intoxicating and can lend itself to the creation of a new class of supervictims who can feel the pea of victimization under twenty mattresses. Preferential treatment rewards us for being underdogs rather than for moving beyond that status—a misplacement of incentives that, along with its deepening of our doubt, is more a yoke than a spur.

But, I think, one of the worst prices that blacks pay for preference has to do with an illusion. I saw this illusion at work recently in the mother of a middle-class black student who was going off to his first semester of college. "They owe us this, so don't think for a minute that you don't belong there." This is the logic by which many blacks, and some whites, justify affirmative action—it is something "owed," a form of reparation. But this logic overlooks looks a much harder and less digestible reality, that it is impossible to repay blacks living today for the historic suffering of the race. If all blacks were given a million dollars tomorrow morning it would not amount to a dime on the dollar of three centuries of oppression, nor would it obviate the residues of that oppression that we still carry today. The concept of historic reparation grows out of man's need to impose a degree of justice on the world that simply does not exist. Suffering can be endured and overcome; it cannot be repaid. Blacks cannot be repaid for the injustice done to the race, but we can be corrupted by society's guilty gestures of repayment.

Affirmative action is such a gesture. It tells us that racial preferences can do for us what we cannot do for ourselves. The corruption here is in the hidden incentive *not* to do what we believe preferences will do. This is an incentive to be reliant on others just as we are struggling for self-reliance. And it keeps alive the illusion that we can find some deliverance in repayment. The hardest thing for any sufferer to accept is that his suffering excuses him from very little and never has enough currency to restore him. To think otherwise is to prolong the suffering.

Several blacks I spoke with said they were still in favor of affirmative action because of the "subtle" discrimination blacks were subject to once on the job. One photojournalist said, "They have ways of ignoring you." A black female television producer said, "You can't file a lawsuit when your boss doesn't invite you to the insider meetings without ruining your career. So we still need affirmative action." Others mentioned the infamous "glass ceiling" through which blacks can see the top positions of authority but never reach them. But I don't think racial preferences are a protection against this subtle discrimination; I think they contribute to it.

In any workplace, racial preferences will always create two-tiered populations composed of preferreds and unpreferreds. This division makes automatic a perception of enhanced competence for the unpreferreds and of questionable competence for the preferreds—the former earned his way, even though others were given preference, while the latter made it by color as much as by competence. Racial preferences implicitly mark whites with an exaggerated superiority just as they mark blacks with an exaggerated inferiority. They not only reinforce America's oldest racial myth but, for blacks, they have the effect of stigmatizing the already stigmatized.

I think that much of the "subtle" discrimination that blacks talk about is often (not always) discrimination against the stigma of questionable competence that affirmative action delivers to blacks. In this sense, preferences scapegoat the very people they seek to help. And it may be that at a certain level employers impose a glass ceiling, but this may not be against the race so much as against the race's reputation for having advanced by color as much as by competence. Affirmative action makes a glass ceiling virtually necessary as a protection against the corruptions of preferential treatment. This ceiling is the point at which corporations shift the emphasis from color to competency and stop playing the affirmative action game. Here preference backfires for blacks and becomes a taint that holds them back. Of course, one could argue that this taint, which is, after all, in the minds of whites, becomes nothing more than an excuse to discriminate against blacks. And certainly the result is the same in either case—blacks don't get past the glass ceiling. But this argument does not get around the fact that racial preferences now taint this color with a new theme of suspicion that makes it even more vulnerable to the impulse in others to discriminate. In this crucial yet gray area of perceived competence, preferences make whites look better than they are and blacks worse, while doing nothing whatever to stop the very real discrimination that blacks may encounter. I don't wish to justify the glass ceiling here, but only to suggest the very subtle ways that affirmative action revives rather than extinguishes the old rationalizations for racial discrimination.

In education, a revolving door; in employment, a glass ceiling.

I believe affirmative action is problematic in our society because it tries to function like a social program. Rather than ask it to ensure equal opportunity we have demanded that it create parity between the races. But preferential treatment does not teach skills, or educate, or instill motivation. It only passes out entitlement by color, a situation that in my profession has created an unrealistically high demand for black professors. The social engineer's assumption is that this high demand will inspire more blacks to earn Ph.D.'s and join the profession. In fact, the number of blacks earning Ph.D.'s has declined in recent years. A Ph.D. must be developed from preschool on. He requires family and community support. He must acquire an entire system of values that enables him to work hard while delaying gratification. There are social programs, I believe, that can (and should) help blacks *develop* in all these areas, but entitlement by color is not a social program; it is a dubious reward for being black. . . .

I would also like to see affirmative action go back to its original purpose of enforcing equal opportunity—a purpose that in itself disallows racial preferences. We cannot be sure that the discriminatory impulse in America has yet been shamed into extinction, and I believe affirmative action can make its greatest contribution by providing a rigorous vigilance in this area. It can guard constitutional rather than racial rights, and help institutions evolve standards of merit and selecting that are appropriate to the institution's needs yet as free of racial bias as possible (again, with the understanding that racial imbalances are not always an indication of racial bias). One of the most important things affirmative action can do is to define exactly what racial discrimination is and how it might manifest itself within a specific institution. The impulse to discriminate *is* subtle and cannot be ferreted out unless its many guises are made clear to people. Along with this there should be monitoring of institutions and heavy

sanctions brought to bear when actual discrimination is found. This is the sort of affirmative action that America owes to blacks and to itself. It goes after the evil of discrimination itself, while preferences only sidestep the evil and grant entitlement to its *presumed* victims.

But if not preferences, then what? I think we need social policies that are committed to two goals: the educational and economic development of disadvantaged people, regardless of race, and the eradication from our society—through close monitoring and severe sanctions—of racial, ethnic, or gender discrimination. Preferences will not deliver us to either of these goals, since they tend to benefit those who are not disadvantaged—middle-class blacks—and attack one form of discrimination with another. Preferences are inexpensive and carry the glamour of good intentions—change the numbers and the good deed is done. To be against them is to be unkind. But I think the unkindest cut is to bestow on children like my own an undeserved advantage while neglecting the development of those disadvantaged children on the East Side of my city who will likely never be in a position to benefit from a preference. Give my children fairness; give disadvantaged children a better shot at development— better elementary and secondary schools, job training, safer neighborhoods, better financial assistance for college, and so on. Fewer blacks go to college today than ten years ago; more black males of college age are in prison or under the control of the criminal justice system than in college. This despite racial preferences.

The mandates of black power and white absolution out of which preferences emerged were not wrong in themselves. What was wrong was that both races focused more on the goals of these mandates than on the means to the goals. Blacks can have no real power without taking responsibility for their own educational and economic development. Whites can have no racial innocence without earning it by eradicating discrimination and helping the disadvantaged to develop. Because we ignored the means, the goals have not been reached, and the real work remains to be done.

Suggestions for Further Reading

For a good collection of articles (although somewhat dated) on the issue of reverse discrimination, see *Equality and Preferential Treatment,* edited by Marshall Cohen, Thomas Nagel, and Thomas Scanlon (Princeton, NJ: Princeton University Press, 1977).

For a review of a number of recent books on affirmative action, see Andrew Hacker, "Goodbye to Affirmative Action?" *The New York Review of Books* 43 (July 11, 1996): 21–29. Hacker argues that politically there seems to be little hope for affirmative action programs, but research reveals that they have been the most effective way yet devised to achieve racial and sexual equality. The AAUP has issued a report of the action of the Board of Regents of the University of California to end affirmative action admission policies. See "The Board of Regents of the University of California, Governance, and Affirmative Action," *Academe* 82 (July–August 1996): 61–66.

In Chapter 5 of *Race Matters* (Boston: Beacon Press, 1993), Cornel West deals with affirmative action as it relates to race, and in *A Darker Shade of Crimson: Odyssey of a Harvard Chicano* (New York: Bantam Books, 1993) Ruben Navarette, Jr. recounts his experiences as a Mexican American at Harvard. He argues that most affirmative action programs serve only a few high-achieving Latinos.

Videos

Affirmative Action Versus Reverse Discrimination (60 minutes; produced by Annenberg) examines charges that affirmative action policies amount to reverse discrimination. See your Media Services Catalog for more information.

Legislating Morality: Affirmative Action and the Burden of History (26 minutes) explores whether affirmative action promotes racial balance (Films for the Humanities and Sciences, PO Box 2053, Princeton, NJ 08543).

6.6 The Animal Rights Debate

Do other-than-human animals have moral rights? That is, do we as humans have a moral obligation or duty to animals that are not human?

At first you might be inclined to answer, "Yes." After all, if someone has a pet cat or dog and they neglect or mistreat that animal, we hold them both morally and legally responsible for their actions. What if my neighbor kicks or injures my dog Arthur? Isn't that wrong, and can I not call on the police to prosecute my neighbor for animal abuse?

Why do we hold people responsible for pet abuse? "Well," you might say, "because to harm a pet harms the owner of the pet or at least harms the interests that humans have in that pet and its safety." Does it not, however, harm the animal too? If we only argue that it is wrong to harm animals because it is in the interests of human animals not to do so, we would be assuming that animals have no intrinsic or inherent rights, and we have only indirect duties to them.

Do we not have direct obligations? Isn't it wrong to harm pets, not only because it harms human interests in having healthy and happy other-than-human companions, but also because it inflicts suffering on our pets directly, and they have a right to be free from suffering?

Some of you might view pets as a special case. While it is true many societies punish and forbid pet abuse, many societies also permit painful medical, cosmetic, and chemical research to be done on dogs, cats, rabbits, monkeys and other animals (although we forbid such research on human animals). We allow farmers to raise calves in confined quarters in order to produce better quality veal, and we allow slaughterhouses to kill and butcher animals so people can eat them, not to mention permitting hunters to hunt them, trappers to trap them, and furriers to skin them. Society clearly allows quite a bit of animal suffering to occur legally, so maybe we do not have any moral obligations to animals in general—only to our pets and the pets of others. But why single out one group? If we have direct moral obligations to some animals, why not to all animals—human and other-than-human alike? Can the case be made that all or most animals have rights? How might we go about developing that sort of argument?

In the first selection that follows, Tom Regan, professor of philosophy at North Carolina State University, explores how we might develop a strong moral argument for animal rights. In the second selection, Mary Anne Warren, professor of philosophy at San Francisco State University, raises some critical questions and offers some counterarguments to Regan's position.

Reading Questions

1. How do the concepts of direct duties and indirect duties relate to the debate about animal rights?
2. What is wrong with the contractarian and utilitarian moral theories?
3. How does the rights view of morality support the case for animal rights?
4. According to Warren, what is wrong with Regan's strong animal rights position?
5. How does Warren make the case that animal rights are weaker than human rights?
6. Who do you think makes the most persuasive case, Regan or Warren? Why?

The Case for Animal Rights

TOM REGAN

I REGARD MYSELF as an advocate of animal rights—as a part of the animal rights movement. That movement, as I conceive it, is committed to a number of goals, including:

- the total abolition of the use of animals in science;
- the total dissolution of commercial animal agriculture;

- the total elimination of commercial and sport hunting and trapping.

There are, I know, people who profess to believe in animal rights but do not avow these goals. Factory farming, they say, is wrong—it violates animals' rights—but traditional animal agriculture is all right. Toxicity tests of cosmetics on animals violates their rights, but important medical

From In Defence of Animals, *edited by Peter Singer, Oxford: Basil Blackwell, 1985, pp. 13–26. Reprinted by permission of the author and the publisher.*

research—cancer research, for example—does not. The clubbing of baby seals is abhorrent, but not the harvesting of adult seals. I used to think I understood this reasoning. Not any more. You don't change unjust institutions by tidying them up.

What's wrong—fundamentally wrong—with the way animals are treated isn't the details that vary from case to case. It's the whole system. The forlornness of the veal calf is pathetic, heart wrenching; the pulsing pain of the chimp with electrodes planted deep in her brain is repulsive; the slow, torturous death of the raccoon caught in the leg-hold trap is agonizing. But what is wrong isn't the pain, isn't the suffering, isn't the deprivation. These compound what's wrong. Sometimes—often—they make it much, much worse. But they are not the fundamental wrong.

The fundamental wrong is the system that allows us to view animals as *our resources,* here for *us*—to be eaten, or surgically manipulated, or exploited for sport or money. Once we accept this view of animals—as our resources—the rest is as predictable as it is regrettable. Why worry about their loneliness, their pain, their death? Since animals exist for us, to benefit us in one way or another, what harms them really doesn't matter—or matters only if it starts to bother us, makes us feel a trifle uneasy. . . .

In the case of animals in science, whether and how we abolish their use . . . are to a large extent political questions. People must change their beliefs before they change their habits. Enough people, especially those elected to public office, must believe in change—must want it—before we will have laws that protect the rights of animals. This process of change is very complicated, very demanding, very exhausting, calling for the efforts of many hands in education, publicity, political organization and activity, down to the licking of envelopes and stamps. As a trained and practicing philosopher, the sort of contribution I can make is limited but, I like to think, important. The currency of philosophy is ideas—their meaning and rational foundation—not the nuts and bolts of the legislative process, say, or the mechanics of community organization. That's what I have been exploring over the past ten years or

so in my essays and talks and, most recently, in my book, *The Case for Animal Rights.* I believe the major conclusions I reach in the book are true because they are supported by the weight of the best arguments. I believe the idea of animal rights has reason, not just emotion, on its side.

In the space I have at my disposal here I can only sketch, in the barest outline, some of the main features of the book. Its main themes—and we should not be surprised by this—involve asking and answering deep, foundational moral questions about what morality is, how it should be understood and what is the best moral theory, all considered. I hope I can convey something of the shape I think this theory takes. The attempt to do this will be (to use a word a friendly critic once used to describe my work) cerebral, perhaps too cerebral. But this is misleading. My feelings about how animals are sometimes treated run just as deep and just as strong as those of my more volatile compatriots. Philosophers do—to use the jargon of the day—have a right side to their brains. If it's the left side we contribute (or mainly should), that's because what talents we have reside there.

How to proceed? We begin by asking how the moral status of animals has been understood by thinkers who deny that animals have rights. Then we test the mettle of their ideas by seeing how well they stand up under the heat of fair criticism. If we start our thinking in this way, we soon find that some people believe that we have no duties directly to animals, that we owe nothing to them, that we can do nothing that wrongs them. Rather, we can do wrong acts that involve animals, and so we have duties regarding them, though none to them. Such views may be called indirect duty views. By way of illustration: suppose your neighbor kicks your dog. Then your neighbor has done something wrong. But not to your dog. The wrong that has been done is a wrong to you. After all, it is wrong to upset people, and your neighbor's kicking your dog upsets you. So you are the one who is wronged, not your dog. Or again: by kicking your dog your neighbor damages your property. And since it is wrong to damage another person's property, your neighbor has done something wrong—to you, of course, not to your dog. Your neighbor no more wrongs your dog than your car would be wronged if the windshield were smashed. Your neighbor's duties involving your dog are indirect duties to you. More generally, all of our duties regarding animals are indirect duties to one another—to humanity.

How could someone try to justify such a view? Someone might say that your dog doesn't feel anything and so isn't hurt by your neighbor's kick, doesn't care about the pain since none is felt, is as unaware of anything as is your windshield. Someone might say this, but no rational person will, since, among other considerations, such a view will commit anyone who holds it to the position that no human being feels pain either—that human beings also don't care about what happens to them. A second possibility is that though both humans and your dog are hurt when kicked, it is only human pain that matters. But, again, no rational person can believe this. Pain is pain wherever it occurs. If your neighbor's causing you pain is wrong because of the pain that is caused, we cannot rationally ignore or dismiss the moral relevance of the pain that your dog feels.

Philosophers who hold indirect duty views—and many still do—have come to understand that they must avoid the two defects just noted: that is, both the view that animals don't feel anything as well as the idea that only human pain can be morally relevant. Among such thinkers the sort of view now favored is one or other form of what is called *contractarianism*.

Here, very crudely, is the root idea: morality consists of a set of rules that individuals voluntarily agree to abide by, as we do when we sign a contract (hence the name contractarianism). Those who understand and accept the terms of the contract are covered directly; they have rights created and recognized by, and protected in, the contract. And these contractors can also have protection spelled out for others who, though they lack the ability to understand morality and so cannot sign the contract themselves, are loved or cherished by those who can. Thus young children, for example, are unable to sign contracts and lack rights. But they are protected by the contract nonetheless because of the sentimental interests of others, most notably their parents. So we have, then, duties involving these children, duties regarding them, but no duties to them. Our duties in their case are indirect duties to other human beings, usually their parents.

As for animals, since they cannot understand contracts, they obviously cannot sign; and since they cannot sign, they have no rights. Like children, however, some animals are the objects of the sentimental interest of others. You, for example, love your dog or cat. So those animals that enough people care about (companion animals, whales, baby seals, the American bald eagle), though they lack rights themselves, will be protected because of the sentimental interests of people. I have, then, according to contractarianism, no duty directly to your dog or any other animal, not even the duty not to cause them pain or suffering; my duty not to hurt them is a duty I have to those people who care about what happens to them. As for other animals, where no or little sentimental interest is present—in the case of farm animals, for example, or laboratory rats—what duties we have grow weaker and weaker, perhaps to vanishing point. The pain and death they endure, though real, are not wrong if no one cares about them.

When it comes to the moral status of animals, contractarianism could be a hard view to refute if it were an adequate theoretical approach to the moral status of human beings. It is not adequate in this latter respect, however, which makes the question of its adequacy in the former case, regarding animals, utterly moot. For consider: morality, according to the (crude) contractarian position before us, consists of rules that people agree to abide by. What people? Well, enough to make a difference—enough, that is, *collectively* to have the power to enforce the rules that are drawn up in the contract. That is very well and good for the signatories but not so good for anyone who is not asked to sign. And there is nothing in contractarianism of the sort we are discussing that guarantees or requires that everyone will have a chance to participate equally in framing the rules of morality. The result is that this approach to ethics could sanction the most blatant forms of social, economic, moral and political injustice, ranging from a repressive caste system to systematic racial or sexual discrimination. Might, according to this theory, does make right. Let those who are the victims of injustice suffer as they will. It matters not so long as no one else—no contractor, or too few of them—cares about it. Such a theory takes one's moral breath away . . . as if, for example, there would be nothing wrong with apartheid in South Africa if few white South Africans were upset by it. A theory with so little to recommend it at the level of the ethics of our treatment of our fellow humans cannot have anything more to recommend it when it comes to the ethics of how we treat our fellow animals.

The version of contractarianism just examined is, as I have noted, a crude variety, and in fairness to those of a contractarian persuasion it must be noted that much more refined, subtle and ingenious varieties are possible. For example, John Rawls, in his *A Theory of Justice*, sets forth a version of contractarianism that forces contractors to ignore the accidental features of being a human being—for example, whether one is white or black, male or female, a genius or of modest intellect. Only by ignoring such features, Rawls believes, can we ensure that the principles of justice that contractors would agree upon are not based on bias or prejudice. Despite the improvement a view such as Rawls's represents over the cruder forms of contractarianism, it remains deficient: it systematically denies that we have direct duties to those human beings who do not have a sense of justice—young children, for instance, and many mentally retarded humans. And yet it seems reasonably certain that, were we to torture a young child or a retarded elder, we would be doing something that wronged him or her, not something that would be wrong if (and only if) other humans with a sense of justice were upset. And since this is true in the case of these humans, we cannot rationally deny the same in the case of animals.

Indirect duty views, then, including the best among them, fail to command our rational assent. Whatever ethical theory we should accept rationally, therefore, it must at least recognize that we have some duties directly to animals, just as we have some duties directly to each other. . . .

Some people think that the theory we are looking for is utilitarianism. A utilitarian accepts two moral principles. The first is that of equality: everyone's interests count, and similar interests must be counted as having similar weight or importance. White or black, American or Iranian, human or animal—everyone's pain or frustration matter[s], and matter[s] as much as the equivalent pain or frustration of anyone else. The second principle a utilitarian accepts is that of utility: do the act that will bring about the best balance between satisfaction and frustration for everyone affected by the outcome.

As a utilitarian, then, here is how I am to approach the task of deciding what I morally ought to do: I must ask who will be affected if I choose to do one thing rather than another, how much each individual will be affected, and where the best results are most likely to lie—which option, in other words, is most likely to bring about the best results, the best balance between satisfaction and frustration. That option, whatever it may be, is the one I ought to choose. That is where my moral duty lies.

The great appeal of utilitarianism rests with its uncompromising *egalitarianism:* everyone's interests count and count as much as the like interests of everyone else. The kind of odious discrimination that some forms of contractarianism can justify—discrimination based on race or sex, for example—seems disallowed in principle by utilitarianism, as is speciesism, systematic discrimination based on species membership.

The equality we find in utilitarianism, however, is not the sort an advocate of animal or human rights should have in mind. Utilitarianism has no room for the equal moral rights of different individuals because it has no room for their equal inherent value or worth. What has value for the utilitarian is the satisfaction of an individual's interests, not the individual whose interests they are. A universe in which you satisfy your desire for water, food and warmth is, other things being equal, better than a universe in which these desires are frustrated. And the same is true in the case of an animal with similar desires. But neither you nor the animal have any value in your own right. Only your feelings do.

Here is an analogy to help make the philosophical point clearer. A cup contains different liquids, sometimes sweet, sometimes bitter, sometimes a mix of the two. What has value are the liquids: the sweeter the better, the bitterer the worse. The cup, the container, has no value. It is what goes into it, not what they go into, that has value. For the utilitarian you and I are like the cup; we have no value as individuals and thus no equal value. What has value is what goes into us, what we serve as receptacles for; our feelings of satisfaction have positive value, our feelings of frustration negative value.

Serious problems arise for utilitarianism when we remind ourselves that it enjoins us to bring about the best consequences. What does this mean? It doesn't mean the best consequences for me alone, or for my family or friends, or any other person taken individually. No, what we must do is, roughly, as follows: we must add up (somehow!) the separate satisfactions and frustrations of everyone likely to be affected by our choice, the satisfactions in one column, the frustrations in the other. We must total each column for each of the options before us. That is what it means to say the theory is aggregative. And then we must choose that option which is most likely to bring about the best balance of totaled satisfactions over totaled frustrations. Whatever act would lead to this outcome is the one we ought morally to perform—it is where our moral duty lies. And that act quite clearly might not be the same one that would bring about the best results for me personally, or for my family or friends, or for a lab animal. The best aggregated consequences for everyone concerned are not necessarily the best for each individual.

That utilitarianism is an aggregative theory—different individuals' satisfactions or frustrations are added, or summed, or totaled—is the key objection to this theory. My Aunt Bea is old, inactive, a cranky, sour person, though not physically ill. She prefers to go on living. She is also rather rich. I could make a fortune if I could get my hands on her money, money she intends to give me in any event, after she dies, but which she re-

fuses to give me now. In order to avoid a huge tax bite, I plan to donate a handsome sum of my profits to a local children's hospital. Many, many children will benefit from my generosity, and much joy will be brought to their parents, relatives and friends. If I don't get the money rather soon, all these ambitions will come to naught. The once-in-a-lifetime opportunity to make a real killing will be gone. Why, then, not kill my Aunt Bea? Oh, of course I *might* get caught. But I'm no fool and, besides, her doctor can be counted on to cooperate (he has an eye for the same investment and I happen to know a good deal about his shady past). The deed can be done . . . professionally, shall we say. There is *very* little chance of getting caught. And as for my conscience being guilt-ridden, I am a resourceful sort of fellow and will take more than sufficient comfort—as I lie on the beach at Acapulco—in contemplating the joy and health I have brought to so many others.

Suppose Aunt Bea is killed and the rest of the story comes out as told. Would I have done anything wrong? Anything immoral? One would have thought that I had. Not according to utilitarianism. Since what I have done has brought about the best balance between totaled satisfaction and frustration for all those affected by the outcome, my action is not wrong. Indeed, in killing Aunt Bea the physician and I did what duty required.

This same kind of argument can be repeated in all sorts of cases, illustrating, time after time, how the utilitarian's position leads to results that impartial people find morally callous. It *is* wrong to kill my Aunt Bea in the name of bringing about the best results for others. A good end does not justify an evil means. Any adequate moral theory will have to explain why this is so. Utilitarianism fails in this respect and so cannot be the theory we seek.

What to do? Where to begin anew? The place to begin, I think, is with the utilitarian's view of the value of the individual—or, rather, lack of value. In its place, suppose we consider that you and I, for example, do have value as individuals—what we'll call *inherent value*. To say we have such value is to say that we are something more than, something different from, mere receptacles. Moreover, to ensure that we do not pave the way for such injustices as slavery or sexual discrimination, we must believe that all who have inherent value have it equally, regardless of their sex, race, religion, birthplace and so on. Similarly to be discarded as irrelevant are one's talents or skills, intelligence and wealth, personality or pathology, whether one is loved and admired or despised and loathed. The genius and the retarded child, the prince and the pauper, the brain surgeon and the fruit vendor, Mother Teresa and the most unscrupulous used-car salesman—all have inherent value, all possess it equally, and all have an equal right to be treated with respect, to be treated in ways that do not reduce them to the status of things, as if they existed as resources for others. My value as an individual is independent of my usefulness to you. Yours is not dependent on your usefulness to me. For either of us to treat the other in ways that fail to show respect for the other's independent value is to act immorally, to violate the individual's rights.

Some of the rational virtues of this view— what I call the rights view—should be evident. Unlike (crude) contractarianism, for example, the rights view *in principle* denies the moral tolerability of any and all forms of racial, sexual or social discrimination; and unlike utilitarianism, this view *in principal* denies that we can justify good results by using evil means that violate an individual's rights—denies, for example, that it could be moral to kill my Aunt Bea to harvest beneficial consequences for others. That would be to sanction the disrespectful treatment of the individual in the name of the social good, something the rights view will not—categorically will not— ever allow.

The rights view, I believe, is rationally the most satisfactory moral theory. It surpasses all other theories in the degree to which it illuminates and explains the foundation of our duties to one another—the domain of human morality. On this score it has the best reasons, the best arguments, on its side. Of course, if it were possible to show that only human beings are included within its scope, then a person like myself, who believes in animal rights, would be obliged to look elsewhere.

But attempts to limit its scope to humans only can be shown to be rationally defective. Animals, it is true, lack many of the abilities humans possess. They can't read, do higher mathematics, build a bookcase or make *baba ghanoush*. Neither can many human beings, however, and yet we don't (and shouldn't) say that they (these humans) therefore have less inherent value, less of a right to be treated with respect, than do others. It is the *similarities* between those human beings who most clearly, most non-controversially have such value (the people reading this, for example), not our differences, that matter most. And the really crucial, the basic similarity is simply this: we are each of us the experiencing subject of a life, a conscious creature having an individual welfare that has importance to us whatever our usefulness to others. We want and prefer things, believe and feel things, recall and expect things. And all these dimensions of our life, including our pleasure and pain, our enjoyment and suffering, our satisfaction and frustration, our continued existence or our untimely death—all make a difference to the quality of our life as lived, as experienced, by us as individuals. As the same is true of those animals that concern us, . . . they too must be viewed as the experiencing subjects of a life, with inherent value of their own.

Some there are who resist the idea that animals have inherent value. "Only humans have such value," they profess. How might this narrow view be defended? Shall we say that only humans have the requisite intelligence, or autonomy, or reason? But there are many, many humans who fail to meet these standards and yet are reasonably viewed as having value above and beyond their usefulness to others. Shall we claim that only humans belong to the right species, the species *Homo sapiens*? But this is blatant speciesism. Will it be said, then, that all—and only—humans have immortal souls? Then our opponents have their work cut out for them. I am myself not illdisposed to the proposition that there are immortal souls. Personally, I profoundly hope I have one. But I would not want to rest my position on a controversial ethical issue on the even more controversial question about who or what has an immortal soul. That is to dig one's hole deeper, not to climb out. Rationally, it is better to resolve moral issues without making more controversial assumptions than are needed. The question of who has inherent value is such a question, one that is resolved more rationally without the introduction of the idea of immortal souls than by its use.

Well, perhaps some will say that animals have some inherent value, only less than we have. Once again, however, attempts to defend this view can be shown to lack rational justification. What could be the basis of our having more inherent value than animals? Their lack of reason, or autonomy, or intellect? Only if we are willing to make the same judgment in the case of humans who are similarly deficient. But it is not true that such humans—the retarded child, for example, or the mentally deranged—have less inherent value than you or I. Neither, then, can we rationally sustain the view that animals, like them in being the experiencing subjects of a life, have less inherent value. *All* who have inherent value have it *equally,* whether they be human animals or not.

Inherent value, then, belongs equally to those who are the experiencing subjects of a life. Whether it belongs to others—to rocks and rivers, trees and glaciers, for example—we do not know and may never know. But neither do we need to know, if we are to make the case for animal rights. We do not need to know, for example, how many people are eligible to vote in the next presidential election before we can know whether I am. Similarly, we do not need to know how many individuals have inherent value before we can know that some do. When it comes to the case for animal rights, then, what we need to know is whether the animals that, in our culture, are routinely eaten, hunted and used in our laboratories, for example, are like us in being subjects of a life. And we do know this. We do know that many—literally, billions and billions—of these animals are the subjects of a life in the sense explained and so have inherent value if we do. And since, in order to arrive at the best theory of

our duties to one another, we must recognize our equal inherent value as individuals, reason—not sentiment, not emotion—reason compels us to recognize the equal inherent value of these animals and, with this, their equal right to be treated with respect.

That, *very* roughly, is the shape and feel of the case for animal rights. Most of the details of the supporting argument are missing. They are to be found in the book to which I alluded earlier. Here, the details go begging, and I must, in closing, limit myself to four final points.

The first is how the theory that underlies the case for animal rights shows that the animal rights movement is a part of, not antagonistic to, the human rights movement. The theory that rationally grounds the rights of animals also grounds the rights of humans. Thus those involved in the animal rights movement are partners in the struggle to secure respect for human rights—the rights of women, for example, or minorities, or workers. The animal rights movement is cut from the same moral cloth as these.

Second, having set out the broad outlines of the rights view, I can now say why its implications for . . . science, among other fields, are both clear and uncompromising. In the case of the use of animals in science, the rights view is categorically abolitionist. Lab animals are not our tasters; we are not their kings. Because these animals are treated routinely, systematically as if their value were reducible to their usefulness to others, they are routinely, systematically treated with a lack of respect, and thus are their rights routinely, systematically violated. This is just as true when they are used in trivial, duplicative, unnecessary or unwise research as it is when they are used in studies that hold out real promise of human benefits. We can't justify harming or killing a human being (my Aunt Bea, for example) just for these sorts of reason. Neither can we do so even in the case of so lowly a creature as a laboratory rat. It is not just refinement or reduction that is called for, not just larger, cleaner cages, not just more generous use of anesthetic or the elimination of multiple surgery, not just tidying up the system. It is complete replacement. The best we can do when it comes to using animals in science is—not to use them. That is where our duty lies, according to the rights view. . . .

My last two points are about philosophy, my profession. It is, most obviously, no substitute for political action. The words I have written here and in other places by themselves don't change a thing. It is what we do with the thoughts that the words express—our acts, our deeds—that changes things. All that philosophy can do, and all I have attempted, is to offer a vision of what our deeds should aim at. And the why. But not the how.

Finally, I am reminded of my thoughtful critic, the one I mentioned earlier, who chastised me for being too cerebral. Well, cerebral I have been: indirect duty views, utilitarianism, contractarianism—hardly the stuff deep passions are made of. I am also reminded, however, of the image another friend once set before me—the image of the ballerina as expressive of disciplined passion. Long hours of sweat and toil, of loneliness and practice, of doubt and fatigue: those are the discipline of her craft. But the passion is there too,

the fierce drive to excel, to speak through her body, to do it right, to pierce our minds. That is the image of philosophy I would leave with you, not "too cerebral" but *disciplined passion*. Of the discipline enough has been seen. As for the passion: there are times, and these not infrequent, when tears come to my eyes when I see, or read, or hear of the wretched plight of animals in the hands of humans. Their pain, their suffering, their loneliness, their innocence, their death. Anger. Rage. Pity. Sorrow. Disgust. The whole creation groans under the weight of the evil we humans visit upon these mute, powerless creatures. It *is* our hearts, not just our heads, that call for an end to it all, that demand of us that we overcome, for them, the habits and forces behind their systematic oppression. All great movements, it is written, go through three stages: ridicule, discussion, adoption. It is the realization of this third stage, adoption, that requires both our passion and our discipline, our hearts and our heads. The fate of animals is in our hands. God grant we are equal to the task.

Difficulties with the Strong Animal Rights Position

MARY ANNE WARREN

TOM REGAN HAS PRODUCED what is perhaps the definitive defense of the view that the basic moral rights of at least some non-human animals are in no way inferior to our own. In *The Case for Animal Rights,* he argues that all normal mammals over a year of age have the same basic moral rights.[1] Non-human mammals have essentially the same right not to be harmed or killed as we do. I shall call this "the strong animal rights po-

sition," although it is weaker than the claims made by some animal liberationists in that it ascribes rights to only some sentient animals.[2]

I will argue that Regan's case for the strong animal rights position is unpersuasive and that this position entails consequences which a reasonable person cannot accept. I do not deny that some non-human animals have moral rights;

1. Tom Regan, *The Case for Animal Rights* Rights (Berkeley: University of California Press, 1983). All page references are to this edition.

2. For instance, Peter Singer, although he does not like to speak of rights, includes all sentient beings under the protection of his basic utilitarian principle of equal respect for like interests. (*Animal Liberation* [New York: Avon Books, 1975], p. 3.)

From Between the Species 2, No. 4. (Fall 1987): 163–73. Reprinted by permission of the author and the publisher.

indeed, I would extend the scope of the rights claim to include all sentient animals, that is, all those capable of having experiences, including experiences of pleasure or satisfaction and pain, suffering, or frustration.[3] However, I do not think that the moral rights of most non-human animals are indentical in strength to those of persons.[4] The rights of most non-human animals may be overridden in circumstances which would not justify overriding the rights of persons. There are, for instance, compelling realities which sometimes require that we kill animals for reasons which could not justify the killing of persons. I will call this view "the weak animal rights" position, even though it ascribes rights to a wider range of animals than does the strong animal rights position.

I will begin by summarizing Regan's case for the strong animal rights position and noting two problems with it. Next, I will explore some consequences of the strong animal rights position which I think are unacceptable. Finally, I will outline the case for the weak animal rights position.

Regan's Case

Regan's argument moves through three stages. First, he argues that normal, mature mammals are not only sentient but have other mental capacities, as well. These include the capacities for emotion, memory, belief, desire, the use of general concepts, intentional action, a sense of the future, and some degree of self-awareness. Creatures with such capacities are said to be subjects-of-a-life. They are not only alive in the biological sense but have a psychological identity over time and

an existence which can go better or worse for them. Thus, they can be harmed or benefitted. These are plausible claims, and well defended. One of the strongest parts of the book is the rebuttal of philosophers, such as R. G. Frey, who object to the application of such mentalistic terms to creatures that do not use a human-style language.[5] The second and third stages of the argument are more problematic.

In the second stage, Regan argues that subjects-of-a-life have inherent value. His concept of inherent value grows out of his opposition to utilitarianism. Utilitarian moral theory, he says, treats individuals as "mere receptacles" for morally significant value, in that harm to one individual may be justified by the production of a greater net benefit to other individuals. In opposition to this, he holds that subjects-of-a-life have a value independent of both the value they may place upon their lives or experiences and the value others may place upon them.

Inherent value, Regan argues, does not come in degrees. To hold that some individuals have more inherent value than others is to adopt a "perfectionist" theory, i.e., one which assigns different moral worth to individuals according to how well they are thought to exemplify some virtue(s), such as intelligence or moral autonomy. Perfectionist theories have been used, at least since the time of Aristotle, to rationalize such injustices as slavery and male domination, as well as the unrestrained exploitation of animals. Regan argues that if we reject these injustices, then we must also reject perfectionism and conclude that all subjects-of-a-life have equal inherent value. Moral agents have no more inherent value than moral patients, i.e., subjects-of-a-life who are not morally responsible for their actions.

In the third phase of the argument, Regan uses the thesis of equal inherent value to derive strong moral rights for all subjects-of-a-life. This thesis underlies the Respect Principle, which forbids us to treat beings who have inherent value as mere receptacles, i.e., mere means to the production of the greatest overall good. This

---

3. The capacity for sentience, like all of the mental capacities mentioned in what follows, is a disposition. Dispositions do not disappear whenever they are not currently manifested. Thus, sleeping or temporarily unconscious persons or non-human animals are still sentient in the relevant sense (i.e., still capable of sentience), so long as they still have the neurological mechanisms necessary for the occurrence of experiences.

4. It is possible, perhaps probable that some non-human animals—such as cetaceans and anthropoid apes—should be regarded as persons. If so, then the weak animal rights position holds that these animals have the same basic moral rights as human persons.

5. See R. G. Frey, *Interests and Rights: The Case Against Animals* (Oxford: Oxford University Press, 1980).

principle, in turn, underlies the Harm Principle, which says that we have a direct *prima facie* duty not to harm beings who have inherent value. Together, these principles give rise to moral rights. Rights are defined as valid claims, claims to certain goods and against certain beings, i.e., moral agents. Moral rights generate duties not only to refrain from inflicting harm upon beings with inherent value but also to come to their aid when they are threatened by other moral agents. Rights are not absolute but may be overridden in certain circumstances. Just what these circumstances are we will consider later. But first, let's look at some difficulties in the theory as thus far presented.

The Mystery of Inherent Value

Inherent value is a key concept in Regan's theory. It is the bridge between the plausible claim that all normal, mature mammals—human or otherwise—are subjects-of-a-life and the more debatable claim that they all have basic moral rights of the same strength. But it is a highly obscure concept, and its obscurity makes it ill-suited to play this crucial role.

Inherent value is defined almost entirely in negative terms. It is not dependent upon the value which either the inherently valuable individual or anyone else may place upon that individual's life or experiences. It is not (necessarily) a function of sentience or any other mental capacity, because, Regan says, some entities which are not sentient (e.g., trees, rivers, or rocks) may, nevertheless, have inherent value (p. 246). It cannot attach to anything other than an individual; species, eco-systems, and the like cannot have inherent value.

These are some of the things which inherent value is not. But what is it? Unfortunately, we are not told. Inherent value appears as a mysterious non-natural property which we must take on faith. Regan says that it is a *postulate* that subjects-of-a-life have inherent value, a postulate justified by the fact that it avoids certain absurdities which he thinks follow from a purely utilitarian theory (p. 247). But why is the postulate that *subjects-of-a-life* have inherent value? If the inherent value

of a being is completely independent of the value that it or anyone else places upon its experiences, then why does the fact that it has certain sorts of experiences constitute evidence that it has inherent value? If the reason is that subjects-of-a-life have an existence which can go better or worse for them, then why isn't the appropriate conclusion that all sentient beings have inherent value, since they would all seem to meet that condition? Sentient but mentally unsophisticated beings may have a less extensive range of possible satisfactions and frustrations, but why should it follow that they have—or may have—no inherent value at all?

In the absence of a positive account of inherent value, it is also difficult to grasp the connection between being inherently valuable and having moral rights. Intuitively, it seems that value is one thing, and rights are another. It does not seem incoherent to say that some things (e.g., mountains, rivers, redwood trees) are inherently valuable and yet are not the sorts of things which can have moral rights. Nor does it seem incoherent to ascribe inherent value to some things which are not individuals, e.g., plant or animal species, though it may well be incoherent to ascribe moral rights to such things.

In short, the concept of inherent value seems to create at least as many problems as it solves. If inherent value is based on some natural property, then why not try to identify that property and explain its moral significance, without appealing to inherent value? And if it is not based on any natural property, then why should we believe in it? That it may enable us to avoid some of the problems faced by the utilitarian is not a sufficient reason, if it creates other problems which are just as serious.

Is There a Sharp Line?

Perhaps the most serious problems are those that arise when we try to apply the strong animal rights position to animals other than normal, mature mammals. Regan's theory requires us to divide all living things into two categories: those which have the same inherent value and the same basic moral rights that we do, and those which have no inherent value and presumably no moral rights. But wherever we try to draw the line, such a sharp division is implausible.

It would surely be arbitrary to draw such a sharp line between normal, mature mammals and all other living things. Some birds (e.g., crows, magpies, parrots, mynahs) appear to be just as mentally sophisticated as most mammals and thus are equally strong candidates for inclusion under the subject-of-a-life criterion. Regan is not in fact advocating that we draw the line here. His claim is only that normal, mature mammals are clear cases, while other cases are less clear. Yet, on his theory, there must be such a sharp line *somewhere,* since there are no degree of inherent value. But why should we believe that there is a sharp line between creatures that are subjects-of-a-life and creatures that are not? Isn't it more likely that "subjecthood" comes in degrees, that some creatures have only a little self-awareness, and only a little capacity to anticipate the future, while some have a little more, and some a good deal more?

Should we, for instance, regard fish, amphibians, and reptiles as subjects-of-a-life? A simple yes-or-no answer seems inadequate. On the one hand, some of their behavior is difficult to explain without the assumption that they have sensations, beliefs, desires, emotions, and memories; on the other hand, they do not seem to exhibit very much self-awareness or very much conscious anticipation of future events. Do they have enough mental sophistication to count as subjects-of-a-life? Exactly how much is enough?

It is still more unclear what we should say about insects, spiders, octopi, and other invertebrate animals which have brains and sensory organs but whose minds (if they have minds) are even more alien to us than those of fish or reptiles. Such creatures are probably sentient. Some people doubt that they can feel pain, since they lack certain neurological structures which are crucial to the processing of pain impulses in vertebrate animals. But this argument is inconclusive, since their nervous systems might process pain in ways different from ours. When injured,

they sometimes act as if they are in pain. On evolutionary grounds, it seems unlikely that highly mobile creatures with complex sensory systems would not have developed a capacity for pain (and pleasure), since such a capacity has obvious survival value. It must, however, be admitted that we do not *know* whether spiders can feel pain (or something very like it), let alone whether they have emotions, memories, beliefs, desires, self-awareness, or a sense of the future.

Even more mysterious are the mental capacities (if any) of mobile microfauna. The brisk and efficient way that paramecia move about in their incessant search for food *might* indicate some kind of sentience, in spite of their lack of eyes, ears, brains, and other organs associated with sentience in more complex organisms. It is conceivable—though not very probable—that they, too, are subjects-of-a-life.

The existence of a few unclear cases need not pose a serious problem for a moral theory, but in this case, the unclear cases constitute most of those with which an adequate theory of animal rights would need to deal. The subject-of-a-life criterion can provide us with little or no moral guidance in our interactions with the vast majority of animals. That might be acceptable if it could be supplemented with additional principles which would provide such guidance. However, the radical dualism of the theory precludes supplementing it in this way. We are forced to say that either a spider has the same right to life as you and I do, or it has no right to life whatever—and that only the gods know which of these alternatives is true.

Regan's suggestion for dealing with such unclear cases is to apply the "benefit of the doubt" principle. That is, when dealing with beings that may or may not be subjects-of-a-life, we should act as if they are.[6] But if we try to apply this principle to the entire range of doubtful cases, we will find ourselves with moral obligations which we cannot possibly fulfill. In many climates, it is

---

6. See, for instance, p. 319, where Regan appeals to the benefit of the doubt principle when dealing with infanticide and late-term abortion.

virtually impossible to live without swatting mosquitoes and exterminating cockroaches, and not all of us can afford to hire someone to sweep the path before we walk, in order to make sure that we do not step on ants. Thus, we are still faced with the daunting task of drawing a sharp line somewhere on the continuum of life forms—this time, a line demarcating the limits of the benefit of the doubt principle.

The weak animal rights theory provides a more plausible way of dealing with this range of cases, in that it allows the rights of animals of different kinds to vary in strength. . . .

Why Are Animal Rights Weaker Than Human Rights?

How can we justify regarding the rights of persons as generally stronger than those of sentient beings which are not persons? There are a plethora of bad justifications, based on religious premises or false or unprovable claims about the differences between human and non-human nature. But there is one difference which has a clear moral relevance: people are at least sometimes capable of being moved to action or inaction by the force of reasoned argument. Rationality rests upon other mental capacities, notably those which Regan cites as criteria for being a subject-of-a-life. We share these capacities with many other animals. But it is not just because we are subjects-of-a-life that we are both able and morally compelled to recognize one another as beings with equal basic moral rights. It is also because we are able to "listen to reason" in order to settle our conflicts and cooperate in shared projects. This capacity, unlike the others, may require something like a human language.

Why is rationality morally relevant? It does not make us "better" than other animals or more "perfect." It does not even automatically make us more intelligent. (Bad reasoning reduces our effective intelligence rather than increasing it.) But it is morally relevant insofar as it provides greater possibilities for cooperation and for the nonviolent resolution of problems. It also makes us more dangerous than non-rational beings can ever be. Because we are potentially more dangerous and

less predictable than wolves, we need an articulated system of morality to regulate our conduct. Any human morality, to be workable in the long run, must recognize the equal moral status of all persons, whether through the postulate of equal basic moral rights or in some other way. The recognition of the moral equality of other persons is the price we must each pay for their recognition of our moral equality. Without this mutual recognition of moral equality, human society can exist only in a state of chronic and bitter conflict. The war between the sexes will persist so long as there is sexism and male domination; racial conflict will never be eliminated so long as there are racist laws and practices. But, to the extent that we achieve a mutual recognition of equality, we can hope to live together, perhaps as peacefully as wolves, achieving (in part) through explicit moral principles what they do not seem to need explicit moral principles to achieve.

Why not extend this recognition of moral equality to other creatures, even though they cannot do the same for us? The answer is that we cannot. Because we cannot reason with most non-human animals, we cannot always solve the problems which they may cause without harming them—although we are always obligated to try. We cannot negotiate a treaty with the feral cats and foxes, requiring them to stop preying on endangered native species in return for suitable concessions on our part.

> If rats invade our houses . . . we cannot reason with them, hoping to persuade them of the injustice they do us. We can only attempt to get rid of them.[7]

Aristotle was not wrong in claiming that the capacity to alter one's behavior on the basis of reasoned argument is relevant to the full moral status which he accorded to free men. Of course, he was wrong in his other premise, that women and slaves by their nature cannot reason well enough to function as autonomous moral agents. Had that premise been true, so would his conclusion that women and slaves are not quite the

---

7. Bonnie Steinbock, "Speciesism and the Idea of Equality," *Philosophy* 53 (1978): 253.

moral equals of free men. In the case of most non-human animals, the corresponding premise is true. If, on the other hand, there are animals with whom we can (learn to) reason, then we are obligated to do this and to regard them as our moral equals.

Thus, to distinguish between the rights of persons and those of most other animals on the grounds that only people can alter their behavior on the basis of reasoned argument does not commit us to a perfectionist theory of the sort Aristotle endorsed. There is no excuse for refusing to recognize the moral equality of some people on the grounds that we don't regard them as quite as rational as we are, since it is perfectly clear that most people can reason well enough to determine how to act so as to respect the basic rights of others (if they choose to), and that is enough for moral equality.

But what about people who are clearly not rational? It is often argued that sophisticated mental capacities such as rationality cannot be essential for the possession of equal basic moral rights, since nearly everyone agrees that human infants and mentally incompetent persons have such rights, even though they may lack those sophisticated mental capacities. But this argument is inconclusive, because there are powerful practical and emotional reasons for protecting non-rational human beings, reasons which are absent in the case of most non-human animals. Infancy and mental incompetence are human conditions which all of us either have experienced or are likely to experience at some time. We also protect babies and mentally incompetent people because we care for them. We don't normally care for animals in the same way, and when we do—e.g., in the case of much-loved pets—we may regard them as having special rights by virtue of their relationship to us. We protect them not only for their sake but also for our own, lest we be hurt by harm done to them. Regan holds that such "side-effects" are irrelevant to moral rights, and perhaps they are. But in ordinary usage, there is no sharp line between moral rights and those moral protections which are not rights. The extension of strong moral protections to infants and the mentally impaired in no way proves that non-human animals have the same basic moral rights as people.

Why Speak of "Animal Rights" at All?

If, as I have argued, reality precludes our treating all animals as our moral equals, then why should we still ascribe rights to them? Everyone agrees that animals are entitled to some protection against human abuse, but why speak of animal *rights* if we are not prepared to accept most animals as our moral equals? The weak animal rights position may seem an unstable compromise between the bold claim that animals have the same basic moral rights that we do and the more common view that animals have no rights at all.

It is probably impossible to either prove or disprove the thesis that animals have moral rights by producing an analysis of the concept of a moral right and checking to see if some or all animals satisfy the conditions for having rights. The concept of a moral right is complex, and it is not clear which of its strands are essential. Paradigm rights holders, i.e., mature and mentally competent persons, are *both* rational and morally autonomous beings and sentient subjects-of-a-life. Opponents of animal rights claim that rationality and moral autonomy are essential for the possession of rights, while defenders of animal rights claim that they are not. The ordinary concept of a moral right is probably not precise enough to enable us to determine who is right on purely definitional grounds.

If logical analysis will not answer the question of whether animals have moral rights, practical considerations may, nevertheless, incline us to say that they do. The most plausible alternative to the view that animals have moral rights is that, while they do not have *rights,* we are, nevertheless, obligated not to be cruel to them. Regan argues persuasively that the injunction to avoid being cruel to animals is inadequate to express our obligations towards animals, because it focuses on the mental states of those who cause animal suffering, rather than on the harm done to the animals themselves (p. 158). Cruelty is inflicting pain or suffering and either taking pleasure in that pain or suffering or being more or less in-different to it. Thus, to express the demand for the decent treatment of animals in terms of the rejection of cruelty is to invite the too easy response that those who subject animals to suffering are not being cruel because they regret the suffering they cause but sincerely believe that what they do is justified. The injunction to avoid cruelty is also inadequate in that it does not preclude the killing of animals—for any reason, however trivial—so long as it is done relatively painlessly.

The inadequacy of the anti-cruelty view provides one practical reason for speaking of animal rights. Another practical reason is that this is an age in which nearly all significant moral claims tend to be expressed in terms of rights. Thus, the denial that animals have rights, however carefully qualified, is likely to be taken to mean that we may do whatever we like to them, provided that we do not violate any human rights. In such a context, speaking of the rights of animals may be the only way to persuade many people to take seriously protests against the abuse of animals.

Why not extend this line of argument and speak of the rights of trees, mountains, oceans, or anything else which we may wish to see protected from destruction? Some environmentalists have not hesitated to speak in this way, and, given the importance of protecting such elements of the natural world, they cannot be blamed for using this rhetorical device. But, I would argue that moral rights can meaningfully be ascribed only to entities which have some capacity for sentience. This is because moral rights are protections designed to protect rights holders from harms or to provide them with benefits which matter *to them*.

Only beings capable of sentience can be harmed or benefitted in ways which matter to them, for only such beings can like or dislike what happens to them or prefer some conditions to others. Thus, sentient animals, unlike mountains, rivers, or species, are at least logically possible candidates for moral rights. This fact, together with the need to end current abuses of animals—e.g., in scientific research . . .—provides a plausible case for speaking of animal rights.

Conclusion

I have argued that Regan's case for ascribing strong moral rights to all normal, mature mammals is unpersuasive because (1) it rests upon the obscure concept of inherent value, which is defined only in negative terms, and (2) it seems to preclude any plausible answer to questions about the moral status of the vast majority of sentient animals. . . .

The weak animal rights theory asserts that (1) any creature whose natural mode of life includes the pursuit of certain satisfactions has the right not to be forced to exist without the opportunity to pursue those satisfactions; (2) that any creature which is capable of pain, suffering, or frustration has the right that such experiences not be deliberately inflicted upon it without some compelling reason; and (3) that no sentient being should be killed without good reason. However, moral rights are not an all-or-nothing affair. The strength of the reasons required to override the rights of a non-human organism varies, depending upon—among other things—the probability that it is sentient and (if it is clearly sentient) its probable degree of mental sophistication. . . .

Suggestions for Further Reading

Of special interest is Tom Regan's *The Case for Animal Rights* (Berkeley: University of California Press, 1983), which has become a classic in the field.

Peter Singer's *Animal Liberation: A New Ethics for Our Treatment of Animals* (New York: Avon Books, 1975) is the "bible" of the animal rights movement.

Tom Regan and Peter Singer have edited a collection of essays covering many important topics in the field. See *Animal Rights and Human Obligations*, 2nd Edition (Englewood Cliffs, NJ: Prentice-Hall, 1989).

Peter Carruthers counters Regan's position in *The Animal Issue: Moral Theory in Practice* (New York: Cambridge University Press, 1992).

Robert Garner in *Animals, Politics, and Morality* (New York: St. Martin's Press, 1993) argues that humans have a limited right to use animals, provided "no unnecessary suffering" occurs.

David DeGrazia in *Taking Animals Seriously: Mental Life and Moral Status* (New York: Cambridge University Press, 1996) provides a detailed discussion of issues relating to equal consideration.

On the specific issue of animal experimentation, see the collection of essays in *Animal Experimention: The Moral Issues* edited by Robert M. Faird and Stuart E. Rosenbaum (Amherst, NY: Prometheus Books, 1991).

Videos

Their Future in Your Hands (13 minutes; produced by Animal Aid) is an introduction to the issue of animal rights and the ethical treatment of animals. Also the *Animal Film* (135 minutes; Cinema Guild) lays out the issues and argues for animal rights. Your Media Services Catalog will provide more information.

Animal Rights and Their Human Consequences (28 minutes) explores the potential conflict between humans and animals that can arise from equal consideration (Films for the Humanities and Sciences, PO Box 2053, Princeton, NJ 08543).

6.7 Environmental Ethics

Have you heard of Love Canal, the cloud of poison at Bhopal, the meltdown at Chernobyl, the Exxon Valdez oil spill, the depletion of the ozone layer, the greenhouse effect, global warming, and the disappearing Amazonian rainforests? You cannot, it seems, read a newspaper or watch the news on television without hearing about one environmental disaster or another. They seem to be increasing in both number and scope.

As we begin the twenty-first century, many people are alarmed and frightened about what lies ahead with respect to the progressive deterioration of our environment. There is an apprehension in the air, a fear, that it may be too late for our environment. Humans have already started processes that will, in time, destroy the earth. We are doomed to environmental death and destruction. Or so it seems to many.

One of the first reactions to an environmental disaster is to re-evaluate policies and decisions. What many thought cost effective and safe at one time (for example, supertankers carrying huge amounts of crude oil) now, after a disaster, seems not only unwise, but criminally negligent. Another response, more delayed and philosophical than the first, is to reconsider our attitudes toward nature and the role our inherited religious and philosophical concepts of the environment have played in shaping our values and actions. Perhaps humans should not treat nature as a resource to be exploited for human good. Perhaps we should see nature as part of our community and, like other members of our community, deserving of respect, care, and nurture. Maybe the way we think about the planet on which we live has something to do with the fear we now feel about our future here.

J. Baird Callicott and Thomas W. Overholt, both professors of philosophy at the University of Wisconsin at Stevens Point, argue that religious and philosophical attitudes toward the environment do matter. The nature of these attitudes and the philosophical history that has shaped them can be clarified by contrasting traditional European views of nature with Native American views. These contrasting views help us understand how we may have gotten into this environmental mess, and, more importantly, how we might get out of it.

Reading Questions

1. How can we know what North American natives thought about nature prior to the coming of Europeans?
2. What are the primary elements in the "Western worldview," and what are its implications for our attitudes toward nature?
3. What is animism, and what role does it play in Native American thought?
4. What is the relationship between Native American attitudes toward their environment and Leopold's land ethic?
5. How do the authors deal with the issue of whether cultural attitudes affect behavior?
6. Do you think the authors' evidence and arguments are sufficient to support their claim that Native American attitudes toward the environment would support the development of a stronger land ethic? Why, or why not?

Traditional American Indian Attitudes Toward Nature

J. BAIRD CALLICOTT AND THOMAS W. OVERHOLT

Problems of Unity and Method

HERE WE SKETCH, in broadest outline, the picture of nature endemic to pre-Columbian North America. And, more specifically, we argue that the view of nature typical of traditional American Indian peoples has included and supported an environmental ethic that helped to prevent them from overexploiting the ecosystems in which they lived.

We do not enter into this discussion unaware of the difficulties and limitations lying in ambush at the very outset. In the first place, there is no *one* thing that can be called *the* American Indian belief system. The aboriginal peoples of the North American continent lived in environments quite different from one another and culturally

adapted to these environments in quite different ways. For each tribe there were a cycle of myths and a set of ceremonies, and from these materials one might abstract *for each* a particular view of nature.

However, recognition of the diversity and variety of American Indian cultures should not obscure a complementary unity to be found among them. Despite great differences there were common characteristics that culturally united American Indian peoples. Joseph Epes Brown claims that

> this common binding thread is found in beliefs and attitudes held by the people in the quality of their relationships to the natural environment. All American Indian peoples possessed

From Africa to Zen: An Invitation to World Philosophy, *edited by Robert C. Solomon and Kathleen M. Higgins, Lanham, MD: Rowman & Littlefield Publishers, 1993, pp. 57–78. Footnotes edited. Copyright © 1993 by Rowman & Littlefield Publishers, Inc. Reprinted by permission.*

what has been called a metaphysic of nature; and manifest a reverence for the myriad forms and forces of the natural world specific to their immediate environment; and for all, their rich complexes of rites and ceremonies are expressed in terms which have reference to or utilize the forms of the natural world.[1]

Calvin Martin has more recently confirmed Brown's conjecture:

> What we are dealing with are two issues: the ideology of Indian land-use and the practical results of that ideology. Actually, there was a great diversity of ideologies, reflecting distinct cultural and ecological contexts. It is thus more than a little artificial to identify a single, monolithic ideology, as though all Native Americans were traditionally inspired by a universal ethos. Still, there were certain elements which many if not all these ideologies seemed to share, the most outstanding being a genuine respect for the welfare of other life-forms.[2]

A second obvious difficulty bedeviling any discussion of American Indian views of nature is our limited ability to accurately reconstruct the cognitive—as opposed to the material—culture of New World peoples prior to their contact with (and influence by) Europeans. Arrowheads, bone awls, and other cultural artifacts that were made before 1492 still exist and can be carefully examined. But documentary records of precontact Indian thought do not.

American Indian metaphysics was embedded in oral traditions. Left alone, an oral culture may be very tenacious and persistent. If radically stressed, it may prove to be very fragile and liable to total extinction. Hence, *contemporary* accounts by contemporary American Indians of *traditional* American Indian philosophy are vulnerable to the charge of inauthenticity, in that for several generations American Indian cultures, cultures preserved in the living memory of their members, have been both ubiquitously and violently disturbed by transplanted European civilization.

Perhaps we ought, therefore, to rely where possible upon the earliest written observations of Europeans concerning American Indian belief. The accounts of the North American "savages" by sixteenth-, seventeenth-, and eighteenth-century Europeans are, however, invariably distorted by ethnocentrism, which today appears so hopelessly benighted as to be more entertaining than illuminating. The written observations of Europeans who first encountered American Indian cultures provide, rather, an instructive record of the implicit European metaphysic. Because Indians were not loyal to the Christian religion, it was assumed that they had to be conscious servants of Satan, and that the spirits about which they talked and the powers their shamans attempted to direct had to be so many demons from hell. Concerning the Feast of the Dead among the Huron, Jean de Brébeuf wrote in the *Jesuit Relations* of 1636 that "nothing as ever better pictured for me the confusion among the damned."[3] His account, incidentally, is very informative and detailed concerning the physical requirements and artifacts of this ceremony, but the rigidity of his own system of belief makes it impossible for him to enter sympathetically into that of the Huron.

Reconstructing the traditional Indian attitude toward nature is, therefore, to some extent a speculative matter. On the other hand, we must not abandon the inquiry as utterly hopeless. Postcontact American Indians do tell of their traditions and conceptual heritage, and the critical ear can filter out the European noise in such accounts. Among the best of these nostalgic memoirs is John G. Neihardt's classic, *Black Elk Speaks,* one of the most important and authentic sources available for the reconstruction of an American Indian attitude toward nature.[4] The explorers', missionaries', and fur traders' accounts of

---

1. Joseph E. Brown, "Modes of Contemplation Through Action: North American Indians," *Main Currents in Modern Thought* 30 (1973–74): 60.
2. Calvin Martin, *Keepers of the Game,* p. 186.
3. Quoted in W. Vernon Kinietz, *Indians of the Western Great Lakes, 1615–1760* (Ann Arbor: University of Michigan Press, 1965), p. 115.
4. John G. Neihardt, *Black Elk Speaks: Being the Life Story of a Holy Man of the Oglala Sioux* (New York: William Morrow, 1932). For its authenticity, see Raymond J. DeMallie, *The Sixth Grandfather: Black Elk's Teachings Given to John G. Neihardt* (Lincoln: University of Nebraska Press, 1984).

woodland Indian attitudes are also useful, despite their ethnocentrism, since we may also critically correct for the distortion of their biases and prejudices.

Further, disciplined and methodical modern ethnographers have recorded an American Indian oral narrative heritage, a diverse body of myths and stories that convey the cognitive structure and values of the people who told and retold them, generation after generation. Folktales have a life of their own and may survive the demise of the material culture in which they originated. Consider the fairy tales we Euro-Americans tell our children. They are set an ocean away in a material culture of castles and knights-in-shining-armor that no longer exists. Yet they remain relatively unchanged when we retell them in our present world of skyscrapers, fast-food joints, and TV. From them we might learn something about the enchanted-thought world of our medieval ancestors. Similarly, American Indian folktales may represent a relatively transparent window on the pre-Columbian mind-set of Stone Age North America.

Using these three sorts of sources—first-contact European records, transcribed personal recollections of tribal beliefs by spiritually favored Indians, and Native American folktales—we may achieve a fairly reliable reconstruction of traditional Indian attitudes toward nature.[5]

The Western Worldview as an Intellectual Foil

The distinct flavor of the typical American Indian conception of nature may be brought out most vividly by contrasting it with the typical Western European concept of nature, which now also prevails in North America and has, until recently, eclipsed native thought.

The European style of thought was set by the Greeks of classical antiquity. Whatever else it may have come to be, modern science is a con-

tinuation and extrapolation of certain concepts originating with the Greeks of the sixth, fifth, and fourth centuries B.C.

Salient among the originally Greek notions of nature to find its way into modern science is the atomic theory of matter. The ancient atomists imagined all material things to be composed of indestructible and internally changeless particles, of which they supposed there were infinitely many. Each of these atoms was believed to be solid and to have a shape and a relative size. All other qualities of things normally disclosed by perception exist, according to the atomic theory, only by "convention," not by "nature." In the terms of later philosophical jargon, characteristics of things such as flavor, odor, color, and sound were regarded as *secondary* qualities, the privately experienced effects of the primary qualities on the sensory subject. The atoms move about haphazardly in the "void" or space. Macroscopic objects are assemblages of atoms; they are wholes exactly equal to the sum of their parts. Such objects come into being and pass away, but process and change were conceived as the association and dissociation of the eternally existing and unchanging atomic parts. The atomists claimed to reduce all the phenomena of nature to a simple dichotomy, variously expressed: the "full" and the "empty," "thing" and "no-thing," the atom and space.

The eventual Newtonian worldview of modern science included as one of its cornerstones the atomists' concept of free space, thinly occupied by moving particles or "corpuscles," as the early moderns called them. It was one of Newton's greatest achievements to supply a quantitative model of the regular motion of the putative material particles. These famous "laws of motion" made it possible to represent phenomena not only materially but also mechanically: All change could be reduced to bits of matter moving through space impacting on other bits.

That the *order* of nature can be successfully disclosed only by means of a quantitative description is an idea that also originated in sixth century B.C. Greece and is attributed to Pythagoras. The prevailing modern concept of nature might be oversimply, but nonetheless not incorrectly,

5. For a more complete discussion of the methodological problem of reconstructing American Indian worldviews, see J. Baird Callicott, "American Indian Land Wisdom?: Sorting Out the Issues," *Journal of Forest History* 33 (1989): 35–42.

portrayed as a merger of the Pythagorean idea that the order of nature is mathematical with the atomists' ontology of void space (so very amenable to geometrical analysis) and material particles.

As Paul Santmire characterizes the modern European concept of nature that took root in North America,

> Nature is analogous to a machine; or in the more popular version nature *is* a machine. Nature is composed of hard, irreducible particles which have neither color nor smell nor taste, . . . Beauty and value in nature are in the eye of the beholder. Nature is the dead *res extensa,* perceived by the mind, which observes nature from a position of objective detachment. Nature in itself is basically a self-sufficient, self-enclosed complex of merely physical forces acting on colorless, tasteless, and odorless particles of hard, dead matter. That is the mechanical view of nature as it was popularly accepted in the circles of the educated [Euro-Americans] in the nineteenth century.[6]

Santmire is careful to mention the nineteenth century because developments in twentieth-century science—the general theory of relativity, quantum theory, and ecology—have begun to replace the modern mechanical model of nature with another paradigm. A cultural worldview, however, lags behind the leading edge of intellectual development and so most Westerners still apprehend nature through a mechanistic-materialistic lens, blissfully unaware that the Newtonian worldview is obsolete. In any case, Santmire's comments bring to our attention a complementary feature of the prevailing (albeit theoretically defunct) modern classical European and Euro-American worldview of particular interest to our overall discussion. If no qualms were felt about picturing rivers and mountains, trees, and even animals as inert, material, mechanical "objects," only a few hard-nosed materialists (Democritus among the ancients and Hobbes among the moderns) were willing to try to provide a wholly mechanical account of mental activity.

6. H. Paul Santmire, "Historical Dimensions of the American Crisis," reprinted from *Dialog* (Summer 1970) in *Western Man and Environmental Ethics,* ed. Ian G. Barbour (Menlo Park, Calif.: Addison-Wesley, 1973), pp. 70–71.

The conception of the soul as not only separate and distinct from the body but as essentially alien to it (that is, of an entirely different, antagonistic nature) also was first introduced into Western thought by Pythagoras. Pythagoras conceived the soul to be a fallen divinity, incarcerated in the physical world as retribution for some unspecified sin. The goal in life for the Pythagoreans was to earn the release of the soul from the physical world upon death and to reunite the soul with its proper (divine) companions. The Pythagoreans accomplished this by several methods: asceticism, ritual purification, and intellectual exercise, particularly in mathematics.

Plato adopted Pythagoras's concept of the soul as immortal, otherworldly, and essentially alien to the physical environment. Influenced by Plato, Saint Paul introduced it into Christianity. Although Plato and Pythagoras had not restricted the soul to human beings, but believed that all sorts of animals are inhabited by one too, Christian orthodoxy limited the earthly residence of souls to human bodies. The "father of modern philosophy," René Descartes, reiterated in especially strong terms both the ancient Pythagorean/Platonic dualism and the Judeo-Christian insistence that only human beings are ensouled. Thus the essential self, in the eventual modern Western worldview, the part of a person by means of which he or she perceives and thinks, and in which resides virtue or vice, is less a citizen of Earth than of Heaven; and while living here on Earth we are lonely strangers in a strange land. Worse, the natural world is the place of trial and temptation for the quasi-divine human soul, its moral antipode.

So what attitude to nature does modern classical European natural philosophy convey? In sum, nature is an inert, material and mechanical plenum completely describable by means of the arid formulae of pure mathematics. In relation to nature, human beings are lonely exiles sojourning in a strange and hostile world, alien not only to their physical environment but to their own bodies, both of which they are encouraged to fear and to attempt to conquer. These Christian-Cartesian ideas were added to the core concepts, thoroughly criticized by Lynn White, Jr., Ian

McHarg, and others, forthrightly set out in Genesis: God created man in his own image to have dominion over nature and to subdue it. The result, the Judeo-Christian/Cartesian-Newtonian worldview, was a very volatile mixture of ingredients that exploded during the nineteenth and twentieth centuries in an all-out European and Euro-American war on nature, a war that, as we rush headlong into the third millennium, has very nearly been won. (To the victors, of course, belong the spoils!)

The prevailing Western worldview, rooted in ancient Greek natural philosophy, is in fact doubly atomistic. Plato accounted for the existence of distinct species by means of his theory of ideal and abstract forms. Each individual or specimen "participated," according to Plato, in a certain essence or form, and it derived its specific characteristics from the form in which it participated. The impression of the natural world conveyed by Plato's theory of forms is that the various species are determined by the static logical-mathematical order of the formal domain, and then the individual organisms (each with its preordained essence) are loosed into the physical arena to interact adventitiously, catch-as-catch-can.

Nature is thus represented as like a room full of furniture, a collection, a mere aggregate of individuals of various types, relating to one another in an accidental and altogether external fashion. This picture of the world is an atomism of a most subtle and insidious sort. It breaks the highly integrated functional ecosystem into separate, discrete, and functionally unrelated sets of particulars. Pragmatically, approaching the world through this model—which we might call "conceptual" in contradistinction to "material" atomism—it is possible to radically rearrange parts of the landscape without the least concern for upsetting its functional integrity and organic unity. Certain species may be replaced by others (for example, wildflowers by grain in prairie biomes) or removed altogether (for example, predators) without consequence, theoretically, for the function of the whole.

Plato's student Aristotle rejected the otherworldliness of Plato's philosophy, both his theory of the soul and his theory of forms. Aristotle, moreover, was a sensitive empirical biologist and did as much to advance biology as a science as Pythagoras did for mathematics. Aristotle's system of classification of organisms according to species, genus, family, order, class, phylum, and kingdom (as modified and refined by Linnaeus) remains a cornerstone of the modern life sciences. This hierarchy of universals was not real or actual, according to Aristotle; only individual organisms fully existed. However, Aristotle's taxonomical hierarchy, as it was formulated long before the development of evolutionary and ecological theory, resulted in a view of living nature that was no less compartmentalized than was Plato's. Relations among things again are, in Aristotle's biological theory, accidental and inessential. A thing's essence is determined by its logical relations within the taxonomical schema rather than, as in ecological theory, by its working relations with other things in its environment—its trophic niche, its thermal and chemical requirements, and so on.

Evolutionary and ecological theory suggest, rather, that the essences of things, the specific characteristics of species, are a function of their relations with other things. Aristotle's taxonomical view of the biotic world, untransformed by evolutionary and ecological theory, thus has the same ecologically misrepresentative feature as Plato's theory of forms: Nature is seen as an aggregate of individuals, divided into various types, that have no functional connection with one another. And the *practical* consequences are the same. The Earth's biotic mantle may be dealt with in a heavy-handed fashion, rearranged to suit one's fancy without danger of dysfunctions. If anything, Aristotle's taxonomical representation of nature has had a more insidious influence on the Western mind than Plato's "real" universals, because the latter could be dismissed, as often they were, as abstracted Olympians in a charming and noble philosophical romance, whereas metaphysical taxonomy went unchallenged as "empirical" and "scientific."

Also, we should not forget another Aristotelian legacy, the natural *hierarchy,* or great chain of being, according to which the world is arranged into "lower" and "higher" forms. Aristotle's belief that everything exists for a purpose resulted in the commonplace Western assumption that the lower forms exist for the sake of the higher forms. Since we human beings are placed at the top of the pyramid, everything else exists for our sakes. The practical tendencies of this idea are too obvious to require further elaboration.

American Indian Animism

The late John Fire Lame Deer, a reflective Sioux Indian, comments, straight to the point, in his biographical and philosophical narrative, *Lame Deer: Seeker of Visions,* that although the "whites" (that is, members of the European cultural tradition) imagine earth, rocks, water, and wind to be dead, they nevertheless "are very much alive."[7] In the previous section we tried to explain in what sense nature is conceived as "dead" in the mainstream of European and Euro-American thought. To say that rocks and rivers are dead is perhaps a little misleading, since to say that something is dead might imply that it was once alive. Rather in the usual Western view of things, such objects are considered inert. But what does Lame Deer mean when he says that they are "very much alive"?

He doesn't explain this provocative assertion as discursively as one might wish, but he provides examples, dozens of examples, of what he calls the "power" in various natural entities. According to Lame Deer, "Every man needs a stone. . . . You ask stones for aid to find things which are lost or missing. Stones can give warning of an enemy, of approaching misfortune."[8] Butterflies, coyotes, grasshoppers, eagles, owls, deer, and especially elk and bear all talk and possess and convey power. "You have to listen to all these creatures, listen with your mind. They have secrets to tell."[9]

It would seem that for Lame Deer the "aliveness" of natural entities (including stones, which to most Europeans are merely "material objects" and epitomize lifelessness) means that they have

a share in the same consciousness that we human beings enjoy. Granted, animals and plants (if not stones and rivers) are recognized to be "alive" by conventional European conceptualization, but they lack awareness in a mode and degree comparable to human awareness. According to Descartes, the most extreme and militant dualist in the Western tradition, even animal behavior is altogether automatic, resembling in every way the behavior of a machine. A somewhat more liberal and enlightened view allows that animals have a dim sort of consciousness, but operate largely by "instinct," a concept altogether lacking a clear definition and one very nearly as obscure as the notorious occult qualities (the "sporific virtues," and so on) of the medieval Scholastic philosophers. Of course, plants, although alive, are regarded as totally lacking in sentience. In any case, we hear that only human beings possess *self*-consciousness, that is, that only we are aware that we are aware and can thus distinguish between ourselves and everything else!

Every sophomore student of philosophy has learned, or should have, that solipsism is an impregnable philosophical position, and corollary to that, that every characterization of other minds—human as well as nonhuman—is a matter of conjecture. The Indian attitude, as represented by Lame Deer, apparently was based on the reasonable consideration that since human beings have a physical body *and* an associated consciousness (conceptually hypostatized or reified as "spirit"), all other bodily things—animals, plants, and, yes, even stones—were similar in this respect. Indeed, this strikes us as an eminently plausible assumption. One can no more directly perceive another human being's consciousness than one can that of an animal or a plant. One *assumes* that another human being is conscious because he or she is very similar to oneself in physical appearance. Anyone not hopelessly prejudiced by the metaphysical apartheid policy of Pauline Christianity, Descartes, and the Western worldview that is their legacy would naturally extend the same consideration to other natural beings. Human beings closely resemble other forms of life in anatomy, physiology, and behavior. The myriad organic forms themselves are

7. Richard Erdoes, *Lame Deer: Seeker of Visions* (New York: Simon and Schuster, 1976), pp. 108–9.
8. Ibid., p. 101.
9. Ibid., p. 124.

obviously closely related, and the organic world, in turn, is continuous with the whole of nature. Thus virtually all things might be supposed, without the least strain upon credence, like ourselves, to be "alive," that is, conscious, aware, or possessed of spirit.

Lame Deer offers a brief, but most revealing and suggestive, metaphysical explanation:

> Nothing is so small and unimportant but it has a spirit given it by *Wakan Tanka*. *Tunkan* is what you might call a stone god, but he is also a part of the Great Spirit. The gods are separate beings, but they are all united in *Wakan Tanka*. It is hard to understand—something like the Holy Trinity. You can't explain it except by going back to the "circles within circles" idea, the spirit splitting itself up into stones, trees, tiny insects even, making them all *wakan* by his ever-presence. And in turn all these myriads of things which make up the universe flowing back to their source, united in one Grandfather Spirit.[10]

This Lakota panentheism (the belief that there exists a single unified holy spirit that is, nevertheless, also manifest in each thing) presents a conception of the world that is, to be sure, dualistic: It posits the existence of a personal spirit in otherwise material bodies. But it is important to emphasize that, unlike the Platonic-Pauline-Cartesian tradition, it is not an *antagonistic* dualism in which body and spirit are conceived in contrary terms and pitted against one another in a moral struggle. Further, and most important for our subsequent remarks, the pervasiveness of spirit in nature, a spirit *in* each thing which is a splinter of the Great Spirit, facilitates a perception of the human and natural realms as akin and alike.

Consider, complementary to this Native American panentheism, the basics of Siouan cosmogony. Black Elk (a Lakota shaman of the generation previous to Lame Deer's) rhetorically asks, "Is not the sky a father and the earth a mother, and are not all living things with feet or wings or roots their children?"[11] Accordingly, he prays, "Give me the strength to walk the soft

earth, a relative to all that is!"[12] Black Elk speaks of the great natural kingdom as, simply, "green things," "the wings of the air," "the four-leggeds," and "the two-legged."[13] Not only does everything have a spirit; in the last analysis, all things are related as members of one universal family, born of one father, the sky, the Great Spirit, and one mother, the Earth herself.

More is popularly known about the Sioux metaphysical vision than about those of most other American Indian peoples. The concept of the Great Spirit and of the Earth Mother and the family-like relatedness of all creatures seems, however, to have been a very common, not to say universal, American Indian idea and, likewise, the concept of a spiritual dimension or aspect to all natural things. Pulitzer Prize-winning American Indian poet and essayist N. Scott Momaday remarked, "'The earth is our mother. The sky is our father.' This concept of nature, which is at the center of the Native American worldview, is familiar to us all. But it may well be that we do not understand entirely what the concept is in its ethical and philosophical implications."[14] And North American ethnomusicologist Ruth Underhill has written that "for the old time Indian, the world did not consist of inanimate materials. . . . It was alive, and everything in it could help or harm him."[15]

Concerning the Ojibwa Indians, who speak an Algonkian language and at the time of first contact maintained only hostile relations with the Lakota, Diamond Jenness reports:

> Thus, then, the Parry Island Ojibwa interprets his own being; and exactly the same interpretation he applies to everything around him. Not only men, but animals, trees, even rocks and water are tripartite, possessing bodies, souls, and shadows. [These Indians, Jenness earlier explains, divided spirit into two aspects—soul

---

10. Ibid., pp. 102–3.
11. Neihardt, *Black Elk Speaks*, p. 3.
12. Ibid., p. 6.
13. Ibid., p. 7.
14. N. Scott Momaday, "A First American Views His Land," *National Geographic* 149 (1976): 14.
15. Ruth M. Underhill, *Red Man's Religion: Beliefs and Practices of the Indians North of Mexico* (Chicago: University of Chicago Press, 1965), p. 40.

and shadow—though, as Jenness admits, the distinction between the soul and shadow was far from clear and frequently confused by the people themselves.] They all have a life like the life in human beings, even if they have all been gifted with different powers and attributes. Consider the animals which most closely resemble human beings; they see and hear as we do, and clearly they reason about what they observe. The tree must have a life somewhat like our own, although it lacks the power of locomotion. . . . Water runs: it too must possess life, it too must have a soul and a shadow. Then observe how certain minerals cause the neighboring rocks to decompose and become loose and friable; evidently rocks too have power, and power means life, and life involves a soul and shadow. All things then have souls and shadows. And all things die. But their souls are reincarnated again, and what were dead return to life.[16]

A. Irving Hallowell has noted an especially significant consequence of the pan-spiritualism among the Ojibwa: "Not only animate properties," he writes, "but even 'person' attributes may be projected upon objects which to us clearly belong to a physical inanimate category."[17] Central to the concept of *person* is the possibility of entering into social relations. Nonhuman persons may be spoken with, may be honored or insulted, may become allies or adversaries, no less than human persons.

The philosophical basis for attributing personhood to nonhuman natural entities also helps to explain the American Indian understanding of dreams. Like eating, getting sick, falling in love, having children, and other such things, dreaming is an experience common to all peoples. But the meaning, the interpretation of the dream state of consciousness differs from culture to culture. A culture's understanding of dreams, no less than its explanation of disease, reflects its more

general worldview. Thus, a culture's representation of dreams can also be very revealing of its more general worldview.

For example, the ancient Greeks, before philosophy had thoroughly undermined their mythic worldview, believed both illness and dreams to be visitations from the gods. In Plato's *Symposium,* to take a case in point, Socrates remarks that the woman who taught him the mysteries of love was believed to have postponed a god-sent plague in Athens by performing certain religious rites; and in the *Phaedo,* Socrates remarks that over the course of his life the same dream had come to him, sometimes wearing one countenance, sometimes another, but always commanding him to work and make music. Most of us modern Europeans and Euro-Americans follow Descartes in believing that to be sick is to experience a mechanical breakdown in our bodies and that dreams are confused phenomena of the mind (though some of us add to this generic idea Freud's more specific hypothesis that dreams are confused manifestations of the unconscious dimension of a person's psyche).

The French fur traders and missionaries of the seventeenth century in the Great Lakes region were singularly impressed by the devotion to dreams of the "savages" with whom they lived. According to Vernon Kinietz, Paul Ragueneau, in 1648, first suggested that among the Algonkians, dreams were "the language of the souls."[18] This expression lacks precision, but we think it goes very much to the core of the American Indian understanding of dreams. Through dreams, and most dramatically through visions, one came into direct contact with the spirits of both human and nonhuman persons, as it were, naked of bodily vestments. In words somewhat reminiscent of Ragueneau's, Hallowell comments, "It is in dreams that the individual comes into direct communication with the *atiso'kanak,* the powerful 'persons' of the other-than-human class."[19] Given the animistic or panspiritualistic worldview of the Indians, acute sensitivity and pragmatic response to dreaming make perfectly good sense.

16. Diamond Jenness, *The Ojibwa Indians of Parry Island, Their Social and Religious Life,* Canadian Department of Mines Bulletin no. 78, Museum of Canada Anthropological Series no. 17 (Ottawa, 1935), pp. 20–21.
17. A. Irving Hallowell, "Ojibwa Ontology, Behavior, and World View," *Culture in History: Essays in Honor of Paul Radin,* ed. S. Diamond (New York: Columbia University Press, 1960), p. 26.

18. Kinietz, *Indians of the Western Great Lakes,* p. 126.
19. Hallowell, "Ojibwa Ontology," p. 19.

Dreams and waking experiences are sharply discriminated, but the theater of action disclosed in dreams and visions is continuous with and often the same as the ordinary world. In contrast to the psychologized contemporary Western view in which dreams are images of sorts (like afterimages) existing only "in the mind," the American Indian while dreaming experiences reality, often the same reality as in waking experience, in another form of consciousness—as it were, by means of another sensory modality.

As one lies asleep and experiences people and other animals, places, and so on, it is natural to suppose that one's spirit becomes temporarily dissociated from one's body and moves about encountering other spirits. Or, as Hallowell says, "when a human being is asleep and dreaming his *otcatcakwin* (vital part, soul), which is the core of the self, may become detached from the body (*miyo*). Viewed by another human being, a person's body may be easily located and observed in space. But his vital part may be somewhere else."[20] Dreaming indeed may be one element in the art of American Indian sorcery (called "bear walking" among the Ojibwa in which the sorcerer skulks around at night in the form of a bear, and appears indeed to be a bear to persons unskilled in detecting the subtle differences between a mischievous bear walker up to no good and an ordinary well-meaning bear minding its own business).[21] If the state of consciousness in dreams is seized and controlled, and the phenomenal content of dreams volitionally directed, then sorcerers may go where they wish in order to spy on enemies or perhaps affect them in some malevolent way.

It follows that dreams should have a higher degree of "truth" than ordinary waking experiences, because in the dream experience the person and everyone he or she meets is present in spirit, in essential self. This, notice, is precisely contrary to the European assumption that dreams are "false" or illusory and altogether private or subjective. For instance, in the second of his *Meditations on First Philosophy,* Descartes, casting around for an example of the highest absurdity, says that it is "as though I were to say 'I am awake now, and discern some truth; but I do not see it clearly enough; so I will set about going to sleep, so that my dreams may give me a truer and clearer picture of the fact.'" Yet this, in all seriousness, is precisely what many Indians have done. An episode from Halowell's discussion may serve as illustration. A boy claimed that during a thunderstorm he saw a thunderbird. His elders were skeptical, since to see a thunderbird in such fashion, that is, with the waking eye, was almost unheard of. He was believed, however, when a man who had dreamed of the thunderbird was consulted and the boy's description was *"verified."*![22]

The Ojibwa, the Sioux, and, if we may safely generalize, most American Indians lived in a world that was peopled not only by human persons but by persons and personalities associated with all natural phenomena. In one's practical dealings in such a world it is necessary to one's well-being and that of one's family and tribe to maintain good social relations not only with proximate human persons, one's immediate tribal neighbors, but also with the nonhuman persons abounding in the immediate environment. For example, Hallowell reports that among the Ojibwa "when bears were sought out in their dens in the spring they were addressed, asked to come out so that they could be killed, and an apology was offered to them."[23]

In characterizing the American Indian attitude toward nature, we have tried to limit our discussion to concepts so fundamental and pervasive as to be capable of generalization. In sum, we have claimed that the typical traditional American Indian attitude was to regard all features of the environment as enspirited. These entities were believed to possess a consciousness, reason, and volition no less intense and complete than a human being's. The earth, the sky, the winds, rocks, streams, trees, insects, birds, and all other

20. Ibid., p. 41.
21. See Richard M. Dorson, *Bloodstoppers and Bearwalkers: Folk Traditions of the Upper Peninsula* (Cambridge, Mass.: Harvard University Press, 1952).

22. Hallowell, "Ojibwa Ontology," p. 32.
23. Ibid., p. 35.

animals therefore had personalities and were thus as fully persons as human beings were. In dreams and visions the spirits of things were directly encountered and could become powerful allies to the dreamer or visionary. We may therefore say that the Indians' social circle, their community, included all the nonhuman natural entities in their locales as well as their fellow clan and tribe members.

Now a most significant conceptual connection obtains in all cultures between the concept of a person, on the one hand, and certain behavioral restraints, on the other. Toward persons it is necessary, whether for genuinely ethical or purely prudential reasons, to act in a careful and circumspect manner. Among the Ojibwa, for example, according to Hallowell, "a moral distinction is drawn between the kind of conduct demanded by the primary necessities of securing a livelihood, or defending oneself against aggression, and unnecessary acts of cruelty. The moral values implied document the consistency of the principle of *mutual obligations* which is inherent in all interactions with 'persons' throughout the Ojibwa world." [24]

The implicit overall metaphysic of American Indian cultures locates human beings in a larger *social*, as well as physical, environment. People belong not only to a human community but to a community of all nature as well. Existence in this larger society, just as existence in a family and tribal context, places people in an environment in which reciprocal responsibilities and mutual obligations are taken for granted and assumed without question or reflection. Moreover, a person's basic cosmological representations in moments of meditation or cosmic reflection place him or her in a world all parts of which are united through ties of kinship. All creatures, be they elemental, green, finned, winged, or legged, are children of one father and one mother. One blood flows through all; one spirit has divided itself and enlivened all things with a consciousness that is essentially the same. The world around, though immense and overwhelmingly diversified and complex, is bound together through bonds of kinship, mutuality, and reciprocity. It is a world in which a person might feel at home, a relative to all that is, comfortable and secure, as one feels as a child in the midst of a large family. As Brown reports:

> But very early in life the child began to realize that wisdom was all about and everywhere and that there were many things to know. There was no such thing as emptiness in the world. Even in the sky there were no vacant places. Everywhere there was life, visible and invisible, and every object gave us great interest to life. Even without human companionship one was never alone. The world teemed with life and wisdom, there was no complete solitude for the Lakota (Luther Standing Bear). [25]

The Ethics of the Multispecies Society

In this section we develop a little more formally the hypothesis that the American Indian concept of nature supported an environmental ethic. And we illustrate and document the existence of an American Indian environmental ethic with reference to specific cultural materials.

Aldo Leopold's land ethic has been the contemporary ecology movement's environmental ethic of choice. It may serve thus as a familiar model of environmental ethics with which we may compare the American Indian worldview and its associated environmental attitudes and values.

According to Leopold, "All ethics so far evolved rest upon a single premise: that the individual is a member of a community of interdependent parts. . . . The land ethic simply enlarges the boundaries of the community to include soils, waters, plants and animals, or collectively: the land." [26] Ethics depend ultimately, Leopold suggests, upon a sense of community. One will acknowledge moral obligations only to those persons whom one recognizes as fellow members of one's own society or group. And if one's sense of

---

24. Ibid., p. 47 (emphasis added).

25. Brown, "Modes of Contemplation," p. 64.
26. Aldo Leopold, *A Sand County Almanac: With Essays on Conservation from Round River* (New York: Ballantine Books, 1966), p. 239.

community includes nonhuman natural entities and is coextensive with the whole of nature, one has the cognitive foundations of a land ethic.

What we have already discovered about the American Indian concept of nature amply shows that nonhuman natural entities are personalized. Whereas in the Western worldview only human beings are fully persons, nature in the Indian worldview abounds with other-than-human-persons, among them "plants and animals" and even "soils and waters," as Leopold's specifications for an environmental ethic would require. For Leopold, the personhood of the nonhuman world is a sadly neglected implication of evolutionary biology. We are, from an evolutionary point of view, animals ourselves. Since we experience sensations, feelings, and thoughts, then only pre-Darwinian prejudices about the uniqueness of people would blind us to similar capacities in other animals. The reasoning indeed is not unlike that of the Indians as outlined by Jenness, quoted in the previous section. Leopold summed up the moral implications of the theory of evolution this way:

> It is a century now since Darwin gave us the first glimpse of the origin of species. We know now what was unknown to all the preceding caravan of generations: that men [and women] are only fellow voyagers in the odyssey of evolution. This new knowledge should have given us by this time, a sense of kinship with fellow-creatures; a wish to live and let live; a sense of wonder over the magnitude and duration of the biotic enterprise.[27]

Although it would be presumptuous to think that American Indians had anticipated Darwin in discovering the evolutionary origin of species, the American Indian worldview certainly supported a similar upshot: a continuity among all beings. That nonhuman persons form with us a community or society Leopold inferred from the science of ecology, which represents plants and animals, soils and waters as "all interlocked in one humming community of cooperations and competitions, one biota."[28] Pre-Columbian Ameri-

can Indians were no more informed by scientific ecology than they were by the theory of evolution, but they did regard themselves as members of multispecies socioeconomic communities of interlocked cooperations and competitions. Traditional Ojibwa narratives amply document this aspect of the pre-Columbian American Indian worldview. The stories tell again and again of the transformation of a human being into an animal (or vice versa) and of a marriage between the transformed human (or animal) person with a person of another species.

One especially representative example is "The Woman Who Married a Beaver." In this story, a young woman on her vision quest meets a person "who was," as the narrator puts it, "in the form of a human being."[29] He asks her to come to his attractive and well-appointed home by a lake and to be his wife. The man was a very good provider; the woman was in want of nothing; and their home was very beautiful. For her part, she collected firewood, made mats and bags out of reeds, and kept the house in very neat order. She has two clues that the person she married was not really of her own species: "When they beheld their first young, four was the number of them"; and "sometimes by a human being were they visited, but only round about out of doors would the man pass, not within would the man come." "Now," the story goes, "the woman knew that she had married a beaver."

The meaning of this oft-repeated theme may not be obvious to Westerners, but a little basic anthropological information should help to make it entirely clear. In tribal societies, alliances between different clans (or extended families) are established through marriage. Further, in many tribal societies, clans are distinguished from one another through totem representation. Within a tribal group, in other words, there may be the bear clan, the snake clan, the crane clan, and so on. (Entertaining the notion of interspecies marriages, therefore, would probably seem less weird

27. Ibid., pp. 116–17.
28. Ibid., p. 193.

29. This and all subsequent quotations from this story are taken from Thomas W. Overholt and J. Baird Callicott, *Clothed-in-Fur and Other Tales: An Introduction to an Ojibwa World View* (Washington, D.C.: University Press of America, 1982), pp. 74–75.

to people who think of themselves in terms of totem identities—the bear people, the snake people, the crane people, and so on.) Further, each clan may assume both ceremonial and economic specialties metaphorically associated with their totems. For example, only the bear clan may be permitted to kill bears for the annual bear ceremony, and thus the bear clan may be the principal provider of bear meat and grease for the whole tribe. Or, to take another hypothetical example, the crane clan may specialize in organizing seasonal migrations and gathering wild rice. Intermarriages between clans—what anthropologists call the rule of exogamy or out-marriage—binds them all together in a functioning tribal whole. More especially, it facilitates the exchange of specialized goods and services among all the subgroups. Such exchange of goods and services was typically less a matter of barter than of gift-giving, as would befit clans united by matrimonial ties.[30]

So the basic meaning of "The Woman Who Married a Beaver" and of similar tales seems to be this: The marriage between the two groups, the people and the beavers, establishes an alliance with economic implications. Gifts are exchanged that are mutually beneficial. Our suggestion is confirmed as the plot develops.

The odd couple of this story is very prolific and the beaver-man (though not the woman herself) and their offspring would go home with the human beings who visited them from time to time. "The people would then slay the beavers, yet they really did not kill them; but back home would they come again." When they came home, "All sorts of things would they fetch—kettles and bowls, knives, tobacco, and all the things that are used when a beaver is eaten. Continually were they adding to their great wealth." Here is the clearest possible representation of a mutually beneficial economic relationship between two matrimonially united "clans"—the beaver "people" and the people proper—executed through gift exchange. The beavers give the people all that they have to give, their flesh

and fur, and the people give the beavers what the aquatic rodents could not otherwise obtain: hand-crafted articles (like kettles and knives) and cultivars (like tobacco), which they highly prize.

But of course the animals could not benefit from the gifts they are given in return if they were dead. So the Indians conveniently supposed that they were not really dead. How did that work? We have already seen that in pre-Columbian North America there prevailed a ubiquitous belief in nature spirits. The spirits of the slain animals would, it was assumed, survive the killing of their bodies and, if their bones were not broken or burned and if they were returned to their appropriate element (water in the case of beavers), the bones might be reincarnated and reclothed in fur.

The existence of many taboos respecting the bones of game animals and the preoccupation of many stories with the proper treatment of animal bones may be understood in one or the other of two possible ways: The spirit may reside in or take refuge in the bones. Or at a stage of American Indian thought before the formation of the concept of an immaterial spirit, the immortal thing may have been supposed to be the skeleton—which, after all, is more lasting than the softer parts.

People, obviously, are economically dependent not only on one another but on many other species as well. To people who live largely by hunting and gathering, this dependence is more palpably apparent on a daily basis than it is to us who are insulated from the natural economy by a series of middlepersons. The Ojibwa represented their dependence upon other species through a social metaphor, not altogether unlike that of contemporary ecology. Ecologists draw an analogy between the economic structure of human societies and the "economy" of the "biotic community." The Ojibwa similarly pictured their interspecies economic relationships with beavers, moose, bears, and other creatures in terms of their intraspecies economic relationships with one another. Again, "The Woman Who Married a Beaver" is almost didactically explicit about this:

30. For a full discussion, see Marshall Sahlins, *Stone Age Economics* (Chicago: Aldine Atherton, 1972).

That was the time when very numerous were the beavers, and the beavers were very fond of the people; in the same way as people are when visiting one another, so were the beavers in their mental attitude toward the people. Even though they were slain by the people, yet they were not really dead. They were very fond of the tobacco that was given them by the people; at times they were also given clothing by the people.

Now, as we earlier observed, social interaction among persons is facilitated by ethical protocols. The conclusion of the story of the woman who married a beaver is explicitly moral. Having grown old together, the beaver-man instructs his wife to return to her people, and he departs for another land.

> Thereupon she plainly told the story of what had happened to her while she lived with the beavers. . . . And she was wont to say: "Never speak you ill of a beaver! Should you speak ill of a beaver, you will not be able to kill one."
>
> Therefore such was what the people always did; they never spoke ill of the beavers, especially when they intended hunting them. . . . Just the same as the feelings of one who is disliked, so is the feeling of the beaver. And he who never speaks ill of a beaver is very much loved by it; . . . particularly lucky then is one at killing beavers.

In addition to forging the alliance between the human clan and the beaver clan necessary for the gift exchange of goods and services typical of a tribal economy, the human changeling often serves in such stories as the emissary from the animals about their special requirements and demands. As we have just seen in this story, when the woman who married a beaver returns to her own kind she informs them of the feelings of the beavers and the appropriate attitude of respect that the beavers demand if people wish successfully to engage in this particular form of fur trading. In another story, "Clothed-in-Fur," in addition to reciprocal gift-giving and respect, the moral of the story focuses on the proper treatment of the beavers' bones.

The Practical Implications of the American Indian Worldview

Let us now explore a little more deeply the suggestion made at the beginning of this chapter,

namely, that in its *practical* consequences the traditional American Indian view of nature was on the whole more productive of a cooperative symbiosis of people with their environment than is the view of nature predominant in the prevailing Western European and Euro-American tradition.

Respecting the latter, Ian McHarg writes that "it requires little effort to mobilize a sweeping indictment of the physical environment which is [Western] man's creation [and] it takes little more to identify the source of the value system which is the culprit."[31] According to McHarg, the culprit is "the Judeo-Christian-Humanist view which is so unknowing of nature and of man, which has bred and sustained his simple-minded anthropocentrism."[32]

Since the early 1960s popular ecologists and environmentalists (perhaps most notably Rachel Carson and Barry Commoner, along with McHarg and Lynn White, Jr., and, more recently, Norman Myers, Paul Ehrlich, and Bill McKibben) have, with a grim fascination, recited a litany of environmental ills. They have spoken of "polychlorinated biphenyls," "chlorofluorocarbons," "nuclear tinkering," "acid rain," and "the gratified bulldozer" in language once reserved for detailing the precincts of Hell and abominating its seductive Prince. Given the frequency with which we are reminded of the symptoms of strain in the global biosphere and the apocalyptic rhetoric in which they are usually cast we may be excused if we omit this particular step from the present argument. Let us stipulate that modern technological civilization (European in its origins) has been neither restrained nor especially delicate in manipulating the natural world.

With somewhat more humor than other advocates of environmental reform, Aldo Leopold characterized the modern Western approach to nature thus: "By and large our present problem is one of attitudes and implements. We are remodeling the Alhambra with a steam shovel, and

---

31. Ian McHarg, "Values, Process, Form," from *The Fitness of Man's Environment* (Washington, D.C.: Smithsonian Institution Press, 1968), reprinted in Robert Disch, ed., *The Ecological Conscience* (Englewood Cliffs, N.J.: Prentice-Hall, 1970), p. 25.
32. Ibid., p. 98.

we are proud of our yardage. We shall hardly relinquish the shovel, which after all has many good points, but we are in need of gentler and more objective criteria for its successful use."[33] So far as the historical roots of the environmental crisis are concerned, we have here suggested that the much maligned attitudes arising out of the Judaic aspect of the Judeo-Christian tradition (man's God-given right to subdue nature, and so forth) have not been so potent a force in the work of remodeling as the tradition of Western natural philosophy that originated among the ancient Greeks, insidiously affected Christianity, and fully flowered in modern classical scientific thought. At least Western natural philosophy has been as formative of the cultural milieu (one artifact of which is the steam shovel itself) as have Genesis and the overall Old Testament worldview. In any case, mixed and blended together, they create a mentality in which unrestrained environmental exploitation and degradation could almost have been predicted in advance.

It seems obvious (especially to philosophers and historians of ideas) that attitudes and values *do* directly "determine" behavior by setting goals (for example, to subdue the Earth, to have dominion) and, through a conceptual representation of the world, by providing means (for example, mechanics, optics, and thermodynamics) expressed in technologies (for example, steam shovels and bulldozers). Skepticism regarding this assumption, however, has been forthcoming. Yi-Fu Tuan says in "Discrepancies Between Environmental Attitude and Behavior: Examples from Europe and China":

> We may *believe* that a world-view which puts nature in subservience to man will lead to the exploitation of nature by man; and one that regards man as simply a component in nature will entail a modest view of his rights and capabilities, and so lead to the establishment of a harmonious relationship between man and his natural environment. But is this correct?[34]

33. Leopold, *Sand County,* pp. 263–64.
34. Yi-Fu Tuan, "Discrepancies Between Environmental Attitude and Behavior," in *Ecology and Religion in History,* eds. D. Spring and I. Spring (New York: Harper and Row, 1947), p. 92.

Yi-Fu Tuan thinks not. The evidence from Chinese experience that he cites, however, is ambiguous, while the evidence from European experience that he cites misses an important point that we earlier made about the origins of Western environmental attitudes and values.

According to Tuan, traditional Chinese attitudes toward nature shaped by Taoism and Buddhism are supposed to have been "quiescent" and "adaptive." But, he points out, China's ancient forests were seriously overcut, suggesting that the traditional Chinese were no more concerned about living in harmony with the natural Tao (or Way of nature) or about respecting the Buddhahood of plants and animals than were their European counterparts. On the other hand, Tuan reports that China's first railway was decommissioned because it was believed to have been laid out contrary to the principles of *feng shui*—the art of siting human works in accordance with the flow of rivers, the direction of prevailing winds, and the contours of land forms— thus suggesting that the Chinese *were* in fact more concerned about living in harmony with nature than were their European counterparts. One can hardly imagine a European or American railway being pulled up solely because it was incompatible with principles of environmental aesthetics. Generally speaking, among the Chinese before Westernization, the facts that Yi-Fu Tuan presents indicate as many congruences as discrepancies between the traditional Taoist and Buddhist attitude's toward nature and Chinese environmental behavior.

Concerning European experience, we would expect that the ancient Greeks and Romans— who deified nature—would not have trashed the environment, if they really believed what they said they did *and* if human actions are determined by human belief. But Tuan marshals examples and cases in point of large-scale transformations, imposed, with serious ecological consequences, on the Mediterranean environment by the Greeks and Romans of classical antiquity. He concludes this part of his discussion with the remark that "against this background of the vast transformations of nature in the pagan world, the inroads made in the early centuries of the Christian era were relatively modest." [35]

Our discussion in the second section of this chapter, however, should explain the environmental impact of "pagan" Greek and Roman civilization consistently with the general thesis that worldview substantially affects behavior. The Greeks and Romans of classical antiquity lived in an age of increasing religious skepticism. By the mid-fifth century B.C., materio-mechanistic, dualistic, and humanistic philosophy had undercut and replaced the earlier sincere paganism of the ancient Greeks. The same religious skepticism eventually spread to the ancient Romans, who habitually followed Greek intellectual fashions. In the absence of religious restraint, the ancients exploited, despoiled, and defiled the natural (but no longer sacred) world.

Nevertheless, a simple deterministic model will not suffice with respect to this question: Do cultural attitudes and values really affect the collective behavior of a culture? At the one extreme, it seems incredible to think that *all* our conceptualizations, our representations of the nature of nature, are, as it were, mere entertainment, a sort of Muzak for the mind, while our actions proceed in some blind way from instinctive or genetically programmed sources. After all, our picture of nature defines our theater of action. It defines both the possibilities and the limitations that circumscribe human endeavor. We attempt to do only what we think is possible, while we leave alone what we think is not. Moreover, what we believe human nature to be, and what we take to be our proper place and role in the natural world, represents an ideal that, consciously or not, we strive to realize. At the other extreme, the facts of history and everyday experience do not support any simple cause-and-effect relationship between a given conceptual and valuational set and how people actually behave. Notoriously, we often act in ways that conflict with our sincere beliefs, especially our moral beliefs, and with our values.

Here is our suggestion for understanding the relationship between human environmental attitudes and values, on the one hand, and actual human behavior in respect to nature, on the other. Inevitably, human beings must consume other living things and modify the natural environment. Representations of the order of nature and the proper relationship of people to that order may have either a tempering, restraining effect on our manipulative and exploitative tendencies or an accelerating, exacerbating effect. They also give form and direction to these inherently human drives and thus provide different cultures with their distinctive styles of doing things. It appears, further, that in the case of the predominant European mentality, shaped both by Judeo-Christian and by Greco-Roman images of nature and man, the effect was to accelerate the inherent human disposition to consume "resources" and modify surroundings. A kind of "take-off" or (to mix metaphors) "quantum leap" occurred, and Western European civilization was propelled—for better or worse—into its industrial, technological stage, with a proportional increase in ecological and environmental distress. The decisive ingredient, the sine qua non, may have been the particulars of the European worldview. [36]

If the predominant traditional Chinese view of nature and man has been characterized by Yi-Fu Tuan and others as quiescent and adaptive, the American Indian view of the world has been characterized as in essence "ecological"—for example, by Stewart Udall in *The Quiet Crisis*. The general American Indian worldview (at least the one central part of it to which we have called attention) deflected the inertia of day-to-day, year-to-year subsistence in a way that resulted, on the average, in conservation. Pre-Columbian American Indian conservation of resources may have been a *consciously* posited goal. But probably it was not. Probably conservation was neither a personal ideal nor a tribal policy because the "wise use" of "natural resources" would, ironically, appear to be inconsistent with the spiritual

---

35. Ibid., p. 98.

36. For a full discussion, see J. Baird Callicott and Roger T. Ames, "Epilogue: On the Relation of Idea and Action" in J. B. Callicott and R. T. Ames, eds., *Nature in Asian Traditions of Thought* (Albany: State University of New York Press, 1989), pp. 279–89.

and personal attributes that the Indians regarded as belonging to nature and natural things. So-called natural resources are represented by most conservationists, whose philosophy was shaped by Gifford Pinchot, the nation's first chief forester, as only commodities, subject to scarcity, and therefore in need of prudent "development" and "management." The American Indian posture toward nature was, we suggest, more moral or ethical. Animals, plants, and minerals were treated as persons, and conceived to be coequal members of a natural social order.

Our cautious claim that the American Indian worldview supported and included a distinctly ethical attitude toward nature and the myriad variety of natural entities is based on the following basic points. The American Indians, on the whole, viewed the natural world as enspirited. Natural beings therefore felt, perceived, deliberated, and responded voluntarily as persons. Persons are members of a social order (that is, part of the operational concept of *person* is the capacity for social interaction). Social interaction is limited by (culturally variable) behavioral restraints—rules of conduct—which we call, in sum, good manners, morals, and ethics. Thus, as N. Scott Momaday maintains: "Very old in the Native American world view is the conviction that the earth is vital, that there is a spiritual dimension to it, a dimension in which man rightly exists. It follows logically that there are ethical imperatives in this matter."[37] The American Indians, more particularly, lived in accordance with an "ecological conscience" that was structurally similar to Aldo Leopold's "land ethic."

Examples of wastage—buffalo rotting on the plains under high cliffs or beaver all but trapped out during the fur trade—are supposed to deliver the coup de grace to all romantic illusions of the American Indian's reverence for nature. But examples of murder and war also abound in European history. Must we conclude therefrom that Europeans were altogether without a humanistic ethic of any sort?[38] Hardly. What confounds such facile arguments is a useful understanding of the function of ethics in human affairs.

As philosophers point out, ethics bear a normative relation to behavior. They do not describe how people actually behave. Rather, they set out how people *ought* to behave. People remain free to act either in accordance with a given ethic or not. The fact that on some occasions some do not scarcely proves that, in a given culture, ethical norms do not exist, or that ethics are not on the whole influential and effective behavioral restraints.

The familiar Christian ethic, with its emphasis on the dignity and intrinsic value of human beings, has long been a very significant element of Western culture, and has exerted a decisive influence within European and Euro-American civilization. Certainly, it has inspired noble and even heroic deeds both by individuals and by whole societies. The documented existence and influence of the Christian ethic are not in the least diminished by monstrous crimes on the part of individual Europeans. Nor do shameful episodes of national depravity, like the Spanish Inquisition, and genocide, as in Nazi Germany, refute the assertion that a human-centered ethic has palpably affected average behavior among members of the European culture and substantially shaped the character of Western civilization.

By parity of reasoning, examples of occasional destruction of nature on the pre-Columbian American continent and even the extirpation of species, especially during periods of enormous cultural stress, as in the fur trade era, do not, by themselves, refute the assertion that American Indians lived not only by a tribal ethic but by a land ethic as well. The overall and usual effect of such an ethic was to establish a greater harmony between the aboriginal American peoples and their environment than that enjoyed by their Euro-American successors.

---

37. Momaday, "First American Views," p. 18.
38. The most scurrilous example of this sort of argument with which we are acquainted is Daniel A. Guthrie's "Primitive Man's Relationship to Nature," *BioScience* 21 (July 1971): 721–23. In addition to rotting buffalo, Guthrie cites alleged extirpation of Pleistocene megafauna by Paleo-Indians, ca. 10,000 B.C. (as if that were relevant), and his cheapest shot of all, "the litter of bottles and junked cars to be found on Indian reservations today."

We are living today in a very troubling time, but also a time of great opportunity. The modern mechanistic worldview and its technological expression are collapsing. A new, more organic ecological worldview and a corresponding technological esprit are beginning to take shape. But how can we translate this essentially scientific realization and its technosocial analogue into terms easily grasped by ordinary people so that we may all begin to see ourselves as a part of nature and as dependent on it for our sustenance? Only then can we hope to evolve a sustainable society.

The Indians were hardly evolutionary ecologists, but their outlook on nature was, albeit expressed in the imagery of myth, remarkably similar to the concept of nature emerging from contemporary biology. They saw themselves as plain members and citizens of their respective biotic communities, humbly and dependently participating in the local economy of nature. Hence one way to help popularize the emerging new ecological worldview and its associated life-style would be to turn for help to the indigenous wisdom of the North American continent. American Indian mythology could put imaginative flesh and blood on the dry skeleton of the abstract environmental sciences.

American Indian thought remains an untapped intellectual resource for all contemporary Americans. Euro-Americans cannot undo the past injustices that our forebears inflicted on American Indians. What we can do, however, is to recognize and fully incorporate the cognitive cultural achievements evolved in this hemisphere. So doing would engender respect and honor for the peoples who created them and for their contemporary custodians.

Some may say that "mining" the so-far "untapped" intellectual "resource" represented by traditional American Indian cognitive cultures would only perpetuate the history of exploitation of Native Americans by Euro-Americans.[39] After appropriating Indian lands, now we propose to add insult to injury by appropriating Indian ideas. We disagree. Things of the mind are not diminished when they are shared. Teachers do not diminish their knowledge by sharing it with students. Quite the contrary. Similarly, American Indian thought could only be enlarged and enriched should it become a principal tributary to the mainstream of contemporary North American culture and civilization. And, vice versa, North American culture and civilization could at last become something more than an extension of its European matrix should it mix and merge with the rich legacy of its native peoples.

---

39. A similar complaint about Western intellectual colonialism of Asian traditions of thought has been registered by Gerald James Larson, "'Conceptual Resources' in South Asia for 'Environmental Ethics'" in Callicott and Ames, *Nature in Asian Traditions of Thought*, pp. 267–77.

Suggestions for Further Readings

See *The Environmental Ethics and Policy Book: Philosophy, Ecology, Economics* (Belmont, CA: Wadsworth, 1994) and *People, Penguins, and Plastic Trees: Basic Issues in Environmental Ethics* (Belmont, CA: Wadsworth, 1986), both edited by Donald Van DeVeer and Christine Pierce, for good selections on issues in environmental ethics.

Watersheds: Classic Cases in Environmental Ethics by Lisa H. Newton and Catherine K. Dillingham (Belmont, CA: Wadsworth, 1994) provides an illuminating discussion of specific cases. In the same vein, by the same authors and from the same publisher, is *Watersheds 2: Ten Cases in Environmental Ethics* (1997).

Philosophy Gone Wild: Environmental Ethics by Homes Rolston, III (Buffalo, NY: Prometheus Books, 1989) provides a collection of essays written by a pioneering environmental ethicist and editor of the journal *Environmental Ethics.*

Videos

A Sense of Place (28 minutes) explores the relationship between humans and the global ecology. *Enviroethics* (60 minutes) discusses the rights of future generations. Both are available from Insight Media, 2162 Broadway, New York, NY 10024.

Crisis Planet Earth (30 minutes), *The Fate of Planet Earth* (57 minutes), *Earth Aid: Recycling* (20 minutes), *Finite Oceans* (60 minutes) and *Pollution* (20 minutes) deal with different environmental issues, and all are available from Teacher's Video Company, PO Box WHG-4455, Scottsdale, AZ 85261.

6.8 Development, Environment, and the Third World

Suppose you live in a country that is, on the whole, very poor. It is what many call a "developing country." There is little industry, most people live on farms, only 52% of the population is literate, 35% live below the poverty line, the population is nearly 1 billion and growing, and the environment is in terrible condition and getting worse every day.

Suppose people who live in a very wealthy "developed country" with a 97% literacy rate and a population of a little over 275 million begin to tell you to restrict your growth and curtail development of your natural resources because it will only increase environmental problems. You will surely note with no little resentment the fact that once their own basic needs for food, shelter, and warmth have been amply fulfilled, and after they have become rich by exploiting natural resources (their own and others), resulting in a variety of ecological disasters, they now, in the luxury of their consumer society, have the gall to tell you how to deal with your environment.

Environmental problems are global. What happens to a jungle in India has an impact on people living in Los Angeles. Economies are global. When some get rich, others get poor. The views of the rich about both environmental and economic issues will be, on the whole, very different from those of the poor. Is it possible to develop ecological theories and practices that will benefit all? Is it possible to recognize the different stages of economic development around the world and, at the same time, develop environmental policies that benefit all? What are the prospects for a sustainable relationship between economic and ecological systems? What are the implications for social justice if a balance cannot be struck between economic growth and ecological preservation?

In the next selection, Ramachandra Guha, Indo-American Community Chair Visiting Professor at the University of California, Berkeley, offers a third-world critique of radical environmentalism, particularly the idea of **deep ecology**.

Reading Questions

1. What are Guha's main arguments?
2. What are the tenets of deep ecology?
3. How does Guha critique the views of deep ecology?
4. Do you find any part of Guha's critique of deep ecology convincing? Why, or why not?
5. How would you revise the philosophy of deep ecology in order to accommodate Guha's critique?

Radical American Environmentalism and Wilderness Preservation

RAMACHANDRA GUHA

> Even God dare not appear to the poor man except in the form of bread.
>
> *Mahatma Gandhi*

I. Introduction

THE RESPECTED RADICAL JOURNALIST Kirkpatrick Sale recently celebrated "the passion of a new and growing movement that has become disenchanted with the environmental establishment and has in recent years mounted a serious and sweeping attack on it—style, substance, systems, sensibilities and all." [1] The vision of those whom Sale calls the "New Ecologists"— and what I refer to in this article as deep ecology—is a compelling one. Decrying the narrowly economic goals of mainstream environmentalism, this new movement aims at nothing less than a philosophical and cultural revolution in human attitudes toward nature. In contrast to the conventional lobbying efforts of environmental professionals based in Washington, it proposes a militant defence of "Mother Earth," an unflinching opposition to human attacks on undisturbed wilderness. With their goals ranging from the spiritual to the political, the adherents of deep ecology span a wide spectrum of the American environmental movement. As Sale correctly notes, this emerging strand has in a matter of a few years made its presence felt in a number of fields: from academic philosophy (as in the journal *Environmental Ethics*) to popular environmentalism (for example, the group Earth First!).

In this article I develop a critique of deep ecology from the perspective of a sympathetic outsider. I critique deep ecology not as a general (or even a foot soldier) in the continuing struggle between the ghosts of Gifford Pinchot and John Muir over control of the U.S. environmental movement, but as an outsider to these battles. I speak admittedly as a partisan, but of the environmental movement in India, a country with an ecological diversity comparable to the U.S., but with a radically dissimilar cultural and social history.

My treatment of deep ecology is primarily historical and sociological, rather than philosophical, in nature. Specifically, I examine the cultural rootedness of a philosophy that likes to present itself in universalistic terms. I make two main arguments: first, that deep ecology is uniquely American, and despite superficial similarities in rhetorical style, the social and political goals of radical environmentalism in other cultural contexts (e.g., West Germany and India) are quite different; second, that the social consequences of putting deep ecology into practice on a worldwide basis (what its practitioners are aiming for) are very grave indeed.

II. The Tenets of Deep Ecology

While I am aware that the term *deep ecology* was coined by the Norwegian philosopher Arne Naess, this article refers specifically to the American variant. [2] Adherents of the deep ecological

---

1. Kirkpatrick Sale, "The Forest for the Trees: Can Today's Environmentalists Tell the Difference," *Mother Jones* 11, no. 8 (November 1986): 26.

2. One of the major criticisms I make in this essay concerns deep ecology's lack of concern with inequalities *within* human society. In the article in which he coined the term *deep ecology,* Naess himself expresses concerns about inequalities between and within nations. However, his concern with social cleavages and their impact an resource utilization patterns and ecological destruction is not very visible in the later writings of deep ecologists. See Arne Naess, "The Shallow and the Deep, Long-Range Ecology Movement: A Summary," *Inquiry* 16 (1973): 96 (I am grateful to Tom Birch for this reference).

From Environmental Ethics, *Volume 11 (Spring 1989): 71–83. Reprinted with permission of Ramachandra Guha and* Environmental Ethics. *Edited.*

perspective in this country, while arguing intensely among themselves over its political and philosophical implications, share some fundamental premises about human-nature interactions. As I see it, the defining characteristics of deep ecology are fourfold:

First, deep ecology argues, that the environmental movement must shift from an "anthropocentric" to a "biocentric" perspective. In many respects, an acceptance of the primacy of this distinction constitutes the litmus test of deep ecology. A considerable effort is expended by deep ecologists in showing that the dominant motif in Western philosophy has been anthropocentric—i.e., the belief that man and his works are the center of the universe—and conversely, in identifying those lonely thinkers (Leopold, Thoreau, Muir, Aldous Huxley, Santayana, etc.) who, in assigning man a more humble place in the natural order, anticipated deep ecological thinking. In the political realm, meanwhile, establishment environmentalism (shallow ecology) is chided for casting its arguments in human-centered terms. Preserving nature, the deep ecologists say, has an intrinsic worth quite apart from any benefits preservation may convey to future human generations. The anthropocentric-biocentric distinction is accepted as axiomatic by deep ecologists, it structures their discourse, and much of the present discussion remains mired within it.

The second characteristic of deep ecology is its focus on the preservation of unspoilt wilderness—and the restoration of degraded areas to a more pristine condition—to the relative (and sometimes absolute) neglect of other issues on the environmental agenda. I later identify the cultural roots and portentous consequences of this obsession with wilderness. For the moment, let me indicate three distinct sources from which it springs. Historically, it represents a playing out of the preservationist (read *radical*) and utilitarian (read *reformist*) dichotomy that has plagued American environmentalism since the turn of the century. Morally, it is an imperative that follows from the biocentric perspective; other species of plants and animals, and nature itself, have an intrinsic right to exist. And finally, the preservation of wilderness also turns on a scientific argu-

ment—viz., the value of biological diversity in stabilizing ecological regimes and in retaining a gene pool for future generations. Truly radical policy proposals have been put forward by deep ecologists on the basis of these arguments. The influential poet Gary Snyder, for example, would like to see a 90 percent reduction in human populations to allow a restoration of pristine environments, while others have argued forcefully that a large portion of the globe must be immediately cordoned off from human beings.[3]

Third, there is a widespread invocation of Eastern spiritual traditions as forerunners of deep ecology. Deep ecology, it is suggested, was practiced both by major religious traditions and at a more popular level by "primal" peoples in non-Western settings. This complements the search for an authentic lineage in Western thought. At one level, the task is to recover those dissenting voices within the Judeo-Christian tradition; at another, to suggest that religious traditions in other cultures are, in contrast, dominantly if not exclusively "biocentric" in their orientation. This coupling of (ancient) Eastern and (modern) ecological wisdom seemingly helps consolidate the claim that deep ecology is a philosophy of universal significance.

Fourth, deep ecologists, whatever their internal differences, share the belief that they are the "leading edge" of the environmental movement. As the polarity of the shallow/deep and anthropocentric/biocentric distinctions makes clear, they see themselves as the spiritual, philosophical, and political vanguard of American and world environmentalism.

III. *Toward a Critique*

Although I analyze each of these tenets independently, it is important to recognize, as deep ecologists are fond of remarking in reference to nature, the interconnectedness and unity of these individual themes.

3. Gary Snyder, quoted in Sale, "The Forest for the Trees," p. 32. See also Dave Foreman, "A Modest Proposal for a Wilderness System," *Whole Earth Review*, no. 53 (Winter 1986–87): 42–45.

(1) Insofar as it has begun to act as a check on man's arrogance and ecological hubris, the transition from an anthropocentric (human-centered) to a biocentric (humans as only one element in the ecosystem) view in both religious and scientific traditions is only to be welcomed.[4] What is unacceptable are the radical conclusions drawn by deep ecology, in particular, that intervention in nature should be guided primarily by the need to preserve biotic integrity rather than by the needs of humans. The latter for deep ecologists is anthropocentric, the former biocentric. This dichotomy is, however, of very little use in understanding the dynamics of environmental degradation. The two fundamental ecological problems facing the globe are (i) overconsumption by the industrialized world and by urban elites in the Third World and (ii) growing militarization, both in a short-term sense (i.e., ongoing regional wars) and in a long-term sense (i.e., the arms race and the prospect of nuclear annihilation). Neither of these problems has any tangible connection to the anthropocentric-biocentric distinction. Indeed, the agents of these processes would barely comprehend this philosophical dichotomy. The proximate causes of the ecologically wasteful characteristics of industrial society and of militarization are far more mundane: at an aggregate level, the dialectic of economic and political structures, and at a micro-level, the life style choices of individuals. These causes cannot be reduced, whatever the level of analysis, to a deeper anthropocentric attitude toward nature; on the contrary, by constituting a grave threat to human survival, the ecological degradation they cause does not even serve the best interests of human beings! If my identification of the major dangers to the integrity of the natural world is correct, invoking the bogy of anthropocentrism is at best irrelevant and at worst a dangerous obfuscation.

(2) If the above dichotomy is irrelevant, the emphasis on wilderness is positively harmful when applied to the Third World. If in the U.S. the preservationist/utilitarian division is seen as mirroring the conflict between "people" and "interests," in countries such as India the situation is very nearly the reverse. Because India is a long settled and densely populated country in which agrarian populations have a finely balanced relationship with nature, the setting aside of wilderness areas has resulted in a direct transfer of resources from the poor to the rich. Thus, Project Tiger, a network of parks hailed by the international conservation community as an outstanding success, sharply posits the interests of the tiger against those of poor peasants living in and around the reserve. The designation of tiger reserves was made possible only by the physical displacement of existing villages and their inhabitants; their management requires the continuing exclusion of peasants and livestock. The initial impetus for setting up parks for the tiger and other large mammals such as the rhinoceros and elephant came from two social groups, first, a class of ex-hunters turned conservationists belonging mostly to the declining Indian feudal elite and second, representatives of international agencies, such as the World Wildlife Fund (WWF) and the International Union for the Conservation of Nature and Natural Resources (IUCN), seeking to transplant the American system of national parks onto Indian soil. In no case have the needs of the local population been taken into account, and as in many parts of Africa, the designated wildlands are managed primarily for the benefit of rich tourists. Until very recently, wildlands preservation has been identified with environmentalism by the state and the conservation elite; in consequence, environmental problems that impinge far more directly on the lives of the poor—e.g., fuel, fodder, water shortages, soil erosion, and air and water pollution—have not been adequately addressed.[5]

---

4. See, for example, Donald Worster, *Nature's Economy: The Roots of Ecology* (San Francisco, Sierra Club Books, 1977).

5. See Centre for Science and Environment, *India: The State of the Environment 1982: A Citizens Report* (New Delhi: Centre for Science and Environment, 1982); R. Sukumar, "Elephant-Man Conflict in Karnataka," in Cecil Saldanha, ed., *The State of Karnataka's Environment* (Bangalore: Centre for Taxonomic Studies, 1985). For Africa, see the brilliant analysis by Helge Kjekshus, *Ecology Control and Economic Development in East African History* (Berkeley: University of California Press, 1977).

Deep ecology provides, perhaps unwittingly, a justification for the continuation of such narrow and inequitable conservation practices under a newly acquired radical guise. Increasingly, the international conservation elite is using the philosophical, moral, and scientific arguments used by deep ecologists in advancing their wilderness crusade. A striking but by no means atypical example is the recent plea by a prominent American biologist for the takeover of large portions of the globe by the author and his scientific colleagues. Writing in a prestigious scientific forum, the *Annual Review of Ecology, and Systematics,* Daniel Janzen argues that only biologists have the competence to decide how the tropical landscape should be used. As "the representatives of the natural world," biologists are "in charge of the future of tropical ecology," and only they have the expertise and mandate to "determine whether the tropical agroscape is to be populated only by humans, their mutualists, commensals, and parasites, or whether it will also contain some islands of the greater nature—the nature that spawned humans, yet has been vanquished by them." Janzen exhorts his colleagues to advance their territorial claims on the tropical world more forcefully, warning that the very existence of these areas is at stake: "if biologists want a tropics in which to biologize, they are going to have to buy it with care, energy, effort, strategy, tactics, time, and cash."[6]

This frankly imperialist manifesto highlights the multiple dangers of the preoccupation with wilderness preservation that is characteristic of deep ecology: As I have suggested, it seriously compounds the neglect by the American movement of far more pressing environmental problems within the Third World. But perhaps more importantly, and in a more insidious fashion, it also provides an impetus to the imperialist yearning of Western biologists and their financial sponsors, organizations such as the WWF and IUCN. The wholesale transfer of a movement culturally rooted in American conservation history can only result in the social uprooting of human populations in other parts of the globe.

(3) I come now to the persistent invocation of Eastern philosophies as antecedent in point of time but convergent in their structure with deep ecology. Complex and internally differentiated religious traditions—Hinduism, Buddhism, and Taoism—are lumped together as holding a view of nature believed to be quintessentially biocentric. Individual philosophers such as the Taoist Lao Tzu are identified as being forerunners of deep ecology. Even an intensely political, pragmatic, and Christian influenced thinker such as Gandhi has been accorded a wholly undeserved place in the deep ecological pantheon. Thus the Zen teacher Robert Aitken Roshi makes the strange claim that Gandhi's thought was not human-centered and that he practiced an embryonic form of deep ecology which is "traditionally Eastern and is found with differing emphasis in Hinduism, Taoism and in Theravada and Mahayana Buddhism."[7] Moving away from the realm of high philosophy and scriptural religion, deep ecologists make the further claim that at the level of material and spiritual practice "primal" peoples subordinated themselves to the integrity of the biotic universe they inhabited.

I have indicated that this appropriation of Eastern traditions is in part dictated by the need to construct an authentic lineage and in part a desire to present deep ecology as a universalistic philosophy. Indeed, in his substantial and quixotic biography of John Muir, Michael Cohen goes so far as to suggest that Muir was the "Taoist of the [American] West."[8] This reading of Eastern traditions is selective and does not bother to differentiate between alternate (and changing) religious and cultural traditions; as it stands, it does considerable violence to the historical record.

---

6. Daniel Janzen, "The Future of Tropical Ecology," *Annual Revive of Ecology and Systematics* 17 (1986): 305–06; emphasis added.

7. Robert Aiken Roshi, "Ganдhi, Dogen, and Deep Ecology," reprinted as appendix C in Bill Devall and George Sessions, *Deep Ecology: Living as if Nature Mattered* (Salt Lake City: Peregrine South Books, 1985). For Gandhi's own views on social reconstruction, see the excellent three volume collection edited by Raghavan Iyer, *The Moral and Political Writings of Mahatma Gandhi* (Oxford: Clarendon Press, 1986–87).
8. Michael Cohen, *The Pathless Way* (Madison: University of Wisconsin Press, 1984), p. 120.

Throughout most recorded history the characteristic form of human activity in the "East" has been a finely tuned but nonetheless conscious dynamic manipulation of nature. Although mystics such as Lao Tzu did reflect on the spiritual essence of human relations with nature, it must be recognized that such ascetics and their reflections were supported by a society of cultivators whose relationship with nature was a far more *active* one. Many agricultural communities do have a sophisticated knowledge of the natural environment that may equal (and sometimes surpass) coded "scientific" knowledge; yet, the elaboration of such traditional ecological knowledge (in both material and spiritual contexts) can hardly be said to rest on a mystical affinity with nature of a deep ecological kind. Nor is such knowledge infallible; as the archaeological record powerfully suggests, modern Western man has no monopoly on ecological disasters.

In a brilliant article, the Chicago historian Ronald Inden points out that this romantic and essentially positive view of the East is a mirror image of the scientific and essentially pejorative view normally upheld by Western scholars of the Orient. In either case, the East constitutes the Other, a body wholly separate and alien from the West; it is defined by a uniquely spiritual and nonrational "essence," even if this essence is valorized quite differently by the two schools. Eastern man exhibits a spiritual dependence with respect to nature—on the one hand, this is symptomatic of his prescientific and backward self, on the other, of his ecological wisdom and deep ecological consciousness. Both views are monolithic, simplistic, and have the characteristic effect—intended in one case, perhaps unintended in the other—of denying agency and reason to the East and making it the privileged orbit of Western thinkers.

The two apparently opposed perspectives have then a common underlying structure of discourse in which the East merely serves as a vehicle for Western projections. Varying images of the East are raw material for political and cultural battles being played out in the West; they tell us far more about the Western commentator and his desires than about the "East." Inden's remarks apply not merely to Western scholarship on India, but to Orientalist constructions of China and Japan as well:

> Although these two views appear to be strongly opposed, they often combine together. Both have a similar interest in sustaining the Otherness of India. The holders of the dominant view, best exemplified in the past in imperial administrative discourse (and today probably by that of 'development economics'), would place a traditional, superstition-ridden India in a position of perpetual tutelage to a modern, rational West. The adherents of the romantic view, best exemplified academically in the discourses of Christian liberalism and analytic psychology, concede the realm of the public and impersonal to the positivist. Taking their succour not from governments and big business, but from a plethora of religious foundations and self-help institutes, and from allies in the 'consciousness industry,' not to mention the important industry of tourism, the romantics insist that India embodies a private realm of the imagination and the religious which modern, western man lacks but needs. They, therefore, like the positivists, but for just the opposite reason, have a vested interest in seeing that the Orientalist view of India as "spiritual," "mysterious," and "exotic" is perpetuated.[9]

(4) How radical, finally, are the deep ecologists? Notwithstanding their self-image and strident rhetoric (in which the label "shallow ecology" has an opprobrium similar to that reserved for "social democratic" by Marxist-Leninists), even within the American context their radicalism is limited and it manifests itself quite differently elsewhere.

9. Ronald Inden, "Orientalist Constructions of India," *Modern Asian Studies* 20 (1986): 442. Inden draws inspiration from Edward Said's forceful polemic, *Orientalism* (New York: Basic Books. 1980). It must be noted, however, that there is a salient difference between Western perceptions of Middle Eastern and Far Eastern cultures respectively. Due perhaps to the long history of Christian conflict with Islam. Middle Eastern cultures (as Said documents) are consistently presented in pejorative terms. The juxtaposition of hostile and worshiping attitudes that Inden talks of applies only to Western attitudes toward Buddhist and Hindu societies.

To my mind, deep ecology is best viewed as a radical trend within the wilderness preservation movement. Although advancing philosophical rather than aesthetic arguments and encouraging political militancy rather than negotiation, its practical emphasis—viz., preservation of unspoilt nature—is virtually identical. For the mainstream movement, the function of wilderness is to provide a temporary antidote to modern civilization. As a special institution within an industrialized society, the national park "provides an opportunity for respite, contrast, contemplation, and affirmation of values for those who live most of their lives in the workaday world."[10] Indeed, the rapid increase in visitations to the national parks in postwar America is a direct consequence of economic expansion. The emergence of a popular interest in wilderness sites, the historian Samuel Hays points out, was "not a throwback to the primitive, but an integral part of the modern standard of living as people sought to add new 'amenity' and 'aesthetic' goals and desires to their earlier preoccupation with necessities and conveniences."[11]

Here, the enjoyment of nature is an integral part of the consumer society. The private automobile (and the life style it has spawned) is in many respects the ultimate ecological villain, and an untouched wilderness the prototype of ecological harmony; yet, for most Americans it is perfectly consistent to drive a thousand miles to spend a holiday in a national park. They possess a vast, beautiful, and sparsely populated continent and are also able to draw upon the natural resources of large portions of the globe by virtue of their economic and political dominance. In consequence, America can simultaneously enjoy the material benefits of an expanding economy and the aesthetic benefits of unspoilt nature. The two poles of "wilderness" and "civilization" mutually coexist in an internally coherent whole, and philosophers of both poles are assigned a prominent place in this culture. Paradoxically as it may seem, it is no accident that Star Wars technology and deep ecology both find their fullest expression in that leading sector of Western civilization, California.

Deep ecology runs parallel to the consumer society without seriously questioning its ecological and socio-political basis. In its celebration of American wilderness, it also displays an uncomfortable convergence with the prevailing climate of nationalism in the American wilderness movement. For spokesmen such as the historian Roderick Nash, the national park system is America's distinctive cultural contribution to the world, reflective not merely of its economic but of its philosophical and ecological maturity as well. In what Walter Lippman called the American century, the "American invention of national parks" must be exported worldwide. Betraying an economic determinism that would make even a Marxist shudder, Nash believes that environmental preservation is a "full stomach" phenomenon that is confined to the rich, urban, and sophisticated. Nonetheless, he hopes that "the less developed nations may eventually evolve economically and intellectually to the point where nature preservation is more than a business."[12]

The error which Nash makes (and which deep ecology in some respects encourages) is to equate environmental protection with the protection of wilderness. This is a distinctively American notion, borne out of a unique social and environmental history. The archetypal concerns of radical environmentalists in other cultural contexts are in fact quite different. The German Greens, for example, have elaborated a devastating critique of industrial society which turns on the

10. Joseph Sax. *Mountains Without Handrails: Reflections on the National Parks* (Ann Arbor: University of Michigan Press, 1980), p. 42. Cf. also Peter Schmitt, *Back to Nature: The Arcadian Myth in Urban America* (New York: Oxford University Press, 1969), and Alfred Runte, *National Parks: The American Experience* (Lincoln: University of Nebraska Press, 1979).

11. Samuel Hays, "From Conservation to Environment: Environmental Politics in the United States since World War Two," *Environmental Review* 6 (1982): 21. See also the same author's book entitled *Beauty, Health and Permanence: Environmental Politics in the United States, 1955–85* (New York: Cambridge University Press, 1987).

12. Roderick Nash, *Wilderness and the American Mind,* 3rd ed. (New Haven: Yale University Press, 1982).

acceptance of environmental limits to growth. Pointing to the intimate links between industrialization, militarization, and conquest, the Greens argue that economic growth in the West has historically rested on the economic and ecological exploitation of the Third World. Rudolf Bahro is characteristically blunt:

> The working class here [in the West] is the richest lower class in the world. And if I look at the problem from the point of view of the whole of humanity, not just from that of Europe, then I must say that the metropolitan working class is the worst exploiting class in history. . . . What made poverty bearable in eighteenth or nineteenth-century Europe was the prospect of escaping it through exploitation of the periphery. But this is no longer a possibility, and continued industrialism in the Third World will mean poverty for whole generations and hunger for millions.[13]

Here the roots of global ecological problems lie in the disproportionate share of resources consumed by the industrialized countries as a whole *and* the urban elite within the Third World. Since it is impossible to reproduce an industrial monoculture worldwide, the ecological movement in the West must begin by cleaning up its own act. The Greens advocate the creation of a "no growth" economy, to be achieved by scaling down current (and clearly unsustainable) consumption levels.[14] This radical shift in consumption and production patterns requires the creation of alternate economic and political structures—smaller in scale and more amenable to social participation—but it rests equally on a shift in cultural values. The expansionist character of modern Western man will have to give way to an ethic of renunciation and self-limitation, in which spiritual and communal values play an increasing role in sustaining social life. This revolution in cultural values, however, has as its point of departure an understanding of environmental processes quite different from deep ecology.

Many elements of the Green program find a strong resonance in countries such as India, where a history of Western colonialism and industrial development has benefited only a tiny elite while exacting tremendous social and environmental costs. The ecological battles presently being fought in India have as their epicenter the conflict over nature between the subsistence and largely rural sector and the vastly more powerful commercial-industrial sector. Perhaps the most celebrated of these battles concerns the Chipko (Hug the Tree) movement, a peasant movement against deforestation in the Himalayan foothills. Chipko is only one of several movements that have sharply questioned the nonsustainable demand being placed on the land and vegetative base by urban centers and industry. These include opposition to large dams by displaced peasants, the conflict between small artisan fishing and large-scale trawler fishing for export, the countrywide movements against commercial forest operations, and opposition to industrial pollution among downstream agricultural and fishing communities.[15]

Two features distinguish these environmental movements from their Western counterparts. First, for the sections of society most critically affected by environmental degradation—poor and landless peasants, women, and tribals—it is a question of sheer survival, not of enhancing the quality of life. Second, and as a consequence, the

13. Rudolf Bahro, *From Red to Green* (London: Verso Books, 1984).

14. From time to time, American scholars have themselves criticized these imbalances in consumption patterns. In the 1950s, William Vogt made the charge that the United States, with one-sixteenth of the world's population, was utilizing one-third of the globe's resources. (Vogt, cited in E. F. Murphy, *Nature, Bureaucracy and the Rule of Property* [Amsterdam: North Holland, 1971, p. 29]). More recently, Zero Population Growth has estimated that each American consumes thirty-nine times as many resources as an Indian. See *Christian Science Monitor,* 2 March 1987.

15. For an excellent review, see Anil Agarwal and Sunita Narain, eds., *India: The State of the Environment 1984–85: A Citizens Report* (New Delhi: Centre for Science and Environment, 1985). Cf. also Ramachandra Guha, *The Unquiet Woods: Ecological Change and Peasant Resistance in the Indian Himalaya* (Berkeley: University of California Press, forthcoming).

environmental solutions they articulate deeply involve questions of equity as well as economic and political redistribution. Highlighting these differences, a leading Indian environmentalist stresses that "environmental protection per se is of least concern to most of these groups. Their main concern is about the use of the environment and who should benefit from it."[16] They seek to wrest control of nature away from the state and the industrial sector and place it in the hands of rural communities who live within that environment but are increasingly denied access to it. These communities have far more basic needs, their demands on the environment are far less intense, and they can draw upon a reservoir of cooperative social institutions and local ecological knowledge in managing the "commons"—forests, grasslands, and the waters—on a sustainable basis. If colonial and capitalist expansion has both accentuated social inequalities and signaled a precipitous fall in ecological wisdom, an alternate ecology must rest on an alternate society and polity as well.

This brief overview of German and Indian environmentalism has some major implications for deep ecology. Both German and Indian environmental traditions allow for a greater integration of ecological concerns with livelihood and work. They also place a greater emphasis on equity and social justice (both within individual countries and on a global scale) on the grounds that in the absence of social regeneration environmental regeneration has very little chance of succeeding. Finally, and perhaps most significantly, they have escaped the preoccupation with wilderness preservation so characteristic of American cultural and environmental history.[17]

IV. A Homily

In 1958, the economist J. K. Galbraith referred to overconsumption as the unasked question of the American conservation movement. There is a marked selectivity, he wrote, "in the conservationist's approach to materials consumption. If we are concerned about our great appetite for materials, it is plausible to seek to increase the supply, to decrease waste, to make better use of the stocks available, and to develop substitutes. But what of the appetite itself? Surely this is the ultimate source of the problem. If it continues its geometric course, will it not one day have to be restrained? Yet in the literature of the resource problem this is the forbidden question. Over it hangs a nearly total silence."[18]

The consumer economy and society have expanded tremendously in the three decades since Galbraith penned these words; yet his criticisms are nearly as valid today. I have said "nearly," for there are some hopeful signs. Within the environmental movement several dispersed groups are working to develop ecologically benign technologies and to encourage less wasteful life styles. Moreover, outside the self-defined boundaries of American environmentalism, opposition to the permanent war economy is being carried on by a peace movement that has a distinguished history and impeccable moral and political credentials.

It is precisely these (to my mind, most hopeful) components of the American social scene that are missing from deep ecology. In their widely noticed book, Bill Devall and George Sessions make no mention of militarization or the movements for peace, while activists whose practical focus is on developing ecologically responsible life styles (e.g, Wendell Berry) are derided as

16. Anil Agarwal, "Human-Nature Interactions in a Third World Country," *The Environmentalist* 6, no. 3 (1986): 167.
17. One strand in radical American environmentalism, the bioregional movement, by emphasizing a greater involvement with the bioregion people inhabit, does indirectly challenge consumerism. However, as yet bioregionalism has hardly raised the questions of equity and social justice (international, intranational, and intergenerational) which I argue must be a central plank of radical environmentalism. Moreover, its stress

on (individual) *experience* as the key to involvement with nature is also somewhat at odds with the integration of nature with livelihood and work that I talk of in this paper. Cf. Kirkpatrick Sale, *Dwellers in the Land: The Bioregional Vision* (San Francisco: Sierra Club Books, 1983).
18. John Kenneth Galbraith, "How Much Should a Country Consume?" in Henry Jarrett, ed., *Perspectives on Conservation* (Baltimore: Johns Hopkins Press, 1958), pp. 91–92.

"falling short of deep ecological awareness."[19] A truly radical ecology in the American context ought to work toward a synthesis of the appropriate technology, alternate life style, and peace movements.[20] By making the (largely spurious)

anthropocentric-biocentric distinction central to the debate, deep ecologists may have appropriated the moral high ground, but they are at the same time doing a serious disservice to American and global environmentalism.[21]

19. Devall and Sessions, *Deep Ecology*, p. 122. For Wendell Berry's own assessment of deep ecology, see his "Amplications: Preserving Wildness," *Wilderness* 50 (Spring 1987): 39–40, 50–54.

20. See the interesting recent contribution by one of the most influential spokesmen of appropriate technology—Barry Commoner, "A Reporter at Large: The Environment," *New Yorker*, 15 June 1987. While Commoner makes a forceful plea for the convergence of the environmental movement (viewed by him primarily as the opposition to air and water pollution and to the institutions that generate such pollution) and the peace movement, he significantly does not mention consumption patterns, implying that "limits to growth" do not exist.

21. In this sense, my critique of deep ecology, although that of an outsider, may facilitate the reassertion of those elements in the American environmental tradition for which there is a profound sympathy in other parts of the globe. A global perspective may also lead to a critical reassessment of figures such as Aldo Leopold and John Muir, the two patron saints of deep ecology. As Donald Worster has pointed out, the message of Muir (and, I would argue, of Leopold as well) makes sense only in an American context; he has very little to say to other cultures. See Worster's review of Stephen Fox's *John Muir and His Legacy*, in *Environmental Ethics* 5 (1983): 277–81.

Suggestions for Further Reading

For a basic and useful collection of essays on radical environmentalism with a lead-off selection from Arne Naess, the father of deep ecology, see *Radical Environmentalism: Philosophy and Tactics,* edited by Peter C. List (Belmont, CA: Wadsworth, 1993).

Jeremy Rifkin's *Biosphere Politics: A Cultural Odyssey from the Middle Ages to the New Age* (New York: HarperSanFrancisco, 1991) explores, among other things, environmental issues from a historical and global perspective.

Sources on environmental ethics can be found at http://ecoethics.net/bib/tl-198-a.htm.

Social Ecology edited by R. Guha (Oxford: Oxford University Press, 1999) provides a collection of essays that survey the new and growing field of social ecology. Also *Varieties of Environmentalism: Essays North and South* edited by R. Guha and Juan Martinez-Alier (London: Earthscan, 1997) provides useful information on environmentalism in developing countries.

Ethical Perspective on Environmental Issues in India edited by George A. James (New Delhi: Vadam Books, 1999) discusses some of the most severe problems with India's environment and explores the resources available in Indian religion and philosophy for environmental theory.

6.9 International Business Ethics

Which social institutions have the greatest impact on people's lives and hence the greatest impact on social justice? Do you think it is educational institutions or religious institutions? Do you think it is government or business corporations? However you might answer these questions, most of you would probably agree that business would be near the top of any list. What businesses do—the profits they make, the wages and benefits they give, the goods and services they generate—all these things have an impact on the quality of life for most people living on this globe. Sooner or later, any discussion of social ethics and the problems associated with achieving social justice must turn its attention to the ethics of business.

How much responsibility does the business community have in promoting social justice? Are corporations under any moral obligation at all to make the world a better place for everyone to live in? Should corporations be "good citizens"?

These questions have become even more urgent with the rise of multinational corporations that have no national identity nor any substantial commitment to the country of their origin. Their workforce and production facilities can be located wherever the greatest profits can be made. This reinforces what many have come to call the *canonical view of business ethics.* According to this view, business social responsibility stops with profit maximization and obeying the law. Corporations have no obligation to anyone beyond their shareholders. Those who invest in a corporation deserve to share the profits generated by the business that corporation does and have the right to expect that business will be conducted in such a way as to lawfully maximize profits. Safe working conditions, paying a livable wage, protection of the environment, and other social concerns are secondary, at best, to the primary goal of making money legally.

Some of you may applaud this canonical view and others may find it harsh if not socially irresponsible. Surely more people than the shareholders have an interest in how business is done. What about those people—suppliers, employees, customers, and so on—who may not be shareholders but certainly are stakeholders? Should we not consider their interests? The *stakeholder theory* of corporate moral responsibility sees managers of corporations as agents for all stakeholders. This stakeholder theory of corporate responsibility, in contrast to the canonical view, has very different implications for what corporations ought to do.

In the following selection, David M. Adams of California State Polytechnic University, Pomona, and Edward W. Maine of California State University, Fullerton, explore how the canonical and stakeholder models of corporate social responsibility might deal with the moral issues that two different business scenarios raise for multinational corporations.

Reading Questions

1. What do you think someone who supported the canonical position would say about G. E. Searle's marketing practices?
2. Assume the stakeholder position and comment on G. D. Searle's marketing practices.
3. Do you think a multinational company using the stakeholder model could ever compete effectively against a multinational company using the canonical model? Explain, and justify your answer.

International Competition and Corporate Social Responsibility

DAVID M. ADAMS AND EDWARD W. MAINE

. . . WE BEGIN BY CONSIDERING two scenarios of recent international business practices. The first involves labor practices in Indonesia, the second, sales practices of pharmaceutical firms in poorer nations. Following the scenarios, we suggest how two prominent models of corporate social responsibility might address the moral issues the scenarios raise. Our purpose here is not to define multinational corporate social responsibility, but simply to explore some of the implications of the models.

Scenarios

Nike manufactures and sells fashionable, high-quality athletic equipment and clothing. Its athletic shoe industry accounts for almost $2 billion in sales per annum. Virtually all of its shoe production is done offshore in Asia through independent local contractors. Nike is not unique in this respect. The Indonesian shoe industry, for instance, employs twenty-five thousand workers, who produce shoes for Nike, Reebok, L.A. Gear, and Addidas. The plight of these workers, who are for the most part young girls, is pitiable. They earn less than $0.15 per hour and live in company-run dormitories or settlements, often sharing their small quarters with six other workers. Overtime is mandatory, and often this results in an eleven-hour workday. Workers are subject to abusive treatment by the factory owners, who hold contracts with leading U.S. manufacturers. Labor laws do exist but they are violated with impunity because of the eagerness of the governments to attract foreign capital.

The United States has not been blind to these offenses and recently threatened to repeal tariff preferences if Indonesia did not improve its labor conditions. The threat resulted in an official minimum wage of $1.80 per hour and a decree that forbade the military from intervening in labor disputes (e.g., wildcat strikes). But many factories fail to comply with these dictates, in part because the very same military officers who command the soldiers sit on the boards of directors of the offending factories. These officers stood to benefit from the existing labor practices. Furthermore, the penalties for noncompliance are minimal; failure to comply with the new wage standard, for example, means a fine of $50.

Endorsements paid to Michael Jordan, Nike's spokesperson, exceed what the entire twenty-five-thousand-person workforce earns in a year. In this system of labor, it costs $5.60 to produce a pair of basketball shoes that retail in the United States for more than $70.

In his text *Ethics and the Conduct of Business,* John R. Boatright outlines some of the more widely criticized practices of the pharmaceutical industry when it sells abroad. One problem is lack of information. A study of the Office of Technology Assessment indicated that many American-made drugs had labels with medically important information missing and unsupported claims added. One example is Lomotril, marketed by G. D. Searle. Used for the treatment of diarrhea (which can be a life-threatening condition, particularly for children in poorer countries), the drug treats the symptoms of diarrhea by producing constipation, but it does not treat the causes. The World Health Organization has declared Lomotril to be of no medical value. Furthermore, the drug is dangerous when used by children under two years of age. But Searle has recommended the drug for infants in Hong Kong, Thailand, the Philippines, and Central America.

Boatright also cites a book by Richard J. Barnet and Ronald Muller entitled *Global Reach,* which shows that the market price for tranquilizers in Columbia was more than sixty times higher than in other places in the world. The only reason for this is that the markets will bear these prices.

Multinational Responses

How would a socially responsible multinational respond to cases like these? Let's consider first the canonical position of corporate social responsibility. . . . According to this framework, a multinational should maximize profits while obeying the law. The interesting question in this context is whose law the multinational should use as a limiting condition for profit maximization. Should a company like Nike insist that its Indonesian contractors adhere to U.S. labor laws and practices with respect to wages, hours, and working conditions? Should G. D. Searle provide to Third World markets the same warnings about side effects and indications for a drug that it provides in the United States? Or should these multinationals adopt the standards of the host nation, or do anything they wish in the absence of any host country standards?

Many corporations faced with this decision adopt the second option—the "When in Rome, do as the Romans do" option—with the following justifications.

Using the host nation's standards respects the autonomy of the host nation, for example, its freedom of self-determination. In choosing the host nation's standards, the multinational respects the host nation's freedom to choose for itself those conditions of labor and commerce that it understands to be in the best interests of its citizenry. In addition, a proponent of this justification might add that FDA regulations are not sacred laws, but peculiarities of our own country in which over-regulation is a problem.

As it stands, this justification is weak. It presupposes a kind of moral relativism which . . . is subject to serious criticisms. It is conceivable that the commercial standards of a host nation are consistent with egregious violations of human rights, such as child and forced labor and dangerous working conditions. We do not countenance such practices in our society because of our respect for persons. By parity of reasoning, we should not countenance these practices in another society since the victims are persons also.

The price paid for host nation autonomy in this sense may be a loss of freedom and security for the workers of the host nation. This is a particularly acute problem when the host nation is not a democracy, but a repressive dictatorship or a corrupt plutocracy which shows no regard at all for the interests of its citizenry. Surely the practices of such regimes cannot be defended on the grounds of national autonomy. It might be argued plausibly that if the host nation is not a representative democracy, the multinational has no business seeking it out as a trading partner.

Still there is another common argument that can support morally objectionable labor practices in Indonesia and other parts of the Third World. It may be argued that any reform of the existing practices actually injures the parties whom it is designed to help. Reforms, such as safer working conditions, shorter hours, higher wages, and so forth, result in an imposition of costs on the multinational; it would be more expensive to do business in the host nation. If these costs were great, the reforms could stop investment in the host nation altogether, which in turn would frustrate the host nation's attempts to industrialize and raise the standard of living. Presumably, the heightened standard of living would be enjoyed by the workers, not just their bosses, as the argument would be moot. Still the argument implies that national prosperity depends on members of the society who are most vulnerable to exploitation.

At first glance, this argument seems more like a rationalization for the exploitation of the workers. According to some critics of multinationals, the adoption of host country standards, however repressive, is not founded on "respect"; rather the standards are adopted because they are conducive to multinational profit maximization. But the argument is more subtle than this. It implies that the absence of protective regulation is the price that must be paid by a poorer nation if it is eventually to join the ranks of wealthy nations.

Some people must suffer for the poor nation to become a player in the global market. Without addressing the knotty question of why the burden of suffering must be borne exclusively by the poor, it is interesting to speculate about whether this is a conceptual or a historical claim; that is, are the labor conditions in China, Indonesia, and Central America a necessary condition for industrialization and eventual prosperity, or could these goals be achieved in some other way? It is true that there is a historical precedent for the claim—the labor conditions during the industrial revolution in Britain and the United States were typically harsh. But it is conceivable that moving from a poor agrarian society to a wealthy industrialized one could be accomplished without harming the interests of the workers. For a transition of this kind to occur in our world economy, cooperation of the multinational would be critical. Countries hungry for foreign dollars are only too willing to accede to the demands of multinationals; therefore, part of the responsibility of avoiding the kinds of harms discussed in the foregoing scenarios rests with them. The multinationals' power to effect change is significant. If U.S. shoe manufacturers insisted that their contractors adopt labor standards that improved working conditions, the factory owners would comply or else lose their businesses. Similarly, if the U.S. garment industry refused to deal with Central American facilities that use child labor, the factories would change their labor practices. But none of this is possible if the multinational's goal is simply profit maximization and where the only interests that matter are those of the profit-maximizing shareholders. We conclude that the canonical position in which obeying the law meant relativism would merely perpetuate the existing deplorable conditions.

A second model of multinational corporate social responsibility is *stakeholder theory.* This model differs radically from the canonical view. Here, the scope of social responsibility includes not only the shareholders but also stakeholders, who are "those groups which have a stake or claim on the firm. Specifically . . . suppliers, customers, employees, stockholders, and the local community as well as management in its role as agent for these groups." Stakeholders are those parties whose actions have an effect on or can be affected by the corporation. On this model, management acts as the agent of *all* stakeholders, not just the shareholders, and the interests of those diverse groups must be taken into account when the firm acts. Any traditional manager, of course, does take into account the interests of these parties when considering a corporate action. When she lowers the price of goods, for example, she considers how the action might affect annual returns or how a new product will be received by customers in the market. But stakeholder theory goes further than this. On this account the business of the firm is to be conducted for the benefit of *all* stakeholders; that is, the corporation is an instrument not for profit maximization, but for promoting and coordinating the interests of the stakeholders.

The moral foundation for this theory of the corporation is (typically) Kantian. The individuals who make up the stakeholder groups are persons of intrinsic worth whose interests require respect. Their interests cannot be compromised without serious and proper consideration.

This conception of corporate social responsibility might seem strange, since it gives a radically different answer to the question *For whose benefit does the corporation exist?* But recently (i.e., in the past sixty years), corporations have been made to recognize the legitimate interests of stakeholders other than the shareholders. That recognition is by way of legislation. Corporations are held liable for faulty products, employees have the right to bargain collectively, and communities are protected from industrial pollution by environmental regulation. Legislation like this indicates an unwillingness by society to have its economic institutions directed simply by self-interest and competition. Other interests, for instance in a clean environment, in safety, in a good wage and working conditions, can be frustrated if society relies upon the "invisible hand." But . . . regulation is reactive—demands for it arise only after society has been injured. Stakeholder theory, on the other hand, is proactive and interweaves societal interests into the fabric of the corporation itself.

Stakeholder theory as applied to a multinational would expand the range of individual stakeholders (e.g., individual workers, managers, and customers) to include foreign nationals. Some may object to this extension, but it is a direct implication of the meaning of *stakeholder* according to traditional definitions. For example, workers as a group are an important stakeholder. They are vital to the success and the survival of the firm. But what about contract workers like those in Indonesia? One might argue that they are really not employees of Nike or Reebok, but rather employees of the factory owners with whom they hold their contract. Still they are stakeholders since their actions can affect the well-being of the multinational (e.g., by striking), and reciprocally the multinational can affect their well-being (e.g., by closing up shop). The community is also a traditional stakeholder. It may provide land and infrastructure (e.g., roads and power lines) that are necessary for the operation of a factory. Reciprocally, the factory provides incomes and other benefits that support the community. In the context of our discussion of multinationals, *community* would include communities in the host nation. Applying stakeholder theory to multinationals would mean including constituencies of the host nation; that they live in foreign lands is irrelevant. What is important is that they can affect and be affected by the multinational. In consequence, their interests, like those of domestic management, domestic workers, and the shareholders, would have to be respected.

There are some troubling questions about stakeholder theory. Here we address one obvious question which has both a practical and moral basis. How does a manager direct the corporation for the benefit of all the stakeholders? Suppose Nike decided to require that its contractors give higher wages to their workers. That might mean lower returns to the shareholders or higher costs to Nike's customers. Pharmaceutical firms are charged by critics with selling drugs at much higher prices in South America than retail in the United States. The market there will bear a much greater markup. Clearly, if they dropped prices to their U.S. levels, customers would benefit. But wouldn't profit-minded shareholders (who are also stakeholders) suffer? Because stakeholder theory does not favor the interests of one constituency over another, it is difficult to know how management would settle these conflicts. It seems that some principle, or set of principles is necessary for adjudicating among the conflicting claims of stakeholders.

How would management balance the diverse and often conflicting interests of the stakeholders? Without a framework a manager might find that task impossible. One way of approaching this problem is to attempt to articulate a set of basic and fundamental interests of the stakeholders. Such fundamental interests would be those of the multinational insofar as they are fundamental interests of the stakeholders it comprises. Sacrificing these would mean jeopardizing the moral status of the stakeholder multinational. We will leave it to you to determine just what might compose this list for all the stakeholders. Still, we can suggest what conditions must be satisfied for an interest to be a fundamental stakeholder interest.

For this we turn to Tom Donaldson's discussion of fundamental international rights from his excellent book *The Ethics of International Business*. Donaldson argues that multinationals are morally required to recognize certain fundamental international rights which no corporation may violate. But how are these to be identified? Donaldson suggests that they must satisfy the following conditions:

- They must protect something of very great importance.
- They must be subject to substantial and recurrent threats.
- The obligations that they impose must be affordable and distributed fairly.

From these conditions Donaldson generates a list of individual rights, including the rights to physical security, property, subsistence, and minimal education. The existence of these individual rights imposes significant limitations on the actions of multinationals. For example, the right to physical security would be violated by a multinational's failure to provide safety equipment, and the employment of child labor would be a violation of the right to minimal education.

We believe that a set of conditions similar to Donaldson's might be useful in specifying fundamental stakeholder interests. Like Donaldson's rights they would place limitations on the actions of the multinational and on the competing interests of the stakeholders. A fundamental interest must be of great importance to the stakeholder, must be subject to substantial and recurrent threats, and may impose on other stakeholders only those burdens that are affordable and distributed fairly.

For example, from these conditions it is clear that Indonesian workers have a substantial interest in at least a subsistence wage and tolerable working conditions. This interest is subject to recurrent threat from both investment-poor host nations and profit-maximizing multinationals alike. But could the burdens of supporting this interest be distributed fairly among the other stakeholders? To ameliorate the working conditions would impose costs. Customers might find that athletic shoes are more expensive, and shareholders might find that their returns are diminished. To answer this question, one would have to articulate the fundamental interests of these groups. Here we can only speculate. Shareholders have a fundamental interest in profitability, but not necessarily maximum profitability. Customers have a fundamental interest in high-quality products at competitive prices. It would seem likely that in many cases (certainly the Nike case) the interest in subsistence wages and safe working conditions could be compatible with both the shareholder and customer interests. Ideally, an equilibrium could be struck between the competing interests. The result would be a cost imposition on customers and shareholders which would not be burdensome (perhaps in the Nike case, Nike could defray some of these costs by hiring a spokesperson with a less-inflated salary). The company would still be profitable, and shoes could still be competitively priced. This outcome is preferable to the current situation in which the workers are made to bear the full costs of high earnings and cheap products; it is a fairer distribution. On the other hand, workers could not demand benefits that would make the venture unprofitable, violating the fundamental interest of the investors. Nor could acceding to workers' demands result in products that are not affordable to consumers. Of course, this would also result in the demise of the corporation. A multinational that could not equitably satisfy the fundamental interests of its constituent shareholders would lose its right to be described as a stakeholder firm.

There are certainly some difficult problems that this brief sketch does not address, such as the distinction between profitability and maximum profitability, a clear articulation of fundamental stakeholder interests, and the role of management. Still, the stakeholder theory seems to be a fruitful area for research and is clearly preferable to the canonical view of corporate social responsibility.

Suggestions for Further Reading

There are a legion of good books (and not so good books) on the market, which deal with business ethics. See John R. Boatright's *Ethics and the Conduct of Business,* 2nd Edition (New York: Prentice-Hall, 1997) for starters.

Thomas Donaldson's *The Ethics of International Business* (New York: Oxford University Press, 1989) explores the tough questions raised by globalization.

For an excellent collection of essays dealing with a variety of issues see the beginning chapters in Adams' and Maine's *Business Ethics for the 21st Century* (Mountain View, CA: Mayfield, 1998).

On the web visit http://www.depaul.edu for the Institute for Business and Professional Ethics.

The Centre for Applied Ethics, http://www.ethicsubc.ca is a good source, as is http://www.darden.virginia.edu, where you will find the Olsson Center for Applied Ethics.

Videos

Global Capitalism and the Moral Imperative (30 minutes) explores how policies and programs can be developed to care for the vast number of poor spawned by unchecked global laissez-faire practices. This video, along with *Business Ethics: The Bottom Line* (28 minutes), is available from Films for the Humanities and Sciences, PO Box 2053, Princeton, NJ 08543.

 You can locate InfoTrac-College Edition articles about this chapter by accessing the InfoTrac-College Edition website (http://www.infotrac-college.com/wadsworth/). Using the InfoTrac-College Edition subject guide, enter the search terms relevant to this chapter, and then read abstracts for relevant articles.

Part 3

Epistemology

Chapter 7

Is Knowledge Possible?

> **A heap see,
> but a few know.**
>
> CAROLYN CHASE'S AUNT

7.1 Introduction

HAVE YOU EVER THOUGHT that people didn't really know what they were talking about? Have you ever wondered whether we can trust our intuition? Have you ever thought about the limits of human reason? Are there things that we cannot know? But how could we know that? Have you thought about how we can know what happened before we were born? Does everything we know come from experience? Have you been puzzled by the question, "What is truth?" Have you wondered whether we can be certain about any of our beliefs? Do we need evidence, and if so, what kind, to support our beliefs?

If you have wondered about these kinds of questions, you have been thinking about what philosophers call *epistemology* (the study of knowledge). The epistemologist wants to know how we can distinguish between opinion and knowledge.

We've all had the experience of listening to someone tell us something she thinks she knows. Perhaps we have dismissed what was said with the comment, "Oh, that's *just* your opinion." How do we know it is only her opinion? However we know it, the very fact that we call it opinion indicates that we assume that it is possible to distinguish between opinion and knowledge.

Let's start with a game. How do you know, if you know, the following?

You exist.	This book exists.
It will snow tomorrow.	All fat cats are fat.
It rained yesterday.	Two plus two equals four.
God exists.	Every event has a cause.

I imagine that you said you knew some of the things on this list because of sense experiences you've had. For example, you might have said that you know this book exists because you can see it and touch it. One important epistemological theory is called **empiricism**. According to this theory, we know things because we experience them with our senses. We see, touch, taste, smell, and hear things. That is how we gain knowledge about them. If someone tells me something is true, but what he says is based neither on experience nor verifiable by reference to experience, I would say, if I were an empiricist, "Oh, that's just a matter of opinion."

However, there are some things on the above list that you might say you knew because of reason. For example, you might have said that you know two plus two equals four because that's the way it works out when you add. Addition is a rational activity, one that requires you to reason, and you reason, in this case, by applying the rules of addition. If you apply the rules correctly, the answer has to be four.

If some of you identified reason as the source of knowledge, you would be reflecting the ideas of another important epistemological theory called **rationalism**. According to this theory, we know things by the use of reason. Reason tells us what is true. If someone says he knows there are some fat cats that are not fat because he has seen one, you might want to suggest that this is not merely a matter of opinion. Fat cats, by definition, are fat. Whatever he saw, he is mistaken.

Let us contrast these two basic theories of knowledge a bit more to be sure we grasp how they are different. Empiricism usually claims that the human mind, prior to sense experience, is like a blank slate (**tabula rasa**) or empty tablet. Sensations make impressions on this slate via our senses. It is from these impressions that we learn what is true and false and thereby, over the years, slowly build up a fund of knowledge. Hence, our knowledge is **a posteriori** (after experience). We cannot know anything until after we have had experiences, and if we wish to test or verify what we believe, we do so by checking it against further experiences. Knowledge, according to the empiricist, is also largely inductive because we induce some future events from past or present experiences. Of course our inductions may be wrong. The conclusions we draw are only probable, but probability is the best we can hope for if we want to know something about the world in which we live.

Rationalists reject the idea that the human mind is blank. We have, they usually claim, **innate ideas**, or ideas already built into our minds at birth, like the wiring built into a computer that allows it to compute. We use these innate ideas to make sense of our sensations. How do we know such innate ideas are true? By direct intellectual intuition (reason). Sensation does not tell us that every event has a cause since we cannot experience every event. Reason tells us that. We know it intuitively. Hence, knowledge is **a priori** (prior to or independent from experience). We do know things not learned from sensation, and we can prove things true without reference to sensation. Our proofs are deductive, and we can deduce that a fat cat is fat from the definition of "fat cat." It follows necessarily. It is certain.

Ponder the contrast between the following:

EMPIRICISM	RATIONALISM
tabula rasa	innate ideas
sensation	reason
a posteriori	a priori
inductive	deductive

"But wait," some of you might be saying, "what about those of us who are not sure that anything on that first list can be known at all? After all, you said, 'How do you know, *if you know?*' Well, I don't think some of these things can be known. For example, God. I think we just believe or we don't, but we can't know."

This response raises the issue of **skepticism**. The word *skepticism* comes from a Greek word that means "to reflect on," "consider," or "examine." We often associate the word with doubt or the suspension of judgment. The skeptic is a doubter.

There are various kinds of skepticism. One kind, what we might call **common-sense skepticism**, refers to the activity of doubting or suspending judgment about some things at one time or another. In this sense, we are all skeptics because we have all doubted. This sort of skepticism is healthy. It prevents an overly credulous attitude and is a good antidote to intellectual arrogance. If you are too gullible, you can be manipulated by others who claim to have knowledge when they do not.

Another kind of skepticism is **methodical skepticism**. This is the sort of skepticism that is used by some philosophers and scientists in their search for truth. If, for example, I want to be as certain as I can be that water freezes at 32 degrees Fahrenheit, I might doubt that hypothesis and conduct several experiments under differing circumstances to see if evidence supports it. Such doubt can be enormously constructive, since it stimulates our intellectual curiosity and energizes our search for truth.

There is yet a third kind of skepticism, **absolute skepticism**, which, somewhat ironically, some philosophers have presented as a theory of knowledge. Unlike both rationalism and empiricism, this theory doubts the very possibility of knowledge. Pyrrho of Elis (about 300 BCE) founded a school of philosophers who advocated absolute skepticism. He claimed to be following Socrates and just asking questions. However, he also claimed that every argument cancels out its opposite. In other words, arguments on opposite sides of an issue balance out, thereby canceling any definitive conclusion. Try as we might, we cannot know what is true.

"Well," you might say, "that is ridiculous. If we cannot know what is true, then how can Pyrrho or any other skeptic know that we cannot know?" That is a good question. You are suggesting that absolute skepticism is self-refuting. If it is true that we cannot know anything, then how do we know that it is true that we cannot know anything? If absolute skepticism is true, then it must be false!

Pyrrho himself anticipated a similar criticism. He retorted that he was not certain that he was not certain of anything. Of course, one wonders whether he was not certain that he was not certain that. . . . This conversation could go on forever! Yet self-refuting propositions are puzzling and provocative things. Consider:

The sentence in this box is false.

Think about that. If "the sentence in the box is false" is false, then it must be true. And if it is true, it must be false. However, one claim central to two-valued logics is that sentences must be either true or false. They presumably cannot be both. Here we have, however, a sentence that seems to be both. What are we to make of this? Is the claim of the absolute skeptic another example of a proposition of this sort? Perhaps certainty is simply not possible for humans, and, if we mean by "knowledge" certainty (knowing without the possibility of doubt), then we may have to be more humble when we claim to know something.

7.2 Sufi Mysticism

Abu Hamid Muhammad al-Ghazali was born at Tus, Persia, in 450 AH (1058). He was appointed a professor of Islamic theology at the university in Baghdad at the early age of thirty-three. (See Section 5.2 for general information on Islam.) Four years later, he had an emotional and spiritual crisis and came to believe that his way of life was too worldly. He left his academic post and became an ascetic, studying both the teachings and the practices of Islamic mystics. He later returned to teaching; he died in 505 AH. *Deliverance from Error,* from which the following selection is taken, constitutes al-Ghazali's spiritual and intellectual autobiography.

Al-Ghazali was embarked on a quest for certainty. He studied theology but was disappointed with its intellectual achievements. His quest prompted him to study philosophy, but once again he was disappointed, especially with its unfounded metaphysical claims and with the fact that philosophers held beliefs contrary to Islamic revelation. He turned to the Batiniyah, who taught that truth is attained not by reason, but by accepting the pronouncements of the infallible imam (religious leader). At the time, this teaching had important political implications since it was the official ideology of the Fatimid caliphate with its center in Cairo. However, al-Ghazali found the teachings of the imams to be trivial. He characterized their knowledge as "feeble" and "emaciated." Finally he investigated **Sufism**, an Islamic mystical movement which taught that direct and immediate experience of Allah is possible. It was among the Sufis that his restless soul found peace.

Al-Ghazali was not satisfied with empiricism, rationalism, or skepticism. Hence, he sought to discover a source or means to knowledge that escapes the skeptic's doubts and provides a firmer foundation than either empiricism or rationalism. He believed he found such a source in mystical experience—that is, an experience of intimate union or contact with the Divine.

Of course, al-Ghazali's motivation was not entirely philosophical or scientific. He did not merely want to know about the world that sense experience could show him, nor about the abstract world of mathematics and metaphysics that reason could reveal. Nor was he content to be a doubter. His motivation was also spiritual; he wanted to know about the Divine. His quest may reveal to us something about the limited nature of epistemological theories. Each theory may be appropriate in a limited domain. If you want to know about the world, empiricism is attractive. If you want to know about mathematics or abstract realities, rationalism commends itself. However, what if you want to know about God? Is either empiricism or rationalism adequate?

Al-Ghazali's views are controversial because many would be skeptical about the claim that adequate knowledge can be grounded in some sort of mystical experience. How do we know that mystical experience is not an illusion, just like some sense experiences? Within Islamic philosophy, al-Ghazali was not without his critics. Another Islamic philosopher, Averroes (ibn-Rushid, 1126–1198), wrote a book called *The Incoherence of the Incoherence,* referring to a book al-Ghazali wrote entitled *The Incoherence of the Philosophers.* Averroes attacked al-Ghazali's views, arguing that the philosophic reliance on reason and sense experience is an adequate method for knowing.

Reading Questions

1. How does al-Ghazali define *knowledge?*
2. What leads him to doubt beliefs based on sense perception and on intellect?
3. What is distinctive about mysticism?
4. What *credal principles* were firmly rooted in al-Ghazali after his study of theology and philosophy?

5. What is the *mystic way,* and what did al-Ghazali learn from following it?
6. How does the author distinguish among *knowledge, immediate experience,* and *faith?*
7. What does he mean by *prophetic revelation?* How is it related to other ways of obtaining knowledge? What is the proof of prophecy, and do you find the proof convincing? Why, or why not?
8. What method does he suggest we use to arrive at the knowledge that someone is a prophet? Why is this method better than relying on miracles as proof?
9. How does al-Ghazali answer the question, "Is knowledge possible?"

Deliverance from Error

AL-GHAZALI

TO THIRST AFTER A comprehension of things as they really are was my habit and custom from a very early age. It was instinctive with me, a part of my God-given nature, a matter of temperament and not of my choice or contriving. Consequently as I drew near the age of adolescence the bonds of mere authority (*taqlid*) ceased to hold me and inherited beliefs lost their grip upon me, for I saw that Christian youths always grew up to be Christians, Jewish youths to be Jews and Muslim youths to be Muslims. I heard, too, the Tradition related of the Prophet of God according to which he said: "Everyone who is born is born with a sound nature; it is his parents who make him a Jew or a Christian or a Magian." My inmost being was moved to discover what this original nature really was and what the beliefs derived from the authority of parents and teachers really were. The attempt to distinguish between these authority-based opinions and their principles developed the mind, for in distinguishing the true in them from the false differences appeared.

I therefore said within myself: "To begin with, what I am looking for is knowledge of what

things really are, so I must undoubtedly try to find what knowledge really is." It was plain to me that sure and certain knowledge is that knowledge in which the object is disclosed in such a fashion that no doubt remains along with it, that no possibility of error or illusion accompanies it, and that the mind cannot even entertain such a supposition. Certain knowledge must also be infallible; and this infallibility or security from error is such that no attempt to show the falsity of the knowledge can occasion doubt or denial, even though the attempt is made by someone who turns stones into gold or a rod into a serpent. Thus, I know that ten is more than three. Let us suppose that someone says to me: "No, three is more than ten, and in proof of that I shall change this rod into a serpent"; and let us suppose that he actually changes the rod into a serpent and that I witness him doing so. No doubts about what I know are raised in me because of this. The only result is that I wonder precisely how he is able to produce this change. Of doubt about my knowledge there is no trace.

After these reflections I knew that whatever I do not know in this fashion and with this mode

Extract taken from The Faith and Practice of Al-Ghazali, *trans. by W. Montgomery Watt. Copyright © 1953 by George Allen and Unwin, pp. 21–26, 54–57, 59, 60–68. Reproduced by kind permission of HarperCollins Publishers. Footnotes deleted.*

of certainty is not reliable and infallible knowledge; and knowledge that is not infallible is not certain knowledge.

Preliminaries: Scepticism and the Denial of All Knowledge

Thereupon I investigated the various kinds of knowledge I had, and found myself destitute of all knowledge with this characteristic of infallibility except in the case of sense-perception and necessary truths. So I said: "Now that despair has come over me, there is no point in studying any problems except on the basis of what is self-evident, namely, necessary truths and the affirmations of the senses. I must first bring these to be judged in order that I may be certain on this matter. Is my reliance on sense-perception and my trust in the soundness of necessary truths of the same kind as my previous trust in the beliefs I had merely taken over from others and as the trust most men have in the results of thinking? Or is it a justified trust that is in no danger of being betrayed or destroyed?"

I proceeded therefore with extreme earnestness to reflect on sense-perception and on necessary truths, to see whether I could make myself doubt them. The outcome of this protracted effort to induce doubt was that I could no longer trust sense-perception either. Doubt began to spread here and say: "From where does this reliance on sense-perception come? The most powerful sense is that of sight. Yet when it looks at the shadow (*sc.* of a stick or the gnomon of a sundial), it sees it standing still, and judges that there is no motion. Then by experiment and observation after an hour it knows that the shadow is moving and, moreover, that it is moving not by fits and starts but gradually and steadily by infinitely small distances in such a way that it is never in a state of rest. Again, it looks at the heavenly body (*sc.* the sun) and sees it small, the size of a shilling; yet geometrical computations show that it is greater than the earth in size."

In this and similar cases of sense-perception the sense as judge forms his judgements, but another judge, the intellect, shows him repeatedly to be wrong; and the charge of falsity cannot be rebutted.

To this I said: "My reliance on sense-perception also has been destroyed. Perhaps only those intellectual truths which are first principles (or derived from first principles) are to be relied upon, such as the assertion that ten are more than three, that the same thing cannot be both affirmed and denied at one time, that one thing is not both generated in time and eternal, nor both existent and non-existent, nor both necessary and impossible."

Sense-perception replied: "Do you not expect that your reliance on intellectual truths will fare like your reliance on sense-perception? You used to trust in me; then along came the intellect-judge and proved me wrong; if it were not for the intellect-judge you would have continued to regard me as true. Perhaps behind intellectual apprehension there is another judge who, if he manifests himself, will show the falsity of intellect in its judging, just as, when intellect manifested itself, it showed the falsity of sense in its judging. The fact that such a supra-intellectual apprehension has not manifested itself is no proof that it is impossible."

My ego hesitated a little about the reply to that, and sense-perception heightened the difficulty by referring to dreams. "Do you not see," it said, "how, when you are asleep, you believe things and imagine circumstances, holding them to be stable and enduring, and, so long as you are in that dream-condition, have no doubts about them? And is it not the case that when you awake you know that all you have imagined and believed is unfounded and ineffectual? Why then are you confident that all your waking beliefs, whether from sense or intellect, are genuine? They are true in respect of your present state; but it is possible that a state will come upon you whose relation to your waking consciousness is analogous to the relation of the latter to dreaming. In comparison with this state your waking consciousness would be like dreaming! When you have entered into this state, you will be certain that all the suppositions of your intellect are empty imaginings. It may be that that state is what the Sufis claim as their special 'state' (*sc.* mystic union or ecstasy), for they consider that in their 'states' (or ecstasies), which occur when they have withdrawn into themselves and are absent from their senses, they witness states (or circumstances) which do not tally with these principles of the intellect. Perhaps that 'state' is death; for the Messenger of God (God bless and preserve him) says: 'The people are dreaming; when they die, they become awake.' So perhaps life in this world is a dream by comparison with the world to come; and when a man dies, things come to appear differently to him from what he now beholds, and at the same time the words are addressed to him: 'We have taken off thee thy covering, and thy sight today is sharp'" (Q. 50, 21).

When these thoughts had occurred to me and penetrated my being, I tried to find some way of treating my unhealthy condition; but it was not easy. Such ideas can only be repelled by demonstration; but a demonstration requires a knowledge of first principles; since this is not admitted, however, it is impossible to make the demonstration. The disease was baffling, and lasted almost two months, during which I was a sceptic in fact though not in theory nor in outward expression. At length God cured me of the malady; my being was restored to health and an even balance; the necessary truths of the intellect became once more accepted, as I regained confidence in their certain and trustworthy character.

This did not come about by systematic demonstration or marshalled argument, but by a light which God most high cast into my breast. That light is the key to the greater part of knowledge. Whoever thinks that the understanding of things Divine rests upon strict proofs has in his thought narrowed down the wideness of God's mercy. When the Messenger of God (peace be upon him) was asked about "enlarging" and its meaning in the verse, "Whenever God wills to guide a man, He enlarges his breast for *islām* (i.e. surrender to God)" (Q. 6, 125), he said, "It is a light which God most high casts into the heart." When asked, "What is the sign of it?," he said, "Withdrawal from the mansion of deception and return to the mansion of eternity." It was

about this light that Muhammad (peace be upon him) said, "God created the creatures in darkness, and then sprinkled upon them some of His light." From that light must be sought an intuitive understanding of things Divine. That light at certain times gushes from the spring of Divine generosity, and for it one must watch and wait—as Muhammad (peace be upon him) said: "In the days of your age your Lord has gusts of favour; then place yourselves in the way of them."

The point of these accounts is that the task is perfectly fulfilled when the quest is prosecuted up to the stage of seeking what is not sought (but stops short of that). For first principles are not sought, since they are present and to hand; and if what is present is sought for, it becomes hidden and lost. When, however, a man seeks what is sought (and that only), he is not accused of falling short in the seeking of what is sought. . . .

The Ways of Mysticism

I knew that the complete mystic "way" includes both intellectual belief and practical activity; the latter consists in getting rid of the obstacles in the self and in stripping off its base characteristics and vicious morals, so that the heart may attain to freedom from what is not God and to constant recollection of Him.

The intellectual belief was easier to me than the practical activity. I began to acquaint myself with their belief by reading their books. . . . I thus comprehended their fundamental teachings on the intellectual side, and progressed, as far as is possible by study and oral instruction, in the knowledge of mysticism. It became clear to me, however, that what is most distinctive of mysticism is something which cannot be apprehended by study, but only by immediate experience (*dhawq*—literally "tasting"), by ecstasy and by a moral change. What a difference there is between *knowing* the definition of health and satiety, together with their causes and presuppositions, and *being* healthy and satisfied! What a difference between being acquainted with the definition of drunkenness—namely, that it designates a state arising from the domination of the seat of the intellect by vapours arising from the stomach—and being drunk! Indeed, the drunken man while in that condition does not know the definition of drunkenness nor the scientific account of it; he has not the very least scientific knowledge of it. The sober man, on the other hand, knows the definition of drunkenness and its basis, yet he is not drunk in the very least. Again the doctor, when he is himself ill, knows the definition and causes of health and the remedies which restore it, and yet is lacking in health. Similarly there is a difference between knowing the true nature and causes and conditions of the ascetic life and actually leading such a life and forsaking the world.

I apprehended clearly that the mystics were men who had real experiences, not men of words, and that I had already progressed as far as was possible by way of intellectual apprehension. What remained for me was not to be attained by oral instruction and study but only by immediate experience and by walking in the mystic way.

Now from the sciences I had laboured at and the paths I had traversed in my investigation of the revelational and rational sciences (that is, presumably, theology and philosophy), there had come to me a sure faith in God most high, in prophethood (or revelation), and in the Last Day. These three credal principles were firmly rooted in my being, not through any carefully argued proofs, but by reason of various causes, coincidences and experiences which are not capable of being stated in detail.

It had already become clear to me that I had no hope of the bliss of the world to come save through a God-fearing life and the withdrawal of myself from vain desire. It was clear to me too that the key to all this was to sever the attachment of the heart to worldly things by leaving the mansion of deception and returning to that of eternity, and to advance towards God most high with all earnestness. It was also clear that this was only to be achieved by turning away from wealth and position and fleeing from all time-consuming entanglements.

Next I considered the circumstances of my life, and realized that I was caught in a veritable thicket of attachments. I also considered my activities, of which the best was my teaching and lecturing, and realized that in them I was dealing with sciences that were unimportant and contributed nothing to the attainment of eternal life.

After that I examined my motive in my work of teaching, and realized that it was not a pure desire for the things of God, but that the impulse moving me was the desire for an influential position and public recognition. I saw for certain that I was on the brink of a crumbling bank of sand and in imminent danger of hell-fire unless I set about to mend my ways.

I reflected on this continuously for a time, while the choice still remained open to me. One day I would form the resolution to quit Baghdad and get rid of these adverse circumstances; the next day I would abandon my resolution. I put one foot forward and drew the other back. If in the morning I had a genuine longing to seek eternal life, by the evening the attack of a whole host of desires had reduced it to impotence. Worldly desires were striving to keep me by their chains just where I was, while the voice of faith was calling, "To the road! to the road! What is left of life is but little and the journey before you is long. All that keeps you busy, both intellectually and practically, is but hypocrisy and delusion. If you do not prepare *now* for eternal life, when will you prepare? If you do not now sever these attachments, when will you sever them?" On hearing that, the impulse would be stirred and the resolution made to take to flight. . . .

I left Baghdad, then. I distributed what wealth I had, retaining only as much as would suffice myself and provide sustenance for my children. This I could easily manage, as the wealth of 'Iraq was available for good works, since it constitutes a trust fund for the benefit of the Muslims. Nowhere in the world have I seen better financial arrangements to assist a scholar to provide for his children. . . .

In general, then, how is a mystic "way" (*tariqah*) described? The purity which is the first condition of it (*sc.* as bodily purity is the prior condition of formal Worship for Muslims) is the purification of the heart completely from what is other than God most high; the key to it, which corresponds to the opening act of adoration in prayer, is the sinking of the heart completely in the recollection of God; and the end of it is complete absorption (*fanā'*) in God. At least this is its end relatively to those first steps which almost come within the sphere of choice and personal responsibility; but in reality in the actual mystic "way" it is the first step, what comes before it being, as it were, the ante-chamber for those who are journeying towards it.

With this first stage of the "way" there begin the revelations and visions. The mystics in their waking state now behold angels and the spirits of the prophets; they hear these speaking to them and are instructed by them. Later, a higher state is reached; instead of beholding forms and figures, they come to stages in the "way" which it is hard to describe in language; if a man attempts to express these, his words inevitably contain what is clearly erroneous.

In general what they manage to achieve is nearness to God; some, however, would conceive of this as "inherence," some as "union," and some as "connection." All that is erroneous. In my book, *The Noblest Aim,* I have explained the nature of the error here. Yet he who has attained the mystic "state" need do no more than say:

> Of the things I do not remember, what was, was;
> Think it good; do not ask an account of it.
>
> (Ibn-al-Mu'tazz)

In general the man to whom He has granted no immediate experience at all, apprehends no more of what prophetic revelation really is than the name. The miraculous graces given to the saints are in truth the beginnings of the prophets; and that was the first "state" of the Messenger of God (peace be upon him) when he went out to Mount Hirā', and was given up entirely to his Lord, and worshipped, so that the bedouin said, "Muhammad loves his Lord passionately."

Now this is a mystical "state" which is realized in immediate experience by those who walk in the way leading to it. Those to whom it is not granted to have immediate experience can become assured of it by trial (*sc.* contact with mystics or observation of them) and by hearsay, if they have sufficiently numerous opportunities of associating with mystics to understand that (*sc.* ecstasy) with certainty by means of what accompanies the "states." Whoever sits in their company derives

from them this faith; and none who sits in their company is pained.

Those to whom it is not even granted to have contacts with mystics may know with certainty the possibility of ecstasy by the evidence of demonstration, as I have remarked in the section entitled *The Wonders of the Heart* of my *Revival of the Religious Sciences.*

Certainty reached by demonstration is *knowledge* (*'ilm*); actual acquaintance with that "state" is *immediate experience* (*dhawq*); the acceptance of it as probable from hearsay and trial (or observation) is *faith* (*imān*). These are three degrees. "God will raise those of you who have faith and those who have been given knowledge in degrees (*sc.* of honour)" (Q. 58, 12).

Behind the mystics, however, there is a crowd of ignorant people. They deny this fundamentally, they are astonished at this line of thought, they listen and mock. "Amazing," they say. "What nonsense they talk!" About such people God most high has said: "Some of them listen to you, until, upon going out from you, they say to those to whom knowledge has been given, 'What did he say just now?' These are the people on whose hearts God sets a seal and they follow their passions" (Q. 47, 18). He makes them deaf, and blinds their sight.

Among the things that necessarily became clear to me from my practice of the mystic "way" was the true nature and special characteristics of prophetic revelation. The basis of that must undoubtedly be indicated in view of the urgent need for it.

The True Nature of Prophecy and the Compelling Need of All Creation for It

You must know that the substance of man in his original condition was created in bareness and simplicity without any information about the worlds of God most high. These worlds are many, not to be reckoned save by God most high Himself. As He said, "None knows the hosts of thy Lord save He" (Q. 74, 34). Man's information about the world is by means of perception; and every perception of perceptibles is created so that thereby man may have some acquaintance with a world (or sphere) from among existents. By "worlds (or spheres)" we simply mean "classes of existents."

The first thing created in man was the sense of *touch,* and by it he perceives certain classes of existents, such as heat and cold, moisture and dryness, smoothness and roughness. Touch is completely unable to apprehend colours and noises. These might be non-existent so far as concerns touch.

Next there is created in him the sense of *sight,* and by it he apprehends colours and shapes. This is the most extensive of the worlds of sensibles. Next *hearing* is implanted in him, so that he hears sounds of various kinds. After that *taste* is created in him; and so on until he has completed the world of sensibles.

Next, when he is about seven years old, there is created in him *discernment* (or the power of distinguishing). This is a fresh stage in his development. He now apprehends more than the world of sensibles; and none of these additional factors (*sc.* relations, etc.) exists in the world of sense.

From this he ascends to another stage, and *intellect* (or reason) is created in him. He apprehends things necessary, possible, impossible, things which do not occur in the previous stages.

Beyond intellect there is yet another stage. In this another eye is opened, by which he beholds the unseen, what is to be in the future, and other things which are beyond the ken of intellect in the same way as the objects of intellect are beyond the ken of the faculty of discernment and the objects of discernment are beyond the ken of sense. Moreover, just as the man at the stage of discernment would reject and disregard the objects of intellect were these to be presented to him, so some intellectuals reject and disregard the objects of prophetic revelation. That is sheer ignorance. They have no ground for their view except that this is a stage which they have not reached and which for them does not exist; yet they suppose that it is non-existent in itself. When a man blind from birth, who has not learnt about colours and shapes by listening to people's talk, is told about these things for the first time,

he does not understand them nor admit their existence.

God most high, however, has favoured His creatures by giving them something analogous to the special faculty of prophecy, namely dreams. In the dream-state a man apprehends what is to be in the future, which is something of the unseen; he does so either explicitly or else clothed in a symbolic form whose interpretation is disclosed.

Suppose a man has not experienced this himself, and suppose that he is told how some people fall into a dead faint, in which hearing, sight and the other senses no longer function, and in this condition perceive the unseen. He would deny that this is so and demonstrate its impossibility. "The sensible powers," he would say, "are the causes of perception (or apprehension); if a man does not perceive things (*sc.* the unseen) when these powers are actively present, much less will he do so when the senses are not functioning." This is a form of analogy which is shown to be false by what actually occurs and is observed. Just as intellect is one of the stages of human development in which there is an "eye" which sees the various types of intelligible objects, which are beyond the ken of the senses, so prophecy also is the description of a stage in which there is an eye endowed with light such that in that light the unseen and other supra-intellectual objects become visible.

Doubt about prophetic revelation is either (a) doubt of its possibility in general, or (b) doubt of its actual occurrence, or (c) doubt of the attainment of it by a specific individual.

The proof of the possibility of there being prophecy and the proof that there has been prophecy is that there is knowledge in the world the attainment of which by reason is inconceivable; for example, in medical science and astronomy. Whoever researches in such matters knows of necessity that this knowledge is attained only by Divine inspiration and by assistance from God most high. It cannot be reached by observation. For instance there are some astronomical laws based on phenomena which occur only once in a thousand years; how can these be arrived at by personal observation? It is the same with the properties of drugs.

This argument shows that it is possible for there to be a way of apprehending these matters which are not apprehended by the intellect. This is the meaning of prophetic revelation. That is not to say that prophecy is merely an expression for such knowledge. Rather, the apprehending of this class of extra-intellectual objects is *one* of the properties of prophecy; but it has many other properties as well. The said property is but a drop in the ocean of prophecy. It has been singled out for mention because you have something analogous to it in what you apprehend in dreaming, and because you have medical and astronomical knowledge belonging to the same class, namely, the miracles of the prophets, for the intellectuals cannot arrive at these at all by any intellectual efforts.

The other properties of prophetic revelation are apprehended only by immediate experience from the practice of the mystic way, but this property of prophecy you can understand by an analogy granted you, namely, the dream-state. If it were not for the latter you would not believe in that. If the prophet possessed a faculty to which you had nothing analogous and which you did not understand, how could you believe in it? Believing presupposes understanding. Now that analogous experience comes to a man in the early stages of the mystic way. Thereby he attains to a kind of immediate experience, extending as far as that to which he has attained, and by analogy to a kind of belief (or assent) in respect of that to which he has not attained. Thus this single property is a sufficient basis for one's faith in the principle of prophecy.

If you come to doubt whether a specific person is a prophet or not, certainty can only be reached by acquaintance with his conduct, either by personal observation, or by hearsay as a matter of common knowledge. For example, if you are familiar with medicine and law, you can recognise lawyers and doctors by observing what they are, or, where observation is impossible, by hearing what they have to say. Thus you are not unable to recognise that al-Shāfi'i (God have mercy upon him) is a lawyer and Galen a doctor; and your recognition is based on the facts and not on the judgment of someone else. Indeed, just because you have some knowledge of law and medicine, and examine their books and writings, you arrive at a necessary knowledge of what these men are.

Similarly, if you understand what it is to be a prophet, and have devoted much time to the study of the Qur'an and the Traditions, you will arrive at a necessary knowledge of the fact that Muhammad (God bless and preserve him) is in the highest grades of the prophetic calling. Convince yourself of that by trying out what he said about the influence of devotional practices on the purification of the heart—how truly he asserted that "whoever lives out what he knows will receive from God what he does not know"; how truly he asserted that "if anyone aids an evildoer, God will give that man power over him"; how truly he asserted that "if a man rises up in the morning with but a single care (*sc.* to please God), God most high will preserve him from all cares in this world and the next." When you have made trial of these in a thousand or several thousand instances, you will arrive at a necessary knowledge beyond all doubt.

By this method, then, seek certainty about the prophetic office, and not from the transformation of a rod into a serpent or the cleaving of the moon. For if you consider such an event by itself, without taking account of the numerous circumstances accompanying it—circumstances readily eluding the grasp of the intellect—then you might perhaps suppose that it was magic and deception and that it came from God to lead men astray; for "He leads astray whom He will, and guides whom He will." Thus the topic of miracles will be thrown back upon you; for if your faith is based on a reasoned argument involving the probative force of the miracle, then your faith is destroyed by an ordered argument showing the difficulty and ambiguity of the miracle.

Admit, then, that wonders of this sort are one of the proofs and accompanying circumstances out of the totality of your thought on the matter; and that you attain necessary knowledge and yet are unable to say specifically on what it is based. The case is similar to that of a man who receives from a multitude of people a piece of information which is a matter of common belief. . . . He is unable to say that the certainty is derived from the remark of a single specific person; rather, its source is unknown to him; it is neither from outside the whole, nor is it from specific individuals. This is strong, intellectual faith. Immediate experience, on the other hand, is like actually witnessing a thing and taking it in one's hand. It is only found in the way of mysticism.

This is a sufficient discussion of the nature of prophetic revelation for my present purpose.

Suggestions for Further Reading

See Seyyed Hossein Nasr's *Ideals and Realities of Islam* (Boston: Beacon Press, 1972) for a general introduction to Islamic thought and practice.

Chapter 4 of F. C. Copleston's *Medieval Philosophy* (New York: Harper & Row, 1961) will provide basic information on Islamic philosophy.

Philosophy in the Middle Ages, edited by Arthur Hyman and James J. Walsh (Indianapolis: Hackett, 1973), provides original texts, background summaries, and a good bibliography.

Martin Ling's *What Is Sufism?* (Berkeley: University of California Press, 1977) will give you a good introduction to this fascinating type of mysticism.

A. J. Arberry's *Revelation and Reason in Islam* (London: George Allen & Unwin, 1957) is a standard presentation of the diverse Islamic approaches to this problem.

See W. M. Watt's *Muslim Intellectual: A Study of al-Ghazali* (Edinburgh: University Press, 1963) for an excellent overview of al-Ghazali's thought.

See Averroes, *Tahafut At-Tanafut (The Incoherence of the Incoherence),* translated by Simon Van den Bergh (London: Luzac, 1969), for a critique of al-Ghazali's views by another Islamic philosopher (a secondary discussion and overview can be found in *World Philosophy*).

See http://encarta.msn.com/find/Concise.asp?ti=06126000 for information on the web and links to other sources.

Video

Islamic Mysticism: The Sufi Way by Huston Smith is twenty years old but still offers a good introduction and can be obtained from Hartley Film Foundation, 59 Cat Rock Rd., Cos Cob, CT 06807.

7.3 Is Certainty Possible?

Have you ever been plagued by doubt? Would you like to be certain about something? Have you ever longed for an absolute truth that would never let you down? Have you ever gotten tired of questions, questions, questions?

You might be inclined to answer, "Yes, especially when studying philosophy." Uncertainty is not a pleasant state for anyone, even philosophers. It leaves us up in the air, juggling things that might fall and break at any moment. Uncertainty is unsettling. However, if we really want to know what is true, if we really want absolutely certain knowledge, must we not question and doubt until we find it?

René Descartes (sounds like "day kart") was born in France in 1596 and died in Sweden in 1650. He was a brilliant philosopher and mathematician who has been called "the father" of modern philosophy. Like many of you, and like al-Ghazali (see the previous selection), he sought something about which he could be absolutely certain. He was willing to undergo the turmoil of doubt to find it because he believed that we should accept as true only that which is supported by sound arguments.

Descartes was a methodical skeptic because he employed the method of doubt in his quest for certainty. This method deals with *logical possibility.* He was not concerned with beliefs that people actually doubt or with beliefs that are in fact false. Rather, he was concerned with those beliefs that are logically possible to doubt. If it is possible for a belief to be false, then it is capable of being doubted, whether or not, as a matter of fact, anyone has ever doubted it and whether or not, as a matter of fact, it is false.

However, Descartes could not be content with skepticism. Ultimately he sought knowledge firmly grounded in reason. Like Plato (see Section 9.3) he was a rationalist, holding that beliefs based on sensations are little more than opinions, but beliefs based on reason constitute genuine knowledge. He refined Plato's distinction between opinion and knowledge. By *certainty* he meant that about which logical doubt is impossible. A belief is certain (or "clear and distinct" as Descartes liked to put it) if it is *not* logically possible to doubt its truth. Only such beliefs constitute knowledge. Because it is logically possible to doubt the truth of beliefs based on sensations, such beliefs must constitute opinion, not knowledge.

To grasp Descartes's philosophical project, we must take a brief look at the historical context. Descartes lived at the time when modern science was replacing medieval science, which had been based on the philosophies of Aristotle and Plato. Medieval science assumed as true a theory (ultimately derived from Aristotle) called **direct realism**. According to this theory, there is a reality that exists apart from human sensations, and our senses put us *directly* in touch with this reality.

This theory of direct realism had proved increasingly problematic because it seemed to lead to all sorts of contradictions. I see a house as small from a distance and as large when close up. Is the house both small and large? "Hardly," you say. If, however, our senses put us *directly* in touch with the *real* house, then what else can we conclude?

Galileo Galilei (1564–1642), who had reintroduced the atomistic theory of matter into physical science, also rejected direct realism because it was rather obvious that we do not directly sense atoms. If what is really out there are atoms and if we don't sense them, then we cannot be directly in touch with physical reality via our senses.

So what role do our senses play? Galileo proposed a theory called **indirect** or **representational realism**. According to this theory, our sensations represent physical reality. We are not directly in touch with physical reality; we are only directly in touch with our sensations *of* physical reality.

How did Galileo know that? How did he know, or how does anyone know, that our sensations represent an external reality? We cannot get outside of sensations to see. We cannot compare our image of a fat cat with the real fat cat as we can compare a picture of a fat cat with our sensations of a fat cat. Here we have a problem that seems to undermine the epistemic certainty the new science promises.

Descartes believed that science ought to provide us with certainty. Its great promise was to give us knowledge. Knowledge is certainty as far as Descartes was concerned, but how can science provide us with knowledge if the theory on which it is built, the theory of indirect or representational realism, cannot be proved true? Without a proof of representational realism, science is without a firm foundation, or so Descartes thought.

Descartes wrote his famous *Meditations on First Philosophy* in order to arrive at certainty and to prove representational realism correct. Here you will read only the first two *Meditations* because they deal directly with his epistemological theory.

In the first *Meditation,* Descartes employed the method of doubt to show that all our beliefs based on sensations can be doubted and that we cannot even be sure we have not made a mistake in calculation when we do mathematics. In the second *Meditation,* he showed that one thing cannot be doubted: "I exist as a thinking thing when I think." This is the famous *"cogito, ergo sum"* ("I think, therefore I am") argument (although Descartes did not use that exact language here), and Descartes maintained this is an absolutely certain truth that cannot be doubted. In later *Meditations,* Descartes attempted to rationally deduce the existence of God from his own existence as a thinking thing and to show that God is perfectly good and hence no deceiver.

"So what," you say? Well, if we can be certain that we exist and if we can be certain that God exists and if we can be certain that God is no deceiver, we can also be certain that our sensations must truly represent an external reality. If they did not, we would live in constant error and ignorance, like Plato's prisoners in the cave, and this, surely, a good and gracious God would not allow.

Reading Questions

1. What was Descartes's goal, and what method did he employ to get there?
2. Many of our beliefs are based on sensation. Descartes offered two arguments, the arguments from deception and dreaming, to show that beliefs based on sensations are not trustworthy. State these arguments in your own words.
3. List some examples of occasions when you have been deceived by your senses.
4. Have you ever had a dream that you were totally convinced was true? How do you know you are not now dreaming?
5. Some of our beliefs—for example, that two plus three equals five—are based on reasoning, not sensation. Descartes argued that even arithmetic calculations can be doubted. What is his argument?
6. Descartes ended the first *Meditation* with the famous evil demon argument. What is the point of this argument?
7. Play Descartes's game for a moment and imagine there is an all-powerful force that has nothing better to do than to deceive you. Give this force a name and imagine it, like some mad puppeteer pulling the strings behind the scenes, constantly arranging things so that your beliefs are false. Now ask yourself, "Is there anything about which this wicked force could not deceive me?" If there is anything you can think of, what is it?
8. Descartes concluded that the statement "I am, I exist" must be true whenever he thought it. Why? What reasons support this conclusion?
9. The next step in Descartes's argument is to reach the conclusion that he is a thinking thing. How did he reach that conclusion? Why did he not conclude instead that he was a physical thing?
10. In the final paragraph of *Meditation II,* Descartes listed several things he had learned from his consideration of a piece of wax. What are they, and how did he arrive at these conclusions?
11. If you studied the previous selection, what similarities and differences do you notice between al-Ghazali's quest for knowledge and Descartes's quest?
12. How did Descartes answer the question, "Is knowledge possible?"

Meditations I and II

RENÉ DESCARTES

Meditation I

ON WHAT CAN BE
CALLED INTO DOUBT

FOR SEVERAL YEARS NOW, I've been aware that I accepted many falsehoods as true in my youth, that what I built on the foundations of those falsehoods was dubious, and accordingly that once in my life I would need to tear down everything and begin anew from the foundations if I wanted to establish any stable and lasting knowledge. But the task seemed enormous, and I waited until I was so old that no better time for undertaking it would be likely to follow. I have thus delayed so long that it would be wrong for me to waste in indecision the time left for action. Today, then, having rid myself of worries and having arranged for some peace and quiet, I withdraw alone, free at last earnestly and wholeheartedly to overthrow all my beliefs.

To do this, I don't need to show each of them to be false: I may never be able to do that. But, since reason now convinces me that I ought to withhold my assent just as carefully from what isn't obviously certain and indubitable as from what's obviously false, I can justify the rejection of all my beliefs if in each I can find some ground for doubt. And, to do this, I need not run through my beliefs one by one, which would be an endless task. Since a building collapses when its foundation is cut out from under it, I will go straight to the principles on which all my former beliefs rested.

Of course, whatever I have so far accepted as supremely true I have learned either from the senses or through the senses. But I have occasionally caught the senses deceiving me, and it's prudent never completely to trust those who have cheated us even once.

But, while my senses may deceive me about what is small or far away, there may still be other things which I take in by the senses but which I cannot possibly doubt—like that I am here, sitting before the fire, wearing a dressing gown, touching this paper. And on what grounds might I deny that my hands and the other parts of my body exist?—unless perhaps I liken myself to madmen whose brains are so rattled by the persistent vapors of melancholy that they are sure that they're kings when in fact they are paupers, or that they wear purple robes when in fact they're naked, or that their heads are clay, or that they are gourds, or made of glass. But these people are insane, and I would seem just as crazy if I were to apply what I say about them to myself.

This would be perfectly obvious—if I weren't a man accustomed to sleeping at night whose experiences while asleep are at least as far-fetched as those that madmen have while awake. How often, at night, I've been convinced that I was here, sitting before the fire, wearing my dressing gown, when in fact I was undressed and between the covers of my bed! But now I am looking at this piece of paper with my eyes wide open; the head that I am shaking has not been lulled to sleep; I put my hand out consciously and deliberately and feel. None of this would be as distinct if I were asleep. As if I can't remember having been tricked by similar thoughts while asleep! When I think very carefully about this, I see so plainly that there are no reliable signs by which I can distinguish sleeping from waking that I am stupefied—and my stupor itself suggests that I am asleep!

Suppose, then, that I am dreaming. Suppose, in particular, that my eyes are not open, that my head is not moving, and that I have not put out my hand. Suppose that I do not have hands, or

From René Descarte's Meditations on First Philosophy, *translated by Ronald Rubin (Claremont, CA: Areté Press, 1986), pp. 1–13. Reprinted by permission of Areté Press.*

even a body. I must still admit that the things I see in sleep are like painted images which must have been patterned after real things and, hence, that things like eyes, heads, hands, and bodies are real rather than imaginary. For, even when painters try to give bizarre shapes to sirens and satyrs, they are unable to give them completely new natures; they only jumble together the parts of various animals. And, even if they were to come up with something so novel that no one had ever seen anything like it before, something entirely fictitious and unreal, at least there must be real colors from which they composed it. Similarly, while things like eyes, heads, and hands may be imaginary, it must be granted that some simpler and more universal things are real—the "real colors" from which the true and false images in our thoughts are formed.

Things of this sort seem to include general bodily nature and its extension, the shape of extended things, their quantity (that is, their size and number), the place in which they exist, the time through which they endure, and so on.

Perhaps we can correctly infer that, while physics, astronomy, medicine, and other disciplines that require the study of composites are dubious, disciplines like arithmetic and geometry, which deal only with completely simple and universal things without regard to whether they exist in the world, are somehow certain and indubitable. For, whether we are awake or asleep, two plus three is always five, and the square never has more than four sides. It seems impossible even to suspect such obvious truths of falsity.

Nevertheless, the traditional view is fixed in my mind that there is a God who can do anything and by whom I have been made to be as I am. How do I know that He hasn't brought it about that, while there is in fact no earth, no sky, no extended thing, no shape, no magnitude, and no place, all of these things seem to me to exist, just as they do now? I think that other people sometimes err in what they believe themselves to know perfectly well. Mightn't I be deceived when I add two and three, or count the sides of a square, or do even simpler things, if we can even suppose that there is anything simpler? Maybe it will be denied that God deceives me, since He is said to

be supremely good. But, if God's being good is incompatible with His having created me so that I am deceived always, it seems just as out of line with His being good that He permits me to be deceived sometimes—as he undeniably does.

Maybe some would rather deny that there is an omnipotent God than believe that everything else is uncertain. Rather than arguing with them, I will grant everything I have said about God to be fiction. But, however these people think I came to be as I now am—whether they say it is by fate, or by accident, or by a continuous series of events, or in some other way—it seems that he who errs and is deceived is somehow imperfect. Hence, the less power that is attributed to my original creator, the more likely it is that I am always deceived. To these arguments, I have no reply. I'm forced to admit that nothing that I used to believe is beyond legitimate doubt—not because I have been careless or playful, but because I have valid and well-considered grounds for doubt. Hence, I must withhold my assent from my former beliefs as carefully as from obvious falsehoods if I want to arrive at something certain.

But it's not enough to have noticed this: I must also take care to bear it in mind. For my habitual views constantly return to my mind and take control of what I believe as if our long-standing, intimate relationship has given them the right to do so, even against my will. I'll never break the habit of trusting and giving in to these views while I see them for what they are—things somewhat dubious (as I have just shown) but nonetheless probable, things that I have much more reason to believe than to deny. That's why I think it will be good deliberately to turn my will around, to allow myself to be deceived, and to suppose that all my previous beliefs are false and illusory. Eventually, when I have counterbalanced the weight of my prejudices, my bad habits will no longer distort my grasp of things. I know that there is no danger of error here and that I won't overindulge in skepticism, since I'm now concerned, not with action, but only with gaining knowledge.

I will suppose, then, not that there is a supremely good God who is the source of all truth, but that there is an evil demon, supremely powerful and cunning, who works as hard as he can to deceive me. I will say that sky, air, earth, color, shape, sound, and other external things are just dreamed illusions which the demon uses to ensnare my judgment. I will regard myself as not having hands, eyes, flesh, blood, and senses—but as having the false belief that I have all these things. I will obstinately concentrate on this meditation and will thus ensure by mental resolution that, if I do not really have the ability to know the truth, I will at least withhold assent from what is false and from what a deceiver may try to put over on me, however powerful and cunning he may be. But this plan requires effort, and laziness brings me back to my ordinary life. I am like a prisoner who happens to enjoy the illusion of freedom in his dreams, begins to suspect that he is asleep, fears being awakened, and deliberately lets the enticing illusions slip by unchallenged. Thus, I slide back into my old views, afraid to awaken and to find that after my peaceful rest I must toil, not in the light, but in the confusing darkness of the problems just raised.

Meditation II

ON THE NATURE OF THE HUMAN MIND, WHICH IS BETTER KNOWN THAN THE BODY

Yesterday's meditation has hurled me into doubts so great that I can neither ignore them nor think my way out of them. I am in turmoil, as if I have accidentally fallen into a whirlpool and can neither touch bottom nor swim to the safety of the surface. I will struggle, however, and try to follow the path that I started on yesterday. I will reject whatever is open to the slightest doubt just as though I have found it to be entirely false, and I will continue until I find something certain—or at least until I know for certain that nothing is certain. Archimedes required only one fixed and immovable point to move the whole earth from its place, and I too can hope for great things if I can find even one small thing that is certain and unshakable.

I will suppose, then, that everything I see is unreal. I will believe that my memory is unreliable and that none of what it presents to me ever happened. I have no senses. Body, shape, extension, motion, and place are fantasies. What then is true? Perhaps just that nothing is certain.

But how do I know that there isn't something different from the things just listed which I do not have the slightest reason to doubt? Isn't there a God, or something like one, who puts my thoughts into me? But why should I say so when I may be the author of those thoughts? Well, isn't it at least the case that I am something? But I now am denying that I have senses and a body. But I stop here. For what follows from these denials? Am I so bound to my body and to my senses that I cannot exist without them? I have convinced myself that there is nothing in the world—no sky, no earth, no minds, no bodies. Doesn't it follow that I don't exist? No, surely I must exist if it's me who is convinced of something. But there is a deceiver, supremely powerful and cunning, whose aim is to see that I am always deceived. But surely I exist, if I am deceived. Let him deceive me all he can, he will never make it the case that I am nothing while I think that I am something. Thus having fully weighed every consideration, I must finally conclude that the statement "I am, I exist" must be true whenever I state it or mentally consider it.

But I do not yet fully understand what this "I" is that must exist. I must guard against inadvertently taking myself to be something other than I am, thereby going wrong even in the knowledge that I put forward as supremely certain and evident. Hence, I will think once again about what I believed myself to be before beginning these meditations. From this conception, I will subtract everything challenged by the reasons for doubt which I produced earlier, until nothing remains except what is certain and indubitable.

What, then, did I formerly take myself to be? A man, of course. But what is a man? Should I say a rational animal? No, because then I would need to ask what an animal is and what it is to be rational. Thus, starting from a single question, I would sink into many which are more difficult, and I do not have the time to waste on such subtleties. Instead, I will look here at the thought which occurred to me spontaneously and naturally when I reflected on what I was. The first thought to occur to me was that I have a face, hands, arms, and all the other equipment (also found in corpses) which I call a body. The next thought to occur to me was that I take nourishment, move myself around, sense, and think—that I do things which I trace back to my soul. Either I didn't stop to think about what this soul was, or I imagined it to be a rarified air, or fire, or ether permeating the denser parts of my body. But, about physical objects, I didn't have any doubts whatever: I thought that I distinctly knew their nature. If I had tried to describe my conception of this nature, I might have said this: "When I call something a physical object, I mean that it is capable of being bounded by a shape and limited to a place; that it can fill a space so as to exclude other objects from it; that it can be perceived by touch, sight, hearing, taste, and smell; that it can be moved in various ways, not by itself, but by something else in contact with it." I judged that the powers of self-movement, of sensing, and of thinking did not belong to the nature of physical objects, and, in fact, I marveled that there were some physical objects in which these powers could be found.

But what should I think now, while supposing that a supremely powerful and "evil" deceiver completely devotes himself to deceiving me? Can I say that I have any of the things that I have attributed to the nature of physical objects? I concentrate, think, reconsider—but nothing comes to me; I grow tired of the pointless repetition. But what about the things that I have assigned to soul? Nutrition and self-movement? Since I have no body, these are merely illusions. Sensing? But I cannot sense without a body, and in sleep I've seemed to sense many things that I later realized I had not really sensed. Thinking? It comes down to this: Thought and thought alone cannot be taken away from me. I am, I exist. That much is certain. But for how long? As long as I think—for it may be that, if I completely stopped thinking, I would completely cease to exist. I am not

now admitting anything unless it must be true, and I am therefore not admitting that I am anything at all other than a thinking thing—that is, a mind, soul, understanding, or reason (terms whose meaning I did not previously know). I know that I am a real, existing thing, but what kind of thing? As I have said, a thing that thinks.

What else? I will draw up mental images. I'm not the collection of organs called a human body. Nor am I some rarified gas permeating these organs, or air, or fire, or vapor, or breath—for I have supposed that none of these things exist. Still, I am something. But couldn't it be that these things, which I do not yet know about and which I am therefore supposing to be nonexistent, really aren't distinct from the "I" that I know to exist? I don't know, and I'm not going to argue about it now. I can only form judgments on what I do know. I know that I exist, and I ask what the "I" is that I know to exist. It's obvious that this conception of myself doesn't depend on anything that I do not yet know to exist and, therefore, that it does not depend on anything of which I can draw up a mental image. And the words "draw up" point to my mistake. I would truly be creative if I were to have a mental image of what I am, since to have a mental image is just to contemplate the shape or image of a physical object. I now know with certainty that I exist and at the same time that all images—and, more generally, all things associated with the nature of physical objects—may just be dreams. When I keep this in mind, it seems just as absurd to say "I use mental images to help me understand what I am" as it would to say "Now, while awake, I see something true—but, since I don't yet see it clearly enough, I'll go to sleep and let my dreams present it to me more clearly and truly." Thus I know that none of the things that I can comprehend with the aid of mental images bear on my knowledge of myself. And I must carefully draw my mind away from such things if it is to see its own nature distinctly.

But what then am I? A thinking thing. And what is that? Something that doubts, understands, affirms, denies, wills, refuses, and also senses and has mental images.

That's quite a lot, if I really do all of these things. But don't I? Isn't it me who now doubts nearly everything, understands one thing, affirms this thing, refuses to affirm other things, wants to know much more, refuses to be deceived, has mental images (sometimes involuntarily), and is aware of many things "through his senses?" Even if I am always dreaming, and even if my creator does what he can to deceive me, isn't it just as true that I do all these things as that I exist? Are any of these things distinct from my thought? Can any be said to be separate from me? That it's me who doubts, understands, and wills is so obvious that I don't see how it could be more evident. And it's also me who has mental images. While it may be, as I am supposing, that absolutely nothing of which I have a mental image really exists, the ability to have mental images really does exist and is a part of my thought. Finally, it's me who senses—or who seems to gain awareness of physical objects through the senses. For example, I am now seeing light, hearing a noise, and feeling heat. These things are unreal, since I am dreaming. But it is still certain that I seem to see, to hear, and to feel. This seeming cannot be unreal, and it is what is properly called sensing. Strictly speaking, sensing is just thinking.

From this, I begin to learn a little about what I am. But I still can't stop thinking that I apprehend physical objects, which I picture in mental images and examine with my senses, much more distinctly than I know this unfamiliar "I," of which I cannot form a mental image. I think this, even though it would be astounding if I comprehended things which I've found to be doubtful, unknown, and alien to me more distinctly than the one which I know to be real: my self. But I see what's happening. My mind enjoys wandering, and it won't confine itself to the truth. I will therefore loosen the reins on my mind for now so that later, when the time is right, I will be able to control it more easily.

Let's consider the things commonly taken to be the most distinctly comprehended: physical objects that we see and touch. Let's not consider physical objects in general, since general conceptions are very often confused. Rather, let's consider one, particular object. Take, for example, this piece of wax. It has just been taken from the honeycomb; it hasn't yet completely lost the taste of honey; it still smells of the flowers from which it was gathered; its color, shape, and size are obvious; it is hard, cold, and easy to touch; it makes a sound when rapped. In short, everything seems to be present in the wax that is required for me to know it as distinctly as possible. But, as I speak, I move the wax towards the fire; it loses what was left of its taste; it gives up its smell; it changes color; it loses its shape; it gets bigger; it melts; it heats up; it becomes difficult to touch; it no longer makes a sound when struck. Is it still the same piece of wax? We must say that it is: no one denies it or thinks otherwise. Then what was there in the wax that I comprehended so distinctly? Certainly nothing that I reached with my senses—for, while everything having to do with taste, smell, sight, touch, and hearing has changed, the same piece of wax remains.

Perhaps what I distinctly knew was neither the sweetness of honey, not the fragrance of flowers, nor a sound, but a physical object which once appeared to me one way and now appears differently. But what exactly is it of which I now have a mental image? Let's pay careful attention, remove everything that doesn't belong to the wax, and see what's left. Nothing is left except an extended, flexible, and changeable thing. But what is it for this thing to be flexible and changeable? Is it just that the wax can go from round to square and then to triangular, as I have mentally pictured? Of course not. Since I understand that the wax's shape can change in innumerable ways, and since I can't run through all the changes in my imagination, my comprehension of the wax's flexibility and changeability cannot have been produced by my ability to have mental images. And what about the thing that is extended? Are we also ignorant of its extension? Since the extension of the wax increases when the wax melts, increases again when the wax boils, and increases still more when the wax gets hotter, I will be mistaken about what the wax is unless I believe that it can undergo more changes in extension than I can ever encompass with mental images. I must therefore admit that I do not have an image of what the wax is—that I grasp what it is with only my mind. (While I am saying this about a particular piece of wax, it is even more clearly true about wax in general.) What then is this piece of wax that I grasp only with my mind? It is something that I see, feel, and mentally picture—exactly what I believed it to be at the outset. But it must be noted that, despite the appearances, my grasp of the wax is not visual, tactile, or pictorial. Rather, my grasp of the wax is the result of a purely mental inspection, which can be imperfect and confused, as it was once, or clear and distinct, as it is now, depending on how much attention I pay to the things of which the wax consists.

I'm surprised by how prone my mind is to error. Even when I think to myself non-verbally, language stands in my way, and common usage comes close to deceiving me. For, when the wax is present, we say that we see the wax itself, not that we infer its presence from its color and shape. I'm inclined to leap from this fact about language to the conclusion that I learn about the wax by eyesight rather than by purely mental inspection. But, if I happen to look out my window and see men walking in the street, I naturally say that I see the men just as I say that I see the wax. What do I really see, however, but hats and coats that could be covering robots? I *judge* that there are men. Thus I comprehend with my judgment, which is in my mind, objects that I once believed myself to see with my eyes.

One who aspires to wisdom above that of the common man disgraces himself by deriving doubt from common ways of speaking. Let's go on, then, to ask when I most clearly and perfectly grasped what the wax is. Was it when I first looked at the wax and believed my knowledge of it to come from the external senses—or at any rate from the so-called "common sense," the power of having mental images? Or is it now, after I have carefully studied what the wax is and how I come to know it? Doubt would be silly here. For what was distinct in my original conception of the wax? How did that conception differ from that had by animals? When I distinguish the wax from its external forms—when I "undress" it and view it "naked"—there may still be errors in my judgments about it, but I couldn't possibly grasp the wax in this way without a human mind.

What should I say about this mind—or, in other words, about myself? (I am not now admitting that there is anything to me but a mind.) What is this "I" that seems to grasp the wax so distinctly? Don't I know myself much more truly and certainly, and also much more distinctly and plainly, than I know the wax? For, if I base my judgment that the wax exists on the fact that I see it, my seeing it much more obviously implies that I exist. It's possible that what I see is not really wax, and it's even possible that I don't have eyes with which to see—but it clearly is not possible that, when I see (or, what now amounts to the same thing, when I think I see), the "I" which thinks is not a real thing. Similarly, if I base my judgment that the wax exists on the fact that I feel it, the same fact makes it obvious that I exist. If I base my judgment that the wax exists on the fact that I have a mental image of it or on some other fact of this sort, the same thing can obviously be said. And what I've said about the wax applies to everything else that is outside me. Moreover, if I seem to grasp the wax more distinctly when I detect it with several senses than when I detect it with just sight or touch, I must know myself even more distinctly—for every consideration that contributes to my grasp of the piece of wax or to my grasp of any other physical object serves better to reveal the nature of my mind. Besides, the mind has so much in it by which it can make its conception of itself distinct that what comes to it from physical objects hardly seems to matter.

And now I have brought myself back to where I wanted to be. I now know that physical objects are grasped, not by the senses or the power of having mental images, but by understanding alone. And, since I grasp physical objects in virtue of their being understandable rather than in virtue of their being tangible or visible, I know that I can't grasp anything more easily or plainly than my mind. But, since it takes time to break old habits of thought, I should pause here to allow the length of my contemplation to impress the new thoughts more deeply into my memory.

Suggestions for Further Reading

Start with Chapter 1 of William H. Brenner's little book, *Elements of Modern Philosophy: Descartes Through Kant* (Englewood Cliffs, NJ: Prentice Hall, 1989), for a lucid account and a good list of suggestions for further reading.

The article on Descartes in volume 6 of *Routledge Encyclopedia of Philosophy* edited by Edward Craig (New York: Routledge, 1998, pp. 1–19) will also prove helpful and provides a bibliography.

Volume 2 of *World Philosophy* (Englewood Cliffs, NJ: Salem Press, 1982, p. 828ff.) will give you a summary of the main ideas of the *Meditations.*

You will find O. K. Bouwsma's "Descartes' Evil Genius" in *Philosophical Essays* (Lincoln: University of Nebraska Press, 1965) a real delight. Bouwsma tries to convince you that Descartes's evil demon could not really deceive you without your being aware of it.

See the *Internet Encyclopedia of Philosophy* at http://www.utm.edu/research/iep/ for more information on Descartes.

Useful information on Descartes's epistemology can also be found at *Stanford Encyclopedia of Philosophy* (http://plato.stanford.edu/).

Video

Bernard Williams examines Descartes's theory of knowledge in *Descartes* (45 minutes). Available from Films for the Humanities & Sciences at www.films.com.

7.4 Empiricism and Limited Skepticism

David Hume (1711–1776) was a Scottish philosopher regarded by some as the greatest philosopher to write in the English language. There is little doubt about his brilliance. He graduated from the University of Edinburgh at the ripe old age of fifteen and headed for law school. Deciding he did not like law, he began writing a philosophical work called *A Treatise on Human Nature* (1739–1740), which he hoped would bring him fame and fortune. It did not. Very few people understood what he was talking about. Disappointed, he wrote a more popular version called *An Enquiry Concerning Human Understanding* (1748) from which the following selection is taken. You can judge for yourself how popular this version might have been.

Hume presented an empiricist theory of knowledge: Everything we can know about the world is ultimately derived from our senses. He developed empiricism into a critical tool for checking ideas. If you want to know what an idea or concept means, said Hume, trace it back to the impressions from which it came. For example, in a famous section (VII, not included here) Hume sought to find out what the concept of cause means. This is a basic idea because so much of science and, for that matter, common sense presupposes the law of cause and effect.

Usually people mean three things by *cause*—namely, that event *A* is the cause of event *B* if *A* occurs *before B*, *A* is *contiguous* to *B* in some way, and *A* is *necessarily connected* with *B*. It is this last idea that puzzled Hume. What is a necessary connection? From what impression does it arise? The only impression Hume could find was the impression of *constant conjunction*. We say *A* is the cause of *B* because in our experience *A* and *B* are constantly conjoined. Yet the concept of a necessary connection goes far beyond constant conjunction. If *A* and *B* are necessarily connected, then whenever *A* occurs, *B* will necessarily occur. However, from the fact that *A* and *B* have been constantly conjoined in the past, can we conclude that they will be so connected in the future? It is likely that they will be connected, even highly probable, but high probability is not the same as necessity.

This conclusion shocked the intellectual community of Hume's day because, if Hume was right, a fundamental law of thought and of science was without foundation in experience. This issue of the foundation of knowledge was of central importance to Hume. The rationalists claimed there was a foundation found in reason; the empiricists claimed there was a foundation found in experience. Hume, while sympathetic to empiricism, questioned whether there are in fact any firm foundations on which knowledge rests other than customary and habitual associations of ideas.

Hume brought the assumption that knowledge had a foundation into question by discovering the problem of induction. Although Hume did not call it by this name, the **problem of induction**, simply stated, is the problem of discovering rational foundations for all the conclusions we draw based on experience.

Later philosophers, inspired by Hume, drew a distinction between **analytic statements** such as "All bachelors are unmarried men" and **synthetic statements** such as "My cat is fat." Hume used the terms *relations of ideas* and *matters of fact* for these two kinds of statements because analytic statements are about how ideas are related and synthetic statements are about facts. You can test to see if any given statement is analytic by applying this rule: "If it is not logically possible for the negation of the statement to be true, the statement is analytic." For example, the claim that "some bachelors are married" cannot be true because the word *bachelor* means "unmarried man." You can test to see if a statement is synthetic by applying this rule: "If it is logically possible for the negation of the statement to be true, the statement is synthetic." For example, it is quite possible that, in fact, my cat is not fat.

See if you understand these rules by determining which of these statements are analytic and which synthetic.

1. The sun is round.
2. The lights are on.
3. $2 + 2 = 4$
4. Philosophy is fun.
5. Blind bats cannot see.

Note that statements about the relation of ideas (analytic) are *necessarily true*. That is, they are true by virtue of the meaning of the terms. Statements about matters of fact (synthetic) are *contingently true* because their truth depends on a certain state of affairs actually obtaining. Philosophers have also maintained that the truth of analytic statements is justified a priori by deductive reasoning, whereas the truth of synthetic statements is justified a posteriori by inductive reasoning.

Let us return to the problem of induction. Conclusions based on experience presuppose, according to Hume, that the future will resemble the past. Now how is this presupposition justified?

There are two types of proof: deductive and inductive. We cannot justify the statement "The future will resemble the past" deductively because it is not an analytic statement, but a synthetic statement. It is logically possible that the future will not resemble the past. So what about induction? Well, according to Hume, we cannot justify it inductively because that would be to beg the question (argue in a circle). It amounts to circular reasoning because the inductive method itself *presupposes* this rule (that the future will resemble the past) to be true.

The question of whether there is a foundation of knowledge remains a major philosophical problem. In fact, philosophy today is deeply embroiled in this issue. For Hume, it was important because the then-new physical sciences claimed to provide knowledge of the world based on conclusions drawn from experience. Can such scientific knowledge be philosophically justified?

In the last section (XII, "On the Academical or Skeptical Philosophy") of the *Enquiry* (not included here), Hume admitted it is our natural instinct to believe that our senses provide us with information about an external world. This, however, is a philosophically naive attitude because serious objections can be raised that would lead us to doubt whether we do have access to an external world through our senses. Our senses do not put us directly in touch with external objects. We never see a chair per se, only visual images that we infer to be *of* a chair.

There are two ways to overcome such objections. One way is to argue that assertions about matters of fact (synthetic statements) are justified a posteriori by reference to sense experience or impressions. However, all such proofs are bound to fail because all they can ever prove is that we have sensations. The other way is to try to prove deductively the existence of an external world (remember Descartes?). However, this line of argument is also bound to fail because the most it can prove is that certain relations among ideas (analytic statements) are true a priori. Such arguments tell us what words mean but do not tell us what the world is like.

If critical objections to the naive attitude cannot be overcome by either inductive or deductive reasoning, then skepticism about all claims to knowledge of the external world seems the only logical conclusion to draw. Absolute skepticism, however, can be shown to lead to absurdities. If we really were totally skeptical about all our beliefs based on sensation, then we would never move because there is no proof that we can, nor would we ever eat because there is no proof that food exists or is good for us. Besides, absolute skepticism appears to be self-refuting. So if inductive and deductive arguments fail and if absolute skepticism leads to absurdities, what are we to do?

Hume ends up advocating a limited or *mitigated* skepticism, much like the commonsense skepticism I mentioned in the introduction. We should take claims to knowledge with a grain of salt. We should accept what seems reasonable and useful but keep an open mind. We should avoid dogmatism and beware of a naive credulity. And we should limit our inquiries to subjects that are useful. These include mathematics, which provides us with useful analytic statements justified a priori, and the physical and social sciences, which provide us with synthetic statements justified a posteriori. All other subjects such as metaphysical speculations and theology are best left alone.

Reading Questions

1. Into what two categories can the "perceptions of the mind" be divided, and how are they distinguished from one another? Give an example of each.
2. Hume presented two arguments to prove "all our ideas . . . are copies of our impressions." State these arguments in your own words. What do you think of them? Are they convincing? Why, or why not?

3. What is the difference between *matters of fact* and *relations of ideas?* Provide your own example of each.
4. According to Hume, all reasoning concerning matters of fact is founded on the relation of cause and effect. This relation, Hume argued, is not discoverable by reason, only by experience. Summarize the argument Hume used to support this claim.
5. In answer to the question "What is the foundation of all conclusions from experience?" Hume challenged the reader to supply the foundation for the inference from the fact that I have found objects (like bread) to produce certain effects (like nourishment) in the past to the conclusion that the same will occur in the future. Can you supply the basis for the connection or inference between these two statements? If so, what is it?
6. Why can we not prove the principle "the future will resemble the past" deductively (Hume's term was "by demonstrative reasoning")?
7. Why can we not prove this principle inductively ("by moral reasoning")?
8. How do you think Hume would have answered the question, "Is knowledge possible?" How would his answer differ from the answers given by al-Ghazali and Descartes?

An Enquiry Concerning Human Understanding

DAVID HUME

Section II

OF THE ORIGIN OF IDEAS

EVERY ONE WILL READILY allow, that there is a considerable difference between the perceptions of the mind, when a man feels the pain of excessive heat, or the pleasure of moderate warmth, and when he afterwards recalls to his memory this sensation, or anticipates it by his imagination. These faculties may mimic or copy the perceptions of the senses; but they never can entirely reach the force and vivacity of the original sentiment. The utmost we say of them, even when they operate with greatest vigour, is, that they represent their object in so lively a manner, that we could *almost* say we feel or see it: But, except the mind be disordered by disease or madness, they never can arrive at such a pitch of vivacity, as to render these perceptions altogether indistinguishable. All the colours of poetry, however splendid, can never paint natural objects in such a manner as to make the description be taken for a real landscape. The most lively thought is still inferior to the dullest sensation.

We may observe a like distinction to run through all the other perceptions of the mind. A man in a fit of anger, is actuated in a very different manner from one who only thinks of that emotion. If you tell me, that any person is in love, I easily understand your meaning, and form a just conception of his situation; but never can mistake that conception for the real disorders and agitations of the passion. When we reflect on our past sentiments and affections, our thought is a faithful mirror, and copies its objects truly; but the colours which it employs are faint and dull, in comparison of those in which our original perceptions were clothed. It requires no nice discernment or metaphysical head to mark the distinction between them.

Here therefore we may divide all the perceptions of the mind into two classes or species, which are distinguished by their different degrees of force and vivacity. The less forcible and lively

Excerpts from Sections II and IV of David Hume's An Enquiry Concerning Human Understanding *(Oxford: Clarendon Press, 1748).*

are commonly denominated *Thoughts* or *Ideas*. The other species want a name in our language, and in most others; I suppose, because it was not requisite for any, but philosophical purposes, to rank them under a general term or appellation. Let us, therefore, use a little freedom, and call them *Impressions;* employing that word in a sense somewhat different from the usual. By the term *impression,* then, I mean all our more lively perceptions, when we hear, or see, or feel, or love, or hate, or desire, or will. And impressions are distinguished from ideas, which are the less lively perceptions, of which we are conscious, when we reflect on any of those sensations or movements above mentioned.

Nothing, at first view, may seem more unbounded than the thought of man, which not only escapes all human power and authority, but is not even restrained within the limits of nature and reality. To form monsters, and join incongruous shapes and appearances, costs the imagination no more trouble than to conceive the most natural and familiar objects. And while the body is confined to one planet, along which it creeps with pain and difficulty; the thought can in an instant transport us into the most distant regions of the universe; or even beyond the universe, into the unbounded chaos, where nature is supposed to lie in total confusion. What never was seen, or heard of, may yet be conceived; nor is any thing beyond the power of thought, except what implies an absolute contradiction.

But though our thought seems to possess this unbounded liberty, we shall find, upon a nearer examination, that it is really confined within very narrow limits, and that all this creative power of the mind amounts to no more than the faculty of compounding, transposing, augmenting, or diminishing the materials afforded us by the senses and experience. When we think of a golden mountain, we only join two consistent ideas, *gold,* and *mountain,* with which we were formerly acquainted. A virtuous horse we can conceive; because, from our own feeling, we can conceive virtue; and this we may unite to the figure and shape of a horse, which is an animal familiar to us. In short, all the materials of thinking are derived either from our outward or inward sentiment: the

mixture and composition of these belongs alone to the mind and will. Or, to express myself in philosophical language, all our ideas or more feeble perceptions are copies of our impressions or more lively ones.

To prove this, the two following arguments will, I hope, be sufficient. First, when we analyze our thoughts or ideas, however compounded or sublime, we always find that they resolve themselves into such simple ideas as were copied from a precedent feeling or sentiment. Even those ideas, which, at first view, seem the most wide of this origin, are found, upon a nearer scrutiny, to be derived from it. The idea of God, as meaning an infinitely intelligent, wise, and good Being, arises from reflecting on the operations of our own mind, and augmenting, without limit, those qualities of goodness and wisdom. We may prosecute this enquiry to what length we please; where we shall always find, that every idea which we examine is copied from a similar impression. Those who would assert that this position is not universally true nor without exception, have only one, and that an easy method of refuting it; by producing that idea, which, in their opinion, is not derived from this source. It will then be incumbent on us, if we would maintain our doctrine, to produce the impression, or lively perception, which corresponds to it.

Secondly. If it happen, from a defect of the organ, that a man is not susceptible of any species of sensation, we always find that he is as little susceptible of the correspondent ideas. A blind man can form no notion of colours; a deaf man of sounds. Restore either of them that sense in which he is deficient; by opening this new inlet for his sensations, you also open an inlet for the ideas; and he finds no difficulty in conceiving these objects. The case is the same, if the object, proper for exciting any sensation, has never been applied to the organ. A Laplander or Negro has no notion of the relish of wine. And though there are few or no instances of a like deficiency in the mind, where a person has never felt or is wholly incapable of a sentiment or passion that belongs to his species; yet we find the same observation to take place in a less degree. A man of mild manners can form no idea of inveterate revenge or cruelty; nor can a selfish heart easily conceive the heights of friendship and generosity. It is readily allowed, that other beings may possess many senses of which we can have no conception; because the ideas of them have never been introduced to us in the only manner by which an idea can have access to the mind, to wit, by the actual feeling and sensation. . . .

Section IV

SCEPTICAL DOUBTS CONCERNING THE OPERATIONS OF THE UNDERSTANDING

PART 1. All the objects of human reason or enquiry may naturally be divided into two kinds, to wit, *Relations of Ideas,* and *Matters of Fact.* Of the first kind are the sciences of Geometry, Algebra, and Arithmetic; and in short, every affirmation which is either intuitively or demonstratively certain. *That the square of the hypothenuse is equal to the square of the two sides,* is a proposition which expresses a relation between these figures. *That three times five is equal to the half of thirty,* expresses a relation between these numbers. Propositions of this kind are discoverable by the mere operation of thought, without dependence on what is anywhere existent in the universe. Though there never were a circle or triangle in nature, the truths demonstrated by Euclid would for ever retain their certainty and evidence.

Matters of fact, which are the second objects of human reason, are not ascertained in the same manner; nor is our evidence of their truth, however great, of a like nature with the foregoing. The contrary of every matter of fact is still possible; because it can never imply a contradiction, and is conceived by the mind with the same facility and distinctness, as if ever so conformable to reality. *That the sun will not rise to-morrow* is no less intelligible a proposition, and implies no more contradiction than the affirmation, *that it will rise.* We should in vain, therefore, attempt to demonstrate its falsehood. Were it demonstratively false, it would imply a contradiction, and could never be distinctly conceived by the mind.

It may, therefore, be a subject worthy of curiosity, to enquire what is the nature of that evidence which assures us of any real existence and matter of fact, beyond the present testimony of our senses, or the records of our memory. This part of philosophy, it is observable, has been little cultivated, either by the ancients or moderns; and therefore our doubts and errors, in the prosecution of so important an enquiry, may be the more excusable; while we march through such difficult paths without any guide or direction. They may even prove useful, by exciting curiosity, and destroying that implicit faith and security, which is the bane of all reasoning and free enquiry. The discovery of defects in the common philosophy, if any such there be, will not, I presume, be a discouragement, but rather an incitement, as is usual, to attempt something more full and satisfactory than has yet been proposed to the public.

All reasonings concerning matter of fact seem to be founded on the relation of *Cause and Effect.* By means of that relation alone we can go beyond the evidence of our memory and senses. If you were to ask a man, why he believes any matter of fact, which is absent; for instance, that his friend is in the country, or in France; he would give you a reason; and this reason would be some other fact; as a letter received from him, or the knowledge of his former resolutions and promises. A man finding a watch or any other machine in a desert island, would conclude that there had once been men in that island. All our reasonings concerning fact are of the same nature. And here it is constantly supposed that there is a connexion between the present fact and that which is inferred from it. Were there nothing to bind them together, the inference would be entirely precarious. The hearing of an articulate voice and rational discourse in the dark assures us of the presence of some person: Why? because these are the effects of the human make and fabric, and closely connected with it. If we anatomize all the other reasonings of this nature, we shall find that they are founded on the relation of cause and effect, and that this relation is either near or remote, direct or collateral. Heat and light are collateral effects of fire, and the one effect may justly be inferred from the other.

If we would satisfy ourselves, therefore, concerning the nature of that evidence, which assures us of matters of fact, we must enquire how we arrive at the knowledge of cause and effect.

I shall venture to affirm, as a general proposition, which admits of no exception, that the knowledge of this relation is not, in any instance, attained by reasonings *a priori;* but arises entirely from experience, when we find that any particular objects are constantly conjoined with each other. Let an object be presented to a man of ever so strong natural reason and abilities; if that object be entirely new to him, he will not be able, by the most accurate examination of its sensible qualities, to discover any of its causes or effects. Adam, though his rational faculties be supposed, at the very first, entirely perfect, could not have inferred from the fluidity and transparency of water that it would suffocate him, or from the light and warmth of fire that it would consume him. No object ever discovers, by the qualities which appear to the senses, either the causes which produced it, or the effects which will arise from it; nor can our reason, unassisted by experience, ever draw any inference concerning real existence and matter of fact. . . .

We fancy, that were we brought on a sudden into this world, we could at first have inferred that one Billiard-ball would communicate motion to another upon impulse; and that we needed not to have waited for the event, in order to pronounce with certainty concerning it. Such is the influence of custom, that, where it is strongest, it not only covers our natural ignorance, but even conceals itself, and seems not to take place, merely because it is found in the highest degree.

But to convince us that all the laws of nature, and all the operations of bodies without exception, are known only by experience, the following reflections may, perhaps, suffice. Were any object presented to us, and were we required to pronounce concerning the effect, which will result from it, without consulting past observation; after what manner, I beseech you, must the mind proceed in this operation? It must invent or imagine some event, which it ascribes to the object as its effect; and it is plain that this invention must be entirely arbitrary. The mind can never possibly find the effect in the supposed cause, by the most accurate scrutiny and examination. For the effect is totally different from the cause, and consequently can never be discovered in it. Motion in the second Billiard-ball is a quite distinct event from motion in the first; nor is there anything in the one to suggest the smallest hint of the other. A stone or piece of metal raised into the air, and left without any support, immediately falls: but to consider the matter *a priori,* is there anything we discover in this situation which can beget the idea of a downward, rather than an upward, or any other motion, in the stone or metal?

And as the first imagination or invention of a particular effect, in all natural operations, is arbitrary, where we consult not experience; so must we also esteem the supposed tie or connexion between the cause and effect, which binds them together, and renders it impossible that any other effect could result from the operation of that cause. When I see, for instance, a Billiard-ball moving in a straight line towards another; even suppose motion in the second ball should by accident be suggested to me, as the result of their contact or impulse; may I not conceive, that a hundred different events might as well follow from that cause? May not both these balls remain at absolute rest? May not the first ball return in a straight line, or leap off from the second in any line or direction? All these suppositions are consistent and conceivable. Why then should we give the preference to one, which is no more consistent or conceivable than the rest? All our reasonings *a priori* will never be able to show us any foundation for this preference. . . .

PART II. But we have not yet attained any tolerable satisfaction with regard to the question first proposed. Each solution still gives rise to a new question as difficult as the foregoing, and leads us on to farther enquiries. When it is asked, *What is the nature of all our reasonings concerning matter of fact?* the proper answer seems to be, that they are founded on the relation of cause and effect. When again it is asked, *What is the foundation of all our reasonings and conclusions concerning that relation?* it may be replied in one word, Experience. But if we still carry on our sifting humour, and ask, *What is the foundation of all conclusions from experience?* this implies a new question, which may be of more difficult solution and explication. Philosophers, that give themselves airs of superior wisdom and sufficiency, have a hard task when they encounter persons of inquisitive dispositions, who push them from every corner to which they retreat, and who are sure at last to bring them to some dangerous dilemma. The best expedient to prevent this confusion, is to be modest in our pretensions; and even to discover the difficulty ourselves before it is objected to us. By this means, we may make a kind of merit of our very ignorance.

I shall content myself, in this section, with an easy task, and shall pretend only to give a negative answer to the question here proposed. I say then, that, even after we have experience of the operations of cause and effect, our conclusions from that experience are *not* founded on reasoning, or any process of the understanding. This answer we must endeavour both to explain and to defend.

It must certainly be allowed, that nature has kept us at a great distance from all her secrets, and has afforded us only the knowledge of a few superficial qualities of objects; while she conceals from us those powers and principles on which the influence of those objects entirely depends. Our senses inform us of the colour, weight, and consistence of bread; but neither sense nor reason can ever inform us of those qualities which fit it for the nourishment and support of a human body. Sight or feeling conveys an idea of the actual motion of bodies; but as to that wonderful force or power, which would carry on a moving body for ever in a continued change of place, and which bodies never lose but by communicating it to others; of this we cannot form the most distant conception. But notwithstanding this ignorance of natural powers and principles, we always presume, when we see like sensible qualities, that they have like secret powers, and expect that effects, similar to those which we have experienced, will follow from them. If a body of like colour and consistence with that bread, which we have formerly [eaten], be presented to us, we make no scruple of repeating the experiment, and foresee,

with certainty, like nourishment and support. Now this is a process of the mind or thought, of which I would willingly know the foundation. It is allowed on all hands that there is no known connexion between the sensible qualities and the secret powers; and consequently, that the mind is not led to form such a conclusion concerning their constant and regular conjunction, by anything which it knows of their nature. As to past *Experience,* it can be allowed to give *direct* and *certain* information of those precise objects only, and that precise period of time, which fell under its cognizance: but why this experience should be extended to future times, and to other objects, which for aught we know, may be only in appearance similar; this is the main question on which I would insist. The bread, which I formerly [ate], nourished me; that is, a body of such sensible qualities was, at that time, endued with such secret powers: but does it follow, that other bread must also nourish me at another time, and that like sensible qualities must always be attended with like secret powers? The consequence seems nowise necessary. At least, it must be acknowledged that there is here a consequence drawn by the mind; that there is a certain step taken; a process of thought, and an inference, which wants to be explained. These two propositions are far from being the same, *I have found that such an object has always been attended with such an effect,* and *I foresee, that other objects, which are, in appearance, similar, will be attended with similar effects.* I shall allow, if you please, that the one proposition may justly be inferred from the other: I know, in fact, that it always is inferred. But if you insist that the inference is made by a chain of reasoning, I desire you to produce that reasoning. The connexion between these propositions is not intuitive. There is required a medium, which may enable the mind to draw such an inference, if indeed it be drawn by reasoning and argument. What that medium is, I must confess, passes my comprehension; and it is incumbent on those to produce it, who assert that it really exists; and is the origin of all our conclusions concerning matter of fact.

This negative argument must certainly, in process of time, become altogether convincing, if many penetrating and able philosophers shall turn their enquiries this way and no one be ever able to discover any connecting proposition or intermediate step, which supports the understanding in this conclusion. But as the question is yet new, every reader may not trust so far to his own penetration, as to conclude, because an argument escapes his enquiry, that therefore it does not really exist. For this reason it may be requisite to venture upon a more difficult task; and enumerating all the branches of human knowledge, endeavour to show that none of them can afford such an argument.

All reasonings may be divided into two kinds, namely, demonstrative reasoning, or that concerning relations of ideas, and moral reasoning, or that concerning matter of fact and existence. That there are no demonstrative arguments in the case seems evident; since it implies no contradiction that the course of nature may change, and that an object, seemingly like those which we have experienced, may be attended with different or contrary effects. May I not clearly and distinctly conceive that a body, falling from the clouds, and which, in all other respects, resembles snow, has yet the taste of salt or feeling of fire? Is there any more intelligible proposition than to affirm, that all the trees will flourish in December and January, and decay in May and June? Now whatever is intelligible, and can be distinctly conceived, implies no contradiction, and can never be proved false by any demonstrative argument or abstract reasoning *a priori*.

If we be, therefore, engaged by arguments to put trust in past experience, and make it the standard of our future judgment, these arguments must be probable only, or such as regard matter of fact and real existence, according to the division above mentioned. But that there is no argument of this kind, must appear, if our explication of that species of reasoning be admitted as solid and satisfactory. We have said that all arguments concerning existence are founded on the relation of cause and effect; that our knowledge of that relation is derived entirely from experience; and that all our experimental conclusions proceed upon the supposition that the future will be conformable to the past. To endeavour, therefore, the proof of this last supposition by probable arguments, or arguments regarding existence, must be evidently going in a circle, and taking that for granted, which is the very point in question.

In reality, all arguments from experience are founded on the similarity which we discover among natural objects, and by which we are induced to expect effects similar to those which we have found to follow from such objects. And though none but a fool or madman will ever pretend to dispute the authority of experience, or to reject that great guide of human life, it may surely be allowed a philosopher to have so much curiosity at least as to examine the principle of human nature, which gives this mighty authority to experience, and makes us draw advantage from that similarity which nature has placed among different objects. From causes which appear *similar* we expect similar effects. This is the sum of all our experimental conclusions. Now it seems evident that, if this conclusion were formed by reason, it would be as perfect at first, and upon one instance, as after ever so long a course of experience. But the case is far otherwise. Nothing so like as eggs; yet no one, on account of this appearing similarity, expects the same taste and relish in all of them. It is only after a long course of uniform experiments in any kind, that we attain a firm reliance and security with regard to a particular event. Now where is that process of reasoning which, from one instance, draws a conclusion, so different from that which it infers from a hundred instances that are nowise different from that single one? This question I propose as much for the sake of information, as with an intention of raising difficulties. I cannot find, I cannot imagine any such reasoning. But I keep my mind still open to instruction, if any one will vouchsafe to bestow it on me.

Suggestions for Further Reading

William Brenner's chapter on Hume in *Elements of Modern Philosophy: Descartes Through Kant* (Englewood Cliffs, NJ: Prentice-Hall, 1989) will provide you with a section-by-section commentary on the *Enquiry* as well as introduce you to some of Hume's provocative writings on religion.

Norman Kemp Smith's *The Philosophy of David Hume* (London: Macmillan, 1941) is a classic interpretation, as is H. H. Price's *Hume's Theory of the External World* (Oxford: Oxford University Press, 1940).

For a contemporary discussion of the problem of induction and an attempt to resolve it by showing how it is a pseudoproblem, see Max Black's "The Justification of Induction" in *Philosophy of Science Today,* edited by Sidney Morgenbesser (New York: Basic Books, 1967).

See the *Internet Encyclopedia of Philosophy* at http://www.utm.edu/research/iep/ and *Stanford Encyclopedia of Philosophy* at http://plato.stanford.edu/ for more information on Hume.

Video

John Passmore examines Hume's views on causality and knowledge among other topics in *Hume* (45 minutes). Available from Films for the Humanities & Sciences at www.films.com.

7.5 Should We Believe Beyond the Evidence?

Should you believe something to be true even though you have insufficient evidence that it is true? Do you have a moral obligation to refrain from believing something true or false if the available evidence is not sufficient? Suppose you loan your old car to a friend. You have not checked the brakes in some time, but you dismiss all doubts about the brakes from your mind, confident that they will work because they have in the past. Suppose your friend crashes and dies due to faulty brakes. Are you to blame? Suppose your friend does not crash and die. Are you to blame for putting her life in danger? According to William K. Clifford (1845–1879), if you do not have sufficient evidence that the brakes are in working order, then you are to blame no matter what happens.

Clifford, a British mathematician interested in philosophical and religious topics, wrote an essay entitled "The Ethics of Belief." Clifford's argument reflects an epistemological position called evidentialism. **Evidentialism** holds that we should not accept any statement as true unless we have good evidence to support its truth. Our beliefs about the truth of things—be they moral, religious, or scientific beliefs—must meet appropriate *epistemic* standards. *Practical* standards, such as aiding me in accomplishing certain goals or possibly resulting in my eternal happiness, will not do. William James (1842–1910), an American philosopher, wrote a famous essay in reply to Clifford, called "The Will To Believe." James advocated a philosophy called **pragmatism**.

James characterized pragmatism (from the Greek word *pragma,* meaning "action") as a method for settling philosophical disputes. This method was based on a distinctive theory of truth, called the **pragmatic theory of truth**. According to this theory, some proposition *p* is true if and only if the belief that "*p* is true" works.

"And what does *works* mean," you ask? James used words like "useful," "adaptive," "serviceable," "satisfying," "verifiable," and "agreeing with reality" to try to explain what it means. He also asserted that for any proposition to "work" and hence to be taken as true, it must be consistent with what we already take to be true, and it must be in agreement with our sense experience. Thus, my belief that "my fat, blind cat is on the rug by the fire" works as long as it is consistent with my other beliefs (he is not outside, he is not in the kitchen eating my dinner, he is not in the pool practicing his backstroke, etc.), and when I look at the rug I get "fat-blind-cat" type sensations.

We can grasp James's theory better by contrasting it with two other theories of truth, both of which derive from Plato. They have been the two dominant theories of truth in Western thought. The first is called the **correspondence theory of truth**. According to this theory, *p* is true if and only if *p* corresponds to the facts. My believing *p* to be true or false has nothing to do with the matter of its truth, or so this theory would maintain. "My cat is on the rug" is true if, indeed, that is where the cat is and is false if the cat is not there. Even if I don't look and no matter how I feel or what I believe, it is true or false independent of my actions or beliefs.

The second theory of truth is called the **coherence theory of truth**. According to this view, *p* is true if and only if *p* is logically implied by *q,* where *q* is a true statement, and *q* in turn is logically implied by *r,* and so on. Truth, on this account, is the coherence of a whole system of statements in which each statement is entailed by all the others. We have only fragments of this whole, but when and if we ever discover the entire system, we will have arrived at absolute truth. Thus, "My fat, blind cat is on the rug" is true if a whole host of other propositions are true such as "My cat is blind," "The rug exists," "Cats exist," and so on.

James ascribed both the correspondence and coherence theories to philosophers he called "intellectualists and rationalists." He objected to these theories on the grounds that they present truth as a static property existing prior to and independent of human experience and investigation. James saw truth as something dynamic, something that happens to ideas when they lead humans into ever more satisfactory experiences. The rationalists accused James, in turn, of denying objectivity, reducing truth to a matter of what we want to believe, and making it relative to the context in which we verify propositions.

From James's point of view, Clifford's argument rests in part on a reliance on a static theory of truth, which too narrowly confines our thinking. His insistence on purely epistemic standards, and his refusal to admit practical standards, not only denies the facts involved in how humans come to hold many of their beliefs, but also restricts us to a very narrow range of beliefs and forbids us to have beliefs about some of the most important matters that make human life worth living.

James's argument against evidentialism is often misunderstood because readers ignore the conditions James placed on believing beyond the evidence. In at least three situations, James contended, belief beyond the evidence is justified. First, when you are confronted with what he called a "genuine option" that *cannot be decided on evidential grounds,* you have a right to decide the issue according to your "passional nature." Second, when faced with a situation when belief in a fact is necessary for the existence of that fact, you have the right to believe beyond the evidence. And finally, in a situation when belief in a true proposition is necessary for getting at the evidence in support of its truth, you are entitled to believe.

What follows is a brief selection from both Clifford's essay and James's. Read their arguments and decide for yourself whether we have a right to believe beyond the evidence.

Reading Questions

1. What do the examples of the shipowner and the commission show?
2. Do you agree with Clifford's contention that all of us have a duty to question our beliefs? Why, or why not?
3. Do you agree with Clifford's claim that it is "wrong always, everywhere, and for anyone, to believe anything upon insufficient evidence"? Why, or why not?
4. What do you think Clifford means by "sufficient evidence"? How much evidence is sufficient?
5. What, according to James, is a *genuine option?* Give an example.
6. What is James's thesis?
7. How, according to James, does Clifford's attitude differ from James's with respect to "our first and great commandments as would-be knowers"?
8. How did James support his own attitude? What examples did he use? Do his examples support his thesis? Why, or why not?
9. Who do you think is right, Clifford or James? Why?

The Ethics of Belief

WILLIAM K. CLIFFORD

A SHIPOWNER WAS ABOUT to send to sea an emigrant-ship. He knew that she was old, and not over-well built at the first; that she had seen many seas and climes, and often had needed repairs. Doubts had been suggested to him that possibly she was not seaworthy. These doubts preyed upon his mind, and made him unhappy; he thought that perhaps he ought to have her thoroughly overhauled and refitted, even though this should put him to great expense. Before the ship sailed, however, he succeeded in overcoming these melancholy reflections. He said to himself that she had gone safely through so many voyages and weathered so many storms that it was idle to suppose she would not come safely home from this trip also. He would put his trust in providence, which could hardly fail to protect all these unhappy families that were leaving their fatherland to seek for better times elsewhere. He would dismiss from his mind all ungenerous suspicions about the honesty of builders and contractors. In such ways he acquired a sincere and comfortable conviction that his vessel was thoroughly safe and seaworthy; he watched her departure with a light heart, and benevolent wishes for the success of the exiles in their strange new home that was to be; and he got his insurance-money when she went down in mid-ocean and told no tales.

What shall we say of him? Surely this, that he was verily guilty of the death of those men. It is admitted that he did sincerely believe in the

From Lectures and Essays, *Vol. 2 (London: Macmillan, 1897), pp. 177–188. Footnotes deleted.*

soundness of his ship; but the sincerity of his conviction can in no wise help him, because *he had no right to believe on such evidence as was before him.* He had acquired his belief not by honestly earning it in patient investigation, but by stifling his doubts. And although in the end he may have felt so sure about it that he could not think otherwise, yet inasmuch as he had knowingly and willingly worked himself into that frame of mind, he must be held responsible for it.

Let us alter the case a little, and suppose that the ship was not unsound after all; that she made her voyage safely, and many others after it. Will that diminish the guilt of her owner? Not one jot. When an action is once done, it is right or wrong for ever; no accidental failure of its good or evil fruits can possibly alter that. The man would not have been innocent, he would only have been not found out. The question of right or wrong has to do with the origin of his belief, not the matter of it; not what it was, but how he got it; not whether it turned out to be true or false, but whether he had a right to believe on such evidence as was before him.

There was once an island in which some of the inhabitants professed a religion teaching neither the doctrine of original sin nor that of eternal punishment. A suspicion got abroad that the professors of this religion had made use of unfair means to get their doctrines taught to children. They were accused of wresting the laws of their country in such a way as to remove children from the care of their natural and legal guardians; and even of stealing them away and keeping them concealed from their friends and relations. A certain number of men formed themselves into a society for the purpose of agitating the public about this matter. They published grave accusations against individual citizens of the highest position and character, and did all in their power to injure these citizens in the exercise of their professions. So great was the noise they made, that a Commission was appointed to investigate the facts; but after the Commission had carefully inquired into all the evidence that could be got, it appeared that the accused were innocent. Not only had they been accused on insufficient evidence, but the evidence of their innocence was such as the

agitators might easily have obtained, if they had attempted a fair inquiry. After these disclosures the inhabitants of that country looked upon the members of the agitating society, not only as persons whose judgment was to be distrusted, but also as no longer to be counted honourable men. For although they had sincerely and conscientiously believed in the charges they had made, yet *they had no right to believe on such evidence as was before them.* Their sincere convictions, instead of being honestly earned by patient inquiring, were stolen by listening to the voice of prejudice and passion.

Let us vary this case also, and suppose, other things remaining as before, that a still more accurate investigation proved the accused to have been really guilty. Would this make any difference in the guilt of the accusers? Clearly not; the question is not whether their belief was true or false, but whether they entertained it on wrong grounds. . . .

In the two supposed cases which have been considered, it has been judged wrong to believe on insufficient evidence, or to nourish belief by suppressing doubts and avoiding investigation. The reason of this judgment is not far to seek: it is that in both these cases the belief held by one man was of great importance to other men. But forasmuch as no belief held by one man, however seemingly trivial the belief, and however obscure the believer, is ever actually insignificant or without its effect on the fate of mankind, we have no choice but to extend our judgment to all cases of belief whatever. . . .

It is not only the leader of men, statesman, philosopher, or poet, that owes this bounden duty to mankind. Every rustic who delivers in the village alehouse his slow, infrequent sentences, may help to kill or keep alive the fatal superstitions which clog his race. Every hard-worked wife of an artisan may transmit to her children beliefs which shall knit society together, or rend it in pieces. No simplicity of mind, no obscurity of station, can escape the universal duty of questioning all that we believe. . . .

The harm which is done by credulity in a man is not confined to the fostering of a credulous character in others, and consequent support of false beliefs. Habitual want of care about what I believe leads to habitual want of care in others about the truth of what is told to me. Men speak the truth to one another when each reveres the truth in his own mind and in the other's mind; but how shall my friend revere the truth in my mind when I myself am careless about it, when I believe things because I want to believe them, and because they are comforting and pleasant? Will he not learn to cry, "Peace," to me, when there is no peace? By such a course I shall surround myself with a thick atmosphere of falsehood and fraud, and in that I must live. It may matter little to me, in my cloud-castle of sweet illusions and darling lies; but it matters much to Man that I have made my neighbours ready to deceive. The credulous man is father to the liar and the cheat; he lives in the bosom of this his family, and it is no marvel if he should become even as they are. So closely are our duties knit together, that whoso shall keep the whole law, and yet offend in one point, he is guilty of all.

To sum up: it is wrong always, everywhere, and for anyone, to believe anything upon insufficient evidence. . . .

The Will to Believe

WILLIAM JAMES

LET US GIVE the name of *hypothesis* to anything that may be proposed to our belief; and just as the electricians speak of live and dead wires, let us speak of any hypothesis as either *live* or *dead*. A live hypothesis is one which appeals as a real possibility to him to whom it is proposed. If I ask you to believe in the Mahdi, the notion makes no electric connection with your nature—it refuses to scintillate with any credibility at all. As an hypothesis it is completely dead. To an Arab, however (even if he be not one of the Mahdi's followers), the hypothesis is among the mind's possibilities: it is alive. This shows that deadness and liveness in an hypothesis are not intrinsic properties, but relations to the individual thinker. They are measured by his willingness to act. The maximum of liveness in an hypothesis means willingness to act irrevocably. Practically, that means belief; but there is some believing tendency wherever there is willingness to act at all.

Next, let us call the decision between two hypotheses an *option*. Options may be of several kinds. They may be—1, *living* or *dead*; 2, *forced* or *avoidable*; 3, *momentous* or *trivial*; and for our purposes we may call an option a *genuine* option when it is of the forced, living and momentous kind.

1. A living option is one in which both hypotheses are live ones. If I say to you: "Be a theosophist or be a mahomedan," it is probably a dead option, because for you neither hypothesis is likely to be alive. But if I say "Be an agnostic or be a Christian," it is otherwise: trained as you are, each hypothesis makes some appeal, however small, to your belief.

2. Next, if I say to you: "Choose between going out with your umbrella or without it," I do not offer you a genuine option, for it is not forced. You can easily avoid it by not going out at all. Similarly, if I say "Either love me or hate me," "Either call my theory true or call it false," your option is avoidable. You may remain indifferent to me, neither loving nor hating, and you may decline to offer any judgment as to my theory. But if I say "Either accept this truth or go without it," I put on you a forced option, for there is no

From William James, The Will to Believe and Other Essays in Popular Philosophy *(New York: Henry Holt, 1912), pp. 1–31.*

standing place outside of the alternative. Every dilemma based on a complete logical disjunction, with no possibility of not choosing, is an option of this forced kind.

3. Finally, if I were Dr. Nansen and proposed to you to join my North Pole expedition, your option would be momentous; for this would probably be your only similar opportunity, and your choice now would either exclude you from the North Pole sort of immortality altogether or put at least the chance of it into your hands. He who refuses to embrace a unique opportunity loses the prize as surely as if he tried and failed. *Per contra,* the option is trivial when the opportunity is not unique, when the stake is insignificant, or when the decision is reversible if it later prove unwise. Such trivial options abound in the scientific life. A chemist finds an hypothesis live enough to spend a year in its verification: he believes in it to that extent. But if his experiments prove inconclusive either way, he is quit for his loss of time, no vital harm being done. . . .

The thesis I defend is, briefly stated, this: *Our passional nature not only lawfully may, but must, decide an option between propositions, whenever it is a genuine option that cannot by its nature be decided on intellectual grounds; for to say, under such circumstances, "Do not decide, but leave the question open," is itself a passional decision—just like deciding yes or no—and is attended with the same risk of losing the truth. . . .*

There are two ways of looking at our duty in the matter of opinion—ways entirely different, and yet ways about whose difference the theory of knowledge seems hitherto to have shown very little concern. *We must know the truth;* and *we must avoid error*—these are our first and great commandments as would-be knowers; but they are not two ways of stating an identical commandment, they are two separable laws. Although it may indeed happen that when we believe the truth *A,* we escape as an incidental consequence from believing the falsehood *B,* it hardly ever happens that by merely disbelieving *B* we necessarily believe *A.* We may in escaping *B* fall into believing other falsehoods, *C* or *D,* just as bad as *B;* or we may escape *B* by not believing anything at all, not even *A.*

Believe truth! Shun error!—these, we see, are two materially different laws; and by choosing between them we may end by colouring differently our whole intellectual life. We may regard the chase for truth as paramount, and the avoidance of error as secondary; or we may, on the other hand, treat the avoidance of error as more imperative, and let truth take its chance. Clifford . . . exhorts us to the latter course. Believe nothing, he tells us, keep your mind in suspense forever, rather than by closing it on insufficient evidence incur the awful risk of believing lies. You, on the other hand, may think that the risk of being in error is a very small matter when compared with the blessings of real knowledge, and be ready to be duped many times in your investigation rather than postpone indefinitely the chance of guessing true. I myself find it impossible to go with Clifford. We must remember that these feelings of our duty about either truth or error are in any case only expressions of our passional life. Biologically considered, our minds are as ready to grind out falsehood as veracity, and he who says "Better go without belief forever than believe a lie!" merely shows his own preponderant private horror of becoming a dupe. He may be critical of many of his desires and fears, but this fear he slavishly obeys. He cannot imagine anyone questioning its binding force. For my own part, I have also a horror of being duped; but I can believe that worse things than being duped may happen to a man in this world: so Clifford's exhortation has to my ears a thoroughly fantastic sound. It is like a general informing his soldiers that it is better to keep out of battle forever than to risk a single wound. Not so are victories either over enemies or over nature gained. Our errors are surely not such awfully solemn things. In a world where we are so certain to incur them in spite of all our caution, a certain lightness of heart seems healthier than this excessive nervousness on their behalf. . . .

Wherever the option between losing truth and gaining it is not momentous, we can throw the chance of *gaining truth* away, and at any rate save ourselves from any chance of *believing falsehood,* by not making up our minds at all till objective evidence has come. In scientific questions, this is almost always the case; and even in human affairs in general, the need of acting is seldom so urgent that a false belief to act on is better than no belief at all. Law courts, indeed, have to decide on the best evidence attainable for the moment, because a judge's duty is to make law as well as to ascertain it, and (as a learned judge once said to me) few cases are worth spending much time over: the great thing is to have them decided on *any* acceptable principle, and got out of the way. But in our dealings with objective nature we obviously are recorders, not makers, of the truth; and decisions for the mere sake of deciding promptly and getting on to the next business would be wholly out of place. Throughout the breadth of physical nature facts are what they are quite independently of us, and seldom is there any such hurry about them that the risks of being duped by believing a premature theory need be faced. The questions here are always trivial options, the hypotheses are hardly living (at any rate not living for us spectators), the choice between believing truth or falsehood is seldom forced. The attitude of sceptical balance is therefore the absolutely wise one if we would escape mistakes. . .

[But] are there not somewhere forced options in our speculative questions, and can we (as men who may be interested at least as much in positively gaining truth as in merely escaping dupery) always wait with impunity till the coercive evidence shall have arrived? . . .

Moral questions immediately present themselves as questions whose solution cannot wait for sensible proof. A moral question is a question not of what sensibly exists, but of what is good, or would be good if it did exist. Science can tell us what exists; but to compare the *worths,* both of what exists and of what does not exist, we must consult not science, but what Pascal calls our heart. Science herself consults her heart when she lays it down that the infinite ascertainment of fact and correction of false belief are the supreme goods for man. Challenge the statement and science can only repeat it oracularly, or else prove it by showing that such ascertainment and correction bring man all sorts of other goods which man's heart in turn declares. The question of hav-

ing moral beliefs at all or not having them is decided by our will. Are our moral preferences true or false, or are they only odd biological phenomena, making things good or bad for *us,* but in themselves indifferent? How can your pure intellect decide? If your heart does not *want* a world of moral reality, your head will assuredly never make you believe in one. . . .

Turn now from these wide questions of good to a certain class of questions of fact, questions concerning personal relations, states of mind between one man and another. *Do you like me or not?*—for example. Whether you do or not depends, in countless instances, on whether I meet you half-way, am willing to assume that you must like me, and show you trust and expectation. The previous faith on my part in your liking's existence is in such cases what makes your liking come. But if I stand aloof, and refuse to budge an inch until I have objective evidence, . . . ten to one your liking never comes. How many women's hearts are vanquished by the mere sanguine insistence of some man that they *must* love him! he will not consent to the hypothesis that they cannot. The desire for a certain kind of truth here brings about that special truth's existence; and so it is in innumerable cases of other sorts. Who gains promotions, boons, appointments, but the man in whose life they are seen to play the part of live hypotheses, who discounts them, sacrifices other things for their sake before they have come, and takes risks for them in advance? His faith acts on the powers above him as a claim, and creates its own verification.

A social organism of any sort whatever, large or small, is what it is because each member proceeds to his own duty with a trust that the other members will simultaneously do theirs. Wherever a desired result is achieved by the co-operation of many independent persons, its existence as a fact is a pure consequence of the precursive faith in one another of those immediately concerned. A government, an army, a commercial system, a ship, a college, an athletic team, all exist on this condition, without which not only is nothing achieved, but nothing is even attempted. A whole train of passengers (individually brave enough) will be looted by a few highwaymen, simply because the latter can count on one another, while each passenger fears that if he makes a movement of resistance, he will be shot before anyone else backs him up. If we believed that the whole car-full would rise at once with us, we should each severally rise, and train-robbing would never even be attempted. There are, then, cases where a fact cannot come at all unless a preliminary faith exists in its coming. *And where faith in a fact can help create the fact,* that would be an insane logic which should say that faith running ahead of scientific evidence is the "lowest kind of immorality" into which a thinking being can fall. Yet such is the logic by which our scientific absolutists pretend to regulate our lives!

In truths dependent on our personal action, then, faith based on desire is certainly a lawful and possibly an indispensable thing.

But now, it will be said, these are all childish human cases, and have nothing to do with great cosmical matters, like the question of religious faith. Let us then pass on to that. Religions differ so much in their accidents that in discussing the religious question we must make it very generic and broad. What then do we now mean by the religious hypothesis? Science says things are; morality says some things are better than other things; and religion says essentially two things.

First, she says that the best things are the most eternal things, the overlapping things, the things in the universe that throw the last stone, so to speak, and say the final word. "Perfection is eternal"—this phrase of Charles Secrétan seems a good way of putting this first affirmation of religion, an affirmation which obviously cannot yet be verified scientifically at all.

The second affirmation of religion is that we are better off even now if we believe her first affirmation to be true.

Now let us consider what the logical elements of this situation are *in case the religious hypothesis in both its branches be really true.* (Of course, we must admit that possibility at the outset. If we are to discuss the question at all, it must involve a living option. If for any of you religion be a hypothesis that cannot, by any living possibility be true, then you need go no farther. I speak to the "sav-

ing remnant" alone.) So proceeding, we see, first, that religion offers itself as a *momentous* option. We are supposed to gain, even now, by our belief, and to lose by our non-belief, a certain vital good. Secondly, religion is a *forced* option, so far as that good goes. We cannot escape the issue by remaining sceptical and waiting for more light, because, although we do avoid error in that way *if religion be untrue,* we lose the good, *if it be true,* just as certainly as if we positively chose to disbelieve. It is as if a man should hesitate indefinitely to ask a certain woman to marry him because he was not perfectly sure that she would prove an angel after he brought her home. Would he not cut himself off from that particular angel-possibility as decisively as if he went and married someone else? Scepticism, then, is not avoidance of option; it is option of a certain particular kind of risk. *Better risk loss of truth than chance of error*—that is your faith-vetoer's exact position. He is actively playing his stake as much as the believer is; he is backing the field against the religious hypothesis, just as the believer is backing the religious hypothesis against the field. To preach scepticism to us as a duty until "sufficient evidence" for religion be found, is tantamount therefore to telling us, when in presence of the religious hypothesis, that to yield to our fear of its being error is wiser and better than to yield to our hope that it may be true. It is not intellect against all passions, then; it is only intellect with one passion laying down its law. And by what, forsooth, is the supreme wisdom of this passion warranted? Dupery for dupery, what proof is there that dupery through hope is so much worse than dupery through fear? I, for one, can see no proof; and I simply refuse obedience to the scientist's command to imitate his kind of option, in a case where my own stake is important enough to give me the right to choose my own form of risk. If religion be true and the evidence for it be still insufficient, I do not wish, by putting your extinguisher upon my nature (which feels to me as if it had after all some business in this matter), to forfeit my sole chance in life of getting upon the winning side—that chance depending, of course, on my willingness to run the risk of acting as if my passional need of taking the world religiously might be prophetic and right.

All this is on the supposition that it really may be prophetic and right, and that, even to us who are discussing the matter, religion is a live hypothesis which may be true. Now to most of us religion comes in a still farther way that makes a veto on our active faith even more illogical. The more perfect and more eternal aspect of the universe is represented in our religions as having personal form. The universe is no longer a mere *It* to us, but a *Thou,* if we are religious; and any relation that may be possible from person to person might be possible here. For instance, although in one sense we are passive portions of the universe, in another we show a curious autonomy, as if we were small active centres on our own account. We feel, too, as if the appeal of religion to us were made to our own active goodwill, as if evidence might be forever withheld from us unless we met the hypothesis half-way. To take a trivial illustration: just as a man who in a company of gentlemen made no advances, asked a warrant for every concession, and believed no one's word without proof, would cut himself off by such churlishness from all the social rewards that a more trusting spirit would earn—so here, one who should shut himself up in snarling logicality and try to make the gods extort his recognition willy-nilly, or not get it at all, might cut himself off forever from his only opportunity of making the gods' acquaintance. This feeling, forced on us we know not whence, that by obstinately believing that there are gods (although not to do so would be so easy both for our logic and our life) we are doing the universe the deepest service we can, seems part of the living essence of the religious hypothesis. If the hypothesis *were* true in all its parts, including this one, then pure intellectualism, with its veto on our making willing advances, would be an absurdity; and some participation of our sympathetic nature would be logically required. I, therefore, for one, cannot see my way to accepting the agnostic rules for truth-seeking, or wilfully agree to keep my willing nature out of the game. I cannot do so for this plain reason, that *a rule of thinking which would absolutely prevent me from acknowledging certain kinds of truth if those kinds of truth were really there, would be an irrational rule.* That for me is the long and short of the formal logic of the situation, no matter what the kinds of truth might materially be.

I confess I do not see how this logic can be escaped. But sad experience makes me fear that some of you may still shrink from radically saying with me, *in abstracto,* that we have the right to believe at our own risk any hypothesis that is live enough to tempt our will. I suspect, however, that if this is so, it is because you have got away from the abstract logical point of view altogether, and are thinking (perhaps without realizing it) of some particular religious hypothesis which for you is dead. The freedom to "believe what we will" you apply to the case of some patent superstition; and the faith you think of is the faith defined by the schoolboy when he said, "Faith is when you believe something that you know ain't true." I can only repeat that this is misapprehension. *In concreto,* the freedom to believe can only cover living options which the intellect of the individual cannot by itself resolve; and living options never seem absurdities to him who has them to consider. When I look at the religious question as it really puts itself to concrete men, and when I think of all the possibilities which both practically and theoretically it involves, then this command that we shall put a stopper on our heart, instincts and courage, and *wait*—acting of course meanwhile more or less as if religion were *not* true—till doomsday, or till such time as our intellect and senses working together may have raked in evidence enough—this command, I say, seems to me the queerest idol ever manufactured in the philosophic cave. Were we scholastic absolutists, there might be more excuse. If we had an infallible intellect with its objective certitudes, we might feel ourselves disloyal to such a perfect organ of knowledge in not trusting to it exclusively, in not waiting for its releasing word. But if we are empiricists, if we believe that no bell in us tolls to let us know for certain when truth is in our grasp, then it seems a piece of idle fantasticality to preach so solemnly our duty of waiting for the bell. Indeed we *may* wait if we will—I hope you do not think that I am denying that—but if we do so, we do so at our peril as much as if we believed. In either case we *act,* taking our life in our hands. No one of us ought to issue vetoes to the other, nor should we bandy words of abuse. We ought, on the contrary, delicately and profoundly to respect one another's mental freedom—then only shall we bring about the intellectual republic; then only shall we have that spirit of inner tolerance without which all our outer tolerance is soulless, and which is empiricism's glory; then only shall we live and let live, in speculative as well as in practical things. . . .

Suggestions for Further Reading

A good overview of the positions can be found in *The Ethics of Belief Debate,* edited by Gerald D. McCarthy (Atlanta: Scholars Press, 1986).

Nicholas Wolterstorff has written a careful study, *John Locke and the Ethics of Belief* (Cambridge: Cambridge University Press, 1996), which explores some of the issues long before Clifford and James entered the debate.

A summary of James's argument can be found in Volume 4 of *World Philosophy* (Englewood Cliffs, NJ: Salem Press, 1982) along with a good bibliography.

Also see *The Works of William James: The Will to Believe and Other Essays in Popular Philosophy,* edited by Frederick H. Burkhardt et al. (Cambridge, MA: Harvard University Press, 1979), for a scholarly discussion of the history of the text as well as an interpretation.

See Part 4 of *William James's Radical Reconstruction of Philosophy* by Charlene Haddock Seigfried (Albany: State University of New York Press, 1990) for a discussion of knowledge and truth in James's version of pragmatism.

Also, Chapters 5 and 6 of Ellen Kappy Suckiel's *The Pragmatic Philosophy of William James* (Notre Dame, IN: University of Notre Dame Press, 1982) will be helpful in unpacking the will-to-believe argument and the pragmatic theory of truth.

For contemporay accounts of the coherence and correspondence theories of truth see *Real Knowing: New Versions of the Coherence Theory* by Linda Martin Alcoff (Ithaca, NY: Cornell University Press, 1996) and *A Realist Conception of Truth* by William P. Alston (Ithaca, NY: Cornell University Press, 1996).

Videos

Lecture 3: "James' Pragmatism," from Part 5 of *The Great Minds of the Western Intellectual Tradition,* provides a summary and is available from The Teaching Company, 7405 Alban Station Court, Suite A107, Springfield, VA 22150.

For a broader background, see *The American Pragmatists: C. S. Peirce, William James, John Dewey* (45 minutes). Available from Films for the Humanities and Sciences at www.film.com.

7.6 Classical Indian Epistemology

Some people think of Indian philosophy as "spiritual" and unconcerned with technical issues relating to truth and knowledge. Popular culture associates India with mysticism, meditation, and religion. Students often study about India in religious studies courses but seldom in philosophy classes.

This picture of Indian thought as spiritual is misleading. Among the various schools of Indian philosophy, careful attention is given to logical and epistemological issues. For example, Udayana, an Indian philosopher who lived about 1000, combined two previous schools of philosophy, the Vaisesika and the **Nyaya** ("nyah-yah") schools, into what is usually called **Naiyayika**. This philosophic school advanced an epistemological theory (first developed in Nyaya philosophy) that influenced much of Indian philosophy. According to this theory, the correct causes of knowledge (called ***pramanas***) can be analyzed into four kinds: perception, inference, comparison (analogy), and reliable testimony.

Perceptual knowledge arises from the contact of the senses (eye, ear, nose, etc.) with an object external to the senses, and such contact correctly represents the way the object is. *Inferential knowledge* arises from the inference from a bit of perceptual knowledge (I see smoke) to a correct conclusion concerning what is not immediately seen (there is a fire). *Analogical knowledge* derives from drawing a correct conclusion about an unknown object from the similarities between it and a known object. *Testimonial knowledge* occurs when the person telling you something is honest and reliable, knows what she or he is talking about, and you understand correctly what is said.

Naiyayika philosophers were very much concerned with epistemological issues. They viewed knowledge as a relation between self (subject) and nonself (object). Knowledge, they claimed, is like the light of a lamp that reveals objects. The light is not the object nor the subject, but it makes it possible for an object to be seen by a subject.

Other schools of Indian philosophy also developed epistemological theories. For example, Advaita Vedanta (see Section 9.4 for more information) argued that we do perceive the absence of things. If the Naiyayika theory is correct that perception is dependent upon the contact of the sense organs with an object, then when an object is absent, we can never correctly know this. However, we do perceive, and correctly perceive, things as absent. Hence the Advaitins added nonperception or the perception of the absence of something to the list of *pranamas.*

There were debates, however, not just about the causes of knowledge, but about the nature of knowledge (***prama***) itself. What are the marks of knowledge? If you had to state the characteristics that differentiate knowledge from opinion, what might you say?

In the next selection, D. M Datta (1916–   ), former professor of philosophy at Patna University, discusses some of the controversies in classical Indian philosophy surrounding the question of the marks of knowledge. He compares some of this debate to Western theories of truth (see the previous section) and shows you how complicated these debates can become as one question leads to an answer that in turn produces another question.

Reading Project

1. Write a critical précis (see Section 2.2) on Datta's essay on Indian views of knowledge.
2. If you had difficulty writing your précis, try to figure out the source of your difficulty.

Knowledge and the Methods of Knowledge

D. M. DATTA

THE SANSKRIT WORD JÑĀNA stands for all kinds of cognition irrespective of the question of truth and falsehood. But the word pramā is used to designate only a true cognition . . . as distinct from a false one. . . . In English the word knowledge implies a cognition attended with belief. If, therefore, a cognition turns out to be false, belief in it is immediately withdrawn and as such it should cease to be called knowledge. Consequently knowledge, strictly speaking, should always stand only for a cognition that is true, uncontradicted or unfalsified. The ordinary division of knowledge into true knowledge and false knowledge should, therefore, be considered as an instance of loose thinking; the word true as applied to knowledge would then be a tautology, and the word false positively contradictory—false knowledge being only a name for falsified knowledge, which is another name for no knowledge.

If this logical meaning of the word knowledge be consistently and rigidly adhered to, knowledge will exactly correspond to the word pramā. Pramā is generally defined as a cognition having the twofold characteristics of truth and novelty. . . .

As regards the first characteristic, truth, all schools of Indian philosophy are unanimous. Every philosopher holds that truth should be the differentia of knowledge or pramā. But views as regards the meaning of truth vary, and consequently the mark of a pramā is variously expressed. Broadly speaking there are at least four different views about truth.

According to one view the truth of knowledge consists in its practical value. A true cognition is, therefore, variously defined as that which reveals an object that serves some purpose . . . or leads to the achievement of some end, or which favours a successful volition. . . . This view will at once be seen to resemble the modern pragmatic theory of the West. It is mostly held by the Buddhists, but other writers also occasionally support it.

Another view, that we find chiefly in the Nyāya works, regards truth as the faithfulness with which knowledge reveals its object. True knowledge is, therefore, defined as that which informs us of the existence of something in a place where it really exists, or which predicates of something a character really possessed by it. This view resembles the correspondence theory of Western realists.

A third view, which is incidentally referred to by many writers, regards truth as a harmony of experience. . . . A true knowledge, according to this view, would be one which is in harmony with other experiences. This view again resembles the Western theory of coherence.

The Advaita school of Vedānta, however, favours a fourth view according to which the truth of knowledge consists in its non-contradictedness. . . . The correspondence view of truth cannot directly prove itself. The only way to prove correspondence is to fall back on the foreign method of consilience or coherence . . . —that is to infer the existence of a real correspondence between knowledge and reality from the facts of the harmony of experience. But all that we can legitimately infer from the harmony of knowledge with the rest of our experience up to that time, is not that the knowledge is absolutely free from error, but that it is not yet contradicted. For we do not know that we shall not have in future any experience that can falsify our present knowledge. As regards the pragmatic test of causal efficiency . . . the Advaitins argue that even a false cognition may, and sometimes does, lead to the fulfilment of a purpose. One of the examples they cite to support their view is the case of a distant bright jewel which emits

From D. M. Datta, The Six Ways of Knowing: A Critical Study of the Vedanta Theory of Knowledge, *revised edition, Calcutta: University of Calcutta, 1960, pp. 19–28. Footnotes omitted.*

lustre. We mistake the lustre for the jewel and, desiring to get the mistaken object of our knowledge, approach it and actually get the jewel. In this case, therefore, the knowledge of lustre as the jewel—which is clearly a false cognition—leads to the attainment of the jewel and thereby satisfies our purpose, though eventually we come also to know that the initial cognition which caused our action was itself false. We can multiply instances of this kind. The hypothesis that the earth is stationary and the sun is moving has been working quite satisfactorily for ages; on the basis of this cognition many of our actions are performed and purposes attained. It is only its conflict with astronomical phenomena that enables us to detect its falsity.

It is found, therefore, that the pragmatic view of truth is not tenable. The correspondence view has ultimately to fall back on the consilience or coherence theory which, when subjected to strict scrutiny, has to yield the result that truth, as ascertained by it, consists only in its noncontradictedness.

According to the Advaitins, therefore, pramā or knowledge must have as one of its characteristics truth; and the truth of pramā consists in its content being uncontradicted. . . .

The second characteristic of pramā or knowledge is, as we have already said, novelty. It is not sufficient that knowledge should be true, it is also necessary that the content of knowledge should be new or previously unacquired—anadhigata. On this point, however, not all authorities are unanimous; while some . . . consider it to be an essential part of the differentia of knowledge, others think it unnecessary as unduly narrowing the scope of knowledge. The Vedāntists seem to be rather indifferent to this controversy and unwilling to take sides. The material part of the controversy turns upon the question whether memory should be admitted to have the status of knowledge. If truth be the sole characteristic of knowledge, memory, in so far as it is uncontradicted or undoubted, has to be called knowledge. But there is a peculiarity about memory that deserves special consideration. The only claim of memory to belief lies in its explicit reference to a past experience which it professes to reproduce faithfully. A remembered fact is believed to be true just because it is regarded as identical with the content of a past experience which it claims to represent. This confessed and explicit falling back on the past experience means its self-abdication in favour of its archetype. Thus the question of treating memory as a distinct type of knowledge does not at all arise, being barred *ex hypothesi*. The only kind of knowledge is then the knowledge of the already unacquired. But though memory is not a distinct source of knowledge, it is still a distinct experience that has to be distinguished from knowledge and given a separate name. The experience which reveals the new (i.e. knowledge proper) is called anubhūti, whereas reproduced knowledge is called smṛti. Thus novelty comes to be considered an essential quality of knowledge.

If this be the conception of knowledge (pramā), the question then arises whether in the case of a persistent knowledge of the same object, our experience at every moment during that time can be regarded as knowledge. When I keep looking at a table for some moments continuously, my experience of the first moment, as an acquisition of the "new," is of course to be called knowledge. But what about the experiences of the subsequent moments? Can they also be rightly called knowledge, seeing that they only reveal to me what has been already acquired at the first moment and lack thereby the quality of novelty?

This question is answered in the affirmative by all schools of thinkers. But different reasons are assigned in justification of this answer.

Some say that in a persistent knowledge . . . say of a table, the object is not the same at different moments, as it is ordinarily supposed to be. For even if we grant that the same table persists without any spatial change for a certain period, yet the inevitable temporal change has to be taken into consideration. In other words the table, the object of our knowledge, is determined both spatially and temporally to our consciousness. By perceiving its spatial properties we judge it to be big or small, high or low. Similarly by perceiving its temporal property we judge it to be "present." Without perceiving this time-quality it would be difficult for us to distinguish present knowledge of a table, or its perception, from the past knowledge of a table or its memory. So the table as determined by the first moment of the persistent knowledge is not the same as that determined by the second moment. Every moment we have the knowledge of an object that is different from the object of the previous moment and is, therefore, as good as a new object. The definition of knowledge (pramā), therefore, applies to the case of a persistent cognition as well, the quality of novelty being present also in that case.

This reply is regarded by others as unsatisfactory. These thinkers, while admitting that the time-quality of a percept is also directly perceived, hold that in a persistent perception the different moments, which are infinitely small, are never perceived as such. What we perceive as "present" is not an atomic point of time but a finite span of time. So it is difficult to say that in a persistent perception the time-quality of the object is perceived as new at every moment. The atomic moments are obtained not perceptually, but logically, i.e. by a continuous conceptual analysis of the perceived span. Knowledge remains, therefore, the same during the moments composing this finite span of time, and consequently at each one of these moments, except the first, there is only a repetition of the old knowledge obtained at the first moment.

The disqualification that is pressed against memory is, therefore, equally present in the case of a persistent cognition, and the difficulty in including the latter in the definition of knowledge (pramā), while excluding the former, remains as great as before.

The solution of the difficulty, however, lies in understanding the exact sense of "novelty" . . . as present in the case of knowledge and absent in the case of memory. In memory novelty is said to be absent, in the sense that memory is wholly a reproduction of a past knowledge; it is solely caused by the impression of a past experience. . . . In a persistent knowledge the knowledge of the second moment is not a reproduction of the knowledge of the previous moment; it is caused not by the impression of the previous experience, but by the very objective conditions which cause the first knowledge. So while memory by its very nature falls back on a past experience, and entirely rests thereon for its validity, the knowledge at subsequent moments of a persistent cognition stands by its own right and makes a demand for its independent validity. It is in this important respect that memory has to be distinguished from a persistent cognition, and it is in virtue of this very important distinction that the one has to be excluded from the definition of knowledge and the other has to be included therein. This is the Nyāya solution of the problem.

The Advaitins however hold that in their theory of knowledge, such a problem or difficulty does not at all arise; no defence or explanation, therefore, is necessary. According to them, knowledge persists so long as fresh knowledge does not come to replace it. Whether knowledge changes or remains the same can only be ascertained by determining whether the logical activity of the self, i.e. the judgment affirming the knowledge ("The pot is" or "The pot is perceived"), changes or remains the same.

This problem assumes that in persistent cognition there is separate knowledge at every moment (during the time of persistence), while the content or object of these distinct elements of knowledge is the same, and therefore at every subsequent moment there is only a repetition or reproduction of the knowledge of the first moment. But this assumption is wrong. For if the object of the so-called different elements of knowledge be judged to be identical, they are themselves indistinguishable from each other, i.e. they are but one identical process of knowledge. Thus the question of repetition or reproduction does not arise at all.

This question and the Vedāntin's answer require the consideration of the fundamental problem how one perception is to be distinguished from another. One way of distinguishing one perception from another is, of course, the ascertaining of a distinction between their respective objects. This would mean that the characteristic that distinguishes one perception from another must remain in the object of that knowledge, i.e. the distinguishing characteristic must itself become the object of that very perception. But is this the sole way of distinguishing one perception from another? The Vedāntins say "yes." But those who raise the original question seem to think that there may be some other way of making a distinction; as, for example, by the distinction of their times of happening. In such a case the time characteristic may not have been originally known as an element qualifying the object of the knowledge. At a subsequent time we may infer that as the knowledge persisted for a length of time which was composed of so many different moments, the knowledge of the first moment must differ from the knowledge of the second moment, since the two pieces of knowledge possess two distinct qualifications (viz. "of the first moment" and "of the second moment"). This would be distinguishing knowledge by an external adjective, while the former case consisted in distinguishing knowledge by an essential or internal quality. But it should be noted that a mere distinction based on an external mark does not argue separateness in existence. Edward VII as the King of England can be, for certain purposes, distinguished from Edward VII as the Emperor of India, or the father of George V; but this does not mean that the three as distinguishable must also be separate. Similarly the knowledge of the first moment, though in language or thought distinguishable from the knowledge of the second moment, is not necessarily separate from the second. In order that time-quality may serve as the basis of an inference as to the separateness of one knowledge from another, that quality must enter the knowledge itself as characterising its object. The perception of the table "now" is known to be different or separate from the perception of the table I had an hour ago, from the fact that the "presence" and "pastness" characterize respectively the object of the present perception and that of the past perception. In such a case the second perception contains a novelty (in virtue of its time-quality, viz. "presence") and is, therefore, a full-fledged knowledge.

To return to the original discussion, then, we find that even if "novelty" be regarded as an essential characteristic of knowledge, any real case of knowledge, such as persistent perception, or repeated perception, is not excluded from the definition of knowledge. A pramā or knowledge, therefore, can be accurately regarded as a cognition the object of which is neither contradicted nor already known as an object. . . .

The special source of a particular pramā or knowledge is called pramāna. Pramāna is defined as the karaṇa of a pramā. A karaṇa is conceived as the *unique* or special cause through the *action* of which a particular effect is produced. In the case of perceptual knowledge or pratyakṣa pramā, for example, a sense-organ (in the case of an external perception) or the mind (in the case of an internal perception) is said to be the karaṇa or instrumental cause. There are many causes, e.g. the mind, the sense-organ, etc., the existence of which is necessary for the production of perceptual knowledge of an external object. But of these, the mind is a cause the existence of which is common to all sorts of knowledge, perceptual and inferential; so it cannot be regarded as a special cause. The special cause here is the particular sense-organ involved in that perception, because it is not common to other kinds of knowledge; it is peculiar to external perception alone.

A cause, to be called a karaṇa, must not be merely unique . . . it must also possess some active function. . . . The contact of the sense-organ with its object is undeniably a cause (kāraṇa) of perception. It is also unique; the instrumentality of sense-contact is present in perception alone. But still it is not called the karaṇa of perception, because it is itself a function or action of the sense-organ and as such does not possess a further function. . . .

A pramāna is, then, such an active and unique cause (kāraṇa) of a pramā or knowledge.

Suggestions for Further Reading

For an overview and summary of philosophy in India in a single chapter, see Chapter 2 of Ninian Smart's *World Philosophies* (London: Routledge, 1999).

A classic and influential discussion of Nyaya is S. C. Chatterjee's *The Nyaya Theory of Knowledge* (Calcutta: University of Calcutta Press, 1950).

See John Koller's chapter on "Knowledge and Reality: Nyaya-Vaisheshika" in *Oriental Philosophies* (New York: Scribner, 1985) for an introductory account.

More complex, but also helpful is J. N. Mohanty's *Classical Indian Philosophy* (Lanham, MD: Rowman and Littlefield, 2000).

Karl H. Potter's *Presuppositions of India's Philosophies* (Englewood Cliffs, NJ: Prentice-Hall, 1963) provides a helpful and detailed analysis.

7.7 Afrocentric Feminist Epistemology

Is knowledge universal? If we know what it means to know something in one culture, do we know what it means in all cultures? Who is the subject of knowledge? Who is the knower? Is knowing the knower at all relevant to knowing what knowledge is or whether it is possible? How does the social position of the knower make an impact on the production and transmission of knowledge? Is all knowledge expressible in the form of propositions? Is knowledge the result of the exercise of social power?

These questions are not easy to answer, and even to raise them is somewhat unsettling because they introduce political and social questions into philosophic reflection on the nature and possibility of knowledge. Feminist epistemology, however, has not shied away from asking such questions or from interjecting moral and political considerations into the epistemological project.

Feminist epistemology began as a critique of existing theories of knowledge (for one example see Cole's critique of Descartes in Section 11.3). This critique revealed and continues to reveal how large a role gender has played in supposedly universal and objective theories of knowledge. Genevieve Lloyd (1984) documents how rationality has been associated with males and with masculine qualities in the development of Western philosophy. Men, supposedly, are rational whereas women are emotional. Thus, not only are women excluded from the sacred halls of knowers, but also an unwarranted division is created between knowledge and emotion.

Janice Moulton (1983) argues that philosophy has relied heavily on the *adversary paradigm*. This model pictures rational activity aimed at producing knowledge as one of an opponent defending a belief against an attacker. According to this model, the best way to arrive at the truth is to subject our beliefs to the strongest possible objections.

Undoubtedly, there are advantages to this method, especially in courts of law, but it has severe limitations if it is transposed into a universal model of knowledge-production. Not only is it tainted with sexism insofar as it assumes that aggressive (male-type) thinking is the best thinking, but also the adversary paradigm leads to bad reasoning. By restricting reasoning to an adversarial situation, we ignore the sorts of reasoning that might be appropriate in different situations, such as figuring something out for oneself, exploring a topic among like-minded people, or trying to show how two apparently opposed positions might be in harmony.

It is not enough, however, to unmask the ways traditional theories of knowledge have been tainted by male bias. We must go on, feminist philosophers maintain, to find new frameworks for thinking about problems relating to knowledge. So some feminists argue that a "standpoint" epistemology that frankly acknowledges that all knowing substantially involves the social and historical context of the knowers is a better place to begin our philosophical reflection on the possibility of knowledge. Others point out how the community—as the place where knowledge is generated, stored, and communicated—has been neglected in favor of the traditional views that the "isolated individual" is the epistemic agent. Still others call for a recognition of the significant role that emotions play in the production of knowledge. One thing that all the diverse feminist views on knowledge have in common is the conviction that philosophical reflection on the nature and possibility of knowledge must begin with and remain rooted in the experience of women.

However, in the search for a new starting point, one which recognizes the importance of the experience of women for doing epistemology, many women have come to see that they cannot presume to speak for all women. If concrete human experiences of coming to know must be the starting point, if feminist theories are to be constructed from the bottom up rather than from the top down, then the experiences of white, middle-class, educated, elite women can no more be used to create a "universal" theory of knowledge than the experiences of white, middle-class, educated, elite males can be.

Patricia Hill Collins, author of our next selection and a professor of Afro-American studies at the University of Cincinnati, is a sociologist. Hence, she approaches the question of knowledge from a perspective often referred to as the "sociology of knowledge." Whereas many philosophers have ignored the social conditions of knowledge-production and validation, sociologists of knowledge argue that these social conditions are essential. Philosophers have sought some sort of "pure" theory—some universal and objective picture of the knowing process untainted by the everyday and peculiar experiences of socially and historically situated people. Sociologists want to know the role that class, race, and gender play in the process of coming to know.

Dr. Collins is a sociologist, but she is also an *African-American woman* doing sociology. Hence, she cannot ignore her own experiences, both as a woman and as a black. The result is a fascinating and provocative inquiry into the dimensions of an Afrocentric feminist epistemology.

Reading Questions

1. What is one key epistemological concern facing black female intellectuals?
2. What is wrong with the "Eurocentric, masculinist knowledge validation process" according to Collins?
3. What are, according to Collins, the dimensions of an Afrocentric feminist epistemology?
4. Are the arguments Collins presents adequate to support her claims? Why, or why not?
5. How do you think Collins would answer the question, "Is knowledge possible?"

Toward an Afrocentric Feminist Epistemology

PATRICIA HILL COLLINS

EPISTEMOLOGY IS THE STUDY of the philosophical problems in concepts of knowledge and truth. The techniques I use in this volume to rearticulate a Black women's standpoint and to further Black feminist thought may appear to violate some of the basic epistemological assumptions of my training as a social scientist. In choosing the core themes in Black feminist thought that merited investigation, I consulted established bodies of academic research. But I also searched my own experiences and those of African-American women I know for themes we thought were important. My use of language signals a different relationship to my material than that which currently prevails in social science literature. For example, I often use the pronoun "our" instead of "their" when referring to African-American women, a choice that embeds me in the group I am studying instead of distancing me from it. In addition, I occasionally place my own concrete experiences in the text. To support my analysis, I cite few statistics and instead rely on the voices of Black women from all walks of life. These conscious epistemological choices signal my attempts not only to explore the thematic content of Black feminist thought but to do so in a way that does not violate its basic epistemological framework.

One key epistemological concern facing Black women intellectuals is the question of what constitutes adequate justifications that a given knowledge claim, such as a fact or theory, is true. In producing the specialized knowledge of Black feminist thought, Black women intellectuals often encounter two distinct epistemologies: one representing elite white male interests and the other expressing Afrocentric feminist concerns. Epistemological choices about who to trust, what to believe, and why something is true are not benign academic issues. Instead, these concerns tap

the fundamental question of which versions of truth will prevail and shape thought and action.

The Eurocentric, Masculinist Knowledge Validation Process

Institutions, paradigms, and other elements of the knowledge validation procedure controlled by elite white men constitute the Eurocentric masculinist knowledge validation process. The purpose of this process is to represent a white male standpoint. Although it reflects powerful white males' interest, various dimensions of the process are not necessarily managed by white men themselves. Scholars, publishers, and other experts represent specific interests and credentialing processes, and their knowledge claims must satisfy the political and epistemological criteria of the contexts in which they reside.

Two political criteria influence the knowledge validation process. First, knowledge claims are evaluated by a community of experts whose members represent the standpoints of the groups from which they originate. Within the Eurocentric masculinist process this means that a scholar making a knowledge claim must convince a scholarly community controlled by white men that a given claim is justified. Second, each community of experts must maintain its credibility as defined by the larger group in which it is situated and from which it draws its basic, taken-for-granted knowledge. This means that scholarly communities that challenge basic beliefs held in the culture at large will be deemed less credible than those which support popular perspectives.

When white men control the knowledge validation process, both political criteria can work to suppress Black feminist thought. Given that the general culture shaping the taken-for-granted

Reprinted from Black Feminist Thought: Knowledge, Consciousness, and the Politics of Empowerment, *by Patricia Hill Collins (1990) by permission of the publisher, Routledge: New York and London. Footnotes and references deleted.*

knowledge of the community of experts is permeated by widespread notions of Black and female inferiority, new knowledge claims that seem to violate these fundamental assumptions are likely to be viewed as anomalies. Moreover, specialized thought challenging notions of Black and female inferiority is unlikely to be generated from within a white-male-controlled academic community because both the kinds of questions that could be asked and the explanations that would be found satisfying would necessarily reflect a basic lack of familiarity with Black women's reality.

The experiences of African-American women scholars illustrate how individuals who wish to rearticulate a Black women's standpoint through Black feminist thought can be suppressed by a white-male-controlled knowledge validation process. Exclusion from basic literacy, quality educational experiences, and faculty and administrative positions has limited Black women's access to influential academic positions. While Black women can produce knowledge claims that contest those advanced by the white male community, this community does not grant that Black women scholars have competing knowledge claims based in another knowledge validation process. As a consequence, any credentials controlled by white male academicians can be denied to Black women producing Black feminist thought on the grounds that it is not credible research. . . .

African-American women academicians who persist in trying to rearticulate a Black women's standpoint also face potential rejection of our knowledge claims on epistemological grounds. Just as the material realities of the powerful and the dominated produce separate standpoints, each group may also have distinctive epistemologies or theories of knowledge. Black women scholars may know that something is true but be unwilling or unable to legitimate our claims using Eurocentric, masculinist criteria for consistency with substantial knowledge and criteria for methodological adequacy. For any body of knowledge, new knowledge claims must be consistent with an existing body of knowledge that the group controlling the interpretive context

accepts as true. The methods used to validate knowledge claims must also be acceptable to the group controlling the knowledge validation process.

The criteria for the methodological adequacy of positivism illustrate the epistemological standards that Black women scholars would have to satisfy in legitimating Black feminist thought using a Eurocentric masculinist epistemology. While I describe Eurocentric masculinist approaches as a single process, many schools of thought or paradigms are subsumed under this one process. Moreover, my focus on positivism should be interpreted neither to mean that all dimensions of positivism are inherently problematic for Black women nor that nonpositivist frameworks are better. For example, most traditional frameworks that women of color internationally regard as oppressive to women are not positivist, and Eurocentric feminist critiques of positivism may have less political importance for women of color, especially those in traditional societies than they have for white feminists.

Positivist approaches aim to create scientific descriptions of reality by producing objective generalizations. Because researchers have widely differing values, experiences, and emotions, genuine science is thought to be unattainable unless all human characteristics except rationality are eliminated from the research process. By following strict methodological rules, scientists aim to distance themselves from the values, vested interests, and emotions generated by their class, race, sex, or unique situation. By decontextualizing themselves, they allegedly become detached observers and manipulators of nature. Moreover, this researcher decontextualization is paralleled by comparable efforts to remove the objects of study from their contexts. The result of this entire process is often the separation of information from meaning.

Several requirements typify positivist methodological approaches. First, research methods generally require a distancing of the researcher from her or his "object" of study by defining the researcher as a "subject" with full human subjectivity and by objectifying the "object" of study. A second requirement is the absence of emotions from the research process. Third, ethics and values are deemed inappropriate in the research process, either as the reason for scientific inquiry or as part of the research process itself. Finally, adversarial debates, whether written or oral, become the preferred method of ascertaining truth: the arguments that can withstand the greatest assault and survive intact become the strongest truths.

Such criteria ask African-American women to objectify ourselves, devalue our emotional life, displace our motivations for furthering knowledge about Black women, and confront in an adversarial relationship those with more social, economic and professional power. It therefore seems unlikely that Black women would use a positivist epistemological stance in rearticulating a Black women's standpoint. Black women are more likely to choose an alternative epistemology for assessing knowledge claims, one using different standards that are consistent with Black women's criteria for substantiated knowledge and with our criteria for methodological adequacy. If such an epistemology exists, what are its contours? Moreover, what is its role in the production of Black feminist thought?

The Contours of an Afrocentric Feminist Epistemology

Africanist analyses of the Black experience generally agree on the fundamental elements of an Afrocentric standpoint. Despite varying histories, Black societies reflect elements of a core African value system that existed prior to and independently of racial oppression. Moreover, as a result of colonialism, imperialism, slavery, apartheid, and other systems of racial domination, Black people share a common experience of oppression. These two factors foster shared Afrocentric values that permeate the family structure, religious institutions, culture, and community life of Blacks in varying parts of Africa, the Caribbean, South America, and North America. This Afrocentric consciousness permeates the shared history of people of African descent through the framework of a distinctive Afrocentric epistemology.

Feminist scholars advance a similar argument by asserting that women share a history of gender oppression, primarily through sex/gender hierarchies. These experiences transcend divisions among women created by race, social class, religion, sexual orientation, and ethnicity and form the basis of a women's standpoint with a corresponding feminist consciousness and epistemology.

Because Black women have access to both the Afrocentric and the feminist standpoints, an alternative epistemology used to rearticulate a Black women's standpoint should reflect elements of both traditions. The search for the distinguishing features of an alternative epistemology used by African-American women reveals that values and ideas Africanist sholars identify as characteristically "Black" often bear remarkable resemblance to similar ideas claimed by feminist scholars as characteristically "female." This similarity suggests that the material conditions of race, class, and gender oppression can vary dramatically and yet generate some uniformity in the epistemologies of subordinate groups. Thus the significance of an Afrocentric feminist epistemology may lie in how such an epistemology enriches our understanding of how subordinate groups create knowledge that fosters resistance. . . .

Like a Black women's standpoint, an Afrocentric feminist epistemology is rooted in the everyday experiences of African-American women. In spite of diversity that exists among women, what are the dimensions of an Afrocentric feminist epistemology?

Concrete Experience as a Criterion of Meaning

"My aunt used to say, 'A heap see, but a few know,'" remembers Carolyn Chase, a 31-year-old inner-city Black woman. This saying depicts two types of knowing—knowledge and wisdom—and taps the first dimension of an Afrocentric feminist epistemology. Living life as Black women requires wisdom because knowledge about the dynamics of race, gender, and class oppression has been essential to Black women's survival. African-American women give such wisdom high credence in assessing knowledge.

Allusions to these two types of knowing pervade the words of a range of African-American women. Zilpha Elaw, a preacher of the mid-1800s, explains the tenacity of racism: "The pride of a white skin is a bauble of great value with many in some parts of the United States, who readily sacrifice their intelligence to their prejudices, and possess more knowledge than wisdom." In describing differences separating African-American and white women, Nancy White invokes a similar rule: "When you come right down to it, white women just *think* they are free. Black women *know* they ain't free." Geneva Smitherman, a college professor specializing in African-American linguistics, suggests that "from a black perspective, written documents are limited in what they can teach about life and survival in the world. Blacks are quick to ridicule 'educated fools,' . . . they have 'book learning' but no 'mother wit,' knowledge, but not wisdom." Mabel Lincoln eloquently summarizes the distinction between knowledge and wisdom: "To black people like me, a fool is funny—you know, people who love to break bad, people you can't tell anything to, folks that would take a shotgun to a roach."

African-American women need wisdom to know how to deal with the "educated fools" who would "take a shotgun to a roach." As members of a subordinate group, Black women cannot afford to be fools of any type, for our objectification as the Other denies us the protections that white skin, maleness, and wealth confer. This distinction between knowledge and wisdom, and the use of experience as the cutting edge dividing them, has been key to Black women's survival. In the context of race, gender, and class oppression, the distinction is essential. Knowledge without wisdom is adequate for the powerful, but wisdom is essential to the survival of the subordinate. . . .

Experience as a criterion of meaning with practical images as its symbolic vehicles is a fundamental epistemological tenet in African-American thought systems. "Look at my arm!" Sojourner Truth proclaimed: "I have ploughed, and planted, and gathered into barns, and no man could head me! And ain't I a woman?" By invoking concrete practical images from her own life to symbolize new meanings, Truth deconstructed the prevailing notions of woman. Stories, narratives, and Bible principles are selected for their applicability to the lived experiences of African-Americans and become symbolic representations of a whole wealth of experience. Bible tales are often told for the wisdom they express about everyday life, so their interpretation involves no need for scientific historical verification. The narrative method requires that the story be told, not torn apart in analysis, and trusted as core belief, not "admired as science." . . .

Some feminist scholars offer a similar claim that women as a group are more likely than men to use concrete knowledge in assessing knowledge claims. For example, a substantial number of the 135 women in a study of women's cognitive development were "connected knowers" and were drawn to the sort of knowledge that emerges from first-hand observation. Such women felt that because knowledge comes from experience, the best way of understanding another person's ideas was to develop empathy and share the experiences that led the person to form those ideas.

In valuing the concrete, African-American women invoke not only an Afrocentric tradition but a women's tradition as well. Some feminist theorists suggest that women are socialized in complex relational nexuses where contextual rules versus abstract principles govern behavior. This socialization process is thought to stimulate characteristic ways of knowing. These theorists suggest that women are more likely to experience two modes of knowing: one located in the body and the space it occupies and the other passing beyond it. Through their child-rearing and nurturing activities, women mediate these two modes and use the concrete experiences of their daily lives to assess more abstract knowledge claims.

Although valuing the concrete may be more representative of women than men, social class differences among women may generate differential expression of this women's value. One study of working-class women's ways of knowing found that both white and African-American women rely on common sense and intuition. These forms of knowledge allow for subjectivity between the knower and the known, rest in the women themselves (not in higher authorities), and are experienced directly in the world (not through abstractions). . . .

In traditional African-American communities Black women find considerable institutional support for valuing concrete experience. Black women's centrality in families, churches, and other community organizations allows us to share our concrete knowledge of what it takes to be self-defined Black women with younger, less experienced sisters. "Sisterhood is not new to Black women," asserts Bonnie Thornton Dill, but "while Black women have fostered and encouraged sisterhood, we have not used it as the anvil to forge our political identities." Though not expressed in explicitly political terms, this relationship of sisterhood among Black women can be seen as a model for a whole series of relationships African-American women have with one another.

Given that Black churches and families are both woman-centered, Afrocentric institutions, African-American women traditionally have found considerable institutional support for this dimension of an Afrocentric feminist epistemology. While white women may value the concrete, it is questionable whether white families—particularly middle-class nuclear ones—and white community institutions provide comparable types of support. Similarly, while Black men are supported by Afrocentric institutions, they cannot participate in Black women's sisterhood. In terms of Black women's relationships with one another, African-American women may find it easier than others to recognize connectedness as a primary way of knowing, simply because we are encouraged to do so by a Black women's tradition of sisterhood.

The Use of Dialogue in Assessing Knowledge Claims

"Dialogue implies talk between two subjects, not the speech of subject and object. It is a humanizing speech, one that challenges and resists domination," asserts bell hooks. For Black women new knowledge claims are rarely worked out in isolation from other individuals and are usually developed through dialogues with other members of a community. A primary epistemological assumption underlying the use of dialogue in assessing knowledge claims is that connectedness rather than separation is an essential component of the knowledge validation process.

This belief in connectedness and the use of dialogue as one of its criteria for methodological adequacy has Afrocentric roots. In contrast to Western, either/or dichotomous thought, the traditional African worldview is holistic and seeks harmony. "One must understand that to become human, to realize the promise of becoming human, is the only important task of the person," posits Molefi Asante. People become more human and empowered only in the context of a community, and only when they "become seekers of the type of connections, interactions, and meetings that lead to harmony." The power of the word generally, and dialogues specifically, allows this to happen.

Not to be confused with adversarial debate, the use of dialogue has deep roots in an African-based oral tradition and in African-American culture. Ruth Shays describes the importance of dialogue in the knowledge validation process of enslaved African-Americans:

> They would find a lie if it took them a year. . . . The foreparents found the truth because they listened and they made people tell their part many times. Most often you can hear a lie. . . . Those old people was everywhere and knew the truth of many disputes. They believed that a liar should suffer the pain of his lies, and they had all kinds of ways of bringing liars to judgement.

The widespread use of the call-and-response discourse mode among African-Americans illustrates the importance placed on dialogue. Composed of spontaneous verbal and nonverbal interaction between speaker and listener in which all of the speaker's statements, or "calls," are punctuated by expressions, or "responses," from the listener, this Black discourse mode pervades African-American culture. The fundamental requirement of this interactive network is active participation of all individuals. For ideas to be tested and validated, everyone in the group must participate. To refuse to join in, especially if one really disagrees with what has been said, is seen as "cheating." . . .

Black women's centrality in families and community organizations provides African-American women with a high degree of support for invoking dialogue as a dimension of an Afrocentric feminist epistemology. However, when African-American women use dialogues in assessing knowledge claims, we might be invoking a particularly female way of knowing as well. Feminist scholars contend that men and women are socialized to seek different types of autonomy—the former based on separation, the latter seeking connectedness—and that this variation in types of autonomy parallels the characteristic differences between male and female ways of knowing. For instance, in contrast to the visual metaphors (such as equating knowledge with illumination, knowing with seeing, and truth with light) that scientists and philosophers typically use, women tend to ground their epistemological premises in metaphors suggesting finding a voice, speaking, and listening. The words of the Black woman who struggled for her education at Medgar Evers College resonate with the importance placed on voice: "I was basically a shy and reserved person prior to the struggle at Medgar, but I found my voice—and I used it! Now, I will never lose my voice again!"

While significant differences exist between Black women's family experiences and those of middle-class white women, African-American women clearly are affected by general cultural norms prescribing certain familial roles for women. Thus in terms of the role of dialogue in an Afrocentric feminist epistemology, Black women may again experience a convergence of the values of the African-American community and women's experiences.

The Ethic of Caring

"Ole white preachers used to talk wid dey tongues widdout sayin' nothin', but Jesus told us slaves to talk wid our hearts." These words of an ex-slave suggest that ideas cannot be divorced from the individuals who create and share them. This theme of talking with the heart taps the ethic of caring, another dimension of an alternative epistemology used by African-American women. Just as the ex-slave used the wisdom in his heart to reject the ideas of the preachers who talked "wid dey tongues widdout sayin' nothin'," the ethic of caring suggests that personal expressiveness, emotions, and empathy are central to the knowledge validation process.

One of three interrelated components comprising the ethic of caring is the emphasis placed on individual uniqueness. Rooted in a tradition of African humanism, each individual is thought to be a unique expression of a common spirit, power, or energy inherent in all life. When Alice Walker "never doubted her powers of judgment because her mother assumed they were sound," she invokes the sense of individual uniqueness taught to her by her mother. The polyrhythms in African-American music, in which no one main beat subordinates the others, is paralleled by the theme of individual expression in Black women's quilting. Black women quilters place strong color and patterns next to one another and see the individual differences not as detracting from each piece but as enriching the whole quilt. This belief in individual uniqueness is illustrated by the value placed on personal expressiveness in African-American communities. Johnetta Ray, an inner-city resident, describes this Afrocentric emphasis on individual uniqueness: "No matter how hard we try, I don't think black people will ever develop much of a herd instinct. We are profound individualists with a passion for self-expression."

A second component of the ethic of caring concerns the appropriateness of emotions in dialogues. Emotion indicates that a speaker believes in the validity of an argument. Consider Ntozake Shange's description of one of the goals of her work: "Our [Western] society allows people to be absolutely neurotic and totally out of touch with their feelings and everyone else's feelings, and yet be very respectable. This, to me, is a travesty. . . . I'm trying to change the idea of seeing emotions and intellect as distinct faculties." The

Black women's blues tradition's history of personal expressiveness heals this either/or dichotomous rift separating emotion and intellect. For example, in her rendition of "Strange Fruit," Billie Holiday's lyrics blend seamlessly with the emotion of her delivery to render a trenchant social commentary on southern lynching. Without emotion, Aretha Franklin's cry for "respect" would be virtually meaningless.

A third component of the ethic of caring involves developing the capacity for empathy. Harriet Jones, a 16-year-old Black woman, explains to her interviewer why she chose to open up to him: "Some things in my life are so hard for me to bear, and it makes me feel better to know that you feel sorry about those things and would change them if you could." Without her belief in his empathy, she found it difficult to talk. Black women writers often explore the growth of empathy as part of an ethic of caring. For example, the growing respect that the Black slave woman Dessa and the white woman Rufel gain for one another in Sherley Anne William's *Dessa Rose* stems from their increased understanding of each other's positions. After watching Rufel fight off the advances of a white man, Dessa lay awake thinking: "The white woman was subject to the same ravishment as me; this the thought that kept me awake. I hadn't knowed white mens could use a white woman like that, just take her by force same as they could with us." As a result of her new-found empathy, Dessa observed, "it was like we had a secret between us."

These components of the ethic of caring—the value placed on individual expressiveness, the appropriateness of emotions, and the capacity for empathy—pervade African-American culture. One of the best examples of the interactive nature of the importance of dialogue and the ethic of caring in assessing knowledge claims occurs in the use of the call-and-response discourse mode in traditional Black church services. In such services both the minister and the congregation routinely use voice rhythm and vocal inflection to convey meaning. The sound of what is being said is just as important as the words themselves in what is, in a sense, a dialogue of reason and emotion. As a result it is nearly impossible to filter

out the strictly linguistic-cognitive abstract meaning from the sociocultural psychoemotive meaning. While the ideas presented by a speaker must have validity (i.e., agree with the general body of knowledge shared by the Black congregation), the group also appraises the way knowledge claims are presented.

There is growing evidence that the ethic of caring may be part of women's experience as well. Certain dimensions of women's ways of knowing bear striking resemblance to Afrocentric expressions of the ethic of caring. Belenky et al. point out that two contrasting epistemological orientations characterize knowing: one an epistemology of separation based on impersonal procedures for establishing truth and the other, an epistemology of connection in which truth emerges through care. While these ways of knowing are not gender specific, disproportionate numbers of women rely on connected knowing.

The emphasis placed on expressiveness and emotion in African-American communities bears marked resemblance to feminist perspectives on the importance of personality in connected knowing. Separate knowers try to subtract the personality of an individual from his or her ideas because they see personality as biasing those ideas. In contrast, connected knowers see personality as adding to an individual's ideas and feel that the personality of each group member enriches a group's understanding. The significance of individual uniqueness, personal expressiveness, and empathy in African-American communities thus resembles the importance that some feminist analyses place on women's "inner voice."

The convergence of Afrocentric and feminist values in the ethic of caring seems particularly acute. White women may have access to a women's tradition valuing emotion and expressiveness, but few Eurocentric institutions except the family validate this way of knowing. In contrast, Black women have long had the support of the Black church, an institution with deep roots in the African past and a philosophy that accepts and encourages expressiveness and an ethic of caring. Black men share in this Afrocentric tradition. But they must resolve the contradictions that confront them in searching for Afrocentric models of masculinity in the face of abstract, unemotional notions of masculinity imposed on them. The differences among race/gender groups thus hinge on differences in their access to institutional supports valuing one type of knowing over another. Although Black women may be denigrated within white-male-controlled academic institutions, other institutions, such as Black families and churches, which encourage the expression of Black female power seem to do so, in part, by way of their support for an Afrocentric feminist epistemology.

The Ethic of Personal Accountability

An ethic of personal accountability is the final dimension of an alternative epistemology. Not only must individuals develop their knowledge claims through dialogue and present them in a style proving their concern for their ideas, but people are expected to be accountable for their knowledge claims. Zilpha Elaw's description of slavery reflects this notion that every idea has an owner and that the owner's identity matters: "Oh, the abominations of slavery! . . . Every case of slavery, however lenient its inflictions and mitigated its atrocities, indicates an oppressor, the oppressed, and oppression." For Elaw abstract definitions of slavery mesh with the concrete identities of its perpetrators and its victims. African-Americans consider it essential for individuals to have personal positions on issues and assume full responsibility for arguing their validity.

Assessments of an individual's knowledge claims simultaneously evaluate an individual's character, values, and ethics. African-Americans reject the Eurocentric, masculinist belief that probing into an individual's personal viewpoint is outside the boundaries of discussion. Rather, all views expressed and actions taken are thought to derive from a central set of core beliefs that cannot be other than personal. "Does Aretha really *believe* that Black women should get 'respect,' or is she just mouthing the words?" is a valid question in an Afrocentric feminist epistemology. Knowledge claims made by individuals respected for their moral and ethical connections to their ideas will carry more weight than those offered by less respected figures.

An example drawn from an undergraduate course composed entirely of Black women which I taught might help to clarify the uniqueness of this portion of the knowledge validation process. During one class discussion I asked the students to evaluate a prominent Black male scholar's analysis of Black feminism. Instead of severing the scholar from his context in order to dissect the rationality of his thesis, my students demanded facts about the author's personal biography. They were especially interested in concrete details of his life, such as his relationships with Black women, his marital status, and his social class background. By requesting data on dimensions of his personal life routinely excluded in positivist approaches to knowledge validation, they invoked concrete experience as a criterion of meaning. They used this information to assess whether he really cared about his topic and drew on this ethic of caring in advancing their knowledge claims about his work. Furthermore, they refused to evaluate the rationality of his written ideas without some indication of his personal credibility as an ethical human being. The entire exchange could only have occurred as a dialogue among members of a class that had established a solid enough community to employ an alternative epistemology in assessing knowledge claims.

The ethic of personal accountability is clearly an Afrocentric value, but is it feminist as well? While limited by its attention to middle-class, white women, Carol Gilligan's work suggests that there is a female model for moral development whereby women are more inclined to link morality to responsibility, relationships, and the ability to maintain social ties. If this is the case, then African-American women again experience a convergence of values from Afrocentric and female institutions.

The use of an Afrocentric feminist epistemology in traditional Black church services illustrates the interactive nature of all four dimensions and also serves as a metaphor for the distinguishing features of an Afrocentric feminist way of knowing. The services represent more than dialogues between the rationality used in examining biblical texts and stories and the emotion inherent in the use of reason for this purpose. The rationale for such dialogues involves the task of examining concrete experiences for the presence of an ethic of caring. Neither emotion nor ethics is subordinated to reason. Instead, emotion, ethics, and reason are used as interconnected, essential components in assessing knowledge claims. In an Afrocentric feminist epistemology, values lie at the heart of the knowledge validation process such that inquiry always has an ethical aim.

Alternative knowledge claims in and of themselves are rarely threatening to conventional knowledge. Such claims are routinely ignored, discredited, or simply absorbed and marginalized in existing paradigms. Much more threatening is the challenge that alternative epistemologies offer to the basic process used by the powerful to legitimate their knowledge claims. If the epistemology used to validate knowledge comes into question, then all prior knowledge claims validated under the dominant model become suspect. An alternative epistemology challenges all certified knowledge and opens up the question of whether what has been taken to be true can stand the test of alternative ways of validating truth. The existence of a self-defined Black women's standpoint using an Afrocentric feminist epistemology calls into question the content of what currently passes as truth and simultaneously challenges the process of arriving at the truth.

Suggestions for Further Reading and References

See Genevieve Lloyd's *The Man of Reason: "Male" and "Female" in Western Philosophy* (Minneapolis: University of Minnesota Press, 1984) and Janice Moulton's "A Paradigm of Philosophy: The Adversary Method" in *Discovering Reality,* edited by Sandra Harding and Merill B. Hintikka (Dordrecht: Reidel, 1983), for a feminist critique of traditional male-dominated epistemology.

For a good collection of articles dealing with various aspects of feminist epistemology, see *Feminist Epistemologies,* edited by Linda Alcoff and Elizabeth Potter (New York: Routledge, 1993).

Also, *Women and Reason,* edited by Elizabeth D. Harvey and Kathleen O. Kruhlik (Ann Arbor: University of Michigan Press, 1992), gathers together some significant writing on the topic. Lorraine Code's two books—*What Can She Know? Feminist Theory and the Construction of Knowledge* (Ithaca, NY: Cornell University Press, 1991) and *Rhetorical Spaces: Essays on Gendered Locations* (New York: Routledge, 1995)—while demanding, will repay the effort.

Chandra Talpade Mohanty, Ann Russo, and Lourdes Torres have edited a collection of essays, *Third World Women and the Politics of Feminism* (Bloomington: Indiana University Press, 1991), relating to a wide variety of issues in the women's liberation movement in the third world.

See Nicholas Rescher, *Objectivity: The Obligations of Impersonal Reason* (Notre Dame, IN: Notre Dame University Press, 1997), for arguments against the relativism Rescher sees lurking in feminist and other "postmodern" types of analysis.

 You can locate InfoTrac-College Edition articles about this chapter by accessing the InfoTrac-College Edition website (http://www.infotrac-college.com/wadsworth/). Using the InfoTrac-College Edition subject guide, enter the search terms relevant to this chapter, and then read abstracts for relevant articles.

Chapter 8

Does Science Tell Us the Whole Truth and Nothing but the Truth?

> "[F]alsehood is as likely to follow truth as the reverse."
>
> JORGE J. E. GRACIA

8.1 Introduction

AS IS OUR PHILOSOPHICAL CUSTOM, a custom I trust you have all become accustomed to, let us begin by asking some questions about science. What are the similarities and differences between common sense and science? Does science progress at a steady pace, carefully building on previous discoveries? Is science objective? Is it value-free? What is the place of science in human life? Should it be subordinated to ethical and religious concerns? What is the relationship between scientific thinking and traditional modes of problem solving? Are scientific explanations and religious explanations logically similar?

These questions raise some of the issues we will explore in this chapter and some of the issues associated with an area of philosophical research known as the **philosophy of science**. This branch of philosophy centers on a critical analysis of the various sciences, such as the physical, life, and behavioral sciences. To the extent that all of these sciences (physics, biology, psychology, and so on) share certain assumptions about the production of knowledge, the philosophy of science often focuses on methodological issues generally associated with all the sciences. Philosophers of science concern themselves with such topics as theory formation, the nature of hypotheses, the role of observation and experiment in the processes of verification and falsification, and the nature of explanation.

Clearly the philosophy of science is closely related to epistemology because of its concern with the role science plays in generating true statements that constitute knowledge about ourselves and the world in which we live. Questions about the nature of truth and the nature of knowledge inevitably arise as philosophical reflection on science proceeds. One cannot long ponder what is meant by such talk as "verifying a hypothesis" without wondering about truth and its possibility.

We live in a time and a place that puts a great deal of trust in science to tell us the truth and nothing but the truth. Many of our decisions, both public and private, are based on scientific information. We are wowed and amazed at the technological spin-offs scientific research engenders. Today we can do what only yesterday seemed like magic. We can travel in outer space and communicate within seconds with people on the other side of the earth.

Many people also mistrust science. They are uncertain about how reliable scientific theory is, what the limits of science are, and whether the technological marvels are ultimately conducive to living a better life. Some scholars warn of **scientism**, a kind of blind faith in the power of science to determine all truth. Still others worry about the religious and moral implications of the trust many have in science.

8.2 Science and Common Sense

What exactly is science? What do we mean when we call an idea or a theory scientific? How does a scientific idea differ from the ideas of common sense? Certainly one can make a case that science is nothing but just plain, good common sense. Do not both science and common sense share the same goals?

In thinking about these questions I am sure the concept of explanation came to your mind. Science explains things. It answers the "why" and the "how" questions about natural events. It explains what causes what. In good philosophical fashion, however, we must press further and ask what an explanation is.

Many (but not all) philosophers of science subscribe to the **deductive-nomological model** (also called the **covering law model**) of explanation. According to this model, an explanation of an event consists in "covering" or "subsuming" the event under some law. In other words, explaining something requires that a description of it is deducible from the relevant laws of nature. One might explain, for example, the expansion of some metal by appealing to some law such as "metal expands when heated." (Note: this is a highly simplified and nontechnical version of the physical laws involved. One can still ask why heat causes expansion.)

So science is concerned with laws, the laws of nature as some would say. Here science seems to go beyond common sense. Scientists discover and formulate natural laws, and science allows us to accomplish much more than common sense allows. The concept of law is important in science because it makes predictions possible, and predictions make control possible. If I can predict exactly how much a metal will expand when heated to such and such a degree, I have much greater control over the behavior of, let us say, a combustion engine, than I would otherwise. So philosophers of science need to ponder the nature of natural laws and how they are discovered. They must explore how scientists construct scientific concepts.

In addition to problems about the nature of explanation and the construction of scientific concepts like natural law, the philosopher of science must give some account of how scientific conclusions are validated. How do we know when we have arrived at a scientific truth? Is it significantly different from how we know when we have arrived at a commonsense truth?

Ernest Nagel (1912–1985) was a Czech-born American philosopher whose ideas had a deep impact on the development of the philosophy of science from the 1930s to the 1960s. His many publications include two classics in the field: *Principles of the Theory of Probability* (1939) and *The Structure of Science* (1960). The following selection is from the introduction to the latter book.

Reading Questions

1. According to Nagel, what are some of the similarities and differences between common sense and science?
2. Do you agree with Nagel about the differences between science and common sense? Why, or why not?
3. What does Nagel mean by the scientific method?
4. What is Nagel's definition of a "scientific explanation"?

The Structure of Science

ERNEST NAGEL

LONG BEFORE THE BEGINNINGS of modern civilization, men acquired vast funds of information about their environment. They learned to recognize substances which nourished their bodies. They discovered the uses of fire and developed skills for transforming raw materials into shelters, clothing, and utensils. They invented arts of tilling the soil, communicating, and governing themselves. Some of them discovered that objects are moved more easily when placed on carts with wheels, that the sizes of fields are more reliably compared when standard schemes of measurement are employed, and that the seasons of the year as well as many phenomena of the heavens succeed each other with a certain regularity. John Locke's quip at Aristotle—that God was not so sparing to men as to make them merely two-legged creatures, leaving it to Aristotle to make them rational—seems obviously applicable to modern science. The acquisition of reliable knowledge concerning many aspects of the world certainly did not wait upon the advent of modern science and the self-conscious use of its methods. Indeed, in this respect, many men in every generation repeat in their own lives the history of the race: they manage to secure for themselves skills and competent information, without benefit of

training in the sciences and without the calculated adoption of scientific modes of procedure.

If so much in the way of knowledge can be achieved by the shrewd exercise of native gifts and "common-sense" methods, what special excellence do the sciences possess, and what do their elaborate intellectual and physical tools contribute to the acquisition of knowledge? The question requires a careful answer if a definite meaning is to be associated with the word "science."

The word and its linguistic variants are certainly not always employed with discrimination, and they are frequently used merely to confer an honorific distinction on something or other. Many men take pride in being "scientific" in their beliefs and in living in an "age of science." However, quite often the sole discoverable ground for their pride is a conviction that, unlike their ancestors or their neighbors, they are in possession of some alleged final truth. It is in this spirit that currently accepted theories in physics or biology are sometimes described as scientific, while all previously held but no longer accredited theories in those domains are firmly refused that label. Similarly, types of practice that are highly successful under prevailing physical and

From Ernest Nagel, The Structure of Science, *Indianapolis, IN: Hackett Publishing Company, 1961, pp. 1–14. Reprinted by permission of Hackett Publishing Company. All rights reserved.*

social conditions, such as certain techniques of farming or industry, are occasionally contrasted with the allegedly "unscientific" practices of other times and places. Perhaps an extreme form of the tendency to rob the term "scientific" of all definite content is illustrated by the earnest use that advertisers sometimes make of such phrases as "scientific haircutting," "scientific rug cleaning," and even "scientific astrology." It will be clear, however, that in none of the above examples is a readily identifiable and differentiating characteristic of beliefs or practices associated with the word. It would certainty be ill-advised to adopt the suggestion, implicit in the first example, to limit the application of the adjective "scientific" to beliefs that are indefeasibly true— if only because infallible guaranties of truth are lacking in most if not all areas of inquiry, so that the adoption of such a suggestion would in effect deprive the adjective of any proper use.

The words "science" and "scientific" are nevertheless not quite so empty of a determinate content as their frequently debased uses might indicate. For in fact the words are labels either for an identifiable, continuing enterprise of inquiry or for its intellectual products, and they are often employed to signify traits that distinguish those products from other things. . . . we shall therefore survey briefly some of the ways in which "prescientific" or "common-sense" knowledge differs from the intellectual products of modern science. To be sure, no sharp line separates beliefs generally subsumed under the familiar but vague rubric of "common sense" from those cognitive claims recognized as "scientific." Nevertheless, as in the case of other words whose fields of intended application have notoriously hazy boundaries (such as the term "democracy"), absence of precise dividing lines is not incompatible with the presence of at least a core of firm meaning for each of these words. In their more sober uses, at any rate, these words do in fact connote important and recognizable differences. It is these differences that we must attempt to identify, even if we are compelled to sharpen some of them for the sake of expository emphasis and clarity.

1. No one seriously disputes that many of the existing special sciences have grown out of the practical concerns of daily living: geometry out of problems of measuring and surveying fields, mechanics out of problems raised by the architectural and military arts, biology out of problems of human health and animal husbandry, chemistry out of problems raised by metallurgical and dyeing industries, economics out of problems of household and political management, and so on. To be sure, there have been other stimuli to the development of the sciences than those provided by problems of the practical arts; nevertheless, these latter have had, and still continue to have, important roles in the history of scientific inquiry. In any case, commentators on the nature of science who have been impressed by the historical continuity of common-sense convictions and scientific conclusions have sometimes proposed to differentiate between them by the formula that the sciences are simply "organized" or "classified" common sense.

It is undoubtedly the case that the sciences are organized bodies of knowledge and that in all of them a classification of their materials into significant types or kinds (as in biology, the classification of living things into species) is an indispensable task. It is clear, nonetheless, that the proposed formula does not adequately express the characteristic differences between science and common sense. A lecturer's notes on his travels in Africa may be very well organized for the purposes of communicating information interestingly and efficiently, without thereby converting that information into what has historically been called a science. A librarian's card catalogue represents an invaluable classification of books, but no one with a sense for the historical association of the word would say that the catalogue is a science. The obvious difficulty is that the proposed formula does not specify what *kind* of organization or classification is characteristic of the sciences.

Let us therefore turn to this question. A marked feature of much information acquired in the course of ordinary experience is that, although this information may be accurate enough within certain limits, it is seldom accompanied by any explanation of why the facts are as alleged. Thus societies which have discovered the uses of the wheel usually know nothing of frictional forces, nor of any reasons why goods loaded on vehicles with wheels are easier to move than goods dragged on the ground. Many peoples have learned the advisability of manuring their agricultural fields, but only a few have concerned themselves with the reasons for so acting. The medicinal properties of herbs like the foxglove have been recognized for centuries, though usually no account was given of the grounds for their beneficent virtues. Moreover, when "common sense" does attempt to give explanations for its facts—as when the value of the foxglove as a cardiac stimulant is explained in terms of the similarity in shape of the flower and the human heart—the explanations are frequently without critical tests of their relevance to the facts. Common sense is often eligible to receive the well-known advice Lord Mansfield gave to a newly appointed governor of a colony who was unversed in the law: "There is no difficulty in deciding a case—only hear both sides patiently, then consider what you think justice requires, and decide accordingly; but never give your reasons, for your judgment will probably be right, but your reasons will certainly be wrong."

It is the desire for explanations which are at once systematic and controllable by factual evidence that generates science; and it is the organization and classification of knowledge on the basis of explanatory principles that is the distinctive goal of the sciences. More specifically, the sciences seek to discover and to formulate in general terms the conditions under which events of various sorts occur, the statements of such determining conditions being the explanations of the corresponding happenings. This goal can be achieved only by distinguishing or isolating certain properties in the subject matter studied and by ascertaining the repeatable patterns of dependence in which these properties stand to one another. In consequence, when the inquiry is successful, propositions that hitherto appeared to be quite unrelated are exhibited as linked to each other in determinate ways by virtue of their place in a system of explanations. In some cases, indeed, the inquiry can be carried to remarkable lengths. Patterns of relations may be discovered that are pervasive in vast ranges of fact, so that with the help of a small number of explanatory principles an indefinitely large number of propositions about these facts can be shown to constitute a logically unified body of knowledge. The unification sometimes takes the form of a deductive system, as in the case of demonstrative geometry or the science of mechanics. Thus a few principles, such as those formulated by Newton, suffice to show that propositions concerning the moon's motion, the behavior of the tides, the paths of projectiles, and the rise of liquids in thin tubes are intimately related, and that all these propositions can be rigorously deduced from those principles conjoined with various special assumptions of fact. In this way a systematic explanation is achieved for the diverse phenomena which the logically derived propositions report.

Not all the existing sciences present the highly integrated form of systematic explanation which the science of mechanics exhibits, though for many of the sciences—in domains of social inquiry as well as in the various divisions of natural science—the idea of such a rigorous logical systematization continues to function as an ideal. But even in those branches of departmentalized inquiry in which this ideal is not generally pursued, as in much historical research, the goal of finding explanations for facts is usually always present. Men seek to know why the thirteen American colonies rebelled from England while Canada did not, why the ancient Greeks were able to repel the Persians but succumbed to the Roman armies, or why urban and commercial activity developed in medieval Europe in the tenth century and not before. To explain, to establish some relation of dependence between propositions superficially unrelated, to exhibit systematically connections between apparently miscellaneous items of information are distinctive marks of scientific inquiry.

2. A number of further differences between common sense and scientific knowledge are

almost direct consequences of the systematic character of the latter. A well-recognized feature of common sense is that, though the knowledge it claims may be accurate, it seldom is aware of the limits within which its beliefs are valid or its practices successful. A community, acting on the rule that spreading manure preserves the fertility of the soil, may in many cases continue its mode of agriculture successfully. However, it may continue to follow the rule blindly, in spite of the manifest deterioration of the soil, and it may therefore be helpless in the face of a critical problem of food supply. On the other hand, when the reasons for the efficacy of manure as a fertilizer are understood, so that the rule is connected with principles of biology and soil chemistry, the rule comes to be recognized as only of restricted validity, since the efficiency of manure is seen to depend on the persistence of conditions of which common sense is usually unaware. Few who know them are capable of withholding admiration for the sturdy independence of those farmers who, without much formal education, are equipped with an almost endless variety of skills and sound information in matters affecting their immediate environment. Nevertheless, the traditional resourcefulness of the farmer is narrowly circumscribed: he often becomes ineffective when some break occurs in the continuity of his daily round of living, for his skills are usually products of tradition and routine habit and are not informed by an understanding of the reasons for their successful operation. More generally, common-sense knowledge is most adequate in situations in which a certain number of factors remain practically unchanged. But since it is normally not recognized that this adequacy does depend on the constancy of such factors—indeed, the very existence of the pertinent factors may not be recognized—common-sense knowledge suffers from a serious incompleteness. It is the aim of systematic science to remove this incompleteness, even if it is an aim which frequently is only partially realized.

The sciences thus introduce refinements into ordinary conceptions by the very process of exhibiting the systematic connections of propositions about matters of common knowledge. Not only are familiar practices thereby shown to be explicable in terms of principles formulating relations between items in wide areas of fact; those principles also provide clues for altering and correcting habitual modes of behavior, so as to make them more effective in familiar contexts and more adaptable to novel ones. This is not to say, however, that common beliefs are necessarily mistaken, or even that they are inherently more subject to change under the pressure of experience than are the propositions of science. Indeed, the age-long and warranted stability of common-sense convictions, such as that oaks do not develop overnight from acorns or that water solidifies on sufficient cooling, compares favorably with the relatively short life span of many theories of science. The essential point to be observed is that, since common sense shows little interest in systematically explaining the facts it notes, the range of valid application of its beliefs, though in fact narrowly circumscribed, is not of serious concern to it.

3. The ease with which the plain man as well as the man of affairs entertains incompatible and even inconsistent beliefs has often been the subject for ironic commentary. Thus, men will sometimes argue for sharply increasing the quantity of money and also demand a stable currency; they will insist upon the repayment of foreign debts and also take steps to prevent the importation of foreign goods; and they will make inconsistent judgments on the effects of the foods they consume, on the size of bodies they see, on the temperature of liquids, and the violence of noises. Such conflicting judgments are often the result of an almost exclusive preoccupation with the immediate consequences and qualities of observed events. Much that passes as common-sense knowledge certainly is about the effects familiar things have upon matters that men happen to value; the relations of events to one another, independent of their incidence upon specific human concerns, are not systematically noticed and explored.

The occurrence of conflicts between judgments is one of the stimuli to the development of science. By introducing a systematic explanation of facts, by ascertaining the conditions and consequences of events, by exhibiting the logical relations of propositions to one another, the sciences strike at the sources of such conflicts. Indeed, a large number of extraordinarily able minds have traced out the logical consequences of basic principles in various sciences; and an even larger number of investigators have repeatedly checked such consequences with other propositions obtained as a result of critical observation and experiment. There is no iron-clad guaranty that, in spite of this care, serious inconsistencies in these sciences have been eliminated. On the contrary, mutually incompatible assumptions sometimes serve as the bases for inquiries in different branches of the same science. For example, in certain parts of physics atoms were at one time assumed to be perfectly elastic bodies, although in other branches of physical science perfect elasticity was not ascribed to atoms. However, such inconsistencies are sometimes only apparent ones, the impression of inconsistency arising from a failure to note that different assumptions are being employed for the solution of quite different classes of problems. Moreover, even when the inconsistencies are genuine, they are often only temporary, since incompatible assumptions may be employed only because a logically coherent theory is not yet available to do the complex job for which those assumptions were originally introduced. In any event, the flagrant inconsistencies that so frequently mark common beliefs are notably absent from those sciences in which the pursuit of unified systems of explanation has made considerable headway.

4. As has already been noted, many everyday beliefs have survived centuries of experience, in contradistinction to the relatively short life span that is so often the fate of conclusions advanced in various branches of modern science. One partial reason for this circumstance merits attention. Consider some instance of common-sense beliefs, such as that water solidifies when it is sufficiently cooled; and let us ask what is signified by the terms "water" and "sufficiently" in that assertion. It is a familiar fact that the word "water," when used by those unacquainted with modern science, generally has no clear-cut meaning. It is then frequently employed as a name for a variety

of liquids despite important physicochemical differences between them, but is frequently rejected as a label for other liquids even though these latter liquids do not differ among themselves in their essential physicochemical characteristics to a greater extent than do the former fluids. Thus, the word may perhaps be used to designate the liquids falling from the sky as rain, emerging from the ground in springs, flowing in rivers and roadside ditches, and constituting the seas and oceans; but the word may be employed less frequently if at all for liquids pressed out of fruits, contained in soups and other beverages, or evacuated through the pores of the human skin. Similarly, the word "sufficiently" when used to characterize a cooling process may sometimes signify a difference as great as that between the maximum temperature on a midsummer day and the minimum temperature of a day in midwinter; at other times, the word may signify a difference no greater than that between the noon and the twilight temperatures on a day in winter. In short, in its common-sense use for characterizing temperature changes, the word "sufficiently" is not associated with a precise specification of their extent.

If this example can be taken as typical, the language in which common-sense knowledge is formulated and transmitted may exhibit two important kinds of indeterminacy. In the first place, the terms of ordinary speech may be quite vague, in the sense that the class of things designated by a term is not sharply and clearly demarcated from (and may in fact overlap to a considerable extent with) the class of things not so designated. Accordingly, the range of presumed validity for statements employing such terms has no determinate limits. In the second place, the terms of ordinary speech may lack a relevant degree of specificity, in the sense that the broad distinctions signified by the terms do not suffice to characterize more narrowly drawn but important differences between the things denoted by the terms. Accordingly, relations of dependence between occurrences are not formulated in a precisely determinate manner by statements containing such terms.

As a consequence of these features of ordinary speech, experimental control of common-sense beliefs is frequently difficult, since the distinction between confirming and contradicting evidence for such beliefs cannot be easily drawn. Thus, the belief that "in general" water solidifies when sufficiently cooled may answer the needs of men whose interest in the phenomenon of freezing is circumscribed by their concern to achieve the routine objectives of their daily lives, despite the fact that the language employed in codifying this belief is vague and lacks specificity Such men may therefore see no reason for modifying their belief, even if they should note that ocean water fails to freeze although its temperature is sensibly the same as that of well water when the latter begins to solidify, or that some liquids must be cooled to a greater extent than others before changing into the solid state. If pressed to justify their belief in the face of such facts, these men may perhaps arbitrarily exclude the oceans from the class of things they denominate as water; or, alternatively, they may express renewed confidence in their belief, irrespective of the extent of cooling that may be required, on the ground that liquids classified as water do indeed solidify when cooled.

In their quest for systematic explanations, on the other hand, the sciences must mitigate the indicated indeterminacy of ordinary language by refashioning it. For example, physical chemistry is not content with the loosely formulated generalization that water solidifies if it is sufficiently cooled, for the aim of that discipline is to explain, among other things, why drinking water and milk freeze at certain temperatures although at those temperatures ocean water does not. To achieve this aim, physical chemistry must therefore introduce clear distinctions between various kinds of water and between various amounts of cooling. Several devices reduce the vagueness and increase the specificity of linguistic expressions. Counting and measuring are for many purposes the most effective of these techniques, and are perhaps the most familiar ones. Poets may sing of the infinity of stars which stud the visible heavens, but the astronomer will want to specify their exact number. The artisan in metals may be content with knowing that iron is harder than lead, but the physicist who wishes to explain this fact will require a precise measure of the difference in hardness. Accordingly, an obvious but important consequence of the precision thus introduced is that statements become capable of more thorough and critical testing by experience. Prescientific beliefs are frequently incapable of being put to definite experiential tests, simply because those beliefs may be vaguely compatible with an indeterminate class of unanalyzed facts. Scientific statements, because they are required to be in agreement with more closely specified materials of observation, face greater risks of being refuted by such data.

This difference between common and scientific knowledge is roughly analogous to differences in standards of excellence which may be set up for handling firearms. Most men would qualify as expert shots if the standard of expertness were the ability to hit the side of a barn from a distance of a hundred feet. But only a much smaller number of individuals could meet the more rigorous requirement of consistently centering their shots upon a three-inch target at twice that distance. Similarly, a prediction that the sun will be eclipsed during the autumn months is more likely to be fulfilled than a prediction that the eclipse will occur at a specific moment on a given day in the fall of the year. The first prediction will be confirmed should the eclipse take place during any one of something like a hundred days; the second prediction will be refuted if the eclipse does not occur within something like a small fraction of a minute from the time given. The latter prediction could be false without the former being so, but not conversely; and the latter prediction must therefore satisfy more rigorous standards of experiential control than are assumed for the former.

This greater determinacy of scientific language helps to make clear why so many common-sense beliefs have a stability, often lasting for many centuries, that few theories of science possess. It is more difficult to devise a theory that remains unshaken by repeated confrontation with the outcome of painstaking experimental observation, when the standards are high for the agreement that must obtain between such experimental data and the predictions derived from the theory, than when such standards are lax and the admissible experimental evidence is not required to be established by carefully controlled procedures. The more advanced sciences do in fact specify almost invariably the extent to which predictions based on a theory may deviate from the results of experiment without invalidating the theory. The limits of such permissible deviations are usually quite narrow, so that discrepancies between theory and experiment which common sense would ordinarily regard as insignificant are often judged to be fatal to the adequacy of the theory.

On the other hand, although the greater determinacy of scientific statements exposes them to greater risks of being found in error than are faced by the less precisely stated common-sense beliefs, the former have an important advantage over the latter. They have a greater capacity for incorporation into comprehensive but clearly articulated systems of explanation. When such systems are adequately confirmed by experimental data, they codify frequently unsuspected relations of dependence between many varieties of experimentally identifiable but distinct kinds of fact. In consequence, confirmatory evidence for statements belonging to such a system can often be accumulated more rapidly and in larger quantities than for statements (such as those expressing common-sense beliefs) not belonging to such a system. This is so because evidence for statements in such a system may be obtainable by observations of an extensive class of events, many of which may not be explicitly mentioned by those statements but which are nevertheless relevant sources of evidence for the statements in question, in view of the relations of dependence asserted by the system to hold between the events in that class. For example, the data of spectroscopic analysis are employed in modern physics to test assumptions concerning the chemical structure of various substances; and experiments on thermal properties of solids are used to support theories of light. In brief, by increasing the determinacy of statements and incorporating them into logically integrated systems of explanation, modern science sharpens the discriminating powers of its testing procedure and aug-

ments the sources of relevant evidence for its conclusions.

5. It has already been mentioned in passing that, while common-sense knowledge is largely concerned with the impact of events upon matters of special value to men, theoretical science is in general not so provincial. The quest for systematic explanations requires that inquiry be directed to the relations of dependence between things irrespective of their bearing upon human values. Thus, to take an extreme case, astrology is concerned with the relative positions of stars and planets in order to determine the import of such conjunctions for the destinies of men; in contrast, astronomy studies the relative positions and motions of celestial bodies without reference to the fortunes of human beings. Similarly, breeders of horses and of other animals have acquired much skill and knowledge relating to the problem of developing breeds that will implement certain human purposes; theoretical biologists, on the other hand, are only incidentally concerned with such problems, and are interested in analyzing among other things the mechanisms of heredity and in obtaining laws of genetic development.

One important consequence of this difference in orientation between theoretical and common-sense knowledge, however, is that theoretical science deliberately neglects the immediate values of things, so that the statements of science often appear to be only tenuously relevant to the familiar events and qualities of daily life. To many people, for example, an unbridgeable chasm seems to separate electromagnetic theory, which provides a systematic account of optical phenomena, and the brilliant colors one may see at sunset; and the chemistry of colloids, which contributes to an understanding of the organization of living bodies, appears to be an equally impossible distance from the manifold traits of personality exhibited by human beings.

It must certainly be admitted that scientific statements make use of highly abstract concepts, whose pertinence to the familiar qualities which things manifest in their customary settings is by no means obvious. Nevertheless, the relevance of such statements to matters encountered in the ordinary business of life is also indisputable. It is well to bear in mind that the unusually abstract character of scientific notions, as well as their alleged "remoteness" from the traits of things found in customary experience, are inevitable concomitants of the quest for systematic and comprehensive explanations. Such explanations can be constructed only if the familiar qualities and relations of things, in terms of which individual objects and events are usually identified and differentiated, can be shown to depend for their occurrence on the presence of certain other pervasive relational or structural properties that characterize in various ways an extensive class of objects and processes. Accordingly, to achieve generality of explanation for qualitatively diverse things, those structural properties must be formulated without reference to, and in abstraction from, the individualizing qualities and relations of familiar experience. It is for the sake of achieving such generality that, for example, the temperature of bodies is defined in physics not in terms of directly felt differences in warmth, but in terms of certain abstractly formulated relations characterizing an extensive class of reversible thermal cycles.

However, although abstractness in formulation is an undoubted feature in scientific knowledge, it would be an obvious error to suppose that common-sense knowledge does not involve the use of abstract conceptions. Everyone who believes that man is a mortal creature certainly employs the abstract notions of humanity and mortality. The conceptions of science do not differ from those of common sense merely in being abstract. They differ in being formulations of pervasive structural properties, abstracted from familiar traits manifested by limited classes of things usually only under highly specialized conditions, related to matters open to direct observation only by way of complex logical and experimental procedures, and articulated with a view to developing systematic explanations for extensive ranges of diverse phenomena.

6. Implicit in the contrasts between modern science and common sense already noted is the important difference that derives from the deliberate policy of science to expose its cognitive claims to the repeated challenge of critically probative observational data, procured under carefully controlled conditions. As we had occasion to mention previously, however, this does not mean that common-sense beliefs are invariably erroneous or that they have no foundations in empirically verifiable fact. It does mean that common-sense beliefs are not subjected, as a matter of established principle, to systematic scrutiny in the light of data secured for the sake of determining the accuracy of those beliefs and the range of their validity. It also means that evidence admitted as competent in science must be obtained by procedures instituted with a view to eliminating known sources of error; and it means, furthermore, that the weight of the available evidence for any hypothesis proposed as an answer to the problem under inquiry is assessed with the help of canons of evaluation whose authority is itself based on the performance of those canons in an extensive class of inquiries. Accordingly, the quest for explanation in science is not simply a search for any *prima facie* plausible "first principles" that might account in a vague way for the familiar "facts" of conventional experience. On the contrary, it is a quest for explanatory hypotheses that are genuinely testable, because they are required to have logical consequences precise enough not to be compatible with almost every conceivable state of affairs. The hypotheses sought must therefore be subject to the possibility of rejection, which will depend on the outcome of critical procedures, integral to the scientific quest, for determining what the actual facts are.

The difference just described can be expressed by the dictum that the conclusions of science, unlike common-sense beliefs, are the products of scientific method. However, this brief formula should not be misconstrued. It must not be understood to assert, for example, that the practice of scientific method consists in following prescribed rules for making experimental discoveries or for finding satisfactory explanations for matters of established fact. There are no rules of discovery and invention in science, any more than there are such rules in the arts. Nor must the formula be construed as maintaining that the practice of scientific method consists in the use in all inquiries of some special set of techniques (such as the techniques of measurement employed in physical science), irrespective of the subject matter or the problem under investigation. Such an interpretation of the dictum is a caricature of its intent; and in any event the dictum on that interpretation is preposterous. Nor, finally, should the formula be read as claiming that the practice of scientific method effectively eliminates every form of personal bias or source of error which might otherwise impair the outcome of the inquiry, and more generally that it assures the truth of every conclusion reached by inquiries employing the method. But no such assurances can in fact be given; and no antecedently fixed set of rules can serve as automatic safeguards against unsuspected prejudices and other causes of error that might adversely affect the course of an investigation.

The practice of scientific method is the persistent critique of arguments, in the light of tried canons for judging the reliability of the procedures by which evidential data are obtained, and for assessing the probative force of the evidence on which conclusions are based. As estimated by standards prescribed by those canons, a given hypothesis may be strongly supported by stated evidence. But this fact does not guarantee the truth of the hypothesis, even if the evidential statements are admitted to be true—unless, contrary to standards usually assumed for observational data in the empirical sciences, the degree of support is that which the premises of a valid deductive argument give to its conclusion. Accordingly, the difference between the cognitive claims of science and common sense, which stems from the fact that the former are the products of scientific method, does not connote that the former are invariably true. It does imply that, while common-sense beliefs are usually accepted without a critical evaluation of the evidence available, the evidence for the conclusions of science conforms to standards such that a significant proportion of conclusions supported by similarly structured evidence remains in good agreement with additional factual data when fresh data are obtained.

Further discussion of these considerations must be postponed. However, one brief addendum is required at this point. If the conclusions of science are the products of inquiries conducted in accordance with a definite policy for obtaining and assessing evidence, the rationale for confidence in those conclusions as warranted must be based on the merits of that policy. It must be admitted that the canons for assessing evidence which define the policy have, at best, been explicitly codified only in part, and operate in the main only as intellectual habits manifested by competent investigators in the conduct of their inquiries. But despite this fact the historical record of what has been achieved by this policy in the way of dependable and systematically ordered knowledge leaves little room for serious doubt concerning the superiority of the policy over alternatives to it.

This brief survey of features that distinguish in a general way the cognitive claims and the logical method of modern science suggests a variety of questions for detailed study. The conclusions of science are the fruits of an institutionalized system of inquiry which plays an increasingly important role in the lives of men. Accordingly, the organization of that social institution, the circumstances and stages of its development and influence, and the consequences of its expansion have been repeatedly explored by sociologists, economists, historians, and moralists. However, if the nature of the scientific enterprise and its place in contemporary society are to be properly understood, the types and the articulation of scientific statements, as well as the logic by which scientific conclusions are established, also require careful analysis. This is a task—a major if not exclusive task—that the philosophy of science undertakes to execute. Three broad areas for such an analysis are in fact suggested by the survey just concluded: the logical patterns exhibited by explanations in the sciences; the construction of scientific concepts; and the validation of scientific conclusions. . . .

Suggestions for Further Reading

Peter Kosso presents a short survey of philosophy of science in *Reading the Book of Nature* (Cambridge: Cambridge University Press, 1992) that is geared for beginners.

An *Introduction to the Philosophy of Science* by Anthony O'Hear (Oxford: Oxford University Press, 1989) is also a good place to start.

I have found Robert Klee's *Introduction to the Philosophy of Science: Cutting Nature at Its Seams* (New York: Oxford University Press, 1997) an up-to-date, readable overview that helps to clarify some of the key issues.

A good collection of articles dealing with a variety of topics can be found in Jennifer McErlean, *Philosophies of Science: From Foundations to Contemporary Issues* (Belmont, CA: Wadsworth, 2000).

For clear discussions of technical terms I recommend the articles in *The Cambridge Dictionary of Philosophy* edited by Robert Audi, 2nd Edition (Cambridge: Cambridge University Press, 1999), beginning with the entry on the philosophy of science (p. 700ff).

Video

Hilary Putman of Harvard University examines contemporary issues in *The Philosophy of Science* (45 minutes), which is available from Films for the Humanities and Sciences at www.film.com.

8.3 Scientific Revolutions

If I asked you to tell me something about scientific procedure, you might start talking about the scientific method of observation, which leads to theories from which predictive hypotheses are deduced and then tested by making further observations. This is called the **hypothetico-deductive method** because it involves deducing consequences (predictions) that should hold if the hypothesis is correct and then designing experiments to see if they do indeed hold true.

Your version of the scientific method might also include a belief that science is incremental in the sense that truth slowly accumulates over time. Scientists build on past discoveries and theories. Many people working very carefully, but slowly and surely, add to an ever growing understanding of the way the world operates. Present theories absorb past theories, and each generation makes progress toward the ideal of understanding everything scientifically.

This picture of science is what philosophers often call **normal science** or standard science. It can be contrasted with a picture of science that might be new to you, a picture called **revolutionary science**. According to this picture, scientists sometimes reject traditional, time-honored, and well-established theories of how the world runs in favor of new and incompatible theories. Old problems and puzzles that people worked on so carefully now seem irrelevant, and a host of new problems emerges, clamoring for attention. **Anomalies** or new events that do not fit with prevailing beliefs generate new and deep questions about accepted scientific views. Theories once thought true now appear inadequate, and new theories must be invented.

According to Thomas Kuhn (1922–1996), one of the most influential and controversial philosophers of science in the last century, one of the main differences between normal science and revolutionary science has to do with what he calls paradigms. A **paradigm** is a scientific achievement so deep and impressive that it defines the daily practice for a particular community of scientists. It settles fundamental issues, provides a general set of assumptions, and offers a kind of basic model, thereby generating research puzzles with definite solutions. Normal science works within a paradigm, solving slowly but surely the puzzles and problems the paradigm generates. Within the boundaries of the paradigm, we may speak of scientific progress. Then anomalies occur. Unexpected experimental results that are incompatible with prevailing theory generate a crisis that leads to a paradigm shift. This shift in paradigms is the work of revolutionary science, which tears down established frameworks and creates something new. Once revolutionary science has done its work, a new paradigm reigns and a new round of normal science begins, now operating within the bounds of the new paradigm.

I think you can see that if Kuhn is right, science does not always make gradual and smooth progress. Crises generated by anomalies create shifts in vision. What people see and how they see it changes very much like gestalt shifts in vision that occur when one suddenly sees a figure that first appeared to be a rabbit, now appears to be a duck (or vice versa). These shifts are not built on the old paradigm. In fact the old and new paradigms are **incommensurable**, not only in the sense of being incompatible, but also in the sense that given any two paradigms, we would not be able to say which one is better or more accurate because we lack paradigm-transcending criteria for making such extra-paradigmatic judgments. From the point of view of revolutionary science, science does not progress in a traditional sense: it changes direction.

The following selection comes from Kuhn's most influential book, *The Structure of Scientific Revolutions*. To present the key ideas, I have edited many of the examples that Kuhn uses to support his views (examples that give a thickness to his ideas) so the resulting version may seem overly thin, abstract, and unconnected to familiar scientific theories. Even so, what Kuhn has to say will get you to think about science and its ability to generate knowledge in a way you have not thought about it before.

Reading Questions

1. How does Kuhn describe normal science?
2. What, according to Kuhn, are two essential characteristics of a paradigm?
3. How does the emergence of a new paradigm in a particular field of science affect the structure of the group that practices that field?
4. What is the nature of normal science in relationship to a paradigm?
5. Why are anomalies important in science?
6. What influences the decision to reject a paradigm?
7. What are scientific revolutions, and what is their function in scientific development?
8. What sorts of parallels are there between scientific and political revolutions?
9. In Section X, do you think Kuhn is claiming that both the way the scientist sees the world and the world itself change when a paradigm shift occurs? Why, or why not?
10. How does Kuhn explain scientific progress? Do you think his answer is better than the traditional picture of science as progressing by drawing closer to the truth about the way things are? Why, or why not?
11. Do you think Kuhn's ideas about science imply that knowledge is relative? Why or why not?

The Structure of Scientific Revolutions

THOMAS S. KUHN

II. *The Route to Normal Science*

IN THIS ESSAY, 'normal science' means research firmly based upon one or more past scientific achievements, achievements that some particular scientific community acknowledges for a time as supplying the foundation for its further practice. Today such achievements are recounted, though seldom in their original form, by science textbooks, elementary and advanced. These textbooks expound the body of accepted theory, illustrate many or all of its successful applications, and compare these applications with exemplary observations and experiments. Before such books became popular early in the nineteenth century (and until even more recently in the newly matured sciences), many of the famous classics of science fulfilled a similar function. Aristotle's *Physica*, Ptolemy's *Almagest*, Newton's *Principia* and *Opticks*, Franklin's *Electricity*, Lavoisier's *Chemistry*, and Lyell's *Geology*—these and many other works served for a time implicitly to define the legitimate problems and methods of a research field for succeeding generations of practitioners. They were able to do so because they shared two essential characteristics. Their achievement was sufficiently unprecedented to attract an enduring group of adherents away from competing modes of scientific activity. Simultaneously, it was sufficiently open-ended to leave all sorts of problems for the redefined group of practitioners to resolve.

Achievements that share these two characteristics I shall henceforth refer to as 'paradigms,' a term that relates closely to 'normal science.' By choosing it, I mean to suggest that some accepted examples of actual scientific practice—examples which include law, theory, application, and instrumentation together—provide models from which spring particular coherent traditions of scientific research. These are the traditions which the historian describes under such rubrics as 'Ptolemaic astronomy' (or 'Copernican'), 'Aristotelian dynamics' (or 'Newtonian'), 'corpuscular optics' (or 'wave optics'), and so on. The study of paradigms, including many that are far more specialized than those named illustratively above, is what mainly prepares the student for membership in the particular scientific community with which he will later practice. Because he there joins men who learned the bases of their field from the same concrete models, his subsequent practice will seldom evoke overt disagreement over fundamentals. Men whose research is based on shared paradigms are committed to the same rules and standards for scientific practice. That commitment and the apparent consensus it produces are prerequisites for normal science, i.e., for the genesis and continuation of a particular research tradition. . . .

We shall be examining the nature of this highly directed or paradigm-based research in the next section, but must first note briefly how the emergence of a paradigm affects the structure of the group that practices the field. When, in the development of a natural science, an individual or group first produces a synthesis able to attract most of the next generation's practitioners, the older schools gradually disappear. In part their disappearance is caused by their members' conversion to the new paradigm. But there are always some men who cling to one or another of the older views, and they are simply read out of the profession, which thereafter ignores their work. The new paradigm implies a new and more rigid definition of the field. Those unwill-

From Thomas S. Kuhn, The Structure of Scientific Revolutions, *2nd Edition, enlarged. Chicago, IL: The University of Chicago Press, 1970, pp. 10–11, 18–19, 23–24, 52–53, 64–65, 77–78, 92–96, 109–112, 160–173.*
Footnotes omitted. © *1962, 1970 by the University of Chicago Press. Reprinted by permission.*

ing or unable to accommodate their work to it must proceed in isolation or attach themselves to some other group. Historically, they have often simply stayed in the departments of philosophy from which so many of the special sciences have been spawned. As these indications hint, it is sometimes just its reception of a paradigm that transforms a group previously interested merely in the study of nature into a profession or, at least, a discipline. In the sciences (though not in fields like medicine, technology, and law, of which the principal *raison d'être* is an external social need), the formation of specialized journals, the foundation of specialists' societies, and the claim for a special place in the curriculum have usually been associated with a group's first reception of a single paradigm. At least this was the case between the time, a century and a half ago, when the institutional pattern of scientific specialization first developed and the very recent time when the paraphernalia of specialization acquired a prestige of their own.

III. *The Nature of Normal Science*

What then is the nature of the more professional and esoteric research that a group's reception of a single paradigm permits? If the paradigm represents work that has been done once and for all, what further problems does it leave the united group to resolve? Those questions will seem even more urgent if we now note one respect in which the terms used so far may be misleading. In its established usage, a paradigm is an accepted model or pattern, and that aspect of its meaning has enabled me, lacking a better word, to appropriate 'paradigm' here. But it will shortly be clear that the sense of 'model' and 'pattern' that permits the appropriation is not quite the one usual in defining 'paradigm.' In grammar, for example, '*amo, amas, amat*' is a paradigm because it displays the pattern to be used in conjugating a large number of other Latin verbs, e.g., in producing '*laudo, laudas, laudat.*' In this standard application, the paradigm functions by permitting the replication of examples any one of which could in principle serve to replace it. In a science, on the other hand,

a paradigm is rarely an object for replication. Instead, like an accepted judicial decision in the common law, it is an object for further articulation and specification under new or more stringent conditions.

To see how this can be so, we must recognize how very limited in both scope and precision a paradigm can be at the time of its first appearance. Paradigms gain their status because they are more successful than their competitors in solving a few problems that the group of practitioners has come to recognize as acute. To be more successful is not, however, to be either completely successful with a single problem or notably successful with any large number. The success of a paradigm—whether Aristotle's analysis of motion, Ptolemy's computations of planetary position, Lavoisier's application of the balance, or Maxwell's mathematization of the electromagnetic field—is at the start largely a promise of success discoverable in selected and still incomplete examples. Normal science consists in the actualization of that promise, an actualization achieved by extending the knowledge of those facts that the paradigm displays as particularly revealing, by increasing the extent of the match between those facts and the paradigm's predictions, and by further articulation of the paradigm itself.

Few people who are not actually practitioners of a mature science realize how much mop-up work of this sort a paradigm leaves to be done or quite how fascinating such work can prove in the execution. And these points need to be understood. Mopping-up operations are what engage most scientists throughout their careers. They constitute what I am here calling normal science. Closely examined, whether historically or in the contemporary laboratory, that enterprise seems an attempt to force nature into the preformed and relatively inflexible box that the paradigm supplies. No part of the aim of normal science is to call forth new sorts of phenomena; indeed those that will not fit the box are often not seen at all. Nor do scientists normally aim to invent new theories, and they are often intolerant of those invented by others. Instead, normal-scientific research is directed to the articulation of those phenomena and theories that the paradigm already supplies. . . .

VI. *Anomaly and the Emergence of Scientific Discoveries*

Normal science, the puzzle-solving activity we have just examined, is a highly cumulative enterprise, eminently successful in its aim, the steady extension of the scope and precision of scientific knowledge. In all these respects it fits with great precision the most usual image of scientific work. Yet one standard product of the scientific enterprise is missing. Normal science does not aim at novelties of fact or theory and, when successful, finds none. New and unsuspected phenomena are, however, repeatedly uncovered by scientific research, and radical new theories have again and again been invented by scientists. History even suggests that the scientific enterprise has developed a uniquely powerful technique for producing surprises of this sort. If this characteristic of science is to be reconciled with what has already been said, then research under a paradigm must be a particularly effective way of inducing paradigm change. That is what fundamental novelties of fact and theory do. Produced inadvertently by a game played under one set of rules, their assimilation requires the elaboration of another set. After they have become parts of science, the enterprise, at least of those specialists in whose particular field the novelties lie, is never quite the same again.

We must now ask how changes of this sort can come about, considering first discoveries, or novelties of fact, and then inventions, or novelties of theory. That distinction between discovery and invention or between fact and theory will, however, immediately prove to be exceedingly artificial. Its artificiality is an important clue to several of this essay's main theses. Examining selected discoveries in the rest of this section, we shall quickly find that they are not isolated events but extended episodes with a regularly recurrent structure. Discovery commences with the awareness of anomaly, i.e., with the recognition that nature has somehow violated the paradigm-induced expectations that govern normal science.

It then continues with a more or less extended exploration of the area of anomaly. And it closes only when the paradigm theory has been adjusted so that the anomalous has become the expected. Assimilating a new sort of fact demands a more than additive adjustment of theory, and until that adjustment is completed—until the scientist has learned to see nature in a different way—the new fact is not quite a scientific fact at all. . . .

In the development of any science, the first received paradigm is usually felt to account quite successfully for most of the observations and experiments easily accessible to that science's practitioners. Further development, therefore, ordinarily calls for the construction of elaborate equipment, the development of an esoteric vocabulary and skills, and a refinement of concepts that increasingly lessens their resemblance to their usual common-sense prototypes. That professionalization leads, on the one hand, to an immense restriction of the scientist's vision and to a considerable resistance to paradigm change. The science has become increasingly rigid. On the other hand, within those areas to which the paradigm directs the attention of the group, normal science leads to a detail of information and to a precision of the observation-theory match that could be achieved in no other way. Furthermore, that detail and precision of match have a value that transcends their not always very high intrinsic interest. Without the special apparatus that is constructed mainly for anticipated functions, the results that lead ultimately to novelty could not occur. And even when the apparatus exists, novelty ordinarily emerges only for the man who, knowing *with precision* what he should expect, is able to recognize that something has gone wrong. Anomaly appears only against the background provided by the paradigm. The more precise and far-reaching that paradigm is, the more sensitive an indicator it provides of anomaly and hence of an occasion for paradigm change. In the normal mode of discovery, even resistance to change has a use that will be explored more fully in the next section. By ensuring that the paradigm will not be too easily surrendered, resistance guarantees that scientists will not be lightly distracted and that the anomalies that lead to paradigm change will penetrate existing knowledge to the core. The very fact that a significant scientific novelty so often emerges simultaneously from several laboratories is an index both to the strongly traditional nature of normal science and to the completeness with which that traditional pursuit prepares the way for its own change. . . .

VIII. *The Response to Crisis*

Let us then assume that crises are a necessary precondition for the emergence of novel theories and ask next how scientists respond to their existence. Part of the answer, as obvious as it is important, can be discovered by noting first what scientists never do when confronted by even severe and prolonged anomalies. Though they may begin to lose faith and then to consider alternatives, they do not renounce the paradigm that has led them into crisis. They do not, that is, treat anomalies as counterinstances, though in the vocabulary of philosophy of science that is what they are. In part this generalization is simply a statement from historic fact, based upon examples like those given above and, more extensively, below. These hint what our later examination of paradigm rejection will disclose more fully: once it has achieved the status of paradigm, a scientific theory is declared invalid only if an alternate candidate is available to take its place. No process yet disclosed by the historical study of scientific development at all resembles the methodological stereotype of falsification by direct comparison with nature. That remark does not mean that scientists do not reject scientific theories, or that experience and experiment are not essential to the process in which they do so. But it does mean—what will ultimately be a central point—that the act of judgment that leads scientists to reject a previously accepted theory is always based upon more than a comparison of that theory with the world. The decision to reject one paradigm is always simultaneously the decision to accept another, and the judgment leading to that decision involves the comparison of both paradigms with nature *and* with each other.

There is, in addition, a second reason for doubting that scientists reject paradigms because

confronted with anomalies or counterinstances. In developing it my argument will itself foreshadow another of this essay's main theses. The reasons for doubt sketched above were purely factual; they were, that is, themselves counterinstances to a prevalent epistemological theory. As such, if my present point is correct, they can at best help to create a crisis or, more accurately, to reinforce one that is already very much in existence. By themselves they cannot and will not falsify that philosophical theory, for its defenders will do what we have already seen scientists doing when confronted by anomaly. They will devise numerous articulations and *ad hoc* modifications of their theory in order to eliminate any apparent conflict. Many of the relevant modifications and qualifications are, in fact, already in the literature. If, therefore, these epistemological counterinstances are to constitute more than a minor irritant, that will be because they help to permit the emergence of a new and different analysis of science within which they are no longer a source of trouble. Furthermore, if a typical pattern, which we shall later observe in scientific revolutions, is applicable here, these anomalies will then no longer seem to be simply facts. From within a new theory of scientific knowledge, they may instead seem very much like tautologies, statements of situations that could not conceivably have been otherwise. . . .

IX. *The Nature and Necessity of Scientific Revolutions*

These remarks permit us at last to consider the problems that provide this essay with its title. What are scientific revolutions, and what is their function in scientific development? Much of the answer to these questions has been anticipated in earlier sections. In particular, the preceding discussion has indicated that scientific revolutions are here taken to be those non-cumulative developmental episodes in which an older paradigm is replaced in whole or in part by an incompatible new one. There is more to be said, however, and an essential part of it can be introduced by asking one further question. Why should a change of paradigm be called a revolution? In the face of the vast and essential differences between political and scientific development, what parallelism can justify the metaphor that finds revolutions in both?

One aspect of the parallelism must already be apparent. Political revolutions are inaugurated by a growing sense, often restricted to a segment of the political community, that existing institutions have ceased adequately to meet the problems posed by an environment that they have in part created. In much the same way, scientific revolutions are inaugurated by a growing sense, again often restricted to a narrow subdivision of the scientific community, that an existing paradigm has ceased to function adequately in the exploration of an aspect of nature to which that paradigm itself had previously led the way. In both political and scientific development the sense of malfunction that can lead to crisis is prerequisite to revolution. Furthermore, though it admittedly strains the metaphor, that parallelism holds not only for the major paradigm changes, like those attributable to Copernicus and Lavoisier, but also for the far smaller ones associated with the assimilation of a new sort of phenomenon, like oxygen or X-rays. Scientific revolutions . . . seem revolutionary only to those whose paradigms are affected by them. To outsiders they may, like the Balkan revolutions of the early twentieth century, seem normal parts of the developmental process. Astronomers, for example, could accept X-rays as a mere addition to knowledge, for their paradigms were unaffected by the existence of the new radiation. But for men like Kelvin, Crookes, and Roentgen, whose research dealt with radiation theory or with cathode ray tubes, the emergence of X-rays necessarily violated one paradigm as it created another. That is why these rays could be discovered only through something's first going wrong with normal research.

This genetic aspect of the parallel between political and scientific development should no longer be open to doubt. The parallel has, however, a second and more profound aspect upon which the significance of the first depends. Political revolutions aim to change political institutions in ways that those institutions themselves prohibit. Their success therefore necessitates the partial relinquishment of one set of institutions in favor of another, and in the interim, society is not fully governed by institutions at all. Initially it is crisis alone that attenuates the role of political institutions as we have already seen it attenuate the role of paradigms. In increasing numbers individuals become increasingly estranged from political life and behave more and more eccentrically within it. Then, as the crisis deepens, many of these individuals commit themselves to some concrete proposal for the reconstruction of society in a new institutional framework. At that point the society is divided into competing camps or parties, one seeking to defend the old institutional constellation, the others seeking to institute some new one. And, once that polarization has occurred, *political recourse fails.* Because they differ about the institutional matrix within which political change is to be achieved and evaluated, because they acknowledge no supra-institutional framework for the adjudication of revolutionary difference, the parties to a revolutionary conflict must finally resort to the techniques of mass persuasion, often including force. Though revolutions have had a vital role in the evolution of political institutions, that role depends upon their being partially extrapolitical or extrainstitutional events.

The remainder of this essay aims to demonstrate that the historical study of paradigm change reveals very similar characteristics in the evolution of the sciences. Like the choice between competing political institutions, that between competing paradigms proves to be a choice between incompatible modes of community life. Because it has that character, the choice is not and cannot be determined merely by the evaluative procedures characteristic of normal science, for these depend in part upon a particular paradigm, and that paradigm is at issue. When paradigms enter, as they must, into a debate about paradigm choice, their role is necessarily circular. Each group uses its own paradigm to argue in that paradigm's defense.

The resulting circularity does not, of course, make the arguments wrong or even ineffectual. The man who premises a paradigm when arguing in its defense can nonetheless provide a clear exhibit of what scientific practice will be like for those who adopt the new view of nature. That exhibit can be immensely persuasive, often compellingly so. Yet, whatever its force, the status of the circular argument is only that of persuasion. It cannot be made logically or even probabilistically compelling for those who refuse to step into the circle. The premises and values shared by the two parties to a debate over paradigms are not sufficiently extensive for that. As in political revolutions, so in paradigm choice—there is no standard higher than the assent of the relevant community. To discover how scientific revolutions are effected, we shall therefore have to examine not only the impact of nature and of logic, but also the techniques of persuasive argumentation effective within the quite special groups that constitute the community of scientists.

To discover why this issue of paradigm choice can never be unequivocally settled by logic and experiment alone, we must shortly examine the nature of the differences that separate the proponents of a traditional paradigm from their revolutionary successors. That examination is the principal object of this section and the next. We have, however, already noted numerous examples of such differences, and no one will doubt that history can supply many others. What is more likely to be doubted than their existence—and what must therefore be considered first—is that such examples provide essential information about the nature of science. Granting that paradigm rejection has been a historic fact, does it illuminate more than human credulity and confusion? Are there intrinsic reasons why the assimilation of either a new sort of phenomenon or a new scientific theory must demand the rejection of an older paradigm?

First notice that if there are such reasons, they do not derive from the logical structure of scientific knowledge. In principle, a new phenomenon might emerge without reflecting destructively upon any part of past scientific practice. Though discovering life on the moon would today be destructive of existing paradigms (these tell us things about the moon that seem incompatible with life's existence there), discovering life in some less well-known part of the galaxy would not. By the same token, a new theory does not have to conflict with any of its predecessors. It might deal exclusively with phenomena not previously known, as the quantum theory deals (but, significantly, not exclusively) with subatomic phenomena unknown before the twentieth century. Or again, the new theory might be simply a higher level theory than those known before, one that linked together a whole group of lower level theories without substantially changing any. Today, the theory of energy conservation provides just such links between dynamics, chemistry, electricity, optics, thermal theory, and so on. Still other compatible relationships between old and new theories can be conceived. Any and all of them might be exemplified by the historical process through which science has developed. If they were, scientific development would be genuinely cumulative. New sorts of phenomena would simply disclose order in an aspect of nature where none had been seen before. In the evolution of science new knowledge would replace ignorance rather than replace knowledge of another and incompatible sort.

Of course, science (or some other enterprise, perhaps less effective) might have developed in that fully cumulative manner. Many people have believed that it did so, and most still seem to suppose that cumulation is at least the ideal that historical development would display if only it had not so often been distorted by human idiosyncrasy. There are important reasons for that belief. In Section X we shall discover how closely the view of science-as-cumulation is entangled with a dominant epistemology that takes knowledge to be a construction placed directly upon raw sense data by the mind. . . . Nevertheless, despite the immense plausibility of that ideal image, there is increasing reason to wonder whether it can possibly be an image of *science*. After the preparadigm period the assimilation of all new theories and of almost all new sorts of phenomena has in fact demanded the destruction of a prior paradigm and a consequent conflict between competing schools of scientific thought. Cumulative acquisition of unanticipated novelties proves to be an almost non-existent exception to the rule of scientific development. The man who takes historic fact seriously must suspect that science does not tend toward the ideal that our image of its cumulativeness has suggested. Perhaps it is another sort of enterprise. . . .

By shifting emphasis from the cognitive to the normative functions of paradigms, the preceding examples enlarge our understanding of the ways in which paradigms give form to the scientific life. Previously, we had principally examined the paradigm's role as a vehicle for scientific theory. In that role it functions by telling the scientist about the entities that nature does and does not contain and about the ways in which those entities behave. That information provides a map whose details are elucidated by mature scientific research. And since nature is too complex and varied to be explored at random, that map is as essential as observation and experiment to science's continuing development. Through the theories they embody, paradigms prove to be constitutive of the research activity. They are also, however, constitutive of science in other respects, and that is now the point. In particular, our most recent examples show that paradigms provide scientists not only with a map but also with some of the directions essential for map-making. In learning a paradigm the scientist acquires theory, methods, and standards together, usually in an inextricable mixture. Therefore, when paradigms change, there are usually significant shifts in the criteria determining the legitimacy both of problems and of proposed solutions.

That observation returns us to the point from which this section began, for it provides our first explicit indication of why the choice between competing paradigms regularly raises questions that cannot be resolved by the criteria of normal science. To the extent, as significant as it is incomplete, that two scientific schools disagree about what is a problem and what a solution, they will inevitably talk through each other when debating the relative merits of their respective paradigms. In the partially circular arguments that regularly result, each paradigm will be shown to satisfy more or less the criteria that it dictates for itself and to fall short of a few of those dictated by its opponent. There are other reasons, too, for

the incompleteness of logical contact that consistently characterizes paradigm debates. For example, since no paradigm ever solves all the problems it defines and since no two paradigms leave all the same problems unsolved, paradigm debates always involve the question: Which problems is it more significant to have solved? Like the issue of competing standards, that question of values can be answered only in terms of criteria that lie outside of normal science altogether, and it is that recourse to external criteria that most obviously makes paradigm debates revolutionary. Something even more fundamental than standards and values is, however, also at stake. I have so far argued only that paradigms are constitutive of science. Now I wish to display a sense in which they arc constitutive of nature as well.

X. Revolutions as Changes of World View

Examining the record of past research from the vantage of contemporary historiography, the historian of science may be tempted to exclaim that when paradigms change, the world itself changes with them. Led by a new paradigm, scientists adopt new instruments and look in new places. Even more important, during revolutions scientists see new and different things when looking with familiar instruments in places they have looked before. It is rather as if the professional community had been suddenly transported to another planet where familiar objects are seen in a different light and are joined by unfamiliar ones as well. Of course, nothing of quite that sort does occur: there is no geographical transplantation; outside the laboratory everyday affairs usually continue as before. Nevertheless, paradigm changes do cause scientists to see the world of their research-engagement differently. In so far as their only recourse to that world is through what they see and do, we may want to say that after a revolution scientists are responding to a different world.

It is as elementary prototypes for these transformations of the scientist's world that the familiar demonstrations of a switch in visual gestalt prove so suggestive. What were ducks in the scientist's world before the revolution are rabbits afterwards. The man who first saw the exterior of the box from above later sees its interior from below. Transformations like these, though usually more gradual and almost always irreversible, are common concomitants of scientific training. Looking at a contour map, the student sees lines on paper, the cartographer a picture of a terrain. Looking at a bubble-chamber photograph, the student sees confused and broken lines, the physicist a record of familiar subnuclear events. Only after a number of such transformations of vision does the student become an inhabitant of the scientist's world, seeing what the scientist sees and responding as the scientist does. The world that the student then enters is not, however, fixed once and for all by the nature of the environment, on the one hand, and of science, on the other. Rather, it is determined jointly by the environment and the particular normal-scientific tradition that the student has been trained to pursue. Therefore, at times of revolution, when the normal-scientific tradition changes, the scientist's perception of his environment must be reeducated—in some familiar situations he must learn to see a new gestalt. After he has done so the world of his research will seem, here and there, incommensurable with the one he had inhabited before. That is another reason why schools guided by different paradigms are always slightly at cross-purposes.

In their most usual form, of course, gestalt experiments illustrate only the nature of perceptual transformations. They tell us nothing about the role of paradigms or of previously assimilated experience in the process of perception. But on that point there is a rich body of psychological literature, much of it stemming from the pioneering work of the Hanover Institute. An experimental subject who puts on goggles fitted with inverting lenses initially sees the entire world upside down. At the start his perceptual apparatus functions as it had been trained to function in the absence of the goggles, and the result is extreme disorientation, an acute personal crisis. But after the subject has begun to learn to deal with his new world, his entire visual field flips over, usually after an intervening period in which vision is simply confused. Thereafter, objects are again seen as they had been before the goggles were put on. The assimilation of a previously anomalous visual field has reacted upon and changed the field itself. Literally as well as metaphorically, the man accustomed to inverting lenses has undergone a revolutionary transformation of vision. . . .

XIII. *Progress through Revolutions*

The preceding pages have carried my schematic description of scientific development as far as it can go in this essay. Nevertheless, they cannot quite provide a conclusion. If this description has at all caught the essential structure of a science's continuing evolution, it will simultaneously have posed a special problem: Why should the enterprise sketched above move steadily ahead in ways that, say, art, political theory, or philosophy does not? Why is progress a perquisite reserved almost exclusively for the activities we call science? The most usual answers to that question have been denied in the body of this essay. We must conclude it by asking whether substitutes can be found.

Notice immediately that part of the question is entirely semantic. To a very great extent the term 'science' is reserved for fields that do progress in obvious ways. Nowhere does this show more clearly than in the recurrent debates about whether one or another of the contemporary social sciences is really a science. These debates have parallels in the pre-paradigm periods of fields that are today unhesitatingly labeled science. Their ostensible issue throughout is a definition of that vexing term. Men argue that psychology, for example, is a science because it possesses such and such characteristics. Others counter that those characteristics are either unnecessary or not sufficient to make a field a science. Often great energy is invested, great passion aroused, and the outsider is at a loss to know why. Can very much depend upon a *definition* of 'science'? Can a definition tell a man whether he is a scientist or not? If so, why do not natural scientists or artists worry about the definition of the term? Inevitably one suspects that the issue is more fundamental.

Probably questions like the following are really being asked: Why does my field fail to move ahead in the way that, say, physics does? What changes in technique or method or ideology would enable it to do so? These are not, however, questions that could respond to an agreement on definition. Furthermore, if precedent from the natural sciences serves, they will cease to be a source of concern not when a definition is found, but when the groups that now doubt their own status achieve consensus about their past and present accomplishments. It may, for example, be significant that economists argue less about whether their field is a science than do practitioners of some other fields of social science. Is that because economists know what science is? Or is it rather economics about which they agree?

That point has a converse that, though no longer simply semantic, may help to display the inextricable connections between our notions of science and of progress. For many centuries, both in antiquity and again in early modern Europe, painting was regarded as *the* cumulative discipline. During those years the artist's goal was assumed to be representation. Critics and historians, like Pliny and Vasari, then recorded with veneration the series of inventions from foreshortening through chiaroscuro that had made possible successively more perfect representations of nature. But those are also the years, particularly during the Renaissance, when little cleavage was felt between the sciences and the arts. Leonardo was only one of many men who passed freely back and forth between fields that only later became categorically distinct. Furthermore, even after that steady exchange had ceased, the term 'art' continued to apply as much to technology and the crafts, which were also seen as progressive, as to painting and sculpture. Only when the latter unequivocally renounced representation as their goal and began to learn again from primitive models did the cleavage we now take for granted assume anything like its present depth. And even today, to switch fields once more, part of our difficulty in seeing the profound differences between science and technology must relate to the fact that progress is an obvious attribute of both fields.

It can, however, only clarify, not solve, our present difficulty to recognize that we tend to see as science any field in which progress is marked. There remains the problem of understanding why progress should be so noteworthy a characteristic of an enterprise conducted with the techniques and goals this essay has described. That question proves to be several in one, and we shall have to consider each of them separately. In all cases but the last, however, their resolution will depend in part upon an inversion of our normal view of the relation between scientific activity and the community that practices it. We must learn to recognize as causes what have ordinarily been taken to be effects. If we can do that, the phrases 'scientific progress' and even 'scientific objectivity' may come to seem in part redundant. In fact, one aspect of the redundancy has just been illustrated. Does a field make progress because it is a science, or is it a science because it makes progress?

Ask now why an enterprise like normal science should progress, and begin by recalling a few of its most salient characteristics. Normally, the members of a mature scientific community work from a single paradigm or from a closely related set. Very rarely do different scientific communities investigate the same problems. In those exceptional cases the groups hold several major paradigms in common. Viewed from within any single community, however, whether of scientists or of non-scientists, the result of successful creative work *is* progress. How could it possibly be anything else? We have, for example, just noted that while artists aimed at representation as their goal, both critics and historians chronicled the progress of the apparently united group. Other creative fields display progress of the same sort. The theologian who articulates dogma or the philosopher who refines the Kantian imperatives contributes to progress, if only to that of the group that shares his premises. No creative school recognizes a category of work that is, on the one hand, a creative success, but is not, on the other, an addition to the collective achievement of the group. If we doubt, as many do, that non-scientific fields make progress, that cannot be because individual schools make none. Rather, it must be because there are always competing schools, each of which constantly questions the very foundations of the others. The man who argues that philosophy, for example, has made no progress emphasizes that there are still Aristotelians, not that Aristotelianism has failed to progress.

These doubts about progress arise, however, in the sciences too. Throughout the pre-paradigm period when there is a multiplicity of competing schools, evidence of progress, except within schools, is very hard to find. This is the period described in Section II as one during which individuals practice science, but in which the results of their enterprise do not add up to science as we know it. And again, during periods of revolution when the fundamental tenets of a field are once more at issue, doubts are repeatedly expressed about the very possibility of continued progress if one or another of the opposed paradigms is adopted. Those who rejected Newtonianism proclaimed that its reliance upon innate forces would return science to the Dark Ages. Those who opposed Lavoisier's chemistry held that the rejection of chemical "principles" in favor of laboratory elements was the rejection of achieved chemical explanation by those who would take refuge in a mere name. A similar, though more moderately expressed, feeling seems to underlie the opposition of Einstein, Bohm, and others, to the dominant probabilistic interpretation of quantum mechanics. In short, it is only during periods of normal science that progress seems both obvious and assured. During those periods, however, the scientific community could view the fruits of its work in no other way.

With respect to normal science, then, part of the answer to the problem of progress lies simply in the eye of the beholder. Scientific progress is not different in kind from progress in other fields, but the absence at most times of competing schools that question each other's aims and standards makes the progress of a normal-scientific community far easier to see. That, however, is only part of the answer and by no means the most important part. We have, for example, already noted that once the reception of a common paradigm has freed the scientific community from the need constantly to re-examine its first principles, the members of that community can concentrate exclusively upon with precision and detail. In the process the community will sustain losses. Often some old problems must be banished. Frequently, in addition, revolution narrows the scope of the community's professional concerns, increases the extent of its specialization, and attenuates its communication with other groups, both scientific and lay. Though science surely grows in depth, it may not grow in breadth as well. If it does so, that breadth is manifest mainly in the proliferation of scientific specialties, not in the scope of any single specialty alone. Yet despite these and other losses to the individual communities, the nature of such communities provides a virtual guarantee that both the list of problems solved by science and the precision of individual problem-solutions will grow and grow. At least, the nature of the community provides such a guarantee if there is any way at all in which it can be provided. What better criterion than the decision of the scientific group could there be?

These last paragraphs point the directions in which I believe a more refined solution of the problem of progress in the sciences must be sought. Perhaps they indicate that scientific progress is not quite what we had taken it to be. But they simultaneously show that a sort of progress will inevitably characterize the scientific enterprise so long as such an enterprise survives. In the sciences there need not be progress of another sort. We may, to be more precise, have to relinquish the notion, explicit or implicit, that changes of paradigm carry scientists and those who learn from them closer and closer to the truth.

It is now time to notice that until the last very few pages the term "truth" had entered this essay only in a quotation from Francis Bacon. And even in those pages it entered only as a source for the scientist's conviction that incompatible rules for doing science cannot coexist except during revolutions when the profession's main task is to eliminate all sets but one. The developmental process described in this essay has been a process of evolution *from* primitive beginnings—a process whose successive stages are characterized by an increasingly detailed and refined understanding of nature. But nothing that has been or will be said makes it a process of evolution *toward* anything. Inevitably that lacuna will have disturbed many readers. We are all deeply accustomed to seeing science as the one enterprise that draws constantly nearer to some goal set by nature in advance.

But need there be any such goal? Can we not account for both science's existence and its success in terms of evolution from the community's state of knowledge at any given time? Does it really help to imagine that there is some one full, objective, true account of nature and that the proper measure of scientific achievement is the extent to which it brings us closer to that ultimate goal? If we can learn to substitute evolution-from-what-we-do-know for evolution-toward-what-we-wish-to-know, a number of vexing problems may vanish in the process. Somewhere in this maze, for example, must lie the problem of induction.

I cannot yet specify in any detail the consequences of this alternate view of scientific advance. But it helps to recognize that the conceptual transposition here recommended is very close to one that the West undertook just a century ago. It is particularly helpful because in both cases the main obstacle to transposition is the same. When Darwin first published his theory of evolution by natural selection in 1859, what most bothered many professionals was neither the notion of species change nor the possible descent of man from apes. The evidence pointing to evolution, including the evolution of man, had been accumulating for decades, and the idea of evolution had been suggested and widely disseminated before. Though evolution, as such, did encounter resistance, particularly from some religious groups, it was by no means the greatest of the difficulties the Darwinians faced. That difficulty stemmed from an idea that was more nearly Darwin's own. All the well-known pre-Darwinian evolutionary theories—those of Lamarck, Chambers, Spencer, and the German *Naturphilosophen*—had taken evolution to be a goal-directed process. The "idea" of man and of

the contemporary flora and fauna was thought to have been present from the first creation of life, perhaps in the mind of God. That idea or plan had provided the direction and the guiding force to the entire evolutionary process. Each new stage of evolutionary development was a more perfect realization of a plan that had been present from the start.

For many men the abolition of that teleological kind of evolution was the most significant and least palatable of Darwin's suggestions. The *Origin of Species* recognized no goal set either by God or nature. Instead, natural selection, operating in the given environment and with the actual organisms presently at hand, was responsible for the gradual but steady emergence of more elaborate, further articulated, and vastly more specialized organisms. Even such marvelously adapted organs as the eye and hand of man—or gans whose design had previously provided powerful arguments for the existence of a supreme artificer and an advance plan—were products of a process that moved steadily *from* primitive beginnings but *toward* no goal. The belief that natural selection, resulting from mere competition between organisms for survival, could have produced man together with the higher animals and plants was the most difficult and disturbing aspect of Darwin's theory. What could 'evolution,' 'development,' and 'progress' mean in the absence of a specified goal? To many people, such terms suddenly seemed self-contradictory.

The analogy that relates the evolution of organisms to the evolution of scientific ideas can easily be pushed too far. But with respect to the issues of this closing section it is very nearly perfect. The process described in Section XII as the resolution of revolutions is the selection by conflict within the scientific community of the fittest way to practice future science. The net result of a sequence of such revolutionary selections, separated by periods of normal research, is the wonderfully adapted set of instruments we call modern scientific knowledge. Successive stages in that developmental process are marked by an increase in articulation and specialization. And the entire process may have occurred, as we now suppose biological evolution did, without benefit of a set goal, a permanent fixed scientific truth, of which each stage in the development of scientific knowledge is a better exemplar.

Anyone who has followed the argument this far will nevertheless feel the need to ask why the evolutionary process should work. What must nature, including man, be like in order that science be possible at all? Why should scientific communities be able to reach a firm consensus unattainable in other fields? Why should consensus endure across one paradigm change after another? And why should paradigm change invariably produce an instrument more perfect in any sense than those known before? From one point of view those questions, excepting the first, have already been answered. But from another they are as open as they were when this essay began. It is not only the scientific community that must be special. The world of which that community is a part must also possess quite special characteristics, and we are no closer than we were at the start to knowing what these must be. That problem—What must the world be like in order that man may know it?—was not, however, created by this essay. On the contrary, it is as old as science itself, and it remains unanswered. But it need not be answered in this place. Any conception of nature compatible with the growth of science by proof is compatible with the evolutionary view of science developed here. Since this view is also compatible with close observation of scientific life, there are strong arguments for employing it in attempts to solve the host of problems that still remain.

Suggestions for Further Reading

The essay entitled "Kuhn" by Richard Rorty in *A Companion to the Philosophy of Science*, edited by W. H. Newton-Smith (Oxford: Blackwell, 2000, pp. 203–206), is a good place to start. Rorty's suggestions for further reading will take you deeper into the literature. The other essays in this helpful volume will also aid you in your study of the philosophy of science.

Chapter 7 in Robert Klee's *Introduction to the Philosophy of Science: Cutting Nature at Its Seams* (New York: Oxford University Press, 1997) is an excellent and clear exposition of some of Kuhn's major ideas and the controversies they have generated. Klee's bibliography will also prove helpful.

For a collection of essays dealing with various aspects of Kuhn's philosophy of science, see *World Changes: Thomas Kuhn and the Nature of Science*, edited by Paul Horwich (Cambridge, MA: MIT Press, 1993).

Video

Worlds Without End (52 minutes) raises questions about scientific progress and its implications for multicultural approaches to knowledge. Available from Insight Media, 2162 Broadway, New York, NY 10024.

8.4 Feminism and Science

Reading this title may make you wonder what feminism has to do with science. You may think that feminism is a political movement designed to improve the status of women and that science has nothing to do with politics. Good science is value-free and objective. Bad science is value-laden and subjective. Surely, you may think, to import political concerns about the status of women into the actual doing of science would be to introduce biases that would taint the results.

We need to pause a moment and think about what it means to "import" value judgments into the "actual doing of science." On one level, it is clear that the context in which science is done is often male oriented (androcentric) in contrast to female oriented (gynocentric). Feminist scholars have shown that a good deal of biological, medical, and social research has taken place in an androcentric context that has tainted the results (see Anne Fausto-Sterling's *Myths of Gender: Biological Theories about Women and Men,* 1985). It has been shown that more money is routinely spent on the medical problems men face rather than on the medical problems women face.

You may say that this is not really science, but rather the politics of science. We do not really need to rethink the nature of science, but rather its social context. Thus better control of funding and research may solve the problem. Or you may say that insofar as androcentric value-judgments have tainted scientific results, it is just bad science. Good science is free from all political and moral values, be they androcentric or gynocentric.

Imagine a situation in which all possible observational evidence is compatible with mutually incompatible theories. This situation is frequent enough in science to warrant a name. It is called **underdetermination of theory**. Theories are underdetermined precisely to the extent that available evidence cannot support a choice between them. This constitutes an epistemological impasse. If evidence does not and cannot guide our choice of theories, what can? Some scientists have suggested criteria like accuracy, fruitfulness, breadth, simplicity, and scope. In other words, you pick the one that works best given a whole variety of considerations. Should moral and political interests be part of those considerations? Is, for example, seeking justice a proper goal of science?

You may argue that value-laden inquiry is just plain dishonest. Being true is the best mark, indeed the only trustworthy mark, of a good theory. Science has one and only one goal—the truth. If other sorts of considerations—considerations like justice—are introduced in situations of underdetermination, then theory choice becomes hopelessly subjective, and science will cease its focus on the single goal of truth. It will become oriented toward multiple goals, thereby degenerating into camps of conflicting ideologies. But will it?

Elizabeth Anderson, professor of philosophy at the University of Michigan, gives what may be a surprising answer to that question. In the following selection she makes a case for value-laden scientific inquiry that supports women's concerns. Such inquiry, she maintains, can be both good science and sensitive to issues of justice if it is done properly.

Reading Projects and Question

1. Write a critical précis (see Section 2.2) on Anderson's article.
2. List two background assumptions and two implications of Anderson's ideas.
3. If you read Sections 7.5 and 7.7, what connections do you see between Anderson's views and the ideas discussed in those sections? List the connections as clearly as you can.

Knowledge, Human Interests, and Objectivity in Feminist Epistemology

ELIZABETH ANDERSON

> Apparatchik (impatiently): How much is 2 + 2?
> Mathematician (cautiously): How much do you want it to be?
>
> —*Soviet joke*

1. Making Room for Values in Feminist Epistemology

THIS JOKE from the former Soviet Union aptly captures the dominant view about what happens when social, political, and moral interests shape inquiry: the result is totalitarian thought control, in which those in power force beliefs to conform to their demands and wishes rather than to the facts. No wonder, then, that attempts by feminist epistemologists to legitimate important roles for social and moral values in academic inquiry have been greeted with such alarm in the recent wars over "political correctness." This paper aims to defuse the hysteria over value-laden inquiry by showing how it is based on a misapprehension of the arguments of the most careful advocates of such inquiry, an impoverished understanding of the goals of science, a mistaken model of the interaction of normative and evidential considerations in science, and a singular inattention to the empirical facts about how responsible inquirers go about their business.

Yet, the task of defending value-laden inquiry is a formidable one. For its most careful recent advocates in feminist epistemology have advanced an ambitious agenda. Feminists have long argued that scientific practice[1] should promote women's interests by removing discriminatory barriers that prevent women from participating in research, by developing technologies that empower women (such as safe, inexpensive birth control), and by paying due regard to women's actual achievements in science and other endeavors. Many who attack the idea of value-laden inquiry are willing to accept such political influences on the conduct of inquiry, because such influences are not thought to touch what they see as the core of scientific integrity: the methods and standards of justification for theoretical claims. These influences affect the context of discovery (where the choice of subjects of investigation and of colleagues is open to influence by the interests of the inquirer or of those who fund the research) or the context of practical application (which, involving action, is always subject to moral scrutiny), not the context of justification. But feminist epistemologists argue that feminist values may properly influence scientific method and theory choice. This ambition challenges the core commitments of many scientists and defenders of the ideal of value-neutral science.

Helen Longino has developed the most careful and closely reasoned recent arguments in favor of using "contextual values"—political, moral, and other values taken from the social context in which science is practiced—to guide scientific method and theory choice.[2] Longino

---

1. I use "science" in the inclusive sense of the German "Wissenschaft," which comprehends not just "science" in the English sense of the natural and social sciences, but all disciplined inquiry found in the academy, including the humanities, mathematics, law, public health, and engineering. I often use "science" rather than the generic "inquiry" to signify that my primary interest is in disciplined, systematic inquiry subject to institutionalized means of quality control (e.g., peer review).

2. Helen Longino, *Science as Social Knowledge* (Princeton, N.J.: Princeton University Press, 1980). See also Lynn Hankinson Nelson, *Who Knows: From Quine to a Feminist Empiricism* (Philadelphia: Temple University Press, 1990).

From Elizabeth Anderson, "Knowledge, Human Interests, and Objectivity in Feminist Epistemology," Philosophical Topics, *Volume 23 (Fall 1995): 27–42, 52–58. Footnotes edited. Copyright © 1995 by Elizabeth Anderson. Reprinted by permission of the author.*

observes that hypotheses are logically underdetermined by the data cited in their support. A particular fact provides evidential support for a given hypothesis only in conjunction with other background assumptions. Thus, two inquirers who accept different background assumptions may take the same fact as evidence for conflicting hypotheses. The failure to observe stellar parallax in the seventeenth century was taken as evidence that the earth did not move around the sun by those who assumed that the stars were not far away. But this same fact was taken as evidence that the stars were very far away by those who believed that the earth did move around the sun. In some cases empirical support, independent of the hypothesis being investigated, can be offered for the background assumptions—although only in conjunction with yet further background assumptions. But in many other cases independent evidence for the background assumptions is not available. Furthermore, as we trace back the sources of support for the interlocking background assumptions of a theory, we find that they do not rest on factual claims alone.

This fact is most dramatically revealed in cases where the available data in conjunction with the shared background assumptions of rival researchers are insufficient to justify the choice of one theory or research program over another. In these cases, dissenting scientists often criticize the background assumptions of their rivals and support their own contested background assumptions by appealing to conceptual, epistemological, methodological, or metaphysical considerations that often rest upon contextually specific norms of inquiry.[3] Thus, Einstein initially appealed to thought experiments grounded in empiricist epistemological norms to argue for the superiority of the theory of relativity over classical Newtonian mechanics. Watson appealed to the methodological norm that we ought to count as evidence only interpersonally accessible observations to argue for the superiority of behaviorism over introspectionist psychology. Functionalist explanation in sociology was discredited

partly because it was incompatible with the non-teleological metaphysical framework of modern science: for those who accept this framework, merely pointing out that a social phenomenon promotes social stability does not provide a satisfactory explanation for why it exists. Marginal utility theory in economics triumphed over classical economic theory partly because its hypotheses could be modeled using calculus, which made many economic problems mathematically tractable for the first time. In these cases, normative considerations about the conduct of inquiry, normative constraints on the form of acceptable data and of satisfactory explanations, and normative desiderata of calculative ease proved to be powerful arguments for theory choice. Where the data run out, values legitimately step in to take up the "slack" between observation and theory.[4]

These arguments show that values embedded in background assumptions help determine what counts as evidence and an explanation, how the evidence should be represented, and what direction the evidence points to. So values play a legitimate role in guiding science that is not reducible to the prescription to simply follow where the facts lead. But this is not enough to show that any sort of value may permissibly guide science. A prominent branch of mainstream philosophy of science accepts the argument that underdetermination leaves room for values to play a legitimate role in theory choice, but it insists that the admissible values must be epistemic or cognitive, rather than, say, moral, political, or economic. Acceptable values are "internal" to science; unacceptable ones are "contextual," or borrowed from the social context in which science is practiced. Thus, Kuhn argues that the values that properly guide theory choice are accuracy, consistency, fruitfulness, breadth of scope, and simplicity.[5] These cognitive values don't have any obvious moral or political content.

A crucial question for feminist epistemologists, then, is whether the sharp division between

3. Thomas Kuhn, *The Structure of Scientific Revolutions*, 2d ed. (Chicago: University of Chicago Press, 1970).

4. Nelson, op. cit., 173–174, 248.

5. Thomas Kuhn, "Objectivity, Value Judgment, and Theory Choice," in his *The Essential Tension* (Chicago: University of Chicago Press, 1977), 320–339.

epistemic and moral or political values is tenable. Longino argues that this division breaks down once we look beyond the content of the standards for theory choice and focus attention on the grounds for supporting them.[6] Here we see that epistemic, metaphysical, and practical interests may all help support a given standard of theory choice. Empirical adequacy is important not just on epistemic grounds but because an empirically inadequate theory cannot satisfy our practical interests in predicting and controlling phenomena.[7] What's more, the content of our practical interests helps determine what dimensions of empirical adequacy are demanded of science. This is not surprising if we keep in mind that theories do more than represent facts—they organize them for our use. The interest in control puts a premium on theories that accurately track in quantitative terms the behavior of objects in experimental and technological contexts, where background "interfering" conditions are tightly constrained and objects are manipulated by one or very few factors under the control of the knower. The Aristotelian interest in leading a life devoted to contemplating the natures of things (rather than asserting mastery over them) put a premium on accurately accounting for the qualitative characters of objects in unmanipulated contexts, where things can display their "true natures."[8] The interest in self-understanding and successful communication puts a premium on theories that accurately account for subjects' behavior in terms that the subjects themselves can recognize, affirm, and act on.[9]

Consider, in this light, two of the theoretical virtues that Longino identifies as among those that may properly guide theory choice for feminists.[10] One is "ontological heterogeneity." This is a preference for "splitting" over "lumping"— for emphasizing the qualitative diversity and individuality of subjects of study and the distinctions among properties commonly classified together. One purely cognitive motivation for this is to seek fine-grained descriptive accuracy. Barbara McClintock's revolutionary discovery of genetic transposition, which was based on close observation of the cytological differences among individual seeds on corn cobs, demonstrates that such a focus can yield huge theoretical advances.[11] But there are political reasons for emphasizing heterogeneity as well. Ideologies that purport to scientifically demonstrate the inevitability of male dominance often appeal to theories that assimilate disparate phenomena under vague, global classifications. Feminist primatologist Linda Fedigan showed that the common idea that male primates "dominate" females is ill-conceived, by pointing out that the numerous distinct measures of individual dominance (social rank, aggressiveness, winning conflicts, strength, initiating group movement, directing group movement, suppressing conflicts among others, mobilizing cooperation) do not correlate, shift over time and context, and in some cases apply only to within-sex rather than between-sex interactions. There is no global, unitary sense of "dominance" in which the generalization "male primates dominate females" is true.[12] Another political reason for emphasizing heterogeneity is to reinforce the self-critical practices of feminism itself. Feminist theories that focus on generalizations about "women" all too often have ignored important differences among women. In the U.S. context, this has meant that characteristics common among white, middle-class, heterosexual women have been represented as the norm for women generally, such that other women either are invisible or appear deviant within the theory.[13] What are we to make of the idea that there is something about "women's" cognitive styles that attracts them more to the life sciences then to the physical sciences or mathematics, once we

6. Helen Longino, "In Search of Feminist Epistemology," *Monist* 77 (1994): 472–485.
7. Ibid., 481.
8. Mary Tiles, "A Science of Mars or of Venus?" *Philosophy* 62 (1987): 293—306.
9. Jürgen Habermas, *Knowledge and Human Interests,* tr. Jeremy Shapiro (Boston: Beacon Press, 1971).
10. Longino, "In Search," 477—478.

11. See Evelyn Fox Keller, *A Feeling for the Organism* (New York: Freeman, 1983).
12. Linda Fedigan, *Primate Paradigms* (Chicago: University of Chicago Press, 1992), ch. 7.
13. bell hooks, *Feminist Theory from Margin to Center* (Boston: South End Press, 1983).

consider that black women scientists are twice as likely as white women scientists to choose a mathematical specialty and only half as likely to choose the life sciences?[14] Emphasizing heterogeneity enables feminist theorists to represent diversity among women and humans generally as a potential resource rather than as deviance.

Both cognitive and political reasons can also be offered in support of a second feminist theoretical virtue: "complexity of relationship." This value supports a preference for dynamic, interactive causal models that emphasize multiple causes of phenomena over single-factor linear or reductionist models. For some theorists, this preference is motivated by a metaphysical conviction that the world is complex, multifaceted, and messy. A cognitive interest in capturing the real causal structure of the world would then concur with this preference. But feminist political interests lend other support to the value of complexity. The preference for complexity encourages historians and social theorists to represent an individual's social power as a feature of context or role supported by others rather than as an individual trait. This representation enables the recognition and appreciation of women's activities, by making visible the role of private, domestic work in maintaining the activity and institutions of the "public" sphere.[15] It also opens up opportunities for activists to imagine strategies of resistance to oppression that involve changing the social structure rather than attacking individuals.

Feminists are not the only ones to justify methodological and theoretical standards by appeal to moral or political considerations. Functional explanation in sociology was discredited not just because it didn't offer a satisfactory scheme of explanation but because, by representing phenomena as functional for the social order, it underplayed the significance of social conflict and discouraged criticism of the status quo. A humanist interest in acknowledging and promoting the dignity and freedom of persons has influenced many social scientists. An emerging methodological norm among interpretive anthropologists is to show one's research to the subjects of study and respond to their criticisms. This norm serves the moral interest of respecting the dignity of those one studies. Chomsky argued for the superiority of cognitive psychology over behaviorism on the ground that the behaviorist explanatory framework left no room for representing human creativity in language use, a core ground of our own self-understandings as dignified free agents.[16] Others have launched a similar critique of behaviorist *methods,* arguing that behaviorism's experimental framework is coercive and demeaning, depriving people of opportunities to express their potentialities for taking initiatives and forging creative solutions to problems.[17]

With all of these moral and political interests shaping methodology and standards of theory choice in so many fields and schools of thought, is there any way to salvage some conception of objectivity in science? Longino argues that there is. In the first place, empirical adequacy is not an optional standard for any research program. Although, as we have seen, moral and political interests may help delineate the domains of evidence which a theory must account for or at least be consistent with, every empirical theory is accountable to some body of evidence.[18] In the second place, all scientists are accountable to other scientists. The evidence to which they appeal must be interpersonally accessible. The methodological standards and criteria of theory choice to which they appeal must be justified to and accepted by others. The entire research community must be open to criticism by others, provide opportunities for such criticism, and respond to it by appropriately modifying its methods, claims, and background assumptions when they fall short of commonly recognized stan-

14. Donna Haraway, *Primate Visions* (New York: Routledge, 1989), 296.
15. Longino, "In Search," 478.

16. Noam Chomsky, "Review of B. F. Skinner's *Verbal Behavior,*" *Language* 35 (1959): 26–58.
17. Barry Schwartz and Hugh Lacey, *Behaviorism, Science, and Human Nature* (New York: W. W. Norton, 1982).
18. Helen Longino, "Essential Tensions—Phase Two: Feminist, Philosophical, and Social Studies of Science," in Louise M. Antony and Charlotte Witt, eds., *A Mind of One's Own* (Boulder, Colo.: Westview Press, 1993), 261–263.

dards. Furthermore, the research community must recognize the equality of inquirers, which is to say that it may not censor or disregard what others say simply on account of their social identity or relative lack of social power.[19] These social aspects of scientific practice—the ways in which it makes each inquirer accountable to others' observations and criticism—are what secure the objectivity of science. They are what prevent inquiry from degenerating into a free play of idiosyncratic preference and subjective bias.[20]

2. The Critique of Politically Value-Laden Science

Longino's defense of morally and politically value-laden inquiry strikes at the core self-understandings of many practicing scientists and at the core legitimation stories told about modern science to insulate it from political criticism. Thus it is no surprise that scientists and traditional epistemologists have subjected her work to pointed attacks. Susan Haack's critiques of Longino articulate better than any other the core assumptions behind the ideal of value-neutral inquiry and provide the sharpest response yet to Longino's proposals.[21]

Haack, like other defenders of value-neutral inquiry, sees many great dangers in permitting moral and political values to shape the criteria of theory choice in inquiry. Such a move would allow inquiry to be infected by wishful thinking: people would feel entitled to infer from the fact that they wanted something to be true that it was actually true.[22] It would invite dogmatism: people would feel entitled to attack as pernicious any reasoning or evidence that did not reach a foregone conclusion supported by their political preferences.[23] It would provide a license for dishonest or less than candid research: researchers would be allowed to focus only on evidence that supports "politically correct" conclusions. The result would be the politicization of research along the lines of Nazi science, Lysenkoism, or *1984*, in which disinterested, honest researchers would be hounded out of the academy, which would henceforth be staffed by political propagandists.[24]

Why does Haack think these are the implications of introducing moral and political values into the context of justification? Behind her alarm lies a particular model of the interaction of evidential and political considerations in shaping inquiry. The model supposes that these considerations necessarily *compete* for control of inquiry. Either theory choice is guided by the facts, by observation and evidence, *or* it is guided by moral values and social influences, construed as wishes, desires, or social-political demands. To the extent that moral values and social influences shape theory choice, they *displace* attention to evidence and valid reasoning and hence *interfere* with the discovery of truth. This model depends upon a particular conception of the goals of theoretical inquiry and the nature of the considerations that can justify theory choice. The basic idea is to limit the goals of theory to the articulation of truths, and then to argue that value judgments have no evidential bearing on whether any claim is true. Therefore, value judgments cannot figure in the justification of theoretical claims or in the criteria for theory choice. It is natural to conclude that to the extent that value judgments influence theory choice, they must be diverting attention from the actual evidential support of theories. A simple logical argument supports this model:

---

19. Critics of the equality requirement assume that it tells us to disregard individual differences in expertise and cognitive ability. But the requirement only tells us not to rank the worth of inquirers' contributions on the basis of their social status. For further defense of the equality requirement and its relation to claims of expertise, see Elizabeth Anderson "The Democratic University: The Role of Justice in the Production of Knowledge," *Social Philosophy and Policy* 12 (1995): 186–219.

20. Longino, *Science as Social Knowledge*, ch. 4.

21. Susan Haack, "Epistemological Reflections of an Old Feminist," *Reason Papers* 18 (1993): 31–43 (reprinted, without footnotes, as "Knowledge and Propaganda: Reflections of an Old Feminist," *Partisan Review* 60 [1993]: 556–564); "Science as Social?—Yes and No," in Jack Nelson and Lynn Nelson, eds., *Dialogue on Feminism, Science, and Philosophy of Science* (Netherlands: Kluwer).

22. Haack, "Epistemological Reflections," 35.

23. Haack, "Science as Social?" 9.

24. Haack, "Epistemological Reflections," 38.

1. Significant truth is the sole aim of theoretical inquiry.
2. Whether a theory is justified depends only on features indicative of its truth, not its significance.
3. One shows that a theory is (most probably) true by showing that it is (best) supported by the evidence.
4. A theoretical proposition is supported by the evidence only if there is some valid inference from the evidence (in conjunction with background information) to it.
5. Value judgments take the form "*P* ought to be the case."
6. There is no valid inference from "*P* ought to be the case" to "*P* is the case" (or any other factual truths).
7. There is no valid inference from value judgments to factual truths (5, 6).
8. Value judgments can provide no evidential support for theories (4, 7).
9. Value judgments can play no role in indicating the truth of theories (3, 8).
10. Value judgments can play no role in justifying theories (1, 2, 9).

I believe this argument captures the core assumptions supporting the ideal of value-neutral science.[25] The debate over the value-neutrality of

science has traditionally taken (6) as the crux of the argument. But the argument is not valid as it stands. In fact, it is remarkably hard to find a valid argument against using value judgments to justify theories that hangs on (6). Particular claims are evidence for theories only in conjunction with other background assumptions [premise (4)]. Premise (6), at most, supports the conclusion that value judgments all by themselves cannot provide evidence for theories. In conjunction with background teleological laws of the form "If *P* ought to be the case, then *P* is the case," it would be easy to license an inference from value judgments to factual claims. So the argument covertly relies on a background metaphysical assumption that the universe is not governed by teleological laws. Furthermore, despite Haack's insistence that no one has ever produced a counterexample to (6), many theorists hold that "ought" implies "can"—that is, that one may validly infer from "*M* ought to do *x*" that "*M* can do *x*," which is a factual claim about *M*'s capabilities.

These flaws in the argument are not worth pursuing, however. For few contemporary defenders of value-laden inquiry stake their case on the existence of teleological laws or on the inference from "ought" to "can."[26] And no defender

25. I am less confident that it accurately represents Haack's views. See Susan Haack, *Evidence and Inquiry* (Oxford: Basil Blackwell, 1993). Haack explicitly endorses premises (1), (2), (3), (5), and (6) [premises (1) and (2): *Evidence and Inquiry,* 199, 203–5; premise (3): ibid., 74, 203–5; premises (5) and (6) "Epistemological Reflections," 35, 42 n. 19]. She seems to think, along with most other defenders of value-neutrality, that (6) is crucial to her case. Premise (6) can play a role in the argument only if something like (4) is accepted. For unless the evidentiary relation can be explicated in logical oaths, the lack of any valid logical inference from "ought" to "is" would be irrelevant to the question of whether "ought" claims can provide evidential support for factual claims. But Haack appears to reject the view that logical inference is the basis of evidential relations. She speaks rather of "fitness" between evidence, background information, and conclusions (See "Science as Social?" 4; *Evidence and Inquiry,* 81–84). Haack might reach (8), not via (4)–(7), but through the assumption that value judgments express something like wishes or desires. Then all she needs for (8) is the claim that the wish or desire that *P* provides no evidential support for *P* or for any other proposition. I render the argument using (4)–(7)

because this captures the concerns of those who take (6) to be crucial and because Longino also accepts (4). The argument diverges from Haack's views in a second way. Haack speaks in the idiom of epistemology, Longino in the idiom of philosophy of science. To bring their views into contact, I have cast Haack's premises in terms of "theory," where Haack herself talks of "inquiry" in general. The argument works only if theories are construed in the logical empiricist sense, as sets of propositions which have truth-values. Many theorists, including Longino, construe theories as nonlinguistic models that can't have truth-values. See Longino, "The Fate of Knowledge in Social Theories of Science," in Frederick Schmitt, ed., *Socializing Epistemology* (Lanham, Md.: Rowman and Littlefield, 1994), 146–8. This raises the larger issue, beyond the scope of my paper, of whether truth is an aim of theory-building at all. I set aside this issue and focus on whether truth is the only target of theoretical justification, assuming the logical empiricist picture of theories for the sake of argument.
26. See, however, Peter Railton, "Moral Realism," *Philosophical Review* 95 (1986): 163–207. No one argues any more that teleological laws govern the natural world. But some,

of value-laden inquiry has ever suggested that values figure in inquiry by licensing any direct inference from "*P* ought to be the case" to "*P*."[27] To focus the debates over values in science on premise (6) is therefore to follow a gigantic red herring. The real contests are over premises (1) and (2): the goals of theory and the relation of justification (criteria of theory choice) to those goals. I shall argue that contextual values properly enter into criteria for theory choice because the constitutive goals of scientific theory-building extend beyond the simple accumulation of bare truths and are themselves properly subject to moral and political evaluation.

But I get ahead of myself. Before we scrutinize Haack's key premises, let us consider whether the alarming conclusions she draws about the implications of contextually value-laden inquiry would follow even if her argument were sound. Haack claims that to allow contextual values to shape theory choice would be to invite wishful thinking, dogmatism, dishonesty, and totalitarianism into science. But the most her argument can so far show is that morally value-laden inquiry will not reliably track the truth. What it *will* track depends on one's further understandings of what value judgments are. Here Haack expresses a remarkable, unexamined cynicism about the nature of value judgments. Her claim that value-laden inquiry leads to wishful thinking makes sense only if value judgments express nothing more than idle wishes or desires: propositions one would like to be true, quite independently of whether they or any other propositions are likely or possible. No serious contemporary theorist accepts such a crude account of value judgments. Even

those who believe that value judgments express something more like emotional states than beliefs argue that emotional states can be warranted or not, depending on the facts.[28] So warranted value judgments, too, must be attentive to the facts. Haack's assumption that value-laden inquiry leads to dogmatism makes sense only if value judgments are essentially matters of blind, overbearing assertion, not subject to critical scrutiny or revision in light of arguments and evidence. Again, no serious moral theorist accepts this primitive emotivist view any more. Haack's assumption that value-laden inquiry will be dishonest comes from the thought that morally value-laden inquiry can only be inquiry designed to reach a foregone conclusion, hence inquiry that will neglect, cover up, or misrepresent evidence tending to show that the conclusion is false. Yet, this supposes that honesty is not itself an important moral value that should guide inquiry. Finally, Haack's charge that politically value-laden inquiry will invite totalitarianism supposes that political values are essentially totalitarian. But feminist empiricists, including Longino, are virtually all democrats and aim to extend principles of democracy to scientific practice, notably in insisting on tolerance of diverse value-laden research programs and on the equality of inquirers. Haack's alarm seems based on the nihilistic view that there is no such thing as moral inquiry at all, only arbitrary moral commitment. . . .

None of the alarmist implications Haack wishes to draw from Longino's advocacy of value-laden inquiry follow from her arguments. Longino's own normative constraints on research communities guard against them. Nevertheless, Haack's central argument does express a fundamental challenge to Longino's views. Even if Longino's recommendations don't lead to a totalitarian abyss, they may lead to false belief, and that is bad enough. Longino rests her case for value-laden inquiry on a logical analysis of the evidential relation between data and theory. If, as Haack suggests, this evidential relation is something like the relation "supporting the

---

like Railton, defend the thought that teleological laws might account for human actions—that is, that sometimes the reason why people do things is just because they are right or good or ought to be done.

27. Why do the critics of value-laden inquiry focus so narrowly on the imagined inference from "*P* ought to be the case" to "*P*"? I think the critics obsess over this single possibility because they imagine only one route by which value judgments could ever influence theory acceptance—via the mechanism of wishful thinking. They therefore overlook the possibility that there could be other routes by which value judgments can influence theory choice.

28. See, for example, Allan Gibbard, *Wise Choices, Apt Feelings* (Cambridge, Mass.: Harvard University Press, 1990).

claim to truth," then it is hard to see how value judgments can figure in this relation unless one accepts some kind of inference from "ought" to "is." Thus, Haack reads Longino as arguing that when the choice between rival theories is underdetermined by the available evidence in conjunction with shared background assumptions, then "we should decide which disjunct to accept by asking which would be politically preferable."[29] But surely Haack is right to insist that the fact that the world would be a better place if a theory were true, or the fact that one would like one theory to be true, offers no evidence for the conclusion that it really is true. Haack argues that in such cases of underdetermination one should suspend judgment rather than plump for one side for bad reasons. Even if practical considerations demand that we act on some theory, this does not justify belief in it, merely acceptance of it as if it were true.[30] Longino claims that underdetermination leaves open the permanent possibility that unarticulated moral judgments may be covertly influencing scientists' assessments of the evidence. But Haack argues that even if this is true, it argues for rigorously exposing and expunging these judgments from inquiry, not for allowing them in explicitly.[31]

Longino's arguments thus stand in need of clarification and further defense. We need an account of how value judgments can properly figure in theory choice which does not just come down to choosing a theory because it is politically preferable. Longino argues that criteria of theory choice can be simultaneously supported by epistemic and political considerations. But if epistemic considerations already support the choice of criteria, then aren't the political considerations superfluous?

I shall argue that the key dispute between Haack and Longino concerns the aims of theoretical inquiry. If these aims are broader than the bare accumulation of truths, and the justification of theories is relative to all these aims, then there is an opening for moral, social, and political val-

ues to enter into theory choice. In fact, Haack already admits that theoretical inquiry aims for more than a bare accumulation of truths. Idle inquiry has no need for theory to accumulate trivial truths. Theoretical inquiry aims at some *organized* body of truths that can lay claim to *significance* [premise (1)]. Thus, it is possible for contextual values to figure in determining what counts as significant, even if they don't figure in determining what is true. Haack forestalls this move by claiming that justification is addressed only to the question of truth, not significance [premise (2)]. Against this view, I shall argue in the following section that theoretical justification cannot avoid questions of significance. For not every set of true statements *about* a given phenomenon constitutes an acceptable theory *of* that phenomenon. Some sets offer a distorted, biased representation of the whole. This can make them unworthy representations of a phenomenon even if they contain no falsehoods. But what constitutes an adequate, unbiased representation of the whole is relative to our values, interests, and aims, some of which have moral and political import. Thus, even the project of defining the boundaries of significant phenomena may involve contextual value judgments.

3. *Why Being True May Be No Defense of a Theory*

If epistemologists took murder mysteries and courtroom dramas as seriously as they take their image of science, they would learn a thing or two about the limitations of truth as a defense of an account of events. Mysteries tease theoretical reason by revealing the facts about crucial events in a sequence designed to turn readers' minds first in one direction, then in another, then in another. Although many characters in mysteries lie, the most interesting characters deceive by telling the truth—but only part of it. It is no accident that in the ritual formula of the courtroom oath one swears not only to tell the truth and nothing but the truth, but the "whole" truth. The significance of most truths can be adequately grasped only in the context of the whole truth. Consider, in this light, the controversy over the role of Jews

29. Haack, "Science as Social?" 12.
30. Ibid., 12–13; Haack, "Epistemological Reflections," 35.
31. Haack, "Epistemological Reflections," 36.

in the Atlantic slave system, sparked by the Nation of Islam's notorious book *The Secret Relationship between Blacks and Jews*.[32] The book stresses such claims as these: that Jews had considerable investments in the Dutch West India Company, which played a significant role in the seventeenth-century Atlantic slave trade; that Marranos (people forced by the Portuguese to convert from Judaism to Christianity) were among the major slaveowning sugar planters in Northeast Brazil; that Jews were prominent among the white colonists of Dutch Brazil and bought a large share of the slaves traded by the Dutch from the 1630s to the 1650s; and that a larger percentage of Jews living [in] the U.S. South owned slaves than did Southern whites as a whole.[33] These claims are all true. Yet, put together, these and the many other true claims in *The Secret Relationship* do not add up to an acceptable account of the role of Jews in the Atlantic slave system. As the historian David Brion Davis argues, even if every purported fact in the book were true, it would still offer a biased and distorted picture of the role of Jews in Atlantic slavery.[34]

The problem is not so much falsehood (although this is also present in *The Secret Relationship*) as the failure to put the facts into the larger context that would be required to assess their significance. The share of Jewish investment in the Dutch West India Company was small, and the Dutch played a significant role in the Atlantic slave trade only in the seventeenth century, when the trade was small. Slaveowning Marranos were not in Northeast Brazil by choice: Portugal had forced them to colonize the area and take up sugar production. Nor is there any reason to call them Jews, as their forced conversion had long since eliminated whatever connections they once had to Jewish culture and religion. Jews owned slaves in Dutch Brazil for only a few decades and

were expelled by the Portuguese in the 1650s.[35] A greater proportion of U.S. Southern Jews owned slaves than other Southern whites only because they were concentrated in urban areas, where rates of slave ownership were higher. Moreover, Jewish slaveowners owned fewer slaves per household than the average slaveowner, because urban slaveowners owned fewer slaves than their rural counterparts. And the vast majority of U.S. Jews lived in the nonslaveholding North. Finally, the absolute numbers of Jews involved in U.S. slavery were vanishingly small: the 1830 census records only 120 Jews among the 45,000 individuals owning 20 or more slaves, and it records only 20 Jews among the 12,000 owning 50 or more slaves.[36] How are we to assess the significance of the facts cited in *The Secret Relationship*? Taken in isolation, they suggest that Jews played a special or disproportionate role in the Atlantic slave system or that their participation was more intense than that of other ethnic and religious groups. But in the context of additional facts, such as those just cited, they show that Jewish participation in the slave system was minor in absolute terms and was no different in intensity from similarly situated ethnic and religious groups. The larger context exposes a serious bias or distortion in the way *The Secret Relationship* characterizes the significance of Jewish participation in the Atlantic slave system. The characterization is "partial" in the literal sense that it tells only part of the truth needed to assess the significance of the matters at hand. What matters for assessing significance, then, is not just that an account be true but that it in some sense represent the whole truth, that it be unbiased. Furthermore, the fact that an account is biased or distorted is a good reason to reject it, even if it contains only true statements. Haack's premise (2) is therefore false: to justify acceptance of a theory one must defend its significance, not just its truth.

I have argued that significance, bias, and partiality are features of theories, relevant to their

32. Historical Research Department, Nation of Islam, *The Secret Relationship between Blacks and Jews* (Chicago: Nation of Islam Press, 1991).
33. Ibid., 23, 20, 28–30, 180.
34. David Brion Davis, "The Slave Trade and the Jews," *The New York Review of Books,* 22 December 1994, 14–16.

35. Ibid.
36. Winthrop Jordon. "Slavery and the Jews," *Atlantic Monthly,* September 1995, 109–112, 114.

justification, that need to be judged in relation to the "whole" truth and that cannot be judged simply by testing the truth-value of each claim a given theory upholds. For in offering T as an adequate theory or an account of a phenomenon, one purports something more than that the constitutive sentences of T are true. Theories don't just state facts; they organize them into patterns that purport to be representative of the phenomenon being theorized, patterns that are adequate to answer some question or satisfy some explanatory demand.[37] But what would be the "whole" historical truth about the Atlantic slave system and about the roles of different ethnic groups in it? What would be an "unbiased" representation of this phenomenon?

One might try to offer a value-neutral account of significance and bias, arguing that an unbiased theory—one that does justice to the whole truth—is one that disregards all contextual values in deciding which facts to represent or how to represent them. But what would such an account look like? The whole truth can't be an account that literally represents every fact about the phenomenon being studied. No theory offers anything close to that. Nor should any theory try. Such a representation would end up burying the significant truths in a mass of irrelevant and trivial detail (e.g., how many waves did each slave ship surmount? how many times did each slave blink?). The whole truth can't be one that rules out in advance all facts that bear on the moral assessment of slavery or of those involved in it, or that describes the phenomenon in terms that evade moral judgment. Such a representation would plainly omit most of the features of slavery that arouse our interest in studying it or else would misrepresent these features by Orwellian euphemism (e.g., by describing whipping as a "labor mobilization technique"). Such a representation would constitute collusion with those who wish to evade moral judgment themselves. I see no contextually value-neutral way to characterize the whole truth, or the significant truths, about slavery.

To get a grip on the notions of significance and wholeness, we need a fuller understanding of the goals and context of theoretical inquiry. Theoretical inquiry does not just seek any random truth. It seeks answers to questions. What counts as a significant truth is any truth that bears on the answer to the question being posed. The whole truth consists of all the truths that bear on the answer, or, more feasibly, it consists of a representative enough sample of such truths that the addition of the rest would not make the answer turn out differently. Many of the questions we ask science to answer are motivated by contextual values and interests—that is, moral, political, cultural, economic, and other concerns drawn from the social context in which science is practiced. When these are the interests that motivate the questions we ask, then what counts as a significant truth, and the whole truth, can only be judged in relation to these interests. Thus, when the question driving inquiry is motivated by concerns with moral content, what counts as a significant truth will be whatever is *morally* relevant to addressing those concerns.

Before we can judge whether a theory is biased, then, we need to specify the question it purports to answer in such a form that we can tell whether the answer satisfactorily addresses the motivations for asking the question in the first place. The question that *The Secret Relationship* purports to answer is thus not adequately specified by such seemingly value-neutral questions as "What was the role of the Jews in the Atlantic slave system?" or even "How did Jewish roles in the slave system compare with the roles of other ethnic groups?" For these do not specify which roles and which comparisons are of interest. The question that *The Secret Relationship* implicitly purports to answer is rather "Do Jews deserve special moral opprobrium or blame for their roles in the Atlantic slave system or bear special moral responsibility for that system's operations?" The whole truth about the role of Jews in the Atlantic slave system, relative to this question, therefore consists of all the facts morally relevant to

---

37. It follows that one could be justified in believing every sentence of T but not justified in accepting T as an adequate theory of the phenomenon it purports to be about.

answering this question about blame and responsibility, or enough of them that adding the rest would not change the answer. *The Secret Relationship* offers a biased account with respect to this question, because it ignores facts morally relevant to answering it—for instance, facts that show that the Jews behaved no differently, from a moral point of view, than anyone else who had the opportunity to profit from the slave system.

When the questions driving inquiry are motivated by contextual values, judgments of significance and bias can only be made in relation to these values. Since significance and lack of bias are legitimate criteria of theory choice, it follows that contextual values play a legitimate role in justifying theories. It follows, also, that theories of phenomena can be criticized on the ground that the background value judgments that organize the theory's conception of significant facts are themselves unjustified. Thus, if it is a moral mistake to pass judgments of collective guilt or merit on whole ethnic groups, then there is no justification even to make "Jewish" a significant classification in historical studies of the slave trade that are aimed at addressing questions of responsibility. What justification could there be for singling out Jews as a comparison class in such studies, rather than, say, the class of people who have drooping eyelids? . . .

Historians sometimes contrast biased inquiry with inquiry that does justice to the events bring narrated and to the people involved in them. That the virtue of doing justice corrects bias expresses a superior understanding of the demands of inquiry than the ideal of value-neutrality. To adopt a stance of value-neutrality is to disregard contextual values in assessing the merits of theories. We have seen that insofar as science is driven by contextually value-laden questions, the ideal of value-neutrality leaves one incapable of coherently directed inquiry at all, because it leaves one incapable of distinguishing a significant from an insignificant fact, a biased account from one that does justice to the phenomena. One does justice not by adopting a stance of value-neutrality but by being impartial. Impartiality is not a commitment to disregard all evaluative standards but is a commitment to pass judgment in relation to a set of evaluative standards that transcends the competing interests of those who advocate rival answers to a question: These standards include honesty and fairness in judgment. To the extent that significance is judged in relation to highly contested political and moral questions, fairness demands attention to all the facts and arguments that support or undermine each side's value judgments, not a pose of value-neutrality. . . .

6. A Cooperative Model of the Interaction of Normative and Evidential Considerations in Theory Choice

The critique of contextually value-laden science depends on the assumption that truth is the only goal of science—or at least the only goal relevant to justifying theories. On this assumption, it is practically inevitable that any influence on theory choice other than evidence (considerations that support the claim to truth) must be viewed as *competing* with the evidence for our beliefs. Value judgments, social interests, wishes, and political demands in themselves have no evidentiary status. They do not support claims to truth. Therefore, to the extent that they influence theory choice, they must be seen as displacing attention to the evidence and diverting the search for truth.

I have defended an alternative conception of science, which holds that there are many goals of scientific inquiry. Multiple goals support multiple grounds for criticizing, justifying, and choosing theories besides truth.[38] Because modern science exists in large part to serve human interests, some of these goals and grounds are based on contextual values. I have identified three ways in which contextual values may shape legitimate grounds for theory choice.

First, all inquiry begins with a question. Questions direct inquiry by defining what is to count

---

38. As Longino also stresses, in her own dual-track model of justification. See her "Subjects, Power, and Knowledge," in Linda Alcoff and Elizabeth Potter, eds., *Feminist Epistemologies* (New York: Routledge, 1993), 101–120, 116.

as a significant fact and what is a complete or adequate account of a phenomenon. A significant fact is one that bears on the answer to the question; an adequate account (one that represents the whole truth) is one that captures enough of the phenomenon that the addition of further detail will not change the answer. Many of the questions we ask science to answer come from the social context of science, not from its internal puzzle-generating activities. The constitutive goals of many sciences, such as engineering, medicine, and economics, are so contextually value-laden that it hardly makes sense to suppose that they have an "internal" source of questions independent from the social context in which they operate. When a theory or account of some phenomenon is taken to address some contextually value-laden question, it is therefore subject to criticism on at least three contextually value laden grounds. The theory, although it asserts nothing but truths, may be trivial, insignificant, or beside the point: it doesn't address the contextual interests motivating the question. Or, although it asserts nothing but truths, it may be biased: it offers an incomplete account, one that pays disproportionate attention to those pieces of significant evidence that incline toward one answer, ignoring significant facts that support rival answers. When the question which the theory seeks to answer has moral or political import, the charge of bias can only be made relative to an assessment of the moral and political relevance of the evidence the theory cites. Such assessments of course depend upon moral and political value judgments. Finally, the theory may be objectionable for trying to answer a question that has illegitimate normative presuppositions.

Second, questions based on contextual interests require answers expressed in terms that track those interests. Contextual values come to directly inform the content of theories not simply by delineating the body of significant truths but by shaping how we ought to describe them. Purely epistemic criteria of significance are not sufficient to define our theoretical classifications. The world is complex and messy enough that it is all too easy to come up with taxonomies that meet basic standards of epistemic significance. So which classifications should we pick? The interests behind the questions' driving inquiry tell us which classifications to use: ones that group phenomena that bear a common relation to these interests. It follows that theories embodying such classifications can be criticized on at least two normative grounds. They may misconceive the relevant, legitimate interests, and thereby classify together phenomena that should be separated or exclude phenomena that should be included in a class. Or a theoretical classification may be based on illegitimate contextual values and for that reason should be rejected altogether.

Third, questions based on contextual interests can only be answered by methods adequate to reveal the phenomena those interests classify as significant. A theory can therefore be criticized for relying on methods that foreclose the possibility of discovering that we have certain valuable potentialities or that certain important differences or similarities exist among the subjects being studied.

The introduction of multiple goals of inquiry allows us to model the interaction of normative and evidential considerations as cooperative rather than competitive. Contextual values aid empirical inquiry by identifying relevant facts and sources of evidence, shaping conceptual schemes for describing observations, and inspiring methodological innovations that open new avenues for empirical discovery adequate for answering contextually value-laden questions. This cooperative model of inquiry supports a dual-track model of theoretical justification. On this view, theory choice is properly based on both normative and evidential considerations. Contextual values set the standards of significance and completeness (impartiality, lack of bias) for a theory, and evidence determines whether the theory meets the standards. Contextual values help define what counts as a meaningful classification and the empirical criteria for identifying things falling under it, and evidence determines what, if anything meets these criteria. Contextual values help determine what methods are needed to answer a question, and evidence gathered in accordance with those methods helps answer it. In each case, evidential and normative considerations cooperate; neither usurps the role of the other.

The need for dual justification prevents wishful thinking and dogmatic insistence from counting as evidence for belief. Contextual value judgments do not play the same role that evidence does in supporting truth claims. But they do play a role in determining what the evidence means: what it points to, how it should be described. No advocate of value-laden inquiry argues that when the evidence is insufficient to justify belief in one of two rival theories, one may take the desirability of one conclusion as evidence for its truth. But contextual values do provide grounds for preferring theories that leave open the possibility of representing certain claims as true and for meth-

ods that leave open the possibility of discovering that we have certain valuable capacities.

My defense of value-laden inquiry suggests that good science is morally value-laden in a more global sense as well: it embodies the virtue of justice. Not value-neutrality, but justice, offers the proper model of objectivity in science. Justice includes the demand to do justice to the subjects of study as well as the demand to do justice to other inquirers: to respect them as equals, to respond to their arguments, evidence, and criticisms, to tolerate the diversity of views needed to secure the objectivity of science as a social practice. The lesson of this defense of value-laden science is not totalitarian, but pluralistic and tolerant.

Suggestions for Further Reading

The article, "Feminist Accounts of Science" by Kathleen Okruhlik in *A Companion to the Philosophy of Science,* edited by W. H. Newton-Smith (Oxford: Blackwell, 2000, pp. 134–142), is a clear and concise introduction to the field. Her bibliography is particularly helpful in guiding further inquiry. Also, in the same volume, see W. H. Newton-Smith's "Underdetermination of Theory by Data" (pp. 532–536).

Of particular note is Helen Longino's *Science as Social Knowledge: Values and Objectivity in Scientific Inquiry* (Princeton, NJ.: Princeton University Press, 1990).

Chapter 9, "The Politics of Epistemology" in Robert Klee's *Introduction to the Philosophy of Science: Cutting Nature at Its Seams* (New York: Oxford University Press, 1997) provides a critical overview, discussing the work of Sandra Harding, Helen Longino, and Lynn Hankinson Nelson. The references in Anderson's notes should also be consulted along with Evelyn Fox Keller's *Reflections on Gender and Science* (New Haven, CT: Yale University Press, 1985).

Video

How Scientists Think and Work is a 19-minute video intended to be used in high school classrooms. You can use its portrayal of science to launch a discussion of gender issues, value-laden theories, and the nature of science. It is available from Hawkhill Associates, Inc., 125 East Gilman St., PO Box 1029, Madison, WI 53701.

8.5 Japanese Views of Western Science

Is science the foundation of all genuine knowledge? Would the alleged knowledge produced by science be less trustworthy if science were subordinated to moral and spiritual values?

These two questions return us to themes on which we have already touched. I mentioned scientism in my introduction to this chapter. Scientism holds that science is indeed the foundation of all genuine knowledge. Science is primary and privileged when it comes to knowing things, or so scientism maintains. In the last section we explored some issues related to science and knowing from a feminist viewpoint. This led to an investigation of the relationship between science and value. In the following selection we return to these themes, but in a different context. The context is cultural, and the questions under investigation by Thomas P. Kasulis, professor of philosophy at the Ohio State University in Columbus, have to do with how differing cultural values influence our understanding of science.

Before we look at what Kasulis says, we need to spend a little time thinking about fact and value. David Hume (see Section 7.4) drew a distinction between fact and value when he argued that one cannot derive an "ought" from an "is." From the fact that *x does y,* we cannot infer that *x ought* to do *y* because the first judgment is descriptive whereas the second judgment is evaluative. To describe something is to state how it is (or is not) with respect to some context. To evaluate something is to find it valuable (or not) with respect to some context. Facts involve how things actually are. Values have to do with the worth of things. If Hume is right, facts and values are irreducibly distinct. Facts are objective. Values are subjective. Facts reflect the way the world is. Values reflect human interest and desire. Values cannot be inferred from facts, and facts cannot be inferred from values.

This distinction between fact and value is reflected in empiricist or (as they are sometimes called) positivist views of the nature of science. According to positivism, science has to do with facts, not values. Indeed, any knowledge claiming the exalted title *scientific* must be value-free. If it is not, then subjective human interests and desires have distorted our thinking about the way things really are. In short, science deals in facts, not values. Religion and morality deal with values, not facts. Hence science is objective, whereas religion and morality are subjective. Science is neutral with respect to human interests. Morality and religion are determined by human interests.

This sort of contrast may seem familiar to you and, perhaps, quite right. The fact that it may seem right indicates the extent to which the positivist or empiricist view of science has permeated our culture. However, since the work of Thomas Kuhn (see Section 8.3) and the feminist analysis of people like Elizabeth Anderson (see Section 8.4), the maxim that scientific knowledge is value-laden, not value-free, has come to be accepted among many philosophers of science in Western cultures. The is/ought gap that Hume so skillfully opened up now seems like a myth or strange dream. Facts and values are not nearly as distinct as they once seemed.

This more recent viewpoint among philosophers of science in the West finds advocates among Eastern philosophers as well. In fact, two of the most influential Japanese philosophers of the last century provide valuable insights into how facts and values are interrelated. These insights are not just theory (as some say); they have important implications not only for the way we live, but also for alternative medical technologies.

Reading Questions

1. What conditions had to be met for Japan to assimilate Western ideas and science?
2. Why did the first phase of Westernization in the sixteenth century fail?

3. What has been an issue of major importance in modern Japanese philosophy, arising out of the modern phase of Westernization?

4. What is scientism, and how did the Japanese attitude toward science differ from scientism?

5. In his early philosophy, how does Nishida "solve" the separation of fact and value characteristic of Western science?

6. What are the three *basho,* how do they relate to one another, and how does Nishida's analysis of their logic lead to revealing the unity of science and value?

7. According to Yuasa, what two major assumptions in the Western view of the body need to be rethought?

8. What is the difference between a relativistic and a pluralistic understanding of truth?

9. In your view, would the subordination of science to moral and religious concerns lead to good science or bad science? Why, or why not?

Sushi, Science, and Spirituality*

THOMAS P. KASULIS

JAPAN SEEMS TO PRESENT two profiles to the West. One is that of a Westernized nation that is a major economic power in the world. Seeing the skyscrapers of Tokyo's downtown districts, hearing Western rock or classical music even in village coffee shops, or tasting the French cuisine of its fine restaurants, it is easy for one to think of Japan as part of the Western-based family of cultures. This face of Japan seems to confirm the interpretation of Habermas and others that European rationality is dominating the world. We might be led to expect that with the passage of time, Japan will become, if anything, even more like the West.

Yet, there is also the other, non-Western, profile as well. It appears to the consternation of foreign business people trying to establish Western-like contractual relations with Japanese corporations. It appears to the frustration of social scientists in their attempts to apply to the Japanese context Western models of social, political, or economic analysis. It appears even to philosophers who have tried to study Japanese thought. Charles Moore, the founder of the East-West Philosophers' Conferences half a century ago, felt able to write authoritatively about the "Chinese mind" and the "Indian mind." When he tried to write about the "Japanese mind," however, he could do no better than call it "enigmatic."[1] These reactions raise serious questions

*Japanese personal names that appear in both the text and the notes may be in either traditional Japanese order (family name first) or in Western order (family name last). Also, conventional usage sometimes requires that historical personages be referred to by their *given* rather than their family names. Here are the names as they appear with *given* name for each in italics: *Masao* Abe, *Setsuko* Aihara, Inoue *Enryō,* Inoue *Tetsujirō,* Kuki *Shūzō,* Nagatomo *Shigenori,* Nakayama *Shigeru,* Nishida *Kitarō,* Nishitani *Keiji,* Oda *Nobunaga,* Sakuma *Shōzan, Masayoshi* Sugimoto, Takeuchi *Yoshinori,* Tanabe *Hajime, Kazuaki* Tanahashi, Tanizaki *Jun'ichirō,* Tokugawa *Ieyasu, Toyotomi* Hideyoshi, Yamamoto *Seisaku,* Yuasa *Yasuo.*

1. See Charles A. Moore, ed., *The Indian Mind: Essentials of Indian Philosophy and Culture, The Chinese Mind: Essentials of Chinese Philosophy and Culture,* and *The Japanese Mind: Essentials of Japanese Philosophy* (all Honolulu: East-West Center Press, University of Hawaii Press, 1967). Moore's "Introductions" to each volume are titled, respectively: "The Comprehensive Indian Mind," "The Humanistic Chinese Mind," and simply "Introduction." The first sentence of the Japanese volume starts: "The Japanese thought-and-culture is probably the most enigmatic and paradoxical of all major traditions. . ." (p. 1). The length of the introductions are perhaps also revealing. The Indian volume is sixteen pages of text, the Chinese ten, and the Japanese three.

From Thomas P. Kasulis, "Sushi, Science, and Spirituality: Modern Japanese Philosophy and its Views of Western Science, Philosophy East and West, Volume 45 (April 1995): 227–248. Reprinted by permission.

about how really "Western" Japanese rationality has become.

In short, Japan is a striking example of an Asian nation that has been successful at Western-style industrialization, technological development, and capitalistic expansion. Still, it has somehow also kept much of its own values and modes of behavior. How can this Western thinking and Japanese thinking exist in the same culture? Part of the answer is undoubtedly social or historical and best left to the analyses of specialists in those fields. Part of it is also philosophical, however. Since the major influx of Western ideas and technology into Japan in the latter half of the nineteenth century, Japanese philosophers have often addressed these very issues. In particular, they have asked (1) what the Western form of scientific and technological thinking is and (2) how it might function in Japan without eroding spiritual and moral values traditional to East Asia.

In this essay we will briefly examine two philosophical strategies representative of trends in modern Japanese philosophy. First, we will examine the early twentieth-century thought of Nishida Kitarō and his attempt to put Western science into its place, a logical realm subordinate to that of ethics, spirituality, and aesthetics. Second, we will explore how a contemporary Japanese philosopher, Yuasa Yasuo, has seen a possible complementarity between modern Western science, especially medicine, and traditional Asian thought about the mind-body complex. Before discussing either philosophical approach, however, we need a sketch of the historical and cultural context of the Japanese encounter with Western thought. Only against that background can we clearly frame the problematics of modern Japanese philosophy.

To frame the specifics of the historical circumstances under which Western thought entered modern Japan, it is first useful to consider generally how ideas move from one culture to the next. Often, of course, they are imposed on a culture by a foreign military occupation. Until 1945, Japan was not in such a situation, however, and by then its internal processes of modernization (or Westernization) were already well under way. For that reason, there has been no prominent mod-

ern Japanese philosophy of "decolonization" as there has been in twentieth-century Indian, African, Islamic, and (to a lesser extent) Chinese thought. Even among Japanese critics of Westernization, the rhetoric has usually not been what "they" (Westerners) have done to "us" (Japanese), but what "we" have done to "ourselves."[2]

In short, Westernization was somewhat like an import item for Japan in the free marketplace of ideas. The issue may have been conditioned by external circumstances (most notably, the expansion of Western imperialist powers into Asia and the Pacific), but to some extent, at least, the Japanese welcomed the imported product. The question is: under what circumstances does a culture freely accept foreign ideas? This is too complex an issue to address fully here. It is easy to let such a question drift off into abstract dialectics concerning the logic of intercultural (mis-)understanding, however. So, for our background purposes, let us simply pursue for a bit the marketplace analogy. How does a product penetrate a foreign market? First, there must be a system of distribution: the product must be made available to the foreign market. Second, the product must develop an attractive image in the new culture. Third, the product must meet some need, or generate some need, in the perception of the potential consumers. Last, the product must suit the tastes of its new cultural home.[3]

To explain these basic categories further, let us consider an extended analogy: the rapidly growing number of sushi restaurants in U.S. urban areas. How can we understand this phenomenon in terms of the marketplace principles just outlined?

---

2. A good example of this ambivalence among Japanese intellectuals about the process of modernization is Tanizaki Jun'ichirō's essay, *"In'ei raisan,"* written in 1933. A fine translation is the short book by Tanizaki, *In Praise of Shadows,* trans. Thomas J. Harper and Edward G. Seidensticker (New Haven, Connecticut: Leete's Island Books, 1977).

3. As Tanizaki's *In Praise of Shadows* suggests, there is an aesthetic dimension to the acceptance of foreign ways. Similarly, in his *Iki no kōzō* (The structure of *iki*) (Tokyo: Iwanami Shoten, 1930), Kuki Shūzō typically characterized cultural influences in terms of "hue" and "tint." These examples suggest that Japanese thinkers often thought of the impact of culture in terms of aesthetic rather than logical categories.

It is not simply the inherent taste of sushi that has given it its market niche in the American restaurant industry. Since the 1950s it has been common knowledge in the United States that the Japanese eat raw fish, yet few Americans wanted to try it. The issue, therefore, is what motivated Americans to want to try it. What changed between the 1950s and the 1980s such that a broadening spiral of supply and demand could develop?

The most obvious difference, of course, was the emergence of Japan as a powerful economic presence in the world generally and in the U.S. specifically. This economic change caused more Japanese business executives to reside temporarily in the United States, thereby establishing the demographic base in large cities for economically supporting a small number of local sushi restaurants. At the same time, more Americans visited Japan for business reasons, often sampling the local fare as part of the hospitality extended by Japanese business associates. Hence, availability increased. Furthermore, as Japan became one of the richest countries in the world, Americans came to admire its power. Americans began to think it worthwhile to emulate the Japanese, not merely observe them from afar as a land of exotica. Hence, we find the principles of availability/distribution and positive image.

One Japanese quality Americans admired was their health. The average Japanese male's life expectancy was almost a decade longer than the average American's. One factor in maintaining that health might be the Japanese low-fat, low-cholesterol diet. As the young American professionals of the baby boom years approached middle age and began to worry about heart disease, the "power lunch" of raw beef and egg so fashionable on Wall Street in the early 1980s was increasingly replaced by foods like sushi. This data shows that sushi was perceived as fitting a societal need to shift dietary habits. The third criterion of the marketplace was met.

The first three factors combined to create a context in which a significant number of Americans would try eating sushi. Then, the fourth condition could be met. If the Americans would acquire a taste for the new food—if they found sushi to be a desirable dietary option—it would become possible for sushi bars to establish a market niche in the American restaurant business. That is what seems to have happened.

Similar conditions had to be met for Japan to assimilate Western ideas, science, and technology. There were two major periods of influx from the West: the sixteenth century and the modern period starting in the mid- to late nineteenth century. In the first case, Westernization was eventually rejected, whereas in the modern period, it has been accepted. Let us briefly examine each case in terms of the four conditions just outlined.

The first factor is availability. In the sixteenth century, Westernization was offered to Japan primarily via Spanish and Portuguese Jesuits and Franciscans. Following the arrival of the missionaries, there was a moderate amount of trade between those European countries (including the Dutch shortly later) and Japan.

The second factor is the positive image of the host culture. The power trappings of Europeanization and Christianity were dual. First, they brought knowledge of the outside world. Maps helped explain the geopolitical constitution of the lands beyond Asia. These were relevant to assessing the opportunities and dangers of future contact with Europe. The Japanese also found the foreigners fascinating: the aristocrats and samurai experimented with things European, including Portuguese dress. The Japanese admired the European worldliness, including the news, ideas, and goods they brought from afar. It might be noted, however, that the Japanese did find the Europeans rather crude culturally. There was some interest in Western foods (sukiyaki, for example, apparently developed as an attempt to make a Portuguese stew with native ingredients) and some exposure to Western art, but in general the Japanese felt more consternation than admiration for the unbathed, bearded barbarians. Most importantly, however, the Europeans brought new technology: some medical and scientific knowledge, but also the military technology of rifles and cannon. This brings us to the third condition—internal need.

For centuries preceding the arrival of the Westerners, Japan had been in a state of civil war, in which various barons were jockeying for territory and political power. There was the need for unification under a new military-political order. The strife ended with the rise to power of three successive military dictators: Oda Nobunaga (1534–1582), Toyotomi Hideyoshi (1536–1598), and Tokugawa Ieyasu (1542–1616). His mastery of Western firearms helped Nobunaga dominate the country militarily, for example. The new leaders initially respected and encouraged Christianity as an aid to unification. They feared the political and military power of the Buddhist sects, many of them having their own militia of armed monks, often numbering in the thousands. Therefore, conversion of the populace to Christianity was not only tolerated, but to some extent encouraged. In short, the introduction of both Western weaponry and Western religious ideas together served the need of unifying the country under the hegemony of the respective military dictators.

The support for these Western influences soon eroded, however. Ironically, this happened because Christianity and weapons technology no longer served the purposes of protecting the sovereignty of the military elite. Hideyoshi learned that the history of the world outside Japan showed that where European missionaries went, European navies and armies soon followed. That hundreds of thousands of Japanese might have a spiritual bond with priests connected to the imperialist courts of Europe was not an idea that Hideyoshi and Ieyasu relished. Christianity was, therefore, first persecuted and then proscribed.

The Tokugawa shōguns also realized that guns did not serve the purpose of a unified state under an iron-fisted rule. A peasant can be taught to fire a rifle in a few hours and kill a samurai swordsman who has spent decades perfecting his skill. Furthermore, ten men with rifles and cannon could kill a hundred archers and swordsmen. Hence, by the 1630s guns were, in effect, banned.[4] If the Tokugawas could ensure that only the samurai had power and that this power

was strictly controlled by regulating the numbers and locations of the samurai, they could effectively rule the country through a central bureaucracy. They did so for over 250 years. During most of that time, with the exception of a few Dutch traders who visited an outlying island under scrupulous supervision, Japan closed itself off from European contact. Hence, the Europeanization process lasted for less than a century, and its effects were intentionally restricted severely.[5]

The influx of Western scientific ideas nurtured a burgeoning Japanese interest in studying the material world. It might be thought that Japanese intellectuals would be hesitant to relinquish that interest. It is significant, however, that Neo-Confucianism, especially that of Zhu Xi, also entered Japan in the fifteenth and sixteenth centuries, primarily via Zen Buddhist monks who brought back to Japan texts acquired during their pilgrimages to China. In that Neo-Confucian tradition there was also the notion of investigating natural things to understand their laws or principles. So, although there was not the mathematical dimension emergent in the contemporary Western science, Neo-Confucianism did offer an empirical interest in the ways of nature.[6] The Tokugawa shōguns opted to support that East Asian empiricism over its Western counterpart. Why? Partly because Neo-Confucianism framed its naturalism within a social ethic, a dimension of its system that the shogunate could use as part of its state ideology. In short, although Western science and technology were available in the sixteenth century and although they often

4. For a general account of the initial acceptance and later prohibition of firearms in Japan, see Noel Perrin, *Giving Up the Gun: Japan's Reversion to the Sword, 1543–1879* (Boulder, Colorado: Shambala Publications, Inc., 1979).

5. The shōguns did allow and even endorsed a very limited influx of Western scientific works, so-called *rangaku* or "Dutch Learning." These were primarily limited to anatomy, medicine, astronomy (for calendar-making), and gunnery.
6. It is noteworthy that the first translated work of Dutch Learning related to mathematics did not appear until 1857, after the period of seclusion was over. See the table in Masayoshi Sugimoto and David L. Swain, *Science and Culture in Traditional Japan* (Cambridge: MIT Press, 1978; Rutland, Vermont: Charles E. Tuttle Company, 1989), p. 331. The book discusses the influx of Chinese science to Japan in two "waves:" 600–894 and 1401–1639. The two premodern Western "waves" were 1543–1639 and 1720–1854. This detailed study adds important nuance to many of the necessarily generalized historical statements in this essay.

had the right image, their practical need was limited and temporary. They also lacked the ethical orientation to fit the image of the state that the Tokugawa shōguns had wanted to foster. So, it was marginalized.

The second Europeanizing phase in Japan is more pertinent to our philosophical purposes. When Commodore Perry forced Japan to open its ports to trade with the West in 1853, Japan once again encountered Westernization in a dynamic and disturbing way. Accessibility to the West had suddenly become a given. The West was at Japan's doorstep, and unlike the early seventeenth century, Japan was no longer in a position to tell it to go away. Japan felt squeezed and threatened. The United States had expanded across North America and into the Pacific; Britain and France were sweeping across the Asian and African continents; and Japan's nearest mainland neighbors, China and Russia, were countries of continental dimension.

The second condition for developing a taste for the foreign was also clearly present—a respect for the foreign culture. Western technology, including the technology of warfare, had developed enormously since Japan's last direct contact. The Tokugawa shōguns had kept Japan in a basically feudal mode for about 250 years. Japan envisioned two possible destinies: either be a pawn in the imperialist power plays of European and North American expansion or be an imperialist power in its own right through extensive economic, political, social, and technological reconstruction. It chose the latter course. It undertook an extensive program to modernize all sectors of the society: the government, education, industry, and the economy. Much of this movement was obviously a response to the outside threat of imperialist encroachment. At the same time, however, it was a response to an internally generated need—our third condition for accepting the foreign.

The Western intrusion came toward the end of a process of national change. The power of the shōguns had waned over the decades, and thoughts of revolutionary change had been brewing for some time. Through information leaking into the country via the heavily restricted trade

with the Dutch, intellectuals were at least peripherally aware of the scientific, medical, and technological revolution occurring in the West. Hence, the internal desire for political and social reform dovetailed with the fear of foreign encroachment. Together, they supported the modernization movement.

By the early twentieth century, Japan had achieved a marked success. It had defeated both China and Russia in wars and had signed a major pact with Great Britain that treated the two countries more as equals. The development of science and technology had become a high priority in education, politics, and the economy.[7] There could be no turning back. The new Japanese industrial society had an enormous appetite for natural resources not available within its own archipelago. Modeling itself on its Western imperialist mentors, Japan looked to secure its supply of resources overseas on the Asian mainland and throughout the Pacific Basin. Japan had become an imperialist power and had set into motion a sequence of events that would result in the Pacific theater of World War II.

It is clear, therefore, that the first three conditions—accessibility, respect for the foreign culture, and internal need—were met. Japan had had a profound taste of Westernization. The issue was now whether that taste was palatable and desirable. In the early part of the Meiji period (1868–1912), intellectuals had expressed the hope that Japan could modernize without changing its underlying cultural value system. This ideal had been expressed in the slogan "Eastern morality and Western techniques" (*tōyōdōtoku to seiyōgeijutsu*) popularized by Sakuma Shōzan (1811–1864), for example. The more the Japanese intellectuals studied Western culture, however, the more skeptical they grew about the possibility of changing their country's social, economic, and political system without also changing its religious and moral values. Toward the end of the nineteenth century, for example,

---

7. For an excellent institutional history of the development of modern Western science in Japan, see James R. Bartholomew, *The Formation of Science in Japan* (New Haven, Connecticut: Yale University Press, 1989).

there was even an idea that science and Christianity had developed together so intimately in the West that it might be advisable for the Japanese emperor to convert to Christianity. The pro-Christian contingent did not win out in the end, and the emperor remained the chief priest of Shintō. Still, many prominent families in the modernization movement did convert. Even today, although Japan is only one percent Christian, Christianity's influence among higher social and economic classes is inordinately strong.

The examples of Sakuma's slogan and the plan to baptize the emperor are revealing. Obviously, even early on, the Japanese were acutely aware of two philosophically significant points. First, Western science and technology seemed to be packaged with a value system, one that at least appeared inimical to traditional Japanese values. Second, many intellectuals sensed that the historical development of the Western economy and the technological world it governed were somehow related to Christianity. Yet, they also sensed, much to their credit, that the connection between Western science and Western values and the connection between Western economics or politics and Western religion were contingent historical facts, not logical necessities. That is, they did not make the common mistake of assuming that what had happened had to have happened. They would, almost from the start, hope that they could have Western economic and technological development without adopting Western values in religion, ethics, and aesthetics. Was this hope justified? This has been a major issue in modern Japanese philosophy.

In exploring this issue, we must be wary of Western cultural assumptions about science. In the West, one often thinks of scientific thinking as acultural, a universal form of theory and practice transcending national boundaries. Unlike art, religion, society, and even morals, we do not tend to speak of, say, French physics as opposed to Indian physics, or German biology as opposed to Chinese biology. Certainly, there may have been indigenous Asian ideas about physical things or life, but they were not "scientific" in the modern Western sense of a science involving empirical observation, controlled experiment, and mathematical modeling.[8]

Certainly, there is much truth in that view of science. (Only in the past couple of decades has the West undertaken a postmodern critique of science, increasingly treating it as a social and cultural construction.) Yet, it is also true that the view of modern technology in Japan is quite different from the one dominant in the West. We must remember that it is the West that invented the modern scientific method of discovery and the technological principles for applying what was learned. Japan, as it has with so many other things that have become important to itself, imported the very idea of modern Western science. For the West, scientific thinking was a natural culmination of a sequence of ideas and trends in its history. It developed science originally as a way of discovering the laws, at first assumed to be the divine laws, of the universe. Assuming God gave humans the rationality to find the divine pattern, early modern Western scientists reasoned that it was their destiny to use that knowledge to complete the act of creation, to modify the world, to make it a better place.

For the Japanese, however, the modern scientific and technological mode of thinking came from outside only about 150 years ago. With their traditional Buddhist and *yin-yang* notions that the world is always in a process of change, technological alteration was accepted as part of the natural order. Nature is changing, so we must adapt to it. Indeed, we are part of the natural change itself. From the traditional Japanese perspective, human technology is as natural as, say,

---

8. Of course, cultural historians of science have generally pointed out the qualifications that must be made about this view of science as Western. In the case of Chinese science, for example, there has been extensive research by such scholars as Joseph Needham and Nathan Sivin. See, for example, Needham's multivolume *Science and Civilisation in China* (Cambridge: Cambridge University Press, 1954–) and Sivin's *Chinese Alchemy: Preliminary Studies* (Cambridge: Harvard University Press, 1968). Also, see Nakayama Shigeru and Nathan Sivin, eds., *Chinese Science: Explorations of an Ancient Tradition* (Cambridge: The M.I.T. Press, 1973).

the technology of a beaver. It is not part of a divine plan.[9]

This raises doubts about the common Western presupposition that science and technology must destroy traditional, nonmodern, non-Western forms of human rationality, values, and spirituality. We often forget what modern science's own ideology is supposed to maintain: science is essentially value-free. The problem is that the Western tradition has intimately connected science with scientism, that is, with the belief that the scientific way of knowing is somehow primary, foundational, or privileged. We should also note that in our scientism, we tend to collapse science into the realm of physics, that is, the discipline which gives a mathematical model for the forces of the universe. The Galileos, Keplers, and Newtons were interested in finding the key to explaining the universe. Mathematics became that key. To go from the idea that mathematics is the key for all scientific knowledge to the idea that scientific knowledge is the key for all knowledge in general was obviously a great leap, but one that enthusiasm could span. Westerners were seeking a replacement for the medieval science of theology; they wanted a single, holistic theory that would yield the one great, uppercase Truth.[10]

The Japanese, on the other hand, were not traditionally looking for that. They were often interested in having a set of lowercase truths, each getting the job done for the task at hand. For

9. A contemporary example illustrates this poignantly. At some major intersections in many large Japanese cities, there are electronic billboards giving readings of the time of day, the temperature, and the levels of noise and carbon monoxide. As the traffic light changes and the vehicles move, one can see the noise and carbon monoxide numbers zoom upward. If such a sign were to appear on most American or European street corners, it would be a political statement about the danger of pollution. In Japan, however, it seems to be taken often as simply an indicator of what is the case. There is the temperature and there is the carbon monoxide level—two givens. This, I think, is one reason the Japanese, despite their love of nature, were slow to address environmental pollution. Technology was seen as natural, not the human intervention into the natural. Of course, Japan did eventually respond to the environmental crisis and has made tremendous strides, in some cases outstripping the West. But even the cleanup campaign was never posed in the humanity-nature dichotomy. It was simply humans taking part in the natural process of purification. Humanity acted out of the need for self-preservation and health, not out of any sense of moral responsibility to the environment.

10. That the enterprise of technological development can differ in Japan from the West is illustrated by the following anecdote, related to me by a research and development officer of a major U.S. electronics company. Japanese corporations hold all the major patents on the technology for the home videocassette recorder. How did this technological advantage occur? In the 1970s the major American electronics companies held a joint meeting concerning the future of home video equipment. At that time, two possible formats had been developed. First, there was the videotape format: it had the advantage of being able to record as well as to play back prerecorded materials. The second was the videodisk format, which was somewhat better in reproductive quality but lacked the capacity to record. Obviously, the videotape system would be more marketable. The problem, however, was the complexity of the videotape mechanism. In a video recorder, unlike an audio recorder, both the tape heads and the tape surface must be in constant movement. Hence, the mechanism was very fragile and the tape tended to get wound around the tape heads causing a breakdown. Although rugged machines had been developed for professional use, the engineers were skeptical about the prospect of an affordable machine that would stand up to the rough use found in the typical American home. They exchanged data about the physics of the mechanical problem and decided that there could be no practical solution.

Meanwhile, the Sony Corporation engineers were tackling the same problem. Instead of swapping formulas, however, they assigned a team of engineers to study the situation. Their approach was to examine the prototype machine for hours, days, and weeks on end, watching how the tape continually got entangled. Then one of the engineers bent a little piece of wire into an odd shape and inserted it into a crucial point in the tape path. The problem was resolved. The production cost of the piece of wire that made the VCR possible, I was told, is about nineteen cents. The interesting part of the story for our purposes is how the Japanese engineer explained to my informant how they came to their sophisticated, technical solution of the problem. He said that they just watched the tape get entangled over and over again until they saw the way to "help the tape go where it wanted to go." The home VCR was the offspring of a marriage between technology and animism.

Another way of posing this is that the Japanese engineers took the attitude of invention rather than pure science. They "tinkered" with the physical object instead of first placing it under the universal categories of mathematical physics. Ironically, this used to be called "Yankee ingenuity."

them, truths were not monolithic but plural, not holistic but partial. The truth varies with the context. Without context, there is no truth.[11] As Zen Master Dōgen (1200–1253) argued in the "Genjōkōan" chapter of his *Shōbōgenzō,* the fish is correct to see the ocean as a translucent emerald palace. The human being far out at sea is correct to see the ocean as a great circle. The celestial deities are correct to see the ocean as shining like a string of jewels in the sunlight. They are incorrect only if they claim that their view is the only correct view.[12] Therefore, the Japanese had the tendency to accept science without its being a scientism. Science is true within its own context; traditional Japanese values in religion, ethics, and aesthetics are also true within their own contexts. This interpretation of science as no more than one example of multiple, equally valid contextual systems was sometimes found in turn-of-the-century Japanese philosophy.[13]

As students of Western philosophy, however, Japanese thinkers began to see difficulties in a theory of contextual truth that did not articulate any hierarchy or criterion of appropriateness for the different contexts. In such a philosophy, there could be no overall consistency, nor any dialectic progress toward an ever more inclusive system. Surely, it was thought, some forms of rationality necessarily evolve out of others; some forms of thinking are simply of a higher order than others. Once a culture develops science, it does not go back to animism. At least such was the argument of Western thinkers like Comte and Hegel, and the early twentieth-century Japanese philosophers were acutely aware of their theories. Is scientific knowledge somehow higher than, say, religious ways of explaining and assimilating reality? Is scientism—a possible byproduct of Westernization—philosophically justified? If so, Western technique could not logically exist alongside Asian morality.

These concerns were anticipated by Japanese philosophers early in this century. Nishida Kitarō (1870–1945), the founder of the Kyōto School, ruminated about this problem throughout his career. We will consider two major phases of his thought. The first phase was developed mainly in his first book, *An Inquiry into the Good (Zen no kenkyū),* written in 1911.[14] *Inquiry into the Good* was written at the very end of the Meiji period, a time when Japanese national confidence was on the upswing and the country had the opportunity to reflect seriously on the full implication of Westernization. In that pioneering work, indeed in all his works to follow, Nishida struggled with the great philosophical issue of his time—the juxtaposition of Western science and technology with traditional Japanese values. If Japanese values were to coexist alongside Western empiricism, there would have to be a common philosophical structure embracing and grounding the

---

11. There were exceptions to this general tendency to seek contextual truths over a single, comprehensive, systematic Truth. In the early Heian period, for example, Kūkai's esoteric Buddhism tried to develop a comprehensive philosophical system including metaphysics, epistemology, a theory of language, and aesthetics. It did not develop much after him as a continuing tradition, however. In the Tokugawa period, Zhu Xi's Neo-Confucian philosophy also had some tendencies toward developing a single, comprehensive system of truth. It was undermined almost immediately, though, by the more antirationalistic, indigenous development of *kogaku* and *kokugaku.*

12. This work has appeared in various translations. See, for example, Kazuaki Tanahashi, ed., *Moon in a Dewdrop: Writings of Zen Master Dōgen* (San Francisco: North Point Press, 1985). The fascicle "*Genjōkōan*" is translated as "Actualizing the Fundamental Point," and the passage cited is found on page 71.

We may also note in passing that Dōgen's position on this point is akin to the pragmatism of Hilary Putnam's "internal realism," for example. For Putnam, truth or meaning is relative to the concepts in which it is framed. As the conceptual systems change, different propositions or theories will be true, even propositions that, if they had shared the same conceptual system, would be incompatible. Putnam develops this view in, for example, his book *The Many Faces of Realism: The Paul Carus Lectures* (LaSalle, Illinois: Open Court Publishing, 1987). This parallel exemplifies the extent to which Dōgen's type of philosophical stance cannot be discounted as merely "premodern" in the Western sense.

13. On trying to set the contextual domains for realism vs. idealism or science vs. spirituality, see the discussion of Inoue Enryō and Inoue Tetsujirō, in chapter 1 of the dissertation by

Robert J. J. Wargo, "The Logic of Basho and the Concept of Nothingness in the Philosophy of Nishida Kitarō" (Ann Arbor: University of Michigan, 1972).

14. Nishida Kitarō, *An Inquiry into the Good,* trans. Masao Abe and Christopher Ives (New Haven, Connecticut: Yale University Press, 1990).

two. Otherwise, Japan would, intellectually, at least, suffer a cultural schizophrenia.

As a philosopher, Nishida was able to take the issue out of its culture-bound form (such as the question of whether the emperor should become Christian in order to help modernization) and universalize it into the classic Western problem of the relation between fact (*is*) and value (*ought*). In this way, Nishida saw himself addressing a fundamental philosophical question, not just a cultural problem. One option open to Nishida was to follow the route of Hume and Kant, bifurcating fact and value into two separate domains and (for Kant) two different kinds of reasoning. This approach would, of course, affirm the possibility of separating Western science from Japanese values. But at what cost? Nishida knew that such a separation of *is* and *ought* was itself a divergence from the Eastern tradition. It was, in the final analysis, a Western approach to the problem, and it would indeed seem strange that only a foreign way of thinking could justify preserving Japanese values.

So Nishida tried to bring fact and value, empiricism and morality (or religion or art), back together in a way consonant with the Asian tradition. At the same time, he thought his theory should be Western enough in form to serve the needs of an increasingly Westernized society. Here Nishida, like his childhood and lifelong friend D. T. Suzuki, found the writing of William James particularly provocative.[15] Rather than analyze science and value as two unrelated systems of reason, Nishida used James' notion of "pure experience" to articulate the common experiential flow toward unity underlying both the scientific and valuational enterprises. The surface differences notwithstanding, on a deeper level, science, morality, art, and religion share a single preconceptual drive (or "will") to unity. On the intellectual level, Nishida called this process "the intellectual intuition." Such was the basic thrust of his maiden philosophical work.

This solution to the fact/value, or is/ought, dilemma also satisfied Nishida as a practicing Zen Buddhist. Zen's ideal is the achievement of a preconceptual state of experiential purity ("no-mind") that becomes enacted pragmatically in various concrete ways, including thought.[16] For both James and Zen, thought is the temporary response to a break in the original unity of experience, a response which is itself intended to bring back the original unity of the experience. As Nishida put it, "pure experience is the alpha and omega of thought."

Inquiry into the Good became immediately popular among Japanese intellectuals and is probably today still the best-known work in modern philosophy among the Japanese. It is questionable how many of those intellectuals actually fathomed the nuances of Nishida's theory, but the major point for them was that Nishida had made Western-style philosophizing into something Japanese. His writing style had a Western ring to it, yet its fundamental insights were consistent with Japanese tradition. With *Inquiry into the Good,* modern Japanese philosophy—the so-called Kyōto or Nishida School—was born.

As Nishida's philosophical thinking further matured, however, he grew dissatisfied with *Inquiry into the Good*—not with its purpose, but with its philosophical form, its structural presuppositions. In particular, he criticized its psychologism (or "mysticism," as he sometimes called it). At the heart of his uneasiness was that *Inquiry into the Good* had attempted to solve the problem of the science/value split by appealing to a kind of experience, asserting it to be the ground of both the *is* and the *ought*. Nishida's readings in the Neo-Kantians during the period shortly after the publication of *Inquiry into the Good* made him sensitive to the problem of how forms of judgment, rather than strata of experience, interrelate.[17] That is, his

15. Suzuki tended to focus on James' *Varieties of Religious Experience,* whereas Nishida was more interested in the *Psychology* and *Essays on Radical Empiricism.* This suggests the fundamental difference in their orientations: Suzuki was more religious and mystical, Nishida more psychological and epistemological.

16. For an account of Zen Buddhism that emphasizes this aspect, see my *Zen Action/Zen Person* (Honolulu: University of Hawaii Press, 1981).

17. For a highly edited translation of Nishida's journals on his reading of the Neo-Kantians, see his *Intuition and Reflection in Self-consciousness,* trans. Valdo H. Viglielmo with Takeuchi Yoshinori and Joseph S. O'Leary (Albany, New York: State University of New York Press, 1987).

concerns shifted from philosophical psychology to epistemology.

Throughout his life, Nishida constructed and subsequently razed his own attempts at systematic philosophy. He was an adamant critic of his own work and never seemed satisfied with the mode of explanations he had developed thus far. So the second phase of his thought rejected the idea that *Inquiry into the Good* had explained anything at all; it had simply described the drive of consciousness toward unification. One problem was that the psychologistic standpoint could only trace the evolution of thought in the individual's experiential process. It could, for example, describe how the desire for unity would lead to the emergence of scientific, moral, and religious thinking. But what about the fields of science, morality, and religion themselves? How can we analyze the interrelation of their claims without limiting them to modes in the biography of a particular person's own experience? It is, after all, one matter to say that my empirical, moral, aesthetic, and religious experiences relate to each other, and quite another matter to say that science, morality, art, and religion are related. The first is to connect experiences within myself, the latter to connect kinds of judgments about what is right. Nishida was impressed with the Neo-Kantian attempts to articulate and explain the rationale of judgments and came to believe his earlier, Jamesian view to be overly subjectivistic.

This new interest led Nishida to examine more closely the structure of judgmental form, what he called its "logic" (*ronri*). The fundamental insight he explored was that any judgment necessarily arises out of a particular contextual field, place, or *topos*. The Japanese word for this contextual field is *basho*. There may be a plurality of truths and contexts, but how do those contexts interrelate? In effect, Nishida wanted to argue for the priority of the religious over both the idealist and empiricist, over both the psychologistic and the scientific. Although his argument was complex and refined or revised over many years, we can briefly summarize his point here in order at least to suggest how his line of thought developed.

Nishida analyzed closely the logical structure of judgmental form. Because he believed that any judgment necessarily arises out of a particular contextual field or place, his task in his later years was to explain the logic of those fields (*basho no ronri*). One way this system came to be formulated was in terms of the three *basho* of being, relative nothingness, and absolute nothingness. Roughly speaking, these corresponded to the judgmental fields of empiricism, idealism, and what he called the field of the "acting intuition" (*kōiteki chokkan*).[18]

Nishida's "logic of *basho*" is a complex system always in flux and under revision. Still, it represents Nishida's most integrated and systematic attempt to deal with the issues of fact and value. To see the overall structure of Nishida's logic of *basho*, we can consider a simple empirical judgment—for example, "this table is brown." Scientific statements are generally of this form. They seem to express pure objectivity; the observer is so neutralized that he or she does not even enter into the judgment per se. They are statements about what is, statements about being (hence, the nomenclature "*basho* of being").

Yet, Nishida asked in what contextual field (*basho*) is such an objective judgment made? Where does one stand in making such a judgment about being? Nishida argued that such a judgment actually also makes judgments about our own consciousness. To neutralize the role of the observer as ordinary empirical judgments do is to say something about the observer—its role can be neutralized and ignored. This is an odd thing to say, however, since the larger contextual field of the judgment "the table is brown" is something more like "I see a brown table, and because what I see is real and external to my self, I can delete any reference to the self." So, Nishida maintains, the field or place of empirical judgments is really within the encompassing field of judgments about self-consciousness. Empiricism is actually dependent on, stands within, a field of judgments about self and its relation to the ob-

18. The best treatment of this aspect of Nishida's thought is the dissertation by Robert J. J. Wargo, cited in note 13 above. The dissertation's Appendix includes a translation of Nishida's "General Summary" in his *The System of Self Consciousness of the Universal,* a crucial formulation of Nishida's position at this stage of his thought.

jects of experience. Since empirical judgments, as empirical judgments, ignore the being of the self, treating it as a nothing, this encompassing field can be called the "*basho* of relative nothingness." The self is, relative to empirical judgments, treated as a nothing. Of course, from the standpoint of the *basho* of relative nothingness, the self is very much a something, the very thing empiricism assumes, yet ignores. This insight, when taken literally, becomes the basis for idealism, theories that maintain that all knowledge is based in the mind.

Yet, Nishida was no idealist either. He criticized idealists (including Kant, Hegel, and Husserl) for not recognizing the true character of the *basho* within which their theories were formulated. The mistake of the idealists, according to Nishida, is that they think of the self as a thing, either a substance or a transcendental ego. Nishida claimed that the "I" in the previously stated judgment "I see a brown table and . . ." is not an agent, but an action, what he called the "acting intuition." So the *basho* of idealism that sees the self as both subject and object is itself encompassed by a third *basho*, the contextual field of "absolute nothingness." The acting intuition is both an active involvement in the world and an intuitive reception of information about that world. It is a process, not a thing, so it can never be either the subject or the object of itself. It can never be the gist of judgment—it is absolutely a nothing when it comes to any judgment. Hence, it is called "absolute nothingness."

The acting-intuiting process (the absolute nothingness) is, therefore, the true basis of judgments about both fact and value. On the surface level, fact is, as it were, the intuiting side, whereas value is the acting side. Yet, one never exists without the other. The two are moments or profiles of a single process. The facts we discover are influenced by what we value, and what we value is influenced by what we discover. Thus, as Yuasa Yasuo has explained in his analysis of Nishida,[19]

the intuition is also active (informed by value) and the acting is also passive (as response to data received). The two poles of the process are totally inseparable.

For Nishida, therefore, science cannot replace spirituality, nor can it be separated from questions of value. Within its own terms, in its own *basho*, science can advocate an impersonal, value-free objectivity. But what makes science possible is the scientist—a person with interests, values, and creativity. It is human intention that cordons off a place within which science can function.

Furthermore, human intentionality can he explained within its own mentalistic or idealistic terms, as we do in phenomenology, psychoanalysis, and some forms of psychology. In taking the self as their starting point, these disciplines have a clearly demarcated field within which to function. Yet, Nishida asks, what makes that field possible? Even "self" is a construction. It is not a given, but a product. As the idealists recognize, the self creates values that direct human activities like science. Nishida noted, however, that focusing an analysis on the self, indeed the very idea that there is a self, is itself a value. Nishida maintains that there is something more basic than self that constitutes the self—a responsive and creative process. That there is something more basic than self is a fundamental insight related to religious, ethical, and (sometimes) aesthetic values. It is this ineffable ground that is the basis for both self and the empirical world as known through science. At least such was Nishida's argument.

To sum up, in Japan, science did not have to break free of religious roots. It did not have to establish its hegemony. Rather, science and technology were foreign imports used to meet a set of practical needs related to political, military, and economic necessity. The traditional Japanese understanding of religion in terms of responsiveness and creativity was not displaced or successfully challenged by a new way of knowing. It did not have to be. The spiritual could continue to be a cornerstone of Japanese values, and, as Nishida tried to show, science could be seen as a special contextual extension of it, rather than a challenger to it.

19. Yuasa Yasuo, *The Body: Toward an Eastern Mind-Body Theory*, ed. T. P. Kasulis, trans. Nagatomo Shigenori and T. P. Kasulis (Albany, New York: State University of New York Press, 1987), chap. 2.

Of course, not every Japanese philosopher agreed with Nishida. Yet, his impact has continued to be significant in Japan. In preparation for the college entrance examinations, only one book of Japanese philosophy is required reading: Nishida's *Inquiry into the Good*. Nishida's philosophical system is significant as an early, prewar philosophical struggle to articulate how it was possible to maintain "Asian values" and still develop "Western technique." His theory, in effect, justified what was already the social practice of giving science its "place" alongside the "places" of traditional religious and moral values. His philosophical theory showed, if nothing else, a distinctively Japanese way of accepting science without paying homage to the totem of scientism.

Has this tradition continued into more recent Japanese philosophy? The Kyōto School of philosophy founded by Nishida remains one of the most vigorous traditions in Japanese thought today.[20] Even philosophers who are not directly connected with the school still appreciate Nishida's pioneering work. We may wonder, therefore, whether there can be some fruitful interaction between Japanese and Western thought in the future. Yuasa Yasuo (1925–) is a Japanese philosopher who has been giving this issue some extensive thought over the past two decades, especially in terms of philosophical and medical views of the body. Since his works are beginning to be available in English translation,[21] let us

briefly discuss his theory and its implications for our present theme.

Yuasa notes that, like science in general, Western and Asian medical traditions arose out of a radically different set of assumptions. He especially focuses on contrasting models of the body. With the birth of modern science in the West, the metaphor of the body as mechanism has become highly influential. Against this background, the West has tended to understand the living body's relation to the dead body as analogous to a machine that is either operative or turned off. Hence, modern Western medicine derives to a great extent from the anatomical information learned through the dissection of corpses or vivisection of animals, neither of which allows access to the functions of the conscious human body. More recently, the model was enhanced by the study of physiology in terms of organs and their biochemical functions. For Yuasa, what is significant is that most of this information was amassed under the assumption that the body can be understood independently of the mind, the physical mechanism independently of consciousness.

Asian forms of medicine such as Chinese acupuncture, on the other hand, developed out of the study of living, conscious human beings. The operative assumption is that the mind-body forms a single energy system responsive to the field in which it functions. To a traditional Asian medical theorist, it would be counterintuitive to study a dead or unconscious human body. It would be like trying to study electromagnetism with the electric current turned off.

Because of this difference in philosophical assumptions, Asian and Western medical traditions developed expertise in radically different aspects of human health and disease. Acupuncture developed highly sophisticated procedures for controlling pain, for example. (It is hard to study pain by dissecting a corpse.) On the other hand, Western medicine became expert at the physical manipulation of the body through surgery, for instance. (Surgery would not develop very far in

20. Two other prominent members of the Kyōto School interested in the place of science were Tanabe Hajime (1885–1962) and Nishitani Keiji (1900–1990). Some of their works have become available in English: Tanabe Hajime, *Philosophy as Metanoetics*, trans. Takeuchi Yoshinori (Berkeley: University of California Press, 1986); Nishitani Keiji, *Religion and Nothingness*, trans. Jan Van Bragt (Berkeley: University of California Press, 1982); Nishitani Keiji, *The Self-Overcoming of Nihilism*, trans. Graham Parkes and Setsuko Aihara (Albany, New York: State University of New York Press, 1990); Nishitani Keiji, *Nishida Kitarō*, trans. Yamamoto Seisaku and James W. Heisig (Berkeley: University of California Press, 1991).

21. So far, three book-length works have appeared: Yuasa Yasuo, *The Body* (see note 19 above); David Edward Shaner, Shigenori Nagatomo, and Yuasa Yasuo, *Science and Comparative Philosophy: Introducing Yuasa Yasuo* (Leiden: E. J. Brill,

1989); and Yuasa Yasuo, *The Body, Self-cultivation, and Ki-energy*, trans. Shigenori Nagatomo and Monte S. Hull (Albany, New York: State University of New York Press, 1993).

a culture where patients were conscious and unanesthetized.)

In recent decades, Western medicine has developed increasingly sophisticated instruments for studying the living, conscious human being. There has been, therefore, a concurrent interest in psychosomatic and holistic approaches to medicine. Conversely, Asians have been learning Western medical techniques and have shown an interest in Western surgical, pharmaceutical, and diagnostic approaches. So, we are finding a situation in which two different conceptual schemes—and their correspondingly different claims about the body—are being brought into conjunction. Can the two systems influence and enrich each other? Yuasa claims they can, but only if each side is willing to call into question some of its most treasured assumptions. Since the Western tradition is more familiar to most of us, let us list just two major assumptions that Yuasa believes must be rethought in the Western view of the body.

According to Yuasa, the modern West has generally tended to assume that the relationship between the mind and the body is fixed and universal. That is, Western theorists tend to ask, "What is *the* relationship between the mind and the body?" Yuasa points out that, in contrast, most Asian traditions assume there is a range of interaction and integration between mind and body. For example, as I learned to type or play the piano, the relationship between my mind and my fingers changed. Originally, my mind had to "tell" my fingers what to do in a separate, self-conscious act. The fingers responded slowly, awkwardly, and imprecisely. Now my fingers are more the extension of my mind when I type or play the piano. This suggests modification in the mind-body system.

Yuasa also points out that traditional Asian medicine retained its intimate relation with Asian spiritual disciplines. The Indian yogin is a good example of how the integration of mind and body is considered to be both a spiritually and medically healthy goal. As we noted already, modern Western science had to separate itself from religion in order to develop. Fasting, contemplation, prayer, chanting, and repetitive ritual exercises

can all shed light on aspects of our bodies as well as our souls, but these activities have fallen outside the concerns of the Western scientific study of the body. Modern Western medicine has only recently begun to explore the therapeutic benefits of biofeedback, relaxation exercises, visualization techniques, and so forth. In effect, these originally spiritual exercises are beginning to find their way back into our Western understanding of the body.

The second assumption that Yuasa believes Western mind-body theories should reexamine concerns what he sometimes calls the "third entity" that is neither mental nor somatic, but the basis of both. Taking physics for its paradigm, modern Western science has drawn too strong a bifurcation between matter and energy. If we were to take biology, not physics, to be the ground of science (as Asian cultures did, in many respects), then we would see the need for this third term. In fact, we would be asking not about matter and energy's applicability to biology, but rather about this third term's relation to non-human phenomena. Yuasa believes that in East Asia, the Chinese concept of *qi* (*ki* in Japanese) is just such a third term. It is interesting that it is foundational to East Asian theories of acupuncture, artistry, electricity, and cosmology alike. What Yuasa calls for is a more Western physical study of this phenomenon that is not even as yet recognized as a category in the West. Such research is, in fact, under way in both China and Japan.

From the examples of Nishida and Yuasa, what summary statements can we make about the modern Japanese philosophical views of science and technology?

1. A non-European culture can accept Western science and technology without necessarily destroying the roots of its traditional value systems. The opposition of science and spirituality, the bifurcation of *is* and *ought,* is a consequence of historical developments in the West and need not apply to other cultural traditions with different histories. For these oppositions not to occur, however, science must not degenerate into a scientism, the belief that only the scientific form of knowledge is valid or that scientific knowledge is

the ground of all legitimate forms of knowing. The evidence suggests that the Japanese have been able to accept science without falling prey to scientism. Nishida's and Yuasa's philosophies give two prominent rationales for keeping science distinct from the assumptions of scientism.

2. The Japanese philosophical tradition for centuries has resisted the idea of developing a single monolithic ontology implying the existence of a single, all-embracing Truth. Rather, the Japanese have traditionally emphasized a world of multiple truths, each dependent on its context. This is not, it should be noted, a relativism, but a pluralism. Relativism would maintain that there is no standpoint by which to judge truth. Pluralism maintains that truth can only be judged from one standpoint at a time, and the standpoints themselves can be judged as appropriate to the questions asked. Within a given context, things are absolutely true or false, not just relatively so.

The Japanese view lends itself to seeing Western logic and scientific thinking as a pragmatic tool for addressing certain problems, rather than as an attempt to explain all things within one supersystem. The god of Western logic and empiricism can only be a henotheistic god, not the monotheistic god that scientism tries to make of it.

3. Following on the previous point, we can wonder about the relation between pluralism and philosophy or religion. Today there seems a need to express our philosophical and religious commitments within a pluralistically open context. Does the Japanese view of truth better lend itself to that enterprise than do the more monolithic, system-building approaches inherited from our Christian and modern Western philosophical traditions? Is part of the success of the Japanese economy related to the culture's capacity to recognize the dependence of truth on context and to move freely and flexibly among different contexts and seemingly different truths? As the world becomes economically, politically, and even philosophically and scientifically more interdependent, the alternatives seem to be either the enforcement of a hegemonic uniformity or the development of the capacity to live within an increasingly pluralistic context. If the latter alternative is preferred—and I would argue it is— might the West learn something from the Japanese experience and the philosophies developing out of it?

Suggestions for Further Reading

Kasulis's references will lead you into the relevant literature on and by Japanese philosophers. Also see Masao Abe's "Religion and Science in the Global Age—Their Essential Character and Mutual Relationship," *Zen and Western Thought,* edited by William R. LaFleur (Honolulu: University of Hawaii Press, 1985, pp. 241–249).

Ernan McMullin's "Values in Science" (pp. 550–560) and W. H. Newton-Smith's "Hume," (pp. 165–168) in *Companion to the Philosophy of Science,* edited by W. H. Newton-Smith (Oxford: Blackwell, 2000) will help you to think through the fact/value distinction and provide background information on Hume's contribution to empiricist views of science.

8.6 Science and Traditional Thought

Do you believe in spirits? Do you think that if you got ill, you could go to a shrine, have a priest sacrifice a chicken, and get well? If you think this would work, why? If you do not think going to spirit-shrines and sacrificing chickens would cure illness, why not?

Do you think false beliefs can survive for long periods of time? If you think there are no spirits who cure people in response to sacrificed chickens, why do you think some people believe there are? Let us suppose that the people who believe there are indeed such spirits have held this view for centuries, and that in fact there are no such spirits. What sustains false beliefs in healing spirits over centuries? Why do they persist if they are false?

I am going to call something a traditional religious belief if it is based on positing spirit-agents as causes of events. You go to the priest, she sacrifices a chicken, and you get well. The priest, who holds traditional religious beliefs, would say that the spirit of the shrine healed you. Is this traditional religious belief scientific? Why, or why not?

Suppose you go to a medical doctor and, instead of the doctor sacrificing a chicken, she gives you a shot and you get well. The medical doctor, who holds scientific beliefs, tells you that you have a bacterial infection and that the antibiotic she has just given you will destroy the bacteria. How is this scientific belief different from a traditional religious belief? Is there a significant difference between the two explanations of why you got well?

Some African people build granaries on poles to store their harvests above the ground so mice will not get into the grain. When it is hot, people sometimes sit under these granaries to get shade and sometimes, because termites weaken the supports, these granaries fall and kill or injure some of the people. If you ask why the granaries fell and people were injured, you would be told it was because of witchcraft. Witches did it! Everyone knows about the termites, and they know what termites have done to the supports, yet they still explain this unfortunate event by appealing to witchcraft. Witchcraft is their **theodicy** or answer to the problem of evil. It explains why bad things happen. Is it a scientific explanation? Why, or why not?

Suppose a friend, a religious and good person, is suddenly killed in an auto accident caused by a drunk driver. At the funeral the minister asks why bad things happen to good people and answers, "I believe this tragic event is part of God's plan." Everyone knows the accident was caused by a drunk driver, yet the minister says it is part of God's plan. Is this a scientific explanation of the tragic accident? Is it an explanation at all? If it is, what kind of explanation is it?

Kwame Anthony Appiah, professor of philosophy at Harvard University and author of the following selection, is a person of "two worlds." Before earning his Ph.D. from Cambridge University, he was trained in Africa to be a leader of the Asante. His farther, a British barrister, was from the royal house of the Asante, the most powerful kinship group in Ghana, and his mother, a published author, a member of the British establishment. One of his worlds is the world of traditional African belief and thought. The other world is the world of modern European scientific belief and thought. Here he offers some intriguing philosophical reflections on the relationship between these worlds.

Reading Questions

1. What is Durkheim's argument for treating religion as symbolic?
2. Why, according to Appiah, is Durkheim wrong?
3. Why are the concepts of "underdetermination" and "theory-laden" important in this context?
4. What is the analogy between traditional religion and natural science?
5. How, according to Horton, do traditional religious beliefs differ from natural science, and why?

6. Which sort of explanation is missing in Horton's account, and why?

7. Explain what Appiah means when he says that the "differences between traditional religious theory and the theories of the sciences reside in the social organization of inquiry." Do you think he is right about this? Why, or why not?

8. What is the difference between an "adversarial style" and an "accommodative style," and why is this difference important?

9. According to Appiah, what accounts for modern scientific cultures being adversarial and traditional religious cultures being accommodative?

Old Gods, New Worlds

KWAME ANTHONY APPIAH

IN COMING TO TERMS with what it means to be modern, Western and African intellectuals have interests they should share. . . . [A]s I shall suggest, neither of us will understand what modernity is until we understand each other. . . .

[O]ne of the marks of traditional life is the extent to which beliefs, activities, habits of mind, and behavior in general are shot through with what Europeans and Americans would call "religion." . . . Most intellectuals outside . . . [traditional societies] think they know, after all, that there are no such spirits [as can be summoned by sacrificing, for example, gold or sheep and chickens at a shrine]. That, for all the requests in the priest's prayer, no unseen agent will come to inhabit the shrine; no one will answer the questions "What made this person ill?" or "Would we win if we went to war?" or "How should we cure the king's elder?" Yet here is a culture [Asante] where, for at least several hundred years, people have been setting up just such shrines and asking them just such questions and asking the spirits they believe are in them to perform just such tasks. Surely by now they should know, if they are rational, that it won't work? . . . And if we press the question how these beliefs can be sustained in the face of a falsity that is obvious, at

least to us, we shall return, in the end, to the question whether we have really understood what is going on. . . .

[W]e need, I think, to bear in mind at least these three separate types of understanding: first, understanding the ritual and the beliefs that underlie it; second, understanding the historical sources of both ritual and belief; and, third, understanding what sustains them.

[T]o understand these ritual acts what is necessary is what is necessary in the understanding of any acts: namely to understand what beliefs and intentions underlie them, so that we know what the actors think they are doing, what they are trying to do. Indeed if we cannot do this we cannot even say what the ritual is. To say that what is going on here is that these people are inviting a spirit to take up its place in a shrine is already to say something about their beliefs and their intentions. It is to say, for example, that they believe that there is a spirit, Ta Kwesi, and believe too that asking the spirit to do something is a way of getting that spirit to do it; it is to say that they want the spirit to inhabit the shrine. . . .

But if we are to face the question of the rationality of traditional belief we must turn, finally, to my third set of questions: those about what keeps

From Kwame Anthony Appiah, In My Father's House: Africa in the Philosophy of Culture. *Oxford: Oxford University Press, © 1992 by Anthony Appiah, pp. 107–136. Reprinted by permission of the author and the publisher. Notes edited.*

these beliefs, which outsiders judge so obviously false, alive.

It is in asking these questions that some have been led by another route to treating religion symbolically. The British anthropologist John Beattie, for example, has developed a "symbolist" view of Africa's traditional religions, whose "central tenet," as Robin Horton (a philosopher-anthropologist, who is a British subject and a longtime Nigerian resident) puts it, "is that traditional religious thought is basically different from and incommensurable with Western scientific thought"; so that the symbolists avoid "comparisons with science and turn instead to comparisons with symbolism and art. . . ."[1] Simply put, the symbolists are able to treat traditional believers as reassuringly rational only because they deny that traditional people mean what they say. Now Robin Horton has objected—correctly— that . . . [i]t is peculiarly unsatisfactory to treat a system of propositions as symbolic when those whose propositions they are appear to treat them literally and display, in other contexts, a clear grasp of the notion of symbolic representation.

I have mentioned Durkheim . . . and it is in his work that we can find the clearest statement of the connection between the urge to treat religion as symbolic and the question why such patently false beliefs survive. For Durkheim cannot allow that religious beliefs are false, because he thinks that false beliefs could not survive. Since if they are false they would not have survived, it follows that they must be true: and since they are not literally true, they must be symbolically true.[2] This argument is based on a misunderstanding of the relationship between the rationality of beliefs, their utility and their truth; it is important to say why.

Rationality is best conceived of as an ideal, both in the sense that it is something worth aiming for and in the sense that it is something we are incapable of realizing. It is an ideal that bears an important internal relation to that other great cognitive ideal, Truth. And, I suggest, we might say that rationality in belief consists in being disposed so to react to evidence and reflection that you change your beliefs in ways that make it more likely that they are true. . . .[3]

With such an account of reasonableness, we can see why the apparently obvious falsehood of the beliefs of the Asante priest might be regarded as evidence of his unreasonableness. For how could he have acquired and maintained such beliefs if he was following the prescription always to try to change his beliefs in ways that made it more likely that they were true? The answer is simple. The priest acquired his beliefs in the way we all acquire the bulk of our beliefs: by being told things as he grew up. As Evans-Pritchard says of the Zande people, they are "born into a culture with ready-made patterns of belief which have the weight of tradition behind them."[4] And of course, so are we. On the whole, little has happened in his life to suggest they are not true. So too, in our lives.

Now it may seem strange to suggest that accepting beliefs from one's culture and holding onto them in the absence of countervailing evidence can be reasonable, if it can lead to having beliefs that are, from the point of view of West-

---

1. Robin Horton, "Spiritual Beings and Elementary Particles—A Reply to Mr. Pratt," *Second Order* 1, No. 1 (1972), p. 30.

2. John Skorupski has persuaded me that Durkheim does indeed offer this apparently crude argument; see Skorupski's *Symbol and Theory* (Cambridge: Cambridge University Press, 1976), chap. 2, for an excellent discussion.

3. . . . This conception of rationality belongs to a family of recent proposals that treat a concept as being defined by the *de re* relations of agents to the world. . . . As Gettler [1963] showed. a belief can be justified and true, but not a piece of knowledge, because the justification fails to be appropriately related *de re* to the facts. . . . Similarly, I want to say a belief can be reasonable (subjectively), but irrational (objectively). Since questions of rationality, therefore, raise questions about how other people stand in relation to reality; and since these questions cannot be answered while leaving open, as I wish to do, questions about who is right, I shall talk from now on about reasonableness rather than rationality. Someone is reasonable, on my view, if they are trying to be rational: if they are trying to act so as to maximize the chance of their beliefs being true.

4. Evans-Pritchard, *Witchcraft, Oracles and Magic among the Azande* (Oxford: Oxford University Press, 1976), p. 202.

ern intellectuals, so wildly false. And this is especially so if you view reasonableness as a matter of trying to develop habits of belief acquisition that make it likely that you will react to evidence and reflection in ways that have a tendency to produce truth. . . .

We may also fail to see how reasonable the priest's views should seem, because, in assessing the religious beliefs of other cultures, we start, as is natural enough, from our own. But it is precisely the absence of this, our alien, alternative point of view in traditional culture, that makes it reasonable to adopt the "traditional" worldview. The evidence that spirits exist is obvious: priests go into trance, people get better after the application of spiritual remedies, people die regularly from the action of inimical spirits. The reinterpretation of this evidence, in terms of medical-scientific theories or of psychology, requires that there be such alternative theories and that people have some reason to believe in them; but again and again, and especially in the area of mental and social life, the traditional view is likely to be confirmed. We have theories explaining some of this, the theory of suggestion and suggestibility, for example, and if we were to persuade traditional thinkers of these theories, they might become skeptical of the theories held in their own culture. But we cannot begin by asking them to assume their beliefs are false, for they can always make numerous moves in reasonable defense of their beliefs. [Blaming some extant auxiliary hypothesis or adding some excusing auxiliary, for example.] It is this fact that entitles us to oppose the thesis that traditional beliefs are simply unreasonable. . . .

Philosophers of science have names for this: they say that theory is "underdetermined" by observation, and that observation is "theory-laden." And they mean by underdetermination the fact that French philosopher-physicist Pierre Duhem noticed in the early part of this century: that the application of theory to particular cases relies on a whole host of other beliefs, not all of which can be checked at once. By the theory-ladenness of observation, relatedly, they mean that our theories both contribute to forming our experience

and give meaning to the language we use for reporting it. Sir Karl Popper's claim that science should proceed by attempts at falsification, as we all know after reading Thomas Kuhn, is incorrect. If we gave up every time an experiment failed, scientific theory would get nowhere. The underdetermination of our theories by our experience means that we are left even by the most unsuccessful experiment with room for maneuver. The trick is not to give up too soon or go on too long. In science, as everywhere else, there are babies and there is bathwater. . . .

[T]raditional religious theory is in certain respects more like modern natural science . . . which we may summarize in the slogan "explanation, prediction, and control." It is his systematic development of the analogy between natural science and traditional religion that has made the work of Robin Horton so important in the philosophy of African traditional religions, and it will be useful to begin with him.[5]

Horton's basic point is just the one I made earlier: the fundamental character of these religious systems is that the practices arise from the belief, literal and not symbolic, in the powers of invisible agents. Horton argues persuasively, and I believe correctly, that spirits and such function in explanation, prediction, and control much as do other theoretical entities: they differ from those of natural science in being persons and not material forces and powers, but the logic of their function in explanation and prediction is the same.

Horton's view, then, is that religious beliefs of traditional peoples constitute explanatory theories and that traditional religious actions are reasonable attempts to pursue goals in the light of these beliefs—attempts, in other words, at prediction and control of the world. In these respects, Horton argues, traditional religious belief and action are like theory in the natural sciences

---

5. Horton's most famous paper is his "African Traditional Religion and Western Science." . . . All my thought on these questions has been stimulated and enlivened by reading and talking with him, and so many of the ideas I shall be offering are his that I make now a general acknowledgement.

and the actions based on it. . . . Horton's thesis is not that traditional religion is a kind of science but that theories in the two domains are similar in these crucial respects. The major difference in the contents of the theories, he argues, is that traditional religious theory is couched in terms of personal forces, while natural scientific theory is couched in terms of impersonal forces. The basic claim strikes me as immensely plausible. . . .

Horton himself is, of course, aware that traditional religious beliefs are certainly unlike those of natural science in at least two important respects. First of all, as I have already insisted, he points out that the theoretical entities invoked are agents and not material forces. . . . And he offers us an account of why this might be. He suggests that this difference arises out of the fundamental nature of explanation as the reduction of the unfamiliar to the familiar. In traditional cultures nature, the wild, is untamed, alien, and a source of puzzlement and fear. Social relations and persons are, on the contrary, familiar and well understood. Explaining the behavior of nature in terms of agency is thus reducing the unfamiliar forces of the wild to the familiar explanatory categories of personal relations.

In the industrial world, on the other hand, industrialization and urbanization have made social relations puzzling and problematic. We move between social environments—the rural and the urban, the workplace and the home—in which different conventions operate; in the new, urban, factory, market environment we deal with people whom we know only through our common productive projects. As a result the social is relatively unfamiliar. On the other hand, our relations with objects in the city are relations that remain relatively stable across all these differing social relations. Indeed, if factory workers move between factories, the skills they take with them are precisely those that depend on a familiarity not with other people but with the workings of material things. It is no longer natural to try to understand nature through social relations; rather, we understand it through machines, through matter whose workings we find comfortably familiar. It is well known that the understanding of

gases in the nineteenth-century was modeled on the behavior of miniature billiard balls—for nineteenth-century scientists in Europe know the billiard table better than they knew, for example, their servants. Alienation is widely held to be the characteristic state of modern man: the point can be overstated, but it cannot be denied. . . . [Horton's] story works so well that is it hard not to feel that there is something right about it; it would indeed explain the preference for agency over matter, the first of the major differences Horton acknowledges between traditional religion and science.

And yet this *cannot* be quite right. All cultures—in modest mood, I might say, all the cultures I have knowledge of—have the conceptual resources for at least two fundamental sorts of explanation. On the one hand, all have some sort of notion of what Aristotle called "efficient" causation: the causality of push and pull through which we understand the everyday interactions of material objects and forces. On the other, each has a notion of explanation that applies paradigmatically to human action, the notion that the American philosopher Daniel Dennett has characterized as involving the "intentional stance."[6] This sort of explanation relates actions to beliefs, desires, intentions, fears, and so on—the so-called propositional attitudes—and is fundamental . . . to folk psychology. We might say, analogously, that efficient causality is central to what cognitive psychologists now call "naive" or "folk physics."

These kinds of explanations are, of course, interconnected: when I explain the death of the elephant by talking of your need for food, your hunt, your firing the gun, there are elements of folk physics and of folk psychology involved in each stage on this narrative. To say that mechanical explanation is unfamiliar to preindustrial peoples is, of course, to say something true. Mechanical explanation is explanation in terms of machines, which are, of course, exactly what

6. See Daniel Dennett's *The Intentional Stance* (Cambridge, Mass.: Bradford Books, 1987).

preindustrial cultures do not have. But mechanical explanation is by no means the only kind of nonintentional explanation: there is more to folk physics than a view of machines. And the fact is that the stability of the causal relations of objects in the preindustrial world is surely quite substantial: not only do people make tools and utensils, using the concepts of efficient causation, but their regular physical interactions with the world—in digging, hunting, walking, dancing—are as stable and as well understood as their familial relations. More than this, preindustrial Homo is already Homo Faber, and the making of pots and of jewelry, for example, involves intimate knowledge of physical things and an expectation of regularity in their behavior. . . .

What we need to bring back into view here is a kind of explanation that is missing from Horton's story: namely, functional explanation, which we find centrally (but by no means uniquely) in what we might call "folk biology." Functional explanation is the sort of explanation that we give when we say that the flower is there to attract the bee that pollinates it; that the liver is there to purify the blood; that the rain falls to water the crops.

This sort of explanation is missing from Horton's story for a very good reason—namely, that the positivist philosophy of science on which Horton relies sought either to eradicate functional explanation or to reduce it to other sorts of explanation, in large part because it reeked of teleology—of the sort of Aristotelian "final" causation that positivism took to have been shown to be hopeless by the failure of vitalism in nineteenth-century biology. And, surely, what is most striking about the "unscientific" explanations that most precolonial African cultures offer is not just that they appeal to agency but that they are addressed to the question "Why?" understood as asking what the event in question was for. Evans-Pritchard in his account of Zande belief insists that the Azande do not think that "unfortunate events" ever happen by chance:[7] their frequent appeal to witchcraft—in the ab-

sence of other acceptable explanations of misfortune—demonstrates their unwillingness to accept the existence of contingency. But to reject the possibility of the contingent is exactly to insist that everything that happens serves some purpose: a view familiar in Christian tradition in such formulas as "And we know that all things work together for good to them that love God" (Rom. 8:28), or in the deep need people feel—in Europe and America as in Africa—for answers to the question "Why do bad things happen to good people?" Zande witchcraft beliefs depend on an assumption that the universe is in a certain sort of evaluative balance; in short, on the sort of assumption that leads monotheistic theologians to develop theodicies.

What Zande people will not accept, as Evans-Pritchard's account makes clear, is not that "unfortunate events" have no explanation—the granary falls because the termites have eaten through the stilts that support it—but that they are meaningless; that there is no deeper reason why the person sitting in the shade of the granary was injured. And in that sense they share an attitude that we find in Christian theodicy from Irenaeus to Augustine to Karl Barth: that the cosmos works to a plan. Precolonial African cultures, pre- and nonscientific thinkers everywhere, are inclined to suppose that events in the world have meaning; they worry not about the possibility of the unexplained (what has no efficient cause nor agent explanation) but of the meaningless (what has no function, no point). And this marks those who accept the scientific worldview—a minority, of course, even in the industrialized world—from almost all other humans throughout history. For it is a distinctive feature of that scientific worldview that it accepts that not everything that happens has a human meaning. To explain this difference between scientific and nonscientific visions we need, I think, to begin with the fact that the world, as the sciences conceive of it, extends so hugely far beyond the human horizon, in time as in space. As Alexandre Korye indicated in the title of his well-known study of the birth of modern celestial physics, the Newtonian revolution took the intellectual path *From the Closed World to the Infinite Universe,*

7. See Evans-Pritchard, *Witchcraft, Oracles and Magic among the Azande,* chap. 2.

and the Victorian dispute between science and religion had at its center a debate about the age of the earth, with geology insisting that the biblical time scale of thousands of years since the creation radically underestimated the age of our planet. Copernicus turned European scientists away from a geocentric to a heliocentric view of the universe and began a process, which Darwin continued, that inevitably displaced humankind from the center of the natural sciences. A recognition that the universe does not seem to have been made simply for us is the basis of the radically nonanthropocentric character of scientific theories of the world. This nonanthropocentrism is part of the change in view that develops with the growth of capitalism, of science, and of the modern state. the change to which, for example, Weber's account of modernization was addressed, and it contributes profoundly to the sense of the universe as disenchanted that Weberians have taken to be so central a feature of modernity (a claim that makes more sense as a claim about the life of professional intellectuals than as one about the culture as a whole). . . .

But Horton in his original work made, as I said, a second important claim for difference: he summarized it by calling the cognitive world of traditional cultures "closed" and that of modern cultures "open." "What I take to be the key difference is a very simple one," he writes. "It is that in traditional cultures there is no developed awareness of alternatives to the established body of theoretical tenets; whereas in scientifically oriented cultures, such an awareness is highly developed." . . . And it is here, when we turn from questions about the content and logic of traditional and scientific explanation to the social contexts in which those theories are constructed and mobilized, that Horton's account begins to seem less adequate. . . .

Remember the answer the priest gave to the question about the gold dust . . . "We do it because the ancestors did it." In the open society this will no longer do as a reason. The early modern natural scientists, the natural philosophers of the Renaissance, stressed often the unreasonableness of appeals to authority. And if modern scholarship suggests that they overstressed the

extent to which their predecessors were bound by a hidebound traditionalism, it is still true that there is a difference—if only in degree—in the extent to which modernity celebrates distance from our predecessors, while the traditional world celebrates cognitive continuity.

Now Horton's account of the sense in which the traditional worldview is closed has—rightly—been challenged. The complexities of war and trade, dominance and clientage, migration and diplomacy, in much of precolonial Africa are simply not consistent with the image of peoples unaware that there is a world elsewhere. . . .

It is also possible to find first-rate speculative thinkers in traditional societies whose individual openness is not to be denied. I think here of Ogotemmêli, whose cosmology Griaule has captured . . . and Barry Hallen has provided evidence from Nigerian sources of the existence, within African traditional modes of thought, of styles of reasoning that are open neither to Wiredu's stern strictures nor to Horton's milder ones. . . .[8] Horton's original stress on the "closed" nature of traditional modes of thought does look less adequate in the face of Africa's complex history of cultural exchanges and of Hallen's babalawo, or in the presence of the extraordinary metaphysical synthesis of the Dogon elder, Ogotemmêli. . . . In a recent book—written with the Nigerian philosopher J. O. Sodipo—Hallen insists on the presence among Yoruba doctors of theories of witchcraft rather different from those of their fellow countrymen.[9] Here, then, among doctors, speculation inconsistent with ordinary folk belief occurs. . . .

Horton has recently come—in response, in part, to Hallen's critique—to speak not of the closedness of traditional belief systems but, borrowing a term from Wole Soyinka, of their being "accommodative." He discusses work by

8. Barry Hallen, "Robin Horton on Critical Philosophy and Traditional Thought." . . . Wiredu, of course, does not deny the existence of skeptics in traditional cultures. See pp. 20–21, 37, 143 of *Philosophy and an African Culture* (London: Cambridge University Press, 1980).
9. Barry Hallen and J. Sodipo, *Knowledge, Belief and Witchcraft: Analytic Experiments in African Philosophy* (London: Ethnographica, 1986)—summarized here in Chapter 9.

students of Evans-Pritchard that not only addresses the kind of static body of belief that is captured in Evans-Pritchard's picture of the Azande thought world but also stresses the dynamic and—as Horton admits—"open" way in which they "devise explanations for novel elements in . . . experience," and "their capacity to borrow, re-work and integrate alien ideas in the course of elaborating such explanations." "Indeed" he continues, "it is this 'open-ness' that has given the traditional cosmologies such tremendous durability in the face of immense changes that the 20th century has brought to the African scene." Horton then contrasts this accommodative style with the "adversary" style of scientific theory, which is characterized by the way in which the main stimulus to change of belief is not "novel experience but rival theory." [10]

And it seems to me that this change from the Popperian terminology of "open" and "closed" allows Horton to capture something important about the difference between traditional religion and science; something to do not with individual cognitive strategies but with social ones. If we want to understand the significance of social organization in differentiating traditional religion and natural science, we can do no better than to begin with those of Evans-Pritchard's answers to the question why the Azande do not see the falsity of their magic beliefs that mention social facts about the organization of those beliefs.

Evans-Pritchard wrote:

> Scepticism, far from being smothered, is recognized, even inculcated. But it is only about certain medicines and certain magicians. By contrast it tends to support other, medicines and other magicians. . . . Each man and each kinship group acts without cognizance of the actions of others. People do not pool their ritual experiences. . . . They are not experimentally inclined. . . . Not being experimentally inclined, they do not test the efficacy of their medicines.[11]

And, he added, "Zande beliefs are generally vaguely formulated. A belief, to be easily contradicted by experience . . . must be clearly shared and intellectually developed." [12]

Whatever the practices of imperfect scientists are actually like, none of these things is supposed to be true of natural science. In our official picture of the sciences, skepticism is encouraged even about foundational questions—indeed, that is where the best students are supposed to be directed. . . . The scientific community is experimentally inclined, and, of course, scientific theory is formulated as precisely as possible in order that those experiments can be carried out in a controlled fashion. . . . [S]cience *is*, crucially, adversarial, and the norms of publication and reproducibility of results, even though only imperfectly adhered to, are explicitly intended to lay theories and experimental claims open to attack by one's peers, and thus make competition from the adventurous "young Turk" possible.

More important than the hugely oversimplified contrast between an experimental, skeptical, science and an unexperimental, "dogmatic" traditional mode of thought is the difference in images of knowledge that are represented in the differences in the social organization of inquiry in modern as opposed to "traditional" societies. Scientists, like the rest of us, hold onto theories longer than they may be entitled to; suppress, unconsciously or half consciously, evidence they

---

10. This work is in the paper, "Traditional Thought and the Emerging African Philosophy Department: A Reply to Dr. Hallen," unpublished manuscript.

11. This is not to say that they do not have the concepts necessary to understand the idea of an experiment, merely to say

that they are not interested in disinterested experimentation simply to find out how things work. For the Azande are very aware, for example, that an oracle needs to be run carefully if it is to be reliable. They therefore test its reliability on every occasion of its use. There are usually two tests: *bambata sima* and *gingo;* the first and second tests. Generally, in the first test, the question is asked so the death of a chicken means yes and in the second so that death means no; but it may be the other way round. Inconsistent results invalidate the procedure. The Azande also have a way of confirming that an oracle is not working; namely to ask it a question to which they already know the answer. Such failures can be explained by one of the many obstacles to an oracle's functioning properly: breach of taboo; witchcraft; the fact that the benge poison used in the oracle has been "spoiled" (as the Azande believe) because it has been near a menstruating woman.

12. Evans-Pritchard, *Witchcraft, Oracles and Magic and Magic among the Azande,* 202–4.

do not know how to handle; lie a little. In pre-colonial societies there were, we can be sure, individual doubters who kept their own counsel, resisters against the local dogma. But what is interesting about modern modes of theorizing is that they are organized around an image of constant change: we expect new theories, we reward and encourage the search for them, we believe that today's best theories will be revised beyond recognition if the enterprise of science survives. My ancestors in Asante never organized a specialized activity that was based around this thought. They knew that some people know more than others, and that there are things to be found out. But they do not seem to have thought it necessary to invest social effort in working out new theories of how the world works, not for some practical end (this they did constantly) but, as we say, for its own sake.

The differences between traditional religious theory and the theories of the sciences reside in the social organization of inquiry, as a systematic business, and it is differences in social organization that account, I think, both for the difference we feel in the character of natural scientific and traditional religious theory—they are products of different kinds of social process—and for the spectacular expansion of the domain of successful prediction and control, an expansion that characterizes natural science but is notably absent in traditional society. Experimentation, the publication and reproduction of results, the systematic development of alternative theories in precise terms, all these ideals, however imperfectly they are realized in scientific practice, are intelligible only in an organized social enterprise of knowledge.

But what can have prompted this radically different approach to knowledge? Why have the practitioners of traditional religion, even the priests, who are the professionals, never developed the organized "adversarial" methods of the sciences? There are, no doubt, many historical sources. A few, familiar suggestions strike one immediately.

Social mobility leads to political individualism, of a kind that is rare in the traditional polity; political individualism allows cognitive authority to shift, also, from priest to king to commoner; and social mobility is a feature of industrial societies.

Or, in traditional societies, accommodating conflicting theoretical views is part of the general process of accommodation necessary for those who are bound to each other as neighbors for life. . . . In Ghana, but not in America, it is impolite to disagree, to argue, to confute. And this accommodating approach to conversation is part of the same range of attitudes that leads to theoretical accommodations. . . .

[I]t seems to me that there is one other fundamental difference between traditional West African culture and the culture of the industrial world, and that it plays a fundamental role in explaining why the adversarial style never established itself in West Africa. And it is that these cultures were largely nonliterate.

Now literacy has, as Jack Goody has pointed out in his influential book *The Domestication of the Savage Mind,* important consequences; among them is the fact that it permits a kind of consistency that oral culture cannot and does not demand. Write down a sentence and it is there, in principle, forever; that means that if you write down another sentence inconsistent with it, you can be caught out. It is this fact that is at the root of the possibility of the adversarial style. How often have we seen Perry Mason—on television in Ghana or the United States or England (for television, at least, there is only one world)—ask the stenographer to read back from the record? In the traditional culture the answer can only be: "What record?" In the absence of written records, it is not possible to compare the ancestors' theories in their actual words with ours; nor, given the limitations of quantity imposed by oral transmission, do we have a detailed knowledge of what those theories were. We know more about the thought of Isaac Newton on one or two subjects than we know about the entire population of his Asante contemporaries.

The accommodative style is possible because orality makes it hard to discover discrepancies. And so it is possible to have an image of knowledge as unchanging lore, handed down from the ancestors. It is no wonder, with this image of knowledge, that there is no systematic research:

nobody need ever notice that the way that traditional theory is used requires inconsistent interpretations. It is literacy that makes possible the precise formulation of questions that we have just noticed as one of the characteristics of scientific theory, and it is precise formulation that points up inconsistency. This explanation, which we owe to Horton, is surely very plausible. . . .

Suggestions for Further Reading

There are good collections of essays on African philosophy available dealing with a wide variety of issues including traditional belief systems in relationship to scientific belief systems. See *African Philosophy: A Classical Approach,* edited by Parker English and Kibujjo M. Kalumba (Upper Saddle River, NJ: Prentice-Hall, 1996); *The African Philosophy Reader,* edited by P. H. Coetzee and A. P. J. Roux (New York: Routledge, 1998); *African Philosophy: Selected Readings,* edited by Albert G. Mosley (Englewood Cliffs, NJ: Prentice-Hall, 1995); and Part V "On Knowledge and Science" in *African Philosophy: An Anthology,* edited by Emmanuel Chukwudi Eze (Malden, MA: Blackwell, 1998).

Stanley Jeyaraja Tambiah's *Magic, Science, Religion, and the Scope of Rationality* (Cambridge: Cambridge University Press, 1990) analyzes some anthropological theories on this topic.

Peter Winch's "Understanding a Primitive Society," in Bryan R. Wilson's *Rationality* (Oxford: Basil Blackwell, 1979) is a widely discussed classic in the field.

Kwame Gyekye's *An Essay on African Philosophical Thought: The Akan Conceptual Scheme* (Cambridge: Cambridge University Press, 1987) will also prove helpful.

 You can locate InfoTrac-College Edition articles about this chapter by accessing the InfoTrac-College Edition website (http://www.infotrac-college.com/wadsworth/). Using the InfoTrac-College Edition subject guide, enter the search terms relevant to this chapter, and then read abstracts for relevant articles.

Metaphysics

Chapter 9

What Is Really Real?

> If the doors of perception were cleansed everything would appear to man as it is, infinite.
>
> WILLIAM BLAKE

9.1 Introduction

HAVE YOU EVER WONDERED if what you *think* is real is *actually* real? Someone has undoubtedly asked you, with a smile, "If a tree falls in a forest and no one is there, does it make a sound?" What do you think? Have you ever thought about the question, "Why is there something rather than nothing?" Have you ever thought, "Is the world we experience real or an illusion?" Have you ever been puzzled by the question, "What are time and space?" Do you think something can come from nothing? What are ideas made of? Is nature all there is, or is there some sort of supernatural reality?

If you have wondered about these sorts of questions, you have been concerned with what philosophers call *metaphysics.* Metaphysics has to do with the construction and criticism of theories about what is truly real. Metaphysics deals with abstract issues, but its concerns arise out of everyday experiences. For example, you may have been traveling down a road and seen, ahead on the highway, what looked like an animal; but when you got closer, you discovered that it was really a bush. It appeared to be one thing and turned out to be another. The question about what is *genuinely or really* real presupposes a distinction between appearance and reality. Metaphysics generalizes that distinction and asks, "If some things in the world appear to be real but turn out not to be, what about the world itself? Is the universe appearance or reality?"

Some philosophers maintain that the chief part of metaphysics is what they call **ontology** (literally, "the study of being"). One ontological concern has to do with the *kinds* of things that exist. For example, try to categorize the items in the following list into two general groups, material and immaterial:

chairs	trees	cats	ideas
seeing	anger	stones	atoms
God	space	time	you

Did you have a hard time sorting these? One problem is that some things seem to be a mixture of the material and the immaterial. For example, you have a body, which is material, but you also have a mind, which some would claim to be immaterial. Another problem has to do with definitions. What do we mean by *material* and *immaterial?* How can we classify things until we know how to distinguish between them?

This last question leads us directly into a second concern of ontology, namely the *definition* of different kinds of being. For example, some philosophers have argued that material beings can be distinguished from immaterial beings according to the following characteristics:

MATERIAL	IMMATERIAL
spatial	nonspatial
public	private
mechanical	teleological

According to this list, material things like chairs take up space (hence are spatial), but immaterial things like ideas do not take up space (hence are nonspatial). It makes good sense to ask how wide a chair is, but does it make any sense to ask how wide my *idea* of a chair is? Material things are also public in the sense that they can be viewed by different people. I can see a chair or a tree, and so can you. However, I can not see your *idea* of a chair or a tree. Your idea is private; it is not open to public inspection. Finally, material objects are causally determined in a purely **mechanistic** way. They are nonintentional—that is, they behave not according to purposes but according to the laws of physics. That chair is in the corner of the room not because it *wants* to be there, but because it was *placed* there by external forces. But what about you? Is your behavior purely mechanistic (machinelike)? Or is your behavior teleological, that is, governed by goals and purposes? Are you in the corner of the room because of external forces, or are you there because you want to leave and the door is located there?

A third concern of ontology has to do with what is *ultimately* real. Once we have discovered all the kinds of beings that seem to exist and have adequately defined each of the kinds, which if any of these kinds are really real? Is matter the really real? If you answer yes, you would be an advocate of materialism. **Materialism** is the metaphysical theory that matter is truly real and immaterial things are not. Note that we should not confuse materialism with physical science. Physical science is clearly concerned with matter and the study of physical things. The claim, however, that *only* physical things are real is not a scientific claim, it is a metaphysical claim. It is a claim about the *whole* of reality.

Some of you might be inclined to argue that being, or reality, is fundamentally immaterial. One widespread philosophical version of this theory is called idealism. The metaphysical theory of **idealism** asserts that ideas (in the broad sense of thoughts, concepts, minds) are ultimately real. Do not confuse idealism as a metaphysical doctrine with idealism as a moral theory about ideals. Idealism, as I am using that term here, has to do with ideas, not ideals.

One major problem with idealism, as you might expect, is to explain our experience of things that seem both material and real. The chair I am sitting on seems physical, solid, and real to me, and I certainly hope it is. Could it be that this chair is nothing more than a bundle of sensations or ideas? If materialism needs to explain the mental in terms of the physical, idealism must explain the physical in terms of the mental.

Maybe you want to suggest that both these sorts of things (the material and the immaterial) are genuinely real. This dualistic approach seems reasonable. It certainly escapes the problems of explaining away chairs, bodies, minds, and ideas. **Dualism** is the theory that reality is both material and immaterial. My body is real, and the material chair it is sitting on is real (what a relief), but my mind and its ideas are also real (that's good to know, too). However, if reality is both material and immaterial, how are the two related? How, for example, are our minds related to our brains? The major problem of dualism is to relate the material and the immaterial.

Those who argue that being, or reality, is fundamentally of one nature avoid this problem. They are called monists, and their theory (in contrast to dualism) is called monism. **Monism** holds that there is a single reality. Notice that a monist can be either a materialist or an idealist. The contrast here is between monism and dualism, not between materialism and idealism.

Discussions of dualism versus monism soon lead to the **problem of the one and the many**. Is there one reality, or are there many different real things that cannot be reduced to a single thing? **Pluralism** is the position that there are many different real things. This question of one or many, along with the question about what is really real, constitute two fundamental metaphysical problems.

I am sure you have had enough of terminology and questions for now. It is time to look at some of the metaphysical views philosophers hold and at some of the arguments they use to try to convince others that they are right.

9.2 The Dao

The name "Daoism" (Wade-Giles spelling is Taoism) was first coined by Han scholars to refer to the philosophy developed by Laozi. As the name implies, central to this philosophical view is the notion of **Dao**, often translated as the "way of nature." Laozi is the alleged author of a book popularly known as the *Dao De Jing* (Wade-Giles *Tao Te Ching*).

We have legends about Laozi and when he lived, but we have very little firm historical information. According to tradition he was a contemporary of Confucius (551–479 BCE), but most scholars have placed his book later, during the Warring States Period (403–221 BCE).

The *Dao De Jing* is a classic of world literature. Each time you come back to it, you will find something new and profound. However, the first time you read it you are likely to find it obscure. This is why I have included the translator's comments along with the translation.

You may find it obscure for a variety of reasons. First, it is written in a poetic and cryptic style. Poetry employs symbols and metaphors, uses paradoxes and unexpected contrasts in order to stimulate thought. It thrives on ambiguity. Second, this is a translation from ancient Chinese, and our English words often do not convey the richness of the Chinese concepts. Third, although 80 percent of the book deals with ethics (how one should live) and politics (what is the best way to govern), the rest deals with difficult metaphysical issues about the basic principles of reality, and it is these metaphysical portions of the text that are included here.

According to Aristotelian logic, a good definition should be positive and not negative. You should state what something is, not what it is not. Telling you that a pencil is "not a cat" does not help much if you do not know what a pencil is. However, what if there are realities that transcend the definitional abilities of human language? In such cases (and the *Dao* is such a case), the best we might hope for are negative indications, analogies, metaphors, and symbols.

Daoism has been characterized as a process ontology in contrast to a substance ontology. **Process ontologies** emphasize change and becoming as fundamentally real. In addition, they often emphasize the interrelatedness of an everflowing reality in which nothing is totally independent. **Substance ontologies** emphasize permanence and unchanging being as fundamentally real. Reality, a substantialist asserts, is made up of one or more substances that can exist independently.

Before you plunge into this bewildering, fascinating, and thought-provoking book about the *Dao,* it may be helpful to say something about some of the key concepts of Daoism. Let us begin with the word *Dao* itself.

The word *Dao* means "road" or "way" in Chinese. Before Laozi, the word had been used by the Confucians (see Section 3.3) to refer to the way of humans, that is, the proper way that human beings ought to live. Laozi extends the term and gives it a cosmic and metaphysical meaning (at least according to some interpreters). It now becomes the way of the universe and the source of all reality. Reality consists of all the sorts of things we think exist (which we can classify as being) as well as what we take to be nonexistent (which we can classify as nonbeing). Already we encounter something odd from a traditional Western perspective. How can the nonexistent be real? Where we tend to identify the real with what exists (being) and the unreal with what does not (nonbeing), the Daoist distinguishes between reality and existence so that both the existent and nonexistent can be classified as real.

The *Dao,* because it is the source of all reality, is not *a* thing (a being or a substance). It is beyond distinctions and hence beyond the definitional powers of language. To define is to distinguish. However, how do you define that which is the source of all distinctions? So the *Dao* is called "the nameless," that is, the indefinable.

This negative designation suggests that the *Dao* is closer to nonbeing than to being, and indeed, Daoists say that the *Dao* is nonbeing. It is, however, not nonbeing in the Western sense of total nothingness. It is nonbeing in the sense of "no-thingness." It is real, but not *a* thing. Laozi compares it to a *positive emptiness,* that is, an emptiness (like the hollow of a bowl) that makes being (the usefulness of the bowl) possible. This notion of nonbeing as positive and creative is a unique insight of the *Dao De Jing.* For the Greeks, and much of the Western tradition since the Greeks, something cannot come from nothing. Nothing is absolute nothingness. It is a totally negative void. Laozi sees things differently. Something *can* come from nothing; indeed, this whole marvelous universe did come from the no-thing—that is the way of all things.

De can be translated as "virtue," "power," or "excellence," so the title of Laozi's mind-expanding poem has been translated as "The Book of the Way and Its Power." It is a book (*jing*) about the excellence or power of the *Dao. De* is sometimes thought of as the *Dao* itself viewed from the perspective of individual things. The excellence (perfection, power) of each thing is called its *de,* and this is the *Dao* manifesting itself on the individual level. To actualize the potential of one's nature in an excellent way is to exhibit *de*. For humans (as for all natural things), this actualization occurs by living in accord with the *Dao*.

Wuwei literally means "no action" and refers to the manner in which the *Dao* acts. The way that is no-thing acts by not acting. Now there is a bit of philosophy on which to chew! Let me repeat it. The way that is no-thing acts by not acting. This rather mysterious claim can be elucidated somewhat by looking at the various levels of meaning of *wuwei*. Laozi provides advice to rulers in his book. He tells them to govern according to *wuwei*. In this political context, *wuwei* means that rulers should not interfere unnecessarily in the lives of the people. In other words, the less government, the better. On a moral level, *wuwei* means acting unselfishly and spontaneously, free of all selfish attachment to the consequences of our actions. And on the cosmic level, *wuwei* refers to the way nature acts—spontaneously, freely, and naturally. There is nothing artificial in natural events. Nature does not calculate how to act, it just acts.

Finally, we need to speak of the Daoist use of the **yin/yang** concept. The Daoists adopted this concept to characterize the universe that stems from the *Dao*. *Yin* and *yang* stand for complementary opposites: *yin* for all things that manifest a passive or receptive force; *yang* for all things that manifest an active or aggressive force. The passive and the active are complementary opposites; you cannot have one without the other.

There is a little bit of *yang* in *yin* and a little bit of *yin* in *yang*. In time, opposites will change into each other. Hence, the universe is essentially a vast, harmonious process. This can be illustrated by the seasonal cycle. Winter is the most *yin* season because it is cold and dark, and life processes are slow. However, winter contains an element of *yang*, which expands over time until we reach spring with its warmth, light, and flourishing life. *Yang* continues to expand and reaches its zenith in summer. Yet summer contains an element of *yin*, which expands into fall and eventually winter again. Such is the operation of *Dao* by means of *yin* and *yang*.

So the *Dao*, which is not a thing, acts naturally, freely, spontaneously, unselfishly, without force, thereby producing and sustaining a universe of harmonious processes in such a way that it is possible for each individual thing to manifest its own excellence. This is the way of nature, the way of genuine reality. I hope this profound vision of reality whets your appetite for more. Read on, and as you do, see if you can answer the following questions.

Reading Questions

1. What does it mean to say that the *Dao* (*Tao*) is nameless, and why do you think it is "named" that?
2. What is the main idea that Chapter 2 conveys about the nature of opposites?
3. How is it possible for the sage (wise person) to act without acting and teach without speaking?
4. What do you think the comparison between the *Dao* and a bowl implies about the relationship between the substance of a thing and its function?
5. Analogies are drawn between the *Dao* and a valley, a female, water, the hub of a wheel, a utensil, and a room. What do these analogies tell us about the *Dao*?
6. If the *Dao* is invisible, inaudible, and formless, how can it be known?
7. How does the *Dao* "run" the universe?
8. What does it mean to say that "reversion is the action of *Dao*"?

9. Is Daoist metaphysics a materialism, idealism, dualism, monism, or something that these categories fail to express adequately? Provide evidence to support your answer.

Dao De Jing

LAOZI

1

The Tao that can be told of is not the eternal Tao;
The name that can be named is not the eternal
*   name.*
The Nameless is the origin of Heaven and Earth;
The Named is the mother of all things.

Therefore let there always be non-being, so we may
*   see their subtlety,*
And let there always be being, so we may see their
*   outcome.*
The two are the same,
But after they are produced, they have different
*   names.*
They both may be called deep and profound.
Deeper and more profound,
The door of all subtleties!

COMMENT

This is the most important of all chapters, for in one stroke the basic characteristics of Tao as the eternal, the nameless, the source, and the substance of all things are explicitly or implicitly affirmed. It is no wonder the opening sentences are among the most often quoted or even chanted sayings in Chinese.

The key Taoist concepts of the named and the nameless are also introduced here. The concept of name is common to all ancient Chinese philosophical schools, but Taoism is unique in this respect. Most schools insist on the correspondence of names and actualities and accept names as necessary and good; Taoism, on the contrary, re-jects names in favor of the nameless. This, among other things, shows its radical and unique character. To Lao Tzu, Tao is nameless and is the simplicity without names; when names arise, that is, when the simple oneness of Tao is split up into individual things with names, it is time to stop.

The cardinal ideas of being and non-being are also important here, for in Taoism the nameless (*wu-ming*) is equivalent to non-being and the named (*yu-ming*) is equivalent to being. For this reason, when he comments on the saying about the named and the nameless, Wang Pi says, "All being originated in non-being." As students of Chinese thought well know, the ideas of being and non-being have been dominant throughout the history of Chinese philosophy. They are central concepts in Neo-Taoism, Chinese Buddhism, and also Neo-Confucianism. It was the importance of these concepts, no doubt, that led the Neo-Confucianist Wang An-shih to deviate from tradition and punctuate the phrases "always be no desires" and "always be desires" to read "Let there always be non-being, so we may . . . ," and "Let there always be being, so we may. . . ."

Wang's punctuation not only underlines the importance of these ideas; it also shows the new metaphysical interest in Neo-Confucianism. Confucianism had been fundamentally ethical in tradition, but under the impact of Buddhist and Taoist metaphysics, the Neo-Confucianists developed Confucianism along metaphysical lines. In this case, in substituting the ideas of being and non-being for the ideas of having desires and having no desires, Wang shows a greater recognition of the philosophical content of the *Lao Tzu,* as it deserves.

2

When the people of the world all know beauty as
   beauty,
There arises the recognition of ugliness.
When they all know the good as good,
There arises the recognition of evil.
Therefore:
   Being and non-being produce each other;
   Difficult and easy complete each other;
   Long and short contrast each other;
   High and low distinguish each other;
   Sound and voice harmonize each other;
   Front and behind accompany each other.

Therefore the sage manages affairs without
   action
And spreads doctrines without words.
All things arise, and he does not turn away
   from them.
He produces them but does not take possession
   of them.
He acts but does not rely on his own ability.
He accomplishes his task but does not claim credit
   for it.
It is precisely because he does not claim credit
   that his
accomplishment remains with him.

COMMENT

That everything has its opposite, and that these opposites are the mutual causations of each other, form a basic part of Chuang Tzu's philosophy and later Chinese philosophy. It is important to note that opposites are here presented not as irreconcilable conflicts but as complements. The traditional Chinese ideal that opposites are to be synthesized and harmonized can be said to have originated with Lao Tzu.

   The idea of teaching without words anticipated the Buddhist tradition of silent transmission of the mystic doctrine, especially in the Zen (Ch'an) school. This is diametrically opposed to the Confucian ideal, according to which a superior man acts and thus "becomes the model of the world," and speaks and thus "becomes the pattern for the world." It is true that Confucianists say that a superior man "is truthful without any words," but they would never regard silence itself as a virtue. . . .

4

Tao is empty (like a bowl).
   It may be used but its capacity is never exhausted.
It is bottomless, perhaps the ancestor of all things.
It blunts its sharpness,
It unties its tangles.
It softens its light.
It becomes one with the dusty world.
Deep and still, it appears to exist forever.
I do not know whose son it is.
It seems to have existed before the Lord.

COMMENT

This chapter, on the substance and function of Tao, shows clearly that in Taoism function is no less important than substance. Substance is further described in chapters 14 and 21, but here, as in chapters 11 and 45, function (*yung,* also meaning "use") is regarded with equal respect. There is no deprecation of phenomena, as is the case with certain Buddhist schools. To describe the world as dusty may suggest a lack of enthusiasm for it; indeed both Buddhism and later Taoism employ the word "dust" to symbolize the dirty world from which we should escape. It is significant to note, however, that Taoism in its true sense calls for identification with, not escape from, such a world. . . .

6

The spirit of the valley never dies.
   It is called the subtle and profound female.
The gate of the subtle and profound female
   Is the root of Heaven and Earth.
It is continuous, and seems to be always existing.
Use it and you will never wear it out.

COMMENT

The valley and the female, like the infant and water, are Lao Tzu's favorite symbols for Tao. The symbol of the valley is employed again and again.

There is nothing mysterious about it or its spirit; it simply stands for vacuity, vastness, openness, all-inclusiveness, and lowliness or humility, all of which are outstanding characteristics of Tao. This is the interpretation of Wang Pi, and commentators, with only a few exceptions, have followed him. To understand the "continuous" operation as breathing, or the valley as the belly or the Void, and then to interpret the whole passage as one on the yoga technique of breathing, or to single out the characteristic of stillness of the valley and then to present it as an evidence of Taoist quietism, is to fail to interpret the passages in the context of the whole. These interpretations are not supported by the symbolic meaning of the valley elsewhere in the book.

The spirit of the chapter is far from quietism. Instead, it involves the idea of natural transformation and continuous creation. As Chu Hsi has said, "The valley is vacuous. As sound reaches it, it echoes. This is the spontaneity of spiritual transformation. To be subtle and profound means to be wonderful. The female is one who receives something and produces things. This is a most wonderful principle and it has the meaning of production and reproduction." . . .

8

The best (man)[1] *is like water.*
  Water is good; it benefits all things and does not
    compete with them.
It dwells in (lowly) places that all disdain.
This is why it is so near to Tao.
(The best man) in his dwelling loves the earth.
In his heart, he loves what is profound.
In his associations, he loves humanity.

---

1. Most commentators and translators have understood the Chinese phrase literally as the highest good, but some commentators and translators, including Lin Yutang, Cheng Lin, and Bynner, have followed Wang Pi and taken the phrase to mean the best man. Both interpretations are possible. The former interpretation has a parallel in chapter 38, which talks about the highest virtue, while the latter has a parallel in chapter 17, where both Wang Pi and Ho-shang Kung interpret "the best" to mean the best ruler. I have followed Wang Pi, not only because his commentary on the text is the oldest and most reliable, but also because the *Lao Tzu* deals with man's way of life more than abstract ideas.

In his words, he loves faithfulness.
In government, he loves order.
In handling affairs, he loves competence.
In his activities, he loves timeliness.
It is because he does not compete that he is without
  reproach.

COMMENT

Water is perhaps the most outstanding among Lao Tzu's symbols for Tao. The emphasis of the symbolism is ethical rather than metaphysical or religious. It is interesting to note that, while early Indian philosophers associated water with creation and the Greek philosophers looked upon it as a natural phenomenon, ancient Chinese philosophers, whether Lao Tzu or Confucius, preferred to learn moral lessons from it. Broadly speaking, Western thought, derived chiefly from the Greeks, has been largely interested in metaphysical and scientific problems, Indian thought largely interested in religious problems, and Chinese thought largely interested in moral problems. It is not too much to say that these different approaches to water characterize the Western, the Indian, and the Chinese systems of thought. . . .

11

Thirty spokes are united around the hub to make a
  wheel,
  But it is on its non-being that the utility of the
    carriage depends.
Clay is molded to form a utensil,
  But it is on its non-being that the utility of the
    utensil depends.
Doors and windows are cut out to make a room,
  But it is on its non-being that the utility of the
    room depends.
Therefore turn being into advantage, and turn
  non-being into utility.

COMMENT

Nowhere else in Chinese philosophy is the concept of non-being more strongly emphasized. This chapter alone should dispel any idea that Taoism is negativistic, for non-being—the hole in the hub, the hollowness of a utensil, the empty space in the room—is here conceived not as nothingness but as something useful and advantageous.

The Taoist interest in non-being has counteracted the positivistic tendency in certain Chinese philosophical schools, especially the Legalist and Confucian, which often overlook what seems to be nonexistent. It has prepared the Chinese mind for the acceptance of the Buddhist doctrine of Emptiness, although neither the Taoist concept of non-being nor that of vacuity is identical with that of the Buddhist Void. In addition, it was because of the Taoist insistence on the positive value of non-being that empty space has been utilized as a constructive factor in Chinese landscape painting. In this greatest art of China, space is used to combine the various elements into an organic whole and to provide a setting in which the onlooker's imagination may work. By the same token, much is left unsaid in Chinese poetry, for the reader must play a creative role to bring the poetic idea into full realization. The Zen Buddhists have developed to the fullest the themes that real existence is found in the nonexistent and that true words are spoken in silence, but the origin of these themes must be traced to early Taoism. . . .

14

We look at it and do not see it;
  Its name is The Invisible.
We listen to it and do not hear it;
  Its name is The Inaudible.
We touch it and do not find it;
  Its name is The Subtle (formless).

These three cannot be further inquired into,
And hence merge into one.
Going up high, it is not bright, and coming down
  low, it is not dark.
Infinite and boundless, it cannot be given any name;
It reverts to nothingness.
This is called shape without shape,
Form without objects.
It is The Vague and Elusive.
Meet it and you will not see its head.
Follow it and you will not see its back.
Hold on to the Tao of old in order to master the
  things of the present.

From this one may know the primeval beginning (of
  the universe).
This is called the bond[2] of Tao.

COMMENT

Subtlety is an important characteristic of Tao and is more important than its manifestations. The Confucianists, on the other hand, emphasize manifestation. There is nothing more manifest than the hidden (subtle), they say, and "a man who knows that the subtle will be manifested can enter into virtue." The Buddhists and Neo-Confucianists eventually achieved a synthesis, saying that "there is no distinction between the manifest and the hidden."

To describe reality in terms of the invisible, the inaudible, and the subtle is an attempt to describe it in terms of non-being. Because the three Chinese words are pronounced *i, hsi,* and *wei,* respectively, they have been likened to *Jod, Heh, Vav,* indicating the name Jehovah, and to the Hindu god Ishvara, but any similarity is purely accidental. The threefold description does not suggest any idea of trinity either. Basically, Taoist philosophy is naturalistic, if not atheistic, and any idea of a god is alien to it. . . .

16

Attain complete vacuity.
Maintain steadfast quietude.

All things come into being,
And I see thereby their return.
All things flourish,
But each one returns to its root.
This return to its root means tranquillity.
It is called returning to its destiny.
To return to destiny is called the eternal (Tao).
To know the eternal is called enlightenment.
Not to know the eternal is to act blindly to result in
  disaster.
He who knows the eternal is all-embracing.
Being all-embracing, he is impartial.
Being impartial, he is kingly (universal).

2. *Chi,* literally, "a thread," denotes tradition, discipline, principle, order, essence, etc. Generally it means the system, principle, or continuity that binds things together.

Being kingly, he is one with Nature.
Being one with Nature, he is in accord with Tao.
Being in accord with Tao, he is everlasting
And is free from danger throughout his lifetime.

COMMENT

The central idea here is returning to the root, which is to be achieved through tranquillity. Generally speaking, in Taoist philosophy Tao is revealed most fully through tranquillity rather than activity. Under its influence, Wang Pi has commented on the hexagram *fu* (to return) in the *Book of Changes* in the same light. He says, "Although Heaven and Earth are vast, possessing the myriad things in abundance, where thunder moves and winds circulate, and while there is an infinite variety of changes and transformations, yet its original [substance] is absolutely quiet and perfect non-being. Therefore only with the cessation of activities within Earth can the mind of Heaven and Earth be revealed."

This Taoistic position is directly opposed by the Neo-Confucianists, who insist that the mind of Heaven and Earth is to be seen in a state of activity. As Ch'eng I says, "Former scholars all said that only in a state of tranquillity can the mind of Heaven and Earth be seen. They did not realize that the mind of Heaven and Earth is found in the beginning of activity." . . .

22

To yield is to be preserved whole.
To be bent is to become straight.
To be empty is to be full.
To be worn out is to be renewed.
To have little is to possess.
To have plenty is to be perplexed.
Therefore the sage embraces the One
And becomes the model of the world.
He does not show himself; therefore he is luminous.
He does not justify himself; therefore he becomes prominent.
He does not boast of himself; therefore he is given credit.
He does not brag; therefore he can endure for long.

It is precisely because he does not compete that the world cannot compete with him.

Is the ancient saying, "To yield is to be preserved whole," empty words?
Truly he will be preserved and (prominence and credit) will come to him.

COMMENT

Taoism seems to be advocating a negative morality. In this respect, it is not much different from the Christian doctrine taught in the Sermon on the Mount, which extols meekness, poverty, and so forth. Whatever negativism there may seem to be, it pertains to method only; the objective is entirely positive. . . .

25

There was something undifferentiated and yet complete,
Which existed before heaven and earth.
Soundless and formless, it depends on nothing and does not change.
It operates everywhere and is free from danger.
It may be considered the mother of the universe.
I do not know its name; I call it Tao.
If forced to give it a name, I shall call it Great.
Now being great means functioning everywhere.
Functioning everywhere means far-reaching.
Being far-reaching means returning to the original point.

Therefore Tao is great.
Heaven is great.
Earth is great.
And the king[3] *is also great.*
There are four great things in the universe, and the king is one of them.
Man models himself after Earth.
Earth models itself after Heaven.
Heaven models itself after Tao.
And Tao models itself after Nature.

3. The Fu I and Fan Ying-yüan texts have "man" in place of "king." This substitution has been accepted by Hsi T'ung, Ma Hsü-lun, Ch'en Chu, Jen Chi-yü, and Ch'u Ta-kao. They have been influenced, undoubtedly, by the concept of the trinity of Heaven, Earth, and man, without realizing that the king is considered here as representative of men. Moreover, in chapters 16 and 39, Heaven, Earth, and the king are spoken of together.

COMMENT

Taoist cosmology is outlined here simply but clearly. In the beginning there is something un-differentiated, which is forever operating; it produces heaven and earth and then all things. In essence this cosmology is strikingly similar to that of the *Book of Changes*. In the system of Change, the Great Ultimate produces the Two Modes (yin and yang), which in turn produce all things. We don't know to what extent Taoist thought has influenced the *Book of Changes,* which the Confucianists have attributed to their ancient sages, chiefly Confucius. At any rate, this naturalistic philosophy has always been prominent in Chinese thought, and later contributed substantially to the naturalistic pattern of Neo-Confucian cosmology, especially through Chou Tun-i. As will be noted, he has added the concept of the Non-ultimate to the philosophy of the *Book of Changes* in order better to explain the originally undifferentiated. It is to be noted that the term "Non-ultimate" comes from the *Lao Tzu. . . .*

34

The Great Tao flows everywhere.
It may go left or right.
All things depend on it for life, and it does not turn
away from them.
It accomplishes its task, but does not claim credit
for it.
It clothes and feeds all things but does not claim to
be master over them.
Always without desires, it may be called The Small.
All things come to it and it does not master them; it
may be called The Great.
Therefore (the sage) never strives himself for the
great, and thereby the great is achieved.

COMMENT

In commenting on this chapter, Yen Fu says that the left and the right, the small and the great, are relative terms, and that Tao in its original substance transcends all these relative qualities. Of greater significance, however, is the paradoxical character of Tao. This character is affirmed more than once in the *Lao Tzu*. In Neo-Confucianism, principle is both immanent and transcendent, as is the Christian God. Ultimate being or reality is by nature paradoxical. . . .

37

Tao invariably takes no action, and yet there is
nothing left undone.
If kings and barons can keep it, all things will
transform spontaneously.
If, after transformation, they should desire to be
active,
I would restrain them with simplicity, which has
no name.
Simplicity, which has no name, is free of desires.
Being free of desires, it is tranquil.
And the world will be at peace of its own accord.

COMMENT

"Transform spontaneously" seems to be a passing remark here, but the idea became a key concept in the *Chuang Tzu* and later formed a key tenet in the Neo-Taoism of Kuo Hsiang. In the *Lao Tzu*, things transform themselves because Tao takes no action or leaves things alone. Chuang Tzu goes a step further, saying that everything is in incessant change and that is self-transformation. In his commentary on the *Chuang Tzu,* Kuo Hsiang goes even further, stressing that things transform themselves spontaneously because they are self-sufficient, and there is no Nature behind or outside of them. Nature, he says, is but a general name for things. . . .

40

Reversion is the action of Tao.
Weakness is the function of Tao.
All things in the world come from being.
And being comes from non-being.[4]

4. Cf. chapter 1. This seems to contradict the saying, "Being and non-being produce each other," in chapter 2. But to produce means not to originate but to bring about.

COMMENT

The doctrine of returning to the original is a prominent one in the *Lao Tzu*.[5] It has contributed in no small degree to the common Chinese cyclical concept, according to which the Chinese believe that both history and reality operate in cycles. . . .

42

Tao produced the One.
The One produced the two.
The two produced the three.
And the three produced the ten thousand things.
The ten thousand things carry the yin and embrace the yang, and through the blending of the material force they achieve harmony.

5. The doctrine is also encountered in one sense or another in chapters 14, 16, 25, 28, 30, and 52. To D. C. Lau, returning to the root is not a cyclical process. According to him, the main doctrine of the *Lao Tzu* is the preservation of life, which is to be achieved through "abiding by softness." Softness is real strength, because when strength is allowed to reach its limit, it falls, whereas softness preserves itself. Thus opposites are neither relative nor paradoxical, and their process is not circular but a gradual development to the limit and then an inevitable and sudden decline. This idea may be implied in the *Lao Tzu* but there is no explicit passage to support Lau's theory. See his "The Treatment of Opposites in Lao Tzu," *Bulletin of the School of Oriental and African Studies*, XXI (1958), 349–50, 352–7.

People hate to be children without parents, lonely people without spouses, or men without food to eat,
And yet kings and lords call themselves by these names.
Therefore it is often the case that things gain by losing and lose by gaining.

What others have taught, I teach also:
"Violent and fierce people do not die a natural death."
I shall make this the father of my teaching.

COMMENT

It is often understood that the One is the original material force of the Great Ultimate, the two are yin and yang, the three are their blending with the original material force, and the ten thousand things are things carrying yin and embracing yang. The similarity of this process to that of the *Book of Changes*, in which the Great Ultimate produces the Two Forces (yin and yang) and then the myriad things, is amazing. The important point, however, is not the specific similarities, but the evolution from the simple to the complex. This theory is common to nearly all Chinese philosophical schools.

It should be noted that the evolution here, as in the *Book of Changes*, is natural. Production (*sheng*) is not personal creation or purposeful origination, but natural causation.

Suggestions for Further Reading

You should read the entire *Dao De Jing*. The selection I have made here is only a small portion of the text and focuses almost exclusively on its metaphysical parts. This selection is somewhat misleading since the book is as much a book about political philosophy and ethics as it is about metaphysics. Chan's translation reflects excellent scholarship, and his introduction will provide you with more background. You may wish to compare his translation to the many others available (along with the Bible, this is one of the world's most translated books). A popular version that is very readable but takes great liberties with the literal meaning of the text is Stephen Mitchell's *Tao Te Ching* (New York: Harper & Row, 1988).

Also see Michael LaFargue's *The Tao of the Tao Te Ching: A Translation and Commentary* (New York: State University of New York Press, 1992). LaFargue rejects a metaphysical reading of the text and argues for an ethical and political reading. He contends that the text embodies a worldview that stresses a philosophy of "organic harmony."

For more background information, check Ninian Smart's chapter on Chinese philosophies in *World Philosophies* (London: Routledge, 1999). His bibliography can guide you further.

On Chinese philosophy in general see Fung Yu-Lan's *A Short History of Chinese Philosophy* (New York: The Free Press, 1966).

If you wish to explore the possible relationships between the Daoist vision of reality and modern physics, see Fritjof Capra's *The Tao of Physics: An Exploration of the Parallels Between Modern Physics and Eastern Mysticism* (Berkeley: Shambhala, 1975) and Gary Zukav's *The Dancing Wu Li Masters: An Overview of the New Physics* (New York: Morrow, 1979).

Links to information on Daoism on the Web can be found at http://www.nauticom.net/ www/asti/history.htm and brief background information is available at http://his.com/ ~merkin/DaoBrief.html.

Video

Taoism (25 minutes; Insight Media, 2162 Broadway, New York, NY 10024) presents the story of Laozi and his book.

9.3 Platonic Dualism

We have encountered Plato and Socrates before (see Chapter 3). Plato (428–347 BCE) was Socrates' star pupil and one of the most creative and influential minds in the whole history of Western philosophy. He lived in Athens, founded the first "university" (called the Academy) in the West, and wrote a number of dialogues in which Socrates frequently appeared.

Alfred North Whitehead, a twentieth-century British-American philosopher, remarked that "all Western philosophy is but a footnote to Plato." This might be overstating the case for Plato's importance, but there can be little doubt that his ideas have influenced and still influence the thoughts and values of people who do not even know his name.

Do you believe in the immortality of the soul? Do you think that there is a material reality and an immaterial or spiritual reality and that the latter is more important than the former? Do you think logical and mathematical methods of reasoning are ideal models for arriving at truth? Do you believe that things have an essential nature? Do you believe you ought to control your passions by the use of reason? Do you think politicians ought to have the good of the people in mind? Do you think virtue is its own reward? If you answered some of these questions in the affirmative, you are reflecting ideas that Plato articulated almost twenty-four centuries ago.

Plato wrote on almost every aspect of philosophy. Here we are concerned primarily with his metaphysical ideas. Plato's metaphysics has been classified as dualistic because he argued that reality could be divided into two radically different sorts of things. There is the reality of matter characterized by change (becoming) and the reality of what he called the **Forms**, or Ideas characterized by permanence (being). Being is immaterial and of greater value than the material.

Along with this general ontological dualism between being and becoming, Plato taught a soul–body dualism. Human beings are composed of bodies and souls. One power that our souls have is the power of thought (the mind), and this is by far our most valuable thing. Our minds and souls are immaterial in contrast to our material bodies.

Plato's metaphysics is also classified as an idealism because it centers on the **theory of Forms** (Ideas) and because, although the reality of matter is not denied, matter is regarded as less real than the immaterial Forms. What is the theory of Forms? The English word *form* is often used to translate the Greek word for idea or concept. So, in the first instance, a form is the mental concept or idea we have of something. For example, how do you recognize a table as a table when you see one? After all, each table is different. How are you able to classify a whole group of different-looking objects into the class "table"? Well, you can do this, we might say, because you have the concept or idea of a table. If someone asked you what a table is, you could give a definition. This definition would constitute the expression of your concept.

Your definition (if it were the "correct" definition in Socrates' sense) would also express the essential nature of table. That is, it would not tell us what this or that *particular* table is, but it would tell us what *all* tables are insofar as they are tables. So, in the second place, a form is an essence.

Now most of us think that the concepts of things exist only in human minds and the essences of things (if there are such) either exist in our minds or somehow exist in the things themselves. If we might use the word *tableness* to designate the Form of tables, then most of us would be inclined to say that if there were no tables, there would be no tableness. Not so Plato. Or at least, not so Plato as interpreted by his star pupil, Aristotle. For Plato, according to Aristotle, essences (Forms) exist objectively apart from the minds that think them and the objects that instantiate them. They constitute ideals, perfect models if you will, that are even more real than the material things that reflect them.

Think of a square. Any particular material square you can draw will be imperfect. Its angles and lines will not be exact. But the square as such (squareness or the pure abstract geometric shape that we can define with mathematical precision) is another matter. It is perfect, and its definition will never change. Is not that which is perfect and permanent more real than that which is imperfect and ever-changing? Plato answers yes.

The selection that follows is from Plato's most famous dialogue, *The Republic*. This is one of the masterpieces of Western literature, and someday you should read all of it. It is filled with stories, myths, striking analogies, and political ideas that are still debated. For now, we will have to be content with just a little bit. However, to appreciate this little bit, some idea of what the whole is about will help.

Socrates, along with others, has been invited to the home of Cephalus. The question "What is justice?" arises and after examining and finding fault with several definitions, Thrasymachus (pronounced Thra-*sim*-a-kus) argues that justice is whatever is in the interest of the stronger party. Socrates disagrees and argues that power and knowledge must be combined since the art of government, like other arts, requires skill and knowledge. In particular, it requires knowledge of what is good for people since government ought to serve the needs of those who are governed, not merely the interests of the strongest.

In Book 2, Glaucon and Adeimantus press Socrates to prove that the just life is worth living. Socrates argues that virtue is its own reward and begins an analysis of political justice. The ideal state needs philosopher-kings (wisdom-loving rulers), guardians (soldiers and police), and producers (artisans, tradesmen, farmers). When each class does its proper business without interfering with the others, political justice is achieved. By analogy with the state, Socrates argues that the just person is one in whom the three basic elements of human nature—the rational, the spirited, and the appetitive—are properly ordered. Proper order consists of the rule of rationality or reason over the spirited and appetitive parts of the soul.

Books 3–5 describe in some detail Socrates' vision of the ideal state. In the ideal republic, the classes are carefully controlled by breeding, education, and selection. Just as reason should rule in the individual if personal justice is to be realized, so the "lovers of wisdom" (philosophers) should rule the state. This means that the rulers (philosopher-kings) need to know what is good and so must be properly educated. These ideas lead to a discussion of what the good is and what the proper education of the guardians should be. This discussion takes place in Books 6 and 7, from which the following selection comes.

Socrates admits that the good itself is the proper object of the philosopher's quest, but he cannot say directly what the good is. He offers three analogies. The first compares the good to the Sun. The second, called the simile of the divided line, compares *opinion* (which derives from sensations of material objects) with *knowledge* (which derives from knowing the Forms via reason and understanding). The third, called the allegory of the cave, compares the philosopher to a prisoner who has escaped from a cave and seen the light of the real world.

The last three books of *The Republic* deal with political change, the decline of the state, and various forms of government. *The Republic* closes with an argument for the immortality of the soul. By loving justice (i.e., by harmonizing reason, spirit, and appetite under the rule of rationality), we can keep our souls healthy and thereby prosper forever.

You should read what follows slowly and carefully, pausing to think about what Socrates is saying. Socrates is the main speaker. In this translation, the words of the speaker who responds to Socrates are sometimes indicated only by a dash (—). The following questions should help you catch the main ideas.

Reading Questions

1. What is the difference between the *many things* and the *Forms?*
2. In what ways are the Sun and the Good alike?
3. Give examples of what Socrates means by *images* and by *objects of sense.*
4. What is the difference between *reasoning* and *understanding?*
5. What do you think the allegory of the cave means?
6. What is the relationship between the image of the divided line and the story about the cave?
7. What conclusion about education does Socrates draw from the allegory of the cave?
8. Are you inclined to agree with Plato about the existence of some higher, immaterial, intelligible reality beyond this material world? Why, or why not?
9. How would Plato answer the question, "What is really real?"

The Republic

PLATO

. . . But you also, Socrates, must tell us whether you consider the good to be knowledge, or pleasure, or something else.

What a man! I said. It has been clear for some time that the opinion of others on this subject would not satisfy you.

Well, Socrates, he said, it does not seem right to me to be able to tell the opinions of others and not one's own, especially for a man who has spent so much time as you have occupying himself with this subject.

Why? said I. Do you think it right to talk about things one does not know as if one knew them? Not as if one knew them, he said, but for a man who has an opinion to say what that opinion is.

And have you not noticed that opinions not based on knowledge are ugly things? The best of them are blind; or do you think that those who express a true opinion without knowledge are any different from blind people who yet follow the right road?—They are no different.

Do you want to contemplate ugly, blind, and crooked things when you can hear bright and beautiful things from others?

By Zeus, Socrates, said Glaucon, do not stand off as if you had come to the end. We shall be satisfied if you discuss the Good in the same fashion as you did justice, moderation, and the other things.

That, my friend, I said, would also quite satisfy me, but I fear I shall not be able to do so, and that in my eagerness I shall disgrace myself and make myself ridiculous. But, my excellent friends, let us for the moment abandon the quest for the nature of the Good itself, for that I think is a larger question than what we started on, which was to ascertain my present opinion about it. I am willing to tell you what appears to be the offspring of the Good and most like it, if that is agreeable to you. If not, we must let the question drop.

Well, he said, tell us. The story of the parent remains a debt which you will pay us some other time.

I wish, I said, that I could pay it in full now, and you could exact it in full and not, as now, only receive the interest.[1] However, accept then this offspring and child of the Good. Only be careful that I do not somehow deceive you unwillingly by giving a counterfeit account of this offspring.—We shall be as careful as we can. Only tell us.

I will, I said, after coming to an agreement with you and reminding you of the things we said before, and also many times elsewhere.—What are these things?

We speak of many beautiful things and many good things, and we say that they are so and so define them in speech.—We do.

And Beauty itself and Goodness itself, and so with all the things which we then classed as many; we now class them again according to one Form of each, which is one and which we in each case call that which is.—That is so.

And we say that the many things are the objects of sight but not of thought, while the Forms are the objects of thought but not of sight.—Altogether true.

With what part of ourselves do we see the objects that are seen?—With our sight.

And so things heard are heard by our hearing, and all that is perceived is perceived by our other senses?— Quite so.

---

1. Plato is punning on the Greek word *tokos* which means a child, and in the plural was used also of the interest on capital, a pleasant and common metaphor.

Have you considered how very lavishly the maker of our senses made the faculty of seeing and being seen?—I cannot say I have.

Look at it this way: do hearing and sound need another kind of thing for the former to hear and the latter to be heard, and in the absence of this third element the one will not hear and the other not be heard.—No, they need nothing else.

Neither do many other senses, if indeed any, need any such other thing, or can you mention one?—Not I.

But do you not realize that the sense of sight and that which is seen do have such a need?—How so?

Sight may be in the eyes, and the man who has it may try to use it, and colours may be present in the objects, but unless a third kind of thing is present, which is by nature designed for this very purpose, you know that sight will see nothing and the colours remain unseen.—What is this third kind of thing?

What you call light, I said.—Right.

So to no small extent the sense of sight and the power of being seen are yoked together by a more honourable yoke than other things which are yoked together, unless light is held in no honour.—That is far from being the case.

Which of the gods in the heavens can you hold responsible for this, whose light causes our sight to see as beautifully as possible, and the objects of sight to be seen?—The same as you would, he said, and as others would; obviously the answer to your question is the sun.

And is not sight naturally related to the sun in this way?—Which way?

Sight is not the sun, neither itself nor that in which it occurs which we call the eye.—No indeed.

But I think it is the most sunlike of the organs of sense.—Very much so.

And it receives from the sun the capacity to see as a kind of outflow.—Quite so.

The sun is not sight, but is it not the cause of it, and is also seen by it?—Yes.

Say then, I said, that it is the sun which I called the offspring of the Good, which the Good begot as analogous to itself. What the Good itself is in the world of thought in relation to the in-

telligence and things known, the sun is in the visible world, in relation to sight and things seen.—How? Explain further.

You know, I said, that when one turns one's eyes to those objects of which the colours are no longer in the light of day but in the dimness of the night, the eyes are dimmed and seem nearly blind, as if clear vision was no longer in them.—Quite so.

Yet whenever one's eyes are turned upon objects brightened by sunshine, they see clearly, and clear vision appears in those very same eyes?—Yes indeed.

So too understand the eye of the soul: whenever it is fixed upon that upon which truth and reality shine, it understands and knows and seems to have intelligence, but whenever it is fixed upon what is mixed with darkness—that which is subject to birth and destruction—it opines and is dimmed, changes its opinions this way and that, and seems to have no intelligence.—That is so.

Say that what gives truth to the objects of knowledge, and to the knowing mind the power to know, is the Form of Good. As it is the cause of knowledge and truth, think of it also as being the object of knowledge. Both knowledge and truth are beautiful, but you will be right to think of the Good as other and more beautiful than they. As in the visible world light and sight are rightly considered sun-like, but it is wrong to think of them as the sun, so here it is right to think of knowledge and truth as Good-like, but wrong to think of either as the Good, for the Good must be honoured even more than they.

This is an extraordinary beauty you mention, he said, if it provides knowledge and truth and is itself superior to them in beauty. You surely do not mean this to be pleasure!

Hush! said I, rather examine the image of it in this way.—How?

You will say, I think, that the sun not only gives to the objects of sight the capacity to be seen, but also that it provides for their generation, increase, and nurture, though it is not itself the process of generation.—How could it be?

And say that as for the objects of knowledge, not only is their being known due to the Good, but also their reality being, though the Good is not being but superior to and beyond being in dignity and power.

Glaucon was quite amused and said: By Apollo, a miraculous superiority!

It is your own fault, I said, you forced me to say what I thought about it.

Don't you stop, he said, except for a moment, but continue to explain the similarity to the sun in case you are leaving something out.

I am certainly leaving out a good deal, I said.—Don't omit the smallest point.

Much is omitted, I said. However, as far as the explanation can go at present, I will not omit anything.—Don't you!

Understand then, I said, that, as we say, there are those two, one reigning over the intelligible kind and realm, the other over the visible (not to say heaven, that I may not appear to play the sophist about the name[2]). So you have two kinds, the visible and the intelligible.—Right.

It is like a line divided[3] into two unequal parts, and then divide each section in the same ratio, that is, the section of the visible and that of the in-

telligible. You will then have sections related to each other in proportion to their clarity and obscurity. The first section of the visible consists of images—and by images I mean shadows in the first instance, then the reflections in water and all those on close-packed, smooth, and bright materials, and all that sort of thing, if you understand me.—I understand.

In the other section of the visible, place the models of the images, the living creatures around us, all plants, and the whole class of manufactured things.—I so place them.

Would you be willing to say that, as regards truth and untruth, the division is made in this proportion: as the opinable is to the knowable so the image is to the model it is made like?—Certainly.

Consider now how the section of the intelligible is to be divided.—How?

In such a way that in one section the soul, using as images what before were models, is compelled to investigate from hypotheses, proceeding from these not to a first principle but to a conclusion. In the second section which leads to a first principle that is not hypothetical, the soul proceeds from a hypothesis without using the images of the first section, by means of the Forms themselves and proceeding through these.—I do not, he said, quite understand what you mean.

Let us try again, I said, for you will understand more easily because of what has been said. I think you know that students of geometry, calculation, and the like assume the existence of the odd and the even, of figures, of three kinds of angles, and of kindred things in each of their studies, as if they were known to them. These they make their hypotheses and do not deem it necessary to give any account of them either to themselves or to others as if they were clear to all; these are their starting points, and going through the remaining steps they reach an agreed conclusion on what they started out to investigate.— Quite so, I understand that.

You know also that they use visible figures and talk about them, but they are not thinking about them but about the models of which these are likenesses; they are making their points about the square itself, the diameter itself, not about the

2. He means play on the similarity of sound between *ouranos,* the sky, and *horaton,* visible.

3. It is clear that Plato visualizes a vertical line . . . with *B* as the highest point in the scale of reality and *A* as the lowest form of existence. The main division is at *C. AC* is the visible, *CB* being the intelligible world, *AD* is the world of images (and perhaps, though Plato does not say so, works of art), mathematical realities are contained in *CE*, the Platonic Forms in *EB*, with the Good presumably at *B*.

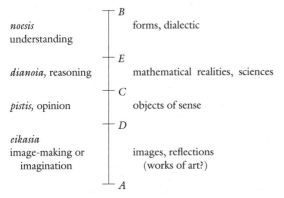

noesis
understanding — *B* — forms, dialectic

dianoia, reasoning — *E* — mathematical realities, sciences

pistis, opinion — *C* — objects of sense

eikasia
image-making or imagination — *D* — images, reflections (works of art?)

— *A* —

The names of the four mental processes—*noesis, dianoia, pistis,* and *eikasia*—are more or less arbitrary, and Plato does not use them regularly in these precise senses in the rest of the *Republic.*

diameter which they draw, and similarly with the others. These figures which they fashion and draw, of which shadows and reflections in the water are images, they now in turn use as images, in seeking to understand those others in themselves, which one cannot see except in thought.— That is true.

This is what I called the intelligible class, and said that the soul is forced to use hypotheses in its search for it, not travelling up to a first principle, since it cannot reach beyond its hypotheses, but it uses as images those very things which at a lower level were models and which, in comparison with their images, were thought to be clear and honoured as such.—I understand, he said, that you mean what happens in geometry and kindred sciences.

Understand also that by the other section of the intelligible I mean that which reason itself grasps by the power of dialectic. It does not consider its hypotheses as first principles, but as hypotheses in the true sense of stepping stones and starting points, in order to reach that which is beyond hypothesis, the first principle of all that exists. Having reached this and keeping hold of what follows from it, it does come down to a conclusion without making use of anything visible at all, but proceeding by means of Forms and through Forms to its conclusions which are Forms.

I understand, he said, but not completely, for you seem to be speaking of a mighty task—that you wish to distinguish the intelligible reality contemplated by the science of dialectic as clearer than that viewed by the so-called sciences, for which their hypotheses are first principles. The students of these so-called sciences are, it is true, compelled to study them by thought and not by sense perception, yet because they do not go back to a first principle but proceed from hypotheses, you do not think that they have any clear understanding of their subjects, although these can be so understood if approached from a first principle. You seem to me to call the attitude of mind of geometers and such reasoning but not understanding, reasoning being midway between opinion and understanding.

You have grasped this very satisfactorily, I said. There are four such processes in the soul, corresponding to the four sections of our line: understanding for the highest, reasoning for the second; give the name of opinion to the third, and imagination to the last. Place these in the due terms of a proportion and consider that each has as much clarity as the content of its particular section shares in truth.—I understand, and I agree and arrange them as you say.

Book VII

Next, I said, compare the effect of education and the lack of it upon our human nature to a situation like this: imagine men to be living in an underground cave-like dwelling place, which has a way up to the light along its whole width, but the entrance is a long way up. The men have been there from childhood, with their neck and legs in fetters, so that they remain in the same place and can only see ahead of them, as their bonds prevent them turning their heads. Light is provided by a fire burning some way behind and above them. Between the fire and the prisoners, some way behind them and on a higher ground, there is a path across the cave and along this a low wall has been built, like the screen at a puppet show in front of the performers who show their puppets above it.—I see it.

See then also men carrying along that wall, so that they overtop it, all kinds of artifacts, statues of men, reproductions of other animals in stone or wood fashioned in all sorts of ways, and, as is likely, some of the carriers are talking while others are silent.—This is a strange picture, and strange prisoners.

They are like us, I said. Do you think, in the first place, that such men could see anything of themselves and each other[4] except the shadows

---

4. These shadows of themselves and each other are never mentioned again. A Platonic myth or parable, like a Homeric simile, is often elaborated in considerable detail. These contribute to the vividness of the picture but often have no other function, and it is a mistake to look for any symbolic meaning in them. It is the general picture that matters.

which the fire casts upon the wall of the cave in front of them?—How could they, if they have to keep their heads still throughout life?

And is not the same true of the objects carried along the wall?—Quite.

If they could converse with one another, do you not think that they would consider these shadows to be the real things?—Necessarily.

What if their prison had an echo which reached them from in front of them? Whenever one of the carriers passing behind the wall spoke, would they not think that it was the shadow passing in front of them which was talking? Do you agree?—By Zeus I do.

Altogether then, I said, such men would believe the truth to be nothing else than the shadows of the artifacts?—They must believe that.

Consider then what deliverance from their bonds and the curing of their ignorance would be if something like this naturally happened to them. Whenever one of them was freed, had to stand up suddenly, turn his head, walk, and look up toward the light, doing all that would give him pain, the flash of the fire would make it impossible for him to see the objects of which he had earlier seen the shadows. What do you think he would say if he was told that what he saw then was foolishness, that he was now somewhat closer to reality and turned to things that existed more fully, that he saw more correctly? If one then pointed to each of the objects passing by, asked him what each was, and forced him to answer, do you not think he would be at a loss and believe that the things which he saw earlier were truer than the things now pointed out to him?—Much truer.

If one then compelled him to look at the fire itself, his eyes would hurt, he would turn round and flee toward those things which he could see, and think that they were in fact clearer than those now shown to him.—Quite so.

And if one were to drag him thence by force up the rough and steep path, and did not let him go before he was dragged into the sunlight, would he not be in physical pain and angry as he was dragged along? When he came into the light, with the sunlight filling his eyes, he would not be

able to see a single one of the things which are now said to be true.—Not at once, certainly.

I think he would need time to get adjusted before he could see things in the world above; at first he would see shadows most easily, then reflections of men and other things in water, then the things themselves. After this he would see objects in the sky and the sky itself more easily at night, the light of the stars and the moon more easily than the sun and the light of the sun during the day.—Of course.

Then, at last, he would be able to see the sun, not images of it in water or in some alien place, but the sun itself in its own place, and be able to contemplate it.—That must be so.

After this he would reflect that it is the sun which provides the seasons and the years, which governs everything in the visible world, and is also in some way the cause of those other things which he used to see.—Clearly that would be the next stage.

What then? As he reminds himself of his first dwelling place, of the wisdom there and of his fellow prisoners, would he not reckon himself happy for the change, and pity them?—Surely.

And if the men below had praise and honours from each other, and prizes for the man who saw most clearly the shadows that passed before them, and who could best remember which usually came earlier and which later, and which came together and thus could most ably prophesy the future, do you think our man would desire those rewards and envy those who were honoured and held power among the prisoners, or would he feel, as Homer put it, that he certainly wished to be "serf to another man without possessions upon the earth"[5] and go through any suffering, rather than share their opinions and live as they do?—Quite so, he said, I think he would rather suffer anything.

Reflect on this too, I said. If this man went down into the cave again and sat down in the

---

5. *Odyssey* 11, 489–90, where Achilles says to Odysseus, on the latter's visit to the underworld, that he would rather be a servant to a poor man on earth than king among the dead.

same seat, would his eyes not be filled with darkness, coming suddenly out of the sunlight?—They certainly would.

And if he had to contend again with those who had remained prisoners in recognizing those shadows while his sight was affected and his eyes had not settled down—and the time for this adjustment would not be short—would he not be ridiculed? Would it not be said that he had returned from his upward journey with his eyesight spoiled, and that it was not worthwhile even to attempt to travel upward? As for the man who tried to free them and lead them upward, if they could somehow lay their hands on him and kill him, they would do so.—They certainly would.

This whole image, my dear Glaucon, I said, must be related to what we said before. The realm of the visible should be compared to the prison dwelling, and the fire inside it to the power of the sun. If you interpret the upward journey and the contemplation of things above as the upward journey of the soul to the intelligible realm, you will grasp what I surmise since you were keen to hear it. Whether it is true or not only the god knows, but this is how I see it, namely that in the intelligible world the Form of the Good is the last to be seen, and with difficulty; when seen it must be reckoned to be for all the cause of all that is right and beautiful, to have produced in the visible world both light and the fount of light, while in the intelligible world it is itself that which produces and controls truth and intelligence, and he who is to act intelligently in public or in private must see it.—I share your thought as far as I am able.

Come then, share with me this thought also: do not be surprised that those who have reached this point are unwilling to occupy themselves with human affairs, and that their souls are always pressing upward to spend their time there, for this is natural if things are as our parable indicates.—That is very likely.

Further, I said, do you think it at all surprising that anyone coming to the evils of human life from the contemplation of the divine behaves awkwardly and appears very ridiculous while his eyes are still dazzled and before he is sufficiently adjusted to the darkness around him, if he is com-

pelled to contend in court or some other place about the shadows of justice or the objects of which they are shadows, and to carry through the contest about these in the way these things are understood by those who have never seen Justice itself?—That is not surprising at all.

Anyone with intelligence, I said, would remember that the eyes may be confused in two ways and from two causes, coming from light into darkness as well as from darkness into light. Realizing that the same applies to the soul, whenever he sees a soul disturbed and unable to see something, he will not laugh mindlessly but will consider whether it has come from a brighter life and is dimmed because unadjusted, or has come from greater ignorance into greater light and is filled with a brighter dazzlement. The former he would declare happy in its life and experience, the latter he would pity, and if he should wish to laugh at it, his laughter would be less ridiculous than if he laughed at a soul that has come from the light above.—What you say is very reasonable.

We must then, I said, if these things are true, think something like this about them, namely that education is not what some declare it to be; they say that knowledge is not present in the soul and that they put it in, like putting sight into blind eyes.—They surely say that.

Our present argument shows, I said, that the capacity to learn and the organ with which to do so are present in every person's soul. It is as if it were not possible to turn the eye from darkness to light without turning the whole body; so one must turn one's whole soul from the world of becoming until it can endure to contemplate reality, and the brightest of realities, which we say is the Good.—Yes.

Education then is the art of doing this very thing, this turning around, the knowledge of how the soul can most easily and most effectively be turned around; it is not the art of putting the capacity of sight into the soul; the soul possesses that already but it is not turned the right way or looking where it should. This is what education has to deal with.—That seems likely.

Now the other so-called virtues of the soul seem to be very close to those of the body—they really do not exist before and are added later by habit and practice—but the virtue of intelligence belongs above all to something more divine, it seems, which never loses its capacity but, according to which way it is turned, becomes useful and beneficial or useless and harmful. Have you never noticed in men who are said to be wicked but clever, how sharply their little soul looks into things to which it turns its attention? Its capacity for sight is not inferior, but it is compelled to serve evil ends, so that the more sharply it looks the more evils it works.— Quite so.

Yet if a soul of this kind had been hammered at from childhood and those excrescences had been knocked off it which belong to the world of becoming and have been fastened upon it by feasting, gluttony, and similar pleasures, and which like leaden weights draw the soul to look downward—if, being rid of these, it turned to look at things that are true, then the same soul of the same man would see these just as sharply as it now sees the things towards which it is directed.—That seems likely.

Further, is it not likely, I said, indeed it follows inevitably from what was said before, that the uneducated who have no experience of truth would never govern a city satisfactorily, nor would those who are allowed to spend their whole life in the process of educating themselves; the former would fail because they do not have a single goal at which all their actions, public and private, must aim; the latter because they would refuse to act, thinking that they have settled, while still alive, in the faraway islands of the blessed.—True.

It is then our task as founders, I said, to compel the best natures to reach the study which we have previously said to be the most important, to see the Good and to follow that upward journey. When they have accomplished their journey and seen it sufficiently, we must not allow them to do what they are allowed to do today.—What is that?

To stay there, I said, and to refuse to go down again to the prisoners in the cave, there to share both their labours and their honours, whether these be of little or of greater worth.

Suggestions for Further Reading

There is so much written on Plato that this list could go on for pages. I will make just a few suggestions, each of which contains bibliographies that will take you as deep into the scholarship as you wish to go. Of course, there is no substitute for reading the primary sources, which are widely available in a number of different translations.

For a summary with interpretative comments on the *Republic* see *Masterpieces of World Philosophy* edited by Frank N. Magill (New York: HaperCollins, 1990).

The article on Plato in *The Cambridge Dictionary of Philosophy,* edited by Robert Audi, 2nd edition (New York: Cambridge University Press, 1999), will provide basic background information.

Of the many works on Plato, G. M. A. Grube's *Plato's Thought* (Indianapolis: Hackett, 1980) is an old standby that provides an excellent introduction to the whole of Plato's philosophy.

For all kinds of information on Plato on the web start with Bernard Suzanne's site at http://phd.evansville.edu/plato.htm.

Videos

The Cave (10 minutes; available from Insight Media, 2162 Broadway, New York, NY 10024) explores the meaning of Plato's parable.

Plato (45 minutes; Films for the Humanities and Sciences, PO Box 2053, Princeton, NJ 08543) explores, under the guidance of Cambridge philosopher Miles Burnyear, many core platonic notions including the theory of forms.

9.4 Nondualism

Shankara (ca. 788–820) is one of the most important figures in Indian philosophy. In his short life, he traveled extensively, founded four monasteries, and made major contributions to the development of philosophical and religious ideas. He wrote extensive commentaries interpreting important Hindu scriptures and became the leading advocate for a school of philosophy known as **Advaita** (nondual) **Vedanta** (end of the *Vedas*). Shankara preferred to be thought of as a *nondualist* rather than a monist because he taught that ultimate reality is an undifferentiated unity beyond all positive predication. Hence, it can only be defined by saying what it is not.

Brahman was the word used by Shankara for ultimate reality. The word **Atman** had been used for the true Self (the real identity behind our individual egos). Shankara thought of the Atman as pure consciousness (consciousness per se) and identified it with the Brahman. Hence, Atman is the word used for the Brahman "within," and Brahman is the word used for the Atman "without." But, of course, since they are identical and since there is no other absolute reality, ultimately there is no division between within and without. Philosophically, Shankara struggled to articulate more precisely what these ideas mean and to understand how they are related. Religiously, he sought to discover the way to experience the identity of Atman and Brahman.

Like Plato, Shankara believed that the more permanent something is, the more real it is. That which is absolutely permanent is absolutely real. Everything else is but an appearance of this eternal reality. The supposed "reality" of the impermanent is nothing but an illusion. We must learn how to discriminate between the permanent and the impermanent if we want to know what is really real.

To distinguish things, we need a principle of discrimination, which we can term *sublation.* **Sublation** is the act of correcting a previous judgment in light of a subsequent one. For example, when I think the shiny surface up ahead on the road is water but decide, as I get closer, that it is only the sun reflecting off the asphalt, I am engaging in an act of sublation and thereby discriminating appearance from reality. Sublatability is the quality a thing has that allows us to correct our judgment about it. If something is sublatable, it must be impermanent. If the "water" I saw up ahead were permanent, when I got closer I would still see water. It would not be a temporary mirage.

Shankara defines *reality* as that which cannot be sublated, *appearance* as that which can be sublated, and *unreality* as neither sublatable nor unsublatable because it does not exist. Armed with these distinctions and the principle of sublation, our task is to examine all the sorts of things we think are real to see if they really are real or just the appearance of what is real.

In the selection from *The Crest-Jewel of Discrimination* that follows, Shankara, speaking as the master, leads a disciple through an examination of various "coverings" in search of the true Self (Atman). The master then claims that the Atman, which is unsublatable, is the same as the Brahman, the really real.

Some scholars do not believe Shankara is the author of this text. Nevertheless, tradition has attributed it to him, and it undoubtedly expresses ideas associated with his philosophy, even if he did not write it.

Read the text slowly and carefully, keeping in mind that to qualify as really real, something must be permanent and unsublatable. I have added footnotes at key points to explain technical terms. Be sure to read them; they will help.

Reading Questions

1. What does *discrimination* mean?
2. Why do you think renunciation, tranquillity, self-control, faith, self-surrender, the longing for liberation, and devotion are necessary to gain knowledge of the Atman?
3. Shankara says all kinds of things about the Atman and yet claims that it cannot be defined. Is this a contradiction? Why?
4. What is *ignorance,* and how is it overcome?
5. Why is your body (physical covering) not your true Self?
6. What are the differences among the fool, the intelligent person, and the wise person?
7. Why are the vital covering, the mental covering, and the covering of the intellect not the Atman?
8. Do you agree that the "mind of the experiencer creates all the objects which he experiences" while in the waking *and* the dreaming state? Why?
9. How does the master answer the disciple's question, "How, then, can there be an existence which the wise man may realize as one with his Atman?" Do you find the answer convincing? Why?
10. How is the universe related to Brahman?
11. If you were in a debate with Shankara, what would be the major objection you would make to his ideas? How do you think he would defend himself?

The Crest-Jewel of Discrimination

SHANKARA

A MAN SHOULD BE intelligent and learned, with great powers of comprehension, and able to overcome doubts by the exercise of his reason. One who has these qualifications is fitted for knowledge of the Atman.

He alone may be considered qualified to seek Brahman who has discrimination, whose mind is turned away from all enjoyments, who possesses tranquillity and the kindred virtues, and who feels a longing for liberation.

In this connection, the sages have spoken of four qualifications for attainment. When these are present, devotion to the Reality will become complete. When they are absent, it will fail.

First is mentioned discrimination between the eternal and the non-eternal. Next comes renunciation of the enjoyment of the fruits of action,

here and hereafter. Then come the six treasures of virtue, beginning with tranquillity. And last, certainly, is the longing for liberation.

Brahman is real; the universe is unreal. A firm conviction that this is so is called *discrimination* between the eternal and the non-eternal.

Renunciation is the giving-up of all the pleasures of the eyes, the ears, and the other senses, the giving-up of the desire for a physical body as well as for the highest kind of spirit-body of a god.

To detach the mind from all objective things by continually seeing their imperfection, and to direct it steadfastly toward Brahman, its goal—this is called *tranquillity.*

To detach both kinds of sense-organs—those of perception and those of action—from objective things, and to withdraw them to rest in their

From Shankara's *Crest-Jewel of Discrimination with a Garland of Questions and Answers, translated by Swami Prabhavananda and Christopher Isherwood (New York: New American Library, 1970), pp. 37–39; 52–61; 65–69. Reprinted by permission of Vedanta Press, 1946 Vedanta Pl., Hollywood, CA 90068.*

respective centers—this is called *self-control*. True *mental poise* consists in not letting the mind react to external stimuli.

To endure all kinds of afflictions without rebellion, complaint or lament—this is called *forbearance*.

A firm conviction, based upon intellectual understanding that the teachings of the scriptures and of one's master are true—this is called by the sages the *faith* which leads to realization of the Reality.

To concentrate the intellect repeatedly upon the pure Brahman and to keep it fixed there always—this is called *self-surrender*. This does not mean soothing the mind, like a baby, with idle thoughts.

Longing for liberation is the will to be free from the fetters forged by ignorance—beginning with the ego-sense and so on, down to the physical body itself—through the realization of one's true nature.

Even though this longing for liberation may be present in a slight or moderate degree, it will grow intense through the grace of the teacher, and through the practice of renunciation and of virtues such as tranquillity, etc.: And it will bear fruit.

When renunciation and the longing for liberation are present to an intense degree within a man, then the practice of tranquillity and the other virtues will bear fruit and lead to the goal.

Where renunciation and longing for liberation are weak, tranquillity and the other virtues are a mere appearance, like the mirage in the desert.

Among all means of liberation, devotion is supreme. To seek earnestly to know one's real nature—this is said to be devotion.

In other words, devotion can be defined as the search for the reality of one's own Atman. The seeker after the reality of the Atman, who possesses the above-mentioned qualifications, should approach an illumined teacher from whom he can learn the way to liberation from all bondage. . . .

Now I shall tell you the nature of the Atman. If you realize it, you will be freed from the bonds of ignorance, and attain liberation.

There is a self-existent Reality, which is the basis of our consciousness of ego. That Reality is the witness of the three states of our consciousness, and is distinct from the five bodily coverings.[1]

That Reality is the knower in all states of consciousness—waking, dreaming and dreamless sleep. It is aware of the presence or absence of the mind and its functions. It is the Atman.

That Reality sees everything by its own light. No one sees it. It gives intelligence to the mind and the intellect, but no one gives it light.

That Reality pervades the universe, but no one penetrates it. It alone shines. The universe shines with its reflected light.

Because of its presence, the body, senses, mind and intellect apply themselves to their respective functions, as though obeying its command.

Its nature is eternal consciousness. It knows all things, from the sense of ego to the body itself. It is the knower of pleasure and pain and of the sense-objects. It knows everything objectively—just as a man knows the objective existence of a jar.

This is the Atman, the Supreme being, the ancient. It never ceases to experience infinite joy. It is always the same. It is consciousness itself. The organs and vital energies function under its command.

Here, within this body, in the pure mind, in the secret chamber of intelligence, in the infinite universe within the heart, the Atman shines in its captivating splendour, like a noonday sun. By its light, the universe is revealed.

It is the knower of the activities of the mind and of the individual man. It is the witness of all the actions of the body, the sense-organs and the vital energy. It seems to be identified with all these, just as fire appears identified with an

---

1. [The five bodily coverings will be discussed later. They are the physical, the vital, the mental, the intellectual, and the covering of bliss. These are called "coverings" because Shankara pictures them as progressively thinner bodies or sheaves (like those dolls within dolls) that cover the Atman. This is based on the idea that matter extends from a gross level (the physical body as we think of it) to subtler or finer levels. Notice that things like mind and intellect, which in the West have usually been thought of as immaterial, are here thought of as material (but matter of a finer sort).—Ed.]

iron ball. But it neither acts nor is subject to the slightest change.

The Atman is birthless and deathless. It neither grows nor decays. It is unchangeable, eternal. It does not dissolve when the body dissolves. Does the ether cease to exist when the jar that enclosed it is broken?

The Atman is distinct from Maya,[2] the primal cause, and from her effect, the universe. The nature of the Atman is pure consciousness. The Atman reveals this entire universe of mind and matter. It cannot be defined. In and through the various states of consciousness—the waking, the dreaming and the sleeping—it maintains our unbroken awareness of identity. It manifests itself as the witness of the intelligence.

The Mind

With a controlled mind and an intellect which is made pure and tranquil, you must realize the Atman directly, within yourself. Know the Atman as the real I. Thus you cross the shoreless ocean of worldliness, whose waves are birth and death. Live always in the knowledge of identity with Brahman, and be blessed.

Man is in bondage because he mistakes what is non-Atman for his real Self. This is caused by ignorance. Hence follows the misery of birth and death. Through ignorance, man identifies the Atman with the body, taking the perishable for the real. Therefore he nourishes this body, and anoints it, and guards it carefully. He becomes enmeshed in the things of the senses like a caterpillar in the threads of its cocoon.

Deluded by his ignorance, a man mistakes one thing for another. Lack of discernment will cause a man to think that a snake is a piece of rope. When he grasps it in this belief he runs a great risk. The acceptance of the unreal as real constitutes the state of bondage. Pay heed to this, my friend.

The Atman is indivisible, eternal, one without a second. It is eternally made manifest by the power of its own knowledge. Its glories are infinite. The veil of tamas[3] hides the true nature of the Atman, just as an eclipse hides the rays of the sun.

When the pure rays of the Atman are thus concealed, the deluded man identifies himself with his body, which is non-Atman. Then rajas, which has the power of projecting illusory forms, afflicts him sorely. It binds him with chains of lust, anger and the other passions.

His mind becomes perverted. His consciousness of the Atman is swallowed up by the shark of total ignorance. Yielding to the power of rajas, he identifies himself with the many motions and changes of the mind. Therefore he is swept hither and thither, now rising, now sinking, in the boundless ocean of birth and death, whose waters are full of the poison of sense-objects. This is indeed a miserable fate.

The sun's rays bring forth layers of cloud. By them, the sun is concealed; and so it appears that the clouds alone exist. In the same way, the ego, which is brought forth by the Atman, hides the true nature of the Atman; and so it appears that the ego alone exists.

On a stormy day the sun is swallowed up by thick clouds; and these clouds are attacked by sharp, chill blasts of wind. So, when the Atman is enveloped in the thick darkness of tamas, the terrible power of rajas attacks the deluded man with all kinds of sorrows.

Man's bondage is caused by the power of these two—tamas and rajas. Deluded by these, he mistakes the body for the Atman and strays on to the path that leads to death and rebirth.

Man's life in this relative world may be compared to a tree. Tamas is the seed. Identification of the Atman with the body is its sprouting forth.

---

2. [*Maya* is sometimes translated as "illusion" and sometimes as "appearance." It refers to the illusions done by magicians, and Shankara uses this analogy to indicate the nature of the pluralistic universe we usually experience. In general, *Maya* is the impermanent that appears to be real but is not. It stands in contrast to the permanence of Atman-Brahman, which is what is truly real.—Ed.]

3. [*Tamas* are one of the three *gunas* that make up all material things. *Gunas* are qualities. In ancient Hindu cosmology, it was thought that everything material is made up of some combination or mixture of the *gunas*. *Tamas* is the quality of stupor, laziness, stupidity, heaviness, and inaction in general. *Rajas*, another *guna*, is the active principle and hence the opposite of *tamas*. *Sattva*, the third *guna*, is associated with the pure, the fine, and the calm.—Ed.]

The cravings are its leaves. Work is its sap. The body is its trunk. The vital forces are its branches. The sense-organs are its twigs. The sense-objects are its flowers. Its fruits are the sufferings caused by various actions. The individual man is the bird who eats the fruit of the tree of life.

The Atman's bondage to the non-Atman springs from ignorance. It has no external cause. It is said to be beginningless. It will continue indefinitely until a man becomes enlightened. As long as a man remains in this bondage it subjects him to a long train of miseries—birth, death, sickness, decrepitude, and so forth.

This bondage cannot be broken by weapons, or by wind, or by fire, or by millions of acts. Nothing but the sharp sword of knowledge can cut through this bondage. It is forged by discrimination and made keen by purity of heart, through divine grace.

A man must faithfully and devotedly fulfill the duties of life as the scriptures prescribe. This purifies his heart. A man whose heart is pure realizes the supreme Atman. Thereby he destroys his bondage to the world, root and all.

Wrapped in its five coverings, beginning with the physical, which are the products of its own Maya, the Atman remains hidden, as the water of a pond is hidden by a veil of scum.

When the scum is removed, the pure water is clearly seen. It takes away a man's thirst, cools him immediately and makes him happy.

When all the five coverings are removed, the pure Atman is revealed. It is revealed as God dwelling within; as unending, unalloyed bliss; as the supreme and self-luminous Being.

The wise man who seeks liberation from bondage must discriminate between Atman and non-Atman. In this way, he can realize the Atman, which is Infinite Being, Infinite Wisdom and Infinite Love. Thus he finds happiness.

The Atman dwells within, free from attachment and beyond all action. A man must separate this Atman from every object of experience, as a stalk of grass is separated from its enveloping sheath. Then he must dissolve into the Atman all those appearances which make up the world of name and form. He is indeed a free soul who can remain thus absorbed in the Atman alone.

The Body

This body is the "physical covering." Food made its birth possible; on food it lives; without food it must die. It consists of cuticle, skin, flesh, blood, bone and water. It cannot be the Atman, the ever-pure, the self-existent.

It did not exist before birth, it will not exist after death. It exists for a short while only, in the interim between them. Its very nature is transient, and subject to change. It is a compound, not an element. Its vitality is only a reflection. It is a sense-object, which can be perceived, like a jar. How can it be the Atman—the experiencer of all experiences?

The body consists of arms, legs and other limbs. It is not the Atman—for when some of these limbs have been cut off, a man may continue to live and function through his remaining organs. The body is controlled by another. It cannot be the Atman, the controller.

The Atman watches the body, with its various characteristics, actions and states of growth. That this Atman, which is the abiding reality, is of another nature than the body, must be self-evident.

The body is a bundle of bones held together by flesh. It is very dirty and full of filth. The body can never be the same as the self-existent Atman, the knower. The nature of the Atman is quite different from that of the body.

It is the ignorant man who identifies himself with the body, which is compounded of skin, flesh, fat, bone and filth. The man of spiritual discrimination knows the Atman, his true being, the one supreme reality, as distinct from the body.

The fool thinks, "I am the body." The intelligent man thinks, "I am an individual soul united with the body." But the wise man, in the greatness of his knowledge and spiritual discrimination, sees the Atman as reality and thinks, "I am Brahman."

O fool, stop identifying yourself with this lump of skin, flesh, fat, bones and filth. Identify yourself with Brahman, the Absolute, the Atman in all beings. That is how you can attain the supreme peace.

The intelligent man may be learned in Vedanta and the moral laws. But there is not the least hope of his liberation until he stops mistakenly identifying himself with the body and the sense-organs. This identification is caused by delusion.

You never identify yourself with the shadow cast by your body, or with its reflection, or with the body you see in a dream or in your imagination. Therefore you should not identify yourself with this living body, either.

Those who live in ignorance identify the body with the Atman. This ignorance is the root-cause of birth, death and rebirth. Therefore you must strive earnestly to destroy it. When your heart is free from this ignorance, there will no longer be any possibility of your rebirth. You will reach immortality.

That covering of the Atman which is called "the vital covering" is made up of the vital force and the five organs of action. The body is called "the physical covering." It comes to life when it is enveloped by the vital covering. It is thus that the body engages in action.

This vital covering is not the Atman—for it is merely composed of the vital airs. Air-like, it enters and leaves the body. It does not know what is good or bad for itself, or for others. It is always dependent upon the Atman.

Purification

The mind, together with the organs of perception, forms the "mental covering." It causes the sense of "I" and "mine." It also causes us to discern objects. It is endowed with the power and faculty of differentiating objects by giving them various names. It is manifest, enveloping the "vital covering."

The mental covering may be compared to the sacrificial fire. It is fed by the fuel of many desires. The five organs of perception serve as priests. Objects of desire are poured upon it like a continuous stream of oblations. Thus it is that this phenomenal universe is brought forth.

Ignorance is nowhere, except in the mind. The mind is filled with ignorance, and this causes the bondage of birth and death. When, in the enlightenment of the Atman, a man transcends the mind, the phenomenal universe disappears from him. When a man lives in the domain of mental ignorance, the phenomenal universe exists for him.

In dream, the mind is emptied of the objective universe, but it creates by its own power a complete universe of subject and object. The waking state is only a prolonged dream. The phenomenal universe exists in the mind.

In dreamless sleep, when the mind does not function, nothing exists. This is our universal experience. Man seems to be in bondage to birth and death. This is a fictitious creation of the mind, not a reality.

The wind collects the clouds, and the wind drives them away again. Mind creates bondage, and mind also removes bondage.

The mind creates attachment to the body and the things of this world. Thus it binds a man, as a beast is tied by a rope. But it is also the mind which creates in a man an utter distaste for sense-objects, as if for poison. Thus it frees him from his bondage.

The mind, therefore, is the cause of man's bondage and also of his liberation. It causes bondage when it is darkened by rajas. It causes liberation when it is freed from rajas and tamas, and made pure.

If discrimination and dispassion are practiced, to the exclusion of everything else, the mind will become pure and move toward liberation. Therefore the wise man who seeks liberation must develop both these qualities within himself.

That terrible tiger called an impure mind prowls in the forest of the sense-objects. The wise man who seeks liberation must not go there.

The mind of the experiencer creates all the objects which he experiences, while in the waking or the dreaming state. Ceaselessly, it creates the differences in men's bodies, color, social condition and race. It creates the variations of the gunas. It creates desires, actions and the fruits of actions.

Man is pure spirit, free from attachment. The mind deludes him. It binds him with the bonds of the body, the sense-organs and the life-breath. It creates in him the sense of "I" and "mine." It makes him wander endlessly among the fruits of the actions it has caused.

The error of identifying Atman with non-Atman is the cause of man's birth, death and rebirth. This false identification is created by the mind. Therefore, it is the mind that causes the misery of birth, death and rebirth for the man who has no discrimination and is tainted by rajas and tamas.

Therefore the wise, who know Reality, have declared that the mind is full of ignorance. Because of this ignorance, all the creatures of the universe are swept helplessly hither and thither, like masses of cloud before the wind.

Therefore, the seeker after liberation must work carefully to purify the mind. When the mind has been made pure, liberation is as easy to grasp as the fruit which lies in the palm of your hand.

Seek earnestly for liberation, and your lust for sense-objects will be rooted out. Practice detachment toward all actions. Have faith in the Reality. Devote yourself to the practice of spiritual disciplines, such as hearing the word of Brahman, reasoning and meditating upon it. Thus the mind will be freed from the evil of rajas.

The "mental covering," therefore, cannot be the Atman. It has a beginning and an end, and is subject to change. It is the abode of pain. It is an object of experience. The seer cannot be the thing which is seen.

The Covering of Intellect

The discriminating faculty with its powers of intelligence, together with the organs of perception, is known as the "covering of intellect." To be the doer is its distinguishing characteristic. It is the cause of man's birth, death and rebirth.

The power of intelligence that is in the "covering of intellect" is a reflection of the Atman, the pure consciousness. The "covering of intellect" is an effect of Maya. It possesses the faculty of knowing and acting. It always identifies itself entirely with the body, sense-organs, etc.

It has no beginning. It is characterized by its sense of ego. It constitutes the individual man. It is the initiator of all actions and undertakings. Impelled by the tendencies and impressions formed in previous births, it performs virtuous or sinful actions and experiences their results.

It gathers experiences by wandering through many wombs of higher or lower degree. The states of waking and dreaming belong to this "covering of intellect." It experiences joy and sorrow.

Because of its sense of "I" and "mine," it constantly identifies itself with the body, and the physical states, and with the duties pertaining to the different stages and orders of life. This "covering of intellect" shines with a bright light because of its proximity to the shining Atman. It is a garment of the Atman, but man identifies himself with it and wanders around the circle of birth, death and rebirth because of his delusion.

The Atman, which is pure consciousness, is the light that shines in the shrine of the heart, the center of all vital force. It is immutable, but it becomes the "doer" and "experiencer" when it is mistakenly identified with the "covering of intellect."

The Atman assumes the limitations of the "covering of intellect" because it is mistakenly identified with that covering, which is totally different from itself. This man, who is the Atman, regards himself as being separate from it, and from Brahman, who is the one Atman in all creatures. An ignorant man, likewise, may regard a jar as being different from the clay of which it was made.

By its nature, the Atman is forever unchanging and perfect. But it assumes the character and nature of its coverings because it is mistakenly identified with them. Although fire is formless, it will assume the form of red-hot iron. . . .

Atman Is Brahman

The Disciple: Master, if we reject these five coverings as unreal, it seems to me that nothing remains but the void. How, then, can there be an existence which the wise man may realize as one with his Atman?

The Master: That is a good question, O prudent one. Your argument is clever. Nevertheless, there must be an existence, a reality, which perceives the ego-sense and the coverings and is also aware of the void which is their absence. This reality by itself remains unperceived. Sharpen your discrimination that you may know this Atman, which is the knower.

He who experiences is conscious of himself. Without an experiencer, there can be no self-consciousness.

The Atman is its own witness, since it is conscious of itself. The Atman is no other than Brahman.

The Atman is pure consciousness, clearly manifest as underlying the states of waking, dreaming and dreamless sleep. It is inwardly experienced as unbroken consciousness, the consciousness that I am I. It is the unchanging witness that experiences the ego, the intellect and the rest, with their various forms and changes. It is realized within one's own heart as existence, knowledge and bliss absolute. Realize this Atman within the shrine of your own heart.

The fool sees the reflection of the sun in the water of a jar, and thinks it is the sun. Man in the ignorance of his delusion sees the reflection of Pure Consciousness upon the coverings, and mistakes it for the real I.

In order to look at the sun, you must turn away from the jar, the water, and the sun's reflection in the water. The wise know that these three are only revealed by the reflection of the self-luminous sun. They are not the sun itself.

The body, the covering of intellect, the reflection of consciousness upon it—none of these is the Atman. The Atman is the witness, infinite consciousness, revealer of all things but distinct from all, no matter whether they be gross or subtle. It is the eternal reality, omnipresent, all-pervading, the subtlest of all subtleties. It has neither inside nor outside. It is the real I, hidden in the shrine of the heart. Realize fully the truth of the Atman. Be free from evil and impurity, and you shall pass beyond death.

Know the Atman, transcend all sorrows, and reach the fountain of joy. Be illumined by this knowledge, and you have nothing to fear. If you wish to find liberation, there is no other way of breaking the bonds of rebirth.

What can break the bondage and misery of this world? The knowledge that the Atman is Brah-man. Then it is that you realize Him who is one without a second, and who is the absolute bliss.

Realize Brahman, and there will be no more returning to this world—the home of all sorrows. You must realize absolutely that the Atman is Brahman.

Then you will win Brahman for ever. He is the truth. He is existence and knowledge. He is absolute. He is pure and self-existent. He is eternal, unending joy. He is none other than the Atman.

The Atman is one with Brahman: this is the highest truth. Brahman alone is real. There is none but He. When He is known as the supreme reality there is no other existence but Brahman.

The Universe

Brahman is the reality—the one existence, absolutely independent of human thought or idea. Because of the ignorance of our human minds, the universe seems to be composed of diverse forms. It is Brahman alone.

A jar made of clay is not other than clay. It is clay essentially. The form of the jar has no independent existence. What, then, is the jar? Merely an invented name!

The form of the jar can never be perceived apart from the clay. What, then, is the jar? An appearance! The reality is the clay itself.

This universe is an effect of Brahman. It can never be anything else but Brahman. Apart from Brahman, it does not exist. There is nothing beside Him. He who says that this universe has an independent existence is still suffering from delusion. He is like a man talking in his sleep.

"The universe is Brahman"—so says the great seer of the Atharva Veda. The universe, therefore, is nothing but Brahman. It is superimposed upon Him. It has no separate existence, apart from its ground.

If the universe, as we perceive it, were real, knowledge of the Atman would not put an end to our delusion. The scriptures would be untrue. The revelations of the Divine Incarnations would make no sense. These alternatives cannot be considered either desirable or beneficial by any thinking person.

Sri Krishna, the Incarnate Lord, who knows the secret of all truths, says in the Gita: "Although I am not within any creature, all creatures exist within me. I do not mean that they exist within me physically. That is my divine mystery. My Being sustains all creatures and brings them to birth, but has no physical contact with them."

If this universe were real, we should continue to perceive it in deep sleep. But we perceive nothing then. Therefore it is unreal, like our dreams.

The universe does not exist apart from the Atman. Our perception of it as having an independent existence is false, like our perception of blueness in the sky. How can a superimposed attribute have any existence, apart from its substratum? It is only our delusion which causes this misconception of the underlying reality.

No matter what a deluded man may think he is perceiving, he is really seeing Brahman and nothing else but Brahman. He sees mother-of-pearl and imagines that it is silver. He sees Brahman and imagines that it is the universe. But this universe, which is superimposed upon Brahman, is nothing but a name.

I Am Brahman

Brahman is supreme. He is the reality—the one without a second. He is pure consciousness, free from any taint. He is tranquillity itself. He has neither beginning nor end. He does not change. He is joy for ever.

He transcends the appearance of the manifold, created by Maya. He is eternal, for ever beyond reach of pain, not to be divided, not to be measured, without form, without name, undifferentiated, immutable. He shines with His own light. He is everything that can be experienced in this universe.

The illumined seers know Him as the uttermost reality, infinite, absolute, without parts—the pure consciousness. In Him they find that knower, knowledge and known have become one.

They know Him as the reality which can neither be cast aside (since He is ever-present within the human soul) nor grasped (since He is beyond the power of mind and speech). They know Him immeasurable, beginningless, endless, supreme in glory. They realize the truth: "I am Brahman."

Suggestions for Further Reading

For a summary with interpretative comments on Shankara's *Crest Jewel* see *Masterpieces of World Philosophy*, edited by Frank N. Magill (New York: HarperCollins, 1990).

For more background information, see Chapter 2 of Ninian Smart's *World Philosophies* (London: Routledge, 1999).

A brief historical survey of Indian philosophies can be found in *The Pulse of Wisdom: The Philosophies of India, China, and Japan* by Michael C. Brannigan, 2nd edition (Belmont, CA: Wadsworth, 2000).

Eliot Deutsch's *Advaita Vedanta: A Philosophical Reconstruction* (Honolulu: East-West Center Press, 1966) is a real gem, managing to make sense out of complicated arguments in a way the beginning student can grasp.

The Britannica article on the web will provide general information and links to much more at http://www.britannica.com/bcom/eb/article/idxref/4/0,5716,415497,00.html.

Video

Absorption in Brahman: The Story of Hinduism (30 minutes; produced by Video Outlines) summarizes the religious viewpoints of ancient India. See your Media Services Catalog for more information.

9.5 Subjective Idealism

George Berkeley was born in 1685 in Kilkenny, Ireland. At age fifteen he went to Trinity College, Dublin, where he studied classics, mathematics, and the then-new and controversial physics of Newton. In 1704, after graduation, he became a Fellow of his college and was ordained to the ministry. By the age of twenty-five, he had worked out the basic ideas of his philosophy in reaction to the philosophy of John Locke (1632–1704). He saw himself as a defender of common sense in a skeptical age and a defender of religion against a science that pictured the universe as a vast machine operating according to blind natural laws. Berkeley lived in the American colonies for a while, married in 1728, and was appointed Bishop of Cloyne in south Ireland in 1734 after his attempt to found a college in Bermuda to educate colonists, Native Americans, and Africans failed due to lack of funding. He died at Oxford in 1753.

Berkeley's metaphysics is called **subjective idealism**. His views constitute a variety of idealism because he argued that reality consists of finite or created minds, an infinite mind (God), and the ideas (thoughts, feelings, and sensations) these minds have. All of these things are immaterial. This idealism is termed *subjective* because physical objects do not exist apart from some subject (mind) who perceives them. This kind of idealism stands in contrast to **objective idealism**, which holds that although reality is mental, it does exist independently of the human knower because it is a manifestation of an absolute mind. Objective idealism is usually monistic (or at least nondualistic), maintaining that there is one absolute mind and the universe is a manifestation of it. Berkeley's subjective idealism, though nondualistic in the sense of asserting that all reality is mental or immaterial, is pluralistic in the sense that there are many finite minds independent of God's mind.

The denial of the objective or independent existence of physical objects seems so utterly fantastic that one wonders how Berkeley could view himself as a champion of common sense. Indeed, when he published his views in 1710, many thought him insane. However, Berkeley's rejection of matter seems more plausible if we understand the historical circumstances that led him to that conclusion.

We must return, for a moment, to Plato (see Section 9.3). Plato was a dualist, arguing that reality is twofold: material and immaterial. This dualism was revived and given a modern formulation by the French philosopher René Descartes (see Section 7.3) in the early seventeenth century. Descartes argued for a position known as indirect or representational realism. His position is called **realism** because he believed objects can exist apart from any knower or mind. It is called *indirect* or *representational* because he also argued that sensations indirectly represent objects that exist outside the mind. This sort of realism stands in contrast to direct or naive realism, which holds that we are directly in touch with real objects via our senses.

John Locke, an English philosopher, combined Descartes's realism with empiricism. Empiricism (see Section 7.1) is the view that knowledge derives from sense experience and that knowledge claims are tested by reference to sense experience. If empiricism is true, then all we can know *directly* or immediately are the ideas or sensations that occur in our minds. Although these ideas are themselves mental, they resemble and are caused by nonmental or physical objects existing outside the mind, or so the indirect realist claims. Hence, according to Locke, there are two substances: *immaterial substances* or minds, that have ideas *caused* by *material substances*.

This distinction between ideas and the physical objects they represent was accompanied by a distinction between primary and secondary qualities. **Primary qualities** are characteristics that constitute the properties of physical objects. Locke believed them to be extension, figure, motion, rest, solidity, and number. **Secondary qualities** are characteristics of our *sensation* of physical objects: color, flavor, odor, texture, sound, hot, cold, and the like. The theory of indirect realism combined with the distinction between secondary and primary qualities allowed Locke to explain, for example, how it is that an object looks a different color in different light or feels cold to one person but hot to another. Direct realism was unable to explain such common experiences, because if we are *directly* in touch with real physical objects via our senses, an object would have to be both blue and green or hot and cold if it were so experienced. However, if we are *indirectly* in touch with objects, and if color and heat sensation are secondary qualities, then we can say that the object *appears* both blue and green or feels both hot and cold, but *in fact* it is simply in a certain state of motion.

Berkeley pondered Locke's ideas as an undergraduate and found them nonsensical. He felt that since all we can really know are immaterial ideas, there is no way of knowing that they represent anything at all outside the mind. To know that this picture is a likeness of my friend, I can look at my friend and compare that image to the picture image. However, I cannot do that with sensations because I can never get outside of sensations to compare them with the physical objects that supposedly caused them.

Locke, Berkeley thought, had created a duplex world. We have a world of physical objects duplicated by a world of mental images. It also turns out that there are problems involved in trying to explain how physical objects can cause nonphysical sensations. Why not just simplify things by getting rid of physical objects? Isn't it true that we only know for sure that ideas or sensations exist, but we have no way of knowing for sure that physical objects do? What we *do* know is that what we call a physical object is for us a bundle of sensations (colors, odors, flavors, etc.). Since sensations cannot exist without being sensed, why not say the obvious, that nothing can exist without being experienced. Hence, Berkeley concluded that "*esse* is *percipi*"— that is, *to be is to be perceived.* We don't really need the materialistic hypothesis— or so Berkeley argued.

Notice how Berkeley's argument is heavily dependent on an empirical epistemological theory. This may surprise you, because many people associate empiricism with materialism. Berkeley argued that this association is wrong. If empiricism is right in claiming that the only thing we can know are things that appear to our minds such as sensations, feelings, and ideas, then why assume we can know matter or some physical reality apart from what appears to our minds. Notice further how epistemological arguments and metaphysical assertions come together. The philosophical concern with knowledge will, sooner or later, lead us into metaphysical territory and theories of reality.

Reading Questions

1. Give an example of each of the three kinds of ideas that constitute, according to Berkeley, the objects of human knowledge.
2. What is the difference between *ideas* and the *mind*?

3. Why does Berkeley assert that the existence (*esse*) of the objects of knowledge consists in their being perceived (*percipi*)?

4. How would Berkeley answer that old question, "If a tree fell in the forest and no one was there to hear it, would it make a sound?"

5. How does Berkeley respond to the claim that things exist apart from minds (unthinking or material substances), which our ideas copy or resemble? Do you find his response convincing? Why, or why not?

6. Why does Berkeley reject the distinction between primary and secondary qualities, and why does he claim that the very notion of matter is contradictory?

7. In Sections 16–20, Berkeley advances a series of arguments against the idea that material objects exist outside our minds. Briefly summarize the main ideas of these arguments.

8. Do you find any of these arguments convincing? If so, which ones, and why? If you find them all unconvincing, why?

9. If you got into a debate with Berkeley, what sort of objections would you raise against his claim that matter does not exist? How do you think he would respond to your objections?

10. Formulate and answer a question comparing Berkeley's views with any of the other metaphysical views you have studied in this chapter. How are they the same, and how are they different?

The Principles of Human Knowledge

GEORGE BERKELEY

Part I

1. IT IS EVIDENT to anyone who takes a survey of the objects of human knowledge, that they are either *ideas* actually imprinted on the senses; or else such as are perceived by attending to the passions and operations of the mind; or lastly, *ideas* formed by help of memory and imagination—either compounding, dividing, or barely representing those originally perceived in the aforesaid ways.—By sight I have the ideas of light and colours, with their several degrees and variations. By touch I perceive hard and soft, heat and cold, motion and resistance, and of all these more and less either as to quantity or degree. Smelling furnishes me with odours; the palate with tastes; and hearing conveys sounds to the mind in all their variety of tone and composition.—And as several of these are observed to accompany each other, they come to be marked by one name, and so to be reputed as one thing. Thus, for example, a certain colour, taste, smell, figure and consistence having been observed to go together, are accounted one distinct thing, signified by the name *apple;* other collections of ideas constitute a stone, a tree, a book, and the like sensible things—which as they are pleasing or disagreeable excite the passions of love, hatred, joy, grief, and so forth.

2. But, besides all that endless variety of ideas or objects of knowledge, there is likewise something which knows or perceives them; and exercises divers operations, as willing, imagining, remembering, about them. This perceiving, active being is what I call mind, spirit, soul, or myself.

From George Berkeley, A Treatise Concerning the Principles of Human Knowledge *(1710), Sections 1–10; 14–20.*

By which words I do not denote any one of my ideas, but a thing entirely distinct from them, wherein they exist, or, which is the same thing, whereby they are perceived—for the existence of an idea consists in being perceived.

3. That neither our thoughts, nor passions, nor ideas formed by the imagination, exist without the mind, is what everybody will allow.—And to me it is no less evident that the various sensations, or *ideas imprinted on the sense,* however blended or combined together (that is, whatever *objects* they compose), cannot exist otherwise than in a mind perceiving them—I think an intuitive knowledge may be obtained of this by anyone that shall attend to *what is meant by the term exist when applied to sensible things.* The table I write on I say exists, that is, I see and feel it; and if I were out of my study I should say it existed—meaning thereby that if I was in my study I might perceive it, or that some other spirit actually does perceive it. There was an odour, that is, it was smelt; there was a sound, that is, it was heard; a colour or figure, and it was perceived by sight or touch. This is all that I can understand by these and the like expressions.—For as to what is said of the absolute existence of unthinking things without any relation to their being perceived, that is to me perfectly unintelligible. Their *esse* is *percipi,* nor is it possible they should have any existence out of the minds or thinking things which perceive them.

4. It is indeed an opinion strangely prevailing amongst men, that houses, mountains, rivers, and in a word all sensible objects, have an existence, natural or real, distinct from their being perceived by the understanding. But, with how great an assurance and acquiescence soever this principle may be entertained in the world, yet whoever shall find in his heart to call it in question may, if I mistake not, perceive it to involve a manifest contradiction. For, what are the forementioned objects but the things we perceive by sense? and what do we perceive besides our own ideas or sensations? and is it not plainly repugnant that any one of *these,* or any combination of them, should exist unperceived?

5. If we thoroughly examine this tenet it will, perhaps, be found at bottom to depend on the doctrine of *abstract ideas.* For can there be a nicer strain of abstraction than to distinguish the *existence* of sensible objects from their *being perceived,* so as to conceive them existing unperceived? Light and colours, heat and cold, extension and figures—in a word the things we see and feel—what are they but so many sensations, notions, ideas, or impressions on the sense? and is it possible to separate, even in thought, any of these from perception? For my part, I might as easily divide a thing from itself. I may, indeed, divide in my thoughts, or conceive apart from each other, those things which, perhaps, I never perceived by sense so divided. Thus, I imagine the trunk of a human body without the limbs, or conceive the smell of a rose without thinking on the rose itself. So far, I will not deny, I can abstract—if that may properly be called *abstraction* which extends only to the conceiving separately such objects as it is possible may really exist or be actually perceived asunder. But my conceiving or imagining power does not extend beyond the possibility of real existence or perception. Hence, as it is impossible for me to see or feel anything without an actual sensation of that thing, so is it impossible for me to conceive in my thoughts any sensible thing or object distinct from the sensation or perception of it.

6. Some truths there are so near and obvious to the mind that a man need only open his eyes to see them. Such I take this important one to be, viz. that all the choir of heaven and furniture of the earth, in a word all those bodies which compose the mighty frame of the world, have not any subsistence without a mind—that their *being* is *to be perceived or known;* that consequently so long as they are not actually perceived by me, or do not exist in my mind or that of any other created spirit, they must either have no existence at all, or else subsist in the mind of some Eternal Spirit—it being perfectly unintelligible, and involving all the absurdity of abstraction, to attribute to any single part of them an existence independent of a spirit. To be convinced of which,

the reader need only reflect, and try to separate in his own thoughts the *being* of a sensible thing from its *being perceived*.

7. From what has been said it is evident there is not any other Substance than SPIRIT, or *that which perceives*. But, for the fuller demonstration of this point, let it be considered the sensible qualities are colour, figure, motion, smell, taste, &c., *i.e.* the ideas perceived by sense. Now, for an idea to exist in an unperceiving thing is a manifest contradiction; for to have an idea is all one as to perceive; that therefore wherein colour, figure, &c. exist must perceive them; hence it is clear there can be no unthinking substance or *substratum* of those ideas.

8. But, say you, though the ideas themselves do not exist without the mind, yet there may be things like them, whereof they are copies or resemblances, which things exist without the mind in an unthinking substance. I answer, an idea can be like nothing but an idea; a colour or figure can be like nothing but another colour or figure. If we look but never so little into our own thoughts, we shall find it impossible for us to conceive a likeness except only between our ideas. Again, I ask whether those supposed originals or external things, of which our ideas are the pictures or representations, be themselves perceivable or no? If they are, then they are ideas and we have gained our point; but if you say they are not, I appeal to anyone whether it be sense to assert a colour is like something which is invisible; hard or soft, like something which is intangible; and so of the rest.

9. Some there are who make a distinction betwixt *primary* and *secondary* qualities. By the former they mean extension, figure, motion, rest, solidity or impenetrability, and number; by the latter they denote all other sensible qualities, as colours, sounds, tastes, and so forth. The ideas we have of these they acknowledge not to be the resemblances of anything existing without the mind, or unperceived, but they will have our ideas of the primary qualities to be patterns or images of things which exist without the mind, in an unthinking substance which they call *matter*. By *matter*, therefore, we are to understand an in-

ert, senseless substance, in which extension, figure, and motion do actually subsist. But it is evident, from what we have already shewn, that extension, figure, and motion are only ideas existing in the mind, and that an idea can be like nothing but another idea, and that consequently neither they nor their archetypes can exist in an unperceiving substance. Hence, it is plain that the very notion of what is called *matter* or *corporeal substance,* involves a contradiction in it.

10. They who assert that figure, motion, and the rest of the primary or original qualities do exist without the mind in unthinking substances, do at the same time acknowledge that colours, sounds, heat, cold, and such like secondary qualities, do not—which they tell us are sensations existing in the mind alone, that depend on and are occasioned by the different size, texture, and motion of the minute particles of matter. This they take for an undoubted truth, which they can demonstrate beyond all exception. Now, if it be certain that those original qualities are inseparably united with the other sensible qualities, and not, even in thought, capable of being abstracted from them, it plainly follows that they exist only in the mind. But I desire any one to reflect and try whether he can, by any abstraction of thought, conceive the extension and motion of a body without all other sensible qualities. For my own part, I see evidently that it is not in my power to frame an idea of a body extended and moving, but I must withal give it some colour or other sensible quality which is acknowledged to exist only in the mind. In short, extension, figure, and motion, abstracted from all other qualities, are inconceivable. Where therefore the other sensible qualities are, there must these be also, to wit, in the mind and nowhere else. . . .

14. I shall farther add, that, after the same manner as modern philosophers prove certain sensible qualities to have no existence in matter, or without the mind, the same thing may be likewise proved of all other sensible qualities whatsoever. Thus, for instance, it is said that heat and cold are affections only of the mind, and not at all patterns of real beings, existing in the corporeal

substances which excite them, for [the reason] that the same body which appears cold to one hand seems warm to another. Now, why may we not as well argue that figure and extension are not patterns or resemblances of qualities existing in matter, because to the same eye at different stations, or eyes of a different texture at the same station, they appear various, and cannot therefore be the images of anything settled and determinate without the mind? Again, it is proved that sweetness is not really in the sapid [tasty] thing, because the thing remaining unaltered the sweetness is changed into bitter, as in case of a fever or otherwise vitiated palate. Is it not as reasonable to say that motion is not without the mind, since if the succession of ideas in the mind become swifter, the motion, it is acknowledged, shall appear slower without any alteration in any external object?

15. In short, let any one consider those arguments which are thought manifestly to prove that colours and tastes exist only in the mind, and he shall find they may with equal force be brought to prove the same thing of extension, figure, and motion. Though it must be confessed this method of arguing does not so much prove that there is no extension or colour in an outward object, as that we do not know by sense which is the true extension or colour of the object. But the arguments foregoing plainly shew it to be impossible that any colour or extension at all, or other sensible quality whatsoever, should exist in an unthinking subject without the mind, or in truth, that there should be any such thing as an outward object.

16. But let us examine a little the received opinion.—It is said extension is a mode or accident of Matter, and that Matter is the *substratum* that supports it. Now I desire that you would explain to me what is meant by Matter's *supporting* extension. Say you, I have no idea of Matter and therefore cannot explain it. I answer, though you have no positive, yet, if you have any meaning at all, you must at least have a relative idea of Matter; though you know not what it is, yet you must be supposed to know what relation it bears to accidents, and what is meant by its supporting

them. It is evident "support" cannot here be taken in its usual or literal sense—as when we say that pillars support a building; in what sense therefore must it be taken?

17. If we inquire into what the most accurate philosophers declare themselves to mean by *material substance,* we shall find them acknowledge they have no other meaning annexed to those sounds but the idea of *being in general,* together with the relative notion of its *supporting accidents.* The general idea of Being appeareth to me the most abstract and incomprehensible of all other; and as for its supporting accidents, this, as we have just now observed, cannot be understood in the common sense of those words; it must therefore be taken in some other sense, but what that is they do not explain. So that when I consider the two parts or branches which make the signification of the words *material substance,* I am convinced there is no distinct meaning annexed to them. But why should we trouble ourselves any farther, in discussing this material *substratum* or "support" of figure, and motion, and other sensible qualities? Does it not suppose *they* have an existence without the mind? And is not this a direct repugnancy, and altogether inconceivable?

18. But, though it were possible that solid, figured, moveable *substances* may exist without the mind, corresponding to the ideas we have of bodies, yet how is it possible for us to know this? Either we must know it by Sense or by Reason.—As for our senses, by them we have the knowledge only of our sensations, ideas, or those things that are immediately perceived by sense, call them what you will: but they do not inform us that things exist without the mind, or unperceived, like to those which are perceived. This the Materialists themselves acknowledge.—It remains therefore that if we have any knowledge at all of external things, it must be by Reason inferring their existence from what is immediately perceived by sense. But what reason can induce us to believe the existence of bodies without the mind, from what we perceive, since the very patrons of Matter themselves do not pretend there is any *necessary* connexion betwixt them and our ideas? I say it is granted on all hands—and what hap-

pens in dreams, frenzies, and the like, puts it beyond dispute—that it is possible we might be affected with all the ideas we have now, though there were no bodies existing without resembling them. Hence, it is evident the supposition of external bodies is not necessary for producing our ideas; since it is granted they are produced sometimes, and might possibly be produced always in the same order we see them in at present, without their concurrence.

19. But, though we might possibly have all our sensations without them, yet perhaps it may be thought easier to conceive and explain the manner of their production, by supposing external bodies in their likeness rather than otherwise; and so it might be at least probable there are such things as bodies that excite their ideas in our minds. But neither can this be said; for, though we give the materialists their external bodies, they by their own confession are never the nearer knowing *how* our ideas are produced; since they own themselves unable to comprehend in what manner body can act upon spirit, or how it is possible it should imprint any idea in the mind. Hence it is evident the production of ideas or sensations in our minds can be no reason why we should suppose Matter or corporeal substances,

since *that* is acknowledged to remain equally inexplicable with or without this supposition. If therefore it were possible for bodies to exist without the mind, yet to hold they do so must needs be a very precarious opinion; since it is to suppose, without any reason at all, that God has created innumerable beings that are entirely useless, and serve to no manner of purpose.

20. In short, if there were external bodies, it is impossible we should ever come to know it; and if there were not, we might have the very same reasons to think there were that we have now. Suppose—what no one can deny possible—an intelligence *without the help of external bodies,* to be affected with the same train of sensations or ideas that you are, imprinted in the same order and with like vividness in his mind. I ask whether that intelligence hath not all the reason to believe the existence of corporeal substances, represented by his ideas, and exciting them in his mind, that you can possibly have for believing the same thing? Of this there can be no question—which one consideration were enough to make any reasonable person suspect the strength of whatever arguments he may think himself to have, for the existence of bodies without the mind.

Suggestions for Further Reading

The article "Berkeley, George" in *The Cambridge Dictionary of Philosophy* edited by Robert Audi, 2nd edition (Cambridge: Cambridge University Press, 1999) will prove a good starting point for those who wish to pursue Berkeley's philosophy.

Chapter 5 in William H. Brenner's *Elements of Modern Philosophy: Descartes Through Kant* (Englewood Cliffs, NJ: Prentice-Hall, 1989) also provides a good overview for the beginner.

For a collection of critical essays on Berkeley and the other classical empiricists see *The Empiricists: Critical Essays on Locke, Berkeley and Hume,* edited by Margaret Atherton (Lanham, MD: Rowman and Littlefield, 1999).

G. J. Warnock's introduction to Berkeley's *The Principles of Human Knowledge* (Cleveland: World, 1963) provides excellent background information.

Berkeley further explicates and defends his views in *Three Dialogues Between Hylas and Philonous,* published in 1713.

The *Internet Encyclopedia of Philosophy* provides basic information at http://www.utm .edu/ research/iep/b/berkeley.htm.

Another useful site in the virtual reality of the web (somehow I think Berkeley would like this idea of a virtual reality) is http://www.knuten .liu.se/~bjoch509/philosophers/ber.html.

Videos

The Enlightenment and Its Critics (12 lectures in all, 45 minutes each) begins with Locke's theories of knowledge and then investigates Berkeley's idealism and his critique of materialism among other philosophical views. These are available from Insight Media, 2162 Broadway, New York, NY 10024.

   Locke and Berkeley (45 minutes) features Michael Ayers discussing the differences between the ideas of these two British empiricists. Available from Films for the Humanities and Sciences, P.O. Box 2053, Princeton, NJ 08543.

9.6 *Materialism*

George Berkeley (see above) tried to dismiss the notion of matter as self-contradictory in order to support idealism. As we said in the introduction to this chapter, anyone who champions an idealistic metaphysics, must explain why matter seems so real to us and we are so wrong about that. We also said that anyone who champions a monistic materialism must explain why mental states seem so real and yet we are so wrong about their immaterial reality.

   We will deal with the mind–body problem in Chapter 11, but here we will anticipate some of that discussion by looking at a modern materialistic theory of mind. There are a variety of ways to support a materialistic metaphysics, and one important way is to show that the sorts of things we think are immaterial (minds, sensations, feelings, ideas, and so on) are perfectly understandable on materialistic grounds.

   Let me give you a problem. Suppose most people think there are two different things in a black box, but you believe there is only one thing. How would you convince those who think there is more than one?

   "Open the box and look," you might say.

   Quite so. However, let's make the problem a bit more complex. Suppose we cannot open the box to look inside. You might be inclined to use a little of your newfound philosophical abilities and ask for definitions of these two things. Then you might try to show that what we know about analogous situations involving similar things leads us to believe that one of these two things can be eliminated.

   There are different kinds of materialism, as we shall soon see, but one kind is called **eliminative materialism**. According to eliminative materialism, there are no such things as mental phenomena. If one of the things you think is in the black box is an immaterial mind, then you are mistaken. What you call a mind and its associated immaterial phenomena are naïve folkways of talking about neurological events in brains.

   "Just a minute," you might cry. "I thought you said we could not look in the black box. Now it turns out that the two things in the box, mind and matter or mind and brains, can be seen. I can see your brain and, while I cannot see your mind, I directly experience (observe if you will) my own mind." "False analogy," you charge.

   You have an important point. My analogy is misleading. So how can anyone eliminate something so directly observable as my own mental states. Professor Churchland, author of the next selection, tries to offer further analogies from the history of science that may convince you.

   Paul M. Churchland is a professor of philosophy at the University of California at San Diego. He has written extensively in the philosophy of mind and cognitive sciences. The selection below is from his influential 1988 book, *Matter and Consciousness*.

Reading Questions

1. What is philosophical behaviorism?
2. What are the two major flaws of philosophical behaviorism?
3. What is reductive materialism (the identity theory)?
4. What is "intertheoretic reduction," and why is it important in the philosophical understanding of reductive materialism?
5. Summarize the arguments for the identity theory.
6. Why does eliminative materialism lead to doubts about the truth of the identity theory?
7. Summarize the arguments for eliminative materialism.
8. What are the arguments against eliminative materialism, and why are they not decisive?
9. Has Churchland convinced you that some type of materialism—either the reductive, eliminative or "revisionary"—will eventually replace the "folk" psychological belief in immaterial mental states? Why, or why not?

Eliminative Materialism

PAUL M. CHURCHLAND

Philosophical Behaviorism

PHILOSOPHICAL BEHAVIORISM reached the peak of its influence during the first and second decades after World War II. It was jointly motivated by at least three intellectual fashions. The first motivation was a reaction against dualism. The second motivation was the Logical Positivists' idea that the meaning of any sentence was ultimately a matter of the observable circumstances that would tend to verify or confirm that sentence. And the third motivation was a general assumption that most, if not all, philosophical problems are the result of linguistic or conceptual confusion, and are to be solved (or dissolved) by careful analysis of the language in which the problem is expressed.

In fact, philosophical behaviorism is not so much a theory about what mental states are (in their inner nature) as it is a theory about how to analyze or to understand the vocabulary we use to talk about them. Specifically, the claim is that talk about emotions and sensations and beliefs and desires is not talk about ghostly inner episodes, but is rather a shorthand way of talking about actual and potential patterns of *behavior*. In its strongest and most straightforward form, philosophical behaviorism claims that any sentence about a mental state can be paraphrased, without loss of meaning, into a long and complex sentence about what observable behavior *would* result if the person in question were in this, that, or the other observable circumstance.

A helpful analogy here is the dispositional property, *being soluble*. To say that a sugar cube is soluble is not to say that the sugar cube enjoys some ghostly inner state. It is just to say that *if* the sugar cube were put in water, then it *would* dissolve. More strictly,

"*x* is water soluble"

is equivalent by definition to

"if *x* were put in unsaturated water,
x would dissolve."

This is one example of what is called an "operational definition." The term "soluble" is defined in terms of certain operations or tests that would reveal whether or not the term actually applies in the case to be tested.

According to the behaviorist, a similar analysis holds for mental states such as "wants a Caribbean holiday," save that the analysis is much richer. To say that Anne wants a Caribbean holiday is to say that (1) if asked whether that is what she wants, she would answer yes, and (2) if given new holiday brochures for Jamaica and Japan, she would peruse the ones for Jamaica first, and (3) if given a ticket on this Friday's flight to Jamaica, she would go, and so on and so on. Unlike solubility, claims the behaviorist, most mental states are *multitracked* dispositions. But dispositions they remain.

There is therefore no point in worrying about the "relation" between the mind and the body, on this view. To talk about Marie Curie's mind, for example, is not to talk about some "thing" that she "possesses"; it is to talk about certain of her extraordinary capacities and dispositions. The mind-body problem, concludes the behaviorist, is a pseudoproblem.

Behaviorism is clearly consistent with a materialist conception of human beings. Material objects can have dispositional properties, even multitracked ones, so there is no necessity to embrace dualism to make sense of our psychological vocabulary. (It should be pointed out, however, that behaviorism is strictly consistent with dualism also. Even if philosophical behaviorism were true, it would remain possible that our multitracked dispositions are grounded in immaterial mind-stuff rather than in molecular structures. This is not a possibility that most behaviorists took seriously, however, for the many reasons outlined at the end of the preceding section.)

Philosophical behaviorism, unfortunately, had two major flaws that made it awkward to believe, even for its defenders. It evidently ignored, and even denied, the "inner" aspect of our mental states. To have a pain, for example, seems to be not merely a matter of being inclined to moan, to wince, to take aspirin, and so on. Pains also have an intrinsic qualitative nature (a horrible one) that is revealed in introspection, and any theory of mind that ignores or denies such *qualia* is simply derelict in its duty.

This problem received much attention from behaviorists, and serious attempts were made to solve it. The details take us deeply into semantical problems, however.

The second flaw emerged when behaviorists attempted to specify in detail the multitracked disposition said to constitute any given mental state. The list of conditionals necessary for an adequate analysis of "wants a Caribbean holiday," for example, seemed not just to be long, but to be indefinitely or even infinitely long, with no finite way of specifying the elements to be included. And no term can be well-defined whose *definiens* is open-ended and unspecific in this way. Further, each conditional of the long analysis was suspect on its own. Supposing that Anne does want a Caribbean holiday, conditional (1) above will be true only if she isn't *secretive* about her holiday fantasies; conditional (2) will be true only if she isn't already *bored* with the Jamaica brochures; conditional (3) will be true only if she doesn't *believe* the Friday flight will be hijacked, and so forth. But to repair each conditional by adding in the relevant qualification would be to reintroduce a series of *mental* elements into the business end of the definition, and we would no longer be defining the mental solely in terms of publicly observable circumstances and behavior.

So long as behaviorism seemed the only alternative to dualism, philosophers were prepared to struggle with these flaws in hopes of repairing or defusing them. However, three more materialist theories rose to prominence during the late fifties and sixties, and the flight from behaviorism was swift.

(I close this section with a cautionary note. The *philosophical* behaviorism discussed above is to be sharply distinguished from the *methodological* behaviorism that has enjoyed such a wide influence within psychology. In its bluntest form, this latter view urges that any new theoretical terms invented by the science of psychology *should be* operationally defined, in order to guarantee that psychology maintains a firm contact with empirical reality. Philosophical behaviorism, by contrast, claims that all of the common-sense psychological terms in our prescientific vocabulary *already* get whatever meaning they have from (tacit) operational definitions. The two views are logically distinct, and the methodology might be a wise one, for new theoretical terms, even though the correlative analysis of common-sense mental terms is wrong.)

Reductive Materialism (The Identity Theory)

Reductive materialism, more commonly known as *the identity theory,* is the most straightforward of the several materialist theories of mind. Its central claim is simplicity itself: Mental states *are* physical states of the brain. That is, each type of mental state or process is *numerically identical with* (is one and the very same thing as) some type of physical state or process within the brain or central nervous system. At present we do not know enough about the intricate functionings of the brain actually to state the relevant identities, but the identity theory is committed to the idea that brain research will eventually reveal them.

Historical Parallels

As the identity theorist sees it, the result here predicted has familiar parallels elsewhere in our scientific history. Consider sound. We now know that sound is just a train of compression waves traveling through the air, and that the property of being high pitched is identical with the property of having a high oscillatory frequency. We have learned that light is just electromagnetic waves, and our best current theory says that the color of an object is identical with a triplet of reflectance efficiencies the object has, rather like a musical chord that it strikes, though the

"notes" are struck in electromagnetic waves instead in sound waves. We now appreciate that the warmth or coolness of a body is just the energy of motion of the molecules that make it up: warmth is identical with high average molecular kinetic energy, and coolness is identical with low average molecular kinetic energy. We know that lightning is identical with a sudden large-scale discharge of electrons between clouds, or between the atmosphere and the ground. What we now think of as "mental states," argues the identity theorist, are identical with brain states in exactly the same way.

Intertheoretic Reduction

These illustrative parallels are all cases of successful *intertheoretic reduction.* That is, they are all cases where a new and very powerful theory turns out to entail a set of propositions and principles that mirror perfectly (or almost perfectly) the propositions and principles of some older theory or conceptual framework. The relevant principles entailed by the new theory have the same structure as the corresponding principles of the old framework, and they apply in exactly the same cases. The only difference is that where the old principles contained (for example) the notions of "heat," "is hot," and "is cold," the new principles contain instead the notions of "total molecular kinetic energy," "has a high mean molecular kinetic energy," and "has a low mean molecular kinetic energy."

If the new framework is far better than the old at explaining and predicting phenomena, then we have excellent reason for believing that the theoretical terms of the *new* framework are the terms that describe reality correctly. But if the old framework worked adequately, so far as it went, and if it parallels a portion of the new theory in the systematic way described, then we may properly conclude that the old terms and the new terms refer to the very same things, or express the very same properties. We conclude that we have apprehended the very same reality that is incompletely described by the old framework, but with a new and more penetrating conceptual framework. And we announce what philosophers of science call "intertheoretic identities": light *is* electromagnetic waves, temperature *is* mean molecular kinetic energy, and so forth.

The examples of the preceding two paragraphs share one more important feature in common. They are all cases where the things or properties on the receiving end of the reduction are *observable* things and properties within our *common-sense* conceptual framework. They show that intertheoretic reduction occurs not only between conceptual frameworks in the theoretical stratosphere: common-sense observables can also be reduced. There would therefore be nothing particularly surprising about a reduction of our familiar introspectible mental states to physical states of the brain. All that would be required would be that an explanatorily successful neuroscience develop to the point where it entails a suitable "mirror image" of the assumptions and principles that constitute our common-sense conceptual framework for mental states, an image where brain-state terms occupy the positions held by mental-state terms in the assumptions and principles of common sense. If this (rather demanding) condition were indeed met, then, as in the historical cases cited, we would be justified in announcing a reduction, and in asserting the identity of mental states with brain states.

Arguments for the Identity Theory

What reasons does the identity theorist have for believing that neuroscience will eventually achieve the strong conditions necessary for the reduction of our "folk" psychology? There are at least four reasons, all directed at the conclusion that the correct account of human-behavior-and-its-causes must reside in the physical neurosciences.

We can point first to the purely physical origins and ostensibly physical constitution of each individual human. One begins as a genetically programmed monocellular organization of molecules (a fertilized ovum), and one develops from there by the accretion of further molecules whose structure and integration is controlled by the information coded in the DNA molecules of the cell nucleus. The result of such a process would

be a purely physical system whose behavior arises from its internal operations and its interactions with the rest of the physical world. And those behavior-controlling internal operations are precisely what the neurosciences are about.

This argument coheres with a second argument. The origins of each *type* of animal also appear exhaustively physical in nature. The argument from evolutionary history lends further support to the identity theorist's claim, since evolutionary theory provides the only serious explanation we have for the behavior-controlling capacities of the brain and central nervous system. Those systems were selected for because of the many advantages (ultimately, the reproductive advantage) held by creatures whose behavior was thus controlled. Again our behavior appears to have its basic causes in neural activity.

The identity theorist finds further support in the argument, discussed earlier, from the neural dependence of all known mental phenomena. This is precisely what one should expect, if the identity theory is true. Of course, systematic neural dependence is also a consequence of property dualism, but here the identity theorist will appeal to considerations of simplicity. Why admit two radically different classes of properties and operations if the explanatory job can be done by one?

A final argument derives from the growing success of the neurosciences in unraveling the nervous systems of many creatures and in explaining their behavioral capacities and deficits in terms of the structures discovered. The preceding arguments all suggest that neuroscience should be successful in this endeavor, and the fact is that the continuing history of neuroscience bears them out. Especially in the case of very simple creatures (as one would expect), progress has been rapid. And progress has also been made with humans, though for obvious moral reasons exploration must be more cautious and circumspect. In sum, the neurosciences have a long way to go, but progress to date provides substantial encouragement to the identity theorist.

Even so, these arguments are far from decisive in favor of the identity theory. No doubt they do provide an overwhelming case for the idea that the causes of human and animal behavior are essentially physical in nature, but the identity theory claims more than just this. It claims that neuroscience will discover a taxonomy of neural states that stand in a one-to-one correspondence with the mental states of our common-sense taxonomy. Claims for intertheoretic identity will be justified only if such a match-up can be found. But nothing in the preceding arguments guarantees that the old and new frameworks will match up in this way, even if the new framework is a roaring success at explaining and predicting our behavior. Furthermore, there are arguments from other positions within the materialist camp to the effect that such convenient match-ups are rather unlikely.

Eliminative Materialism

The identity theory was called into doubt not because the prospects for a materialist account of our mental capacities were thought to be poor, but because it seemed unlikely that the arrival of an adequate materialist theory would bring with it the nice one-to-one match-ups, between the concepts of folk psychology and the concepts of theoretical neuroscience, that intertheoretic reduction requires. The reason for that doubt was the great variety of quite different physical systems that could instantiate the required functional organization. *Eliminative materialism* also doubts that the correct neuroscientific account of human capacities will produce a neat reduction of our common-sense framework, but here the doubts arise from a quite different source.

As the eliminative materialists see it, the one-to-one match-ups will not be found, and our common-sense psychological framework will not enjoy an intertheoretic reduction, *because our common-sense psychological framework is a false and radically misleading conception of the causes of human behavior and the nature of cognitive activity.* On this view, folk psychology is not just an incomplete representation of our inner natures; it is an outright *mis*representation of our internal states and activities. Consequently, we cannot expect a truly adequate neuroscientific account of our inner lives to provide theoretical categories that match up nicely with the categories of our common-sense framework. Accordingly, we must expect that the older framework will simply be eliminated, rather than be reduced, by a matured neuroscience.

Historical Parallels

As the identity theorist can point to historical cases of successful intertheoretic reduction, so the eliminative materialist can point to historical cases of the outright elimination of the ontology of an older theory in favor of the ontology of a new and superior theory. For most of the eighteenth and nineteenth centuries, learned people believed that heat was a subtle *fluid* held in bodies, much in the way water is held in a sponge. A fair body of moderately successful theory described the way this fluid substance—called "caloric"—flowed within a body, or from one body to another, and how it produced thermal expansion, melting, boiling, and so forth. But by the end of the last century it had become abundantly clear that heat was not a substance at all, but just the energy of motion of the trillions of jostling molecules that make up the heated body itself. The new theory—the "corpuscular/kinetic theory of matter and heat"—was much more successful than the old in explaining and predicting the thermal behavior of bodies. And since we were unable to *identify* caloric fluid with kinetic energy (according to the old theory, caloric is a material *substance;* according to the new theory, kinetic energy is a form of *motion*), it was finally agreed that there is *no such thing* as caloric. Caloric was simply eliminated from our accepted ontology.

A second example. It used to be thought that when a piece of wood burns, or a piece of metal rusts, a spiritlike substance called "phlogiston" was being released: briskly, in the former case, slowly in the latter. Once gone, that "noble" substance left only a base pile of ash or rust. It later came to be appreciated that both processes involve, not the loss of something, but the *gaining* of a substance taken from the atmosphere: oxygen. Phlogiston emerged, not as an incomplete description of what was going on, but as a radical misdescription. Phlogiston was therefore not suitable for reduction to or identification with some notion from within the new oxygen chemistry, and it was simply eliminated from science.

Admittedly, both of these examples concern the elimination of something nonobservable, but our history also includes the elimination of certain widely accepted "observables." Before Copernicus' views became available, almost any human who ventured out at night could look up at *the starry sphere of the heavens,* and if he stayed for more than a few minutes he could also see that it *turned,* around an axis through Polaris. What the sphere was made of (crystal?) and what made it turn (the gods?) were theoretical questions that exercised us for over two millennia. But hardly anyone doubted the existence of what everyone could observe with their own eyes. In the end, however, we learned to reinterpret our visual experience of the night sky within a very different conceptual framework, and the turning sphere evaporated.

Witches provide another example. Psychosis is a fairly common affliction among humans, and in earlier centuries its victims were standardly seen as cases of demonic possession, as instances of Satan's spirit itself, glaring malevolently out at us from behind the victims' eyes. That witches exist was not a matter of any controversy. One would occasionally see them, in any city or hamlet, engaged in incoherent, paranoid, or even murderous behavior. But observable or not, we eventually decided that witches simply do not exist. We concluded that the concept of a witch is an element in a conceptual framework that misrepresents so badly the phenomena to which it was standardly applied that literal application of the notion should be permanently withdrawn. Modern theories of mental dysfunction led to the elimination of witches from our serious ontology.

The concepts of folk psychology—belief, desire, fear, sensation, pain, joy, and so on—await a similar fate, according to the view at issue. And when neuroscience has matured to the point where the poverty of our current conceptions is apparent to everyone, and the superiority of the new framework is established, we shall then be able to set about reconceiving our internal states and activities, within a truly adequate conceptual framework at last. Our explanations of one another's behavior will appeal to such things as our neuropharmacological states, the neural activity in specialized anatomical areas, and whatever other states are deemed relevant by the new theory. Our private introspection will also be transformed, and may be profoundly enhanced by reason of the more accurate and penetrating framework it will have to work with—just as the astronomer's perception of the night sky is much enhanced by the detailed knowledge of modern astronomical theory that he or she possesses.

The magnitude of the conceptual revolution here suggested should not be minimized: it would be enormous. And the benefits to humanity might be equally great. If each of us possessed an accurate neuroscientific understanding of (what we now conceive dimly as) the varieties and causes of mental illness, the factors involved in learning, the neural basis of emotions, intelligence, and socialization, then the sum total of human misery might be much reduced. The simple increase in mutual understanding that the new framework made possible could contribute substantially toward a more peaceful and humane society. Of course, there would be dangers as well: increased knowledge means increased power, and power can always be misused.

Arguments for Eliminative Materialism

The arguments for eliminative materialism are diffuse and less than decisive, but they are stronger than is widely supposed. The distinguishing feature of this position is its denial that a smooth intertheoretic reduction is to be expected—even a species-specific reduction—of the framework of folk psychology to the framework of a matured neuroscience. The reason for this denial is the eliminative materialist's conviction that folk psychology is a hopelessly primitive and deeply confused conception of our internal activities. But why this low opinion of our common-sense conceptions?

There are at least three reasons. First, the eliminative materialist will point to the widespread explanatory, predictive, and manipulative failures of folk psychology. So much of what is central and familiar to us remains a complete mystery from within folk psychology. We do not know what *sleep* is, or why we have to have it, despite spending a full third of our lives in that condition. (The answer, "For rest," is mistaken. Even if people are allowed to rest continuously, their need for sleep is undiminished. Apparently, sleep serves some deeper functions, but we do not yet know what they are.) We do not understand how *learning* transforms each of us from a gaping infant to a cunning adult, or how differences in *intelligence* are grounded. We have not the slightest idea how *memory* works, or how we manage to retrieve relevant bits of information instantly from the awesome mass we have stored. We do not know what *mental illness* is, nor how to cure it.

In sum, the most central things about us remain almost entirely mysterious from within folk psychology. And the defects noted cannot be blamed on inadequate time allowed for their correction, for folk psychology has enjoyed no significant changes or advances in well over 2,000 years, despite its manifest failures. Truly successful theories may be expected to reduce, but significantly unsuccessful theories merit no such expectation.

This argument from explanatory poverty has a further aspect. So long as one sticks to normal brains, the poverty of folk psychology is perhaps not strikingly evident. But as soon as one examines the many perplexing behavioral and cognitive deficits suffered by people with *damaged* brains, one's descriptive and explanatory resources start to claw the air. As with other humble theories asked to operate successfully in unexplored extensions of their old domain (for example, Newtonian mechanics in the domain of velocities close to the velocity of light, and the classical gas law in the domain of high pressures or temperatures), the descriptive and explanatory inadequacies of folk psychology become starkly evident.

The second argument tries to draw an inductive lesson from our conceptual history. Our early folk theories of motion were profoundly confused, and were eventually displaced entirely by more sophisticated theories. Our early folk theories of the structure and activity of the heavens were wildly off the mark, and survive only as historical lessons in how wrong we can be. Our folk theories of the nature of fire, and the nature of life, were similarly cockeyed. And one could go on, since the vast majority of our past folk conceptions have been similarly exploded. All except folk psychology, which survives to this day and has only recently begun to feel pressure. But the phenomenon of conscious intelligence is surely a more complex and difficult phenomenon than any of those just listed. So far as accurate understanding is concerned, it would be a *miracle* if we had got *that* one right the very first time, when we fell down so badly on all the others. Folk psychology has survived for so very long, presumably, not because it is basically correct in its representations, but because the phenomena addressed are so surpassingly difficult that any useful handle on them, no matter how feeble, is unlikely to be displaced in a hurry.

A third argument attempts to find an a priori advantage for eliminative materialism over the identity theory and functionalism. It attempts to counter the common intuition that eliminative materialism is distantly possible, perhaps, but is much less probable than either the identity theory or functionalism. The focus again is on whether the concepts of folk psychology will find vindicating match-ups in a matured neuroscience. The eliminativist bets no; the other two bet yes.

The eliminativist will point out that the requirements on a reduction are rather demanding. The new theory must entail a set of principles and embedded concepts that mirrors very closely the specific conceptual structure to be reduced. And the fact is, there are vastly many more ways of being an explanatorily successful neuroscience while *not* mirroring the structure of folk psychology, than there are ways of being an explanatorily successful neuroscience while also *mirroring* the very specific structure of folk psychology. Accordingly, the a priori probability of eliminative materialism is not lower, but substantially *higher* than that of either of its competitors. One's initial intuitions here are simply mistaken.

Granted, this initial a priori advantage could be reduced if there were a very strong presumption in favor of the truth of folk psychology—true theories are better bets to win reduction. But according to the first two arguments, the presumptions on this point should run in precisely the opposite direction.

Arguments Against Eliminative Materialism

The initial plausibility of this rather radical view is low for almost everyone, since it denies deeply entrenched assumptions. That is at best a question-begging complaint, of course, since those assumptions are precisely what is at issue. But the following line of thought does attempt to mount a real argument.

Eliminative materialism is false, runs the argument, because one's introspection reveals directly the existence of pains, beliefs, desires, fears, and so forth. Their existence is as obvious as anything could be.

The eliminative materialist will reply that this argument makes the same mistake that an ancient or medieval person would be making if he insisted that he could just see with his own eyes that the heavens form a turning sphere, or that witches exist. The fact is, all observation occurs within some system of concepts, and our observation judgments are only as good as the conceptual framework in which they are expressed. In all three cases—the starry sphere, witches, and the familiar mental states—precisely what is challenged is the integrity of the background conceptual frameworks in which the observation judgments are expressed. To insist on the validity of one's experiences, *traditionally interpreted,* is therefore to beg the very question at issue. For in all three cases, the question is whether we should *re*conceive the nature of some familiar observational domain.

A second criticism attempts to find an incoherence in the eliminative materialist's position. The bald statement of eliminative materialism is

that the familiar mental states do not really exist. But that statement is meaningful, runs the argument, only if it is the expression of a certain *belief,* and an *intention* to communicate, and a *knowledge* of the language, and so forth. But if the statement is true, then no such mental states exist, and the statement is therefore a meaningless string of marks or noises, and cannot be true. Evidently, the assumption that eliminative materialism is true entails that it cannot be true.

The hole in this argument is the premise concerning the conditions necessary for a statement to be meaningful. It begs the question. If eliminative materialism is true, then meaningfulness must have some different source. To insist on the "old" source is to insist on the validity of the very framework at issue. Again, an historical parallel may be helpful here. Consider the medieval theory that being biologically *alive* is a matter of being ensouled by an immaterial *vital spirit.* And consider the following response to someone who has expressed disbelief in that theory.

> My learned friend has stated that there is no such thing as vital spirit. But this statement is incoherent. For if it is true, then my friend does not have vital spirit, and must therefore be *dead.* But if he is dead, then his statement is just a string of noises, devoid of meaning or truth. Evidently, the assumption that antivitalism is true entails that it cannot be true! Q.E.D.

This second argument is now a joke, but the first argument begs the question in exactly the same way.

A final criticism draws a much weaker conclusion, but makes a rather stronger case. Eliminative materialism, it has been said, is making mountains out of molehills. It exaggerates the defects in folk psychology, and underplays its real successes. Perhaps the arrival of a matured neuroscience will require the elimination of the occasional folk-psychological concept, continues the criticism, and a minor adjustment in certain folk-psychological principles may have to be endured. But the large-scale elimination forecast by the eliminative materialist is just an alarmist worry or a romantic enthusiasm.

Perhaps this complaint is correct. And perhaps it is merely complacent. Whichever, it does bring out the important point that we do not confront two simple and mutually exclusive possibilities here: pure reduction versus pure elimination. Rather, these are the end points of a smooth spectrum of possible outcomes, between which there are mixed cases of partial elimination and partial reduction. Only empirical research can tell us where on that spectrum our own case will fall.

Perhaps we should speak here, more liberally, of "revisionary materialism," instead of concentrating on the more radical possibility of an across-the-board elimination. Perhaps we should. But it has been my aim in this section to make it at least intelligible to you that our collective conceptual destiny lies substantially toward the revolutionary end of the spectrum.

Suggestions for Further Reading

Classical materialism (atomism) was given influential expression in Lucretius's famous poem, *On the Nature of Things.*

Thomas Hobbes gave materialism a seventeenth-century update in *Leviathan.*

Carvaka is an Indian philosophical school that supported a materialistic interpretation of reality—see page 227ff. in *A Sourcebook in Indian Philosophy,* edited by S. Radhakrishnan and Charles A. Moore (Princeton, NJ: Princeton University Press, 1957).

See Edgar Wilson's *The Mental as Physical* (London: Routledge & Kegan Paul, 1979) for a detailed argument in support of physicalism and its implications for notions like free will.

See John O'Connor's collection of readings in *Modern Materialism: Readings on Mind–Body Identity* (New York: Harcourt, Brace & World, 1969) for a good sampling of views as they relate to the mind–body problem.

The Ontology of Mind: Events, Processes and States by Hellen Steward (New York: Oxford University Press, 1997) and *Deconstructing the Mind* by Stephen P. Stich (New York: Oxford University Press, 1996) both explore eliminative materialism.

Video

Heroic Materialism (52 minutes, Number 13 in the Civilization Series) deals with the rise of modern materialism. See your Media Services Catalog for more information.

How the Human Mind Works (30 minutes) features Patricia Smith Churchland discussing with Bill Moyers issues relating to neurophilosophy. Available from Films for the Humanities and Sciences, P.O. Box 2053, Princeton, NJ 08543. You can get more information at www.films.com.

9.7 Pre-Columbian Cosmologies

From Paul Churchland's predictions that the advances in neuroscience will confirm the truth of a materialistic metaphysics to pre-Columbian cosmologies of ancient peoples is a big leap. However, it is a leap we are about to make as we consider Mesoamerican metaphysics in the wider global context of the Western philosophical tradition.

Cultural critiques have often lamented the fragmentation of modern life. Many think this fragmentation stems from modern scientific developments that have slowly chipped away at a more integrated view of the cosmos. Others lay the blame at the doorstep of modern metaphysical views, which deny the interconnectedness of fact and values, mind and matter, faith and science.

Comparisons can be illuminating. In fact, comparing one thing to another is one of the primary ways we add depth to our understanding. I would hope that the comparisons you have read in this book between feminists and nonfeminist views of ethics (see Section 4.5), Native American and European views of nature (see Section 6.7), Afrocentric and Eurocentric views of epistemology (see Section 7.7), Japanese and Western views of science (see Section 8.5), and the like have shown you the value of comparing and contrasting viewpoints for increasing our insight into important matters.

However helpful comparisons can be, they can also be misleading. Sometimes we view the "other" in the comparison as inferior to ourselves or to some viewpoint we prefer. Sometimes we view the "other" as superior, romanticizing a past no longer existent, but one for which we long. Comparisons are particularly difficult when comparing the views of a culture that has conquered another culture or when comparing existing cultural viewpoints with those that no longer exist. In such situations we must imagine the "other," and imagination—as we all know—can be both helpful and misleading.

Jorge Valadez, author of the next selection, teaches philosophy at Marquette University. His research focuses on ontology, social and political philosophy, and pre-Columbian philosophy. The selection that follows is part of a larger essay that includes a discussion of the Maya, Aztec, and Inca worldviews along with the changes that took place in the colonial and post-colonial period in Latin America.

Valadez is convinced that the metaphysical views of ancient Mesoamerican cultures have not been fully appreciated because of the Eurocentricism brought by the conquering Spanish. When we think of these cultures we think of wild-eyed priests in feathered headdresses brutally sacrificing humans to their sun god. However dreadful the practice of human sacrifice may be, it was embedded in a metaphysical view that we need to understand. We must not lose sight of the more positive elements that might be found in this ancient metaphysic, especially when compared to modern views.

Reading Projects

1. Write a critical précis (see Section 2.2) on "Pre-Columbian Philosophical Perspectives."
2. Compare your précis with one written by a classmate and note the similarities and differences in your impressions of Valadez's essay.

Pre-Columbian Philosophical Perspectives

JORGE VALADEZ

NOTHING IN THE EXPERIENCE of the much-traveled soldiers of Hernán Cortés's invading army could have prepared them for what they saw when they marched into Tenochtitlán, the ancient site of present-day Mexico City, in 1519. They encountered great buildings and ceremonial centers, vast and beautiful floating gardens, splendid murals, impressive sculptures and other works of art, and large and well-organized markets. The Spaniards were witnessing the splendors of one of the greatest civilizations in history. Their amazement was magnified by the fact that this civilization was so utterly foreign and unexpected. The Spaniards were denizens of the Old World, where diverse cultures had interacted and influenced one another for thousands of years. But here was a civilization that had evolved in isolation from the rest of the world and yet was highly advanced in astronomy and agriculture, had created architectural wonders, practiced sophisticated types of surgery, and developed complex and unique systems of religious belief and social organization.

This unprecedented and extraordinary encounter of two diverse cultures was destined to have catastrophic consequences for the people of the Americas. In less than two centuries diseases like smallpox and diphtheria, which the inhabitants of the New World had no defenses against because of their genetic isolation, decimated approximately two-thirds of the population of the Americas. In Mesoamerica (a region covering the southern two-thirds of Mexico and Guatemala, El Salvador, Belize, and certain areas of Nicaragua, Honduras, and Costa Rica), tens of millions of native people died either in battles with the technologically superior invading army or, more commonly, as the result of infection with these new diseases. The Spaniards eventually conquered the Aztec capital, Tenochtitlán, plundered it for its gold and silver (melting many pieces of jewelry and religious figurines into gold bullion), and enslaved many of its inhabitants.

But there was another kind of destruction that the Spaniards were to wreak on the Aztecs and other people of Mesoamerica—the almost wholesale destruction of their culture. The social, religious, and political organization of early Mesoamerican society—including the structure of its large urban centers, forms of religious ritual, cultural customs, artistic styles, philosophy of education, and architectural forms—were all based on a religious and cosmological perspective that was completely foreign and incomprehensible to the Europeans.

The worldview of the Spaniards was determined by their Christian beliefs, and hence they were at once amazed and repulsed by what they saw: human sacrifices, rituals involving bloodletting, adoration of pagan gods, cannibalism, sculptures of what they considered monstrous creatures, and so on. According to their Christian metaphysical perspective there was a clear and straightforward way to categorize these practices; they were to be considered evil and the work of the Devil. One of the most famous chroniclers of the native culture, the Spanish Franciscan priest Bernardino de Sahagun, firmly believed that the existence of Aztec religious beliefs and customs was an ingenious and elaborate manifestation of the power of Satan's influence. Thus, the religious practices of the Aztecs not only had no claim to cultural legitimacy, they had to be stopped at whatever cost. Bolstered by such ethical and cultural chauvinism, the Spaniards undertook what is perhaps the most extensive and systematic (and certainly the most large-scale) destruction of a civilization in the world's history. In that the civilizations of Mesoamerica were essentially grounded in a radically different religious and cosmological vision, this conquest was nothing less than an attempt at metaphysical annihilation, that is, an attempt to destroy the worldviews of the native people. Nevertheless, despite the efforts of the Spaniards to eradicate the cosmological roots of these cultures, we shall see that some important features of the ancient worldviews can still be found in some contemporary Mesoamerican cultures.

Given their imperialistic orientations and the closed nature of their religious perspective, it was perhaps inevitable that the Spaniards would fail so completely to understand the Aztec culture and the other cultures of ancient Mesoamerica. In fact, it is only in the latter half of the twentieth century that it has been possible, through a variety of archaeological sources and different kinds of interpretive techniques, to understand the religious and metaphysical worldview of early Mesoamerican cultures.

This essay will present a systematic exposition of some of the central concepts and principles of the early Mesoamerican cosmological perspectives, . . . I will draw contrasts and comparisons between the Mesoamerican metaphysical perspectives and some perspectives that have been of predominant importance in the Western philosophical tradition. These comparisons will help us to appreciate more fully the uniqueness and depth of the ancient Mesoamerican worldviews and will further our understanding of some of the Western European philosophical perspectives by placing them within a wider global cultural context.

Precolonial Latin American Cosmologies

Cultures throughout history have developed a variety of answers to certain fundamental and perennial questions: What place do human beings have in the universe? What is the structure of the cosmos? How can we explain or account for the origin of the world? The cultures of Mesoamerica developed complex and fascinating answers to such questions. In order to provide a general understanding of how they approached these questions, we will look first at some central metaphysical principles common to the Mayan and Aztec cosmologies, and then examine the structure of each of these worldviews in more detail.

One of the most striking features of the Mesoamerican metaphysical perspective was the remarkable degree to which it interconnected or integrated different aspects or components of reality. Four different kinds of integration characterized its cosmology: (1) the internal structural interconnection of the different components of the universe, (2) the integration of fundamental dualities that were perceived as complementary instead of oppositional, (3) the holistic integration of astronomical science and religious beliefs, and, most important, (4) the integration of everyday life with the cycles and rhythms of the cosmos through the practice of rituals that were perceived as necessary for sustaining the very existence of the universe. To arrive at a unified view of the Mesoamerican metaphysical perspective, we must understand each of these four aspects of Mesoamerican cosmology. . . .

THE INTERACTIVE UNIVERSE

The people of Mesoamerica believed that the universe consisted of three different planes or levels: a celestial plane, a terrestrial plane, and an underworld plane. There were further divisions within the celestial and underworld levels. (The Aztecs, for example, believed that there were thirteen celestial levels and nine underworld levels.) There was also a constant interaction of supernatural forces or powers among these levels, which was made possible by the existence of spiral-shaped channels called *mallinalis.* These supernatural forces were thought to enter the terrestrial level through caves, sunlight, fire, and animals. Some of the rituals of the Mesoamerican cultures were designed to tap and redirect or harness these supernatural cosmic forces. Thus their universe was not a static universe, but rather an interactive one, with three dynamic levels of reality.

Time itself also existed at different planes or levels: human or terrestrial time; the time of myth; and the transcendent time in which the gods dwelled. Terrestrial time originated in the interaction of cosmic forces from the celestial and underworld levels converging at the terrestrial level. In other words, human time originated in the interaction of forces from two distinct spatial planes.

Myth time existed prior to terrestrial time, and in it the actions of the gods, as they were depicted in their myths, took place. For example, in one of the Mayan myths about death, two heroic twin brothers descend to the underworld to challenge the Lords of Death. After a long series of trials and ordeals, the brothers defeat the Lords of the Underworld and emerge victorious. This myth is an expression of the Mayan belief that death represents a challenge which, through courage and fortitude, can be overcome. It was also during this myth time, which still progresses and has not ceased to be, that many supernatural beings who exert cyclical influences on humans at the terrestrial level were born or created.

In transcendent time lived the most powerful gods at the apex of the divine hierarchy who created and grounded the universe. (Apparently these powerful creator gods existed in two temporal dimensions, namely, mythic and transcendent time.) The gods and supernatural beings that inhabited transcendent time, like those that lived in mythic time, had periodic or cyclical influences on the events and beings that existed in terrestrial time. The early Mesoamerican calendars marked the occasions during the year when these periodic influences occurred.

Thus, in the Mesoamerican worldview, space and time were not understood as existing independently of one another; instead, they formed a complex, unified whole. . . . For the ancient Mesoamericans, the world was replete with cosmic forces resulting from the intersection of the various spatial and temporal levels that comprised the universe.

In addition, their universe did not consist of isolated, discrete entities; rather, it consisted of entities, events, and forces that were in constant interaction with one another and that existed in different spaciotemporal planes. Absolute space, conceived as an empty vacuum in which entities exist and events take place, and absolute time, understood as an infinite linear progression of moments, had no reality in the Mesoamerican cosmological perspective. For the people of early Mesoamerica, space and time constituted the very fabric of existence; that is, they affected, shaped, and determined everything that exists. This is why Mesoamerican cultures were so preoccupied with developing accurate calendars and astronomical techniques for measuring time, determining the spatial location of celestial bodies, and anticipating the occurrence of astronomical events. The capacity to measure and predict the solar, lunar, planetary, and astral cycles enabled them to understand the various complex cosmic forces that they believed affected human events at the terrestrial level. By knowing the particular times at which certain cosmic forces affected events at the human level, they tried to mediate and channel these forces through rituals. From such observations we can appreciate the great extent to which the different components of the Mesoamerican universe were interrelated and interconnected with one another.

COMPLEMENTARY DUALITIES

The second kind of integration in Mesoamerican cosmology concerns the complementary nature of fundamental dualities. Dualities such as life/death, celestial world/underworld, male/female, night/day, and so forth were of central importance in the Mesoamerican worldview. These dualities were not conceived as being oppositional in nature; instead, they were understood as being different and necessary aspects of reality. One of the clearest examples of this type of nonoppositional duality was the supreme dual god of the Aztecs, Ometeotl. This supreme deity, who was the ultimate originator of all that exists, had a dual male and female nature. Ometeotl was sometimes called Tonacatecuhtli-Tonacacihuatl, which means "lord and lady of our maintenance," and often he/she was referred to as "our mother, our father." The dual nature of Ometeotl enabled him/her to beget other beings and the universe from his/her own essence. It is clear that the Aztecs wanted to incorporate both the male and the female principle within a single supreme entity and that they saw no contradiction in a deity who was simultaneously male and female.

It is interesting and instructive to compare the conception of a male/female dual god with the monotheistic God of the Judeo-Christian tradition. Traditionally, the Christian god has been characterized primarily as having male qualities and has been referred to in explicitly male terms. For example, the first two substantive terms in the expression "the father, the son, and the holy ghost" refer to God in terms that are unequivocally male, while the third substantive term, "the holy ghost," has traditionally never been spoken of in female terms. And historically, rarely if ever have we heard the Christian God referred to by the female pronoun "she" or by the phrase "holy mother." He is usually characterized by predominantly male qualities that emphasized his power and authority instead of, say, his nurturance and unconditional acceptance. Some contemporary theologians have argued that these gender-specific characterizations of the Christian God deny women full spiritual participation in the Christian religious tradition. In any case, we can see that the Aztec conceptualization of the supreme deity Ometeotl incorporates the two aspects of the male/female duality into a single divine entity.

We find another case of the Mesoamerican tendency to think in terms of nonoppositional dualities in the Mayan understanding of the life/death duality. From the Mayan perspective, death, whether of humans or of plants, was an integral part of a never-ending life cycle of birth, death, and regeneration. Death was not seen as the discontinuity of life, but rather as a necessary phase in the regeneration of life. Upon death, humans went to the underworld of Xibalba, where they experienced various ordeals and struggles

with the supernatural entities of the underworld. Then they would be reborn and ascend to the celestial or terrestrial level, where they might become a part of a heavenly body, an ancestral spiritual entity, or a maize plant. Through this transformation and process of rebirth, individuals would be integrated into one of the eternal life cycles of the universe. In similar fashion, the death of plant life in the seasonal and agricultural cycles was merely one phase in the recurring pattern of sowing, sprouting, dying, and regenerating. One of the central ideas in the Mayan cosmology was that the earth was a living entity that was continually in the process of regeneration, and that the death of plant life was an integral part of this process.

In short, death was not seen as the negation, or as the polar opposite, of life. Rather, death was a process that either (1) made possible the continuation of the life process or (2) allowed for the integration of the life of the individual into the eternal cosmic cycles. In the plant world, the death of plants enabled new vegetation to sprout and develop; that is, death was an integral part of the process of regeneration. In the human realm, death was, as we have seen, a process in which the individual would eventually become a part of the astral or earthly cycles of the universe. In contrast to some Western views on death, in which the soul of the individual continues to exist in an otherworldly spiritual realm, in the early Mesoamerican cosmology the spirits of the dead return to become a part of the world we can see, touch, and feel. That is, they became part of the world of everyday experience.

A SCIENTIFIC-RELIGIOUS WORLDVIEW

The third kind of structural integration that characterizes the Mesoamerican cosmology concerns the intimate linkage between Mesoamerican scientific and religious perspectives. Astronomy was by far the most fully developed science of the cultures of Mesoamerica. The accuracy of their calendars equaled or surpassed those of other cultures in the world at that time, and their astronomical observations were as extensive and accurate as those of any other civilization. Insofar as they possessed a scientific, empirically validated form of knowledge, it was their astronomy. This was the knowledge that allowed them to correctly predict celestial events, carry out extensive and accurate calendrical computations (some of which involved dates many millions of years into the future), and measure agricultural cycles. But their astronomical science was also closely interconnected with their religious ideas and beliefs, especially the fundamentally important concept of the renewal or regeneration of agricultural and human life cycles. They believed that the influences of the supernatural forces and beings that permeated the earth and supported these life cycles could be tracked and predicted by their calendars. In addition, they maintained that through religious rituals they could harness and successfully mediate these cosmic forces.

Thus, the intense interest of the people of ancient Mesoamerica in astronomical observation and the measurement of time was not motivated merely by the desire to acquire knowledge for its own sake; the continuation of the life cycles of the universe depended on the performance of the appropriate religious rituals at specific points in time. Their scientifically validated observations were united with their fundamental religious ideas and with the rituals they believed were crucial for the continued existence of the cosmos. This unification of their two most basic kinds of knowledge gave rise to a holistic conceptual unity in their thinking that is difficult for us to understand and appreciate. The reason this conceptual integration is so foreign to us is that there is a fundamental fragmentation in modern thought between scientific knowledge and religious belief.

Science tells us that reality consists of physical entities and forces that exist independently of human consciousness and that are utterly indifferent to the human search for meaning and cosmic significance. According to the contemporary scientific worldview, everything that occurs in the universe is explainable in terms of universal physical laws, not in terms of the acts of a divine will. Because according to this worldview it is physics,

and not the will of God, that explains why events occur, modern scientific knowledge conflicts with the age-old reliance on a supernatural, spiritual being to explain what happens in the universe. And if, as the modern scientific perspective tells us, reality consists exclusively of impersonal physical forces and entities governed by universal laws, where in such a universe can we find a basis for human spiritual meaning and significance? This scientific perspective has also deeply influenced nonreligious, philosophical attempts to find a basis for the meaning of human existence. For the past several centuries (a period coinciding with the emergence of modern science and the decline of the religious worldview), Western philosophers have wrestled with questions concerning the meaning of life. Here again the problem has been to find a basis for grounding existential significance and human values in an indifferent, impersonal universe consisting solely of objective physical forces and entities. In short, a basic dilemma has arisen in modern Western thought as a result of the scientific view of the universe as an objectively existing physical realm in which there is no room for the principles of human subjective experience as expressed in religious and philosophic thought. By contrast, in the Mesoamerican cosmological view there was no conflict between science and religion; on the contrary, Mesoamerican scientific and religious worldviews complemented and reinforced one another.

COSMIC RESPONSIBILITY

We have already alluded to the fourth kind of integration characteristic of the Mesoamerican metaphysical perspective. It concerns the belief that religious rituals were of central importance for maintaining the existence of the cosmos. Perhaps the clearest expression of this belief can be found in the Aztec Legend of the Four Suns. According to this legend, there have been four ages that have been dominated by four different suns. Each of these ages—which correspond to each of the four directions, east, south, west, and north—had ended in a catastrophic manner with the destruction of the human race and the world.

The Aztecs believed that they lived in the age of the Fifth Sun, which was created at Tenochtitlán, the ancient site of Mexico City, as the result of the self-sacrifice of the gods Nanahuatzin and Tecuciztecatl. After the destruction of the Fourth Sun, all was darkness except for the divine hearth (the *teotexcalli*), where the gods gathered to create the new sun that would usher in the new age. The gods ordered Tecuciztecatl to leap into the great fire, but he was unable to do so out of fear. After Tecuciztecatl attempted and failed four times to leap into the fire, the gods ordered Nanahuatzin to sacrifice himself in the giant blaze. Nanahuatzin braced himself, closed his eyes, and threw himself in. Upon seeing this, Tecuciztecatl finally gained enough courage to jump into the fire. As the result of his courage and sacrifice, Nanahuatzin reemerges from the east as the new, blazing red sun.

The Legend of the Suns expresses some central ideas of the Aztec cosmology. One of these is the centrality of cataclysmic change in the evolution of the universe. Each of the previous four ages had been destroyed by sudden, catastrophic disasters and the present age was also susceptible to an abrupt, massive destruction. The Aztec universe was thus highly unstable and vulnerable to extinction. Another prominent theme in this myth is that of sacrifice. The Aztecs believed that the present age began with a sacrifice by the gods, and that in order to prevent this age from ending they had continually to provide the sun with life-sustaining blood and with the energy concentrated in certain parts of the body of sacrificial victims. This is the primary explanation for the religious rituals involving human sacrifice.

The need for sacrificial victims demanded the continued capture of enemy warriors and the creation of a warrior class to satisfy this need. This sense of cosmic responsibility reinforced certain authoritarian orientations in Aztec culture. Theirs was a society that did not tolerate a great deal of individual freedom or challenges to the established social order.

Human actions had great significance in the cosmology of the Aztecs, because the very existence of the universe depended on the proper performance of religious rituals, including human sacrifice. Without a doubt, most of us would find the practice of human sacrifice, and the extent to which it was practiced by the Aztecs, to be morally objectionable and repugnant in the extreme. Nevertheless, this practice was based on a religious doctrine that was of central importance in the Aztec cosmological perspective. Within their worldview, human sacrifice was not only justified, it was absolutely essential. Indeed, the profound sense of cosmic responsibility that was so central to the Aztec worldview was a double-edged sword. It provided them with an unquestioned faith in their relevance and importance as a people, but it also burdened them with the heavy obligation of maintaining the existence of the cosmos. It can truly be said that the Aztecs elaborated a highly imaginative, though severe, answer to the question concerning the role and relevance of human existence in the universe. . . .

Suggestions for Further Reading

David Carrasco's *Religions of Mesoamerica* (San Francisco: Harper and Row, 1990) and Miguel Leon-Portilla's *Aztec Thought and Culture* (Norman: University of Oklahoma Press, 1963) will provide useful background information.

Dennis Tedlock's translation of *Popul Vuh: The Definitive Edition of the Mayan Book of Dawn of Life and the Glories of Gods and Kings* (New York: Simon and Schuster, 1985) provides interesting source material.

The Fifth Sun: Aztec Gods, Aztec World by Burr C. Brundage (Austin: University of Texas Press, 1979) and *Quetzalcoatl and the Irony of Empire: Myths and Prophecies in the Aztec Tradition* by David Carrasco (Chicago: University of Chicago Press, 1982) will take you deeper into the worldview of Mesoamericans.

The concept of a "worldview" is a broader notion than "metaphysics." Metaphysical ideas are one part but not the only part of a worldview. On worldview analysis in a crosscultural context, see Ninian Smart's *Worldviews: Crosscultural Explorations of Human Beliefs,* 2nd Edition (Englewood Cliffs, NJ: Prentice-Hall, 1995).

9.8 So What Is Real?

Philosophers from around the world have wondered about whether there is some Archimedian point, some firm and solid foundation, some privileged perspective from which we can distinguish with confidence dreaming from waking, good from bad, reality from appearance. Some have claimed to have found such a foundation; others have claimed it does not exist. Is there some sort of "God's-eye view" that humans can adopt that will allow them to see things as they really are? What do you think?

"Not that question again," I hear some of you say. Wondering can be frustrating business, and being constantly challenged to think for ourselves can be intimidating. Yet thinking is what philosophy is about. Of course, from time to time we all wonder what we have accomplished by all this thought. Sometimes it seems we just go in circles, but the circles get bigger and after a while begin to form a spiral. New ideas arise. Fresh distinctions emerge. Questions are refined and plateaus of clarity reached. You may not be in a position to say with absolute certainty exactly what is really real, but think about all you have learned in thinking about metaphysical issues in conversation with others from around the world.

I do hope that this experience encourages you to continue to wonder because wondering has given birth to some of the greatest of human accomplishments. I also hope that you have come to value the ideas and insights from different countries and cultural groups. It is good to learn what the world looks like from a different perspective. Different viewpoints enrich our own and open up new paths for further exploration. As we move deeper into the twenty-first century, it will become ever more necessary to understand the perspectives and values of others. Philosophy needs to become a global conversation that is stimulating, productive, and edifying. Each of you has something of value to contribute to this emerging global conversation, and I hope what you have learned has helped you begin to find your voice in these matters.

I close this chapter with a tale of dreaming by Jorge Luis Borges (1899–1986), Argentina's greatest writer and a man with an active, ever-probing mind and imagination who lived in constant wonder. He uses fiction to raise philosophical issues worth pondering. Can we ever be certain that our perspective is the right one? Can we ever be confident that our way of distinguishing appearance from reality is the one correct way? And if we cannot, then what?

Reading Projects

1. Write a one-page interpretative essay on what you think the tale of "The Circular Ruins" means. What is Borges' point?
2. Compare your interpretative essay with one written by a classmate and discuss the differences in your interpretations.

The Circular Ruins

JORGE LUIS BORGES

And if he left off dreaming about you . . .
—*Through the Looking Glass*, VI

No one saw him disembark in the unanimous night. No one saw the bamboo canoe running aground on the sacred mud. But within a few days no one was unaware that the taciturn man had come from the South and that his home had been one of the infinity of hamlets which lie upstream, on the violent flank of the mountain, where the Zend language is uncontaminated by Greek, and where leprosy is infrequent. The certain fact is that the anonymous gray man kissed the mud, scaled the bank without pushing aside (probably without even feeling) the sharp-edged sedges lacerating his flesh, and dragged himself, bloody and sickened, up to the circular enclosure whose crown is a stone colt or tiger, formerly the color of fire and now the color of ash. This circular clearing is a temple, devoured by ancient conflagration, profaned by the malarial jungle, its god unhonored now of men. The stranger lay beneath a pedestal. He was awakened, much later, by the sun at its height. He was not astonished to find that his wounds had healed. He closed his pale eyes and slept, no longer from weakness of the flesh but from a determination of the will. He knew that this temple was the place required by his inflexible purpose; he knew that the incessant trees had not been able to choke the ruins of another such propitious temple down river, a temple whose gods also were burned and dead; he knew that his immediate obligation was to dream. The disconsolate shriek of a bird awoke him about midnight. The prints of bare feet, some figs, and a jug told him that the people of the region had reverently spied out his dreaming and solicited his protection or feared his magic. He felt the cold chill of fear, and sought in the dilapidated wall for a sepulchral niche where he concealed himself under some unfamiliar leaves.

The purpose which impelled him was not impossible though it was supernatural. He willed to dream a man. He wanted to dream him in minute totality and then impose him upon reality. He had spent the full resources of his soul on this magical project. If anyone had asked him his own name or about any feature of his former life, he would have been unable to answer. The shattered and deserted temple suited his ends, for it was a minimum part of the visible world, and the nearness of the peasants was also convenient, for they took it upon themselves to supply his frugal needs. The rice and fruits of the tribute were nourishment enough for his body, given over to the sole task of sleeping and dreaming.

At first his dreams were chaotic. A little later they were dialectical. The stranger dreamt he stood in the middle of a circular amphitheater which was in some measure the fired temple; clouds of taciturn students wearied the tiers; the faces of the last rows looked down from a distance of several centuries and from a stellar height, but their every feature was precise. The dreamer himself was delivering lectures on anatomy, cosmography, magic: the faces listened anxiously and strove to answer with understanding, as if they guessed the importance of that examination, which would redeem one of them from his insubstantial state and interpolate him into the real world. In dreams or in waking the man continually considered the replies of his phantoms; he did not let himself be deceived by the impostors; in certain paradoxes he sensed an expanding intelligence. He was seeking a soul worthy of participating in the universe.

At the end of nine or ten nights he realized, with a certain bitterness, that he could expect nothing from those students who accepted his teaching passively, but that he could of those who sometimes risked a reasonable contradiction. The former, though deserving of love and affection, could never rise to being individuals; the latter already existed to a somewhat greater degree. One afternoon (now even the afternoons were tributaries of the dream; now he stayed awake for only a couple of hours at daybreak) he dismissed the entire vast illusory student body for good and retained only one pupil. This pupil was a silent, sallow, sometimes obstinate boy, whose sharp features repeated those of his dreamer. The sudden elimination of his fellow students did not disconcert him for very long; his progress, at the end of a few private lessons, made his master marvel. And nevertheless, catastrophe came. One day the man emerged from sleep as from a viscous desert, stared about at the vain light of evening, which at first he took to be dawn, and realized he had not dreamt. All that night and all the next day the intolerable lucidity of insomnia broke over him in waves. He was impelled to explore the jungle, to wear himself out; he barely managed some quick snatches of feeble sleep amid the hemlock, shot through with fugitive visions of a rudimentary type: altogether unserviceable. He strove to assemble the student body, but he had scarcely uttered a few words of exhortation before the college blurred, was erased. Tears of wrath scalded his old eyes in his almost perpetual vigil.

He realized that the effort to model the inchoate and vertiginous stuff of which dreams are made is the most arduous task a man can undertake, though he get to the bottom of all the enigmas of a superior or inferior order: much more arduous than to weave a rope of sand or mint coins of the faceless wind. He realized that an initial failure was inevitable. He vowed to forget the enormous hallucination by which he had been led astray at first, and he sought out another approach. Before essaying it, he dedicated a month to replenishing the forces he had squandered in delirium. He abandoned all premeditation concerned with dreaming, and almost at once managed to sleep through a goodly part of the day. The few times he did dream during this period he took no notice of the dreams. He waited until the disk of the moon should be perfect before taking up his task again. Then, on the eve, he purified himself in the waters of the river, worshiped the planetary gods, pronounced the lawful syllables of a powerful name and went to sleep. Almost at once he dreamt of a beating heart.

He dreamt it active, warm, secret, the size of a closed fist, garnet-colored in the half-light of a human body that boasted as yet no sex or face. He dreamt this heart with meticulous love, for fourteen lucid nights. Each night he saw it more clearly. He never touched it, but limited himself to witnessing it, to observing it or perhaps rectifying it with a glance. He watched it, lived it, from far and from near and from many angles. On the fourteenth night he ran his index finger lightly along the pulmonary artery, and then over the entire heart, inside and out. The examination satisfied him. The next night, he deliberately did not dream. He then took up the heart again, invoked the name of a planet, and set about to envision another one of the principal organs. Before the year was up he had reached the skeleton, the eyelids. The most difficult task, perhaps, proved to be the numberless hairs. He dreamt a whole man, a fine lad, but one who could not stand nor talk nor open his eyes. Night after night he dreamt him asleep.

In the Gnostic cosmogonies, demiurges fashion a red Adam who never manages to get to his feet: as clumsy and equally as crude and elemental as this dust Adam was the dream Adam forged by the nights of the wizard. One afternoon, the man almost destroyed all his work, but then changed his mind. (It would have been better for him had he destroyed it.) Having expended all the votive offerings to the numina of the earth and the river, he threw himself at the feet of the effigy, which was perhaps a tiger or perhaps a colt, and implored its unknown help. That evening, at twilight, he dreamt of the statue. He dreamt it alive, tremulous: it was no atrocious bastard of a tiger and a colt, but both these vehement creatures at once and also a bull, a rose, a tempest. This multiple god revealed to him that its terrestrial name was Fire, that in this same circular temple (and in others like it) it once had been offered sacrifices and been the object of a cult, and that now it would magically animate the phantom dreamt by the wizard in such wise that all creatures—except Fire itself and the dreamer—would believe the phantom to be a man of flesh and blood. It directed that once the phantom was instructed in the rites, he be sent to the other broken temple, whose pyramids persisted down river, so that some voice might be raised in glorification in that deserted edifice. In the dream of the man who was dreaming, the dreamt man awoke.

The wizard carried out the directives given him. He dedicated a period of time (which amounted, in the end, to two years) to revealing the mysteries of the universe and the cult of Fire to his dream creature. In his intimate being, he suffered when he was apart from his creation. And so every day, under the pretext of pedagogical necessity, he protracted the hours devoted to dreaming. He also reworked the right shoulder, which was perhaps defective. At times, he had the uneasy impression that all this had happened before. . . . In general, though, his days were happy ones: as he closed his eyes he would think: *Now I shall be with my son.* Or, more infrequently: *The son I have engendered is waiting for me and will not exist if I do not go to him.*

Little by little he got his creature accustomed to reality. Once, he ordered him to plant a flag on a distant mountain top. The next day the flag was fluttering on the peak. He tried other analogous experiments, each one more audacious than the last. He came to realize, with a certain bitterness, that his son was ready—and perhaps impatient—to be born. That night he kissed his child for the first time, and sent him to the other temple, whose remains were whitening down river, many leagues across impassable jungle and swamp. But first, so that his son should never know he was a phantom and should think himself a man like other men, he imbued him with total forgetfulness of his apprentice years.

His triumph and his respite were sapped by tedium. In the twilight hours of dusk or dawn he would prostrate himself before the stone figure, imagining his unreal child practicing identical rites in other circular ruins downstream. At night

he did not dream, or dreamt as other men do. The sounds and forms of the universe reached him wanly, pallidly: his absent son was being sustained on the diminution of the wizard's soul. His life's purpose had been achieved; the man lived on in a kind of ecstasy. After a time—which some narrators of his story prefer to compute in years and others in lustra—he was awakened one midnight by two boatmen: he could not see their faces, but they told him of a magical man at a temple in the North, who walked on fire and was not burned. The wizard suddenly recalled the words of the god. He remembered that of all the creatures composing the world, only Fire knew his son was a phantom. This recollection, comforting at first, ended by tormenting him. He feared lest his son meditate on his abnormal privilege and somehow discover his condition of mere simulacrum. Not to be a man, to be the projection of another man's dream—what incomparable humiliation, what vertigo! Every father is concerned with the children he has procreated (which he has permitted) in mere confusion or felicity: it was only natural that the wizard should fear for the future of his son, thought out entrail by entrail and feature by feature on a thousand and one secret nights.

The end of his caviling was abrupt, but not without forewarnings. First (after a long drought) a remote cloud, light as a bird, appeared over a hill. Then, toward the South, the sky turned the rosy color of a leopard's gums. Smoke began to rust the metallic nights. And then came the panic flight of the animals. And the events of several centuries before were repeated. The ruins of the fire god's sanctuary were destroyed by fire. One birdless dawn the wizard watched the concentric conflagration close around the walls: for one instant he thought of taking refuge in the river, but then he understood that death was coming to crown his old age and to absolve him of further work. He walked against the florid banners of the fire. And the fire did not bite his flesh but caressed and engulfed him without heat or combustion. With relief, with humiliation, with terror, he understood that he, too, was all appearance, that someone else was dreaming him.

Suggestions for Further Reading

The Mythmaker by Carter Wheelock (Austin: University of Texas Press, 1969) discusses "The Circular Ruins" in various places; see pages 48–53 in particular. Wheelock also provides an excellent bibliography.

Emir Rodríguez Monegal provides useful background information in *Jorge Luis Borges: A Literary Biography* (New York: Dutton, 1978).

On the web visit the Borges Center at http://www.hum.au.dk/romansk/borges/english.htm for more information. For a biography and other information visit http://www.sccs.swarthmore.edu/~pwillen1/lit/index3.htm.

 You can locate InfoTrac-College Edition articles about this chapter by accessing the InfoTrac-College Edition website (http://www.infotrac-college.com/wadsworth/). Using the InfoTrac-College Edition subject guide, enter the search terms relevant to this chapter, and then read abstracts for relevant articles.

Are We Free or Determined?

10.1 Introduction

Determinism (sometimes called simple determinism in order to distinguish it from other types) refers to the idea that all events are caused. For every event there is a set of conditions such that if the conditions were repeated, the event would recur. Simple determinism implies that the universe and what happens in it is lawful, that is, that the law of causality (or law of cause and effect) governs events. Hence, we can assume that any given event is determined (caused) by some set of antecedent events even if we are not fully aware of what those antecedent events are.

Simple determinism should not be confused with fatalism nor with predestination. **Fatalism** is the belief that events are predetermined by some impersonal cosmic force or power; **predestination** is the belief that events are predetermined by some personal power. Although fatalism and predestination differ about what predetermines events, they share the idea that if an event or action is fated or predestined, it will happen *no matter what.*

Simple determinism does not claim that events or actions are predetermined by personal or impersonal cosmic powers, nor does it claim that events will happen no matter what. Rather, it holds that events happen *only if* particular causes of those events occur. If the causes of a possible event do not occur, that event will not occur.

Although there are important differences among simple determinism, fatalism, and predestination, all three positions clearly raise questions about human freedom. If all events are caused (whether their cause be fate, a god, or some set of antecedent events), how can any human actions (assuming human actions are events), like your act of reading these words, be free? This is one way of formulating what philosophers call the **problem of freedom and determinism** (sometimes called the *problem of free will*).

This problem is important for a number of reasons. One of the most important has to do with moral responsibility. If the choices we make and the actions we perform are not free, it seems to make no sense to praise or blame people for what they do. Indeed, why bother to search for how one should live, or how to make correct moral choices, or how to create a just society if, in fact, all our choices are determined by antecedent factors over which we have no control?

The issue of moral responsibility allows us to probe more deeply the problem of freedom and determinism by formulating that problem as a dilemma.

1. Human choice is either free, or it is not free.
2. If it is free, then the law of causality is false.
3. If it is not free, then people are not responsible for their actions.
4. Therefore, either the law of causality is false, or people are not responsible for their actions.

Neither of the choices given in conclusion (4) is very attractive. On the one hand, we want to believe in the law of causality. All of science and technology depend on it. Surely, if there are uncaused events, then there are events that can never be explained, or predicted. So why search for a cure for cancer, or why try to eliminate crime, or why try to invent a pollution-free form of rapid transportation? There may be no causes for these things and hence no means of prediction or control. If the law of causality is false, the universe appears chaotic, disordered, unreliable, and events seem unexplainable.

On the other hand, we want to hold people morally responsible for what they do. What sense would praise or blame make if we aren't responsible? If you are not free and hence not responsible for what you do, then what sense does it make to say you *earned* a good grade in philosophy, or you *merited* a promotion, or you *ought* to be punished for behaving badly? Indeed, what sense would morality make if people cannot freely choose what they do?

In this chapter, we explore some of the solutions people have proposed to the problem of freedom and determinism. As we explore these solutions, our understanding of the problem will grow, and alternatives that may not have occurred to us will present themselves.

10.2 We Are Determined

One proposed solution to the problem of freedom and determinism is called **hard determinism**. Hard determinism holds that every event has a cause and that this fact is *incompatible* with free will. Nothing happens for which there is no sufficient reason; hence, free will is an illusion. People should not be held morally responsible for their actions since a given act is unavoidable if the appropriate antecedent conditions obtain. If we want to change people's behavior, we need to develop a science of behavior that will show us how to manipulate the causes of human behavior.

Notice that hard determinism is a form of simple determinism insofar as it holds that every event has a cause. However, *unlike* simple determinism, hard determinism claims, in addition, that determinism and free will are *incompatible,* that free will is an illusion, and that humans are *not* in fact responsible for what they do in the sense that they could have made choices other than they did.

Supporters of this position usually appeal to the physical sciences and concepts like "natural law" to back up their views. Science seeks to give a description of objective facts. It also seeks to discover uniformity in nature. That is, it seeks to explain facts by discovering the networks of cause and effect according to which events are ordered.

Robert Blatchford (1851–1943) believed in hard determinism and crusaded in England for that position. He argued that heredity and environment determine human behavior. Hence rewards and punishments should not be linked to the notion of responsibility. His arguments are aimed against a particular conception of free will, namely, that humans are free to do other than what their heredity and environment cause them to do. He did not deny that humans make choices and that they even make choices in accord with their wishes, desires, likes, and dislikes. Nor did he deny that many of the choices humans make are voluntary in the sense that no other person forced them to make a particular choice. All he denied is that humans are free to somehow rise above heredity and environment.

Reading Questions

1. According to Blatchford, what is the "point" that the free will discussion turns on?
2. What is Blatchford's main point?
3. What arguments does Blatchford present to support his main point?
4. Why, according to Blatchford, should we not blame someone for his or her conduct?
5. Present the best counterargument you can to Blatchford's position.
6. If what you believe about the existence of free will is determined (as Blatchford claims) by heredity and environment, why would Blatchford even try to convince you that hard determinism is true?

Not Guilty

ROBERT BLATCHFORD

THE FREE WILL DELUSION has been a stumbling block in the way of human thought for thousands of years. Let us try whether common sense and common knowledge cannot remove it. Free will is a subject of great importance to us in this case; and it is one we must come to with our eyes wide open and our wits wide awake; not because it is very difficult, but because it has been tied and twisted into a tangle of Gordian knots by twenty centuries full of wordy but unsuccessful philosophers.

The free will party claim that man is responsible for his acts, because his will is free to choose between right and wrong.

We reply that the will is not free, and that if it were free man could not know right from wrong until he was taught.

As to the knowledge of good and evil the free will party will claim that conscience is an unerring guide. But I have already proved that conscience does not and cannot tell us what is right and what is wrong: it only reminds us of the lessons we have learnt as to right and wrong.

The "still small voice" is not the voice of God: it is the voice of heredity and environment.

And now to the freedom of the will.

When a man says his will is free, he means that it is free of all control or interference: that it can overrule heredity and environment.

We reply that the will is ruled by heredity and environment.

The cause of all the confusion on this subject may be shown in a few words.

When the free will party say that man has a free will, they mean that he is free to act as he chooses to act.

There is no need to deny that. *But what causes him to choose?*

That is the pivot upon which the whole discussion turns.

The free will party seem to think of the will as something independent of the man, as something outside him. They seem to think that the will decides without the control of the man's reason.

If that were so, it would not prove the man responsible. "The will" would be responsible, and not the man. It would be as foolish to blame a man for the act of a "free" will, as to blame a horse for the action of its rider.

But I am going to prove to my readers, by appeals to their common sense and common knowledge, that the will is not free; and that it is ruled by heredity and environment.

To begin with, the average man will be against me. He knows that he chooses between two courses every hour, and often every minute, and he thinks his choice is free. But that is a delusion: his choice is not free. He can choose, and does choose. But he can only choose as his heredity and his environment cause him to choose. He

never did choose and never will choose except as his heredity and his environment—his temperament and his training—cause him to choose. And his heredity and his environment have fixed his choice before he makes it.

The average man says "I know that I can act as I wish to act." But what causes him to wish? The free will party say, "We know that a man can and does choose between two acts." But what settles the choice?

There is a cause for every wish, a cause for every choice; and every cause of every wish and choice arises from heredity, or from environment.

For a man acts always from temperament, which is heredity, or from training, which is environment.

And in cases where a man hesitates in his choice between two acts, the hesitation is due to a conflict between his temperament and his training, or as some would express it, "between his desire and his conscience."

A man is practising at a target with a gun, when a rabbit crosses his line of fire. The man has his eye and his sights on the rabbit, and his finger on the trigger. The man's will is free. If he presses the trigger the rabbit will be killed.

Now, how does the man decide whether or not he shall fire? He decides by feeling, and by reason.

He would like to fire, just to make sure that he could hit the mark. He would like to fire, because he would like to have the rabbit for supper. He would like to fire, because there is in him the old, old hunting instinct, to kill.

But the rabbit does not belong to him. He is not sure that he will not get into trouble if he kills it. Perhaps—if he is a very uncommon kind of man—he feels that it would be cruel and cowardly to shoot a helpless rabbit.

Well. The man's will is free. He can fire if he likes: he can let the rabbit go if he likes. How will he decide? On what does his decision depend?

His decision depends upon the relative strength of his desire to kill the rabbit, and of his scruples about cruelty, and the law.

Not only that, but, if we knew the man fairly well, we could guess how his free will would act before it acted. The average sporting Briton would kill the rabbit. But we know that there are men who on no account shoot any harmless wild creature.

Broadly put, we may say that the sportsman would will to fire, and that the humanitarian would not will to fire.

Now, as both their wills are free, it must be something outside the wills that makes the difference.

Well. The sportsman will kill, because he is a sportsman: the humanitarian will not kill, because he is a humanitarian.

And what makes one man a sportsman and another a humanitarian? Heredity and environment: temperament and training.

One man is merciful, another cruel, by nature; or one is thoughtful and the other thoughtless, by nature. That is a difference of heredity.

One may have been taught all his life that to kill wild things is "sport"; the other may have been taught that it is inhuman and wrong: that is a difference of environment.

Now, the man by nature cruel or thoughtless, who has been trained to think of killing animals as sport, becomes what we call a sportsman, because heredity and environment have made him a sportsman.

The other man's heredity and environment have made him a humanitarian.

The sportsman kills the rabbit, because he is a sportsman, and he is a sportsman because heredity and environment have made him one.

That is to say the "free will" is really controlled by heredity and environment.

Allow me to give a case in point. A man who had never done any fishing was taken out by a fisherman. He liked the sport, and for some months followed it eagerly. But one day an accident brought home to his mind the cruelty of catching fish with a hook, and he instantly laid down his rod, and never fished again.

Before the change he was always eager to go fishing if invited: after the change he could not be persuaded to touch a line. His will was free all the while. How was it that his will to fish changed to his will not to fish? It was the result of environ-

ment. He had learnt that fishing was cruel. This knowledge controlled his will.

But, it may be asked, how do you account for a man doing the thing he does not wish to do? No man ever did a thing he did not wish to do. When there are two wishes the stronger rules.

Let us suppose a case. A young woman gets two letters by the same post; one is an invitation to go with her lover to a concert, the other is a request that she will visit a sick child in the slums. The girl is very fond of music, and is rather afraid of the slums. She wishes to go to the concert, and to be with her lover; she dreads the foul street and the dirty home, and shrinks from the risk of measles or fever. But she goes to the sick child, and she foregoes the concert. Why?

Because her sense of duty is stronger than her self-love.

Now, her sense of duty is partly due to her nature—that is, to her heredity—but it is chiefly due to environment. Like all of us, this girl was born without any kind of knowledge, and with only the rudiments of a conscience. But she has been well taught, and the teaching is part of her environment.

We may say that the girl is free to act as she chooses, but she *does* act as she has been *taught* that she *ought* to act. This teaching, which is part of her environment, controls her will.

We may say that a man is free to act as he chooses. He is free to act as *he* chooses, but *he* will choose as heredity and environment cause *him* to choose. For heredity and environment have made him that which he is. . . .

As we want to get this subject as clear as we can, let us take one or two familiar examples of the action of the will.

Jones and Robinson meet and have a glass of whisky. Jones asks Robinson to have another. Robinson says, "no thank you, one is enough." Jones says, "all right: have another cigarette." Robinson takes the cigarette. Now, here we have a case where a man refuses a second drink, but takes a second smoke. Is it because he would like another cigarette, but would not like another glass of whisky? No. It is because he knows that it is *safer* not to take another glass of whisky.

How does he know that whisky is dangerous? He has learnt it—from his environment.

"But he *could* have taken another glass if he wished."

But he could not wish to take another, because there was something he wished more strongly—to be safe.

And why did he want to be safe? Because he had learnt—from his environment—that it was unhealthy, unprofitable, and shameful to get drunk. Because he had learnt—from his environment—that it is easier to avoid forming a bad habit than to break a bad habit when formed. Because he valued the good opinion of his neighbors, and also his position and prospects.

These feelings and this knowledge ruled his will, and caused him to refuse the second glass. But there was no sense of danger, no well-learnt lesson of risk to check his will to smoke another cigarette. Heredity and environment did not warn him against that. So, to please his friend, and himself, he accepted.

Now suppose Smith asks Williams to have another glass. Williams takes it, takes several, finally goes home—as he often goes home. Why?

Largely because drinking is a habit with him. And not only does the mind instinctively repeat an action, but, in the case of drink, a physical craving is set up, and the brain is weakened. It is easier to refuse the first glass than the second; easier to refuse the second than the third; and it is very much harder for a man to keep sober who has frequently got drunk.

So, when poor Williams has to make his choice, he has habit against him, he has a physical craving against him, and he has a weakened brain to think with.

"But Williams could have refused the first glass."

No. Because in this case the desire to drink, or to please a friend, was stronger than his fear of the danger. Or he may not have been so conscious of the danger as Robinson was. He may not have been so well taught, or he may not have been so sensible, or he may not have been so cautious. So that his heredity and environment, his temperament and training, led him to take the drink, as surely as Robinson's heredity and environment led him to refuse it.

And now, it is my turn to ask a question. If the will is "free," if conscience is a sure guide, how is it that the free will and the conscience of Robinson caused him to keep sober, while the free will and the conscience of Williams caused him to get drunk?

Robinson's will was curbed by certain feelings which failed to curb the will of Williams. Because in the case of Williams the feelings were stronger on the other side.

It was the nature and the training of Robinson which made him refuse the second glass, and it was the nature of the training of Williams which made him drink the second glass.

What had free will to do with it?

We are told that *every* man has a free will, and a conscience.

Now, if Williams had been Robinson, that is to say if his heredity and his environment had been exactly like Robinson's, he would have done exactly as Robinson did.

It was because his heredity and environment were not the same that his act was not the same. Both men had free wills. What made one do what the other refused to do?

Heredity and environment. To reverse their conduct we should have to reverse their heredity and environment. . . .

And, again, as to that matter of belief. Some moralists hold that it is wicked not to believe certain things, and that men who do not believe those things will be punished.

But a man cannot believe a thing he is told to believe: he can only believe a thing which he *can* believe; and he can only believe that which his own reason tells him is true.

It would be no use asking Sir Roger Ball to believe that the earth is flat. He *could not* believe it.

It is no use asking an agnostic to believe the story of Jonah and the whale. He *could not* believe it. He might pretend to believe it. He might try to believe it. But his reason would not allow him to believe it.

Therefore it is a mistake to say that a man "knows better," when the fact is that he has been told "better" and cannot believe what he has been told.

That is a simple matter, and looks quite trivial; but how much ill-will, how much intolerance, how much violence, persecution, and murder have been caused by the strange idea that a man is wicked because *his* reason *cannot* believe that which to another man's reason seems quite true.

Free will has no power over a man's belief. A man cannot believe by will, but only by conviction. A man cannot be forced to believe. You may threaten him, wound him, beat him, burn him; and he may be frightened, or angered, or pained; but he cannot *believe,* nor can he be made to believe. Until he is convinced.

Now, truism as it may seem, I think it necessary to say here that a man cannot be convinced by abuse, nor by punishment. He can only be convinced by *reason.*

Yes. If we wish a man to believe a thing, we shall find a few words of reason more powerful than a million curses, or a million bayonets. To burn a man alive for failing to believe that the sun goes round the world is not to convince him. The fire is searching, but it does not seem to him to be relevant to the issue. He never doubted that fire would burn; but perchance his dying eyes may see the sun sinking down into the west, as the world rolls on its axis. He dies in his belief. And knows no "better." . . .

We are to ask whether it is true that everything a man does is the only thing he could do, at the instant of his doing it.

This is a very important question, because if the answer is yes, all praise and all blame are undeserved.

All praise and *all* blame.

Let us take some revolting action as a test.

A tramp has murdered a child on the highway, has robbed her of a few coppers, and has thrown her body into a ditch.

"Do you mean to say that tramp could not help doing that? Do you mean to say he is not to blame? Do you mean to say he is not to be punished?"

Yes. I say all those things; and if all those things are not true this book is not worth the paper it is printed on.

Prove it? I have proved it. But I have only instanced venial acts, and now we are confronted with murder. And the horror of murder drives men almost to frenzy, so that they cease to think: they can only feel.

Murder. Yes, a brutal murder. It comes upon us with a sickening shock. But I said in my first chapter that I proposed to defend those whom God and man condemn, and to demand justice for those whom God and man have wronged. I have to plead for the *bottom* dog: the lowest, the most detested, the worst.

The tramp has committed a murder. Man would loathe him, revile him, hang him: God would cast him into outer darkness.

"Not," cries the pious Christian, "if he repent."

I make a note of the repentance and pass on. The tramp has committed a murder. It was a cowardly and cruel murder, and the motive was robbery.

But I have proved that all motives and all powers; all knowledge and capacity, all acts and all words, are caused by heredity and environment. I have proved that a man can only be good or bad as heredity and environment cause him to be good or bad; and I have proved these things because I have to claim that all punishments and rewards, all praise and blame, are undeserved. . . . Punishment has never been just, has never been effectual. Punishment has always failed of its purpose: the greater its severity, the more abject its failure.

Men cannot be made good and gentle by means of violence and wrong. The real tamers and purifiers of human hearts are love and charity and reason. . . .

Suggestions for Further Reading

The articles entitled "Determinism," and "Behaviorism," in *The Cambridge Dictionary of Philosophy,* 2nd Edition, edited by Robert Audi (Cambridge: Cambridge University Press, 1999), will provide general background information.

For arguments in favor of hard determinism and its application to the judicial system, see Clarence Darrow, *Crime and Criminals* (New York: Charles H. Kerr, 1902).

B. F. Skinner, an influential psychologist, has touched on the issues of determinism, freedom, and control in a number of different writings. See his *Walden Two* (New York: Macmillan, 1948, 1976) and *Beyond Freedom and Dignity* (New York: Knopf, 1972) for popular and controversial treatments.

More recent versions of hard determinism are associated with sociobiology. Sociobiology claims that all forms of social behavior can be biologically explained. The literature is extensive, but see E. O. Wilson's *Sociobiology: The New Synthesis* (Cambridge: Belknap, 1975). For a philosophical discussion, a critique, and a good bibliography, see Michael Ruse's *Sociobiology: Sense or Nonsense?*, 2nd Edition (Dordrecht: Reidel, 1985).

For a collection of essays dealing with various positions, see *Determinism and Freedom in the Age of Modern Science,* edited by Sidney Hook (New York: New York University Press, 1958).

Also, Ted Honderich's *How Free Are You? The Determinism Problem* (New York: Oxford University Press, 1993) will take you into deeper waters.

Videos

A Clockwork Orange (137 minutes; produced by Warner Home Video) illustrates, in a futuristic setting, how behavioral techniques can be used to modify destructive behavior. See your Media Services Catalog for more information.

Genetic Prophecy (26 minutes) and *Science, Society, and the Human Genome Project* (46 minutes), both available from Films for the Humanities and Sciences (PO Box 2053, Princeton, NJ 08543), explore the ethical implications of research on genes.

10.3 We Are Free

Some of you may find hard determinism unconvincing. Some of you might still be wondering whether we are free in the sense that our choices are *not* always caused or determined by heredity or environment.

Libertarianism is the position that some human choices, in particular moral choices for which we are responsible, are not determined by antecedent events. (Note: This kind of libertarianism should *not* be confused with the political movement and theory of the same name.) One version of this theory holds that the self (sometimes called "soul") is an agent with a power to choose that transcends heredity and environment in the sense that the self can choose contrary to these factors. Another version holds that humans are radically free in the sense that they are free to create their own self. The self is not a fixed essence determined by heredity, environment, or any other factor except our capacity for choice. We create who we are (our selves) by the choices we make. It follows that humans, when freely deciding to act in a particular way, not only can be but also ought to be held responsible for what they do.

Jean-Paul Sartre (1905–1980) was a French novelist, playwright, and philosopher. In 1939 he was called up by the French army to fight the German invasion. He was captured by the Germans in 1940 but returned to France after the armistice and became active in the resistance movement. After the war, he emerged as a leading French intellectual, a major figure in the philosophical movement called **existentialism**, and he became involved in a number of radical causes. His major philosophical work is *Being and Nothingness* (1943).

In 1945 Sartre gave a lecture that was published the following year as *L'Existentialisme est un Humanisme*. The selection that follows is from that lecture. Sartre is not only concerned with defining existentialism and defending it against its critics, but he is also concerned with free choice. Sartre realizes that, if human nature is not something determined beforehand but is something we create as we make the decisions that come to constitute our lives, we are radically free. This is central to the existentialist view of human beings and, as Sartre also clearly realizes, has important implications for ethics. If you are free to do whatever you wish, if for you everything is permissible, then what will you do?

Reading Questions

1. What does *existence precedes essence* mean?
2. What is the first principle of existentialism?
3. Why does Sartre claim that "In choosing myself, I choose man"?
4. What is meant by *anguish?*
5. What does *forlornness* mean?
6. Do you agree with the contention that "everything is permissible if God does not exist"? Why, or why not?
7. Why does Sartre say we are *condemned* to be free?
8. What is meant by *despair?*
9. If we create moral value and there is no guarantee that our values are correct or will produce good results, why bother to become socially and politically involved at all? How does Sartre answer this question? Do you agree with his answer? Why, or why not?

Existentialism

JEAN-PAUL SARTRE

WHAT IS MEANT BY THE TERM EXISTEN-TIALISM? Most people who use the word would be rather embarrassed if they had to explain it, since, now that the word is all the rage, even the work of a musician or painter is being called existentialist. A gossip columnist in *Clartés* signs himself *The Existentialist,* so that by this time the word has been so stretched and has taken on so broad a meaning that it no longer means anything at all. It seems that for want of an advance-guard doctrine analogous to surrealism, the kind of people who are eager for scandal and flurry

Jean-Paul Sartre, Existentialism, *translated by Bernard Frechtman (New York: The Philosophical Library, 1947), pp. 14–42. Reprinted by permission of The Philosophical Library, Inc.*

turn to this philosophy which in other respects does not at all serve their purposes in this sphere.

Actually, it is the least scandalous, the most austere of doctrines. It is intended strictly for specialists and philosophers. Yet it can be defined easily. What complicates matters is that there are two kinds of existentialist; first, those who are Christian, among whom I would include Jaspers and Gabriel Marcel, both Catholic; and on the other hand the atheistic existentialists, among whom I class Heidegger, and then the French existentialists and myself. What they have in common is that they think that existence precedes essence, or, if you prefer, that subjectivity must be the starting point.

Just what does that mean? Let us consider some object that is manufactured, for example, a book or a paper-cutter: here is an object which has been made by an artisan whose inspiration came from a concept. He referred to the concept of what a paper-cutter is and likewise to a known method of production, which is part of the concept, something which is, by and large, a routine. Thus, the paper-cutter is at once an object produced in a certain way and, on the other hand, one having a specific use; and one can not postulate a man who produces a paper-cutter but does not know what it is used for. Therefore, let us say that, for the paper-cutter, essence—that is, the ensemble of both the production routines and the properties which enable it to be both produced and defined—precedes existence. Thus, the presence of the paper-cutter or book in front of me is determined. Therefore, we have here a technical view of the world whereby it can be said that production precedes existence.

When we conceive God as the Creator, He is generally thought of as a superior sort of artisan. Whatever doctrine we may be considering, whether one like that of Descartes or that of Leibniz, we always grant that will more or less follows understanding or, at the very least, accompanies it, and that when God creates He knows exactly what He is creating. Thus, the concept of man in the mind of God is comparable to the concept of paper-cutter in the mind of the manufacturer, and, following certain techniques and a conception, God produces man, just as the artisan, following a definition and a technique, makes a paper-cutter. Thus, the individual man is the realization of a certain concept in the divine intelligence.

In the eighteenth century, the atheism of the *philosophes* discarded the idea of God, but not so much for the notion that essence precedes existence. To a certain extent, this idea is found everywhere; we find it in Diderot, in Voltaire, and even in Kant. Man has a human nature; this human nature, which is the concept of the human, is found in all men, which means that each man is a particular example of a universal concept, man. In Kant, the result of this universality is that the wild-man, the natural man, as well as the bourgeois, are circumscribed by the same definition and have the same basic qualities. Thus, here too the essence of man precedes the historical existence that we find in nature.

Atheistic existentialism, which I represent, is more coherent. It states that if God does not exist, there is at least one being in whom existence precedes essence, a being who exists before he can be defined by any concept, and that this being is man, or, as Heidegger says, human reality. What is meant here by saying that existence precedes essence? It means that, first of all, man exists, turns up, appears on the scene, and, only afterwards, defines himself. If man, as the existentialist conceives him, is indefinable, it is because at first he is nothing. Only afterward will he be something, and he himself will have made what he will be. Thus, there is no human nature, since there is no God to conceive it. Not only is man what he conceives himself to be, but he is also only what he wills himself to be after this thrust toward existence.

Man is nothing else but what he makes of himself. Such is the first principle of existentialism. It is also what is called subjectivity, the name we are labeled with when charges are brought against us. But what do we mean by this, if not that man has a greater dignity than a stone or table? For we mean that man first exists, that is, that man first of all is the being who hurls himself toward a future and who is conscious of imagining himself as being in the future. Man is at the start a plan which is aware of itself, rather than a patch of moss, a piece of garbage, or a cauliflower; nothing exists prior to this plan; there is nothing in heaven; man will be what he will have planned to be. Not what he will want to be. Because by the word "will" we generally mean a conscious decision, which is subsequent to what we have already made of ourselves. I may want to belong to a political party, write a book, get married; but all that is only a manifestation of an earlier, more spontaneous choice that is called "will." But if existence really does precede essence, man is responsible for what he is. Thus, existentialism's first move is to make every man aware of what he is and to make the full responsibility of his existence rest on him. And when we say that a man is responsible for himself, we do not only mean that he is responsible for his own individuality, but that he is responsible for all men.

The word subjectivism has two meanings, and our opponents play on the two. Subjectivism means, on the one hand, that an individual chooses and makes himself; and, on the other, that it is impossible for man to transcend human subjectivity. The second of these is the essential meaning of existentialism. When we say that man chooses his own self, we mean that every one of us does likewise; but we also mean by that that in making this choice he also chooses all men. In fact, in creating the man that we want to be, there is not a single one of our acts which does not at the same time create an image of man as we think he ought to be. To choose to be this or that is to affirm at the same time the value of what we choose, because we can never choose evil. We always choose the good, and nothing can be good for us without being good for all. If, on the other hand, existence precedes essence, and if we grant that we exist and fashion our image at one and the same time, the image is valid for everybody and for our whole age. Thus, our responsibility is much greater than we might have supposed, because it involves all mankind. If I am a working man and choose to join a Christian trade-union rather than be a communist, and if by being a member I want to show that the best thing for man is resignation, that the kingdom of man is not of this world, I am not only involving my own case—I want to be resigned for everyone.

As a result, my action has involved all humanity. To take a more individual matter, if I want to marry, to have children; even if this marriage depends solely on my own circumstances or passion or wish, I am involving all humanity in monogamy and not merely myself. Therefore, I am responsible for myself and for everyone else. I am creating a certain image of man of my own choosing. In choosing myself, I choose man.

This helps us understand what the actual content is of such rather grandiloquent words as anguish, forlornness, despair. As you will see, it's all quite simple.

First, what is meant by anguish? The existentialists say at once that man is anguish. What that means is this: the man who involves himself and who realizes that he is not only the person he chooses to be, but also a law-maker who is, at the same time, choosing all mankind as well as himself, can not help escape the feeling of his total and deep responsibility. Of course, there are many people who are not anxious; but we claim that they are hiding their anxiety, that they are fleeing from it. Certainly, many people believe that when they do something, they themselves are the only ones involved, and when someone says to them, "What if everyone acted that way?" they shrug their shoulders and answer, "Everyone doesn't act that way." But really, one should always ask himself, "What would happen if everybody looked at things that way?" There is no escaping this disturbing thought except by a kind of double-dealing. A man who lies and makes excuses for himself by saying "not everybody does that," is someone with an uneasy conscience, because the act of lying implies that a universal value is conferred upon the lie.

Anguish is evident even when it conceals itself. This is the anguish that Kierkegaard called the anguish of Abraham. You know the story: an angel has ordered Abraham to sacrifice his son; if it really were an angel who has come and said, "You are Abraham, you shall sacrifice your son," everything would be all right. But everyone might first wonder, "Is it really an angel, and am I really Abraham? What proof do I have?"

There was a madwoman who had hallucinations; someone used to speak to her on the telephone and give her orders. Her doctor asked her, "Who is it who talks to you?" She answered, "He says it's God." What proof did she really have that it was God? If an angel comes to me, what proof is there that it's an angel? And if I hear voices, what proof is there that they come from heaven and not from hell, or from the subconscious, or a pathological condition? What proves that they are addressed to me? What proof is there that I have been appointed to impose my choice and my conception of man on humanity? I'll never find any proof or sign to convince me of that. If a voice addresses me, it is always for me to decide that this is the angel's voice; if I consider that such an act is a good one, it is I who will choose to say that it is good rather than bad. Now, I'm not being singled out as an Abraham, and yet at every moment I'm obliged to perform exemplary acts. For every man, everything happens as if all mankind had its eyes fixed on him and were guiding itself by what he does. And every man ought to say to himself, "Am I really the kind of man who has the right to act in such a way that humanity might guide itself by my actions?" And if he does not say that to himself, he is masking his anguish.

There is no question here of the kind of anguish which would lead to quietism, to inaction. It is a matter of a simple sort of anguish that anybody who has had responsibilities is familiar with. For example, when a military officer takes the responsibility for an attack and sends a certain number of men to death, he chooses to do so, and in the main he alone makes the choice. Doubtless, orders come from above, but they are too broad; he interprets them, and on this interpretation depend the lives of ten or fourteen or twenty men. In making a decision he can not help having a certain anguish. All leaders know this anguish. That doesn't keep them from acting; on the contrary, it is the very condition of their action. For it implies that they envisage a number of possibilities, and when they choose one, they realize that it has value only because it is chosen. We shall see that this kind of anguish, which is the kind that existentialism describes, is explained, in addition, by a direct responsibility to the other men whom it involves. It is not a curtain separating us from action, but is part of action itself.

When we speak of forlornness, a term Heidegger was fond of, we mean only that God does not exist and that we have to face all the consequences of this. The existentialist is strongly opposed to a certain kind of secular ethics which would like to abolish God with the least possible expense. About 1880, some French teachers tried to set up a secular ethics which went something like this: God is a useless and costly hypothesis; we are discarding it; but, meanwhile, in order for there to be an ethics, a society, a civilization, it is essential that certain values be taken seriously and that they be considered as having an *a priori* existence. It must be obligatory, *a priori,* to be honest, not to lie, not to beat your wife, to have children, etc. So we're going to try a little device which will make it possible to show that values exist all the same, inscribed in a heaven of ideas, though otherwise God does not exist. In other words—and this, I believe, is the tendency of everything called reformism in France—nothing will be changed if God does not exist. We shall find ourselves with the same norms of honesty, progress, and humanism, and we shall have made of God an outdated hypothesis which will peacefully die off by itself.

The existentialist, on the contrary, thinks it very distressing that God does not exist, because all possibility of finding values in a heaven of ideas disappears along with Him; there can no longer be an *a priori* Good, since there is no infinite and perfect consciousness to think it. Nowhere is it written that the Good exists, that we must be honest, that we must not lie; because the fact is we are on a plane where there are only men. Dostoievsky said, "If God didn't exist, everything would be possible." That is the very starting point of existentialism. Indeed, everything is permissible if God does not exist, and as a result man is forlorn, because neither within him or without does he find anything to cling to. He can't start making excuses for himself.

If existence really does precede essence, there is no explaining things away by reference to a fixed and given human nature. In other words, there is no determinism, man is free, man is freedom. On the other hand, if God does not exist, we find no values or commands to turn to which legitimize our conduct. So, in the bright realm of values, we have no excuse behind us, nor justification before us. We are alone, with no excuses.

That is the idea I shall try to convey when I say that man is condemned to be free. Condemned, because he did not create himself, yet, in other respects is free; because, once thrown into the world, he is responsible for everything he does. The existentialist does not believe in the power of passion. He will never agree that a sweeping passion is a ravaging torrent which fatally leads a man to certain acts and is therefore an excuse. He thinks that man is responsible for his passion.

The existentialist does not think that man is going to help himself by finding in the world some omen by which to orient himself. Because he thinks that man will interpret the omen to suit himself. Therefore, he thinks that man, with no support and no aid, is condemned every moment to invent man. Ponge, in a very fine article, has said, "Man is the future of man." That's exactly it. But if it is taken to mean that this future is recorded in heaven, that God sees it, then it is false, because it would really no longer be a future. If it is taken to mean that, whatever a man may be, there is a future to be forged, a virgin future before him, then this remark is sound. But then we are forlorn.

To give you an example which will enable you to understand forlornness better, I shall cite the case of one of my students who came to see me under the following circumstances: His father was on bad terms with his mother, and, moreover, was inclined to be a collaborationist; his older brother had been killed in the German offensive of 1940, and the young man, with somewhat immature but generous feelings, wanted to avenge him. His mother lived alone with him, very much upset by the half-treason of her husband and the death of her older son; the boy was her only consolation.

The boy was faced with the choice of leaving for England and joining the Free French Forces—that is, leaving his mother behind—or remaining with his mother and helping her to carry on. He was fully aware that the woman lived only for him and that his going-off—and perhaps his death—would plunge her into despair. He was also aware that every act that he did for his mother's sake was a sure thing, in the sense that it was helping her to carry on, whereas every effort he made toward going off and fighting was an uncertain move which might run aground and prove completely useless; for example, on his way to England he might, while passing through Spain, be detained indefinitely in a Spanish camp; he might reach England or Algiers and be stuck in an office at a desk job. As a result, he was faced with two very different kinds of action: one, concrete, immediate, but concerning only one individual; the other concerned an incomparably vaster group, a national collectivity, but for that very reason was dubious, and might be interrupted en route. And, at the same time, he was wavering between two kinds of ethics. On the one hand, an ethics of sympathy, of personal devotion; on the other, a broader ethics, but one whose efficacy was more dubious. He had to choose between the two.

Who could help him choose? Christian doctrine? No. Christian doctrine says, "Be charitable, love your neighbor, take the more rugged path, etc." But which is the more rugged path? Whom should he love as a brother? The fighting man or his mother? Which does the greater good, the vague act of fighting in a group, or the concrete one of helping a particular human being to go on living? Who can decide *a priori*? Nobody. No book of ethics can tell him. The Kantian ethics says, "Never treat any person as a means, but as an end." Very well, if I stay with my mother, I'll treat her as an end and not as a means; but by virtue of this very fact, I'm running the risk of treating the people around me who are fighting, as means; and, conversely, if I go to join those who are fighting, I'll be treating them as an end, and, by doing that, I run the risk of treating my mother as a means.

If values are vague, and if they are always too broad for the concrete and specific case that we are considering, the only thing left for us is to trust our instincts. That's what this young man tried to do; and when I saw him, he said, "In the end, feeling is what counts. I ought to choose whichever pushes me in one direction. If I feel that I love my mother enough to sacrifice everything else for her—my desire for vengeance, for action, for adventure—then I'll stay with her. If, on the contrary, I feel that my love for my mother isn't enough, I'll leave."

But how is the value of a feeling determined? What gives his feeling for his mother value? Precisely the fact that he remained with her. I may say that I like so-and-so well enough to sacrifice a certain amount of money for him, but I may say so only if I've done it. I may say "I love my mother well enough to remain with her" if I have remained with her. The only way to determine the value of this affection is, precisely, to perform an act which confirms and defines it. But, since I require this affection to justify my act, I find myself caught in a vicious circle.

On the other hand, Gide has well said that a mock feeling and a true feeling are almost indistinguishable; to decide that I love my mother and will remain with her, or to remain with her by putting on an act, amount somewhat to the same thing. In other words, the feeling is formed by the acts one performs; so, I can not refer to it in order to act upon it. Which means that I can neither seek within myself the true condition which will impel me to act, nor apply to a system of ethics for concepts which will permit me to act. You will say, "At least, he did go to a teacher for advice." But if you seek advice from a priest, for example, you have chosen this priest; you already knew, more or less, just about what advice he was going to give you. In other words, choosing your adviser is involving yourself. The proof of this is that if you are a Christian, you will say, "Consult a priest." But some priests are collaborating, some are just marking time, some are resisting. Which to choose? If the young man chooses a priest who is resisting or collaborating, he has already decided on the kind of advice he's going to get. Therefore, in coming to see me he knew the answer I was going to give him, and I had only one answer to give: "You're free; choose, that is, invent." No general ethics can show you what is to be done; there are no omens in the world. The Catholics will reply, "But there are."

Granted—but, in any case, I myself choose the meaning they have.

When I was a prisoner, I knew a rather remarkable young man who was a Jesuit. He had entered the Jesuit order in the following way: he had had a number of very bad breaks; in childhood, his father died, leaving him in poverty, and he was a scholarship student at a religious institution where he was constantly made to feel that he was being kept out of charity; then, he failed to get any of the honors and distinctions that children like; later on, at about eighteen, he bungled a love affair; finally, at twenty-two, he failed in military training, a childish enough matter, but it was the last straw.

This young fellow might well have felt that he had botched everything. It was a sign of something, but of what? He might have taken refuge in bitterness or despair. But he very wisely looked upon all this as a sign that he was not made for secular triumphs, and that only the triumphs of religion, holiness, and faith were open to him. He saw the hand of God in all this, and so he entered the order. Who can help seeing that he alone decided what the sign meant?

Some other interpretation might have been drawn from this series of setbacks; for example, that he might have done better to turn carpenter or revolutionist. Therefore, he is fully responsible for the interpretation. Forlornness implies that we ourselves choose our being. Forlornness and anguish go together.

As for despair, the term has a very simple meaning. It means that we shall confine ourselves to reckoning only with what depends upon our will, or on the ensemble of probabilities which make our action possible. When we want something, we always have to reckon with probabilities. I may be counting on the arrival of a friend. The friend is coming by rail or street-car; this supposes that the train will arrive on schedule, or that the street-car will not jump the track. I am left in the realm of possibility; but possibilities are to be reckoned with only to the point where my action comports with the ensemble of these possibilities, and no further. The moment the possibilities I am considering are not rigorously involved by my action, I ought to disengage myself from them, because no God, no scheme, can adapt the world and its possibilities to my will. When Descartes said, "Conquer yourself rather than the world," he meant essentially the same thing.

The Marxists to whom I have spoken reply, "You can rely on the support of others in your action, which obviously has certain limits because you're not going to live forever. That means: rely on both what others are doing elsewhere to help you, in China, in Russia, and what they will do later on, after your death, to carry on the action and lead it to its fulfillment, which will be the revolution. You even *have* to rely upon that, otherwise you're immoral." I reply at once that I will always rely on fellow-fighters insofar as these comrades are involved with me in a common struggle, in the unity of a party or a group in which I can more or less make my weight felt; that is, one whose ranks I am in as a fighter and whose movements I am aware of at every moment. In such a situation, relying on the unity and will of the party is exactly like counting on the fact that the train will arrive on time or that the car won't jump the track. But, given that man is free and that there is no human nature for me to depend on, I can not count on men whom I do not know by relying on human goodness or man's concern for the good of society. I don't know what will become of the Russian revolution; I may make an example of it to the extent that at the present time it is apparent that the proletariat plays a part in Russia that it plays in no other nation. But I can't swear that this will inevitably lead to a triumph of the proletariat. I've got to limit myself to what I see.

Given that men are free and that tomorrow they will freely decide what man will be, I can not be sure that, after my death, fellow-fighters will carry on my work to bring it to its maximum perfection. Tomorrow, after my death, some men may decide to set up Fascism, and the others may be cowardly and muddled enough to let them do it. Fascism will then be the human reality, so much the worse for us.

Actually, things will be as man will have decided they are to be. Does that mean that I should abandon myself to quietism? No. First, I should involve myself; then, act on the old saw, "Nothing ventured, nothing gained." Nor does it mean that I shouldn't belong to a party, but rather that I shall have no illusions and shall do what I can. For example, suppose I ask myself, "Will socialization, as such, ever come about?" I know nothing about it. All I know is that I'm going to do everything in my power to bring it about. Beyond that, I can't count on anything. Quietism is the attitude of people who say, "Let others do what I can't do." The doctrine I am presenting is the very opposite of quietism, since it declares, "There is no reality except in action." Moreover, it goes further, since it adds, "Man is nothing else than his plan; he exists only to the extent that he fulfills himself; he is therefore nothing else than the ensemble of his acts, nothing else than his life."

According to this, we can understand why our doctrine horrifies certain people. Because often the only way they can bear their wretchedness is to think, "Circumstances have been against me. What I've been and done doesn't show my true worth. To be sure, I've had no great love, no great friendship, but that's because I haven't met a man or woman who was worthy. The books I've written haven't been very good because I haven't had the proper leisure. I haven't had children to devote myself to because I didn't find a man with whom I could have spent my life. So there remains within me, unused and quite viable, a host of propensities, inclinations, possibilities, that one wouldn't guess from, the mere series of things I've done."

Now, for the existentialist there is really no love other than one which manifests itself in a person's being in love. There is no genius other than one which is expressed in works of art; the genius of Proust is the sum of Proust's works; the genius of Racine is his series of tragedies. Outside of that, there is nothing. Why say that Racine could have written another tragedy, when he didn't write it? A man is involved in life, leaves his impress on it, and outside of that there is nothing. To be sure, this may seem a harsh thought to someone whose life hasn't been a success. But, on the other hand, it prompts people to understand that reality alone is what counts, that dreams, expectations, and hopes warrant no more than to define a man as a disappointed dream, as miscarried hopes, as vain expectations. In other words, to define him negatively and not positively. However, when we say, "You are nothing else than your life," that does not imply that the artist will be judged solely on the basis of his works of art; a thousand other things will contribute toward summing him up. What we mean is that a man is nothing else than a series of undertakings, that he is the sum, the organization, the ensemble of the relationships which make up these undertakings.

When all is said and done, what we are accused of, at bottom, is not our pessimism, but an optimistic toughness. If people throw up to us our works of fiction in which we write about people who are soft, weak, cowardly, and sometimes even downright bad, it's not because these people are soft, weak, cowardly, or bad; because if we were to say, as Zola did, that they are that way because of heredity, the workings of environment, society, because of biological or psychological determinism, people would be reassured. They would say, "Well, that's what we're like, no one can do anything about it." But when the existentialist writes about a coward, he says that this coward is responsible for his cowardice. He's not like that because he has a cowardly heart or lung or brain; he's not like that on account of his physiological makeup; but he's like that because he has made himself a coward by his acts. There's no such thing as a cowardly constitution; there are nervous constitutions; there is poor blood, as the common people say, or strong constitutions. But the man whose blood is poor is not a coward on that account, for what makes cowardice is the act of renouncing or yielding. A constitution is not an act; the coward is defined on the basis of the acts he performs. People feel, in a vague sort of way, that this coward we're talking about is guilty of being a coward, and the thought frightens them. What people would like is that a coward or a hero be born that way.

One of the complaints most frequently made about *The Ways of Freedom** can be summed up as follows: "After all, these people are so spineless, how are you going to make heroes out of them?" This objection almost makes me laugh, for it assumes that people are born heroes. That's what people really want to think. If you're born cowardly, you may set your mind perfectly at rest; there's nothing you can do about it; you'll be cowardly all your life, whatever you may do. If you're born a hero, you may set your mind just as much at rest; you'll be a hero all your life; you'll drink like a hero and eat like a hero. What the existentialist says is that the coward makes himself cowardly, that the hero makes himself heroic. There's always a possibility for the coward not to be cowardly any more and for the hero to stop being heroic. What counts is total involvement; some one particular action or set of circumstances is not total involvement.

Thus, I think we have answered a number of the charges concerning existentialism. You see that it can not be taken for a philosophy of quietism, since it defines man in terms of action; nor for a pessimistic description of man—there is no doctrine more optimistic, since man's destiny is within himself; nor for an attempt to discourage man from acting, since it tells him that the only hope is in his acting and that action is the only thing that enables a man to live. Consequently, we are dealing here with an ethics of action and involvement. . . .

**Les Chemins de la Liberté*. M. Sartre's projected trilogy of novels, two of which, *L'Age de Raison* (*The Age of Reason*) and *Le Sursis* (*The Reprieve*) have already appeared.—Translator's note.

Suggestions for Further Reading

On the Web you can find useful background information on Sartre at http://www.blupete.com/Literature/Biographies/Philosophy/Sartre.

The Philosophy of Jean-Paul Sartre, edited and introduced by Robert Denoon Cumming (New York: Random House, 1965), provides a good collection of primary sources and a helpful introduction to major themes in Sartre's philosophy.

For in-depth analysis and an excellent bibliography see volume XVI in *The Library of Living Philosophers* devoted to *The Philosophy of Jean-Paul Sartre* edited by Paul Arthur Schilpp (Chicago: Open Court, 1990).

For a different sort of libertarian position, one that views human freedom as far more limited than Sartre, see Susan L. Anderson, "The Libertarian Conception of Freedom," *International Philosophical Quarterly* 21 (1981): 391–404. Her bibliography will lead you into the standard philosophical literature on the topic.

The article on the "Free Will Problem" in *The Cambridge Dictionary of Philosophy,* 2nd Edition, edited by Robert Audi (Cambridge: Cambridge University Press, 1999), will provide a good overview.

For a discussion of different varieties of libertarianism as well as other issues related to the free will problem see Laura Waddell Ekstrom, *Free Will: A Philosophical Study* (Boulder, CO: Westview Press, 2000).

Videos

Existentialism (35 minutes) surveys the ideas of Kierkegaard, Nietzsche, Sartre, and Camus. *No Excuses: Existentialism and the Meaning of Life* (8 lectures, 45 minutes each) features Robert Solomon discussing existentialist philosophy. These are available from Insight Media, 2162 Broadway, New York, NY 10024.

Films for the Humanities and Sciences (PO Box 2053, Princeton, NJ 08543) offers a four-part series (52 minutes each) on *French Intellectuals in the 20th Century.*

10.4 Karma and Freedom

The contemporary Western discussion of the problem of freedom and determinism usually takes place in the context of the natural and social sciences. Many philosophers believe that some type of determinism is one of the basic assumptions of science. If it is, then the scene is set for a conflict between a scientific view and the moral or religious view of human freedom and responsibility. The law of causality, as understood by science, is an amoral law. That is, it operates regardless of moral considerations. The social or behavioral sciences (psychology, sociology, anthropology, economics, and history) have extended this view to human behavior. They assume that human action, like physical action, is understandable only when the causal factors determining such action are described and explained by reference to some kind of "natural" law.

In the Asian (primarily Indian) context, the discussion of the problem of freedom and determinism often takes place in a moral and religious context. The law of causality that concerns much Indian and Buddhist philosophy is moral, not amoral. Very early in Indian philosophy (500 BCE?), the idea of the *law of karma* developed. This law states that as each of us sows, so shall we reap. If this law is valid, then your past and present actions determine your future spiritual, moral, and physical conditions. If there is a life beyond this one, then your actions also determine it.

The teaching of karma posits the existence of a perfect law of moral justice that operates automatically within the universe. Habitual liars in this life, for example, will pay for lying in the future. Perhaps they will be falsely accused at some future date or, when reborn, will have relatives who lie, cheat, and deceive them. In contrast, an honest person will be treated honestly by others.

The law of karma provides a good deal of comfort. It assures us that the universe is a just place. It tells us that evil people and good people will eventually get their just deserts. However, the notion of karma also raises questions about human freedom. If what is happening to me now is the effect of my own actions in the past, how can I be free? Are not my life and the circumstances of my life determined? It seems to be the case, according to the law of karma, that, for example, if you are poor, this condition is due to what you did in the past, and hence, it would seem, you are no more in control of your poverty than you are in control of the orbit of Earth.

Some Indian philosophers have drawn fatalistic conclusions from the doctrine of karma and have denied human freedom. The majority of Indian philosophers, however, have affirmed human freedom and argued that freedom and karma are compatible ideas. One such philosopher was Sarvepalli Radhakrishnan (1888–1975), a scholar and statesman who held chairs of philosophy at several Indian universities and was president of India from 1962 until 1967. He was a leading exponent of neo-Hinduism, maintaining that all religions are but different expressions of one truth and that spiritual reality is more fundamental than material reality. The following selection comes from his book *An Idealist View of Life,* which contains his Hibbert lectures given in 1929 and 1930.

Radhakrishnan supports a type of libertarianism. Though he believes that human action is determined to a large extent (and hence would not subscribe to Sartre's radical libertarianism), he also believes in self-determination. If a choice is caused by the whole self, rather than part of the self (such as character or environment), such choice is free. In other words, he subscribes to what is often called *agent causation.* When your self (not a part of your self but your whole self) is the agent that causes you to choose and act, then you are free. A crucial question now becomes, what is the self?

Reading Questions

1. According to Radhakrishnan, what is the law of karma?
2. What are the two aspects of karma?
3. How does Radhakrishnan define *freedom of the will?*
4. What does he mean by *self-determination?*
5. How does he respond to the argument that self-determination is not really freedom?
6. How does he define *choice?*
7. Does the author's assertion that even though "the self is not free from the bonds of determination, it can subjugate the past to a certain extent and turn it into a new course" make sense?
8. Do you think Radhakrishnan's analogy with a game of bridge is a good one? Why, or why not?
9. Name one thing you learned from reading this selection that you did not know before.

Karma and Freedom

SARVEPALLI RADHAKRISHNAN

THE TWO PERVASIVE features of all nature, connection with the past and creation of the future, are present in the human level. The connection with the past at the human stage is denoted by the word "Karma" in the Hindu systems. The human individual is a self-conscious, efficient portion of universal nature with his own uniqueness. His history stretching back to an indefinite period of time binds him with the physical and vital conditions of the world. Human life is an organic whole where each successive phase grows out of what has gone before. We are what we are on account of our affinity with the past. Human growth is an ordered one and its orderedness is indicated by saying that it is governed by the law of Karma.

Karma literally means action, deed. All acts produce their effects which are recorded both in the organism and the environment. Their physical effects may be short-lived but their moral effects (samsskāra) are worked into the character of the self. Every single thought, word and deed enters into the living chain of causes which makes us what we are. Our life is not at the mercy of blind chance or capricious fate. The conception is not peculiar to the Oriental creeds. The Christian Scriptures refer to it. "Be not deceived; God is not mocked: for whatsoever a man soweth, that shall he also reap." Jesus is reported to have said on the Mount, "Judge not that ye be not judged, for with what judgment ye judge, ye shall be judged, and with what measure ye mete, it shall be measured to you again."

Karma is not so much a principle of retribution as one of continuity. Good produces good, evil, evil. Love increases our power of love, hatred our power of hatred. It emphasizes the great importance of right action. Man is continuously shaping his own self. The law of Karma is not to be confused with either a hedonistic or a juridical theory of rewards and punishments. The reward for virtue is not a life of pleasure nor is the punishment for sin pain. Pleasure and pain may govern the animal nature of man but not his human. Love which is a joy in itself suffers; hatred too often means a perverse kind of satisfaction. Good and evil are not to be confused with material well-being and physical suffering.

All things in the world are at once causes and effects. They embody the energy of the past and exert energy on the future. Karma or connection with the past is not inconsistent with creative freedom. On the other hand it is implied by it. The law that links us with the past also asserts that it can be subjugated by our free action. Though the past may present obstacles, they must all yield to the creative power in man in proportion to its sincerity and insistence. The law of Karma says that each individual will get the return according to the energy he puts forth. The universe will respond to and implement the demands of the self. Nature will reply to the insistent call of spirit. "As is his desire, such is his purpose; as is his purpose, such is the action he performs; what action he performs, that he procures for himself." "Verily I say unto you that whoever shall say to this mountain, 'Be lifted up and cast into the sea,' and shall not doubt in his heart but believe fully that what he says shall be, it shall be done for him." When Jesus said, "Destroy this temple and I will raise it again in three days" he is asserting the truth that the spirit within us is mightier than the world of things. There is nothing we cannot achieve if we want it enough. Subjection to spirit is the law of universal nature. The principle of Karma has thus two aspects, a retrospective and a prospective,

From S. Radhakrishnan's An Idealist View of Life *(London: George Allen & Unwin, 1932), pp. 218–223. Reproduced by kind permission of Unwin Hyman, an imprint of HarperCollins Publishers Limited. Footnotes deleted.*

continuity with the past and creative freedom of the self.

The urge in nature which seeks not only to maintain itself at a particular level but advance to a higher becomes conscious in man who deliberately seeks after rules of life and principles of progress. "My father worketh hitherto, and I work." Human beings are the first among nature's children who can say "I" and consciously collaborate with the "father," the power that controls and directs nature, in the fashioning of the world. They can substitute rational direction for the slow, dark, blundering growth of the subhuman world. We cannot deny the free action of human beings however much their origin may be veiled in darkness. The self has conative tendencies, impulses to change by its efforts the given conditions, inner and outer, and shape them to its own purpose.

The problem of human freedom is confused somewhat by the distinction between the self and the will. The will is only the self in its active side and freedom of the will really means the freedom of the self. It is determination by the self.

It is argued that self-determination is not really freedom. It makes little difference whether the self is moved from without or from within. A spinning top moved from within by a spring is as mechanical as one whipped into motion from without. The self may well be an animated automaton. A drunkard who takes to his glass habitually does so in obedience to an element in his nature. The habit has become a part of his self. If we analyze the contents of the self, many of them are traceable to the influence of the environment and the inheritance from the past. If the individual's view and character are the product of a long evolution, his actions which are the outcome of these cannot be free. The feeling of freedom may be an illusion of the self which lives in each moment of the present, ignoring the determining past. In answer to these difficulties, it may be said that the self represents a form of relatedness or organization, closer and more intimate than that which is found in animal, plant or atom. Self-determination means not determination by any fragment of the self's nature but by the whole of it. Unless the individual employs his whole nature, searches the different possibilities and selects one which commends itself to his whole self, the act is not really free.

Sheer necessity is not to be found in any aspect of nature; complete freedom is divine and possible only when the self becomes co-extensive with the whole. Human freedom is a matter of degree. We are most free when our whole self is active and not merely a fragment of it. We generally act according to our conventional or habitual self and sometimes we sink to the level of our subnormal self.

Freedom is not caprice, nor is Karma necessity. Human choice is not unmotivated or uncaused. If our acts were irrelevant to our past, then there would be no moral responsibility or scope for improvement. Undetermined beginnings, upstart events are impossible either in the physical or the human world. Free acts cannot negate continuity. They arise within the order of nature. Freedom is not caprice since we carry our past with us. The character, at any given point, is the condensation of our previous history. What we have been enters into the "me" which is now active and choosing. The range of one's natural freedom of action is limited. No man has the universal field of possibilities for himself. The varied possibilities of our nature do not all get a chance and the cosmic has its influence in permitting the development of certain possibilities and closing down others. Again, freedom is dogged by automatism. When we make up our mind to do a thing, our mind is different from what it was before. When a possibility becomes an actuality, it assumes the character of necessity. The past can never be cancelled, though it may be utilized. Mere defiance of the given may mean disaster, though we can make a new life spring up from the past. Only the possible is the sphere of freedom. We have a good deal of present constraint and previous necessity in human life. But necessity is not to be mistaken for destiny which we can neither defy nor delude. Though the self is not free from the bonds of determination, it can subjugate the past to a certain extent and turn it into a new course. Choice is the assertion of freedom over necessity by which it converts necessity to its own use and thus frees itself from it. "The human agent is free." He is not the plaything of fate or driftwood on the tide of uncontrolled events. He can actively mould the future instead of passively suffering the past. The past may become either an opportunity or an obstacle. Everything depends on what we make of it and not what it makes of us. Life is not bound to move in a specific direction. Life is a growth and a growth is undetermined in a measure. Though the future is the sequel of the past, we cannot say what it will be. If there is no indetermination, then human consciousness is an unnecessary luxury.

Our demand for freedom must reckon with a universe that is marked by order and regularity. Life is like a game of bridge. The cards in the game are given to us. We do not select them. They are traced to past Karma but we are free to make any call as we think fit and lead any suit. Only we are limited by the rules of the game. We are more free when we start the game than later on when the game has developed and our choices become restricted. But till the very end there is always a choice. A good player will see possibilities which a bad one does not. The more skilled a player the more alternatives does he perceive. A good hand may be cut to pieces by unskillful play and the bad play need not be attributed to the frowns of fortune. Even though we may not like the way in which the cards are shuffled, we like the game and we want to play. Sometimes wind and tide may prove too strong for us and even the most noble may come down. The great souls find profound peace in the consciousness that the stately order of the world, now lovely and luminous, now dark and terrible, in which man finds his duty and destiny, cannot be subdued to known aims. It seems to have a purpose of its own of which we are ignorant. Misfortune is not fate but providence.

The law of Karma does not support the doctrine of predestination. There are some who believe that only the predestination of certain souls to destruction is consistent with divine sovereignty. God has a perfect right to deal with his creatures even as a potter does with his clay.

St. Paul speaks of "vessels of wrath fitted to destruction." Life eternal is a gracious gift of God. Such a view of divine sovereignty is unethical. God's love is manifested in and through law.

In our relations with human failures, belief in Karma inclines us to take a sympathetic attitude and develop reverence before the mystery of misfortune. The more understanding we are, the less do we pride ourselves on our superiority. Faith in Karma induces in us the mood of true justice or charity which is the essence of spirituality. We realize how infinitely helpless and frail human beings are. When we look at the warped lives of the poor, we see how much the law of Karma is true. If they are lazy and criminal, let us ask what chance they had of choosing to be different. They are more unfortunate than wicked. Again, failures are due not so much to "sin" as to errors which lead us to our doom. In Greek tragedy man is held individually less responsible and circumstances or the decisions of Moira [Fate] more so. The tale of Oedipus Rex tells us how he could not avoid his fate to kill his father and marry his mother, in spite of his best efforts. The parting of Hector and Andromache in Homer is another illustration. In Shakespeare again, we see the artist leading on his characters to their destined ends by what seems a very natural development of their foibles, criminal folly in Lear or personal ambition in Macbeth. The artist shows us these souls in pain. Hamlet's reason is puzzled, his will confounded. He looks at life and at death and wonders which is worse. Goaded by personal ambition, Macbeth makes a mess of it all. Othello kills his wife and kills himself because a jealous villain shows him a handkerchief. When these noble souls crash battling with adverse forces we feel with them and for them; for it might happen to any of us. We are not free from the weaknesses that broke them, whatever we call them, stupidity, disorder, vacillation or, if you please, insane ambition and self-seeking. Today the evil stars of the Greek tragedians are replaced by the almighty laws of economics. Thousands of young men the world over are breaking their heads in vain against the iron walls of society like trapped birds in cages. We see in them the essence of all tragedy, something noble breaking down, something sublime falling with a crash. We can only bow our heads in the presence of those broken beneath the burden of their destiny. The capacity of the human soul for suffering and isolation is immense. Take the poor creatures whom the world passes by as the lowly and the lost. If only we had known what they passed through, we would have been glad of their company. It is utterly wrong to think that misfortune comes only to those who deserve it. The world is a whole and we are members one of another, and we must suffer one for another. In Christianity, it needed a divine soul to reveal how much grace there is in suffering. To bear pain, to endure suffering, is the quality of the strong in spirit. It adds to the spiritual resources of humanity.

Suggestions for Further Reading

See the article on "Karma" in *The HarperCollins Dictionary of Religion*, edited by Jonathan Z. Smith (San Francisco: HarperSanFrancisco and The American Academy of Religion, 1995).

A. L. Herman's *An Introduction to Indian Thought* (Englewood Cliffs, NJ: Prentice-Hall, 1976, p. 130ff.) provides a good discussion.

In *Religious Reason* (New York: Oxford University Press, 1978, pp. 203–222) Ronald M. Green tackles the issue of karma and freedom, arguing that the idea of moral freedom is "an implicit assumption" of the law of karma.

For a detailed discussion, see Bruce R. Reichenbach, *The Law of Karma: A Philosophical Study* (Honolulu: University of Hawaii Press, 1990).

For a classic discussion from a Western viewpoint see A. C. Campbell's *On Selfhood and Godhood* (London: Allen & Unwin, 1967) and Harry G. Frankfurt's "Freedom of the Will and the Concept of a Person," *Journal of Philosophy*, Vol. LXVIII, (Jan. 1971).

10.5 We Are Both Free and Determined

You might be thinking, "Hard determinism seems awfully hard. Human beings are not just pawns in the hands of heredity and environment. We are free. I am free. Indeed, right now, I can continue reading this book or I can stop, whichever is my pleasure. Yet Sartre's views seem unrealistic. I am not totally free. Heredity and environment clearly play some role. However, Radhakrishnan's ideas, though less radical than Sartre's with respect to the scope of human freedom, require me to believe in some kind of metaphysical notions about the self and reincarnation. I don't find that attractive. I don't, however, want to deny the law of causality. There must be some way to reconcile freedom and determinism."

If these are your thoughts, then you might like another answer that has been proposed to the problem of freedom and determinism, an answer called **soft determinism**. This position holds that every event has a cause, and this fact is *compatible* with human freedom. Hence, another name for soft determinism is **compatibilism**. According to the compatibilist, even if determinism is true, people ought to be held morally responsible for those actions they do voluntarily. Indeed, many compatibilists argue that moral responsibility makes no sense unless determinism is true because it makes no sense to hold anyone responsible for uncaused (undetermined) actions.

Notice that soft determinism is, like hard determinism, a kind of determinism. Both the soft and hard determinists agree that every event has a cause. However, they disagree about whether this is compatible with human freedom and about the implications for moral responsibility.

As you might imagine, the harmony between freedom and determinism that the compatibilist wishes to defend is based on a particular understanding of human freedom. Compatibilists do *not* define a free event as an uncaused event. The issue, according to many compatibilists, is not a question of events being caused or uncaused, rather it is a question of what kind of cause we are talking about. If my behavior is coerced or forced by circumstances over which I have no control, then I am not free and my behavior is involuntary. But if my behavior is caused by circumstances over which I do have control, it is free or voluntary.

Raymond M. Smullyan, author of the next selection, gives a slightly different twist to the compatibilist argument. In an imaginative dialogue between a "mortal" and "God" (here used to symbolize *Dao*), Smullyan applies his understanding of Daoism (see Section 9.2) to the issue of free will and determinism. Daoism maintains that the Dao is the way of nature that harmonizes all opposites. If we follow this idea to its logical conclusion, then, Smullyan thinks, it makes sense to say that free choice is just built into the causal order of the universe. The so-called laws of nature do not literally "determine" anything in the sense of forcing events. They simply describe the regularities we can observe in nature. Hence, there can be no conflict between our wills and the way of nature because one of the ways nature operates is via the human will. In the final analysis, there is no problem of free will at all!

Is this a reasonable solution? Does it really answer the question, "Could we have done other that we did, all other conditions remaining the same?" Some philosophers argue that this is really the crucial question in the debate and that compatibilistic answers do not adequately address it. Read this fun dialogue and freely (?) decide for yourself.

Reading Questions

1. The dialogue opens with the mortal requesting that God take away its free will. But very soon the mortal is refusing to let God take its free will away. What happened to cause such a reversal?
2. What is the "double bind" the mortal finds himself in?
3. What is the "double bind" God finds herself in?
4. What argument does the mortal present supporting the conclusion that God should not have given free will to humans in the first place?
5. Why does the mortal finally wish that a replica of himself be created with free will?
6. What is wrong with the word *determined* as used in the controversy over free will?
7. How does God show determinism and free will compatible? What do you think of the argument? Is it convincing? Why, or why not?

Is God a Taoist?

RAYMOND M. SMULLYAN

Mortal: AND THEREFORE, O God, I pray thee, if thou hast one ounce of mercy for this thy suffering creature, absolve me of *having* to have free will!

God: You reject the greatest gift I have given thee?

Mortal: How can you call that which was forced on me a gift? I have free will, but not of my own choice. I have never freely chosen to have free will. I have to have free will, whether I like it or not!

God: Why would you wish not to have free will?

Mortal: Because free will means moral responsibility, and moral responsibility is more than I can bear!

God: Why do you find moral responsibility so unbearable?

Mortal: Why? I honestly can't analyze why; all I know is that I do.

God: All right, in that case suppose I absolve you from all moral responsibility but leave you still with free will. Will this be satisfactory?

Mortal (after a pause): No, I am afraid not.

God: Ah, just as I thought! So moral responsibility is not the only aspect of free will to which you object. What else about free will is bothering you?

Mortal: With free will I am capable of sinning, and I don't want to sin!

God: If you don't want to sin, then why do you?

Mortal: Good God! I don't know why I sin, I just do! Evil temptations come along, and try as I can, I cannot resist them.

God: If it is really true that you cannot resist them, then you are not sinning of your own free will and hence (at least according to me) not sinning at all.

Mortal: No, no! I keep feeling that if only I tried harder I could avoid sinning. I understand that the will is infinite. If one wholeheartedly wills not to sin, then one won't.

God: Well now, you should know. Do you try as hard as you can to avoid sinning or don't you?

Mortal: I honestly don't know! At the time, I feel I am trying as hard as I can, but in retrospect, I am worried that maybe I didn't!

God: So in other words, you don't really know whether or not you have been sinning. So the possibility is open that you haven't been sinning at all!

Mortal: Of course this possibility is open, but maybe I have been sinning, and this thought is what so frightens me!

God: Why does the thought of your sinning frighten you?

Mortal: I don't know why! For one thing, you do have a reputation for meting out rather gruesome punishments in the afterlife!

God: Oh, that's what's bothering you! Why didn't you say so in the first place instead of all this peripheral talk about free will and responsibility? Why didn't you simply request me not to punish you for any of your sins?

Mortal: I think I am realistic enough to know that you would hardly grant such a request!

God: You don't say! *You* have a realistic knowledge of what requests I will grant, eh? Well, I'll tell you what I'm going to do! I will grant you a very, very special dispensation to sin as much as you like, and I give you my divine word of honor that I will never punish you for it in the least. Agreed?

Mortal (in great terror): No, no, don't do that!

God: Why not? Don't you trust my divine word?

Mortal: Of course I do! But don't you see, I don't want to sin! I have an utter abhorrence of sinning, quite apart from any punishments it may entail.

God: In that case, I'll go you one better. I'll remove your abhorrence of sinning. Here is a magic pill! Just swallow it, and you will lose all *abhorrence* of sinning. You will joyfully and merrily sin away, you will have no regrets, no abhorrence and I still promise you will never be punished by me, or yourself, or by any source whatever. You will be blissful for all eternity. So here is the pill!

Mortal: No, no!

God: Are you not being irrational? I am even removing your abhorrence of sin, which is your last obstacle.

Mortal: I still won't take it!

God: Why not?

Mortal: I believe that the pill will indeed remove my future abhorrence for sin, but my present abhorrence is enough to prevent me from being willing to take it.

God: I command you to take it!

Mortal: I refuse!

God: What, you refuse of your own free will?

Mortal: Yes!

God: So it seems that your free will comes in pretty handy, doesn't it?

Mortal: I don't understand!

God: Are you not glad now that you have the free will to refuse such a ghastly offer? How would you like it if I forced you to take this pill, whether you wanted it or not?

Mortal: No, no! Please don't!

God: Of course I won't; I'm just trying to illustrate a point. All right, let me put it this way. Instead of forcing you to take the pill, suppose I grant your original prayer of removing your free will—but with the understanding that the moment you are no longer free, then you *will* take the pill.

Mortal: Once my will is gone, how could I possibly choose to take the pill?

God: I did not say you would choose it; I merely said you would take it. You would act, let us say, according to purely deterministic laws which are such that you would as a matter of fact take it.

Mortal: I still refuse.

God: So you refuse my offer to remove your free will. This is rather different from your original prayer, isn't it?

Mortal: Now I see what you are up to. Your argument is ingenious, but I'm not sure it is really correct. There are some points we will have to go over again.

God: Certainly.

Mortal: There are two things you said which seem contradictory to me. First you said that one cannot sin unless one does so of one's own free will. But then you said you would give me a pill which would deprive me of my own free will, and then I could sin as much as I liked. But if I no longer had free will, then, according to your first statement, how could I be capable of sinning?

God: You are confusing two separate parts of our conversation. I never said the pill would deprive you of your free will, but only that it would remove your abhorrence of sinning.

Mortal: I'm afraid I'm a bit confused.

God: All right, then let us make a fresh start. Suppose I agree to remove your free will, but with the understanding that you will then commit an enormous number of acts which you now regard as sinful. Technically speaking, you will not then be sinning since you will not be doing these acts of your own free will. And these acts will carry no moral responsibility, nor moral culpability, nor any punishment whatsoever. Nevertheless, these acts will all be of the type which you presently regard as sinful; they will all have this quality which you presently feel as abhorrent, but your abhorrence will disappear; so you will not *then* feel abhorrence toward the acts.

Mortal: No, but I have present abhorrence toward the acts, and this present abhorrence is sufficient to prevent me from accepting your proposal.

God: Hm! So let me get this absolutely straight. I take it you no longer wish me to remove your free will.

Mortal (reluctantly): No, I guess not.

God: All right, I agree not to. But I am still not exactly clear as to why you now no longer wish to be rid of your free will. Please tell me again.

Mortal: Because, as you have told me, without free will I would sin even more than I do now.

God: But I have already told you that without free will you cannot sin.

Mortal: But if I choose now to be rid of free will, then all my subsequent evil actions will be sins, not of the future, but of the present moment in which I choose not to have free will.

God: Sounds like you are pretty badly trapped, doesn't it?

Mortal: Of course I am trapped! You have placed me in a hideous double bind! Now whatever I do is wrong. If I retain free will, I will continue to sin, and if I abandon free will (with your help, of course), I will now be sinning in so doing.

God: But by the same token, you place me in a double bind. I am willing to leave you free will or remove it as you choose, but neither alternative satisfies you. I wish to help you, but it seems I cannot.

Mortal: True!

God: But since it is not my fault, why are you still angry with me?

Mortal: For having placed me in such a horrible predicament in the first place!

God: But, according to you, there is nothing satisfactory I could have done.

Mortal: You mean there is nothing satisfactory you can now do, but that does not mean that there is nothing you could have done.

God: Why? What could I have done?

Mortal: Obviously you should never have given me free will in the first place. Now that you have given it to me, it is too late—anything I do will be bad. But you should never have given it to me in the first place.

God: Oh, that's it! Why would it have been better had I never given it to you?

Mortal: Because then I never would have been capable of sinning at all.

God: Well, I'm always glad to learn from my mistakes.

Mortal: What!

God: I know, that sounds sort of self-blasphemous, doesn't it? It almost involves a logical paradox! On the one hand, as you have been taught, it is morally wrong for any sentient being to claim

that I am capable of making mistakes. On the other hand, I have the right to do anything. But I am also a sentient being. So the question is, Do I or do I not have the right to claim that I am capable of making mistakes?

Mortal: That is a bad joke! One of your premises is simply false. I have not been taught that it is wrong for any sentient being to doubt your omniscience, but only for a mortal to doubt it. But since you are not mortal, then you are obviously free from this injunction.

God: Good, so you realize this on a rational level. Nevertheless, you did appear shocked when I said, "I am always glad to learn from my mistakes."

Mortal: Of course I was shocked. I was shocked not by your self-blasphemy (as you jokingly called it), not by the fact that you had no right to say it, but just by the fact that you did say it, since I have been taught that as a matter of fact you don't make mistakes. So I was amazed that you claimed that it is possible for you to make mistakes.

God: I have not claimed that it is possible. All I am saying is that *if* I make mistakes, I will be happy to learn from them. But this says nothing about whether the *if* has or ever can be realized.

Mortal: Let's please stop quibbling about this point. Do you or do you not admit it was a mistake to have given me free will?

God: Well now, this is precisely what I propose we should investigate. Let me review your present predicament. You don't want to have free will because with free will you can sin, and you don't want to sin. (Though I still find this puzzling; in a way you must want to sin, or else you wouldn't. But let this pass for now.) On the other hand, if you agreed to give up free will, then you would now be responsible for the acts of the future. Ergo, I should never have given you free will in the first place.

Mortal: Exactly!

God: I understand exactly how you feel. Many mortals—even some theologians—have complained that I have been unfair in that it was I, not they, who decided that they should have free will, and then I hold *them* responsible for their actions. In other words, they feel that they are expected to live up to a contract with me which they never agreed to in the first place.

Mortal: Exactly!

God: As I said, I understand the feeling perfectly. And I can appreciate the justice of the complaint. But the complaint arises only from an unrealistic understanding of the true issues involved. I am about to enlighten you as to what these are, and I think the results will surprise you! But instead of telling you outright, I shall continue to use the Socratic method.

To repeat, you regret that I ever gave you free will. I claim that when you see the true ramifications you will no longer have this regret. To prove my point, I'll tell you what I'm going to do. I am about to create a new universe—a new space-time continuum. In this new universe will be born a mortal just like you—for all practical purposes, we might say that you will be reborn. Now, I can give this new mortal—this new you— free will or not. What would you like me to do?

Mortal (in great relief): Oh, please! Spare him from having to have free will!

God: All right, I'll do as you say. But you do realize that this new *you* without free will, will commit all sorts of horrible acts.

Mortal: But they will not be sins since he will have no free will.

God: Whether you call them sins or not, the fact remains that they will be horrible acts in the sense that they will cause great pain to many sentient beings.

Mortal (after a pause): Good God, you have trapped me again! Always the same game! If I now give you the go-ahead to create this new creature with no free will who will nevertheless commit atrocious acts, then true enough he will not be sinning, but I again will be the sinner to sanction this.

God: In that case, I'll go you one better! Here, I have already decided whether to create this new *you* with free will or not. Now, I am writing my decision on this piece of paper and I won't show it to you until later. But my decision is now made and is absolutely irrevocable. There is nothing you can possibly do to alter it; you have no responsibility in the matter. Now, what I wish to know is this: Which way do you hope I

have decided? Remember now, the responsibility for the decision falls entirely on my shoulders, not yours. So you can tell me perfectly honestly and without any fear, which way do you hope I have decided?

Mortal (after a very long pause): I hope you have decided to give him free will.

God: Most interesting! I have removed your last obstacle! If I do not give him free will, then no sin is to be imputed to anybody. So why do you hope I will give him free will?

Mortal: Because sin or no sin, the important point is that if you do not give him free will, then (at least according to what you have said) he will go around hurting people, and I don't want to see people hurt.

God (with an infinite sigh of relief): At last! At last you see the real point!

Mortal: What point is that?

God: That sinning is not the real issue! The important thing is that people as well as other sentient beings don't get hurt!

Mortal: You sound like a utilitarian!

God: I am a utilitarian!

Mortal: What!

God: Whats or no whats, I am a utilitarian. Not a unitarian, mind you, but a utilitarian.

Mortal: I just can't believe it!

God: Yes, I know, your religious training has taught you otherwise. You have probably thought of me more like a Kantian than a utilitarian, but your training was simply wrong.

Mortal: You leave me speechless!

God: I leave you speechless, do I! Well, that is perhaps not too bad a thing—you have a tendency to speak too much as it is. Seriously, though, why do you think I ever did give you free will in the first place?

Mortal: Why did you? I never have thought much about why you did; all I have been arguing for is that you shouldn't have! But why did you? I guess all I can think of is the standard religious explanation: Without free will, one is not capable of meriting either salvation or damnation. So without free will, we could not earn the right to eternal life.

God: Most interesting! *I* have eternal life; do you think I have ever done anything to merit it?

Mortal: Of course not! With you it is different. You are already so good and perfect (at least allegedly) that it is not necessary for you to merit eternal life.

God: Really now? That puts me in a rather enviable position, doesn't it?

Mortal: I don't think I understand you.

God: Here I am eternally blissful without ever having to suffer or make sacrifices or struggle against evil temptations or anything like that. Without any of that type of "merit," I enjoy blissful eternal existence. By contrast, you poor mortals have to sweat and suffer and have all sorts of horrible conflicts about morality, and all for what? You don't even know whether I really exist or not, or if there really is any afterlife, or if there is, where you come into the picture. No matter how much you try to placate me by being "good," you never have any real assurance that your "best" is good enough for me, and hence you have no real security in obtaining salvation. Just think of it! I already *have* the equivalent of "salvation"—and have never had to go through this infinitely lugubrious process of earning it. Don't you ever envy me for this?

Mortal: But it is blasphemous to envy you!

God: Oh come off it! You're not now talking to your Sunday school teacher, you are talking to *me*. Blasphemous or not, the important question is not whether you have the right to be envious of me but whether you are. Are you?

Mortal: Of course I am!

God: Good! Under your present world view, you sure should be most envious of me. But I think with a more realistic world view, you no longer will be. So you really have swallowed the idea which has been taught you that your life on earth is like an examination period and that the purpose of providing you with free will is to test you, to see if you merit blissful eternal life. But what puzzles me is this: If you really believe I am as good and benevolent as I am cracked up to be, why should I require people to merit things like happiness and eternal life? Why should I not grant such things to everyone regardless of whether or not he deserves them? . . .

God: [But] [w]e have gotten sidetracked as it is, and I would like to return to the question of what you believed my purpose to be in giving you free will. Your first idea of my giving you free will in order to test whether you merit salvation or not may appeal to many moralists, but the idea is quite hideous to me. You cannot think of any nicer reason—any more humane reason—why I gave you free will?

Mortal: Well now, I once asked this question to an Orthodox rabbi. He told me that the way we are constituted, it is simply not possible for us to enjoy salvation unless we feel we have earned it. And to earn it, we of course need free will.

God: That explanation is indeed much nicer than your former but still is far from correct. According to Orthodox Judaism, I created angels, and they have no free will. They are in actual sight of me and are so completely attracted by goodness that they never have even the slightest temptation towards evil. They really have no choice in the matter. Yet they are eternally happy even though they have never earned it. So if your rabbi's explanation were correct, why wouldn't I have simply created only angels rather than mortals?

Mortal: Beats me! Why didn't you?

God: Because the explanation is simply not correct. In the first place, I have never created any ready made angels. All sentient beings ultimately approach the state which might be called "angelhood." But just as the race of human beings is in a certain stage of biologic evolution, so angels are simply the end result of a process of Cosmic Evolution. The only difference between the so-called *saint* and the so-called *sinner* is that the former is vastly older than the latter. Unfortunately it takes countless life cycles to learn what is perhaps the most important fact of the universe—evil is simply painful. All the arguments of the moralists—all the alleged reasons why people *shouldn't* commit evil acts—simply pale into insignificance in light of the one basic truth that *evil is suffering*. No, my dear friend, I am not a moralist. I am wholly a utilitarian. That I should have been conceived in the role of a moralist is one of the great tragedies of the human race. My role in the scheme of things (if one can use this misleading expression) is neither to punish nor reward, but to aid the process by which all sentient beings achieve ultimate perfection. . . .

Mortal: Anyway, putting all these pieces together, it occurs to me that the only reason you gave free will is because of your belief that with free will, people will tend to hurt each other—and themselves—less than without free will.

God: Bravo! That is by far the best reason you have yet given! I can assure you that had I *chosen* to give free will that would have been my very reason for so choosing.

Mortal: What! You mean to say you did not choose to give us free will?

God: My dear fellow, I could no more choose to give you free will than I could choose to make an equilateral triangle equiangular. I could choose to make or not to make an equilateral triangle in the first place, but having chosen to make one, I would then have no choice but to make it equiangular.

Mortal: I thought you could do anything!

God: Only things which are logically possible. As St. Thomas said, "It is a sin to regard the fact that God cannot do the impossible, as a limitation on His powers." I agree, except that in place of his using the word *sin* I would use the term *error.*

Mortal: Anyhow, I am still puzzled by your implication that you did not choose to give me free will.

God: Well, it is high time I inform you that the entire discussion—from the very beginning—has been based on one monstrous fallacy! We have been talking purely on a moral level—you originally complained that I gave you free will, and raised the whole question as to whether I should have. It never once occurred to you that I had absolutely no choice in the matter.

Mortal: I am still in the dark!

God: Absolutely! Because you are only able to look at it through the eyes of a moralist. The more fundamental *metaphysical* aspects of the question you never even considered.

Mortal: I still do not see what you are driving at.

God: Before you requested me to remove your free will, shouldn't your first question have been whether as a matter of fact you *do* have free will?

Mortal: That I simply took for granted.

God: But why should you?

Mortal: I don't know. Do I have free will?

God: Yes.

Mortal: Then why did you say I shouldn't have taken it for granted?

God: Because you shouldn't. Just because something happens to be true, it does not follow that it should be taken for granted.

Mortal: Anyway, it is reassuring to know that my natural intuition about having free will is correct. Sometimes I have been worried that determinists are correct.

God: They are correct.

Mortal: Wait a minute now, do I have free will or don't I?

God: I already told you you do. But that does not mean that determinism is incorrect.

Mortal: Well, are my acts determined by the laws of nature or aren't they?

God: The word *determined* here is subtly but powerfully misleading and has contributed so much to the confusions of the free will versus determinism controversies. Your acts are certainly in accordance with the laws of nature, but to say they are *determined* by the laws of nature creates a totally misleading psychological image which is that your will could somehow be in conflict with the laws of nature and that the latter is somehow more powerful than you, and could "determine" your acts whether you liked it or not. But it is simply impossible for your will to ever conflict with natural law. You and natural law are really one and the same.

Mortal: What do you mean that I cannot conflict with nature? Suppose I were to become very stubborn, and I *determined* not to obey the laws of nature. What could stop me? If I became sufficiently stubborn, even you could not stop me!

God: You are absolutely right! *I* certainly could not stop you. Nothing could stop you. But there is no need to stop you, because you could not even start! As Goethe very beautifully expressed it, "In trying to oppose Nature, we are in the very process of doing so, acting according to the laws of nature!" Don't you see, that the so-called "laws of nature" are nothing more than a description of how in fact you and other beings *do* act. They are merely a description of how you act, not a prescription of how you should act, nor a power or force which compels or determines your acts. To be valid a law of nature must take into account how in fact you do act, or, if you like, how you choose to act.

Mortal: So you really claim that I am incapable of determining to act against natural law?

God: It is interesting that you have twice now used the phrase "determined to act" instead of "chosen to act." This identification is quite common. Often one uses the statement "I am determined to do this" synonymously with "I have chosen to do this." This very psychological identification should reveal that determinism and choice are much closer than they might appear. Of course, you might well say that the doctrine of free will says that it is *you* who are doing the determining, whereas the doctrine of determinism appears to say that your acts are determined by something apparently outside you. But the confusion is largely caused by your bifurcation of reality into the "you" and the "not you." Really now, just where do you leave off and the rest of the universe begin? Or where does the rest of the universe leave off and you begin? Once you can see the so-called "you" and the so-called "nature" as a continuous whole, then you can never again be bothered by such questions as whether it is you who are controlling nature or nature who is controlling you. Thus the muddle of free will versus determinism will vanish. If I

may use a crude analogy, imagine two bodies moving toward each other by virtue of gravitational attraction. Each body, if sentient, might wonder whether it is he or the other fellow who is exerting the "force." In a way it is both, in a way it is neither. It is best to say that it is the configuration of the two which is crucial.

Mortal: You said a short while ago that our whole discussion was based on a monstrous fallacy. You still have not told me what this fallacy is.

God: Why, the idea that I could possibly have created you without free will! You acted as if this were a genuine possibility, and wondered why I did not choose it! It never occurred to you that a sentient being without free will is no more conceivable than a physical object which exerts no gravitational attraction. (There is, incidentally, more analogy than you realize between a physical object exerting gravitational attraction and a sentient being exerting free will!) Can you honestly even imagine a conscious being without free will? What on earth could it be like? I think that one thing in your life that has so misled you is your having been told that I gave man the *gift* of free will. As if I first created man, and then as an afterthought endowed him with the extra property of free will. Maybe you think I have some sort of "paint brush" with which I daub some creatures with free will, and not others. No, free will is not an "extra"; it is part and parcel of the very essence of consciousness. A conscious being without free will is simply a metaphysical absurdity. . . .

Suggestions for Further Reading

See "The Compatibility of Freedom and Determinism" in *Reason and Practice* by Kai Nielsen (New York: Harper & Row, 1971) for a sophisticated defense of soft determinism. Nielsen summarizes many of the contributions to the discussion by such modern philosophers as Hobbes, Hume, Mill, Schlick, and Ayer.

Daniel Dennett's *Elbow Room: Varieties of Free Will Worth Wanting* (Cambridge, MA: MIT Press, 1983) provides a well-reasoned defense of compatibilism.

Also see W. T. Stace's *Religion and the Modern* (New York: J. B. Lippincott, 1952), pp. 279–291, for a defense of compatibilism.

See Richard Taylor's *Metaphysics,* 3rd Edition (Englewood Cliffs, NJ: Prentice-Hall, 1983), for a discussion of all three positions (hard and soft determinism along with libertarianism) and an argument in favor of libertarianism.

Peter van Inwagen's *An Essay on Free Will* (Oxford: Oxford University Press, 1983) is one of the best critiques of compatibilism available. It is not easy going, however.

See Gary Watson's *Free Will* (Oxford: Oxford University Press, 1982) for a good collection of articles on the subject.

 You can locate InfoTrac-College Edition articles about this chapter by accessing the InfoTrac-College Edition website (http://www.infotrac-college.com/wadsworth/). Using the InfoTrac-College Edition subject guide, enter the search terms relevant to this chapter, and then read abstracts for relevant articles.

Chapter 11

What Am I?
Who Am I?

> **Don't think of who I once was. Reflect on who you are now, and who you would like to be in the future.**
>
> A TOMBSTONE FOUND NEAR STRASBOURG

11.1 Introduction

THE TWO QUESTIONS IN THIS CHAPTER TITLE ask about different but related things. The first asks about the "stuff" out of which you are made. The second asks about personal identity. We will spend most of our time in this chapter exploring the first question, but the answers we will look at are relevant to answering the second one. Let's begin with the first question and ask to what the word *I* refers.

You might want to say that the word *I* refers to your body. This would mean that you are your body, and I am my body. That seems simple enough. Notice, however, the words *your* body or *my* body. Why do we say *my* body as if the body were something the *I* possessed? This way of talking seems to imply that we make a distinction between ourselves and our bodies. And, of course, we can lose parts of our bodies or even have parts of them replaced without losing or replacing ourselves.

Maybe "I" doesn't refer to the body but to something that goes on inside the body, like thoughts or sensations. So you are what you think, perceive, and feel. However, we run into the same problem, don't we? We speak of *my* thoughts, *my* perceptions, and *my* feelings. Also, these things are constantly changing, but is the "I" constantly changing? Are you a different person every time you have a different thought, feeling, or sensation?

If "I" does not refer to my body or my thoughts, perceptions, and feelings, maybe it refers to my mind. My mind is what *has* thoughts, perceptions, and feelings, so you might say it possesses them. And since my mind tells my body what to do, you might even say that my body is possessed by my mind. Or, at least, my mind inhabits my body.

As the above bit of thinking about the question "What am I?" indicates, the discussion sooner or later leads one to talk about the mind and the body. This seems natural enough since we normally think of ourselves as human beings, and we commonly think of humans as having minds and bodies. However, what precisely are the mind and the body, and how are they related to each other? These questions constitute what philosophers call the **mind–body problem**.

Generally speaking, the proposed solutions to the mind–body problem fall into two groups: dualistic and monistic. Dualistic theories hold that the mind and the body are two different substances. The mind is conscious, nonspatial, and private (only you have direct access to your own mind). The body is unconscious, spatial, and public (it can be viewed by others). How do these two substances, so defined, relate?

One theory, usually associated with René Descartes (see Section 7.3), is called **interactionism**. According to this theory, mind and body causally interact in the sense that mental events (e.g., thoughts) can cause physical events (e.g., walking) and physical events (e.g., taking a sleeping pill) can cause mental events (e.g., feeling sleepy). This seems plausible enough at first, but the problem of how two substances so radically different can causally affect each other has led to considerable controversy as well as to the development of other theories.

Some dualists who reject the idea of causal interactionism subscribe to **parallelism**. The German philosopher Gottfried Leibniz (1646–1716), for example, argued that a preestablished harmony exists between mental and physical events so that they run in parallel, like two clocks set to tick together. Mind and body appear to interact, but in fact they do not. A physical event occurs (e.g., a blow to the arm), and parallel to that event, but uncaused by it, a mental event (e.g., pain) occurs.

This seems somewhat fantastic, so other dualists have been led to yet a third theory called **epiphenomenalism**. According to this theory, mental events are by-products of physical events, as smoke is a by-product of fire. This means that physical events cause mental events, but mental events cannot cause physical events. Mental events are just things that happen when certain brain activities take place. The brain activity is what is primary; the mental activity is secondary.

Monistic solutions to the mind–body problem deny that the mind and the body are two different substances. For example, *materialism* (see Section 9.6), or *physicalism* as it is sometimes called, holds that so-called mental events are not different from physical events. There is no such thing as a mental substance above and beyond the physical. There are several varieties of materialism, but a popular version, called the **identity theory**, proposes that mental events are identical with brain processes in much the same way as lightning flashes are identical with electrical discharges.

Whereas some versions of materialism attempt to reduce mind to matter, *idealism* (see Section 9.5) attempts to reduce matter to mind. If you read Berkeley, you may recall how such an argument progresses. Berkeley argues that since all we ever experience are sensations and since sensations are mental, matter is an unwarranted and unneeded inference. Only minds and mental events exist.

A third kind of monism is called the **double-aspect theory**. This view, maintained by the Dutch philosopher Baruch Spinoza (1632–1677), proposes that we rethink what we mean by mind and body (matter). Instead of thinking of these as things or *substances,* we should think of them as qualities, characteristics, or aspects. There is one substance, Spinoza argued, that in itself is neither mental nor physical but has at least two different aspects or qualities called mind and body. A modern version of this theory was suggested by the famous British philosopher Bertrand Russell (see Section 1.3). Russell called his theory **neutral monism** and characterized it as the view that what exists is neither mental nor physical but neutral with respect to these distinctions.

The question about what I am leads to questions about the nature of human beings, about what they are made of or what constitutes their being. It also leads to other questions, in particular questions about what a person is. It is here that the question of what begins to shade off into the question of who? Who are we? We are persons. Simple enough, right?

We must be careful to distinguish the concept of "person" from the concept "human being." Human being refers to a biological species, one to which we happen to belong. Person, on the other hand, is not a biological concept. We can bring out the distinction by pointing to the example of the space alien E.T. It would appear that E.T. is a person, but certainly not a human being in the biological sense. This distinction is central to much of the debate about abortion since many claim that while a fetus belongs to the biological species human being, it is not a person, but only potentially a person.

To say that something is potentially a person indicates that personhood is something that may not always be present. Of course we all know that persons can and do change. The fact that being a person is dynamic (a changing and developing process) leads to the issue of the identity of persons through time. Consider this puzzle: Are you the same person today as you were when you were five years old? If we mean by "same" a kind of strict identity such that if *A* is identical with *B*, then *A* and *B* have the same characteristics, the answer is obviously no. You have a different set of qualities today (such as size and age) than you did when you were five years old. If we mean by "same" similar, but not absolutely identical characteristics, then the answer is yes.

But is similarity good enough? If I am only similar to my former self, then I have changed. And if I have changed, how much have I changed? For example, does it make sense to hold the person I am today responsible for the act of stealing cookies at age five? If my mother suddenly discovered that I, not my sister, stole the cookies and I lied about it, should she call me up and scold me many years later?

The questions about what and who we are lead, as we just have seen, to issues about the nature of human beings, about the existence of minds and bodies, about the relationship between minds and bodies, about how to define a person, and issues about personal identity through time. These sorts of issues, however, may seem awfully abstract and academic. "Are they of any practical consequence?" you might well ask.

The answer is yes. There is a host of moral questions, such as abortion and euthanasia, surrounding the issue of personhood. But there are also important questions about the possibility of life after death that are directly related to these abstract questions.

I am sure you have wondered if there is life after death. Do we live on after the death of our bodies? What is death? When does it happen? Do I die when my body does, or my brain, or when my influence on subsequent generations ceases? Is there a heaven or hell? What about reincarnation? Can I move from one body to another? If I don't remember my past lives, how can I really claim they are *my* past lives? Is there an immortal soul? What is life like apart from the body? Does the idea of a resurrection of the body make any sense? Is it probable that at death I will just go to sleep and then wake up with a new body? Would it still be me if my body is different?

The problem of survival is closely related to the mind–body problem and the problem of personal identity. For example, if we define the person as a mental substance and if we assume that death occurs when the body and brain die, then we might argue that our soul or mind survives death. If souls exist and if souls can live without bodies, then perhaps life after death consists of the **immortality of the soul**. And even if souls cannot live or at least not live for long without bodies, then maybe some sort of **reincarnation** is possible—souls moving from one body to another after the death of the last body. Conversely, if we identify the person or mind with the body or some part of it like the brain, then it seems clear we do not survive death (assuming once again that death means death of the body–brain complex) because it is evident that the body, including the brain, ceases to function at what we call death and eventually decays. However, as we will see, perhaps some kinds of materialism are compatible with survival.

Or maybe you aren't your soul or body exclusively, but a combination of things— a mind, a body, a personality. If that combination could be re-created after the first combination died, could we not say that you survived death? The idea of a **resurrection of the body**, while open to a variety of interpretations, seems to indicate that life in a new body after the death of this one is possible.

However, maybe death is too much of a trauma. Maybe the person cannot survive. If so, does that make life pointless? Is this life worth living only if there is some other afterlife? Maybe this life is valuable in itself. Maybe living forever would get boring. Then again, maybe not.

Questions about what and who we are have led us quite far afield—from talking about minds to talking about life after death. There is, however, still more to talk about (it seems philosophers always have more to say). If we refocus our attention on the question, "Who am I?" and ask it fully aware that people do not live in social vacuums, we are plunged into a whole series of interesting issues about what we can call the social self. This concept of a social self brings to the fore problems about the role our cultural, historical, ethnic, family, and other relationships play in identity formation. These relational aspects of self-formation are particularly complex in the modern, mobile world of the twenty-first century in which national and cultural borders have become more porous than at any time in the past.

There is not space in this chapter to look at all of the issues surrounding the seemingly simple questions, What am I?/Who am I? We will, however, sample some thoughts about some proposed answers. We begin with a look at mind–body dualism.

11.2 You Are Your Mind

We return once again to Descartes, in particular to the last chapter of his *Meditations*. Let me remind you of his argument so far. Descartes was concerned with proving representational realism true. That is, he wanted to show for certain that physical objects really do exist outside our minds. He began by using his method of doubt to show that all our beliefs about an external world based on our sensations can be doubted. Hence, the most direct way to know the external world—namely, by sensation—is blocked by doubt. He then discovered that he could not doubt that he existed as a thinking thing as long as he was thinking because every time he doubted (thought) that he existed he proved that he existed (thought). So he found a certain foundation from which to begin, but he was trapped in his own mind.

Our selection in Section 7.3 ended with the second meditation and with Descartes knowing for certain that he existed as a thinking thing, but knowing nothing else. In the subsequent meditations, he sought a way out of his own mind by showing that God exists. If he could prove that God exists, he could be certain that at least one thing outside his own mind exists. He attempted this proof in *Meditation V* with his famous argument from perfection. Descartes argued that by God we mean a perfect being. A perfect being has all perfections. Existing is a perfection and, since a perfect being has all perfections, God must exist (see the ontological argument in Section 12.5 for a version of this sort of argument). Furthermore, God cannot be a deceiver since a perfect being must also have the perfection of goodness and a perfectly good being would not deceive.

Along the way Descartes also tried to establish a rule for distinguishing true ideas from false. Ideas that are clear and distinct are true. He also thought he discovered the cause of error. We can use our will to choose to believe things that our understanding does not completely grasp. Hence, we can be confident that God is good and not the source of error. He also tried to show that material things are essentially different from mental things. Matter is extended in space and mind is not. So Descartes believed he had established with absolute certainty the existence of his own mind as a mental substance and the existence of a perfectly good God. How did he get from there to a world made up of physical objects external to our minds? In the *Meditation* that follows, Descartes made that move.

He argued that physical objects outside his mind exist because there are only three possible causes of his perception of such objects:

1. His mind caused the perceptions.
2. God caused them.
3. Physical objects caused them.

We have, Descartes argued, a strong inclination to believe that (3) is true. If it were not true, then God who is perfectly good and who has given us this strong inclination, would be a deceiver since it is neither evident nor certain that our mind causes our perceptions of physical objects or that God does. Since he proved (at least to his satisfaction) that God is perfectly good, then it follows that God is not a deceiver, and hence (3) is true.

Central to Descartes's view is a sharp distinction between the mind, which is a nonphysical substance (not extended in space and private), and objects outside the mind, which are physical substances (extended in space and public). One of these outside objects is our own body. However, unlike rocks (so far as we know), persons are a unique combination of the nonphysical (the mind) and the physical (the body). In addition, it appears that human minds can cause their bodies to act in certain ways and that bodies can cause certain mental events.

The standard interpretation of Descartes is that he not only establishes a mind–body dualism but also supports a theory of interactionism. According to this theory, the mind and body can causally interact even though one is a mental substance and the other is a physical substance. Recently, some philosophers have questioned whether Descartes did in fact support interactionism. Descartes corresponded about this very issue with Princess Elisabeth of Bohemia in May and June of 1643. Elisabeth was puzzled about how interactive causation might happen since causation is a mechanical process requiring contact between bodies extended in space. But the mind is not extended in space and hence can have no contact with a physical body. So *how* do you raise your arm if your mind can have no contact with the muscles in your arm?

Reading Questions

1. What two reasons does Descartes give in support of the proposition that material objects *can* exist?
2. What is the difference between having a *mental image* and having a *pure understanding?* Give an example of each.
3. According to Descartes, is having a mental image essential to one's self? Why, or why not?
4. Summarize in your own words Descartes's summary of the reasoning that led him to doubt whether his sensations could prove the existence of external physical objects.
5. Descartes says he no longer believes that he ought to "call it all into doubt." Why has he changed his mind?
6. At one point Descartes concludes that he is "really distinct from my body and can exist without it," and at another point he says that "my whole self . . . consists of a body and a mind." Do these two claims contradict one another? Why, or why not?
7. How do the mind and body differ, according to Descartes?
8. In the first *Meditation,* Descartes was skeptical about how confident we can be in distinguishing dreaming from waking. Then he became more confident about making the distinction. According to Descartes, how can dreaming be distinguished from waking? Do you agree? Why, or why not?
9. What are the issues at stake in the correspondence between Princess Elisabeth and Descartes?
10. Do you think Descartes successfully answers Princess Elisabeth's questions? Why, or why not?

Meditation VI

RENÉ DESCARTES

On the Existence of Material Objects and the Real Distinction of Mind from Body

IT REMAINS FOR ME to examine whether material objects exist. Insofar as they are the subject of pure mathematics, I now know at least that they can exist, because I grasp them clearly and distinctly. For God can undoubtedly make whatever I can grasp in this way, and I never judge that something is impossible for Him to make unless there would be a contradiction in my grasping the thing distinctly. Also, the fact that I

From René Descartes's Meditations on First Philosophy, *translated by Ronald Rubin (Claremont, CA: Areté Press, 1986), pp. 40–53. Reprinted by permission of Areté Press.*

find myself having mental images when I turn my attention to physical objects seems to imply that these objects really do exist. For, when I pay careful attention to what it is to have a mental image, it seems to me that it's just the application of my power of thought to a certain body which is immediately present to it and which must therefore exist.

To clarify this, I'll examine the difference between having a mental image and having a pure understanding. When I have a mental image of a triangle, for example, I don't just understand that it is a figure bounded by three lines; I also "look at" the lines as though they were present to my mind's eye. And this is what I call having a mental image. When I want to think of a chiliagon, I understand that it is a figure with a thousand sides as well as I understand that a triangle is a figure with three, but I can't imagine its sides or "look" at them as though they were present. Being accustomed to using images when I think about physical objects, I may confusedly picture some figure to myself, but this figure obviously is not a chiliagon—for it in no way differs from what I present to myself when thinking about a myriagon or any other many sided figure, and it doesn't help me to discern the properties that distinguish chiliagons from other polygons. If it's a pentagon that is in question, I can understand its shape, as I can that of the chiliagon, without the aid of mental images. But I can also get a mental image of the pentagon by directing my mind's eye to its five lines and to the area that they bound. And it's obvious to me that getting this mental image requires a special mental effort different from that needed for understanding—a special effort which clearly reveals the difference between having a mental image and having a pure understanding.

It also seems to me that my power of having mental images, being distinct from my power of understanding, is not essential to my self or, in other words, to my mind—for, if I were to lose this ability, I would surely remain the same thing that I now am. And it seems to follow that this ability depends on something distinct from me. If we suppose that there is a body so associated with my mind that the mind can "look into" it at

will, it's easy to understand how my mind might get mental images of physical objects by means of my body. If there were such a body, the mode of thinking that we call imagination would only differ from pure understanding in one way: when the mind understood something, it would turn "inward" and view an idea that it found in itself, but, when it had mental images, it would turn to the body and look at something there which resembled an idea that it had understood by itself or had grasped by sense. As I've said, then, it's easy to see how I get mental images, if we suppose that my body exists. And, since I don't have in mind any other equally plausible explanation of my ability to have mental images, I conjecture that physical objects probably do exist. But this conjecture is only probable. Despite my careful and thorough investigation, the distinct idea of bodily nature that I get from mental images does not seem to have anything in it from which the conclusion that physical objects exist validly follows.

Besides having a mental image of the bodily nature which is the subject-matter of pure mathematics, I have mental images of things which are not so distinct—things like colors, sounds, flavors, and pains. But I seem to grasp these things better by sense, from which they seem to come (with the aid of memory) to the understanding. Thus, to deal with these things more fully, I must examine the senses and see whether there is anything in the mode of awareness that I call sensation from which I can draw a conclusive argument for the existence of physical objects.

First, I'll remind myself of the things that I believed really to be as I perceived them and of the grounds for my belief. Next, I'll set out the grounds on which I later called this belief into doubt. And, finally, I'll consider what I ought to think now.

To begin with, I sensed that I had a head, hands, feet, and the other members that make up a human body. I viewed this body as part, or maybe even as all, of me. I sensed that it was influenced by other physical objects whose effects could be either beneficial or harmful. I judged these effects to be beneficial to the extent that I felt pleasant sensations and harmful to the extent that I felt pain. And, in addition to sensations of pain and pleasure, I sensed hunger, thirst, and other such desires—and also bodily inclinations towards cheerfulness, sadness, and other emotions. Outside me, I sensed, not just extension, shape, and motion, but also hardness, hotness, and other qualities detected by touch. I also sensed light, color, odor, taste, and sound—qualities by whose variation I distinguished such things as the sky, earth, and sea from one another.

In view of these ideas of qualities (which presented themselves to my thought and were all that I really sensed directly), I had some reason for believing that I sensed objects distinct from my thought—physical objects from which the ideas came. For I found that these ideas came to me independently of my desires so that, however much I tried, I couldn't sense an object when it wasn't present to an organ of sense or fail to sense one when it was present. And, since the ideas that I grasped by sense were much livelier, more explicit, and (in their own way) more distinct than those I deliberately created or found impressed in my memory, it seemed that these ideas could not have come from me and thus that they came from something else. Having no conception of these things other than that suggested by my sensory ideas, I could only think that the things resembled the ideas. Indeed, since I remembered using my senses before my reason, since I found the ideas that I created in myself to be less explicit than those grasped by sense, and since I found the ideas that I created to be composed largely of those that I had grasped by sense, I easily convinced myself that I didn't understand anything at all unless I had first sensed it.

I also had some reason for supposing that a certain physical object, which I viewed as belonging to me in a special way, was related to me more closely than any other. I couldn't be separated from it as I could from other physical objects; I felt all of my emotions and desires in it and because of it; and I was aware of pains and pleasant feelings in it but in nothing else. I didn't know why sadness goes with the sensation of pain or why joy goes with sensory stimulation. I didn't know why the stomach twitchings that I call hunger warn me that I need to eat or why dry-

ness in my throat warns me that I need to drink. Seeing no connection between stomach twitchings and the desire to eat or between the sensation of a pain-producing thing and the consequent awareness of sadness, I could only say that I had been taught the connection by nature. And nature seems also to have taught me everything else that I knew about the objects of sensation—for I convinced myself that the sensations came to me in a certain way before having found grounds on which to prove that they did.

But, since then, many experiences have shaken my faith in the senses. Towers that seemed round from a distance sometimes looked square from close up, and huge statues on pediments sometimes didn't look big when seen from the ground. In innumerable such cases, I found the judgments of the external senses to be wrong. And the same holds for the internal senses. What is felt more inwardly than pain? Yet I had heard that people with amputated arms and legs sometimes seem to feel pain in the missing limb, and it therefore didn't seem perfectly certain to me that the limb in which I feel a pain is always the one that hurts. And, to these grounds for doubt, I've recently added two that are very general: First, since I didn't believe myself to sense anything while awake that I couldn't also take myself to sense in a dream, and since I didn't believe that what I sense in sleep comes from objects outside me, I didn't see why I should believe what I sense while awake comes from such objects. Second, since I didn't yet know my creator (or, rather, since I supposed that I didn't know Him), I saw nothing to rule out my having been so designed by nature that I'm deceived even in what seems most obviously true to me.

And I could easily refute the reasoning by which I convinced myself of the reality of sensible things. Since my nature seemed to impel me towards many things which my reason rejected, I didn't believe that I ought to have much faith in nature's teachings. And, while my will didn't control my sense perceptions, I didn't believe it to follow that these perceptions came from outside me, since I thought that the ability to produce these ideas might be in me without my being aware of it.

Now that I've begun to know myself and my creator better, I still believe that I oughtn't blindly to accept everything that I seem to get from the senses. Yet I no longer believe that I ought to call it all into doubt.

In the first place, I know that everything that I clearly and distinctly understand can be made by God to be exactly as I understand it. The fact that I can clearly and distinctly understand one thing apart from another is therefore enough to make me certain that it is distinct from the other, since the things could be separated by God if not by something else. (I judge the things to be distinct regardless of the power needed to make them exist separately.) Accordingly, from the fact that I have gained knowledge of my existence without noticing anything about my nature or essence except that I am a thinking thing, I can rightly conclude that my essence consists solely in the fact that I am a thinking thing. It's possible (or, as I will say later, it's certain) that I have a body which is very tightly bound to me. But, on the one hand, I have a clear and distinct idea of myself insofar as I am just a thinking and unextended thing, and, on the other hand, I have a distinct idea of my body insofar as it is just an extended and unthinking thing. It's certain, then, that I am really distinct from my body and can exist without it. In addition, I find in myself abilities for special modes of awareness, like the abilities to have mental images and to sense. I can clearly and distinctly conceive of my whole self as something that lacks these abilities, but I can't conceive of the abilities' existing without me, or without an understanding substance in which to reside. Since the conception of these abilities includes the conception of something that understands, I see that these abilities are distinct from me in the way that a thing's properties are distinct from the thing itself.

I recognize other abilities in me, like the ability to move around and to assume various postures. These abilities can't be understood to exist apart from a substance in which they reside any more than the abilities to imagine and sense, and they therefore cannot exist without such a substance. But it's obvious that, if these abilities do exist, the substance in which they reside must

be a body or extended substance rather than an understanding one—for the clear and distinct conceptions of these abilities contain extension but not understanding.

There is also in me, however, a passive ability to sense—to receive and recognize ideas of sensible things. But, I wouldn't be able to put this ability to use if there weren't, either in me or in something else, an active power to produce or make sensory ideas. Since this active power doesn't presuppose understanding, and since it often produces ideas in me without my cooperation and even against my will, it cannot exist in me. Therefore, this power must exist in a substance distinct from me. And, for reasons that I've noted, this substance must contain, either formally or eminently, all the reality that is contained subjectively in the ideas that the power produces. Either this substance is a physical object (a thing of bodily nature which contains formally the reality that the idea contains subjectively), or it is God or one of His creations which is higher than a physical object (something which contains this reality eminently). But, since God isn't a deceiver, it's completely obvious that He doesn't send these ideas to me directly or by means of a creation which contains their reality eminently rather than formally. For, since He has not given me any ability to recognize that these ideas are sent by Him or by creations other than physical objects, and since He has given me a strong inclination to believe that the ideas come from physical objects, I see no way to avoid the conclusion that He deceives me if the ideas are sent to me by anything other than physical objects. It follows that physical objects exist. These objects may not exist exactly as I comprehend them by sense; in many ways, sensory comprehension is obscure and confused. But these objects must at least have in them everything that I clearly and distinctly understand them to have—every general property within the scope of pure mathematics.

But what about particular properties, such as the size and shape of the sun? And what about things that I understand less clearly than mathematical properties, like light, sound, and pain? These are open to doubt. But, since God isn't a deceiver, and since I therefore have the

God-given ability to correct any falsity that may be in my beliefs, I have high hopes of finding the truth about even these things. There is undoubtedly some truth in everything I have been taught by nature—for, when I use the term "nature" in its general sense, I refer to God Himself or to the order that He has established in the created world, and, when I apply the term specifically to *my* nature, I refer to the collection of everything that God has given *me*.

Nature teaches me nothing more explicitly, however, than that I have a body which is hurt when I feel pain, which needs food or drink when I experience hunger or thirst, and so on. Accordingly, I ought not to doubt that there is some truth to this.

Through sensations like pain, hunger, and thirst, nature also teaches me that I am not present in my body in the way that a sailor is present in his ship. Rather, I am very tightly bound to my body and so "mixed up" with it that we form a single thing. If this weren't so, I—who am just a thinking thing—wouldn't feel pain when my body was injured; I would perceive the injury by pure understanding in the way that a sailor sees the leaks in his ship with his eyes. And, when my body needed food or drink, I would explicitly understand that the need existed without having the confused sensations of hunger and thirst. For the sensations of thirst, hunger, and pain are just confused modifications of thought arising from the union and "mixture" of mind and body.

Also, nature teaches me that there are other physical objects around my body—some that I ought to seek and others that I ought to avoid. From the fact that I sense things like colors, sounds, odors, flavors, temperatures, and hardnesses, I correctly infer that sense perceptions come from physical objects which vary as widely (though perhaps not in the same way) as the perceptions do. And, from the fact that some of these perceptions are pleasant while others are unpleasant, I infer with certainty that my body—or, rather, my whole self which consists of a body and a mind—can be benefited and harmed by the physical objects around it.

There are many other things which I seem to have been taught by nature but which I have really accepted out of a habit of thoughtless judgment. These things may well be false. Among them are the judgments that a space is empty if nothing in it happens to affect my senses; that a hot physical object has something in it resembling my idea of heat; that a white or green thing has in it the same whiteness or greenness that I sense; that a bitter or sweet thing has in it the same flavor that I taste; that stars, towers, and other physical objects have the same size and shape that they present to my senses; and so on. If I am to avoid accepting what is indistinct in these cases, I must more carefully explain my use of the phrase "taught by nature." In particular, I should say that I am now using the term "nature" in a narrower sense than when I took it to refer to the whole complex of what God has given me. This complex includes much having to do with my mind alone (such as my grasp of the fact that what is done cannot be undone and of the rest of what I know by the light of nature) which does not bear on what I am now saying. And the complex also includes much having to do with my body alone (such as its tendency to go downwards) with which I am not dealing now. I'm now using the term "nature" to refer only to what God has given me insofar as I am a composite of mind and body. It is this nature which teaches me to avoid that which occasions painful sensations, to seek that which occasions pleasant sensations, and so on. But this nature seems not to teach me to draw conclusions about external objects from sense perceptions without first having examined the matter with my understanding—for true knowledge of external things seems to belong to the mind alone, not to the composite of mind and body. . . .

. . . I'll note that mind differs importantly from body in that body is by its nature divisible while mind is indivisible. When I think about my mind—or, in other words, about myself insofar as I am just a thinking thing—I can't distinguish any parts in me; I understand myself to be a single, unified thing. Although my whole mind seems united to my whole body, I know that cutting off a foot, arm, or other limb would not take anything away from my mind. The abilities to will, sense, understand, and so on can't be called parts, since it's one and the same mind that wills, senses, and understands. On the other hand, whenever I think of a physical or extended thing, I can mentally divide it, and I therefore understand that the object is divisible. This single fact would be enough to teach me that my mind and my body are distinct, if I hadn't already learned that in another way.

Next, I notice that the mind isn't directly affected by all parts of the body, but only by the brain—or maybe just by the small part of the brain containing the so-called "common sense." Whenever this part of the brain is in a given state, it presents the same thing to the mind, regardless of what is happening in the rest of the body (as is shown by innumerable experiments that I need not review here).

In addition, I notice that the nature of body is such that, if a first part can be moved by a second that is far away, the first part can be moved in exactly the same way by something between the first and second without the second part's being affected. For example, if A, B, C, and D are points on a cord, and if the first point (A) can be moved in a certain way by a pull on the last point (D), then A can be moved in the same way by a pull on one of the middle points (B or C) without D's being moved. Similarly, science teaches me that, when my foot hurts, the sensation of pain is produced by nerves distributed throughout the foot which extend like cords from there to the brain. When pulled in the foot, these nerves pull the central parts of the brain to which they are attached, moving those parts in ways designated by nature to present the mind with the sensation of a pain "in the foot." But, since these nerves pass through the shins, thighs, hips, back, and neck on their way from foot to brain, it can happen that their being touched in the middle, rather than at the end in the foot, produces the same motion in the brain as when the foot is hurt and, hence, that the mind feels the same pain "in the foot." And the point holds for other sensations as well.

Finally, I notice that, since only one sensation can be produced by a given motion of the part of the brain that directly affects the mind, the best conceivable sensation for it to produce is the one that is most often useful for the maintenance of the healthy man. . . .

I know that sensory indications of what is good for my body are more often true than false; I can almost always examine a given thing with several senses; and I can also use my memory (which connects the present to the past) and my understanding (which has now examined all the causes of error). Hence, I need no longer fear that what the senses daily show me is unreal. I should reject the exaggerated doubts of the past few days as ridiculous. This is especially true of the chief ground for these doubts—namely, my inability to distinguish dreaming from being awake. For I now notice that dreaming and being awake are importantly different: the events in dreams are not linked by memory to the rest of my life like those that happen while I am awake. If, while I'm awake, someone were suddenly to appear and then immediately to disappear without my seeing where he came from or went to (as happens in dreams), I would justifiably judge that he was not a real man but a ghost—or, better, an apparition created in my brain. But, if I distinctly observe something's source, its place, and the time at which I learn about it, and if I grasp an unbroken connection between it and the rest of my life, I'm quite sure that it is something in my waking life rather than in a dream. And I ought not to have the slightest doubt about the reality of such things if I have examined them with all my senses, my memory, and my understanding without finding any conflicting evidence. For, from the fact that God is not a deceiver, it follows that I am not deceived in any case of this sort. Since the need to act does not always allow time for such a careful examination, however, we must admit the likelihood of men's erring about particular things and acknowledge the weakness of our nature.

Correspondence with Princess Elisabeth, Concerning the Union of Mind and Body

RENÉ DESCARTES AND PRINCESS ELISABETH

Elisabeth to Descartes

May 6–16, 1643

. . . ⟨I ASK⟩ YOU TO TELL ME how man's soul, being only a thinking substance, can determine animal spirits so as to cause voluntary actions. For every determination of movement seems to come about either by the propelling of the thing moved, by the manner in which it is propelled by that which moves it, or else by the quality and shape of the surface of the latter. Now contact is required for the first two conditions, and extension for the third. But you exclude extension entirely from the notion you have of the soul, and contact seems to me incompatible with something which is immaterial. Therefore I ask you for a more explicit definition of the soul than you give in your metaphysics, i.e., of its substance, apart from its action, thought. For even if we suppose that soul and thought are, like the attributes of God, inseparable, a thesis difficult enough anyway to establish [for the child] in the mother's womb and in fainting spells, still we can acquire a more perfect idea of them if we consider them separately. . . .

Descartes to Elisabeth

May 21, 1643

. . . [T]he question which your Highness raises seems to me one which can most reasonably be asked as a consequence of my published writings. For there are two aspects of the human soul upon which depends all knowledge we can have of its nature. One of these is that it thinks; the other, that, united to the body, it can act and suffer with the body. I said almost nothing of the latter aspect, for I was interested in expounding the first clearly. My principal objective was to establish the distinction between soul and body, and for that purpose only the first characteristic of the soul was useful, and the other would not have been at all helpful. But since your Highness sees so clearly, that no one can dissemble anything from you, I will try to explain how I conceive the union of the soul with the body, and how the soul has the power to move the body. First, I hold that there are in us certain primitive notions, which are like the models on whose pattern we form all other knowledge. There are very few of these notions. After the most general— being, number, duration, etc., which apply to all that we could know—we have, specifically for body, only the notion of extension, from which are derived the notions of figure and motion. And for the soul alone, we have only the notion of thought, in which are included the conceptions of the understanding and the inclinations of the will. Finally, for soul and body together, we have only the notion of their union, from which are derived our notions of the power which the soul has to move the body, and of the body to act on the soul, to cause feelings and passions.

I believe too that all human knowledge consists in nothing else but in distinguishing these notions clearly and in attributing each of them correctly to the thing to which it applies. For when we want to explain some difficulty by means of a notion which is not appropriate to it, we cannot fail to be mistaken. Similarly we should err if we try to explain one of these notions in terms of another. For they are primitive, and each can be understood only in terms of itself. Now our senses have made the notions of extension, figure, and motion much more familiar than the others. Thus the main cause of our errors is that we ordinarily try to use these notions to explain things to which they are inappropriate, as when we want to use imagination to conceive of the nature of the soul, or, in trying to conceive the manner in which the soul moves the body, we think of it as similar to the way in which a body is moved by another body.

In the *Meditations,* which your Highness has so kindly read, I tried to explain the notions which belong to the soul only, distinguishing them from those which belong only to the body. Consequently the matter that I must next explain is the manner of conceiving those notions which apply to the union of the soul with the body, apart from those which belong only to body or only to the soul. In this regard it seems to me that what I wrote at the end of my *Replies to the Sixth Objections* could well be of use here. For we cannot expect to find these notions anywhere except in our soul, which contains all of them in itself, by its nature, but which does not always adequately distinguish them one from another, nor does it attribute them to the objects to which we should attribute them.

Thus I believe that we have in the past confused the notion of the power by which the soul acts in the body with that by which one body acts in another; and that we have attributed both of these, not to the soul, which we did not yet know, but to the different qualities of body, that is, to gravity, to heat, and to other qualities which we supposed to be real, that is, to have an existence distinct from that of body and therefore to be substances, even though we called them qualities. To conceive them we have sometimes used notions which are in us to know body and sometimes those which are in us to know the soul, according to whether that which we have attributed to them has been material or immaterial. For example, in supposing that gravity is a real quality, of which we have no other knowledge than that it has the power to move the body in which it is toward the center of the earth, we have no difficulty in conceiving how it moves this body nor how it is joined to it. We do not suppose that this occurs by any actual contact of one surface with another, but rather we experience in ourselves that we have a particular notion which enables us to understand this. Yet I hold that we misuse this notion in applying it to gravity (something which is not really distinct from body, as I hope to show in my *Physics*). For this notion has been given us to conceive the manner by which soul moves body. . . .

Elisabeth to Descartes

June 10–20, 1643

I must confess that . . . I find in myself all the causes of error which you mention in your letter, and I am unable to banish them entirely, because the life I am constrained to lead does not permit me enough time at my disposal to acquire a habit of meditation according to your rules. From time to time the interests of my House, which I must not neglect, or the conversations and amusements that I cannot evade, beset my feeble mind so strongly with annoyances and boredom that it becomes, for a long time thereafter, useless for anything else. This will serve, I hope, as an excuse for my stupidity in being unable to understand the idea by which we must judge how the soul (unextended and immaterial) can move the body, in terms of the notion which you previously had of gravity. Nor do I see why this power of moving a body toward the center of the earth, which you once erroneously attributed to the body under the name of quality, should be likely to convince us that a body can be impelled by something immaterial. It is more likely that the demonstration of a contrary truth ⟨about gravity⟩, which you promise in your *Physics,* would strengthen our belief in the impossibility ⟨of soul moving body⟩; chiefly because our idea ⟨of gravity⟩ (which cannot claim the same perfection and objective reality as that of God) might have been invented out of ignorance of that which really moves these bodies toward the center ⟨of the earth⟩. And since no material cause is present to the senses, we would have attributed it to its opposite, the immaterial. Yet I have never been able to conceive of the immaterial except as a negation of matter with which it can have no communication.

I confess that it would be easier for me to concede matter and extension to the soul, than the capacity to move a body and to be moved, to an immaterial being. For if the first ⟨moving a body⟩ is brought about by ⟨transfer of ⟩ information, it would be necessary that the ⟨animal⟩ spirits which cause movements be intelligent. But you do not attribute intelligence to anything corporeal. And even though in your *Meditations on Metaphysics* you show the possibility of the second ⟨body moving soul⟩, it is yet very difficult to understand how a soul, as you have described it, when it has the faculty and habit of reasoning, can lose all that because of some ⟨bodily⟩ vapors. And it is difficult also to understand how the soul, which is able to exist without the body, and has nothing in common with it, yet should be thus governed by the body. . . .

Descartes to Elisabeth

June 28, 1643

Madame,

I am very much obliged to your Highness because, after you have seen that I explained myself badly in my previous letters on the question it pleased you to ask me, you still accord me the patience to listen to me again on the same subject, and that you afford me the occasion to note the things which I omitted. The chief omissions seem to me to be the following. After I distinguished three types of ideas or primitive notions, each of which is known to us individually and not by a comparison of one with another, i.e., the notions we have of the soul, of the body, and that of the union of the soul with the body, I should have explained the differences in these three sorts of notions, and in the operations of the soul by which we come to have these notions, and I should explain the means by which we make each of these easy and familiar to ourselves. I should have explained also why I utilized the comparison with gravity, and I should have made clear that even though we might want to consider the soul as material (which we do when we conceive properly its union with the body) we do not thereby cease to know that it is separable from the body. These are, I think, all the problems that your Highness has set for me to deal with here.

First of all, then, I discern a great difference in these three sorts of notions, in that the soul cannot be conceived other than by the pure understanding; body (that is, extension, figure, and motion) may also be known by the understanding alone, but can be known much better by the understanding when it is aided by imagination. Finally, the notions which apply to the union of soul and body can be known only obscurely by the understanding alone, and no better by the understanding aided by the imagination; but they can be known very clearly by the senses: Hence it follows that those who never philosophize and who use only their senses do not doubt that the soul moves the body and that the body acts on the soul. But they consider the two as a single thing, that is, they consider the union of the two and to consider the union between two things is to consider them as one single thing. Metaphysical thoughts, which exercise only the pure understanding, are of use in rendering the notion of the soul familiar to us. The study of mathematics, which exercises in the main the imagination in the consideration of figures and motions, accustoms us to form very distinct notions of body. But it is by means of ordinary life and conversations and in abstaining from meditation and from studying things which exercise the imagination, that one learns to conceive the union of soul and body.

I'm almost afraid that your Highness may think that I am not speaking seriously here, but that would be contrary to the respect I owe you, and which I shall never fail to pay. And I can say, truthfully, that the chief rule that I have always observed in my studies, and that which I think has been most useful to me in acquiring knowledge, has been that I have devoted only a very few hours each day to thoughts which occupy imagination, and a very few hours each year, to those which occupy the understanding alone, and I have given all the rest of my time to the relaxation of the senses and to the repose of my mind. I count here among the exercises of the imagination all serious conversations and everything to which we must pay attention. It is this which has led me to withdraw to the country. Even though in the busiest city in the world I could have as many hours to myself as I employ now in study, nonetheless I could not employ them so efficiently when my intellect would be tired by the attention that the bustle of life requires.

For that reason I take the liberty of expressing here to your Highness my true appreciation of your ability, among the affairs and cares which are never lacking to those who are at the same time of great mind and of great birth, to find leisure to attend to those meditations which are requisite to understanding fully the distinction between the soul and the body. But I am of the opinion that it was these meditations, rather than the thoughts which require less attention, which cause you to find some obscurity in the notion that we have of their union. It does not seem to me that the human mind is capable of conceiving very distinctly, and at the same time, both the distinction between mind and body, and their union. To do that, it is necessary to conceive them as a single thing and at the same time consider them two things, which is self-contradictory.

In explaining this matter I assumed that your Highness had reasons which prove the distinction of the mind and body still very much in mind, and I did not at all intend to furnish you with reasons to put them aside, to represent to yourself the notion of the union which everyone experiences in himself without philosophizing; that is to say, that there is a single person who has at the same time a body and a thought which are of such a nature that this thought can move the body and can experience the events which happen to the body. Thus in an earlier letter when I used the comparison of gravity and other qualities which we imagine commonly to be united to bodies just as thought is united to ours, I did not bother

much that the comparison was not quite apt, because these qualities are not real in the way that we suppose they are, because I thought that your Highness was already entirely persuaded that the soul is a substance distinct from the body.

But since your Highness remarks that it is easier to attribute matter and extension to soul than to attribute to it the capacity to move a body and to be moved by it, without being material itself, I would ask your Highness to feel free in attributing this matter and extension to the soul, for this is nothing else than to conceive it united to the body. And after having considered this and experienced the union in yourself it will be easy for you to consider that the matter which you have attributed to thought is not thought itself, and that the extension of matter is of a different nature from the extension of thought. For the first ⟨extension of matter⟩ is determined at a certain location, and excludes from that location every other corporeal extension, which the second ⟨extension of thought⟩ does not. Thus your Highness will be able to recover easily the knowledge of the *distinction* of the soul and body, even though she has considered their union.

Finally, although I believe it is quite necessary to have understood, once in one's life, the principles of metaphysics, because it is through them that we receive knowledge of God and of our soul, I believe too that it would be very harmful to devote one's understanding to meditations about these principles, because we cannot attend as well to the functions of imagination and the senses. It is better to be content with retaining in memory and in belief the conclusions that one has at one time drawn, and to employ the rest of the time that one has for study for thoughts in which the understanding acts with the imagination and the senses. . . .

Suggestions for Further Reading

Colin McGinn in *The Character of Mind* (Oxford: Oxford University Press, 1982) provides a concise introduction to the mind–body problem, as does Chapter 4 of *Philosophical Problems and Arguments: An Introduction* by James Cornman and Keith Lehrer (New York: Macmillan, 1982).

The article on "Philosophy of Mind" and "Descartes" in *The Cambridge Dictionary of Philosophy,* edited by R. Audi, 2nd Edition (Cambridge: Cambridge University Press, 1999), will provide a helpful overview.

For a classic attack on mind–body dualism, see *The Concept of Mind* by Gilbert Ryle (New York: Harper and Row, 1949), especially Chapter 1.

For a classic defense, see Curt Ducasse, "In Defense of Dualism," from *Dimensions of Mind,* edited by Sidney Hook (New York: University Press, 1960).

Videos

Does Mind Matter? The Mind–Body Problem (30 minutes) features Julian Isaacs arguing that a materialistic view of mind is not compatible with the latest scientific evidence. *Is Mind Distinct from Body?* (30 minutes) examines how Descartes's dualism has been criticized. Both are available from Insight Media, 2162 Broadway, New York, NY 10024.

The Nature of Human Nature (58 minutes) and *Consciousness* (58 minutes) explore issues relating to the mind and the brain (available from Films for the Humanities and Sciences, PO Box 2053, Princeton, NJ 08543).

11.3 You Are an Embodied Self

Descartes's notion that the mind causally interacts with the body has been criticized for a variety of reasons. One has to do with the mysterious nature of the supposed causality. How can an immaterial substance that is nonspatial cause a material substance (the spatial body) to do anything? Causality requires some sort of contact. But how can this contact take place? This was the worry Princess Elisabeth expressed.

Another problem has to do with a physical law called the *conservation of energy.* According to this well-established law in current physical theory, the amount of energy in the universe is constant. However, if minds can act on physical bodies, new energy is created every time the mind causes the body to act. So interactionism appears to stand in direct contradiction to known physical laws.

A more recent line of criticism derives from mounting evidence about the brain and how it operates. Many scientists and philosophers now believe that it is only a matter of time until we can explain human behavior in physical terms. The more we learn about the brain and how it works, the more it seems evident that so-called mental states totally depend on the way the brain functions. If we had never seen a computer and suddenly discovered one, we might suppose that it was operated by some little person inside. However, as we learn more about the computer and how it works, we realize that there is no little person, or self, inside. The computations it performs are due to a complex mechanical arrangement and a program that provides instructions. So too, the argument goes, is the human brain.

Another recent criticism of Descartes's notion of the self as mind does not focus on the issue of interactionism but attacks the very idea of the self that underlies the theory of interaction. Cartesian dualism is a refined and sophisticated version of Plato's soul–body dualism (see Section 9.3). Both types of dualism have been immensely influential in Western culture. In fact, most of us were raised to believe in some kind of dualism. The very way we talk about ourselves reflects a dualistic viewpoint. We talk and think about our bodies as if they were shells or containers we just happen to inhabit. In other words, being in a body is not a necessary or essential characteristic of who we are.

However, imagine a world in which we had no eyes or ears, no sense of touch or smell or taste. What would such a world be like? "We would be very isolated," you might plausibly respond. Quite so. And isn't Descartes's mind quite isolated as well?

In the next selection, Eve Browning Cole, professor of philosophy at the University of Minnesota, Duluth, summarizes a critique of Descartes that stems from feminist philosophy. She argues that Descartes's procedure and his notion of the self pays insufficient attention to the fact that the self is embodied and exists in a network of relations with others. This fault has led to sexism insofar as it has reinforced a masculine notion of the self as autonomous, detached, and dominant over matter.

Reading Questions

1. What are some of the motivations, according to Cole, behind the philosophical discomfort with the physical body?
2. In what sense, according to Cole, is Descartes setting himself an artificial task?
3. Cole claims that if Descartes were working in collaboration with others, he could not easily entertain such radical doubts. Why?
4. What is the main point of the section entitled "The Uncertain Body"?
5. What is meant by "the relational self," and what difference would it have made if Descartes had begun his thought there?
6. In what sense is the concept of a radically isolated subject incoherent?
7. What does it mean to say that "the Cartesian ego is quintessentially *masculine*" and to say that "the relational self . . . is more aligned with feminine identity development"? What do you think about these two claims?
8. According to Cole, how is the "appearance obsession" related to Descartes's views about the relationship between mind and body?
9. What does Cole mean by the "embodied self"?
10. In light of what Descartes says in his correspondence with Princess Elisabeth about the "union" of the soul and body as a primitive notion, do you think Cole is right when she criticizes Descartes for not sufficiently acknowledging the importance of the fact that the self is embodied? Why, or why not?

Body, Mind, and Gender

EVE BROWNING COLE

WE HAVE ALREADY had occasion to observe that much of Western philosophy has displayed a definite discomfort with the fact that human minds come in human *bodies*, that consciousness and the thought processes it underlies are embodied in more or less gross matter. It is not very difficult to understand some of the motivations behind this discomfort. For thoughts do not seem to be subject to the same limitations as ordinary physical objects; in imagination, I can accomplish things which seem to transcend the limits of space and time. Vivid memories defy the irrecoverability of the past, seeming to bring to life dead friends, bringing into the present past scenes, meals, and dreams. Dreams themselves are a powerful impetus toward regarding the mind as something more than or different from the physical "container" which it "inhabits" (though we shall soon see reasons to question these terms). And personal identity, the "I" who is the location of my consciousness, stretches back in time to embrace the child I was, the adolescent I became, and the woman I am now, even though in the physical sense I can only claim to be exactly what I now am (the past being no longer present).

Thus there are certain *prima facie* reasons for at least questioning how consciousness, thought, dreams, and identity relate to the physical world. But we will see that quite often philosophers have gone much further than questioning the relationship, to the extent of privileging the mental over the physical, derogating the physical and the human body along with it to a secondary ontological status, counseling efforts to transcend the body in order to apprehend truth, and even regarding the fact that mental events can cause physical events as a miracle performed by God on a daily basis! While this last, far from being a majority view, seems to have been instead a desperate expedient recommended only by one philosopher (Malebranche), it is symptomatic of something having gone badly wrong at the philosophical starting point.

Let us look more closely at the way in which the relation between body and mind, and the status of the body in the grand scheme of things, become problematic for philosophy. As our companion in this inquiry we will choose René Descartes—whose philosophical outlook, especially as represented in the designedly popular work *Meditations on First Philosophy* (published in 1641), proved enormously influential and remains a standard component of introductory studies of Western philosophy today.

Solitary Meditations, Radical Doubts

Descartes's work came at an extremely crucial juncture for Western philosophy. He entered a philosophical milieu still largely dominated by the medieval scholastic tradition, itself based heavily on a theologized and incomplete digestion of the legacy of the ancient Greeks. Studying with the Jesuits at the college of La Flèche, he received a "classical" and rather intellectually conservative education. Descartes made a radical break with this tradition, however, and set institutional philosophy off in a wholly new direction. Seeking to provide a philosophical method which would be accessible to all who possess common sense, providing a set of "rules for the direction of the mind" which would be so simple that "even women" would be able to follow them, his contributions to philosophy were revolutionary and of inestimable worth and influence. His contribution to the topic of this chapter, however, is highly problematic; and the difficulties he bequeathed to subsequent modern Western thought are enormous.

The full title of Descartes's *Meditations* is *Meditations on First Philosophy: In Which the Existence of God and the Distinction Between Mind and Body Are Demonstrated*. This full title is instructive as to how Descartes himself viewed his purpose in the work, which is often read in modern terms as a refutation of skepticism or an essay in foundationalism. By his own description, it is a work of *metaphysics*.

Descartes begins by confessing that he has long been aware that false beliefs have formed a part of his world view, and that a general and total mental "housecleaning" would need to be undertaken, in order to discover which of his views should be retained and which discarded. The procedure for this belief-testing, which he now proposes to undertake (since he is at present free "from every care" and "happily agitated by no passions") is that of *doubting*. He will attempt to cast doubt on each of his present beliefs; only those that survive the doubt ordeal will be retained. Rather than holding up individual beliefs for scrutiny, however, he proposes to address their general bases:

> . . . [I]t will not be requisite that I should examine each [belief] in particular, which would be an endless undertaking; for owing to the fact that the destruction of the foundations of necessity brings with it the downfall of the rest of the edifice, I shall only in the first place attack those principles upon which all my former opinions rested.

This project raises several interesting issues. First, Descartes is firmly committed to a *hierarchical* view of the structure of his belief system. The metaphor of the edifice of opinion, an ordered structure in which there is a top-down organization of architectural form, is an epistemological image to which we return . . . when we discuss images of belief systems, and the power of the metaphors we choose to represent cognition.

But note also the extreme *solitude* of Descartes's project here. He is proposing to take apart and rebuild his entire belief structure in isolation from the rest of the world, and particularly from other human beings. The idea that an epistemological value test could reliably be applied in complete isolation from other knowers, that one's own relations of knowing the world could be tested through demolition and then rebuilt to stringent specifications entirely of one's own devising, is extraordinary. When we consider the contexts in which knowing takes place, in which knowledge is sought and constructed, few of these appear to be ones in which isolation is afforded or even desirable (we might think of archeological digs, science labs, classrooms, reading groups, research institutes, fact-finding missions to other countries, courtrooms, and other typical situations in which knowledge is found and formed in human minds; none is an individual-based project).

Thus Descartes is setting himself an *artificial* kind of task, in the dual sense that his knowledge-seeking environment is atypical and that the envisioned "new and improved" cognitive structure or edifice of opinion will be his *own* individual artifact.

But the solitariness of Descartes's project has also another implication/motivation. Only in radical isolation from the rest of the human social world can Descartes *fully* explore the reliability of his entire belief system. For if he were exploring in collaboration with others, if the meditations he undertakes were the work of a Cartesian task force, he would have to make concessions to the reliability of certain beliefs before the task force could begin its work. He would have to trust that the others were thinkers, perhaps even thinkers on a par with himself; that they were working with him rather than against him, that they could have and work toward a common goal, that their words could be understood, trusted, believed, taken more or less at face value. In other words, the Cartesian project could not motivate total doubt if it were not so solitary. The powerful skeptical doubts which Descartes is about to summon into existence will answer only to the call of an isolated individual human mental voice. They are creatures of solitude. Descartes's individualistic starting point has lasting and dramatic effects on his total project and its overall outcomes.

The Uncertain Body

As the doubt program progresses, Descartes discards his trust in his senses as a source of reliable belief. Since (he reasons) the senses have deceived him in the past, it is advisable to suspend belief in sensory information for the duration of his meditations until he can uncover some justification for their occasional reliable operations. But the senses have been the source of his belief that he is an embodied creature, that he exists in or as a physical organism, in addition to being an originator of thoughts. Thus he must suspend his belief in the existence of the embodied Descartes and conceive of himself only as a locus of thoughts and other mental events, possibly not embodied at all, possibly embodied very differently from the way he has always pictured and experienced himself:

> I shall . . . suppose, not that God who is supremely good and the fountain of truth, but

some evil genius not less powerful than deceitful, has employed his whole energies in deceiving me; I shall consider that the heavens, the earth, colors, figures, sound, and all the other external things are nought but the illusions and dreams of which this genius has availed himself in order to lay traps for my credulity; I shall consider myself as having no hands, no eyes, no flesh, no blood, nor any senses, yet falsely believing myself to possess all these things; I shall remain obstinately attached to this idea. . . .

Descartes will conceive of "himself" as something independent of his body, and will discover in this incorporeal consciousness the one indubitable truth which will function for him as an Archimedean immovable point, from which his belief structure can be rebuilt. This point is the certain truth of his own existence.

Descartes has effectively divided himself, and his belief structure, into two components: the certain mind, the component in which he will repose confidence at least as to its existence, and the uncertain body, about whose reality he will remain in a state of doubt until complex argumentation proves a limited trustworthiness, a constricted and carefully policed reliability.

Armed with the certainty of his own existence (as an insular node of consciousness which may or may not be embodied), Descartes goes on to demonstrate the existence of God, the fact that God is neither a grand deceiver nor the kind of being who would tolerate such massive deception of his creatures, and finally infers that the senses' urgings toward belief are not in themselves so awfully unreliable after all.

But the body, on Descartes's showing, remains forever only a probability, never a certainty. Since certainty is the Cartesian Holy Grail, this means that the body is irredeemably a second-class citizen in the metaphysical scheme of things. First rank in Descartes's universe is held by "thinking things," nodes of consciousness that can through purely rational processes follow deductive argumentation to absolutely certain conclusions. The body cannot participate in this process with its own humble abilities, here conceived as sensation and perception; it either impedes the rational process or, tamed and disciplined, stands dumbly by and lets knowledge happen. Highest epistemological honors go to the elements of deductive reasoning processes: mathematical laws, logical principles, indubitable truths. These construct the knowable core of the world, and to them in human experience is superadded a "flesh" of more dubious nature: bodies, colors, touches, smells, and the entire organic contents of the universe.

This theme, the privileging of the mental over the physical, does not originate with Descartes by any means. It is familiar to readers of Plato, who describes the relationship of soul to body in vivid terms:

> . . . [W]hen the soul uses the instrumentality of the body for any inquiry, whether through sight or hearing or any other sense—because using the body implies using the senses—it is drawn away by the body into the realm of the variable, and loses its way and becomes confused and dizzy, as though it were fuddled, through contact with things of a similar nature. . . . But when it investigates by itself, it passes into the realm of the pure and everlasting and immortal and changeless. . . . [*Phaedo* 79c–d]

Here the body is cast in the role of a bad companion, bad company for the soul to keep, company that drags it down to its own level and impedes its effective functioning. A nonphysical form of knowing, in which the soul or mind operates "by itself," is much to be preferred.

Two features of this way of discussing the relation of mind to body, common to Plato and Descartes, should be noted. First, it is striking how easily both drop into the mode of thought in which a human being becomes not one but two, and two *different*, kinds of entity. There quickly emerges a kind of logical and metaphysical distance between mind and body, an alienation that provokes disagreement about what to believe, what to seek, how to behave. But secondly, this is not a disagreement among equals. The mind or soul is in Descartes's view the locus of certainty and value, in Plato's view the part of the human composite akin to the "pure" and "divine." Its relationship to the body is to be one of dominance; the body is to be subordinated and ruled.

An individual human being contains within the self, therefore, a fundamental power dialectic in which mind must triumph over body and must trumpet its victory in flourishes of "pure" rationality by means of which its soundness is demonstrated and ratified. Far from being an isolated peculiarity of a small handful of philosophers, moreover, this general dialectic is seen being set up and played out in many theaters of Western culture, from religion to popular morality, from Neoplatonism to existentialism. . . .

Feminist Critiques

We have already noted the extraordinary isolation of Descartes's metaphysical musings; he cuts off not only the instructions of his perceptive faculties, but also the entirety of his human social surroundings, to seek a certainty accessible only to the lone and insular conscious node "I." A feminist critique of Cartesian method might well begin with just this feature of his project.

The Cartesian ego, rather than being the ground for certainty and the Archimedean point which some philosophers have taken it to be, may in fact be the result of a mistaken abstraction. Feminist philosophers such as Caroline Whitbeck and Lorraine Code have convincingly argued that a preferable starting point for understanding the contents of human consciousness is *the relational self,* the self presented as involved in and importantly constituted by its connectedness to others. Each of us at this moment is connected as it were by invisible threads to an indefinite number of specific other human beings. In some cases, these connections are relatively remote; for example, we are all members of the same species and have biological similarities. Similarity is a relationship; therefore we are all related. Western culture has not tended to place much weight on this species relationship, however, and in some notorious institutions such as chattel slavery the reality of the relationship has been implicitly or explicitly denied. In other cases, the relationships in which we now stand are of deep significance in defining who we are, how we think, and how we act.

Starting with the concept of the relational self would greatly have changed the course of Descartes's meditations. If other persons are not just colorful wallpaper the design of which I contemplate from inside a mental fishbowl but actually part of who I am, then distancing myself from them in thought and supposing that I am the only consciousness in the universe becomes, if not impossible, extremely illogical. What would I hope to accomplish? If on the other hand I begin by granting them mentality and humanity, I will proceed by considering the specific ways in which their contributions to my mental life are made.

Paula Gunn Allen writes that, in Native American cultures, the question "Who is your mother?" is another and more profound way of asking who one is. In asking, one is inquiring about one of the most significant parts of a person's identity, for the influence of the mother and the mother's contribution to the child's self is considerable. In much the same way, we might begin a metaphysics of the self by asking "To whom am I related? In what ways? What contributions to my consciousness are presently being made, and by whom?" Such a beginning acknowledges the fundamental importance of sociality in human existence.

Here it might be objected that Descartes's . . . methodological skepticism about the existence and reality of other minds remains a possible position even for a relational self. Haven't we merely sidestepped the skeptical possibility by granting the mentality and humanity of the others? Doesn't it really still seem possible that they are all phantasms, or robots, or results of direct C-fiber stimulation by a mad scientist on a distant planet?

Yes, skeptical possibilities remain and cannot be ruled out. But taking the standpoint of the relational self allows us to affirm that such possibilities *do not matter.* What matters is that relationships are granted metaphysical priority over isolated individuals, so that the embeddedness of the self in a social world becomes its primary reality. The exact nature of the individuals involved becomes a matter of secondary importance. I grant at the outset that others make constitutive contributions to my experience, and I to theirs. This mutual interrelation becomes the ground for any further inquiry rather than functioning as a more or less uncertain inductive conclusion. Thus, to return to the problem of other minds, we can see that the philosopher's uncertainty about the mentality of the "foreign body" at the bus stop is a symptom of a flawed starting point rather than a genuine puzzle attending our reflective lives. The philosopher's mistake is to begin from isolation and attempt to reason himself back into society; we in fact begin in society and this is not an accidental but a deep truth about us.

We might go even further and argue that the concept of a radically isolated subject as the seat of consciousness is simply incoherent. We do not begin to think and speak in solitude, but in concert with our culture and with the specific representatives of the culture in whose care we find ourselves. We form ourselves in a collective process that is ongoing; our thoughts are never entirely our own, intersubjectivity is basic, while individual subjectivity is secondary and an abstraction.

Some feminist philosophers have analyzed the isolation of the ego and the "fishbowl" syndrome of some philosophy of mind in terms of differences between masculine and feminine gender socialization. Developmental psychologists have suggested that the structure and dynamics of relationships with other human beings differ profoundly for traditionally socialized men and women. Due largely to the fact that, in most cultures and historical epochs, women function as the primary caregiver for children of both sexes while men enter into the life of the family in a more intermittent way, it is to be expected that male children will form their earliest sense of themselves by *distinguishing* themselves from their female caregiver, realizing that they are members of the group from which the (distant, absent, or intermittently present) male family members derive. Female children will form their sense of themselves by *identifying* with the female caregiver, realizing that they share with her membership in the group of female family members. This early direction of the sense of self, either to distinguish oneself and differ from, or to identify oneself and resemble, leaves a lasting legacy in the child's heart and mind. The adult character which emerges from the social-

ization process is marked by the tendency toward either clear and stark ego boundaries (if male) or flexible and mobile ego boundaries (if female). A whole constellation of dispositions and traits goes alongside this basic distinction. The masculine ego, formed at a distance from its primary role exemplar, displays a lifelong tendency toward independence, distancing from others, and endless acts of "proving" the masculinity which it modeled, with some uncertainty, on the distant fellow *man*. The feminine ego, formed in close proximity to its primary role exemplar, has lifelong tendencies toward identifying with others, reciprocating feelings, being dependent on others and relating to them easily even confusing its own needs with those of others—since it early on perceived that part of being a woman was to place others first, as a primary caregiver must frequently do.

This developmental thesis about gender identity, though impossible to demonstrate empirically and almost certainty *not* cross-culturally or cross-racially, offers a tempting explanation for the philosophical model of the isolated self we have traced in Descartes and seen lurking behind the problem of other minds. The Cartesian ego is quintessentially *masculine* in its solitary doubting program, in its self-confidence about its quest, in its ambition ("proving" itself all on its own resources), and in its uneasiness. . . .

By contrast, the relational self which some feminist philosophers have proposed as an alternative starting point for philosophy of mind, and for grounding our understanding of human experience generally, is more aligned with feminine identity development.

In addition to proposing that philosophers start from a conception of the human self as relational, as situated within a web of cultural and personal relationships which not only shape but do much to constitute its being and its thought, feminist philosophers have also criticized the Cartesian legacy for the relation between mind and body which it conveys.

We saw above that Descartes (and others) operate from a position that separates mind, self, consciousness, ego from the physical body these are said to "inhabit" or . . . "animate." In Descartes, the distinction is so drastic that mind and body are said to share no attributes whatsoever; they are oppositionally defined and thus, metaphysically speaking, mutually exclusive. Consciousness is nonphysical, nonextended, and inhabits an order of being completely distinct from that in which the body lives. The body is a machine, operated by the mind in the case of the human being, mindless and purely mechanical in the case of other animals.

This drastic dualism is vulnerable to criticism from many different directions; feminist critics begin with the observation that in Western culture and throughout its history, we can observe a tendency to identify women with the natural, the physical, the bodily. Nature is personified as a female, a "mother"; women are portrayed as more closely linked to nature, less completely integrated into civilization and the cultural order, than men. Men are rational agents, makers of order and measure, controllers of history; women are emotional vessels, subjects of orders and measures, passive observers of history. No one describes this more clearly or more influentially for modern psychology than Sigmund Freud, who writes:

> The fact that women must be regarded as having little sense of justice is no doubt related to the predominance of envy in their mental life; for the demand for justice is a modification of envy and lays down the condition subject to which we can lay envy aside. We also regard women as weaker in their social interests and as having less capacity for sublimating their instincts than men.

Freud subsumes women into the domain of the natural, where instinct rules and justice is foreign.

Now, if man is to mind as woman is to body, as appears from much of the literature and iconography of Western culture throughout historical time, and if we adhere to a generally Cartesian view of the self as a purely mental entity, then the self of the woman becomes deeply problematic. Can women have Cartesian egos? Genuine selves? It would appear to be impossible if woman's essence is located in the domain of

the bodily. Clearly some other and less dichotomously dualistic conception of the self must be sought. The associations between woman and body in Western culture have had a decidedly negative aspect, which feminist critics have stressed. The reduction of a woman's value to the culturally inscribed value of a certain feminine appearance and protest against that reduction have been strong themes of feminist criticism for several decades. Nevertheless, the appearance obsession which women are encouraged to develop in our culture, according to which a more-or-less single standard of feminine beauty applies to all women, no matter their age, race, build, or lifestyle, is as strong as ever and, some argue, gaining strength. In addition now to being slim, youthful, cosmetically adorned to the correct degree, fashionably dressed, and as light-skinned as possible (with of course a healthy tan to indicate white-skinned class-privilege), women must ideally have "hard bodies" with muscle-definition acquired by hours of grueling workouts and aerobic routines. That this formula cannot be met by the poor, those who don't have the time to devote to the pursuit of beauty, or those whose bodies resist the mold for whatever reason, does not mean that the standard does not hold its pristine severity over all women's heads equally. (Sadly, the appearance obsession does seem to be extending to men as well, but still seems to pertain to them in lesser degree.)

In a recent classroom discussion of trends in advertising, one young female student spoke out with sincere enthusiasm: "I can't wait till I get older! I'm going to eat whatever I want, wear whatever I want, and just not care!" An older female student turned to her and said, "Why wait? It isn't any easier to look different at age fifty than at age twenty." This exchange was instructive in many ways. There was anger in the second woman's voice; she heard herself as older being dismissed somehow from the class of viable potential beauties. There was a strange assumption behind the first woman's statements, to the effect that until some unspecified age, women are under an obligation to eat and to dress in ways other than those they would choose if not constrained. And there was in the second speaker's choice of the word *different* to describe an undisciplined woman the implicit admission that the *norm,* what it means to be *non*different, is precisely the cultural ideal of the dieting and carefully dressed youthful appearance. But this is clearly false, as a simple glance at the immense variety of actual women's bodies in any real-life situation will immediately confirm. The so-called *norm* is in fact extremely rare. Yet an enormous amount of women's energy is devoted to its pursuit. Constant dieting, eating disorders such as anorexia and bulimia, compulsive exercising, and (not least of all) enormous cash investments in beauty and fashion, are all symptomatic of the power of the cultural ideal.

To connect with our previous discussion of the gendered distinction between mind and body, men generally do not in our culture tend to identify themselves and their worth as persons with the details of their physical bodies' appearances. While in recent years the standards of male attractiveness have undoubtedly become more exacting, men clearly feel more relaxed about not meeting these standards.

Let us summarize the contribution which the dualistic Platonic–Cartesian model of the self has made to our cultural conceptions of body and mind: (1) The body's relationship to the mind, in any given human being, is one of unruly bondage or servitude; mind properly dominates its body and directs its actions, while body properly obeys. (2) Mind's behavior and dispositions are, however, described in terms more appropriate to masculine gender identity (activity, ruling or hegemony, capacity for abstraction and objectivity, distanced contemplation, dispassionate analysis), while body's configurations tend toward feminine (passivity, subordination, unconscious physicality, sensuous and emotional implication, confusion). (3) Thus, while rationality becomes defined as a mostly masculine project, an adorned and disciplined physicality becomes the feminist project—leading to the contemporary obsession of middle-class women with weight and appearance generally. Women are given the cultural prescription to be docile bodies, adorned and available for participation in the rational schemes of the male-dominated social

order. Thus the fact that in some basic respects the Cartesian ego is a masculine ego can be seen to have enormous reverberations throughout modern life. It is of no small significance to recognize that a certain outlook in the philosophy of mind provides a perfect recipe for male dominance and women's subordination.

Several important qualifications need to be made here, however. First, the neat gender dichotomy we have drawn in the ratio of proportion:

Male : Mind :: Female : Body

does not appear to hold cross-racially. That is, nonwhite males in a white-dominated culture will be treated in much the same way as bodies are treated by minds in the Cartesian framework: They will be dominated, ruled, directed, used. Furthermore, white females will participate in this domination and rule, functioning as "minds" in a bureaucratic manner; and white women will benefit from skin privilege at the expense of the dominated nonwhite men and women. The nonwhite populations will be accorded *mental* attributes that correspond to the physical attributes of the body in the Cartesian scheme; they will be considered less than fully rational, emotional, "natural" or savage, sensuous, weak-willed, and so forth. So the factor of race does much to complicate a mind–body value map which takes *only* gender into account. This has led some feminist philosophers to hypothesize that *both* sexism and racism are more about power than they are about either sex or race.

A second qualification concerns the relationship between what, for want of a clearer word, we could call ideology and social reality. The rational man and the physical woman, intellectual masculinity and corporeal femininity, are creatures of ideology. This means that they are intensely value-laden concepts structuring culture and its expectations, rather than empirical generalizations drawn from observation of real women and real men. But ideology and reality touch one another at multiple points and reciprocally influence each other at these points of contact. It may be a strange-sounding philosophical thesis that rationality has been interpreted in terms defined as masculine, but it takes on a gruesomely real shape when a Berkeley philosophy professor announces to his classes that women can't do logic, or when another philosophy professor writes to the secretary of the American Philosophical Association that white women and black people of both sexes display analytical capabilities inferior to those of white men. This is ideology shaping social reality with a vengeance.

Believing that the drastic dualism of the traditional picture of body's relation to mind, along with the inbuilt evaluatively hierarchical model of dominance and subordination which gives the model its working directives, are both deeply flawed, feminist philosophers look for alternatives.

A beginning point is to conceive of the human self as intrinsically embodied: An *embodied self* can displace the only questionably embodied Cartesian ego, the uncomfortably body-trapped Platonic soul, as a foundation for further inquiry into the nature of human experience. To conceive of the self as essentially or intrinsically embodied means to acknowledge the centrality of the physical in human psychology and cognition, for one thing. It means opening the door to the possibility of a bodily wisdom, to revaluing the physical human being, in ways that promise both better metaphysical schemes and more ethical models for human interaction. Breaking down the valuational hierarchy between mind and body, attempting to think of them as woven and melded together into what constitutes who we are and who we ought to be, eliminates the perhaps primary internal oppression model of mind over body. As a culture, however, we have learned to think of the body, and of those primarily identified with it, in terms of scorn (even when those latter people are ourselves). We have learned to

privilege the "rational" over the emotional (conceived as proceeding from physical sources), the basely corporeal, the manual and tactile; to weigh technorationality over the mute testimony of nature and our own bodies. Those of us who are women have at times been encouraged to view our bodies with contempt when we perceive them as falling short of the beauty ideal or when we are addressed rudely in sexual terms by strangers. How can we begin to approach the relation of mind and body not as a *problem* but as a source of liberatory insight and joy?

French feminist philosophers, building on their national intellectual tradition, which placed the phenomenology of *lived experience* at center stage, have made exciting progress in constructing the basis for a liberatory philosophy of the body. They have argued that the dominant tradition in Western philosophy has made women's bodies problematic in two contradictory ways: In one way, woman and body are equated as essentially physical, and women's entire personalities become sexualized (think of the late Victorian habit of referring to women as a group with the phrase "the sex," as if men were "the nonsex"). In another direction, however, the sexualized woman is either ignored in philosophy, so complete is her subsumption under the rubric *Nature,* or she is philosophized about in male terms, and her (now highlighted in neon) sexuality is described in terms appropriate only to a certain specific cultural construction of *male* sexuality. She is thus obscured as a subject, discussed as an object.

This means that, for a genuinely liberatory philosophy of the body to be developed, women must reclaim in theory and in practice their own physicality, their own sexuality. . . .

Suggestions for Further Reading

In *The Flight to Objectivity: Essays on Cartesianism and Culture* (Albany: State University of New York Press, 1987), Susan Bordo develops in more detail some of the ideas summarized here.

Also see Lynda Lange, "Sexist Dualism: Its Material Sources in the Exploitation of Reproductive Labor," *Praxis International* 9 (1990): 400–407.

Rosemary Radford Ruether has developed this line of criticism from a theological perspective in "Body–Soul and Subject–Object Dualism as the Model of Oppression" in *Liberation Theology: Human Hope Confronts Christian History and American Power* (New York: Paulist Press, 1972).

Caroline Whitbeck develops a nondualistic viewpoint from a feminist perspective in "A Different Reality: Feminist Ontology" in *Women, Knowledge, and Reality: Explorations in Feminist Philosophy,* edited by Ann Garry and Marilyn Pearsall (Boston: Unwin Hyman, 1989).

See *The Nature of the Self* by Risieri Frondizi (Carbondale: Southern Illinois University Press, 1953) for a critique of Descartes and the development of a relational and functional view of the self.

Video

The Social Brain (58 minutes; Films for the Humanities and Sciences, PO Box 2053, Princeton, NJ 08543) explores how desire to relate to others is rooted in the brain.

The Doors of Perception (58 minutes) explores the relationship between the internal world of mind and the external world. Available from Insight Media, 2162 Broadway, New York, NY, 10024.

11.4 There Is No Self

Buddhism developed in India around 500 BCE and quickly came into conflict with some of the basic ideas of Hindu philosophy. Among the areas of conflict was the issue of the existence of the self. Hinduism and Buddhism gave very different answers to the question "What am I?" Some Hindu philosophers answered, "You are the Atman" (for a discussion of the Atman, see Section 9.4), and Buddhism responded with the assertion "There is no Atman." This is called **anatta** (also *Anatman*), or the no-self doctrine.

To understand this teaching, we must back up a moment to another Buddhist teaching called **anicca**, or impermanence. The doctrine of impermanence is a logical implication of the doctrine of dependent origination. If everything that exists is dependent on something else for its existence (as the thesis of dependent origination holds), there can be no independently existing things. This amounts to a denial of the existence of substances since substances are usually thought of as independently existing things. It also amounts to a denial of eternally permanent essences. And it is quite clear that some Indian philosophers regarded the Atman as an independently existing thing that is eternal and permanent.

If there are no substances and if everything is impermanent, it follows that what exists is in constant process. In contrast to Plato's essentialist metaphysics (see Section 9.3), Buddhism teaches a process view of reality. There are no Forms or essences, only ever-changing processes. Hence, according to Buddhist thought, we are wrong if we think of the *jiva* (individual soul or ego) as a permanent substance the way Plato did, or if we think of the Atman (universal Self) as a permanent substance the way some Hindu thinkers did. There is no soul, no ego, no Self, if we mean by any of those terms some independently existing substance or essence.

Note that Buddhists are not denying that you or I exist. They are only denying a particular philosophical view about our natures, the view that the word *I* refers to some unchanging substance called the self or soul. According to Buddhist philosophy, humans are made up of what they call the **five aggregates**. These consist of physical form, sensation, conceptualization, dispositions to act, and consciousness. There is no substance over and above these aggregates.

"What," I hear you say, "I am nothing but a collection of elements! How disappointing." It seems so to those of us raised with the idea that what is most important about us is our souls. If we have no souls, then we have no value, or so our culture has taught us. However, our cultural conditioning in this regard may blind us to the value of the Buddhist concept of *anatta*.

The no-self teaching had particular moral and religious value for Buddhism because once we are clear about the fact that there is no substantial self, we can be released from suffering and motivated to act with compassion. Suffering and selfishness arise from desiring things and clinging to them (see Section 3.2). However, if there is no self, then selfish desiring and clinging amount to one vast illusion, a dream from which those who know the truth about the self can awake. What appears at first glance to be a negative doctrine becomes positive once its moral and religious implications are understood.

What does all of this have to do with the mind–body problem? Unlike Western concerns, the problem that concerns Buddhists is how to overcome suffering. So the question "What am I?" inevitably leads them down a different path. Even so, it is interesting to note that of the five aggregates, all but the first one refer to what Western philosophers would call mental events. The mind–body problem can be stated in Buddhist terms, but it is not a problem about how two totally different substances can causally interact. Rather, it is a problem about how differing processes can causally affect each other. Since both mental processes and physical processes are dependent on each other, the sharp separation of totally different substances characteristic of dualism does not enter the picture. This does not mean that Buddhist philosophers faced no problems in working out the details of how the aggregates might be related, but the dualist and substantialist assumptions so characteristic of the mind–body problem in the West did not shape the problem for them.

The Buddhist thesis of no-self is not without its parallels in the West. According to C. D. Broad (see his *The Mind and Its Place in Nature* published by Littlefield, Adams, 1960, p. 558), two theories about the self developed in Western philosophy. One he calls the center theory. According to this theory, the unity of the mind is constituted by a center that is not identical with any of one's thoughts, feelings, or sensations, but thoughts, feelings, and sensations can be characterized as states of this center. This center, or self, is thought of by Descartes as an immaterial substance. The other theory can be called either the non-center theory or the bundle theory. According to this theory, there is no center (self) over and above mental events. All we are is a bundle of mental events, and our unity consists in the fact that these mental events are interrelated in certain characteristic ways. David Hume (see Section 7.4) is often interpreted as holding the bundle theory. According to Hume, when he examines his mental life, all he ever finds is a series of thoughts, feelings, and sensations. Hard as he looks, he can find no self, or soul, above and beyond his changing mental events. The self, or soul, is a fiction we construct to characterize the unity we feel binds these bundles together.

It is tempting to characterize the Buddhist idea of the no-self and the five aggregates as yet another version of the bundle, or non-center, theory. And indeed it does seem to be related insofar as it denies there is a substantive, immaterial center of consciousness that has mental states but is not identical with such states. However, there is also a difference, at least a difference with the way Hume articulates the bundle theory. The bundle Hume is concerned with is a purely mental bundle of thoughts, feelings, and sensations. The five aggregates the Buddhists speak of include more than this. We are not just a unified bundle of mental events but a unified aggregate that includes our physical bodies as well.

I think it would be a mistake to interpret the no-self doctrine (at least as it is presented in the following selection) as yet another theory (like the bundle theory) of the self. This so-called theory is not really a theory of the self but a critique of the substantive theory. Its intention is not to create a new theory but to show what is wrong with existing theories.

The first selection comes from the *Digha Nikaya* and is attributed to the Buddha himself. It deals with teachings about the permanence and existence of the soul found in Hindu philosophy. Buddhist monks found themselves in debate with Hindus on these issues, and this selection instructs them on how they can argue with their opponents and thereby show their opponents' views about the soul to be false. It is the classic expression of the sorts of arguments refined and elaborated in latter Buddhism.

Note that this selection ends with a statement about the afterlife. Clearly one advantage of the doctrine that there is a soul is that one can explain life after death and reincarnation in terms of this soul persisting after the death of the body. However, if there is no soul, what, if anything, persists? Interestingly, the Buddhists affirmed a doctrine of continuity from one life to the next but denied there is a soul that is reborn or reincarnated. Rather what connects this life to the past or to the future is *karma* (see Section 10.4). You are the result of what you have done.

The second selection is the famous simile of the chariot found in the *Milindapanha*. It would seem that if there is no soul, then all kinds of absurd things follow. King Menander, a Greek who ruled northwestern India in the second century BCE, was quick to point out these absurdities when the Buddhist monk Nagasena denied that his personal name referred to a permanent individual substance. Nagasena counterargued, using the king's own logic and the example of a chariot, to show that the king himself believed there is no chariot above and beyond its parts, yet he saw no problem in using the term *chariot* as a practical designation. So too with the word *I*. It is just a convenient way of talking, a mere sound, without any reference to something substantial.

As an interesting multicultural footnote on this ancient debate, I should call your attention to the fact that here Greek culture (represented by King Menander) encountered Indian Buddhist culture (represented by Nagasena) in public debate (there was an audience of Greeks and Indian monks who witnessed the exchange). Greek philosophers were fond of an argument called "turning the tables." One turns the table on one's debate opponents by using their own assumptions and arguments against them. So Socrates (see Section 3.4) turned the table on a famous sophist named Protagoras by showing that his relativistic principle that stated "Man is the measure of all things" led to the conclusion that Protagoras's philosophical principle was false because Socrates (a man) thought (measures) it false. Supposedly the Greeks invented the technique of "turning the tables," but in this passage a Buddhist monk successfully used it on a Greek, much to the pleasure of the other monks and the grudging admiration of the assembled Greeks.

Reading Questions

1. What is wrong with maintaining that the soul is sentient (conscious)?
2. What is wrong with maintaining that the soul is not sentient?
3. What is wrong with maintaining that consciousness, or sentience, is a property or characteristic of the soul?
4. Since the notions of the soul and of surviving death are closely related, what must a Buddhist monk who rejects these theories of the soul believe about a perfected being who has died?
5. How does King Menander argue against Nagasena's assertion that the name Nagasena is only a practical designation and does not refer to any permanent individual?
6. How does Nagasena counter the King's argument?
7. Who do you think wins this debate, Nagasena or King Menander? Why?
8. What unanswered questions do these readings leave you with? Can you figure out how to answer them?

False Doctrines About the Soul
and the Simile of the Chariot

False Doctrines About the Soul

AGAIN THE SOUL MAY BE thought of as sentient or insentient, or as neither one nor the other but having sentience as a property. If someone affirms that his soul is sentient you should ask, "Sentience is of three kinds, happy, sorrowful, and neutral. Which of these is your soul?" For when you feel one sensation you don't feel the others. Moreover these sensations are impermanent, dependent on conditions, resulting from a cause or causes, perishable, transitory, vanishing, ceasing. If one experiences a happy sensation and thinks "This is my soul," when the happy sensation ceases he will think "My soul has departed." One who thinks thus looks on his soul as something impermanent in this life, a blend of happiness and sorrow with a beginning and end, and so this proposition is not acceptable.

If someone affirms that the soul is not sentient, you should ask, "If you have no sensation, can you say that you exist?" He cannot, and so this proposition is not acceptable.

And if someone affirms that the soul has sentience as a property you should ask, "If all sensations of every kind were to cease absolutely there would be no feelings whatever. Could you then say 'I exist'?" He could not, and so this proposition is not acceptable.

When a monk does not look on the soul as coming under any of these three categories . . . he refrains from such views and clings to nothing in the world; and not clinging he does not tremble, and not trembling he attains Nirvāna. He knows that rebirth is at an end, that his goal is reached, that he has accomplished what he set out to do, and that after this present world there is no other for him. It would be absurd to say of such a monk, with his heart set free, that he believes that the perfected being survives after death—or indeed that he does not survive, or that he does and yet does not, or that he neither

From The Buddhist Tradition in India, China and Japan, *edited by Wm. Theodore De Bary. Copyright © 1969 by Wm. Theodore De Bary. Reprinted by permission of The Modern Library, a Division of Random House Inc., pp. 20–23.*

does nor does not. Because the monk is free his state transcends all expression, predication, communication, and knowledge.

[From *Digha Nikāya,* pp. 2.64 ff.]

The Simile of the Chariot

Then King Menander went up to the Venerable Nāgasena, greeted him respectfully, and sat down. Nāgasena replied to the greeting, and the King was pleased at heart. Then King Menander asked: "How is your reverence known, and what is your name?"

"I'm known as Nāgasena, your Majesty, that's what my fellow monks call me. But though my parents may have given me such a name . . . it's only a generally understood term, a practical designation. There is no question of a permanent individual implied in the use of the word."

"Listen, you five hundred Greeks and eighty thousand monks!" said King Menander. "This Nāgasena has just declared that there's no permanent individuality implied in his name!" Then, turning to Nāgasena, "If, Reverend Nāgasena, there is no permanent individuality, who gives you monks your robes and food, lodging and medicines? And who makes use of them? Who lives a life of righteousness, meditates, and reaches Nirvāna? Who destroys living beings, steals, fornicates, tells lies, or drinks spirits? . . . If what you say is true there's neither merit nor demerit, and no fruit or result of good or evil deeds. If someone were to kill you there would be no question of murder. And there would be no masters or teachers in the [Buddhist] Order and no ordinations. If your fellow monks call you Nāgasena, what then is Nāgasena? Would you say that your hair is Nāgasena?" "No, your Majesty."

"Or your nails, teeth, skin, or other parts of your body, or the outward form, or sensation, or perception, or the psychic constructions, or con-

sciousness? Are any of these Nāgasena?" "No, your Majesty."

"Then are all these taken together Nāgasena?" "No, your Majesty."

"Or anything other than they?" "No, your Majesty."

"Then for all my asking I find no Nāgasena. Nāgasena is a mere sound! Surely what your Reverence has said is false!"

Then the Venerable Nāgasena addressed the King.

"Your Majesty, how did you come here—on foot, or in a vehicle?"

"In a chariot."

"Then tell me what is the chariot? Is the pole the chariot?" "No, your Reverence."

"Or the axle, wheels, frame, reins, yoke, spokes, or goad?" "None of these things is the chariot."

"Then all these separate parts taken together are the chariot?" "No, your Reverence."

"Then is the chariot something other than the separate parts?" "No, your Reverence."

"Then for all my asking, your Majesty, I can find no chariot. The chariot is a mere sound. What then is the chariot? Surely what your Majesty has said is false! There is no chariot! . . . "

When he had spoken the five hundred Greeks cried "Well done!" and said to the King, "Now, your Majesty, get out of that dilemma if you can!" "What I said was not false," replied the King. "It's on account of all these various components, the pole, axle, wheels, and so on, that the vehicle is called a chariot. It's just a generally understood term, a practical designation."

"Well said, your Majesty! You know what the word 'chariot' means! And it's just the same with me. It's on account of the various components of my being that I'm known by the generally understood term, the practical designation Nāgasena."

[From *Milindapanha* (Trenckner ed.), pp. 25 ff.]

Suggestions for Further Reading

For a detailed study of Buddhist views on the self see Paul J. Griffiths's *On Being Mindless: Buddhist Meditation and the Mind–Body Problem* (La Salle, IL: Open Court, 1986). The concluding chapter provides a concise summary of the major philosophical issues.

See also Chapters 2 and 6 of Walpola Rahula's *What the Buddha Taught* (New York: Grove, 1959); Joaquin Perez-Remon's *Self and Non-Self in Early Buddhism* (The Hague: Mouton, 1980); and Steven Collens's *Selfless Persons: Imagery and Thought in Theravada Buddhism* (London: Cambridge University Press, 1982).

See "The No-Self Theory: Hume, Buddhism, and Personal Identity," *Philosophy East and West: A Quarterly of Comparative Philosophy* 43 (April 1993): 175–200, for a presentation of the view that the no-self theory is not a new theory of the self analogous to reductionism or versions of the bundle theory.

See *Self as Body in Asian Theory and Practice,* edited by Thomas P. Kasulis et al. (Albany: State University of New York Press, 1993), for a good collection of essays on Asian thought about the self and body in general.

In *The Body: Toward an Eastern Mind–Body Theory,* edited by T. P. Kasulis (Albany: State University of New York Press, 1987), Yuasa Yasuo argues that the Eastern approach to the mind–body problem is not ontological but practical. Mind–body unity is something we achieve rather than something that is innate.

Video

See *Mind as a Myth* (30 minutes; J. Krishnamurti, Thinking Allowed Productions) in which Krishnamurti argues, in Buddhist fashion, that the notion of the mind or self existing as an entity apart from our thoughts about it is mistaken.

11.5 What Is Consciousness?

It is tempting to make an analogy between movies and consciousness. We can think of consciousness as a sort of movie-in-the brain. This movie, however, is much richer than the ones we see in theaters. There are not only visual and auditory effects; there are also tactile, olfactory, and many other types of events that philosophers call **qualia**. Qualia are the qualities of what it is like to have a feeling or sensation. Phenomenal properties of consciousness such as seeing green, hearing a dog bark, and feeling a pain are examples of qualia.

Consciousness can be characterized not only by qualia but also by **intentionality**. Conscious states are directed toward some object. They are "of" or "about" something. They represent to us other things, either things in the mind—such as thoughts—or things we think are outside of the mind—such as trees. This state of being about something is what philosophers call intentionality.

It seems clear to most of us that our brains have a lot to do with being conscious. If our brains malfunction, our consciousness changes. The "movie" looks and feels different. However, what have brain cells and their activity to do with conscious experiences like seeing red? How do qualia arise from brain activity? How can consciousness, which is a subjective first-person experience, result from objective electrical activity in the brain that can be measured and observed by third parties? How can brain cells be "about" anything? How can intentional states arise from nonintentional brain activity?

As I pointed out in the introduction to this chapter, one set of answers to the mind–body problem is called *monism* because it denies that humans are made up of two radically different things, minds and bodies. One version of monism, usually called *materialism* or *physicalism* claims that only bodies (matter) exist. The problem this answer must explain is why we have a conscious mental life (thoughts, feelings, sensations) that appears to be nonphysical in nature, that is, made up of qualia and intentionality. In attempting to solve this problem, various kinds of physicalistic theories have been proposed. I briefly mentioned the identity theory in the introduction. According to this theory, mental states are identical with brain states. When we think a certain kind of thought or dream a certain sort of dream, certain sorts of physical events are happening in various parts of our brain, which can be observed and studied by science.

One problem with this theory is that mental states seem to have characteristics different from physical states. For one thing, they are private while physical states are publicly observable. For another, it appears unlikely that the same kind of brain state accompanies the same kind of thought or sensation. For example, I feel pain, you feel pain, and the other day Peanut, my fat blind cat, also felt pain when I accidentally stepped on his tail. Now my brain and yours may be sufficiently alike so that our brain states may also be sufficiently alike. But the brain of my cat, and indeed the brains of many other animals, is quite different, and it seems unlikely that—even though we might have similar mental states (e.g., feeling pain)—we would have identical brain states.

Further, for two things to be identical, they must have identical properties. A brain state, being physical, is located in space. But where in space is my feeling of being sorry that I stepped on my cat's tail? Is it 3 inches to the right of my left ear? Is it possible for a brain scientist to observe some kind of electrical event in my brain (a brain state) and read my thoughts? When I see Arthur the dog chasing Peanut the cat, can some scientist looking at my brain activity see the same thing? Hardly!

There are alternatives to materialistic theories, as we saw in our introduction and as we are about to see again in the following selection. However, the serious question remains: Are any of the theories of consciousness we presently have adequate to explain what consciousness is and how it happens.

Colin McGinn, a professor of philosophy at Rutgers University, specializes in the philosophy of mind. In this selection he reviews two books. One is by John Searle, a professor of philosophy at the University of California, Berkeley, titled *Mind, Language, and Society: Philosophy in the Real World* (New York: Basic Books, 1999), and the other is by Paul and Patricia Churchland (see Section 9.6) titled *On the Contrary: Critical Essays, 1987–1997* (Cambridge, MA: MIT Press, 1999).

Reading Project and Question

1. Write a critical précis (see Section 2.2) of the following review.
2. Assuming that McGinn is right about our lack of a theory to understand consciousness, do you think it will be possible to have such a theory some day? Why, or why not?

Can We Ever Understand Consciousness?

COLIN MCGINN

1.

CONSCIOUSNESS IS HARD TO MISS but easy to avoid, theoretically speaking. Nothing could be more present to you than your current state of consciousness—all those vivid sensations, pressing thoughts, indomitable urges. But it has proved only too easy for theorists of mind to turn a blind eye to what gives them a sense of sight to start with. Thus for most of the century consciousness has been comparable to sex in Victorian England: everyone knew it was there, throbbing away, but it was not a fit subject for polite conversation, or candid investigation. With the rise of behaviorism, in both philosophy and psychology, consciousness was deemed the "ghost in the machine," an ethereal legacy of Cartesianism that could be neither observed nor measured, a purely private realm of no conceivable relevance to objective science.

Neither did neurophysiologists find it necessary to recognize the scientific legitimacy of consciousness: they did just fine by regarding the brain as a wholly physical system, a complex of neurons and their biochemistry. Even the nascent computer-based theories of the mind had no place for consciousness, since computers can perform their information-processing operations without benefit of conscious awareness. Consciousness seemed like a phenomenon it was not necessary to consider, and hence possible to deny—common sense notwithstanding. Other subjects took up the intellectual space that one might have thought would be occupied by consciousness: overt physical behavior, environmental "stimuli," internal states of the nervous system, abstract computations. In principle, as they have defined "principle," the sciences of human nature need make no reference to consciousness and suffer no explanatory or predictive inadequacy.

Yet to any sensible person consciousness is the essence of mind: to have a mind precisely is to endure or enjoy conscious states—inner, subjective awareness. Recently consciousness has leaped naked from the closet, streaking across the intellectual landscape. People are conscious—all of them! The deep, dark secret is out. Even animals carry their own distinctive quantum of consciousness, their own inner life. You can almost hear the sigh of relief across the learned world as theorists let loose and openly acknowledge what they have repressed for so long. The Nineties are to consciousness what the Sixties were to sex.

Why this has occurred is somewhat obscure, as intellectual revolutions often are. Post-positivist disenchantment with behavioristic and materialistic reductionism began to grow in the Seventies, abetted by a greater willingness to return to the deep old problems of philosophy. Philosophers became less ready to assume that a recalcitrant philosophical problem could be diagnosed as mere conceptual confusion, as a pseudoquestion. At the same time neuroscientists began trying to build connections from the neural to the mental, acknowledging that the brain is nothing if not the seat of the mind. It was only a matter of time until they faced up to the fact that the brain is also the organ of conscious awareness. Instead of shunning consciousness as prescientific, maybe it could be approached as the holy grail of brain science, from which many a Nobel Prize might be harvested.

But there is a price to pay for all this theoretical liberation: once consciousness is admitted as a real and distinctive phenomenon in the natural world we have to find a place for it in our scheme

From Colin McGinn, *"Can We Ever Understand Consciousness?"* The New York Review of Books, *XLVI* *(June 10, 1999), 44–48. Reprinted with permission from* The New York Review of Books. *Copyright © 1999* *NYREV Inc.*

of things; we have to give an explanation of its nature. How does consciousness fit into the scientific world-picture so laboriously constructed since the seventeenth century? How does it relate to the physical world of atoms, space, and fields of force? How is it that the organ known as the brain contrives to usher consciousness into existence? These are the troubling questions that arise once our state of denial is exposed for what it is.

There was a reason for all that denial: consciousness is threatening. It looks like an anomaly in our conception of the universe, a place where our usual methods of understanding run out of steam. How can the objective sciences of the natural world, dealing with particles and their modes of aggregation, find a place for the subjective phenomenon of consciousness? How do the biological cells of the brain give rise to experiences of seeing red and emotions of despair? Must we suppose that consciousness exists outside the realm accessible to the natural sciences? Is the long-rejected dualism of mind and body the right position after all? Has the ghost come back to haunt the machine? Worse, is the machine really a ghost in disguise? Is our entire conception of the material world suspect in the light of the fact that full-blown consciousness does have its ghostly roots in the nature of matter? Is matter less material than we thought?

All these questions, and others, become pressing once the reality and uniqueness of consciousness is forthrightly acknowledged. I believe myself that the new interest in consciousness represents the next big phase in human thought about the natural world, as large as the determination to understand the physical world that gathered force in the seventeenth century. We are now beginning to face up to the aspect of nature we do not understand. Whether this phase will be crowned with the same success as our efforts to understand matter in motion is not at all clear.

Certainly it is not that consciousness has gained recognition and respect because we have established a consensus about what it is and how it arises. Quite the opposite: discussion of consciousness is marked by divergences of opinion

as wide as can be found anywhere. John Searle's *Mind, Language, and Society* and Paul and Patricia Churchland's *On the Contrary* (an appropriate title given the radical lack of consensus) exemplify this divergence. Searle takes consciousness to be incontrovertibly real and fundamentally irreducible to the familiar terms of brain science — neurons, electrochemical impulses, synaptic gaps. All the neurophysiology in the world, he argues, will not provide an adequate account of the very nature of consciousness, even though neural processes operate as the causal basis of conscious processes. He also takes consciousness to be a central issue in the science and philosophy of mind.

The Churchlands, on the other hand, waver between denying that consciousness exists altogether and claiming that it is completely reducible to their own preferred neurophysiological theory. This difference between Searle and the Churchlands is as great as that which separates flat-earthers from round-earthers or Darwinists from Creationists. For my part, I differ from both points of view — and there are others with yet other doctrines to defend. We are in the uncomfortable position of having admitted a topic into discussion about which we cannot agree, even about the basics.

Searle's book aims to be a synthesis and summary of his major philosophical preoccupations over the last forty-odd years, centering on the philosophy of mind. After a preliminary discussion, in which Searle defends the Enlightenment vision of our gradually accumulating knowledge of an objective external world, he squares up to his main positive target: consciousness. His position here combines three principal theses: (1) Consciousness consists of inner, qualitative, subjective states and processes, such as experiences of red, thoughts of skiing, feelings of pain. (2) Consciousness cannot be reduced to the "third-person phenomena" investigated by the neurosciences. (3) Consciousness is nevertheless a "biological process," a higher-order natural feature of the organic brain.

Searle encourages us to reject the traditional Cartesian frame for thinking about these questions, which takes the world to be divided into a physical part and a mental part that are mutually exclusive. This is the root of all our confusion, he thinks, and once it is abandoned we can state the solution to the mind–body problem with gratifying simplicity. After listing his three theses he writes: "But that is it. That is our account of the metaphysical relations between consciousness and the brain. Nowhere do we even raise the questions of dualism and materialism. They have simply become obsolete categories."

Searle calls this solution to the mind–body problem "biological naturalism" and summarizes it thus: "Consciousness is caused by brain processes and is a higher-order feature of the brain system." The idea is that the third-person phenomena of the brain—neurons and their activities—operate to cause higher-level subjective processes that have what Searle calls "first-person ontology," i.e., they exist only insofar as they are experienced by a conscious subject. He writes:

> Grant me that consciousness, with all its subjectivity, is caused by processes in the brain, and grant me that conscious states are themselves higher-level features of the brain. Once you have granted these two propositions, there is no metaphysical mind–body problem left. The traditional problem arises only if you accept the vocabulary with its mutually exclusive categories of mental and physical, mind and matter, spirit and flesh.
>
> Of course, consciousness is still special among biological phenomena. Consciousness has a first-person ontology and so cannot be reduced to, or eliminated in favor of, phenomena with a third-person ontology. But that is just a fact about how nature works. It is a fact of neurobiology that certain brain processes cause conscious states and processes. I am urging that we should grant the facts without accepting the metaphysical baggage that traditionally goes along with the facts.

This view has a beguiling simplicity and there is much about it that seems to me clearly on the right track. Conscious processes are indeed different in kind from standard physical processes in the brain, being defined by what they are like for their subject. They are also biological processes in at least three senses: (1) they characteristically occur in organic systems, unlike computer programs; (2) they must have resulted from the process of natural selection and not from intentional design, unlike CDs and bell-bottoms; (3) they are genetically based rather than learned or acquired, unlike knowledge of history and typing skills. (Searle in fact says almost nothing about what he means by "biological," but I take it he has in mind some such theses as these.) Further, brain states surely operate to cause conscious states and are preconditions for the existence of conscious states. Finally, conscious states are higher-level properties of the brain in the sense that they do not belong to the primary components of the brain in isolation but somehow result from combining these elements into a complex organ.

The question is: Is that really the solution to the mind–body problem? Let us first note a concession Searle makes. After likening consciousness to other higher-level macrophenomena that depend upon lower-level microphenomena—solidity, liquidity, photosynthesis, digestion—he notes, correctly enough, that these phenomena are wholly explicable in terms of the microprocesses that underlie them. There is nothing more to the liquidity of water, say, than is contained in a description of its constituent molecules and the chemical bonds that obtain between them; liquidity is not something over and above these underlying chemical facts.

But, as Searle acknowledges, indeed urges, consciousness is something over and above the neurophysiological facts that "cause" it; consciousness is not reducible to its underlying causal basis. This is a radical asymmetry between the two kinds of cases, and it implies that the conceptually uncontroversial nature of other higher-level properties cannot be adduced to make us more comfortable with the dependence of consciousness on brain processes. Those other cases are straightforward precisely because they permit reduction: we have no difficulty seeing how molecules and the forces that bind them can give rise to impenetrability in macroscopic objects, for example. In the case of consciousness, by contrast, what we have is an unexplained mode of dependence, and one that is unique in nature—a dependence of subjective facts on objective facts. And the question is: How can this be? Suppose we are told that a visual experience of red causally depends upon X-neurons firing thus and so in the occipital cortex. The following question then cries out for an answer: How could a subjective experience like that owe its very being to the electrochemical activity of mere biological cells? What has a cell got to do with an experience?

Searle says nothing about the concept of "supervenience" in his book, and this is a crucial omission. Supervenience entails that a person's conscious mental state is wholly determined by his or her physical brain state: if your neurons are firing thus and so, then your consciousness must be internally such and such. Presumably Searle would agree with this rather modest thesis, but it immediately raises the question, *in virtue of what* does such supervenience hold? What *is* there about neurons that enables them to determine consciousness in this way? It can hardly be a brute fact. To that central question Searle offers us no answer, and indeed he doesn't really ever raise the question. But to many of us that is the mind–body problem. I think that what Searle offers as the solution to the problem is really just a statement of it. The problem, precisely, is how it is that the higher-level biological process of consciousness results from lower-level physical properties of neurons. Searle assures us that it is a fact of nature that consciousness is so produced. I agree, but it is a fact that demands some kind of explanation. How can subjective consciousness result from the operations of little gray cells all bunched together into a few pounds of bland-tasting meat?

I can guess what Searle might say to this objection, though he does not say it in his book. He might say that this is a purely scientific question, not a metaphysical or philosophical one. He has done all the philosophical work when he states his main theses; it is now up to empirical science to discover the actual mode of dependence that links consciousness to the brain. But this reply will not do at all. It doesn't much matter whether we label the problem "scientific" or "philosophical," the fact remains that it is a profound and unsolved theoretical problem—a

problem we have no inkling even of how to set about solving. We have no conception of what it is about neurons, as distinct from (say) cells in the kidneys, that could explain their remarkable ability to generate or constitute an episode of conscious awareness. Neurophysiologists find correlations between brain states and conscious states, but nothing in neurophysiology even begins to explain such correlations; there isn't even an explanation of why organisms with brains have a capacity for sensation or feeling to begin with.

The reason philosophers are interested in this problem, as opposed to the mechanical problem of how to derive liquidity from water molecules, is precisely that it is a conceptual problem, in the sense that it seems to test our very conception of mind and brain. The concepts of consciousness and the brain seem intrinsically unsuited to permit a smooth explanatory theory that links them—unlike the concepts of liquidity and molecular bonding. There is nothing more to liquidity than molecular bonding, but there is vastly more to consciousness than neural firings—and it is this more that demands explanation.

Consciousness is not even an observable phenomenon! We cannot see a person's conscious states when we peer into her brain, observing all those gray fissures and biochemical reactions, because conscious states are not the kind of thing that can be so observed; yet the underlying causative brain processes are apparently just ordinary observable physical events. This is the kind of peculiarity that sets consciousness apart from other higher-level phenomena; and it is not a peculiarity that goes away once we assert, however confidently, that consciousness is a higher-level biological phenomenon. My response to such an assertion is, "So what?" That is the beginning of the problem, not the end.

Much the same objection applies to Searle's treatment of "intentionality." This technical use of the term has no specific connection with intentions in the ordinary sense. Intentionality is the capacity of the mind to be *about* things, to have meaning or content, to point beyond itself. There are many kinds of intentionality: my belief that London is dingy is about London; my desire to go skiing is directed toward skiing; my fear of heights has heights as its reference; my sensation of red takes redness as its object. Intentionality is the capacity of the mind to connect with and represent the external world, and hence distinguishes symbolizing animals from those that merely exist *in* the world. In a broad sense, intentionality is what makes an animal a semantic being, a repository of representational states. It is also what underlies the meaning of spoken languages.

Searle has done as much as anyone to make a case for the importance of intentionality and has said many insightful things about it over the years. But he is a philosopher with an inbuilt resistance to admitting he is stumped (he is by no means alone in this). Many philosophers in recent years have attempted to "naturalize" intentionality, to render it explicable by reducing it to something more familiar—causality, biological function, computational structure. In this way intentionality will emerge as nothing but a special case of something we already have on our list of scientifically acceptable facts.

Searle will have none of this, but he claims to have his own explanation of the nature of intentionality. Instead of offering to reduce intentionality to something else, as other writers do, he declares it irreducible, while nevertheless proposing to explain it in such a way as to render it "biologically natural." By way of illustration he gives a textbook account of the physiological processes that underlie thirst: a lack of water in the body causes the hypothalamus, via certain biochemical mechanisms, to increase its rate of neuron firing, this in turn causing the animal to feel a conscious desire to drink. Since the desire to drink is an intentional state—it is directed toward the act of drinking—this is held to provide an explanation of one mode of conscious intentionality. And the same kind of story could be told, Searle thinks, about other forms of intentionality—perceptual, cognitive, etc. Thus we render intentionality biologically explicable.

But this is not a genuine naturalistic explanation of intentionality per se; it merely tells us the physiological mechanisms that underlie intentionality. What philosophers interested in intentionality have wanted is some kind of account

of what the intentional relation itself consists in—what it is for the mind to be directed onto things outside itself when we are thinking or desiring or perceiving. What is this mysterious relation of "aboutness" that our various mental states exhibit? What is the nature of mental representation?

Searle's textbook summary gives us no account of this; it merely describes what causes a state that exhibits this kind of intentionality. And this leaves the conceptual problem where it was: How can a brain succeed in giving rise to mental states that represent the external world? What is it about bunches of neurons that makes them into symbols with reference? Kidney cells have no intentionality, so why do brain cells? What relation between cells in my brain and London makes it the case that I am thinking *about* London? It is not so much that Searle's proposal is false; it is simply irrelevant to the question. It would be better for him to stick with his claim of the irreducibility of intentionality and not attempt to "explain" it; but then of course there would remain the puzzling question of how intentionality is possible in a physical system. Searle is trying to have it both ways: declare a conceptually perplexing phenomenon irreducible but not incur the charge that he has left something unexplained.

The remainder of *Mind, Language, and Society* is taken up with a discussion of the meaning of "speech acts," such as asserting and commanding and questioning, and with a restatement of the view of social facts Searle developed in *The Construction of Social Reality*.[1] The temperature of the book goes down considerably during these chapters. The basic idea is to exploit intentionality, specifically intentions themselves, in the explanation of how symbols get their meaning and how institutions like money come to exist. The intention to treat pieces of paper as having economic value has intentionality, since this intention is about paper and value, and such intentions underlie the capacity of the pieces of paper

---

1. The Free Press, 1995. I wrote about this book in *The New Republic*, May 22, 1995; this review is reprinted in my *Minds and Bodies: Philosophers and Their Ideas* (Oxford University Press, 1997).

to *have* economic value. Thus the institution of money exists because people have intentions that treat certain physical objects in a certain way. Social facts, Searle argues, result from underlying intentional facts. Here he presents a clear discussion of institutions and intentions that does not depend on the view of consciousness I have criticized.

2.

Most of the papers in *On the Contrary* are written by Paul Churchland and I shall focus on these (though Patricia Churchland appears to share his views). Paul Churchland is best known for his advocacy of the doctrine of "eliminative materialism," a view maintained in the Sixties by Richard Rorty and Paul Feyerabend and prefigured by J. B. Watson at the turn of the century. Churchland has revived this view, coupling it with attention to the details of contemporary work in neuroscience. The view, put baldly, is that mental states do not exist. We *talk* as if they do when we use what has come to be called "folk psychology," the kind of explanation we use to account for human action: we commonsensically refer to beliefs and desires, sensations, thoughts, decisions, and so forth. For example, we might explain a person's dialing a phone number by attributing to him both a desire to speak to his girlfriend and a belief that dialing that number is a means to satisfying his desire. This is the kind of psychological explanation of human action we use all the time—hence "folk" psychology—and it involves ascribing certain kinds of inner mental states to people.

Folk psychology describes people as beings with desires and beliefs and intentions and feelings. It is common throughout human cultures and periods. It is the way we ordinarily understand each other. But this is all empty talk, according to Churchland's eliminativism; in reality there are no such things, any more than there are witches or ghosts or spirits in the weather. Accordingly, we should eliminate all such psychological talk as outmoded error and replace it with descriptions of the nervous system and its physical processes. It is highly probable that our in-

herited folk psychology is a radically false theory, destined to be replaced by a mature neuroscience—just as folk physics has been jettisoned in favor of the scientific physics of Newton and Einstein.

We don't yet have the replacement theory in full, Churchland acknowledges, and we cannot at present be sure that there are no mental states, but he supposes that elimination is the most likely theoretical development as science progresses. His position is that folk psychology was cobbled together in an earlier, pre-scientific age, as a speculative theory of what causes people's behavior, and it is high time to examine it critically with a view to finding a more streamlined theory of our inner workings. The familiar conceptions of belief and desire, and the accompanying mental states, are about to go the way of weather gods and fairies—there simply are no such things. It is not merely that folk psychology gives the wrong theory of human desire and belief; Churchland wants to claim it is mistaken to suppose that anyone has *any* desires and beliefs. It is folk psychology itself that is at fault, not the specific details of this or that psychological explanation. The superior theory that replaces folk psychology will not preserve its ontology—the mental entities it assumes to exist—but will replace this ontology with something radically different. Instead of referring to beliefs and desires it will work with patterns of activation in populations of neurons. Mental states as we now articulate them will go the way of phlogiston, the mythical substance that earlier theorists mistakenly thought to be released when something burns.

According to Churchland, the folk-psychological understanding of people in terms of beliefs and desires is a degenerate theory that suffers from the following defects: (1) it is objectionably partial in its treatment of the mind, providing no explanation of sleep, learning, memory, madness, etc.; (2) it is dogmatically resistant to change over time, having remained roughly the same since before the ancient Greeks; (3) it refuses to be integrated with the developing studies of human nature, such as evolutionary biology, neuroscience, biochemistry. Since the concept of consciousness is at the heart of folk psychology, we can look forward to the day when we no longer speak of it at all, being content to describe what is actually whirring away deep in our neural circuitry. The mind is a myth.

I will forgo the usual expressions of incredulity that are elicited by this doctrine (though I share them) and confine myself to some obvious objections to it. To begin with, the arguments offered in support of eliminativism are remarkably weak. Without undertaking a full-scale criticism of them, we can note the following: First, it is no argument for the falsity of folk psychology that it does not cover everything about the mind; partiality does not entail error. With respect to the second objection, the constancy of folk psychology over time could as well be explained by its obvious truth, not its inherent dogmatism; compare the stability of elementary arithmetic since the ancient Greeks. As for Churchland's third objection, it is tendentious at best to suppose folk psychology not to be capable of integration with the sciences of human nature, since the standard contemporary model of cognitive science is arguably continuous with the apparatus of folk psychology. The Rutgers philosopher Jerry Fodor, for example, has argued convincingly that the conception of the mind as a symbol-manipulating information processor fits smoothly with the folk-psychological picture of the mind as consisting of a range of "propositional attitudes" like belief and desire.[2] So none of these arguments shows that folk psychology is radically on the wrong track about what makes us tick.

Churchland, moreover, severely underplays the first-person aspect of folk psychology. Folk psychology is not just a "speculative theory" we apply to others; it is also the means by which we directly report on our own mental states. And such first-person reporting carries special privileges: my knowledge that I am thinking about philosophy right now is as secure as any knowledge can be—well-nigh incorrigible, as Descartes pointed out. But Churchland holds that this kind of first-person knowledge is no knowl-

edge at all, since I do not *have* thoughts, according to the eliminativist doctrine: folk psychology for him is a false speculative theory, not the vehicle of incorrigible first-person knowledge. But once we acknowledge the first-person privileges of folk psychology, it becomes inconceivable that we could be simply wrong about having mental states. The simple truth is that evolution equipped us with both mental states and the conceptual apparatus to describe those states in a uniquely privileged way. Hence the well-grounded conviction, *contra* eliminativism, that we simply know that we have beliefs and desires and all the rest.

One of Churchland's recurrent themes is that the neural dynamics that underlie what we are pleased to call the mind do not involve symbolic representations of a sentencelike kind. The brain is not to be construed as a device for processing internal sentences that underlie our cognitive capacities. Instead, he writes that the neurons choreograph themselves into "activation vectors," patterns of activity that do not involve anything that looks like a sentence or proposition. Yet folk psychology insists on describing the mind by using the language of propositions: Sally believes *that* Clinton will be impeached, Jack hopes *that* he won't be. But, Churchland thinks, there is nothing in the brain itself that corresponds to the propositional apparatus of folk psychology, and so folk psychology is trafficking in illusions.

I will make only two points about this, though many more could be made. First, we haven't been convinced by Churchland or anyone else that folk psychology is not simply providing a description of the brain that abstracts from the details of what the neurons are doing, as a software description of a computer abstracts from its hardware description. After all, from the perspective of basic physics the brain does not have "activation vectors" either, being merely a collection of subatomic particles. Reality comes in levels, and what is invisible at one level might be salient at another. Second, Churchland studiously avoids confronting the question of language processing itself. But surely when we understand speech we must suppose that our mental dynamics involve

2. See Jerry Fodor, *The Language of Thought* (Crowell, 1975); *A Theory of Content and Other Essays* (MIT Press, 1990).

the manipulation of sentencelike structures, since speech consists of sentences. And if propositional attitudes like beliefs and desires are bound up with language, they too will involve internal sentencelike structures.

It may indeed be true that the representational machinery of the brain can at one level be described without reference to sentencelike symbols, but it does not follow that such symbols play no part in our mental functioning. And once it is admitted that they do, then folk psychology can claim vindication by reference to an established science of the brain. (This is precisely the position of theorists like Jerry Fodor, who subscribe to a "language of thought.")

Churchland's insistence on the nonpropositional character of neural representation leads to a strange result, namely that it is more plausible that computers think than that human beings do. He observes that the standard architecture of computers consists in the serial manipulation of sentencelike structures, while the brain (he claims) works by means of parallel nonpropositional neural activations (what are nowadays called connectionist networks). Thus computers display the kind of internal machinery that folk psychology demands, while human brains display a quite different kind of machinery. The result is that eliminativism is more likely to be true of us than of our computers! By Churchland's skewed lights the computer I am typing on has a greater claim to be a thinker than I do. I take this to be a *reductio ad absurdum* of his position. He does not notice this consequence of his arguments explicitly, but he hands the reader the materials with which to draw the strange conclusion.

Signs that Churchland does not take his eliminativism quite as seriously as he invites us to take it are evident in a certain inconsistency that pervades the essays in this book. Once I started to notice this inconsistency I became increasingly irritated by it. On the one hand, he preaches the eliminativist gospel, bravely announcing that folk psychology is on its last legs; on the other hand, we find him elsewhere arguing that this or that aspect of folk psychology is *reducible* to processes in the brain. But you can't have it both ways: if eliminativism is true, then there is *nothing to re-*

duce. Yet here is Churchland blithely arguing that he can explain the notion of sameness of concept within his neural network scheme, that "qualia"—the subjective features of sensory experiences—can be identified with certain patterns in the nervous system, that consciousness itself is a phenomenon we need to know more about.

But none of these claims is available to a consistent eliminativist, any more than a reduction of phlogiston to atomic physics is an option for someone who denies the existence of phlogiston—since if phlogiston is identical to particular existent physical facts, then it must exist after all. Churchland is perfectly aware of the logical tension between reductionism and eliminativism, and indeed is careful to explain the distinction when he is espousing eliminativism. But then he inconsistently slides into reductionism when it suits him to do so.

I can find no explanation of this inconsistency or recognition of it in his text. But I think I understand the psychology behind it: Churchland doesn't want to be left out of the fun, which is what his professed eliminativism would require. He *wants* to theorize about the nature of concepts and consciousness, about reasoning and perceptual experience; so he conveniently forgets that according to his official eliminativist position there is nothing to talk about here. I suppose we could surmise that his good sense has triumphed over his theoretical pronouncements, but he owes it to us to qualify his eliminativism, if that is his true position. Otherwise he is playing a duplicitous game.

3.

Searle and Churchland represent opposite ends of the philosophical spectrum. Searle takes our common-sense view of the mind seriously and resists attempts to reduce or eliminate it in favor of a materialistic metaphysics; Churchland regards the very idea that human beings have beliefs and desires as a false theory of how our brains work, soon to be replaced by a better theory that describes us according to neuroscience. Is there any middle ground? My own view is that these two extremes are intelligible—though mistaken—responses to a genuine conceptual and explanatory problem. The problem is how to integrate the conscious mind with the physical brain—how to reveal a unity beneath this apparent diversity. That problem is very hard, and I do not believe anyone has any good ideas about how to solve it.

In view of this gap in our understanding, two kinds of response might be expected: either that there is no unification of mind and brain to be had or that there is no mind to unify with the brain. Thus we get dualistic antireductionism, of which Searle's position is an example (though I am sure he will not welcome the description). Or we get Churchland's kind of eliminativism, perhaps inconsistently combined with an attempt to reduce mental phenomena to our *current* understanding of the brain. My own position is that there is a theory that unifies conscious minds with physical brains, but we do not have any idea what that theory is. In *reality* there is an underlying unity here, even though *we* have no understanding of it.

There has to be natural underlying unity here, for if there is not, we have to postulate miraculous kinds of emergence in the biological world; consciousness cannot just spring into existence from matter like a djinn from a lamp. But our modes of access to consciousness and the brain—by means of introspection and sensory perception, respectively—do not, as a matter of principle, disclose the hidden structure of this indispensable nexus. I know that I am in pain by feeling my pain from the inside, and I can know that my neurons are activated thus and so by using scientific methods to observe that they are; but I have no awareness of the necessary links that bind sensation and brain process together—nor any method for extrapolating to these links. We cannot deduce brain states from our inner awareness of consciousness and we cannot deduce consciousness from our sensory awareness of the brain; so the manner of their association remains elusive to our cognitive faculties.

We can apprehend each side of the great divide between mind and body, but we have no faculty that reveals how they slot seamlessly together. That is the root of our troubles in trying to form a theory of what could connect consciousness to the brain. But it is hardly surprising to find that not every aspect of the natural world comes within the scope of our powers of understanding. We do not expect other evolved species to be omniscient, so why assume that our intelligence has evolved with the capacity to solve every problem that can be raised about the universe of which we are such a small and contingent part? But even if this strong unknowability thesis is mistaken—and I have only sketched my reasons for maintaining it here[3]—we should surely allow for the possibility that our knowledge of the mind and brain is severely limited, thus producing the impression that the association is brute and inexplicable. There may be an explanatory theory of the psychophysical link somewhere in Plato's heaven; it is just that our minds are miles away from grasping what this theory looks like. So we are apt to flail around in ignorance, going from one implausible extreme to another. If this is right, then antireductionism is wrong as a claim about all possible theories of the brain, and eliminativism is not necessary after all. But one can at least understand why people might be tempted by these unsatisfactory views: both are misguided, though intelligible, reactions to matters about which human beings are still deeply ignorant.

3. I discuss this view further in *The Problem of Consciousness* (Basil Blackwell, 1991), *Problems in Philosophy* (Basil Blackwell, 1993), and *The Mysterious Flame* (Basic Books, 1999).

Suggestions for Further Reading

For a clear and concise introductory account of some key issues in the debate about the mind, see Chapter 12 ("Bodies and Minds") in Jeffry Olen's *Persons and Their World: An Introduction to Philosophy* (New York: Random House, 1983).

For a collection of essays on philosophy of mind see Brian Cooney, *The Place of Mind* (Belmont, CA: Wadsworth, 2000).

Also William Lyons has edited a collection of essays that represent the various positions. See his *Modern Philosophy of Mind* (London: Dent, 1995).

See Daniel C. Dennett's *Brainstorms: Philosophical Essays on Mind and Psychology* (Boston: Bradford Books, 1978) for a lively presentation of some controversial views.

David J. Chalmers, *The Conscious Mind: In Search of a Fundamental Theory* (New York: Oxford University Press, 1996), attempts to develop a theory that is compatible with our scientific knowledge of the brain, yet avoids reducing the mind to the brain.

In "How the Brain Creates the Mind," *Scientific American* (December 1999), 112–117, Antonio R. Damasio presents the reasons he thinks that the problem of how the brain creates consciousness will be solved by 2050.

José Luis Bermúdez tackles the special problems associated with self-consciousness in *The Paradox of Self Consciousness* (Cambridge, MA: Bradford/MIT Press, 1998).

Jonathan Shear has edited a useful volume focusing on the most difficult problems titled *Explaining Consciousness: The Hard Problems* (Cambridge, MA: Bradford/MIT, 1997).

Ned Block, Owen Flanagan, and Güven Güseldere (editors) lead you through some of the philosophical issues in *The Nature of Consciousness: Philosophical Debates* (Cambridge, MA: Bradford/MIT Press, 1996).

Videos

The third in the series, *A Glorious Accident: Understanding Our Place in the Cosmic Puzzle,* features an interview with Daniel C. Dennett. This video is available from Films for the Humanities and Sciences, PO Box 2053, Princeton, NJ 08543.

Also *The Conscious Mind,* which is part of the series "No Dogs or Philosophers Allowed," features Verna Gehring, Daniel Kolak, and Bruce Umbaugh debating some of the issues relating to consciousness. For more information see www.nodogs.org.

11.6 How Much Can I Change and Still Be Me?

I imagine most of you have seen *Star Trek* and watched Captain Kirk and the others get beamed into and out of the transporter room. Although it is unclear precisely how this machine works, it seems to dismantle the crew molecule by molecule and reassemble them molecule by molecule at a different location. Would you say that Captain Kirk and the others are the same people when they are reassembled? My guess is you would say yes.

However, let's imagine that it doesn't quite work like that on the home trip. Let's say molecules can stand just so many transports and that whereas they can be beamed from the transporter room to some planet, the only thing beamed back on the return trip is a molecule blueprint. Fresh atoms from the well-stocked transporter room's reservoirs are then used to recreate the crew according to the blueprint. Would you say that the crew members are the same persons? This question may be a bit harder to answer because the atoms have been changed and only the blueprint remains the same. Is that enough to make the crew the same? (I owe this provocative example to Daniel Dennett; see the introduction to *The Mind's I.*)

Jeffry Olen, author of our next selection and professor of philosophy at the University of Wisconsin at Stevens Point, connects the issues of what is a person, personal identity, and personal survival by discussing the interesting fictional case of John Badger and Joe Everglade, who apparently and mysteriously change identities. He argues that the idea of one continuing person must involve the idea of one continuing stream of consciousness. Can such continuity carry over from one body to another? Olen thinks so, provided we adopt a functionalist viewpoint.

There are different varieties of **functionalism**, but in general this theory holds that mental states are defined completely by their functions or causal relations. A mind is what a brain does. Theoretically, something other than a brain could function as a mind—for example, a computer.

The slogan of functionalism is *not* the cry of the identity theorist that "the mind is nothing but the brain." Rather, in an analogy with computers, the slogan is "the mind is to the brain as a computer's software is to its hardware." The behavior of a computer is not explained, or at least not explained completely, by its physics and chemistry (hardware). It is explained by its program or "software" that describes the tasks the computer performs. The software of a computer is not identical with its hardware. Neither are our minds identical with our brains. Nevertheless, the brain is a kind of computing machine, and the mind is the brain's program.

Olen uses this functionalist theory to tackle the problem of identity and even the thorny issue of life after the death of our present brain. He argues that just as different computers can process the same information and run the same programs, so we might imagine it is possible to survive in another body/brain (computer) as long as our personalities and memories (software) are preserved.

Reading Questions

1. What are Olen's main points?
2. What are his key terms, and how does he define them?
3. What are Olen's basic assumptions?
4. What sorts of arguments does he give to support his views?
5. Is what Olen writes clear? If not, why are you puzzled? Over which points?
6. Does Olen overlook any important aspects of the topic that you can think of?
7. Do you agree or disagree with what Olen says? Be specific and say why you agree or disagree.

Personal Identity and Life After Death

JEFFRY OLEN

IT IS SUNDAY NIGHT. After a long night of hard drinking, John Badger puts on his pajamas, lowers the heat in his Wisconsin home to fifty-five degrees and climbs into bed beneath two heavy blankets. Meanwhile, in Florida, Joe Everglade kisses his wife goodnight and goes to sleep.

From Persons and Their World: An Introduction to Philosophy *by Jeffry Olen. Copyright © 1983 Random House, pp. 231–237; 239–240; 243–247. Reprinted by permission of McGraw-Hill Publishing Company.*

The next morning, two very confused men wake up. One wakes up in Wisconsin, wondering where he is and why he is wearing pajamas, lying under two heavy blankets, yet shivering from the cold. He looks out the window and sees nothing but pine trees and snow. The room is totally unfamiliar. Where is his wife? How did he get to this cold, strange place? Why does he have such a terrible hangover? He tries to spring out of bed with his usual verve but feels an unaccustomed aching in his joints. Arthritis? He wanders unsurely through the house until he finds the bathroom. What he sees in the mirror causes him to spin around in sudden fear. But there is nobody behind him. Then the fear intensifies as he realizes that it was his reflection that had stared back at him. But it was the reflection of a man thirty years older than himself, with coarser features and a weather-beaten face.

In Florida, a man awakens with a young woman's arm around him. When she too awakens, she snuggles against him and wishes him good morning. "Who are you?" he asks. "What am I doing in your bed?" She just laughs, then tells him that he will have to hurry if he is going to get in his ten miles of jogging. From the bathroom she asks him about his coming day. None of the names or places she mentions connect with anything he can remember. He climbs out of bed, marveling at the ease with which he does so, and looks first out the window and then into the mirror over the dresser. The sun and swimming pool confound him. The handsome young man's reflection terrifies him.

Then the phone rings. The woman answers it. It is the man from Wisconsin. "What happened last night, Mary? How did I get here? How did I get to look this way?"

"Who is this?" she asks.

"Don't you recognize my voice, Mary?" But he knew that the voice was not his own. "It's Joe."

"Joe who?"

"Your husband."

She hangs up, believing it to be a crank call. When she returns to the bedroom, the man in her husband's robe asks how he got there from Wisconsin, and why he looks as he does.

Personal Identity

What happened in the above story? Who woke up in Joe Everglade's bed? Who woke up in John Badger's? Which one is Mary's husband? Has Badger awakened with Everglade's memories and Everglade with Badger's? Or have Badger and Everglade somehow switched bodies? How are we to decide? What considerations are relevant?

To ask such questions is to raise the problem of *personal identity*. It is to ask what makes a person the same person he was the day before. It is to ask how we determine that we are dealing with the same person that we have dealt with in the past. It is to ask what constitutes personal identity over time. It is also to ask what we mean by the *same person*. And to answer this question, we must ask what we mean by the word "person."

Persons

In the previous chapter, we asked what a human being is. We asked what human beings are made of, what the nature of the human mind is, and whether human beings are part of nature or distinct from it.

To ask what a *person* is, however, is to ask a different question. Although we often use the terms "person" and "human being" interchangeably, they do not mean the same thing. If we do use them interchangeably, it is only because all the persons we know of are human beings, and because, as far as we know, whenever we are confronted with the same human being we are confronted with the same person.

But the notion of a human being is a *biological* notion. To identify something as a human being is to identify it as a member of *Homo sapiens,* a particular species of animal. It is a type of organism defined by certain physical characteristics.

The notion of a person, on the other hand, is *not* a biological one. Suppose, for instance, that we find life on another planet, and that this life is remarkably like our own. The creatures we discover communicate through a language as rich as our own, act according to moral principles, have a legal system, and engage in science and art. Suppose also that despite these cultural similarities, this form of life is biologically different from human life. In that case, these creatures would be persons, but not humans. Think, for example, of the alien in *E.T.* Since he is biologically different from us, he is not human. He is, however, a person.

What, then, is a person? Although philosophers disagree on this point, the following features are relatively noncontroversial.

First, a person is an intelligent, rational creature. Second, it is a creature capable of a peculiar sort of consciousness—self-consciousness. Third, it not only has beliefs, desires, and so forth, but it has beliefs *about* its beliefs, desires, and so forth. Fourth, it is a creature to which we ascribe moral responsibility. Persons are responsible for their actions in a way that other things are not. They are subject to moral praise and moral blame. Fifth, a person is a creature that we treat in certain ways. To treat something as a person is to treat it as a member of our own moral community. It is to grant it certain rights, both moral and legal. Sixth, a person is a creature capable of reciprocity. It is capable of treating us as members of the same moral community. Finally, a person is capable of verbal communication. It can communicate by means of a *language*, not just by barks, howls, and tail-wagging.

Since, as far as we know, only human beings meet the above conditions, only human beings are considered to be persons. But once we recognize that to be a person is not precisely the same thing that it is to be a human being, we also recognize that other creatures, such as the alien in *E.T.,* is also a person. We also recognize that perhaps not all human beings are persons—human fetuses, for example, as some have argued. Certainly, in the American South before the end of the Civil War, slaves were not considered to be persons. We might also mention a remark of D'Artagnan, in Richard Lester's film version of *The Three Musketeers.* Posing as a French nobleman, he attempted to cross the English Channel with a companion. When a French official remarked that his pass was only for one person, D'Artagnan replied that he was only one person—his companion was a servant.

Moreover, once we recognize the distinction between human beings and persons, certain questions arise. Can one human being embody more than one person, either at the same time or successive times? In the example we introduced at the beginning of this chapter, has Badger's body become Everglade's and Everglade's Badger's? Can the person survive the death of the human being? Is there personal survival after the death of the body?

THE MEMORY CRITERION AND THE BODILY CRITERION

Concerning identity through time in general, two issues must be distinguished. First, we want to know how we can *tell* that something is the same thing we encountered previously. That is, we want to know what the *criteria* are for establishing identity through time. Second, we want to know what *makes* something the same thing it was previously. That is, we want to know what *constitutes* identity through time.

Although these issues are related, they are not the same, as the following example illustrates. We can *tell* that someone has a case of the flu by checking for certain symptoms, such as fever, lack of energy, and sore muscles. But having these symptoms does not *constitute* having a case of the flu. It is the presence of a flu virus—not the symptoms—that makes an illness a case of the flu.

We commonly use two criteria for establishing personal identity. The first is the *bodily criterion,* the second the *memory criterion.* How do we apply them?

We apply the bodily criterion in two ways. First, we go by physical resemblance. If I meet someone on the street who looks, walks, and sounds just like Mary, I assume that it is Mary. Since the body I see resembles Mary's body exactly, I assume that it is Mary. Since the body I see resembles Mary's body exactly, I assume that the person I see is Mary. But that method can sometimes fail us, as in the case of identical twins.

In such cases, we can apply the bodily criterion in another way. If I can discover that there is a continuous line from one place and time to another that connects Mary's body to the body I now see, I can assume that I now see Mary. Suppose, for example, that Mary and I went to the beach together, and have been together all afternoon. In that case, I can say that the person I am now with is the person I began the day with.

There are, however, times when the bodily criterion is not available. If Mary and Jane are identical twins, and I run across one of them on the street, I may have to ask who it is. That is, I may have to rely on Mary's memory of who she is. And, if I want to make sure that I am not being fooled, I may ask a few questions. If Mary remembers things that I believe only Mary can remember, and if she remembers them as happening to *her,* and not to somebody else, then I can safely say that it really is Mary.

Generally, the bodily criterion and the memory criterion do not conflict, so we use whichever is more convenient. But what happens if they do conflict? That is what happened in our imagined story. According to the bodily criterion, each person awoke in his own bed, but with the memories of someone else. According to the memory criterion, each person awoke in the other's bed with the body of someone else. Which criterion should we take as decisive? Which is fundamental, the memory criterion or the bodily criterion?

THE CONSTITUTION OF PERSONAL IDENTITY

To ask the above questions is to ask what *constitutes* personal identity. What is it that makes me the same person I was yesterday? What makes the author of this book the same person as the baby born to Sam and Belle Olen in 1946? Answers to these questions will allow us to say which criterion is fundamental.

Perhaps the most widely discussed answer to our question comes from John Locke (1632–1704), whose discussion of the topic set the stage for all future discussions. According to Locke, the bodily criterion cannot be fundamental. Since the concept of a person is most importantly the con-

cept of a conscious being who can be held morally and legally responsible for past actions, it is *continuity of consciousness* that constitutes personal identity. The bodily criterion is fundamental for establishing sameness of *animal,* but not sameness of *person.*

Suppose, for instance, that John Badger had been a professional thief. If the person who awoke in Badger's bed could never remember any of Badger's life as his own, but had only Everglade's memories and personality traits, while the man who awoke in Everglade's bed remembered all of Badger's crimes as his own, would we be justified in jailing the man who awoke in Badger's bed while letting the man who awoke in Everglade's go free? Locke would say no. The person who awoke in Badger's bed was not Badger.

If we agree that it is sameness of consciousness that constitutes personal identity, we must then ask what constitutes sameness of consciousness. Some philosophers have felt that it is sameness of *mind,* where the mind is thought of as a continuing nonphysical substance. Although Locke did not deny that minds are nonphysical, he did not believe that sameness of nonphysical substance is the same thing as sameness of consciousness. If we can conceive of persons switching *physical* bodies, we can also conceive of persons switching *non*physical ones.

Then what does Locke take to be crucial for personal identity? *Memory.* It is my memory of the events of Jeffry Olen's life as happening to *me* that makes me the person those events happened to. It is my memory of his experiences as *mine* that makes them mine.

Although Locke's answer seems at first glance a reasonable one, many philosophers have considered it inadequate. One reason for rejecting Locke's answer is that we don't remember everything that happened to us. If I don't remember anything that happened to me during a certain period, does that mean that whoever existed "in" my body then was not me? Hardly.

Another reason for rejecting Locke's answer is that memory is not always accurate. We often sincerely claim to remember things that never happened. There is a difference, then, between *genuine* memory and *apparent* memory. What marks this difference is the *truth* of the memory claim. If what I claim to remember is not true, it cannot be a case of genuine memory.

But that means that memory cannot constitute personal identity. If I claim to remember certain experiences as being my experiences, that does not make them mine, because my claim may be a case of apparent memory. If it is a case of genuine memory, that is because it is true that the remembered experiences are mine. But the memory does not *make* them mine. Rather, the fact that they *are* mine makes it a case of genuine memory. So Locke has the situation backward. But if memory does not constitute personal identity, what does?

Some philosophers have claimed that, regardless of Locke's views, it *must* be sameness of mind, where the mind is thought of as a continuing nonphysical entity. This entity can be thought of as the self. It is what makes us who we are. As long as the same self continues to exist, the same person continues to exist. The major problem with this answer is that it assumes the truth of mind–body dualism, a position we found good reason to reject in the previous chapter. But apart from that, there is another problem.

In one of the most famous passages in the history of philosophy, David Hume (1711–1776) argued that there is no such self—for reasons that have nothing to do with the rejection of dualism. No matter how hard we try, Hume said, we cannot discover such a self. Turning inward and examining our own consciousness, we find only individual experiences—thoughts, recollections, images, and the like. Try as we might, we cannot find a continuing self. In that case, we are justified in believing only that there are *experiences*—not that there is a continuing *experiencer*. Put another way, we have no reason to believe that there is anything persisting through time that underlies or unifies these experiences. There are just the experiences themselves.

But if we accept this view, and still require a continuing nonphysical entity for personal identity, we are forced to the conclusion that there is no such thing as personal identity. We are left, that is, with the position that the idea of a person existing through time is a mere fiction, however useful in daily life. And that is the position that Hume took. Instead of persons, he said, there are merely "bundles of ideas."

Thus, the view that personal identity requires sameness of mind can easily lead to the view that there is no personal identity. Since this conclusion seems manifestly false, we shall have to look elsewhere. But where?

THE PRIMACY OF THE BODILY CRITERION

If neither memory nor sameness of mind constitutes personal identity, perhaps we should accept the view that sameness of *body* does. Perhaps it is really the bodily criterion that is fundamental.

If we reflect on the problem faced by Locke's theory because of the distinction between genuine and apparent memory, it is tempting to accept the primacy of the bodily criterion. Once again, a sincere memory claim may be either genuine memory or apparent memory. How can we tell whether the claim that a previous experience was mine is genuine memory? By determining whether I was in the right place in the right time to have it. And how can we determine that? By the bodily criterion. If my *body* was there, then *I* was there. But that means that the memory criterion must rest on the bodily criterion. Also, accepting the primacy of the bodily criterion gets us around Hume's problem. The self that persists through and has the experiences I call mine is my physical body.

This answer also has the advantage of being in keeping with materialism, a view accepted in the previous chapter. If human beings are purely physical, then persons must also be purely physical, whatever differences there may be between the notion of a person and the notion of a human being. But if persons are purely physical, what makes me the same person I was yesterday is no different in kind from what makes my typewriter the same typewriter it was yesterday. In both cases, we are dealing with a physical object existing through time. In the latter case, as long as we have the same physical materials (allowing for change of ribbon, change of keys, and the like) arranged in the same way, we have the same typewriter. So it is with persons. As long as we have the same physical materials (allowing for such changes as the replacement of cells) arranged in the same way, we have the same person.

Although this answer is a tempting one, it is not entirely satisfactory. Suppose that we could manage a brain transplant from one body to another. If we switched two brains, so that all the memories and personality traits of the persons involved were also switched, wouldn't we conclude that the persons, as well as their brains, had switched bodies? When such operations are performed in science-fiction stories, they are described this way.

But this possibility does not defeat the view that the bodily criterion is fundamental. It just forces us to hold that the bodily criterion must be applied to the brain, rather than the entire body. Personal identity then becomes a matter of brain identity. Same brain, same person. Unfortunately, even with this change, our answer does not seem satisfactory. Locke still seems somehow right. Let us see why.

BADGER AND EVERGLADE
RECONSIDERED

Returning to our tale of Badger and Everglade, we find that some troubling questions remain. If Mrs. Everglade continues to live with the man who awoke in her bed, might she not be committing adultery? Shouldn't she take in the man who awoke in Badger's bed? And, once again assuming that Badger was a professional thief, would justice really be served by jailing the man who awoke in his bed? However we answer these questions, one thing is certain—the two men would always feel that they had switched bodies. So, probably, would the people who knew them. Furthermore, whenever we read science-fiction stories describing such matters, we invariably accept them as stories of switched bodies. But if we accept the bodily criterion as fundamental, we are accepting the impossible, and the two men in our story, Mrs. Everglade, and their friends are mistaken in their beliefs. How, then, are we to answer our questions?

If we are unsure, it is because such questions become very tricky at this point. Their trickiness seems to rest on two points. First, cases like the Badger–Everglade case do not happen in this world. Although we are prepared to accept them in science-fiction tales, we are totally unprepared to deal with them in real life.

Second, and this is a related point, we need some way of *explaining* such extraordinary occurrences. Unless we know how the memories of Badger and Everglade came to be reversed, we will be unable to decide the answers to our questions. In the movies, it is assumed that some nonphysical substance travels from one body to another, or that there has been a brain transplant of some sort. On these assumptions, we are of course willing to describe what happens as a change of body. This description seems to follow naturally from such explanations.

What explains what happened to Badger and Everglade? We can rule out change of nonphysical substance, because of what was said in the previous chapter and earlier in this chapter. If we explain what happened as the product of a brain switch, then the bodily criterion applied to the brain allows us to say that Badger and Everglade did awaken in each other's bed, and that Mrs. Everglade would be committing adultery should she live with the man who awoke in her bed.

Are there any other possible explanations? One that comes readily to mind is hypnotism. Suppose, then, that someone had hypnotized Badger and Everglade into believing that each was the other person. In that case, we should not say that there had been a body switch. Badger and Everglade awoke in their own beds, and a wave of the hypnotist's hand could demonstrate that to everyone concerned. Their memory claims are not genuine memories, but apparent ones.

But suppose it was not a case of hypnotism? What then? At this point, many people are stumped. What else could it be? The strong temptation is to say nothing. Without a brain transplant or hypnotism or something of the sort, the case is impossible.

Suppose that we accept this conclusion. If we do, we may say the following: The memory criterion and the bodily criterion cannot really conflict. If the memories are genuine, and not apparent, then whenever I remember certain experiences as being mine, it is possible to establish that the same brain is involved in the original experiences and the memory of them. Consequently, the memory criterion and the bodily criterion are equally fundamental. The memory criterion is fundamental in the sense that consciousness determines what part of the body is central to personal identity. Because sameness of consciousness requires sameness of brain, we ultimately must apply the bodily criterion to the brain. But the bodily criterion is also fundamental, because we assume that some physical object—the brain—must remain the same if the person is to remain the same.

THE MEMORY
CRITERION REVISITED

Although the answer given above is a tidy one, it may still seem unsatisfactory. Perhaps it is a cheap trick just to dismiss the Badger–Everglade case as mere fantasy and then ignore it. After all, if we can meaningfully describe such cases in books and films, don't we have to pay some attention to them? As long as we can imagine situations in which two persons can switch bodies without a brain transplant, don't we need a theory of personal identity to cover them?

Philosophers are divided on this point. Some think that a theory of personal identity has to account only for what can happen in this world, while others think it must account for whatever can happen in any conceivable world. Then again, some do not believe that there is any conceivable world in which two persons could change bodies without a brain switch, while there are others who are not sure that such things are impossible in the actual world.

Without trying to decide the matter, I can make the following suggestion for those who demand a theory of personal identity that does not rely on the assumption that genuine memory is tied to a particular brain.

In the previous chapter, I concluded that functionalism is the theory of mind most likely

to be true. To have a mind, I said, is to embody a psychology. I also said that we don't merely move our bodies, but write poetry, caress the cheek of someone we love, and perform all sorts of human actions. I might have expressed this point by saying that we are not just human beings, but persons as well. What makes a human being a person? We are persons because we embody a psychology.

If that is true, then it may also be true that we are the persons we are because of the psychologies we embody. If it is a psychology that makes a human being a person, then it is a particular psychology that makes a particular human being a particular person. Sameness of psychology constitutes sameness of person. In that case, we can agree with this much of Locke's theory—it is continuity of consciousness that constitutes personal identity. But what is continuity of consciousness, if not memory?

An answer to this question is provided by the contemporary British philosopher Anthony Quinton. At any moment, we can isolate a number of mental states belonging to the same momentary consciousness. Right now, for instance, I am simultaneously aware of the sound and sight and feel of my typewriter, plus the feel and taste of my pipe, plus a variety of other things. Such *momentary* consciousnesses belong to a continuous *series*. Each one is linked to the one before it and the one following it by certain similarities and recollections. This series is my own *continuity* of consciousness, my own *stream* of consciousness. It is this stream of consciousness that makes me the same person I was yesterday.

If we accept Quinton's theory, we can then say that the memory criterion, not the bodily criterion, is fundamental. We can also say that, even if in this world continuity of consciousness requires sameness of brain, we can conceive of worlds in which it does not. To show this, let us offer another possible explanation of the Badger–Everglade situation.

Suppose a mad computer scientist has discovered a way to reprogram human beings. Suppose that he has found a way to make us the embodiment of any psychology he likes. Suppose further that he decided to experiment on Badger and

Everglade, giving Badger Everglade's psychology and Everglade Badger's and that is why the events of our story occurred. With this explanation and the considerations of the previous paragraphs, we can conclude that Badger and Everglade did change bodies. By performing his experiment, the mad scientist has made it possible for a continuing stream of consciousness to pass from one body to another. He has, in effect, performed a body transplant.

Should we accept Quinton's theory? There seems to be no good reason not to. In fact, there are at least two good reasons for accepting it. First, it seems consistent with a functionalist theory of the mind. Second, it allows us to make sense of science-fiction stories while we continue to believe that in the real world to be the same person we were yesterday is to have the same brain.

Life After Death

Is it possible for the person to survive the death of the body? Is there a sense in which *we* can continue to live after our bodies have died? Can there be a personal life after death?

According to one popular conception of life after death, at the death of the body the soul leaves the body and travels to a realm known as heaven. Of course, this story must be taken as metaphorical. Does the soul literally leave the body? How? Out of the mouth? Ears? And how does it get to heaven? By turning left at Mars? Moreover, if the soul remains disembodied, how can it perceive anything? What does it use as sense organs? And if all souls remain disembodied, how can one soul recognize another? What is there to recognize?

As these questions might suggest, much of this popular story trades on a confusion. The soul is thought of as a translucent physical substance, much like Casper the ghost, through which other objects can pass as they do through air or water. But if the soul is *really* nonphysical, it can be nothing like that.

If this story is not to be taken literally, is there some version of it that we can admit as a possibility? Is there also the possibility of personal survival through reincarnation as it is often understood—the re-embodiment of the person without memory of the former embodiment?

MATERIALISM AND THE DISEMBODIED SOUL

So far, we have considered both the mind and the body as they relate to personal identity. Have we neglected the soul? It may seem that we have, but philosophers who discuss the mind–body question and personal identity generally use the terms "mind" and "soul" interchangeably. Is the practice legitimate, or is it a confusion?

The practice seems to be thoroughly legitimate. If the soul is thought to be the crucial element of the person, it is difficult to see how it could be anything but the mind. If it is our character traits, personality, thoughts, likes and dislikes, memories, and continuity of experience that makes us the persons we are, then they must belong to the soul. If they are taken to be crucial for one's personal identity, then it seems impossible to separate them from one's soul.

Moreover, people who accept some version of the popular conception of life after death noted above believe in certain continuities between earthly experiences and heavenly ones. In heaven, it is believed, we remember our earthly lives, we recognize friends and relatives, our personalities are like our earthly personalities, and we are judged by God for our actions on earth. But if we believe any of this, we must also believe that the soul cannot be separated from the mind.

If that is the case, it is difficult to accept the continued existence of a disembodied soul. Once we accept some form of materialism, we seem compelled to believe that the soul must be embodied. Does that rule out the possibility of any version of the popular story being true?

Some philosophers think that it does. Suppose, for instance, that the mind–brain identity theory is true. In that case, when the brain dies, so does the mind. Since the mind is the repository of memory and personality traits, it is identical with the soul. So when the brain dies, so does the soul.

This is a powerful argument, and it has convinced a number of people. On the other hand, it has also kept a number of people from accepting materialism of any sort. If it is felt that materialism and life after death are incompatible, and if one is firmly committed to the belief in life after death, then it is natural for one to reject materialism.

Is there a way of reconciling materialism and life after death? I think so.

Although it seems necessary that persons must be embodied, it does not seem necessary that the same person must be embodied by the same body. In our discussion of personal identity, we allowed that Badger and Everglade might have changed bodies, depending on our explanation of the story. Let us try a similar story.

Mary Brown is old and sick. She knows she will die within a couple of weeks. One morning she does die. At the same time, in some other world, a woman wakes up believing herself to be Mary. She looks around to find herself in a totally unfamiliar place. Someone is sitting next to her. This other woman looks exactly like Mary's mother, who died years earlier, and believes herself to be Mary's mother. Certainly, she knows everything about Mary that Mary's mother would know.

Before the woman believing herself to be Mary can speak, she notices some surprising things about herself. She no longer feels old or sick. Her pains are gone, and her mind is as sharp as ever. When she asks where she is, she is told heaven. She is also told that her husband, father, and numerous old friends are waiting to see her. All of them are indistinguishable from the persons they claim to be. Meanwhile, back on earth, Mary Brown is pronounced dead. Is this woman in "heaven" really Mary Brown? How could we possibly explain the phenomenon?

Suppose we put the story in a religious context. Earlier, we saw that one possible explanation of the Badger–Everglade case is that some mad computer scientist had reprogrammed the two so that each embodied the psychology of the other. Suppose we replace the mad scientist with God, and say that God had kept a body in heaven for the purpose of embodying Mary's psychology when she died, and that the person believing herself to be Mary is the new embodiment of Mary's psychology. Would this count as a genuine case of life after death?

If we accept the Badger–Everglade story, appropriately explained, as a case of two persons switching bodies, there seems no reason to deny that Mary has continued to live "in" another body. But even if we are unsure of the Badger–Everglade case, we can approach Mary Brown's this way. What is it that we want to survive after death? Isn't it our memories, our consciousness of self, our personalities, our relations with others? What does it matter whether there is some nonphysical substance that survives? If that substance has no memories of a prior life, does not recognize the souls of others who were important in that earlier life, what comfort could such a continuing existence bring? In what sense would it be the survival of the *person?* How would it be significantly different from the return of the lifeless body to the soil?

If we assume that our story is a genuine case of personal survival of the death of the body, we may wonder about another point. Is it compatible with Christian belief? According to John Hick, a contemporary British philosopher who imagined a similar story, the answer is yes. In I Corinthians 15, Paul writes of the resurrection of the body—not of the physical body, but of some spiritual body. Although one *can* think of this spiritual body as a translucent ghostlike body that leaves the physical body at death, Hick offers another interpretation.

The human being, Hick says, becomes extinct at death. It is only through God's intervention that the spiritual body comes into existence. By the resurrection of this spiritual body, we are to understand a *recreation* or *reconstitution* of the person's body in heaven. But that is precisely what happened in our story.

Thus, a materialist view of the nature of human beings is not incompatible with the Christian view of life after death. Nor, for that matter, is it incompatible with the belief that the spiritual body is nonphysical. If we can make sense of the claim that there might be such things as nonphysical bodies, then there is no reason why a nonphysical body could not embody a psychology. Remember—according to functionalism, an abstract description such as a psychology is independent of any physical description. Just as we can play chess using almost anything as chess pieces, so can a psychology be embodied by almost anything, assuming that it is complex enough. So if there can be nonphysical bodies, there can be nonphysical persons. Of course, nothing said so far assures us that the Christian story—or any other story of life after death— is true. . . .

REINCARNATION

Much of what has been said so far does, however, rule out the possibility of reincarnation as commonly understood. If human beings are purely physical, then there is no nonphysical substance that is the person that can be reincarnated in another earthly body. Moreover, even if there were such a substance, it is difficult to see how its continued existence in another body could count as the reincarnation of a particular person, *if* there is no other continuity between the old life and the new one. Once again, personal survival requires some continuity of consciousness. It is not sameness of *stuff* that constitutes personal identity, but sameness of consciousness. This requirement is often overlooked by believers in reincarnation.

But suppose that there is some continuity of consciousness in reincarnation. Suppose that memories and the rest do continue in the next incarnation, but that they are not easily accessible. Suppose, that is, that the slate is not wiped completely clean, but that what is written on it is hard to recover. In that case, the passage of the soul into a new incarnation would count as personal survival *if* there were such a soul to begin with.

Assuming, again, that there is not, what can we say about the possibility of reincarnation? To conceive of such a possibility, we must conceive of some very complicated reprogramming by God or some mad scientist or whatever. I shall leave it to you to come up with such a story, but I shall say this much. There does not seem to be any good reason to think that any such story is remotely plausible, least of all true.

The Final Word?

. . . [W]e looked at two closely related questions: What constitutes personal identity? And is it possible for a person to survive the death of her own body?

The answer to the second question depended on the first. If we had concluded that the basis of personal identity is sameness of body, then we would have been forced to conclude that life after death is impossible. And there did seem to be good reason to come to these conclusions. How, we asked, could we assure that any memory claim is a case of genuine memory? Our answer was this. In the cases likely to confront us in our daily lives, we must establish some physical continuity between the person who had the original experience and the person who claims to remember it.

But the problem with this answer is that it is too limited. Because we can imagine cases like the Everglade–Badger example, and because our science-fiction tales and religious traditions offer stories of personal continuity without bodily continuity, we can say the following. Regardless of what happens in our daily lives, our concept of a person is a concept of something that does not seem tied to a particular body. Rather, our concept of a person seems to be tied to a particular stream of consciousness. If there is one continuing stream of consciousness over time, then there is one continuing person. Our question, then, was whether we can give a coherent account of continuity of consciousness from one body to another.

The answer was yes. Using the computer analogy of the functionalist, we can explain such continuity in terms of programming. If it is possible to "program" another brain to have the same psychology as the brain I now have, then it is possible for me to change bodies. And if it is possible for me to change bodies, then it is also possible for me to survive the death of my body.

Suggestions For Further Reading

See Jerry Fodor's *Representations: Philosophical Essays on the Foundations of Cognitive Science* (Cambridge, MA: MIT Press, 1983) for an exposition and defense of functionalism.

The Mind's I: Fantasies and Reflections on Self and Soul, edited by Douglas R. Hofstadter and Daniel C. Dennett (New York: Basic Books, 1981), provides a collection of stimulating articles probing the puzzles of personhood.

A volume edited by Amelie Oksenberg Rorty, *The Identities of Persons* (Berkeley: University of California Press, 1976), will prove challenging as it takes you deeper into the mystery of personal identity.

Also see Derek Parfit, *Reasons and Persons* (Oxford: Clarendon Press, 1984) for a revisionist view of the nature of persons and much more. John Hick, in his *Philosophy of Religion,* 4th Edition (Englewood Cliffs, NJ: Prentice-Hall, 1990), develops the replica theory in his presentation of what he takes to be a plausible philosophical account of the Christian idea of resurrection.

If you are interested in material promoting reincarnation and the work of Dr. Ian Stevenson see http://www.childpastlives.org/stevenson.htm.

11.7 Social Identity

How many languages do you speak? One? Two? Three or more? You probably speak more than you think.

"So why do you ask?" you might be thinking. I ask because when we focus on the question, "Who am I?" the issues relating to personal identity arise. This means that issues of ethnic and linguistic identity must soon be explored since our personal identities are shaped in a cultural and linguistic environment.

Recall that Eve Cole (see Section 11.3) takes Descartes to task for not only ignoring the embodied nature of the self, but also for ignoring the relational self. She suggests that we might even begin a "metaphysics of the self" by asking, "To whom am I related?" Communication of some kind is essential to establishing relationships, and, for most of us, that means language is the vehicle by which we relate. You have all heard the slogan, "You are what you eat." Is it going to far to say, "You are your language?"

If you have grown up monolinguistic and securely centered within clear cultural borders, the slogan about you being your language may seem strange. However, if you have grown up in a borderland, between cultures, and multilinguistic, the slogan may not seem so strange. If we add to that experiences that have made you feel ashamed of your native tongue, then you can see more clearly how personal identity and language can be so closely related.

In the selection that follows, Gloria Anzaldúa explores issues of identity and language based on her own personal experience as a Chicana. In the preface to the book from which this selection is taken, the author writes, "I am a border woman. I grew up between two cultures, the Mexican (with a heavy Indian influence) and the Anglo (as a member of a colonized people in our own territory). I have been straddling that *tejas*-Mexican border, and others, all my life."

As a poet and writer of fiction who has taught at various universities, Anzaldúa brings a particular insightful passion to her explorations of identity in a borderland.

As you can imagine, borderlands are not always comfortable places. The discomfort and contradictions that often characterize life on the border not only shape one's identity, they make one more aware of the subtle ways our personal self is a social self.

Reading Project and Questions

1. Write a critical précis (see Section 2.2) on this selection.
2. Did you have difficulty writing the précis? Why?
3. What did you learn about identity from reading this selection that you had not thought about before?

How to Tame a Wild Tongue

GLORIA ANZALDÚA

"WE'RE GOING TO HAVE TO CONTROL your tongue," the dentist says, pulling out all the metal from my mouth. Silver bits plop and tinkle into the basin. My mouth is a motherlode.

The dentist is cleaning out my roots. I get a whiff of the stench when I gasp. "I can't cap that tooth yet, you're still draining," he says.

"We're going to have to do something about your tongue," I hear the anger rising in his voice. My tongue keeps pushing out the wads of cotton, pushing back the drills, the long thin needles. "I've never seen anything as strong or as stubborn," he says. And I think, how do you tame a wild tongue, train it to be quiet, how do you bridle and saddle it? How do you make it lie down?

"Who is to say that robbing a people of
its language is less violent than war?"
—Ray Gwyn Smith

I remember being caught speaking Spanish at recess—that was good for three licks on the knuckles with a sharp ruler. I remember being sent to the corner of the classroom for "talking back" to the Anglo teacher when all I was trying to do was tell her how to pronounce my name.

"If you want to be American, speak 'American.' If you don't like it, go back to Mexico where you belong."

"I want you to speak English. *Pa' hallar buen trabajo tienes que saber hablar el inglés bien. Qué vale toda tu educación si todavía hablas inglés con un* 'accent,'" my mother would say, mortified that I spoke English like a Mexican. At Pan American University, I, and all Chicano students were required to take two speech classes. Their purpose: to get rid of our accents.

Attacks on one's form of expression with the intent to censor are a violation of the First Amendment. *El Anglo con cara de inocente nos arrancó la lengua.* Wild tongues can't be tamed, they can only be cut out.

Overcoming the Tradition of Silence

*Ahogadas, escupimos el oscuro.
Peleando con nuestra propia sombra
el silencio nos sepulta.*

En boca cerrada no entran moscas. "Flies don't enter a closed mouth" is a saying I kept hearing when I was a child. *Ser habladora* was to be a gossip and a liar, to talk too much. *Muchachitas bien*

From Gloria Anzaldúa, Borderlands/La Frontera: The New Mestiza. *San Francisco, CA: aunt lute books, 1987. Copyright © 1987 by Gloria Anzaldúa. Notes omitted. Reprinted by permission.*

criadas, well-bred girls don't answer back. *Es una falta de respeto* to talk back to one's mother or father. I remember one of the sins I'd recite to the priest in the confession box the few times I went to confession: talking back to my mother, *hablar pa' 'tras, repelar. Hocicona, repelona, chismosa,* having a big mouth, questioning, carrying tales are all signs of being *mal criada.* In my culture they are all words that are derogatory if applied to women—I've never heard them applied to men.

The first time I heard two women, a Puerto Rican and a Cuban, say the word *"nosotras,"* I was shocked. I had not known the word existed. Chicanas use *nosotros* whether we're male or female. We are robbed of our female being by the masculine plural. Language is a male discourse.

And our tongues have become
dry   the wilderness has
dried out our tongues   and
we have forgotten speech.

—Irena Klepfisz

Even our own people, other Spanish speakers *nos quieren poner candados en la boca.* They would hold us back with their bag of *reglas de academia.*

*Oyé como ladra: el lenguaje de la frontera
Quien tiene boca se equivoca.*

—Mexican saying

"*Pocho,* cultural traitor, you're speaking the oppressor's language by speaking English, you're ruining the Spanish language," I have been accused by various Latinos and Latinas. Chicano Spanish is considered by the purist and by most Latinos deficient, a mutilation of Spanish.

But Chicano Spanish is a border tongue which developed naturally. Change, *evolución, enriquecimiento de palabras nuevas por invención o adopción* have created variants of Chicano Spanish, *un nuevo lenguaje. Un lenguaje que corresponde a un modo de vivir.* Chicano Spanish is not incorrect, it is a living language.

For a people who are neither Spanish nor live in a country in which Spanish is the first language; for a people who live in a country in which English is the reigning tongue but who are not Anglo; for a people who cannot entirely identify with either standard (formal, Castillian) Spanish nor standard English, what recourse is left to them but to create their own language? A language which they can connect their identity to, one capable of communicating the realities and values true to themselves—a language with terms that are neither *español ni inglés,* but both. We speak a patois, a forked tongue, a variation of two languages.

Chicano Spanish sprang out of the Chicanos' need to identify ourselves as a distinct people. We needed a language with which we could communicate with ourselves, a secret language. For some of us, language is a homeland closer than the Southwest—for many Chicanos today live in the Midwest and the East. And because we are a complex, heterogeneous people, we speak many languages. Some of the languages we speak are:

1. Standard English
2. Working class and slang English
3. Standard Spanish
4. Standard Mexican Spanish
5. North Mexican Spanish dialect
6. Chicano Spanish (Texas, New Mexico, Arizona and California have regional variations)
7. Tex-Mex
8. *Pachuco* (called *caló*)

My "home" tongues are the languages I speak with my sister and brothers, with my friends. They are the last five listed, with 6 and 7 being closest to my heart. From school, the media and job situations, I've picked up standard and working class English. From Mamagrande Locha and from reading Spanish and Mexican literature, I've picked up Standard Spanish and Standard Mexican Spanish. From *los recién llegados,* Mexican immigrants, and *braceros,* I learned the North Mexican dialect. With Mexicans I'll try to speak either Standard Mexican Spanish or the North Mexican dialect. From my parents and Chicanos living in the Valley, I picked up Chicano Texas Spanish, and I speak it with my mom, younger brother (who married a Mexican and who rarely mixes Spanish with English), aunts and older relatives.

With Chicanas from *Nuevo México* or *Arizona* I will speak Chicano Spanish a little, but often they don't understand what I'm saying. With most California Chicanas I speak entirely in English (unless I forget). When I first moved to San Francisco, I'd rattle off something in Spanish, unintentionally embarrassing them. Often it is only with another Chicana *tejana* that I can talk freely.

Words distorted by English are known as anglicisms or *pochismos*. The *pocho* is an anglicized Mexican or American of Mexican origin who speaks Spanish with an accent characteristic of North Americans and who distorts and reconstructs the language according to the influence of English. Tex-Mex, or Spanglish, comes most naturally to me. I may switch back and forth from English to Spanish in the same sentence or in the same word. With my sister and my brother Nune and with Chicano *tejano* contemporaries I speak in Tex-Mex.

From kids and people my own age I picked up *Pachuco*. *Pachuco* (the language of the zoot suiters) is a language of rebellion, both against Standard Spanish and Standard English. It is a secret language. Adults of the culture and outsiders cannot understand it. It is made up of slang words from both English and Spanish. *Ruca* means girl or woman, *vato* means guy or dude, *chale* means no, *simón* means yes, *churro* is sure, talk is *periquiar*, *pigionear* means petting, *que gacho* means how nerdy, *ponte águila* means watch out, death is called *la pelona*. Through lack of practice and not having others who can speak it, I've lost most of the *Pachuco* tongue.

Chicano Spanish

Chicanos, after 250 years of Spanish/Anglo colonization have developed significant differences in the Spanish we speak. We collapse two adjacent vowels into a single syllable and sometimes shift the stress in certain words such as *maíz/maiz*, *cohete/cuete*. We leave out certain consonants when they appear between vowels: *lado/lao*, *mojado/mojao*. Chicanos from South Texas pronounce *f* as *j* as in *jue* (*fue*). Chicanos use "archaisms," words that are no longer in the Spanish language, words that have been evolved out. We say *semos*, *truje*, *haiga*, *ansina*, and *naiden*. We retain the "archaic" *j*, as in *jalar*, that derives from an earlier *h* (the French *halar* or the Ger-

manic *halon* which was lost to standard Spanish in the 16th century), but which is still found in several regional dialects such as the one spoken in South Texas. (Due to geography, Chicanos from the Valley of South Texas were cut off linguistically from other Spanish speakers. We tend to use words that the Spaniards brought over from Medieval Spain. The majority of the Spanish colonizers in Mexico and the Southwest came from Extremadura—Hernán Cortés was one of them—and Andalucía. Andalucians pronounce *ll* like a *y*, and their *d*'s tend to be absorbed by adjacent vowels: *tirado* becomes *tirao*. They brought *el lenguaje popular, dialectos y regionalismos*.)

Chicanos and other Spanish speakers also shift *ll* to *y* and *z* to *s*. We leave out initial syllables, saying *tar* for *estar, toy* for *estoy, hora* for *ahora* (*cubanos* and *puertorriqueños* also leave out initial letters of some words). We also leave out the final syllable such as *pa* for *para*. The intervocalic *y*, the *ll* as in *tortilla, ella, botella*, gets replaced by *tortia* or *tortiya, ea, botea*. We add an additional syllable at the beginning of certain words: *atocar* for *tocar, agastar* for *gastar*. Sometimes we'll say *lavaste las vacijas*, other times *lavates* (substituting the *ates* verb endings for the *aste*).

We use anglicisms, words borrowed from English: *bola* from ball, *carpeta* from carpet, *máchina de lavar* (instead of *lavadora*) from washing machine. Tex-Mex argot, created by adding a Spanish sound at the beginning or end of an English word such as *cookiar* for cook, *watchar* for watch, *parkiar* for park, and *rapiar* for rape, is the result of the pressures on Spanish speakers to adapt to English.

We don't use the word *vosotros/as* or its accompanying verb form. We don't say *claro* (to mean yes), *imagínate*, or *me emociona*, unless we picked up Spanish from Latinas, out of a book, or in a classroom. Other Spanish-speaking groups are going through the same, or similar, development in their Spanish.

Linguistic Terrorism

Deslenguadas. Somos los del español deficiente.
We are your linguistic nightmare, your linguis-

tic aberration, your linguistic *mestisaje,* the subject of your *burla.* Because we speak with tongues of fire we are culturally crucified. Racially, culturally and linguistically *somos huér-fanos—we speak an orphan tongue.*

Chicanas who grew up speaking Chicano Spanish have internalized the belief that we speak poor Spanish. It is illegitimate, a bastard language. And because we internalize how our language has been used against us by the dominant culture, we use our language differences against each other.

Chicana feminists often skirt around each other with suspicion and hesitation. For the longest time I couldn't figure it out. Then it dawned on me. To be close to another Chicana is like looking into the mirror. We are afraid of what we'll see there. *Pena.* Shame. Low estimation of self. In childhood we are told that our language is wrong. Repeated attacks on our native tongue diminish our sense of self. The attacks continue throughout our lives.

Chicanas feel uncomfortable talking in Spanish to Latinas, afraid of their censure. Their language was not outlawed in their countries. They had a whole lifetime of being immersed in their native tongue; generations, centuries in which Spanish was a first language, taught in school, heard on radio and TV, and read in the newspaper.

If a person, Chicana or Latina, has a low estimation of my native tongue, she also has a low estimation of me. Often with *mexicanas y latinas* we'll speak English as a neutral language. Even among Chicanas we tend to speak English at parties or conferences. Yet, at the same time, we're afraid the other will think we're *agringadas* because we don't speak Chicano Spanish. We oppress each other trying to out-Chicano each other, vying to be the "real" Chicanas, to speak like Chicanos. There is no one Chicano language just as there is no one Chicano experience. A monolingual Chicana whose first language is English or Spanish is just as much a Chicana as one who speaks several variants of Spanish. A Chicana from Michigan or Chicago or Detroit is just as much a Chicana as one from the Southwest. Chi-cano Spanish is as diverse linguistically as it is regionally.

By the end of this century, Spanish speakers will comprise the biggest minority group in the U.S., a country where students in high schools and colleges are encouraged to take French classes because French is considered more "cultured." But for a language to remain alive it must be used. By the end of this century English, and not Spanish, will be the mother tongue of most Chicanos and Latinos.

So, if you want to really hurt me, talk badly about my language. Ethnic identity is twin skin to linguistic identity—I am my language. Until I can take pride in my language, I cannot take pride in myself. Until I can accept as legitimate Chicano Texas Spanish, Tex-Mex and all the other languages I speak, I cannot accept the legitimacy of myself. Until I am free to write bilingually and to switch codes without having always to translate, while I still have to speak English or Spanish when I would rather speak Spanglish, and as long as I have to accommodate the English speakers rather than having them accommodate me, my tongue will be illegitimate.

I will no longer be made to feel ashamed of existing. I will have my voice: Indian, Spanish, white. I will have my serpent's tongue—my woman's voice, my sexual voice, my poet's voice. I will overcome the tradition of silence.

> My fingers
> move sly against your palm
> Like women everywhere, we speak in
>   code. . . .
>
> —Melanie Kaye/Kantrowitz

"Vistas," corridos, y comida: *My Native Tongue*

In the 1960s, I read my first Chicano novel. It was *City of Night* by John Rechy, a gay Texan, son of a Scottish father and a Mexican mother. For days I walked around in stunned amazement that a Chicano could write and could get published. When I read *I Am Joaquín* I was surprised to see a bilingual book by a Chicano in print. When I saw poetry written in Tex-Mex for the first time, a feeling of pure joy flashed through me. I felt like we really existed as a people. In 1971, when I started teaching High School English to Chicano students, I tried to supplement the required texts with works by Chicanos, only to be reprimanded and forbidden to do so by the principal. He claimed that I was supposed to teach "American" and English literature. At the risk of being fired, I swore my students to secrecy and slipped in Chicano short stories, poems, a play. In graduate school, while working toward a Ph.D., I had to "argue" with one advisor after the other, semester after semester, before I was allowed to make Chicano literature an area of focus.

Even before I read books by Chicanos or Mexicans, it was the Mexican movies I saw at the drive-in—the Thursday night special of $1.00 a carload—that gave me a sense of belonging. "*Vámonos a las vistas,*" my mother would call out and we'd all—grandmother, brothers, sister and cousins—squeeze into the car. We'd wolf down cheese and bologna white bread sandwiches while watching Pedro Infante in melodramatic tearjerkers like *Nosotros los pobres,* the first "real" Mexican movie (that was not an imitation of European movies). I remember seeing *Cuando los hijos se van* and surmising that all Mexican movies played up the love a mother has for her children and what ungrateful sons and daughters suffer when they are not devoted to their mothers. I remember the singing-type "westerns" of Jorge Negrete and Miquel Aceves Mejía. When watching Mexican movies, I felt a sense of homecoming as well as alienation. People who were to amount to something didn't go to Mexican movies, or *bailes* or tune their radios to *bolero, rancherita,* and *corrido* music.

The whole time I was growing up, there was *norteño* music sometimes called North Mexican border music, or Tex-Mex music, or Chicano music, or *cantina* (bar) music. I grew up listening to *conjuntos,* three- or four-piece bands made up of folk musicians playing guitar, *bajo sexto,* drums and button accordion, which Chicanos had borrowed from the German immigrants who had come to Central Texas and Mexico to farm and build breweries. In the Rio Grande Valley, Steve Jordan and Little Joe Hernández were popular, and Flaco Jiménez was the accordian king. The rhythms of Tex-Mex music are those of the polka, also adapted from the Germans, who in turn had borrowed the polka from the Czechs and Bohemians.

I remember the hot, sultry evenings when *corridos*—songs of love and death on the Texas-Mexican borderlands—reverberated out of cheap amplifiers from the local *cantinas* and wafted in through my bedroom window.

Corridos first became widely used along the South Texas/Mexican border during the early conflict between Chicanos and Anglos. The *corridos* are usually about Mexican heroes who do valiant deeds against the Anglo oppressors. Pancho Villa's song, "*La cucaracha,*" is the most famous one. *Corridos* of John F. Kennedy and his death are still very popular in the Valley. Older Chicanos remember Lydia Mendoza, one of the great border *corrido* singers who was called *la Gloria de Tejas.* Her "*El tango negro,*" sung during the Great Depression, made her a singer of the people. The everpresent *corridos* narrated one hundred years of border history, bringing news of events as well as entertaining. These folk musicians and folk songs are our chief cultural mythmakers, and they made our hard lives seem bearable.

I grew up feeling ambivalent about our music. Country-western and rock-and-roll had more status. In the 50s and 60s, for the slightly educated and *agringado* Chicanos, there existed a sense of shame at being caught listening to our music. Yet I couldn't stop my feet from thumping to the music, could not stop humming the words, nor hide from myself the exhilaration I felt when I heard it.

There are more subtle ways that we internalize identification, especially in the forms of images and emotions. For me food and certain smells are tied to my identity, to my homeland. Woodsmoke curling up to an immense blue sky; woodsmoke perfuming my grandmother's clothes, her skin. The stench of cow manure and the yellow patches on the ground; the crack of a .22 rifle and the reek of cordite. Homemade white cheese sizzling in a pan, melting inside a folded *tortilla*. My sister Hilda's hot, spicy *menudo, chile colorado* making it deep red, pieces of *panza* and hominy floating on top. My brother Carito barbequing *fajitas* in the backyard. Even now and 3,000 miles away, I can see my mother spicing the ground beef, pork and venison with *chile*. My mouth salivates at the thought of the hot steaming *tamales* I would be eating if I were home.

Si le preguntas a mi mamá, "¿Qué eres?"

> "Identity is the essential core of who we are as individuals, the conscious experience of the self inside."
>
> —Kaufman

Nosotros los Chicanos straddle the borderlands. On one side of us, we are constantly exposed to the Spanish of the Mexicans, on the other side we hear the Anglos' incessant clamoring so that we forget our language. Among ourselves we don't say *nosotros los americanos, o nosotros los españoles, o nosotros los hispanos*. We say *nosotros los mexicanos* (by *mexicanos* we do not mean citizens of Mexico; we do not mean a national identity, but a racial one). We distinguish between *mexicanos del otro lado* and *mexicanos de este lado*. Deep in our hearts we believe that being Mexican has nothing to do with which country one lives in. Being Mexican is a state of soul—not one of mind, not one of citizenship. Neither eagle nor serpent, but both. And like the ocean, neither animal respects borders.

> *Dime con quien andas y te diré quien eres.*
> (Tell me who your friends are and I'll tell you who you are.)
>
> —Mexican saying

Si le preguntas a mi mamá, "¿Qué eres?" te dirá, "Soy mexicana." My brothers and sister say the same. I sometimes will answer *"soy mexicana"* and at others will say *"soy Chicana"* o *"soy tejana."* But I identified as *"Raza"* before I ever identified as *"mexicana"* or "Chicana."

As a culture, we call ourselves Spanish when referring to ourselves as a linguistic group and when copping out. It is then that we forget our

predominant Indian genes. We are 70–80% Indian. We call ourselves Hispanic or Spanish-American or Latin American or Latin when linking ourselves to other Spanish-speaking peoples of the Western hemisphere and when copping out. We call ourselves Mexican-American to signify we are neither Mexican nor American, but more the noun "American" than the adjective "Mexican" (and when copping out).

Chicanos and other people of color suffer economically for not acculturating. This voluntary (yet forced) alienation makes for psychological conflict, a kind of dual identity—we don't identify with the Anglo-American cultural values and we don't totally identify with the Mexican cultural values. We are a synergy of two cultures with various degrees of Mexicanness or Angloness. I have so internalized the borderland conflict that sometimes I feel like one cancels out the other and we are zero, nothing, no one. *A veces no soy nada ni nadie. Pero hasta cuando no lo soy, lo soy.*

When not copping out, when we know we are more than nothing, we call ourselves Mexican, referring to race and ancestry; *mestizo* when affirming both our Indian and Spanish (but we hardly ever own our Black ancestory); Chicano when referring to a politically aware people born and/or raised in the U.S.; *Raza* when referring to Chicanos; *tejanos* when we are Chicanos from Texas.

Chicanos did not know we were a people until 1965 when Caesar Chavez and the farmworkers united and *I Am Joaquín* was published and *la Raza Unida* party was formed in Texas. With that recognition, we became a distinct people. Something momentous happened to the Chicano soul—we became aware of our reality and acquired a name and a language (Chicano Spanish) that reflected that reality. Now that we had a name, some of the fragmented pieces began to fall together—who we were, what we were, how we had evolved. We began to get glimpses of what we might eventually become.

Yet the struggle of identities continues, the struggle of borders is our reality still. One day the inner struggle will cease and a true integration take place. In the meantime, *tenémos que hacer la lucha. ¿Quién está protegiendo los ranchos de mi gente? ¿Quién está tratando de cerrar la fisura entre la india y el blanco en nuestra sangre? El Chicano, si, el Chicano que anda como un ladrón en su propia casa.*

Los Chicanos, how patient we seem, how very patient. There is the quiet of the Indian about us. We know how to survive. When other races have given up their tongue, we've kept ours. We know what it is to live under the hammer blow of the dominant *norteamericano* culture. But more than we count the blows, we count the days the weeks the years the centuries the eons until the white laws and commerce and customs will rot in the deserts they've created, lie bleached. *Humildes* yet proud, *quietos* yet wild, *nosotros los mexicanos-Chicanos* will walk by the crumbling ashes as we go about our business. Stubborn, persevering, impenetrable as stone, yet possessing a malleability that renders us unbreakable, we, the *mestizas* and *mestizos,* will remain.

Suggestions for Further Reading

You should read the whole book (see credit line) from which this selection is taken in order to get a deeper sense of the issues the author is exploring.

Jack D. Forbes, *Aztecas del Norte: The Chicanos of Aztlán* (Greenwich, CT: Fawcett, 1973), is dated but still valuable for background as is John R. Chávez, *The Lost Land: The Chicano Images of the Southwest* (Albuquerque: University of New Mexico Press, 1984).

Jorge J. E. Gracia and Mireya Camurati have edited a useful book titled *Philosophy and Literature in Latin America: A Critical Assessment of the Current Situation* (Albany: State University of New York Press, 1989).

Historical background on Chicana feminist thought can be found in a book edited by Alma M. García called *Chicana Feminist Thought: The Basic Historical Writings* (New York: Routledge, 1997.

You can find more information on the web relating to borders and identity at http://www.cas.ilstu.edu/english/strickland/border/abstracts/crisler.htm.

For a brief bio and links to other sources see http://www.mankato.msus.edu/depts/worldsot/anza.htm.

 You can locate InfoTrac-College Edition articles about this chapter by accessing the InfoTrac-College Edition website (http://www.infotrac-college.com/wadsworth/). Using the InfoTrac-College Edition subject guide, enter the search terms relevant to this chapter, and then read abstracts for relevant articles.

Chapter 12

Is There a God?

> **Why can't everybody just make up their own religion?**
>
> A Student

12.1 Introduction

HAVE YOU EVER WONDERED whether God exists? Of course; most people have. But have you wondered whether God's existence can be proved? Are there arguments that would convince any reasonable person? Is there evidence, I mean real hard-core scientific evidence, that God exists? When I ask my students how many of them believe God exists, almost all of them raise their hands. But when I ask them how many think God's existence can be *proved,* most are skeptical. "It is," they say, "a matter of faith."

The existence of God is a metaphysical question central to a branch of philosophy called the **philosophy of religion**. As the name implies, this area of philosophy applies philosophical methods to the study of a wide variety of religious issues, including the existence of God. Philosophy of religion should be clearly distinguished from a type of theology called revealed theology. **Theology** literally means the "study of God." **Revealed theology** is a type of theology that claims human knowledge of God comes through special revelations such as the Bible or the Qur'an. St. Thomas Aquinas (see Section 12.2 below) said that revealed theology provides "saving knowledge"—that is, knowledge that will result in our salvation.

Another kind of theology, called **natural theology**, has to do with the knowledge of God that is possible based on the use of "natural" reason—that is, reason unaided by special revelations. St. Thomas says that this sort of theology can provide us with some knowledge of God's nature and can demonstrate that God exists, but it cannot provide saving knowledge because, after all, even devils know that God exists.

Natural theology is sometimes called *rational theology* or *philosophical theology.* As this last name indicates, this kind of theology is more closely related to the philosophy of religion than is revealed theology. Both natural theology and the philosophy of religion rely solely on the use of human reason in their attempts to discover something about the divine. They do not assume the truth of some special revelation; they allow only what reason can prove.

Although both philosophy of religion and natural theology rely on reason rather than on revelation, they differ in the range of topics considered. Philosophy of religion studies a wide range of religious issues and different notions of what constitutes ultimate reality. Theism is just one sort of religious notion of ultimate reality. The *Tao* or Brahman-Atman, for example (see Chapter 9), both present conceptions of ultimate reality that appear quite different from theistic ideas. Needless to say, *nontheistic* philosophies have not been overly concerned with the issue of God's existence even though they have been concerned with the nature and existence of some kind of ultimate reality. However, *theistic* philosophies and the cultures—both Eastern and Western—influenced by theistic religions have regarded the topic of God's existence as an issue of immense significance.

Although the questions "What is God like?" and "Does God exist?" are different, nevertheless they are closely related. The answer to the first question tells us something about God's nature; for example, that God or the Divine, if there is such a being, is the creator of the universe, is all-powerful and all-knowing, is perfectly good and loving, and so on. The answer to the second question tells us whether a being of this sort exists. But these answers blend into each other because every argument for God's existence or nonexistence is an argument for the existence or nonexistence of a God *of a certain sort*. So, for example, those who argue that the existence of complex order and beauty in the universe is evidence that God created it and hence exists imply that God's nature is that of an intelligent being capable of producing beauty and complex order.

Arguments for God's existence fall into two broad types: a posteriori and a priori. A posteriori arguments attempt to demonstrate the existence of God by appealing to sense experience. Typically, they argue from some feature of our experience of the world to the conclusion that God exists. We will be looking at two examples in what follows: the cosmological argument and the teleological argument. A priori arguments attempt to show that God exists independently of any appeal to sense experience. Typically, they proceed from some definition of God's nature to the conclusion that God exists. We will look at one example, the ontological argument of St. Anselm.

12.2 Cosmological Arguments

How many of you have thought "there must be a God because the universe just couldn't happen by itself? Something must have caused it. Things don't just pop into existence out of nothing." If you have had thoughts like this, you have been thinking along the lines of a cosmological argument. **Cosmological arguments** (there are several varieties) argue from the existence of the universe (world or cosmos) to the existence of God as its cause, its creator, or its explanation.

Cosmological arguments are very old, being found among ancient Greek and Indian philosophers. The Greek versions were most influential on Western thought. Since the Greeks believed the universe was eternal (i.e., it had no beginning and has no end), they did not believe that God created it out of nothing. However, they did believe that there had to be an explanation for the universe. After all, why should there be something, even if that something is not created and has been around forever? They especially thought that motion, a basic characteristic of the universe, needed an explanation.

Aristotle (see Section 3.5) argued from the existence of motion to the existence of an Unmoved Mover as the explanation of motion. This Unmoved Mover he called "*ho theos*" (the god), in part because it was unmoved (i.e., nothing caused it to move) but was responsible for the motion of other things. It is, if you will, a *prime* mover. Aristotle's argument was based on three principles that operate as assumptions in practically all cosmological arguments: (1) Something cannot be the cause of itself, (2) something cannot come from nothing, and (3) there cannot be an infinite series of causes and effects.

Christian and Islamic theologians inherited the Greek thinking on these matters, but most could not accept the notion that the universe was uncreated and hence eternal. God, they believed, must be absolute, and the existence of the world must be completely dependent on him. God alone is uncreated. Therefore, they interpreted the story of creation found in Genesis (the first book of the Bible) in a manner compatible with the doctrine of *creatio ex nihilo,* creation out of nothing. God, they argued, created the universe out of nothing, and hence the universe is not eternal but began to exist at some point.

Kalam, which means "speech" in Arabic, came to denote the statement of points in theological doctrine. Eventually, it was used as a name for a movement in Islamic thought, which, among other things, was much concerned with the problems involved in demonstrating God's existence. Islamic theologians rejected the Greek idea that the world is uncreated and so formulated the cosmological argument to explicitly recognize a created universe. A simple version of the *Kalam* cosmological argument is the following:

1. Whatever begins to exist has a cause of its existence.
2. The universe began to exist.
3. Therefore, the universe has a cause of its existence, and this is Allah.

The first version of the cosmological argument that follows is from Moses ben Maimon, better known as Maimonides. He was born in Cordova, Spain, in 4895 (1135 in the Christian calendar) and died in 4964 (1204) at the age of sixty-nine. Maimonides was a great Jewish theologian and philosopher who inherited both the Greek and Islamic thinking about cosmological proofs. "From Moses to Moses there is none like Moses" is a famous phrase showing how important Maimonides is in Jewish thought. The first Moses is the prophet through whom the Law or Torah was given. The second Moses is Maimonides, who reconciled the Torah with the science and philosophy of his day. In 1190 he published a book called *Guide for the Perplexed* that showed Jews, who were perplexed by the relationship of Jewish tradition and law to science and philosophy, how to harmonize their religious tradition and scientific thinking.

Maimonides was critical of the Greek arguments because he thought the Greeks were unable to prove that the universe was uncreated (i.e., eternal), and their proofs depended on that assumption. However, he was also critical of the *Kalam* arguments because he believed their assumption—namely, that the universe was created—also could not be proven. He therefore developed a version of the argument that attempts to prove that God exists no matter which assumption we make.

His argument makes reference to a "fifth essence" (better translated as "element") and to "heavenly spheres" because the science of his day taught that Earth was at the center of the universe, surrounded by various spheres where the stars were located. The material bodies within the terrestrial realm (everything below the Sun and Moon), it was thought, were made of various combinations of earth, air, fire, and water, and could move up and down. The heavenly bodies, however, were made out of a fifth element called "ether" because they moved in a circle and did not move up or down—that is, fall toward the center (Earth) or move away from it.

His argument begins with a list of "propositions," which he took to be proven true. These propositions constitute the fundamental ideas of the physical science of his time, a science adopted from the Greek physical theories of Aristotle. They provide an interesting contrast to modern physical science (see Section 12.3 below) and show how radically our conception of the universe has changed from the Middle Ages.

The second set of cosmological arguments comes from St. Thomas Aquinas (ca. 1225–1274). St. Thomas was born in the family castle near Naples, Italy. His father, the Count of Aquino, hoped for a military career for his son. Thomas, however, became a monk instead and pursued a teaching career in theology at the University of Paris and elsewhere. He was largely responsible for harmonizing Christian theology with the then recently discovered scientific and philosophical ideas of Aristotle. His major work is the *Summa Theologica,* which treats all the major theological issues of the day. Thomas was made a saint of the Roman Catholic Church in 1323, and in 1879 his ideas were proclaimed by Pope Leo XIII to be the official philosophy and theology of the Roman Catholic Church.

In the *Summa,* Thomas gives five separate arguments for God's existence, called the Five Ways. The selection included here presents two of these arguments, the second and third ways. It is evident that Thomas is heavily indebted to both Islamic and Jewish theology, not to mention the Greek philosophy of Aristotle.

The idea of an efficient cause, which plays a major role in his argument, is taken from Aristotle's idea of **four causes**. Things, Aristotle taught, had four causes: (1) efficient, (2) material, (3) formal, and (4) final. For example, the efficient cause of a statue is the agent (sculptor) and agency (sculpting) by which it is made. The material cause is the stuff (marble) out of which it is made. The formal cause is some set of essential characteristics *without* which this statue would not be this statue (let us say a statue of Socrates), but some other statue or no statue at all, and the final cause is the outcome or result, that is, the statue of Socrates.

St. Thomas also borrows the ideas of *necessity* and *contingency.* Something is contingent if its existence is dependent on something else, and it is necessary if its existence does not depend on anything else. In one of the most influential versions of the cosmological argument, Thomas argues that the universe is contingent and hence dependent on something besides itself for existence.

Reading Questions

1. Of the twenty-six propositions listed by Maimonides, which ones do you not understand? Discuss them in class.
2. At the beginning of Chapter 1, Maimonides presents a long argument to show that the efficient motion of the sphere must be incorporeal (without a body) and separate from the sphere. Summarize that argument in your own words.
3. What is the conclusion of Maimonides' argument for God's existence presented in Chapter 2? Underline it.
4. Why must God be the creator of the spheres if the spheres are transient (i.e., temporal), and why must God be the cause of the perpetual motion of the spheres if they are eternal?

5. According to St. Thomas, why is it not possible for the order of efficient causes to proceed to infinity?
6. Must a first efficient cause of the universe be God? Why, or why not?
7. Why, according to St. Thomas, is it impossible for *all* things that exist to be capable of not existing?
8. If there was a time when nothing existed, why, according to St. Thomas, would it be impossible for anything to begin to exist?
9. How would St. Thomas answer the question, "Who caused God to exist?"
10. Do you think any of these arguments prove the existence of God? Why, or why not? Can you formulate a better argument?
11. Just because everything *in* the universe has a cause and is contingent, does it follow that the universe itself, *taken as whole*, has a cause and is contingent?

Guide for the Perplexed

MAIMONIDES

Part II

INTRODUCTION

TWENTY-FIVE of the propositions which are employed in the proof for the existence of God, or in the arguments demonstrating that God is neither corporeal nor a force connected with a material being, or that He is One, have been fully established, and their correctness is beyond doubt. Aristotle and the Peripatetics who followed him have proved each of these propositions. There is, however, one proposition which we do not accept—namely, the proposition which affirms the Eternity of the Universe, but we will admit it for the present, because by doing so we shall be enabled clearly to demonstrate our own theory.

PROPOSITION I

The existence of an infinite magnitude is impossible.

PROPOSITION II

The coexistence of an infinite number of finite magnitudes is impossible.

PROPOSITION III

The existence of an infinite number of causes and effects is impossible, even if these were not magnitudes; if, e.g., one Intelligence were the cause of a second, the second the cause of a third, the third the cause of a fourth, and so on, the series could not be continued *ad infinitum*.

PROPOSITION IV

Four categories are subject to change:

1. *Substance.* Changes which affect the substance of a thing are called genesis and destruction.
2. *Quantity.* Changes in reference to quantity are increase and decrease.

From Moses Maimonides, The Guide for the Perplexed, *translated by M. Friedlander (London: Routledge &*
Kegan Paul, Ltd., 1904), Part 2, Chapters 1 and 2, pp. 145–151, 154–155.

3. *Quality.* Changes in the qualities of things are transformations.
4. *Place.* Change of place is called motion.

The term "motion" is properly applied to change of place, but is also used in a general sense of all kinds of changes.

PROPOSITION V

Motion implies change and transition from potentiality to actuality.

PROPOSITION VI

The motion of a thing is either essential or accidental; or it is due to an external force, or to the participation of the thing in the motion of another thing. This latter kind of motion is similar to the accidental one. An instance of essential motion may be found in the translation of a thing from one place to another. The accident of a thing, as, e.g., its black color, is said to move when the thing itself changes its place. The upward motion of a stone, owing to a force applied to it in that direction, is an instance of a motion due to an external force. The motion of a nail in a boat may serve to illustrate motion due to the participation of a thing in the motion of another thing; for when the boat moves, the nail is said to move likewise. The same is the case with everything composed of several parts: when the thing itself moves, every part of it is likewise said to move.

PROPOSITION VII

Things which are changeable are, at the same time, divisible. Hence everything that moves is divisible, and consequently corporeal; but that which is indivisible cannot move, and cannot therefore be corporeal.

PROPOSITION VIII

A thing that moves accidentally must come to rest, because it does not move of its own accord; hence accidental motion cannot continue forever.

PROPOSITION IX

A corporeal thing that sets another corporeal thing in motion can only effect this by setting itself in motion at the time it causes the other thing to move.

PROPOSITION X

A thing which is said to be contained in a corporeal object must satisfy either of the two following conditions: it either exists through that object, as is the case with accidents, or it is the cause of the existence of that object; such is, e.g., its essential property. In both cases it is a force existing in a corporeal object.

PROPOSITION XI

Among the things which exist through a material object, there are some which participate in the division of that object, and are therefore accidentally divisible, as, e.g., its color, and all other qualities that spread throughout its parts. On the other hand, among the things which form the essential elements of an object, there are some which cannot be divided in any way, as, e.g., the soul and the intellect.

PROPOSITION XII

A force which occupies all parts of a corporeal object is finite, that object itself being finite.

PROPOSITION XIII

None of the several kinds of change can be continuous, except motion from place to place, provided it be circular.

PROPOSITION XIV

Locomotion is in the natural order of the several kinds of motion the first and foremost. For genesis and corruption are preceded by transformation, which, in its turn, is preceded by the approach of the transforming agent to the object which is to be transformed. Also, increase and decrease are impossible without previous genesis and corruption.

PROPOSITION XV

Time is an accident that is related and joined to motion in such a manner that the one is never found without the other. Motion is only possible in time, and the idea of time cannot be conceived otherwise than in connection with motion; things which do not move have no relation to time.

PROPOSITION XVI

Incorporeal bodies can only be numbered when they are forces situated in a body; the several forces must then be counted together with substances or objects in which they exist. Hence purely spiritual beings, which are neither corporeal nor forces situated in corporeal objects, cannot be counted, except when considered as causes and effects.

PROPOSITION XVII

When an object moves, there must be some agent that moves it, from without, as, e.g., in the case of a stone set in motion by the hand; or from within, e.g., when the body of a living being moves. Living beings include in themselves, at the same time, the moving agent and the thing moved; when, therefore, a living being dies, and the moving agent, the soul, has left the body, i.e., the thing moved, the body remains for some time in the same condition as before, and yet cannot move in the manner it has moved previously. The moving agent, when included in the thing moved, is hidden from, and imperceptible to, the senses. This circumstance gave rise to the belief that the body of an animal moves without the aid of a moving agent. When we therefore affirm, concerning a thing in motion, that it is its own moving agent, or, as is generally said, that it moves of its own accord, we mean to say that the force which really sets the body in motion exists in that body itself.

PROPOSITION XVIII

Everything that passes over from a state of potentiality to that of actuality, is caused to do so by some external agent; because if that agent existed in the thing itself, and no obstacle prevented the transition, the thing would never be in a state of potentiality, but always in that of actuality. If, on the other hand, while the thing itself contained that agent, some obstacle existed, and at a certain time that obstacle was removed, the same cause which removed the obstacle would undoubtedly be described as the cause of the transition from potentiality to actuality [and not the force situated within the body]. Note this.

PROPOSITION XIX

A thing which owes its existence to certain causes has in itself merely the possibility of existence; for only if these causes exist, the thing likewise exists. It does not exist if the causes do not exist at all, or if they have ceased to exist, or if there has been a change in the relation which implies the existence of that thing as a necessary consequence of those causes.

PROPOSITION XX

A thing which has in itself the necessity of existence cannot have for its existence any cause whatever.

PROPOSITION XXI

A thing composed of two elements has necessarily their composition as the cause of its present existence. Its existence is therefore not necessitated by its own essence; it depends on the existence of its two component parts and their combination.

PROPOSITION XXII

Material objects are always composed of two elements [at least], and are without exception subject to accidents. The two component elements of all bodies are substance and form. The accidents attributed to material objects are quantity, geometrical form, and position.

PROPOSITION XXIII

Everything that exists potentially, and whose essence includes a certain state of possibility, may at some time be without actual existence.

PROPOSITION XXIV

That which is potentially a certain thing is necessarily material, for the state of possibility is always connected with matter.

PROPOSITION XXV

Each compound substance consists of matter and form, and requires an agent for its existence, *viz.,* a force which sets the substance in motion, and thereby enables it to receive a certain form. The force which thus prepares the substance of a certain individual being is called the immediate motor.

Here the necessity arises of investigating into the properties of motion, the moving agent and the thing moved. But this has already been explained sufficiently; and the opinion of Aristotle may be expressed in the following proposition: Matter does not move of its own accord—an important proposition that led to the investigation of the Prime Motor (the first moving agent).

Of these foregoing twenty-five propositions some may be verified by means of a little reflection and the application of a few propositions capable of proof, or of axioms or theorems of almost the same force, such as have been explained by me. Others require many arguments and propositions, all of which, however, have been established by conclusive proofs partly in the Physics and its commentaries, and partly in the Metaphysics and its commentary. I have already stated that in this work it is not my intention to copy the books of the philosophers or to explain difficult problems, but simply to mention those propositions which are closely connected with our subject, and which we want for our purpose.

To the above propositions one must be added which enunciates that the universe is eternal, and which is held by Aristotle to be true, and even more acceptable than any other theory. For the present we admit it, as a hypothesis, only for the purpose of demonstrating our theory. It is the following proposition:—

PROPOSITION XXVI

Time and motion are eternal, constant, and in actual existence.

In accordance with this proposition, Aristotle is compelled to assume that there exists actually a body with constant motion, *viz.,* the fifth element. He therefore says that the heavens are not subject to genesis or destruction, because motion cannot be generated nor destroyed. He also holds that every motion must necessarily be preceded by another motion, either of the same or of a different kind. The belief that the locomotion of an animal is not preceded by another motion, is not true; for the animal is caused to move, after it had been in rest, by the intention to obtain those very things which bring about that locomotion. A change in its state of health, or some image, or some new idea can produce a desire to seek that which is conducive to its welfare and to avoid that which is contrary. Each of these three causes sets the living being in motion, and each of them is produced by various kinds of motion. Aristotle likewise asserts that everything which is created must, before its actual creation, have existed *in potentiâ.* By inferences drawn from this assertion he seeks to establish his proposition, *viz.,* The thing that moves is finite, and its path finite; but it repeats the motion in its path an infinite number of times. This can only take place when the motion is circular, as has been stated in Proposition XIII. Hence follows also the existence of an infinite number of things which do not coexist but follow one after the other.

Aristotle frequently attempts to establish this proposition; but I believe that he did not consider his proofs to be conclusive. It appeared to him to be the most probable and acceptable proposition. His followers, however, and the commentators of his books, contend that it contains not only a probable but a demonstrative proof, and that it has, in fact, been fully established. On the other hand, the Mutakallemim try to prove that the proposition cannot be true, as, according to their opinion, it is impossible to conceive how an infinite number of things could even come into existence successively. They assume this impossibility as an axiom. I, however, think that this proposition is admissible, but neither demonstrative, as the commentators of Aristotle assert, nor, on the other hand, impossible, as the Mutakallemim say. We have no intention to explain here the proofs given by Aristotle, or to show our doubts concerning them, or to set forth our opinions on the creation of the universe. I here simply desire to mention those propositions which we shall require for the proof of the three principles stated above. Having thus quoted and admitted these propositions, I will now proceed to explain what may be inferred from them.

Chapter 1

According to Proposition XXV, a moving agent must exist which has moved the substance of all existing transient things and enabled it to receive Form. The cause of the motion of that agent is found in the existence of another motor of the same or of a different class, the term "motion," in a general sense, being common to four categories (Prop. IV). This series of motions is not infinite (Prop. III); we find that it can only be continued till the motion of the fifth element is arrived at, and then it ends. The motion of the fifth element is the source of every force that moves and prepares any substance on earth for its combination with a certain form, and is connected with that force by a chain of intermediate motions. The celestial sphere [or the fifth element] performs the act of locomotion which is the first of the several kinds of motion (Prop. XIV), and all locomotion is found to be the indirect effect of the motion of this sphere; e.g., a stone is set in motion by a stick, the stick by a man's hand, the hand by the sinews, the sinews by the muscles, the muscles by the nerves, the nerves by the natural heat of the body, and the heat of the body by its form. This is undoubtedly

the immediate motive cause, but the action of this immediate cause is due to a certain design, e.g., to bring a stone into a hole by striking against it with a stick in order to prevent the draught from coming through the crevice. The motion of the air that causes the draught is the effect of the motion of the celestial sphere. Similarly it may be shown that the ultimate cause of all genesis and destruction can be traced to the motion of the sphere. But the motion of the sphere must likewise have been effected by an agent (Prop. XVII) residing either without the sphere or within it; a third case being impossible. In the first case, if the motor is without the sphere, it must either be corporeal or incorporeal; if incorporeal, it cannot be said that the agent is *without* the sphere; it can only be described as *separate* from it; because an incorporeal object can only be said metaphorically to reside without a certain corporeal object. In the second case, if the agent resides within the sphere, it must be either a force distributed throughout the whole sphere so that each part of the sphere includes a part of the force, as is the case with the heat of fire; or it is an indivisible force, e.g., the soul and the intellect (Props. X and XI). The agent which sets the sphere in motion must consequently be one of the following four things: a corporeal object without the sphere; an incorporeal object separate from it; a force spread throughout the whole of the sphere; or an indivisible force [within the sphere].

The first case, *viz.*, that the moving agent of the sphere is a corporeal object without the sphere is, impossible, as will be explained. Since the moving agent is corporeal, it must itself move while setting another object in motion (Prop. IX), and as the sixth element would likewise move when imparting motion to another body, it would be set in motion by a seventh element, which must also move. An infinite number of bodies would thus be required before the sphere could be set in motion. This is contrary to Proposition II.

The third case, *viz.,* that the moving object be a force distributed throughout the whole body, is likewise impossible. For the sphere is corporeal, and must therefore be finite (Prop. I); also the force it contains must be finite (Prop. XII), since each part of the sphere contains part of the force (Prop. XI): the latter can consequently not produce an infinite motion, such as we assumed according to Proposition XXVI, which we admitted for the present.

The fourth case is likewise impossible, *viz.,* that the sphere is set in motion by an indivisible force residing in the sphere in the same manner as the soul resides in the body of man. For this force, though indivisible, could not be the cause of infinite motion by itself alone; because if that were the case the prime motor would have an accidental motion (Prop. VI). But things that move accidentally must come to rest (Prop. VIII), and then the thing comes also to rest which is set in motion. [The following may serve as a further illustration of the nature of accidental motion. When man is moved by the soul, i.e., by his form, to go from the basement of the house to the upper storey, his body moves directly, while the soul, the really efficient cause of that motion, participates in it accidentally. For through the translation of the body from the basement to the upper storey, the soul has likewise changed its place, and when no fresh impulse for the motion of the body is given by the soul, the body which has been set in motion by such impulse comes to rest, and the accidental motion of the soul is discontinued.] Consequently the motion of that supposed first motor must be due to some cause which does not form part of things composed of two elements, *viz.,* a moving agent and an object moved; if such a cause is present the motor in that compound sets the other element in motion; in the absence of such a cause no motion takes place. Living beings do therefore not move continually, although each of them possesses an indivisible motive element; because this element is not constantly in motion, as it would be if it produced motion of its own accord. On the contrary, the things to which the action is due are separate from the motor. The action is caused either by desire for that which is agreeable, or by aversion from that which is disagreeable, or by some image, or by some ideal when the moving being has the capacity of conceiving it. When any of these causes are present then the motor acts; its motion is accidental, and must therefore come to an end (Prop. VIII). If the motor of the sphere were of this kind the sphere could not move *ad infinitum.* Our opponent, however, holds that the spheres move continually *ad infinitum;* if this were the case, and it is in fact possible (Prop. XIII), the efficient cause of the motion of the sphere must, according to the above division, be of the second kind, *viz.,* something incorporeal and separate from the sphere.

It may thus be considered as proved that the efficient cause of the motion of the sphere, if that motion be eternal, is neither itself corporeal nor does it reside in a corporeal object; it must move neither of its own accord nor accidentally; it must be indivisible and unchangeable (Prop. VII and Prop. V). This Prime Motor of the sphere is God, praised be His name! . . .

Chapter 2

The fifth essence, i.e., the heavenly spheres, must either be transient, and in this case motion would likewise be temporary, or, as our opponent assumes, it must be eternal. If the spheres are transient, then God is their Creator; for if anything comes into existence after a period of nonexistence, it is self-evident that an agent exists which has effected this result. It would be absurd to contend that the thing itself effected it. If, on the other hand, the heavenly spheres be eternal, with a regular perpetual motion, the cause of this perpetual motion, according to the Propositions enumerated in the Introduction, must be something that is neither a body, nor a force residing in a body, and that is God, praised be His name! We have thus shown that whether we believe in the *Creatio ex Nihilo,* or in the Eternity of the Universe, we can prove by demonstrative arguments the existence of God, i.e., an absolute Being, whose existence cannot be attributed to any cause, or admit in itself any potentiality.

Summa Theologica

ST. THOMAS AQUINAS

The Second Way: The Argument from Causation

THE SECOND WAY is taken from the idea of the Efficient cause. (1) For we find that there is among material things a regular order of efficient causes. (2) But we do not find, nor indeed is it possible, that anything is the efficient cause of itself, for in that case it would be prior to itself, which is impossible. (3) Now it is not possible to proceed to infinity in efficient causes. (4) For if we arrange in order all efficient causes, the first is the cause of the intermediate, and the intermediate the cause of the last, whether the intermediate be many or only one. (5) But if we remove a cause the effect is removed; therefore, if there is no *first* among efficient causes, neither will there be a last or an intermediate. (6) But if we proceed to infinity in efficient causes there will be no first efficient cause, and thus there will be no ultimate effect, nor any intermediate efficient causes, which is clearly false. Therefore it is necessary to suppose the existence of some first efficient cause, and this men call God.

The Third Way: The Argument from Contingency

The Third Way rests on the idea of the "contingent" and the "necessary" and is as follows:

(1) Now we find that there are certain things in the Universe which are capable of existing and of not existing, for we find that some things are brought into existence and then destroyed, and consequently are capable of being or not being. (2) But it is impossible for all things which exist to be of this kind, because anything which is capable of not existing, at some time or other does not exist. (3) If therefore *all* things are capable of not existing, there was a time when nothing existed in the Universe. (4) But if this is true there would also be nothing in existence now; because anything that does not exist cannot begin to exist except by the agency of something which has existence. If therefore there was once nothing which existed, it would have been impossible for anything to begin to exist, and so nothing would exist now. (5) This is clearly false. Therefore all things are not contingent, and there must be something which is necessary in the Universe. (6) But everything which is necessary either has or has not the cause of its necessity from an outside source. Now it is not possible to proceed to infinity in necessary things which have a cause of their necessity, as has been proved in the case of efficient causes. Therefore it is necessary to suppose the existence of something which is necessary in itself, not having the cause of its necessity from any outside source, but which is the cause of necessity in others. And this "something" we call God.

From Thomas Aquinas, Summa Theologica, *translated by Lawrence Shapcotte (London: O. P. Benziger Brothers, 1911). Part 1, Article 3.*

Suggestions for Further Reading

For more on the philosophy of religion, including the arguments for God's existence, see Gary E. Kessler, *Philosophy of Religion: Toward a Global Perspective* (Belmont, CA: Wadsworth, 1999).

For information on the world's religions along with primary texts, see *Way of Being Religious* by Gary E. Kessler (Mountain View, CA: Mayfield, 2000).

Articles on Maimonides and St. Thomas can be found in *The Cambridge Dictionary of Philosophy*, edited by Robert Audi, 2nd Edition (Cambridge: Cambridge University Press, 1999).

On the Web, see the relevant articles in the *Stanford Encyclopedia of Philosophy* at http://plato.stanford.edu.

For a Web page that will link you to all kinds of information on Aquinas see http://www.pagesz.net/~stevek/intellect/aquinas.html.

Donald R. Burrill has edited a useful collection of readings in *The Cosmological Arguments* (Garden City, NY: Anchor Books, 1967), and you can find a somewhat advanced discussion in William L. Rowe's *The Cosmological Argument* (Princeton, NJ: Princeton University Press, 1975).

Richard Taylor has provided an introductory and sympathetic approach to the cosmological argument in the third edition of his *Metaphysics* (Englewood Cliffs, NJ: Prentice-Hall, 1983).

For a detailed discussion and defense of the *Kalam* version, see William Lane Craig's *The Kalam Cosmological Argument* (London: Macmillan, 1979). The seven ways of Udayana can be found in his *Nyayakusumanjali*, translated by José Perelra, in *Hindu Theology: A Reader* (New York: Doubleday, 1976).

Videos

Age of Faith to Age of Reason, a twelve-part lecture series (45 minutes each) made in 1992, begins with a discussion of Aquinas's *Summa* and ends with the philosophy of Leibniz. *Does God Exist?* (30 minutes) discusses not only cosmological arguments but also the ontological argument and the teleological argument as well. Both are available from Insight Media, 2162 Broadway, New York, NY 10024.

Anthony Kenny and Bryan Magee discuss St. Thomas's views in *Medieval Philosophy: Thomas Aquinas* (45 minutes), a BBC production available from Films for the Humanities & Sciences (www.films.com).

12.3 The Origin of the Universe According to Modern Science

Victor Weisskopf, the author of the next essay, is the Institute Professor Emeritus at MIT. In 1988 he was awarded the Enrico Fermi Award from the U.S. Department of Energy for outstanding scientific achievement. He is one of the premier physicists of our age. The selection that follows is based on a talk he gave to the American Academy of Arts and Sciences.

You may be asking yourself, "What is an essay by a physicist on the origin of the universe doing in a chapter having to do with God's existence? What does religion have to do with science?" These are good questions. For many, religion is akin to poetry and myth. It speaks in metaphors and symbols. It expresses values and feelings. Science is fact. It speaks literally and realistically. It expresses what we *know about* the world, not how we *feel about* being in the world.

There is much to be said in favor of a sharp distinction between religion and science. They are very different. And yet, throughout history, especially modern history, they have repeatedly come into conflict. For example, Galileo (1564–1642) was prosecuted for heresy by the Roman Catholic Church for teaching heliocentrism (the view that the Sun, not Earth, is the center of our solar system). And most of you are probably aware of the present-day conflict between fundamentalist Christians and biologists over evolution and creationism.

The cosmological argument seems to beg for comparisons with scientific views. It is a theory about the origin of the universe and, insofar as science is interested in the origin of the universe, it seems inevitable that scientific theories and this argument should meet at some point. Indeed, the versions of the cosmological arguments presented in the last section all depended heavily on the science of their day. However, science has changed. Geocentrism has been replaced by heliocentrism, and the idea that matter is made up of earth, air, fire, and water has been replaced by the atomic theory of matter. No longer do we believe that the stars are made out of ether. We have also discovered that they are not attached to spheres that rotate in a perfect circle. In fact, the universe is expanding. Stars and planets are moving away from a "center."

Modern science is strongly influenced by **naturalism**, the theory that the universe is a self-existing, self-regulating, and homogeneous system (its parts differ in degree but not in kind). Pierre Laplace (1749–1827), the famous and influential French mathematician and astronomer, when asked why God played no role in scientific theories about the origin of the universe, remarked, "We have no need of that hypothesis." He believed that science can explain the universe quite well without recourse to anything outside the universe. This is a good example of a naturalistic attitude.

Of course, there have been attempts to develop ideas of God that are compatible with scientific theories. Many scientists have been attracted, for example, to a deistic theory of God. **Deism** is the view that God started the universe and established natural laws (the laws of physics) according to which it operates. It now runs on its own without God's interference or help. Such a view of God implies that there are no miracles, if what you mean by a miracle is God intervening in world affairs in violation of natural laws. Still others have been attracted to **pantheism**, the theory that nature is God. According to pantheism, God does not transcend the universe; God is the universe.

Both deistic and pantheistic views of God appear to conflict with theism. **Theism** is the view that God is an infinite, self-existent, all-powerful, all-knowing, perfectly good, and personal being who created the universe out of nothing and controls it. Both Maimonides and St. Thomas had this theistic sort of God in mind when they presented their cosmological arguments. But do their arguments prove the existence of a theistic God, rather than the God of deists or of pantheists? Do they prove the existence of God, any sort of God, at all?

Some people believe that some versions of the cosmological argument conflict with modern science. One of the laws of energy is called the law of the conservation of energy. According to this law, energy can be neither created nor destroyed (although it can be transformed). This would seem to directly contradict the view that God created the universe out of nothing.

Many of you may have heard of the Big Bang. This is the notion that the universe began as a huge explosion. The Big Bang has been treated as a physical singularity, that is, as an occurrence whose physics is not understood. A physical singularity marks the limits of the conceptual resources of a theory. Singularities must be thought of as a kind of arbitrary initial condition or as a phenomenon awaiting explanation.

Science is not content with singularities, and recently, new theories have been developed to explain the singularity of the Big Bang according to known physical laws. These theories are highly speculative and tentative, but they do show how scientists might explain the origin of the universe without recourse to the "God hypothesis."

These theories raise the issue of what constitutes a sufficient explanation of the universe. To have a sufficient explanation, do we need a concept like God as a stopping point in an otherwise infinite regress? Or will certain physical phenomena like "fluctuations" in a vacuum do just as well? Read this fascinating and lucid account of recent cosmogonic theory and decide.

Reading Questions

1. What is the *quantum ladder?*
2. How do we know that matter must have been very compressed at the time of the Big Bang?
3. What is the *cosmic horizon?*
4. How does Weisskopf define *cosmology?*
5. How does a false vacuum differ from a true vacuum, and what is the Big Bang?
6. How did the Big Bang start?
7. Why might we conclude that our universe is not the only universe?
8. Even though Weisskopf says that some aspects of the present scientific view complement religious views, he never mentions God as the creator of the universe. Does the scientific picture he paints support, contradict, or complement the cosmological argument? Why, or why not?
9. Try to restate the cosmological argument in modern scientific terms. Can you do it?

The Origin of the Universe

VICTOR WEISSKOPF

1.

HOW DID THE UNIVERSE begin about 12 billion years ago? The question concerns the very large—space, galaxies, etc.—but also the very small, namely the innermost structure of matter. The reason is that the early universe was very hot, so that matter was then decomposed into its constituents. These two topics hang together, and this is what makes them so interesting.

One must start with a few words about the innermost structure of matter. The sketch in Figure 1 indicates, on the very left, a piece of metal. It is made of atoms. To the right of it you see one of the atoms symbolically designed with a nucleus in the middle and with electrons around it. Here we proceed toward the innermost structure of matter in steps. That's why I call it the quantum ladder. Further to the right you see the nucleus, consisting of protons and neutrons, which I will call nucleons from now on. We have found out that the nucleons themselves are composite; they are made up of quarks, as seen in Figure 1.

Let us look at the forces that keep the constituents together in the four steps of the quantum ladder. The deeper you go, the stronger the forces become. In the piece of metal, the chemical force that keeps the atoms together has the

Victor Weisskopf, "The Origin of the Universe," The New York Review of Books *XXXVI (February 16, 1989),*
10–14. Reprinted with permission from The New York Review of Books. *Copyright © 1989 Nyrev Inc.*

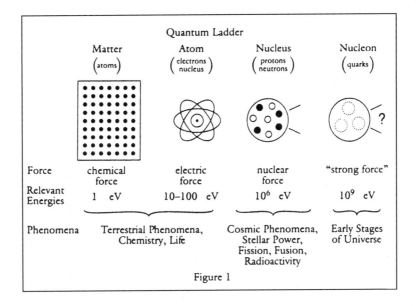

Figure 1

strength of a few electron volts (this is a measure of force strength). In the atom, the electrons are bound to the nucleus by a few tens of electron volts. The protons and neutrons are bound within the nucleus by millions of electron volts, and the forces between the quarks in a nucleus are in the billions of electron volts. This leads us to the concept of conditional elementarity. When we apply small amounts of energy, we cannot overcome the forces that keep the constituents together. For example, if energies of less than a few electron volts are available, atoms cannot be decomposed into electrons and nuclei. They seem to be elementary, which means stable, or unchangeable. When energies above a few hundred but below a million electron volts are available, atoms may be decomposed, but nuclei and electrons seem elementary. For energies over a million electron volts, nuclei are decomposed, but the protons and neutrons are elementary. At a billion electron volts, the nucleons appear to be composed of quarks. Electrons, so far, have never been shown to be composite.

It will be important later on to understand the connection between energy and temperature. Heating a piece of material is equivalent to increasing the energy of motion of the constituents of that piece, be they atoms or electrons or other particles. In a hot material, the atoms or the electrons perform all kinds of motions, oscillations, straight flights, etc. The greater the temperature, the higher the energy of the motions. Thus, temperature is equivalent to energy. For example, one electron volt corresponds to about 12,000 degrees Celsius (about 22,000 degrees Fahrenheit). The temperature at which atomic nuclei decompose is about 20 billion degrees. A billion electron volts would be about 20 trillion degrees Celsius.

On the last rung of the quantum ladder, when billions of electron volts are available—by means of accelerators or when the universe was very hot—new phenomena appear. Let us call it the sub-nuclear realm. Antimatter plays an important role at that stage. What is it? In the last fifty years it was discovered that there is an antiparticle to every particle; an antielectron called a positron, an antiproton and antineutron, an antiquark. They carry the opposite charge of the actual particle. Thus there ought to exist antiatoms, antimolecules, antimatter of all sorts, made of antielectrons and antinuclei. Why do we not find antimatter in our environment? Because of an important fact: when an antiparticle hits a particle, they "annihilate." A small explosion occurs, and the two entities disappear in a burst of light energy or other forms of energy. This is in agreement with the famous Einstein formula

$E = mc^2$, which says that mass—in this case, the masses of the particle and the antiparticle—is a form of energy. The opposite process also occurs: a high concentration of energy can give rise to the birth of a particle and antiparticle. This is called pair creation.

To summarize the quantum ladder, let me quote a prophetic statement by Newton, who wrote three hundred years ago; it describes Figure 1 from the right to the left, as it were:

> Now the smallest particles of matter may cohere by the strongest attractions, and compose bigger particles of weaker virtue. And many of these may cohere, and compose bigger particles whose virtue is still weaker. And so on for diverse successions, until the progression ends in the biggest particles on which the operation in chemistry and the colors of natural bodies depend, which by cohering compose bodies of a sensible magnitude. . . .

He foresaw the ideas of the structure of matter that were developed centuries after his time.

2.

Let us now turn to our main subject: the universe. Let's first look at the universe as we see it today. There are six facts that are important to us. First, most of the stars we see in the universe consist of 93 percent hydrogen, 6 percent helium, and only 1 percent all other elements. This has been determined by analyzing the light from the stars. Here on earth, things—including our bodies—consist mainly of other elements besides hydrogen. But this is a special case; the stars are made mostly of hydrogen. I have to mention something of which astronomers should be very much ashamed. It turned out that visible matter, the one that sends light to us, is only 10 percent of the total matter. Ninety percent of the matter of the universe is what is now called dark matter—dark because we don't see it; dark because we don't know what it is. How do we know that it is there? The dark matter, like any matter, attracts other matter by gravity. One has found motions of stars and galaxies that could not be explained by the gravitational attraction of the visible, luminous matter. For example, stars in the

neighborhood of galaxies move much faster than they would if they were attracted only by the visible stars. So far the nature of that dark matter is unknown. We do not have the slightest idea of what 90 percent of the world is made of.

The second fact concerns the distribution of matter in space. We know that it is very uneven. We see stars, but nothing in between; we see galaxies and clusters of galaxies. However, if we average over a large part of space containing many stars and galaxies, we find that luminous matter is very thinly distributed, only about one hydrogen atom per cubic meter. To this we must add ten times as much dark matter.

The third fact is the expansion of the universe. The following astounding observation was made about sixty years ago, first by the American astronomer E. P. Hubble. It was Hubble who found that faraway objects like galaxies move away from us; the greater the distance, the faster they move away. For example, a galaxy that is as far as one million light years moves away from us with a speed of about twenty kilometers per second. Another galaxy, at a distance of two million light years, moves away at forty kilometers per second; another, at three million light years, moves away at sixty kilometers per second; and so on. As a consequence, the distances between objects in space increase as time goes on. The universe gets more dilute with time. It is a kind of decompression of matter.

A most dramatic conclusion must be drawn from this: if we go backward in time, we conclude that galaxies were nearer to each other in the past. Therefore, at a certain time in the far distant past, the matter in the universe must have been extremely dense. Matter must have been highly compressed, far more than any compression achievable on earth by technical means. At that time there were no galaxies or stars: matter was so thoroughly compressed that everything merged. A little calculation shows that this happened about 12 billion years ago.

In this calculation, one has taken into account that the expansion was faster at an earlier time, since the gravitational attraction acts like a brake and slows down the expansion. Today's rate of expansion, the so-called Hubble constant, is not very well established. It could be fifteen or thirty, instead of twenty, kilometers per second at a million light years. Therefore, the time of extreme compression—this is the time of the beginning of our universe, of the Big Bang—may not have been 12 billion years ago, but perhaps 10 or 15 billion years ago. Still, we can introduce a new chronology: the zero time is the time of extreme compression, the time of the Big Bang. Today is about 12 billion years since the beginning.

We now approach the fourth point regarding our present universe. How far can we see into space? Since the universe is about 12 billion years old, we cannot see farther than about 12 billion light years. We call this distance the cosmic horizon of today. As we will see later in more detail, the Big Bang was a tremendous explosion in which space expanded almost infinitely fast, creating matter over a region probably much larger than what is visible today. Light from those farther regions has not had enough time to reach us today but may do so in the future.

There is another interesting consequence: the farther we look within the cosmic horizons, the younger are the objects we see. After all, it took time for the light to reach us. The light we see of a galaxy, say, 100 million light years away, was emitted 100 million years ago. A picture of the galaxy shows how it was 100 million years back. Figure 2 shows this schematically. The outer circle is the cosmic horizon. The broken circle is about six billion light years away, and objects there appear to us only six billion years old. What about objects at or very near the horizon? What we see there is matter in its first moments, matter just or almost just born. Thus, if we had very good telescopes, we could see the whole history of matter in the universe, starting far out and ending near us.

Beware of the following misunderstanding. One could wrongly argue that, say, the regions that are six billion light years away were much nearer to us when they did send out their light, and therefore we should see them earlier than six billion years after emission. This conclusion is false, because the light velocity must be understood as relative to the expanding space. Seen from a nonexpanding frame, a light beam run-

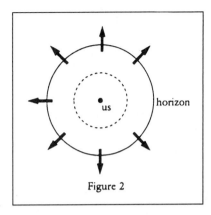

Figure 2

ning against the expansion—that is, toward us—moves slower than the usual light velocity. As it were, light is dragged along with the expansion.

Our fifth question has to do with the temperature in the universe. How hot is it out there? Let us consider a kiln, such as potters use, to understand the situation. Take a kiln and heat it up. First you can see no light, but the kiln radiates microwaves. When it gets hotter it radiates infrared radiation, which we do not see but can feel as heat radiation. At higher temperatures it becomes red, then yellow and white, then ultraviolet; at millions of degrees it will radiate X-rays.

Today, in the immediate surroundings within a few million light years, the temperature is very low in space. It was measured a few decades ago when two Princeton physicists, A. Penzias and R. Wilson, found a very cool microwave radiation in space corresponding to heat radiation of only five degrees above absolute zero—the lowest possible temperature, which is minus 460 degrees F. An appropriate measure of very low temperatures is the Kelvin scale. Zero degree Kelvin is absolute zero. The Kelvin scale uses Celsius degrees above absolute zero. Thus, the space temperature in our neighborhood is 3 degrees K. This is the temperature in space between the stars. The stars are much hotter inside, but there is so much space between them that their higher temperature does not count.

Was the temperature always 3 degrees K? No, it was much warmer at earlier times, a fact that is related to the expansion of the universe. Let us go back to the kiln again. Imagine a kiln made in such a way that we can expand or contract its volume at will. The laws of physics tell us that the temperature of a kiln drops when it expands and rises when it contracts. Thus, we must conclude that the expansion of the universe lowers the temperature. It must have been hotter at earlier times. For example, about six million years ago, the temperature was roughly twice as high—that is, near 6 degrees K. At the very beginning, about 12 billion years ago, when space was extremely contracted, the temperature must have been extremely high. This has interesting consequences.

We know from the physics of radiation that matter is transparent for light when the temperature is below 1,000 degrees C. This is true only for very dilute matter, such as that found in the space between the stars. Matter of ordinary density, such as a piece of iron or wood, is not transparent, of course. But if the temperature is raised from 1,000 degrees C, even very dilute matter becomes opaque. Thus light from those outer regions near the cosmic horizon, which are so young that the temperature is over 1,000 degrees C, cannot penetrate space and will not reach us. We should emphasize that these regions are very near the cosmic horizon. A temperature of 1,000 degrees C was reached when the universe was about 300,000 years old, an age that is very young compared with 12 billion years. Hence, light reaches us not from the cosmic horizon but from a distance that is almost as far as the cosmic horizon. We see only matter older than 300,000 years, which is nevertheless pretty young. Even younger matter, younger than that, is hidden by the opaque space.

Figure 3 illustrates this schematically. The outermost circle is the cosmic horizon, where matter is just born at extreme density and extreme heat. But already a little nearer to us at the center, the temperature has fallen to and below 1,000 degrees C, and we can see it, since space inside that second circle is transparent.

But why do we not see that part of the universe glowing white-hot at 1,000 degrees C? The reason is the famous Doppler effect. That part of the universe moves away from us at a terrific speed according to the law of expansion, which states

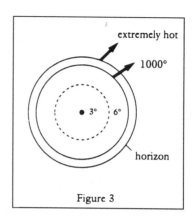

Figure 3

that the greater the distance of an object, the faster it moves away from us. The Doppler effect reduces the frequency of light if the emitting object moves away from us. Everybody has observed how the whistle of a fire engine lowers its pitch as the engine moves away. Reducing the frequency is equivalent to lowering the temperature. Red's frequency is lower than yellow's and much lower than violet's. Therefore, the heat radiation from that faraway region of 1,000 degrees K is much cooled down because it moves away from us so fast. Indeed, it is cooled down from 1,000 degrees K to 3 degrees K. Thus, the cool radiation that Penzias and Wilson have observed is indeed the radiation from the hot universe 300,000 years after the Big Bang. The 3 degrees K radiation can be considered the optical reverberation of the Big Bang. This is not quite correct, because it was emitted a little later. That is the explanation of the cool radiation of today.

3.

So far we have discussed the present state of the universe and what one can deduce from it as to its past. Now we will recount the speculations and hypotheses as to the history of the universe from the Big Bang to today, and perhaps also what was before the Big Bang. Usually history does not enter physics. One studies the properties of matter as it is today. Other sciences, such as geology, anthropology, and biology, are historical sciences; the first one deals with the history of the earth, anthropology with the history of the human animal, and biology with the history of animal and plant species.

When physics becomes historical, it deals with the history of matter—that is, with the history of the universe. It is then called cosmology. It must be emphasized that most of the conclusions are much less reliable than those in other fields of physics. Facts are scarce and not known with any accuracy. The Russian physicist Lev Landau said that the cosmologists have very weak facts to work with but very strong convictions about what they think is going on. Whatever will be told here may turn out to be wrong in the near future. Nevertheless, it is so impressive that it is worth reporting.

As we have seen, our universe is expanding and cooling down. We are in principle able to see parts of the universe in earlier periods just by looking at distant objects. We have seen that this is possible to a point in time in the past 300,000 years after the Big Bang. Let us therefore call the time from 300,000 years after the Bang up to today the period of observable history. Of course, the history is observable only in principle. Actually, our instruments are not good enough to get detailed information regarding very distant objects.

We will not say much about that period; the preobservable history is more interesting. At the beginning of observable history the temperature was around 1,000 degrees K, which was low enough so that atoms were not destroyed and robbed of their electrons. Therefore, space was filled mainly with hydrogen and helium atoms forming a hot gas. The density of things never was completely uniform. There were gas accumulations here and more dilute parts somewhere else. The accumulations grew because of gravity. They had more concentration of mass and therefore attracted the surrounding gas more strongly than the dilute parts. The further this accumulative process went, the more effective the gravitational pull became. Such accumulations finally formed "protostars" of much higher density than elsewhere. These protostars also became much hotter than the rest, since compression produces heat. When it became hot enough at the center of such protostars, nuclear reactions were ignited,

producing even more energy. The protostar became a real star like the sun, whose radiation energy comes from the nuclear reactions at the center. Furthermore, the early deviations from complete uniformity caused the stars to be not uniformly distributed but to form agglomerations that we see today as galaxies.

The nuclear reactions inside a star produce helium out of hydrogen. When a star has used up its primary nuclear fuel—hydrogen—at its center, other nuclear processes form heavier elements, such as carbon, oxygen, up to iron. Finally the star explodes and becomes a supernova. In this process most other elements are formed and expelled into space. Then new accumulations and protostars are formed from the gases in space, which now contain traces of other heavier elements, such as oxygen, carbon, iron, gold, and uranium. The sun is an example of a "second-generation" star. Some of the stars are surrounded by planets like the sun. In some of the planets, such as the earth, heavier elements are present in higher concentration. This is because most hydrogen and helium atoms escape from smaller planets, since those atoms are light and planets exert only weak gravitational pull. The hydrogen found on earth is bound in molecules to heavier atoms. Life may develop under the mild warming of the nearby star. So much for the observable history.

Now let us turn to the period between the Big Bang and the onset of observable history at about 300,000 years. Let us call it preobservable history. Nothing about that period can be observed; space was opaque because the temperature was higher than 1,000 degrees C. But we are able to conclude from our knowledge of physics what happened during that period, at least for times that are not too near to the Big Bang. Pursuing the picture of an expanding and cooling universe, one comes to the conclusion that a microsecond after the Big Bang, the temperature must have reached about 10 trillion degrees, or a thermal energy of a billion electron volts. Our present knowledge is good enough that we can guess what has happened in the universe between a microsecond and 300,000 years. But conclusions about events at earlier times, when the energy concentrations were higher, are very uncertain.

Let us tell the story in reverse, going back in time from 300,000 years to a microsecond. In that inverse sense, the universe must be regarded as contracting and getting hotter. When the temperature was hotter than 10,000 degrees K, the atoms were decomposed and formed a "plasma," a dense gas of nuclei and electrons. The plasma was bathed in shining light, visible light, during the time when the temperature was between a thousand and a few ten thousand degrees.

That light was more and more ultraviolet (that is, of a higher frequency) at earlier times, when the temperature was higher. This radiation should be considered the same as today's 3 degrees K radiation but enormously compressed at the early seconds of the expansion. Compression makes light hotter and of higher frequency. Going back in time, we come to a moment at about one second after the Big Bang, when the temperature was about 10 billion degrees, corresponding to an energy concentration of about a few million electron volts. At that point the thermal energy is high enough for creating pairs of electrons and antielectrons (positrons). This is the process of matter–antimatter formation mentioned before. Hence, at one second and earlier, when the temperature was even higher, space was filled by a plasma composed not only of hydrogen and helium nuclei and their electrons but also of a rather dense gas of electrons and positrons.

At a fraction of a second after the Bang, the temperature was high enough to split the helium and nuclei into neutrons and protons. Finally, when our backward history reaches the microsecond after the Bang, the heat and the corresponding energy concentration were high enough not only to decompose protons and neutrons into quarks but also to produce quark–antiquark pairs. At this point of our backward journey in time, the universe was filled with hot, dense gases of quarks and antiquarks, electrons and positrons, and a very intense, high-frequency thermal light radiation. There was also a hot, dense gas of neutrinos, which survived the whole evolution and should be present even today, though much less hot and dense, together with the cool three-degree light radiation. We stop at this point, which is a millionth of a second after the Big Bang. We are practically at it anyway.

The prehistory described here is based on a relatively firm knowledge of the properties of matter at energy concentrations up to several billion electron volts. This knowledge stems from experiments made with accelerators producing particle beams at these energies. The largest of these machines, the ones in Geneva, Switzerland, and in Batavia, Illinois, have reached energies of several hundred billion electron volts. It would be hard to guess what happened much earlier than a microsecond, since the energy concentrations were much higher than the ones reached with our accelerators, and we have no way to know how matter behaves at these enormous compressions and temperatures.

1.

We now have reached the point where we should ask the great questions: What was the Big Bang? What caused it? And what existed before? When facing these exciting questions, it must be said that we have no reliable answers. There are speculation, guesswork led by intuition, and a great deal of imagination that may turn out to be wrong in a few years. However, the answers that are discussed in these days are so unusual and impressive that it is worthwhile to describe them in simple terms. The underlying ideas came mostly from four persons whom one might call the four apostles of the new story of Genesis: Alan Guth of MIT, Alexander Vilenkin of Tufts University, Andrei Linde in the USSR, and Stephen Hawking in England. Paul Steinhardt of the University of Pennsylvania also contributed to it.

In order to understand the basic ideas, we must introduce a concept that is suggested by some of the latest developments in particle physics. It is the so-called false vacuum. According to these ideas, there are two types of vacuum: the true vacuum and the false vacuum. The true one is very much what one would imagine: it is empty space, empty of matter and empty of energy. The false vacuum, however, is also empty of matter, but not of energy. The energy of the false vacuum is supposed to be none of the ordinary forms of energy, such as electric fields or gravity fields. It is imagined to be a new kind of field, of a type encountered in the current theories of radioactive processes. The most characteristic feature of the false vacuum follows directly from Einstein's general relativity theory. A region filled with energy but not with matter is bound to expand suddenly and explosively, filling more and more space with false vacuum. Alan Guth has called it, succinctly, an inflationary expansion, with a speed very much faster than the previously considered expansion of our universe at any time in its development. According to our four apostles, this sudden explosion is nothing else but the Big Bang.

How does this sudden inflationary expansion of a false vacuum start? Before the event, all space was in the state of a true vacuum. "The world was without form and void, and darkness was upon the face of the deep," as the Bible says. Now we must introduce a concept that is typical for quantum mechanics. According to the fundamental tenets of this well-established theory, there is nothing in nature that remains quiet. Everything, including the true vacuum, is subject to fluctuations—in particular to energy fluctuations. The field that provides the energy to the false vacuum is absent in the true vacuum, but not completely. There must be fluctuations of the field. Thus, at one moment a small region somewhere in space may have fluctuated into a false vacuum. It would happen very rarely but cannot be excluded. That region almost instantly expands tremendously and creates a large space filled with energy according to the properties of a false vacuum. That is supposed to be the Big Bang!

One might wonder where the energy comes from that fills the expanding false vacuum. There is no need to worry about conservation of energy. According to Einstein, energy is subject to gravity. The newly created energies interact via gravity, an effect that produces negative energy, so that the net energy remains essentially constant.

When a certain large size is reached, the inflationary explosion stops and a true vacuum emerges. But the vast amount of energy contained in the false vacuum must have shown up in some form. It filled the true vacuum with hot light, quark–antiquark pairs, electron–antielectron pairs, neutrinos, etc.—in other words, with all the stuff we have described as filling the space at a microsecond after the Big Bang. Our universe is born, the slow expansion takes over, the temperature falls, and the pre-observable history develops and is followed by the observable history.

In short, the history of our universe started with a fluctuation of the empty true vacuum into a small region of false vacuum, which exploded, almost immediately, into a very much larger region of false vacuum. That was the primal Bang. Then it changed to a true vacuum, but the energy of the false vacuum created all light, all particles and antiparticles, which developed into what existed at about a microsecond after the explosion. Then the ordinary expansion of the universe took over; it cooled down; quarks and antiquarks as well as electrons and antielectrons were annihilated, but a few supernumerary quarks and electrons remained. The quarks formed protons and neutrons. Then some of these nucleons formed helium nuclei. After 300,000 years it was cool enough that the protons and helium nuclei could grab and retain electrons and become atoms. A hot gas of hydrogen and helium appeared. The gas of atoms condensed to protostars, which became hot inside, allowing nuclear processes to start. Stars were born, grouping themselves in galaxies. The nuclear reactions in the center of the stars and in exploding supernovas produced heavier elements. The expelled gases of exploding stars condensed to protostars and then to stars containing traces of all elements, not only hydrogen and helium. The sun is one of these second-generation stars. It is surrounded by planets, some of which—such as the earth—are special concentrations of heavier elements, benignly supplied with energy from the nearby sun, so that life can start and develop the strange human animal that pretends to understand the whole process. An interesting conclusion follows from this view of the birth of our universe, as the consequence of an energy fluctuation in the true vacuum. Such intense fluctuations creating a speck of false vacuum are very rare, but it may have happened at other places in infinite space at other times and may have developed into other universes. Thus, we may conclude that our universe is not the only one. It is not the center and the stage of everything in this world. There may be other universes much older or much younger or even not yet born somewhere else. Remember that our universe today is most probably considerably larger than our present cosmic horizon of about 12 billion light years, but there is room and time enough for many other universes. Maybe, in a few billion years, another universe will penetrate ours. Until then we cannot check this hypothesis. Our own universe, of which we see only a small part today, may not be unique. Its beginning is not the beginning of everything. Other universes may exist at an earlier or later stage.

It must be emphasized again that these are unproven hypotheses. They may turn out to be pure fantasies, but the ideas are impressively grandiose.

The origin of the universe is not only of scientific interest. It always was the subject of mythology, art, and religion. Such approaches are complementary to scientific ones. Most familiarly, the Old Testament describes the beginning of the world with the creation of light on the first day. It seemed contradictory that the sun, our terrestrial source of light, was only created on day four, but it turns out to be in line with current scientific thought, according to which the early universe was full of various kinds of radiation long before the sun appeared.

Those first days have been depicted in various forms, in pictures and poetry, but to me, Franz Josef Haydn's oratorio *The Creation* is the most remarkable rendition of the Big Bang. At the beginning we hear a choir of angels singing mysteriously and softly, "And God Said Let There Be Light." And at the words "And There Was Light" the entire choir and the orchestra explode into a blazing C major chord. There is no more beautiful and impressive presentation of the beginning of everything.

Suggestions for Further Reading

Try Ronald C. Pine's *Science and the Human Prospect* (Belmont, CA: Wadsworth, 1989) for starters. You will learn a good deal about science and the philosophy of science.

Stephen W. Hawking's *A Brief History of Time: From the Big Bang to Black Holes* (New York: Bantam Books, 1988) is a real gem by one of the greatest scientific minds of our time.

Milton K. Munitz has edited a useful but now somewhat dated collection: *Theories of the Universe: From Babylonian Myth to Modern Science* (New York: Free Press, 1957). Munitz's *The Question of Reality* (Princeton, NJ: Princeton University Press, 1990) presents an updated discussion of the philosophical and religious implications of modern cosmology.

For an interpretation of Big Bang theory that is at odds with theism and rejects the cosmological argument visit the following site: http://www.secularhumanism.org/library/fi/smith_18_2.html.

For all kinds of neat pictures from outer space and tons of information, see NASA's Structure and Evolution of Universe at http://universe.gsfc.nasa.gov/.

Videos

Universe: Man's Changing Perceptions (28 minutes; produced by Howard Preston Films, 1978; distributed by Kinetic Film Enterprise) traces the development of cosmological thought through 5000 years. *Soul* is a three-part (50 minutes each) BBC series featuring

Stephen Hawking and others discussing how the universe began and the relationship between science and religion (Insight Media, 2162 Broadway, New York, NY 10024).

The Expanding Universe (36 minutes) is an updated (1997) version of a two-part series dealing with the history of astronomy and the formation of planets, stars, and galaxies available from Hawkhill Associates, Inc., 125 East Gilman Street, PO Box 1029, Madison, WI 53701.

12.4 Creationism vs. Evolution

In addition to the cosmological argument (see above) another type of a posteriori argument for God's existence is the **teleological argument**, or the argument from design. This kind of argument begins with the premise that the universe exhibits order and draws the conclusion that a supreme, divine intelligence is responsible for the order of the universe.

Versions of the teleological argument are very old, but William Paley (1743–1805), a defender of the Christian evangelical cause in England, popularized it in his 1802 publication *Natural Theology*. Paley was under the influence of Newtonian physics, which pictured the universe as a vast machine operating in accord with well-known laws. In addition, he was much taken by the naturalist's descriptions of the complex order of various plant and animal life. It seemed to Paley that the universe was one vast, harmonious, interconnected order designed for a purpose. It seemed to him much like a watch, an intricately designed machine with all its parts working in harmony for a common goal.

Although David Hume (see Section 7.4) lived before Paley and published posthumously in 1779 his *Dialogues Concerning Natural Religion,* in which he severely criticized the teleological argument, Paley seems to be unaware of his work. Among Hume's several objections to the argument, three stand out. First Hume argues, through a fictional character named Philo, a skeptic, that the universe is not sufficiently like the productions of human design to support the argument. The things between which the analogy is drawn (the world and designed objects) are the same in some respects and different in others. Although the universe may share some things in common with houses, ships, watches, and the like, it is also vastly different. For one thing it is bigger than anything any human has ever made. Second, Philo points out that we have no other universes with which to compare this one, and we would need to make comparisons in order to decide if it were the kind of thing that was designed or simply grew on its own. Would you know, if you had never seen a cut diamond and found one by accident on a beach, that this stone was designed (cut according to a pattern) and the other stones were not? Third, Philo argues that an effect must be proportionate to its cause. Since the universe is imperfect (evil and suffering occur), its cause must be imperfect. But no theologian wishes to admit that God is anything less than perfect.

While many philosophers thought Hume's objections to the teleological argument fatal, the argument, in one form or another, continued to be popular. Perhaps its continued popularity was due to the fact that Hume could provide no convincing alternative explanations for the observed order because there was no body of scientific evidence and theory to which Hume could point. At least there was no evidence or theory until the nineteenth century.

In 1859, some 58 years after Paley's *Natural Theology* was published, Charles Darwin published *On the Origin of the Species.* This book revolutionized the biological sciences by showing how the order nature exhibits is the result of evolutionary processes. According to Aristotle, species are fixed. This idea supported the sort of creationism Paley promoted: that God is the original creator and designer of species, which then proliferate by reproductive means. However, by Darwin's time, the fossil record and mounting biological evidence no longer supported the fixed-species idea. Species change, develop, and evolve, Darwin claimed, and they do so by a mechanism he called *natural selection.*

The theory of evolution has undergone considerable refinement since Darwin first formulated it. In one form or another, it has emerged as the dominant theory of modern biology. Since Paley had argued that only a divine intelligence was a sufficient explanation for the order found in nature, evolutionary theory appears to offer a direct challenge to his views. It provides not only an alternative explanation, but also one far more sufficient from a scientific viewpoint.

The reaction to the theory of evolution on the part of those who believe in a divine creative intelligence has been both varied and intense. A theory of *instantaneous creation* has been advanced by those who reject the theory of evolution. According to this view, God is responsible for the immediate and direct creation of all distinct forms of life. Supporters of this outlook have been very persistent in attempting to get the public schools to teach what they call "creation science" in addition to evolution. *Guided evolution* is a theory advanced by those who wish to combine evolution and belief in a creator God. In this view, God creates and designs the order in the world, but the means God uses is natural selection.

Evolutionary theory has had an impact on the way modern versions of the teleological argument are formulated. Recent versions of the argument tend to emphasize the idea of probability. In effect, they claim that evolutionary explanations ultimately boil down to notions of chance. The next move is to point out the tremendous odds against the complexity of life evolving by chance. Someone has suggested, for example, that the odds against life evolving on this planet in its present form by chance alone are about as great as the chances of a tornado assembling the parts of a Boeing 747 scattered over a field into a functioning airplane. If your choice is between chance and intelligent design and if the odds are against chance and in favor of design, which constitutes the most plausible explanation?

How much does chance have to do with the order we find? The next selection is by Richard Dawkins, a zoologist who has taught at Berkeley and Oxford. He was born in Nairobi, Kenya, in 1941 and moved to England in 1949. He is best known for his book *The Selfish Gene* (1976). Dawkins argues against Paley and in support of neo-Darwinian views of evolution. He maintains that the critics of evolution have misunderstood the mechanism by which life evolves. It does not evolve by chance (or at least the more complex forms do not), but by a nonrandom process he calls *cumulative selection* in contrast to *single-step selection.* Single-step selection sorts or filters all items once and for all. It is like filtering sand through a sieve once and looking at the formation that results. Cumulative selection filters repeatedly, thus passing on some of the first results of the filtering to the next process of selection. In other words, the first pile of sand resulting from the first filtering is filtered again, with a finer sieve. Hence, the result will be different from the first result (smaller bits of sand will result). If this process is repeated over and over again, the result will be that the finest bits of sand survive each filtering, and the larger pieces do not. If natural selection operated as single-step selection, then the odds *against* getting a heap of the finest sand the first time around would be very high. It would largely be a matter of chance. But if natural selection operates as a cumulative selection (and it does according to evolutionary theory), the odds of eventually getting a heap of the finest sand would greatly increase.

As the genetic traits of one generation are filtered by natural selection and passed on to the next, and again filtered and passed on to the next, and so on for many many generations, the chances of ending up with a complex, adaptive order increase greatly. Dawkins also argues that the major alternatives to neo-Darwinism are fatally flawed. Evolution remains the only viable scientific hypothesis for explaining the natural order.

You may have noted how discussions of both the cosmological and teleological arguments seem to return again and again to the issue of what constitutes a sufficient explanation. All parties agree that the existence of the universe and the order of life on Earth require an explanation, but they disagree about what constitutes a sufficient one. Perhaps there can be no agreement on this matter, since what counts as sufficient depends on the conceptual scheme (see Kuhn's idea of a paradigm in Section 8.3) from which you approach the issue. Or does it?

Reading Project and Questions

1. Write a critical précis (see Section 2.2) on Dawkins's argument.
2. What do you find most puzzling about what Dawkins says?
3. What do you find most plausible about what Dawkins says?

The Blind Watchmaker

RICHARD DAWKINS

THIS BOOK IS WRITTEN in the conviction that our own existence once presented the greatest of all mysteries, but that it is a mystery no longer because it is solved. Darwin and Wallace solved it, though we shall continue to add footnotes to their solution for a while yet. I wrote the book because I was surprised that so many people seemed not only unaware of the elegant and beautiful solution to this deepest of problems but, incredibly, in many cases actually unaware that there was a problem in the first place!

The problem is that of complex design. The computer on which I am writing these words has an information storage capacity of about 64 kilobytes (one byte is used to hold each character of text). The computer was consciously designed and deliberately manufactured. The brain with which you are understanding my words is an array of some ten million kiloneurones. Many of these billions of nerve cells have each more than a thousand "electric wires" connecting them to other neurones. Moreover, at the molecular

From Richard Dawkins, The Blind Watchmaker, *1986, pp. ix–xii; 4–6; 43–49; 316–318. Reprinted by permission of W. W. Norton. Copyright © 1986 by Richard Dawkins.*

genetic level, every single one of more than a trillion cells in the body contains about a thousand times as much precisely-coded digital information as my entire computer. The complexity of living organisms is matched by the elegant efficiency of their apparent design. If anyone doesn't agree that this amount of complex design cries out for an explanation, I give up. No, on second thought I don't give up, because one of my aims in the book is to convey something of the sheer wonder of biological complexity to those whose eyes have not been opened to it. But having built up the mystery, my other main aim is to remove it again by explaining the solution.

Explaining is a difficult art. You can explain something so that your reader understands the words, and you can explain something so that the reader feels it in the marrow of his bones. To do the latter, it sometimes isn't enough to lay the evidence before the reader in a dispassionate way. You have to become an advocate and use the tricks of the advocate's trade. This book is not a dispassionate scientific treatise. Other books on Darwinism are, and many of them are excellent and informative and should be read in conjunction with this one. Far from being dispassionate, it has to be confessed that in parts this book is written with a passion which, in a professional scientific journal, might excite comment. Certainly it seeks to inform, but it also seeks to persuade and even—one can specify *aims* without presumption—to inspire. I want to inspire the reader with a vision of our own existence as, on the face of it, a spine-chilling mystery; and simultaneously to convey the full excitement of the fact that it is a mystery with an elegant solution which is within our grasp. More, I want to persuade the reader, not just that the Darwinian world-view *happens* to be true, but that it is the only known theory that *could,* in principle, solve the mystery of our existence. This makes it a doubly satisfying theory. A good case can be made that Darwinism is true, not just on this planet but all over the universe wherever life may be found.

In one respect I plead to distance myself from professional advocates. A lawyer or a politician is paid to exercise his passion and his persuasion on behalf of a client or a cause in which he may not privately believe. I have never done this and I never shall. I may not always be right, but I care passionately about what is true and I never say anything that I do not believe to be right. I remember being shocked when visiting a university debating society to debate with creationists. At dinner after the debate, I was placed next to a young woman who had made a relatively powerful speech in favour of creationism. She clearly couldn't *be* a creationist, so I asked her to tell me honestly why she had done it. She freely admitted that she was simply practising her debating skills, and found it more challenging to advocate a position in which she did not believe. Apparently it is common practice in university debating societies for speakers simply to be *told* on which side they are to speak. Their own beliefs don't come into it. I had come a long way to perform the disagreeable task of public speaking, because I believed in the truth of the motion that I had been asked to propose. When I discovered that members of the society were using the motion as a vehicle for playing arguing games, I resolved to decline future invitations from debating societies that encourage insincere advocacy on issues where scientific truth is at stake.

For reasons that are not entirely clear to me, Darwinism seems more in need of advocacy than similarly established truths in other branches of science. Many of us have no grasp of quantum theory, or Einstein's theories of special and general relativity, but this does not in itself lead us to *oppose* these theories! Darwinism, unlike "Einsteinism," seems to be regarded as fair game for critics with any degree of ignorance. I suppose one trouble with Darwinism is that, as Jacques Monod perceptively remarked, everybody *thinks* he understands it. It is, indeed, a remarkably simple theory; childishly so, one would have thought, in comparison with almost all of physics and mathematics. In essence, it amounts simply to the idea that nonrandom reproduction, where there is hereditary variation, has consequences that are far-reaching if there is time for them to be cumulative. But we have good grounds for believing that this simplicity is deceptive. Never forget that, simple as the theory may seem, nobody thought of it until Darwin and Wallace in the mid-nineteenth century, nearly 200 years after Newton's *Principia,* and more than 2,000 years after Eratosthenes measured the Earth. How could such a simple idea go so long undiscovered by thinkers of the calibre of Newton, Galileo, Descartes, Leibniz, Hume and Aristotle? Why did it have to wait for two Victorian naturalists? What was *wrong* with philosophers and mathematicians that they overlooked it? And how can such a powerful idea go still largely unabsorbed into popular consciousness?

It is almost as if the human brain were specifically designed to misunderstand Darwinism, and to find it hard to believe. Take, for instance, the issue of "chance," often dramatized as *blind* chance. The great majority of people that attack Darwinism leap with almost unseemly eagerness to the mistaken idea that there is nothing other than random chance in it. Since living complexity embodies the very antithesis of chance, if you think that Darwinism is tantamount to chance you'll obviously find it easy to refute Darwinism! One of my tasks will be to destroy this eagerly believed myth that Darwinism is a theory of "chance." Another way in which we seem predisposed to disbelieve Darwinism is that our brains are built to deal with events on radically different *timescales* from those that characterize evolutionary change. We are equipped to appreciate processes that take seconds, minutes, years or, at most, decades to complete. Darwinism is a theory of cumulative processes so slow that they take between thousands and millions of decades to complete. All our intuitive judgments of what is probable turn out to be wrong by many orders of magnitude. Our well-tuned apparatus of scepticism and subjective probability-theory misfires by huge margins, because it is tuned—ironically, by evolution itself—to work within a lifetime of a few decades. It requires effort of the imagination to escape from the prison of familiar timescale, an effort that I shall try to assist.

A third respect in which our brains seem predisposed to resist Darwinism stems from our great success as creative designers. Our world is dominated by feats of engineering and works of art. We are entirely accustomed to the idea that complex elegance is an indicator of premeditated, crafted design. This is probably the most powerful reason for the belief, held by the vast majority of people that have ever lived, in some kind of supernatural deity. It took a very large leap of the imagination for Darwin and Wallace to see that, contrary to all intuition, there is another way and, once you have understood it, a far more plausible way, for complex "design" to arise out of primeval simplicity. A leap of the imagination so large that, to this day, many people seem still unwilling to make it. It is the main purpose of this book to help the reader to make this leap. . . .

The watchmaker of my title is borrowed from a famous treatise by the eighteenth-century theologian William Paley. His *Natural Theology—or Evidences of the Existence and Attributes of the Deity Collected from the Appearances of Nature,* published in 1802, is the best-known exposition of the "Argument from Design," always the most influential of the arguments for the existence of a God. It is a book that I greatly admire, for in his own time its author succeeded in doing what I am struggling to do now. He had a point to make, he passionately believed in it, and he spared no effort to ram it home clearly. He had a proper reverence for the complexity of the living world, and he saw that it demands a very special kind of explanation. The only thing he got wrong—admittedly quite a big thing!—was the explanation itself. He gave the traditional religious answer to the riddle, but he articulated it more clearly and convincingly than anybody had before. The true explanation is utterly different, and it had to wait for one of the most revolutionary thinkers of all time, Charles Darwin.

Paley begins *Natural Theology* with a famous passage:

> In crossing a heath, suppose I pitched my foot against a *stone,* and were asked how the stone came to be there; I might possibly answer, that, for anything I knew to the contrary, it had lain there for ever: nor would it perhaps be very easy to show the absurdity of this answer. But suppose I had found a *watch* upon the ground, and

it should be inquired how the watch happened to be in that place; I should hardly think of the answer which I had before given, that for anything I knew, the watch might have always been there.

Paley here appreciates the differences between natural physical objects like stones, and designed and manufactured objects like watches. He goes on to expound the precision with which the cogs and springs of a watch are fashioned, and the intricacy with which they are put together. If we found an object such as a watch upon a heath, even if we didn't know how it had come into existence, its own precision and intricacy of design would force us to conclude

> that the watch must have had a maker: that there must have existed, at some time, and at some place or other, an artificer or artificers, who formed it for the purpose which we find it actually to answer; who comprehended its construction, and designed its use.

Nobody could reasonably dissent from this conclusion, Paley insists, yet that is just what the atheist, in effect, does when he contemplates the works of nature, for:

> every indication of contrivance, every manifestation of design, which existed in the watch, exists in the works of nature; with the difference, on the side of nature, of being greater or more, and that in a degree which exceeds all computation.

Paley drives his point home with beautiful and reverent descriptions of the dissected machinery of life, beginning with the human eye, a favourite example which Darwin was later to use and which will reappear throughout this book. Paley compares the eye with a designed instrument such as a telescope, and concludes that "there is precisely the same proof that the eye was made for vision, as there is that the telescope was made for assisting it." The eye must have had a designer, just as the telescope had.

Paley's argument is made with passionate sincerity and is informed by the best biological scholarship of his day, but it is wrong, gloriously and utterly wrong. The analogy between telescope and eye, between watch and living organ-

ism, is false. All appearances to the contrary, the only watchmaker in nature is the blind forces of physics, albeit deployed in a very special way. A true watchmaker has foresight: he designs his cogs and springs, and plans their interconnections, with a future purpose in his mind's eye. Natural selection, the blind, unconscious, automatic process which Darwin discovered, and which we now know is the explanation for the existence and apparently purposeful form of all life, has no purpose in mind. It has no mind and no mind's eye. It does not plan for the future. It has no vision, no foresight, no sight at all. If it can be said to play the role of watchmaker in nature, it is the *blind* watchmaker.

I shall explain all this, and much else besides. But one thing I shall not do is belittle the wonder of the living "watches" that so inspired Paley. On the contrary, I shall try to illustrate my feeling that here Paley could have gone even further. When it comes to feeling awe over living "watches" I yield to nobody. I feel more in common with the Reverend William Paley than I do with the distinguished modern philosopher, a well-known atheist, with whom I once discussed the matter at dinner. I said that I could not imagine being an atheist at any time before 1859, when Darwin's *Origin of Species* was published. "What about Hume?" replied the philosopher. "How did Hume explain the organized complexity of the living world?" I asked. "He didn't," said the philosopher. "Why does it need any special explanation?"

Paley knew that it needed a special explanation; Darwin knew it, and I suspect that in his heart of hearts my philosopher companion knew it too. In any case it will be my business to show it here. As for David Hume himself, it is sometimes said that that great Scottish philosopher disposed of the Argument from Design a century before Darwin. But what Hume did was criticize the logic of using apparent design in nature as *positive* evidence for the existence of a God. He did not offer any *alternative* explanation for apparent design, but left the question open. An atheist before Darwin could have said, following Hume: "I have no explanation for complex biological design. All I know is that God isn't a good explanation, so we must wait and hope that somebody comes up with a better one." I can't help feeling that such a position, though logically sound, would have left one feeling pretty unsatisfied, and that although atheism might have been *logically* tenable before Darwin, Darwin made it possible to be an intellectually fulfilled atheist. I like to think that Hume would agree, but some of his writings suggest that he underestimated the complexity and beauty of biological design. The boy naturalist Charles Darwin could have shown him a thing or two about that, but Hume had been dead 40 years when Darwin enrolled in Hume's university of Edinburgh. . . .

We have seen that living things are too improbable and too beautifully "designed" to have come into existence by chance. How, then, did they come into existence? The answer, Darwin's answer, is by gradual, step-by-step transformations from simple beginnings, from primordial entities sufficiently simple to have come into existence by chance. Each successive change in the gradual evolutionary process was simple enough, *relative to its predecessor,* to have arisen by chance. But the whole sequence of cumulative steps constitutes anything but a chance process, when you consider the complexity of the final end-product relative to the original starting point. The cumulative process is directed by nonrandom survival. The purpose of this chapter is to demonstrate the power of this *cumulative selection* as a fundamentally nonrandom process.

If you walk up and down a pebbly beach, you will notice that the pebbles are not arranged at random. The smaller pebbles typically tend to be found in segregated zones running along the length of the beach, the larger ones in different zones or stripes. The pebbles have been sorted, arranged, selected. A tribe living near the shore might wonder at this evidence of sorting or arrangement in the world, and might develop a myth to account for it, perhaps attributing it to a Great Spirit in the sky with a tidy mind and a sense of order. We might give a superior smile at such a superstitious notion, and explain that the arranging was really done by the blind forces of physics, in this case the action of waves. The waves have no purposes and no intentions, no tidy mind, no mind at all. They just energetically throw the pebbles around, and big pebbles and small pebbles respond differently to this treatment so they end up at different levels of the beach. A small amount of order has come out of disorder, and no mind planned it.

The waves and the pebbles together constitute a simple example of a system that automatically generates nonrandomness. The world is full of such systems. The simplest example I can think of is a hole. Only objects smaller than the hole can pass through it. This means that if you start with a random collection of objects above the hole, and some force shakes and jostles them about at random, after a while the objects above and below the hole will come to be nonrandomly sorted. The space below the hole will tend to contain objects smaller than the hole, and the space above will tend to contain objects larger than the hole. Mankind has, of course, long exploited this simple principle for generating nonrandomness, in the useful device known as the sieve.

The solar system is a stable arrangement of planets, comets and debris orbiting the Sun, and it is presumably one of many such orbiting systems in the universe. The nearer a satellite is to its sun, the faster it has to travel if it is to counter the sun's gravity and remain in stable orbit. For any given orbit, there is only one speed at which a satellite can travel and remain in that orbit. If it were travelling at any other velocity, it would either move out into deep space, or crash into the Sun, or move into another orbit. And if we look at the planets of our solar system, lo and behold, every single one of them is travelling at exactly the right velocity to keep it in its stable orbit around the Sun. A blessed miracle of provident design? No, just another natural "sieve." Obviously all the planets that we see orbiting the Sun must be travelling at exactly the right speed to keep them in their orbits, or we wouldn't see them there because they wouldn't be there! But equally obviously this is not evidence for conscious design. It is just another kind of sieve.

Sieving of this order of simplicity is not, on its own, enough to account for the massive amounts of nonrandom order that we see in living things. Nowhere near enough. Remember the analogy of the combination lock. The kind of nonrandomness that can be generated by simple sieving is roughly equivalent to opening a combination lock with one dial: it is easy to open it by sheer luck. The kind of nonrandomness that we see in living systems, on the other hand, is equivalent to a gigantic combination lock with an almost uncountable number of dials. To generate a biological molecule like haemoglobin, the red pigment in blood, by simple sieving would be equivalent to taking all the amino-acid building blocks of haemoglobin, jumbling them up at random, and hoping that the haemoglobin molecule would reconstitute itself by sheer luck. The amount of luck that would be required for this feat is unthinkable, and has been used as a telling mind-boggler by Isaac Asimov and others.

A haemoglobin molecule consists of four chains of amino acids twisted together. Let us think about just one of these four chains. It consists of 146 amino acids. There are 20 different kinds of amino acids commonly found in living things. The number of possible ways of arranging 20 kinds of thing in chains 146 links long is an inconceivably large number, which Asimov calls the "haemoglobin number." It is easy to calculate, but impossible to visualize the answer. The first link in the 146-long chain could be any one of the 20 possible amino acids. The second link could also be any one of the 20, so the number of possible 2-link chains is 20×20, or 400. The number of possible 3-link chains is $20 \times 20 \times 20$, or 8,000. The number of possible 146-link chains is 20 times itself 146 times. This is a staggeringly large number. A million is a 1 with 6 noughts after it. A billion (1,000 million) is a 1 with 9 noughts after it. The number we seek, the "haemoglobin number," is (near enough) a 1 with 190 noughts after it! This is the chance against happening to hit upon haemoglobin by luck. And a haemoglobin molecule has only a minute fraction of the complexity of a living body. Simple sieving, on its own, is obviously nowhere near capable of generating the amount of order in a living thing. Sieving is an essential ingredient in the generation of living order, but it is very far from being the whole story. Something else is needed. To explain the point, I shall

need to make a distinction between "single-step" selection and "cumulative" selection. The simple sieves we have been considering so far in this chapter are all examples of single-step selection. Living organization is the product of cumulative selection.

The essential difference between single-step selection and cumulative selection is this. In single-step selection the entities selected or sorted, pebbles or whatever they are, are sorted once and for all. In cumulative selection, on the other hand, they "reproduce"; or in some other way the results of one sieving process are fed into a subsequent sieving, which is fed into . . . , and so on. The entities are subjected to selection or sorting over many "generations" in succession. The end-product of one generation of selection is the starting point for the next generation of selection, and so on for many generations. It is natural to borrow such words as "reproduce" and "generation," which have associations with living things, because living things are the main examples we know of things that participate in cumulative selection. They may in practice be the only things that do. But for the moment I don't want to beg that question by saying so outright.

Sometimes clouds, through the random kneading and carving of the winds, come to look like familiar objects. There is a much published photograph, taken by the pilot of a small aeroplane, of what looks a bit like the face of Jesus, staring out of the sky. We have all seen clouds that reminded us of something—a sea horse, say, or a smiling face. These resemblances come about by single-step selection, that is to say by a single coincidence. They are, consequently, not very impressive. The resemblance of the signs of the zodiac to the animals after which they are named, Scorpio, Leo, and so on, is as unimpressive as the predictions of astrologers. We don't feel overwhelmed by the resemblance, as we are by biological adaptations—the products of cumulative selection. We describe as weird, uncanny or spectacular, the resemblance of, say, a leaf insect to a leaf or a praying mantis to a cluster of pink flowers. The resemblance of a cloud to a weasel is only mildly diverting, barely worth calling to the attention of our companion. Moreover, we are quite likely to change our mind about exactly what the cloud most resembles.

> *Hamlet:* Do you see yonder cloud that's almost in shape of a camel?
> *Polonius:* By the mass, and 'tis like a camel, indeed.
> *Hamlet:* Methinks it is like a weasel.
> *Polonius:* It is backed like a weasel.
> *Hamlet:* Or like a whale?
> *Polonius:* Very like a whale.

I don't know who it was first pointed out that, given enough time, a monkey bashing away at random on a typewriter could produce all the works of Shakespeare. The operative phrase is, of course, given enough time. Let us limit the task facing our monkey somewhat. Suppose that he has to produce, not the complete works of Shakespeare but just the short sentence "Methinks it is like a weasel," and we shall make it relatively easy by giving him a typewriter with a restricted keyboard, one with just the 26 (capital) letters, and a space bar. How long will he take to write this one little sentence?

The sentence has 28 characters in it, so let us assume that the monkey has a series of discrete "tries," each consisting of 28 bashes at the keyboard. If he types the phrase correctly, that is the end of the experiment. If not, we allow him another "try" of 28 characters. I don't know any monkeys, but fortunately my 11-month-old daughter is an experienced randomizing device, and she proved only too eager to step into the role of monkey typist. Here is what she typed on the computer.

UMMK JK CDZZ F ZD DSDSKSM
S SS FMCV PU I DDRGLKDXRRDO
RDTE QDWFDVIOY UDSKZWDCCVYT
H CHVY NMGNBAYTDFCCVD D
RCDFYYYRM N DFSKD LD K WDWK
JJKAUIZMZI UXDKIDISFUMDKUDXI

She has other important calls on her time, so I was obliged to program the computer to simulate a randomly typing baby or monkey:

WDLDMNLT DTJBKWIRZREZLMQCO P
Y YVMQKZPGJXWVHGLAWFVCHQYOPY

MWR SWTNUXMLCDLEUBXTQHNZVJQF
FU OVAODVYKDGXDEKYVMOGGS VT
HZQZDSFZIHIVPHZPETPWVOVPMZGF
GEWRGZRPBCTPGQMCKHFDBGW ZCCF

And so on and on. It isn't difficult to calculate how long we should reasonably expect to wait for the random computer (or baby or monkey) to type METHINKS IT IS LIKE A WEASEL. Think about the total number of *possible* phrases of the right length that the monkey or baby or random computer *could* type. It is the same kind of calculation as we did for haemoglobin, and it produces a similarly large result. There are 27 possible letters (counting "space" as one letter) in the first position. The chance of the monkey happening to get the first letter—M—right is therefore 1 in 27. The chance of it getting the first two letters—ME—right is the chance of it getting the second letter—E—right (1 in 27) *given that* it has also got the first letter—M—right, therefore $1/27 \times 1/27$, which equals $1/729$. The chance of it getting the first word—METHINKS—right is $1/27$ for each of the 8 letters, therefore $(1/27) \times (1/27) \times (1/27) \times (1/27) \ldots$, etc. 8 times, or $(1/27)$ to the power 8. The chance of it getting the entire phrase of 28 characters right is $(1/27)$ to the power 28, i.e. $(1/27)$ multiplied by itself 28 times. These are very small odds, about 1 in 10,000 million million million million million. To put it mildly, the phrase we seek would be a long time coming, to say nothing of the complete works of Shakespeare.

So much for single-step selection of random variation. What about cumulative selection; how much more effective should this be? Very very much more effective, perhaps more so than we at first realize, although it is almost obvious when we reflect further. We again use our computer monkey, but with a crucial difference in its program. It again begins by choosing a random sequence of 28 letters, just as before:

WDLMNLT DTJBKWIRZREZLMQCO P

It now "breeds from" this random phrase. It duplicates it repeatedly, but with a certain chance of random error—"mutation"—in the copying. The computer examines the mutant nonsense phrases, the "progeny" of the original phrase, and chooses the one which, *however slightly*, most resembles the target phrase, METHINKS IT IS LIKE A WEASEL. In this instance the winning phrase of the next "generation" happened to be:

WDLTMNLT DTJBSWIRZREZLMQCO P

Not an obvious improvement! But the procedure is repeated, again mutant "progeny" are "bred from" the phrase, and a new "winner" is chosen. This goes on, generation after generation. After 10 generations, the phrase chosen for "breeding" was:

MDLDMNLS ITJISWHRZREZ MECS P

After 20 generations it was:

MELDINLS IT ISWPRKE Z WECSEL

By now, the eye of faith fancies that it can see a resemblance to the target phrase. By 30 generations there can be no doubt:

METHINGS IT ISWLIKE B WECSEL

Generation 40 takes us to within one letter of the target:

METHINKS IT IS LIKE I WEASEL

And the target was finally reached in generation 43. A second run of the computer began with the phrase:

Y YVMQKZPFJXWVHGLAWFVCHQXYOPY,

passed through (again reporting only every tenth generation):

Y YVMQKSPFTXWSHLIKEFV HQYSPY
YETHINKSPITXISHLIKEFA WQYSEY
METHINKS IT ISSLIKE A WEFSEY
METHINKS IT ISBLIKE A WEASES
METHINKS IT ISJLIKE A WEASEO
METHINKS IT IS LIKE A WEASEP

and reached the target phrase in generation 64. In a third run the computer started with:

GEWRGZRPBCTPGQMCKHFDBGW ZCCF

and reached METHINKS IT IS LIKE A WEASEL in 41 generations of selective "breeding."

The exact time taken by the computer to reach the target doesn't matter. If you want to know, it completed the whole exercise for me, the first time, while I was out to lunch. It took about half an hour. (Computer enthusiasts may think this unduly slow. The reason is that the program was written in BASIC, a sort of computer baby-talk. When I rewrote it in Pascal, it took 11 seconds.) Computers are a bit faster at this kind of thing than monkeys, but the difference really isn't significant. What matters is the difference between the time taken by *cumulative* selection, and the time which the same computer, working flat out at the same rate, would take to reach the target phrase if it were forced to use the other procedure of *single-step selection:* about a million million million million million years. This is more than a million million million times as long as the universe has so far existed. Actually it would be fairer just to say that, in comparison with the time it would take either a monkey or a randomly programmed computer to type our target phrase, the total age of the universe so far is a negligibly small quantity, so small as to be well within the margin of error for this sort of back-of-an-envelope calculation. Whereas the time taken for a computer working randomly but with the constraint of *cumulative selection* to perform the same task is of the same order as humans ordinarily can understand, between 11 seconds and the time it takes to have lunch.

There is a big difference, then, between cumulative selection (in which each improvement, however slight, is used as a basis for future building), and single-step selection (in which each new "try" is a fresh one). If evolutionary progress had had to rely on single-step selection, it would never have got anywhere. If, however, there was any way in which the necessary conditions for *cumulative* selection could have been set up by the blind forces of nature, strange and wonderful might have been the consequences. As a matter of fact that is exactly what happened on this planet, and we ourselves are among the most recent, if not the strangest and most wonderful, of those consequences.

It is amazing that you can still read calculations like my haemoglobin calculation, used as though they constituted arguments *against* Darwin's theory. The people who do this, often expert in their own field, astronomy or whatever it may be, seem sincerely to believe that Darwinism explains living organization in terms of chance—"single-step selection"—alone. This belief, that Darwinian evolution is "random," is not merely false. It is the exact opposite of the truth. Chance is a minor ingredient in the Darwinian recipe, but the most important ingredient is cumulative selection which is quintessentially *non*random. . . .

We have dealt with all the alleged alternatives to the theory of natural selection except the oldest one. This is the theory that life was created, or its evolution master-minded, by a conscious designer. It would obviously be unfairly easy to demolish some particular version of this theory such as the one (or it may be two) spelled out in Genesis. Nearly all peoples have developed their own creation myth, and the Genesis story is just the one that happened to have been adopted by one particular tribe of Middle Eastern herders. It has no more special status than the belief of a particular West African tribe that the world was created from the excrement of ants. All these myths have in common that they depend upon the deliberate intentions of some kind of supernatural being.

At first sight there is an important distinction to be made between what might be called "instantaneous creation" and "guided evolution." Modern theologians of any sophistication have given up believing in instantaneous creation. The evidence for some sort of evolution has become too overwhelming. But many theologians who call themselves evolutionists, for instance the Bishop of Birmingham quoted in Chapter 2, smuggle God in by the back door: they allow him some sort of supervisory role over the course that evolution has taken, either influencing key moments in evolutionary history (especially, of course, *human* evolutionary history), or even meddling more comprehensively in the day-to-day events that add up to evolutionary change.

We cannot disprove beliefs like these, especially if it is assumed that God took care that his interventions always closely mimicked what would be expected from evolution by natural se-

lection. All that we can say about such beliefs is, firstly, that they are superfluous and, secondly, that they *assume* the existence of the main thing we want to *explain,* namely organized complexity. The one thing that makes evolution such a neat theory is that it explains how organized complexity can arise out of primeval simplicity.

If we want to postulate a deity capable of engineering all the organized complexity in the world, either instantaneously or by guiding evolution, that deity must already have been vastly complex in the first place. The creationist, whether a naive Bible-thumper or an educated bishop, simply *postulates* an already existing being of prodigious intelligence and complexity. If we are going to allow ourselves the luxury of postulating organized complexity without offering an explanation, we might as well make a job of it and simply postulate the existence of life as we know it! In short, divine creation, whether instantaneous or in the form of guided evolution, joins the list of other theories we have considered in this chapter. All give some superficial appearance of being alternatives to Darwinism, whose merits might be tested by an appeal to evidence. All turn out, on closer inspection, not to be rivals of Darwinism at all. The theory of evolution by cumulative natural selection is the only theory we know of that is in principle *capable* of explaining the existence of organized complexity. Even if the evidence did not favour it, it would *still* be the best theory available! In fact the evidence does favour it. But that is another story.

Let us hear the conclusion of the whole matter. The essence of life is statistical improbability on a colossal scale. Whatever is the explanation for life, therefore, it cannot be chance. The true explanation for the existence of life must embody the very antithesis of chance. The antithesis of chance is nonrandom survival, properly understood. Nonrandom survival, improperly understood, is not the antithesis of chance, it is chance itself. There is a continuum connecting these two extremes, and it is the continuum from single-step selection to cumulative selection. Single-step selection is just another way of saying pure chance. This is what I mean by nonrandom survival improperly understood. *Cumulative selection,* by slow and gradual degrees, is the explanation, the only workable explanation that has ever been proposed, for the existence of life's complex design.

The whole book has been dominated by the idea of chance, by the astronomically long odds against the spontaneous arising of order, complexity and apparent design. We have sought a way of taming chance, of drawing its fangs. "Untamed chance," pure, naked chance, means ordered design springing into existence from nothing, in a single leap. It would be untamed chance if once there was no eye, and then, suddenly, in the twinkling of a generation, an eye appeared, fully fashioned, perfect and whole. This is possible, but the odds against it will keep us busy writing noughts till the end of time. The same applies to the odds against the spontaneous existence of any fully fashioned, perfect and whole beings, including—I see no way of avoiding the conclusion—deities.

To "tame" chance means to break down the very improbable into less improbable small components arranged in series. No matter how improbable it is that an X could have arisen from a Y in a single step, it is always possible to conceive of a series of infinitesimally graded intermediates between them. However improbable a large-scale change may be, smaller changes are less improbable. And provided we postulate a sufficiently large series of sufficiently finely graded intermediates, we shall be able to derive anything from anything else, without invoking astronomical improbabilities. We are allowed to do this only if there has been sufficient time to fit all the intermediates in. And also only if there is a mechanism for guiding each step in some particular direction, otherwise the sequence of steps will career off in an endless random walk.

It is the contention of the Darwinian worldview that both these provisos are met, and that slow, gradual, cumulative natural selection is the ultimate explanation for our existence. If there are versions of the evolution theory that deny slow gradualism, and deny the central role of natural selection, they may be true in particular cases. But they cannot be the whole truth, for they deny the very heart of the evolution theory, which gives it the power to dissolve astronomical improbabilities and explain prodigies of apparent miracle.

Suggestions for Further Reading

Read David Hume's *Dialogues Concerning Natural Religion* for the classic refutation of the teleological argument and Richard Swinburne's *The Existence of God* (Oxford: Oxford University Press, 1979) for a contemporary defense.

R. R. Tennant also provides a version of the argument that takes Hume's objections into account in his *Philosophical Theology* (Cambridge: Cambridge University Press, 1928).

Thomas McPherson's *The Argument from Design* (London: Macmillan, 1972) provides an introduction to various forms of the argument.

See Chapter 4 of William Rowe's *Philosophy of Religion: An Introduction,* 2nd Edition (Belmont, CA: Wadsworth, 1993) for a good discussion of the issues.

See L. Stafford Betty and Bruce Cordell's article "God and Modern Science: New Life for the Teleological Argument," *International Philosophical Quarterly* 27 (December 1987): 409–435, for a discussion of arguments for God's existence in light of recent scientific theories about the origin of the universe and of life. They argue in favor of a theistic explanation.

For a critical review of Dawkins's book, see *Dialogue and Alliance: A Journal of the International Religious Foundation* 1 (Winter 1987–1988): 85–87.

The literature on the creation-versus-evolution debate is vast. See Niles Eldredge's *The Monkey Business: A Scientist Looks at Creationism* (New York: Washington Square Press, 1982) for a vigorous defense of evolution, and see Duane Gish's *Evolution? The Fossils Say No!* (San Diego: Institute for Creation Research, 1973) for an attack on evolutionary theory.

The case for intelligent design independent of religious claims about God and the case against Darwin can be found at http://www.darwinsmistake.com/Domains/darwins_mistake/design.htm.

Videos

God, Darwin, and Dinosaurs (58 minutes, 1993) explores the debate about teaching evolution and creationism in the public schools, *The Creationist Argument* (26 minutes, 1993) lets Luther Sutherland have his say, and *The Evidence for Evolution* (26 minutes, 1993) presents the case for evolution. *A Glorious Accident: Understanding Our Place in the Cosmic Puzzle* is an eight-part series presenting discussions with the likes of Rupert Sheldrake, Stephen Toulmin, and Stephen Jay Gould. All of the above are available from Films for the Humanities & Sciences (www.films.com).

12.5 An Ontological Argument for God's Existence

Cosmological and teleological arguments for the existence of God are a posteriori. They argue from our experience of the universe to the existence of God as the cause, creator, designer, or explanation for the universe or some important feature of it. **Ontological arguments** are a priori. They argue from a definition of God (*ontological* means "the study of being") to God's existence.

St. Anselm (1033–1109) is credited with having invented the ontological argument. He reasoned that, by definition, God must be that than which nothing greater can be thought. In other words, God is the greatest possible being of which we can conceive. Now, if that is so, it follows necessarily that God must exist. Why? Well, let us assume, contrary to fact, that the greatest possible being of which we can conceive does not exist outside of our minds that think it. If it does not, then we can image something still greater, namely, the greatest possible being of which we can conceive that *does* exist outside of our thoughts about it. However, there can be, by definition, nothing greater than the greatest possible being of which we can think because then the greatest possible being of which we can think would *not* be the greatest possible being. That is clearly a contradiction. So, if assuming "the greatest possible being of which we can conceive does not exist outside our conception of it" leads to a contradiction, then the opposite must be true, namely, the greatest possible being of which we can conceive does exist both as a thought in our minds as well as outside.

You may have found that a little hard to follow because the reasoning is what logicians call a *reductio ad absurdum* (reduction to absurdity) and hence the argument amounts to an indirect proof. It supports its conclusion by showing that the *negation* of its conclusion leads to a logical absurdity. If the assumption that God, defined in a certain way, does *not* exist *leads to a contradiction,* then it logically follows that God does exist.

You might well think there is something fishy going on here. Can we just define things into existence? A contemporary of Anselm, a Christian monk named Gaunilo, also thought something fishy was going on here. Suppose, he says, there is an island that no one knows about. Further suppose that this is the greatest possible island, the ultimate island if you will. Should we conclude that it must exist just because it is the greatest possible island?

Anselm is not left speechless by Gaunilo's response, as you shall soon see, but Gaunilo did spark attempts at refutation that have continued since the Middle Ages. Immanuel Kant (see Section 4.2), for example, said that the problem with the ontological argument stems from Anselm's mistaken belief that existence is a real predicate.

Real predicates are those that add some descriptive information about the subject. For example, "My dog Arthur loves to take walks" adds information to our *descriptive* understanding of Arthur the dog. We now know something about the dog named Arthur we did not know before. However, we do not add to the *description* of a thing when we say it exists. To say something exists is to say that there is something in reality that corresponds to our description. It answers the question "Is there any?" but it does not answer the question "What is It?" The question "what is it" is logically distinct from the question "Are there any?" Hence, according to Kant, the answer to the first question about the nature of something does not provide an answer to the second question, the question about its existence. Anselm mistakenly thinks that, at least in the case of God, it does.

In addition, Kant argued that existence is an all or nothing situation. Either the blind cat Peanut exists or he does not. Real predicates, however, are not all or nothing. They are a matter of degree. Blindness, for example, is not necessarily the total loss of sight, but it falls within a range of a reduction in the power of vision. Thus, Kant concludes that Anselm's ingenious argument mistakenly treats existence as a real predict.

Just as Anselm was not left speechless by Gaunilo, so supporters of the ontological argument have not been left speechless by Kant's refutation. A lively debate about the adequacy of the argument broke out in the latter half of the twentieth century. This is not surprising because, unlike the cosmological and teleological arguments (see above) for God's existence, the conclusion of the ontological argument leads to the other great-making characteristics we often associate with God. If a perfect being (the greatest possible for thought) exists, then such a being must also be perfect in power, goodness, and knowledge. To use traditional language, it must be omnipotent (all-powerful), omnibenevolent (all-good), omniscient (all-knowing). The most the cosmological argument proves, if it proves anything at all, is that the cosmos has a cause that some call divine. It does not prove that this cause is perfect in power, goodness, and knowledge. Likewise, the most the teleological argument proves, assuming it proves something, is that there is an intelligent designer of the universe. It tells us very little about the goodness, power, and knowledge of this designer as David Hume pointed out more than 200 years ago.

Reading Projects and Question

1. Summarize Anselm's argument in your own words.
2. Summarize Gaunilo's response in your own words.
3. Summarize Anselm's rejoinder in your own words.
4. Whose arguments do you find most persuasive, Anselm's or Gaunilo's? Why?

A Debate

ST. ANSELM AND GAUNILO

Truly there is a God, although the fool hath said in his heart, There is no God.

AND SO, Lord, do thou, who dost give understanding to faith, give me, so far as thou knowest it to be profitable, to understand that thou art as we believe; and that thou art that which we believe. And, indeed, we believe that thou art a being than which nothing greater can be conceived. Or is there no such nature, since the fool hath said in his heart, there is no God? (Psalms xiii, 1). But, at any rate, this very fool, when he hears of this being of which I speak—a being than which nothing greater can be conceived—understands what he hears, and what he understands is in his understanding; although he does not understand it to exist.

For, it is one thing for an object to be in the understanding, and another to understand that the object exists. When a painter first conceives of what he will afterwards perform, he has it in his understanding, but he does not yet understand it to be, because he has not yet performed it. But after he has made the painting, he both has it in his understanding, and he understands that it exists, because he has made it.

Hence, even the fool is convinced that something exists in the understanding, at least, than which nothing greater can be conceived. For, when he hears of this, he understands it. And whatever is understood, exists in the understanding. And assuredly that, than which nothing greater can be conceived, cannot exist in the understanding alone. For, suppose it exists in the understanding alone: then it can be conceived to exist in reality; which is greater.

Therefore, if that, than which nothing greater can be conceived, exists in the understanding alone, the very being, than which nothing greater can be conceived, is one, than which a greater can be conceived. But obviously this is impossible. Hence, there is no doubt that there exists a being, than which nothing greater can be conceived, and it exists both in the understanding and in reality.

God cannot be conceived not to exist.—God is that, than which nothing greater can be conceived.—That which can be conceived not to exist is not God.

And it assuredly exists so truly, that it cannot be conceived not to exist. For, it is possible to conceive of a being which cannot be conceived not to exist; and this is greater than one which can be conceived not to exist. Hence, if that, than which nothing greater can be conceived, can be conceived not to exist, it is not that, than which nothing greater can be conceived. But this is an irreconcilable contradiction. There is, then, so truly a being than which nothing greater can be conceived to exist, that it cannot even be conceived not to exist: and this being thou art, O Lord, our God.

So truly, therefore, dost thou exist, O Lord, my God, that thou canst not be conceived not to exist; and rightly. For, if a mind could conceive of a being better than thee, the creature would rise above the Creator; and this is most absurd. And, indeed, whatever else there is, except thee alone, can be conceived not to exist. To thee alone, therefore, it belongs to exist more truly than all other beings, and hence in a higher degree than all others. For, whatever else exists does not exist so truly, and hence in a less degree it belongs to it to exist. Why, then, has the fool said in his heart, there is no God (Psalms xiii, 1), since it is so evident, to a rational mind, that thou dost

Reprinted by permission of Open Court Publishing Company, a division of Carus Publishing Company, Peru, IL, from Anselm's Basic Writings, *2d ed. Translated by S. W. Deane. Copyright ©1962 by Open Court Publishing Company.*

exist in the highest degree of all? Why, except that he is dull and a fool?

> How the fool has said in his heart what cannot be conceived.—A thing may be conceived in two ways: (1) when the word signifying it is conceived: (2) when the thing itself is understood. As far as the word goes, God can be conceived not to exist; in reality he cannot.

But how has the fool said in his heart what he could not conceive; or how is it that he could not conceive what he said in his heart? since it is the same to say in the heart, and to conceive.

But, if really, nay, since really, he both conceived, because he said in his heart; and did not say in his heart, because he could not conceive; there is more than one way in which a thing is said in the heart or conceived. For, in one sense, an object is conceived, when the word signifying it is conceived; and in another, when the very entity, which the object is, is understood.

In the former sense, then, God can be conceived not to exist; but in the latter, not at all. For no one who understands what fire and water are can conceive fire to be water, in accordance with the nature of the facts themselves, although this is possible according to the words. So, then, no one who understands what God is can conceive that God does not exist; although he says these words in his heart, either without any or with some foreign, signification. For, God is that than which a greater cannot be conceived. And he who thoroughly understands this, assuredly understands that this being so truly exists, that not even in concept can it be non-existent. Therefore, he who understands that God so exists, cannot conceive that he does not exist.

I thank thee, gracious Lord, I thank thee: because what I formerly believed by thy bounty, I now so understand by thine illumination, that if I were unwilling to believe that thou dost exist, I should not be able not to understand this to be true.

Gaunilo's Criticism

For example: it is said that somewhere in the ocean is an island, which, because of the difficulty, or rather the impossibility, of discovering what does not exist, is called the lost island. And they say that this island has an inestimable wealth of all manner of riches and delicacies in greater abundance than is told of the Islands of the Blest; and that having no owner or inhabitant, it is more excellent than all other countries, which are inhabited by mankind, in the abundance with which it is stored.

Now if some one should tell me that there is such an island, I should easily understand his words, in which there is no difficulty. But suppose that he went on to say, as if by a logical inference: "You can no longer doubt that this island which is more excellent than all lands exists somewhere, since you have no doubt that it is in your understanding. And since it is more excellent not to be in the understanding alone, but to exist both in the understanding and in reality, for this reason it must exist. For if it does not exist, any land which really exists will be more excellent than it; and so the island already understood by you to be more excellent will not be more excellent."

If a man should try to prove to me by such reasoning that this island truly exists, and that its existence should no longer be doubted, either I should believe that he was jesting, or I know not which I ought to regard as the greater fool: myself, supposing that I should allow this proof; or him, if he should suppose that he had established with any certainty the existence of this island. For he ought to show first that the hypothetical excellence of this island exists as a real and indubitable fact, and in no wise as any unreal object, or one whose existence is uncertain, in my understanding.

St. Anselm's Rejoinder

> A criticism of Gaunilo's example, in which he tries to show that in this way the real existence of a lost island might be inferred from the fact of its being conceived.

But, you say, it is as if one should suppose an island in the ocean, which surpasses all lands in its fertility, and which, because of the difficulty, or rather the impossibility, of discovering what does not exist, is called a lost island; and should say that there can be no doubt that this island truly exists in reality, for this reason, that one who hears it described easily understands what he hears.

Now I promise confidently that if any man shall devise anything existing either in reality or in concept alone (except that than which a greater cannot be conceived) to which he can adapt the sequence of my reasoning, I will discover that thing, and will give him his lost island, not to be lost again.

But it now appears that this being than which a greater is inconceivable cannot be conceived not to be, because it exists on so assured a ground of truth; for otherwise it would not exist at all.

Hence, if any one says that he conceives this being not to exist, I say that at the time when he conceives of this either he conceives of a being than which a greater is inconceivable, or he does not conceive at all. If he does not conceive, he does not conceive of the non-existence of that of which he does not conceive. But if he does conceive, he certainly conceives of a being which cannot be even conceived not to exist. For if it could be conceived not to exist, it could be conceived to have a beginning and an end. But this is impossible.

He, then, who conceives of this being conceives of a being which cannot be even conceived not to exist; but he who conceives of this being does not conceive that it does not exist; else he conceives what is inconceivable. The non-existence, then, of that than which a greater cannot be conceived is inconceivable.

Suggestions for Further Reading

There is a vast literature on the ontological argument. Part 1(c) of Louis P. Pojman's (ed.) *Philosophy of Religion: An Anthology,* 2nd Edition (Belmont, CA: Wadsworth, 1994) provides a good selection of different viewpoints.

Alvin Plantinga's (ed.) *The Ontological Argument: From St. Anselm to Contemporary Philosophers* (Garden City, NY: Anchor Books, 1965) offers a useful compendium of materials.

Also see Colin Grant's "Anselm's Argument Today," *Journal of the American Academy of Religion* 57, no. 4 (Winter 1989): 791–806, for an excellent overview of the controversy surrounding St. Anselm's argument. Grant highlights the way the basic assumptions of St. Anselm's "age of faith" differ from the assumptions of the "modern age of reason."

Believe it or not there is much on the WWW about the ontological argument and other arguments for God's existence. For links see the Hutchinson Encyclopedia at http://ukdb .web.aol.com/hutchinson/encyclopedia/77/M0044177.htm.

12.6 The Gender of God

There is an old story about the reporter who was granted an interview with God. When the reporter returned, people eagerly asked, "Well, tell us. What is God like?"

"You will have to wait until I write my article," the reporter replied, "but I can tell you this much, she is black."

The punch line makes us smile because it is unexpected. But why is it unexpected? Why shouldn't God be female and black?

We have all been raised with certain images of God and the dominant one in Western culture has been the image of a white male (usually old and bearded!). Although the arguments for God's existence make no mention of God's sex, many who read the arguments undoubtedly imagine a male deity as the reference of these arguments. How many of you, as you read the arguments and read the word *God* thought of a male deity? If you did, you can understand how these arguments reinforce, perhaps unconsciously and unintentionally, the idea that masculinity is creative, powerful, perfect, and intelligent.

Mary Daly, professor of theology at Boston College until her forced retirement because of a controversy about allowing males to take some of her classes, understands the goal of Christianity as the liberation of all humans. She thinks that traditional Christian images of God as Father do not promote the liberation of females. Therefore, she argues, we must get beyond the notion of God as Father. In the introduction to the book from which this selection is taken (a book that has become a classic statement in the field), she sets forth her presuppositions as follows:

1. Women exist in a sexual "caste" system subordinate to and dominated by men.
2. Sex-role socialization perpetuates this system by convincing women to accept their "inferior" status and men to accept their "superior" status.
3. Women's lower status is disguised by sex-role segregation ("women are 'equal' but different") and by providing them derivative status as a consequence of their relationships with men (Mr. and *Mrs. John* Gibbons).
4. Judaism, Christianity, and Islam (to mention only three of the major world religions) have helped maintain women's subordination to men by their teachings about marriage, reproduction, and the roles women can assume in their respective religious organizations.
5. People try to avoid acknowledging the issue of sexual caste by trivializing it ("After all there are more important issues, like war or racism"), by particularizing it ("It's a problem for Muslims or Hindus or Jews, but not for Christians"), or by universalizing it ("The real problem is *human* liberation, so let's concentrate on that").

Daly's purpose is to show that the women's movement is a "spiritual revolution" that points us beyond the idolatries of a sexist society and religion. Her method, she writes, derives from the Biblical insight that "to exist humanly is to name the self, the world, and God. The method of evolving spiritual consciousness of women is nothing less than this beginning to speak humanly—reclaiming of the right to name. The liberation of language is rooted in the liberation of ourselves." For Daly, feminism is the attempt to gain equal opportunity and status for women. She does *not* believe God causes sexism, but she does believe human symbols and concepts of God have reinforced sexism.

Daly is not concerned with arguments for God's existence. Rather she is concerned with what humans think about the nature of God and how they conceptualize God. We express our concepts in language, so God-talk becomes a natural focus for those who would argue, as Daly does, that our ordinary concepts of God are sexist.

Reading Questions

1. How has the symbol of God as Father rendered service to male-dominated (patriarchal) societies?
2. How does Daly respond to the criticism that the liberation of women will not basically change the structures, ideologies, and values of society?
3. What are the differences between the masculine and the feminine stereotypes?
4. What do you think Daly means by "androgynous human persons"?

5. What is inadequate about popular preaching about God?
6. Why won't calling God "she" and stressing God's maternal qualities help the situation?
7. Why does the women's revolution even need to speak about God at all?
8. How does Daly interpret the "image of God"?
9. Who are the false deities (idols), and why are they false? Do you agree with Daly that there are false images of God? Why, or why not?
10. What are some of the important implications of Daly's argument?

Beyond God the Father

MARY DALY

> The first step in the elevation of women under all systems of religion is to convince them that the great Spirit of the Universe is in no way responsible for any of these absurdities.
> —Elizabeth Cady Stanton

THE BIBLICAL AND POPULAR image of God as a great patriarch in heaven, rewarding and punishing according to his mysterious and seemingly arbitrary will, has dominated the imagination of millions over thousands of years. The symbol of the Father God, spawned in the human imagination and sustained as plausible by patriarchy, has in turn rendered service to this type of society by making its mechanisms for the oppression of women appear right and fitting. If God in "his" heaven is a father ruling "his" people, then it is in the "nature" of things and according to divine plan and the order of the universe that society be male-dominated.

Within this context a mystification of roles takes place: the husband dominating his wife represents God "himself." The images and values of a given society have been projected into the realm of dogmas and "Articles of Faith," and these in turn justify the social structures which have given rise to them and which sustain their plausibility. The belief system becomes hardened and objectified, seeming to have an unchangeable independent existence and validity of its own. It resists social change that would rob it of its plausibility. Despite the vicious circle, however, change can occur in society, and ideologies can die, though they die hard.

As the women's movement begins to have its effect upon the fabric of society, transforming it from patriarchy into something that never existed before—into a diarchal situation that is radically new—it can become the greatest single challenge to the major religions of the world, Western and Eastern. Beliefs and values that have held sway for thousands of years will be questioned as never before. This revolution may well be also the greatest single hope for survival of spiritual consciousness on this planet.

The Challenge: Emergence of Whole Human Beings

There are some who persist in claiming that the liberation of women will only mean that new characters will assume the same old roles, and that nothing will change essentially in structures, ideologies, and values. This supposition is often based on the observation that the very few women in "masculine" occupations often behave much as men do. This kind of reasoning is not at all to the point, for it fails to take into account the fact that tokenism does not change stereotypes or social systems but works to preserve them, since it dulls the revolutionary impulse. The minute proportion of women in the United States who occupy such roles (such as senators, judges, business executives, doctors, etc.) have been trained by men in institutions defined and designed by men, and they have been pressured subtly to operate according to male rules. There are no alternate models. As sociologist Alice Rossi has suggested, this is not what the women's movement in its most revolutionary potential is all about.

What *is* to the point is an emergence of woman-consciousness such as has never before taken place. It is unimaginative and out of touch with what is happening in the women's movement to assume that the becoming of women will simply mean uncritical acceptance of structures, beliefs, symbols, norms, and patterns of behavior that have been given priority by society under male domination. Rather, this becoming will act as catalyst for radical change in our culture. It has been argued cogently by Piaget that structure is maintained by an interplay of transformation laws that never yield results beyond the system and never tend to employ elements external to the system. This is indicative of what *can* effect basic alteration in the system, that is, a potent influence *from without*. Women who reject patriarchy have this power and indeed *are* this power of transformation that is ultimately threatening to things as they are.

The roles and structures of patriarchy have been developed and sustained in accordance with an artificial polarization of human qualities into the traditional sexual stereotypes. The image of the person in authority and the accepted understanding of "his" role has corresponded to the eternal masculine stereotype, which implies hyperrationality (in reality, frequently reducible to pseudo-rationality), "objectivity," aggressivity, the possession of dominating and manipulative attitudes toward persons and the environment, and the tendency to construct boundaries between the self (and those identified with the self) and "the Other." The caricature of human being which is represented by this stereotype de-

pends for its existence upon the opposite caricature—the eternal feminine. This implies hyper-emotionalism, passivity, self-abnegation, etc. By becoming whole persons women can generate a counterforce to the stereotype of the leader, challenging the artificial polarization of human characteristics into sex-role identification. There is no reason to assume that women who have the support of each other to criticize not only the feminine stereotype but the masculine stereotype as well will simply adopt the latter as a model for ourselves. On the contrary, what is happening is that women are developing a wider range of qualities and skills. This is beginning to encourage and in fact demand a comparably liberating process in men—a phenomenon which has begun in men's liberation groups and which is taking place every day within the context of personal relationships. The becoming of androgynous human persons implies a radical change in the fabric of human consciousness and in styles of human behavior.

This change is already threatening the credibility of the religious symbols of our culture. Since many of these have been used to justify oppression, such a challenge should be seen as redemptive. Religious symbols fade and die when the cultural situation that gave rise to them and supported them ceases to give them plausibility. Such an event generates anxiety, but it is part of the risk involved in a faith which accepts the relativity of all symbols and recognizes that clinging to these as fixed and ultimate is self-destructive and idolatrous.

The becoming of new symbols is not a matter that can be decided arbitrarily around a conference table. Rather, symbols grow out of a changing communal situation and experience. This does not mean that we are confined to the role of passive spectators. The experience of the becoming of women cannot be understood merely conceptually and abstractly but through active participation in the overcoming of servitude. Both activism and creative thought flow from and feed into the evolving woman-consciousness. The cumulative effect is a surge of awareness beyond the symbols and doctrines of patriarchal religion.

The Inadequate God of Popular Preaching

The image of the divine Father in heaven has not always been conducive to humane behavior, as any perceptive reader of history knows. The often cruel behavior of Christians toward unbelievers and toward dissenters among themselves suggests a great deal not only about the values of the society dominated by that image, but also about how that image itself functions in relation to behavior. There has been a basic ambivalence in the image of the heavenly patriarch—a split between the God of love and the jealous God who represents the collective power of "his" chosen people. As historian Arnold Toynbee has indicated, this has reflected and perpetuated a double standard of behavior. Without debating the details of his historical analysis, the insight is available on an experiential level. The character of Vito Corleone in *The Godfather* is a vivid illustration of the marriage of tenderness and violence so intricately blended in the patriarchal ideal. The worshippers of the loving Father may in a sense love their neighbors, but in fact the term applies only to those within a restricted and unstable circumference, and these worshippers can "justifiably" be intolerant and fanatic persecutors of those outside the sacred circle.

How this God operates is illustrated in contemporary American civil religion. In one of the White House sermons given during the first term of Richard Nixon, Rabbi Louis Finkelstein expressed the hope that a future historian may say "that in the period of great trials and great tribulations, the finger of God pointed to Richard Milhous Nixon, giving the vision and the wisdom to save the world and civilization; and also to open the way for our country to realize the good that the twentieth century offers mankind." Within this context, as Charles Henderson has shown, God is an American and Nixon is "his" anointed one. The preachers carefully selected for the White House sermons stress that this nation is "under God." The logical conclusion is that its politics are right. Under God, the President becomes a Christ figure. In 1969, the day the astronauts would set foot on the moon, and when the President was preparing to cross the Pacific "in search of peace," one of these preachers proclaimed:

> And my hope for mankind is strengthened in the knowledge that our intrepid President himself will soon go into orbit, reaching boldly for the moon of peace. God grant that he, too, may return in glory and that countless millions of prayers that follow him shall not have been in vain.

A fundamental dynamic of this "theology" was suggested by one of Nixon's speech writers, Ray Price, who wrote:

> Selection of a President has to be an act of faith. . . . This faith isn't achieved by reason: it's achieved by charisma, by a feeling of trust. . . .

Price also argued that the campaign would be effective only "if we can get people to make the *emotional* leap, or what theologians call 'leap of faith.'" This is, of course, precisely the inauthentic leap that Camus labeled as philosophical suicide. It is the suicide demanded by a civil religion in which "God," the Savior-President, and "our nation" more or less merge. When the "leap" is made, it is possible simply not to see what the great God-Father and his anointed one are actually doing. Among the chosen ones are scientists and professors who design perverse methods of torture and death such as flechette pellets that shred the internal organs of "the enemy" and other comparable inhumane "anti-personnel" weapons. Also among the elect are politicians and priests who justify and bestow their blessing upon the system that perpetrates such atrocities. "Under God" are included the powerful industrialists who are making the planet uninhabitable.

Sophisticated thinkers, of course, have never intellectually identified God with a Superfather in heaven. Nevertheless it is important to recognize that even when very abstract conceptualizations of God are formulated in the mind, images survive in the imagination in such a way that a person can function on two different and even apparently contradictory levels at the same time.

Thus one can speak of God as spirit and at the same time imagine "him" as belonging to the male sex. Such primitive images can profoundly affect conceptualizations which appear to be very refined and abstract. So too the Yahweh of the future, so cherished by the theology of hope, comes through on an imaginative level as exclusively a He-God, and it is consistent with this that theologians of hope have attempted to develop a political theology which takes no explicit cognizance of the devastation wrought by sexual politics.

The widespread conception of the "Supreme Being" as an entity distinct from this world but controlling it according to plan and keeping human beings in a state of infantile subjection has been a not too subtle mask of the divine patriarch. The Supreme Being's plausibility and that of the static worldview which accompanies this projection has of course declined, at least among the more sophisticated, as Nietzsche prophesied. This was a projection grounded in specifically patriarchal societal structures and sustained as subjectively real by the usual processes of producing plausibility such as preaching, religious indoctrination, and cult. The sustaining power of the social structure has been eroded by a number of developments in recent history, including the general trend toward democratization of society and the emergence of technology. However, it is the women's movement which appears destined to play the key role in the overthrow of such oppressive elements in traditional theism, precisely because it strikes at the source of the societal dualism that is reflected in traditional beliefs. It presents a growing threat to the plausibility of the inadequate popular "God" not so much by attacking "him" as by leaving "him" behind. Few major feminists display great interest in institutional religion. Yet this disinterest can hardly be equated with lack of spiritual consciousness. Rather, in our present experience the woman-consciousness is being wrenched free to find its own religious expression.

It can legitimately be pointed out that the Judeo-Christian tradition is not entirely bereft of elements that can foster intimations of transcendence. Yet the liberating potential of these elements is choked off in the surrounding atmosphere of the images, ideas, values, and structures of patriarchy. The social change coming from radical feminism has the potential to bring about a more acute and widespread perception of qualitative differences between the conceptualizations of "God" and of the human relationship to God which have been oppressive in their connotations, and the kind of language that is spoken from and to the rising woman-consciousness.

Castrating "God"

I have already suggested that if God is male, then the male is God. The divine patriarch castrates women as long as he is allowed to live on in the human imagination. The process of cutting away the Supreme Phallus can hardly be a merely "rational" affair. The problem is one of transforming the collective imagination so that this distortion of the human aspiration to transcendence loses its credibility.

Some religious leaders, notably Mary Baker Eddy and Ann Lee, showed insight into the problem to some extent and tried to stress the "maternal" aspect of what they called "God." A number of feminists have referred to "God" as "she." While all of this has a point, the analysis has to reach a deeper level. The most basic change has to take place in women—in our being and self-image. Otherwise there is danger of settling for mere reform, reflected in the phenomenon of "crossing," that is, of attempting to use the oppressor's weapons against him. Black theology's image of the Black God illustrates this. It can legitimately be argued that a transsexual operation upon "God," changing "him" to "her," would be a far more profound alteration than a mere pigmentation change. However, to stop at this level of discourse would be a trivialization of the deep problem of human becoming in women. . . .

Why Speak About "God"?

It might seem that the women's revolution should just go about its business of generating a new consciousness, without worrying about God. I suggest that the fallacy involved in this would be an overlooking of a basic question that is implied in human existence and that the pitfall in such an oversight is cutting off the radical potential of the movement itself.

It is reasonable to take the position that sustained effort toward self-transcendence requires keeping alive in one's consciousness the question of ultimate transcendence, that is, of God. It implies recognition of the fact that we have no power *over* the ultimately real, and that whatever authentic power we have is derived from *participation in* ultimate reality. This awareness, always hard to sustain, makes it possible to be free of idolatry even in regard to one's own cause, since it tells us that all presently envisaged goals, life-styles, symbols, and societal structures may be transitory. This is the meaning that the question of God should have for liberation, sustaining a concern that is really open to the future, in other words, that is really ultimate. Such a concern will not become fixated upon limited objectives. Feminists in the past have in a way been idolatrous about such objectives as the right to vote. Indeed, this right is due to women in justice and it is entirely understandable that feminists' energies were drained by the efforts needed to achieve even such a modicum of justice. But from the experience of such struggles we are in a position now to distrust token victories within a societal and structural framework that renders them almost meaningless. The new wave of feminism desperately needs to be not only many faceted but cosmic and ultimately religious in its vision. This means reaching outward and inward toward the God beyond and beneath the gods who have stolen our identity.

The idea that human beings are "to the image of God" is an intuition whose implications could hardly be worked through under patriarchal conditions. If it is true that human beings have projected "God" in their own image, it is also true that we can evolve beyond the projections of earlier stages of consciousness. It is the creative potential itself in human beings that is the image of God. As the essential victims of the archaic God-projections, women can bring this process of creativity into a new phase. This involves iconoclasm—the breaking of idols. Even—and per-

haps especially—through the activity of its most militantly atheistic and areligious members, the movement is smashing images that obstruct the becoming of the image of God. The basic idol-breaking will be done on the level of internalized images of male superiority, on the plane of exorcising them from consciousness and from the cultural institutions that breed them.

One aspect of this expurgation is dethronement of false Gods—ideas and symbols of God that religion has foisted upon the human spirit (granted that the human spirit has created the religions that do this). I have already discussed this to some extent, but it might be well to focus specifically upon three false deities who still haunt the prayers, hymns, sermons, and religious education of Christianity. The three usurpers I have in mind have already been detected and made the targets of attack by liberal male theologians, but the point in mentioning them here is to indicate the specific relevance of feminism to their demise.

One of the false deities to be dethroned is the God of explanation, or "God as a stop-gap for the incompleteness of our knowledge," as Bonhoeffer called him. This serves sometimes as the legitimation of anomic occurrences such as the suffering of a child, a legitimation process which Peter Berger lucidly analyzes in discussing the problem of theodicy. Such phenomena are "explained" as being God's will. So also are socially prevailing inequalities of power and privilege, by a justifying process which easily encourages masochistic attitudes. Clearly, this deity does not encourage commitment to the task of analyzing and eradicating the social, economic, and psychological roots of suffering. As marginal beings who are coming into awareness, women are in a situation to see that "God's plan" is often a front for men's plans and a cover for inadequacy, ignorance, and evil. Our vantage point offers opportunities for dislodging this deity from its revered position on the scale of human delusions.

Another idol is the God of otherworldliness. The most obvious face of this deity in the past has been that of the Judge whose chief activity consists in rewarding and punishing after death. As de Beauvoir indicated, women have been the major consumers of this religious product. Since there has been so little self-realization possible by the female sex "in this life," it was natural to focus attention on the next. As mass consumers of this image, women have the power to remove it from the market, mainly by living full lives here and now. I do not mean to advocate a mere re-utterance of the "secularization" theology that was so popular in the sixties. This obvious shape of the God of otherworldliness has after all been the target of male theologians for some time, and the result has often been a kind of transla-tion of religion into humanism to such an extent that there is a kind of "self-liquidation of theol-ogy." What I see beginning to happen with women coming into their own goes beyond this secularization. The rejection of the simplistic God of otherworldliness does not mean necessar-ily reduction to banal secularism. If women can sustain the courage essential to liberation this can give rise to a deeper "otherworldliness"—an awareness that the process of creating a counter-world to the counterfeit "this world" presented to consciousness by the societal structures that oppress us is participation in eternal life.

It should be noted that the God lurking be-hind some forms of Protestant piety has func-tioned similarly to the otherworldly God of pop-ular Roman Catholic piety. In his analysis of the effects of Luther's doctrine of salvation by faith alone, Max Weber uncovers serious problems of ethical motivation, involving a complicated se-ries of phenomena: "Every rational and planned procedure for achieving salvation, every reliance on good works, and above all every effort to sur-pass normal ethical behavior by ascetic achieve-ment is regarded by religion based on faith as a wicked preoccupation with purely human pow-ers." Transworldly asceticism and monasticism tend to be rejected when salvation by faith is stressed, and as a result there may be an in-creased emphasis upon vocational activity within the world. However, as Weber explains, empha-sis upon personal religious relationship to God tends to be accompanied by an attitude of indi-vidualism in pursuit of such worldly vocational activity. One consequence is an attitude of pa-tient resignation regarding institutional struc-tures, both worldly and churchly. It is precisely this schizophrenic attitude that combines per-sonal vocational ambition within the prevailing set of social arrangements and passive acceptance of the system that radical feminism recognizes as destructive.

A third idol, intimately related to those de-scribed above, is the God who is the Judge of "sin," who confirms the rightness of the rules and roles of the reigning system, maintaining false consciences and self-destructive guilt feel-ings. Women have suffered both mentally and physically from this deity, in whose name they have been informed that birth control and abor-tion are unequivocally wrong, that they should be subordinate to their husbands, that they must be present at rituals and services in which men have all the leadership roles and in which they are degraded not only by enforced passivity but also verbally and symbolically. Although this is most blatant in the arch-conservative religions, the God who imposes false guilt is hardly absent from liberal Protestantism and Judaism, where his presence is more subtle. Women's growth in self-respect will deal the death blow to this as well as to the other demons dressed as Gods.

Suggestions for Further Reading

Some have argued that before masculine symbolism was used for the divine, feminist sym-bolism was used. See Merlin Stone's *When God Was a Woman* (New York: Harcourt Brace Jovanovich, 1976) and Carol Ochs, *Behind the Sex of God* (Boston: Beacon Press, 1977) for starters.

See also Rosemary Radford Ruether's *New Women, New Earth: Sexist Ideologies and Human Liberation* (New York: Seabury, 1975).

Mary Daly's *Pure Lust: Elemental Feminist Philosophy* (Boston: Beacon Press, 1984) develops a new feminist vocabulary.

For a philosophy of religion written from a feminist perspective, see *A Feminist Philosophy of Religion* by Pamela Sue Anderson (Oxford: Blackwell, 1998).

See also the collection of essays from *Womanspirit Rising: A Feminist Reader in Religion,* as well as the more pluralistic sequel *Weaving the Visions: New Patterns in Feminist Spirituality,* both edited by Judith Plaskow and Carol P. Christ (San Francisco: Harper & Row, 1989).

For a study of Buddhism and patriarchy, see Rita M. Gross, *Buddhism After Patriarchy: A Feminist History, Analysis, and Reconstruction of Buddhism* (Albany: State University of New York Press, 1993).

There is a lot of information on Mary Daly and her views on the Web. You can begin with http://www.womanandmoney.com/mary_daly/ and follow the links to more information.

Videos

Films for the Humanities & Sciences (www.films.com) offers several videos on the topic of women and religion. See *Elaine Pagels: Guilt and Suffering in Christianity* (52 minutes), *The Need to Know: Women and Religion* (47 minutes), *The Forbidden Goddess* (28 minutes), *Women and Islam* (30 minutes), and *Shackled Women: Abuses of a Patriarchal World* (41 minutes) for starters.

 You can locate InfoTrac-College Edition articles about this chapter by accessing the InfoTrac-College Edition website (http://www.infotrac-college.com/wadsworth/). Using the InfoTrac-College Edition subject guide, enter the search terms relevant to this chapter, and then read abstracts for relevant articles.

Appendix I

Glossary

absolute skepticism. *See* skepticism.

Advaita Vedanta. A school of Hindu philosophy that teaches that reality is nondual (*advaita*).

aesthetics. A subdivision of the field of axiology (value theory) that has to do with philosophical reflection on a range of concepts relevant to art, such as beauty, harmony, structure, plot, texture, narrative, fiction, composition, and so on.

Allah. The Muslim name for God. Allah is viewed as a unitary sovereign, creator God of infinite mercy and goodness whose will is absolute.

altruism. The view holding that one ought to do what is in the best interest of others.

ambiguity. The word *ambiguity* refers to instances when linguistic meaning is unclear. For example, the word "bank" is ambiguous because without specified context it is unclear whether it refers to a place to keep money, the side of a river, or a type of shot in pool.

analytic statement. A statement that is necessarily true by virtue of the meaning of the words. According to Hume, such statements are about the relations of ideas, and it is not logically possible for their negation to be true. They are the opposite of synthetic statements.

anarchism. The political theory that governments, by their very nature, are immoral and should not be formed. It is based on the idea that only the individual has ultimate moral authority.

***anatta* (Anatman).** A Buddhist term meaning "no-self," refers to the Buddhist doctrine that there is no Atman. It is the denial of the notion that a substance exists that constitutes the human self or soul.

anicca. A Buddhist term meaning "impermanence." According to this teaching, there are no eternal substances, essences, or ideal Forms (as in Plato's theory of Forms).

anomalies. New events that are inconsistent with prevailing laws and theories.

a posteriori. Latin meaning "following from" or "after," characterizes reasoning based on sense experience and identifies human experience as the place from which ideas come. Knowledge that comes from experience is called a posteriori.

a priori. Latin meaning "prior to" or "before," refers to reasoning based on reason (in contrast to sense experience) and identifies ideas as innate (acquired *prior* to sense experience) or as valid independent of experience. Mathematical knowledge is frequently characterized as a priori because its truth does not depend on sense experience.

atheism. The belief that God does not exist.

Atman. Usually translated "Self." According to some schools of Hindu philosophy, it is pure consciousness or consciousness itself and constitutes the essence of all reality. It is to be distinguished from the ego, or individual self.

axiology. A branch of philosophy concerned with developing a theory of value. Ethics (moral value) and aesthetics (artistic value) are two main subdivisions.

behaviorism. The view that mental states are either equivalent to the behaviors of an organism or the dispositions to behave.

Brahman. A Sanskrit term that can refer to the creator God or, as in Shankara, to the source and essence of all reality. Sometimes translated as "Godhead," indicating the essence of the divine.

categorical imperative. A command or law that is unconditional. Such a law instructs us to do something regardless of the consequences. According to Kant, this is the principle of all morality. Kant characterized it as the highest moral law and formulated it in several ways, one of which states that humans should be treated as ends, not means.

cognitive relativism. The view that truth and standards of knowledge are relative rather than absolute. (*See* relativism.)

coherence theory of truth. *See* truth.

commonsense skepticism. *See* skepticism.

communism. A political and economic theory that rejects private ownership and maintains that the ideal society is classless.

compatibilism. *See* soft determinism.

compensatory justice. The sort of justice that demands the correct distribution of benefits to those who have suffered unfair hardship. Affirmative action programs are often justified on these grounds.

constructivists. Critics of foundationalism (see below) who maintain that rationality is a social construction.

correspondence theory of truth. *See* truth.

cosmological argument. An a posteriori argument from the existence of the universe (cosmos) to God as the cause, creator, or explanation of the universe's existence.

covering law model. A concept of explanation in the philosophy of science which holds that science explains events by reference to some natural law that includes (covers) the events.

Dao (Tao). A concept central to Chinese philosophy, usually translated as "The Way." It has a variety of meanings but often refers to the way of nature or the way reality functions.

de (te). A Chinese word meaning "excellence" or "power," often translated as "virtue."

deductive-nomological model. Another name for the covering law model (see above).

deep ecology. An ethical view that advocates forms of identification with the nonhuman world as essential to the development of a responsible environmental ethic.

deism. A view of God that emphasizes God's remoteness from the creation. God is a first cause who starts the universe running according to natural laws and does not interfere in its operation.

democracy. The political theory stating that the people are sovereign and have the right to rule.

deontological ethical theory. A theory (such as Kant's) that stresses the importance of the motive of doing one's duty as a determining factor in assessing the moral value of actions. It is the motive for, not the consequences of, actions that morally count.

descriptive. A concept that is usually contrasted with normative (what ought to be) and is used to refer to a type of reflection that seeks to describe the way things are in *fact*.

determinism. Also called simple determinism, the belief that every event has a cause—that is, for every event, there is a set of conditions such that, if the conditions are repeated, the event is repeated.

dharma. A Sanskrit term meaning "duty," "teachings," or "doctrines." In Hindu philosophy, it often refers to the moral law and order believed to be inherent in nature.

direct realism. *See* realism.

distributive justice. The fair distribution of benefits such as wealth, privileges, rights, and honors among the members of a society.

divine command theory. A position holding that what makes an action morally right is the fact that God commands or wills it.

doctrine of the mean. A Confucian concept referring to a universal moral order that consists in the harmony of all things. Also the title of a Confucian book developing this idea.

double-aspect theory. The view that the mind and body are two different aspects of one substance, which is itself neither mental nor physical. *See* neutral monism.

dualism. A metaphysical theory that two fundamentally different things, usually characterized as mind and matter (body), are real.

egalitarianism. The view that all persons, just because they are persons, should share equally in all benefits and burdens.

Eightfold Path. The way of attaining enlightenment as taught by Buddhism; this path consists of right views, right thought, right speech, right action, right livelihood, right effort, right mindfulness, and right concentration.

eliminative materialism. In the philosophy of mind, the metaphysical thesis that there are no mental phenomena.

empiricism. An epistemological theory holding that (1) knowledge derives from sense experience and (2) knowledge claims are verified by reference to sense experience.

epiphenomenalism. Refers to a theory that mental events are by-products of physical events.

epistemology. A branch of philosophy concerned with developing a theory of knowledge and truth.

ethical absolutism. *See* objectivism.

ethical egoism. The belief that what is good for oneself is of primary moral value and ought to be chosen over what is primarily good for others (ethical altruism).

ethical emotivism. The view that moral value derives from how people feel.

ethical nihilism. The view that moral value has no basis.

ethical relativism. *See* relativism.

ethical skepticism. The position that the existence of moral truth and the possibility of ethical knowledge is doubtful.

ethics. A subdivision of axiology concerned with the study of moral value.

eudaimonia. Usually translated as "happiness" or "living well" and can be thought of as self-realization. Aristotle uses the concept to refer to the final good or purpose of human action, namely, to realize or actualize essential human nature.

evidentialism. The view that we should have good evidence in support of a position before we accept it as true.

existentialism. A philosophical movement that takes as its starting point reflection on the concrete existence of humans and what it means to be a human being living in the sort of world in which we actually live.

fatalism. The view that some or all events are predetermined by an impersonal force or power.

five aggregates. These are physical form, sensation, conceptualization, dispositions to act, and consciousness. According to Buddhism, they constitute the processes that make up the individual.

five pillars of Islam. These are the five central practices of Islam: (1) witnessing that there is no God but Allah and that Muhammad is his Apostle; (2) *salat*, or mandatory prayers;

(3) *zakat,* or mandatory alms; (4) fasting during the holy month of Ramadan; and (5) *hajj,* or pilgrimage to Mecca.

formal principle of justice. People ought to be treated fairly with respect to relevantly similar (or relevantly different) traits.

Forms. *See* theory of Forms.

foundationalism. The claim that rationality and knowledge rest on a firm foundation of self-evident truths.

four causes. Aristotle's theory that existing things have four causes: (1) an efficient cause or agency by which they are made, (2) a material cause or stuff out of which they are made, (3) a formal cause (the idea or essence) according to which they are made, and (4) a final cause or end for which they are made.

Four Noble Truths. The name for the heart of the Buddha's teaching: (1) life is suffering; (2) the cause of suffering is craving; (3) suffering can be overcome; and (4) the Eightfold Path, or the Middle Way, of right understanding, thought, speech, action, livelihood, effort, mindfulness, and concentration is the way to attain release from suffering.

functionalism. A theory about the mind, holding that mental states are completely defined as functions of physical processes.

hard determinism. The theory that every event has a cause and that this fact is incompatible with the existence of free will. Hence, human beings should not be held morally responsible for their actions because it is impossible for them to do other than what they do.

hedonism. A moral theory holding that the highest or greatest good is pleasure.

hypothetico-deductive method. Sometimes called the "scientific method" because it involves deducing predictions that can be experimentally tested in order to check some hypothesis.

incommensurable. A term that means not only incompatibility but also a degree of difference so fundamental that no value judgments are possible about incompatible views because they are based on a completely different set of assumptions.

idealism. A metaphysical theory that only ideas (minds and mental events) are real or that they are more real, valuable, and enduring than material things. In an ethical context, *idealistic* is sometimes used to refer to a person who lives by ideals or to a view based on principle.

identity theory. The view that mental events are identical with brain events.

immortality of the soul. The view that the soul, which constitutes the essence of a person, lives forever and can exist apart from a physical body.

indirect realism. *See* realism.

innate ideas. Refers to ideas we are born with, a concept used by rationalists to characterize the state of the human mind prior to sense experience.

interactionism. The theory that the mind and body, though they are two distinct and different substances, nevertheless can causally affect one another.

kalam. An Arabic word used to refer to theology in general and, in particular, that part of theology concerned with cosmological arguments for God's existence.

karma. From a Sanskrit word meaning "action"; it often refers to the consequences of actions and the natural moral law that governs actions called the law of karma ("You reap what you sow").

karma yoga. Refers to practices of detachment from consequences that allegedly allows one to escape karma (the results of actions) and hence to escape the cycle of reincarnation.

laissez-faire capitalism. An economic theory based on the idea of a totally free market.

law of noncontradiction. A cannot be A *and* not-A in the same respect and at the same time.

li. A Confucian concept meaning order, ceremony, custom, and propriety.

libertarianism. The theory that human choice is not caused (determined) by antecedent events. Human beings are free agents with the power to decide contrary to the influence of character and inclination. Hence, when deciding freely, humans can and should be held morally responsible. This term is also used in a political context to name a movement that supports the idea that the role of government ought to be severely restricted and individual freedom ought to be maximized.

materialism. Also called physicalism, the metaphysical view holding that matter alone is real. Negatively, it is the denial of the existence of immaterial, mental, and spiritual reality. In an ethical context, also refers to a value system that prizes material goods and possessions above other things.

material principle of justice. Refers to some specific trait on which decisions of distribution, retribution, and compensation are made—for example, all those who work 2 years get a 10 percent bonus.

mechanism. The view that the universe operates like a machine according to the law of cause and effect. It is the opposite of a teleological view.

metaphysics. A major branch of philosophy concerned with developing a theory of what is genuinely real.

methodical skepticism. *See* skepticism.

Middle Way. This term is used in general to characterize Buddhist teaching and practice as a middle way between extremes. It also has a variety of specialized meanings, such as specific reference to the Fourth Noble Truth or the Eightfold Path.

mind–body problem. The problem of defining what mind and body are and stating clearly how they are related.

monism. A metaphysical theory holding that reality is one.

Muslim. Literally it means "one who submits to Allah's will" and refers to the members of the Islamic religion.

naïve realism. Same as direct realism. *See* realism.

Naiyayika. An Indian school of philosophy concerned with a whole range of philosophical issues, but most often associated with advancing a theory of knowledge called *pramana* (*see* *pramana*).

naturalism. The view that the universe is a self-existing, self-regulating, homogeneous system.

natural theology. *See* theology.

neutral monism. The view that what exists is neither mental nor physical, but neutral with respect to these properties. (*See* double-aspect theory.)

nirvana. A Buddhist term meaning "release from suffering." Attaining nirvana is the goal of life for a Buddhist.

normal science. A term referring to the practice of accumulating knowledge by careful applications of scientific methods working within a given model or paradigm.

normative. This concept, often contrasted with descriptive, refers to a type of reflection that seeks to discover the way things *ought* to be. It has to do with norms (rules for correct behavior).

Nyaya. A school of Hindu philosophy that emphasizes logic and holds that there are four sources of knowledge: correct perception, correct inference, correct comparison, and correct testimony.

objective idealism. The view that reality is a manifestation of an absolute mind.

objectivism. The view that there is some permanent, transcultural, and transhistorical framework for determining rationality, knowledge, truth, reality, and moral value. The opposite of relativism.

Occam's Razor. Advocated by William Occam, a principle that advises us not to multiply entities beyond necessity. That is, when inventing explanations for an event, we should posit as existing only those things necessary to explain the event.

ontological argument. An a priori argument for God's existence that attempts to deduce God's existence from a definition of God's nature.

ontology. A major subdivision of metaphysics, the study of being as such.

pantheism. The view that God is the infinite, unitary, and self-existing cause of all existence and is the same as nature.

paradigm. A scientific achievement so deep and impressive that it defines the daily practice for a particular community of scientists.

parallelism. The theory that mental and physical events parallel one another in a coordinated manner but do not causally interact.

philosophy. From the Greek word for "love of wisdom," it has been defined in a variety of ways, one of which is the notion that philosophy is the rational attempt to formulate, understand, and answer fundamental questions.

philosophy of religion. The use of philosophical methods to study a variety of religious issues such as the relation of faith to reason, God's existence, life after death, and the nature of religious experience.

philosophy of science. The use of philosophical methods to critically analyze the assumptions and key concepts of science.

pluralism. The metaphysical theory holding that there are many different realities and that they are not reducible to a single reality or to only two basic realities. Also used in a different context to refer to a society characterized by a variety of different cultural groups.

political philosophy. Philosophical reflection on the nature and justification of government.

positivism. A view holding that modern science and its methods are the sole trustworthy guide to the truth.

pragmatic theory of truth. *See* truth.

pragmatism. A philosophical movement, which developed in the United States, stressing that, in determining both the meaning and truth of our beliefs, we must pay attention to their implications for our behavior.

prakriti. A Sanskrit term usually translated as "matter" or "nature," refers to that which is not conscious.

pramana. The means of knowledge developed in Indian philosophy: correct perception, correct inference, correct comparison (analogy), and reliable testimony.

predestination. The belief that some or all events (including the salvation of some people) are predetermined by a personal divine power.

primary qualities. *See* secondary qualities.

problem of evil. In the broad sense, the problem of explaining and making sense of evil. In the theological sense, the difficulty of reconciling the existence of evil with the existence of a perfectly good, all-powerful, creator God.

problem of freedom and determinism. If all events are caused, how can human actions be free?

problem of induction. The problem of providing a rational justification for inductive reasoning. Hume claimed we could not provide such a justification, and so our trust in inductive reasoning was rooted in custom or habit, not reason.

problem of the one and many. Is reality fundamentally one thing or many things?

process ontology. The view that change is a basic feature of reality and that all aspects of reality are interrelated.

Purusha. A Sanskrit term meaning "person," "self," or "pure consciousness."

rationalism. An epistemological theory holding that all genuine knowledge derives from reason and is justified a priori (independent of sense experience). It is the opposite of empiricism.

realism. The view that objects exist apart from a mind that knows them. *Representational* or *indirect realism* holds that sensations put us indirectly in touch with the real objects that they represent; *direct realism* holds that we are directly in touch with physical objects via our senses.

reincarnation. The view that souls or karmic effects can become attached to successive physical bodies and hence be reborn over and over again.

relativism. Found in both ethics and epistemology, a view that denies the existence of objective, transcultural moral values and/or standards of rationality. The only moral values and standards of rationality that exist are relative to either individuals (*individual relativism*) or societies (*social relativism*).

Ren (jen). A Confucian concept commonly translated as "benevolence" or "humanity," it refers to the highest human virtue or excellence.

representational realism. *See* realism.

resurrection of the body. The view that after death a person is re-created and constitutes the same person who lived before death.

retributive justice. A corrective distribution of burdens to persons who undeservedly enjoy benefits or to those who are guilty of failing to fulfill their responsibilities. Legal penalties for breaking the law are examples of the application of this principle.

revealed theology. *See* theology.

samsara. A Buddhist and Hindu concept referring to the life of suffering and the constant round of birth, death, and rebirth in which we are trapped.

scientism. The strong belief that science can solve all or almost all of the problems that plague human existence.

secondary qualities. The objects of the five senses (sounds, colors, odors, flavors, textures) are called secondary because they exist in the mind. *Primary qualities* (extension, figure, motion, rest, solidity, and number) are traits of physical objects that exist apart from the mind.

Shi'i. A branch of Islam that believes Allah gave the right to rule to the religious leaders (*imams*).

simple determinism. *See* determinism.

skepticism. In its absolute form, an epistemological theory contending that knowledge is not possible. *Commonsense skepticism* and *methodical skepticism* are not so absolute. The former doubts some but not all knowledge claims, and the latter uses doubt as a tool in the search for truth.

social contract. A theory of political sovereignty claiming that the authority of government derives from a voluntary agreement among all the people of a society to form a political community and to obey the laws laid down by the government they collectively select.

socialism. An economic system based on collective ownership of the means of production, rational economic planning, and the equal distribution of goods and services.

social philosophy. The study of issues relating to social policy and justice.

Socratic method. The method of critical analysis Socrates developed in an effort to uncover the essential qualities of various concepts.

soft determinism. Also called compatibilism because, according to this theory, determinism (the fact that every event has a cause) is compatible with the existence of human freedom. Human beings can and should be held morally responsible for whatever they voluntarily do.

subjective idealism. The view that physical objects do not exist apart from their perception.

sublation. Literally meaning "to carry or wipe away," often used in logic for the activity of contradicting, negating, or correcting. The concept is used by Shankara in conjunction with the distinction between appearance and reality. Appearance is sublatable, but reality is not.

substance ontology. A view holding that permanence is the basic feature of reality and that one or more substances exist independently in the sense that they would exist even if other things did not.

Sufism. A mystical movement in Islam that teaches the possibility of a direct and immediate experience of Allah.

Sunni. A branch of Islam that believes Allah gave the right to rule to the whole community.

synthetic statement. A statement whose truth value depends on the way the world is. According to Hume, they are about matters of fact, and it is possible for their negation to be true. They are the opposite of analytic statements.

tabula rasa. Meaning "blank tablet or slate," a term some empiricists use to characterize the state of the human mind prior to sense experience. It stands in contrast with the concept of innate ideas.

teleological argument. An a posteriori argument for God's existence, begins with the premise that the world exhibits purposeful order and concludes that this order is the result of the actions of a divine intelligence.

teleological ethical theory. A theory maintaining that good consequences constitute the moral rightness of an action.

teleology. The word comes from the Greek *telos* (goal, purpose, or end) and *logos* (word, reason, study), hence, literally, "the study of ends or goals." It often refers to the position that the universe has a goal, purpose, or final cause and that everything that happens contributes toward achieving that goal or outcome. In ethics, refers to those theories stressing that the consequences or outcomes of actions are what determines their moral value.

theism. The view that God is the infinite, unitary, all-powerful, perfectly good, self-existent cause of all things and is a personal being who created the universe out of nothing and directs it according to teleological laws.

theocracy. The political theory holding that God is and ought to be the ruler of human societies and the government must rule according to God's laws and through God's representatives.

theodicy. In the broad sense, any proposed solution to the problem of evil. In the narrow sense, any solution to the problem of evil that reconciles the existence of evil with the existence of God.

theology. The study of divine reality or God, sometimes divided into *natural theology,* which deals with possible knowledge about God based on the use of reason alone, and *revealed theology,* which claims knowledge about God based on special revelations.

theory of Forms. A Platonic theory claiming that Forms or concepts constitute essences that exist in their own right, as entities independent of the world of appearances in which they may be manifest.

totalitarianism. A political theory claiming that the state's entitlement to rule extends to all aspects of life and that the authority of the state is beyond question.

truth. Three theories that have determined philosophical discussion: (1) the *pragmatic theory,* which holds that "*p* is true if and only if believing that *p* is true works"; (2) the *correspondence theory,* which holds that "*p* is true if and only if *p* corresponds to the facts"; and (3) the *coherence theory,* which holds that "*p* is true, if and only if *p* is logically implied by *q,* and *q* is true."

underdetermination of theory. This refers to an epistemological impasse in which all the possible relevant evidence is compatible with different incompatible theories.

utilitarianism. A moral theory holding that the value of an action resides in its utility or use for the production of pleasure or happiness.

vagueness. Linguistic meaning is vague when the range of applicability is unclear. For example, the word "bald" is vague because it is unclear precisely how much hair must be missing before the word applies.

wuwei. A Chinese word meaning "no action," refers to acting unselfishly, naturally, and spontaneously.

xiao (hsiao). The Confucian virtue of filial love, loyalty, obedience, and piety.

yi. The Confucian term for what is fitting or appropriate.

yin and yang. A Chinese concept referring to the basic opposites that make up reality and are complementary. Yin is the passive force, and yang the active force.

Pronunciation Guides

Chinese

Two methods are in wide use today for romanticizing (translating into a Latin-based alphabetical system) Chinese words. One is called Wade-Giles and the other Pinyin. I have used Pinyin instead of Wade-Giles because that is, today, the official romanticization system endorsed by the Chinese government. However, my selections use the older Wade-Giles spelling, which requires a pronunciation guide because some of the sounds indicated by the letters do not, to an English speaker, correspond to the sounds in Chinese.

a as in father	ch pronounced as j
e as in end	k pronounced as g
i as in the initial e in eve	p pronounced as b
o as in go	t pronounced as d
u as in rude	ts or tz pronounced as tz or dz
ü as in menu	hs pronounced as sh
ai as in ice	j pronounced as r
ao as in out	ch', k', p', ts', tz' pronounced as in English
ou as in obey	

Sanskrit

VOWELS

1. *e, ai, o,* and *au* are long and are pronounced as in *gray, aisle, open,* and *cow.*
2. *ā, ī, ū,* with lines over them (macrons) are long and are pronounced as in *father, machine,* and *rude.*
3. The same vowels without macrons are short as in *but, tin,* and *full.*
4. *ṛ* is sounded as in *rill* and is lightly trilled.

CONSONANTS

5. *c* as in *church, j* as in *jungle, ṣ* as in *ship, s* as in *sun,* and *jn* as in *gyana.*
6. Aspirated consonants should be pronounced distinctly: thus *bh* as in *caB-House, dh* as in *maD-House, gh* as in *doG-House, jh* as in *fudGE-House, kh* as in *rocK-House, ph* as in *toP-Hat,* and *th* as in *goaT-Herd.*

ACCENT

7. Words of two syllables are accented on the first syllable: *GIta*.
8. Words of more than two syllables are accented on the penult (second syllable from end) when the penult is long or has a short vowel followed by two or more consonants: *veDANta*.
9. Words of more than two syllables are accented on the antepenult (third syllable from the end) in cases where the penult is short and *not* followed by two consonants: *UpaniSHAD*

Arabic

Letters are pronounced in the usual English manner unless indicated otherwise in the following list.

a	fl*a*t	o	n*o*t
ah	f*a*ther	oo	f*oo*d
ay	p*ay*	ōō	f*oo*t
ee	s*ee*	ow	h*ow*
e	l*e*t	u	b*u*t
i	h*i*gh	a	*a*bout
i	p*i*ty	izm	tribal*ism*
ō	n*o*	j	*j*et

SOME EXAMPLES

caliphs (*kay* lifs)	salat (sa *laht*)
dhikr (*dhi* kar)	Qur'an (kor *an*)
faqih (fa *kee*)	Shi'i (*Shee* ee)